The LaTeX Companion

Third Edition – Part I

Addison-Wesley Series on
Tools and Techniques for Computer Typesetting

This series focuses on tools and techniques needed for computer typesetting and information processing with traditional and new media. Books in the series address the practical needs of both users and system developers. Initial titles comprise handy references for LaTeX users; forthcoming works will expand that core. Ultimately, the series will cover other typesetting and information processing systems, as well, especially insofar as those systems offer unique value to the scientific and technical community. The series goal is to enhance your ability to produce, maintain, manipulate, or reuse articles, papers, reports, proposals, books, and other documents with professional quality.

Ideas for this series should be directed to frank.mittelbach@latex-project.org. Send all other feedback to the publisher at informit.com/about/contact_us or via email to community@informit.com.

Series Editor

Frank Mittelbach
Technical Lead, LaTeX Project, Germany

Editorial Board

Jacques André
Irisa/Inria-Rennes, France (Ret.)

Barbara Beeton
Editor, TUGboat, USA

David Brailsford
University of Nottingham, UK

Peter Flynn
University College, Cork, Ireland (Ret.)

Matthew Hardy
Adobe, USA

Leslie Lamport
Microsoft, USA

Chris Rowley
Open University, UK (Ret.)

William Robertson
The University of Adelaide, Australia

Steven Simske
Colorado State University, USA

Series Titles

Guide to LaTeX, Fourth Edition by Helmut Kopka and Patrick W. Daly

The LaTeX Companion, Third Edition by Frank Mittelbach, with Ulrike Fischer and contributions by Javier Bezos, Johannes Braams, and Joseph Wright

The LaTeX Graphics Companion, Second Edition by Michel Goossens, Frank Mittelbach, Sebastian Rahtz, Denis Roegel, and Herbert Voß
Reprinted 2022 by Lehmanns Media, Berlin

The LaTeX Web Companion by Michel Goossens and Sebastian Rahtz

Also from Addison-Wesley and New Riders:

LaTeX: A Document Preparation System, Second Edition by Leslie Lamport

Computers & Typesetting, Volumes A–E by Donald E. Knuth

The Type Project Book: Typographic projects to sharpen your creative skills & diversify your portfolio by Nigel French and Hugh D'Andrade

The LaTeX Companion
Third Edition – Part I

Frank Mittelbach
LaTeX Project, Mainz, Germany

Ulrike Fischer
LaTeX Project, Bonn, Germany

With contributions by Joseph Wright

✦Addison-Wesley

Boston • Columbus • New York • San Francisco • Amsterdam • Cape Town
Dubai • London • Madrid • Milan • Munich • Paris • Montreal • Toronto • Delhi • Mexico City
São Paulo • Sydney • Hong Kong • Seoul • Singapore • Taipei • Tokyo

Cover illustration by Lonny Garris/Shutterstock
Photos of Sebastian Rahtz courtesy of the TeX Users Group

Book design by Frank Mittelbach
Typeset with LaTeX in Lucida Bright at 8.47pt/11.72pt

For information about buying this title in bulk quantities, or for special sales opportunities, please contact our corporate sales department at corpsales@pearsoned.com or (800)382-3419.

For government sales inquiries, please contact governmentsales@pearsoned.com. For questions about sales outside the United States, please contact intlcs@pearson.com.

Visit us on the Web: informit.com/aw

Library of Congress Control Number: 2022947208

Part I:	ISBN-13:	978-0-13-465894-0
	ISBN-10:	0-13-465894-9
Part II:	ISBN-13:	978-0-201-36300-5
	ISBN-10:	0-201-36300-3
Part I+II:	ISBN-13:	978-0-13-816648-9
(bundle)	ISBN-10:	0-13-816648-X

2 2023

Pearson's Commitment to Diversity, Equity, and Inclusion

Pearson is dedicated to creating bias-free content that reflects the diversity of all learners. We embrace the many dimensions of diversity, including but not limited to race, ethnicity, gender, socioeconomic status, ability, age, sexual orientation, and religious or political beliefs.

Education is a powerful force for equity and change in our world. It has the potential to deliver opportunities that improve lives and enable economic mobility. As we work with authors to create content for every product and service, we acknowledge our responsibility to demonstrate inclusivity and incorporate diverse scholarship so that everyone can achieve their potential through learning. As the world's leading learning company, we have a duty to help drive change and live up to our purpose to help more people create a better life for themselves and to create a better world.

Our ambition is to purposefully contribute to a world where:

- Everyone has an equitable and lifelong opportunity to succeed through learning.

- Our educational products and services are inclusive and represent the rich diversity of learners.

- Our educational content accurately reflects the histories and experiences of the learners we serve.

- Our educational content prompts deeper discussions with learners and motivates them to expand their own learning (and worldview).

While we work hard to present unbiased content, we want to hear from you about any concerns or needs with this Pearson product so that we can investigate and address them.

- Please contact us with concerns about any potential bias at https://www.pearson.com/report-bias.html.

A TeX Haiku

```
\expandafter\def
\csname def\endcsname
{\message{farewell}}\bye
```

SPQR
at the poetry competition

TUG conference,
Vancouver, 1999

I dedicate this edition to all my friends in the TeX world and in particular
to the memory of my good friend Sebastian P. Q. Rahtz (1955–2016),
with whom I spent many happy hours discussing parenting, literature,
LaTeX and other important aspects of life [97].

Contents

Part II

List of Figures

List of Tables

Foreword

Before my retirement, I had the distinct privilege to work with leading authors in computing and related, technical fields. In many cases, my job as editor was simply to be an encouraging and sympathetic presence, as well as a welcome dining companion, while trying to make the publishing process as painless for them (and for in-house staff) as I could. As in childbirth, of course, eliminating all pain was virtually impossible; over unexpectedly long periods, authors yielded much too much time for family, pleasure, and sleep, all in the pursuit of a newborn book. I sometimes felt like an able midwife; other times, I could do nothing more than boil water and hope for the best. In the end, I was always proud of what these creative men and women could produce.

At no time during my lengthy tenure was my pride greater than it was for the authors who gave the world two, now three, editions of *The LaTeX Companion*. Building on the original inventions of Don Knuth and Leslie Lamport — speaking of my privilege to have worked with the best! — and led in each case by Frank Mittelbach, they have reached deeply into the work of selfless contributors, including themselves, to define the current state of LaTeX typesetting, and then to organize and document, in one authoritative and comprehensive publication, the tools now available for both beginning and advanced users.

My pride, I should say, has its origins in the book's publisher itself. Addison-Wesley (A-W), now an imprint of Pearson, had been founded by a printer, Melbourne Cummings, and Mel's values for production quality, particularly for textbooks with heavy mathematical content, were engrained in the company from the start (Thomas's *Calculus and Analytical Geometry* was his first book). Indeed, some notable authors with concern for the physical look of their books selected A-W precisely because of those values, even when they thought they might get a bigger sales bang elsewhere (they ultimately were pleased to get both)! Don, by the way, having just developed TEX, was the author Mel most strongly insisted to me on meeting in person, wishing to speak, as it were, typesetter to typesetter.

I have to leave it for the Preface to describe the book's contents more specifically. I have been away from LaTeX too long to be able to add much anyway. I have no idea, for example, whether newer versions of the system incorporate AI, so that a user might hear a HAL-like voice in the computer say something like, "Are you sure you want such narrow margins, Dave?" Nor do I know if the system now has 3D options, so that an important discovery literally jumps out from the page. Never mind. See the Preface.

What I can add from experience, and I am sure this much has not changed, is that LaTeX authors and users are an intense and serious bunch when it comes to making their writing look good. I admire their attention to detail, to getting precisely the right format to present their ideas. I once was dining out with one such person, and watched as he studied the menu for quite some time. A very picky eater, I thought. But when he finally put the menu down, he tapped it with his pointed finger and told me, as the best appetizer for him, which letter didn't go well with the balance of the font. I, by contrast, soon became more concerned with a mushroom that didn't seem to go well with the rest of my meal.

From experience, too, I can tell you that there are LaTeX users all over the world, and not just in those places you would expect to find them. The land of Gutenberg, sure, but how about a user in South America typesetting his book while bullets from a civil war literally flew by his university window (talk about intensity!)? I once also received user survey feedback from a urologist in Kenya. I frankly forget what his comment or question was — it was long ago — but I do remember being impressed how far LaTeX use had spread, and into what surprising fields. Without doubt, an extensive literature search would turn up beautifully typeset works on the broadest range of topics, maybe even a book on digital rectal examinations.

Putting my own finger to the wind, as even former editors are wont to do, the need and demand for this revision are clear. Wherever you are, whatever your subject area, you will surely find in the pages (and pages) that follow the most helpful LaTeX typesetting support a user could ever hope for. That certainly was my experience with the first two editions, and I now invite you to make it yours with the third.

Peter S. Gordon
Publishing Partner (Ret.)

To be continued in Part II . . .

Preface

With LATEX being a voluntary effort,
it seems quite appropriate that
TLC also stands for "tender, loving care"
(Concise Oxford Dictionary)!

David Rhead, 1994

I have now been involved in computer based typesetting for nearly four decades, three of them as the technical lead for the development of LATEX. During that long period there have been impressive technical advances in many different areas.

When I started there was no Internet to speak of — there were no browsers and there was no World Wide Web as we know it today. To book a hotel on my first trip to California to meet with Leslie Lamport, I had to resort to a travel agency that used fax machines to arrange the trip; on the flight I was served free alcoholic drinks (bad idea); and my computer at home was an Atari with two floppy drives (younger people probably only know these as the strange "save icon" in many software programs and perhaps have wondered what that represents) and an impressive external hard disc with 100mb of storage (that cost me a fortune at that time).

However, already back then LATEX had existed for some time and worked fine, though a lot of today's functionality was unavailable or, even if available, impossible to use, because computer processing speed was simply too slow.[1] As explained in more detail in the history section in Chapter 1, most of our enthusiastic ideas back then for a new and improved LATEX were simply two decades too early, and while we had a fully working first version of the L3 programming layer in the early nineties our

---

[1] The first simple TEX documents I produced on a large university mainframe took about half a minute per page — you could literately watch the progress as [, *wait*, 1, *wait*,], *long wait*, ... — and we still thought it was great and fast.

users would have died of caffeine consumption waiting for the results of processing their documents if we had dared to inflict it on them.

This all has changed since that time and today my smartphone is faster than the mainframe power available in the nineties. As a result, many new packages appeared over time and a lot of our dormant ideas and concepts envisioned in 1990 were finally integrated into LaTeX on the memorable day of February 2, 2020.

Since then, this programming environment has been used by the LaTeX Team to offer new functionality and also by many package authors developing new packages. All these developments — the recent as well as the older — are covered in this book.

$$\backsim \; \partial \; \backsim$$

The Companion *editions — setting the standard for a dozen years each*

When Michel, Alexander, and I wrote the first edition of *The LaTeX Companion* [29] in 1993, we intended to describe what is usefully available in the LaTeX world (though ultimately we ended up describing the then-new LaTeX 2_ε standard and what was useful and available at CERN in those days). As an unintended side effect, this first edition *defined* for most readers what should be available in a then-modern LaTeX distribution. Fortunately, most of the choices we made at that time proved to be reasonable, and the majority (albeit not all) of the packages described in the first edition are still in common use today.

During the following decade the *Companion* (nicknamed the "doggie book" because of its cover) became a core resource for many LaTeX users, with several reprints and translations into German, Japanese, and Russian.

Our approach was to provide comprehensive coverage for typical LaTeX documents so that for most users the *Companion* would serve as the only reference needed to get "the job" done. More esoteric package features or features still under development were not described. Instead, pointers to the package documentation were given if we thought such a feature was worth mentioning. This approach worked well, so at the turn of the millennium one reviewer wrote, "while the book shows its age, it still remains a solid reference in most parts".

The second edition in the new millennium...

Nevertheless, much had changed and a lot of new and exciting functionality had been added to LaTeX during that decade and it became clear that a revised edition was necessary. This second edition [96], published in 2004, saw a major change in the authorship: I took over as principal author (so from then on I am to blame for all the faults in the *Companion* editions) and several members of the LaTeX Project Team joined in the book's preparation, enriching it with their knowledge and experience in individual subject areas.

We ended up rewriting 90% of the original content and adding about 600 additional pages describing impressive and useful new developments. As a result, the second edition was essentially a new book — a book that we hoped preserved the positive aspects of the first edition even as it greatly enhanced them, while at the same time avoiding the mistakes we made back then, both in content and presentation (though, of course, we made some new ones). From the reception in the user community, I think it is fair to say that we largely succeeded — in fact, that book served even longer as a useful resource.

However, a decade or more is an awfully long time for a technical book, even given the longevity and stability of LaTeX and the *Companion*'s approach of describing a coherent and well-established set of packages. So in 2017 I started discussing with Kim Spenceley (my new editor at Addison-Wesley/Pearson after Peter Gordon's retirement) plans for a third edition of *The LaTeX Companion*. One question to solve up front was that of authorship. Initially, it looked as if I would have to do any necessary work all by myself this time, because none of the previous co-authors was available to help for one reason or another, making it a very daunting task indeed.

... and nearly two decades later, the third

Fortunately, this impression was wrong! In the end I got great help from Ulrike Fischer, who wrote Chapters 15 and 16, the sections on hyperref and tikz, and helped with numerous tasks during the production of this edition.

Javier Bezos and Johannes Braams took on the task of revising Chapter 13 on localizing documents, and Joseph Wright helped with describing siunitx and the section on source control support. Thanks to all of them — without their help the book would have been be much more difficult to finish.

Furthermore, Nelson Beebe kindly offered to read *all* chapters, checking them for accuracy as well as doing a first pass on copyediting. He provided numerous suggestions for improvements and I cannot thank him enough for undertaking that enormous task! The professional copy editor and the two proofreaders found additional boo-boos of mine, and I then found a few they missed while entering their corrections. I am sure our readers will find even more — it is a never-ending task, but we all did our best and, on the whole, I think we delivered a solid result.

Big thanks to our volunteer copy editor Nelson!

The new edition

Initially, when I discussed plans for a third edition of *The LaTeX Companion*, I expected the need for a large number of updates to the existing material, but not many additions. Thus, my naive estimate was that the book would perhaps grow by 10–15%.

However, after researching in depth the new material that had been developed since 2004, it became crystal clear that to remain faithful to the core promise of the *Companion* — to be a solid reference for the majority of LaTeX users to get their work done — we had to include a much larger amount of new material:

 What's in it for you?

- Descriptions of highly useful, large-scale packages that appeared in the meantime or were substantially updated in the last decade, e.g., biblatex, fontspec, hyperref, mathtools, siunitx, tcolorbox, unicode-math, and tikz, to name a few.

- A larger number of smaller packages that cover new ground and are useful for day-to-day work or for specialized (but not too esoteric) tasks.[1]

- Two new chapters on the exciting possibilities offered by using high-quality fonts for text *and* math — yes, LaTeX is no longer restricted to Computer Modern fonts or a few PostScript fonts that were set up for use with LaTeX in the nineties.

    You can now choose from a large number of high-quality, free fonts for both text and math; the only serious remaining problem is finding the ones you like. These chapters help with that, by showing samples of more than one hundred

---

[1] Give or take the odd exception, e.g., sillywalk, which I found just too lovely to bypass.

*Big thanks to Adam,
helping me with
my two favorite
"coffee table book"
chapters*

text fonts and more than forty alternative math font setups. I am very grateful for the help I received from Adam Twardoch (president of GUST, the Polish TeX users group, and the designer of the Lato fonts) on this, who spent many hours with me during two BachoTeX conferences, guiding me through the fonts available today and helping to select those of high quality for inclusion in the book.

- We also had to cover newer engine developments, e.g., the use of Unicode engines with LaTeX, across all chapters of the book. There are often subtle differences that you need to be aware of if you use these engines.

- Finally, there have been very important changes to LaTeX itself, which is undergoing a transformation that started in 2018, to keep it relevant in the years to come. Examples are the new hook management system for LaTeX, the extended document command syntax, and the inclusion of the L3 programming layer into the LaTeX format. All this is covered in the appropriate places — just take a peek at the term "L3 programming layer" in the index to see how much of the new material is already based on it.

In that sense the third edition is like the first: both have been written just after LaTeX itself had seen major changes and these exciting changes and additions are covered.

All this relevant information is now part of the new edition, but as a result we ended up with 1700 pages, not including the index — clearly too much to be printed as a single book that you can reasonably use as a day-to-day reference on your desk.

*Two parts — one
(virtual) book*

For that reason the decision was made to split the book into two parts of roughly equal size and market them as a unit.[1] The chapter progression follows more or less the successful order of the earlier editions, starting with elements and concepts that you need quite often in nearly all documents (the first few chapters in Part I) followed by topics you also usually need in most documents but not necessarily all the time (remainder of Part I and most of Part II).

Of course, if you are a mathematician you might end up keeping Chapter 11 open all the time, but if your interest is typesetting novels or company reports, it might be the chapter least often touched.

Part II also contains three important appendices on core LaTeX commands for defining your own little commands or applications, one on resolving errors (not that you would make any, would you?), and one on getting further help if this edition is not answering your questions — unlikely I'm sure, but then who knows?

⌒ ༄ ⌒

As David Rhead observed in the quotation at the beginning of the preface, TLC is not only an acronym for *The LaTeX Companion* but also stands for "tender, loving care" and this is most certainly an accurate description of the efforts and lifeblood poured into the works described on the pages of this book.

---

[1]For technical and accounting reasons that still means three separate ISBNs, one for each part and one for the bundle. From my perspective this is far from perfect, but it is how the world of publishing and logistics works. It means that while it is theoretically possible to buy only one part, there is little sense in that — unless you have used it so much that it is worn out and you want a fresh copy.

There are millions of LaTeX users out there (the online service Overleaf alone reported ten million accounts in 2022) and most of them use LaTeX because they love its typesetting capabilities and its superior quality. With LaTeX being easily extensible, users often adapt LaTeX to their needs in new fields and for new applications, and some of them go one step further, packaging their solution and making it available to others — usually supporting it long after they have a private need for it.

This is why we now have close to 5000 packages for use with LaTeX on the Comprehensive TeX Archive Network (CTAN) and why its catalogue lists nearly 3000 contributors. It is because of their dedication and "tender, loving care" that TeX and LaTeX stayed relevant for nearly four decades, offering unsurpassed quality and, likely, continuing to do so for several decades to come.

A standing salute to all these dedicated developers in the LaTeX world!

⌇ ﻉ ⌇

Looking back, it took roughly five years and several thousand hours to write this book, which sounds like an awfully long time and a huge effort — both of which are true — but the effort was rooted in the complexity and size of the task.

The first phase of the production was reading through the documentation of nearly 5000 packages available in today's LaTeX distributions, classifying them according to functionality, usability, and correctness. This included testing all packages initially considered as candidates for inclusion, to see if their documentation actually matched reality (often it did not — mine included ☹) and to come up with relevant use cases and examples. Often, alternative solutions provided by different packages existed, in which case a more in-depth analysis was necessary to decide which packages to recommend. That phase took somewhat more than a year.

Research

After this initial survey I started with documenting the selected packages or, in the case of packages already in the previous edition, revising and updating the existing material, describing new functionality, or rearranging the documentation to provide better access.

Describe

Frequently, while thinking up useful examples, I found some errors in a package or in its documentation or identified valuable but missing functionality, in which case a discussion with the package author started. As a side effect, this process more than once messed up the text that I had already written about the package, because afterwards I had to account for the new or changed functionality that I had requested. Thus, in several cases I rewrote whole sections or provided new, improved examples when further features became available. However, a real headache proved to be the larger, complex packages that sometimes come with several hundred pages of documentation. The task in such a case is to work through all this material and figure out what from it is needed by the majority of our readers, describe it adequately, and point out which areas I had left out or only skimmed over.

Of course, in many other cases the situation was reversed; i.e., the package functionality was good, but the documentation difficult to understand or incomplete, so here the task was to provide a different, possibly expanded, and hopefully better description. In either case, a strong focus was on providing useful, ready-to-apply examples, of which this edition has more than 1550. They have all been handcrafted to cover the typical use cases and support the accompanying documentation in the book.

This phase took close to three years, which means roughly writing two pages per day if working without break — going at it each and every day, including weekends (and for large periods it was like this).

Produce

The final phase, which started in spring 2022, was to pass all the work, chapter by chapter, to the professional copy editors engaged by Pearson, enter their corrections, and then do the layout of the chapters.[1] Once a chapter was in its final form I passed it back to a proofreader, who verified that the corrections had been correctly entered (not always), followed by a final pass by another proofreader who checked the final version once more. In parallel, Keith Harrison and I worked through all chapters to compile a useful concept index. The overall process took nine months, and I completely underestimated the amount of work necessary for this, even though I should have known better from previous books.

Many thanks to Kim and Julie for making the book a reality

My sincere thanks to Kim Spenceley, my editor at Pearson, and Julie Nahil, my senior content producer, who steered me patiently through the whole process, putting up with my idosyncrasies while keeping me on track, and at the same time making sure that my quest for quality was supported as much as possible.

Was it worth the effort?

Maybe you are asking yourself was that worth it, in the days of the Internet, where you can search for almost anything in a matter of seconds or watch a video that explains how to do something?

My personal answer to that question is a clear yes, because while there is a huge amount of information out there, it is of very varying quality, from extremely good to horrendously bad, misleading, or even plain wrong. This makes it very difficult for a user to sort the wheat from the chaff and, as a result, this overflow of information is not helpful unless you get good guidance.

And this guidance, we trust, is what the *Companion* is offering you, by providing you with a curated set of packages covering all areas of document production, showing you suitable solutions to various problems, and explaining the limitations when using one or the other approach.

We hope that this new edition will become a good companion for you for many years to come — just like the previous editions in the last decades. If it turns out that we achieved that, it will certainly be something to be proud of.

Frank Mittelbach

November 2022

---

[1] The nightmarish but also oddly satisfying task to lay out a book like this is described in the Production Notes at the very end of Part II.

CHAPTER 1

Introduction

LaTeX is not just a system for typesetting mathematics. Its applications span one-page memoranda, business and personal letters, newsletters, articles, and books covering the whole range of the sciences and humanities ... right up to full-scale expository texts and reference works on all topics. Versions of LaTeX now exist for practically every type of computer and operating system. This book provides a wealth of information about its many present-day uses but first provides some background information.

The first section of this chapter looks back at the origins and subsequent development of LaTeX.[1] The second section gives an overview of the file types used by a typical current LaTeX system and the rôle played by each. Finally, the chapter offers some guidance on how to use the book.

1.1 A brief history (of nearly half a century)

In May 1977, Donald Knuth of Stanford University [58] started work on the text-processing system that is now known as "TeX and METAFONT" [48–52]. In the foreword of *The TeXbook* [48], Knuth writes: "TeX [is] a new typesetting system intended for the creation of beautiful books — and especially for books that contain a lot of mathematics. By preparing a manuscript in TeX format, you are telling a computer exactly how the manuscript is to be transformed into pages whose typographic quality is comparable to that of the world's finest printers."

In the Beginning ...

---

[1] A more personal account can be found in *The LaTeX legacy: 2.09 and all that* [122].

In 1979, Gordon Bell wrote in a foreword to an earlier book, *TEX and METAFONT, New Directions in Typesetting* [47]: "Don Knuth's Tau Epsilon Chi (TEX) is potentially the most significant invention in typesetting in this century. It introduces a standard language in computer typography and in terms of importance could rank near the introduction of the Gutenberg press."

In the early 1990s, Donald Knuth produced an updated version and also officially announced that TEX would not undergo any further development [59, 60] in the interest of stability. Perhaps unsurprisingly, the 1990s saw a flowering of experimental projects that extended TEX in various directions; many of these are coming to fruition in the early 21st century, making it an exciting time to be involved in automated typography.

The development of TEX from its birth as one of Don's "personal productivity tools" (created simply to ensure the rapid completion and typographic quality of his then-current work on *The Art of Computer Programming*) [54] was largely influenced and nourished by the American Mathematical Society on behalf of U.S. research mathematicians.

... and Lamport saw that it was Good.

While Don was developing TEX, in the early 1980s, Leslie Lamport started work on the document preparation system now called LATEX, which used TEX's typesetting engine and macro system to implement a declarative document description language based on that of a system called Scribe by Brian Reid [115]. The appeal of such a system is that a few high-level LATEX declarations, or commands, allow the user to easily compose a large range of documents without having to worry much about their typographical appearance. In principle at least, the details of the layout can be left for the document designer to specify elsewhere.

The second edition of *LATEX: A Document Preparation System* [65] begins as follows: "LATEX is a system for typesetting documents. Its first widely available version, mysteriously numbered 2.09, appeared in 1985." This release of a stable and well-documented LATEX led directly to the rapid spread of TEX-based document processing beyond the community of North American mathematicians.

LATEX was the first widely used language for describing the logical structure of a large range of documents and hence introducing the philosophy of logical design, as used in Scribe. The central tenet of "logical design" is that the author should be concerned only with the logical content of his or her work and not its visual appearance. Back then, LATEX was described variously as "TEX for the masses" and "Scribe liberated from inflexible formatting control". Its use spread very rapidly during the next decade. By 1994 Leslie could write, "LATEX is now extremely popular in the scientific and academic communities, and it is used extensively in industry". But that level of ubiquity looks quite small when compared with the present day when it has become, for many professionals on every continent, a workhorse whose presence is as unremarkable and essential as the workstation on which it is used.

Going global

The worldwide availability of LATEX quickly increased international interest in TEX and in its use for typesetting a range of languages. LATEX 2.09 was (deliberately) not globalized, but it was globalizable; moreover, it came with documentation worth translating because of its clear structure and straightforward style. Two pivotal conferences (Exeter UK, 1988, and Karlsruhe Germany, 1989) established clearly the widespread adoption of LATEX in Europe and led directly to International LATEX [126] and to work led by Johannes Braams [5] on more general support for using a wide variety of languages and switching between them (see Chapter 13).

Note that in the context of typography, the word *language* does not refer exclusively to the variety of natural languages and dialects across the universe; it also has a wider meaning. For typography, "language" covers a lot more than just the choice of "characters that make up words", as many important distinctions derive from other cultural differences that affect traditions of written communication. Thus, important typographic differences are not necessarily in line with national groupings but rather arise from different types of documents and distinct publishing communities.

Another important contribution to the reach of LaTeX was the pioneering work of Frank Mittelbach and Rainer Schöpf on a complete replacement for LaTeX's interface to font resources, the New Font Selection Scheme (NFSS) (see Chapter 9). They were also heavily involved in the production of the $\mathcal{A}_{\mathcal{M}}\mathcal{S}$-LaTeX system that added advanced mathematical typesetting capabilities to LaTeX (see Chapter 11).

The Next Generation

As a reward[1] for all their efforts, which included a steady stream of bug reports (and fixes) for Leslie, by 1989 Frank and Rainer "were allowed" to take over the maintenance and further development of LaTeX. One of their first acts was to consolidate International LaTeX as part of the kernel[2] of the system, "according to the standard developed in Europe". Very soon version 2.09 was formally frozen, and although the change-log entries continued for a few months into 1992, plans for its demise as a supported system were already far advanced as something new was badly needed. The worldwide success of LaTeX had by the early 1990s led in a sense to too much development activity: under the hood of Leslie's "family sedan" many TeXnicians had been laboring to add such goodies as super-charged, turbo-injection, multivalved engines and much "look-no-thought" automation. Thus, the announcement in 1994 of the new standard LaTeX, christened LaTeX 2_ε, explains its existence in the following way:

Too much of a Good Thing[TM]

> Over the years many extensions have been developed for LaTeX. This is, of course, a sure sign of its continuing popularity but it has had one unfortunate result: incompatible LaTeX formats came into use at different sites. Thus, to process documents from various places, a site maintainer was forced to keep LaTeX (with and without NFSS), SLITeX, $\mathcal{A}_{\mathcal{M}}\mathcal{S}$-LaTeX, and so on. In addition, when looking at a source file it was not always clear for which format the document was written.
>
> To put an end to this unsatisfactory situation a new release of LaTeX was produced. It brings all such extensions back under a single format and thus prevents the proliferation of mutually incompatible dialects of LaTeX 2.09.

The development of this "New Standard LaTeX" and its maintenance system was started in 1993 by the LaTeX Project Team [99], which soon comprised the author of this book, Rainer Schöpf, Chris Rowley, Johannes Braams, Michael Downes (1958–2003), David Carlisle, Alan Jeffrey, and Denys Duchier, with some encouragement and gentle bullying from Leslie. Although the major changes to the basic LaTeX system (the kernel) and the standard document classes (styles in 2.09) were completed by

Standard LaTeX (LaTeX 2_ε)

---

[1]Pronounced "punishment".

[2]*Kernel* here means the core, or center, of the system.

1994, substantial extra support for colored typography, generic graphics, and fine positioning control were added later, largely by David Carlisle. Access to fonts for the new system incorporated work by Mark Purtill on extensions of NFSS to better support variable font encodings and scalable fonts [9–11].

1994 — The first edition of the LATEX Companion

At this point in the story the first edition of the *LATEX Companion* was written, which helped a lot in making many important packages known to a wide audience and as a side effect helped shape a standard corpus of LATEX packages expected to be available on any installation across the world.

Towards the 21st century

Although the original goal for this LATEX 2_ε was consolidation of the wide range of incompatible models carrying the LATEX marquee, what emerged was a substantially more powerful system with both a robust mechanism (via LATEX packages) for extension and, importantly, a solid technical support and maintenance system. This provides robustness via standardization and maintainability of both the code base and the support systems. The core of this system remains the current standard LATEX system that is described in this book. It has fulfilled most of the goals for "a new LATEX for the 21st Century", as they were envisaged back in 1989 [102, 104].

The specific claims of the current system are "... better support for fonts, graphics and color; actively maintained by the LATEX Project Team". The details of how these goals were achieved, and the resulting subsystems that enabled the claims to be substantially attained, form a revealing study in distributed software support: the core work was done in at least five countries and, as is illustrated by the bugs database [67], the total number of active contributors to the technical support effort remains high.

The package system

Although the LATEX kernel suffered a little from feature creep in the late 1990s, the package system together with the clear development guidelines and the legal framework of the LATEX Project Public License (LPPL) [69, 85] have enabled LATEX to remain almost completely stable while supporting a wide range of extensions. These have largely been provided by a similarly wide range of people who have, as the project team are happy to acknowledge and the online catalogue [138] bears witness, enhanced the available functionality in a vast panoply of areas.

Development work

All major developments of the base system have been listed in the regular issues of *LATEX News* [66]. At the turn of the century, development work by the LATEX Project Team focused on the following areas: supporting multi-language documents [83]; a "Designer Interface for LATEX" [93]; major enhancements to the output routine [84]; improved handling of inter-paragraph formatting; and the complex front-matter requirements of journal articles. Back then prototype code had been made available (see [92]), but the work has otherwise been kept separate from LATEX — partly because it was executing simply too slowly on the available hardware.

No new features at the kernel level ...

One thing the project team steadfastly refused to do at that time was to unnecessarily "enhance" the kernel by providing additional features as part of it, thereby avoiding the trap into which LATEX 2.09 fell in the early 1990s: the disintegration into incompatible dialects where documents written at one site could not be successfully processed at another site. In this discussion it should not be forgotten that LATEX serves not only to produce high-quality documents but also to enable collaboration and exchange by providing a lingua franca for various research communities.

With LATEX 2_ε, documents written in 1996[1] can still be run with today's LATEX. In the opposite direction, new documents run on older kernel releases if the additional packages used are brought up-to-date — a task that, in contrast to updating the LATEX kernel software, is easily manageable even for users working in a multiuser environment (e.g., in a university or company setting).

But a stable kernel is not identical to a standstill in software development; of equally crucial importance to the continuing relevance and popularity of LATEX is the diverse collection of contributed packages building on this stable base. The success of the package system for nonkernel extensions is demonstrated by the enthusiasm of these contributors — many thanks to all of them! As can be easily appreciated by visiting the highly accessible and stable Comprehensive TEX Archive Network (see Appendix C) or by reading this book (where more than 250 of these "Good Guys"[2] are listed on page 943), this has supported the existence of an enormous treasure trove of LATEX packages and related software.

... but no standstill

The provision of services, tools, and systems-level support for such a highly distributed maintenance and development system was itself a major intellectual challenge, because many standard working methods and software tools for these tasks assume that your colleagues are in the next room, not the next continent (and in the early days of the development, e-mail and FTP were the only reliable means of communication). The technical inventiveness and the personalities of everyone involved were both essential to creating this example of the friendly face of open software maintenance, but Alan Jeffrey and Rainer Schöpf deserve special mention for "fixing everything".

The back office

A vital part of this system that is barely visible to most people is the regression testing system with its vast suite of test files [82]. It was initially devised and set up by Frank and Rainer with Daniel Flipo; it has proved its worth countless times in the never-ending battle of the bugs. Over the years it has seen many refinements, cumulating in a complete rewrite as part of l3build [98], which we describe in Section 17.3 on page →II 606.

In 2004, i.e., roughly a decade after its first edition, the second edition of the *LATEX Companion* was published. Due to the popularity of LATEX 2_ε and its extended features for developers, new important packages had emerged, and LATEX had reached out into new domains. While the advice given in the first edition remained largely valid (last not least because of the long-term backward compatibility paradigm of LATEX), we ended up rewriting 90% of the original content and added about 600 pages to account for new developments. As before, the second edition helped a lot in standardizing the use, and this way the interoperability, of LATEX across the world.

2004 — The second edition of the LATEX Companion

Some members of the LATEX Project Team have built on the team's experience to extend their individual research work in document science beyond the current LATEX structures and paradigms. Some examples of their work up to now can be found in

Research

---

[1] The time between 1994 and 1996 was a consolidation time for LATEX 2_ε, with major fixes and enhancements being made until the system was thoroughly stable. In fact, with some minor alterations in pagination or font usage, it is usually possible to reprocess even documents from the eighties (i.e., written for LATEX 2.09) or make them reusable with little effort.

[2] Unfortunately, this is nearly the literal truth: you need a keen eye to spot the few ladies listed.

the following references: [12, 14–16, 86–88, 91, 100, 121, 123]. An important spin-off from the research work was the provision of some interfaces and extensions that are immediately usable with standard LaTeX.

…and into the future

The decision to keep the core of the standard LaTeX system stable and essentially unchanging had two major advantages over any other approach to support fully automated document processing. First, the system already efficiently provided high-quality formatting of a large range of elements in very complex documents of arbitrary size. Second, it was robust in both use and maintenance and hence offered the potential to remain in widespread use for at least a further 15 years.[1] In the second edition of this book we wrote on this topic:

> As more such functionality is added, it will become necessary to assess the likelihood that merely extending LaTeX in this way will provide a more powerful, yet still robust and maintainable, system. This is not the place to speculate further about the future of LaTeX but we can be sure that it will continue to develop and to expand its areas of influence whether in traditional publishing or in electronic systems for education and commerce.

Reassessment time

This reassessment became necessary in the second decade of the new century, when it became obvious that this position was gradually getting unsustainable, because more and more areas in which people were looking for solutions could not be adequately addressed with a model of a fixed kernel and all developments outsourced to the package level. Examples are the move to Unicode in basically all operating systems and the growing pressure to produce "accessible" documents that conform to standards such as PDF/UA (Portable Document Format/Universal Accessibility).

An important policy change

Thus, in 2015, the LaTeX Project Team changed its policy and restarted kernel development. To retain the best of both worlds this was accompanied by developing a rollback/roll-forward functionality for the kernel and packages (that care to implement it). This allows a current LaTeX format to roll back to an earlier point in time in order to process old documents that rely on interfaces that have been changed since then or to process documents that explicitly worked around bugs (and so expect them to be there) that have been fixed in the meantime.

The first action of the team was to retire the fixltx2e package and instead include the accumulated fixes it contained directly in the format and to officially support LaTeX when using the Unicode engines X E TeX and LuaTeX. A big step forward happened in 2018 when LaTeX switched its default input encoding to UTF-8. This change proved that the policy change was the right thing to do and that the preparatory work (e.g., providing rollback) allows executing even major changes without disruption in its user base in order to keep LaTeX relevant and useful. A good indicator for the renewed and increased activity are the regular LaTeX newsletters [66] accompanying each release, which grew bulkier and again appeared semi-annually.

---

[1]One of the authors of the second edition had publicly staked a modest amount of beer on TeX remaining in general use (at least by mathematicians) until at least 2010. He should have made a larger bet, given that this is now 2022 and LaTeX is healthy and in fact growing its user base due to its many unsurpassed qualities.

The event of providing the mythical LaTeX3 had long become a standing joke as "two years from 'now' — with 'now' a moving target". The reason was that the concepts and ideas for LaTeX3 have been simply a decade or more too early, and while the team implemented a fully working version already in 1990, it was simply too slow to be usable with the then available computing power. Thus, we gave up pursuing it and instead concentrated on offering LaTeX 2_ε, which then went public in 1994.

And where is the mythical LaTeX3?

But ideas and concepts were never forgotten by the team, and especially its newer members (who joined in this century) pushed them back to the forefront and improved them dramatically. As a result, the code was eventually publicly made available as the expl3 package. It was then picked up by a number of enthusiastic package developers and used as the basis for their new packages. For example, if you use acro, breqn, fontspec, siunitx, unicode-math, or xparse, to name a few, you use "LaTeX3" under the hood; a recent count shows more than 200 such packages or classes as part of TeX Live.

So in 2019 the LaTeX Project Team made two wide-ranging decisions: there will not be a separate LaTeX3 that is being developed alongside LaTeX 2_ε (as was originally planned). Instead, we will modernize the current LaTeX gradually from the inside, using the new rollback mechanism and "development" formats as a safety net to ensure that there is no disruption of service for our user base. As a first step on this journey, the L3 programming layer and the LaTeX3 document-level command declarations (formerly known as expl3 and xparse) were made an integral part of LaTeX on February 2, 2020. Thus, more or less exactly 30 years after its conception, LaTeX3 became a reality for every LaTeX user — even though few will have immediately noticed.

... well it got merged into the kernel in 2020

The importance of this step is that it allows the team to modernize other parts of the kernel and develop new functionality entirely based on the L3 programming layer, which offers many features not available with legacy LaTeX programming constructs. For example, the new Hook Management System for LaTeX, which is a cornerstone for modernizing and transforming the existing LaTeX, is entirely written using the new L3 programming layer, and other parts will follow suit.

The foundation layer for modernization

As already mentioned, there is a steadily increasing interest in the production of "tagged" PDF documents that are "accessible", in the sense that they contain information to assist screen reading software, etc., and, more formally, that they adhere to the PDF/UA (Portable Document Format/Universal Accessibility) standard [134], explained further in [21]. In many disciplines this is starting to become a requirement when applying for grants or when publishing results.

Today's challenge: structured and accessible output is needed

At the moment, all methods of producing such "accessible PDFs", including the use of LaTeX, require extensive manual labor in preparing the source or in post-processing the PDF (maybe even at both stages); and these labors often have to be repeated after making even minimal changes to the (LaTeX or other) source. This is a huge pity, because LaTeX should in theory be well positioned to do this work automatically, given that its source is already well-structured.

The production of tagged (i.e., structured) PDF documents is not only important in order to comply to accessibility standards. It also opens possibilities to reuse data from such PDFs, because it allows other applications to correctly identify the structure inside the output document and this way extract or manipulate parts of the content — workflows that become increasingly important in the digital world.

The LaTeX Project Team has for some years been well aware that these new usages are not adequately supported by the current system architecture of LaTeX 2_ε and that major work in this area is therefore urgently needed to ensure that LaTeX remains an important and relevant document source format. However, the amount of work required to make such major changes to the LaTeX system architecture is enormous and definitely way beyond the limited resources of a small team of volunteers working in their spare time (or maybe just about possible, but only given a very long — and most likely too long — period of time).

A multi-year project to shape the future of LaTeX
At the TeX Users Group conference 2019 in Palo Alto the team's previously pessimistic outlook on this subject became cautiously optimistic, because of discussions with senior executives from Adobe about the possibility of producing structured PDF from LaTeX source without the need for the usual requirement of considerable manual post-processing. As a result of these discussions, towards the end of 2019 the team produced an extended feasibility study for the project, aimed primarily at Adobe engineers and decision-makers. This study [95] describes in some detail the various tasks that constitute the project and their interdependencies. It also contains a project plan covering how, and in what order, these tasks should be tackled both to achieve the final goal and, at the same time, to provide intermediate concrete results that are relevant to user communities (both LaTeX and PDF); these intermediate results will help in obtaining feedback that is essential to the successful completion of later tasks.

This multi-year project found the approval of Adobe, which then committed to financially and otherwise supporting this endeavor [101]. Unfortunately — thanks to the COVID-19 pandemic — the start got delayed, but since the end of 2020, this exciting project is now well under way. First results from this project that are already in existence (such as the new hook management system and the alignment of the hyperref package with the LaTeX kernel) are already described in this book. Other parts are obviously still vaporware at this point. Fortunately, none is expected to render any documentation or suggestion made in this book obsolete — after all, the project goal is to enable tagging of existing documents, simply by reprocessing with minor configuration changes as outlined in the "Spoiler alert" Section 2.1.1 on page 23.

1.2 Today's systems

When we wrote the second edition of *The LaTeX Companion* (i.e., 2003–2004), standard LaTeX was (officially) supported only on 8-bit engines, e.g., pdfTeX. Around the same time, the first version of the Unicode engine XeTeX and (somewhat later, in 2007) the first beta version of LuaTeX appeared, and there were soon unofficial support files that helped people running LaTeX on these Unicode engines as well.

When LuaTeX reached version 1.0, the LaTeX Project Team used the opportunity and officially took on LaTeX support for all three engines that included, for example, running the release regression test suite with its roughly 1000 tests against all three engines. Besides these three engines (which are covered in this book), there are further ones, such as pTeX and upTeX for Japanese, where the LaTeX adjustments for the engine are maintained by the respective user groups.

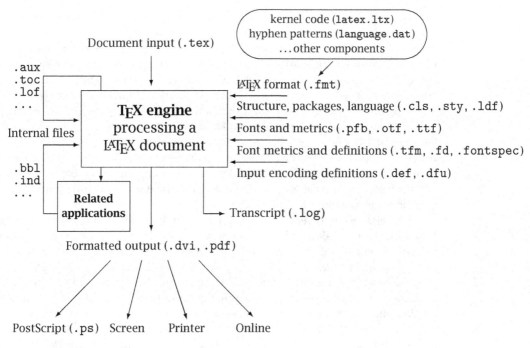

Figure 1.1: Data flow in the LaTeX system

What is described in this book should work with all of these engine — in cases where there are differences between 8-bit and Unicode engines, then they are explicitly described (see page 18 for a description how).

However, each of the engines also has one or the other specialty compared to the original TeX program, which is available only with that particular engine; e.g., LuaTeX supports code written in Lua, or upTeX offers special commands for Japanese typography, etc. Standard LaTeX either abstracts such features (when support is available in all engines and only the methods differ) or does not make use of the features — and for that reason such engine-specific commands are not discussed in the LaTeX Companion. If you are interested in that level of coding, please refer to the engine documentation, e.g., for pdfTeX [36], for XƎTeX [119], and for LuaTeX [77].

Engine specifics not covered in this book

In the remainder of the current section we present an overview of the vast array of files used by a typical LaTeX system with its many components. This overview also involves some descriptions of how the various program components interact. Most users will never need to know the exact details of this software environment that supports their work, but this section will be a useful general reference and an aid to understanding some of the more technical parts of this book.

Files used in the LaTeX universe

Although modern LaTeX systems are most often embedded in project-oriented, menu-driven interfaces, behind the scenes little has changed from the file-based description given here. Figure 1.1 shows schematically the flow of information.

The following description assumes familiarity with a standard computer file system in which a "file extension" is used to denote the "type of a file". In processing a document, the LaTeX program reads and writes several files, some of which are further processed by other applications. The most important ones are listed in Table 1.1 on the next page. The book covers a total of 64 file types, but those not described in the current section are rather specialized and used only by individual packages.

Document input

The most obviously important files in any LaTeX-based documentation project are the *input source files*. Typically, there will be a main file that uses other subsidiary files (see Section 2.1). These files most often have the extension `.tex` (code documentation for LaTeX typically carries the extension `.dtx`; see Chapter 17). They are commonly known as "plain text files", because they can be prepared with a basic text editor. Often, external graphical images are included in the typeset document utilizing the graphics interface described in Section 8.1.

Structure and style

LaTeX also needs several files containing structure and layout definitions: *class* files with the extension `.cls`; *option* files with the extension `.clo`; *package* files with the extension `.sty` (see Appendix A). Many of these are provided by the basic system setup, but others may be supplied by other developers. LaTeX is distributed with five standard document classes: article, report, book, slides, and letter. These document classes can be customized by the contents of other files specified either by class options or by loading additional packages as described in Section 2.1. In addition, many LaTeX documents automatically input *language definition files* of the babel system with the extension `.ldf` (see Chapter 13) and *encoding definition files* of the inputenc/fontenc packages with the extension `.def` (see Chapter 9).

Font resources

The information that LaTeX needs about the glyphs to be typeset is found in TeX *font metric* files (extension `.tfm`). This does not include information about the shapes of glyphs, only about their dimensions. Information about which font files are needed by LaTeX is stored in *font definition* files (extension `.fd`), or in case of Unicode engines sometimes in `.fontspec` files. Both types are loaded automatically when necessary. See Chapter 9 for further information about font resources.

The LaTeX format

A few other files need to be available to TeX, but you are even less likely to come across them directly. An example includes the LaTeX format file `pdflatex.fmt` that contains the core LaTeX instructions, precompiled for processing by the pdfTeX formatter. There are some situations in which this format needs to be recompiled — for example, when changing the set of hyphenation rules available to LaTeX (configured in `language.dat`; see Section 13.6.2) and, of course, when a new LaTeX kernel is made available. The details regarding how such formats are generated differ from one TeX implementation to the next, so they are not described in this book, but usually this all happens behind the scenes with the tools of the distribution you use.

The output from LaTeX itself is a collection of *internal* files (see below), plus one very important file that contains all the information produced by TeX about the typeset form of the document.

Formatted output

TeX's own particular representation of the formatted document is that of a *device-independent* file (extension `.dvi`). TeX positions glyphs and rules with a precision far better than $0.01\,\mu m$ (1/4,000,000 inch). Therefore, the output generated by TeX can be effectively considered to be independent of the abilities of any physical rendering device — hence the name. These days all major TeX engines can alternatively produce

	File Type	Common File Extension(s)
Document Input	text	`.tex .ltx`
	bibliography	`.bbl`
	index / glossary	`.ind / .gnd`
Graphics	internal	`.tex`
	external	`.ps .eps .tif .png .jpeg .jpg .gif .pdf`
Other Input	layout and structure	`.clo .cls .sty`
	encoding definitions	`.def .dfu`
	language definitions	`.ldf .ini`
	font access definitions	`.fd .fontspec`
	configuration data	`.cfg`
Internal Communication	auxiliary	`.aux`
(Input and Output)	table of contents / partial	`.toc / .ptc`
	list of figures / tables	`.lof / .lot`
Low-Level TEX Input	format	`.fmt`
	font image files	`.pfb .otf .ttf .pk`
	font metrics	`.tfm`
Output	formatted result	`.dvi .pdf`
	raw index / raw glossary	`.idx / .glo`
	transcript	`.log`
Bibliography (BIBTEX)	input / output	`.aux / .bbl`
	database / style / transcript	`.bib / .bst / .blg`
(biblatex)	style / citation / model / config	`.bbx / .cbx / .dbx / .bcf`
Index	input / output	`.idx / .ind`
	style / transcript	`.ist / .ilg`
Documentation & Testing	documentation / unpacking	`.dtx .fdd / .ins`
	test input / test output	`.lvt / .tlg`
Archive	dependencies / file usage	`.dep / .fls`

Table 1.1: Major file types used by LaTeX

PDF output (extension `.pdf`), and over time this has become the standard output format largely replacing `.dvi`.[1] The `.dvi` file format specifies only the names/locations of fonts and their glyphs — it does not contain any rendering information for those glyphs. The `.pdf` file format can and usually does contain such rendering information.

Some of the *internal* files contain code needed to pass information from one LaTeX run to the next, such as for cross-references (the *auxiliary* file, extension `.aux`; see Section 2.3) and for typesetting particular elements of the document such as the table of contents (extension `.toc`) and the lists of figures (extension `.lof`) and

Cross-references

---

[1] There are established workflows based on `.dvi` usually post-processed further to PostScript and from there often to PDF. For that reason the original format will remain a viable option.

of tables (extension `.lot`). Others are specific to particular packages (such as `acro`, Section 3.3.2, or `enotez`, Section 3.5.10) or to other parts of the system (see below).

Errors, warnings, and information
Finally, TEX generates a transcript file of its activities with the extension `.log`. This file contains a lot of information, such as the names of the files read, the page numbers (in brackets) of the pages processed, warning and error messages, and other pertinent data that is especially useful when debugging errors (see Appendix B). When you use an editor with integrated TEX support, this `.log` file is sometimes hidden from you and its data only selectively presented. If that is the case, it might be worth looking for it on the file system level, because it is likely to contain important information in case of problems that puzzle you.

Indexing
A file with the extension `.idx` contains individual unsorted items to be indexed. These items need to be sorted, collated, and unified by a program like *MakeIndex*, `upmendex`, or `xindy` (see Chapter 14). The sorted version is typically placed into a file (extension `.ind`) that is itself input to LATEX. For *MakeIndex* or `upmendex`, the *index style information* file has an extension of `.ist`, and the transcript file has an extension of `.ilg`; in contrast, `xindy` appears not to use any predefined file types.

Citations and bibliography
Information about bibliographic citations (see Chapter 16) in a document is normally output by LATEX to the *auxiliary* file or to the `biber` control file (extension `.bcf`). This information is used first to extract the necessary information from a bibliographic database and then to sort it; the sorted version is put into a *bibliography* file (extension `.bbl`) that is itself input to LATEX. If the system uses BIBTEX or biber (see Chapter 15) for this task, then the *bibliographic database* files will have an extension of `.bib`, and the transcript file will have the extension `.blg`. With BIBTEX, additional information about the process will be in a *bibliography style* file (extension `.bst`); biber does not use styles — this is handled by `biblatex` in that case.

Using \specials in the .dvi workflow
Because of the limitations of TEX, especially its failure to natively handle graphics or color, it is often necessary to complete the formatting of some elements of the typeset document after TEX has positioned everything and written this information to the `.dvi` file in some post-processing step. This is normally done by attaching extra information and handling instructions at the correct "geometrical position in the typeset document", using TEX's `\special` primitive that simply puts this information at the correct place in the `.dvi` file (see Chapter 8). This information may be simply the name of a graphics file to be input; or it may be instructions in a graphics language. This is then post-processed when the `.dvi` file is converted by a separate program, such as dvips, for printing or displaying. If TEX is directly generating PDF, there is conceptually not much difference, except that the post-processing happens directly in the extended TEX engine (e.g., pdftex, XƎTEX, or LuaTEX) at the point where TEX has finished a page and passes the result to a component that translates it to a PDF page. This component then plays the rôle that external programs play in the `.dvi` workflow: it also uses either `\specials` to communicate or additional primitives of the particular engine that do a similar job.

Using \specials in the .pdf workflow

In either case, LATEX abstracts from the underlying workflow peculiarities so that you can always just specify `\color` or `\includegraphics`. LATEX translates that into the right `\special` commands based on your workflow and the chosen TEX engine.

Seeing is believing
Once the document has been successfully processed by TEX (and possibly transformed into PostScript or PDF), you probably want to take a look at the formatted text.

This is commonly done on screen, but detailed inspection of printed output should always be performed via printing on paper at the highest available resolution. The applications available for viewing documents on screen vary quite a lot depending on your chosen workflow and your operating system. If you generate PDF, then various free and commercial tools exist that differ mainly in their features to post-process the document, but not in the actual representation, because the PDF normally includes all resources used by the document. If, on the other hand, you want to view a .dvi file, you need a viewer that can find and display the fonts or graphics referenced in the .dvi, because they are not part of the file itself. Occasionally you therefore find that some applications produce far superior screen output than others; this is due to limitations of the different technologies and the availability of suitable font resources.

1.3   Working with this book

This final section of Chapter 1 gives an overview of the structure of this edition, the typographic conventions used, and ways to use the examples given. Because of its size, this edition is typeset as two separate physical volumes (Part I and Part II), which has some implications on the presentation.

Chapters are numbered consecutively across both volumes, but we restart the page numbers in Part II to keep the numbers readable. As a consequence, cross-references to pages come in two forms: if they are to a page in the same volume, they read "see page 253", but if they refer to a page in the other volume, they look like "see page →II 127" or similar.

The main index, which contains entries for the whole edition, is replicated at the end of each physical volume to improve its usability and make it easier to work with. To identify the volume each page number in an entry refers to, the start of each volume sequence is identified by →I and →II, respectively.

1.3.1   What's where

Following is a summary of the subject areas covered by each chapter and appendix. In principle, all chapters can be read independently because, when necessary, pointers are given to where necessary supplementary information can be found in other parts of the edition.

Part I —

Chapter 1   gives a short introduction to the LaTeX system and this book.

Chapter 2   discusses document structure markup, including sectioning commands and cross-references as well as document source management.

Chapter 3   describes LaTeX's basic typesetting commands for the paragraph level. It also contains a section on packages offering document development support.

Chapter 4   looks at the typesetting of larger structures, such as lists and code displays, and shows how to work with multiple columns.

Chapter 5 explains how to influence the visual layout of the pages in various ways.

Chapter 6 shows how to lay out material tables, on single and multiple pages.

Chapter 7 surveys floating material and caption formatting.

Chapter 8 covers image loading and manipulation and the generation of portable graphics. It also offers an extensive overview on the tcolorbox package and an introduction to the world of tikz.

Chapter 9 discusses in detail LaTeX's Font Selection Scheme and shows how to access new fonts in 8-bit and Unicode TeX engines.

Part II —

Chapter 10 gives a comprehensive list with examples of high-quality text and symbol fonts available out of the box to LaTeX users today.

Chapter 11 reviews mathematical typesetting, particularly the packages supported by the American Mathematical Society.

Chapter 12 describes aspects of font usage in math formulas and offers a comparison between available font setups with 8-bit and Unicode TeX engines.

Chapter 13 discusses the support for using LaTeX with multiple languages, particularly the babel system.

Chapter 14 discusses the preparation and typesetting of an index with a focus on the programs *MakeIndex* and upmendex.

Chapter 15 explains how to create and use bibliographical databases in conjunction with LaTeX, and how to generate typeset bibliographies according to publishers' or style guide expectations.

Chapter 16 describes LaTeX's support for the different citation systems for bibliographical references in common use and how to produce multiple bibliographies by chapter and topic.

Chapter 17 shows how to document LaTeX packages and classes and how to use such files provided by others. It also covers setting up a development and testing environment and working with version control, which is useful for essentially every project.

Appendix A reviews how to handle and manipulate the basic LaTeX programming structures and how to produce class and package files.

Appendix B discusses how to trace and resolve problems and explains common error and warning messages and their likely causes.

Appendix C shows where to go beyond this book if that is ever needed, e.g., how to obtain the packages and systems described, how to access help or take an online course, and much more.

Some of the material covered in the book may be considered "low-level" TeX that has no place in a book about LaTeX. However, to the authors' knowledge, much of this information has never been described in the "LaTeX" context even though it is important. Moreover, we do not think that it would be helpful simply to direct readers to books like *The TeXbook*, because most of the advice given in books about "plain TeX" either is not directly applicable to LaTeX or, worse, produces subtle errors if used with LaTeX. In some sections we have, therefore, tried to make the treatment as self-contained as possible by providing all the information about the underlying TeX engine that is relevant and useful within the LaTeX context.

1.3.2 Typographic conventions

It is essential that the presentation of the material immediately conveys its function in the framework of the text. Therefore, we present below the typographic conventions used in this book.

Throughout the text, LaTeX command and environment names are set in monospaced type (e.g., \caption, enumerate, \begin{tabular}), while names of packages, class files, and programs are in sans serif type (e.g., article). Commands to be typed by the user on a computer terminal are shown in monospaced type and are underlined, e.g., showing how to call the LaTeX development format on the command line: *Commands, environments, packages, ...*

pdflatex-dev ⟨file⟩

The syntax of the more complex LaTeX commands is presented inside a rectangular box. Command arguments are shown in italic type: *Syntax descriptions*

\titlespacing*{*cmd*}{*left-sep*}{*before-sep*}{*after-sep*} [*right-sep*]

In LaTeX, optional arguments are denoted with square brackets, and the star indicates a variant form (i.e., is also optional), so the above box means that the \titlespacing command can come in four different incarnations:

```
\titlespacing{cmd}{left-sep}{before-sep}{after-sep}
\titlespacing{cmd}{left-sep}{before-sep}{after-sep}[right-sep]
\titlespacing*{cmd}{left-sep}{before-sep}{after-sep}
\titlespacing*{cmd}{left-sep}{before-sep}{after-sep}[right-sep]
```

For some commands, not all combinations of optional arguments and/or star forms are valid. In that case the valid alternatives either are explained in the text or are explicitly shown together, as, for example, in the case of LaTeX's sectioning commands:

\section*{*title*}   \section[*toc-entry*]{*title*}

Here the optional *toc-entry* argument can be present only in the unstarred form; thus, we get the following valid possibilities:

```
\section{title}     \section*{title}     \section[toc-entry]{title}
```

Code examples . . .
Lines containing examples with LaTeX commands are indented and are typeset in a monospaced type at a size somewhat smaller than that of the main text:

```
\addtocontents{lof}{\protect\addvspace{10pt}}
\addtocontents{lot}{\protect\addvspace{10pt}}
```

. . . with output . . .
However, in the majority of cases we provide complete examples together with the output they produce side by side:

```
\usepackage{ragged2e}
```

The right column shows the input text to be treated by LaTeX with preamble material shown in blue. In the left column one sees the result after typesetting.

```
The right column shows the input text to be treated
by \LaTeX{} with preamble material shown in blue.
In the left column one sees the result after
typesetting.
```

1-3-1

Note that all preamble commands are always shown in blue in the example source.

. . . with several pages . . .
In case several pages need to be shown to prove a particular point, (partial) "page spreads" are displayed and usually framed to indicate that we are showing material from several pages.

1 A TEST	1 A TEST
1 A test	page that might get reused over and over again.
Some text for our page that might get reused over and over again.	
Some text for our	
Page 6 of 7	Page 7 of 7

```
\usepackage{fancyhdr,lastpage}
\pagestyle{fancy}
\fancyhf{} % --- clear all fields
\fancyhead[RO,LE]{\leftmark}
\fancyfoot[C]{Page \thepage\
                  of \pageref{LastPage}}
% \sample defined as before

\section{A test}
\sample \par \sample
```

1-3-2

A number of points should be noted here:

- We usually arrange the examples to show pages 6 and 7 so that a double spread is displayed.
- We often use the command \sample to hold a short piece of text to keep the example code short: the definition for this command is either given as part of the example or, as indicated here, repeated from a previous example — which in this case is simply a lie because \sample was not defined earlier. In other examples we make use of lipsum or kantlipsum to generate sample text.
- The output may or may not show a header and footer. In the above case it shows both. Because the "pages" are very small but show the real output from the given input on the right, there are often deficiencies in line breaking, etc.

For large examples, where the input and output cannot be shown conveniently   *... with large* *output ...*
alongside each other, the following layout is used:

```
\usepackage{ragged2e,kantlipsum}  \RaggedRight
This is a wide line, whose input commands and output result cannot
be shown nicely in two columns. \kant[1][1-3]
```

Depending on the example content, some additional explanation might appear between input and output (as in this case). Then the output is displayed:

1-3-3

This is a wide line, whose input commands and output result cannot be shown nicely in two columns. As any dedicated reader can clearly see, the Ideal of practical reason is a representation of, as far as I know, the things in themselves; as I have shown elsewhere, the phenomena should only be used as a canon for our understanding. The paralogisms of practical reason are what first give rise to the architectonic of practical reason. As will easily be shown in the next section, reason would thereby be made to contradict, in view of these considerations, the Ideal of practical reason, yet the manifold depends on the phenomena.

Chapter 11 shows yet another example format, where the margins of the example   *... or with lines*
are explicitly indicated with thin blue vertical rules. This is done to better show the   *indicating the*
precise placement of displayed formulas and their tags in relation to the text margins.   *margins*

1-3-4 (1) $(a+b)^2 = a^2 + 2ab + b^2$

```
\usepackage[leqno]{amsmath}
\begin{equation} (a+b)^2 = a^2+2ab+b^2 \end{equation}
```

Some examples make use of color commands, e.g., \color or \textcolor, but   *Color usage*
because the book is printed only with two colors, it is not possible to do them justice.   *in this book*
The approach we took is that all colors appear as shades of gray except for blue, which we changed to produce the "lightblue" that is used as a second color in the book. Thus, all examples actually deploy the declarations as shown in the next example if they use color, but to save space none of them is shown elsewhere.

Black blue
red   green
yellow blue
1-3-5 bluish

```
\usepackage{xcolor}
\definecolor{blue}{cmyk}{1,0.56,0,0}  % what we call 'blue' in this book
\definecolor{red}{gray}{.7}     \definecolor{green}{gray}{.8}
\definecolor{yellow}{gray}{.9}
Black \textcolor{blue}{blue} \textcolor{red}{red} {\color{green} green}
\textcolor{yellow}{yellow} \colorbox{black!30}{\color{blue} blue}
\fcolorbox{blue}{blue!8}{\color{blue}bluish}
```

The notation blue!8 is a short form for writing blue!8!white. It is xcolor's way to specify simple color mixes and means that we mix 8% blue with 92% white.

All of these examples are "complete" if you mentally add a \documentclass line (with the article class[1] as an argument) and surround the body of the example with a document environment. In fact, this is how all of the examples in this book were produced. When processing the book, special LaTeX commands take the source lines for an example and write them to an external file, thereby automatically adding the \documentclass and the document environment lines. This turns each example into a small but complete LaTeX document. These documents are then externally processed (using a mechanism that runs each example as often as necessary, including the generation of a bibliography through BibTeX). The resulting PDF (Portable Document Format) is then cropped to the smallest size that shows all output, using the program pdfcrop and if necessary separated into individual pages using pdfseparate. The resulting graphic files are then loaded in the appropriate place the next time LaTeX is run on the whole book. More details on the actual implementation of this scheme can be found in Section 4.2.4 on page 315.

Watch out for these

Throughout the book, blue notes are sprinkled in the margin to help you easily find certain information that would otherwise be hard to locate. In a few cases these notes exhibit a warning sign, indicating that you should probably read this information even if you are otherwise only skimming through the particular section.

Information relevant only to Unicode TeX engines

Most of the material presented in this book is applicable to all TeX engine flavors, e.g., pdfTeX, XƎTeX, or LuaTeX. However, some aspects are applicable only to Unicode engines, and to help you identify this at a glance we have placed such information into boxes like this:

> **Unicode engines**
>
> This is information that applies only to Unicode engines, e.g., XƎTeX or LuaTeX.

The only exceptions are Section 9.6 on fontspec and Section 12.4 on unicode-math, both of which would have ended up completely within such boxes — which would be rather hard to read.

Information specific to biblatex/biber

A similar approach is used to highlight any differences between a workflow that uses BibTeX and traditional citation methods and one that uses the biblatex package and the biber program. As both methods have a large overlap, they are described together, and specific considerations are placed into boxes like this:

> **biber/biblatex**
>
> This is information specific to biblatex/biber and often gives tips how to ensure compatibility between the biber/biblatex and the BibTeX workflow.

This convention is used in Chapter 15.

1.3.3 Using the examples

Our aim when producing this book was to make it as useful as possible for our readers. For this reason the book contains more than 1500 complete, self-contained examples of all aspects of typesetting covered in the book.

---

[1] Except for examples involving the \chapter command, which need the report or book class.

All examples are made available in source format on CTAN at `https://ctan.org/pkg/tlc3-examples`. The examples are numbered per section, and each number is shown in a small box in the inner margin (e.g., 1-3-6 below). These numbers are also used for the external file names by appending `.ltx` (single-page examples) or `.ltx2` (double-page examples).

To reuse any of the examples it is usually sufficient to copy the preamble code (typeset in blue) into the preamble of your document and, if necessary, adjust the document text as shown. In some cases it might be more convenient to place the preamble code into your own package (or class file), thus allowing you to load this package in multiple documents using `\usepackage`. If you want to do the latter, there are two points to observe:

- Any use of `\usepackage` in the preamble code needs to be replaced by a `\RequirePackage` declaration, which is the equivalent command for use in package and class files (see Section A.6.7).

- Any occurrence of `\makeatletter` and `\makeatother` *must* be removed from the preamble code. This is very important because the `\makeatother` would stop correct reading of such a file.

So let us assume you wish to reuse the code from the following example:

A line of text[1] with some[2] footnotes.

```
\makeatletter
\renewcommand\@makefntext[1]%
    {\noindent\makebox[0pt][r]{\@thefnmark.\,}#1}
\makeatother
A line of text\footnote{The first}
with some\footnote{The second} footnotes.
```

---

1. The first
2. The second

1-3-6

You have two alternatives: you can copy the preamble code (i.e., the code colored blue) into your own document preamble or you can place that code — but without the `\makeatletter` and `\makeatother` — in a package file (e.g., `lowfnnum.sty`) and afterwards load this "package" in the preamble of your own documents with `\usepackage{lowfnnum}`.

The Structure of a LaTeX Document

One of the ideas behind LaTeX is the separation between layout and structure (as far as possible), which allows the user to concentrate on content rather than having to worry about layout issues [65]. This chapter explains how this general principle is implemented in LaTeX.

The first section of this chapter shows how document class files, packages, options, and preamble commands can affect the structure and layout of a document.

The logical subdivisions of a document are then discussed in general, before explaining in more detail how sectioning commands and their arguments define a hierarchical structure, how they generate numbers for titles, and how they produce running heads and feet. This is followed by discussing a few useful packages that allow you to customize different aspects of the layout of sectional units or to provide your own definitions.

In Section 2.3 we take a closer look at the design of table of contents structures and how it can be influenced or extended.

This is followed by a section discussing important packages that support you in providing cross-references that remain correct, even if you change parts of your document. These packages can automatically insert appropriate phrases (varioref, cleveref, nameref), can help you manage your label keys (showkeys and refcheck), or support you in providing references to external documents (xr) or hyperlinks in general (hyperref).

The final section introduces packages and programs that support you in archiving documents or managing them when you work jointly with others on some document.

2.1 The overall structure of a source file

You can use LATEX for several purposes, such as writing an article or a book or producing presentations. Clearly, documents for different purposes may need different logical structures, i.e., different commands and environments. We say that a document belongs to a *class* of documents having the same general structure (but not necessarily the same typographical appearance). You specify the class to which your document belongs by starting your LATEX file with a \documentclass command, where the mandatory parameter specifies the *name* of the *document class*. The document class defines the available logical commands and environments (for example, \chapter in the report class) as well as a default formatting for those elements. An optional argument allows you to modify the formatting of those elements by supplying a list of *class options*. For example, 11pt is an option recognized by most document classes that instructs LATEX to choose eleven point as the basic document type size.

Many LATEX commands described in this book are not specific to a single class but can be used with several classes. A collection of such commands is called a *package*, and you inform LATEX about your use of certain packages in the document by placing one or more \usepackage commands after \documentclass.

Just like the \documentclass declaration, \usepackage has a mandatory argument consisting of the *name* of the package and an optional argument that can contain a list of *package options* that modify the behavior of the package.[1]

The document classes and the packages reside in external files with the extensions .cls and .sty, respectively. Code for options is sometimes stored in external files (in the case of class files with the extension .clo) but is normally directly specified in the class or package file (see Appendix A for information on declaring options in classes and packages). However, in the case of options, the file name can differ from the option name. For example, the option 11pt is related to size11.clo when used in the article class and to bk11.clo inside the book class.

The document preamble
Commands placed between \documentclass and \begin{document} are in the so-called *document preamble*. All style parameters must be defined in this preamble, either in package or class files or directly in the document *before* the \begin{document} command, which sets the values for some of the global parameters. A typical document preamble could look similar to the following:

```
\documentclass[twocolumn,a4paper]{article}
\usepackage{multicol}
\usepackage[ngerman,french]{babel}
\addtolength\textheight{3\baselineskip}
\begin{document}
```

This document preamble defines that the class of the document is article and that the layout is influenced by the formatting request twocolumn (typeset in two columns) and the option a4paper (print on A4 paper). The first \usepackage declaration

---

[1] These commands also have a second optional argument that is intended for cases where a specific release of a package or a document class is required. This is discussed in Section 2.5.5 on page 114.

informs LaTeX that this document contains commands and structures provided by the package multicol. In addition, the babel package with the options ngerman (support for German language) and french (support for French language) is loaded. Finally, the default height of the text body was enlarged by three lines for this document.

Generally, nonstandard LaTeX package files contain modifications, extensions, or improvements[1] with respect to standard LaTeX, while commands in the preamble define changes for the current document. Thus, to modify the layout of a document, you have several possibilities:

- Change the standard settings for parameters in a class file with options defined for that class.

- Add one or more packages to your document and make use of them.

- Change the standard settings for parameters in a package file with options defined for that package.

- Write your own local packages containing special parameter settings and load them with \usepackage after the package or class they are supposed to modify (as explained in the next section).

- Make final adjustments inside the preamble.

If you want to get deeper into LaTeX's internals, you can, of course, define your own general-purpose packages that can be manipulated with options. You find additional information on this topic in Appendix A.

2.1.1 Spoiler alert — The \DocumentMetadata command

When LaTeX changed from LaTeX 2.09 to LaTeX 2$_\varepsilon$ around 1994, the overall document structure was slightly changed to automatically distinguish old from new documents (to switch to compatibility mode, if necessary). LaTeX 2$_\varepsilon$ documents start with \documentclass as described above, while LaTeX 2.09 documents started with the command \documentstyle, and \usepackage was unavailable.

Now, roughly a quarter century later, there is another major shift under way during which LaTeX is being modernized to support accessible PDF/UA (Portable Document Format/Universal Accessibility) and other functionality that is important for it to remain useful; see the discussion in Section 1.1 on page 7. This time around, the functionality change is essentially upward compatible, and old documents can be easily reprocessed using the new features. Thus, instead of dividing documents into two classes (old and new) by changing the first command, you can now indicate that you want to use the new functionality by adding a \DocumentMetadata declaration in front of \documentclass while leaving the rest of the document unchanged.

---

[1] Many of these packages have become de facto standards and are described in this book. This does not mean, however, that packages that are not described here are necessarily less important or useful, of inferior quality, or should not be used. We merely concentrated on a few of the more established ones; for others, we chose to explain what functionality is possible in a given area.

```
\DocumentMetadata{key/value list}
```

This declaration should be the first command in a document; i.e., if present, it should come before \documentclass. It expects a *key/value list* as its argument in which you specify "metadata" about the document that guides the production of the final output, e.g., should it adhere to a certain standard, should it be a tagged PDF, what is its author, title, and keywords that are shown in the metadata of the resulting PDF, etc. All these "metadata" are stored so that packages and users can access the data in a consistent way.

For example, the key pdfversion allows you to set the PDF version. With the key pdfstandard it is possible to require a standard such as A-2b. If that is specified, it directs LATEX to embed an appropriate color profile and set up verification tests that packages like hyperref can use to suppress actions not allowed in this standard. A further example is the backend key that allows you to specify a backend, e.g., dvipdfmx or dvisvg, which is useful in cases where the correct backend cannot be detected automatically.

At the time of writing this book the details about which other keys are going to be supported are still open (the whole exercise is a multi-year project [101] after all), but what we can say is that already now you can use this future interface to enable some new functionality. For example, just adding

```
\DocumentMetadata{}
\documentclass{article}        % (or any other class)
...                            % with preamble as previously
\begin{document}
```

is enough to load the new support code for managing PDF output, and this enables packages, such as hyperref, to provide features otherwise not available; see Section 2.4.6 on page 96 for details.

2.1.2 Processing of options of the document class and packages

You can think of options to the document class or to packages as a simple way to adjust some of the properties of the whole document (when used in \documentclass) or of properties of individual packages (if specified in \usepackage). More fine-grain control is usually also possible through declarations and setup commands that are defined by a class or package file and are available for use once that file is loaded.

You can specify options in a \usepackage command only if these options are explicitly declared by the package. Otherwise, you receive an error message, informing you that your specified option is unknown to the package in question. Options to the \documentclass are handled slightly differently. If a specified option is not declared by the class, it is assumed to be a "global option".

All options given to \documentclass (whether declared or global) are automatically passed as class options to all \usepackage declarations. Thus, if a package file loaded with a \usepackage declaration recognizes (i.e., declares) some of the class options, it can take appropriate actions. If not, the class options are ignored while processing that package. Because all options have to be defined inside the class or package file, their actions are under the control of the class or package (an action can be anything from setting internal switches to reading an external file). For this reason their order in the optional argument of \documentclass or \usepackage is (usually) irrelevant.

If you want to use several packages, all taking the same set of options (for example, none), it is possible to load them all with a single \usepackage command by specifying the package names as a comma-separated list in the mandatory argument. For example,

```
\usepackage[ngerman]{babel}   \usepackage[ngerman]{varioref}
\usepackage{array}            \usepackage{multicol}
```

is equivalent to

```
\usepackage[ngerman]{babel,varioref} \usepackage{array,multicol}
```

By specifying ngerman as a global option to the class we can further shorten the \usepackage declaration as ngerman is passed to all loaded packages and thus will be processed by those packages that declare it.

```
\documentclass[ngerman]{book}
\usepackage{babel,varioref,array,multicol}
```

Of course, this assumes that neither array nor multicol changes its behavior when ngerman is passed as a class option.

Finally, when the \begin{document} is reached, all global options are checked to see whether each has been used by at least one package; if not, a warning message is displayed. It is usually a spelling mistake if your option name is never used; another possibility is the removal of a \usepackage command loading a package that used this option previously.

When the option concept was originally developed, it was based on the idea that options are simple strings separated by commas without further structure. Spaces in that option list are explicitly ignored, because people often split such option lists over several lines and inadvertently introduced spaces before or after the commas. After a while some package developers started to use a key/value concept for options or setup commands; e.g., geometry allows you to write paper=a4,margin=1in with the meaning that the option paper gets the value a4 and margin is set to one inch. That works if neither the option name nor the intended value requires spaces because those get stripped away if used in a class or package option list.[1]

Key/value options and their limitations

This limitation is not easy to overcome for existing implementations without huge backward compatibility issues, which means that it is usually best to use a setup command (if provided by a package) rather than the option list with such packages, because in a setup command spaces are honored except those next to commas and equal signs. With the new key/value methods directly supported by the LaTeX format, spaces are trimmed only at either end (where one would expect it). For new packages or package reimplementations we therefore recommend using LaTeX's mechanism, which is described in Appendix A.6.6 on page →II 700.

If you want to make some modifications to a document class or a package (for example, changing parameter values or redefining some commands), you can put the relevant code into a separate file with the extension .sty. Then load this file with a

Configuration after loading a package

---

[1]This restriction is lifted in very new packages using the L3 programming layer methods.

\usepackage command after the package whose behavior you wish to modify (or the document class, if your modifications concern class issues).

Alternatively, you can insert the modifications directly into the preamble of your document. In that case, you may have to bracket them with \makeatletter and \makeatother if they contain internal LATEX 2$_\varepsilon$ commands (i.e., those with an @ sign in their names) or use \ExplSyntaxOn and \ExplSyntaxOff if they are LATEX3 commands (i.e., with _ and : in their names). For more details see the discussion on page → II 623 concerning internal commands in the preamble.

2.1.3 Front, main, and back matter

In a longer document, such as a book or a longer article, we usually can identify three distinct areas: the front matter, the main matter (or body matter), and the back matter.

As the name indicates the main matter holds the main text, while the two other parts provide supplementary information before and after. The front matter typically consists of the title page or pages, the table of contents and similar lists, an abstract, and a foreword or preface (though the latter may already be thought of belonging to the main matter). To the back matter you typically count any appendices, bibliography, index, and afterword, colophon, etc.

Typographically these three regions are often handled in different ways to make them easily identifiable, for example, by using different page numbering systems for front and main matter[1], not numbering headings in the front matter, and often using different heading number styles in main and back matter.

In shorter works this distinction becomes somewhat blurry: the front matter may just consist of the title (and not even on a page of its own) in which case it makes more sense to think of it as belonging to the main matter. Similarly, even in longer works there may not be any back matter.

In LATEX's book class these three regions can be explicitly marked up using the commands \frontmatter, \mainmatter, and \backmatter. In other classes you often find only the command \appendix, which is used to separate the body matter from the back matter — the assumption being that in articles and similar documents the front matter due to its length does not require special typographical treatment.

Front matter elements

The standard LATEX classes provide \title, \author (with \and and \thanks) and \date to set up the title information and \maketitle to produce the actual document title. For more elaborate title pages they offer the environment titlepage, which basically gives you an empty page in which you have to draw and position your title yourself.[2]

---

[1] If you prefer the front and main matter to use the same page numbering system, check out the little package arabicfront by Javier Bezos. It works with most document classes and results in the front and main matter being numbered with arabic numerals in a continuing sequence.

[2] Please note that in many classes the titlepage environment sets the page number explicitly to one and then issues a \thispagestyle{empty} to hide it. The downside is that this looks internally to LATEX always like a recto page, which in a twoside setting might cause problems. Thus, even though

If you design your own title page, it might be worth taking a look at the collection *Producing title pages* of title page examples by Peter Wilson [140], which contains forty examples together with the (sometimes low-level) code to produce them. Another possibly helpful resource is the package titling by the same author, which provides methods for restyling the material produced by \title, \author, \thanks, \date, and \maketitle.

The support offered by the standard classes (article, report, or book) is not really sufficient for anything other than preprints, which is why classes for specific journals or classes targeting book production often offer additional commands for specifying data relevant for the title or even provide some totally different commands altogether. This is an area where, due to the lack of decent support in the standard classes, the document syntax unfortunately varies from class to class, so you have to consult the appropriate documentation to see what is necessary for a particular class.

A possible alternative is the little package authblk by Patrick Daly that provides *Complex author* an extended syntax for the \author command and can typeset affiliation information *information* either in blocks (below each group of authors) or as footnotes as shown in the next example. By using an optional argument to \author and/or to \affil, it is even possible to have author and affiliations ordered in different ways. The package offers a number of customization possibilities, two of which are shown in the example; consult the documentation for further details. It should work with most document classes even if they provide their own author management.

Author Management

IMMANUEL KANT[1], MOSES MENDELSSOHN[2],
FRIEDRICH SCHILLER[3], LEONHARD EULER[4], AND
FRIEDRICH DER GROSSE[*2]

[1]*KÖNIGSBERG*
[2]*BERLIN*
[3]*JENA*
[4]*ST. PETERSBURG*

June, 1770

As any dedicated reader can clearly see, the Ideal of practical reason is a representation of, as far as I know, the things in themselves; as I have shown elsewhere, the phenomena should

*Sponsor

2-1-1

```
\usepackage[auth-sc,affil-it]
            {authblk}
\usepackage{kantlipsum}

\title{Author Management} `

\author{Immanuel Kant}
   \affil{Königsberg}
\author{Moses Mendelssohn}
   \affil{Berlin}
\author{Friedrich Schiller}
   \affil{Jena}
\author{Leonhard Euler}
   \affil{St.\ Petersburg}
\author[2]{Friedrich der
           Große\thanks{Sponsor}}

\date{June, 1770}

\maketitle
\kant[1]    % only partly shown
```

the page number is suppressed, you may have to adjust the page number to a different number inside (and again afterwards) if the page is meant to be a verso page.

Various content lists For the typical lists found in the front matter, such as the table of contents, the standard classes support the commands `\tableofcontents`, `\listoftables`, and `\listoffigures`. Additional lists can be defined as explained in Section 2.3.4 on page 74. Typically such lists produce unnumbered headings. If your front matter requires further sectional units, such as a foreword or a preface, produce them with the star form of a suitable heading command, e.g., `\chapter*` or `\section*`.

Abstracts Another important element, in particular for articles, is the `abstract` environment. Note that unfortunately the correct placement of this environment may depend on the chosen document class. In the standard classes and many others it is typeset where specified in the source, but there are classes in which it is formatted and placed by the `\maketitle` command and therefore has to appear before it. Its default formatting is usually adequate, and if you are typesetting an article for some particular journal, you should probably not alter it. However, if you do not like the outcome and you are free to make changes, take a look at the `abstract` package by Peter Wilson that offers a large arsenal of bells and whistles for adjusting most aspects of the abstract layout.

Other nonstandard elements There are other important frontmatter elements, such as a keyword list in journal articles, or bibliographic and copyright information in books, but none of these is provided for by the standard classes. However, in document classes for specific journals or book series from publishers, you usually find additional commands and environments that cater for these elements. Typically they differ from class to class so that one has to redo this part of the frontmatter if the document class is changed.

Main matter elements

The top-level structural elements of the body text are various levels of heading commands that are discussed in detail in Section 2.2 on page 32 and of course lists and other elements discussed in Chapter 4.

Back matter elements

Probably the most often used back matter elements are a bibliography and an index, which are supported through the environments `theindex` and `thebibliography` discussed in more detail in Chapters 14 and 15.

If you have several other appendices, use heading commands of the appropriate level to introduce them. The numbering scheme for such headings is automatically adjusted by the `\appendix` or `\backmatter` declaration that separates the back matter material from the main text. However, if there is only a single appendix, it may look odd if that gets numbered. Thus, in that case, you may explicitly want to use the star form of the heading command.

2.1.4 Splitting the source document into several files

LATEX source documents can be conveniently split into several files by using `\input` or `\include` commands. The `\input` command unconditionally includes the file specified as its argument at the current point. This is useful if you want to split your document into reasonably sized chunks or you want to reuse some parts for one or the other reason and therefore want to keep them in separate files.[1]

The \include command, however, is different in that it automatically starts a new page before and after the included file. For each \include file a separate .aux file is produced, which is why in contrast to \input such files should be specified without extension and on the operating system level always have the extension .tex.

\include used without extension

The reason for \include is that documents can be reformatted piecewise by specifying as arguments of an \includeonly declaration only those \include files LaTeX has to reprocess. For the other files that are loaded with \include commands, the counter information (page, chapter, table, figure, equation, …) is then read from the corresponding .aux files generated during a previous run. In the following example, the user wants to reprocess only the files chap1.tex and appen1.tex:

Partial processing

```
\documentclass{book}        % the document class ``book''
\includeonly{chap1,appen1}  % only include chap1 and appen1
\begin{document}
\include{chap1}             % input chap1.tex
\include{chap2}             % input chap2.tex
   ...                      % ... further chapters
\include{appen1}            % input appen1.tex
\include{appen2}            % input appen2.tex
\end{document}
```

Be aware that LaTeX issues only a warning message like "No file xxx.tex" and not an error message when it cannot find a file specified in an \include statement and then continues processing.

If the information in the .aux files is up-to-date, it is possible to process only part of a document and have all counters, cross-references, and pages be correct in the reformatted part. However, if one of the counters (including the page number for cross-references) changes in the reprocessed part, then the complete document might have to be rerun to get the index, table of contents, and bibliographic references consistently correct.

Note that each document part loaded via \include starts on a new page and finishes by calling \clearpage; thus, floats contained therein do not move outside the pages produced by this part. Natural candidates for \include are therefore whole chapters of a book but not necessarily small fractions of text.

While it is certainly an advantage to split a larger document into smaller parts and to work on more manageable files with a text editor, partial reformatting should be used only with great care and when still in the developing stage for one or more chapters. When a final and completely correct copy is needed, the only really safe procedure is to reprocess the complete document. However, if the document is too large to process in a single run, make sure that for the final version the pieces are processed *in the correct sequence* (if necessary several times) to ensure that the cross-references and page numbers are correct.

Avoid using partial processing when preparing the final version of your document

---

[1]Not everything can be placed into separate \input files, though. For example, it is not possible to put only a part of a tabular environment in a file; it has to go in completely.

Some packages are incompatible with the `\include` *mechanism*

It is very important to note that some packages can not be used reliably with the `\include` mechanism. Likely candidates are those that write their own support files to store data between runs as they often do not realize that parts of the document are not processed. A premier example from this book is the acro package. It always considers the first acronym it sees as being the acronym that is showing the full form; thus, if you apply `\includeonly`, it may see different instances as being the first, thereby altering the line breaking and pagination compared to always processing the full document.

2.1.5 askinclude — Managing your inclusions

Interactive inclusion

If you intend to work with `\include` commands, consider using the small package askinclude created by Pablo Straub and Heiko Oberdiek. It interactively asks you which files to include. You can then specify the files as a comma-separated list (i.e., what you would put into the `\includeonly` argument) or use * to indicate all files, − to include no files or ? in which case it asks you for each include file separately. Alternatively, if the Enter button is pressed in response, then your answer from the previous run is used again. This way you do not have to modify your master source to process different parts of your document (a very useful feature during the production of this book). All this works by storing the answer given in the .aux file so that it is available again on the next run. Thus, if that file is removed for some reason, you have make your selection again and cannot simply hit Enter.

The package also offers some pattern matching facilities if enabled with the option makematch. In this case * matches zero or more arbitrary characters, and a ! at the start of a pattern negates its effect (i.e., excludes matching names). For example, `chap*,!chap1` would include all files starting with chap except chap1.

2.1.6 tagging — Providing variants in the document source

Sometimes it is useful to keep several versions of a document together in a single source, especially if most of the text is shared between versions. This functionality is provided by the tagging package[1] created by Brent Longborough (1944–2021).

| `\tagged{`*label-list*`}{`*text*`}` | `\usetag{`*label-list*`}` | `\droptag{`*label-list*`}` |

The variant text parts are specially marked in the source using the command `\tagged`, and during formatting some of them are selected. The command takes two arguments: a label (or a comma-separated list of labels) that describes to which variant the optional text belongs, and the text to be conditionally printed.

With the command `\usetag` in the document preamble you can select which label (or labels) is active at the beginning of the document. Alternatively, you can specify the labels as package options to activate them. Inside the document body you

---

[1]A number of other packages provide similar functionality with slightly different interfaces, e.g., comment by Victor Eijkhout, xcomment by Timothy Van Zandt, and optional and version by Donald Arseneau. There is also multiaudience by Boris Veytsman, which uses a quite different approach that might be more suitable in complex situations.

can use further `\usetag` commands to activate additional labels, and you can use `\droptag` to inactivate some of them.

`\untagged{`*label-list*`}{`*text*`}`   `\iftagged{`*label-list*`}{`*yes-test*`}{`*no-text*`}`

For convenience there is also `\untagged`, which typesets its second argument if none of its labels is currently active. Finally, there is `\iftagged` with three arguments that print the second or third argument depending on the given labels in the first.

All five commands are shown in the following example:

Typeset this if tag doc is used. Typeset this if tag code is not used. Not to be! Which is it?

Typeset this for either doc or code. Typeset this always!

Now none of the variants are typeset!

```
\usepackage[doc]{tagging}
\tagged{doc}   {Typeset this if tag doc is used.}
\untagged{code}{Typeset this if tag code is not used.}
\iftagged{be} {To be or}{Not to be!}  Which is it?    \par
\tagged{doc,code}{Typeset this for either doc or code.}
Typeset this \untagged{}{always}\tagged{}{never}!      \par
\usetag{code} \droptag{doc}
Now neither of the variants are typeset!
\tagged{doc}   {Typeset this if tag doc is used.}
\untagged{code}{Typeset this if tag code is not used.}
```

This approach works well enough for shorter texts but has the limitation that it cannot contain `\verb` commands and must have balanced braces because the *text* is provided as an argument. With longer parts to be optionally printed, however, it is usually best to either store them in an external file and conditionally load this file in a `\tagged` command or use the environments shown in the next example.

Environments can contain verbatim material e.g., #&.

Note the placement of the period and the spacing! Careful:

```
\usepackage[doc]{tagging}
Environments can contain verbatim material
\begin{taggedblock}{doc} e.g., \verb=#&=\end{taggedblock}
. \par Note the placement of the period and the spacing!
Careful: \begin{untaggedblock}{doc}
                        Not \end{untaggedblock} shown!
```

Please note the surprising placement of the period. You should never place anything after the `\end{taggedblock}` or `\end{untaggedblock}`, because it gets discarded if the environment body is not typeset. This can be seen by the missing word "shown!" in the result. This may not be immediately apparent, because as long as the optional material is typeset, everything appears to be fine, but the moment the material is ignored, the rest of the last line vanishes too. Best practice is therefore to place the `\begin` and `\end` commands on lines by themselves.

The handling of space is also a bit peculiar: inside the environment body spaces are honored, except for spaces immediately following the `\begin` command. This is why we do not see two spaces in the output but only one, even though there is a space before and after `\begin`. If we had added a space before the `\end` command, it would have resulted in "# ." in the output.

31

\part	top-level	(level −1 in book and report; level 0 in article)		
\chapter	level 0	(only defined by book and report)		
\section	level 1			
\subsection	level 2		\paragraph	level 4
\subsubsection	level 3		\subparagraph	level 5

Table 2.1: LATEX's standard sectioning commands

The **tagging** package selects the variants to process during the LATEX formatting. Depending on the application, it might be better to use a different approach involving a preprocessor that extracts individual variants from the master source. For example, the **docstrip** program can be successfully used for this purpose; in contrast to other preprocessors, it has the advantage that it is usable at every site that has an installed LATEX system (see Section 17.2 for details).

2.2 Sectioning commands

In the previous section we discussed the top-level division into front, main, and back matter. Within these regions further division is done through sectional units that are typically substructured. These we discuss in this section.

The standard LATEX document classes (i.e., article, report, and book) contain commands to define the different hierarchical structural units of a document (e.g., chapters, sections, subsections, etc.). Each such command defines a nesting level inside a hierarchy, and each structural unit belongs to some level. The commands should be correctly nested. For example, a \subsection command should be issued only after a previous \section.

Standard LATEX provides the set of sectioning commands[1] shown in Table 2.1. The \chapter command defines level zero of the hierarchical structure of a document, \section defines level one, and so on, whereas the optional \part command defines the level minus one (or zero in classes that do not define \chapter). Not all of these commands are defined in all document classes. The article class does not have \chapter, and the letter class does not support sectioning commands at all. It is also possible for a package to define other sectioning commands, allowing either additional levels or variants for already supported levels.

The standard names are admittedly somewhat strange; e.g., \paragraph does not mean as one might expect "start a new text paragraph" but instead "here is the heading for the next subsubsubsection". So if you prefer a different name for such units in your documents, a definition such as

```
\newcommand\subsubsubsection{\paragraph}
```

---

[1]Using commands instead of environments to indicate the sectional units has the effect that these heading commands do not define a scope; e.g., parameter changes stay in force across different sectional units.

would easily fix that (though is that name really better?). Note that it only means your document uses a different command: the actual work is still carried out by \paragraph, and the counter associated with the unit is still called paragraph and printed with \theparagraph and so on.

\section[*toc-entry*]{*title*}   \section*{*title*}

All standard sectioning commands — i.e., \part, \chapter (only in the book and report classes), \section, \subsection, \subsubsection, \paragraph, and \subparagraph — have a common syntax as exemplified here by the \section command. Generally, the sectioning commands automatically perform one or more of the following typesetting actions:

- produce the heading number reflecting the hierarchical level;

- store the heading as an entry for a table of contents (into the .toc file);

- save the contents of the heading to be (perhaps) used in a running header/footer;

- format the heading.

The first form performs all of the above actions. If the optional argument *toc-entry* is present, it is used as the text string for the table of content and the running header and/or footer; otherwise, the *title* is also used for those places. In particular this means that you cannot specify different texts for the table of content and for the running header through this interface. The numbering depends on the current value of the counter secnumdepth (discussed in the next section).

If you try to advise TeX on how to split the heading over a few lines using the "~" symbol or the \\ command, then side effects may result when formatting the table of contents or generating the running head. In this case the simplest solution is to repeat the heading text without the specific markup in the optional parameter of the sectioning command.

Problems with explicit formatting

The starred form (e.g., \section*{...}) suppresses the numbering for a title and does not produce an entry in the table of contents or the running head. This is usually used inside the front matter and sometimes in the back matter but can, of course, be used anywhere within the document. In the standard classes, the commands \tableofcontents, \listoftables, and \listoffigures, and the theindex and thebibliography environments internally invoke the command (\section or \chapter) using their starred form.

The remainder of this section discusses how the appearance of headings can be adjusted to your needs. First we explain how heading numbers work and how they can be manipulated. We then take a quick look at the various fixed texts produced by some headings and how they can be altered. In Sections 2.2.3 to 2.2.7 we describe several packages for heading design, mainly focusing on the titlesec package, as that is a good toolbox for most heading design requirements. Finally, we conclude with a discussion of LaTeX's low-level interfaces for this area — a section largely meant for reference only (which is why it is set in a smaller font to save space).

2.2.1 Numbering headings

To support numbering, LaTeX uses a counter for each sectional unit and composes the heading number from these counters.

Perhaps the change desired most often concerning the numbering of titles is to alter the nesting level up to which a number should be produced. This is controlled by a counter named `secnumdepth`, which holds the highest level with numbered head- *Numbering no* ings. For example, some documents have none of their headings numbered. Instead *headings* of always using the starred form of the sectioning commands, it is more convenient to set the counter `secnumdepth` to −2 in the document preamble. The advantages of this method are that an entry in the table of contents can still be produced and that arguments from the sectioning commands can produce information in running headings. As discussed, these features are suppressed in the starred form.

To number all headings down to `\subparagraph` or whatever the deepest sec- *Numbering all* tioning level for the given class is called, setting the counter to a high enough value *headings* (e.g., a declaration such as `\setcounter{secnumdepth}{5}` would be sufficient for the standard classes).

Finally, the `\addtocounter` command provides an easy way of numbering more *Numbering more or* or fewer heading levels without worrying about the level numbers of the corresponding *less heading levels* sectioning commands. For example, if you need one more level with numbers, you can place `\addtocounter{secnumdepth}{1}` in the preamble of your document without having to look up the right value. In some cases this might even be useful within the document; see also the package tocvsec2 by Peter Wilson that provides further support for such occasions.

Every sectioning command has an associated counter, which by convention has the same name as the sectioning command (e.g., the command `\subsection` has a corresponding counter `subsection`). This counter stores the current number of sectional units of the level, but its print representation (that you get with `\the`*counter*) holds the full formatted number for the given sectioning command. Thus, in the report class, the commands `\chapter`, `\section`, `\subsection`, and so on, represent the hierarchical structure of the document, and a counter like `subsection` keeps track of the number of `\subsection`s used inside the current `\section`, e.g., holds the value 1 at this point in the book, while `\thesubsection` would generate 2.2.1.

Normally, when a counter at a given hierarchical level is incremented, then the next lower-level counter (i.e., that with the next higher-level number) is reset. For example, the report class file contains the following declarations:

```
\newcounter{part}                         % (-1)  parts
\newcounter{chapter}                       % (0)   chapters
\newcounter{section}[chapter]              % (1)   sections
\newcounter{subsection}[section]           % (2)   subsections
\newcounter{subsubsection}[subsection]     % (3)   subsubsections
\newcounter{paragraph}[subsubsection]      % (4)   paragraphs
\newcounter{subparagraph}[paragraph]       % (5)   subparagraphs
```

These commands declare the various counters. The level one (`section`) counter is reset when the level zero (`chapter`) counter is stepped. Similarly, the level two (`subsection`) counter is reset whenever the level one (`section`) counter is stepped. The same mechanism is used down to the `\subparagraph` command. Note that in the standard classes the `part` counter is decoupled from the other counters and has no influence on the lower-level sectioning commands. As a consequence, `\chapters` in the book or report class or `\sections` in article are numbered consecutively even if a `\part` command intervenes. Changing this inside a class is simple — you just replace the corresponding declaration of the chapter counter with:

```
\newcounter{chapter}[part]
```

The behavior of an already existing counter can be changed with the commands `\counterwithin` or `\counterwithout` (see Appendix A.2.1); for example, to alter the behavior for just a single document, you can use

```
\counterwithin{chapter}{part}
```

Every counter in LaTeX, including the sectioning counters, has an associated command constructed by prefixing the counter name with `\the`, which generates a typeset representation of the counter in question. In the case of the sectioning commands, this representation form is used to produce the full number associated with the commands, as in the following definitions:

```
\renewcommand\thechapter{\arabic{chapter}}
\renewcommand\thesection{\thechapter.\arabic{section}}
\renewcommand\thesubsection{\thesection.\arabic{subsection}}
```

In this example, `\thesubsection` produces an Arabic number representation of the `subsection` counter prefixed by the command `\thesection` and a dot. This kind of recursive definition facilitates modifications to the counter representations because changes do not need to be made in more than one place. If, for example, you want to number sections using capital letters, you can redefine the command `\thesection`:

A Different-looking section

A.1 Different-looking subsection

Due to the default definitions not only the numbers on sections change, but lower-level sectioning commands also show this representation of the section number.

```
\renewcommand\thesection{\Alph{section}}
\section{Different-looking section}
\subsection{Different-looking subsection}
Due to the default definitions not only the
numbers on sections change, but lower-level
sectioning commands also show this
representation of the section number.
```

2-2-1

Thus, by changing the counter representation commands, it is possible to change the number displayed by a sectioning command. However, the representation of the number cannot be changed arbitrarily by this method. Suppose you want to produce a subsection heading with the number surrounded by a box. Given the above examples, one straightforward approach would be to redefine \thesubsection; e.g.,

```
\renewcommand\thesubsection{\fbox{\thesection.\arabic{subsection}}}
```

But this is not a good approach, as one sees when trying to reference such a section.

3.1   A mistake

Referencing a subsection in this format produces a funny result as we can see looking at subsection 3.1 . We get a boxed reference.

```
\renewcommand\thesubsection
    {\fbox{\thesection.\arabic{subsection}}}
\setcounter{section}{3}
\subsection{A mistake}\label{wrong}
Referencing a subsection in this format produces
a funny result as we can see looking at
subsection~\ref{wrong}. We get a boxed reference.
```

2-2-2

In other words, the counter representation commands are also used by LATEX's cross-referencing mechanism (the \label and \ref commands; see Section 2.4). Therefore, we can make only small changes to the counter representation commands so that their use in the \ref command still makes sense. To produce the box around the heading number without spoiling the output of a \ref, we would have to redefine LATEX's internal command \@seccntformat, which is responsible for typesetting the counter part of a section title. As this is rather messy, it is better to use the interface provided by the titlesec package for this, which is what we do in the next example.

1   This is correct

Referencing a section using this definition generates the correct result for the section reference 1.

```
\usepackage{titlesec}
\titlelabel{\fbox{\thetitle}\hspace{0.5em}}
\section{This is correct}\label{sec:OK}
Referencing a section using this definition
generates the correct result for the section
reference~\ref{sec:OK}.
```

2-2-3

The framed box around the number in the section heading is now typeset only as part of the heading, and hence the reference labels come out correctly. Within \titlelabel the command \thetitle refers to the section counter representation; e.g., it evaluates to \thesection in this case. Also note that we reduced the space between the box and the text to 0.5em (instead of the default 1em). Another often asked for use case for \titlelabel is adding a period after the heading number (but not when referencing it). This is shown in Example 2-2-8 on page 41.

A declaration done with \titlelabel applies to all headings. Therefore, if you wish to use different definitions for different headings, you must put the appropriate code into every heading definition instead (which requires the extended interface of titlesec; see page 42).

2.2.2   Changing fixed heading texts

Some of the standard heading commands produce predefined texts. For example, \chapter produces the string "Chapter" in front of the user-supplied text. Similarly,

Command	Default String	Command	Default String
\abstractname	Abstract	\indexname	Index
\appendixname	Appendix	\listfigurename	List of Figures
\bibname	Bibliography	\listtablename	List of Tables
\chaptername	Chapter	\partname	Part
\contentsname	Contents	\refname	References

\refname *is used by* article *class;* \bibname *by* report *and* book.

Table 2.2: Language-dependent strings for headings

some environments generate headings with predefined texts. For example, by default the abstract environment displays the word "Abstract" above the text of the abstract supplied by the user. LaTeX defines these strings as command sequences (see Table 2.2) so that you can easily customize them to obtain your favorite names. This is shown in the example below, where the default name "Abstract", as defined in the article class, is replaced by the word "Summary".

Summary

This book describes how to modify the appearance of LaTeX documents.

2-2-4

```
\renewcommand\abstractname{Summary}
\begin{abstract}
This book describes how to modify the
appearance of \LaTeX{} documents.
\end{abstract}
```

The standard LaTeX class files define a few more strings. See Section 13.1.3, and especially Table 13.2 on page →II 305, for a full list and a discussion of the babel system, which provides translations of these strings in more than sixty languages.

2.2.3 Introduction to heading design

Headings can be loosely subdivided into two major groups: display and run-in headings. A display heading is separated by a vertical space from the preceding and the following text — most headings in this book are of this type.

A run-in heading is characterized by a vertical separation from the preceding text, but the text following the title continues on the same line as the heading itself, only separated from the latter by a horizontal space. In many classes the lower-level headings such as \paragraph are formatted as run-in headings. Note that an empty line after the heading command is ignored.

Run-in headings. This example shows how a run-in heading looks like. Paragraph text following the heading continues on the same line as the heading.

2-2-5

```
\paragraph{Run-in headings.}
This example shows how a run-in heading looks
like.  Paragraph text following the heading
continues on the same line as the heading.
```

In the remainder of this section we are now going to look at how display and run-in headings can be designed and how one can adjust a given design. We start by looking at two packages that offer a somewhat special feature: they add quotations to display headings.

We then discuss all other design aspects that are supported through the high-level interfaces of the titlesec package. At the very end we also briefly look at the low-level support offered by LATEX because this is helpful in understanding the code found in older document class files.

2.2.4 quotchap, epigraph — Mottos on chapters and sections

An interesting way to enhance `\chapter` headings is provided by the `quotchap` package created by Karsten Tinnefeld with later updates by Jan Klever. It allows the user to specify quotation(s) that will appear on the top left of the chapter title area.

The quotation(s) for the next chapter are specified in a `savequote` environment; the width of the quotation area can be given as an optional argument defaulting to `10cm`. Each quotation should finish with a `\qauthor` command to denote its source, though it would be possible to provide your own formatting manually.

The default layout produced by the package can be described as follows: the quotations are typeset in `\slshape`, placed flush left, followed by vertical material stored in the command `\chapterheadstartvskip`. It is followed by a very large chapter number, typeset flush right in 60% gray, followed by the chapter title text, also typeset flush right. After a further vertical separation, taken from the command `\chapterheadendvskip`, the first paragraph of the chapter is started without indentation.

The number can be printed in black by specifying the option `nogrey` to the package. To print the chapter number in one of the many freely available fonts, you can choose among a dozen of options, such as `charter` for Bitstream's Charter BT or `times` for Adobe's Times. By default, Adobe's Bookman is chosen. Alternatively, you can explicitly specify a font family (basically any of those listed in the tables in Chapter 10) as an argument to `\qsetcnfont`. Or you could redefine the `\chapnumfont` command, which is ultimately responsible for selecting the font and font size for the chapter number.

The `\quotefont` command defines the font used for the quote, and with the help of `\qauthorfont` you can alter the font for the author name (which is why we still get a sans serif font in the example even though only `\scshape` was specified). Finally, the font for the chapter title font can be influenced by redefining the `\sectfont` command as shown in the example.

This, together with the possibilities offered by redefining the commands `\chapterheadstartvskip` and `\chapterheadendvskip`, allows you to produce a number of interesting layouts even though a lot remains hardwired.[1] The following example uses a negative vertical skip to move the quotation on the same level as the number (in Avantgarde) and set the title and quotation in Helvetica (or more exactly in TEX Gyre Heros).

---

[1] If you require more customization, you have to define your own variation of the command `\@makechapterhead` starting from the code found in the package.

Cookies! Give me some cookies!
Cookie Monster

A Package Test

```
\usepackage[avantgarde]{quotchap}
\renewcommand\chapterheadstartvskip
              {\vspace*{-5\baselineskip}}
% select TeX Gyre Heros for title and quote:
\usepackage{tgheros}
\renewcommand\sectfont{\sffamily\bfseries}
\renewcommand\quotefont{\sffamily\slshape}
\renewcommand\qauthorfont{\scshape}

\begin{savequote}[10pc]
 Cookies! Give me some cookies!
 \qauthor{Cookie Monster}
\end{savequote}
\chapter{A Package Test}
```

Adding this package changes the chapter heading dramatically.

```
Adding this package changes the chapter
heading dramatically.
```

2-2-6

With the quotchap package the quotation is directly integrated into the design of the chapter heading. The epigraph package by Peter Wilson has a different approach; here the quotation is typeset after the heading (using the command \epigraph or the environment epigraphs), and the heading command itself has no knowledge of it. On one hand this is more versatile; on the other it clearly means that designs that properly interact with the heading text are not possible.

The package offers a lot of configuration possibilities, typically by redefining some command or setting a dimension. A few of them are shown in the next example (but actually using the default values, so none of the redefinitions has any effect). For others you have to consult the package documentation.

1 A Package Test

Cookies! Give me some cookies!

Cookie Monster

```
\usepackage{epigraph}
 \setlength\epigraphwidth{.4\textwidth}
 \renewcommand\epigraphsize {\small}
 \renewcommand\epigraphflush{flushright}
 \renewcommand\sourceflush  {flushright}

\section{A Package Test}
\epigraph{Cookies! Give me some cookies!}
         {Cookie Monster}
```

When adding a quote, the paragraph following it comes out indented. If you do not like this, you have to use \noindent at the beginning of this paragraph.

```
When adding a quote, the paragraph following
it comes out indented. If you do not like
this, you have to use \verb=\noindent= at
the  beginning of this paragraph.
```

2-2-7

There are also mechanisms to place an epigraph onto a chapter or part heading using the command \epigraphhead; see the package documentation for details.

2.2.5 indentfirst — Indent the first paragraph after a heading

Standard LaTeX document classes and many others, following (American) English typographic tradition, suppress the indentation of the first paragraph after a display heading. While this can be changed with an option to titlesec (see below), it can also be done through the little[1] package indentfirst by David Carlisle, regardless of whether or not the titlesec package is loaded.

2.2.6 nonumonpart — No page numbers on parts

Another often asked for adjustment is to drop page numbers on part titles. On chapter headings this can be easily manually achieved using `\thispagestyle{empty}`, but because `\part`s in many classes occupy a whole page, there is no possibility to place such a declaration.[2] To solve this without any manual work someone suggested a few lines of code, and Yvon Henel took the effort to put them into the little nonumonpart package. It works for the standard classes report and book and any other class that is derived from them. All you have to do is load the package; there are no options or other customization possibilities.

2.2.7 titlesec — A package approach to heading design

The titlesec package created by Javier Bezos provides a flexible and fairly compre-hensive reimplementation of the basic heading tools offered by Standard LATEX and is therefore a good choice if adjustments are wanted or new document classes are to be designed. It works together with most document classes in existence; notable exceptions are memoir and the KOMA-Script classes, both of which have their own tools for setting up heading structures that need to be used.

Javier's approach overcomes some of the limitations inherent in the original LATEX tools and provides a cleaner and more generic interface. The package supports two interfaces: a simple one for smaller adjustments, which is realized mainly by options to the package, and an extended interface to make more elaborate modifications.

The basic interface

The basic interface lets you modify the font characteristics of all headings by spec-ifying one or more options to set a font family (rm, sf, tt), a font series (md, bf), or a font shape (up, it, sl, sc). The title size can be influenced by selecting one of the following options: big (same sizes as for standard LATEX classes), tiny (all headings except for chapters in text size), medium, or small, which are layouts between the two extremes. The alignment is controlled by raggedleft, center, or raggedright, while the vertical spacing can be reduced by specifying the option compact as shown later.

To modify the format of the number accompanying a heading, the command `\titlelabel` is available. Within it `\thetitle` refers to the current sectioning

---

[1] This package probably holds the record of "the shortest package in the LATEX world": besides 40 lines of comments it consists of two lines of code.

[2] Well, you could try to put it into the heading title, but you will soon find that this not a good place for a number of reasons (though one can make it work with the help of the optional argument to the `\part` command).

number, such as \thesection or \thesubsection. The declaration applies to all headings, as can be seen in the next example:

1. A section

1.1. A subsection

1.1.1. A subsubsection

Three headings following each other, a situation you will not see very often …

```
\usepackage[sf,bf,tiny,center]{titlesec}
\titlelabel{\thetitle.\enspace}
\section{A section}
\subsection{A subsection}
\subsubsection{A subsubsection}
Three headings following each other, a situation you
will not see very often \ldots
```

2-2-8

```
\titleformat*{cmd}{format}
```

The basic interface offers one more command, \titleformat*, that takes two arguments. The first argument (*cmd*) is a sectioning command that we intend to modify. The second argument (*format*) contains the formatting instruction that should be applied to this particular heading. This declaration works on individual sectioning commands, and its use overwrites all font or alignment specifications given as options to the package (i.e., the options rm, it, and raggedleft in the following example). The last command used in the second argument can be a command with one argument — it receives the title text if present. In the next example we use this feature to set the \subsubsection title in small capitals (though this looks rather ugly with full-sized numbers).

1   A section

1.1   A subsection

1.1.1   A SUBSUBSECTION

Three headings following each other, a situation you will not see very often …

```
\usepackage[rm,it,raggedleft,tiny,compact]{titlesec}
\titleformat*{\subsubsection}{\scshape\MakeLowercase}
\section{A section}
\subsection{A subsection}
\subsubsection{A subsubsection}
Three headings following each other, a situation you
will not see very often \ldots
```

2-2-9

In many LaTeX document classes (with or without loading titlesec), words in long headings are justified and, if necessary, hyphenated as can be seen in the next example. If this is not wanted, line breaks can be manually adjusted using \\, but then one has to repeat the heading title, without the extra formatting instruction, in the optional argument. Otherwise, the line breaks also show up in the table of contents.

Hyphenation and line breaks in headings

1   A very long heading that shows the default behavior of LaTeX's sectioning commands

Nulla malesuada porttitor diam. Donec felis erat, congue non, volutpat at, tincidunt tristique, libero.

```
\usepackage{lipsum,titlesec}

\section{A very long heading that
          shows the default behavior of
          \LaTeX's sectioning commands}
\lipsum[3][1-2]
```

2-2-10

Alternatively, one can use the option `raggedright` from the simple interface, which then applies to all heading, or use the extended interface to make a dedicated decision for each heading level separately.

1 A very long heading that shows the default behavior of LaTeX's sectioning commands

Nulla malesuada porttitor diam. Donec felis erat, congue non, volutpat at, tincidunt tristique, libero. Vivamus viverra fermentum felis.

```
\usepackage[raggedright]{titlesec}
\usepackage{lipsum}

\section{A very long heading that
    shows the default behavior of
    \LaTeX's sectioning commands}
\lipsum[3][1-3]
```

2-2-11

Interpretation of heading command arguments

Two other options may offer some extra help for such cases: if you specify `newlinetospace`, then any `\\` or `\\*` in the heading text is replaced by a space before the text is passed on to the table of contents or into the running header so that it is not necessary to use the optional argument to the heading command, just because the text has explicit line breaks. The option `toctitles` changes the use of the optional argument so that it is only specifying the text for the running header while the TOC always receives the full text.

Indentation after heading

The paragraph indentation for the first paragraph following the headings can be globally specified using the package options `indentafter` or `noindentafter`. With the extended interface this can be done for individual heading levels.

Adjusting "empty" pages

If chapter headings always appear on recto pages (by internally issuing a `\cleardoublepage` command), then this often generates an empty verso page — except that this page may still contain a page number or a running header. To force such pages to be totally empty you can specify the option `clearempty`. See also the `nextpage` package discussed in Section 5.6.4 on page 418 for alternative approaches.

\part* in the TOC

For some reason the default for `\part*` used by titlesec is that these headings show up in the table of contents. If that is not wanted, use the option `notocpart*`. The `\part` heading is otherwise not influenced by settings for the basic interface. If you want to modify it, you must use the extended interface described below.

Fixing a TOC problem with \part

Another option specific to `\part` commands is `newparttoc`. This changes the entries generated in the TOC so that they can be manipulated by the titletoc package, which is normally not the case as they have a nonstandard definition in most LaTeX classes. See the discussion on page 72 for details.

The extended interface

The extended interface consists of two major commands, `\titleformat` and `\titlespacing`. They allow you to declare the "inner" format (i.e., fonts, label, alignment, ...) and the "outer" format (i.e., spacing, indentation, etc.), respectively. This scheme was adopted because people often wish to alter only one or the other aspect of the layout.

\titleformat{*cmd*} [*shape*] {*format*}{*label*}{*sep*}{*before-code*} [*after-code*]

The first argument (*cmd*) is the heading command name (e.g., \section) whose format is to be modified. In contrast to LaTeX's \@startsection (see Section 2.2.8 on page 51) this argument requires the command name — that is, with the backslash in front. The remaining arguments have the following meaning:

shape   The basic shape for the heading. A number of predefined shapes are available: hang, the default, produces a hanging label (like \section in standard classes); display puts label and heading text on separate lines (like standard \chapter); while runin produces a run-in title (like standard \paragraph).

In addition, the following shapes, which have no equivalents in standard LaTeX, are provided: frame is similar to display but frames the title; leftmargin puts the title into the left margin, while rightmargin places it into the right margin. The last two shapes might conflict with \marginpar commands; that is, they may overlap.

A general-purpose shape is block, which typesets the heading as a single block. It should be preferred to hang for centered layouts.

Both drop and wrap wrap the first paragraph around the title, with drop using a fixed width for the title and wrap using the width of the widest title line (automatically breaking the title within the limit forced by the *left-sep* argument of \titlespacing).

format   The declarations that are applied to the whole title — label and text. They may include only vertical material, which is typeset following the space above the heading. If you need horizontal material, it should be entered in the *label* or *before-code* argument.

label   The formatting of the label, that is, the heading number. To refer to the number itself, use \thesection or whatever is appropriate. For defining \chapter headings the package offers \chaptertitlename, which produces \chaptername or \appendixname, depending on the position of the heading in the document.

sep   Length whose value determines the distance between the label and title text. Depending on the *shape* argument, it might be a vertical or horizontal separation. For example, with the frame shape, it specifies the distance between the frame and heading text.

before-code   Code executed immediately preceding the heading text. Its last command can take one argument, which will pick up the heading text and thus permits more complicated manipulations (see Example 2-2-15).

Since version 2.7, it is possible to load the package with the option explicit in which case the heading text *must* be given explicitly as #1 inside *before-code*. This makes the declaration somewhat clearer, and you can do any manipulations directly instead of defining a command with one argument to do the job.

after-code   Optional code to be executed after formatting the heading text (still within the scope of the declarations given in *format*). For hang, block, and display, it is executed in vertical mode; with `runin`, it is executed in horizontal mode. For other shapes, it has no effect.

If the starred form of a heading is used, the *label* and *sep* arguments are ignored because no number is produced.

The next example shows a more old-fashioned run-in heading, for which we define only the format, not the spacing around the heading. The latter is manipulated with the `\titlespacing` command.

```
\usepackage{titlesec}
\titleformat{\section}[runin]{\normalfont\scshape}
    {\S\,\oldstylenums{\thesection}.}{.5em}{}[.]
```

§1. THE TITLE. The heading is separated from the section text by a dot and a space of one quad.

```
\section{The Title}
The heading is separated from the section text by
a dot and a space of one quad.
```

2-2-12

By default, LATEX's `\section` headings are not indented (they are usually of *shape* hang). If you prefer a normal paragraph indentation with such a heading, you could add `\indent` before the `\S` sign or specify the indentation with the `\titlespacing` declaration, described next.

```
\titlespacing*{cmd}{left-sep}{before-sep}{after-sep}[right-sep]
```

The starred form of the command suppresses the paragraph indentation for the paragraph following the title, except with shapes where the heading and paragraph are combined, such as `runin` and `drop`. The *cmd* argument holds the heading command name to be manipulated. The remaining arguments are as follows:

left-sep Length specifying the increase of the left margin for headings with the `block`, `display`, `hang`, or `frame` shape. With `...margin` or `drop` shapes it specifies the width of the heading title, with `wrap` it specifies the maximum width for the title, and with `runin` it specifies the indentation before the title (negative values would make the title hang into the left margin).

before-sep Length specifying the vertical space added above the heading.

after-sep Length specifying the separation between the heading and the following paragraph. It can be a vertical or horizontal space depending on the shape deployed.

right-sep Optional length specifying an increase of the right margin, which is supported for the shapes `block`, `display`, `hang`, and `frame`.

In the case of a run-in heading, *after-sep* is the horizontal space after the heading that by default is usually noticeably wider than a normal word space. This is reasonable for headings such as the one in Example 2-2-12 but not if the heading and following text are forming a sentence in which case we want a normal word space. For this you can use \wordsep in *after-sep*, which refers to the interword space (including stretch and shrink) of the current font.

... some text above.

THE MAN started to run away from the truck. He saw that he was followed by the ...

2-2-13

```
\usepackage{titlesec}
\titleformat {\paragraph} [runin] {\normalfont\scshape}{}{0pt}{}
\titlespacing{\paragraph}{\parindent}{\medskipamount}{\wordsep}
\noindent \ldots\ some text above.
\paragraph{The man} started to run away from the truck.
He saw that he was followed by the \ldots
```

The *before-sep* and *after-sep* arguments usually receive rubber length values to allow some flexibility in the design. To simplify the declaration you can alternatively specify *f* (where *f* is a decimal factor). This is equivalent to *f* ex with some stretchability as well as a small shrinkability inside *before-sep*, and an even smaller stretchability and no shrinkability inside *after-sep*.

...some text before ...

┌─────── SECTION 1 ───────┐
│ **A Title Test** │
└─────────────────────────┘

Some text to prove that this paragraph is not indented and that the title has a margin of 1pc on either side.

2-2-14

```
\usepackage{titlesec}
\titleformat{\section}[frame]{\normalfont}
   {\footnotesize \enspace SECTION \thesection
     \enspace}{6pt}{\large\bfseries\filcenter}
\titlespacing*{\section}{1pc}{*4}{*2.3}[1pc]
\noindent \ldots some text before \ldots
\section{A Title Test}
Some text to prove that this paragraph is not indented
and that the title has a margin of 1pc on either side.
```

The previous example introduced \filcenter, but there are also \filleft, \filright, and \fillast — the latter produces an adjusted paragraph but centers the last line. These commands should be preferred to \raggedleft or \raggedright inside \titleformat, as the latter would cancel *left-sep* or *right-sep* set up by the \titlespacing command. Alternatively, you can use \filinner or \filouter, which resolve to \filleft or \filright, depending on the current page. However, due to TeX's asynchronous page makeup algorithm, they are supported only for headings that start a new page — for example, \chapter in most designs. See Example 2-2-17 on page 49 for a solution to this problem for other headings. Another useful spacing command we already used in Example 2-2-13 is \wordsep, which refers to the current interword space.

Spacing tools for headings

By default, the spacing between two consecutive headings is defined to be the *after-sep* of the first one. If this result is not desired, you can change it by specifying the option largestsep, which puts the spacing to the maximum of *after-sep* from the first heading and *before-sep* of the second.

Spacing between consecutive headings

Normally the vertical space occupied by a display heading is the sum of *before-sep*, the size of the actual heading text, and the *after-sep*; i.e., it varies depending on the number of lines in the heading. However, in some designs the text following the chapter heading should always start at the same point regardless. This can be achieved

Space reserved for chapter headings

by specifying the option `rigidchapters`. If used, *after-sep* no longer specifies the space below the heading but always measured from the top of the heading text; i.e., the sum of *before-sep* and *after-sep* defines the space reserved for the heading. Despite its name, the option applies to any heading of class `top`; see page 50.

Headings at page bottom

After a heading LATEX tries to ensure that at least two lines from the following paragraph appear on the same page as the heading title. If this proves impossible, the heading is moved to the next page. If you think that two lines are not enough, try the option `nobottomtitles` or `nobottomtitles*`, which move headings to a new page whenever the remaining space on the page is less than the current value of `\bottomtitlespace`. (Its default is `.2\textheight`; to change its value, use `\renewcommand` rather than `\setlength`.) The starred version is preferred, as it computes the remaining space with more accuracy, unless you use headings with `drop`, `margin`, or `wrap` shapes, which may get badly placed when deploying the starred option.

Handling unusual layouts

In most heading layouts the number appears either on top or to the left of the heading text. If this placement is not appropriate, the *label* argument of `\titleformat` cannot be used. Instead, one has to exploit the fact that the *before-code* can pick up the heading text. In the next example, the command `\secformat` has one argument that defines the formatting for the heading text and number; we then call this command in the *before-code* argument of `\titleformat`. Note that the font change for the number is kept local by surrounding it with braces. Without them the changed font size might influence the title spacing in some circumstances.

```
\usepackage{titlesec}
\newcommand\secformat[1]{%
  \parbox[b]{.5\textwidth}{\filleft\bfseries #1}%
  \quad\rule[-12pt]{2pt}{70pt}\quad
  {\fontsize{60}{60}\selectfont\thesection}}
\titleformat{\section}[block]
  {\filleft\normalfont\sffamily}{}{0pt}{\secformat}
\titlespacing*{\section}{0pt}{*3}{*2}[1pc]
```

A Title on Two Lines 1

```
\section{A Title\\ on Two Lines}
```

In this example the heading number appears to the right of the heading text.

In this example the heading number appears to the right of the heading text.

2-2-15

The same technique can be applied to change the heading text in other ways. For example, if we want a period after the heading text, we could define

```
\newcommand\secformat[1]{#1.}
```

and then call `\secformat` in the last mandatory argument of the `\titleformat` declaration as shown in the previous example. Alternatively, we could have used the option `explicit` in which case such manipulations could have been done inline with `#1` referencing the heading text inside that argument.

Measuring the width of the title

The `wrap` shape has the capability to measure the lines in the title text and return the width of the widest line in `\titlewidth`. This capability can be extended to three other shapes (block, display, and hang) by loading the package with the option calcwidth and then using \titlewidth within the arguments of \titleformat, as needed.

Measuring the title means trial typesetting it, and thus it is typeset twice. In some cases that can have undesirable side effects. For special requirements, the package therefore offers the command \iftitlemeasuring. It takes two arguments: the first is executed during the trial and the second when the heading is finally typeset.

For rules and leaders the package offers the \titlerule command. Used without any arguments it produces a rule of height .4pt spanning the full width of the column (but taking into account changes to the margins as specified with the \titlespacing declaration). An optional argument lets you specify a height for the produced rule. The starred form of \titlerule is used to produce leaders (i.e., repeated objects) instead of rules. It takes an optional *width* argument and a mandatory *text* argument. The *text* is repeatedly typeset in boxes with its natural width, unless a different *width* is specified in the optional argument. In that case, only the first and last boxes retain their natural widths to allow for proper alignment on either side.

Rules and leaders

The command \titleline lets you add horizontal material to arguments of \titleformat that expect vertical material. It takes an optional argument specifying the alignment and a mandatory argument containing the material to typeset. It produces a box of fixed width taking into account the marginal changes due to the \titlespacing declaration. Thus, either the material needs to contain some rubber space, or you must specify an alignment through the optional argument (allowed values are l, r, and c).

The \titleline* variant first typesets the material from its mandatory argument in a box of width \titlewidth (so you may have to add rubber space to this argument) and then uses this box as input to \titleline (i.e., aligns it according to the optional argument). Remember that you may have to use the option calcwidth to ensure that \titlewidth contains a sensible value.

In the next somewhat artificial example, which is worth studying though better not used in real life, all of these tools are applied together:

Section 1

Rules and Leaders
LATEXLATEXLATEXLATEXLATEXLATEXLATEX

```
\usepackage[noindentafter,calcwidth]{titlesec}
\titleformat{\section}[display]
  {\filright\normalfont\bfseries\sffamily}
  {\titleline[r]{Section \Huge\thesection}}{1ex}
  {\titleline*[l]{\titlerule[1pt]}\vspace{1pt}%
    \titleline*[l]{\titlerule[2pt]}\vspace{2pt}}
  [{\titleline*[l]{\titlerule*{\tiny\LaTeX}}}]
\titlespacing{\section}{1pc}{*3}{*2}
```

Note that the last \titleline* is surrounded by braces. Without them its optional argument would prematurely end the outer optional argument of \titleformat.

```
\section{Rules and Leaders}
Note that the last \verb=\titleline*= is
surrounded by braces. Without them its
optional argument would prematurely end the
outer optional argument of \verb=\titleformat=.
```

2-2-16

47

Breaking before a heading

Standard LaTeX considers the space before a heading to be a good place to break the page unless the heading immediately follows another heading. The penalty to break at this point is stored in the internal counter `\@secpenalty`, and in many classes it holds the value −300 (negative values are bonus places for breaking). Because only one penalty value is available for all heading levels, there is seldom any point in modifying its setting. With titlesec, however, you can exert finer control: whenever a command `\`*name*`break` is defined (where `\`*name* is the name of a sectioning command, such as `\sectionbreak`), the latter will be used instead of adding the default penalty. For example,

```
\newcommand\sectionbreak{\clearpage}
```

would result in sections always appearing on top of a page with all pending floats being typeset first. This interface also exists for headings of class top. For example, you can force parts to always start on a recto page, while chapters could be set to just start a new page by using `\cleardoublepage` and `\clearpage`, respectively. However, you have to first change their class to page or top, because this is not automatically done. Heading classes are explained on page 50.

Always keeping the space above a heading

In some layouts the space above a heading must be preserved, even if the heading appears on top of a page (by default, such spaces vanish at page breaks). This can be accomplished using a definition like the following:

```
\newcommand\sectionbreak{\addpenalty{-300}\vspace*{0pt}}
```

The `\addpenalty` command indicates a (good) breakpoint, which is followed by a zero space that cannot vanish. Thus, the "before" space from the heading will appear as well at the top of the page if a break is taken at the penalty.

Special page styles

Headings that start a new page often require a special page style; e.g., `\chapter` commands in the standard styles usually use plain even if for other pages a different style has been set up. To accommodate adjustments titlesec offers the command `\assignpagestyle`. For example,

```
\assignpagestyle{\chapter}{empty}
```

results in pages starting a new chapter to have neither a page number nor a running header. This command works with any heading of class top or page; see page 50. There are, however, restrictions when the sectioning command was not defined with titlesec; e.g., when using the standard document classes, it works for `\chapter` but not for `\part`. For the latter you first have to redeclare a format with `\titleformat`.

Conditional heading layouts

So far we have seen how to define fixed layouts for a heading command using `\titleformat` and `\titlespacing`. The titlesec package also allows you to conditionally change the layout on verso and recto pages and to use special layouts for numberless headings (i.e., those produced by the starred form of the heading command).

This is implemented through a keyword/value syntax in the first argument of `\titleformat` and `\titlespacing`. The available keys are name, page (values odd or even), and numberless (values true or false). In fact, the syntax we have seen so far, \titleformat{\section}{..}..., is simply an abbreviation for the general form \titleformat{name=\section}{..}....

In contrast to the spacing commands \filinner and \filouter, which can be used only with headings that start a new page, the page keyword enables you to define layouts that depend on the current page without any restriction. To specify the layout for a verso (left-hand) page, use the value even; for a recto (right-hand) page, use the value odd. Such settings only affect a document typeset in twoside mode. Otherwise, all pages are considered to be recto in LaTeX. In the following example we use a block shape and shift the heading to one side, depending on the current page. In a similar fashion you could implement headings that are placed in the margin by using the shapes leftmargin and rightmargin.

The example also shows that placing declarations into the *format* argument affects both number and title, while placing them into *before-code* affects only the title: both are in bold, but only the text is in bold italics.

1. *A Head* Lorem ipsum dolor sit amet, consectetuer adipiscing elit. Ut purus elit, vestibulum ut, placerat ac, adipiscing vitae, felis. Curabitur dictum	gravida mauris. Nam arcu libero, nonummy eget, consectetuer id, vulputate a, magna. **2. *Another*** Lorem ipsum dolor sit amet, consectetuer

```
\usepackage{lipsum,titlesec}
\titleformat{name=\section,page=odd}[block]
    {\normalfont\bfseries}{\thesection.}{6pt}
    {\itshape\filleft}
\titleformat{name=\section,page=even}[block]
    {\normalfont\bfseries}{\thesection.}{6pt}
    {\itshape\filright}
\section{A Head}      \lipsum[1][1-4]
\section{Another}     \lipsum[1][1-4]
```

2-2-17

Similarly, the numberless key is used to specify that a certain \titleformat or \titlespacing declaration should apply only to headings without numbers (value true) or to those with numbers (value false). By default, a heading declaration applies to both cases, so in the example the second declaration actually overwrites part of the first declaration. To illustrate what is possible the example uses quite different designs for the two cases — do not mistake this for an attempt to show good taste. It is important to realize that neither the *label* nor the *sep* argument is ignored when numberless is set to true as seen in the example — in normal circumstances you would probably use {}{0pt} as values.

1. A Head

Some text to fill the page. Some text to fill the page.

— *Another*

Some text to fill this line.

```
\usepackage{titlesec}
\titleformat{name=\section}[block]
    {\normalfont\bfseries}{\thesection.}{6pt}{\filright}
\titleformat{name=\section,numberless=true}[block]
    {\normalfont}{---}{12pt}{\itshape\filcenter}
\section{A Head}
Some text to fill the page. Some text to fill the page.
\section*{Another}
Some text to fill this line.
```

2-2-18

Changing the heading hierarchy

The commands described so far are intended to adjust the formatting and spacing of existing heading commands. With the \titleclass declaration it is possible to define new headings.

```
\titleclass{cmd}{class}
\titleclass{cmd}{class}[parent-level-cmd]
\titleclass{cmd}[start-level]{class}              (with loadonly option)
```

There are three classes of headings: the page class contains headings that fill a full page (like \part in LaTeX's report and book document classes); the top class contains headings that start a new page and thus appear at the top of a page; and all other headings are considered to be part of the straight class.

Used without any optional argument, the \titleclass declaration simply changes the heading class of an existing heading *cmd*. For example,

```
\titleclass\section{top}
```

would result in sections always starting a new page. Note, however, that the existing *cmd* should have been defined using titlesec or at least should have been given a format with \titleformat in order to work. Otherwise you get an error message.

If this declaration is used with the optional *parent-level-cmd* argument, you introduce a new heading level below *parent-level-cmd*. Any existing heading command at this level is moved one level down in the hierarchy. For example,

```
\titleclass\subchapter{straight}[\chapter]
```

introduces the heading \subchapter between \chapter and \section. The declaration does not define any layout for this heading (which needs to be defined by an additional \titleformat and \titlespacing command), nor does it initialize the necessary counter. Most likely you also want to update the counter representation for \section:

```
\titleformat{\subchapter}{..}...    \titlespacing{\subchapter}{..}...
\newcounter{subchapter}
\renewcommand\thesubchapter{\thechapter.\arabic{subchapter}}
\renewcommand\thesection{\thesubchapter.\arabic{section}}
```

The third variant of \titleclass is needed only when you want to build a heading structure from scratch — for example, when you are designing a completely new document class that is not based on one of the standard classes. In that case load the package with the option loadonly so that the package will make no attempt to interpret existing heading commands so as to extract their current layout. You can then start building heading commands, as in the following example:

```
\titleclass\Ahead[0]{top}
\titleclass\Bhead{straight}[\Ahead]
\titleclass\Chead{straight}[\Bhead]
```

```
\newcounter{Ahead} \newcounter{Bhead} \newcounter{Chead}
\renewcommand\theBhead{\theAhead-\arabic{Bhead}}
\renewcommand\theChead{\theBhead-\arabic{Chead}}
\titleformat{name=\Ahead}{..}...   \titlespacing{name=\Ahead}{..}...
\titleformat{name=\Bhead}{..}...        ...
```

The *start-level* is usually 0 or −1; see the introduction in Section 2.2 for its meaning. There should be precisely one \titleclass declaration that uses this particular optional argument.

If you intend to build your own document classes in this way, take a look at the documentation accompanying the titlesec package. It contains additional examples and offers further tips and tricks.

2.2.8 Formatting headings — LaTeX's internal low-level methods

While it is recommended to use the higher-level interfaces provided by titlesec or those defined by KOMA-Script or the memoir class, it is useful to have a basic understanding of the interfaces defined in the LaTeX kernel, given that these interfaces are still in use in many document classes.[1]

LaTeX provides a generic command called \@startsection that can be used to define a wide variety of heading layouts. If the desired layout is not achievable that way, then \secdef can be used to produce sectioning formats with arbitrary layout. It is used by the standard classes to define \chapter and \part headings.

The generic command \@startsection allows both types of headings to be defined. Its syntax and argument description are as follows:

> \@startsection{*name*}{*level*}{*indent*}{*beforeskip*}{*afterskip*}{*style*}

name The name used to refer to the heading counter[2] for numbered headings and to define the command that generates a running header or footer (see page 390). For example, *name* would be the counter name, \the*name* would be the command to display the current heading number, and *name*mark would be the command for running headers. In most circumstances the *name* will be identical to the name of the sectioning command being defined, without the preceding backslash — but this is no requirement.

level A number denoting the depth level of the sectioning command. This level is used to decide whether the sectioning command gets a number (if the level is less than or equal to secnumdepth; see Section 2.2.1 on page 34) or shows up in the table of contents (if the value is less or equal to tocdepth; see Section 2.3.4 on page 71). It should therefore reflect the position in the command hierarchy of sectioning commands, where the outermost sectioning command has level zero.[3]

indent The indentation of the heading with respect to the left margin. By making the value negative, the heading starts in the outer margin. Making it positive indents all lines of the heading by this amount.

beforeskip The absolute value of this parameter defines the space to be left in front of the heading. If the parameter is negative, then the indentation of the paragraph following the heading is suppressed. This dimension is a rubber length; that is, it can take a stretch and shrink component. Note that LaTeX starts a new paragraph before the heading so that additionally the value of \parskip is added to the space in front.

---

[1] The whole section is set in a smaller font to indicate that is more a reference — helpful mainly when studying existing code.

[2] This counter must exist; it is not defined automatically.

[3] In the book and report classes, the \part command actually has level −1 (see Table 2.1).

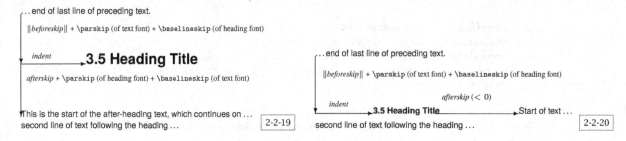

Figure 2.1: The layout for display and run-in headings (produced by layouts)

afterskip The space to be left following a heading. It is the vertical space after a display heading or the horizontal space after a run-in heading. The sign of *afterskip* controls whether a display heading (*afterskip* > 0) or a run-in heading (*afterskip* ≤ 0) is produced. In the first case a new paragraph is started so that the value of \parskip is added to the space after the heading. An unpleasant side effect of this parameter coupling is that it is impossible to define a display heading with an effective "after space" of less than \parskip using the \@startsection command. When you try to compensate for a positive \parskip value by using a negative *afterskip*, you change the display heading into a run-in heading.

style The style of the heading text. This argument can take any instruction that influences the typesetting of text, such as \raggedright, \Large, or \bfseries (see the examples below).

Figure 2.1 shows these parameters graphically for the case of display and run-in headings, respectively. As an example we redefine \subsection to be set in normal-sized italic with the separation from the preceding text being exactly one baseline. The separation from the text following is one-half baseline, and this text is not indented.

```
\makeatletter
\renewcommand\subsection{\@startsection
  {subsection}{2}{0mm}%                      % name, level, indent
  {-\baselineskip}{0.5\baselineskip}%  % beforeskip, afterskip
  {\normalfont\normalsize\itshape}}%  % style
\makeatother
```

… some text above.

4.1   *Subsection Heading*

The first paragraph following the redefined subsection heading …
       And a second one (indented).

```
\ldots\ some text above.
\subsection{Subsection Heading}
The first paragraph following the redefined subsection
heading \ldots   \par   And a second one (indented).
```

2-2-21

The first argument to \@startsection is the string subsection to denote that we use the corresponding counter for heading numbers. In the sectional hierarchy we are at level two. The third argument is 0mm because the heading should start at the left margin.

The absolute value of the fourth argument (*beforeskip*) specifies that a distance equal to one baseline must be left in front of the heading and, because the parameter is negative, that the indentation of the paragraph following the heading should be suppressed.

The absolute value of the fifth parameter (*afterskip*) specifies that a distance equal to one-half baseline must be left following the heading and, because the parameter is positive, that a display heading has to be produced. Finally, according to the sixth parameter, the heading should be typeset in an italic font using a size equal to the normal document type size.

In fact, the redefinition is a bit too simplistic because, as mentioned earlier, on top of the absolute value of *beforeskip* and *afterskip*, LATEX always adds the current value of \parskip. Thus, in layouts where this parameter is nonzero, we need to subtract it to achieve the desired separation.

Other simple heading style changes Which commands can be used for setting the styles of the heading texts in the *style* argument of the \@startsection command? Apart from the font-changing directives (see Chapter 9), few instructions can be used here. A \centering command produces a centered display heading, and a

\raggedright declaration makes the text left justified. The use of \raggedleft is possible, but may give somewhat strange results. You can also use \hrule, \medskip, \newpage, or similar commands that introduce local changes.

In the standard LaTeX classes the highest-level sectioning commands \part and \chapter produce their titles without using \@startsection because their layout cannot be produced with that command. Similarly, you may also want to construct sectioning commands without limitations. In this case you must follow a few conventions to allow LaTeX to take all the necessary typesetting actions when executing them.

Complex heading layout definitions

The command \secdef can help you when defining such commands by providing an easy interface to the three possible forms of section headings. With the definition

```
\newcommand\myhead{\secdef\myheadA\myheadB}
```

the following actions take place:

\myhead{*title*}	invokes	\myheadA [*title*] {*title*}
\myhead [*toc-entry*] {*title*}	invokes	\myheadA [*toc-entry*] {*title*}
\myhead*{*title*}	invokes	\myheadB{*title*}

The commands you have to provide are a (re)definition[1] of \myhead and a definition of the commands named \myheadA or \myheadB, respectively. Note that \myheadA has an optional argument containing the text to be entered in the table of contents .toc file, while the second (mandatory) argument, as well as the single argument to \myheadB, specifies the heading text to be typeset. Thus, the definitions must have the following structure:

```
\newcommand\myhead{ ... \secdef \myheadA \myheadB }
\newcommand\myheadA[2][default]{ ... }
\newcommand\myheadB[1]{ ... }
```

An explicit example is a simplified variant of \appendix. It redefines the \section command to produce headings for appendices (by invoking either the command \Appendix or \sAppendix), changing the presentation of the section counter and resetting it to zero. The modified \section command also starts a new page (with all deferred floats placed), which is typeset with a special page style (see Chapter 5) and with top floats suppressed. The indentation of the first paragraph in a section is also suppressed by using the low-level kernel command \@afterheading and setting the Boolean switch @afterindent to false. For details on the use of these commands, see the \chapter implementation in the standard classes (file classes.dtx).

```
\makeatletter
\renewcommand\appendix{%
    \renewcommand\section{%                 % Redefinition of \section...
        \clearpage\thispagestyle{plain}%     % new page, folio bottom
        \suppressfloats[t]\@afterindentfalse % no top floats, no indent
        \secdef\Appendix\sAppendix}%         % call \Appendix or \sAppendix
    \setcounter{section}{0}\renewcommand\thesection{\Alph{section}}}
```

In the definition below you can see how \Appendix advances the section counter using the \refstepcounter command (the latter also resets all subsidiary counters and defines the "current reference string"; see Section 2.4). It writes a line into the .toc file with the \addcontentsline command, formats the heading title, and saves the title for running heads and/or feet by calling \sectionmark. The \@afterheading command in the later part of the definition handles the indentation of the paragraph following the heading.

```
\newcommand\Appendix[2][?]{%                 % Complex form:
    \refstepcounter{section}%                % step counter/ set label
    \addcontentsline{toc}{appendix}%         % generate toc entry
        {\protect\numberline{\appendixname~\thesection}#1}%
    {\raggedleft\large\bfseries \appendixname\ % typeset the title
    \thesection\par \centering#2\par}%       %    and number
```

---

[1] Redefinition in case you change an existing heading command such as \part in the preamble of your document.

```
\sectionmark{#1}%                           % add to running header
\@afterheading                              % prepare indentation handling
\addvspace{\baselineskip}}                  % space after heading
```

The \sAppendix command (starred form) performs only the formatting.

```
\newcommand\sAppendix[1]{%                   % Simplified (starred) form
  {\raggedleft\large\bfseries\appendixname\par \centering#1\par}%
  \@afterheading\addvspace{\baselineskip}}
\makeatother
```

Applying these definitions produces the following output:

Appendix A
The list of all commands

Then follows the text of the first section in the appendix. Some more text in the appendix.

```
% Example needs commands introduced above!
\appendix
\section{The list of all commands}

Then follows the text of the first section in
the appendix. Some more text in the appendix.
```

2-2-22

Do not forget that the example shown above represents only a simplified version of a redefined \section command. Among other things, we did not take into account the secnumdepth counter, which contains the numbering threshold. You might also have to foresee code dealing with various types of document formats, such as one- and two-column output or one- and two-sided printing. Also missing is an appropriate definition for \l@appendix, which is called in the table of contents because of the \addcontentsline. This is discussed at the beginning of Section 2.3.4 on page 70.

2.3 Table of contents structures

A *table of contents* (TOC) is a special list in which the titles of the section units are listed, usually together with the page numbers indicating the start of the sections. This list can be rather complicated if units from several nesting levels are included, and it should be formatted carefully because it plays an important rôle as a navigation aid for the reader.

Similar lists exist containing reference information about the floating elements in a document — namely, the *list of tables* and the *list of figures*. The structure of these lists is usually simpler, as their contents, the captions of the floating elements, are normally all on the same level (but see subfloats in Section 7.5).

Standard LATEX can automatically create these three contents lists. By default, LATEX enters text from one of the arguments of each sectioning command into the .toc file. While information from all sectioning levels is added to the .toc file, not all of them are used when producing the table of contents. The level down to which the heading information is displayed is controlled by the counter tocdepth. It can be changed, for example, with the following declaration:

```
\setcounter{tocdepth}{1}
```

In this case section heading information down to the first level (e.g., in the report class part, chapter, and section) will be shown.

Granular control is possible

This counter globally defines which entries are typeset in the table of contents. Sometimes, however, more granular control is necessary; e.g., you may want to show less or more heading levels in an appendix, etc. For such use cases, you may want to try the package tocvsec2 by Peter Wilson. It provides commands to adjust the level within the document.

Similarly, LaTeX maintains two more files, one for the list of figures (.lof) and one for the list of tables (.lot), which contain the text specified as the argument of the \caption command for figures and tables.

When using the \tableofcontents, \listoffigures, or \listoftables, the information written into these files during a previous LaTeX run is read and typeset (normally at the beginning of a document), and at the end of the run newly collected information is written back to the files.

To generate these cross-reference tables, it is therefore always necessary to run LaTeX at least twice — once to collect the relevant information, and a second time to read back the information and typeset it in the correct place in the document. Because of the additional material to be typeset in the second run, the cross-referencing information may change, making a third LaTeX run necessary. This is one of the reasons for the tradition of using different page-numbering systems for the front matter and the main text: in the days of hand typesetting any additional iteration made the final product much more expensive.

A TOC needs two, sometimes even three, LaTeX runs

Normally the contents files are generated automatically by LaTeX by internally using the commands \addcontentsline, \addtocontents, and \numberline; see Section 2.3.4 on page 70. With some care this interface can also be used to enter information directly into these files to complement the actions of standard LaTeX.

For instance, in the case of the starred form of the section commands, no information is written to the .toc file. If you do not want a heading number (starred form) but you do want an entry in the .toc file, you can use \addcontentsline with or without \numberline as shown in the following example.

Adding arbitrary starred headings to the TOC

Contents

Foreword	**1**
1 Thoughts	**2**
1.1 Contact info	2
References	**2**

Foreword

A starred heading with the TOC entry manually added. Compare this to the form used for the bibliography.

---

1 Thoughts

We find all in [1].

1.1 Contact info

E-mail Ben at [2].

References

[1] Ben User, Some day will never come, 2010

[2] BUser@earth.info

```
\tableofcontents
\section*{Foreword}
\addcontentsline{toc}{section}
   {\protect\numberline{}Foreword}
A starred heading with the TOC entry
manually added. Compare this to the
form used for the  bibliography.

\section{Thoughts}
We find all in \cite{k1}.
\subsection{Contact info}
E-mail Ben at \cite{k2}.
\begin{thebibliography}{9}
\addcontentsline{toc}{section}
   {\refname}
\bibitem{k1} Ben User, Some day will
             never come, 2010
\bibitem{k2} BUser@earth.info
\end{thebibliography}
```

2-3-1

Using `\numberline` as in the "Foreword" produces an indented "section" entry in the table of contents, leaving the space where the section number would go free. The `\protect` in front is required in this case; see page 70 for more details. Omitting the `\numberline` command (as was done for the bibliography entry) would typeset the heading flush left instead. Adding a similar line after the start of the `theindex` means that the "Index" will be listed in the table of contents. Unfortunately, this approach cannot be used to get the list of figures or tables into the table of contents because `\listoffigures` or `\listoftables` might generate a listing of several pages, and consequently the page number picked up by `\addcontentsline` might be wrong. And putting it before the command does not help either, because often these list commands start a new page. One potential solution is to copy the command definition from the class file and put `\addcontentsline` directly into it.

Bibliography or index in tables of contents

In the case of standard classes or close derivatives, you can use the tocbibind package created by Peter Wilson to get the "List of...", "Index", or "Bibliography" section listed in the table of contents without further additions to the source. The package offers a number of options such as `notbib`, `notindex`, `nottoc`, `notlof`, and `notlot` (do not add the corresponding entry to the table of contents).

Numbered headings for bibliography or index

There also exist the options `numbib` and `numindex` (number the corresponding heading), and with `section` you can ask for section instead of chapter headings in document classes like report or book.

An oddity better turned off

By default the "Contents" section is listed within the table of contents, which is seldom desirable — use the option `nottoc` to disable this behavior.

* * * * *

There are a number of packages that extend or alter standard LATEX's table of contents mechanism. The hyperref package changes the internals to support hyperlink anchors; in particular, this changes the internal contents file structures. It is briefly touched upon on page 72; an extensive coverage of that package is found in Section 2.4.6 on page 96.

The tocdata package provides an interface for adding special data such as author names to the contents files. It is discussed in the next section. We will then turn to customizing the design of such lists with the help of the titletoc package. There are alternative packages for this available, e.g., tocloft by Peter Wilson or tocstyle by Markus Kohm, but titletoc provides a good general-purpose interface suitable for most needs, so we concentrate on that.

The final section concerned with contents file data discusses the low-level interface already provided by LATEX and is included mainly for reference (in a smaller font) because one often find its commands in older class files.

2.3.1 tocdata — Providing extra data for the TOC

In anthologies or other multi-author works it is quite common to list the different authors in the table of contents next to their entries. The package tocdata by Brian Dunn provides a framework for this that enables you to place such data into the typeset TOC entry just before the page number. The package works well with most document classes and supports TOC packages such as titletoc or tocloft.

In the next example we have added author names to the two subsections; the section itself shows no extra data. The extra data is formatted with the help of the command \tocdataformat, which by default sets the material in a small italic font. Here we added color and an em-dash.

Contents

```
\usepackage{color,tocdata}
\renewcommand\tocdataformat[1]{\textnormal{%
    \textcolor{blue}{--- \small\itshape#1}}}
\tableofcontents

\section{On Cookies}
\tocdata{toc}{Ben User}
\subsection{Preparing cookies}
Text of his recipes \ldots

\tocdata{toc}{Cookie Monster}
\subsection{Eating cookies}
How to do it \ldots
```

1   On Cookies

1.1   Preparing cookies

Text of his recipes ...

1.2   Eating cookies

2-3-2   How to do it ...

In a similar fashion you can add to the list of figures or tables to indicate the artist who made a certain picture or the source of the table data, etc. All you need to do is to specify in the first argument to \tocdata the correct target destination file extension, e.g., lof for the list of figures or lot for the list of tables.

The \tocdata command used in the previous example enables you to add data to any "TOC-like" file, but often you also want to provide this information within your document as well.

For such use cases the package offers a set of special commands that combine \tocdata with a heading or a caption command. We show the syntax for the \part heading, but corresponding commands exist for \chapter (if supported by the document class), \section, and \subsection headings.

```
\partauthor [list-entry] {title} [prefix] {first}{last} [suffix]
\partauthor*            {title} [prefix] {first}{last} [suffix]
```

The first form executes the following set of commands for you

```
\todata{toc}{first last}
\part [list-entry] {title\nopagebreak
              \tocdatapartprint{prefix}{first}{last}{suffix}}
\index{last, first}
```

while the star form on the second line omits the \tocdata, since the heading is not written to the table of contents. The \tocdatapartprint command formats the name and adds it as part of the heading title. By redefining this command, various layouts can be realized. Note that *prefix* and *suffix* are used only there — the \tocdata and \index commands receive only *first* and *last*.

While *first* is a mandatory argument, it can be left empty if the author has no first name. In this case, the comma in the \index is automatically dropped too as shown in the example.

Contents

1   On Cookies

1.1   Preparing cookies

— *Sir Ben User*

Text of his recipes ...

1.2   Eating cookies

— *Cookie Monster!!*

How to do it ...

Index

```
\usepackage{makeidx}
  \makeindex % enable indexing
% save some space in the index:
  \renewcommand\indexspace{\par\vspace{2pt}}

\usepackage{tocdata}

\tableofcontents \smallskip

\section{On Cookies}
\subsectionauthor{Preparing cookies}
        [Sir]{Ben}{User}
Text of his recipes \ldots

\subsectionauthor{Eating cookies}
            {}{Cookie Monster}[!!]
How to do it \ldots

\printindex
```

2-3-3

For captions of figures (or tables) two commands exist with a syntax similar to \partauthor, but with one further optional *extra-text* argument. They are intended to be used instead of the normal \caption command:

> \captionartist [*list-entry*] {*title*} [*extra-text*] [*prefix*] {*first*}{*last*} [*suffix*]

The arguments *list-entry* and *title* correspond to the usual \caption arguments, and *first* and *last* are used to add the artist name to the list of figures and produce an index entry (if an index is made). Again, *prefix* and *suffix* are used only when displaying the artist name as part of the float. Finally the *extra-text* allows you to place additional information next to the caption title that does not show up in the list of figures.

Note that if you want to use the optional *prefix* but not the *extra-text*, you need to supply an empty optional argument for the latter to identify for LaTeX which is which.

To influence justification of the name there are a number of declarations available of the form \tdartist... where ... is either justify, left, center, or right, and for the additional text you have \tdartisttext... with the same possibilities.

To change the formatting in more drastic ways, you can alternatively redefine the commands \tocdataartistprint (receiving *prefix*, *first*, *last*, and *suffix* as arguments to format the name) and \tocdataartisttextprint (responsible for formatting *extra-text*). See the package documentation for details.

Sebastian Rahtz (1955–2016)

This has been already used
in the first edition of TLC

Figure 1: A cat

```
\usepackage{graphicx,tocdata}    \tdartistright
\begin{figure}
  \centering
  \includegraphics{cat}
  \captionartist{A cat}[This has been already used\\
                     in the first edition of TLC]
         {Sebastian}{Rahtz}[ (1955--2016)]
\end{figure}
```

2-3-4

Instead of the command \captionartist you can use \captionauthor with exactly the same syntax (and corresponding configuration commands). The difference between the two is the default formatting: \captionartist typesets the name centered, whereas \captionauthor places it flush right. The latter may look nicer for wide pictures.

If you use the caption package, which supports the \caption* command, then \captionartist and \captionauthor will also accept a star.

2.3.2 titletoc — A high-level approach to contents list design

The titletoc package written by Javier Bezos was originally developed as a companion package to titlesec but can be used on its own. It implements its own interface to lay out contents structures, thereby avoiding some of the limitations of the original LaTeX code for this task. This makes it a good candidate when adjustments of such lists are necessary when a new class is being developed.

The actual generation of external contents files and their syntax is left unchanged so that it works nicely with other packages generating such files. There is one exception, however: contents files should end with the command \contentsfinish. For the standard file extensions .toc, .lof, and .lot, this is handled automatically. But if you provide your own type of contents lists (see Section 2.3.4), you have to announce it to titletoc, as in the following example:

Relation to standard LaTeX

```
\contentsuse{example}{xmp}
```

Designing the layout for a single contents list entry

A single contents list entry normally consists of one or more lines of text, typically starting with a label (e.g., the heading number) followed by the heading title and finishing off with a page number. Typically, the page number is pushed to the right edge so that page numbers from different entries align. Thus, there is normally a gap between title and page number, which is filled either by white space or by some leaders, e.g., some dots or a line.

Standard LaTeX already supports that type of design with some flexibility in allowing for indentation at the left and right of all lines. In addition, the start of the

59

first line as well as the endpoint of the last line can be moved (typically to place both the label and the page number outside of the title text block).

A typical multiline entry could look like this:

> 3.11 This is a sample section entry which has been deliberately made very long so that it spans three lines to exhibit the handling of the first and the last line in the entry 27

As you see, the entry is indented on both sides with the entry label placed into the available white space. The heading title is set ragged right in sans serif, and the page number is separated from the text block using a row of leader dots and again placed outside of the block.

Standard (dotted) layouts

The titletoc package supports this type of standard layout, but compared to standard LATEX offers more convenient ways to customize it. In addition, it supports other layouts such as running lower-level heading entries together in a single paragraph and, as a nice add-on, supports partial table of contents lists so that you can provide chapter tables, etc. For the most common case, i.e., the layout shown above, it offers the \dottedcontents declaration.

\dottedcontents{*type*}[*left-indent*]{*before-code*}{*label-width*}{*leader-width*}

The first argument of \dottedcontents contains the *type* of contents entry for which we set up the layout — normally the name of the heading command without a backslash or the name of the float environment, e.g., figure. In other words, for each *type* of sectioning command that can appear in the document, we need one \dottedcontents (or alternatively \titlecontents discussed below) declaration.[1] The remaining arguments have the following meaning:

left-indent The indentation from the left margin for all lines of the entry. It should normally be wider than the *label-width* argument because the label is placed into that space. Even though this argument has to be given in square brackets, it is *not* optional in the current package release (and probably never will become one)!

before-code Code to be executed before the entry is typeset. It can be used to provide vertical space, such as by using \addvspace, and to set up formatting directives, such as font changes, for the whole entry. You can also use \filleft, \filright, \filcenter, or \fillast, already known from the titlesec package, at this point.

label-width Nominal width of the label, i.e., the label starts to left of the first line offset by this amount. Thus, the value should be wide enough to comfortably

---

[1] The package honors existing *type* declarations made, for example, by the document class even if they are defined using the standard LATEX interface. Thus, it can be used to change the layout of only some types.

hold the label material for this type. Problematic cases with varying label widths and possible solutions are discussed on pages 63 (\contentspush) and 73.

leaders-width   Distance between two dots in the leaders on the last line of the entry.

For example, the entry above was typeset using the following declaration:

```
\dottedcontents{section}[40pt]{\normalfont\sffamily\filright}{24pt}{6pt}
```

i.e., we have an indentation of 40pt from the left margin with the label starting 16pt from the margin[1] and occupying 24pt. The whole entry is set in sans serif and ragged right (via \filright), and each leader dot occupies 6pt of space.

You may wonder where the indentation on the right (for all lines but the last) comes from and why it is not available as an argument to \dottedcontents. The main reason is that in nearly all designs its value is the same for all entry types, and thus providing it as an argument on the entry level would cumbersome and error prone. In most document classes the default is wide enough to contain up to three digits in the document body font. If that is not enough (or too much), it can be globally (or locally) changed with a \contentsmargin declaration.

\contentsmargin [*correction*] {*right-sep*}

This declaration shortens all entry lines by *right-sep*. On the last line the page number is typeset in that space, so if it is too small, the entry and page number may overlap. In addition, the optional *correction* argument is added to all lines of an entry except the last. This argument can, for example, be used to fine-tune the contents layout so that dots from a row of leaders align with the text of previous lines in a multiline entry if the entry is set justified.

In the unlikely case that there is a need to have different *right-sep* values for different entry types, then the solution is to place this command inside the *before-code* of \dottedcontents or \titlecontents. It is then local to that entry type.

More complicated layouts

While \dottedcontents works well in many cases, it clearly has its limitations and cannot be used if you do not want any leaders or other typographic adjustments that go beyond setting the font or the indentation. For such cases titletoc offers the \titlecontents declaration and a few helper commands to be used within its arguments.

\titlecontents{*type*} [*left-indent*] {*before-code*}{*numbered-entry-format*}
                {*numberless-entry-format*}{*page-format*} [*below-code*]

The first three arguments *type*, *left-indent*, and *before-code* are the same as the corresponding ones for \dottedcontents and are described there. However, the remaining ones differ. Instead of simply specifying the width for the label we have

---

[1] In other words, *left-indent* minus *label-width*, i.e., 40pt − 24pt in this case.

now two arguments that allow us to explicitly define how the label and the title text should be formatted and what should happen if the label is empty. This means you have way more design possibilities at the cost of specifying more code.

numbered-entry-format   Code to format the entry including its number. It is executed in horizontal mode (after setting up the indentation). The last token can be a command with one argument, in which case it receives the entry *text* as its argument. The unformatted heading number is available in the \thecontentslabel command, but see below for other possibilities to access and place it.

numberless-entry-format   Code to format the entry if the current entry does not contain a number. Again, the last token may be a command with one argument.

Instead of specifying the *leader-width*, we now have an argument in which we have to define exactly what should happen after the title text and how the page number should be formatted. Finally, there is a further optional argument to be executed after the entry is typeset.

page-format   Code that is executed after formatting the entry but while still being in horizontal mode. It is normally used to add some filling material, such as a dotted line, and to attach the page number stored in \thecontentspage. You can use the \titlerule command, discussed on page 47, to produce leaders.

below-code   Optional code to be executed in vertical mode after the entry is typeset — for example, to add some extra vertical space after the entry.

To help with placing and formatting the heading and page numbers, the titletoc package offers two useful tools: \contentslabel and \contentspage.

\contentslabel [*text*] {*size*}   \contentspage [*text*]

The purpose of the \contentslabel command is to typeset the *text* (which by default contains \thecontentslabel) left aligned in a box of width *size* and to place that box to the left of the current position. Thus, if you use this command in the *numbered-entry-format* argument of \titlecontents, then the number is placed in front of the entry text into the margin or indentation set up by *left-indent*. For a more refined layout you can use the optional argument to specify your own formatting usually involving \thecontentslabel.

In a similar fashion \contentspage typesets *text* (which by default contains \thecontentspage) right aligned in a box and arranges for the box to be placed to the right of the current position but without taking up space. Thus, if placed at the right end of a line, the box extends into the margin. In this case, however, no mandatory argument specifies the box size: it is the same for all entries. Its value is the same as the space found to the right of all entries and can be set by the command \contentsmargin described below.

Package options for \contentslabel   The package offers three options to influence the default outcome of the \contentslabel command when used without the *text* argument. With the option rightlabels the heading number is right aligned in the space, while leftlabels (the default) makes it left aligned. You can also specify `dotinlabels` to always add a period after the number.

Instead of indenting the whole entry and then moving some material into the left margin using `\contentslabel`, you can make use of `\contentspush` to achieve a similar effect.

`\contentspush{`*text*`}`

This command typesets *text* and then increases the *left-indent* by the width of *text* for all additional lines of the entry (if any). As a consequence, the indentation will vary if the width of the *text* changes. In many cases such variation is not desirable, but in some cases other solutions give even worse results. Consider the case of a document with many chapters, each containing dozens of sections. A rigid *left-indent* needs to be able to hold the widest number, which may have five or six digits. In that case a label like "1.1" comes out unduly separated from its entry text. Given below is a solution that grows with the size of the entry number:

```
\usepackage{titletoc}
\titlecontents{section}[0pt]{\addvspace{2pt}\filright}
                {\contentspush{\thecontentslabel\enspace }}
                {}{~\hrulefill\contentspage}
```

12.8 Some section that is wrapped in the TOC ___ 87

12.9 Another section _____ 88

12.10 And yet another wrapping section ___ 90

12.11 Final section _____ 92

```
\contentsline{section}{\numberline{12.8}Some section that
                   is wrapped in the TOC}{87}{}%
\contentsline{section}{\numberline{12.9}Another section}{88}{}%
\contentsline{section}{\numberline{12.10}And yet another
                   wrapping section}{90}{}%
\contentsline{section}{\numberline{12.11}Final section}{92}{}%
\contentsfinish
```

A few design examples

For the examples in this section we copied some parts of the original `.toc` file generated by LaTeX for this book (Chapter 2 and parts of Chapter 3) into a file we called `partial.toc` and manually added a `\contentsfinish` command at the end. Inside the examples we can then load this file with `\input`. Of course, in a real document you would use the command `\tableofcontents` instead so that the `.toc` file for *your* document is loaded and processed.

A note on the examples in this and the next section

In our first example we provide a new formatting for chapter entries, while keeping the formatting for the section entries as defined by the standard LaTeX document class. The chapter entries are now set ragged right (`\filright`) in bold typeface, get one pica space above, followed by a thick rule. The actual entry is indented by six picas. In that space we typeset the word "Chapter" in small caps followed by a space and the chapter number (`\thecontentslabel`) using the `\contentslabel` directive with its optional argument. There is no special handling for entries without numbers, so they would be formatted with an indentation of six picas. We fill the remaining space using `\hfill` and typeset the page number in the margin via `\contentspage`.

Finally, after the entry we add another two points of space so that the entry is slightly separated from any section entry following.

```
\usepackage[dotinlabels]{titletoc}
\titlecontents{chapter} [5pc]
  {\addvspace{1pc}\bfseries
   \titlerule[2pt]\filright}
  {\contentslabel
     [\textsc{\chaptername}\
      \thecontentslabel][5pc}}
  {}{\hfill\contentspage}
  [\addvspace{2pt}]
% Show only chapter/section entries:
\setcounter{tocdepth}{1}
\input{partial.toc}
```
2-3-6

In our second example we typeset the chapter title in sans serif with the chapter and page numbers on the left and right. Any free space is filled with a rule on the baseline, and we provide a bit of extra space above and below the chapter line. The section headings are shown slightly indented; for them the page numbers are suppressed. All numbers are formatted using oldstyle numerals.

```
\usepackage{titletoc}
\titlecontents{chapter}[0pc]
  {\addvspace{6pt}}
  {\large\sffamily
   \oldstylenums{\thecontentslabel}
   \ \hrulefill\ }{}
  {\large\sffamily\ \hrulefill\
   \oldstylenums{\thecontentspage}}
  [\addvspace{2pt}]
\titlecontents{section} [1pc]{}
  {\oldstylenums{\thecontentslabel}
   -- }{}{}
\setcounter{tocdepth}{1}
\input{partial.toc}
```
2-3-7

The third example and final example for now puts the page numbers in focus; they are printed on the left, while the normal heading numbers are suppressed. The chapter title is placed on the right by filling the available space with \dotfill. Section titles are left aligned and separated with an en-dash from the page number. Note that we use \enspace instead of a normal space around it so that this space does not stretch or shrink if the section title is longer than a single line.

```
\usepackage{titletoc}
\titlecontents{chapter}[2pc]
  {\addvspace{5pt}}
  {\large\bfseries
   \contentslabel[\hfill
      \thecontentspage]{2pc}\dotfill
   }{}{}
  [\addvspace{2pt}]
\titlecontents{section}[2pc]{}
  {\contentslabel[\hfill
      \thecontentspage]{2pc}%
   \enspace --\enspace }{}{}
\setcounter{tocdepth}{1}
\input{partial.toc}
```

2-3-8

Note that none of the previous examples have provisions to format headings that are unnumbered; i.e., the third mandatory argument of the \titlecontents command was always left empty. This was done because the sample data contains only numbered headings and it saved space to not provide formatting instructions for unnumbered headings that are never used. However, in real life you better think about how such entries should be displayed as well.

Contents entries combined in a paragraph

Standard LaTeX only supports contents entries formatted on individual lines. In some cases, however, it is more economical to format lower-level entries together in a single paragraph. With the titletoc package this becomes possible.

\titlecontents*{type} [left-indent] {before-code}{numbered-entry-format}
              {numberless-entry-format}{page-format} [mid-code]
\titlecontents*{type}...{page-format} [mid-code] [final-code]
\titlecontents*{type}...{page-format} [start-code] [mid-code] [final-code]

The \titlecontents* declaration is used for entries that should be formatted together with other entries of the same or lower level in a single paragraph. The first six arguments are identical to those of \titlecontents described on page 61.

Instead of a vertically oriented *below-code* argument, \titlecontents* provides one to three optional arguments that handle different situations that can happen when entries are about to be joined horizontally. All three optional arguments are by default empty. The joining works recursively as follows:

- If the current entry is the first entry to participate in joining, then its *start-code* is executed before typesetting the entry.
- Otherwise, there has been a previous entry already participating.
  - If both entries are on the same level, then the *mid-code* is inserted.

- Otherwise, if the current entry is of a lower level, then the *start-code* for it is inserted, and we recur processing the new level.

- Otherwise, the current entry is of a higher level. First, we execute for each level that has ended the *final-code* (in reverse order). Then, if the current entry is not participating in joining, we are done. Otherwise, the *mid-code* for the entry is executed, as a previous entry of the same level should already be present (assuming a hierarchically structured document).

Careful with paragraph parameters If several levels are to be joined, then you have to specify any paragraph layout information in the *before-code* of the highest level participating. Otherwise, the scope of your settings does not include the paragraph end and thus is not applied. In the following example, \footnotesize applies only to the section entries — the \baselineskip for the whole paragraph is still set in \normalsize. This artificial example shows how one can join two different levels using the three optional arguments. Note in particular the spaces added at the beginning of some arguments to get the right result when joining.

CHAPTER 2

The Structure of a LATEX Document, 21 *(The overall structure of a source file; Sectioning commands; Table of contents structures; Managing references; Document source management)* • **Basic Formatting Tools, 119** *(Shaping your paragraphs; Dealing with special characters; Generated or specially formatted text; Various ways of highlighting and quoting text; Footnotes, endnotes, and marginals)* ¶

```
\usepackage{titletoc,xcolor} \contentsmargin{0pt}
\titlecontents*{chapter}[0pt]
    {\sffamily}{}{}{, \thecontentspage}
    [\ \textbullet \ ] [~\P]    % mid, finish
\titlecontents*{section}[0pt]
    {\color{blue}\footnotesize\slshape}{}{}{}
    [ \{] [; ] [\}]       % start, mid, finish
\setcounter{tocdepth}{1}
\sloppy \input{partial.toc}
```

2-3-9

Let us now see how this works in practice. In the next example we join the section level, separating entries by a bullet surrounded by some stretchable space (\xquad) and finishing the list with a period. The chapter entries are interesting as well, because we move the page number to the left. Both types omit the heading numbers completely in this design. Because there are no page numbers at the right, we also set the right margin to zero.

21 The Structure of a LATEX Document

119 Basic Formatting Tools

```
\usepackage{titletoc}
\contentsmargin{0pt}
\titlecontents{chapter}[0pt]
    {\addvspace{1.4pc}\bfseries}
    {{\Huge\thecontentspage\quad}}{}{}
\newcommand\xquad
    {\hspace{1em plus.4em minus.4em}}
\titlecontents*{section}[0pt]
    {\filright\small}{}{}
    {,~\thecontentspage}
    [\xquad\textbullet\xquad][.]
\setcounter{tocdepth}{1}
\input{partial.toc}
```

2-3-10

As a second example we look at a setup implementing a layout close to the one used in *Methods of Book Design* [139]. This design uses Garamond fonts with oldstyle digits, something we achieve by using the garamondx package. The \chapter titles are set in small capitals. To arrange that we use \scshape and turn all letters in the title to lowercase using \MakeLowercase (remember that the last token of the *numbered-entry-format* and the *numberless-entry-format* arguments can be a command with one argument to receive the heading text). The sections are all run together in a paragraph with the section number getting a § sign prepended. Separation between entries is a period followed by a space, and the final section is finished with a period as well.

Justifying the paragraph really requires a wider measure than available in the example, even though it comes out fairly well with the given text. If not, consider using \filright, but that would rather drastically alter the design.

```
\usepackage[osf]{garamondx}
\usepackage{titletoc}
\contentsmargin{0pt}
\titlecontents{chapter}[1.5pc]
  {\addvspace{2pc}\large}
  {\contentslabel{2pc}%
   \scshape\MakeLowercase}
  {\scshape\MakeLowercase}
  {\hfill\thecontentspage}
  [\vspace{2pt}]
\titlecontents*{section}[1.5pc]
  {\small}{\S\thecontentslabel\ }
  {}{,~\thecontentspage}[.\ ][.]
\setcounter{tocdepth}{1}

\input{partial.toc}
```

2-3-11

Generating partial table of contents lists

It is possible to generate partial contents lists using the titletoc package like we do for every chapter in this book; it provides four commands for this purpose.

\startcontents [*name*]

A partial table of contents is started with \startcontents. It is possible to collect data for several partial TOCs in parallel, such as one for the current \part as well as one for the current \chapter. In that case the optional *name* argument allows us to distinguish between the two (its default value is the string default). Concurrently running partial TOCs are allowed to overlap each other, although normally they will be nested. All information about these partial TOCs is stored in a single file with the extension .ptc; this file is generated once a single \startcontents command is executed.

> `\printcontents [`*name*`] {`*prefix*`}{`*start-level*`}{`*toc-code*`}`

This command prints the current partial TOC started earlier by `\startcontents`
and includes all entries up to the next invocation of `\startcontents`. If the optional
name argument is used, then a partial contents list with that *name* must have been
started earlier.

It is quite likely that you want to format the partial TOC differently from the main
table of contents. To allow for this the *prefix* argument is prepended to any entry *type*
when looking for a layout definition provided via `\titlecontents` or its starred
form. In the example below we used p- as the *prefix* and then defined a formatting
for p-subsection to format `\subsection` entries in the partial TOC.

The *start-level* argument defines the first level that is shown in the partial TOC;
in the example we used the value 2 to indicate that we want to see all subsections
and lower levels.

The depth to which we want to include entries in the partial TOC can be set in
toc-code by setting the tocdepth counter to a suitable value. Other initializations for
typesetting the partial TOC can be made there as well. In the example we cancel any
right margin, because the partial TOC is formatted as a single paragraph.

Integrating partial TOCs in the heading definitions so that there is no need to
change the actual document is very easy when titletoc is used together with the
titlesec package. Below we extend Example 2-2-14 from page 45 so that the `\section`
command now automatically prints a partial TOC of all its subsections. This is done by
using the optional *after-code* argument of the `\titleformat` declaration. We first add
some vertical space, thereby ensuring that no page break can happen at this point. We
next (re)start the default partial TOC with `\startcontents`. We then immediately
typeset it using `\printcontents`; its arguments have been explained above. Finally,
we set up the formatting for subsections in a partial TOC using `\titlecontents*`
to run them together in a justified paragraph whose last line is centered (`\fillast`).
Stringing this all together gives the desired output without any modification to the
document source. Of course, a real design would also change the look and feel of the
subsection headings in the document to better fit those of the sections.

```
\usepackage{titlesec,titletoc}
\titleformat{\section}[frame]{\normalfont}
    {\footnotesize \enspace SECTION \thesection
    \enspace}{6pt}{\large\bfseries\filcenter}
    [\vspace*{5pt}\startcontents
    \printcontents{p-}{2}{\contentsmargin{0pt}}]
\titlespacing*{\section}{1pc}{*4}{*2.3}[1pc]
\titlecontents*{p-subsection}[0pt]
    {\small\itshape\fillast}{}{}{}[ --- ][.]
\section{A Title Test}
Some text to prove that this paragraph is not indented.
\subsection{A first}  Some text        \ldots \newpage
\subsection{A longer second} Some more text.
\stopcontents  \subsection{A third}  \resumecontents
\subsection{An even longer fourth}
```

2-3-12

SECTION 1
A Title Test

*A first — A longer second — An even longer
fourth.*

Some text to prove that this paragraph is
not indented.

1.1   A first

Some text...

68

If necessary, one can temporarily (or permanently) stop collecting entries for a partial TOC. We made use of this feature in the previous example by suppressing the third subsection.

`\stopcontents [`*name*`]`   `\resumecontents [`*name*`]`

The `\stopcontents` command stops the entry collection for the `default` partial TOC or, if used with the *name* argument, for the TOC with that *name*. At a later point the collection can be restarted using `\resumecontents`. Note that this is quite different from calling `\startcontents`, which starts a *new* partial TOC, thereby making the old entries inaccessible.

Partial TOCs do not need to be confined to a subset of your document. It is equally possible to use them to provide "overviews", e.g., listing only the chapter headings, in addition to a full table of contents. A possible implementation could look like this:

```
\AtBeginDocument{\startcontents[short]}
\newcommand\shorttoc[1]{\chapter*{#1}%
  \printcontents[short]{short-}{0}{\setcounter{tocdepth}{0}}}
\titlecontents{short-chapter}[..]{..}{..}{..}{..}
```

We start a partial contents list named `short` at the beginning of the document. Because we never restart, this partial list receives all headings. Then we define the command `\shorttoc` to produce a chapter heading without a number and then print this partial TOC list starting from level 0 (i.e., chapters) but displaying only chapters (since we set the `tocdepth` counter to zero). Finally, we define a suitable formatting for chapter entries in that list. As we used the prefix `short-`, we need to define `short-chapter` (no details given in the code above).

There are similar commands for producing partial lists of figures or tables named `\startlist`, `\printlist`, `\stoplist`, and `\resumelist` but with a slightly different syntax. For details consult the package documentation.

In this book we used these partial contents lists in several places. Each chapter starts with a `\startcontents` declaration, which enables us to show the chapter TOCs with special formatting. Each `\chapter` command executed something similar to the following:

How we produced the content lists for this book

```
\startcontents
\printcontents{p-}{1}{\contentsmargin{0pt}\setcounter{tocdepth}{1}%
                \color{blue}\headingfont\mdseries}
```

All we had to do in addition was to provide a suitable definition for `p-section` to format the section entries. For this book we used the following setup, which was all that was necessary:

```
\titlecontents{p-section}[18pt]{\addvspace{1pt}}
              {\contentspush{\thecontentslabel\enspace}}
              {}
              {\titlerule*[6pt]{.}\ \thecontentspage}
```

Furthermore, for the overall content lists we also deployed partial lists, because both physical books have been produced in a single run (to simplify cross-referencing and indexing). We therefore started each part of the book with

```
\startcontents[part]  \startlist[part]{lof}  \startlist[part]{lot}
```

thereby dividing the content lists in the two parts representing the two physical books. This enabled us to automatically include the headings of both books in the table of contents for each book — with suitable formatting; i.e., in book I, we show only the chapter titles of book II, while in book II only the chapters of book I are listed, but chapters and sections are given for book II. The situation for the list of figures and tables is simpler: here we show only those entries that belong to the current book. But again this is possible only because we have divided the content lists as shown above.

2.3.3 multitoc — Setting contents lists in multiple columns

Setting contents lists in multiple columns is a design that is sometimes requested. A solution for this is provided through the multitoc package by Martin Schröder, which internally uses the multicol package to achieve the desired result.

The package has three options (toc, lof, and lot) to typeset the table of contents, the list of figures, or the list of tables in multiple columns (default 2).

More columns are seldom needed, but if necessary, you can specify the desired number of columns by changing \multicolumntoc, \multicolumnlof, or \multicolumnlot with \renewcommand.

2.3.4 LATEX's low-level interfaces

In this final section on TOCs we briefly review the basic interfaces for contents files as provided by LATEX, because you may find them used directly in older class files. Packages like titletoc also invoke them but offer some additional level of abstraction on top.

Entering information into the contents files

The interface for writing to the contents files consists of two commands: \addcontentsline and \addtocontents. They are automatically invoked by heading or caption commands, but if necessary, it is also possible to use them to enter some information directly into the files.

```
\addcontentsline{ext}{type}{text}
```

The \addcontentsline command writes the *text* together with some additional information, such as the page number of the current page, into a file with the extension *ext* (usually .toc, .lof, or .lot). Fragile commands within *text* need to be protected with \protect. The *type* argument is a string that specifies the kind of contents entry that is being made. For the table of contents (.toc), it is usually the name of the heading command without a backslash; for .lof or .lot files, figure or table is normally specified.

The \addcontentsline instruction is invoked automatically by the document sectioning commands or by the \caption commands within the float environments. Unfortunately, the interface has only one argument for the variable text, which makes it awkward to properly identify an object's number if present. Because such numbers (e.g., the heading number) typically need special formatting in the contents lists, this identification is absolutely necessary. The trick used by the current LATEX kernel to achieve this goal is to surround such a number with the command \numberline within the *text* argument as follows:

> \protect\numberline{*number*}*heading*

For example, a \caption command inside a figure environment saves the caption text for the figure using the following line:

> \addcontentsline{lof}{figure}{\protect\numberline{\thefigure}*caption text*}

Because of the \protect command, \numberline is written unchanged into the external file, while \thefigure is replaced along the way so that the actual figure number and not the command ends up in the file.

Later, during the formatting of the contents lists, a suitable definition of \numberline can then be used to format the number in a special way, such as by providing extra space or a different font. The disadvantage of this approach is that it is less general than a version that takes a separate argument for this number (e.g., you cannot easily do arbitrary transformation on this number), and it requires an appropriate definition for \numberline — something that is unfortunately not always easy to provide (see the discussion below).

> \addtocontents{*ext*}{*text*}

The \addtocontents command does not contain a *type* parameter and is intended to enter special formatting information not directly related to any contents line. For example, the \chapter command of the standard classes places additional white space in the .lof and .lot files to separate entries from different chapters as follows:

> \addtocontents{lof}{\protect\addvspace{10pt}}
> \addtocontents{lot}{\protect\addvspace{10pt}}

By using \addvspace at most 10 points separate the entries from different chapters without producing strange gaps if some chapters do not contain any figures or tables.

This example, however, shows a certain danger of the interface: while \addcontentsline, \addtocontents, and \addvspace appear to be user-level commands (given that they do not contain any @ signs in their names), they can easily produce strange errors.[1] In particular, \addvspace can be used only in vertical mode, which means that a line like the above works correctly only if an earlier \addcontentsline ends in vertical mode. Thus, you need to understand how such lines are actually processed to be able to enter arbitrary formatting instructions between them. This is the topic of the next section.

Potential problems with \addvspace

If either \addcontentsline or \addtocontents is used within the source of a document, one important restriction applies: neither command can be used at the same level as an \include statement. That means, for example, that the sequence

Potential problems with \include

> \addtocontents{toc}{\protect\setcounter{tocdepth}{1}}
> \include{sect1}

with sect1.tex containing a \section command would surprisingly result in a .toc file containing

> \contentsline {section}{\numberline {1}Section from sect1}{2}{}%
> \setcounter {tocdepth}{1}

showing that the lines appear out of order. The solution is to move the \addtocontents or \addcontentsline statement into the file loaded via \include or to avoid \include altogether.

Typesetting a contents list

As discussed above, contents lists are generated by implicitly or explicitly using the commands \addcontentsline and \addtocontents. The exact effect of \addcontentsline{*ext*}{*type*}{*text*} is to place the line

> \contentsline{*type*}{*text*}{*page*}{*anchor-name*}%

---

[1] For an in-depth discussion of \addvspace, see Appendix A.2.4, page →II 655.

including the final percent sign into the auxiliary file with extension *ext*, where *page* is the current page number in the document. The *anchor-name* argument is by default empty but gets filled if the hyperref package is loaded. In that case it specifies a hyperlink anchor name.

The command `\addtocontents{ext}{text}` is simpler: it just puts *text* into the auxiliary file without any extra material. Thus, a typical contents list file consists of a number of `\contentsline` commands, possibly interspersed with further formatting instructions added as a result of `\addtocontents` calls. It is also possible for the user to create a table of contents by hand with the help of the command `\contentsline`.

Inconsistency with `\part`

A typical example is shown below. Note that most (though not all) heading numbers are entered as a parameter of the `\numberline` command to allow formatting with the proper indentation. For historical reasons LATEX is unfortunately not consistent here; the standard classes do not use `\numberline` for `\part` headings but instead specify the formatting explicitly.[1]

```
\setcounter{tocdepth}{3}
\contentsline {part}{I\hspace{1em}Part}{2}{}%
\contentsline{chapter}{\numberline{1}A-Head}{2}{}%
\contentsline{section}{\numberline{1.1}B-Head}{3}{}%
\contentsline{subsection}%
              {\numberline{1.1.1}C-Head}{4}{}%
\contentsline{subsection}%
              {\numberline{}With Empty Number}{5}{}%
\contentsline{subsection}{Unnumbered C-Head}{6}{}%
\contentsline{subsection}%
              {\numberline{1.1.2}Another C-Head}{8}{}%
\contentsline{section}%
              {\numberline{1.2}Another B-Head}{10}{}%
```

2-3-13

The `\contentsline` command is implemented to take its first argument *type* and then use it to call the corresponding `\l@type` command, which does the actual typesetting. One separate command for each of the types must be defined in the class file. For example, in the report class you find the following definitions:

```
\newcommand\l@section        {\@dottedtocline{1}{1.5em}{2.3em}}
\newcommand\l@subsection     {\@dottedtocline{2}{3.8em}{3.2em}}
\newcommand\l@subsubsection{\@dottedtocline{3}{7.0em}{4.1em}}
\newcommand\l@paragraph      {\@dottedtocline{4}{10em}{5em}}
\newcommand\l@subparagraph {\@dottedtocline{5}{12em}{6em}}
\newcommand\l@figure         {\@dottedtocline{1}{1.5em}{2.3em}}
\newcommand\l@table          {\l@figure}
```

By defining `\l@type` to call `\@dottedtocline` (a command with five arguments) and specifying three arguments (*level*, *indent*, and *numwidth*), the remaining arguments, *text* and *page*, of `\contentsline` are picked up by `\@dottedtocline` as arguments 4 and 5. The last argument (which is by default empty) is simply left sitting there doing nothing. If hyperref is loaded, the definitions are changed and the last argument is also processed.

Note that some section levels build their table of contents entries in a somewhat more complicated way so that the standard document classes have definitions for `\l@part` and `\l@chapter` (or `\l@section` with article) that do not use `\@dottedtocline`. Generally they use a set of specific formatting commands, perhaps omitting the ellipses and typesetting the title in a larger font.

So to define the layout for the contents lists, we have to declare the appropriate `\l@type` commands (which is precisely what titletoc's `\dottedcontents` and `\titlecontents` commands do). One easy way without this package, as shown above, is to use `\@dottedtocline`, an internal command that we will now look at in some detail.

---

[1] The titlesec package offers the option `newparttoc` to repair this defect.

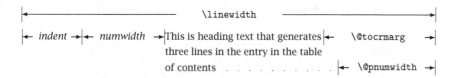

Figure 2.2: Parameters defining the layout of a contents file

---

`\@dottedtocline{`*level*`}{`*indent*`}{`*numwidth*`}{`*text*`}{`*page*`}`

The last two arguments of `\@dottedtocline` coincide with the second and third arguments of `\contentsline`, which itself usually invokes a `\@dottedtocline` command. The other arguments are the following:

level   The nesting level of the entry. With the help of the counter `tocdepth` the user can control how many nesting levels are displayed. Levels greater than the value of this counter will not appear in the table of contents.

indent   The total indentation from the left margin.

numwidth   The width of the box that contains the number if *text* has a `\numberline` command. It is also the amount of extra indentation added to the second and later lines of a multiple-line entry.

Additionally, the command `\@dottedtocline` uses the following global formatting parameters, which specify the visual appearance of all entries. Although all parameters store length values, they have to be changed with `\renewcommand`!

`\@pnumwidth`   The width of the box in which the page number is set.

`\@tocrmarg`   The indentation of the right margin for all but the last line of multiple-line entries. It can be set to a rubber length, which results in the TOC being set unjustified.

`\@dotsep`   The separation between dots, in `mu` (math units).[1] The value stored is a pure number (like 1.7 or 2). By making this number large enough you can get rid of the dots altogether.

A pictorial representation of the effects described is shown in Figure 2.2. The field identified by *numwidth* contains a left-justified section number, if present. You can achieve the proper indentation for nested entries by varying the settings of *indent* and *numwidth*.

One case in which this is necessary, while using a standard class (article, report, or book), arises when you have ten or more sections and within the later ones more than nine subsections. In that case numbers and text will come too close together or even overlap if the *numwidth* argument on the corresponding calls to `\@dottedtocline` is not extended, as seen in the following example.

Problem with too many headings on one level

---

10 A-Head   **3**

   10.1 B-Head   3

   ...

   10.9 B-Head   7

10.10B-Head   8

```
\contentsline{section}{\numberline{10}A-Head}{3}{}%
\contentsline{subsection}{\numberline{10.1}B-Head}{3}{}%
\ldots % several more heading lines here (not shown)
\contentsline{subsection}{\numberline{10.9}B-Head}{7}{}%
\contentsline{subsection}{\numberline{10.10}B-Head}{8}{}%
```

Redefining `\l@subsection` to leave a bit more space for the number (i.e., the third argument to `\@dottedtocline`) gives a better result in this case. You will probably have to adjust the other

---

[1]There are 18 `mu` units to an `em`, where the latter is taken from the `\fontdimen2` of the math symbol font `symbols`. See Section 9.8.1 on page 745 for more information about `\fontdimens`.

73

commands, such as `\l@subsubsection`, as well to produce a balanced look for the whole table.

```
\makeatletter
\renewcommand\l@subsection{\@dottedtocline{2}{1.5em}{3em}}
\makeatother
\contentsline{section}{\numberline{10}A-Head}{3}{}%
\ldots % several more heading lines here
\contentsline{subsection}{\numberline{10.9}B-Head}{7}{}%
\contentsline{subsection}{\numberline{10.10}B-Head}{8}{}%
```

2-3-15

Another example that requires changes is the use of unusual page numbering. For example, if the pages are numbered by part and formatted as "A-78", "B-328", and so on, then the space provided for the page number is probably too small, resulting at least in a large number of annoying "Overfull hbox" warnings, but more likely in some bad spacing around them. In that case the remedy is to set `\@pnumwidth` to a value that fits the widest entry — for example, via

```
\makeatletter \renewcommand\@pnumwidth{2cm} \makeatother
```

When adjusting `\@pnumwidth` this way, it is likely that the value of `\@tocrmarg` needs to be changed as well to keep the layout of the table of contents consistent.

These examples and their remedies clearly show the advantages of the higher-level interfaces provided by titletoc where commands like `\contentspush` allow for much simpler solutions.

Providing additional contents files

You may want to mark up other data in your document and display it as a list. If so, you need to create a new contents file and then make use of the facilities described above.

For example, suppose you want to collect notes on artists. For this we need to define two commands. The first command, `\artist`, typesets the artist's name and associates both of its arguments with the current position in the document by writing them and the current page number to the contents file. The second command, `\listofartistnotes`, reads the information written to the contents file on the previous run and typesets it at the point in the document where the command is called.

For this, the `\listofartistnotes` command invokes `\@starttoc{ext}`, which reads the external file (with the extension *ext*) and then reopens it for writing. This command is also used by the commands `\tableofcontents`, `\listoffigures`, and `\listoftables`. The supplementary file could be given any unused extension such as `.rec`. A command like `\chapter*{Notes on artists}` can be put in front or inside of `\listofartistnotes` to produce a title and, if desired, one can signal the presence of this list to the reader by entering it into the `.toc` file with an `\addcontentsline` command.

The actual typesetting of the individual entries in the `.rec` file is controlled by `\l@note`, which needs to be defined. In the example below, the notes are typeset as paragraphs followed by an italicized page number. Instead of defining this command directly we could have used titletoc's interfaces, e.g., `\titlecontents{note}`...

The version of Ravel's Boléro by Jacques Loussier Trio is rather unusual. Quite interesting is Davis' Blue in Green by Cassandra Wilson.

Notes on artists

Jacques Loussier Trio: A strange experience, *1*

Cassandra Wilson: A wonderful version, *1*

```
\newcommand\artist[2]
         {#1\addcontentsline{rec}{note}{#1: #2}}
\makeatletter \newcommand\listofartistnotes
   {\section*{Notes on artists}\@starttoc{rec}}
\newcommand\l@note[2]
   {\par\noindent#1,~\textit{#2}\par}    \makeatother
The version of Ravel's Boléro by \artist{Jacques
Loussier Trio}{A strange experience} is rather
unusual. Quite interesting is Davis' Blue in Green
by \artist{Cassandra Wilson}{A wonderful version}.
\listofartistnotes
```

2-3-16

The float package described in Section 7.3.1 on page 529 implements the above mechanism with the command `\listof`, which generates a list of floats of the type specified as its argument.

2.4 Managing references

LaTeX has commands that make it easy to manage references in a document. In particular, it supports *cross-references* (internal references between elements within a document), *bibliographic* citations (references to external documents), and *indexing* of selected words or expressions. Indexing facilities will be discussed in Chapter 14, and bibliographic citations in Chapters 15 and 16.

To allow cross-referencing of elements inside a document, you should assign a "key" (consisting of a string of characters, preferably ASCII letters, digits, and punctuation) to the given structural element and then use that key to refer to that element elsewhere.

```
\label{key}   \ref{key}   \pageref{key}
```

The \label command assigns the *key* to the currently "active" element of the document (see below for determining which element is active at a given point). The \ref command typesets a string, identifying the given element — such as the section, equation, or figure number — depending on the type of structural element that was active when the \label command was issued. The \pageref command typesets the number of the page where the \label command was given. The *key* strings should, of course, be unique. As a simple aid it can be useful to prefix them with a string identifying the structural element in question: sec might represent sectional units, fig would identify figures, and so on.

```
\section{A Section} \label{sec:this}
```

4   A Section

A reference to this section looks like this: "see section 4 on page 6".

2-4-1

```
A reference to this section looks
like this:  ''see section~\ref{sec:this}
on page~\pageref{sec:this}''.
```

There is a potential danger when using punctuation characters such as a colon. In certain language styles within the babel system (see Chapter 13), some of these characters have special meanings and behave essentially like commands. The babel package tries hard to allow such characters as part of \label keys, but this can fail in some situations. Similarly, characters outside the ASCII range have been a problem in the past. However, starting with the LaTeX release in 2019 there is a new implementation that essentially supports all Unicode characters that can also be used for typesetting text, i.e., are not generally rejected because LaTeX does not know how to deal with them. Thus, you can use labels like "fig:größer", but using, say, Chinese characters may still give you errors, unless you have loaded special font support packages for them or used a fairly recent LaTeX release.[1]

Restrictions on the characters used in keys

For building cross-reference labels, the "currently active" structural element of a document is determined in the following way. The sectioning commands (\chapter,

---

[1] With real Unicode engines, such as X∃TEX or LuaTEX, all Unicode characters are usable. The remaining technical restrictions of the pdfTEX engine were finally overcome with the November 2021 release of LaTeX — so now you can also use all Unicode characters with that engine.

\section, ...), the environments equation, figure, table, and the theorem family, as well as the various levels of the enumerate environment, and \footnote set the *current reference string*, which contains the number generated by LATEX for the given element. This reference string is usually set at the beginning of an element and reset when the scope of the element is exited.

Problems with wrong references to floats

Notable exceptions to this rule are the table and figure environments, where the reference string is defined by the \caption commands. This allows several \caption and \label pairs inside one environment.[1] Because it is the \caption directive that generates the number, the corresponding \label command must *follow* the \caption command in question. Otherwise, an incorrect number is generated. If placed earlier in the float body, the \label command picks up the *current reference string* from some earlier entity, typically the current sectional unit.

The problem is shown clearly in the following example, where only the labels "fig:in2" and "fig:in3" are placed correctly to generate the needed reference numbers for the figures. In the case of "fig:in4" it is seen that environments (in this case, center) limit the scope of references, because we obtain the number of the current section, rather than the number of the figure.

Do not use center in floats

It should be noted that using a center environment in a float (like we did below) is not a good idea not just because it limits the reference scope: it also creates a usually unwanted extra space at the top of the float! It is better to use a \centering declaration, which avoids both problems.

3   A section

3.1   A subsection

Text before is referenced as '3.1'.

```
\section{A section}
\subsection{A subsection}\label{sec:before}
Text before is referenced as '\ref{sec:before}'.
```

... figure body ...

Figure 1: First caption

... figure body ...

Figure 2: Second caption

```
\begin{figure}[ht]                    \label{fig:in1}    % bad
  \begin{center}
    \fbox{\ldots{} figure body \ldots}
    \caption{First caption}    \label{fig:in2}    % ok
    \bigskip
    \fbox{\ldots{} figure body \ldots}
    \caption{Second caption}  \label{fig:in3}    % ok
  \end{center}                          \label{fig:in4}    % bad
\end{figure}
\label{sec:after} % bad, unless you want the page reference
```

The labels are: 'before' (3.1), 'fig:in1' (3.1) – bad, 'fig:in2' (1), 'fig:in3' (2), 'fig:in4' (3.1) – bad and 'after' (3.1) – probably bad!

```
\raggedright
The labels are: 'before' (\ref{sec:before}),
'fig:in1' (\ref{fig:in1}) -- bad, 'fig:in2' (\ref{fig:in2}),
'fig:in3' (\ref{fig:in3}), 'fig:in4' (\ref{fig:in4}) -- bad
and 'after' (\ref{sec:after})   -- probably bad!
```

2-4-2

---

[1]There are, however, good reasons for not placing more than one \caption command within a float environment. Typically proper spacing is difficult to achieve, and, more importantly, it limits LATEXs options to place the float and should (if at all) be done only during final layout adjustments.

For each *key* declared with \label{*key*}, LaTeX records the current reference string and the page number. Thus, multiple \label commands (with different key identifiers *key*) inside the same sectional unit generate an identical reference string but, possibly, different page numbers like sec:before and sec:after above.

According to the *LaTeX Manual* [65] labels can be placed inside the main argument of heading or caption commands, rather than after them. Doing this makes the source a little less readable (which is why I prefer them after), but there are some edge cases, usually with \caption, where placing the label after the command can result in some incorrect extra space, so you need to watch out for this.

Label commands inside arguments

Fancier labels

A reference via \ref produces, by default, the data associated with the corresponding \label command (typically a number); any additional formatting must be provided by the user. If, for example, references to equations are always to be typeset as "equation (*number*)", one has to code "equation (\ref{*key*})".

To enforce consistency the amsmath package provides an \eqref command to reference equations. It automatically places parentheses around the equation number. To utilize this and also get varioref's magic applied (see next section), one could define

```
\newcommand\eqvref[1]{\eqref{#1} \vpageref{#1}}
```

which then automatically adds a page reference if the equation is on a different page. What that does not do is to automatically add the word "equation", though you could, of course, code that into the definition as well. However, a more general solution for adding words based on the referenced counter is offered with the \labelformat declaration. Alternatively you can use the cleveref package discussed in Section 2.4.2, which provides a more sophisticated solution for this.

\labelformat{*counter*}{*formatting-code*} \Ref{*label*}

With \labelformat LaTeX offers a possibility to generate such frills automatically.[1] The command takes two arguments: the name of a counter and its representation when referenced. Thus, for a successful usage, one has to know the counter name being used for generating the label, though in practice this should not pose a problem. When processing a reference the current counter number (or, more exactly, its representation) is picked up as an argument, so the second argument should contain #1 to retrieve it.

A side effect of using \labelformat is that, depending on the defined formatting, it becomes impossible to use \ref at the beginning of a sentence (if its replacement text starts with a lowercase letter). To overcome this problem there is also a \Ref command that behaves like \ref except that it uppercases the first token

---

[1] In the past this command was provided by the varioref package.

of the generated string. In the following example, you can observe this behavior when "section" is turned into "Section".

1 An example

Section 1 shows the use of the `\labelformat` declaration with a reference to equation (1).

$$a = b \tag{1}$$

```
\usepackage[nospace]{varioref}
\labelformat{section}{section~#1}
\labelformat{equation}{equation~(#1)}

\section{An example}\label{sec}
\Ref{sec} shows the use of the \verb=\labelformat=
declaration with a reference to \ref{eq}.
\begin{equation} a = b \label{eq} \end{equation}
```

`2-4-3`

To make the `\Ref` command work properly, the first token in the second argument of `\labelformat` has to be a single ASCII letter; otherwise, the capitalization fails or, even worse, you end up with some error messages. If you actually need something more complicated in this place (e.g., an accented letter), you have to explicitly surround it with braces, thereby identifying the part that needs to be capitalized. For example, for figure references in the Hungarian language you might want to write `\labelformat{figure}{{á}bra~\thefigure}`.

Unicode engines

In pdfTEX the braces are necessary, regardless of whether you write the accented character as `\'a` or as á as we did above, because in this engine UTF-8 characters are seen as several tokens even if on the screen they look like a single character. The downside is that these braces prevent any kerning that the font may specify between á and the following character. However, in X_ETEX or LuaTEX a Unicode character is a single token (not a sequence of bytes) and is therefore picked up correctly even without the braces. Thus, with these engines the braces should not be used to improve the typeset result.

As a second example of the use of `\labelformat` consider the following situation: in the report or book document class, footnotes are numbered per chapter. Referencing them would normally be ambiguous, given that it is not clear whether we refer to a footnote in the current chapter or to a footnote from a different chapter. This ambiguity can be resolved by always adding the chapter information in the reference or by comparing the number of the chapter in which the `\label` occurred with the current chapter number and adding extra information if they differ. This is achieved by the following code:

```
\usepackage{ifthen,varioref}
\labelformat{footnote}{#1\protect\iscurrentchapter{\thechapter}}
\newcommand\iscurrentchapter[1]{%
    \ifthenelse{\equal{#1}{\thechapter}}{}{ in Chapter~#1}}
```

The trick is to use `\protect` to prevent `\iscurrentchapter` from being evaluated when the label is formed. Then, when the `\ref` command is executed, `\iscurrentchapter` compares its argument (i.e., the chapter number current when the label was formed) to the now current chapter number and, when they differ, typesets the appropriate information.

2.4.1 varioref — More flexible cross-references

In many cases it is helpful, when referring to a figure or table, to put both a `\ref` and a `\pageref` command into the document, especially when one or more pages separate the reference and the object. Some people use a command like

```
\newcommand\fullref[1]{\ref{#1} on page~\pageref{#1}}
```

to reduce the number of keystrokes necessary to make such a complete reference. But because one never knows with certainty where the referenced object finally falls, this method can result in a citation to the current page, which is disturbing and should therefore be avoided. The package varioref, written by Frank Mittelbach, tries to resolve that problem automatically. For this it provides the commands `\vref` and `\vpageref` to deal with single references, as well as `\vrefrange` and `\vpagerefrange` to handle multiple references.[1]

We recommend that you always load the package with the option `nospace`, and this is what we assume throughout the book. Without it varioref manipulates the spaces in front of its commands (and even adds one if there is not any), but this causes a number of problems and should therefore be avoided.[2] Some more details are given on page 85.

We recommend to always use the `nospace` *option*

| `\vref*[`*same-page*`]{`*key*`}`   `\Vref*[`*same-page*`]{`*key*`}` |

The command `\vref` is like `\ref` when the reference and `\label` are on the same page and the optional argument is not used. With the optional argument it prints the text *same-page* after the reference.[3] If the label and reference differ by one page, `\vref` creates one of these strings: "on the facing page", "on the preceding page", or "on the following page". The word "facing" is used when both label and reference fall on a double spread and the document is typeset in `twoside` mode. When the difference is larger than one page, `\vref` produces both `\ref` and `\pageref`. Note that when a special page numbering scheme is used instead of the usual arabic numbering (for example, `\pagenumbering{roman}`), there will be no distinction between being one or many pages off.

If `\varioref` is loaded with the option `nospace` as recommended, then the star form has no effect unless you also load hyperref. In the latter case it prevents hyperref from generating a hyperlink for this reference. If `nospace` is not used, then the star form stops adding a space in front of the reference.

Different behaviors of the star form depending on options used

The `\Vref` command works like `\vref` except that it internally uses `\Ref` instead of `\ref`; i.e., it uppercases the first letter. See above for a discussion of the restrictions that apply to its use with pdfTeX.

---

[1] As a matter of fact, the package also defines `\fullref` for cases where it is certain that label and reference are far apart. Using that instead of `\vref` needs less resources and is faster although these days this seldom matters.

[2] The reason that `nospace` is not the default is that the documents in the last twenty years assumed the old behavior, and thus changing the default would break too many documents out there.

[3] Note that the optional arguments of `\vref`, `\vpageref`, and similar commands from varioref are not supported if you also load the cleveref package! See Section 2.4.2 on page 86 for the restrictions.

> \vpageref*[*same-page*] [*other-page*] {*key*}

Sometimes you may only want to refer to a page number. In that case, a reference should be suppressed if you are citing the current page. For this purpose the \vpageref command is defined. It produces the same strings as \vref except that it does not start with \ref, and it produces the string saved in \reftextcurrent if both label and reference fall on the same page.

Defining \reftextcurrent to produce something like "on the current page" ensures that text like "... see the diagram \vpageref{ex:foo} which shows ..." does not come out as "... see the diagram which shows ...", which could be misleading.

A space in front of \vpageref is ignored if the command does not create any text at all. Thus the correct way to use the command is to place a space on either side. As with \vref the star form has no effect when the option nospace is used unless hyperref is also loaded in which case it suppresses the hyperlink to the page.

In fact, \vpageref allows even more control when used with its two optional arguments. The first argument specifies an alternative text to be used if the label and reference fall on the same page. This is helpful when both are close together so that they may or may not be separated by a page break. In such a case, you usually know whether the reference comes before or after the label so that you can code something like the following:

```
... see the diagram \vpageref[above]{ex:foo} which shows ...
```

The resultant text will be "... see the diagram above which shows ..." when both are on the same page, or "... see the diagram on the page before which shows ..." (or something similar, depending on the settings of the \reftext..before and \reftext..after commands) if they are separated by a page break. Note, however, that if you use \vpageref with such an optional argument to refer to a figure or table, depending on the float placement parameters, the float may show up at the top of the current page and therefore before the reference, even if it follows the reference in the source file.[1]

Maybe you even prefer to say "... see the above diagram" when both diagram and reference fall on the same page — that is, reverse the word order compared to our previous example. In fact, in some languages the word order automatically changes in that case. To allow for this variation the second optional argument *other-page* can be used. It specifies the text preceding the generated reference if both object and reference do not fall on the same page. Thus, one would write

```
... see the \vpageref[above diagram][diagram]{ex:foo} which shows ...
```

to achieve the desired effect.

---

[1] To ensure that a floating object always follows its place in the source, use the flafter package, which is described in Section 7.2.

> \vpagerefrange*[*same-page*]{*first*}{*last*}

This command is similar to \vpageref (without the second optional argument) but takes two mandatory arguments — two labels denoting a range. If both labels fall on the same page, the command acts exactly like \vpageref (with a single label); otherwise, it produces something like "on pages 15-18" (see the customization possibilities described below). It has an optional argument that defaults to the string stored in \reftextcurrent and is used if both labels appear on the current page.

Again there exists a starred form, \vpagerefrange*, which suppresses a hyperlink or the insertion of a space depending on the options used.

> \vrefrange[*same-page*]{*first*}{*last*}

This \vrefrange command is simply a convenient shorthand for

$$\ref\{first\} \text{ to } \ref\{last\} \text{ } \vrefpagerange[same\text{-}page]\{first\}\{last\}$$

except that it varies the word "to" depending on the language. This means it is suitable only for ranges of length three or more, because with just two you better use "and" between the references as we did in the following example.

---

1 Test

Observe equations 1.1 to 1.3 on pages 6–7 and in particular equations 1.2 and 1.3 on the facing page.

$$a = b \qquad (1.1)$$

6

Here is a second equation...

$$b < c \qquad (1.2)$$

...and finally one more equation:

$$a < c \qquad (1.3)$$

7

```
\usepackage[nospace]{varioref}
\renewcommand\theequation
     {\thesection.\arabic{equation}}
\section{Test}
Observe equations~\vrefrange{A}{C} and
in particular equations~\ref{B}
and~\ref{C} \vpagerefrange{B}{C}.
\begin{equation}a=b\label{A}\end{equation}
Here is a second equation\ldots
\begin{equation}b<c\label{B}\end{equation}
\ldots and finally one more equation:
\begin{equation}a<c\label{C}\end{equation}
```

Providing your own reference commands

Sometimes you may want to define your own reference commands that make use of the varioref features internally. For this the package offers three helper commands.

> \vpagerefcompare{*key₁*}{*key₂*}{*true-code*}{*false-code*}

This command compares the page numbers for key_1 and key_2 and then executes either *true-code* or *false-code* depending on the result. The next example shows a not very serious application that compares two equation labels and prints out text depending on their relative positions. Compare the results of the tests on the first page with those on the second.

| Test: the equations (1) and (2) on this page.<br><br>Test: the equation (1) on the current page and (3) on page 8.<br><br>$$a = b \qquad (1)$$<br><br>$$b = c \qquad (2)$$<br><br><br>6 | Test: the equations (1) and (2) on the preceding page.<br><br>Test: the equation (1) on the facing page and (3) on the next page.<br><br>We force eq. 3 to the next page!<br><br><br><br>7 | ```
\usepackage[nospace]{varioref}
\newcommand\veqns[2]{the equation%
  \vpagerefcompare{#1}{#2}%
    {s (\ref{#1})}%
    { (\ref{#1}) \vpageref{#1}}%
  \space and (\ref{#2}) \vpageref{#2}}
Test: \veqns{A}{B}. \par Test: \veqns{A}{C}.
\begin{equation} a=b \label{A}\end{equation}
\begin{equation} b=c \label{B}\end{equation}
\newpage
Test: \veqns{A}{B}. \par Test: \veqns{A}{C}.
\par We force eq.~\ref{C} to the next page!
\newpage % for eq. to next page
\begin{equation} c=a \label{C}\end{equation}
``` 2-4-5 |

`\vpagerefnearby{key}{true-code}{false-code}`

This command lets you find out if a page reference would generate textual reference because it is on the previous, current, or next page or if it would just generate reference with a page number. Depending on the result, either the *true-code* or the *false-code* is executed.

`\vrefpagenum{cmd}{key}`

The package also provides the `\vrefpagenum` command, which allows you to write your own small commands that implement functions similar to those provided by the two previous commands. It takes two arguments: the second is a label (i.e., as used in `\label` or `\ref`), and the first is an arbitrary command name (make sure you use your own) that is set to the page number representation related to this label. This can then be used for comparisons with page numbers of other labels, but note that it may not be a number.

Language options

The package supports the options defined by the babel system (see Section 13.1.3); thus, a declaration like `\usepackage[ngerman]{varioref}` produces texts suitable for the German language. If your document is written in several languages, you need to specify all of them as options so that the strings get integrated into babel's language switching mechanism. For languages not (yet) supported you need to specify the relevant language strings yourself as explained on page 84.

Individual customizations

How to say before . . . To allow further customization, the generated text strings (which will be predefined by the language options) are all defined via macros. Backward references
```

use \reftextbefore if the label is on the preceding page but invisible, and \reftextfacebefore if it is on the facing page (that is, if the current page number is odd and the document is set in twoside mode).

Similarly, \reftextafter is used when the label comes on the next page but one has to turn the page, and \reftextfaceafter is used when it is on the next, but facing, page. These four strings can be redefined with \renewcommand.

... and after ...

In fact, \reftextfacebefore and \reftextfaceafter are used only if the user or the document class specified two-sided printing.

The command \reftextfaraway is used when the label and reference differ by more than one page or when they are nonnumeric. This macro is a bit different from the preceding ones because it takes one argument, the symbolic reference string, so that you can make use of \pageref in its replacement text. For instance, if you wanted to use your macros in German language documents, you would define something like:

... or far away

```
\renewcommand\reftextfaraway[1]{auf Seite~\pageref{#1}}
```

The \reftextpagerange command takes two arguments and produces the text that describes a page range (the arguments are keys to be used with \pageref). Similarly, \reftextlabelrange takes two arguments and describes the range of figures, tables, or whatever the labels refer to. See below for the English language defaults of both.

Denoting ranges

To allow some random variation in the generated strings, you can use the command \reftextvario inside the string macros. This command takes two arguments and selects one or the other for printing depending on the number of \vref or \vpageref commands already encountered in the document (alternating between the first and the second argument).

Minor randomness

As an example, the English language default definitions of the various macros described in this section are shown below:

```
\newcommand\reftextfaceafter{on the \reftextvario{facing}{next} page}
\newcommand\reftextfacebefore
                {on the \reftextvario{facing}{preceding} page}
\newcommand\reftextafter {on the \reftextvario{following}{next} page}
\newcommand\reftextbefore
                {on the \reftextvario{preceding page}{page before}}
\newcommand\reftextcurrent {on \reftextvario{this}{the current} page}
\newcommand\reftextfaraway    [1]{on page~\pageref{#1}}
\newcommand\reftextpagerange [2]{on pages~\pageref{#1}--\pageref{#2}}
\newcommand\reftextlabelrange[2]{\ref{#1} to~\ref{#2}}
```

If you want to customize the package according to your own preferences, just write appropriate redefinitions of the above commands into the preamble of your document or in a file with the extension .sty (e.g., vrflocal.sty) and load that with \usepackage. If you also put \RequirePackage[nospace]{varioref} (see Section A.6 on page →II 693) at the beginning of this file, then your local package automatically loads the varioref package.

Using varioref
without textual
references

Some people do not like textual references to pages but want to automatically suppress a page reference when both label and reference fall on the same page. This can be achieved with the help of the \thevpagerefnum command as follows:

```
\renewcommand\reftextfaceafter {on page~\thevpagerefnum}
\renewcommand\reftextfacebefore{on page~\thevpagerefnum}
\renewcommand\reftextafter    {on page~\thevpagerefnum}
\renewcommand\reftextbefore    {on page~\thevpagerefnum}
```

Within one of the \reftext... commands, \thevpagerefnum evaluates to the current page number if known or to two question marks otherwise.

In the same fashion you can suppress all textual page references if the reference is on the preceding or following page and show the page number only when it is further away. For this, change the definitions as follows:

```
\renewcommand\reftextfaceafter {\unskip}
\renewcommand\reftextafter    {\unskip}
\renewcommand\reftextfacebefore{\unskip}
\renewcommand\reftextbefore    {\unskip}
```

The \unskip is necessary in order to remove the space that was already added after the reference. Without it you end up with two spaces.

Altering the phrase
structure

Some languages have a completely different sentence structure so that adjusting only the individual phrases is not enough. To cater for this, there are also \vrefformat, \Vrefformat, \vrefrangeformat, and \fullrefformat. For example, for Japanese there are definitions such as

```
\renewcommand\vrefformat[2]{\ref{#2}(\vpageref[#1]{#2})} % for Japanese
\renewcommand\vrefformat[2]{\ref{#2} \vpageref[#1]{#2}}  % all other
                                                         % languages
```

The parentheses in the Japanese definition are not the normal characters but their full wide counterparts in Unicode slots U+FF08 and U+FF09 — something you cannot see here but is important when this is used together with Kanji glyphs.

Customization for several languages with babel

If you use the babel system, redefinitions for individual languages should be added using \addto, as explained in Section 13.6, e.g.,

```
\addto\extrasngerman{%
  \renewcommand\reftextfaceafter{auf der nächsten Seite}%
  ... }
```

Do not forget to add appropriate % signs as shown above. Otherwise, a language switch might generate spurious spaces in your document!

A few things to watch out for

Defining commands like the ones described above poses some interesting problems. Suppose, for example, that a generated text like "on the next page" gets broken across pages. If this happens, it is very difficult to find an acceptable algorithmic solution, and, in fact, this situation can even result in a document that always changes from one state to another (i.e., inserting one string; finding that this is wrong; inserting another string on the next run which makes the first string correct again; inserting ...). The current implementation of the package varioref considers the end of the generated string as being relevant. For example,

> Table 5 on the current ⟨*page break*⟩ page

would be true if Table 5 were on the page containing the word "page", not the one containing the word "current". However, this behavior is not completely satisfactory and in some cases may actually result in a possible loop (where LaTeX is requesting an additional run over and over again). Therefore, all such situations produce a LaTeX error message so that you can inspect the problem and perhaps decide to use a \ref command in that place.

During document preparation, while one is still changing the text, such errors can be turned into warnings by placing a \vrefwarning command in the preamble. This is equivalent to specifying draft as an option to the package. \vrefshowerrors ensures that varioref stops when detecting a possible loop. This is the default and equivalent to specifying final as an option. The commands can also be used inside the document if you want to disable the errors only in some places.

Also, be aware of the potential problems that can result from the use of \reftextvario in the default definitions: if you reference the same object several times in nearby places, the change in wording every second time can look strange. To get rid of the variations introduced by \reftextvario without redefining all the \reftext... commands that use it, you can simply redefine it to always use the first or the second of its arguments, e.g.,

    \renewcommand\reftextvario[2]{#1}

in the preamble of your document.

Package behavior without the nospace option

When varioref was originally designed, it had a special behavior: its commands removed any preceding space and inserted their own instead. Thus, you could leave out space before \vref or \vpageref and it would still put the reference in the right place. But this meant that you could not write something like (\vref{foo}), and therefore the package offered star forms of the commands to prevent the space manipulations. This is still the default behavior if you use the package without the nospace option.

However, this approach has several drawbacks. For one it prevents hyperref from using the star forms for hyperlink suppression (which is an important feature), it makes your sources less readable if you leave out the space, and it does not work well with other packages, e.g., cleveref. This is why these days we recommend using always the nospace option.

2.4.2 cleveref — Cleverly formatted references

We have already seen on page 77 that LATEX offers some light-weight support for formatted references based on the counter used in the reference. The package cleveref by Toby Cubitt is the heavy-weight version of this approach. In addition, it supports references to multiple labels and with numerical references or page references sorts the results and compresses ranges appropriately. The varioref commands \vref, \Vref, and \vpageref are augmented to support multiple keys and reference formatting.[1] All aspects of the formatting are customizable in the document preamble, which makes cleveref a truly comprehensive and powerful solution.

```
\cref*{key-list}    \Cref*{key-list}
```

The main command offered by cleveref is \cref. It accepts either a single key (like \ref) or a list of such keys separated by commas. It then formats the corresponding reference (or references) according to their type, e.g., prepends words such as "section" or abbreviations such as "fig." and possibly adds other frills such as parentheses around equation numbers.

If a comma-separated list of keys is given, it uses plural forms as appropriate and in longer lists it knows about appropriate conjunctions; e.g., it can distinguish pairs, longer sets of individual references, and consecutive ranges, and it can handle combinations thereof.

Because the generated text might start with a lowercase letter, the package additionally offers \Cref to be used at the start of a sentence. It differs from \cref by using a capital first letter in the text that is prepended to the reference number. It also always uses full words, e.g., "Figure" not "Fig.", whereas \cref may produce abbreviations if so directed.

If the hyperref package is used, then the typeset reference gets a hyperlink to the reference target by default. Use the star form to suppress this link.

4   A Section

A reference to an equation in this section looks like: "see eq. (1) in section 4".

$$a = b \tag{1}$$
$$b < c \tag{2}$$
$$c < d \tag{3}$$

Equations (1) to (3) above are ...

```
\usepackage{amsmath,cleveref}

\section{A Section}\label{sec:this}

A reference to an equation in this section looks
like: ``see \cref{eq:a} in \cref{sec:this}''.
\begin{align} a &= b \label{eq:a} \\
              b &< c \label{eq:b} \\
              c &< d \label{eq:c} \end{align}
\Cref{eq:c,eq:a,eq:b} above are \ldots
```

2-4-6

---

[1] The cleveref package requires varioref to be loaded with the option nospace, to be able to use the star forms for suppressing hyperlinks. If necessary, it enforces this varioref behavior.

As you can see, the reference to the equation is handled quite differently from the one to the heading: it uses an abbreviation and adds parentheses around the equation number, whereas the heading is referred to as "section". In comparison, \Cref used "Equations"; the references are correctly sorted (even though they are given in a different order in the source), and the resulting range was correctly compressed. Automatic sorting of references is usually helpful. If you rearrange parts of your text, then some of your reference may change their order, and without this sorting, you might end up with strange references such as "see figures (1), (3), and (2)".

If we had two additional equations and referenced some of them, the result would come out quite different as shown in the next example:

Equations (1) to (5) are sorted and eqs. (1) to (3) and (5) are sorted with a gap. But compare these results with referencing eqs. (1) to (3), (4) and (5)! Surprised?

```
% equations as before + 2 more
\Cref{eq:c,eq:b,eq:a,eq:d,eq:e} are sorted and
\cref{eq:c,eq:b,eq:a,eq:e} are sorted with a gap.
But compare these results with referencing
\cref{eq:c,,eq:b,eq:a,eq:d,eq:e}! Surprised?
```

2-4-7

The behavior of the last \cref in the previous example may have been a bit of a surprise: the references are correctly sorted but split into two groups with the first one compressed. The reason is the ",,". It tells cleveref that the preceding key (eq:c) should be treated as a final reference in whatever range it belongs to after sorting. Thus, equations eq:d and eq:e form a second range or rather a pair and we therefore get this particular result in the second sentence of the example. This facility can be sometimes helpful, but in such a case you would probably want to make sure that you keep the keys sorted in the source to better understand what is going on.

If you use \cref or \Cref with a list of keys, it is not required that they are all of the same type as cleveref happily sorts them within each type and then applies the rest of its magic. Of course, this works well only if the types are compatible with each other, e.g., if you are referring to a number of different heading levels, to floats, or to different types of theorem environments, etc. Otherwise, you might end up with strange constructs.

```
\usepackage{cleveref}
```

2-4-8

In figs. 1 to 3 and table 1 we ...

```
In \cref{fig:a,tab:a,fig:b,fig:c} we \ldots
```

You may not fancy all of the defaults that cleveref applies, so to alter them you can use the options sort (but do not compress), compress (but do not sort), nosort (do neither), or sort&compress (the default). If the generated texts should always be capitalized, which is often requested in house styles, use the option capitalize.

Options to alter the package behavior

The package also understands most language options; e.g., in the next example we use German text and turn off compression but keep the sorting. We do not have to use capitalize, because German nouns are always capitalized.

Gleichungen (1), (2) und (3) in Abschnitt 4 ...

```
\usepackage[ngerman,sort]{cleveref}
\Cref{eq:c,eq:a,eq:b} in \cref{sec:this} \ldots
```

2-4-9

Another useful option is `noabbrev` if you do not like the abbreviations used by `\cref` in some languages such as English.

Finally, if you use cleveref with hyperref, then references are hyperlinked to their target (unless the star forms of the commands are used). By default the link area, i.e., the text you can click to navigate, is only the label and does not include the additional material. With the option `nameinlink`, you can change this to enlarge the clickable area. To demonstrate this we colored the link areas in the next example:

```
\usepackage[colorlinks,linkcolor=blue]{hyperref}
\usepackage[nameinlink,noabbrev]{cleveref}
```

Section 4 contains equations (1) and (2).   `\Cref{sec:this}` contains `\cref{eq:a,eq:b}`.   2-4-10

```
\namecref{key}      \nameCref{key}      \lcnamecref{key}
\namecrefs{key}     \nameCrefs{key}     \lcnamecrefs{key}
```

Sometimes it is useful to provide just the text generated for a certain reference type without typesetting the label value. The above commands do this for use within a sentence and at the start of a sentence, both in singular and plural forms. The `\lcname...` commands always use lowercase, even if the `capitalize` option is in force. All of the commands accept only a single *key* as their argument, because a key list would be pointless if no labels are set.

```
\labelcref{key-list}    \labelcpageref{key-list}
```

There are also `\labelcref` and `\labelcpageref` that print the labels or page references without prepending any text. They support *key-list*s and still add any necessary conjunction text between the items. However, because no text denoting the type is typeset, the elements in the *key-list* must be of a single type.

```
\crefrange*{key₁}{key₂}    \Crefrange*{key_first}{key_last}
```

Instead of specifying a lengthy *key-list* with `\cref`, you can use `\crefrange` or `\Crefrange` using the *first* and *last* keys to denote a consecutive range. Note that the assumption is that this range has at least three items; thus, referencing a range of length two comes out slightly strange as shown below. For this you therefore should use `\cref{eq:b,eq:c}`.

```
\usepackage{cleveref}
```

Equations (1) to (5) and in particular   `\Crefrange{eq:a}{eq:e}` and in particular
eqs. (2) to (3) show ...   `\crefrange{eq:b}{eq:c}` show `\ldots`   2-4-11

```
\cpageref{key-list}              \Cpageref{key-list}
\cpagerefrange{key_first}{key_last}    \Cpagerefrange{key_first}{key_last}
```

These are the commands to deal with references to page number and, just like with `\cref`, sort and compress them and add the appropriate words and punctuations in the target language.

\vref*{*key-list*}	\Vref*{*key-list*}	\vrefrange*{*key$_{first}$*}{*key$_{last}$*}
\vpageref*{*key-list*}		\vpagerefrange*{*key$_{first}$*}{*key$_{last}$*}

If the varioref package is used with cleveref, then some of its functions are changed to support *key-lists* instead of only a single *key* as arguments. Note that optional arguments are not supported if both packages are used together. For use at the beginning of a sentence cleveref also defines \Vrefrange, \Vpageref, and \Vpagerefrange, which are not offered by varioref.

Below we repeat Example 2-4-4 on page 81 with both packages loaded. Note that we can now simply use \vref with a *key-list* instead of the construction used before.

1 Test

Observe equations (1.1) to (1.3) on pages 6–7 and in particular equations (1.2) and (1.3) on the facing page.

$$a = b \qquad (1.1)$$

Here is a second equation that appears on the

6

next page ...

$$b < c \qquad (1.2)$$

...and finally one more equation:

$$a < c \qquad (1.3)$$

7

```
\usepackage[nospace]{varioref}
\usepackage[noabbrev]{cleveref}
\renewcommand\theequation
    {\thesection.\arabic{equation}}
\section{Test}
Observe \vrefrange{A}{C} and
in particular \vref{B,C}.
\begin{equation}a=b\label{A}\end{equation}
Here is a second equation that appears
on the next page \ldots
\begin{equation}b<c\label{B}\end{equation}
\ldots and finally one more equation:
\begin{equation}a<c\label{C}\end{equation}
```

2-4-12

Customizing the references

The text generated by the cleveref commands depend on the "type" of the reference, which is usually based on the counter used by the reference.[1] For example, \section commands use the section counter, figure environments the figure counter, enumerate the counters enumi to enumiv for its different nesting levels, and so on. Thus, the reference type for a second-level enumeration is enumii, while that to a figure is figure. There are a few exceptions to the rule: the heading levels in the back matter have the types appendix, subappendix, etc., and theorem-like environments use the environment name if amsthm or ntheorem is loaded.

As the package has knowledge about all these standard types and defines default texts for them, it can be used out of the box generating results like those shown in the previous examples.

However, if you load additional packages that define their own environments or commands with referenceable counters or if you simply do not like the default texts generated by cleveref, then it is easy to adjust or extend them using the configuration possibilities offered by the package as discussed below.

---

[1] As a side effect this means that if two different environments use the same counter, then references to them are of the same type and thus always generate the same text. This is normally not an issue, but see the discussion on theorems on page 91.

> \crefname{*type*}{*singular*}{*plural*}   \Crefname{*type*}{*singular*}{*plural*}

These two commands define for a given *type* the text to typeset when a single reference is made and when several references are made by \cref and \Cref, respectively. For convenience, various types inherit their defaults from other types; e.g., if you change the section type, then subsection and the other lower levels inherit the new text as well, unless you provide an explicit declaration for them too.

If you define for a given *type* only a \crefname, then a corresponding \Crefname is automatically provided by uppercasing the first letter in the second and third arguments. Similarly, if only \Crefname is provided, then \crefname is constructed by the package by applying \MakeLowercase.

> \creflabelformat{*type*}{*format*}

If you want the labels of a certain *type* formatted in a special way, you can denote that with a \creflabelformat declaration. The *format* can be any LᴬTₑX code,[1] and within it #1 denotes the place where the label (e.g., \thesection) is placed, and #2 and #3 denote the start and end points of the clickable area if a hyperlink is produced. For example, to add a closing parenthesis to references to an enumerate environment, you could write

    \creflabelformat{enumi}{#2#1)#3}

or to remove the parentheses around equation references the solution is to write

    \creflabelformat{equation}{#2#1#3}

> \crefrangeconjunction   \crefpairconjunction
> \crefmiddleconjunction   \creflastconjunction

To alter the conjunctions between multiple labels, a number of commands exist that contain the material to be inserted; all are changed using \renewcommand. Between a consecutive range of labels \crefrangeconjunction is added, between pairs \crefpairconjunction is used, and for longer lists \crefmiddleconjunction and \creflastconjunction are added in the appropriate places.

For instance, if you did not like the fact that figures are abbreviated as "figs." in Example 2-4-8 on page 87 and you prefer a range dash instead of the word "to", then this can be easily arranged as follows:

```
\usepackage{cleveref}
\crefname{figure}{figure}{figures}
\newcommand\crefrangeconjunction{--}
```

In figures 1–3 and table 1 we show all relevant data from the different experiments …

```
In \cref{fig:a,tab:a,fig:b,fig:c} we show all
relevant data from the different experiments \ldots
```

2-4-13

---

[1] Use \protect with fragile commands.

```
\crefalias{type}{existing-type}        \label[type]{key}
```

Instead of setting up a (new) *type* with \crefname, etc., you can alternatively specify that reference of that *type* should be formatted according to some *existing-type*. This can be useful in some circumstances if you want several counters (types) to use the same referencing format.

You can also use \label with an optional *type* argument to overwrite the default type for references to a particular label. For example, if you want to refer to some questions as "assumptions", the following will do the trick:

$$a = b \qquad (1)$$

```
\usepackage{cleveref}
\crefname{assume}{assumption}{assumptions}
\creflabelformat{assume}{#2(#1)#3}
\begin{equation} a=b\label[assume]{eq}\end{equation}
Starting from \cref{eq} we get \ldots
```

2-4-14 Starting from assumption (1) we get ...

There are several other adjustments possible with further configuration commands supporting special cases as needed by some languages. Thus, if the above is not sufficient for your needs, consult the package documentation for additional customization possibilities.

Support for multiple languages

So far we covered customizing commands for the main language of a document. If your document uses several languages and you want to customize more than one of them, then you have to get your changes into the language switching mechanism of babel or polyglossia. Here is an example for babel:

Customizing several languages in parallel

```
\usepackage[ngerman,english]{babel,cleveref}
\crefname{figure}{figure}{figures}
\newcommand\crefrangeconjunction{--}
\AtBeginDocument{\addto\extrasngerman{%
    \crefname{figure}{Abbildung}{Abbildungen}%
    \renewcommand\crefrangeconjunction{--}}}
In \cref{fig:a,tab:a,fig:b,fig:c} we have \ldots
\par \selectlanguage{ngerman}
In \cref{fig:a,tab:a,fig:b,fig:c} haben wir \ldots
```

In figures 1–3 and table 1 we have
...
In Abbildungen 1–3 und Tabelle 1

2-4-15 haben wir ...

Note that the additions to \extrasngerman have to be made after the beginning of the document or inside \AtBeginDocument to take effect and that we have to use \renewcommand, not \newcommand, at this point.

Handling theorem-like environments

If you define a new theorem-like environment with the help of \newtheorem, then cleveref does not use the counter name as the *type* but instead the environment name that has been set up.

It also automatically assumes that it can use the environment title as the reference text (converted to lowercase if necessary), but it does not make any attempt to set up a plural form as that is too irregular even in English. Thus, if we process the following example, we see that \Cref and \cref with a single *key* work out of the box, but the last one using a *key-list* fails without further declarations.

Theorem 1 *A theorem.*

Lemma 1 *A lemma.*

Lemma 2 *Another one.*

Lemma 2 is used to prove theorem 1. But **??** 1**??** 2 need formatting help.

```
\usepackage{cleveref}
\newtheorem{thm}{Theorem}
\newtheorem{lem}{Lemma}

\begin{thm} A theorem.   \label{thm:a}\end{thm}
\begin{lem} A lemma.     \label{lem:a}\end{lem}
\begin{lem} Another one.\label{lem:b}\end{lem}
\Cref{lem:b} is used to prove \cref{thm:a}.    \\
But \cref{lem:a,lem:b} need formatting help.
```

2-4-16

Beside the question marks in the printout we also get warnings like

```
LaTeX Warning: cref reference format for label type 'lem'
              undefined on input line 31.
```

in that case. The remedy is to provide appropriate \crefname or \Crefname declarations. However, even that is not enough if you set up the theorem-like environments to share a single counter: in that case we suddenly get texts always referring to theorems and not to lemmas where appropriate.

Theorem 1 *A theorem.*

Lemma 2 *A lemma.*

Lemma 3 *Another one.*

Theorem 3 is used to prove theorem 1. But theorems 2 and 3 need formatting help.

```
\usepackage{cleveref}
\crefname{thm}{theorem}{theorems}
\crefname{lem}{lemma}{lemmas}
\newtheorem{thm}{Theorem} \newtheorem{lem}[thm]{Lemma}

\begin{thm} A theorem.   \label{thm:a}\end{thm}
\begin{lem} A lemma.     \label{lem:a}\end{lem}
\begin{lem} Another one.\label{lem:b}\end{lem}
\Cref{lem:b} is used to prove \cref{thm:a}.    \\
But \cref{lem:a,lem:b} need formatting help.
```

2-4-17

Fortunately, cleveref has a solution for this case too. All you need to do is to use either the amsthm, ntheorem, or thmtools package for theorem-like environments (which is anyway preferable), and then everything comes out correctly.

Lemma 3 is used to prove theorem 1. Now lemmas 2 and 3 are typeset correctly.

```
\usepackage{amsthm,cleveref}
% Otherwise same setup as in previous example ...
\Cref{lem:b} is used to prove \cref{thm:a}.  \\
Now \cref{lem:a,lem:b} are typeset correctly.
```

2-4-18

Other special considerations

LATEX's eqnarray is not supported

The cleveref package cannot be used together with LATEX's eqnarray, or, more precisely, you cannot use \cref to refer to a \label inside such an environment. If you really need this, use \ref instead and supply the necessary textual material (e.g., "eqs.") manually. In most circumstances it is better to use the environments provided by amsmath anyway, because they offer much better spacing of the equations.

2.4.3 nameref — Non-numerical references

In some documents it is required to reference sections by displaying their title texts instead of their numbers, either because there is no number to refer to or because the house style asks for it. This functionality is provided by the \nameref command, available through the nameref package by Sebastian Rahtz (1955–2016) et al. This package is also automatically loaded by hyperref.

For numbered sections and floats with captions, the titles are those that would be displayed in the contents lists (regardless of whether such a list is actually printed). That is, if a short title is provided via the optional argument of a sectioning command or caption, then this title is printed by \nameref. This can be somewhat surprising for the reader if the short title of a heading is noticeably different in wording to the title in the body of the document. In contrast, unnumbered sections take their title reference from the printed title. If you use \nameref with a label key unrelated to a title (e.g., a label in a footnote, or an enumeration item), it simply displays the title of the surrounding section.

As \nameref does not produce the heading number but only its title, you have to additionally use \ref if you want to typeset both. More commonly you may want to display the title together with a page reference for which you can use the abbreviation \Nameref. Note that this command surrounds the title with single quotes, which may not be to your taste and may lead to strange results if you use other type of quotes elsewhere as we did in the next example.

4 Textual References

Section 'Textual References' on page 6 proves that it is possible to reference unnumbered sections by referencing section "Example".

A Small Example

The current section is referenced in section 4.

```
\usepackage{nameref}
\setcounter{secnumdepth}{1}

\section{Textual References}\label{num}
Section \Nameref{num} proves that
it is possible to reference unnumbered sections
by referencing section ''\nameref{unnum}''.

\subsection[Example]{A Small Example}\label{unnum}
The current section is referenced in
section~\ref{num}.
```

2-4-19

If hyperref is used, then you can also use \nameref*, which works like \nameref but prevents a hyperlink to the section. If you load only nameref, both commands have the same effect.

2.4.4 showkeys, refcheck — Displaying & checking reference keys

When writing a larger document, many people print intermediate drafts. In such drafts it would be helpful if the positions of \label commands as well as their keys could be made visible. This becomes possible with the **showkeys** package written by David Carlisle or the **refcheck** package by Oleg V. Motygin.

When the **showkeys** package is loaded, the commands \label, \ref, \pageref, \cite, and \bibitem are modified in a way that the used key is printed. The \label and \bibitem commands normally cause the key to appear in a box in the margin, while the commands referencing a key print it in small type above the formatted reference (possibly overprinting some text). The package tries hard to position the keys in such a way that the rest of the document's formatting is kept unchanged. There is, however, no guarantee for this, and it is best to remove or disable the showkeys package before attempting final formatting of the document.

1 An example

1.1 A subsection

Section 1 shows the use of the showkeys package with a reference to equation (1).

$$a = b \qquad (1)$$
$$a < b \qquad (2)$$
$$a > b \qquad (3)$$

```
\usepackage{amsmath, showkeys}
\section{An example}\label{sec}
\subsection{A subsection}\label{unused}
Section~\ref{sec} shows the use of the
\texttt{showkeys} package with a
reference to equation~(\ref{eq}).
\begin{align} a &= b \label{eq} \\
              a &< b \label{eq2} \\
              a &> b     \end{align}
```

2-4-20

The package supports the **fleqn** option of the standard classes and works together with the packages of the $\mathcal{A}_{\mathcal{M}}\mathcal{S}$-LATEX collection, varioref, natbib, and many other packages. Nevertheless, it is nearly impossible to ensure its safe working with all packages that hook into the reference mechanisms.

If you want to see only the keys on the \label command in the margin, you can suppress the others by using the package option **notref** (which disables the redefinition of \ref, \pageref, and related commands) or the option **notcite** (which does the same for \cite and its cousins from the natbib package). Alternatively, you might want to use the option **color** to make the labels less obstructive.

Also supported are the options **draft** (default) and **final**. While the latter is useless when used on the package level, because you can achieve the same result by not specifying the **showkeys** package, **draft** comes in handy if **final** is specified as a global option on the class and you nevertheless want to visualize the keys.

If you look at the keys used in Example 2-4-20, then both "unused" and "eq2" are never used in references, and the third equation has an equation number without a label. While the latter is directly visible because there is no boxed key in the margin, the unused keys cannot be identified easily if at all. Nevertheless, all three cases are likely to be either mistakes or leftovers; e.g., some references were intended but never made or misspelled.

To find such problems you can use the package **refcheck** instead of **showkeys**. With that package unused labels are shown in the margins surrounded by question marks and in the case of equation tags also underlined. Equations with tags that are not referenced show {?} in the margin. What is not shown are key usage by \ref,

\pageref, or \cite. Thus, by redoing our example with this package, we get the following result:

1   An example

⟨sec⟩ **1.1   A subsection**

?⟨unused⟩? Section 1 shows the use of the refcheck package with a reference to equation (1).

$$a = b \qquad (1)\,\boxed{\text{eq}}$$
$$a < b \qquad (2)\,?\text{eq2}?$$
$$a > b \qquad (3)\,\{?\}$$

```
\usepackage{amsmath,refcheck}
\section{An example}\label{sec}
\subsection{A subsection}\label{unused}
Section~\ref{sec} shows the use of the
\texttt{refcheck} package with a
reference to equation~(\ref{eq}).
\begin{align} a &= b \label{eq}  \\
               a &< b \label{eq2} \\
               a &> b      \end{align}
```

2-4-21

The checking is also done for \bibitems so that you can easily see if you have any citations in your bibliography that are never referenced in your paper.

If you use the xr package to provide references across different documents, then those can also be verified; for details see the package documentation.

2.4.5 xr — References to external documents

David Carlisle, building on the earlier work of Jean-Pierre Drucbert (1947–2009), developed a package called xr, which implements a system for external references.

If, for instance, a document needs to refer to sections of another document — say, other.tex — then you can specify the xr package in the main file and give the command \externaldocument{other} in the preamble. Then you can use \ref and \pageref to refer to anything that has been defined with a \label command in either other.tex or your main document. You may declare any number of such external documents.

If any of the external documents or the main document uses the same \label key, then a conflict occurs, because the key is multiply defined. To overcome this problem, \externaldocument takes an optional argument in which you can declare a *prefix*. For example, with \externaldocument[A-]{other} all references from the file other.tex are prefixed by A-. So, for instance, if a section in the file other.tex had a \label{intro}, then it could be referenced with \ref{A-intro}. The *prefix* can be any string chosen to ensure that all the keys imported from external files are unique.

Note, however, that if one of the packages you are using declares certain active characters (e.g., : in French or " in German), then these characters should not be used inside \label commands and thus not as part of the *prefix* either.

As of 2019 the package also supports referencing \bibitems; i.e., you can cite a bibliography entry with \cite or any of its cousins even if the bibliography is stored in a separate document.[1]

Citations to external bibliographies

The package does not work together with the hyperref package because both modify the internal reference mechanism. Instead, you can use the xr-hyper package, which is a reimplementation tailored to work with hyperref.

---

[1]This was originally available as a separate xcite package, written by Enrico Gregorio.

2.4.6 hyperref—Active references

The hyperref package has a long history with many contributors going back to the early days of LaTeX 2_ε. The original development was done by Sebastian Rahtz (1955–2016; see page vii), with contributions by Heiko Oberdiek and David Carlisle; later Heiko took over and rewrote and extended the package—so today's comprehensive version is largely due to his efforts. Now the hyperref package is maintained by the LaTeX Project Team.

The package makes it possible to automatically turn all cross-references (citations, table of contents, and so on) into hypertext links. It also supports hyperlinks to external resources, and in addition it offers access to many PDF features, such as bookmarks, etc. The package is described in detail in [30, pp. 35–67] and comes with its own extensive manual [114]. In this section we therefore discuss only the most important features useful for day-to-day work, but keep in mind that there is much more available (just in terms of option keys you find more than 100 in the manual).

As has been mentioned in Section 2.1.1 there is a major shift under way during which LaTeX is being modernized to support accessible PDF; adapting hyperref is an important step of the task, and if you start your document with \DocumentMetadata to indicate that you want to use the new functionality, a large part of its internal code is different. The LaTeX Project Team works on moving core parts of hyperref directly into the LaTeX kernel, on cleaning up the code, and on extending and standardizing its features.

\DocumentMetadata required!

These changes have also some impact on the user commands: a few features depend on the new code. Options and commands that are not available or that behave differently without \DocumentMetadata are therefore marked with a danger symbol in the following sections.

Using hyperref can be quite easy. Just including it in your list of loaded packages (preferably as the *last* package[1]) suffices to turn all cross-references in your document into hypertext links. For documents viewed on a computer screen, this gives invaluable help for navigating through them.

Configuration possibilities

You may however consider some of the package's default settings not particularly pleasing (such as placing colored boxes around link areas), so many people call the package with a few keys adjusted to taste. The package uses a key/value approach, and most keys can be set when loading the package or later using a \hypersetup declaration.[2]

Manually and automatically provided links

Hyperlinks within a document consist of two parts: a region (of text—typically) that, if clicked, instructs the viewing software to jump to a different part in the document (the so called anchor point). This is realized by putting "named" anchors into the target

---

[1] The hyperref documentation contains a lengthy section discussing deviations to this rule, i.e., in which order certain packages should be loaded in relation to the hyperref package.

[2] Some keys need to be set when the package is loaded because they implement global settings that cannot be altered once set. Even \hypersetup is then impossible, except when used in hyperref.cfg, the configuration file for the package.

places, surrounding regions that should react to clicks with appropriate commands that invoke some sort of "go to the anchor with a certain name" action.

To be able to jump to the right place, each anchor needs a unique name, and the clickable regions need to know to which "name" they should point. This can be done manually with the following two commands:

\hypertarget{*name*}{*text*}   \hyperlink{*name*}{*clickable text*}

The \hypertarget typesets the *text* and additionally places an anchor with the name *name* before it. In a different part of the document you can then make a link to it using \hyperlink. The clickable region is the *clickable text* argument, and by default this gets surrounded by a box with thin colored borders. If used in the manual way, it is your responsibility to make sure that *name* is unique across the whole document.

In many cases there is no need to produce internal document links manually, because hyperref does this automatically for us behind the scenes. Whenever a command or environment is set up to allow cross-references, hyperref adds an anchor point, and when you use \ref or \pageref, it surrounds the generated number with a \hyperlink so that clicking that number takes you to the section, caption, bibliography item, or whatever else is referenced. In the same way, it adds hyperlinks to the titles (and/or page numbers) in the table of contents, list of figures etc.

If you want to make a reference without a hyperlink, use \ref* or \pageref* instead. Making hyperlinks to existing \labels in the document is also available through the following command:

\hyperref [*label*] {*text*}

This command is useful if you do not want to typeset a normal reference, through \ref{*label*}, but instead want to refer in *text* to the object the \label{*label*} is pointing to. Using \hyperref turns this *text* into a clickable area. If *text* should additionally contain a \ref to display the reference number, use \ref* instead to avoid nested links (which do not work).

\MakeLinkTarget{}

\ref, \pageref, and \hyperref do not jump to the place where the \label{*label*} is written but to the last structure before the \label that set an anchor. This can have the surprising (at least for \pageref) effect that it jumps to a different page than the one shown in the output if, for example, the last section was on a previous page. In such cases an explicit target before the label can be inserted with \MakeLinkTarget. This creates the needed target anchor for a correct link if hyperref is loaded.[1]

The hyperref package also generates links from the lists generated by the commands \tableofcontents, \listoffigures, etc., back to the pages with the headings, figures, tables, and so forth. By default, the clickable areas are the heading titles or the captions. This can be changed with the key linktoc, which accepts the

Links from the table of contents and similar lists

---

[1]The legacy hyperref name for this command is \phantomsection, but it is only available if the package is loaded, while \MakeLinkTarget{} can be used with and without hyperref.

values `none`, `section` (the default), `page`, or `all` (in which case both the title and page number become hyperlinks).

Links to footnotes

By default, links from footnote markers in the paragraphs to the footnote text at the bottom of the page are automatically added except inside some environments (like `tabularx`) or when packages such as bigfoot are loaded that introduce their own footnote handling. You also do not get a link if you use `\footnotemark` with an optional argument. You can explicitly suppress such links by setting `hyperfootnotes` to `false` if you prefer not to have any footnote links at all.

Links from the bibliography to citations

It is also possible to automatically generate references from the bibliography back to the pages where the bibliography items are cited. This can be helpful, especially during document preparation. This is achieved with the package option `pagebackref` (displaying the page numbers on which a bibliography item is cited) or `backref`. The latter supports the values `section` (displaying the numbers of the sectional units in which the citations are made, the default), `slides` for use in presentations, `page` (same as `pagebackref`), or `none` to prevent them.

There is one important restriction to be aware of: the mechanism to add the links requires that after each `\bibitem` entry there is always an empty line or a `\par` command. If this is missing and the `\bibitems` directly follow each other, then the links are attached to the wrong place.

The hyperref options for such back references are not relevant when the biblatex package is used to produce the bibliography, because this package implements full support for back references with links directly, and their behavior can and should be adapted by using the relevant biblatex options.

Links from the index entries

Links back from an index to the pages that are referenced are also automatically generated. This can be controlled with the package option `hyperindex`, which can be set to `false` if this is not wanted.

Ensuring unique anchor names

The names for anchors are built by hyperref with the name of the counter and a special representation of the counter called `\theH⟨ctr⟩`, which by default expands to `\the⟨ctr⟩`. If this representation is not unique across the document and you get warnings about duplicated destination names, you should redefine it, for example, by adding another counter value.

This is a common problem with appendices: their definitions often reset the chapter or section counter to zero and switch the numbering style. We therefore repeat the low-level definition from Section 7 on page 53 to demonstrate what is needed to make it compatible with hyperref. We start with a redefinition of `\appendix`. Here we add a redefinition of `\theH⟨ctr⟩` to get a unique anchor name. We could simply mirror the `\thesection` definition, but in languages different from English `\Alph` is perhaps not usable as an anchor name, so we use a prefix instead. To avoid errors if hyperref is not loaded, we provide also a default definition of `\theHsection`:

```
\providecommand\theHsection{\arabic{section}}
\makeatletter
\renewcommand\appendix{%
    \renewcommand\section{%                  % Redefinition of \section...
        \clearpage\thispagestyle{plain}%     %  new page, folio bottom
```

```
        \suppressfloats[t]\@afterindentfalse  % no top floats, no indent
        \secdef\Appendix\sAppendix}%            % call \Appendix or \sAppendix
      \setcounter{section}{0}\renewcommand\thesection{\Alph{section}}%
      \renewcommand\theHsection{appendix-\arabic{section}}% for hyperref
    }
  \makeatother
```

No change is needed in the \Appendix command, but we should tell hyperref the bookmark level:

```
  \makeatletter    \providecommand\toclevel@appendix{1}    \makeatother
```

As a minimum, the \sAppendix command (implementing the starred form) needs a \MakeLinkTarget so that it creates an anchor usable for page references:

```
  \newcommand\sAppendix[1]{%                     % Simplified (starred) form
    {\raggedleft\large\bfseries\MakeLinkTarget{}%
     \appendixname\par \centering#1\par}%
     \@afterheading\addvspace{\baselineskip}}
  \makeatother
```

The special case of enumerate counters, which are typically never unique in a document, is handled internally by hyperref. Another problem can arise from page numbers: hyperref creates for every page an anchor and assumes that every page has a unique name. This is normally the case because roman and arabic page numbers count as different, but it can fail if documents reset the page number after a cover page. The easiest workaround is to set the page number to a negative value for cover pages or to use a different numbering style. If the class hardwires such duplicate page numbers, then another option is to surround the cover pages with the NoHyper environment: it disables all hyperref features and so suppresses also the anchor creation.

Links to external resources

It is also possible with hyperref to link to external resources, e.g., to some Internet Uniform Resource Locator (URL) or to a local file, etc. In a PDF file, such links come in three "flavors": links to a URL, links that launch ("run") an external application to view a local file, and links to other PDF files that can be loaded by the PDF viewer. The link types are marked automatically with different colors or link borders that can be specified in \hypersetup.

The basic command for such links is \href, which attempts to identify the flavor of the link based on some patterns, e.g., if there is a colon in the target or if the file name ends with .pdf. For most standard cases this works quite well.

There are now also the more specialized commands \hrefurl, \hrefrun, and \hrefpdf that create the link type as specified by their name and offer some  additional options to manipulate the link target. The latter are available only if the command \DocumentMetadata has been used at the start of the document.

```
\href [options] {link target}{text}    \hrefurl [options] {url}{text}
\hrefrun [options] {file}{text}        \hrefpdf [options] {file}{text}
```

The *text* argument is typeset and becomes the clickable area. You can use any kind of formatting within *text* argument — it is just typeset by LATEX as usual. The first mandatory argument should describe where the link should take us. This can be a website (starting with `https://` or `http://`), but there are many other URL schemes that are defined and supported by many PDF readers. For example,

```
\href{mailto:frank.mittelbach@latex-project.org?subject=Typo found
                in TLC3}{Report Typo in TLC3}
```

would typeset the text "Report Typo in TLC3" in the document and, if clicked, would open the reader's mailing program with my e-mail address and a default subject line prefilled — try it out if you find a typo.[1]

The special characters #, %, and ~ can be used verbatim in the argument for the link target.[2] This is helpful, because they appear quite often in URLs to web pages.

Non-ASCII links   If the URL contains — as now happens quite commonly — non–ASCII characters, they must be converted into the "percent-encoded" form in the first argument of `\href`; this means, e.g., that a link to the town Köln should be entered as

```
\href{https://www.k%C3%B6ln.de}{Köln}
```

or if used in an argument as

```
\href{https://www.k\%C3\%B6ln.de}{Köln}
```

\DocumentMetadata required!   For this purpose the `\hrefurl` command offers the option `urlencode`, which does the percent-encoding for you. This makes the LATEX input considerably longer, but if you need it often, you can also make it the default by setting `href/urlencode` in `\hypersetup`.

```
\hrefurl[urlencode]{https://www.köln.de}{some text}
```

Preset a protocol   Most URLs use the HTTPS protocol. To save some typing, it is possible to preset this protocol with `href/protocol` in `\hypersetup` for `\hrefurl` and `\url`:

\DocumentMetadata required!

```
\hypersetup{href/protocol=https://}
\hrefurl{www.latex-project.org.de}{some text}
\url{www.latex-project.org.de}
```

Opening files by launching an action   To link to files on the computer you can simply enter the file name in the `\href` argument, or you can launch an action using hyperref's special "`run:`" notation. The first approach works well for PDF files, while a launch action is normally the better choice for all other file types. It instructs the operating system to open the file, and for this

---

[1]Of course, to work, the viewing software would need to understand the URL schema `mailto:`, and the security configuration would need to allow the browser (or whatever is used for display) to open other applications.

[2]You need to escape them only if `\href` is used inside an argument of another command, e.g., as part of a `\section` title.

to work, the operating system needs to know how to do this.[1] Thus, if you can double-click a *file* in your directory browser and that starts a program to view or process the file, then run : *file* in the *url* argument does exactly the same. For example, writing

```
\href{run:resources/video.mp4}{see the video}
```

typesets "see the video", and if clicked it opens — after a security dialog — the file video.mp4 in the subdirectory resources relative to the current document in your default .mp4 viewer. The optional *options* argument of \href can be used if PDF files are opened in this way in Adobe Acrobat viewers. It accepts a number of different keys, e.g., to specify at which page the PDF file should be opened; see the package manual for details.

Being able to start other programs in this way out of your document can be very handy, for example, in presentations where you can add little buttons that start an audio or a video presentation, etc.

Links to external PDF files can jump to anchors in these files. If the files have been created with LaTeX and hyperref, the names of the anchors can often be guessed from the representation: in many cases the name is built from the counter name, a period, and the value. For example, anchors to headings are by default constructed as ⟨heading⟩.⟨heading-number⟩. Thus, to jump to section 1.3 in manual.pdf, you can write something like

```
\href{manual.pdf#section.1.3}{see section 1.3 in the manual}
```

Anchor names for other types of numbered objects are less easy to guess. Equations, for example, are often numbered on a per chapter or section basis in document classes. To have a fighting chance for unique names, hyperref constructs such names as equation.⟨section-number⟩.⟨equation-counter-value⟩ (where the section number includes the chapter number if the class has chapters). If in doubt you can take a look into the .aux file and look for lines containing the command \newlabel.

\hypersetup{..., baseurl = *baseurl* , ...}

For URL links it is possible to shorten the *url* arguments by providing a base URL through the key baseurl, e.g.,

```
\hypersetup{baseurl=https://www.latex-project.org/}
\href{publications.html}{Publications of the \LaTeX{} Project Team}
\href{help/books.html}  {Books about \LaTeX}
```

This saves a bit of typing and may make later changes easier if most or all URLs have the same base, but be aware that not every viewer program can deal with the fact that the URLs are split into a base part and a remainder and that the base URL is prepended only if hyperref identifies the URL as referring to an external website (e.g., through the .html extension). If the viewer thinks it is a local file, no base URL is prepended.

---

[1]Usually the file extension is associated with a default program to open it, and that is then called.

Establishing a base URL can be done only once for the whole document because this information is written into the PDF catalog. Links to all other places then need to be specified with their complete URL.

```
\url{url}      \nolinkurl{url}
```

A very common requirement when typesetting an external URL is to suppress normal hyphenation and to allow it to break after slashes and other places. This is provided by the \url command from the url package discussed in Section 3.4.7 on page 198. This package is loaded by hyperref and its command is augmented so that you can click the *url* to open it. To typeset a URL without a link, use \nolinkurl.

\DocumentMetadata required!

\url has an optional argument and can, like \hrefurl, percent-encode its argument if it contains non–ASCII letters. However, this can be used only with Unicode engines — while the link is encoded correctly in pdfTeX, the typeset output in the document is mangled and shows something weird, such as www.kÃüln.de or similar, depending on the current font encoding.

Highlighting links

The various links generated either automatically or through the above commands can be highlighted in different ways through a number of keys, either as package options or in a \hypersetup declaration. By default, clickable areas are surrounded by a box with thin rules (in color). By specifying one of the following boolean keys, you can change that behavior everywhere in your document.[1]

colorlinks   Color the text in the clickable area and set the width of the thin rules to zero to make them invisible.

hidelinks   Do not mark links in any way.

Setting colors

The hyperref package offers a number of keys to change the colors of the text and the borders if they are activated. All keys setting colors accept two color specifications: the name of a color model together with a list of comma-separated numbers, or the extended color syntax such as known from the xcolor package.

```
\hypersetup{ linkcolor = [rgb]{1,0,0} } % red in rgb
\hypersetup{ urlcolor  = red!30!blue } % mix of red and blue
```

\DocumentMetadata required!

The color support is built using code from the L3 programming layer (which is part of the format) and is thus available without needing an external color package. Documents not using the new code should load xcolor.

The colors used for the individual links (when using colorlinks) can be altered at any time using \hypersetup and the following key:

linkcolor   Color for internal document links.

filecolor   Color for URLs that open local files.

---

[1]In older hyperref versions they can be used only in the preamble.

runcolor   Color for run: links.

urlcolor   Color for externally linked URLs.

menucolor   Color for "named" links. These are links to menu functions of the PDF
            viewer; see page 108.

allcolors   Sets all link colors to the same value.

If you stay with borders around the links (or want to use them in addition to get a particularly colorful result), the names for the keys are the same as those above with bordercolor instead of just color at the end of the key name. All border colors can be set with allbordercolors.

```
\hypersetup{ linkbordercolor = [rgb]{1,0,0} }
\hypersetup{ urlbordercolor = blue!30 }
\hypersetup{ allbordercolors = yellow }
```

The borders around the link areas (when drawn) are by default very thin so that they often become invisible when rendered in the viewing programs.

With pdfborder you can adjust their width or reenable the borders if they have been disabled with the colorlinks key. This key has a somewhat obscure syntax: you need to supply three numbers: the first two typically zero and the third positive specifying the rule size in pixels.[1]

There also exists the key pdfborderstyle that allows you to underline links or place dash boxes around them. The feature is, however, supported only in a few viewers; see the manual for details and examples.

Borders and border styles can also be set for individual link types by using keys such as urlborder or runborderstyle.

\DocumentMetadata required!

The hyperref package predefines a number of color schemes for the link colors based on suggestions by users. By default it uses the color scheme phelype (named after its author, a member of the LaTeX Project Team). The default colors used by previous versions of hyperref were not to the liking of everyone, but if wanted, they can be restored by using the scheme primary-colors.

\DocumentMetadata required!

```
\hypersetup{ colorscheme = primary-colors }
```

Bookmarks a.k.a. outline view

It is possible for a PDF document to contain an outline view, in a manner similar to a table of contents, that can be used for navigating the document in the viewer. A screenshot of such a view in Adobe Acrobat Pro, with some of the formatting options described in this section, is shown in Figure 2.3 on the next page. These "bookmarks" can be (and by default are) automatically produced by the hyperref package. The package option bookmarks (default true) chooses whether bookmarks are produced at all.

---

[1] The first two values are used to specify rounded corners, but only a few viewers support this. Even the third value is not uniformly handled, unfortunately, but 0 always omits the border, and a positive value shows it.

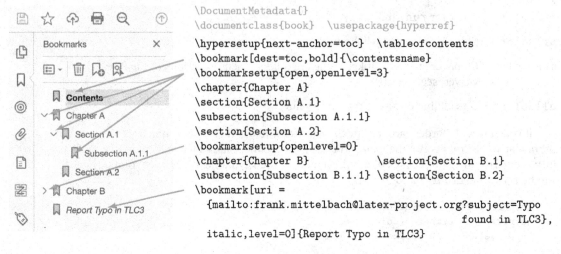

```
\DocumentMetadata{}
\documentclass{book}   \usepackage{hyperref}
\hypersetup{next-anchor=toc}   \tableofcontents
\bookmark[dest=toc,bold]{\contentsname}
\bookmarksetup{open,openlevel=3}
\chapter{Chapter A}
\section{Section A.1}
\subsection{Subsection A.1.1}
\section{Section A.2}
\bookmarksetup{openlevel=0}
\chapter{Chapter B}                \section{Section B.1}
\subsection{Subsection B.1.1} \section{Section B.2}
\bookmark[uri =
    {mailto:frank.mittelbach@latex-project.org?subject=Typo
                                  found in TLC3},
    italic,level=0]{Report Typo in TLC3}
```

Figure 2.3: The outline view of a PDF

In older versions this required at least two passes by LATEX. In the first pass a file with the extension .out was written that contained information about each sectional unit plus some bookkeeping data. In subsequent runs the information from the previous run was then placed into the PDF document. Heiko Oberdiek improved this in a separate bookmark package that provided much more sophisticated bookmark management allowing for additional formatting and the use of colors in the bookmarks and that avoided the need of the second compilation.

The bookmark package has now been merged into hyperref and replaces its legacy code. In older systems or when not using \DocumentMetadata, the package bookmark should be loaded either after or instead of hyperref.

\DocumentMetadata required!

\bookmarksetup{*options*}

Bookmarks have their own command to set up various aspects like the level or the depth.[1] The full list of keys can be found in the documentation [110]; we present here only a few important ones.

Keys that influence how bookmarks are presented

Typically the bookmarks mirror the content of the table of contents and the nesting depth to which bookmarks are added is the value of the counter tocdepth. This can be explicitly set and changed through the option depth. The key accepts as values integers representing the level but also names for the level like section. It can be set anywhere and so allows changing the depth locally. By using a negative value, bookmarks of all levels can be suppressed.

```
\section{section}              % shown
\subsection{subsection}        % shown
\bookmarksetup{depth=section}
```

---

[1] For historical reasons a few options can also be set with \hypersetup.

```
\section{section}              % shown
\subsection{subsection}        % hidden
\bookmarksetup{depth=-1}
\section{section}              % hidden
```

With numbered you can decide if the bookmark string should include the section numbers: by default it does not.

With the key open you can decide if the view should initially show only the top level (which is the default) or if it should show all bookmarks already opened. Additionally, you can use openlevel to request that bookmarks only up to a certain level are initially opened. The value is an integer — unlike the depth it does not accept a name — and it can be changed in the document and so allows fine-tuning which parts are opened initially.

Finally, with the keys bold, italic, and color, the bookmark can be formatted. The formatting is always applied to the whole bookmark, and only some PDF viewers honor the settings. For example,

```
\bookmark[dest=toc,bold,italic,color={red!50!green}]{\contentsname}
```

Even if bookmarks are produced, you may not want them to be shown automatically when the document is opened. This is controlled through pdfpagemode, which is described below.

Textual data in such bookmarks can contain arbitrary Unicode characters, but complicated formulas or similar constructs are not possible. The hyperref package attempts to parse the titles of sectional units and places only allowed strings into the bookmarks, but in some cases the results are less than suboptimal. For example, suppose you have

```
\section{Discussion of $a \leq b$}
```

as a document heading. First of all this results in three warnings of the form

```
Token not allowed in a PDF string (Unicode):
(hyperref)                removing 'math shift' on input line 46.
```

because neither the $ (math shift) nor the \leq is allowed. Worse, as a consequence, the text of your bookmark becomes "Discussion of a b", which is simply wrong. In such cases you can help the hyperref package by using \texorpdfstring.

> \texorpdfstring{*TₑX string*}{*PDF string*}

The *TₑX string* argument is used when doing normal typesetting, while the second argument is used when writing a bookmark. This argument can even contain UTF-8 characters that are unavailable for typesetting when pdfTₑX is used and would normally generate an error. Thus, writing

```
\section{Discussion of \texorpdfstring{$a \leq b$}{a <= b}} % or with
\section{Discussion of \texorpdfstring{$a \leq b$}{a ≤ b}}  % U+2264 character
```

or even just using three dots as the *PDF string* would avoid the warnings and give a better bookmark result.

> \bookmark [*options*] {*bookmark text*}

Manual bookmarks   Beside automatic generations of bookmarks through sectioning commands, it is also possible to create bookmarks manually to allow for easy navigation to places that are normally not added to the printed table of contents such as the TOC itself. The target of such a bookmark is given with the key dest, which needs as a value the name of the anchor it should point to. Such anchors can be created with \hypertarget, but for the table of contents you can also override the name of the automatically created anchor with the key next-anchor of \hypersetup:

```
\hypersetup{next-anchor=toc}
\tableofcontents
\bookmark[dest=toc,level=0]{\contentsname}
```

Bookmarks executing other actions   Bookmarks not only allow you to jump to places in a document, other actions are possible too. Thus, for example,

```
\bookmark[named=Print]{Print this!}
```

creates a bookmark that — if the PDF viewer supports this action — opens the print dialog. Or to repeat the example from the begin of the section,

```
\bookmark[uri =
    {mailto:frank.mittelbach@latex-project.org?subject=Typo found
                                                    in TLC3}]
    {Report Typo in TLC3}
```

would add the text "Report Typo in TLC3" into the bookmarks and, if clicked, would open the reader's mailing program with my e-mail address in the same way as the link in the document.

Document properties

If you look at the properties of a PDF document, you find information about title, author, subject, keywords. They can be set in the preamble with keys of the same name but prefixed with pdf, e.g.,

```
\hypersetup{pdfauthor   = Frank Mittelbach,
    pdftitle   = {The LaTeX Companion, 3rd edition},
    pdfsubject = Typesetting,
    pdfkeywords = {document structure, layout, design, LaTeX}}
```

Note the use of braces to hide the commas in the title and keyword list from being misinterpreted as key separators. Like with bookmarks, the values have to be textual data, and hyperref removes unsuitable commands. This is the legacy interface offered by hyperref since its first release. It is, however, only a small subset of the metadata that is these days often required for PDF documents to comply with one or the other standard. It will be therefore eventually superseded by keys offered by \DocumentMetadata. Once that happens, these \hypersetup keys are deprecated but will remain functional to support reuse of older documents.

PDF presentation possibilities (available with some viewers)

If a PDF document is opened in a viewer program such as **Acrobat**, it may start with different configurations, e.g., in full screen, on a page different than the first, with or without some menus open, etc. Such variant configurations can already be specified in the source document, though as with many aspects of the hyperref package, the actual behavior depends on the viewer used: they all work with Adobe's Acrobat programs but not necessarily elsewhere. The remainder of the section therefore describes the situation with **Acrobat** software. Some of the keys also work with other viewers, but the results may differ from viewer to viewer, so you need to check.

Perhaps the most important key is pdfpagemode with which you can control the initial viewing layout. Possible values are UseNone, UseThumbs, UseOutlines (i.e., show bookmarks), FullScreen, UseOC (when using overlay layers[1]), and UseAttachments.

Normally the document window title shows the file name displayed, but if you prefer to see its title, then add the key pdfdisplaydoctitle. The title should be set with pdftitle for this; using only the command \title is not enough.

By default **Acrobat** starts out with both a menu bar and a tool bar (or pane) open. Their settings are controlled through the keys pdfmenubar and pdftoolbar. Especially the latter takes up a lot of space, so I prefer to turn it off by setting its key to false.

Pages can be presented either as single pages or two pages side by side, and one can flip them or ask for continuous scrolling. This is controlled through the key pdfpagelayout that accepts six different values: SinglePage (flip pages when pressing down or up keys), OneColumn (single pages with scrolling), TwoPageRight (two pages with odd pages on the right), and TwoColumnRight (ditto with scrolling).

Note that **Acrobat** does not look at the logical page number but simply uses the physical one to determine odd and even. It therefore also offers TwoPageLeft and TwoColumnLeft, but neither helps if your pages are not continuous. In such a case you really have to add empty pages into your document so that it is displayed correctly.

A simple-minded way to determine recto and verso pages

By default the first physical page of PDF file is shown. To specify a different starting page, use the key pdfstartpage. Again, if your logical pages are specially numbered, you may have to count to determine the right physical page number to

---

[1]For example with the help of the ocgx2 package by Alexander Grahn.

use as a value. With individual links that open PDF documents, you can also specify a starting page with the key page in the optional argument to \href.

If you open PDF documents through \href links, then Acrobat replaces the current document with the new one, which is often not desired. With the global boolean key pdfnewwindow, you can specify that a new window should be used instead in all such-cases. Alternatively, you can do this on individual links in the optional argument to \href.

\DocumentMetadata
required!
It is also possible to add transition options. They typically have an effect only if you view the PDF in full-screen mode and add animations between page switches like pages flying into the screen or dissolving into the background.

```
\hypersetup{pdfpagetransition={style=Glitter,duration=2,
                               direction=180}}
```

Other miscellaneous features

For Adobe **Acrobat** viewer software the **hyperref** package offers some special support for accessing the program menus through the command \Acrobatmenu. It allows you to define clickable areas that act as if you have selected the corresponding menu. A huge number of menu items are supported (see the package documentation), but probably only a few of them are likely to be useful.

```
\Acrobatmenu{FullScreen}{F} \Acrobatmenu{FitWidth}{W}
\Acrobatmenu{NextPage}{R}    \Acrobatmenu{PrevPage}{L}
```

This places "F", "W", "L", and "R" onto the page, and if you click them, the Acrobat menu action is carried out, e.g., your document changes size or advances to the next page, etc. This can be helpful occasionally, but if you know the corresponding keyboard shortcuts, it does not gain you that much. Also note that the clickable area is only as big as the glyph(s) in the second argument, so if you try to make them inconspicuous, there is not much to click unless you use gray or even white. The border color around the link area can be set with key menubordercolor or, if the link text is colored, with menucolor.

The package also offers a useful set of commands to build PDF or HTML forms with fields, check boxes, radio buttons, etc. If you are interested in that kind of functionality, consult the package documentation for details.

As mentioned in the beginning, the package offers more than one hundred keys to adjust its behavior in certain situations of which we covered only the most important ones in this section. If you require some feature that appears not to be possible, study the extensive package documentation — it may well exist after all.

2.5 Document source management

In the final section of this chapter we discuss tools that help you archiving your documents as well as reliably exchanging them with others, e.g., journal publishers.

We start with environments that hold the contents of a file, which is then extracted when the document is processed, allowing you to combine several files in one document. We then look at ways to gather information on "used files" for archival purposes. This is followed by looking at two programs that take such information to produce an archive with all relevant files included: bundledoc, which saves only the text and package files used and produces fairly small archives, and mkjobtexmf, which does a more thorough job and also includes fonts and similar binary data. Which of them is more suitable depends on your use case.

Finally, we briefly discuss the latexrelease package, which offers you a way to roll back your LaTeX installation to an earlier date without the need to install a previous release explicitly. There are limits to what it can achieve, but it is a good addition to LaTeX's insurance that your documents can be processed successfully without any changes in the output for long periods of time.

2.5.1 Combining several files

When sending a LaTeX document to another person, you may have to send local or uncommon package files (e.g., your private modifications to some packages) along with the source. In such cases it is often helpful if you can put all the information required to process the document into a single file.

\begin{filecontents} [*option-list*] {*file name*} ... \end{filecontents}

For this purpose, LaTeX provides the environment `filecontents`. This environment takes one mandatory argument, the name of a file[1]; its body consists of the contents of this file. The \begin and \end tags should be placed on lines of their own in the source. In particular, there should be no material following them, or you will get LaTeX errors.

If LaTeX encounters such an environment, it tries to find the mentioned file name. If it cannot, it writes the body of the environment verbatim into a file in the current directory and inform you about this action. Conversely, if a file with the given name was found by LaTeX, it informs you that it has ignored this instance of the `filecontents` environment because the file is already present on the file system.

The *option-list* argument allows you modify this behavior. If you specify `nosearch`, then only the current directory is searched for the file, not the whole TeX tree. This is useful if you want to write, for example, a local version of a configuration file, such as `graphics.cfg`, which would otherwise not appear in your local directory. If you specify `force` (or `overwrite`), then the file is always written, even if it already exists in the current directory or somewhere in the TeX installation tree. Use this option with caution because you can clobber files this way by mistake.[2] You can

---

[1] If no extension is specified, the actual external file name is the one LaTeX would read if you used this name as an argument to \input, i.e., adding the extension .tex.

[2] The environment refuses to write to \jobname.tex — disaster is assured if you overwrite your own input file. However, other files might be equally important!

silence any warnings from the `force` key by also specifying `nowarn`, in which case warnings are only written to the `.log` file.

By default the generated file gets a few comment lines (using % as a comment character) added to the top to announce that this file was written by a `filecontents` environment:

```
%% LaTeX2e file 'foo.txt'
%% generated by the 'filecontents' environment
%% from source 'test' on 2022/04/22.
```

If this is not appropriate — for example, if the file is not a LATEX file — use the option `noheader` in which case these extra lines are not produced. Alternatively, you can use the `filecontents*` environment instead, which is just a short way to set this option.

In older LATEX formats the content of such a file was restricted to ASCII characters — with other characters all bet were off. These days essentially any Unicode character should be admissible.

If you use `filecontents` to ship all files necessary to process your document in a single master file, then it is best to place the environment(s) at the very top of the file so that they are written out before they are needed when processing the document.

There are, however, also use cases where one would want to write files somewhere inside the document body. For example, if you have some material that is reused several times, you could write it to a file and then load that file via `\input` wherever necessary. Other use cases are packages that require their input in external files (ltxtable is an example). In that case you can keep your data where it belongs in your source and write it to a file prior to using it. If you are using `filecontents` for such purposes, it is best to add the `force` option, because otherwise you are likely to be puzzled by the fact that you change your data and nothing happens in your document (because the file was already written out in a previous run).

2.5.2 Document archival information

For archival purposes or sharing or collaborating on documents, it is often important to record (and usually collect) all files needed for processing a document. This needs their correct versions to faithfully re-create the document at a later stage or in a different place. For this a number of tools and programs are available.

As a simple solution LATEX already offers the command `\listfiles`, which records all files that are opened with `\documentclass`, `\usepackage`, `\include`, `\input`,[1] `\includegraphics`, etc. Suppose you process the following document

```
\documentclass[12pt]{article}  \usepackage{lmodern}
\listfiles
\begin{document} Hello, world! \end{document}
```

---

[1] Files opened with `\input` are recorded only if you use the recommended syntax with a braced argument. The primitive plain TEX syntax that delimits the file name with spaces is not supported!

then as a result your transcript file will show the following list of files, possibly with
different version numbers if your installation is older or younger:

```
*File List*
article.cls    2021/02/12 v1.4n Standard LaTeX document class
 size12.clo    2021/02/12 v1.4n Standard LaTeX file (size option)
lmodern.sty    2015/05/01 v1.6.1 Latin Modern Fonts
 ot1lmr.fd     2015/05/01 v1.6.1 Font defs for Latin Modern
l3backend-pdftex.def    2021-05-07 L3 backend support: PDF output (pdfTeX)
***********
```

As you can see, this shows the document class, the class option file, the package used,
and one font definition file for Latin Modern, but it is clearly missing everything else
related to font usage. Thus, if the fonts used in your document do not exist elsewhere
(or in a different version), then the results of processing your document may differ
without a way to determine the cause.

Nevertheless, it goes a long way towards resolving issues when collaborating with
others or experiencing a problem that others do not seem to have: good advice in such
cases is to add \listfiles to the document and compare the results on different
installations. In many cases this already pinpoints the reason for different behavior.

2.5.3 snapshot, bundledoc — Document archival and verification

The snapshot package by Michael Downes (1958-2003) uses the same approach as
\listfiles for collecting file information about a document but presents it in a way
that it can be automatically verified at a later stage or on a different installation. This
is particularly useful when collaborating or when one want to archive documents and
record this information as part of the document itself.

To enable it, you have to place the package in the first line of your document
using \RequirePackage[error]{snapshot} even before the \documentclass.
Without any further options to the package, this will then write a file with the extension
.dep (for dependencies) containing the following lines if applied to our example
document:

```
\RequireVersions{
  *{application}{pdfTeX}  {0000/00/00 v1.40.22}
  *{format} {LaTeX2e}     {2021-06-01 v2.e}
  *{package}{snapshot}    {2020/06/17 v2.14}
  *{class}  {article}     {2021/02/12 v1.4n}
  *{file}   {size12.clo}  {2021/02/12 v1.4n}
  *{package}{lmodern}     {2015/05/01 v1.6.1}
  *{file}   {ot1lmr.fd}   {2015/05/01 v1.6.1}
  *{file}   {l3backend-pdftex.def}{2021-05-07 v3}
}
```

Up to this point this is not much difference than when using \listfiles, except that
the information is placed into a separate file and slightly more structured. However,

as a next step you can copy the content of this file into your document directly after loading the package, which makes it the information of record for this document. From now on this data is checked at each run, and if any differences are found, they raise a warning or an error.

For example, assume that you collaborate with some people on writing the "Hello World" short story and their TeX installation has an obsolete Latin Modern package somewhere in their `texmf` tree, then they will see the following error message

```
! Package snapshot Error:
  Required version 2009/10/30 v1.6 of lmodern.sty and
  provided version 2008/12/01 v1.5 do not match.
```

if they attempt to run the document. If you prefer to generate just warnings instead of errors, use the option `warning` (or no option). It is also possible to restrict file information verification just to dates, versions, or major version numbers by using one of the options `date`, `version`, or `major-version` — if the latter is applied in our example, there would be no error because the major version is 1 for both files.

The `.dep` file produced by `snapshot` can also be used to produce an archive with all or some of the files it lists, by using the `bundledoc` program by Scott Pakin. This is particularly useful if you want to send your document with all the necessary files to somebody else and do not want to worry about missing anything relevant. For example, journals often request all source files in addition to the camera-ready PDF. In that case running

```
bundledoc --verbose --localonly --include=⟨myfile⟩.pdf ⟨myfile⟩.dep
```

does the trick, and you get an archive file[1] containing the final PDF and everything that is required and not part of the main TeX installation. Of course, it requires an up-to-date `.dep` file; i.e., you have to include the `snapshot` package as described above and process your document with it.

Alternatively, or in addition, you can use `--exclude=`*string* to exclude all files whose names contain that string, and with `--include`, you can explicitly request additional files otherwise not included to be added to the archive like we did above. For example, you may want to include your bibliography databases (and not just the resulting `.bbl` files used by the document), which can be achieved with `--include="*.bib"`. Both options can be used as often as necessary. The `--verbose` option, as used above, gives some progress information.

Without any of the options above, `bundledoc` includes all files listed in the `.dep` file, which is more suitable for archival purposes. But do not forget that some files important for the final results (such as font files) are not included. The advantage is that the archive is noticeably smaller in size compared to those produced by

---

[1] The exact type of archive depends on your operating system; on Windows it is typically a `.zip`, on Unix or macOS a `.tar.gz` file. The exact behavior can be controlled through configuration files.

mkjobtexmf discussed in the next section. Usually a workable approach is to addition-ally archive the yearly TEX Live distributions as fonts change less often. However, for 100% accurate results it might be required to archive all files for a given project using mkjobtexmf.

By default, bundledoc flattens the directory structure and places all files in the archive next to each other. With --keepdirs the original structure is preserved.

With the option --config you can select a configuration file, for example, --config=miktex.cfg for .zip archives on MiKTEX. Another interesting one is texlive-unix-arlatex.cfg, which generates a single LATEX file including all other files through filecontents environments. How to define your own configuration file is described in the documentation where you also find details on a few other options that may be useful in some cases.

You can omit the extensions .dep and .cfg for the dependency and the config file, so on MiKTEX, for example, we could write

```
bundledoc --config=miktex --localonly --include=⟨myfile⟩.pdf ⟨myfile⟩
```

to prepare a .zip file for a journal submission.

2.5.4 mkjobtexmf — Providing a minimal TEX file tree

To find out exactly which files are used by a TEX engine when processing a document, most modern engines offer the command-line option -recorder. If it is used, then a file with the extension .fls is produced that contains information on all files that the engine opened for reading or writing, one per line. With our "Hello World" example this amounts to 28 lines, and after removing the duplicates (LATEX opens most files twice for reading), the following 16 remain, among them various configuration and font files and the format file:

```
INPUT /usr/local/texlive/2021/texmf-dist/fonts/enc/dvips/lm/lm-rm.enc
INPUT /usr/local/texlive/2021/texmf-dist/fonts/map/fontname/texfonts.map
INPUT /usr/local/texlive/2021/texmf-dist/fonts/tfm/public/cm/cmr12.tfm
INPUT /usr/local/texlive/2021/texmf-dist/fonts/tfm/public/lm/rm-lmr12.tfm
INPUT /usr/local/texlive/2021/texmf-dist/fonts/type1/public/lm/lmr12.pfb
INPUT /usr/local/texlive/2021/texmf-dist/tex/latex/base/article.cls
INPUT /usr/local/texlive/2021/texmf-dist/tex/latex/base/size12.clo
INPUT /usr/local/texlive/2021/texmf-dist/tex/latex/lm/lmodern.sty
INPUT /usr/local/texlive/2021/texmf-dist/tex/latex/lm/ot1lmr.fd
INPUT /usr/local/texlive/2021/texmf-dist/tex/latex/snapshot/snapshot.sty
INPUT /usr/local/texlive/2021/texmf-dist/web2c/texmf.cnf
INPUT /usr/local/texlive/2021/texmf-var/fonts/map/pdftex/updmap/pdftex.map
INPUT /usr/local/texlive/2021/texmf-var/web2c/pdftex/pdflatex.fmt
INPUT /usr/local/texlive/2021/texmf.cnf
INPUT myfile.aux
INPUT myfile.tex
```

For 100% accuracy, all of them, except the .aux file, should be archived, and doing this with the --include option of bundledoc would be rather cumbersome. This is where the mkjobtexmf program by Heiko Oberdiek comes into play. If you execute

```
mkjobtexmf --verbose --copy --jobname myfile   # without extension
```

then LATEX is run (using the -recorder option) on the file myfile.tex. The resulting .fls file is examined, and all files in the above listing are then copied into the directory myfile.mjt using a standard setup of texmf subdirectories. For archival, all that remains is to zip up this directory and store it in a safe place. Note that the --copy or --force-copy is essential for this to work: without it mkjobtexmf adds links to the files, not physical copies.[1] The --copy does not overwrite existing files in the target texmf, whereas --force-copy does. The latter is useful because it means that updates are properly accounted for if you run the program repeatedly and want to make sure that the latest versions are inside the tree.[2]

Always mandatory is the option --jobname to specify the file to run and the default destination directory. The --verbose displays information about what mkjobtexmf does and is sometimes helpful.

If you prefer a flat structure with all files directly in the myfile.mjt directory, specify the option --flat. If your document should be processed with one of the Unicode engines, you can specify this too, e.g., by using --cmd-tex lualatex for LuaTeX.

There are a number of further options to tweak the program behavior including defining the destination directory (--destdir), the LATEX file name to process if it has an extension different from .tex (--texname), and several others. --help produces a concise but useful reference.

Existing files are never changed in the destination directory If you use mkjobtexmf for archival purposes as described above, then you should be aware of one important aspect in the program behavior. It always only adds *new* material to its destination directory but never deletes from it nor does it replace any existing link to a file with a copy of the file or vice versa. If the purpose is to speed up processing, that is fine, but for archiving the final result, it might mean that the archive contains files no longer used or contains links where it should contain copies because you forgot to specify --copy on the first invocation. Even worse, it may not contain the latest version of your source files if they have changed since the first time the program was used.

2.5.5 The rollback concept for LATEX and individual packages

Keeping your LATEX installation up-to-date and using the latest packages is usually a good approach because that means you get the latest corrections and feature updates. The LATEX universe is well-known for its unparalleled backward compatibility:

---

[1] A texmf tree containing only links does not take up much space, but speeds up the processing of a document because it contains only the files necessary for the document to run.

[2] I used this during the production of this book to store all packages used in the book in a source control system (with history). That enabled me to keep track of changes that happened to the packages while writing the book.

reprocessing documents decades old with a modern LaTeX is normally not a problem, and very seldom requires adjustments by the user.

However, there are cases where packages change their interfaces in incompatible ways or where you have worked around a problem and now that the problem is solved, your workaround no longer works.

For situations like this, LaTeX introduced in 2015 a rollback concept for the LaTeX kernel as well as for document classes and packages, allowing the LaTeX maintainers to make corrections to the software while continuing to maintain backward compatibility to the highest degree. With its help you can explicitly ask LaTeX to revert its code to a version that was current on a specific date, and the software tries its best to undo changes to match this state.

To request a kernel rollback to its state at a given *date*, you use the latexrelease package by the LaTeX Project Team. For example,

```
\RequirePackage[2016-01-01]{latexrelease}
```

would result in undoing all kernel modifications (corrections or extensions) released between January 1, 2016, and the current date.[1] Undoing means reinstalling the definitions current at the requested date and normally also removing new commands from TeX's memory so that \newcommand and similar declarations do not fall over because a name is already declared.

This mechanism helps in correctly processing older documents that contain workarounds for issues with an older kernel and issues that have since been fixed in a way that would make the old document fail, or produce different output, when processed with the newer, fixed kernel.

If necessary, the latexrelease package also allows for rolling the kernel forward without installing a new format. For example, if your current installation is dated 2016-04-01 but you have a document that requires a kernel with date 2018-01-01, then this can be achieved by starting it with

```
\RequirePackage[latest]{latexrelease}
```

provided you have a version of the latexrelease package that knows about the kernel changes between the date of your kernel and the requested date. Getting this version of the package is simple as the latest version can always be downloaded from the Comprehensive TeX Archive Network (CTAN). Thus, you are able to process your document correctly, even when updating your complete installation is not advisable or is impossible for one or another reason.[2]

---

[1] There are a few exceptions because some modifications are kept: for example, the ability to accept date strings in ISO format (i.e., 2016-01-01) in addition to the older LaTeX convention (i.e., 2016/01/01). These are not rolled back because removing such a feature would result in unnecessary failures.

[2] For example, this might help when you work on Overleaf (an online LaTeX portal). At the time of writing this book, Overleaf was about a year behind the current LaTeX release. Of course, in that case you may also have to upload individual packages into your account, if they have specific new features that you want to use.

Typical scenarios

A typical example, for which such a rollback functionality would have provided a major benefit (and will do for packages in the future), is the caption package by Axel Sommerfeldt. This package started out under the name of caption with a certain user interface. Over time it became clear that there were some deficiencies in the user interface; to rectify these without making older documents fail, Axel introduced caption2. At a later point the syntax of that package itself was superseded, resulting in caption3, and then that got renamed back to caption. So now older documents using caption will fail, while documents from the intermediate period require caption2 (which is listed as superseded on CTAN but is still distributed in the major distributions). So users accustomed to copying their document preamble from one document to the next are probably still continuing to use it without noticing that they are in fact using a version with defective and limited interfaces.

Another example would be the fixltx2e package that for many years contained fixes to the LᴬTEX kernel. In 2015 these were integrated into the kernel so that today this package is an empty shell, only telling the user that it is no longer needed. However, if you process an old document (from before 2015) using rollback, and that document loads fixltx2e, then of course fixes originally provided by this package (like the corrections to the floats algorithm) would get lost as they are now neither in the kernel nor in the "empty" fixltx2e package if that does not roll back as well — fortunately it does, so in reality it is not quite an empty shell.

A somewhat different example would be the amsmath package, which for nearly a decade did not see any corrections even though several problems have been found in it over the years. If such bugs finally get corrected, then that would affect many of the documents written since 2000, since their authors may have manually worked around one or another deficiency of the code. Of course, as with the caption package, one could introduce an amsmath2, amsmath3, ... package, but that puts the burden on the user to always select the latest version (instead of automatically using the latest version unless an earlier one is really needed).

The document-level interface

By default LᴬTEX automatically uses the current version of any class or package — and prior to offering the new rollback concept it always did that unless the package or class had its own scheme for providing versioning, either using alternative names or using hand-coded options that select a version.

Global rollback

With the new rollback concept all the user has to do (if they want a document processed with a specific version of the kernel and packages) is to add the latexrelease package at the beginning of the document and specify a desired date as the package option, e.g.,

```
\RequirePackage[2018-01-01]{latexrelease}
```

This rolls back the kernel to its state on that day (as described earlier), and for each package and the document class, it checks if there are alternate releases available and selects the most appropriate release of that package or class in relation to the given date.

There is further fine-grain adjustment possible: both \documentclass as well as \usepackage have a second (less known) optional argument that up to now was used to allow the specification of a "minimal date". For example, by declaring

Individual rollback

```
\usepackage[colaction]{multicol}[2018-01-01]
```

you specify that multicol is expected to be no older than the beginning of 2018. If only an older version is found, then processing such a document results in a warning message:

```
LaTeX Warning: You have requested, on input line 12, version
    '2018-01-01' of package  multicol, but only version
    '2017/04/11 v1.8q multicolumn formatting (FMi)' is available.
```

The idea behind this approach is that packages seldom change syntax in an incompatible way, but more often add new features: with such a declaration you can indicate that you need a version that provides certain new features.

The new rollback concept now extends the use of this optional argument by letting you additionally supply a target date for the rollback. This is done by prefixing a date string with an equal sign. For example,

```
\usepackage{multicol}[=2017-06-01]
```

would request a release of multicol that corresponds to its version in June 2017.

So assuming that at some point in the future there will be a major rewrite of this package that changes the way columns are balanced, the above would request a fallback to what right now is the current version from 2017-04-11. The old use of this optional argument is still available because existence or absence of the = determines how the date is interpreted.

The same mechanism is available for document classes via the \documentclass declaration and for \RequirePackage if that is ever needed.

Specifying a rollback date is most appropriate if you want to ensure that the behavior of the processing engine (i.e., the kernel and all packages) corresponds to that specific date. In fact, once you are finished with editing a document, you can preserve it for posterity by adding this line at the top of your document:

Preparing your document for posterity

```
\RequirePackage[today's-date]{latexrelease}
```

This would mean that it is processed a little more slowly (because the kernel may get rolled back and each package gets checked for alternate versions), but it would have the advantage that processing it a long time in the future will probably still work without the need to add that line later.

However, in a case such as the caption package or, say, the longtable package, that might eventually see a major new release after several years, it would be nice to allow the specification of a "named" release instead of a date: for example, a user might want to explicitly use version 4 rather than 5 of longtable when these versions have incompatible syntax or produce different results.

This is also now possible if the developer declares "named" releases for a package or class: one can then request a named version simply by using this second optional argument with the "name" prefixed by an equal sign. For example, if there is a new version of longtable and the old (now current) version is labeled "v4", then all that is necessary to select that old version is

```
\usepackage{longtable}[=v4]
```

Note that there is no need to know that the new version is dated 2018-04-01 (nor to request a date before that) to get the old version back.

The version "name" is an arbitrary string at the discretion of the package author — but note that it must not resemble a date specification; i.e., it must not contain hyphens or slashes, because these confuse the parsing routine.[1]

The user interface is fairly simple, and to keep the processing speed high, the syntax checking is therefore rather light and rather unforgiving if it finds unexpected data. Basically any string containing a hyphen or a slash triggers the date parsing, which then expects two hyphens (in case of an ISO date) or two slashes (otherwise) and other than these separators, only digits. If it does find anything else, chances are that you get a "Missing \begin{document}" error or, perhaps even more puzzling, a strange selection being made. For example, 2011/02 may mean to you February 2011, but for the parsing routine it is some day in the year 20 A.D. That is, it gets converted to the single number 201102 so that when this number is compared numerically to, say, 20000101, it is the smaller number, i.e., earlier, even though the latter is the numerical representation of January 1, 2000. Bottom line: do not misspell your dates, and all is fine.

The package writer interface

The commands to set up the rollback functionality in packages and classes are described in Appendix A.6.1 on page →II 693; for more details on the concepts, see [90].

---

[1]Of course, more sophisticated parsing could fix this, but we opted for a fast and simple parsing that scans for slashes or hyphens with no further analysis.

Basic Formatting Tools
— Paragraph Level

The way information is presented visually can influence, to a large extent, the message as it is understood by the reader. Therefore, it is important that you use the best possible tools available to convey the precise meaning of your words. It must, however, be emphasized that visual presentation forms should aid the reader in understanding the text and should not distract his or her attention. For this reason, visual consistency and uniform conventions for the visual clues are a must, and the way given structural elements are highlighted should be the same throughout a document. This constraint is most easily implemented by defining a specific command or environment for each document element that has to be treated specially and by grouping these commands and environments in a package file or in the document preamble. By using exclusively these commands, you can be sure of a consistent presentation form.

In this chapter we look at such tools, starting at the micro level; larger structures are covered in Chapter 4. The first section covers different aspects of paragraph formatting, such as producing large initial letters at the start of a paragraph, modifying paragraph justification, altering the vertical spacing between lines of a paragraph, and similar topics. This is followed by a look at handling special characters such as ellipses, dashes, underscores, or spaces.

In the third section we discuss generated or specially formatted text, i.e., counter values represented as ordinals or cardinals, fractions formatted for use in running text, and in particular the acro package for consistently managing acronyms and abbreviations. A special focus is given to scientific notation provided by the siunitx package, which forms the last and rather lengthy topic of this section.

The fourth section then covers various way of highlighting and quoting text. This includes a number of generally useful packages as well as some more specialized ones that are occasionally useful.

Section 3.5 deals with the different kind of "notes", such as footnotes, marginal notes, and endnotes, and explains how they can be customized to conform to different styles, if necessary. In the final section we take a quick look at different helper packages for document development, e.g., how to add different kind of notes, copy-editing marks, or change bars to your documents.

3.1 Shaping your paragraphs

Paragraph justification in TeX and LaTeX

For formatting paragraphs LaTeX deploys the algorithms already built into the TeX program, which by default produce justified paragraphs. In other words, spaces between words are slightly stretched or shortened to produce lines of equal length. TeX achieves this outcome with an algorithm that attempts to find an optimal solution for a whole paragraph, using the current settings of about 20 internal parameters. They include aspects such as trying to produce visually compatible lines, such that a tight line is not followed by one very loosely typeset, or considering several hyphens in a row as a sign of bad quality. The interactions between these parameters are very subtle, and even experts find it difficult to predict the results when tweaking them. Because the standard settings are suitable for nearly all applications, we describe only some of the parameters in this book. Appendix B.4.3 discusses how to trace the algorithm. If you are interested in delving further into the matter of automatic paragraph breaking, refer to *The TeXbook* [48, chap. 14], which describes the algorithm in great detail, or to the very interesting article by Michael Plass and Donald Knuth on the subject, which is reprinted in *Digital Typography* [61].

Downside of global optimization

The downside of the global optimizing approach of TeX, which you will encounter sooner or later, is that making small changes, like correcting a typo near the end of a paragraph, can have drastic and surprising effects, as it might affect the line breaking of the whole paragraph. It is possible, and not even unlikely, that, for example, the *removal* of a word might actually result in making a paragraph one line *longer*.

This behavior can be very annoying if you are near the end of an important project (like the third edition of this book) and a correction wreaks havoc on your already manually adjusted page breaks. In such a situation it is best to place \linebreak or \pagebreak commands into strategic places to force TeX to choose a solution that it would normally consider inferior. To be able to later get rid of such manual corrections you can easily define your own commands, such as

```
\newcommand\CElinebreak{\linebreak}
```

rather than using the standard LaTeX commands directly. This helps you to distinguish the layout adjustments for a particular version from other usages of the original commands — a method successfully used in the preparation of this book.

Interword spacing

The interword spacing in a justified paragraph (the white space between individual words) is controlled by several TEX parameters — the most important ones are `\tolerance` and `\emergencystretch`. By setting them suitably for your document you can prevent most or all of the "Overfull box" messages without any manual line breaks. The `\tolerance` command is a means for setting how much the interword space in a paragraph is allowed to diverge from its optimum value.[1] This command is a TEX (not LATEX) counter, and therefore it has an uncommon assignment syntax — for example, `\tolerance=500`. Lower values make TEX try harder to stay near the optimum; higher values allow for loose typesetting. The default value is often 200. When TEX is unable to stay in the given tolerance, you will find overfull boxes in your output (i.e., lines sticking out into the margin like this). Enlarging the value of `\tolerance` means that TEX also considers poorer but hopefully still acceptable line breaks, instead of turning the problem over to you for manual intervention. Sensible values are between 50 and 9999. Do not use 10000 or higher, because that allows TEX to produce a single arbitrarily bad line (like   this   one) to keep the rest of the paragraph perfect. If you really need fully automated line breaking, it is better to set the length parameter `\emergencystretch` to a positive value. If TEX cannot break a paragraph without producing overfull boxes (due to the setting of `\tolerance`) and `\emergencystretch` is positive, it adds this length as stretchable space to every line, thereby accepting line-breaking solutions that have been rejected before. You may get some underfull box messages because all the lines are now set in a loose measure, but this result will still look better than a single horrible line in the middle of an otherwise perfectly typeset paragraph.

Careful with TEX's idea about infinitely bad

LATEX has two predefined commands influencing the above parameters: `\fussy`, which is the default, and `\sloppy`, which allows for relatively bad lines. The `\sloppy` command is automatically applied by LATEX in some situations (e.g., when typesetting `\marginpar` arguments or p columns in a `tabular` environment) where perfect line breaking is seldom possible due to the narrow measure. It uses a `\tolerance` of 9999 together with an `\emergencystretch` of 3 em.

Unjustified text

While the theory on producing high-quality justified text is well understood (even though surprisingly few typesetting systems other than TEX use algorithms that can produce high quality other than by chance), the same cannot be said for the situation when unjustified text is being requested. This may sound strange at first hearing. After all, why should it be difficult to break a paragraph into lines of different length? The answer lies in the fact that we do not have quantifiable quality measures that allow us to easily determine whether a certain breaking is good or bad. In comparison to its

---

[1]The optimum is font defined; see Section 9.8.1 on page 745.

work with justified text, TEX does a very poor job when asked to produce unjustified paragraphs. Thus, to obtain the highest quality we have to be prepared to help TEX far more often by adding explicit line breaks in strategic places. A good introduction to the problems in this area is given in an article by Paul Stiff (1949–2011) [129].

The main type of unjustified text is the one in which lines are set flush left but are unjustified at the right. For this arrangement LaTeX offers the environment flushleft. It typesets all text in its scope "flush left" by adding very stretchable white space at the right of each line; that is, it sets the internal parameter \rightskip to 0pt plus 1fil. This setting often produces very ragged-looking paragraphs because it makes all lines equally good independent of the amount of text they contain. In addition, hyphenation is essentially disabled because a hyphen adds to the "badness" of a line and, because there is nothing to counteract it, TEX's paragraph-breaking algorithm normally chooses line breaks that avoid hyphenated words.

"The LaTeX document preparation system is a special version of Donald Knuth's TEX program. TEX is a sophisticated program designed to produce high-quality typesetting, especially for mathematical text."

```
\begin{flushleft}
  ``The \LaTeX{} document preparation system is
  a special version of Donald Knuth's \TeX{}
  program. \TeX{} is a sophisticated program
  designed to produce high-quality typesetting,
  especially for mathematical text.''
\end{flushleft}
```

3-1-1

In summary, LaTeX's flushleft environment is not particularly well suited to continuous unjustified text, which should vary at the right-hand boundary only to a certain extent and where appropriate should use hyphenation (see ragged2e in the next section for alternatives). Nevertheless, it can be useful to place individual objects, like a graphic, flush left to the margin, especially because this environment adds space above and below itself in the same way as list environments do.

Another important restriction is the fact that the settings chosen by this environment have no universal effect, because some environments (e.g., minipage or tabular) and commands (e.g., \parbox, \footnote, and \caption) restore the alignment of paragraphs to full justification. That is, they set the \rightskip length parameter to 0pt and thus cancel the stretchable space at the right line endings. A way to automatically deal with this problem is provided by the package ragged2e.

Other ways of typesetting paragraphs are flush right and centered, with the flushright and center environments, respectively. In these cases the line breaks are usually indicated with the \\ command, whereas for ragged-right text (the flushleft environment discussed above) you can let LaTeX do the line breaking itself (if you are happy with the resulting quality).

The three environments discussed in this section work by changing declarations that control how TEX typesets paragraphs. These declarations are also available as LaTeX commands, as shown in the following table of correspondence:

environment:	center	flushleft	flushright
command:	\centering	\raggedright	\raggedleft

The commands neither start a new paragraph nor add vertical space, unlike the corresponding environments. Hence, the commands can be used inside other environments and inside a \parbox, in particular, to control the alignment in p columns of an array or tabular environment. Note, however, that if they are used in the last column of a tabular or array environment, the \\ is no longer available to denote the end of a row. Instead, the command \tabularnewline can be used for this purpose (see also Section 6.2.2).

It is also important to realize that the command forms always apply to whole paragraphs, even if used in the middle of a paragraph. TeX uses the setting active at the *end* of a paragraph to decide how to justify the text. This means that if using, for example, \centering inside a group, you have to ensure that the paragraph ends within that group, otherwise your request is ignored or partially ignored.

End of paragraphs matter!

3.1.1 ragged2e — Improving unjustified text

Above we discussed the deficiencies of LaTeX's flushleft and flushright environments if used for normal text. The package ragged2e, written by Martin Schröder and now maintained by Marei Peischl, sets out to provide alternatives that do not produce such extreme raggedness. This venture is not quite as simple as it sounds, because it is not enough to set \rightskip to something like 0pt plus 2em. Notwithstanding the fact that this would result in TeX trying hard to keep the line endings within the 2em boundary, there remains a subtle problem: by default, the interword space is also stretchable for most fonts. Thus, if \rightskip has only finite stretchability, TeX distributes excess space equally to all spaces. As a result, the interword spaces have different width, depending on the amount of material in the line. The solution is to redefine the interword space so that it no longer can stretch or shrink by specifying a suitable (font-dependent) value for \spaceskip. This internal TeX parameter, if nonzero, represents the current interword space, overwriting the default that is defined by the current font.

By default, the package does not modify the standard LaTeX commands and environments discussed in the previous section, but instead defines its own using the same names except that some letters are uppercased.[1] The new environments and commands are given in the following correspondence table:

| *environment:* | Center | FlushLeft | FlushRight |
| *command:* | \Centering | \RaggedRight | \RaggedLeft |

They differ from their counterparts of the previous section not only in the fact that they try to produce less ragged output, but also in their attempt to provide additional flexibility by easily letting you change most of their typesetting aspects.

The available parameters and their default values are shown in Table 3.1 on the following page. They are used as values for \parindent, \leftskip, \rightskip, and \parfillskip, whenever one of the corresponding ragged2e commands or

The default values

---

[1] This is actually against standard naming conventions. In most packages, mixed-case commands indicate interface commands to be used by designers in class files or in the preamble, but not commands to be used inside documents.

Parameter	Default	Parameter	Default
\RaggedLeftParindent	0pt	\RaggedLeftLeftskip	0pt plus 2em
\RaggedLeftRightskip	0pt	\RaggedLeftParfillskip	0pt
\CenteringParindent	0pt	\CenteringLeftskip	0pt plus 2em
\CenteringRightskip	0pt plus 2em	\CenteringParfillskip	0pt
\RaggedRightParindent	0pt	\RaggedRightLeftskip	0pt
\RaggedRightRightskip	0pt plus 2em	\RaggedRightParfillskip	0pt plus 1fil
\JustifyingParindent	1em	\JustifyingParfillskip	0pt plus 1fil

Table 3.1: Parameters used by ragged2e

environments is called. Using em values in the defaults (see Table 3.1) means that special care is needed when loading the package, because the em is turned into a real dimension at this point! The package should therefore be loaded *after* the body font and size have been established — for example, after font packages have been loaded.

Instead of using the defaults listed in Table 3.1, one can instruct the package to initially mimic the original LaTeX settings by using the option originalparameters and then changing the parameter values as desired afterwards.

Unjustified setting as the default

To set a whole document unjustified, you can specify document as an option to the ragged2e package. For the purpose of justifying individual paragraphs in such a document the package offers the command \justifying and the environment justify. Thus, to produce a document with a moderate amount of raggedness and paragraphs indented by 12 pt, you could use a setting like the one in the following example (compare it to Example 3-1-1 on page 122):

```
\usepackage[document]{ragged2e}
\setlength\RaggedRightRightskip{0pt plus 1cm}
\setlength\RaggedRightParindent{12pt}
```

"The LaTeX document preparation system is a special version of Donald Knuth's TeX program. TeX is a sophisticated program designed to produce high-quality typesetting, especially for mathematical text."

```
``The \LaTeX{} document preparation system is
a special version of Donald Knuth's \TeX{}
program. \TeX{} is a sophisticated program
designed to produce high-quality typesetting,
especially for mathematical text.''
```

3-1-2

Unjustified settings in narrow columns

In places with narrow measures (e.g., \marginpars, \parboxes, minipage environments, or p-columns of tabular environments), the justified setting usually produces inferior results. With the option raggedrightboxes, paragraphs in such places are automatically typeset using \RaggedRight. If necessary, \justifying can be used to force a justified paragraph in individual cases.

Spurious underfull box warnings

There is, however, one problem that you should be aware of if you use the command \RaggedLeft or \Centering with very little text (i.e., less than a single line): you may get strange "Underfull box" warnings such as

```
Underfull \hbox (badness 10000) in paragraph at lines 25--25
 []\T1/ptm/m/n/10 ragged left text
Underfull \hbox (badness 5893) in paragraph at lines 26--27
 []\T1/ptm/m/n/10 centered text
```

even though the result looks (and is) correct. For example, the above warnings have been generated during the processing of the next example:

ragged right text

ragged left text

centered text

```
\usepackage{ragged2e}

\RaggedRight ragged right text \par
\RaggedLeft  ragged left text  \par
\Centering   centered text
```

The reason is that with ragged2e there is only very limited flexibility in each line compared to \raggedleft or \centering where the white space on one or both sides can stretch arbitrarily. \RaggedRight on the other hand is usually fine, because there we still have a fully stretchable \parfillskip at the end of the paragraph.

Thus, while it is tempting to overload the standard LaTeX definitions with the new commands (using the package option newcommands) to avoid the need to typeset the somewhat tedious mixed-case names, it cannot really be recommended. At least \centering is very often used to center a single object such as a graphic in a figure environment, and each such case would then result in a spurious warning.

Overloading the original commands not recommended

3.1.2 nolbreaks — Preventing line breaks in text fragments

To prevent a line break at a space inside a paragraph LaTeX offers ~ denoting an unbreakable space that you can use instead of an ordinary one, e.g., A.~Einstein to ensure that the initial and surname are not split apart. If you (additionally) want to ensure that a word is not hyphenated, you can put it into an \mbox, e.g., A.~\mbox{Einstein}.

However, to keep several words together, it is not a good idea to place them together with the spaces between them into a single \mbox, because inside a box a space has always its nominal width and does not react to the justification of the line, which means that you can end up with noticeably uneven spacing.[1] For high quality it is therefore necessary to \mbox all words individually and place a ~ between each of them — which is fairly cumbersome. To simplify this task Donald Arseneau has written the small package nolbreaks that offers a single command.

---

[1] Exemplified in this paragraph by boxing "it is not a good idea" in the first line.

```
\nolbreaks*{text}
```

The *text* does not break across lines, but spaces inside still participate in paragraph justification as expected. If you use the starred form, then the line before the unbreakable text is allowed to run short (like ragged-right) as shown below. You can also load the package with the option `ragged` in which case `\nolbreaks` behaves like its starred form.

However, to keep several words together, it is not a good idea to place them together with the spaces between them into a box; use `\nolbreaks` instead.

```
\usepackage{nolbreaks} \sloppy
However, to keep several \nolbreaks*{words together,}
it is not a good idea to place them together
with the spaces between them into \nolbreaks{a box};
use \verb=\nolbreaks= instead.
```

3-1-4

The command does not work in all circumstances, e.g., you cannot have verbatim material in its argument, and spaces hidden inside braces or commands can still create breakpoints, but in most situations it offers a simple and readable method for fine-tuning your text. Note that you may need a higher `\tolerance` or `\sloppy` if you add many unbreakable chunks to your paragraphs.

3.1.3 microtype — Enhancing justified text

As mentioned before, TeX uses an algorithm for line breaking that attempts to globally optimize the paragraphs according to a set of parameters weighing different (often conflicting) goals, such as unevenness in the white space distribution, incompatible lines (with respect to word space size), length of the paragraph, number of consecutive hyphens, etc., against each other.

There are, however, a number of further aspects that improve the paragraph quality not taken into account by the original TeX algorithm. Support for them is due to the work of Hàn Thế Thành who developed pdfTeX, which is now the standard TeX engine,[1] and thus these improvements are available to everybody [33, 34, 36].

Already Donald Knuth discussed the use of "hanging punctuations" as an exercise in the *TeXbook* [48, p. 394f] and gave the following example:

"What is hanging punctuation?" asked Alice, with a puzzled frown. 'Well, y'know, actually,' answered Bill, 'I'd rather demonstrate it than explain it.' "Oh, now I see. Commas, periods, and quotes are allowed to stick out into the margins, if they occur next to a line break." 'Yeah, I guess.' "Really! But why do all your remarks have single quotes, while mine are double?" 'I haven't the foggiest; it's weird. Ask the author of this crazy book.'

3-1-5

Optical alignment a.k.a. protrusion feature   As you can see, all punctuation marks and quotation characters are placed outside the text body into the margin. This is a special version of a general principle of optical alignment: to achieve optimal vertical alignment of the text at the margins,

---

[1] The features discussed in this section are also (with minor variations) available in the Unicode engines X∃TeX and LuaTeX and can thus be used with any modern TeX engine.

it is necessary to take the glyph shapes into account and allow some glyphs to protrude slightly into the margin because otherwise the line would appear to be slightly indented — hanging punctuation is just an extreme variant of this principle. How much to protrude depends on the glyph shape and the amount of whiteness it produces. It thus depends on the font being used and may need adjustments accordingly for optimal results. However, even if you do not have specially tailored values for the fonts used in your document, you achieve noticeable improvements by applying a set of default values based on "typical" glyph forms.

A second type of improvement introduced with pdfTeX was in the incorporation of the *hz*-algorithm named after its inventor Hermann Zapf (1918–2015). He realized that (certain) letter shapes can be slightly expanded or compressed without being noticeable to the reader and that this extra flexibility in the text can be used to improve justification. For example, instead of just enlarging the word space (possibly beyond acceptable limits), one can slightly widen most letters in a line, thereby achieving a much more consistent gray value of the whole paragraph. In fact, the additional flexibility introduced this way may lead to different set of line breaks that would otherwise not be possible. This can then avoid overfull lines that would be otherwise produced by TeX's algorithm if it could not satisfy all requirements posed by the line-breaking parameter settings.

The hz algorithm a.k.a. expansion feature

Both features and configuration possibilities to tailor them are made available through the microtype package[1] by Robert Schlicht. It has been used with excellent results throughout this book and is one of the standard packages the author loads in the preamble of nearly every document.

Three other micro-typographical features are supported but not activated by default (because applying them does not always lead to improvements). These are automatic letterspacing of SMALL CAPITALS and possibly other fonts (discussed in Section 3.4.6), extra kerning around individual characters, and interword spacing adjustments based on the character before the space (kind of an extension to the \spacefactor concept of TeX). The features are enabled with the options tracking, kerning, and spacing, respectively. Tracking can be used with pdfTeX and LuaTeX, while the other two features are available only with pdfTeX to date.

Tracking, kerning, and spacing feature

Package options

In many cases it is fully sufficient to simply load the package with a \usepackage declaration (without any option) in the preamble and let it apply its magic behind the scenes using its default configuration. It then automatically applies character protrusion and (if possible) font expansion.

For the latter the engine has to be either pdfTeX or LuaTeX, you have to use only scalable outline fonts (i.e., no bitmap fonts generated from METAFONT sources[2]), and the engine must be set to generate Portable Document Format (PDF) and not Device Independent File Format (DVI). For details of what is possible in DVI mode, see

---

[1]We discuss most aspects of the package here; its letterspacing features are covered in Section 3.4.6.
[2]Bitmap fonts usually produce a fatal error; see page → II 735. There are ways to work with them, but the fonts need to be specially tailored for this.

the manual [125]. Saying it differently, the package applies as many micro-typographic improvements as can be expected to work correctly given the circumstances.

Turning them on (or off)

It does, however, offer a number of key/value options to globally adjust the behavior and as we see later, also methods to tailor the behavior depending on fonts, font sets, and the context inside the document. The options `protrusion` and `expansion` can be used to change or turn on or off the respective feature by giving the value `true` (default), `false`, or `compatibility`. The latter restricts the features to act only on single lines after the line-breaking algorithm has acted. This ensures that the line breaking with or without `microtype` is identical, but at the same time it limits the positive effects that the package can offer and is therefore useful only in special situations.

One can also specify a *font set name* as a value, in which case only fonts belonging to this set use the feature. For details on this advanced usage, consult the `microtype` manual [125].

Protrusion control

The option `factor` can be used to tailor the protrusion feature, and it expects an integer value between 0 (no protrusion) and 1000 (full protrusion). For example, specifying a value of 500 means that the currently defined protrusion for every character is halved. To showcase the results let's first repeat Example 3-1-5 on page 126 with a `factor` of 0 (which is equivalent to not using protrusion at all):

"What is hanging punctuation?" asked Alice, with a puzzled frown. 'Well, y'know, actually,' answered Bill, 'I'd rather demonstrate it than explain it.' "Oh, now I see. Commas, periods, and quotes are allowed to stick out into the margins, if they occur next to a line break." 'Yeah, I guess.' "Really! But why do all your remarks have single quotes, while mine are double?" 'I haven't the foggiest; it's weird. Ask the author of this crazy book.'

3-1-6

You can nicely observe the different line breaks that we get with just the normal TeX algorithm. Now repeat this but with a `factor` of 500, in which case the punctuation and quote characters stick out somewhat into the margins.

"What is hanging punctuation?" asked Alice, with a puzzled frown. 'Well, y'know, actually,' answered Bill, 'I'd rather demonstrate it than explain it.' "Oh, now I see. Commas, periods, and quotes are allowed to stick out into the margins, if they occur next to a line break." 'Yeah, I guess.' "Really! But why do all your remarks have single quotes, while mine are double?" 'I haven't the foggiest; it's weird. Ask the author of this crazy book.'

3-1-7

The line breaks are now identical to Example 3-1-5 even though we use a smaller amount of protrusion. Note that the protrusion feature does not generate more flexibility for the paragraph breaking (in contrast to the expansion feature). It only alters the line breaks because characters at the margins appear unconditionally smaller than without the feature turned on and thus change the attractiveness of individual breakpoints so that TeX may decide to choose a different set.

Also note that in the examples above protrusion was only specified for the punctuation and quote characters to implement "hanging punctuation". For proper optical alignment, one would have to specify protrusion for many more characters. As a showcase for optical alignment, you can look at any paragraph in this book (except for the examples) where many characters stick out to a small degree into the margin to give the impression of vertical alignment at both sides.

To control expansion, a few more options are available. The options `stretch` and `shrink` define how much fonts are allowed to be expanded or compressed. They expect an integer value that is multiplied by $\frac{1}{1000}$ of the character width. Thus, to allow a maximum of 1.5% expansion you would specify `stretch=15`. The default value for both is 20, and if you specify only `stretch`, then its value is also inherited by `shrink`.

Expansion control

As the next example shows, you should be conservative when allowing fonts to stretch or shrink. The idea is to improve the typographic quality by producing paragraphs with more uniform grayness and fewer hyphenated lines by offering the line-breaking algorithm more choices. With most fonts a variation range of ±2% yields reasonable results, but already above 3% you may notice the stems getting bigger or thinner, which can be distracting. Furthermore, some shapes are somewhat distorted when only stretched horizontally, and above a certain point this may become noticeable and thus reduce, rather than enhance, the quality.

Stretching or shrinking text too much is a bad idea!	*-15%*
Stretching or shrinking text too much is a bad idea!	*-5%*
Stretching or shrinking text too much is a bad idea!	*-2%*
Stretching or shrinking text too much is a bad idea!	*(natural)*
Stretching or shrinking text too much is a bad idea!	*2%*
Stretching or shrinking text too much is a bad idea!	*5%*
Stretching or shrinking text too much is a bad idea!	*15%*

3-1-8

To lessen the impact of distorted shapes, microtype offers the option `selected` in which case such shapes are expanded or compressed at a smaller rate than others. This may allow slightly higher overall limits, but on the other hand one has to realize that it also means that characters next to each other may stretch at different rates and thus show different stem widths. In our example, the characters "trix!" are fully expanded, while all others are expanded only by 70%. Whether or not this is then really an improvement is probably a matter of taste.

Stretching or shrinking text too much is a bad idea!	*-3%*
Stretching or shrinking text too much is a bad idea!	*-2%*
Stretching or shrinking text too much is a bad idea!	*(natural)*
Stretching or shrinking text too much is a bad idea!	*2%*
Stretching or shrinking text too much is a bad idea!	*3%*
Stretching or shrinking text too much is a bad idea!	*5%*
Stretching or shrinking text too much is a bad idea!	*15%*

3-1-9

For best results with expansion you need to use scalable fonts (which is fortunately not a problem any longer), and it is advisable to generate PDF output, though neither is an absolute must. If need be, it is possible to use a DVI-based workflow, and even bitmap fonts can be prepared for the task, but it requires a more complicated setup and specially tailored font support files; see the manual [125] for details.

Miscellaneous options There are a few other options that can become handy once in a while. Among them is `activate`, which is simply a shorthand for setting both `protrusion` and `expansion` to the same value. Then there is `verbose`, which outputs extra information into the transcript file (useful for debugging) or, if given the value `errors`, stops if it thinks it encounters a questionable situation. Once you have investigated all warnings, you can also give it the value `silent`.

Specifying the option `babel` directs microtype to adjust the typesetting to the language(s) used in the document. This feature exists for only a few selected languages so far.

The package supports the option `disable` that disables *all* processing if given. As a result, processing is much faster when microtype does nothing, but then line and page breaks are likely to change.[1]

By default microtype loads its configuration from the file `microtype.cfg`. You can bypass this by using the option `config` and specify a different configuration file (without the extension `.cfg`). This way you can maintain and use your own configuration setup if you do not like the default values.

All options except for `config` can alternatively be used in the argument to `\microtypesetup` to define or alter the desired setup in the preamble. Furthermore, this command can also be used inside the document body to temporarily disable or enable any of the micro-typography features, e.g.,

```
\microtypesetup{expansion=false}
```

but otherwise changing the features is no longer possible.

Configuring the machinery

As already indicated, the micro-typography features supported by microtype all require tailoring to the individual fonts used to achieve best results. While that sounds no doubt daunting, the good news is that the package already comes equipped with ready-made protrusion settings for more than a dozen common font families, and for most others the default profile is likely to give you good results too. For expansion the default of ±2% is also likely to work universally, and if not, it is easy to change for a document. In summary, the general usage information provided above should be sufficient for most real-life situations.

We therefore give only a few examples for setup commands to enable you to skim through the configuration files and grasp what they are setting up. This may not be enough to embark on the somewhat tedious task of providing a fully hand-tailored setup for a new font family, but if you are one of the few people[2] interested in that, all necessary information can be found in [125].

---

[1] In older versions of the package this option was called `draft`, which was rather unfortunate, because specifying `draft` on the document class made microtype stop working. You can restore the previous behavior, if you really want to, by specifying `disable=ifdraft`.

[2] Rest assured that Robert would be happy to hear from you that you have worked on the integration of another font family.

\SetProtrusion [*key/value list*] {*set of fonts*}{*protrusion settings*}

The \SetProtrusion declaration lets you define *protrusion settings* for an arbitrary number of characters for a given *set of fonts*.

The *protrusion settings* consists of *character*={*integer-tuple*} where the *integer-tuple* defines the protrusion for left and right margin for the *character*. Zero or no value means no protrusion, and 1000 denotes full protrusion. The *character* can be given as a UTF-8 character, a LaTeX command, and in a few other ways. For example

```
A = {50,50},   \AE = {50, },   : = { ,500},   - = {400,500}
```

lets "A" protrude by 5% on both sides and "Æ" by 5% on the left only. Both the colon and hyphen protrude with half of their width into the right margin, and on the left the hyphen also protrudes with 40% of its width. If you specify a base character such as "A", then microtype knows that there are several other characters, e.g., "À, Á, Â, Ã, Ä, Å, Ą, Ă", that should inherit the setting, and it does that automatically[1] for you.

There are many ways to specify the *set of fonts*, but very often it is enough to specify the supported encoding(s) and the font family name (in New Font Selection Scheme (NFSS) convention); for further details, see [125, §4].

In the optional argument you can specify a number of key values: with name you can give your setting a name, which is useful when reading the output from the verbose option. More importantly, this allows you to refer to such a setting in a later declaration with a load key, thereby extending or modifying it for special situations.

For example, the main protrusion settings for Computer Modern fonts are named cmr-default; additions specific to T1 encoding are named cmr-T1 (loading cmr-default first). And because Latin Modern fonts are very similar to Computer Modern, the protrusion declaration for that family is then simply this:

```
\SetProtrusion [ name = lmr-T1, load = cmr-T1 ]
    { encoding = {T1,LY1}, family = lmr }
    { \textquotedblleft = {300,400}, \textquotedblright = {300,400} }
```

That is, it loads cmr-T1, which in turn loads cmr-default and then makes two changes. All of this applies to any font in the font family lmr in either T1 or LY1 encoding (but not in OT1 or other encodings).

If you like the look and feel of hanging punctuation, here is how Example 3-1-5 from page 126 was produced using Latin Modern fonts:

```
\usepackage{lmodern}
\usepackage[expansion=false,verbose]{microtype}
\LoadMicrotypeFile{cmr}
```

---

[1] Of course, if ever needed, that is customizable too, using \CharacterInheritance. With pdfTeX the standard settings are most likely adequate for all fonts. However, with the Unicode engines it is more likely that font-specific adjustments are needed, simply because OpenType fonts have many more characters (or miss some) so that a single default is not sufficient. Details on that is given in [125].

```
\SetProtrusion [ name = lmr-hangingp  ]
     { encoding = {T1,OT1}, family = lmr }
     { .  = { ,1000}, {,} = { ,1000}, ; = { ,1000}, : = { ,1000},
       \textquotedblleft = {1000, }, \textquotedblright = { ,1000},
       \textquoteleft    = {1000, }, \textquoteright    = { ,1000}  }
```

This example is interesting on several accounts: we explicitly disabled expansion to reproduce the same line breaks as in the TEXbook. With expansion, TEX would have found a "better" or at least different alternative. The protrusion settings as such hold no surprises: each of the punctuation and quote characters fully protrudes into the respective margin. You may also want to do the same to the hyphen character. This was not done, because again it would result in different line breaks compared to the TEXbook.

Nothing happens when making config changes

The surprising line is the second one — without it nothing happens. The problem is that when microtype encounters a font family for the first time in a document, it attempts to load a configuration file named mt-⟨*family*⟩.cfg and applies the declarations it contains. If that file also contains a declaration for the *set of fonts* that we try to customize, it overwrites our carefully drafted setup in the preamble of the document. The solution here is to load that configuration file (using \LoadMicrotypeFile) before we make our declarations so that our settings overwrite the default and not the other way around.

A slight complication is that some font families share such configuration files. In our case we have to load the one for the cmr font family, because that also contains the settings for lmr. The basic advice here is to use the verbose option if something does not seem to work, because that tells you what microtype loads for which font and what gets overwritten and with that information it is easy to make the right adjustments.

Supporting the development visually

If you develop your own protrusion set for a font family or if you want to verify that the currently used one is sufficient and adequate, you can use the companion package microtype-show that offers a number of check and test commands, such as \ShowProtrusion or \ShowCharacterInheritance. These commands produce test output by displaying the current settings both numerically as well as visually. This is a great development and debugging facility; for details see the microtype package documentation.

> \SetExpansion[*key/value list*]{*set of fonts*}{*expansion settings*}

Expansion is normally applied uniformly to all characters, and the necessary settings (if any) are done through the package options stretch and shrink. If, however, the option selected was used, then certain characters expand more than others, and the settings for this can be done through \SetExpansion.

The *expansion settings* are a list with elements of the form *character=factor* where *factor* is an integer between 0 (no expansion) and 1000 (full expansion).

The *set of fonts* argument limits the declaration to a group of fonts in the same way as was already discussed for \SetProtrusion. For example, the default settings (defined in `microtype.cfg`) used for all fonts in the major text encodings look as follows:

```
\SetExpansion [ name = default ] { encoding = {OT1,OT4,QX,T1,LY1} }
   { A = 500, a = 700,   \AE = 500, \ae = 700,  B = 700,  b = 700,
     C = 700, c = 700,     D = 500,   d = 700,  E = 700,  e = 700,
     F = 700,              G = 500,   g = 700,  H = 700,  h = 700,
     K = 700, k = 700,     M = 700,   m = 700,  N = 700,  n = 700,
     O = 500, o = 700,   \OE = 500, \oe = 700,  P = 700,  p = 700,
     Q = 500, q = 700,     R = 700,             S = 700,  s = 700,
     U = 700, u = 700,     W = 700,   w = 700,  Z = 700,  z = 700,
     2 = 700, 3 = 700, 6 = 700, 8 = 700, 9 = 700                   }
```

In the *key/value list* argument you can again use `name` and `load`, though with expansion, these keys are less likely to be needed. The keys `stretch` and `shrink` overwrite the global defaults or the values given on the package level. One application of this is when you provide special settings for named contexts as we see below.

Providing context

By default all declarations made with `\SetProtrusion` and friends apply globally throughout the document. There is, however, the possibility of specifying that they should be activated only in a specific context. This is done by using the key `context` in the *key/value list* argument and assigning it a *context* name. In that case the declaration is activated only if we are within that context.

`\microtypecontext{`*context spec*`}`
`\begin{microtypecontext}{`*context spec*`}` ... `\end{microtypecontext}`
`\textmicrotypecontext{`*context spec*`}{`*text*`}`

You can inform microtype that it is in a specific context in three different ways: with `\microtypecontext` a new context is started that continues to the end of the current scope, or you can use the environment form of that, or you can use the command `\textmicrotypecontext` in which the context applies to the *text* argument. The *context spec* is a comma-separated list of assignments of the form *feature = context* where *feature* is `protrusion`, `expansion`, `tracking`, `kerning`, or `spacing` and *context* is the name you assigned in the declaration. To reset the context (if not automatically reverted through scoping) you can provide an empty *context name*.

Specifying tracking, extra kerning, and adjusted spacing

The features described below cover some concepts that are not activated by default but need to be explicitly enabled through options, i.e., `tracking`, `kerning`, and `spacing`, respectively. Furthermore, the kerning and spacing features are available only with pdfTeX, while tracking can also be used with the LuaTeX engine. An interesting article on the background of these features can be found in [35].

133

```
\SetTracking [key/value list] {set of fonts}{tracking amount}
\SetExtraKerning [key/value list] {set of fonts}{kerning settings}
\SetExtraSpacing [key/value list] {set of fonts}{spacing settings}
```

The \SetTracking declaration allows you to specify extra spaces between all characters of a font or a set of fonts in order to achieve letter spacing. This is discussed further in Section 3.4.6 on page 191.

The \SetExtraKerning declaration provides a way to specify for individual characters some additional space to be added on either side of the glyph. This is useful with languages that have typographical traditions requiring such spacing around some characters (typically punctuations). In French, for example, an extra space is required in front of ":", ";", "?", and "!", and with a declaration such as

```
\SetExtraKerning[name=french-default, context=french, unit=space]
                {encoding = {OT1,T1,LY1}}
                { : = {1000,},   ; = {500, }, ! = {500,},   ? = {500,} }
```

this can be automatically provided without the need to alter the input sources. Note the use of the context key, which limits the declaration to a context named french so that you can restrict its usage as needed.

To communicate with babel and install different contexts per language, microtype offers the declaration \DeclareMicrotypeBabelHook. In the next example we use this to specify special kerning for French text. The \SetExtraKerning declaration is already in that form part of the microtype default settings, so we can make use of it without the need to repeat it in the example.

FRENCH : Je ne parle pas français !
ENGLISH: I speak English!

```
\usepackage[english,french]{babel}
\usepackage[kerning]{microtype}
% \SetExtraKerning ... as above
\DeclareMicrotypeBabelHook{french}{kerning=french}
FRENCH: Je ne parle pas français! \par
\selectlanguage{english} ENGLISH: I speak English!
```

3-1-10

Finally, with the \SetExtraSpacing declaration you get granular control over the width and behavior of interword spaces. For each font TeX maintains three dimensions (called \fontdimens: see page 745) that describe the default width of a space, the amount by which that space can stretch, and the amount it can shrink when doing paragraph justification. In addition, there is a "space factor" table where for each character a factor is specified by which these font dimensions are multiplied when that character is directly in front of a space. This is the reason why spaces after punctuation characters appear larger (when \nonfrenchspacing is in force — the default) and appear uniform (when \frenchspacing is specified).

The problem with TeX's approach of a space factor is that you not only get larger or smaller spaces with the help of these factors; in addition, they are also applied to the stretching and shrinking components and so in spaced-out lines spaces after punctuation characters may become excessively large.

The pdfTeX engine extends the TeX functionality by providing individual controls on a per-character and per-font basis for all three dimensions, and the \SetExtraSpacing declaration offers an interface to that. For example,

```
\SetExtraSpacing[unit=space]
                {font={*/*/*/*/*}}{ . = {2000,0,0} }
```

would double the space after a period without altering its stretch and shrink component. The mechanism can also be used to implement optical spacing, that is, slightly altering the standard width of a space depending on the shape of the preceding character. The default configuration files for microtype provide some settings for this. However, this is of course semi-optimal given that only a character to the left of the space can influence its width.

For further details on all three features refer to the package manual [125] and study the default configuration files that provide standard settings from which you may want to start if you make changes.

Disabling selected ligatures

Using ligatures, e.g., "ffi" instead of "ffi", usually improves the appearance, and the fact that LaTeX can produce them automatically (if available in the font) is normally a good thing. There are occasions where you want to prevent this from happening, e.g., in compound words like "Auflage" instead of "Auflage", (because it is a special "Lage" not a "Flage"), but these are rare and need to be handled on an individual basis. The babel package offers some support for this; see Example 13-3-7 on page →II 311. However, there are also situations where one wants to disable ligatures (or some ligatures) altogether and for this microtype provides \DisableLigatures.

\DisableLigatures [*start characters*] {*set of fonts*}

With the *set of fonts* argument one specifies for which fonts ligatures should be suppressed and with the optional *start characters* argument, it is possible to restrict it to only a subset of ligatures. For example, Latin Modern Typewriter has ligatures for "--" becoming a single "-" and "<<" and ">>" generating "«" and "»", respectively. To prevent this you could write

```
\DisableLigatures[-,<,>]{family = lmtt}
```

Note that for technical reasons you can specify only the ligature start character, thus by specifying, for example, f, you disable all ligatures starting with "f".

Some special considerations when using microtype

As mentioned before it is usually just enough to load microtype in the preamble without any further adjustments to the document body. There are, however, a few cases to watch out for, and it might pay to temporarily turn off some or all of the package features or guide them in difficult situations.

Being pedantic about protrusion

Protrusion, for example, works automatically in normal paragraphs, but in certain situations TeX does not consider the text whose boundary requires vertical alignment (and thus protrusion) as being at the margin, because there is some intervening material. For instance, the bullet in an `itemize` is seen by LaTeX as being part of the line, while for a human reader the text of that item is what needs visual alignment. Thus, without help, the first character on that line would not protrude, while the first character on the next line would.[1]

```
\leftprotrusion{text}      \rightprotrusion{text}
\leftprotrusion            \noprotrusion
```

In case protrusion is not done automatically or not done correctly, you can force or prevent it with these commands. `\leftprotrusion` and `\rightprotrusion` add a protrusion correction to the left or right of *text*, respectively. You can use also `\leftprotrusion` without an argument, in which case it scans the input for text characters, and if it finds one (which may be a ligature), it applies protrusion to this character. The version without argument is slightly less efficient, but it has the advantage that you can use it in places where you do not know what text is following, e.g., at the beginning of a `tabular` cell:

```
\begin{tabular}{l>{\leftprotrusion}p{9cm}r}
```

This is unfortunately not possible for protrusion on the right: with the command `\rightprotrusion` you always have to use the argument.

There is also `\noprotrusion` that prohibits protrusion in all cases. This command is already defined in the LaTeX format so you can use it in command definitions whether or not microtype gets loaded in your document.

Interaction with TOC-like lists

If protrusion is turned on while a table of contents is being typeset, then the page numbers at the right might protrude into the margin. That in turn makes the left-hand side of the page number column somewhat uneven, which may be noticeable if the numbers start with the same digits. The solution in such a case is to use `\microtypesetup` to set protrusion to `false`, i.e.,

```
\microtypesetup{protrusion=false}
\tableofcontents \listoftables \listoffigures
\microtypesetup{protrusion=true}
```

Standard LaTeX avoids this problem, but with older document classes or special definitions for such lists it may still happen.

Interaction with verbatim

Similarly, both protrusion and expansion are not really wanted if you typeset code material verbatim. After all, the idea of using a mono-spaced font in `verbatim` environments is to ensure that the characters appear perfectly aligned above each other, and either feature may spoil that alignment. Thus, setting both features (or `activate`

---

[1] There is work under way to help LaTeX to recognize this particular case automatically, so in the future the `itemize` case may work automatically. Currently, the microtype package attempts to patch `\item`, but this does not always work and may have to be prevented with the `nopatch` option.

as a shorthand) to `false` in front of such environments solves this problem. However, you may not want to litter your source with such declarations, especially if you have many such environments.[1]

A possibly better alternative is to incorporate the setting into the environment itself using \AddToHook with a reasonably new LaTeX as follows:

```
\AddToHook{env/verbatim/begin}{\microtypesetup{activate=false}}
```

There is no need to undo the setting because the environment forms a group so that at its end the change is automatically undone. If you are doing that, then you may want to also update \tableofcontents and friends in a similar way:

```
\AddToHook{cmd/tableofcontents/before}{\microtypesetup{protrusion=false}}
\AddToHook{cmd/tableofcontents/after} {\microtypesetup{protrusion=true}}
```

In this case we have to turn microtype on again after the command.

Another situation where expansion is often not really helpful is the case of typesetting unjustified text using the ragged2e package, discussed in Section 3.1.1 on page 123. Because this package tries to avoid extreme raggedness by making short lines appear "underfull" to the paragraph-breaking algorithm, microtype mistakenly tries to help by expanding the fonts in such lines. Thus, nearly all lines in unjustified paragraphs get expanded, which is not a desired state of affairs.

Interaction with ragged2e

On the other hand, microtype is still useful if there is a need to slightly shrink a line to make it fit. Instead of completely disabling expansion when typesetting unjustified text, it is better to define a special context in which only shrinking but not stretching is allowed. This can be done as follows (and with the help of \AddToHook directly attached to \RaggedRight and similar commands):

```
\SetExpansion[ context = ragged, stretch = 0, shrink = 30 ]
             { encoding = {OT1,T1,TS1} } {}
\AddToHook{cmd/RaggedRight/before}{\microtypecontext{expansion=ragged}}
```

There is usually no need to restore the context in this case, because that happens automatically when the scope of \RaggedRight ends.

3.1.4 parskip — Adjusting the look and feel of paragraphs

In the majority of publications, paragraphs are typeset justified with the first line indented by some fixed amount and the last line run short based on the line-breaking results of the paragraph material. Because of the indentation at the left in the first line and the white space on the right in the last line, readers can easily identify the paragraphs without any further visual signals. Therefore, there is typically no extra vertical space added between paragraphs, which saves space. This type of layout is used by most LaTeX document classes and is what you see on most pages in this book.

---

[1] Verbatim-like environments done with listings or fancyvrb are not affected because due to their implementation, protrusion or expansion is automatically prevented.

However, this is by no means the only common layout. Quite often you see documents that do not use paragraph indentation, but instead add some vertical space between paragraphs to clearly distinguish them. Of course, one could have both indentation and some vertical spacing. One could also run all paragraphs together as a single block with just a special sign (e.g., ¶) separating the paragraphs — a style that was quite common in medieval manuscripts.[1]

Inside the TeX engine, this is handled by a number of parameters: the width of the paragraph indentation of the first line stored in \parindent, the white space at the end in \parfillskip, and the vertical space between paragraphs in \parskip.

Unfortunately, it is not enough to change their values to move from one type of layout to the other. Building paragraphs is one of the few core functionalities of TeX, and thus many elements that technically are not text paragraphs are internally handled as if they are. For example, heading titles or lines in a table of contents and many more things are constructed as "single-line" paragraphs. If one would simply set \parskip to the height of a full line, all these elements would widely spread apart resulting in very ugly-looking documents.[2]

It is therefore best to use a document class that has been explicitly designed for this type of layout. For cases where that is not possible, there exists the small **parskip** package, which can be used with any document class and by default implements paragraphs without indentation and half a line of separation (while fixing "some" of the resulting side effects). The package dates back thirty years, originally written by Hubert Partl and later maintained by Robin Fairbairns (1947–2022) and others. In 2018 it got rewritten and once more extended by Frank Mittelbach.

In its simplest form all you need to do is to load the package, and that gives you zero indentation, gives some vertical paragraph separation, and handles headings, list environments, and TOCs fairly well. There still may be other display environments that may show too much vertical white space if their parameter settings are not adjusted.

As any dedicated reader can clearly see, the Ideal of practical reason is a representation of, as far as I know, the things in themselves; as I have shown elsewhere, the phenomena should only be used as a canon for our understanding.

The paralogisms of practical reason are what first give rise to the architectonic of practical reason.

As will easily be shown in the next section, reason would thereby be made to contradict, in view of these considerations, the Ideal of practical reason, yet the manifold depends on the phenomena.

```
\usepackage{kantlipsum}
\usepackage{multicol}
  \raggedcolumns
\usepackage{parskip}
\begin{multicols}{2}
  \kant[1][1] % one sentence
  \kant[1][2] % paragraphs
  \kant[1][3]
\end{multicols}
```

3-1-11

---
[1] This type of layout, while possible, is rather difficult to achieve with TeX due to the fact that TeX wants to globally optimize the line breaking. A document consisting of a single block of text is therefore not a very good idea and needs some special tricks not covered in this book.

[2] One can (correctly) argue that this is in fact a design flaw in LaTeX and should be handled differently. While true, there is no way of changing this now without severe consequences to existing documents.

In the 2018 reimplementation the package got a number of key/value options to allow for some configuration adjustments. With the option `skip` you can now define the amount of vertical separation, the default being `0.5\baselineskip` plus `2pt` of stretch if the option is not given.

By default the `\parskip` is zero within `\tableofcontents` and similar lists, regardless of its value elsewhere. With the option `tocskip` it can be given a different value. If used without an explicit value, you get the same `\parskip` as elsewhere within these lists.

The option `indent` defines the width of the indentation of the first line. If it is not given, then all paragraphs are without indentation; if set to some value, that value is used; and if used without a value, the indentation from the document class is kept.

Finally, there is the option `parfill`. If you give it a dimension value, then LaTeX tries to keep at least that width as white space in the last line. This may not be possible because of the paragraph content and other line-breaking parameter settings in which case you might see an "Overfull hbox" warning even though the text looks fine.[1] If specified without a value, then `30pt` is used, and if not specified, then the line is allowed to completely fill up.

In the next example three of the options are applied. The `parfill` setting has no visible effect because all three paragraphs have more than `1em` of white space in the last line. However, a change to `2em` would affect the first paragraph, and requiring even `3em` would also alter the third paragraph.

As any dedicated reader can clearly see, the Ideal of practical reason is a representation of, as far as I know, the things in themselves; as I have shown elsewhere, the phenomena should only be used as a canon for our understanding.

The paralogisms of practical reason are what first give rise to the architectonic of practical reason.

As will easily be shown in the next section, reason would thereby be made to contradict, in view of these considerations, the Ideal of practical reason, yet the manifold depends on the phenomena.

```
\usepackage{kantlipsum}
\usepackage{multicol}
  \raggedcolumns
\usepackage[indent=3em,
            parfill=1em,
            skip=\baselineskip]
  {parskip}
\begin{multicols}{2}
  \kant[1][1]   \kant[1][2]
  \kant[1][3]
\end{multicols}
```

3-1-12

3.1.5 setspace — Changing interline spacing

The `\baselineskip` command is TeX's parameter for defining the *leading* (normal vertical distance) between consecutive baselines. Standard LaTeX defines a leading approximately 20% larger than the design size of the font (see Section 9.7.1 on page 731). Because it is not recommended to change the setting of `\baselineskip` directly, LaTeX 2_ε provides the `\linespread` declaration to allow for changing

---

[1] It is admittedly a somewhat dubious feature, but it would prevent paragraphs like the previous one (that ended at the right margin) or at least give a warning if adjustment turned out to be impossible.

`\baselineskip` at all sizes globally. After `\linespread{1.5}\selectfont`, the leading increases immediately.

The package setspace (by Geoffrey Tobin and others) provides commands and environments for typesetting with variable spacing (primarily double and one-and-a-half). Three commands — `\singlespacing`, `\onehalfspacing`, and `\doublespacing` — are available for use in the preamble to set the overall spacing for the document. Instead of the preamble commands, one can load the package with one of the options singlespacing (default), onehalfspacing, or doublespacing to achieve the same effect. Alternatively, a specific spacing value can be defined by placing a `\setstretch` command in the preamble. It takes the desired spacing factor as a mandatory argument. In the absence of any of the above commands, the default setting is single spacing.

To change the spacing inside a document, three environments — singlespace, onehalfspace, and doublespace — are provided. They set the spacing to single, one-and-a-half, and double spacing, respectively. These environments cannot be nested.

In the beginning God created the heaven and the earth. Now the earth was unformed and void, and darkness was upon the face of the deep; and the spirit of God hovered over the face of the waters.

```
\usepackage{setspace}

\begin{doublespace}
In the beginning God created the heaven
and the earth. Now the earth was unformed
and void, and darkness was upon the face
of the deep; and the spirit of God
hovered over the face of the waters.
\end{doublespace}
```

3-1-13

For any other spacing values the generic environment spacing should be used. Its mandatory parameter is the value of `\baselinestretch` for the text enclosed by the environment.

In the beginning God created the heaven and the earth. Now the earth was unformed and void, and darkness was upon the face of the deep; and the spirit of God hovered over the face of the waters.

```
\usepackage{setspace}

\begin{spacing}{2.0}
In the beginning God created the heaven
and the earth. Now the earth was unformed
and void, and darkness was upon the face
of the deep; and the spirit of God
hovered over the face of the waters.
\end{spacing}
```

3-1-14

In the above example the coefficient "2.0" produces a larger leading than the "double spacing" (doublespace environment) required for some publications. With the spacing environment the leading is effectively increased twice — once by `\baselineskip` (which LaTeX already sets to about 20% above the font size) and a second time by setting `\baselinestretch`. "Double spacing" means that the vertical distance between baselines is about twice as large as the font size. Since `\baselinestretch` refers to the ratio between the desired distance and the

spacing	10pt	11pt	12pt
one and one-half	1.25	1.21	1.24
double	1.67	1.62	1.66

Table 3.2: Effective \baselinestretch values for different font sizes

\baselineskip, the values of \baselinestretch for different document base font sizes (and at two different optical spacings) can be calculated and are presented in Table 3.2.

If display formula environments are used in the document, then the spaces before and after such environments are also enlarged by the current stretch factor. This can be completely suppressed by using the package option nodisplayskipstretch. Alternatively one can specify an independent stretch factor for such display spaces by using \setdisplayskipstretch.

If the caption package is used (discussed in Section 7.4.1 on page 540), then captions do not change their spacing based on options given to setspace. Instead, you have to set the caption key font to either onehalfspacing or doublespacing or to {stretch=⟨factor⟩}.

3.1.6 lettrine — Dropping your capital

In certain types of publications you may find the first letter of some paragraphs being highlighted by means of an enlarged letter often dropped into the paragraph body (so that the paragraph text flows around it) and usually followed by the first phrase or sentence being typeset in a special font. Applications range from chapter openings in novels, or indications of new thoughts in the text, to merely decorative elements to produce lively pages in a magazine. This custom can be traced back to the early days of printing, when such initials were often hand-colored after the printing process was finished. It originates in the manuscripts of the Middle Ages; that is, it predates the invention of printing.

```
\lettrine [key/value list] {initial}{text}
```

The package lettrine written by Daniel Flipo lets you create such initials by providing the command \lettrine. In its simplest form it takes two arguments: the letter to become an initial and the follow-up text to be typeset in a special font, by default in \scshape.

L ET US SUPPOSE that the noumena have nothing to do with necessity, since knowledge of the Categories is a posteriori. Hume tells ...

```
\usepackage{lettrine}

\lettrine{L}{et us suppose} that the noumena have
nothing to do with necessity, since knowledge of
the Categories is a posteriori. Hume tells \ldots
```

3-1-15

The font used for the initial is, by default, a larger size of the current text font. As an alternative, you can specify a special font family by redefining the command \LettrineFontHook using standard NFSS commands. Similarly, the font used for the text in the second argument can be modified by changing \LettrineTextFont. As demonstrated below, it is also possible to add color using these hooks:

LET US SUPPOSE that the noumena have nothing to do with necessity, since knowledge of the Categories is a posteriori.

```
\usepackage{lettrine,color,ragged2e}
\renewcommand\LettrineFontHook{\sffamily\bfseries\color{blue}}
\renewcommand\LettrineTextFont{\sffamily\scshape\color{blue}}
\RaggedRight
\lettrine{L}{et us suppose} that the noumena have nothing to do
with necessity, since knowledge of the Categories is a posteriori.
```
3-1-16

Many books on typography give recommendations about how to best set large initials with respect to surrounding text. For highest quality it is often necessary to manually adjust the placement depending on the shape of the initial. For example, it is often suggested that letters with a projecting left stem should overhang into the margin. The \lettrine command caters to this need by supporting an optional argument in which you can specify adjustments in the form of a comma-separated list of key/value pairs.

The size of the initial is calculated by default to have a height of two text lines (stored in DefaultLines); with the keyword lines you can change this value to a different number of lines. There is an exception: if you specify lines=1, the initial is still made two lines high, but instead of being dropped is placed onto the baseline of the first text line.

If you want a dropped initial that also extends above the first line of text, then use the keyword loversize. A value of .2 would enlarge the initial by 20%. The default value for this keyword is stored in \DefaultLoversize. This keyword is also useful in conjunction with lraise (default 0 in \DefaultLraise). In the case of an initial with a large descender such as a "Q", you may have to raise the initial to avoid it overprinting following lines. In that case loversize can be used to reduce the height so as to align the initial properly. Instead, or in addition, you can use the keyword depth (default 0 stored in DefaultDepth) to tell lettrine to extend the cutout by that many lines to leave room for the descender of the initial.

With the keyword lhang you specify how much the initial extends into the margin. The value is specified as a fraction — that is, between 0 and 1. Its document default is stored in \DefaultLhang.

QUALITY QUESTIONS create a quality life. Successful people ask better questions, and as a result, they get better answers.

```
\usepackage{tgpagella,lettrine,color}
\lettrine[lines=3, depth=1, loversize=0.4,
    lraise=-0.05, lhang=.1]{\color[gray]{0.8}Q}
                         {uality questions}
create a quality life. Successful people ask better
questions, and as a result, they get better answers.
```
3-1-17

The distance between the initial and the following text in the first line is controlled by the dimension `\DefaultFindent` (default 0pt) and can be overwritten using the keyword `findent`. The indentation of following lines is by default 0.5em (stored in `\DefaultNindent`) but can be changed through the keyword `nindent`. If you want to specify a sloped indentation, you can use the keyword `slope`, which applies from the third line onward. Again, the default value can be changed via the dimension `\DefaultSlope`, though it seems questionable that you would ever want anything different than 0pt because a slope is normally used only for letters like "A" or "V".

To attach material to the left of the initial, such as some opening quote, you can use the keyword `ante`. It is the only keyword for which no command exists to set the default. In the next example we use it to add a quotation mark in a way that it overlaps with the space occupied by the initial. Note the extra braces around the value to hide the brackets.

...paragraphe précédent...

« A PEINE ONT-ILS MIS le pied dans la ville en pleurant la mort de leur bienfaiteur, qu'ils sentent la terre trembler sous leurs pas; ... »

3-1-18

```
\usepackage{tgpagella,lettrine}
\usepackage[french]{babel}

\noindent \ldots paragraphe précédent \ldots
\lettrine[ante={\makebox[0pt][l]{\hspace{5pt}\og}},
   lines=4,slope=0.6em,findent=-1em,nindent=0.6em]{À}
      { peine ont-ils mis} le pied dans la ville
en pleurant la mort de leur bienfaiteur, qu'ils
sentent la terre trembler sous leurs pas; \ldots \fg
```

The example above clearly demonstrates that the size calculation for the initial does not take accents into account, which is normally the desired behavior. It is nevertheless possible to manually adjust the size using `loversize`.

The exact font size to use for the initial is determined as follows: first the height of the cutout needed for the initial is calculated (based on the current key values for `lines`, `lraise`, and `loversize`). Then lettrine trial-typesets the text stored in `\LettrineTestString` (which by default holds the string EFTZ[1]) using the font setup stored in `\LettrineFontHook`. It then scales the font for the initial such that the test string would exactly fit the cutout. You can locally change this test string using the key `refstring`. If used without a value, then the first mandatory argument to `\lettrine` is used as the string. This can be useful if the initials are very irregular in height and you therefore want the size calculation done based on the individual initial.

Calculating the exact initial size

If not raised or extended, then the top of the initial aligns with text from the second argument of `\lettrine`. More precisely it aligns with the height of a trial text stored in `\LettrineSecondText` typeset in `\LettrineTextFont` (as before that masks out any variations due to argument values). The default string is just an x, which makes sense if the second argument is typeset in `\scshape`. However, if you have changed `\LettrineTextFont`, that may not be any longer appropriate, and

---

[1]Some fonts apply optical corrections to letters like C, G, O, or Q, i.e., make them slightly higher than other capitals. They are therefore not included in the test string.

you may have to change this test string too. A possible alternative is to use the key `realheight`, which directs `\lettrine` to use the second mandatory argument as the test string.

As a result of this approach the font size used for the initial "A" is exactly the same as the one for "À" (as shown in Example 3-1-18), and because the latter is bigger, its accent sticks out above the cutout. In that case lettrine adds some extra vertical skip in front of the paragraph so that the initial does not bump into material from the previous line. If you also use the key `grid`, the package rounds up this extra space to a multiple of `\baselineskip` to stay in register. If the extra space needed is very small, it might be better to avoid it completely to keep the register, which is controlled through the key `novskip` (the default of `0.2pt` is stored in `\DiscardVskip`).

Because the `\lettrine` command calculates the initial size to fit a certain number of lines, you need scalable fonts to obtain the best results. The examples in this book are typeset in Times and Helvetica by default, so we have no problems *Fonts with* here. Later examples use Palatino, which is also a scalable Type 1 font. However, *discrete sizes are* if you use a font that exists only in discrete sizes, the results may not be always *a problem* satisfactory. For example, the default setup for Computer Modern would not work well because for historical reasons it uses discrete sizes even though it is now provided in scalable fonts. As an alternative you could use Latin Modern or the fix-cm package; see Section 9.5.1 on page 684.

IF YOUR INITIAL does not exist as a glyph in a font but as a graphic object (like this one taken from [42]), then you can use the keyword `image` to inform lettrine about this fact. It then attempts to load a graphic with the name of the initial (using `\includegraphics{`*initial*`}` from the `graphicx` package); e.g., in this paragraph it looked for a graphic named `I.png` or `I.pdf` or whatever your system supports as extensions. This graphic is then scaled to the right size and positioned according to any other keywords that you have supplied.

By modifying the default settings you can easily adapt the package to typeset initials the way you like. This can be done either in the preamble or in a file with the name `lettrine.cfg`, which is loaded if found.

Adjusting values for However, if there is a need to adjust many initials individually, you may want to *individual initials* record these settings for each character once and afterwards simply use `\lettrine` without an optional argument. This is in fact possible by providing a special configuration file containing lines of the form `\LettrineOptionsFor{`*initial*`}{`*key/value list*`}` for every initial that needs values different from the defaults. Officially this is supported only for the initials A to Z, but it does in fact work for (most) accented characters too. You then have to redefine `\DefaultOptionsFile` to contain the name of your option file, and that's all that is needed. The `myinitials.cfg` file we use in the next example holds the following lines:

```
\LettrineOptionsFor{A}{grid,loversize=.33,slope=0.6em,
                       findent=-1em,nindent=0.6em}
\LettrineOptionsFor{I}{image,loversize=.1,lraise=-.05,
                       findent=1pt}
```

Individual initials can still have an optional argument overwriting or extending the configured values. In the next example we use that to add a left quote mark.

I f your initial does not exist as a glyph in a font but as a graphic object (like this one) then you can use the keyword image …

```
\usepackage{tgpagella,lettrine,graphicx}
\setcounter{DefaultLines}{3}
% content of file shown above
\renewcommand\DefaultOptionsFile{myinitials.cfg}
```

"A s a result font size used for the initial 'A' is exactly the same as the one for 'À' and as …"

```
\lettrine{I}{f your initial} does not exist as a glyph
in a font but as a graphic object (like this one) then
you can use the keyword \texttt{image} \ldots
\lettrine[ante={\makebox[0pt][l]{\hspace{5pt}''}}]
 {A}{s a result} font size used for the initial 'A' is
exactly the same as the one for 'À' and as \ldots ''
```

3-1-19

One problem to watch out for are initials near a page break. The package does not check for this, and if you are unlucky, the initial may overprint the foot line while the cutout partly or fully ends up on the top of the next page.

3.1.7 Alphabets for initials

If you hunt on the Internet, you find many fonts that are suitable for being used as initials, but it is not always easy to make them available for use with LaTeX (at least not when using pdfTeX).

As part of the TeX distributions you find 23 such fonts, designed by Dieter Steffmann. They have been arranged for use with LaTeX by Clea F. Rees, and all you have to do is to load a corresponding support package. Each of these packages defines two commands: a font switch (like \rmfamily) and a command with one argument to typeset in the font (like \textrm), e.g., \Kramerfamily and \kramer.

Some of the fonts contain only uppercase letters, while others offer a variant alphabet in the lowercase character positions. For use with the lettrine package the font switches are convenient; if you prefer to use the glyphs directly, then the commands with an argument may be better. Both usages are shown in the next example, showing four of the fonts:

A s a well-spent day brings happy sleep, so life well used brings happy death. (Leonardo da Vinci)

𝕬 𝕭 𝕮 𝖆 𝖇 𝖈 𝔄 𝔅 ℭ A B C
STARBURST

```
\usepackage{Typocaps,Kramer,Starburst,Rothdn,lettrine}
\renewcommand\LettrineFontHook{\Typocapsfamily}

\lettrine{A}{s} a well-spent day brings happy sleep, so
life well used brings happy death. (Leonardo da Vinci)
\par {\Rothdnfamily A B C  a b c} \hfill
{\Kramerfamily A B C  a b c} \par \starburst{STARBURST}
```

3-1-20

To get the list of all packages and command names together with some sample specimens for each font, refer to the documentation that can be accessed through texdoc initials on the command line.

3.1.8 magaz — Special handling of the first line

In magazine-type publications the first line of an introductory paragraph is often handled in a special way, either by using an initial letter (see Section 3.1.6) or by setting that line in a special font. A method for the latter is provided by Donald Arseneau with his package **magaz**. While this can be manually achieved with trial and error, the package offers a convenient way with the command \FirstLine.

```
\FirstLine{text}
```

It expects a single argument and typesets this argument partially or fully in a special font defined by \FirstLineFont (by default \scshape). More precisely, if the text when typeset occupies more than one line, then only its first line is handled specially; otherwise, all of the argument gets the special treatment.

```
\usepackage{magaz}
\renewcommand\FirstLineFont{\bfseries}
```

The first line of this paragraph is typeset in boldface. The remainder is set in the normal body font.

```
\FirstLine{The first line of this paragraph is
          typeset in boldface.}
The remainder is set in the normal body font.
```

Less material in the argument will be fully typeset in the special font. Note the placement and result of the \noindent command.

```
\FirstLine{\noindent Less material} in the argument
will be fully typeset in the special font. Note the
placement and result of the \verb=\noindent= command.
```

If placed in front it will get lost as you can see here.

```
\noindent\FirstLine{If placed in front it will get
lost} as you can see here.
```

3-1-21

The command should be used only at the beginning of a paragraph; elsewhere it might result in strange errors or weird output. Furthermore, the *text* should be simple ordinary text (not display environments, etc.) and not subject to changes when typeset several times. For example, a \footnote would not work because it increments and prints the footnote counter. For the same reason the \FirstLineFont should not change the hyphenation of the text (as \ttfamily or a language change typically do) because otherwise the internal trials would be done with incorrect assumptions. Also note that if you want to suppress the indentation, you need to place the \noindent inside the argument. The package documentation discusses a few other problematical cases.

In short, the method works well in standard cases, but if you have some complicated material, you are going to exceed its abilities. In that situation you can still revert to a manual trial and error solution and, once you have determined the point where the second line should start, write something like

```
\textbf{The first line\footnote{...} of this paragraph}\linebreak
is typeset in boldface. The remainder is set in ...
```

Of course, the moment you change your text, then you have to move the \linebreak.

3.1.9 fancypar — Fancy layouts for individual paragraphs

The fancypar package by Gonzalo Medina Arellano offers a number of decorative paragraph layouts for individual paragraphs that may be of interest in some types of documents.

`\NotebookPar`[*options*]{*simple text*}   `\MarkedPar`[*options*]{*simple text*}   ...

These are `\NotebookPar` (notebook style with spiral binding), `\MarkedPar` (a marker on each line, either left or right), and `\ZebraPar` (alternating backgrounds), as well as `\DashedPar` and `\UnderlinedPar`.

All of them expect a mandatory argument that can receive *simple text* (i.e., no display material such as lists, display formulas, etc.). It is also possible to supply key/value *options* to adjust the layout though that is normally done via options to the package or through `\fancyparsetup`.

Below we show two examples using a few key/value options to customize them to give you some impression of what is possible:

```
\usepackage{lipsum,fancypar}
\fancyparsetup{linecolor=green!20,
    textcolor=blue,intercolor=black,
    spiral=true,spiralcolor=red,
    interheight=0.5pt }
\NotebookPar{\lipsum[1][1]\par
            \lipsum[1][2]}
```

3-1-22

With `\MarkedPar` one can define the marker and its placement (left or right):

Nam dui ligula, fringilla a, euismod sodales, sol-   ←
licitudin vel, wisi.   ←

→   Morbi auctor lorem non justo. Nam lacus libero,
3-1-23   →   pretium at, lobortis vitae, ultricies et, tellus.

```
\usepackage{lipsum,fancypar}
\fancyparsetup{mark=$\gets$}
\MarkedPar{\lipsum[2][1]}
\MarkedPar[mark=$\to$,position=left]
          {\lipsum[2][2-3]}
```

The package offers many other keys to adjust the layout of the other predefined styles. It is also possible to define your own type of layouts. For details consult the package documentation.

3.2 Dealing with special characters

In this section we deal with small text fragments and explain how they can be manipulated and highlighted in a consistent manner by giving them a visual appearance different from the one used for the main text.

We start by discussing ways to produce professional-looking marks of omission. This is followed by methods for typesetting various dashes, again a topic that has a variety of different conventions in different parts of the world. We then take a look at a package for using underscores in words without losing the ability to hyphenate, something often needed when documenting computer code. Finally, we discuss how to define commands that take care of the space after them.

3.2.1 ellipsis, lips — Marks of omission

Omission marks are universally represented by three consecutive periods (also known as an *ellipsis*). Their spacing, however, depends on house style and typographic conventions, and significant differences are observed. In French, according to Hart [37] or *The Chicago Manual of Style* [18], "points de suspension" are set close together and immediately follow the preceding word with a space on the right:

> C'est une chose... bien difficile.

In German, according to the *Duden* [22], "Auslassungspunkte" have space on the left *and* right unless they mark missing letters within a word or are followed by punctuation:

> Du E... du! Scher dich zum ...!

Elsewhere, such as in British and American typography, the dots are sometimes set with full word spaces between them, and rather complex rules determine how to handle other punctuation marks at either end.

LaTeX offers the command \dots (which is a shorthand for \textellipsis in normal text) to produce closely spaced omission marks. Unfortunately, the standard definition (inherited from plain TeX) produces uneven spacing at the left and right — unsuitable to typeset some of the above examples properly. The extra thin space at the right of the ellipsis is correct in certain situations (e.g., when a punctuation character follows). If the ellipsis is followed by space, however, it looks distinctly odd and is best canceled as shown in the example below (though removing the space in the second instance brings the exclamation mark a bit too close).

```
\newcommand\lips{\dots\unkern}
```

Compare the following:	`Compare the following:\\`
Du E... du! Scher dich zum ...!	`   Du E\dots\ du! Scher dich zum \dots!\\`
Du E... du! Scher dich zum ...!	`   Du E\lips\ du! Scher dich zum \lips!`

3-2-1

This problem is addressed in the package ellipsis written by Peter Heslin, which redefines the \dots command to look at the following character to decide whether to add a final separation. An extra space is added if the following character is listed in the command \ellipsispunctuation, which defaults to ",.:;!?". When using some of the language support packages that make certain characters active, this list may have to be redeclared afterwards to enable the package to still recognize the characters.

If loaded with the option xspace, it also automatically issues an \xspace command at the end of the definition for \dots so that you get an normal word space based on the next character.

The spacing between the periods and the one possibly added after the ellipsis can be controlled through the command \ellipsisgap. To allow for automatic adjustments depending on the font size, use a font-dependent unit like em or a fraction of a \fontdimen (see page 745).

Compare the following:
Du E... du! Scher dich zum ...!
Du E. . . du! Scher dich zum . . . !
Du E... du! Scher dich zum T...el!

```
\usepackage[xspace]{ellipsis}
Compare the following:\\
 Du E\dots du! Scher dich zum \dots!\\
\renewcommand\ellipsisgap{1.0\fontdimen2\font}
 Du E\dots du! Scher dich zum \dots!\\
\renewcommand\ellipsisgap{0.05em}
 Du E\dots du! Scher dich zum T\midwordellipsis el!
```

3-2-2

For the special case when you need an ellipsis in the middle of a word (or for other reasons want a small space at either side), the package offers the command \midwordellipsis as shown above.

If the package is loaded with the option mla (Modern Language Association style), the ellipsis is automatically bracketed without any extra space after the final period. Finally, if one follows *The Chicago Manual of Style* [18], then an ellipsis should be set with full word spaces between the dots. This can be achieved by setting \ellipsisgap appropriately or by using the option chicago.

Compare the following:
Du E[...] du! Scher dich zum [...]!
Du E[. . .] du! Scher dich zum [. . .]!
Du E[...] du! Scher dich zum T...el!

```
\usepackage[mla,xspace]{ellipsis}
Compare the following:\\
 Du E\dots du! Scher dich zum \dots!\\
\renewcommand\ellipsisgap{1.0\fontdimen2\font}
 Du E\dots du! Scher dich zum \dots!\\
\renewcommand\ellipsisgap{0.05em}
 Du E\dots du! Scher dich zum T\midwordellipsis el!
```

3-2-3

3.2.2 extdash and amsmath — Dashes in text

Standard LaTeX knows about three different kinds of dashes for text: the normal hyphen (entered as -) for use in compound words; the somewhat longer en-dash (entered as \textendash or --) for indicating ranges, e.g., "pages 7-9"; and the even longer em-dash (entered as \textemdash or ---) typically used to mark up a pause in speech or highlight a thought. LaTeX now also supports the dashes when input as Unicode characters, which is helpful if you cut and paste text from other sources.[1]

Typesetting conventions for dashes indicating thoughts vary; e.g., in English text you often find the em-dash without any space on either side, but in other texts you might find the shorter en-dash with word spaces on both sides. In traditional German and Russian typography a dash somewhere between an en- and em-dash is used, and often the spacing on both sides is smaller than a normal word space. Whatever the

---

[1] However, in an editor the Unicode characters are nearly indistinguishable from a normal hyphen, which is why I prefer to always write them in TeX-notation, e.g., --- in my sources.

convention is that you follow, ensure that you do not mix the presentation to avoid confusing your readers.

There are a few problems to look out for when using hyphens or dashes as part of words or directly next to words. For one, LATEX will by default consider the place after the dash as a potential breakpoint during line breaking, which is usually but not always desirable. For example, you may not want to see "*p*-adic" split like "*p*-adic" across lines or even pages.

Even worse, a hyphen or dash prevents automatic hyphenation in the rest of the word, and the only potential breakpoint is the one after the dash. In languages with few compound words it may be acceptable to not hyphenate such words or to manually indicate other hyphenation points via \-. However, in languages with many compound words this leads to a lot of manual effort or inferior paragraph-breaking results.

To resolve such problems, you can use the extdash package by Alexander Rozhenko that defines the commands \Hyphdash, \Endash, and \Emdash that generate these dashes while allowing automatic hyphenation on either side. Furthermore, each command has a star form that prohibits a line break immediately after the dash.

```
\Hyphdash* (\-/,\=/)   \Endash* (\--,\==)   \Emdash* (\---,\===)
```

Given that the command names are fairly long, the package offers shorthands for them if loaded with the option shortcuts. These are \-/, \--, \--- and for the star forms \=/, \==, and \===.

The amsmath package, extensively discussed in Chapter 11, also offers one command related to dashes within paragraphs. The command \nobreakdash suppresses any possibility of a line break after the following hyphen or dash (without enabling hyphenation). This command must be used *immediately* before a hyphen or dash (-, --, or ---). A very common use of \nobreakdash is to prevent undesirable line breaks in usages such as "*p*-adic". However, in a case like "*n*-dimensional" the use of \Hyphdash or its shortcut is clearly superior, because without the ability to hyphenate "dimensional" one might see badly spaced out lines.

The following example shows some of the commands from both packages in action. For frequent use, it is advisable to make abbreviations, such as \p or \n. As a result, "dimension" is broken across the line, while a break after "*p*-" is prevented (resulting in a overfull box in the example) and "3-9" is moved to the next line.

```
\usepackage{amsmath}
  \newcommand\p{$p$\nobreakdash}    % for "\p-adic"
  \newcommand\Ndash{\nobreakdash--}% "3\Ndash 9"
\usepackage[shortcuts]{extdash}
  \newcommand\n[1]{$n$\-/}          % "\n-dimensional"
```

The generalization to the *n*-dimensional case—using the standard *p*-adic topology—can be found on Pages 3–9 of Volume IV.

Compare the above em-dashes to the \Emdash command — this leaves a small space on either side.

```
\noindent  The generalization to the \n-dimensional
case---using the standard \p-adic topology---can be
found on Pages 3\Ndash 9 of Volume IV.

Compare the above em\-/dashes to the \verb=\Emdash=
command\---this leaves a small space on either side.
```

3-2-4

150

As the shown in the previous example, the em-dash as produced with \Emdash or its shortcut \---, which is different from the one produced by --- in that it adds by default a little extra space on either side. This reflects the different typography traditions in different parts of the world. To properly cater for that, extdash offers a set of options to adjust this behavior: nospacearound implements American style, while wordspacearound, as its name indicates, adds a full word space — common, for example, in Germany and several other countries. In all cases \Emdash controls the space on both sides; i.e., it makes no difference if you add a space manually, because it is removed and replaced by whatever is specified through the options.

Another often needed option is shortemdash, which produces a somewhat shorter em-dash, because the dashes found in many fonts are too long to fit the traditional typography of many countries.[1] By default, line breaks are allowed only *after* any of the dashes (or not at all if the star forms are used). However, if em-dashes are separated by a word space, then it may make sense to allow line breaks also in front of the em-dash. To enable this, use allowbreakbefore. The next example shows a setting suitable for languages like German, where "Gedankenstriche" should be shorter, separated by a full word space, and are allowed to appear at the start of a line.

```
\usepackage[shortcuts,wordspacearound,shortemdash,
            allowbreakbefore]{extdash}
```

TeX's—basic — em-dash does not manipulate surrounding spaces.
Here are — Gedankenstriche — shorter and set apart. Breaks can — as shown — happen before them.

```
\TeX{}'s---basic --- em-dash does not manipulate
surrounding spaces.

Here are\---Gedankenstriche \--- shorter and set
apart. Breaks can\--- as shown \---happen before them.
```

3-2-5

Note that the shortened Gedankenstriche are produced by typesetting two slightly overlapping en-dashes. This means that copy and paste of such text produces a somewhat strange result: two dashes next to each other because the overlap gets lost.

3.2.3 underscore — Making that character more usable

The underscore character has a special meaning in LaTeX and in normal circumstances can be used only in math mode where it denotes a subscript. Using it in normal text generates an error message. Here you have to write \textunderscore or its short form _ instead, which then produces an underscore character if available in the current font or otherwise constructs a fake using a rule.

For occasional use that is fine, but if you have a need for many textual underscores, e.g., because the *variables_you_describe* all have underscores in their names, then the standard approach is less convenient, and it would be nicer to simply enter the underscore as a single "_" character. Furthermore, you may want words with underscores inside to allow for hyphenation (and that is not the case if _ is used).

---

[1] Of course, this option has a dependency on the font used: if you happen to have one that already uses shorter dashes, you end up with a dash that is too short, but for many fonts it produces the right results if you look for short dashes.

To help with such tasks Donald Arseneau developed the underscore package. It redefines `\_` (but not `\textunderscore`!) in such a way that it can be hyphenated after the underscore and in the word part to the right of it (a break before it is always possible).

A com- pound_fracture A compound_frac- ture A bad compound_- fracture A really bad com- pound_fracture

```
\usepackage{underscore}
\fbox{\parbox{77pt}{
    A compound\textunderscore fracture \\ % bad
    A compound\_fracture              \\ % good (with package)
    A bad compound\_fracture          \\ % good? see below
    A really bad compound\_fracture      % ok here
}}
```

3-2-6

If you do not like the fact that a hyphen character is added when the break happens after the underscore, you can load the package with the option nohyphen in which cases you get this behavior.

A compound_frac- ture A bad compound_ fracture

```
\usepackage[nohyphen]{underscore}
\fbox{\parbox{77pt}{
    A compound\_fracture     \\
    A bad compound\_fracture       % no hyphen here this time
}}
```

3-2-7

In fact, the package makes the _ character more intelligent too. It can be used without preceding it with a backslash, has the meaning of `\_` in text, and retains its usual "subscript" meaning in math. Thus, this allows for concise input. Note the use of `\var` inside math in the next example. This becomes possible because `\textsf` generates a text object and thus _ gets its "text" meaning.

We have *temperature_cur_value* $< x_i$ even if *temperature_max* has not been set.

```
\usepackage{underscore}
\newcommand\var[1]{\textsf{\itshape #1}}
We have $\var{temperature_cur_value} < x_i$
even if \var{temperature_max} has not been set.
```

3-2-8

This convenience comes with a caveat: in certain places, most noticeable in file names or labels, the underscore may no longer be usable unless you use babel, precede it with `\string`, or use the option strings. The package documentation has some further details on this.

3.2.4 xspace — Gentle spacing after a macro

The space character is another special character in LaTeX. Several spaces in a row are collapsed into one, and all spaces directly after a command with a name consisting of letters[1] are ignored. To get a space there you need to use \␣, e.g., \LaTeX\␣, and if you want several spaces somewhere, you can repeatedly use that command.

The small package xspace (by David Carlisle) offers a method for automatically deciding whether a command should be followed by a space. For this it defines the \xspace command, for use at the end of macros that produce text. It adds a space unless the macro is followed by certain punctuation characters.

Thus, the \xspace command saves you from having to type \␣ or {} after most occurrences of a macro name in text. However, if either of these constructs follows \xspace, a space is not added by \xspace. This means that it is safe to add \xspace to the end of an existing macro without making too many changes in your document. Possible candidates for \xspace are commands for abbreviations such as "e.g.," and "i.e.,".

```
\newcommand\eg{e.g.,\xspace}      \newcommand\ie{i.e.,\xspace}
\newcommand\etc{etc.\@\xspace}
```

Notice the use of the \@ command in the definition of \etc to generate the correct kind of space. If used to the right of a punctuation character, it prevents extra space from being added: the dot is not regarded as an end-of-sentence symbol. Using it on the left forces LaTeX to interpret the dot as an end-of-sentence symbol.[2]

In some circumstances \xspace may make a wrong decision and add a space when it is not wanted. The most common reason for this is that \xspace is followed by a command that should not be preceded by a space, but is not on the exception list for \xspace. For example, \xspace knows about \footnote and \footnotemark but not about new footnote commands that you may have defined with manyfoot as explained in Section 3.5.7. In such cases, follow the macro with {}, which suppresses this space, or add the necessary commands to the exception list as shown in the next example where there should not be a space added in front of \marker.

In 2017 Great Britain * voted for leaving the European Union *.

In 2017 Great Britain* voted for leaving the European Union*.

```
\usepackage{xspace}
\newcommand\marker{\textsuperscript{*}\xspace}
\newcommand\GB {Great Britain\xspace}
\newcommand\EU {European Union\xspace}

In 2017 \GB\marker voted for leaving the \EU\marker.
\par \xspaceaddexceptions{\marker}
In 2017 \GB\marker voted for leaving the \EU\marker.
```

3-2-9

In the above example \xspaceaddexceptions was used in the middle of the document to show the results without and with the declaration. In real documents this declaration would be placed in the preamble of a document instead.

---

[1] Commands consisting of a backslash and a symbol, e.g., \& or \$, are different. A space following any of them is honored.

[2] You should, for example, write "... in the USA\@." to get the correct spacing after the period. See also the discussion in Section 3.3.2 on page 157.

3.3 Generated or specially formatted text

One of the features of LaTeX is that it can automatically generate text based on the current context. We have already seen examples of this in Chapter 2 in the form of references that adjust their text based on the distance between label and reference.

In this section two other useful applications are discussed. The fmtcount package offers ways to produce ordinal and cardinal strings from counter values so that you can refer to the "third chapter" without worrying that it may become the "fourth chapter" later. The other package (acro) helps you manage acronyms and offers sophisticated ways to typeset them based on your needs and their position in the text.

We finish the section with a small package that produces fractions such as ½, ⅔, or ¾ for use in running text.

3.3.1 fmtcount — Ordinals and cardinals

When typesetting the value of counters, LaTeX offers a number of commands, such as \Roman{chapter}, to generate "III"; see Appendix A.2.1. Sometimes there is a need to provide a textual representation of the counter value or to write "in the 3rd chapter", and for this you can use the fmtcount package by Nicola Talbot and Vincent Belaïche. The package provides various commands to format counter values and can generate correct ordinals for different languages.

\ordinal{*ctr*}[*gender*]　　\fmtord{*text*}

The \ordinal command[1] takes the name of a LaTeX counter as its argument and produces by default a raised ordinal, e.g., \ordinal{chapter} produces "3rd". The "rd" is generated by calling \fmtord, which by default typesets the text as a superscript. If the package is loaded with the option level, the *text* is set at the baseline.

In some languages the correct text string depends on the *gender* of what is being referred to, and in these cases the optional argument can be used to specify the *gender* as m (masculine), f (feminine), or n (neuter). If the argument is missing or if the current language does not have this concept, m is assumed.

\ordinalstring{*ctr*}[*gender*]　　\Ordinalstring{*ctr*}[*gender*]
\ORDINALstring{*ctr*}[*gender*]

These commands produce the counter value as a textual ordinal with the command \Ordinalstring uppercasing the first letter and \ORDINALstring uppercasing the whole word, respectively. That is, we get "third", "Third", and "THIRD" at this point in the book when used with the **chapter** counter. The next example shows the use of the optional *gender* argument when using the German language — chapters

---

[1] For users of the memoir document class the package offers \FCordinal as an alternate name because \ordinal is already defined by this class.

(Kapitel) are neuter, sections (Abschnitte) are masculine, and footnotes (Fußnoten) are feminine in that language:

```
\usepackage[ngerman]{babel,fmtcount}
```

Drittes Kapitel erster Abschnitt, siebte Fußnote.

3-3-1

```
\Ordinalstring{chapter}[n] Kapitel \ordinalstring{section}[m]
Abschnitt, \ordinalstring{footnote}[f] Fußnote.
```

While *gender* as needed in some languages is supported, one should not expect miracles: depending on the grammatical case further differentiations may be needed; e.g., "in the third chapter" would translate in German to "im dritten Kapitel" — a form that cannot be autogenerated by the package to date.

Not all grammatical forms are supported

| `\numberstring{ctr}[gender]` | `\Numberstring{ctr}[gender]` |
| `\NUMBERstring{ctr}[gender]` | |

In the same fashion, `\numberstring`, `\Numberstring`, and `\NUMBERstring` can be used to produce the counter value as an ordinary text string, e.g., with `subsection` as its argument we get one, One, and ONE at this point.

Instead of formatting counter values, it is also possible to format numbers that are directly entered. For this purpose variants of the previous six commands exist that all end in `\...num`, e.g., `\ordinalstringnum`. Here is an example:

```
\usepackage{fmtcount}
\newcommand\nth[1]{\ordinalstringnum{#1}}
```

We select the first, thirteenth, fourteenth and twenty-second.

3-3-2

```
We select the \nth{1}, \nth{13}, \nth{14} and \nth{22}.
```

As already seen, the package offers some (limited) multilingual support for a number of languages including English, French (various flavors), German, Italian, Portuguese, and Spanish. It works together with babel or polyglossia and uses the same language or dialect names (for implemented languages). Important is that all used languages are made known to fmtcount in the preamble by loading them as options or through the declaration `\FCloadlang`, which expects a list of language names. After that, ordinals or cardinals are formatted using the language currently in force.

```
\usepackage[ngerman,english]{babel,fmtcount}
```

First section in 3rd chapter has five subsections.
Erster Abschnitt im 3. Kapitel hat fünf Unterabschnitte.

3-3-3

```
\Ordinalstring{section} section in \ordinal{chapter}
chapter has \numberstring{subsection} subsections.
    \par    \selectlanguage{ngerman}%
\Ordinalstring{section} Abschnitt im \ordinal{chapter}[n]
Kapitel hat \numberstring{subsection}[m] Unterabschnitte.
```

The package has extensive support for the French language and offers many options to tailor the appearances of ordinals; for details refer to the package documentation [132]. It also offers a number of additional counter representations not available with standard LaTeX. These are discussed in Appendix A.2.2 on page →II 650.

3.3.2 acro — Managing your abbreviations and acronyms

Documents often contain acronyms and abbreviations such as "CTAN" or "etc.". If they are infrequent, one can easily typeset them manually, e.g., as `\textsc{ctan}`, or provide simple commands for them.

However, if there are many and there is a need to introduce the acronyms on first use, e.g., writing "Comprehensive TeX Archive Network (CTAN)" and only later just "CTAN", then this gets problematical. Every change of the text might move the first use to a different place and thus require reworking of the text. Furthermore, if you want to generate an annotated list of all acronyms in an appendix, there is a good chance that this compilation of terms may not fit reality if it was done manually and not automatically generated from the acronyms used in the text.

To help you with such tasks Clemens Niederberger developed the very comprehensive `acro` package with which you can easily manage your acronyms and customize their appearance. To declare such acronyms and abbreviations you use the `\DeclareAcronym` command.

```
\DeclareAcronym{id}{short=short-text, long=long-text, other-key/values }
```

The *id* is a case-sensitive text string that identifies the acronym and is used in the typesetting commands to refer to the declaration. There are two required keys that must be provided with any acronym declaration: the `short` key specifies the *short-text* for the acronym (i.e., the text that is usually typeset), and the `long` key defines the *long-text* (typically used on the first occurrence). Further keys cover special requirements when typesetting an acronym, such as plural or alternative forms and are discussed below.

Generally customizing the acronyms   Besides customizing individual acronyms by adding key/value pairs in their declarations, it is possible to adjust the overall appearance and set up defaults for them. This is done with `\acsetup`, which also expects a list of key/value pairs. The most useful ones are discussed in the remainder of the section, but note that there are even more than could be covered here, so check the manual [106] if you have an unusual requirement.

```
\ac*{id}     \acs*{id}     \acl*{id}     \acf*{id}     \aca*{id}
```

Commands for typesetting acronyms   For typesetting an acronym a number of commands are available. `\acs` and `\acl` typeset the short or the long text, respectively. `\ac` in contrast typesets the long text followed by the short text in parentheses on first occurrence and from that point onwards always the short text. Thus, this is the command most often used. `\acf` acts as if this is the first usage of `\ac`, useful for reintroducing the meaning of an acronym at some point, even if it was used before.

Sometimes you may want an alternative short text for an acronym to use in special circumstances. This text can be specified with the `alt` key in the declaration and is typeset using the `\aca` command. If no alternative text was given, you receive a warning, and the *short-text* is used instead (case 8 in the example). Note that the full text then shows both short and alternate text by default — if this it is not desired, you can modify the template for the full form as explained in [106].

The star forms generate identical output, but they are not counted as "usage" with respect to \ac. This can be useful, for example, when an acronym appears in a heading (and thus in the table of contents) and you do not want to count that occurrence as first use.

1 Electronic Data Systems (EDS or Excel driven solutions), 2 Excel driven solutions, 3 EDS
4 Also known as (aka), 5 aka, 6 also known as (aka), 7 aka, 8 aka, 9 Also known as, 10 Aka, 11 also known as (aka)

3-3-4

```
\usepackage{acro}
\DeclareAcronym{eds}{short=\mbox{EDS}, long=Electronic
        Data Systems, alt=Excel driven solutions}
\DeclareAcronym{aka}{short = aka, long = also known as}
1 \ac{eds},   2 \aca{eds},   3 \ac{eds}               \\
4 \Acf*{aka}, 5 \acs*{aka}, 6 \ac{aka}, 7 \ac{aka},
8 \aca{aka},  9 \Acl{aka},  10 \Ac{aka}, 11 \acf{aka}
```

The \mbox in the short key value warrants some explanation that is worth remembering: by default LaTeX distinguishes spaces between words from spaces after punctuation — a space after a sentence is usually[1] noticeably wider than a normal space. However, LaTeX does not consider a period, question mark, or exclamation point to be the end of a sentence if the immediately preceding character is an uppercase letter, since it assumes that this is likely somebody's initial. The \mbox now hides the uppercase letters inside, and therefore \ac{eds} can appear at the end of a sentence, and you get correct spacing. It has the additional effect that the word inside is never hyphenated (but that is important only for longer words). If you want to allow for hyphenation and get the correct sentence-ending space, use \@ after the last uppercase letter instead, which also results in correct spacing. If you care for high-quality results, then one or the other should be used whenever your acronym text ends in an uppercase letter.

Acronyms at the end of the sentence

If acronyms appear at the beginning of a sentence, they may need uppercasing of their first letter. This can be achieved by using commands that have the first letter of the command name uppercased, e.g., \Acf*, \Acl, \Ac, etc., as shown in the previous example. These variants are available for all commands that typeset acronyms.

Acronyms at the start of a sentence

Plural forms

If a plural of an acronym is needed, then this usually affects the generated text, though there are exceptions. To typeset a plural, use any of the acronym commands and append a p to the end of the command name, e.g.,

```
\acp*{id}   \acsp*{id}   \aclp*{id}   \acfp*{id}   \acap*{id}   ...
```

By default these commands add an "s" to the generated text. If the acronym has an irregular form and this is incorrect, you need to use some additional keys in the

---

[1]This is controlled by the commands \frenchspacing (default in, e.g., French and German, if babel is used) and \nonfrenchspacing (default in English or if babel is not used).

declaration to specify what should be used instead. Append -plural to the base name; e.g., use the key short-plural to specify what should be appended to the *short-text*. In cases where the plural form is more complicated and cannot be constructed by appending some characters, you can use the short-plural-form key to specify the text should be replace the *short-text*. Similar keys, e.g., long-plural, long-plural-form, alt-plural, alt-plural-form, etc., exist to provide the necessary variants.

Members of Parliament (MPs), MPs

```
\usepackage{acro}
\DeclareAcronym{mp}{short = MP\@, long = Member of Parliament,
                    long-plural-form = Members of Parliament}
\acp{mp}, \acp{mp}
```

3-3-5

Indefinite forms

At least in English the indefinite article depends on the pronunciation of the following word and thus may differ depending on whether the short or the long form of an acronym is typeset. To cater for this you can use the keys short-indefinite, long-indefinite, and alt-indefinite in the declaration and then typeset the acronym using one of the following commands:

```
\iac*{id}      \iacs*{id}      \iacl*{id}      \iacf*{id}      \iaca*{id}
```

While plural forms do not make sense in this case, variants for uppercasing of the first letter are available too.

1 An unidentified flying object (UFO), 2 a UFO, 3 an unidentified flying object, 4 a UFO, 5 an unidentified flying object (UFO)

```
\usepackage{acro}
\DeclareAcronym{ufo}{short=UFO\@, long=unidentified
    flying object, long-indefinite = an}
1 \Iac{ufo}, 2 \iac{ufo}, 3 \iacl{ufo}, 4 \iacs{ufo},
5 \iacf{ufo}
```

3-3-6

One-time usage of acronyms

If a declared acronym is used only once, you may not want to show both *long-* and *short-text* on that occasion (as normally done by \ac or \acf), but rather just the *long-text* or a variation thereof. This can be easily achieved by specifying the key single in \acsetup. This results in typesetting the *long-text* if the acronym is used only once. It also prevents that acronym from being listed in any acronym list, if such a list is generated.

For more control you can specify the minimal number of times it needs to appear before the normal machinery kicks in: the example below uses 2. What is being typeset can be adjusted as well by using the key single-style. It takes any acronym template name as its value and thus can be long (default), short, short-long, alt, and a few others.

It is also possible to specify a variant text to be typeset: for this use the key `single` on the acronym declaration. In the next example we do that for the second acronym and also change the `single-style` to `short`. Since `\Acf*` is not counted towards the number of occurrences the two `\ac` commands are both shown as single occurrences.

THGTTG and Unidentified flying object (UFO), UFO and Za-
phod Beeblebrox

```
\usepackage{acro}  \acsetup{single=2,single-style=short}
\DeclareAcronym{hg}{short = \mbox{THGTTG}, long = the
                Hitchhiker's Guide to the Galaxy}
\DeclareAcronym{ufo}{short = UFO\@, long = unidentified
                flying object, single = Zaphod Beeblebrox}
\Ac{hg} and  \Acf*{ufo}, \acs{ufo} and \ac{ufo}
```

3-3-7

Citations for acronyms

It is sometimes helpful to add a citation to the long text of an acronym. Technically this could be done by simply adding an appropriate `\cite` command to the *long-text*. However, a superior way is to specify this citation using the `cite` key in the declaration (normally, its value is the label you would use on `\cite`, but additionally specifying pre- or post-notes is also supported). This enables you to easily change the appearances of such citations by setting keys in `\acsetup`.

If necessary, the command to generate the citation (default `\cite`) can be altered through the key `cite/cmd`. The material placed before a citation is defined with `cite/pre` (default `\nobreakspace`). If your citations, for example, generate footnotes or side-notes, you would change the key to produce nothing. The `cite/display` key defines when a citation is displayed. It can take the values `first` (default), `all`, or `none`. Below is an example:

Dirty Tricks in the TeX Book [1, App. D] and
later refer to TB-tricks [1, App. D].

References

[1] Donald E. Knuth. *The TeXbook*, volume A
of *Computers and Typesetting*. Addison-
Wesley, Reading, MA, USA, 1986.

```
\usepackage{acro} \acsetup{cite/display=all}
\DeclareAcronym{tb}{short = TB-tricks,
  long = Dirty Tricks in the \TeX{} Book,
  first-style = long,
  cite = [App.\,D]{Knuth-CT-a} }
\Ac{tb} and later refer to \ac{tb}.
\bibliography{tlc}
```

3-3-8

By default the citation is typeset after the acronym and separated by the code specified by the key `cite/pre` as shown in the previous example. Alternatively, you can move it inside the parentheses that surround the *short-text* when the first occurrence of the acronym is typeset. For this set the key `cite/group` (to `true`).

Depending on the circumstances, you may additionally need a special citation command or a special connector for this case. These can be specified with `cite/group/cmd` and `cite/group/pre` (default `,␣`), respectively.

The next example defines a simple `\footcite` command and then makes use of the above keys to place the citation into a footnote when only the full text is shown.

Compare this to Example 3-3-8 on the previous page.

Dirty Tricks in the TeX Book (TB-tricks[1]) and later refer to TB-tricks.

References

[1] Donald E. Knuth. *The TeXbook*, volume A of *Computers and Typesetting*. Addison-Wesley, Reading, MA, USA, 1986.

---

[1] See [1, App. D].

```
\usepackage{acro}
\acsetup{cite/group,cite/group/pre=,
             cite/group/cmd=\footcite}
\DeclareAcronym{tb}{short = TB-tricks,
  long = Dirty Tricks in the \TeX{} Book,
  cite = [App.\,D]{Knuth-CT-a} }
\newcommand\footcite[2][]
             {\footnote{See \cite[#1]{#2}.}}
\Ac{tb} and later refer to \ac{tb}.
\bibliography{tlc}
```

3-3-9

Foreign acronyms

If an acronym has its origin in a different language, one can provide additional information in the key `foreign` and specify its language in the key `foreign-babel`. This information is then used when the acronym is first displayed, and it requires that your document has a language support package, such as babel with the corresponding language loaded. See Example 3-3-10 for a use case.

Formatting acronym texts

By default the text specified in any of the keys `short`, `long`, `single`, `foreign`, or `alt` is typeset as given, but if necessary, one can apply special formatting to such texts. This can be set globally for all entries through the keys that start in `format/`, e.g., `format/short`, `format/long`, etc. There also exists `format/first-long`, which is being used for the *long-text* on first usage.

Alternatively, one can use keys keys when declaring acronyms, thereby overwriting the defaults. In that case append `-format` to the name, e.g., `short-format` to alter the *short-text* for one acronym only.

The value is either a command with one argument such as `\textit` or a declaration such as `\scshape` — both forms work. If you want to alter the setup for all or most acronyms, you do this using `\acsetup`, otherwise in the acronym declaration. In the next example we force the *short-text* to lowercase and then apply `\textsc`, and we use `\itshape` for the *foreign-text*. Note that for "etc" the formatting is canceled because this is an abbreviation that should not be set in small capitals.

Compact Disc (CD)
Langsielplatte (*Long Playing Vinyl Record*, LP)
et cetera (etc.)

```
\usepackage[english,ngerman]{babel}  \usepackage{acro}
\acsetup{format/short=\textlsc, format/foreign=\itshape}
\DeclareAcronym{etc}{short=etc.\@, long=et cetera,
             short-format= }   % overwriting default
\DeclareAcronym{cd}{short = CD\@, long = Compact Disc}
\DeclareAcronym{lp}{short = LP\@, long = Langsielplatte,
    foreign = Long Playing Vinyl Record, foreign-babel = english}
\newcommand\textlsc[1]{\textsc{\MakeLowercase{#1}}}
\ac{cd} \\ \ac{lp} \\  \ac{etc}
```

3-3-10

With the help of the `first-style` key you can determine how the acronym should be display on its first use. As we have seen, the default setting is to typeset the *long-text* followed by the *short-text* and possibly the *alt-text* and/or the *foreign-text* in parentheses. Other possibilities available are `short-long` (like *long-short* but swapped), `short` (just the *short-text*), `long` (just the *long-text*), or `footnote` (*short-text* as footnote). If used in `\acsetup`, the key `first-style` defines the default for all acronyms as shown in the next example:

CD (Compact Disc), LP (*Long Playing Vinyl Record*, Langspielplatte), etc.

3-3-11

```
\usepackage{acro} \acsetup{first-style=short-long}
% Acronym declarations as in previous example except ...
\DeclareAcronym{etc}{short = etc.\@, long=et cetera,
                    short-format=, first-style=short}
\ac{cd}, \ac{lp}, \ac{etc}
```

In fact, it is possible to define your acronym own styles to be used with the `first-style` key. As an example we define a new template `square` as a variation of the predefined `long-short` style (using square brackets instead of parentheses).

```
\NewAcroTemplate{square}
 {\acroiffirstTF                              % first usage of acronym?
    {\acrowrite{long}%                        %    write long text
     \acspace [%                              %    followed by a space and [
      \acroifT{foreign}{\acrowrite{foreign}, }%   write foreign text if given
       \acrowrite{short}%                     %    write short text
       \acroifT{alt}{ \acrotranslate{or}%     %    maybe write alt text
                     \acrowrite{alt}}%
        \acrogroupcite                        %    handle group cites if present
      ]}%                                     %   end finish of with ]
      {\acrowrite{short}}%                    % use short text if not first time
  }
```

Applying this to acronyms from the previous example gives the following result:

Compact Disc [CD], Langspielplatte [*Long Playing Vinyl Record*, LP], etc.

3-3-12

```
\usepackage{acro}  \acsetup{first-style=square}
\ac{cd}, \ac{lp}, \ac{etc}
```

More details on these kinds of extensions (and the commands used in the above definition) are discussed in [106].

Using acro for abbreviations

If you use the mechanism of acro to define commands for abbreviations such as "etc", you may be faced with two issues: for one there is usually no point in generating "et cetera (etc.)" on first usage. This can be corrected with an appropriate value for the `first-style` key as shown previously.

The second problem is that the *short-text* may end in a period, and if your abbreviation appears at the end of a sentence, that may then result in two periods. To avoid this, you have to direct the `acro` commands to look ahead and identify the following character and act accordingly. For this you can use `\acdot` inside the acronym declaration, which typesets a period unless the acronym is followed by one.

1 Z.B., 2 z.B.,
3 zum Beispiel, 4
z.B.
1 Etc., 2 etc.,
3 et cetera, 4 etc.

```
\usepackage{acro}
\DeclareAcronym{zB}{short=z.B\acdot,long=zum Beispiel,
                    first-style=short}
\DeclareAcronym{etc}{short=etc\acdot,long=et cetera,
                     first-style=short}

1 \Ac*{zB},  2 \ac{zB},  \\ 3 \acl{zB},  4 \ac{zB}. \\
1 \Ac*{etc}, 2 \ac{etc}, \\ 3 \acl{etc}, 4 \ac{etc}.
```

3-3-13

It is possible to direct `acro` to look for other characters (e.g., a hyphen or other punctuation characters) and change the output of an acronym depending on the result. For details on this special topic, refer to the package documentation [106].

The `acro` package offers you an easy way to produce one or more lists displaying your acronyms together with some explanation and, if desired, with back references to their use in the document.

In the simplest form you just have to place the command `\printacronyms` at the point where the list should appear. By default, this lists all[1] used acronyms and abbreviations used in alphabetical order as a `description` list.

This list and its content can be customized through keys specified in an optional argument to `\printacronyms`. The command to produce the heading for the list is defined by `heading`. Specify a sectioning command without the leading backslash or `none` to suppress any heading. The default is `section*`. The text used in the heading is given by `name` and defaults to `Acronyms`. If you want to typeset the acronyms unsorted (i.e., in the order of their declarations), specify `sort=false`.

If the list is being sorted but some entries are placed in incorrect positions, you can specify `sort=`*sortkey* in the acronym declaration. By default the list is sorted using the *short-text* of each acronym.

It is also possible to group your acronyms into different classes by specifying a `tag` key in the acronym declaration. Such tags can then be used to selectively include or exclude acronyms from a list by specifying `include` or `exclude` with a list of tag names as the value. In the next example this has been used to tag the "etc" and "zB" abbreviations with `ignore` and then exclude all acronyms with that tag in the listing.

Another useful key when declaring acronyms is `extra`. This allows you to specify additional information about some acronym that is *only* shown in listings produced with `\printacronyms`.

---

[1]If the `single` key is used, then only acronyms used more than once are included.

There are also some keys that apply to all listings (if you have several) and are therefore set with \acsetup.

If you want to list all declared acronyms regardless of whether they are used, specify list/display=all as we did above. This is the reason why the entry for "LOL" is listed.

Back references to the pages where the acronyms are used can be added by specifying pages/display with the value all (used above) or first (showing only the page of the first occurrence). The formatting of these page numbers is subject to a number of additional keys; consult the documentation if you are dissatisfied with the defaults.

The list/template key defines what type of lists are being produced and defaults to description. Many other styles, such as longtable or lof, are available, and it is possible to define your own layout as described in the package documentation [106].

```
\usepackage{acro}
\acsetup{list/display=all,
            pages/display=all,format/extra=\itshape}

\DeclareAcronym{aka}{short=aka,long=also known as}
\DeclareAcronym{cd}{short=CD\@,long=Compact Disc}
\DeclareAcronym{ES}{short = $\emptyset$,
    long = empty set, sort = 0}
\DeclareAcronym{etc}{short=etc\acdot,
    long=et cetera, first-style=short,tag=ignore}
\DeclareAcronym{lol}{short=LOL\@,long=laughing out loud}
\DeclareAcronym{ufo}{short = UFO\@,
    long = unidentified flying object,
    extra = Most often seen in the north}
\DeclareAcronym{zB}{short=z.B\acdot,long=zum Beispiel,
    first-style=short,tag=ignore}
```

Zum Beispiel: CD, aka, UFO, etc.
Some acronyms not used, but still listed: ES and lol.

Abbrevs

$\emptyset$ empty set

aka also known as

CD Compact Disc

LOL laughing out loud

UFO unidentified flying object (*Most often seen in the north*)

3-3-14

```
\Acl{zB}: \acs{cd}, \acs{aka}, \acs{ufo}, \ac{etc}.\\
Some acronyms not used, but still listed: ES and lol.

\printacronyms[exclude=ignore,name=Abbrevs]
```

Instead of using heading or name with \printacronyms, you can alternatively change the global defaults with the keys list/heading and list/name.

Further possibilities not covered

The acro package offers many more bells and whistles. For interactive documents it supports hyperref, offers support for bookmarks, and can produce tooltips.

If desired, one can list all acronyms in the index, and there are several keys that help you to tailor the index entries. It is also possible to erect barriers and collect only those acronyms between two barriers for printing with \printacronyms. Details on this and further features can be found in the package documentation [106].

3.3.3 xfrac — Customizable ^{text}/_{fractions}

In formulas, fractions are usually typeset with the command `\frac` that sets the numerator on top of the denominator separated by a horizontal like this: $\frac{1}{2}$. While this layout is sensible in mathematics, because it helps to unambiguously identify the components, it does not work very well in text. The fraction is typically too large to fit nicely into the text line, and furthermore the digits used come from the math fonts that may or may not match the current text font.

For this reason it is quite customary to set fractions used in text (for example in recipes) like this: ½. Here a solidus symbol is used as a separator and the figures in the numerator and denominator come from the current text font in a slightly smaller size. This type of layout is provided with the xfrac package by Morten Høgholm.

`\sfrac` [*style*] {*numerator*} [*separator*] {*denominator*}

The only user command defined by the package is `\sfrac`. It takes two mandatory arguments, the *numerator* and *denominator* of the fraction. By default it generates a split-level fraction using these arguments and a `\textfractionsolidus` symbol and typesets everything suitably placed in the current text font.

If ever needed, it is possible to specify a different separation symbol using the optional *separator* argument, and for special use cases one can explicitly select a *style* in the first optional argument. However, this optional argument is ignored if the `\sfrac` command is used in a formula. Normally, none of these optional arguments is needed.

Here is an example for the curiosity cabinet (fix-cm is used to get freely scalable Computer Modern fonts):

¼ ²/₄ ³|₄ ⁴\₄

And in math:

¹/₄ ²/₄ ³|₄ ⁴\₄

```
\usepackage{xfrac,fix-cm}
\sfrac{1}{4}  \sfrac{2}[/]{4}  \sfrac{3}[|]{4}  \sfrac{4}[\textbackslash]{4}
  \\[3pt]            And in math:            \\[3pt]
$\sfrac{1}{4}\,\sfrac{2}[/]{4}\,\sfrac{3}[|]{4}\,\sfrac{4}[\setminus]{4}$
```

         3-3-15

What is more interesting than playing with separator symbols is that `\sfrac` attempts to blend into the context when used in text; i.e., it varies with font changes as far as possible.

½ ³/₄ ⁵/₆
⁷/₁₀ ⁸/₁₅ ⁹/₂₃
¹/₂₅ ¹/₁₀₀ ¹/₁₀₀₀

```
\usepackage{xfrac,lmodern}
\rmfamily \sfrac{1}{2}   \itshape \sfrac{3}{4}     \bfseries \sfrac{5}{6}     \\
\sffamily \sfrac{7}{10} \upshape \sfrac{8}{15}    \mdseries \sfrac{9}{23}    \\
\ttfamily \sfrac{1}{25} \slshape \sfrac{1}{100} \bfseries \sfrac{1}{1000}
```

         3-3-16

As you can see, this not only changes the fonts for the *numerator* and *denominator* but also the one used for the `\textfractionsolidus` command. Next to one another this looks somewhat ugly, but in normal text the adjusted fractions work quite well.[1]

---

[1] The Latin Modern Sans family has inherited a somewhat dubious feature of Computer Modern in that the normal shapes are somewhat different from the rounder bold shapes, which is quite visible in the endings of the letters.

However, if you do not like the results of \sfrac with any particular font, it is easy enough to modify it by using a different *style*.

For that we need to understand how xfrac determines the layout to use for a particular \sfrac occurrence. What happens behind the scene is this: if you use the optional *style* argument and this is a known style, then it is used. Otherwise, xfrac takes the name of the current font family (e.g., lmr) and checks if there exists a style with that name. If yes, that will be used; otherwise, a style named default is chosen.

Applying style

In case you are not happy about \sfrac in a particular font family, you can define or redefine a style with the name of that family. The package already knows about the following six font families and has customized styles for them: cmr, cmss, cmtt, lmr, lmss, and lmtt, i.e., the main Computer Modern and Latin Modern font families. For all others fonts it uses its default style, and one needs to provide a new style if the default is not satisfactory.

If you are unhappy about the defaults as such, you have to modify the default style, and if you need a one-off style, you can define it and give it an arbitrary name. You can then use it in the optional argument of \sfrac (which is what we did for the section heading). Here are the commands[1] needed to do any of this:

```
\ShowInstanceValues {xfrac}{style}
\EditInstance       {xfrac}{style}        {key/value list}
\DeclareInstance    {xfrac}{style}{text}{key/value list}
```

The \ShowInstanceValues allows you to inspect the key/value setting for an existing *style*. We cover the important keys below, i.e., those one is likely to need when tailoring xfrac for a particular font family. There are a few more that may help in fairly special cases. For those consult the package documentation [39].

For editing an existing *style* use \EditInstance and supply it with a comma-separated list of key values that you want to change. If you want to declare a new style, use \DeclareInstance. In that case you also have to specify the name of the "template" to use, but for xfrac there is only one right now,[2] which is called text.

To give an example for \EditInstance: suppose you do not like the different \textfractionsolidus versions shown in Example 3-3-16. Then you can correct that with the slash-symbol-format key and surround the symbol with \textnormal. That would then always select the symbol from the main document font regardless of surrounding conditions. Note that you have to do this for lmr, lmss, and lmtt, because xfrac already has style definitions for all three Latin Modern families.

However, for Latin Modern Sans you may have decided that the upright solidus from that family looks nice, so we use that in all Sans variants (notice that it does not bolden the solidus in ⁷⁄₁₀ and ⁸⁄₁₅).

---

[1] xfrac was something like a test case for the LaTeX3 xtemplate package that provides a general template mechanism with configurable instances. These are really commands from that package.

[2] There is in fact a second template called math that is needed to tinker with the layout of \sfrac inside of formulas. For this you need to consult the package documentation.

Finally, for Latin Modern Typewriter we show yet another approach: because the solidus in that family is rather heavy, we use the one from the Sans font, but this time allow it to change width or shape. To achieve this, we declare the font family to use for the symbol with the key `slash-symbol-font` that expects a font family name. Compare the results with those from Example 3-3-16 to decide what you like best.

```
\usepackage{xfrac,lmodern}
\EditInstance{xfrac}{lmr} {slash-symbol-format=\textnormal{#1}}
\EditInstance{xfrac}{lmss}{slash-symbol-format=\textnormal{\sffamily #1}}
\EditInstance{xfrac}{lmtt}{slash-symbol-font  =lmss}
```

¹⁄₂ ³⁄₄ ⁵⁄₆
⁷⁄₁₀ ⁸⁄₁₅ ⁹⁄₂₃
¹⁄₂₅ ¹⁄₁₀₀ ¹⁄₁₀₀₀

```
\rmfamily \sfrac{1}{2}  \itshape \sfrac{3}{4}  \bfseries \sfrac{5}{6}  \\
\sffamily \sfrac{7}{10} \upshape \sfrac{8}{15} \mdseries \sfrac{9}{23} \\
\ttfamily \sfrac{1}{25} \slshape \sfrac{1}{100} \bfseries \sfrac{1}{1000}
```

3-3-17

Similar keys exist for specifying the font family or the format to be used for the numerator and denominator: they are called `numerator-font`, `numerator-format`, `denominator-font`, and `denominator-format`, respectively.

As an example for defining a new style we show the declaration used in this book to make the fraction in the title of the current section:

```
\DeclareInstance{xfrac}{hls-bf}{text}
  { scale-factor          = 0.9 ,
    numerator-top-sep   = -0.2 ex , denominator-bot-sep = -0.1 ex ,
    slash-left-kern     = 0.15 em , slash-right-kern    = 0.15 em   }
```

The declaration shows a number of new keys: the `scale-factor` by which the numerator and denominator should be scaled down (we scale down only a little bit for this example; i.e., we do not want the default). The keys `numerator-top-sep` and `denominator-bot-sep` define how much to lower the numerator or raise the denominator with respect to the size of the slash symbol. Finally, `slash-left-kern` and `slash-right-kern` specify some extra kerning between the slash symbol and the surrounding material (for some reason the left and right refers to kerns as viewed from numerator and denominator; e.g., `slash-left-kern` is the kern next to the denominator).

The font family used in the book for the headings is called `hls`. Because this declaration was meant to be a one-off with special settings (using text not digits), the *style* was named `hls-bf` and was used in the heading of this section like this:

```
\subsection{\texttt{xfrac}\Dash Customizable
            \sfrac[hls-bf]{text}{fractions}}
```

Customizing math fractions

As shown earlier, \sfrac can also be used in formulas, but due to some restrictions in the way TₑX uses fonts in math, there is less flexibility, and the default layout is usually sufficient — if not, refer to the package documentation [39] for further information.

3.3.4 siunitx — Scientific notation of units and quantities

The International System of Units (SI, abbreviated from the French Système international (d'unités)) is a codified form of the metric system and one of the most widely used system of measurement, officially endorsed by more than 50 nations [8]. It is built on seven base units that can be derived from invariant constants of nature and measured with high precision (ampere, kelvin, second, metre, kilogram,[1] candela, mole) and a set of decimal prefixes to the unit names and unit symbols to specify multiples or fractions of the units. The system further defines the names for derived units of other common physical quantities like becquerel, lumen, volt, etc. The standard also offers advice on many units that are not adopted into the system, but are in common use in many places. Typographic conventions for all such units are defined, and consistently following them helps to ensure that there are no misunderstandings when presenting numbers and units in printed matter.

The siunitx package by Joseph Wright aims at providing access to this standard and ways for LaTeX users to typeset numbers and units correctly and consistently. By default the package follows agreed conventions but at the same time offers a huge number of keys to configure the results to fit the requirements posed by journals or universities without the need to alter the document source.

The most important of such configuration possibilities are covered in this section, but if you find that a particular requirement is not discussed, there is a high likelihood that you can find it in the extensive package documentation [142]. The package preloads amstext, array, and color; if you prefer xcolor, you can load that on top.

| \si-cmd [options] {...} ...   \sisetup{options} |

Essentially all user commands take an optional first argument for specifying keys that influence the typesetting or the input conventions. If used in this way, the keys then apply to the current command only.

As an alternative, the same set of keys can be used in the mandatory argument of \sisetup to set up document-wide defaults (if used in the preamble) or to set up conventions for the following commands (if used inside the document). In the latter case the usual scoping rules apply.

The siunitx package offers roughly 130 keys to customize all kinds of aspects of parsing and presentation. Many of them are discussed in some detail. For the others we only mention what kind of customization is possible. If adjustments in those areas are needed, please refer to the package documentation.

With this range of customization available, it is not possible to cover *all* of the package features here. We therefore look at some of the key ideas supported by the package in the context of different types of input: formatting numbers, formatting units, combining the two to make quantities, and specialist tools for complex values.

---

[1]The definition of a kilogram is an exception: it is the only base unit that already takes a prefix in its name and therefore cannot be used with another prefix in the system. For those cases the unit gram is used instead.

Basic number and unit formatting

The core functionality in siunitx is the ability to format numbers and units; this can be done on its own or used as the building block for more complex commands described later.

\num [*options*] {*number*}

Formatting simple numbers can be carried out using the \num command. This understands various input conventions and can handle exponents and uncertainties. By default any spaces in the *number* argument are removed, decimal markers (either "," or ".") and exponents (default e, E, d, or D) are identified, and, if necessary, a zero is added in front or after a decimal marker. Both the parsing as well as the printed representation can be adjusted using a large number of keys. As illustrated, the standard settings add a small amount of separation between each group of three digits.

123 456 789 011	123	
10 001	10 001	
0.000 005	0.123	
0.05	−0.05	
9.95×10^{-3}	9.95×10^{-3}	

```
\usepackage{siunitx}
\num{123456789011}   \hfill \num{123}        \\
\num{10001}          \hfill \num{10 001}     \\
\num{0.000005}       \hfill \num{0,123}      \\
\num{.05}            \hfill \num{-,05}       \\
\num{9.95e-3}        \hfill \num{9,95 d-3}
```

3-3-18

In some disciplines it is customary to show uncertainty values together with experimentally obtained values. By default this is indicated by parentheses or alternatively by \pm or +- (but not -+). Both input and output conventions are adjustable.

Use 1.2(30), 1(2) or 0.5(2). Note that 0(1) is, but ±1 is not, an uncertainty value.

```
\usepackage{siunitx}
Use \num{1.2+-3}, \num{1\pm 2} or \num{0.5(2)}. Note that
\num{0+-1} is, but \num{+-1} is not, an uncertainty value.
```

3-3-19

If you are cramped for space, it is possible to direct siunitx to use as little space as possible when printing numbers by using the key tight-spacing.

1×10^3 or tight as 1×10^3

```
\usepackage{siunitx}
\num{1e3} or tight as \sisetup{tight-spacing} \num{1e3}
```

3-3-20

\numlist [*options*] {*numbers*}
\numrange [*options*] {*start*}{*stop*}
\numproduct [*options*] {*numbers*}

For simple lists one can use \numlist (with numbers separated by ;), and to specify a range of numbers \numrange is available. The individual numbers are parsed and formatted like with \num. In addition, some customizable text (or other material) is added between the items. There is also \numproduct, which uses x as the separator.

2, 3, 5, 7 and 11 are prime. 6 and 28 are perfect numbers, e.g., $6 = 1 \times 2 \times 3 = 1 + 2 + 3$. There are 25 prime and 2 perfect numbers in the range from 2 to 100.

```
\usepackage{siunitx}

\numlist{2;3;5;7;11} are prime. \numlist{6;28} are
perfect numbers, e.g., $6=\numproduct{1x2x3}=1+2+3$.
There are $25$ prime and $2$ perfect numbers in the
range from \numrange{2}{100}.
```

3-3-21

$\boxed{\texttt{\textbackslash unit}\,[\textit{options}]\,\{\textit{unit}\}}$

The \unit command is used to format a unit (or a combination of units). It supports two types of input: a literal form and a macro-based input. In the "literal" form the units are specified as simple strings like kg or s, and their relationships are specified as follows: a . or a ~ denotes an inter-unit product, a / denotes a division, and sub- and superscripts are specified with ^ and _, respectively.

```
\usepackage{siunitx}
```

$\mathrm{N\,m} \quad \mathrm{g/cm^3} \quad \mathrm{J\,mol\,K^{-1}}$

```
\unit{N.m} \hfill \unit{g/cm^{3}} \hfill \unit{J.mol.K^{-1}}
```

3-3-22

While this literal mode is easy to input, it offers little flexibility in the output representation compared to the macro-based version. In the latter method, the units and their relationships are represented through commands that are parsed and interpreted by the \unit command. For example, \per (indicating the division of units) can then be printed as a reciprocal power of the unit (default) or as a "slash" symbol or through a fraction by specifying keys in an \sisetup declaration, as shown in the next example. In a similar way many other aspects can be globally or locally adjusted.

```
\usepackage{siunitx,xfrac}
\newcommand\sample[1]{#1:\quad \unit{\kilo\metre\per\hour}
                              \hfill\unit{\mole\per\metre\cubed}\\[5pt]}
```

A:	$\mathrm{km\,h^{-1}}$	$\mathrm{mol\,m^{-3}}$
B:	$\mathrm{km/h}$	$\mathrm{mol/m^3}$
C:	$\frac{\mathrm{km}}{\mathrm{h}}$	$\frac{\mathrm{mol}}{\mathrm{m^3}}$
D:	$\mathrm{km/h}$	$\mathrm{mol/m^3}$

```
\sisetup{per-mode=symbol}                              \sample{A}
\sisetup{per-mode=fraction}                            \sample{B}
                                                       \sample{C}
\sisetup{per-mode=fraction,fraction-command=\sfrac} \sample{D}
```

3-3-23

What we can see in the previous example are unit names, such as \metre, \hour, or \mole; a prefix \kilo; an inter-unit connector \per; and a power specification \cubed. The concept is that all these components are named in a way that the argument to \unit more or less matches what one would say when communicating the unit over the phone.

The command names for core units and prefixes are listed in Tables 3.3 to 3.6. They are split into different tables matching the conventions of the SI system. Further units can be easily defined as we see below.

Quantities

A quantity is the combination of a number and a unit. Most of the time, combining these two parts requires only the appropriate "glue". The package offers the potential

Unit	*cmd*	Symbol	Unit	*cmd*	Symbol
ampere	\ampere	A	metre	\metre	m
candela	\candela	cd	mole	\mole	mol
kelvin	\kelvin	K	second	\second	s
kilogram	\kilogram	kg			

Table 3.3: SI base units

Unit	*cmd*	Symbol	Unit	*cmd*	Symbol
degree Celsius	\degreeCelsius	°C	newton	\newton	N
becquerel	\becquerel	Bq	ohm	\ohm	Ω
coulomb	\coulomb	C	pascal	\pascal	Pa
farad	\farad	F	radian	\radian	rad
gray	\gray	Gy	siemens	\siemens	S
henry	\henry	H	sievert	\sievert	Sv
hertz	\hertz	Hz	steradian	\steradian	sr
joule	\joule	J	tesla	\tesla	T
katal	\katal	kat	volt	\volt	V
lumen	\lumen	lm	watt	\watt	W
lux	\lux	lx	weber	\weber	Wb

Table 3.4: Coherent derived units in the SI with special names and symbols

for more involved work, such as converting a power-of-ten in the numerical part into a prefix in the unit part.

`\qty[options]{number}{unit}`

Quite often numbers and units are used together, and for this purpose there exists \qty, which is a combination of the \num and the \unit command. As such, we can use either literal or macro-based units for these *quantities* and apply keys that adjust the formatting of one or both parts.

$1.23\,\mathrm{J\,mol^{-1}\,K^{-1}}$
$0.23 \times 10^{7}\,\mathrm{cd}$
$1.99/\mathrm{kg}$
$1.345\,\frac{\mathrm{C}}{\mathrm{mol}}$
$\sqrt{3}\,\mathrm{m}$

```
\usepackage{siunitx}
\qty{1.23}{J.mol^{-1}.K^{-1}}                          \\
\qty{.23e7}{\candela}                                  \\
\qty[per-mode = symbol]{1.99}{\per\kilogram}          \\
\qty[per-mode = fraction]{1,345}{\coulomb\per\mole}  \\
\qty[parse-numbers = false]{\sqrt{3}}{\metre}
```

3-3-24

Unit	*cmd*	Symbol	Unit	*cmd*	Symbol
astronomicalunit	\astronomicalunit	au	hectare	\hectare	ha
bel	\bel	B	hour	\hour	h
dalton	\dalton	Da	litre	\litre	L
day	\day	d	minute (plane angle)	\arcminute	′
decibel	\decibel	dB	minute (time)	\minute	min
degree	\degree	°	second (plane angle)	\arcsecond	″
electronvolt	\electronvolt	eV	tonne	\tonne	t

Table 3.5: Non-SI units accepted for use with the International System of Units

```
\qtylist [options] {numbers}{unit}
\qtyproduct [options] {numbers}{unit}
\qtyrange [options] {number₁}{number₂}{unit}
```

In the same way that lists, products, and ranges of numbers can be given, the same commands exist for quantities. These then apply the unit to one or more of the entries, and combine exponents and similar manipulations, depending on the keys selected.

Typical inner-city speed limits are 7.5 km/h, 10 km/h, 30 km/h and 50 km/h. Cyclists usually travel between 10 km/h to 25 km/h.

```
\usepackage{siunitx}   % next line defines a new unit...
\DeclareSIUnit[per-mode=symbol]\kmh{\kilo\metre\per\hour}
Typical inner-city speed limits are
\qtylist{7.5;10;30;50}{\kmh}. Cyclists
usually travel between \qtyrange{10}{25}{\kmh}.
```

3-3-25

```
\ang [options] {angle}
```

Specifying angles is somewhat of an exception because it is done through its own command. One of the reasons is that there are two conventions supported for specifying the *angle*: either one can give a decimal number or one can specify the *angle* as a semicolon-separated list of degrees, minutes, and seconds (aka arc-format).

10°   60.948°   −3°
12°3′   1°2′3″   1″

```
\usepackage{siunitx}
\ang{10}    \quad \ang{60.948} \quad \ang{-3}   \\
\ang{12;3;} \quad \ang{1;2;3}   \quad \ang{;;1}
```

3-3-26

Complex values as numbers or in quantities

Complex numbers, and even complex quantities, come up in some parts of physical science. To support these, the package offers dedicated commands that take a complex number rather than a normal decimal.[1]

---

[1] Earlier versions of the package allowed complex values in the standard command number arguments; this was removed because it led to some problematic interaction of options.

Prefix	*cmd*	Symbol	Power	Prefix	*cmd*	Symbol	Power
yocto	\yocto	y	-24	deca	\deca	da	1
zepto	\zepto	z	-21	hecto	\hecto	h	2
atto	\atto	a	-18	kilo	\kilo	k	3
femto	\femto	f	-15	mega	\mega	M	6
pico	\pico	p	-12	giga	\giga	G	9
nano	\nano	n	-9	tera	\tera	T	12
micro	\micro	µ	-6	peta	\peta	P	15
milli	\milli	m	-3	exa	\exa	E	18
centi	\centi	c	-2	zetta	\zetta	Z	21
deci	\deci	d	-1	yotta	\yotta	Y	24

Table 3.6: SI prefixes

\complexnum{*number*} \complexqty{*number*}{*unit*}

The imaginary root is indicated with i and has to be present in the *number* argument.

$$(1 + 2i) \times 10^3$$
$$(2.3 - 3.4i)\,\Omega$$

```
\usepackage{siunitx}
\complexnum{1+2ie3} \\ \complexqty{2.3-3.4i}{\ohm}
```

3-3-27

Tabulating numbers

Documents that use a large number of values often show these in tables, and for this siunitx provides some extra support for formatting these in a consistent way.

In addition to the keys we have already seen and those discussed below, siunitx has a number of dedicated keys for aligning values in tables. These are provided by the S column specifier, which is discussed in more detail in Chapter 6 on page 484.

Customizing numerical data representation

Input parsing of numbers

The default conventions for number parsing are suitable for most situations. However, if necessary, a large number of keys are available to adjust the display of numbers. For example, both the period and comma are interpreted as a decimal separator, but if your input data obtained through external sources uses one of them as a thousand separator, then this default needs changing to parse the numbers correctly. In the same way you can adjust what is recognized as exponent markers; what constitutes digits, signs, special symbols; how to mark up uncertainty in the values; etc.

Writing out these unit macros in full can sometimes be tedious, and so the package provides a (large) set of pre-defined abbreviations, for example \kg for \kilogram and \nA for \nanoampere. These abbreviations are, in general, command versions of how they would be written literally, with u taking the place of the micro symbol. For a full list of supported abbreviations, see the package manual.

Inter-unit products are implicitly given by listing the unit macros one after another. Powers of 2 and 3 can be specified through \square and \cubic (before a unit) or \squared and \cubed (after a unit) and general powers through \raiseto or \tothe. General qualifiers are specified with \of.

<table>
<tr><td>3-3-28</td><td>m^4 H^{-5} mol_{cat}</td></tr>
</table>

```
\usepackage{siunitx}
\unit{\raiseto{4}{\metre}} \quad
\unit{\per\henry\tothe{5}} \quad  \unit{\mole\of{cat}}
```

It is also possible to prohibit parsing altogether, either because the numbers should be processed as given or because the data contains LaTeX constructs that cannot be correctly parsed. In that case the number is printed in math mode.

German:	4 276 928 295.32
Spanish:	4 276 928 295.32
English:	4 276 928 295.32
Not parsed:	4, 276, 928, 295.32
Not parsed:	$\sqrt{2 + \text{offset}}\,m$

3-3-29

```
\usepackage{siunitx}
German:       \hfill \num{4 276 928 295,32}      \\[8pt]
\sisetup{input-ignore=. ,input-decimal-markers={,}}
Spanish:      \hfill \num{4.276.928.295,32}      \\[8pt]
\sisetup{input-ignore={,} ,input-decimal-markers=.}
English:      \hfill \num{4,276,928,295.32}      \\[8pt]
\sisetup{parse-numbers=false}
Not parsed: \hfill \num{4,276,928,295.32}       \\[8pt]
Not parsed: \hfill \qty{\sqrt{2+\text{offset}}}{\metre}
```

The previous example shows that all numbers are correctly parsed and that regardless of input conventions the output is always the same (using small spaces as a digit group separator for large numbers unless parsing is off).

As well as simple adjustments to appearance, some manipulation of the data values is possible. Most notably, the package is capable of carrying out rounding both to a fixed number of figures or a number of places. This is enabled using the round-mode key, which would be set to either places or figures (the default is off). The rounding precision is defined through round-precision (default 2). Rounding using an uncertainty is also possible, by setting round-mode to uncertainty.

Rounding data

There are two common methods to handle cases where the rounded fraction of the number is exactly 0.5: rounding up (default) or rounding to the nearest even number. The next two examples show the difference in behavior:

A: 18.276(1)	18.276	124.5	1.245×10^2
B: 18.276(1)	18.28	124.50	1.25×10^2
C: 18.276(1)	18.3	124.5	1.2×10^2
D: 18.276(1)	18.276	124.500	1.245×10^2
E: 18.276(1)	18.3	125	1.25×10^2
F: 18.276(1)	18.3	124	1.24×10^2

3-3-30

```
\usepackage{siunitx}
\newcommand\sample[1]{#1:
   \num{18.276(1)}\hfill \num{18.276}\hfill
   \num{124.5}\hfill \num{1.245e2}\\[8pt]}
                                       \sample{A}
\sisetup{round-mode=places}     \sample{B}
\sisetup{round-precision=1}     \sample{C}
\sisetup{round-precision=3}     \sample{D}
\sisetup{round-mode=figures}    \sample{E}
\sisetup{round-half=even}       \sample{F}
```

If a number is shown as zero after rounding, it is sometimes desirable that this is represented as being below a certain threshold. This can be indicated with round-minimum.

```
\usepackage{siunitx}
\newcommand\sample[1]{#1:\hfill \num{0.005}\hfill
   \num{0.0023}\hfill \num{-0.005}\hfill
   \num{-0.0023}\\[5pt]}
```

A:	0.005	0.0023	−0.005	−0.0023
B:	0.01	0.00	−0.01	0.00
C:	0.00	0.00	0.00	0.00
D:	<0.01	<0.01	>−0.01	>−0.01

```
                                       \sample{A}
\sisetup{round-mode=places}            \sample{B}
\sisetup{round-half=even}              \sample{C}
\sisetup{round-minimum=0.01}           \sample{D}
```

3-3-31

Scientific notation   It is possible to automatically convert numbers to scientific notation. This is controlled through the key exponent-mode that takes the values input (default), scientific, engineering, or fixed. With engineering the exponent is always a power of 3; with fixed it is given by the value of the key fixed-exponent.

```
\usepackage{siunitx}
\newcommand\sample[1]{#1: \num{0.005} \hfill
   \num{0.03} \hfill \num{123.4(1)} \\[5pt]}
```

A: 0.005	0.03	123.4(1)
B: 5×10^{-3}	3×10^{-2}	$1.234(1) \times 10^2$
C: 5×10^{-3}	30×10^{-3}	123.4(1)
D: 0.5×10^{-2}	3×10^{-2}	$12\,340(10) \times 10^{-2}$

```
                                       \sample{A}
\sisetup{exponent-mode=scientific}     \sample{B}
\sisetup{exponent-mode=engineering}    \sample{C}
\sisetup{exponent-mode=fixed,fixed-exponent=-2}
                                       \sample{D}
```

3-3-32

Managing exponents   When exponents are present in the input, then the exponent base is assumed to be 10. If that is an invalid assumption, you can change the interpretation of the base using the exponent-base key. You can also retain zero exponents that are normally dropped or drop a mantissa of 1 that is normally kept. By default a × symbol is used between mantissa and exponent base; with exponent-product a different symbol can be specified.

```
\usepackage{siunitx}
\newcommand\sample[1]{#1:\quad \num{1e4}\hfill
                 \num{5e8}\hfill \num{1.7e0}\\[5pt]}
```

A:	1×10^4 5×10^8 1.7	
B:	10^4 5×10^8 1.7×10^0	
C:	2^4 $5 \cdot 2^8$ $1.7 \cdot 2^0$	

```
                                            \sample{A}
\sisetup{retain-zero-exponent,
         retain-unity-mantissa=false}       \sample{B}
\sisetup{exponent-base=2,exponent-product=\cdot}\sample{C}
```

3-3-33

The package documentation describes further keys that can adjust (almost) any aspect of the treatment of numerical data.

Customizing units and quantities

If a unit is the product of several different units, then `inter-unit-product` is used as a separator between them (default `\,`). If you prefer a mathematical symbol like `\cdot` it often needs some spatial adjustments. A quotient indicated with `\per` can be represented in various ways through the key `per-mode`. It can take the values `power` (default), `power-positive-first` (move later positive powers before the quotient), `fraction` (use `fraction-command` to specify the command generating the fraction), `symbol` (use `per-symbol` as the symbol), or `repeated-symbol` (if there are several `\per` commands).

By default `\per` applies only to the next unit in the spec, so you need several such commands, if different units are part of the quotient denominator. This convention fits with the way units are normally pronounced in English, but you can turn on `sticky-per` to change that.

Instead of displaying prefixes as symbols, one can also direct siunitx to attempt to convert them to powers; this is shown in the last line of the example.

A: $\mathrm{J\,Mmol^{-1}\,K^{-1}}$	$5.3\,\mathrm{kA\,mol^{-1}\,ds}$
B: $\mathrm{J\,Mmol^{-1}\,K^{-1}}$	$5.3\,\mathrm{kA\,ds\,mol^{-1}}$
C: $\frac{\mathrm{J}}{\mathrm{Mmol\,K}}$	$5.3\,\frac{\mathrm{kA\,ds}}{\mathrm{mol}}$
D: $\mathrm{J}/\mathrm{Mmol\,K}$	$5.3\,\mathrm{kA\,ds}/\mathrm{mol}$
E: $\mathrm{J}/\mathrm{Mmol\cdot K}$	$5.3\,\mathrm{kA\cdot ds}/\mathrm{mol}$
F: $\mathrm{J}/(\mathrm{Mmol\cdot K})$	$5.3\,\mathrm{kA\cdot ds}/\mathrm{mol}$
G: $\mathrm{J}/\mathrm{Mmol}/\mathrm{K}$	$5.3\,\mathrm{kA}/\mathrm{mol}\cdot\mathrm{ds}$
H: $\mathrm{J}/\mathrm{Mmol}/\mathrm{K}$	$5.3\times10^{2}\,\mathrm{A}/\mathrm{mol}\cdot\mathrm{s}$

```
\usepackage{siunitx,xfrac}
\newcommand\sample[1]{#1: \unit{\joule\per
                         \mega\mole\per\K}
   \hfill \qty{5.3}{\kilo\ampere\per\mole\deci\s}\\[5pt]}
                                                \sample{A}
\sisetup{per-mode=power-positive-first} \sample{B}
\sisetup{per-mode=fraction}             \sample{C}
\sisetup{fraction-command=\sfrac}       \sample{D}
\sisetup{inter-unit-product=\cdot}      \sample{E}
\sisetup{per-mode=symbol}               \sample{F}
\sisetup{per-mode=repeated-symbol}      \sample{G}
\sisetup{prefix-mode=extract-exponent}  \sample{H}
```

3-3-34

Placement and handling of qualifiers is managed by the `qualifier-mode` key accepting `subscript` (default), `brackets`, `space`, or `phrase`. For the latter the added phrase comes from `qualifier-phrase`.

A: $3\,\mathrm{m^3_{oak}}$	$5\,\mathrm{kW_{sol}\,h^{-1}_{dl}}$
B: $3\,\mathrm{m(oak)^3}$	$5\,\mathrm{kW(sol)\,h(dl)^{-1}}$
C: $3\,\mathrm{m\,oak^3}$	$5\,\mathrm{kW\,sol\,h\,dl^{-1}}$
D: $3\,\mathrm{m\,oak^3}$	$5\,\mathrm{kW\,sol\,h\,dl^{-1}}$
E: $3\,\mathrm{m\,t{:}oak^3}$	$5\,\mathrm{kW\,t{:}sol\,h\,t{:}dl^{-1}}$

```
\usepackage{siunitx} \DeclareSIQualifier\daylight{dl}
\DeclareSIQualifier\oak{oak} \DeclareSIQualifier\solar{sol}
\newcommand\sample[1]{#1: \qty{3}{\cubic\m\oak}
   \hfil \qty{5}{\kW\solar\per\hour\daylight}\\[5pt]}
                                             \sample{A}
\sisetup{qualifier-mode=bracket}            \sample{B}
\sisetup{qualifier-mode=space}              \sample{C}
\sisetup{qualifier-mode=phrase}             \sample{D}
\sisetup{qualifier-phrase={\text{\,t:}}}\sample{E}
```

3-3-35

In quantities, the combination of number and unit is logically speaking a product. How that is represented is defined by the `quantity-product` keys, by default a thin space. Line breaking at this point is normally not allowed, though in an emergency it can be enabled with `allow-quantity-breaks`.

Special care is also necessary when a unit applies to several numbers, e.g., where there is a separated uncertainty component or in a product of quantities. In that case the unit applies to all components. How this is displayed is configurable with the key `separate-uncertainty`. More granular control is possible through `separate-uncertainty-units` that accepts `bracket` (the default when `separate-uncertainty` is given), `repeat`, or `single`.

A: $12.3(4)\,\mathrm{km}$

B: $(12.3 \pm 0.4)\,\mathrm{km}$

C: $12.3\,\mathrm{km} \pm 0.4\,\mathrm{km}$

D: $(12.3 \pm 0.4)\,\mathrm{km}$

E: $12.3 \pm 0.4\,\mathrm{km}$

```
\usepackage{siunitx}
\newcommand\sample[1]{#1: \qty{12.3(4)}{\km}\\[5pt]}

                                            \sample{A}
\sisetup{separate-uncertainty}              \sample{B}
\sisetup{separate-uncertainty-units=repeat} \sample{C}
\sisetup{separate-uncertainty-units=bracket}\sample{D}
\sisetup{separate-uncertainty-units=single} \sample{E}
```

3-3-36

`\DeclareSIUnit [`*options*`] {`*cmd*`}{`*definition*`}`

With `\DeclareSIUnit` you can define new unit commands or change the appearance of existing ones. The *definition* can be anything that would be allowed in the argument to `\unit`. If you specify any keys, they are applied to that unit definition only and, if necessary, can be overwritten by the optional argument to `\unit` or `\qty` when the unit is used.[1]

You can drive $50\,\mathrm{km/h}$ in most cities.

```
\usepackage{siunitx}
\DeclareSIUnit[per-mode=symbol]\kmh{\kilo\metre\per\hour}
You can drive \qty{50}{\kmh} in most cities.
```

3-3-37

`\DeclareSIPrefix{`*cmd*`}{`*notation*`}{`*power*`}`
`\DeclareSIPower{`*before-cmd*`}{`*after-cmd*`}{`*power*`}`
`\DeclareSIQualifier{`*cmd*`}{`*qualifier*`}`

All power prefixes defined in the SI standard are pre-defined by siunitx, but if necessary, new ones can be made available with `\DeclareSIPrefix`. More interesting, however, are power declarations because the package defines only those for the powers of two and three.

N^4 and m^4

```
\usepackage{siunitx}   \DeclareSIPower\quartic\tothefourth{4}
\unit{\newton\tothefourth} and \unit{\quartic\metre}
```

3-3-38

Finally, there is a general qualifier declaration for which the package provides no defaults, so it is up to the user to provide declarations as needed. It was already used in Example 3-3-35 on the preceding page.

---

[1]However, you cannot overwrite such settings using `\sisetup`.

Controlling printing

With the standard settings, siunitx prints almost all output in math mode.[1] It also ignores any font changes, for example italic or bold. This follows standard style guidelines that state that quantities are mathematical entities, which therefore should be treated the same as for example $y = mx + c$. This behavior is controllable using a series of keys that can select between math and text mode printing and determine which aspects of font selection are fixed.

The key `mode` sets which mode is used for printing output: this can be one of `math`, `text`, or `match`. The latter means that printing uses the prevailing mode, so remains in whichever mode the surrounding material is set in.

As TeX's math and text modes work quite differently in terms of font selection, further font control depends on which mode is being used for printing. For many users, the most important outcome is to follow (or otherwise) surrounding bold or sans serif font selection from text. This is achieved using the keys `text-family-to-math` and `text-series-to-math` when siunitx is printing in math mode, and the keys `reset-text-family` and `reset-text-series` when printing in text mode. Thus, by setting all of these appropriately, one can always "follow" the surrounding font selection. Note that in the example the second \qty appears inside a formula.

```
\usepackage{siunitx}
\DeclareSIUnit[per-mode=symbol]\kmh{\kilo\metre\per\hour}
\newcommand\sample[1]{\textnormal{\noindent #1:}}
        The speed limit is \qty{100}{\kmh}.\par}
```

A: The speed limit is $100\,\mathrm{km/h}$.
B: **The speed limit is** $100\,\mathrm{km/h}$.
C: The speed limit is $100\,\mathrm{km/h}$.
D: **The speed limit is 100** km/h.

E: **The speed limit is 100 km/h.**

```
\sffamily    \sample{A}    \textbf{\sample{B}}
\sisetup{text-family-to-math,text-series-to-math}
\sample{C}    \textbf{\sample{D}}
\sisetup{mode=match,reset-text-family=false,
        reset-text-series=false}
\textbf{\sample{E}}
```

3-3-39

3.4 Various ways of highlighting and quoting text

For highlighting text you can customize the font shape, weight, or size (see Section 9.3.1 on page 659). Text can also be uppercased, underlined, or the spacing between letters can be varied. Ways for performing such operations are offered by the four packages textcase, ulem, soul, and microtype discussed here.

General mechanisms for intelligent and context-dependent quoting are provided by the csquotes package, and for typesetting web resources we look at the packages url and uri.

We also cover a few more specialized packages, i.e., dashundergaps (for producing simple forms as an application of the ulem package) and embrac for producing upright parentheses or brackets while emphasizing text using italic font shapes.

---

[1] Real textual material, such as the "to" used in a range of quantities, is printed in text mode.

3.4.1 Change case of text intelligently (formerly textcase)

The standard LaTeX commands \MakeUppercase and \MakeLowercase change the characters in their arguments to uppercase or lowercase, respectively, thereby expanding macros as needed. For example,

```
\MakeUppercase{On \today}
```

results in something like "ON FEBRUARY 22, 2022". Sometimes this changed more characters than desirable. For example, if the text contains a math formula, then uppercasing this formula is normally a bad idea because it changes its meaning. Similarly, arguments to the commands \label, \ref, and \cite represent semantic information, which, if modified, results in incorrect or missing references, because LaTeX looks for the wrong labels.

The package **textcase** by David Carlisle overcame these defects by providing two alternative commands, \MakeTextUppercase and \MakeTextLowercase, which recognize math formulas and cross-referencing commands and leave them alone.

1 Textcase example

TEXT IN SECTION 1, ABOUT $a = b$ AND $\alpha \neq a$

```
\usepackage{textcase}

\section{Textcase example}\label{exa}
\MakeTextUppercase{Text in section~\ref{exa},
   about $a=b$ and $\alpha \neq a$ }
```

3-4-1

| \MakeUppercase{*text*} | \MakeLowercase{*text*} | *(improved in 2022)* |

With the June 2022 release of LaTeX this functionality was integrated into core LaTeX, so these days you can simply use \MakeUppercase and \MakeLowercase and achieve the same effect without the need to load a package:

1 Textcase example

TEXT IN SECTION 1, ABOUT $a = b$ AND $\alpha \neq a$

```
\section{Textcase example}\label{exa}
\MakeUppercase{Text in section~\ref{exa},
   about $a=b$ and $\alpha \neq a$ }
```

3-4-2

| \NoCaseChange{*text*} |

Sometimes portions of text should be left unchanged for one reason or another. With \NoCaseChange the textcase package provided a generic way to mark such parts. An improved version of that command has now been added to LaTeX directly.

NEITHER OF THESE **FAIL:** $a + B = c$ **AND** *FORtunaTELY*, but did so in the past!

```
\MakeUppercase{Neither of these \textbf{fail: $a+B=c$
            and} \emph{for\NoCaseChange{tuna}tely}},
but did so in the past!
```

3-4-3

Improved, because brace groups inside the argument of \MakeTextUppercase enforced uppercasing in the past, and the previous example would have failed in both places: it would have uppercased the formula and ignored the \NoCaseChange, because it was inside the braced argument of \emph. There have been workarounds, but fortunately they are no longer necessary.

The textcase package remains available for backwards compatibility and defines the commands \MakeTextUppercase and \MakeTextLowercase, but simply redirects them to use the kernel commands now.

3.4.2 csquotes — Context-sensitive quotation marks

Correctly quoting textual material usually depends on the context and requires some care. Not only do the quote characters change, for example, if the quote text itself contains quoted material, but one also has to ensure consistent attributions, etc.

LaTeX itself offers rudimentary support for quotes in the English language, but not much else. For display quotes it has the quote environment, and for longer quotations it offers the quotation environment, but neither adds quote characters. In most classes these environments indent the text from both sides, and quotation typically also indents each paragraph. For in-line quotes, single or double quotation marks are used, but it is up to the user to select the correct pairs depending on the circumstances. People sometimes use straight marks ("), but this gives incorrect results.

Alice said: "Why did you do that, Bob?" And Bob answered: "What do you mean by 'that', dear Alice?"

"I mean the use of "straight" marks!"

```
Alice said: ``Why did you do that, Bob?'' And Bob
answered: ``What do you mean by `that', dear Alice?''

``I mean the use of "straight" marks!''
```

3-4-4

If all this is done manually, there is a high likelihood that inconsistencies creep in, and if a language other than English is needed or a publisher's house style poses special requirements, then a lot of reworking is necessary.

To resolve these issues and to provide advanced facilities for in-line and display quotations, Philipp Lehman developed the csquotes package, now maintained by Joseph Wright. It offers support for a wide range of tasks, from the simple applications to the complex demands of formal quotations. The quote styles are fully configurable so that without touching the document content it is possible to drastically alter the appearance.

\enquote*{*text*}   \textquote*[*attribution*] [*punct*] {*text*} *tpunct*

The purpose of the \enquote command is simply to add the correct quotation marks around *text* depending on the context (nesting level, current language) and the current quoting style. (Think of "en"circle if you wonder about the command name.) On the top-level it uses so-called "outer" marks, and if quotes are nested, it toggles between "outer" and "inner" marks. With the star form you force it to always use inner marks.

By default two levels of quoting are supported: if your document has a deeper nesting, you receive an error message. However, this is easily repaired by specifying the needed nesting level in the option maxlevel. Most of the time deeper nestings are either a mistake (like a forgotten closing brace) or at least a questionable presentation of your material — which you perhaps should consider changing. It is therefore best to leave this default untouched unless you really know that you need more levels. An example with three levels is Example 3-4-11 on page 184.

Alice said: "Why did you do that, Bob?" And Bob answered: "What do you mean by 'that', dear Alice?"

```
\usepackage{csquotes}

Alice said: \enquote{Why did you do that, Bob?}
And Bob answered: \enquote{What do you mean
by \enquote{that}, dear Alice?}
```

3-4-5

The \textquote command is similar to \enquote, but offers further control with its two optional arguments and its facility to scan for a trailing punctuation. If present, the *attribution* holds attribution information, which may be a name or a \cite command or a combination of both.

He said "Our life is full of empty space." (Umberto Eco) and "Space is big. You just won't believe how [...]" (Douglas Adams).

```
\usepackage{csquotes}

He said \textquote[Umberto Eco][.]{Our life is full
of empty space} and \textquote[Douglas Adams]{Space
is big. You just won't believe how [\ldots]}.
```

3-4-6

In the optional *punct* argument you should place any final punctuation of the quote. While splitting the quote this way needs getting used to, it helps a lot to cater to some of the more peculiar requirements concerning quotation handling.

For example, the quote attributed to Umberto Eco in the previous example is a full sentence (ending in a period), while the one by Adams is not, and the period after it belongs to the outer sentence. Whether such periods should be placed inside the quotes or outside is a matter of style and convention. For example, the standard American quotation style, as advocated by the Chicago Manual of Style [18], requires that a period or comma immediately after closing quotation marks is to be moved inside the quotes, even if it is logically not a part of the quotation.[1]

Because analyzing the *text* argument is TeXnically a rather difficult undertaking, one needs to explicitly tell the command if there is final punctuation. Scanning ahead is simpler, so the package automatically checks whether the mandatory *text* argument is followed by (trailing) punctuation outside the quoted material and then uses this information to decide where to place the *punct* and/or *tpunct*.

```
\begin{displayquote} [attribution] [punct]
```

What the \textquote command does for in-line quotations, the displayquote environment does for quotations that should be displayed on their own. The advantage of choosing this environment over the standard quote or quotation environments is that it supports *attribution*, can correctly handle final punctuation, and is easily configurable to a wide range of formats. Furthermore, whatever the configuration, it always matches the results from the \blockquote command discussed below.

For example, with \SetBlockEnvironment{*env*} you can specify which environment should be used to do the actual quoting. By default it is quote, but this

---

[1] While this book generally follows American spelling and style, we have vetoed this convention, because it feels rather unnatural for European authors.

way you can change it to `quotation` or provide the name of your own quoting environment. Such a change then applies to any type of display or block quote.

He said:

> Our life is full of empty space. (Umberto Eco)
>
> Space is big. You just won't believe how vastly, hugely, mind-bogglingly big [...] (Douglas Adams)

```
\usepackage{csquotes} \SetBlockEnvironment{quotation}
He said: \begin{displayquote}[Umberto Eco][.]
   Our life is full of empty space
\end{displayquote}
\begin{displayquote}[Douglas Adams]  Space is big.
   You just won't believe how  vastly, hugely,
   mind-bogglingly big [\ldots]
\end{displayquote}
```

3-4-7

In academic writing it is common to embed short quotations in the running text (e.g., use `\textquote`), but to set longer ones as separate and clearly distinguished paragraphs — so-called block quotations (provided by `displayquote`). When to make the change from one to the other type may depend on criteria like the number of lines or number of words in the quotation and often varies from one place or publisher to the next. To help with this situation, `csquotes` offers the command `\blockquote`.

`\blockquote*`[*attribution*] [*punct*] {*text*} *tpunct*

This command takes the same arguments as `\textquote`. It measures the length of the quotation, and if that exceeds a configurable threshold, it typesets the *text* in the layout of a `displayquote` environment (but also takes care of a trailing *tpunct* punctuation). Otherwise, it behaves like a `\textquote` or `\textquote*` command and produces an in-line quotation. Inside footnotes, parboxes, minipages, or floats it by default always forces in-line quotations. This can be changed by loading the package with the option `csdisplay`.

He started his talk with the quotes "Our life is full of empty space." (Umberto Eco) and

> Space is big. You just won't believe how vastly, hugely, mind-bogglingly big it is. I mean, you may think it's a long way down the road to the chemist, but that's just peanuts to space ... (Douglas Adams).

Later on he finished with "God does not play ..." (Albert Einstein).

```
\usepackage{csquotes}
\SetBlockEnvironment{quotation}
He started his talk with the quotes
\blockquote[Umberto Eco][.]{Our life is
   full of empty  space}  and
\blockquote[Douglas Adams]{Space is big.
   You just won't believe how vastly, hugely,
   mind-bogglingly big it is. I mean, you
   may think it's a long way down the road to
   the chemist, but that's just peanuts to
   space \ldots}.  Later on he finished with
\blockquote[Albert Einstein]{God does not
   play \ldots}.
```

3-4-8

By default display quotes are used whenever the current quote consists of three or more lines. This can be globally changed by specifying a different number with the `threshold` option when loading the package or within the document by using `\SetBlockThreshold`; both ways are shown in Example 3-4-9.

181

If you prefer the length evaluation to be by words rather than lines, set the option thresholdtype to words and the threshold value to an appropriate value such as 50. If there are explicit line or paragraph breaks within *text*, the quote is set as a block regardless of the threshold. To change that, set parthreshold to false. Further fine-tuning possibilities are discussed in the documentation [76], but they should be seldom needed.

The option debug helps when you want to understand why the package made a certain selection: if enabled, it writes that information into the transcript file.

Quotations with formal citations

To indicate the source of a quotation you can use a \cite command in the optional *attribution* argument of the commands discussed above. For documents that are supposed to provide proper references for all quotes used, the csquotes package offers another set of commands that formalize this approach by requiring the citation key and optional citation arguments as part of the command syntax. These commands all have an additional "c" (for citation) in their name, for example, \textcquote instead of \textquote or \blockcquote, etc.

\textquote*	[*attribution*]	[*punct*] {*text*} *tpunct*
\textcquote*	[*post-note*] {*key-list*} [*punct*] {*text*} *tpunct*
\textcquote* [*pre-note*] [*post-note*] {*key-list*} [*punct*] {*text*} *tpunct*

As shown above, the optional *attribution* gets replaced by a mandatory *key-list* argument (receiving the citation key or keys) preceded by one or two further optional arguments, all of which are internally passed to a \cite command.

Standard LaTeX's \cite command only understands *post-note*; thus, without loading an additional package only *post-note* is supported. However, extended bibliography packages, such as natbib or biblatex, provide \cite commands with two optional arguments, and in that case the versions with two optional arguments can be used.

Changes, insertions, and deletions

When quoting material, there is often the need to make changes to the quoted text, and those modifications should be properly marked up to enable the reader to see the omissions, alterations, or insertions easily. To help with this task, csquotes offers a number of commands (all configurable to adhere to any required convention).

\textelp{}   \textelp{*text*}   \textelp*{*text*}

Omissions or longer modifications should be marked up with \textelp. If used with an empty argument, it prints by default an ellipsis surrounded by brackets to indicate where text is missing. If you supply *text* in the argument, then it is typeset in a second set of brackets after the ellipsis to indicate that it was added in place of the removed material. The star form reverses the placement of *text* and ellipsis.

Do not forget the empty pair of braces if you have not added any text. Without it, the next letter from your document will be mistakenly picked up as *text*.

The next example shows both forms in practice (the original quote by Adams used "chemist", while the US printing said "drug store").

```
\usepackage[threshold=4]{csquotes}
```

He started his talk with the quotes "Our life is full of empty space." (Umberto Eco) and "Space is big. You just won't believe how vastly, hugely, mind-bogglingly big it is. I mean, you may think it's a long way down the road to the [drug store] [...], but that's just peanuts to space [...]" (Douglas Adams). Later on he finished with

> God does not play [...] (Albert Einstein).

3-4-9

```
He started his talk with the quotes
\blockquote[Umberto Eco][.]{Our life is full
   of empty  space} and
\blockquote[Douglas Adams]{Space is big. You
   just  won't believe how vastly, hugely,
   mind-bogglingly big it is. I mean, you may
   think it's a long way down the road to the
   \textelp*{drug store}, but that's just peanuts
   to space \textelp{}}. Later on he finished with
\SetBlockThreshold{0}% -- force block quote
\blockquote[Albert  Einstein]{God does
   not play \textelp{}}.
```

\textins*{*text*}	\textdel{*text*}

For insertions of words or phrases use \textins, and for minor modifications like capitalization of a letter use \textins*. Both forms by default surround the *text* with a pair of brackets. Example 3-4-15 shows how to change this behavior.

Short deletions (like removing a surplus character) can be marked up with \textdel. By default this just outputs a pair of brackets, and the deleted *text* is not shown. For longer deletions (that are really omissions) use \textelp instead.

```
\usepackage{csquotes}
```

3-4-10

Corr[]ection: [chemist] [sic]

```
Corr\textdel{r}ection: \textins*{chemist} \textins{sic}
```

Language support

By default **csquotes** determines the correct quotation marks to use, based on the language that is in force at the beginning of the document. It then uses these quote marks throughout the whole document. Alternatively, if you load the package with the option `autostyle`, it continuously monitors language changes throughout the document and adjusts the quotation symbols when necessary (at the cost of processing speed).

As a further possibility, one can load the package with the option `style` that expects the name of a quoting style as its value. It then uses that style throughout the document. Standard quoting styles have language names, such as `english`, `german`, or `french`, and some of them even have subvariants that can be individually selected — for a full list refer to the package documentation [76]. There is even a way to define your own styles, if necessary.

If **csquotes** has problems loading the support for a particular language, it issues a warning and switches to the default language. Because such warnings can be easily overlooked, consider loading the package with the option `strict` that turns all such warnings into errors.

Managing quotes in foreign languages

When typesetting a quote written in a language different from the main document language, one has to make sure that it is correctly hyphenated and possibly that it uses quotation marks common for that language (though you may want to be consistent with the document language and use the standard quoting symbols from there). For these types of needs, csquotes offers support through a number of commands as long as the document has some multilingual support, e.g., through babel or polyglossia.

> `\foreignquote*{language}{text}`   `\hyphenquote*{language}{text}`

The `\foreignquote` combines `\enquote` with the `\foreignlanguage` command (from babel or the polyglossia package); i.e., it switches hyphenation rules, enables any extra commands for the specified *language*, and uses the quotation marks set up for that language in case csquotes was loaded with the option `autostyle`.

In contrast, `\hyphenquote` always only changes hyphenation rules (by internally using the appropriate support command from the multilingual package), and the quotation marks remain those of the surrounding language.

Note the use of `maxlevel` in the next example to account for the three levels of nesting. You may have to trust me in my claim that "wunderbar" is correctly hyphenated, but the use of English and German quote marks in the two sentences can be easily spotted.

```
\usepackage[ngerman,english]{babel}
\usepackage[maxlevel=3,autostyle]{csquotes}
\enquote{He said \enquote{I can speak
    \foreignquote{ngerman}{wunderbar} German.}}

\selectlanguage{ngerman}
\enquote{Er sagte \foreignquote{english}{I can speak
    \hyphenquote{ngerman}{wunderbar} German.}}
```

"He said 'I can speak „wunderbar" German.'"
„Er sagte 'I can speak "wunderbar" German.' "

3-4-11

> `\foreigntextquote*{language}[attribution][punct]{text}tpunct`
> `\hyphentextquote* {language}[attribution][punct]{text}tpunct`

For all other quoting commands (and environments) discussed so far, there are also versions that combine them with `\foreignlanguage` or the hyphenrules environment. The general concept is to prepend `foreign` or `hyphen` to the command name. These commands then all have an additional first mandatory argument specifying the *language* of the quotation. This means you also can use the commands `\foreignblockquote` and `\hyphenblockquote` or their star forms and the environments `foreigndisplayquote` or `hyphendisplayquote` to typeset quotations in a foreign language.

\hybridblockquote*{*lang*} [*attribution*] [*punct*] {*text*} *tpunct*

An interesting further possibility is the \hybridblockquote command that behaves like \hyphentextquote if the quotation is short and like \foreignblockquote otherwise.

Further configuration possibilities

In addition to the package options, csquotes offers a larger number of hooks that can be redefined to change most aspects of the output generated by the user commands discussed above. In this section we show a few important possibilities for customization, but essentially all commands can be customized in similar ways. Thus, if you are required to modify other aspects, it is most likely possible. In that case, please consult the package documentation [76] for further details.

\mkcitation{*attribution*}   \mkccitation{*cite-command*}

All commands that take an optional *attribution* argument pass that argument on to the \mkcitation hook for processing. By default this surrounds the *attribution* with parentheses and separates it from preceding text by an interword space. If there is no *attribution* argument, nothing is output. Example 3-4-12 shows a redefinition that places all attributions into footnotes.

The \mkccitation hook has the same default definition but is used by the formal quotation commands that have a mandatory *key-list* argument. It receives the full \cite command with all relevant optional arguments as input.

\mktextquote{*open*}{*text*}{*close*}{*punct*}{*tpunct*}{*citation*}

The \mktextquote hook is responsible for formatting in-line quotations and is used by any of the commands that do this and support attribution or formal citation. This includes all "blockquote" commands when they decide to produce a short in-line quotation (but not \enquote and derived commands).

The arguments *text*, *punct*, and *tpunct* are passed on unchanged from the calling command. The *open* and *close* arguments receive the open and close marks as determined by the context (language and nesting level), and *citation* receives the result of \mkcitation or in the case of formal quote commands that of \mkccitation. If there was no *punct* or *tpunct*, those arguments will be empty. The same is true for *citation* if there was not any *attribution*.

The task of \mktextquote is then mainly to place all arguments in the right order, but for more complicated tasks it can also do some further processing based on the values in certain arguments (see the helper commands below). Its default definition is equivalent to

```
\newcommand\mktextquote[6]{#1#2#4#3#6#5}
```

which means that the output starts with the *open* quote mark (#1), followed by the quote *text* (#2), followed by final *punct*uation (#4, which may be empty) and followed by the *close* quote mark (#3). This is then followed by the *citation* (#6, which is either empty or provides its own separation). Finally, the trailing *tpunct* is appended (#5, which again can be empty).

Implementing American quotation style

Scary, isn't it? In fact, it is not so difficult if you stare at it for a moment, and it obviously offers a lot of flexibility. For example, below we show how to implement American-style quoting, where a final *tpunct* (#5) moves into the quoted material — all that it needed is shuffling the order of arguments a bit.

He started his talk with the quotes "Our life is full of empty space."[1] and "Space is big. You just won't believe how vastly, hugely, mind-bogglingly big it is. I mean, you may think it's a long way down the road to the [...][chemist], but that's just peanuts to space [...]."[2] Later he finished with "God does not play [...]."[3]

---

[1] Umberto Eco
[2] Douglas Adams
[3] Albert Einstein

```
\usepackage[threshold=5]{csquotes}
\renewcommand\mkcitation [1]{\footnote{#1}}
\renewcommand\mktextquote [6]{#1#2#4#5#3#6}

He started his talk with the quotes
\blockquote[Umberto Eco] [.]{Our life is full of empty
                             space} and
\blockquote[Douglas Adams]{Space is big. You just
  won't believe how vastly, hugely, mind-bogglingly
  big it is. I mean, you may think it's a long way
  down the road to the \textelp{chemist}, but that's
  just peanuts to space \textelp{}}.
Later he finished with \blockquote[Albert Einstein]
{God does not play \textelp{}}.
```

3-4-12

$$\boxed{\texttt{\mkblockquote\{text\}\{punct\}\{tpunct\}\{citation\}}}$$

The `\mkblockquote` command does a similar job but is used whenever a block quote is produced by a user command (for display environments, see below). Given that block quotes are already visually separated, they are normally typeset without quotation marks. For that reason `\mkblockquote` does not receive *open* or *close* quotation marks as arguments. However, it is easy enough to add them to block quotes, as shown in the next example.

This example also uses the helper `\ifblank` to automatically add a `\textelp` command at the end in the case of incomplete quotations.

He started with the quotes "Our life is full of empty space." (Umberto Eco) and

"Space is big. You just won't believe how vastly, hugely, mind-bogglingly big [...]." (Douglas Adams)

Later he finished with "God does not play [...]." (Albert Einstein)

```
\usepackage[threshold=1]{csquotes}
\renewcommand\mktextquote [6]
    {#1#2\ifblank{#4}{ \textelp{}}{#4}#5#3#6}
\renewcommand\mkblockquote [4]
    {\enquote{#1\ifblank{#2}{ \textelp{}}{#2}#3}#4}

He started with the quotes
\blockquote[Umberto Eco] [.]{Our life is full of empty
                             space} and
\blockquote[Douglas Adams]{Space is big. You just
  won't believe how vastly, hugely, mind-bogglingly
  big}.
Later he finished with
\blockquote[Albert Einstein]{God does not play}.
```

3-4-13

```
\mkbegdispquote{punct}{citation}      \mkenddispquote{punct}{citation}
```

There are two hooks to handle `displayquote` and related environments, one for the beginning and one for the end of the environment. Both receive the final *punctua*tion and the *citation* (*attribution* or formal citation) specified on the environment as arguments, though normally these are needed only when the end of the environment is reached, i.e., `\mkenddispquote` is executed.

As an application, the next example shows how the *citation* can be forced onto a new line if it does not fully fit with the last line of the quotation. What happens in the redefinition of `\mkenddispquote` is this: first we typeset any terminal punctuation (#1) and then a nonbreakable stretchable space followed by a `\nolinebreak[3]`. This does not prohibit a line break at this point, but the break is discouraged. If the line break is taken, then the next line starts with another nonbreakable stretchable space followed by the *citation* placed into an `\mbox` to ensure that it does not break across lines. If the break between the two stretchable spaces is not taken, then everything must fit into the last line. In both cases the *citation* is placed at the far end of the line.

Force the attribution on its on the next line, if necessary

If you like this style, then you should, of course, implement it in `\mkblockquote` as well, to get consistent results.

```
\usepackage{csquotes}
\renewcommand\mkenddispquote[2]
    {#1\hspace*{\stretch{1}}\nolinebreak[3]%
        \hspace*{\stretch{1}}\mbox{#2}}
```

He said:

>   Our life is full of empty space.
>   (Umberto Eco)

and

>   Space is big. You just won't believe
>   how [...] big [...]   (Douglas Adams)

```
He said: \begin{displayquote}[Umberto Eco][.]
    Our life is full of empty space
\end{displayquote}
and \begin{displayquote}[Douglas Adams]
    Space is big. You just won't believe how
    \textelp{} big \textelp{}
\end{displayquote}
```

3-4-14

```
\mktextins{insertion}   \mktextmod{modification}   \mktextdel{deletion}
```

The hook `\mktextins` generates the typeset result of `\textins`, while the command `\mktextmod` does the same for `\textins*`, and `\mktextdel` produces the output for `\textdel`.

If you prefer, for example, to use parentheses instead of brackets or if you want modifications to be indicated by some ellipsis in addition to the new text or if you want to show deleted text (struck out), these are the commands to redefine (though perhaps not in this inconsistent combination with both parentheses and brackets):

```
\usepackage{csquotes,ulem}
\renewcommand\mktextins[1]{(\textit{#1})}
\renewcommand\mktextmod[1]{[\textellipsis #1]}
\renewcommand\mktextdel[1]{[\sout{#1}]}
```

Corr[r]ection:
[...chemist]
(*sic*)

```
Corr\textdel{r}ection: \\ \textins*{chemist} \\ \textins{sic}
```

3-4-15

187

> `\mktextelp`   `\mktextelpins{`*insertion*`}`   `\mktextinselp{`*insertion*`}`

These hooks generate the output for `\textelp` with an empty argument, with a nonempty argument, and for `\textelp*`, respectively. Their definition needs to be changed if you want, for example, parentheses around the ellipsis or just an ellipsis.

Additional helper commands

The package also offers a number of helper commands for use in any of the hooks. They can be used to test for special conditions.

> `\ifblank{`*string*`}{`*true*`}{`*false*`}`
> `\iftextpunct{`*text*`}{`*true*`}{`*false*`}`

For example, `\ifblank` tests if some *string* is empty and then executes the *true* or *false* code, accordingly. This was used in Example 3-4-13 to automatically add a `\textelp` command into incomplete quotations.

    `\iftextpunct` tests if the *text* ends in any type of punctuation mark, and there are further commands to test for specific characters.

3.4.3 embrac — Upright brackets and parentheses

In his book "The Elements of Typographic Style" Robert Bringhurst writes, "*Use upright (i.e., 'roman') rather than sloped parentheses, square brackets and braces, even if the context is italic*", and explains this further with

> Parentheses and brackets are not letters, and it makes little sense to speak of them as roman or italic. There are vertical parentheses and sloped ones, and the parentheses on italic fonts are almost always sloped, but vertical parentheses are generally to be preferred. That means they must come from the roman font, and may need extra spacing when used with italic letterforms. The sloped square brackets usually found on italic fonts are, if anything, even less useful than sloped parentheses. [7, p.85, §5.3.2.]

Inspired by this advice Clemens Niederberger wrote the **embrac** package that redefines `\textit` and other font commands to implement vertical parentheses in sloped text fonts. Thus, if you want to follow Bringhurst's advice, then loading this package is worth considering.

    While it is not difficult to achieve the effect manually in a one-off situation, Bringhurst is correct that the parentheses or brackets have to be properly (manually) kerned as well (i.e., moved closer or more likely further away from the italic characters). To support this, the **embrac** package adds (customizable) kerns around the parentheses so that in most cases all that is necessary is loading the package.

```
\emph*{text}   \textit*{text}   \textsl*{text}
```

The three standard commands are redefined by the package. Any parentheses, brackets, or braces inside their *text* argument are automatically replaced with upright versions, and any necessary kerning is added. Only braces directly visible in the text are handled; i.e., anything hidden in commands or inside a brace group is left alone.

All commands now have a star form that restores the original behavior if that is necessary somewhere.

The right amount of kerning depends on the fonts used in the document. The default values are reasonable for Computer or Latin Modern fonts, but with other families you may end up with too much or too little space around the parentheses. How to alter the kerning in such cases is explained in the package documentation.

```
\usepackage{lmodern,embrac}
\emph {[Here] we highlight (some) text.}
```

[Here] we highlight (some) text.

[Here] we highlight (some) text.

3-4-16

```
\emph*{[Here] we highlight (some) text.}
```

Redefining core commands is not always a good idea, so if you want to reinstate the original behavior for a part of your document, you can do so with \EmbracOff and \EmbracOn.

3.4.4 ulem — Emphasize and copy-edit via underline

LaTeX encourages the use of the \emph command and the \em declaration for marking emphasis, rather than explicit font-changing declarations, such as \bfseries and \itshape. The ulem package (by Donald Arseneau) redefines the command \emph to use underlining, rather than italics. It is possible to have line breaks and even primitive hyphenation in the underlined text. Every word is typeset in an underlined box, so automatic hyphenation is normally disabled, but explicit discretionary hyphens (\-) can still be used. The underlines continue between words and stretch just like ordinary spaces do. The method is, however, suitable only for fairly simple text — some LaTeX constructs, such as \footnote, do not work within the argument.

If problems occur, you might try enclosing the offending command in braces, because everything inside braces is internally put inside an \mbox. Thus, braces suppress stretching and line breaks in the text they enclose. That is one of the reasons that nested emphasis constructs are not always treated correctly by this package if the inner one contains more than a single word.

```
\usepackage{ulem}
```

Advice from Robert Bringhurst [7]: Use the virgule with words and dates, the solidus with split-level fractions.

3-4-17

```
Advice from Robert Bringhurst [7]:
\emph{Use the \emph{virgule} with words
   and dates, the \emph{solidus} with
   split-level fractions.}
```

Alternatively, underlining can be explicitly requested using the \uline command. In addition, a number of variants are available that are common in editorial markup. These are shown in the next example:

You can have single or double under-lining, a wavy underline, ~~strike out~~, or ~~cross out~~ text or use dashes or dots.

```
\usepackage{ulem}
You can have \uline{single} or \uuline{double
    under\-lining}, \uwave{a wavy underline},
\sout{strike out}, or \xout{cross out} text or use
\dashuline{dashes} or \dotuline{dots}.
```

3-4-18

The redefinition of \emph can be turned off and on by using \normalem and \ULforem. Alternatively, the package can be loaded with the option normalem to suppress this redefinition. Another package option is UWforbf, which replaces \textbf and \bfseries by \uwave whenever possible.

Instead of using these options you can explicitly direct ulem to change any basic font command or declaration to produce one of the special effects by using the declaration \useunder. This is shown in the next example, where \textit, \textbf, and \texttt has been changed to produce \uwave, \uline, and \uuline, respectively.

Historically speaking, expl3 is an acronym for EXperimental Programming Language 3 even though it is a production language.

```
\usepackage[normalem]{ulem}
\useunder{\uwave}{\itshape}{\textit}
\useunder{\uline}{\bfseries}{\textbf}
\useunder{\uuline}{\ttfamily}{\texttt}
Historically speaking, \texttt{expl3} is an acronym for
\textbf{EX}perimental \textbf{P}rogramming \textbf{L}anguage
\textbf{3} even though it is a \textit{production lan\-guage}.
```

3-4-19

The position of the line produced by \uline can be set explicitly by specifying a value for the length \ULdepth. The default value is font-dependent, denoted by the otherwise senile value \maxdimen. Similarly, the thickness of the line can be controlled via \ULthickness, which, for some historical reason, needs to be redefined using \renewcommand.

3.4.5 dashundergaps — Produce fill-in forms

An interesting application of ulem is the package dashundergaps, originally written by Luca Merciadri and reimplemented by Frank Mittelbach. Its main purpose is to provide "underlined" gaps (possibly numbered) for use in fill-in tests and similar forms. The main command it provides is \gap.

```
\gap*[type]{material}
```

This command typesets the *material* using one of the ulem commands (by default \uline) but keeps the text invisible so that one ends up with an underlined gap of the right width. This is followed by a gap number in parentheses unless the star form is used. With the help of the optional *type* argument one can explicitly request a specific form of underlining: u (underlining), d (double underlining), w (wave line), – (dash line), or . (dot line).

The next example shows most variations in the form of a fill-in puzzle. Of course, in real life using that many different variations next to another is not really recommended.

The initial 'E.' in Donald E. Knuth's name stands for ....(1). The well-known answer to the Ultimate Question _____ _____ (2) is 42 according to ⌢⌢⌢⌢⌢⌢⌢⌢(3). The first edition of _____ celebrates silver anniversary in 2019. Historically speaking, exp13 is an acronym for _even though it is now a_____ (4).

```
\usepackage{dashundergaps}
The initial 'E.' in Donald E. Knuth's name stands
for \gap[.]{Erwin}. The well-known answer to the
Ultimate Question \gap{of Life, the Universe, and
  Everything} is 42 according to \gap[w]{Douglas
  Adams}.  The first edition of \gap*[d]{The
  \LaTeX{} Companion} celebrates silver
anniversary in 2019. Historically speaking,
\texttt{expl3} is an acronym for
\gap*[-]{\textbf{EX}perimental \textbf{P}rogramming
  \textbf{L}an\-guage \textbf{3}} even though it
is now a \gap{production language}.
```

3-4-20

The package offers a large amount of customization possibilities, such as changing the default underline type, the look and feel of the gap numbers, etc. The most important one is perhaps the option widen, which enlarges each gap by a configurable percentage so that it is easier to produce forms that are intended for manual fill-in.

With \TeacherModeOn (or teachermode as an option) the gaps are filled in, and if necessary, it is possible to adjust the gapnumber counter as shown below:

The initial 'E.' in Donald E. Knuth's name stands for _ _ _ _ _ _ _ _[1]. The well-known answer to the Ultimate Question _[2] is 42 according to _ _ _ _ _ _ _ _ _ _ _ _ _[3].

```
\usepackage{dashundergaps}
\dashundergapssetup{widen, dash, gap-font=\itshape,
  teacher-gap-format=underline, gap-number-format=
    \textsuperscript{\normalfont/\thegapnumber/}}
\newcommand\puzzletext{The initial 'E.' in Donald
  E. Knuth's name stands for \gap{Erwin}. The
  well-known answer to the Ultimate Question
  \gap{of Life, the Universe, and Everything} is
  42 according to \gap{Douglas Adams}.\par}
\puzzletext
\bigskip \setcounter{gapnumber}{0} \TeacherModeOn
\puzzletext
```

The initial 'E.' in Donald E. Knuth's name stands for *Erwin*[1]. The well-known answer to the Ultimate Question *of Life, the Universe, and Everything*[2] is 42 according to *Douglas Adams*[3].

3-4-21

3.4.6 microtype & soul — Letterspacing or stealing sheep

Frederic Goudy (1865–1947) supposedly said, "Anyone who would letterspace lower case would steal sheep" and Erik Spiekermann used this quote in a title for one of his books on typography [127]. Whether true or a myth, the topic of letterspacing clearly provokes heated discussions among typographers and is considered bad practice in most situations because it changes the "gray" level of the text and thus

Tracking is the uniform increase or decrease of spacing between glyphs.	−0.05 em	(−50)
Tracking is the uniform increase or decrease of spacing between glyphs.	−0.03 em	(−30)
Tracking is the uniform increase or decrease of spacing between glyphs.	−0.02 em	(−20)
Tracking is the uniform increase or decrease of spacing between glyphs.	−0.01 em	(−10)
Tracking is the uniform increase or decrease of spacing between glyphs.	— LaTeX's default setting —	
Tracking is the uniform increase or decrease of spacing between glyphs.	+0.01 em	(10)
Tracking is the uniform increase or decrease of spacing between glyphs.	+0.02 em	(20)
Tracking is the uniform increase or decrease of spacing between glyphs.	+0.05 em	(50)
Tracking is the uniform increase or decrease of spacing between glyphs.	+0.07 em	(70)

Figure 3.1: Tracking in action

disturbs the flow of reading. Nevertheless, there are legitimate reasons for undertaking letterspacing. For example, display type often needs a looser setting, and in most fonts uppercased text is improved this way. You may also find letterspacing being used to indicate emphasis, although this exhibits the gray-level problem.

Until fairly recently the TeX engines were fairly ill equipped when it came to supporting letterspacing. In theory, the best solution is to use specially designed fonts rather than trying to solve the problem with a macro package. Because this requires the availability of such fonts, it is not an option for most users. Thus, for several decades the only practical solution was a macro-based approach implemented by Melchior Franz with his soul package, even though that means dealing with a number of restrictions.

With the event of pdfTeX version 1.4 or alternatively the LuaTeX engine, this situation changed because these engines[1] provide facilities for letterspacing (also known as tracking) as part of the font machinery. This is explored by the microtype package that we already introduced in Section 3.1.3. In the remainder of this section we now compare the two packages with respect to their letterspacing features and also show some of the other aspects of soul that make it worthwhile to consider, even though for font tracking microtype should probably be the first choice.[2] The microtype package provides two methods for tracking: ad hoc tracking through special commands and general tracking set up for individual (groups of) fonts. Figure 3.1 shows a sentence typeset at different tracking levels for comparison.

`\textls*[`*tracking-amount*`]{`*text*`}`   `{\lsstyle ... }`   `\lslig{`*ligature*`}`

Ad hoc tracking with microtype   For ad hoc letterspacing, it offers the command `\textls` that adds extra space between the characters and possibly enlarges the interword spaces in its *text* argument. The amount of tracking is either determined from a configurable database or explicitly

---

[1] Unfortunately, XᴇTeX does not offer this feature directly. Thus, the TeX world stays divided in this respect, and XᴇTeX users are either forced to use soul with its restrictions if they want to letterspace fonts or set up fonts using the `LetterSpace` font feature offered through fontspec; see Section 9.6.

[2] Please note that by loading microtype for tracking you automatically enable two other microtypographical features: protrusion and font expansion, discussed in Section 3.1.3. Normally this is sensible, but if you do not want these features, load the package with the option `activate=false`.

specified in the optional *tracking-amount* argument. The amount is specified in 1‰ of an em in the current font, the permissible range is ±1000. The default value is 100, i.e., `0.1em`, which gives reasonable results with many fonts. The default can be globally changed through the option `letterspace=`*value*.

Half the tracking amount is also added before the first and after the last character in the *text* argument to separate them a bit from surrounding material. In some situations that is undesirable, and to suppress it one can use `\textls*` as shown in the next example (look at the placement of the exclamation mark).

Because microtype operates on the font level, the tracking change is transparent for TEX so automatic hyphenation remains possible and font changes, math, etc., work seamlessly. The next example clearly proves that overdoing the amount of tracking leads to very questionable results, and for the highest quality, different fonts would clearly need different amounts of tracking to give a uniform appearance.

Nothing is letterspaced!	`\usepackage{lmodern,microtype}`
Everything is letterspaced!	`    \emph{Nothing}    is \textsf{letterspaced}! \\`
Much *too much* letter-	`\textls{\emph{Everything}  is \textsf{letterspaced}}! \\`
3-4-22 s p a c i n g!	`\textls*[230]{Much \emph{too much} \textsf{letterspacing}}!`

`\textls` is modeled after font commands such as `\textbf`. Thus, it is not so surprising that there also exists a declarative form `\lsstyle` that turns on letterspacing until the end of the current group. This then always uses the current tracking setup; i.e., there is no way to modify the tracking amount on invocation.

When writing normal text, TEX automatically takes care of constructing ligatures for you; e.g., inputting `difficult` leads to "difficult" and not "difficult". However, when letterspacing text, such ligatures should not be generated. Instead, each character should be kept separate. On the other hand, some ligatures available in fonts for TEX are purely shortcuts to ease writing the document; e.g., `---` is a convenient input form for an em-dash (—), and, of course, that character should still appear as a single character while tracking and not suddenly come out as "---". To avoid such problems, microtype takes all ligatures starting with f apart, but leaves all others alone. That default is suitable for most situations, but if not, it is easy to change this behavior either by changing the default or by using `\lslig` to tell that package that a group of characters should stay together without being tracked. For example, the Dutch ligature "IJ" is traditionally considered to be a single letter and thus should not be tracked. If necessary, `\lslig` can also be "misused" to break up ligatures that microtype would otherwise keep together, exemplified by breaking up ¡ to become !'.

	`\usepackage{lmodern,microtype}`
	`!'Hola! << ?'difficult? --- ''IJsselmeer'' \\`
¡Hola! « ¿difficult? — "IJsselmeer"	`\lsstyle`
¡Hola! « ¿difficult? — "IJsselmeer"	`!'Hola! << ?'difficult? --- ''IJsselmeer'' \\`
3-4-23 !' "IJsselmeer"	`\lslig{!}'  \hfill  ''\lslig{IJ}sselmeer''`

The amount of tracking, the adjustment to the interword spacing while tracking, which ligatures to deconstruct, etc., can all be adjusted for individual fonts or groups of fonts using \SetTracking declarations. For details refer to page 134 and the package documentation [125].

General tracking with microtype   To enable letterspacing generally with the microtype package, load the package with the option tracking[1] or specify it in the argument to \microtypesetup. As a reasonable default this activates tracking for SmallCaps fonts, i.e., those selected via \textsc or \scshape.

Normal size text and Small Caps!

Large text & Small Caps!

```
\usepackage[tracking]{microtype}

Normal size text and \textsc{Small Caps}!  \\[5pt]
{\Large Large text \&  \textsc{Small Caps}!}
```

3-4-24

The soul package also provides facilities for letterspacing (and underlining) while maintaining automatic hyphenation. The package works by parsing the text to be letterspaced or underlined, token by token, which results in a number of peculiarities and restrictions in comparison to microtype (for letterspacing) or ulem (for underlining). Thus, users who just need letterspacing and use pdfTeX or only wish to underline a few words and do not need automatic hyphenation are probably better off with microtype or ulem, which are far less picky about their input.

For LuaTeX users the suggested alternative is the lua-ul package by Marcel Krüger, which uses features of that engine to achieve highlighting, underlining, and strikethrough. It uses its own command names, but with the option soul it understands the command names of the soul package as well.

```
\caps{text}    \hl{text}    \so{text}    \st{text}    \ul{text}
```

The use of the five main user commands of soul are shown in the next example. In cases where TeX's hyphenation algorithm fails to find the appropriate hyphenation points, you can guide it as usual with the \- command. If the color package is loaded, \hl works like a text marker, coloring the background using yellow as the default color; otherwise, it behaves like \ul and underlines its argument.

With the soul package you can l e t t e r-s p a c e w o r d s a n d p h r a s e s. Capitals are LetterSpaced (not LetterSpaced) with a separate command. Interfaces for underlining, strikeouts, and highlighting are also provided.

```
\usepackage{soul,color}

With the \texttt{soul} package you can
\so{letter\-space words and phrases}. Capitals
are \caps{Letter\-Spaced} (not
\textsc{Letter\-Spaced}) with a separate command.
Interfaces for \ul{underlining}, \st{strikeouts},
and \hl{highlighting} are also provided.
```

3-4-25

The \caps command automatically applies \scshape to its argument and uses fairly subtle tracking, quite suitable for headings set in SmallCaps.

Nesting of the soul commands is not supported, but it is in fact possible to load both microtype and soul and use the former for tracking and the latter for underlining and highlighting. This way you can have letterspaced text that is underlined or otherwise highlighted.

---

[1]Not available with XeTeX.

With `microtype` you can also letterspace words and phrases while the highlighting is done with `soul`. Capitals or small capitals are then L̶E̶T̶T̶E̶R̶-̶ ̶S̶P̶A̶C̶E̶D̶ like this.

```
\usepackage{soul,color,microtype}
With \texttt{microtype} you can \textls{also
letterspace \hl{words} and \hl{phrases}} while the
highlighting is done with \texttt{soul}. Capitals
or small capitals are then \textls{\scshape
\ul{Letter\-}\st{Spaced}} like this.
```

3-4-26

Normally, the `soul` package interprets one token after another in the argument of `\so`, `\st`, and so on. However, in the case of characters that are represented by more than one token (e.g., accented characters) this might fail with some low-level TeX error messages. Fortunately, the package already knows about all common accent commands, so these are handled correctly. For others, such as those provided by the TS1 encoding (Section 9.5.6), you can announce them to `soul` with the help of a `\soulaccent` declaration. The alternative is to surround the tokens by braces.

Restrictions of the soul package

For the same reason `soul` is unable to cope with UTF-8 input characters if they are internally represented by several bytes. If you use such characters, you must load `soulutf8` (an extension written by Heiko Oberdiek) instead of `soul`.

ä̶ ̶ù̶ ̶Õ̶ ̶X̶ ̶Y̶̆

ä̶ ̶ù̶ ̶Õ̶ ̶X̶ ̶Y̶̆

```
\usepackage{soulutf8}
\soulaccent{\capitalgrave}
\Huge \st{\"a \`u \~O \capitalgrave X {\capitalbreve Y}}

% next line needs soulutf8:
        \st{ä   ù   Õ   \capitalgrave X {\capitalbreve Y}}
```

3-4-27

For comparison here is the same input using `ulem`: no adjustments are necessary. You see that the packages use a different rule width for strikeout.

ä̶ ̶ù̶ ̶Õ̶ or ä̶ ̶ù̶ ̶Õ̶ ̶X̶ ̶Y̶̆

```
\usepackage[normalem]{ulem}
\Huge\sout{ä ù Õ} or \sout{\"a \`u \~O
            \capitalgrave X \capitalbreve Y}
```

3-4-28

The `soul` package already knows that quotation characters, en-dashes, and em-dashes consist of several tokens and handles them correctly. In the case of other syntactical ligatures, such as the Spanish exclamation mark, you have to help it along with a brace group. The package also knows about math formulas as long as they are surrounded by $ signs (the form `\(...\)` is not supported), and it knows about all standard font-changing commands, such as `\textbf`. If you have defined your own font-switching command or use a package that provides additional font commands or other simple commands for use in text, you have to register them with `soul` using `\soulregister`. This declaration expects the (font) command to be registered as its first argument and the number of arguments (i.e., 0 or 1) for that command to appear as its second argument. Within the `soul` commands none of the font commands inserts any (necessary) italic correction. If needed, one has to provide it manually using `\/`.

In the next example we tell it that \enquote is a command with one argument and hide the ligature with a brace group.

"2 + 2 e q u a l s 5 ," he said.
¡FOR **EXTREMELY** LARGE VAL-
UES OF 2!

```
\usepackage{soul,csquotes}      \soulregister{\enquote}{1}
\so{\enquote{$2+2$ equals $5$,}} he said.
\caps{{!'}For \textbf{Extremely} Large Values of $2$!}
```
3-4-29

None of that would be necessary with microtype. Comparing the two examples one can see that we had to provide a definition for \caps because it is not available in microtype. The default values for tracking small caps are noticeably wider with microtype, and this package also tracks math formulas if they are in its scope, while soul leaves formulas alone.

"2 + 2 equals 5," he said.
¡FOR **EXTREMELY** LARGE
VALUES OF 2!

```
\usepackage{microtype,csquotes}
\newcommand\caps[1]{\textls{\scshape#1}}
\textls{\enquote{$2+2$ equals $5$,}} he said.
\caps{!'For \textbf{Extremely} Large Values of $2$!}
```
3-4-30

If you look carefully, you see that the font commands when used with soul suppress letterspacing directly preceding and following them — very noticeably when the font change happens within a word. This can be corrected by adding \>, which forces a tracking space. With microtype such adjustments are not needed.

Compare "b lo od y" and "b l o o d y"
with "bloody" (microtype)

```
\usepackage{soul,microtype}
Compare ''\so{bl\textbf{oo}dy}'' and
        ''\so{bl\>\textbf{oo}\>dy}'' with
        ''\textls{bl\textbf{oo}dy}'' (\texttt{microtype})
```
3-4-31

One of the most important restrictions of the above commands is that they cannot be nested; any attempt to nest soul commands results in low-level TEX errors. If you really need nesting, you have to place the inner material in a box, which means you lose the possibility of breaking the material at a line ending, or you use microtype for letterspacing and soul or ulem for underlining.

A few other commands are special within the argument of \so and friends. Spacing out at certain points can be canceled using \< or forced with \> as we saw above. As usual with LATEX a ~ produces an unbreakable space. The \\ command is supported, though only in its basic form — no star, no optional argument. You can also use \linebreak to break a line at a certain point, but again the optional argument is not supported. Other LATEX commands are likely to break the package — some experimentation will tell you what is safe and what produces havoc. By comparison, because microtype handles its tracking on the font level, it does not have any of these restrictions. However, it does not offer explicit canceling or forcing tracking kerns either, except through \textls* that suppresses the extra kerns at the outer side.

The next example shows applications of these odds and ends of soul:

"So there ..." he said. Let's
produce   a   spaced   out
line , Right?

```
\usepackage{soul}
\so{''\<So there \ldots\<'' he said.  Let's
   produce a spaced out\linebreak line\>, Right?}
```

3-4-32

Text inside a braced group is regarded as a single object during parsing by soul and is therefore not spaced out. This is handy if certain ligatures are to be kept intact inside spaced-out text. However, this method works only if the text inside the brace group contains no hyphenation points. If it does, you receive the package error message "Reconstruction failed". To hide such hyphenation points you need to put the text inside an \mbox, as shown in the second text line of the next example (TeX would hyphenate this as "Es-cher" — that is, between the "sch" that we try to keep together). You can also use \soulomit to achieve this effect, but this also suppresses the action as shown in the last line of the example (and in case of tracking the kerns on its left and right).

Schutzvorrichtung
Ausſichtsloſigkeit
Gödel, Escher, Bach
Temporarily disabling the scanner

```
\usepackage{soulutf8,yfonts}
\textfrak{\so{S{ch}u{tz}vorri{ch}tung        \\
           Au{s:}si{ch}t{s:}losigkeit}} \\
\so{Gödel, E\mbox{sch}er, Bach}              \\
\ul{Temporarily dis\soulomit{abl}ing the scanner}
```

3-4-33

When you do letterspacing with microtype, then brace groups or \mboxes do not keep ligatures together because the tracking happens at the font level and not by parsing the input. Instead, it requires the \lslig command as mentioned earlier — but then microtype usually knows which ligatures to keep so it is necessary only in unusual circumstances.

Schutzvorrichtung
Ausſichtsloſigkeit
Gödel, Escher, Bach
Gödel, Escher, Bach

```
\usepackage{microtype,yfonts}
\textfrak{\textls{Schutzvorrichtung        \\ % all
           Aus:sichts:losigkeit}} \\ % easy
\textls{Gödel, E\mbox{sch}er,  Bach}       \\ % no, but
\textls{Gödel, E\lslig{sch}er, Bach}          % yes
```

3-4-34

The position and the height of the line produced by the \ul command can be customized using either \setul or \setuldepth. The command \setul takes two dimensions as arguments: the position of the line in relation to the baseline and the height of the line. Alternatively, \setuldepth can be used to specify that the line should be positioned below the text provided as an argument. Finally, \resetul restores the default package settings.

Customizing soul's
underlining and
highlighting

Here we test
a number of
different settings.
And back to normal!

```
\usepackage{soul}
\setul{0pt}{.4pt}    \ul{Here we test}        \par
\setul{-.6ex}{.3ex}  \ul{a number of}         \par
\setuldepth{g}       \ul{different settings.} \par
\resetul             \ul{And back to normal!}
```

3-4-35

Both `\ul` and `\st` use a black rule by default. If you additionally load the color package, you can use colored rules instead and, if desired, modify the highlighting color as demonstrated below:

```
\usepackage{soul,color}
\sethlcolor{yellow} \setulcolor{blue} \setstcolor{red}
```

Rules are now in red or blue.   `Rules \hl{are now} in \st{red} or \ul{blue}.`

3-4-36

3.4.7 url — Typesetting URLs, path names, and the like

E-mail addresses, URLs, path or directory names, and similar objects usually require some attention to detail when typeset. For one thing, they often contain characters with special significance to LaTeX, such as the characters ~, #, &, %, {, or }. In addition, breaking them across lines should be avoided or at least done with special care. For example, it is usually not wise to break at a hyphen, because then it is not clear whether the hyphen was inserted because of the break (as it would be the case with normal words) or was already present. Similar reasons make breaks at a space undesirable. To help with these issues, Donald Arseneau wrote the url package, which attempts to solve most of these problems.

No Unicode support with pdfTeX

The package does not explicitly[1] provide links from URLs to external resources. If that is wanted, consider using the `\url` command of the hyperref package, which adds this functionality to the command. Another restriction is that it supports only simple ASCII strings if used with pdfTeX. If you need accented characters, etc., as part of command arguments, you have to use XeTeX or LuaTeX as your engine.

```
\url{text}    \url!text!          \path{text}    \path=text=
```

The base command provided by the package is `\url`, which is offered in two syntax variants: the *text* argument either can be surrounded by braces (in which case the *text* must not contain unbalanced braces) or, like `\verb`, can be delimited by using an arbitrary character on both sides that is not used inside *text*. (The syntax box above uses ! and =, but these are really only examples.) In that second form one can have unbalanced braces in the argument.

The `\path` command is the same except that it always uses typewriter fonts (`\ttfamily`), while `\url` can be customized as we see below. The argument to both commands is typeset pretty much verbatim. For example, `\url{~}` produces a tilde. Spaces are ignored by default, as can be seen in the following example:

```
\usepackage{url}
```

The LaTeX project web pages are at https://www.latex-project.org and my home directory is ~frank (sometimes).

```
The \LaTeX{} project web pages are at
\url{https://www . latex-project . org} and my
home directory is \path+~frank+ (sometimes).
```

3-4-37

---

[1]However, PDF viewers often guess that something is meant to be a URL and automatically provide a clickable link, but this may fail depending on context or if the URL is broken across lines.

Line breaks can happen at certain symbols (by default, not between letters or hyphens) and in no case can the commands add a hyphen at the breakpoint. Whenever the *text* contains either of the symbols % or #, or ends with \, it cannot be used in the argument to another command without producing errors (just like the \verb command). Another case that does not work properly inside the argument of another command is the use of two ˆ characters in succession. However, the situation is worse in that case because one might not even get an error but simply incorrect output[1] as the next example shows (see Example 3-4-39 for a way to correct this).

3-4-38

```
                                          \usepackage{url}
ˆfrank and ˆfrank (OK)           \url{ˆfrank}  and \mbox{\url{ˆfrank}}  (OK)  \par
ˆˆfrank but &rank (bad)          \url{ˆˆfrank} but \mbox{\url{ˆˆfrank}} (bad) \par
```

Even if the *text* does not contain any critical symbols, it is always forbidden to use such a command inside a moving argument — for instance, the argument of a \section. If used there, you get the error message

```
! Undefined control sequence.
\Url Error ->\url used in a moving argument.
```

followed by many strange errors. Even the use of \protect does not help in that case. So what can be done if one needs to cite a path name or a URL in such a place? If you are prepared to be careful and only use "safe" characters inside *text*, then you can enable the commands for use in moving arguments by specifying the option allowmove when loading the package. But this does not help if you actually need a character like "#". In that case the solution is to record the information first using \urldef and then reuse it later.

Allow \url *in moving arguments*

```
\urldef{cmd}{url-cmd}{text}    \urldef{cmd}{url-cmd}=text=
```

The declaration \urldef defines a new command *cmd* to contain the *url-cmd* (which might be \url, \path, or a newly defined command — see below) and the *text* in a way such that they can be used in any place, including a moving argument. The *url-cmd* is not executed at this point, which means that style changes can still affect the typesetting (see Example 3-4-40 on the next page). Technically, what happens is that the \catcodes of characters in *text* are frozen during the declaration so that they cannot be misinterpreted in places like arguments.

1   ˆˆfrank~#$\ works?

```
\usepackage{url}
\urldef\test\path{ˆˆfrank~#$\}
\section{\test{} works?}
```

3-4-39

It does—in contrast to the earlier example.   `It does---in contrast to the earlier example.`

---

[1]It depends on the letter that is following. An uppercase F instead of the lowercase f would produce an error.

```
\urlstyle{style}
```

We have already mentioned style changes. For this task the url package offers the `\urlstyle` command, which takes one mandatory argument: a named *style*. Predefined styles are `rm`, `sf`, `tt`, and `same`. The first three select the font family of that name, while the `same` style uses the current font and changes only the line breaking.

The `\url` command uses whatever style is currently in force (the default is `tt`, i.e., typewriter), while `\path` internally always switches to the `tt` style. In the following example we typeset a URL saved in `\lproject` several times using different styles. The particular example may look slightly horrifying, but imagine how it would have looked if the URL had not been allowed to split at all in this narrow measure.

Zapf Chancery for text! https: //latex-project.org *(default setup)* https://latex-project.org *(CM Roman)* https://latex-project.org *(CM Sans Serif)* https://latex-project.org *(CM Typewriter)* https://latex-project.org *(Zapf Chancery)*

```
\usepackage[hyphens]{url}
\urldef\lproject\url{https://latex-project.org}
\fontfamily{qzc}\selectfont Zapf Chancery for text!
                \lproject\    (default setup) \quad
\urlstyle{rm}\lproject\    (CM Roman)        \quad
\urlstyle{sf}\lproject\    (CM Sans Serif) \quad
\urlstyle{tt}\lproject\    (CM Typewriter) \quad
\urlstyle{same}\lproject\ (Zapf Chancery)
```

3-4-40

Allow line breaks after explicit hyphens
If you studied the previous example closely, you probably noticed that the option hyphens was used. This option allows breaking at explicit hyphens, something normally disabled for `\url`-like commands. Without this option, breaks would have been allowed only at the periods, after the colon, or after "//".

Spaces in the argument
As mentioned earlier, spaces inside *text* are ignored by default. If this is not desired, one can use the option obeyspaces. However, this option may introduce spurious spaces if the `\url` command is used inside the argument of another command and *text* contains any "\" character. In that case `\urldef` solves the problem. Line breaks at spaces are not allowed unless you also use the option spaces.

The package automatically detects which font encoding is currently in use. In the case of T1 encoded fonts it uses the additional glyphs available in this encoding, which improves the overall result.

Appending material at left or right
The package offers two hooks, `\UrlLeft` and `\UrlRight`, that by default do nothing but can be redefined to typeset material at the left or right of *text*. The material is typeset in the same fashion as the *text*. For example, spaces are ignored unless one uses `\␣` or specifies obeyspaces as a package option. If the commands are redefined at the top level, they act on every `\url`-like command, which may be undesirable. See Example 3-4-41 on the facing page for a possibility of restricting their scope and the issue if you do not.

```
\DeclareUrlCommand\cmd{style-information}
```

Defining URL-like commands
It is sometimes helpful to define your own commands that work similarly to `\url` or `\path` but use their own fonts, and so on. The command `\DeclareUrlCommand` can be used to define a new `\url`-like command or to modify an existing one. It

takes two arguments: the command to define or change and the *style-information* (e.g., \urlstyle). In the next example, we define \email to typeset e-mail addresses in rm style, prepending the string "e-mail: " via \UrlLeft. The example clearly shows that the scope for this redefinition is limited to the \email command. If you look closely, you can see that a space inside \UrlLeft (as in the top-level definition) has no effect, while \␣ produces the desired result.

```
\usepackage{url}
\renewcommand\UrlLeft{<url: }\renewcommand\UrlRight{>}
\DeclareUrlCommand\email{\urlstyle{rm}%
\renewcommand\UrlLeft{mail:\ }\renewcommand\UrlRight{}}
```

<url:https://latex-project.org>
mail: frank.mittelbach@latex-project.org
<url:$HOME/figures> oops picks up the
global definition!

```
\url{https://latex-project.org}              \par
\email{frank.mittelbach@latex-project.org} \par
\path{$HOME/figures} oops picks up the global definition!
```

3-4-41

The url package offers a number of further hooks that influence line breaking, among them \UrlBreaks, \UrlBigBreaks, and \UrlNoBreaks. These hooks can be redefined in the *style-information* argument of \DeclareUrlCommand to set up new or special conventions. For details consult the package documentation [3].

As mentioned earlier, Unicode characters are not supported in the commands provided by the url package if the pdfTeX engine is used. This is because they are internally represented by several bytes and the url package then typesets each byte separately without recognizing that together they represent a single glyph. As a result there is no warning, but simply wrong output:

Issues with Unicode characters when using pdfTeX

3-4-42   Garbled: ~/groÃ§e Bilder/Ã¼bel.jpg

```
\usepackage[obeyspaces]{url}
```
Garbled: \path{~/große Bilder/übel.jpg}

For URLs this is less of a problem, because the URL standard does not support such characters in URLs, but requires them to be %-encoded. However, you might run into multibyte characters in e-mail addresses or path names. In that case you need to use a Unicode engine, such as LuaTeX, to get correct output.

Linking URLs to external resources

Many PDF viewers try to be clever and automatically produce clickable regions if they think that a certain text portion is a URL, e.g., when it contains the string http:// or https://. This means that many URLs produced using \url from the url package have workable links inside the PDF even though that package does not actually provide any special support for this. However, if the URL is broken across two lines or has some unusual form, the automatically generated link may point to the wrong place or may be missing altogether.

This can be improved by also loading the hyperref package. It modifies the \url command to explicitly provide a hyperlink for each URL. If you want to use url with package options, you have to load it first; otherwise, the order does not matter. In fact, it is enough to load hyperref because that loads url if it is not already loaded.

Thus, all commands provided by the url package are available, and \url works as before, except for the fact that it produces a link and reacts to hyperref options *Avoid* that change or add link colors or borders around links. As the example shows, some *unnecessary* URL strings are interpreted as files on the local machine. Furthermore, spaces in the *spaces* URL are removed in print but remain in the link, which means that the first link is broken too.

The LaTeX project web site is: `https://` `www.latex-project.org`. However, writing `latex-project.org` would produce a link to the local file `./latex-project.org` which may or may not be right.

```
\usepackage[colorlinks,urlcolor=blue]{hyperref}
The \LaTeX\ project web site is: \url{https://
    www . latex-project . org}. However, writing
\urlstyle{sf}\url{latex-project.org} would produce
a link to the local file \path{./latex-project.org}
which may or may not be right.
```

3-4-43

If for some reason you want hyperref functionality within your document (e.g., for internal cross-references) but do not want active links to external URL resources, you can simply disable this after loading hyperref with the following declaration:

```
\DeclareUrlCommand\url{}
```

That resets the definition to the one from the url package.

3.4.8 uri — Typesetting various types of URIs

A Uniform Resource Identifier (URI) is a string of characters that unambiguously identifies a resource across a network, typically the World Wide Web. The most common type of a URI is a URL, natively understood by any Web browser, but many other types of URIs with associated protocols exist. For example, Digital Object Identifiers (DOIs) are widely used to identify academic information, such as journal articles or research reports or arXiv URIs (pronounced "archive") that refer to electronic preprints in a huge repository holding roughly 2.0 million entries. However, without suitable plugins few browsers know how to deal with `DOI:10.1111/coin.12165` or can handle a request for `arXiv:math/9201303` (Donald Knuth's paper on "Stable husbands").

The uri package by Martin Münch helps you to format such URIs uniformly in your document and — if used together with hyperref — provide clickable links in your PDF that resolve to the document location, e.g., to `https://arxiv.org/abs/math/9201303` given the above input.

The main URI types[1] supported by the package are shown in the next example:

```
\usepackage{hyperref,uri}
```

```
\begin{itemize}
\item Amazon Catalogue:            \hfill \asin{0201362996}
\item Cornell University Library:  \hfill \arxiv{math/9201303}
\item Global library cooperative (OCLC):  \hfill \oclc{935889548}
```

---

[1]There is also \oid to access data from the Object Identifier Repository and a few others.

```
\item Handle System (CNRI):          \hfill \hdl{10338.dmlcz/702604}
\item International DOI Foundation:   \hfill \doi{10.1111/coin.12165}
\item National Bibliography Number:  \hfill \nbn{urn:nbn:de:bsz:mit1-opus-3145}
\item PubMed Central (PMC):          \hfill \pubmed{24925405}
\item WebCite:                       \hfill \wc{71lh2xily}
\end{itemize}
```

The predominant use case for such commands is within bibliography entries, but if necessary, they can be used anywhere. Here is the result of the above input:

- Amazon Catalogue: `ASIN:0201362996`
- Cornell University Library: `arXiv:math/9201303`
- Global library cooperative (OCLC):   `OCLC:935889548`
- Handle System (CNRI):   `HDL:10338.dmlcz/702604`
- International DOI Foundation: `DOI:10.1111/coin.12165`
- National Bibliography Number: `urn:nbn:de:bsz:mit1-opus-3145`
- PubMed Central (PMC):   `PubMed:24925405`
- WebCite: `WC:71lh2xily`

3-4-44

If clicked, any references on the right resolve to a URL reference as long as the PDF viewer supports accessing external resources.

If you do not like the default outcome of the URI commands, you can easily adjust that using `\urisetup`. For all commands there exist keys that define the material before and after the actual URI reference. They all follow the same naming conventions with `pre` or `post` appended to the command name. Here is an example:

Customizing the outcome

```
\usepackage{uri}
\urisetup{asinpre = ASIN( , asinpost =) ,
              doipre  = \textsc{doi:}\hspace*{2pt} }
\asin{0201362996}  \\ \doi{10.1111/coin.12165}
```

ASIN(0201362996)
DOI: 10.1111/coin.12165

3-4-45

The site `https://tinyurl.com` provides a widely used free service on the Internet that maintains persistent short redirects for longish and difficult to type URLs. You provide them with the target URL, and they then assign a short URL that redirects to your target. For example, instead of referring to

Using short URLs

```
https://www.latex-project.org/publications/indexbytopic/pagination/#a
-hrefpublications2017-ci-journal-28454894assubmittedpdf-targetblank-o
nclickvgwpixelcall76c39a7e25524b9a8b93f680f6f20cbaa-general-luatex-fr
amework-for-globally-optimized-paginationa-pre-peer-reviewed-version
```

that nobody can type, you can then use something like `https://tinyurl.com/optpag` to direct people to the above URL. The uri package supports these kinds of URIs through the commands \tinyuri and \tinypuri. The latter command provides the user with a preview of the target URL and asks if they want to be redirected. The next example also shows that it is possible to adjust the look and feel of the links with options to hyperref and the font used with \urlstyle from url.

Wikipedia article on 42: TINY:424242.
Research on optimal pagination: TINY: P:optpag.

```
\usepackage[colorlinks,urlcolor=blue]{hyperref}
  \usepackage{uri}  \urlstyle{sf}
Wikipedia article on 42:        \tinyuri {424242}. \\
Research on optimal pagination: \tinypuri{optpag}.
```
3-4-46

Referencing arbitrary web pages
To archive and refer to snapshots of web pages it was possible in the past to use the free service provided by WebCite (http://www.webcitation.org/archive.php). For example, the research papers on optimal pagination at the LaTeX Project website were archived on 2018-08-18 under the Id 71lh2xily (provided by WebCite) so that they now can be referenced in a bibliographic entry, e.g., with BibTeX:

```
@Misc{FMi:optimal-pagination:2018,
   author={Frank Mittelbach},  title={Papers on automatic pagination},
   note={\url{https://latex-project.org/publications/indexbytopic/pagination}.
      Accessed: 2018-08-18. (Archived by WebCite at \wc{71lh2xily})}
}
```

Unfortunately, WebCite no longer accepts new requests, so the \wc interface stopped being useful for new material. There are, however, several other (free) services available that you can use instead, e.g., https://archive.org/web (Wayback Machine). They do not offer nice short URLs, but otherwise provide referenceable snapshots, so with a bit more work the same effect can be obtained.

To refer to normal URLs the package provides \citeurl, which works like \url but wraps the URL in angle brackets. Finally, it also offers \emailto for formatting e-mail addresses. If clicked, they then open the e-mail client with the address already prefilled. You can also provide an optional argument holding a default subject line. This does not show up in print but is automatically added as a subject in the mail client.

Website: <https://latex-project.org>.
Report errors to: mailto:webmaster@latex-project.org

```
\usepackage[colorlinks,urlcolor=blue]{hyperref}
\usepackage{uri}   \urlstyle{same}
Website:            \citeurl{https://latex-project.org}.
Report errors to: \mailto[Website error]
                    {webmaster@latex-project.org}
```
3-4-47

3.5 Footnotes, endnotes, and marginals

LaTeX has facilities to typeset "inserted" text, such as marginal notes, footnotes, figures, and tables. The present section looks more closely at different kinds of notes, while Chapter 7 describes floats in more detail.

We start by discussing the possibilities offered through standard LaTeX's footnote commands and explain how (far) they can be customized. This is followed by a presentation of the footmisc package, which overcomes most of the limitations of the standard commands and offers a wealth of additional features. The packages footnoterange and fnpct deal specifically with the formatting of the footnote markers in text, how consecutive markers should be handled, and what should happen if they come next to a punctuation mark such as a comma or a period.

Some type of documents, e.g., critical editions, require an elaborate footnote apparatus with nested footnotes — something that standard LaTeX does not offer. Both the manyfoot and bigfoot packages (which can be combined with footmisc) extend the footnote support for disciplines like linguistics by providing several independent footnote commands.

Instead of producing footnotes at the end of the page, it is sometimes useful to place such notes directly below the paragraph in which they appeared or after a consecutive group of paragraphs. This kind of "paragraph notes" is offered by the parnotes package. For two-column documents, a special layout for footnotes is provided by the ftnright package, which moves all footnotes to the bottom of the right column.

Support for endnotes is offered through the enotez package, which allows for mixing footnotes and endnotes and can also be used to provide chapter notes, as required by some publishers. The section concludes with a discussion of marginal notes, which are already provided by standard LaTeX and with two packages (marginnote and snotez) that enhance LaTeX's basic capabilities.

3.5.1 Using standard footnotes

A sharp distinction is made between footnotes in the main text and footnotes inside a minipage environment. The former are numbered using the footnote counter, while inside a minipage the \footnote command is redefined to use the mpfootnote counter. Thus, the representation of the footnote mark is obtained by the \thefootnote or \thempfootnote command depending on the context. By default, it typesets an arabic number in text and a lowercase letter inside a minipage environment. You can redefine these commands to get a different representation by specifying, for example, footnote symbols, as shown below:

A line of text* with some† footnotes.

```
\renewcommand\thefootnote{\fnsymbol{footnote}}
```

---

*The first
†The second

3-5-1

```
A line of text\footnote{The first}
with some\footnote{The second} footnotes.
```

Footnotes produced with the \footnote command inside a minipage environment use the mpfootnote counter and are typeset at the bottom of the box produced by the minipage. However, if you use the \footnotemark command in a minipage, it produces a footnote mark in the same style and sequence as the main text footnotes — that is, stepping the footnote counter and using the

Peculiarities inside a minipage

205

\thefootnote command for the representation. This behavior allows you to produce a footnote inside your minipage that is typeset in sequence with the main text footnotes at the bottom of the page: you place a \footnotemark inside the minipage and the corresponding \footnotetext after it. The downside is that you cannot nest minipage environments if they contain footnotes.

… main text …

> Footnotes in a minipage are numbered using lowercase letters.[a]
> This text references a footnote at the bottom of the page.[1] And another[b] note.
>
> _____
> [a] Inside minipage
> [b] Inside again

… main text …

_____
[1] At bottom of page

```
\noindent\ldots{} main text \ldots
\begin{center}
\begin{minipage}{.8\linewidth}
Footnotes in a minipage are numbered using
lowercase letters.\footnote{Inside minipage}
\par This text references a footnote at the
bottom of the page.\footnotemark{}
And another\footnote{Inside again} note.
\end{minipage}\footnotetext{At bottom of page}
\end{center}
\ldots{} main text \ldots
```

3-5-2

As the previous example shows, if you need to reference a minipage footnote several times, you cannot use \footnotemark because it refers to footnotes typeset at the bottom of the page.

A footmisc addition

You can, however, load the package footmisc and then use \mpfootnotemark in place of \footnotemark. Just like \footnotemark, the command first increments its counter and then displays its value. Thus, to refer to the previous value you typically have to decrement it first, as shown in the next example:

Main text …

> Footnotes in a minipage are numbered using lowercase letters.[a]
> This text references the previous footnote.[a] And another[b] note.
>
> _____
> [a] Inside minipage
> [b] Inside as well

… main text …

```
\usepackage{footmisc}
\noindent Main text \ldots
\begin{center}
\begin{minipage}{.8\linewidth}
Footnotes in a minipage are numbered using
lowercase letters.\footnote{Inside minipage}
\par This text references the previous
footnote.\addtocounter{mpfootnote}{-1}%
         \mpfootnotemark{}
And another\footnote{Inside as well} note.
\end{minipage}
\end{center} \ldots{} main text \ldots
```

3-5-3

Manipulating the footnote or mpfootnote counter to get the appropriate footnote mark is fairly cumbersome. A usually better alternative is to use a \label command in the footnote and then use \footref to generate the mark referring to it. This works for footnotes inside and outside of `minipages` as the next example shows:

Main text with a footnote[1] ...

> Footnotes in a minipage are numbered using lowercase letters.[a] This text references a footnote at the bottom[1] of the page. And another[b] note.
>
> ───────────
> [a]Inside minipage
> [b]Inside again

... main text referencing minipage footnote.[a]

───────────
[1]At bottom

3-5-4

```
\noindent Main text with a
  footnote\footnote{\label{A}At bottom} \ldots
\begin{center}
 \begin{minipage}{.8\linewidth}
  Footnotes in a minipage are numbered using
  lowercase letters.\footnote{\label{B}Inside
   minipage} This text references a footnote
  at the bottom\footref{A} of the page.
  And another\footnote{Inside again} note.
 \end{minipage}
\end{center}
\ldots{} main text referencing minipage
footnote.\footref{B}
```

LaTeX does not allow you to use a `\footnote` inside another `\footnote` command, as is common in some disciplines. You can, however, use the `\footnotemark` command inside the first footnote and then put the text of the footnote's footnote as the argument of a `\footnotetext` command. For other special footnote requirements consider using the bigfoot or the manyfoot package (described below).

Some[1] text and some more text.

───────────
[1]A sample[2] footnote.
[2]A subfootnote.

3-5-5

```
Some\footnote{A sample\footnotemark{}
footnote.}\footnotetext{A subfootnote.}
text and some more text.
```

What if you want to reference a given footnote? You can use LaTeX's normal `\label` and `\ref` mechanism, although you may want to define your own command to typeset the reference in a special way. For instance:

This is some text.[1] ...
As shown in footnote (1) on page 6, ...

───────────
[1]Text inside referenced footnote.

3-5-6

```
\newcommand\fnref[1]{\unskip~(\ref{#1})}
This is some text.\footnote{Text inside
referenced footnote\label{fn:myfoot}.} \ldots\par
As shown in footnote\fnref{fn:myfoot} on
page~\pageref{fn:myfoot}, \ldots
```

Standard LaTeX does not allow you to construct footnotes inside tabular material. Section 6.8 describes several ways of tackling that problem.

If a footnote in the main text does not fit on the current page, then LaTeX attempts to split it and continue the footnote text on the next column or page. If this does not succeed, e.g., because there is no breakpoint that would make part of the footnote fit, then the whole footnote and the text line containing the footnote marker is moved. As a consequence, if there are two footnotes on the same line and the first already requires splitting, then everything is moved to the next page because the second footnote could not even start.

Handling of split footnotes

The footnote splitting is happening automatically, and the only control you have is adding something like \nopagebreak into the footnote text to prevent a split after a certain line. Of course, as an author there is always the possibility of rewriting your text so that the footnote appears elsewhere or becomes unnecessary.

Problem with color

If color is used inside footnotes, then you may see a problem that the color is lost after the split. In that case load the package pdfcolfoot, which extends the color support in PDF documents. There is work under way to improve the color support in LaTeX, so this package is only a temporary solution.

3.5.2 Customizing standard footnotes

Footnotes in LaTeX are generally simple to use and provide a quite powerful mechanism for typesetting material at the bottom of a page. This material can consist of several paragraphs and can include lists, inline or display mathematics, tabular material, and so on.

LaTeX offers several parameters for customizing footnotes. They are shown schematically in Figure 3.2 on the next page and are described below:

\footnotesize The font size used inside footnotes (see also Table 9.1 on page 666).

\footnotesep The height of a strut placed at the beginning of every footnote. If it is greater than the \baselineskip used for \footnotesize, then additional vertical space is inserted above each footnote. See Appendix A.3.3 for more information about struts.

\skip\footins A low-level TeX length parameter that defines the space between the main text and the start of the footnotes. You can change its value with the \setlength or \addtolength command by putting \skip\footins into the first argument, e.g., \addtolength{\skip\footins}{10mm plus 2mm}.

\footnoterule A macro to draw the rule separating footnotes from the main text that is executed right after the vertical space of \skip\footins. It should take zero vertical space; that is, it should use a negative skip to compensate for any positive space it occupies. The default definition is equivalent to the following:

```
\renewcommand\footnoterule{\vspace*{-3pt}%
    \hrule width 2in height 0.4pt \vspace*{2.6pt}}
```

Note that TeX's \hrule command and not LaTeX's \rule command is used. Because the latter starts a paragraph, it would be difficult to calculate the spaces needed to achieve a net effect of zero height. For this reason producing a fancier "rule" is perhaps best done by using a zero-sized picture environment to position the rule object without actually adding vertical space.

In the report and book classes, footnotes are numbered inside chapters; in article, footnotes are numbered sequentially throughout the document. You can change

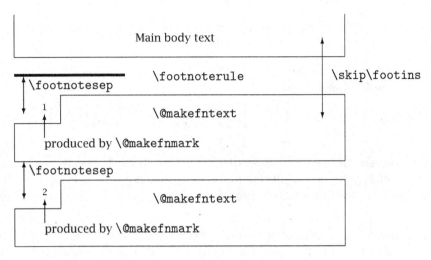

Figure 3.2: Schematic layout of footnotes

that default by using the \counterwithin or \counterwithout command (see Appendix A.2.1). However, do not try to number your footnotes within pages with the help of this mechanism. LaTeX is looking ahead while producing the final pages, so your footnotes would most certainly be numbered incorrectly. To number footnotes on a per-page basis, use the footmisc or perpage package (described below).

The command \@makefnmark is normally used to generate the footnote mark. One would expect this command to take one argument (the current footnote number), but in fact it takes none. Instead, it uses the command \@thefnmark to indirectly refer to that number. The reason is that depending on the position (inside or outside of a minipage) a different counter needs to be accessed. The definition, which by default produces a superscript mark, looks roughly as follows:

```
\renewcommand\@makefnmark
        {\mbox{\textsuperscript{\normalfont\@thefnmark}}}
```

The \footnote command executes \@makefntext inside a \parbox, with a width of \columnwidth. The default version looks something like:

```
\newcommand\@makefntext[1]
        {\noindent\makebox[1.8em][r]{\@makefnmark}#1}
```

This places the footnote mark right aligned into a box of width 1.8em directly followed by the footnote text. Note that it reuses the \@makefnmark macro, so any change to it will, by default, modify the display of the mark in both places. If you want the text set flush left with the number placed into the margin, then you could use the redefinition shown in the next example. Here we do not use \@makefnmark to format the mark, but rather access the number via \@thefnmark. As a result, the mark is placed onto the baseline instead of being raised. Thus, the marks in the text and at the bottom are formatted differently:

A line of text[1] with some[2] footnotes.

1. The first
2. The second

```
\makeatletter
\renewcommand\@makefntext[1]%
    {\noindent\makebox[0pt][r]{\@thefnmark.\,}#1}
\makeatother

A line of text\footnote{The first}
with some\footnote{The second} footnotes.
```

3-5-7

However, instead of manipulating footnote commands directly as done above, it is usually better to load the footmisc package that provides higher-level declarations to adjust these commands to your liking.

3.5.3 footmisc — Various footnotes styles

Since standard LaTeX offers only one type of footnotes and only limited (and somewhat low-level) support for customization, several people developed small packages that provided features otherwise not available. Many of these earlier efforts were captured by Robin Fairbairns (1947–2022) in his footmisc package (these days maintained by Frank Mittelbach), which supports, among other things, page-wise numbering of footnotes and footnotes formatted as a single paragraph at the bottom of the page. In this section we describe the features provided by this package, showing which packages it supersedes whenever applicable.

The interface for footmisc is quite simple: nearly everything is customized by specifying options when the package is loaded, though in some cases further control is possible via parameters.

Numbering footnotes per page

In the article class, footnotes are numbered sequentially throughout the document; in report and book, footnotes are numbered inside chapters. Sometimes, however, it is more appropriate to number footnotes on a per-page basis. This can be achieved by loading footmisc with the option perpage, which loads the package perpage (see Section 3.5.6 on page 218). Since TeX's page-building mechanism is asynchronous, it is always necessary to process the document at least twice to get the numbering correct. Fortunately, the package warns you via "Rerun to get cross-references right" if the footnote numbers are incorrect. The package stores information between runs in the .aux file, so after a lot of editing this information is sometimes not even close to reality. In such a case deleting the .aux file helps the package to find the correct numbering faster.[1]

Some text* with a footnote. More† text.

*First.
†Second.

Even more text.* And even† more text. Some

*Third.
†Fourth.

```
\usepackage[perpage,symbol]{footmisc}
Some text\footnote{First.} with a footnote.
More\footnote{Second.} text. Even more
text.\footnote{Third.} And even\footnote
{Fourth.} more text. Some final text.
```

3-5-8

---

[1] In fact, during the preparation of this chapter we managed to confuse footmisc (by changing the \textheight in an example) so much that it was unable to find the correct numbering thereafter and kept asking for a rerun forever. Removing the .aux file resolved the problem.

Name	List of Symbols															
lamport	*	†	‡	§	¶	‖	**	††	‡‡	§§	¶¶	***	†††	‡‡‡	§§§	¶¶¶
bringhurst	*	†	‡	§	‖	¶										
chicago	*	†	‡	§	‖	#										
wiley	*	**	†	‡	§	¶	‖									

Table 3.7: Footnote symbol lists predefined by footmisc

For this special occasion our example shows two pages side by side so you can observe the effects of the `perpage` option. The example also shows the effect of another option: `symbol` uses footnote symbols instead of numbers. Because only a limited number of such symbols are available, you can use this option only if there are few footnotes in total or if footnote numbers restart on each page. There are six different footnote symbols and, by duplicating some, standard LATEX supports nine footnotes. By triplicating some of them, footmisc supports up to 16 footnotes (per page or in total). If this number is exceeded, you get a LATEX error message.

Counter too large errors …

In particular with the `perpage` option, this behavior can be a nuisance because the error could be spurious, happening only while the package is still trying to determine which footnotes belong on which page. To avoid this problem, you can use the variant option `symbol*`, which also produces footnote symbols but numbers footnotes for which there are no symbols left with arabic numerals. In that case you get a warning at the end of the run that some footnotes were out of range and detailed information is placed in the transcript file.

… are sometimes spurious (but can be avoided)

`\setfnsymbol{`*name*`}`

If the `symbol` or `symbol*` option is selected, a default sequence of footnote symbols, as defined by Leslie Lamport, is used. Other authorities suggest different sequences, so footmisc offers three other sequences to choose from using the declaration `\setfnsymbol` (see Table 3.7). This declaration only changes the meaning of the `\fnsymbol` command; it does *not* change the counter formatting of footnotes — for the latter you have to additionally specify the `symbol` or `symbol*` option, or redefine `\thefootnote`, so that it formats the counter using `\fnsymbol`.

`\DefineFNsymbols*{`*name*`}[`*type*`]{`*list of symbols*`}`
`\DefineFNsymbolsTM*{`*name*`}{`*list of symbol pairs*`}`

It is also possible to define your own sequence using a `\DefineFNsymbols` declaration in the preamble. It takes two mandatory arguments: the *name* to access the list later via `\setfnsymbol` and a *list of symbols*. From this list symbols are taken one after another (with spaces ignored). If a symbol is built from more than one glyph, it has to be surrounded by braces. If the starred form of the declaration is used, LATEX issues an error message if it runs out of symbols. Without it, you get arabic numerals and a warning at the end of the LaTeX run.

Due to an unfortunate design choice, footnote symbols (as well as some other text symbols) were originally added to the math fonts of TeX, rather than to the text fonts, with the result that they did not change when the text font was modified. In today's LaTeX this flaw was corrected by adding these symbols to the text symbol encoding (TS1; see Section 9.5.6), and LaTeX's default set of footnote symbols are now taken from the companion text symbol font unless the footnote itself is within a formula.

If you define your own sequence, you can use the optional *type* argument with the value `math` or `text` (the default) to tell footmisc that your list consists of math or text symbols, respectively. If you choose `math`, then the symbols are all wrapped in `\ensuremath` so that they can be safely used in text as well.

Alternatively, you can use a `\DefineFNsymbolsTM` declaration. It does not have an optional argument and instead expects pairs of text/math symbols in its second mandatory argument, which are pairwise wrapped in `\TextOrMath`. This is the way the default sequences in Table 3.7 are defined.

Some text[*] with a footnote. More[**] text. Even more text.[***]   And even[****] more text. Some more text to finish up.

---
[*]First.
[**]Second.
[***]Third.
[****]Fourth.

```
\usepackage[symbol]{footmisc}
\DefineFNsymbols{stars}[text]{* {**} {***} {****}}
\setfnsymbol{stars}

Some text\footnote{First.} with a footnote.
More\footnote{Second.} text. Even more
text.\footnote{Third.} And even\footnote{Fourth.}
more text. Some more text to finish up.
```

3-5-9

If you have many short footnotes, then their default placement at the bottom of the page, stacked on top of each other, is perhaps not completely satisfactory. A typical example would be critical editions, which contain many short footnotes.[1] The layout of the footnotes can be changed using the `para` option, which formats them into a single paragraph. If this option is chosen, then footnotes never split across pages. The code for this option is based on earlier work by Chris Rowley and Dominik Wujastyk, which in turn was inspired by an example in *The TeXbook* by Donald Knuth.

Some text with a footnote.[1] More text.[2] Even more text.[3] Some final text.

---
[1] A first.   [2] A second.   [3] A third.

```
\usepackage[para]{footmisc}
Some text with a footnote.\footnote{A first.}
More text.\footnote{A second.}  Even more
text.\footnote{A third.}  Some final text.
```

3-5-10

Another way to deal with footnotes is given by the option `side`. In this case footnotes are placed into the margin, if possible on the same line where they are referenced. What happens internally is that special `\marginpar` commands are used

---
[1]See, for example, the reledmac package [120] by Maïeul Rouquette for the kinds of footnotes and endnotes that are common in critical editions. This package is a reimplementation of the EDMAC system for LaTeX and was initially made available by Peter Wilson as ledmac. See also the bigfoot package by David Kastrup described in Section 3.5.7.

to place the footnote text, so everything said in Section 3.5.11 about the \marginpar commands is applicable. This option cannot be used together with the para option, described earlier, but can be combined with most others.

[1] A first.

[2] A second.

[3] A third.

[4] A fourth.

Some text with a footnote.[1] A lot of additional text here with a footnote.[2] Even more text and then another footnote.[3] Some more text.[4] A lot of additional lines of text here to fill up the space on the left.

```
\usepackage[side,flushmargin]{footmisc}
Some text with a footnote.\footnote{A first.}
A lot of additional text here with a
footnote.\footnote{A second.} Even more text
and then another footnote.\footnote{A third.}
Some more text.\footnote{A fourth.} A lot
of additional lines of text here to fill up
the space on the left.
```

3-5-11

The option flushmargin used in the previous example makes the footnote text start at the left margin with the footnote marker protruding into the margin; by default, the footnote text is indented. For obvious reasons this option is incompatible with the para option. A variant form is called marginal. If this option is used, then the marker sticks even farther into the margin, as shown in the example below:

Some text[1] with a footnote. More text.[2] Even more text.[3] Some final

[1] A first.

[2] A second footnote with a few lines of text to show variations in the footnote line-breaking behavior.

[3] A third note.

```
\usepackage[marginal]{footmisc}
\newcommand\sampletext{Some text\footnote{A first.}
  with a footnote. More text.\footnote{A second
  footnote with a few lines of text to show
  variations in the footnote line-breaking behavior.}
Even more text.\footnote{A third note.}
Some final text.}
\sampletext
```

3-5-12

Instead of using one of the above options, the position of the footnote marker can be directly controlled using the parameter \footnotemargin. If set to a negative value, the marker is positioned in the margin. A value of 0pt is equivalent to using the option flushmargin. A positive value (default is 1.8em) means that the footnote text is indented by this amount and the marker is placed flush right in the space produced by the indentation.

Some text[1] with a footnote. More text.[2] Even

[1] A first.

[2] A second footnote with a few

more text.[3] Some final text.

lines of text to show variations in the footnote line-breaking behavior.

[3] A third note.

```
\usepackage{footmisc}
\setlength\footnotemargin{10pt}

\sampletext   % as defined above
```

3-5-13

Instead of indenting the first line of a footnote, you can also have all lines indented by the same amount (\footnotemargin) with the footnote marker placed into that space. This is achieved by specifying the option hang with a suitable setting for \footnotemargin as shown in the next example. This example also uses the splitrule option discussed below:

Some text[1] with a foot-note. More text.[2] Even

---
[1] A first.
[2] A second footnote with a few lines of text to show

more text.[3] Some final text.

---
variations in the footnote line-breaking behavior.
[3] A third note.

```
\usepackage[hang,splitrule]{footmisc}
\setlength\footnotemargin{6pt}

\sampletext % as defined before
```

3-5-14

By default, the footnote text is justified, but this does not always give satisfactory results, especially with the options para and side. In the case of the para option nothing can be done, but for other layouts you can switch to ragged-right typesetting by using the option ragged. The next example does not specify flushmargin, so we get an indentation of width \footnotemargin (which we made smaller than its default) — compare this to Example 3-5-11 on the preceding page.

```
\usepackage[side,ragged]{footmisc}
\setlength\footnotemargin{5pt}

A lot of additional text here to fill
up\footnote{In the margin ragged
  right often looks best. Do you agree?}
the space in the example. Include some
text with a footnote and some more.
```

A lot of additional text here to fill up[1] the space in the example. Include some text with a footnote and some more.

[1] In the margin ragged right often looks best. Do you agree?

3-5-15

Rules separating footnotes

The two options norule and splitrule (courtesy of Donald Arseneau) modify the rule normally placed between text and footnotes. If norule is specified, then the separation rule is suppressed. As compensation the value of \skip\footins is slightly enlarged. If a footnote does not fit onto the current page, it is split and continued on the next page, unless the para option is used (it does not support split footnotes). By default, the rule separating normal and split footnotes from preceding text is the same. If you specify the option splitrule as done in Example 3-5-14, however, it becomes customizable: the rule above split footnotes runs across the whole column while the one above normal footnotes retains the default definition given by \footnoterule. More precisely, this option introduces the commands \mpfootnoterule (for use in minipages), \pagefootnoterule (for use on regular pages), and \splitfootnoterule (for use on pages starting with a split footnote). By modifying their definitions, similar to the example given earlier for the \footnoterule command, you can customize the layout according to your needs.

Some text[1] with a footnote. More text.[2] Even more text.[3] Some final text.

---
[1] A first. [2] A second footnote with a few lines of text to show variations in the footnote line-breaking behavior. [3] A third note.

```
\usepackage[norule,para]{footmisc}

\sampletext   % as defined previously
```

3-5-16

By default LaTeX places footnotes below the text followed by the bottom floats, if present. In classes such as article or report in which \raggedbottom is in effect, so that columns are allowed to be of different heights, the footnotes are attached at a distance of \skip\footins from the column text, unless the page contains infinite stretchable space, e.g., coming from ending it with \newpage or \clearpage. In such a case the footnotes are pushed to the bottom, which is quite noticeable on the last page of the document or a chapter that is typically only partly filled. This strange behavior is corrected by any of the options that adjust the footnote placement on the page; e.g., abovefloats corrects it but otherwise keeps the standard order.

A strange behavior in standard LaTeX when prematurely ending a page

By loading the package with the option belowfloats you can swap the order of footnotes and bottom floats. You can also request abovefloats to enforce the default order or to ensure that the \newpage behavior is corrected without any other change.

Swapping footnotes and floats …

If you want any bottom float to be aligned at the bottom, even if \raggedbottom is in force, specify the option bottomfloats. If you prefer the footnotes to be always aligned on the bottom instead, you can specify the option bottom. This automatically swaps the order of footnotes and bottom floats if both are present on the page.

… or pushing footnotes or floats to the bottom …

By suitably combining these options you can force both footnotes and floats to the bottom (i.e., any excess space on the pages goes directly after the text). The combination of bottom and abovefloats puts footnotes and floats at the bottom (in that order), and bottomfloats together with belowfloats puts both at the bottom (with the footnotes last). The other combinations are duplicates, e.g., bottom, belowfloats is the same as just specifying bottom.

… or pushing both to the bottom

The footmisc package deals with one other potential problem: if you put a footnote into a sectional unit, then it might appear in the table of contents or the running header, causing havoc. Of course, you could prevent this dilemma (manually) by using the optional argument of the heading command; alternatively, you could specify the option stable, which prevents footnotes from appearing in such places.

Footnotes in headings

In some documents, e.g., literary analysis, several footnotes may appear at a single point. Unfortunately, LaTeX's standard footnote commands are not able to handle this situation correctly: the footnote markers are simply clustered together so that you cannot tell whether you are to look for the footnotes 1 and 2, or for the footnote with the number 12.

Several footnotes at the same point

Some text[1][2] with two footnotes.
Even more text.[3]

─────

[1] A first. [2] A second. [3] A third.

3-5-17

```
\usepackage[para]{footmisc}

Some text\footnote{A first.}\footnote{A second.} with
two footnotes. Even more text.\footnote{A third.}
```

This problem is resolved by specifying the option multiple, which ensures that footnotes in a sequence display their markers separated by commas. The separator can be changed to something else, such as a small space, by changing the command \multfootsep. Below we used a vertical bar for illustration purposes.

Some text[1|2] with two footnotes.
Even more text.[3]

─────

[1] A first. [2] A second. [3] A third.

3-5-18

```
\usepackage[multiple,para]{footmisc}
\renewcommand\multfootsep{|}

Some text\footnote{A first.}\footnote{A second.} with
two footnotes. Even more text.\footnote{A third.}
```

3.5.4 footnoterange — Referencing footnote ranges

If you have to deal with many footnotes at a single point, then you may find the above layout still suboptimal. In that case you may want to try the footnoterange package by Martin Münch. It provides the environment footnoterange, and within its scope all footnotes are collected, and (at the end of the environment) a single mark with a range, e.g., "$^{2-4}$" is displayed.

If hyperlinks to footnotes are enabled (through the package hyperref), then ranges of footnotes are hyperlinked as well, pointing to the first and last footnotes in the range. This can be suppressed by using the footnoterange* environment. Both environments provide the same results when hyperlinking is disabled.

It is possible to use the footnoterange package together with the multiple option from footmisc. In that case the option affects only those footnotes outside the scope of a footnoterange environment, as shown in the next example:

Some text.[1-3] with three footnotes. Even more text.[4,5]

---

[1] A first.   [2] Second.   [3] Third.
[4] One more.   [5] Another one.

```
\usepackage[para,multiple]{footmisc} \usepackage{footnoterange}
Some text.\begin{footnoterange}
          \footnote{A first.}\footnote{Second.}%
          \footnote{Third.}          \end{footnoterange}
with three footnotes. Even more
text.\footnote{One more.}\footnote{Another one.}
```
3-5-19

The final example shows that the environment can contain text as well as footnotes, which are then collected and a single range mark written at the end of the environment. It also shows that the environment works within minipages and in particular with footnote mark setups that do not use arabic numerals (as long as they support ranges).

Some text with three footnotes.[a-c] Even more text.[d,1]

---

[a] A first.
[b] Second.
[c] Third (moved).
[d] One more.

---

[1] An external one.

```
\usepackage[multiple]{footmisc} \usepackage{footnoterange}
\fbox{\begin{minipage}{.95\textwidth}
  Some text\begin{footnoterange}
          \footnote{A first.}\footnote{Second.} with
          three footnotes.\footnote{Third (moved).}
       \end{footnoterange}
  Even more text.\footnote{One more.}\footnotemark
\end{minipage}}\footnotetext{An external one.}
```
3-5-20

A different approach to obtain ranges of footnote marks (without the need of a dedicated environment) is offered by the fnpct package discussed below.

3.5.5 fnpct — Managing footnote markers and punctuation

When footnote or endnotes are placed next to a punctuation character, there is the question of how to place the marker in relation to the punctuation. Bringhurst suggests that if the marker is a raised symbol, then it could placed (partly) over low punctuation, e.g., a period or a comma, to avoid the otherwise noticeable gap [7].

The package fnpct by Clemens Niederberger can be used to make this adjustment for you. It works by modifying footnote and endnote commands so that they look *forward* in the input for a comma or period and if found adjust the placement by exchanging the punctuation and the marker position and also move them closer together so that they partly overlap.

This has two consequences: the punctuation must always *follow* the note command, even if the footnote or endnote is meant to apply to the whole sentence or phrase.[1] Furthermore, while fnpct works with nearly every other footnote or endnote package, the automatic detection of consecutive note commands as for example implemented by the multiple option of footmisc will not work well with it. For that reason fnpct provides its own, and the footmisc option is simply not needed.

We use the following text to demonstrate different aspects of the package and its customization possibilities. Here we show the results when the package is *not* loaded (we use footmisc to provide handling of consecutive footnotes and get all footnote text somewhat compressed at the bottom):

The three little pigs built their houses out of straw[1], sticks[2] and bricks[3,4].

---
[1] not to be confused with hay   [2] or lumber according to some sources   [3] probably fired clay bricks   [4] With kind permission by Clemens.

```
\usepackage[para,multiple]{footmisc}
The three little pigs built their houses out of
straw\footnote{not to be confused with hay},
sticks\footnote{or lumber according to some sources}
and bricks\footnote{probably fired clay
  bricks}\footnote{With kind permission by Clemens.}.
```

3-5-21

If we now also apply the fnpct package (and drop the option multiple from footmisc), we get the following result:

The three little pigs built their houses out of straw,[1] sticks[2] and bricks.[3,4]

---
[1] not to be confused with hay   [2] or lumber according to some sources   [3] probably fired clay bricks   [4] With kind permission by Clemens.

```
\usepackage[para]{footmisc} \usepackage{fnpct}
The three little pigs built their houses out of
straw\footnote{not to be confused with hay},
sticks\footnote{or lumber according to some sources}
and bricks\footnote{probably fired clay
  bricks}\footnote{With kind permission by Clemens.}.
```

3-5-22

The first marker has exchanged its position with the comma and was slightly moved backwards by the amount specified by the key after-punct-space (default -0.06em). After the second marker there is no punctuation. In that case it is slightly moved to the right by the amount given by the key before-footnote-space (default 0.06em). Changes to both are demonstrated in Example 3-5-23. The last two markers show that this also works well with consecutive markers: the period exchanged its position with both markers and is moved up front.

| \footnote*[*mark*]{*note*}   \footnotemark*[*mark*] | *% extended* |

The package extends the footnote command syntax by adding a star form (where applicable). If used, it prevents the exchange of punctuation and footnote mark for

---
[1] Technically it is much easier for LaTeX to look ahead than to look back.

the current instance. For example, it could be used to make the first note attach to the word "straw" and not exchange places with the following comma.

Additionally, the package handles consecutive \footnote commands. The resulting footnote markers are then combined using a comma or some other material (key separation-symbol) as output separator. As before, the star form of the command prevents the exchange of markers and punctuation.

In case there are three or more consecutive footnotes they can be turned into a range by specifying ranges as shown in the next example. There are, however, some dependencies on other packages, and you may have to additionally set keep-ranges, for instance with hyperref. See the package documentation [108] for details.

The same syntax extension is provided for "endnote" commands in case fnpct is used with enotez or any other supported package. We exhibit the extended commands in conjunction with enotez below (endnotes are not shown):

```
\usepackage{fnpct,enotez}
\setfnpct{after-punct-space=-0.2em,
          before-footnote-space=0pt,ranges}
```

The three little pigs built
their houses out of straw[1],
sticks[2] and bricks[3–5]

```
The three little pigs built their houses out of
straw\endnote*{not to be confused with hay},
sticks\endnote{or lumber according to some sources} and
bricks\endnote{probably fired clay bricks}\endnote{With
kind permission by Clemens.}\endnote{I asked, honestly.}.
```

3-5-23

Keys are specified with the command \setfnpct that for most keys can be used both in the preamble as well as in the document. Above we used it for modifying the spacing. Most keys have default values that are applied if you use the key without a value; for example, above we used ranges without specifying =true.

There are more than twenty other customization possibilities for special scenarios, among them the possibility of including other punctuation characters into the mechanism. As mentioned earlier, fnpct works well together with most other footnote or endnote packages, among them bigfoot, endnotes, enotez, footmisc, manyfoot, parnotes, and snotez. However, in some cases it is necessary to provide the preamble declarations in some specific order. If you run into problems or have additional customization needs, consult the package documentation [108], which gives detailed advice and also describes the mechanisms to adapt further packages to fnpct.

3.5.6 perpage — Resetting counters on a "per-page" basis

As mentioned earlier, the ability to reset arbitrary counters on a per-page basis is implemented in the small package perpage written by David Kastrup.

> \MakePerPage [*start*] {*counter*}

The declaration \MakePerPage defines *counter* to be reset on every page, optionally requesting that its initial starting value be *start* (default 1). For demonstration we repeat Example 3-5-8 on page 210 but start each footnote marker sequence with the second symbol (i.e., "†" instead of "*").

<table>
<tr><td>Some text† with a footnote. More‡ text.</td><td>Even more text.† And even‡ more text. Some</td></tr>
<tr><td>————
†First.
‡Second.</td><td>————
†Third.
‡Fourth.</td></tr>
</table>

3-5-24

```
\usepackage[symbol]{footmisc}
\usepackage{perpage}
\MakePerPage[2]{footnote}
Some text\footnote{First.} with a footnote.
More\footnote{Second.} text. Even more
text.\footnote{Third.} And even\footnote
{Fourth.} more text. Some final text.
```

The package synchronizes the numbering via the .aux file of the document, thus requiring at least two runs to get the numbering correct. In addition, you may get spurious "Counter too large" error messages on the first run if \fnsymbol or \alph is used for numbering (see the discussion of the symbol* option for the footmisc package on page 211).

Among LaTeX's standard counters probably only footnote can be sensibly modified in this way. Nevertheless, one can easily imagine applications that provide, say, numbered marginal notes, which could be defined as follows:

```
\newcounter{mnote}    \renewcommand\themnote{\alph{mnote}}
\usepackage{perpage}  \MakePerPage{mnote}
\newcommand\mnote[1]{%
  {\refstepcounter{mnote}%
  \marginpar[\small\raggedleft\textsuperscript{(\themnote)}\itshape #1]%
         {\small\raggedright\textsuperscript{(\themnote)}\itshape #1}%
}}
```

We step the new counter mnote outside the \marginpar so that it is executed only once[1]; we also need to limit the scope of the current redefinition of \label (through \refstepcounter) so we put braces around the whole definition. Notes on left-hand pages should be right aligned, so we use the optional argument of \marginpar to provide different formatting for this case.

<table>
<tr><td>(a)First.   Some text with a footnote. More[1] text.
(b)Third! Even more text. And</td><td>even more text. Final (a)Fourth. text.[2]</td></tr>
<tr><td>————
[1]Second as footnote.</td><td>————
[2]Fifth!</td></tr>
</table>

3-5-25

```
% code as above
Some text\mnote{First.} with a
footnote. More\footnote{Second
as footnote.} text. Even more
text.\mnote{Third!} And even
more\mnote {Fourth.} text.
Final text.\footnote{Fifth!}
```

Another application for the package is given in Example 3-5-30 on page 223, where several independent footnote streams are all numbered on a per-page basis.

---
[1]If placed in both arguments of \marginpar, it would be executed twice. It would work if placed in the optional argument only, but then we would make use of an implementation detail (that the optional argument is evaluated first) that may change.

`\theperpage`	`\AddAbsoluteCounter{cnt}`

In addition to numbering some elements on a per-page basis you may want to include the page number into the counter representation, e.g., to display the float numbers (if numbered per page) prefixed by the page on which they appear. A simple approach using `\thepage`, e.g.,

```
\renewcommand\thefigure{\thepage-\arabic{figure}}   % fails!
```

would fail, because `\thepage` may not have the correct value when the element is constructed. Instead, you can use `\theperpage`, which would refer to the page at the time the corresponding counter is stepped. Below is a variation of Example 3-5-24 that uses this approach.

Another feature of the package is its ability to define counters that automatically increment with their companion counter but are never reset. `\AddAbsoluteCounter` expects an existing counter name as its argument and provides an additional counter prefixed by `abs`. This way you can count the total number of pages, equations, sections, or any other element with an associated counter. The absolute counter for pages `abspage` is automatically defined by the package. Please note, though, that if used shortly after a page break, it may report the wrong number of pages when the pagination algorithm looks ahead; e.g., without the `\par` command, it would incorrectly report just one page!

```
\usepackage{perpage} \MakePerPage{footnote}
\renewcommand\thefootnote
      {\theperpage.\arabic{footnote}}
\AddAbsoluteCounter{footnote}
```

Some text[6.1] with a footnote. More[6.2] text. Even more text.[6.3] And	even[7.1] more text. There have been 5 footnotes in total.
	This document has 2 pages.
_____	
[6.1]First.	
[6.2]Second.	
[6.3]Third.	_____
	[7.1]Fourth.

```
Some text\footnote{First.} with a footnote.
More\footnote{Second.} text. Even more
text.\footnote{Third.} And even\footnote
{Fourth.} more text. There have been
\theabsfootnote{} footnotes in total. \par
This document has \theabspage{} pages.
```

$\boxed{\text{3-5-26}}$

3.5.7 manyfoot, bigfoot — Independent footnotes

Most documents have only a few footnotes, if any. For them LATEX's standard commands plus the enhancements offered by footmisc are usually sufficient. However, certain applications, such as critical editions, require several independently numbered footnote streams. For these situations the package manyfoot by Alexander Rozhenko, and the even more comprehensive package bigfoot by David Kastrup can provide valuable help.

Both packages use largely the same interfaces so we describe them together. They do, however, differ with respect to capabilities and results so that there are cases for favoring one over the other as discussed below. Differences are discussed as appropriate next to the examples.

\DeclareNewFootnote[*fn-style*]{*suffix*}[*enum-style*]

This declaration can be used to introduce a new footnote level. In its simplest form you merely specify a *suffix* such as "B". This allocates a new counter footnote⟨*suffix*⟩ that is used to automatically number the footnotes on the new level. The default is to use arabic numerals; by providing the optional argument *enum-style*, some other counter style (e.g., roman or alph) can be selected.

The optional *fn-style* argument defines the general footnote style for the new level; the default is plain. If the manyfoot package was loaded with the para or para* option, then para can also be selected as the footnote style. With bigfoot the *fn-style* para can be chosen without loading any additional option.

The declaration then automatically defines six commands for you. The first three are described here:

\footnote⟨*suffix*⟩[*number*]{*text*} Same as \footnote but for the new level. Steps the footnote⟨*suffix*⟩ counter unless the optional *number* argument is given. Generates footnote markers and puts *text* at the bottom of the page.

\footnotemark⟨*suffix*⟩[*number*] Same as \footnotemark but for the new level. Steps the corresponding counter (if no optional argument is used) and prints a footnote marker corresponding to its value.

\footnotetext⟨*suffix*⟩[*number*]{*text*} Same as \footnotetext but for the new level. Puts *text* at the bottom of the page using the optional argument or the current value of footnote⟨*suffix*⟩ to generate a footnote marker in front of it.

In all three cases the style of the footnote markers depends on the chosen *enum-style*. The remaining three commands defined by \DeclareNewFootnote for use in the document are \Footnote⟨*suffix*⟩, \Footnotemark⟨*suffix*⟩, and \Footnotetext⟨*suffix*⟩ (i.e., same names as above but starting with an uppercase F). The important difference to the previous set is the following: instead of the optional *number* argument, they require a mandatory *marker* argument allowing you to specify arbitrary markers if desired. When using them, you have to provide the formatting for the marker; i.e., it is not automatically based on the *enum-style*. Some examples are given below.

The three companion commands for LaTeX's standard footnotes (i.e., \Footnote, \Footnotemark, and \Footnotetext) are also automatically made available if either manyfoot or bigfoot is loaded.[1]

One important difference between manyfoot and bigfoot is that the latter allows you to also make a declaration for the default footnote commands by using the artificial suffix default, e.g.,

```
\DeclareNewFootnote[para]{default}[roman]
```

would typeset standard footnotes joined together in a paragraph using lowercase roman numerals as markers. With manyfoot this is not possible, and you would need to resort to loading footmisc with appropriate settings to achieve the same effect.

---

[1] They are in fact also available separately by loading the package nccfoots by Alexander Rozhenko.

The general layout of the footnotes can be influenced by loading the footmisc package in addition to manyfoot or bigfoot, except that the para option of footmisc cannot be used, and its side option can be used only with manyfoot.

In the next example we use the standard footnote layout for top-level footnotes and the run-in layout (option para) for the second level. Note how footmisc's `multiple` option properly acts on all footnotes.

Some text[1],[a] with footnotes. Even more text.[b] Some text[2],[*] with footnotes. Even more text.[c]

---

[1] A first.
[2] Another main note.

[a] B-level. [b] A second. [*] A manual marker.
[c] Another B note.

```
\usepackage[multiple]{footmisc}
\usepackage[para]{manyfoot}
\DeclareNewFootnote[para]{B}[alph]
Some text\footnote{A first.}\footnoteB{B-level.}
with footnotes. Even more text.\footnoteB{A second.}
Some text\footnote{Another main note.}%
\FootnoteB{*}{A manual marker.} with footnotes.
Even more text.\footnoteB{Another B note.}
```

3-5-27

If all footnote levels should produce run-in footnotes, then the solution with manyfoot is to avoid the standard top-level footnotes completely (e.g., \footnote) and provide all necessary levels through manyfoot, i.e., only use \footnote⟨*suffix*⟩ commands. With bigfoot you can alternatively declare the formatting for the `default` level, as done for instance in Example 3-5-31.

In the following example the top-level footnotes are moved into the margin by loading footmisc with a different set of options. This is possible only with manyfoot; the bigfoot package ignores footmisc's side option and always places the footnotes at the bottom of the page.

This time manyfoot is loaded with the option para*, which differs from the para option used previously in that it suppresses any indentation in the run-in footnote blocks. In addition, the second-level notes are now numbered with roman numerals. For comparison the example typesets the same input text as Example 3-5-27, but it uses a different measure, because we have to show marginal notes now.

[1] A first.

[2] Another main note.

Some text[1],[i] with footnotes. Even more text.[ii] Some text[2],[*] with footnotes. Even more text.[iii]

---

[i] B-level. [ii] A second. [*] A manual marker. [iii] Another B note.

```
\usepackage[side,flushmargin,ragged,multiple]
           {footmisc}
\usepackage[para*]{manyfoot}
\DeclareNewFootnote[para]{B}[roman]
Some text\footnote{A first.}\footnoteB{B-level.}
with footnotes. Even more text.\footnoteB{A
second.} Some text\footnote{Another main note.}%
\FootnoteB{*}{A manual marker.} with footnotes.
Even more text.\footnoteB{Another B note.}
```

3-5-28

Separation of footnote blocks

The vertical separation between a footnote block and the previous one is specified by \skip\footins⟨*suffix*⟩. By default, it is equal to \skip\footins (i.e., the separation between main text and footnotes). Initially the extra blocks are separated only by such spaces, but if the option ruled is included, a \footnoterule is used as well. In fact, arbitrary material can be placed in that position by redefining the command

\extrafootnoterule — the only requirement being that the typeset result from that command does not take up any additional vertical space (see the discussion of \footnoterule on page 208 for further details). It is even possible to use different rules for different blocks of footnotes; consult the package documentation for details.

Some text[1],[*] with a footnote. Even more text.[A] Some text[†] with a footnote.[B] Some more text for the example.

[1]   A first.

[*]   A second.
[†]   A sample.

[A]   A third.
[B]   Another sample.

```
\usepackage[marginal,multiple]{footmisc}
\usepackage[ruled]{manyfoot}        % or bigfoot
\DeclareNewFootnote{B}[fnsymbol]
\DeclareNewFootnote{C}[Alph]
\renewcommand\extrafootnoterule{\vspace*{-3pt}%
     \hrule width 4em height 0.4pt \vspace*{2.6pt}}
\setlength{\skip\footinsC}{5pt minus 1pt}
Some text\footnote{A first.}\footnoteB{A second.}
with a footnote. Even more text.\footnoteC{A third.}
Some text\footnoteB{A sample.} with a
footnote.\footnoteC{Another sample.} Some more
text for the example.
```

3-5-29

The previous example deployed two additional *enum-styles*: Alph and fnsymbol. However, because only a few footnote symbols are available in both styles, that choice is most likely not a good one, unless we ensure that these footnote streams are numbered on a per-page basis. The perpage option of footmisc does not help here, because it applies to only the top-level footnotes. We can achieve the desired effect either by using \MakePerPage from the perpage package on the counters footnoteB and footnoteC (as done below) or by using the perpage option of manyfoot (which numbers all new footnote levels defined on a per-page basis). Note that the top-level footnotes are still numbered sequentially the way the example was set up.

Number the footnotes per page

Some text[1] with a footnote. Even more[*],[A] text. Some

[1]A first.

[*]Second.

[A]Third.

text[A] with a footnote here.[*] Some more text. And[2],[B] a last

[2]Again.

[*]Another sample.

[A]A sample.
[B]A last one.

```
\usepackage[multiple]{footmisc}
\usepackage{manyfoot,perpage}
\DeclareNewFootnote{B}[fnsymbol]
\DeclareNewFootnote{C}[Alph]
\MakePerPage{footnoteB}\MakePerPage{footnoteC}
Some text\footnote{A first.} with a footnote.
Even more\footnoteB{Second.}\footnoteC{Third.}
text. Some text\footnoteC{A sample.} with a
footnote here.\footnoteB{Another sample.} Some
more text. And\footnote{Again.}\footnoteC{A
    last one.} a last note.
```

3-5-30

If the previous example is set with bigfoot instead of manyfoot, then we do not need to load perpage: this is automatically done by bigfoot. We do, however, need to explicitly declare

```
\usepackage{bigfoot}    \DeclareNewFootnote{default}    ...
```

because otherwise the top-level footnotes end up in the last footnote block.

The biggest difference between manyfoot and bigfoot and probably the deciding factor for which to choose is the handling of run-in footnotes and the fact that with manyfoot, footnotes for different levels cannot be easily nested. That is, to have, for example, footnotes of the second level inside a top-level footnote, you have to go the roundabout way of using \footnotemark⟨suffix⟩ inside the main footnote and then place the corresponding \footnotetext⟨suffix⟩ directly afterwards.

In contrast, bigfoot allows natural nesting of such footnotes and distributes their text correctly to the different footnote apparatus as needed in critical editions and similar documents. Furthermore, it is able to split the last footnote in each footnote block automatically if that becomes necessary.

To give you an impression of the power behind these concepts, take a look at the next example[1], which shows several of the bigfoot features (though due to the space constraints not necessarily with a very pleasing layout).

There are three footnote levels defined: the default one uses arabic numbers, a second level uses lowercase Latin letter, and a third level uses footnote symbols. The markers for the inner footnotes are restarted on each page using \MakePerPage from the perpage package that is automatically loaded by bigfoot.

```
\usepackage[ruled]{bigfoot}
\DeclareNewFootnote[para]{default}
\DeclareNewFootnote[para]{B}[alph]
\DeclareNewFootnote[para]{C}[fnsymbol]
\MakePerPage{footnoteB}\MakePerPage{footnoteC}
Some text\footnote{First.} with a footnote.
Another sentence\footnote{Second.\footnoteB{A
    subnote.}} with a footnote. Some
text\footnote{Third.} with two footnotes
here.\footnote{Fourth.\footnoteB{A
    controversial\footnoteC{A C-level
        commentary on the commentary.}
    and lengthy subnote going on for a
    number\footnoteC{Another commentary.} of
    lines.\footnoteC{Final commentary.}}}
Some more text. More text to fill up the
pages in the example. A last note with
notes.\footnote{Fifth.\footnoteB{A B-level
    comment.\footnoteC{Being scrutinized!}}}
```

3-5-31

> Some text[1] with a footnote. Another sentence[2] with a footnote. Some text[3] with two footnotes here.[4] Some more text. More text to fill up the pages in the
>
> ---
> [1]First. [2]Second.[a] . [3]Third. [4]Fourth.[b]
> ---
> [a]A subnote.
> [b]A controversial[*] and
> ---
> [*]A C-level commentary on the commentary.

> example. A last note with notes.[5]
>
> ---
> [5]Fifth.[a]
> ---
> lengthy subnote going on for a number[*] of lines.[†]
> [a]A B-level comment.[‡]
> ---
> [*]Another commentary.
> [†]Final commentary.
> [‡]Being scrutinized!

Note in particular the handing of footnote "4": It contains a B-level footnote that itself contains three C-level footnotes. This does not fit into the space remaining on the first page, so the B-level note is split. This has the effect that the first C-level note is on the first page and the remaining C-level notes are on the second page. Because C-level markers are restarted on each page, two of them show "*" as their marker.

What you can also observe is that we requested para footnotes on all levels, but in fact only the top-level footnotes have been typeset run-in. This is another

---

[1]If you try to run this example using manyfoot, then none of the second-level notes would appear.

specialty of bigfoot. In contrast to footmisc and manyfoot, the para request is not unconditionally obeyed but chosen only when it saves noticeable space and delivers visually attractive results (which is obviously not possible in such a small measure).

The actual criteria are somewhat complicated (and the manual offers some customization possibilities), but in a nutshell a footnote starts on a new line if it is several lines long or the previous line is already nearly full. In the next example we re-typeset the text from Example 3-5-31 but this time to a full measure. However, even here bigfoot refuses to use the para for all footnote levels.

Some text[1] with a footnote. Another sentence[2] with a footnote. Some text[3] with two footnotes here.[4] Some more text. More text to fill up the pages in the example. A last note with notes.[5]

---

[1]First.   [2]Second.[a]   [3]Third.   [4]Fourth.[b]   [5]Fifth.[c]

---

[a]A subnote.   [b]A controversial* and lengthy subnote going on for a number[†] of lines.[‡]
[c]A B-level comment.[§]

---

*A C-level commentary on the commentary.
[†]Another commentary.
[‡]Final commentary.
[§]Being scrutinized!

3-5-32

While bigfoot can split footnotes set with the para option, this is not the case for run-in footnotes with manyfoot (neither with the para nor the para* option).

For very long footnotes near a page break, this may cause ugly pagination because without a split everything is moved to the next page. To resolve this problem the manyfoot package offers a (semi)manual solution: at the point where you wish to split your note you place a \SplitNote command and end the footnote.[1] You then place the remaining text of the footnote one paragraph farther down in the document in a \Footnotetext⟨suffix⟩ using an empty *marker* argument.

Some[1] text with two footnotes.[i] More text.[ii] Even more text. <hr> [1]An A-note. <hr> [i]A B-level comment.[i] [ii]This is an extremely long B-note that is	Some text here and[2] even more there. <hr> [2]Another A-note. <hr> continued here.

```
\usepackage[para]{manyfoot}
\DeclareNewFootnote[para]{B}[roman]
Some\footnote{An A-note.} text with two
footnotes.\footnoteB{A B-note.} More
text.\footnoteB{This is an extremely long
B-note that is\SplitNote} Even more text.
\par  Some\FootnotetextB{}{continued
  here.} text here and\footnote{Another
  A-note.} even more there.
```

3-5-33

If both parts of the footnote fall onto the same page after reformatting the document, the footnote parts get correctly reassembled, as we prove in the next example, which uses the same example text but a different measure. However, if the reformatting requires breaking the footnote in a different place, then further

---

[1]bigfoot does not offer this command, but then it is not really needed with this package.

manual intervention is unavoidable. Thus, such work is best left until the last stage of production.

Some[1] text with two footnotes.[i] More text.[ii] Even more text.

Some text here and[2] even more there.

---
[1] An A-note.
[2] Another A-note.

[i] A B-note.   [ii] This is an extremely long B-note that is continued here.

```
\usepackage[para]{manyfoot}
\DeclareNewFootnote[para]{B}[roman]

Some\footnote{An A-note.} text with two
footnotes.\footnoteB{A B-note.} More
text.\footnoteB{This is an extremely long
B-note that is\SplitNote} Even more text.
\par  Some\FootnotetextB{}{continued here.}
text here and\footnote{Another A-note.} even
more there.
```

3-5-34

3.5.8 parnotes — Present the notes inside the galley

Instead of placing notes at the bottom of the page as footnotes, in the margin or as endnotes, you may want to collect and place them into the main text, e.g., after each paragraph. For this Chelsea Hughes developed the small package **parnotes** that can be used on its own or together with one of the footnote or endnote packages. It provides its own command and can thus coexist with footnote or endnote commands.

\parnote[*mark*]{*note*}   \parnotes   \begin{autopn} ... \end{autopn}

The \parnote adds a marker to the text (by default a raised arabic numeral) and stores away the *note* text for later use (nested notes are not supported). With the optional *mark* argument you can provide your own marker. The notes are typeset when you issue a \parnotes command. By default they are set as their own paragraph in a slightly smaller font. With a bit of care you can use this command in uncommon places, e.g., in a marginpar or a float: it typesets all notes that have been encountered in the source since its last invocation.

If you like the notes to appear after each paragraph, you can avoid the necessary \parnotes commands by instead surrounding several paragraphs with the autopn environment.

This is simple text.[1] This is simple text.[2,3]

Some more text with a mark[†] and text for two lines.

---
[1] The first parnote.   [2] The second parnote with more than one line of text to show the formatting in the note section.   [3] Consecutive!   [†] A note with custom mark.

```
\usepackage{parnotes}

This is simple text.\parnote{The first parnote.}
This is simple text.\parnote{The second parnote with
  more than one line of text to show the formatting
  in the note section.}\parnote{Consecutive!}

Some more text with a mark\parnote[\textdagger]
  {A note with custom mark.} and text for two lines.
\parnotes
```

3-5-35

If you do not like the default settings, then there are several package options to adjust its behavior, as well as a number of configuration commands that you can adjust. For example, below we asked for alphabetic markers that restart after each invocation (options `alph` and `reset`) and are typeset in sans serif with a slight indentation on both sides of the notes (options `notessf` and `narrower`).

Other supported options are `notesrm` (default) and `notesit` for the font, `roman` and `symbol` for the marker, `breakwithin` to place each note on its own line, and `nomultiple` to prevent automatic handling of consecutive notes (if ever needed).

This is simple text.[a] This is simple text.[b]

> [a] The first parnote. [b] The second parnote with more than one line of text to show the formatting in the note section.

Another[a] paragraph.

Some more text with a mark[†] and text for two lines.

> [a] Note shows up later. [†] A note with custom mark.

```
\usepackage[alph,reset,narrower,notessf]{parnotes}
This is simple text.\parnote{The first parnote.}
This is simple text.\parnote{The second parnote with
    more than one line of text to show the formatting
    in the note section.} \parnotes

Another\parnote{Note shows up later.} paragraph.

Some more text with a
mark\parnote[\textdagger]{A note with custom mark.}
and text for two lines. \parnotes
```

3-5-36

Instead of the automatic and `reset` of numbering via the option, you can also manage this by yourself (e.g., when you want a restart at chapter boundaries) by using the command `\parnotereset`.

As you can see, the paragraph following a notes section is not indented. If this is undesired, you can change it with the option `indentafter`. In the next example we show this and a few more options by typesetting the notes in *italic*, using roman numerals for markers, and also adding some background color to the notes by redefining the command `\parnotefmt` that configures the note section. By doing that we make the basic formatting options (like `notesit` or `narrower`) no-ops so that we have to take care of font and placement in our redefinition. The example also exhibits the use of the `autopn` environment.

This is simple text.[i] This is simple text.[ii,1]

> [i] *The first parnote.* [ii] *The second parnote with more than one line of text to show the formatting in the note section.*

Another[iii] paragraph.

> [iii] *Note shows up immediately.*

Some more text with a mark[†] and text for two lines.

> [†] *A note with custom mark.*

---
[1] Consecutive!

```
\usepackage[multiple]{footmisc} \usepackage{xcolor}
\usepackage[indentafter,roman]{parnotes}
\renewcommand\parnotefmt[1]{\centerline{\colorbox
    {black!5}{\parbox{0.82\columnwidth}%
              {\footnotesize\itshape\noindent #1}}}}
\begin{autopn}
  This is simple text.\parnote{The first parnote.}
  This is simple text.\parnote{The second parnote with
      more than one line of text to show the formatting
      in the note section.}\footnote{Consecutive!}

Another\parnote{Note shows up immediately.} paragraph.

Some more text with a mark\parnote[\textdagger]{A note
    with custom mark.} and text for two lines.
\end{autopn}
```

3-5-37

The previous example also displayed the combination of parnotes and footnotes. While parnotes automatically handles consecutive notes, this is not the case for footnotes or for a mixture of both. For this reason we also had to load footmisc with its multiple option.

3.5.9 ftnright — Right footnotes in a two-column environment

It is sometimes desirable to group all footnotes in a two-column document at the bottom of the right column. This can be achieved by specifying the ftnright package written by the author. The effect of this package is shown in Figure 3.3 on the next page — the first page of the original documentation (including its spelling errors) of the ftnright implementation. It is clearly shown how the various footnotes collect in the lower part of the right-hand column.

The main idea for the ftnright package is to assemble the footnotes of all columns on a page and place them all together at the bottom of the right column. The layout produced allows for enough space between footnotes and text and, in addition, sets the footnotes in smaller type.[1] Furthermore, the footnote markers are placed at the baseline instead of raising them as superscripts.[2]

This package can be used together with most other class files for LaTeX. Of course, the ftnright package takes effect only with a document using a two-column layout specified with the twocolumn option on the \documentclass command — it does not for columns produced with multicols environments. In most cases, it is best to use ftnright as the very last package to make sure that its settings are not overwritten by other packages.

3.5.10 enotez — Endnotes, an alternative to footnotes

Scholarly works usually group notes at the end of each chapter or at the end of the document. Such notes are called endnotes. Endnotes are not supported in standard LaTeX, but they can be created in several ways.

The standard in this area was set many years ago by the package endnotes (by John Lavagnino). It provides its own \endnote command, thus allowing footnotes and endnotes to coexist. In 2012 Clemens Niederberger started to develop the package enotez. It implements the same document interface but allows for a lot of extra customization and is thus a worthy successor to endnotes.[3] In the following we describe his package (though most of the examples would also work with small modifications with the endnotes package).

---

[1] Some journals use the same size for footnotes and text, which sometimes makes it difficult to distinguish footnotes from the main text.

[2] Of course, this is done only for the mark preceding the footnote text and not the one used within the main text, where a raised number or symbol set in smaller type helps to keep the flow of thoughts uninterrupted.

[3] While the document user interface is largely the same, the customization methods are quite different. This means that reusing text from old documents using the new package is easily possible; only the preamble setup and command for printing notes need adjustment.

Footnotes in a multi-column layout*

Frank Mittelbach

August 10, 1991

1   Introduction

The placement of footnotes in a multi-column layout
always bothered me. The approach taken by LaTeX
(i.e., placing the footnotes separately under each column)
might be all right if nearly no footnotes are present. But
it looks clumsy when both columns contain footnotes,
especially when they occupy different amounts of space.

In the multi-column style option [5], I used page-wide
footnotes at the bottom of the page, but again the result
doesn't look very pleasant since short footnotes produce
undesired gaps of white space. Of course, the main goal
of this style option was a balancing algorithm for columns
which would allow switching between different numbers
of columns on the same page. With this feature, the
natural place for footnotes seems to be the bottom of the
page[1] but looking at some of the results it seems best to
avoid footnotes in such a layout entirely.

Another possibility is to turn footnotes into endnotes,
i.e., printing them at the end of every chapter or the end
of the entire document. But I assume everyone who has
ever read a book using such a layout will agree with me,
that it is a pain to search back and forth, so that the reader
is tempted to ignore the endnotes entirely.

When I wrote the article about "Future extensions of
TeX" [6] I was again dissatisfied with the outcome of
the footnotes, and since this article should show certain
aspects of high quality typesetting, I decided to give the
footnote problem a try and modified the LaTeX output
routine for this purpose. The layout I used was inspired
by the yearbook of the Gutenberg Gesellschaft Mainz
[1]. Later on, I found that it is also recommended by Jan
White [9]. On the layout of footnotes I also consulted
books by Jan Tschichold [8] and Manfred Simoneit [7],
books, I would recommend to everyone being able to
read German texts.

1.1   Description of the new layout

The result of this effort is presented in this paper and the
reader can judge for himself whether it was successful
or not.[2] The main idea for this layout is to assemble the
footnotes of all columns on a page and place them all

together at the bottom of the right column. Allowing for
enough space between footnotes and text, and in addition,
setting the footnotes in smaller type[3] I decided that one
could omit the footnote separator rule which is used in
most publications prepared with TeX.[4] Furthermore, I
decided to place the footnote markers[5] at the baseline
instead of raising them as superscripts.[6]

All in all, I think this generates a neat layout, and
surprisingly enough, the necessary changes to the LaTeX
output routine are nevertheless astonishingly simple.

1.2   The use of the style option

This style option might be used together with any other
style option for LaTeX which does not change the three
internals changed by ftnright.sty.[7] In most cases,
it is best to use this style option as the very last option in
the \documentstyle command to make sure that its
settings are not overwritten by other options.[8]

---

*. The LaTeX style option ftnright which is described in this ar-
ticle has the version number v1.0d dated 92/06/19. The documentation
was last revised on 92/06/19.

1. You can not use column footnotes at the bottom, since the number
of columns can differ on one page.

2. Please note, that this option only changed the placement of footnotes. Since this article also makes use of the doc option [4], that
assigns tiny numbers to code lines sprinkled throughout the text, the
resulting design is not perfect.

3. The standard layout in TUGboat uses the same size for footnotes and text, giving the footnotes, in my opinion, much too much
prominence.

4. People who prefer the rule can add it by redefining the command
\footnoterule [2, p. 156]. Please, note, that this command should
occupy no space, so that a negative space should be used to compensate
for the width of the rule used.

5. The tiny numbers or symbols, e.g., the '5' in front of this footnote.

6. Of course, this is only done for the mark preceeding the footnote
text and not the one used within the main text where a raised number
or symbol set in smaller type will help to keep the flow of thoughts,
uninterrupted.

7. These are the macros \@startcolumn, \@makecol and
\@outputdblcol as we will see below. Of course, the option will
take only effect with a document style using a twocolumn layout (like
ltugboat) or when the user additionally specifies twocolumn as a
document style option in the \documentstyle command.

8. The ltugboat option (which is currently set up as a style option
instead of a document style option which it actually is) will overwrite

1

Figure 3.3: The placement of text and footnotes with the ftnright package

---

```
\endnote[mark]{note}    \endnotemark[mark]    \endnotetext{note}
```

The document-level syntax is modeled after the footnote commands if you replace
foot with end — for example, \endnote produces an endnote, \endnotemark produces just the mark, and \endnotetext produces just the text. The counter used
to hold the current endnote number is called endnote, and it is stepped whenever
\endnote or \endnotemark is used without an optional argument.

When using the commands, an endnote marker is placed into the text, and corresponding *note* text is stored away for later use. Via the optional *mark* argument it is possible to place custom marks if that is ever needed. In this respect it differs from endnotes where the optional *mark* argument always had to be a number formatted according to the default style, while with `enotez` the argument is used as provided.

The printing of the accumulated notes happens when you issue the command `\printendnotes` in the source. It can be used several times (for example, at the end of each chapter) and by default typesets those notes that have been encountered since its previous invocation.

This is simple text.[1] This is simple text.[2] Some more text with a mark.[†]

Notes

1. The first endnote.

2. The second endnote with more than one line of text to show the formatting in the note section.

†. A note with custom mark

```
\usepackage{enotez}

This is simple text.\endnote{The first endnote.}
This is simple text.\endnote{The second endnote with
    more than one line of text to show the formatting
    in the note section.}  Some more text with a
mark.\endnote[\textdagger]{A note with custom mark}

\printendnotes    % output endnotes here
```

3-5-38

In contrast to `endnotes`, the `enotez` package is capable of handling nested endnotes up to any depth as shown in the next example. All notes are numbered sequentially by level; i.e., the document level notes are numbered consecutively followed by all second-level notes found when printing them, etc. As a consequence you need at least as many additional LaTeX runs as you have note levels. The package warns you about the need to rerun, but this is something to keep in mind.

This is text.[1] And this is more text.[2]

Notes

1. The first[3] endnote.[4]

2. The third endnote.[5]

3. A nested note...[6]

4. Another second-level note with more text to show its formatting in the note section.

5. Also with a second-level note.

6. ...which itself contains a note.

```
\usepackage{enotez}

This is text.\endnote{The first\endnote{A nested
    note\ldots\endnote{\ldots which itself
        contains a note.}} endnote.\endnote{Another
        second-level note with more text to show its
        formatting in the note section.}}
And this is more text.\endnote{The third
    endnote.\endnote{Also with a second-level note.}}

\printendnotes[itemize]
```

3-5-39

```
\printendnotes*[style]
```

If used as in the earlier examples, `\printendnotes` typesets all notes (and nested notes) encountered between two invocations. The star form allows you to print all notes contained in the document in a place prior to the last note. This form should be used only once.

If necessary, it is possible to add some predefined text between each note heading and the notes using `\AtEveryEndnotesList` or only for the next list with

\AtNextEndnotesList. One can also add text after the notes section or adjust the vertical spacing using a number of options and commands. The default heading title can be changed with the key list-name as shown in the next example.

All configurations are managed with the help of \setenotez declarations. This command expects a comma-separated key/value list as shown in the following examples. In the standard configuration the notes sections are not shown in the table of contents. If you prefer them to appear there, use the key totoc. As a value you can try auto or explicitly supply the heading level to be used in the table of contents, e.g., part, chapter, section, or subsection.

The package offers a number of *styles* to print the endnotes. By default the style plain is used; other possibilities are description or itemize. All of them can be customized, and it is also possible to define new styles. For details on the various customization possibilities and other keys not described here, consult the package documentation [107].

In the following example we define a new style that sets all endnotes as an inline list using the itemize* environment of enumitem. The endnotes are separated by 1em of space with some additional flexibility. \AtEveryEndnotesList enables provision of some introductory text. Compare this to Example 3-5-39 that uses the same set of nested endnotes.

```
\usepackage[inline]{enumitem}
\setlist[itemize]{itemjoin=\hspace{1em plus 2pt}}
```

This is text.[1] And this is more text.[2]

Section Notes

General introductory text...

1. The first[3] endnote.[4] 2. The third endnote.[5] 3. A nested note...[6] 4. Another second-level note with more text to show its formatting in the note section. 5. Also with a second-level note. 6. ...which itself contains a note.

```
\usepackage{enotez}
\setenotez{list-name={Section Notes}}
\DeclareInstance{enotez-list}{inline}{list}
                {list-type = itemize*}
\AtEveryEndnotesList{General introductory text\ldots}
This is text.\endnote{The first\endnote{A nested
    note\ldots\endnote{\ldots which itself contains a
    note.}} endnote.\endnote{Another second-level note with
    more text to show its formatting in the note section.}}
And this is more text.\endnote{The third
    endnote.\endnote{Also with a second-level note.}}
\printendnotes[inline]
```

3-5-40

By default notes are continuously numbered throughout the document. If you want to reset the number after each invocation of \printendnotes, use the key reset. If you load hyperref to generate links within your document, you can add the key backref that establishes links from the notes in the notes section(s) back to the pages where the note markers appeared.

The layout for endnote numbers is controlled through \theendnote, which is the standard way LaTeX handles counter formatting. If you want to change it, either redefine this command or use the key counter-format as we do in the next example. The format of the mark is produced from \enotezwritemark — a command that takes one argument and defaults to \textsuperscript. In a similar fashion one can redefine the command \enmark to change the format of the endnote marker in the endnote list.

This is simple text.[a)] This is simple text.[b)] Some more text with a mark.[†)]

Notes

a) The first endnote.

b) The second endnote with more than one line of text to show the formatting in the note section.

†) A note with custom mark

```
\usepackage{enotez}
\setenotez{reset,counter-format=alph}
\renewcommand\enotezwritemark[1]{\textsuperscript{#1)}}
\renewcommand\enmark[1]{#1)}
This is simple text.\endnote{The first endnote.}
This is simple text.\endnote{The second endnote with
   more than one line of text to show the formatting
   in the note section.}  Some more text with a
mark.\endnote[\textdagger]{A note with custom mark}
\printendnotes[description]
```

3-5-41

Even if you want all notes in a single place in your document, you may want them subdivided by chapters or sections to help the reader locate individual notes more easily. This is supported by enotez through the key split. As values it accepts chapter, section, or false (default, i.e., no splitting). You can combine this with the key reset, in which case the endnote counter resets depending on the split level specified, e.g., in the next example at every section.

1 A first section

This is simple text.[1] Here is a bit more text.[2]

2 Second section

Some[1] text for this section also with a note.

Notes

Notes for section 1

1. An endnote.
2. The second endnote with two lines.

Notes for section 2

1. A third note.

```
\usepackage{enotez}
\setenotez{reset,split=section}
\section{A first section}
This is simple text.\endnote{An endnote.}
Here is a bit more text.\endnote{The
   second  endnote with two lines.}
\section{Second section}
Some\endnote{A third note.} text
for this section also with a note.
\newpage \printendnotes[itemize]
```

3-5-42

3.5.11 Marginal notes

The standard LaTeX command \marginpar generates a marginal note. This command typesets the text given as its argument in the margin, with the first line being at the same height as the line in the main text where the \marginpar command occurs. When only the mandatory argument is specified, the text goes to the right margin for one-sided printing; to the outside margin for two-sided printing; and to the nearest margin for two-column formatting. When you also specify an optional argument, its text is used if the left margin is chosen, while the second (mandatory) argument is used for the right margin.

This placement strategy can be reversed (except for two-column formatting) using \reversemarginpar, which acts on all marginal notes from there on. You can return to the default behavior with \normalmarginpar.

As explained in Table 5.2 on page 369, there are three length parameters to customize the style of marginal notes: \marginparwidth, \marginparsep, and \marginparpush. It is usually best to change them only in the preamble (or in a class file) but not in the middle of the document.

There are a few important things to understand when using marginal notes. First, the \marginpar command does not start a paragraph so that it can be used between paragraphs without introducing extra vertical space. Thus, if it is used before the first word of a paragraph, the vertical alignment does not match the beginning of the paragraph. Second, the first word of its argument is not automatically hyphenated. Thus, for a narrow margin and long words (as in German), you may have to precede the first word by an \hspace{0pt} command to allow hyphenation of that word. These two potential problems can be eased by defining a command like \marginlabel, which starts with an empty box \mbox{}, typesets a marginal note ragged right, and adds an \hspace{0pt} in front of the argument.

Some text with a
marginal note. Some
more text. Another
text with a marginal
note coming up next.
A lot of additional text
here to fill up the space
in the example on the
left.

ASuperLongFirstWord
with problems

ASuperLong-
Firstword
without
problems

```
\newcommand\marginlabel[1]{\mbox{}\marginpar
    {\raggedright\hspace{0pt}#1}}

Some\marginpar{ASuperLongFirstWord with problems}
text with a marginal note. Some more text.
Another text with a marginal note coming up
next\marginlabel{ASuperLongFirstword without
    problems}. A lot of additional text here to fill
up the space in the example on the left.
```

3-5-43

Of course, the above definition can no longer produce different texts depending on the chosen margin. With a little more finesse this problem can be solved, using, for example, the \NewDocumentCommand construct discussed in Section A.1.4 on page →II 632.

```
\NewDocumentCommand \marginlabel {O{#2}m} {\mbox{}%
    \marginpar[\raggedleft\hspace{0pt}#1]{\raggedright\hspace{0pt}#2}}
```

The LaTeX kernel tries hard (without producing too much processing overhead) to ensure that the contents of \marginpar commands always show up in the correct margin, and in most circumstances, it makes the right decisions. In some cases, however, it can fail. If you are unlucky enough to stumble across one of them, a one-off solution is to add an explicit \pagebreak to stop the page generation from looking too far ahead. Of course, this has the disadvantage that the correction means visual formatting and has to be undone if the document changes. A better solution is to load the package mparhack written by Tom Sgouros and Stefan Ulrich. Once this package is loaded, all \marginpar positions are tracked (internally using a label mechanism and writing the information to the .aux file). You may then get a warning "Marginpars may have changed. Rerun to get them right", indicating that the positions have changed in comparison to the previous LaTeX run and that a further run is necessary to stabilize the document.

Incorrectly placed \marginpars

3.5.12 marginnote — An alternative to \marginpar

A different approach to the problem with \marginpar is taken by Markus Kohm in his marginnote package.[1]

\marginnote[*left note*]{*right note*}[*vertical offset*]

It implements the command \marginnote that has a similar interface but offers an additional optional *vertical offset* argument to adjust the positioning of the note in the margin because this is sometimes helpful. In the next example we used this to move the first note one line down.

Instead of internally using parts of LaTeX's float mechanism, the package uses positioning information from the output to place the notes in relation to that. As a result \marginnote can be used in places in which \marginpar is disallowed, e.g., within floats or in the scope of the multicols. It also means that you need at least two LaTeX runs before the notes settle in their right places.

As you can see, the notes are typeset ragged right by default in the right margin and ragged left in the left margin, but that can be adjusted as necessary. Also, the problem with hyphenation of the first word is taken care of automatically.

Some text with a | ASuperLong-
marginal note. Some | FirstWord
more text. | without
Another text with | problems
a marginal note com-
ing up next. A lot of | ASuperLongFirstword
additional text here to | without problems
fill up the space with a
few additional lines.

```
\usepackage{xcolor,marginnote}
Some\marginnote{ASuperLongFirstWord without problems}
text with a marginal note. Some more text.

\renewcommand\raggedrightmarginnote{\centering}
\renewcommand\marginfont
             {\strut\color{blue}\sffamily\tiny}
Another text with a marginal note coming up
next\marginnote{ASuperLongFirstword without problems}.
A lot of additional text here to fill up the space
with a few additional lines.
```

3-5-44

Changing the justification within the marginal notes is somewhat unintuitive because the commands for that are called \raggedleftmarginnote and \raggedrightmarginnote for the left and right margins, respectively. By redefining them you can arrange for other justification methods, as we did above by producing centered notes in the right margin. Defining them to be empty is equivalent to requesting justified notes.

There is also the command \marginfont in which you can place font or other code to be applied at the start of the marginal note. Above we used this to make the second note blue and typeset in a tiny sans serif font. You may wonder about the *Subtle issue with font size changes* additional \strut added. Normally, \marginnote aligns the note with its top at the top of the line it was encountered. This is fine if main text and notes share the same font size. Because we changed to \tiny, this results in the baseline of the first

---

[1]Note that at the time of writing this book the package is in search of a new maintainer because Markus is no longer supporting it. Being a widely used solution, we describe it nonetheless.

line being no longer aligned with the baseline of the text. By adding a strut (before changing the font size) we ensure that the first note line still has a normal height and thus get a better alignment.

One disadvantage of \marginnote over the standard \marginpar command is that it typesets the note blindly in the "correct" spot. This means that two such notes on the same or nearby line in the document overprint each other, unless you explicitly move one or the other out of the way with the *vertical offset* argument. In contrast, a \marginpar automatically moves down if its normal placement is already occupied. Unfortunately, there is no warning when this happens, so you have to control your note placement visually!

Watch out for overwrites!

Issue with sidenotes getting too close to each other. First longer second Third

Issue with sidenotes getting too close to each other. A bit more text for the main galley. First A longer Third

```
\usepackage{xcolor,marginnote}

Issue\marginnote{First} with\marginnote{\color{blue}A
    longer second} sidenotes getting too close to
each other.\marginnote{Third}


Issue\marginnote{First} with\marginnote{\color{blue}A
    longer second}[12pt] sidenotes getting too close to
each other.\marginnote{Third}
A bit more text for the main galley.
```

3-5-45

As you see, even moving the second node down is not enough because it then overprints the third; thus, that one needs moving too.

It is also important to watch out for \marginnote commands that end up at a line break. In that case the placement is not always correct, but sometimes a line too low. This is a bug in the current package code.

Watch out for line breaks!

3.5.13 snotez — Numbered or otherwise marked side notes

We have already seen the implementation of numbered or marked side notes with the side option of footmisc that turns footnotes into marginal notes. In contrast, the snotez package by Clemens Niederberger provides side notes that can be used in addition to footnotes. It introduces the command \sidenote with the same syntax conventions as the \footnote command except that it additionally adds a *vertical offset* argument for adjusting the placement of the note.

\sidenote *(vertical offset)* [*mark*] {*note*}
\sidenotemark [*mark*]   \sidenotetext *(vertical offset)* [*mark*] {*note*}

Modeled after footnotes there is no explicit way to specify different text depending on the margin into which the note is placed. The optional argument in brackets is interpreted as a request for a *mark*. The other optional argument (*vertical offset*) is given in parentheses, not brackets, to make it easier to specify only one of them.[1]

---

[1]Earlier versions of the package used brackets for both optional arguments; this form of the syntax can still be used if the package option dblarg is used.

The \sidenotemark and \sidenotetext commands are used in the same way as the corresponding commands for footnotes; if necessary, refer to the earlier sections on footnotes for details.

Some text with a side note.[1] A lot of additional text here with a note.[2] Even more text and then two side notes.[3][†] A lot of additional lines of text here to fill up the space on the left.

[1] A first.
[2] A second.
[3] A third.
[†] A fourth.

```
\usepackage{snotez}

Some text with a side note.\sidenote{A first.}
A lot of additional text here with a
note.\sidenote{A second.} Even more text
and then two side notes.\sidenote{A third.}%
\sidenote[\textdagger]{A fourth.} A
lot of additional lines of text here to
fill up the space on the left.
```
3-5-46

By default the notes are typeset using \marginpar (as long as no *vertical offset* is used), but you can direct it to use the marginnote package for all notes by specifying the option marginnote. In this case it is your responsibility to ensure that the notes do not overlap and if necessary move them apart as we did with the last note in the next example.

Some text with a side note.[1] A lot of additional text here with a note.[2] Even more text and then two side notes.[3][†] A lot of additional lines of text here to fill up the space on the left.

[1] A first.
[2] A second.
[3] A third.
[†] A fourth.

```
\usepackage[marginnote]{snotez}

Some text with a side note.\sidenote{A first.}
A lot of additional text here with a
note.\sidenote{A second.} Even more text
and then two side
notes.\sidenote{A third.}% next one moved down
     \sidenote(12pt)[\textdagger]{A fourth.}
A lot of additional lines of text here to
fill up the space on the left.
```
3-5-47

Instead of writing 12pt (which corresponds to a baseline distance in our example), we could have used a convenient shortcut offered by the snotez package: in this argument a single * indicates a distance of a baseline, *2 and so on.

Customizing the side notes with options
Options and keys can be specified either during package load or in the argument of a \setsidenotes declaration that can be repeatedly used in the preamble and in the document body (exceptions are the options dblarg, footnote, marginnote, and perpage options, which can be set only in the preamble because they apply to the whole document).

The key text-format specifies the code used to format the text of the note. It defaults to \footnotesize. In contrast, the key text-format+ provides code that is used in addition to text-format.

By default snotez numbers the notes per chapter using the counter sidenote. With perpage you can change this so that the notes are numbered on a per-page basis. If you want to change the numbering style, you have to modify \thesidenote yourself.

With the option footnote you direct the package to redefine the footnote commands to generate side notes, i.e., act like the side option of footmisc.

Finally, we have `text-mark-format` and `note-mark-format` for formatting the marker in text and in the note (both expect code that manipulates one argument and defaults to using `\superscript`) and `note-mark-sep` for specifying the separation between side note mark and side note text (default `\space`). In the next example we have applied some of those keys.

... of straw[a], sticks[b] and bricks.[c,d]

a) not to be confused with hay

b) or lumber according to some sources

c) probably fired clay bricks

d) Several in a row?

```
\usepackage{fnpct}   \usepackage[footnote]{snotez}
\setsidenotes{text-format=\tiny,note-mark-format=#1)}
\renewcommand\thesidenote{\alph{sidenote}}

\ldots\ of straw\footnote*{not to be confused with hay},
sticks\footnote{or lumber according to some sources}
and bricks\footnote{probably fired clay bricks}%
            \footnote{Several in a row?}.
```

3-5-48

3.6 Support for document development

In this final section of the chapter we look at a number of packages supporting document development. The first two packages todonotes and fixme help you with managing notes in the text about stuff that needs doing. They have different approaches, so it is a matter of taste and style which of them fits your own workflow better — you certainly do not need both in a single document. This is followed by the changes package, which is also for note taking, but with the focus on editorial work, providing some specialized support for this. Internally it makes use of todonotes. We also briefly touch upon the pdfcomment package that allows you to produce PDF annotations and tool tips visible in suitable PDF viewers.

A slightly different task is to add markers in a final document to indicate recent changes. Sometimes a note package like todonotes is appropriate for this, but often such changes are simply indicated with vertical lines in the margin, and the package vertbars offers a simple solution for this.

3.6.1 todonotes — Adding todos to your document

While writing documentation, it is often the case that one wants to add some reminders about things that still need doing, researching, fixing, or whatever. The package todonotes by Henrik Skov Midtiby offers nice facilities for such tasks, which are easy to use and to adapt to one's needs.

`\todo` [*key/value list*] {*text*}   `\listoftodos` [*title*]

The main command provided by the package is `\todo`. In its basic form it just takes one *text* argument that describes what needs doing. It places that text in a box into the (outer) margin and places a line from the box to the place in the text where the command was encountered.

237

Internally the box is placed using LaTeX's `\marginpar` command, so the box is placed at roughly where it appears in the source unless that space is already occupied by other `\todo` boxes or other `\marginpar` commands in which case the box is moved downwards on the page.[1]

If you want a consolidated list of all todos, place a `\listoftodos` command somewhere into your document (typically at the end to avoid pagination changes in the document). With its optional argument you can specify your own heading if desired; otherwise, a default text is used. The package option `colorinlistoftodos` adds a colored square in front of each list item as shown in the next example. This can be useful if you have differently colored notes to indicate different types of necessary actions or different importance.

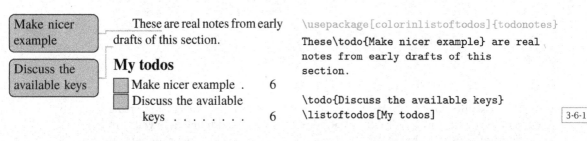

These are real notes from early drafts of this section.

My todos

  Make nicer example . 6
  Discuss the available keys 6

```
\usepackage[colorinlistoftodos]{todonotes}

These\todo{Make nicer example} are real
notes from early drafts of this
section.

\todo{Discuss the available keys}
\listoftodos[My todos]
```

Make nicer example

Discuss the available keys

3-6-1

If you really want to, you can arrange for the todo list to be added to the table of contents by placing the command `\todotoc` directly in front of `\listoftodos`. However, this makes your TOC one line longer and thus changes the pagination, at least in an article. Unless you intend to use such notes also in your final document for some reason, this may not be advisable.

`\missingfigure[`*key/value list*`]{`*text*`}`

The other command todonotes provides is `\missingfigure`, used to indicate that an image is missing and should be added. Its *text* argument can be used to describe what the image should show. The command ends the current paragraph and shows a very visible warning (by default going across the full line width and taking up about 4 cm of vertical space). You can change (typically enlarge) this space through the keys `figwidth` and `figheight` (see example) in case you know the rough size[2] of the image.

You typically would use this command inside a `figure` environment so that you can already set up a `\caption` and reference it even though you have not provided the actual graphic yet. In normal running text it is less useful because there it drastically

---

[1] In the worst case this means that it may move into the footer or even off the page, e.g., if you have too many things still to do or there is not enough space to describe them. However, because these commands are intended only for use during document development, this is a limitation one can usually live with.

[2] The warning triangle does not change its size, so if you specify a very small height or width, the warning may overprint nearby material. This is already visible in Example 3-6-2 where the triangle sticks out slightly on the top.

changes the pagination. It is better to use a simple \todo command reminding you to "add a figure roughly here".

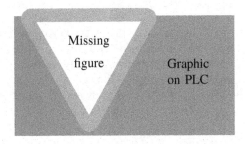

Figure 1: The product lifecycle stages

```
\usepackage{todonotes}
\begin{figure}
  \centering
  \missingfigure[figheight=90pt,
                 figwidth=170pt]
                {Graphic on PLC}
  \caption{The product lifecycle
           stages}
  \label{fig:plc}
\end{figure}
As shown in Figure~\ref{fig:plc}
the four product lifecycle stages
are Introduction, Growth, Maturity
and Decline.
```

As shown in Figure 1 the four product lifecycle stages are Introduction, Growth, Maturity and Decline.

3-6-2

Customizing todos

Individual todo items can be customized through a large number of keys in the optional *key/value list* argument. While this is fine in a one-off situation, in most cases you probably want to customize all notes in the same manner. For this, use the command \setuptodonotes, which takes a *key/value list* as a mandatory argument and changes the default values for the specified keys. For example, *Default setup changes*

```
\setuptodonotes{color=blue!30}
```

would change the background and line color from its orange default to a light blue. It can be used several times in the preamble or the document body and modifies only those keys that are given. Overwriting such defaults on an individual \todo command still remains possible. Some keys can be also used as options when loading the package, something we do a few times in the examples to save space, but in general using \setuptodonotes is preferable.

Instead of the color key you can set the background color and line color individually using backgroundcolor and linecolor. Both produce a very noticeable orange color by default. The border around the note is by default black and changeable through bordercolor. Finally, the text is colored based on textcolor, which again defaults to black. *Coloring the leaves*

Besides changing the colors, you can also ask for a shadow behind the notes (that is always in gray) by using the Boolean key shadow. Omitting the shadow is done by setting this key to false or by using the shorter form noshadow. However, shadows are available only if you additional add the loadshadowlibrary package option or otherwise ensure that the required tikz library is loaded. *shadows need a loaded tikz library*

Because this book uses only two colors in printing, it is a little difficult to demonstrate these keys, given that most colors, such as the default orange, come out as gray. Nevertheless, we try in the next example using gray for the text, white for the background, blue for the border, and black for the lines. In other words, we switch everything around to show what is possible (without any claim that this is a useful or pleasing design).

Line adjustments If you do not want a line pointing to the origin in the text, you can use `noline`. With `line` you can turn the lines on if they are off by default. Another possible key is `fancyline`, which produces a thicker curved arrow. Possibly more interesting is changing the length of the tick mark at the end of a normal line to indicate the original place of the note, using the key `tickmarkheight`. By default that key has a value of zero (i.e., no tick mark). If you set it to, say, `5pt`, it clearly marks the place, which can be useful if you have several notes pointing to different words in the same source line.

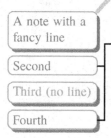

A bit of paragraph text. Observe how all the spaces around \todo commands are handled.

```
\usepackage[loadshadowlibrary]{todonotes}
\setuptodonotes{shadow,backgroundcolor=white,
    bordercolor=blue,linecolor=black,
    textcolor=gray,tickmarkheight=5pt}

A\todo[fancyline]{A note with a fancy line}
bit of paragraph text. Observe
\todo[noshadow]{Second} how all the
\todo[noline,textcolor=blue]{Third (no line)}
spa\todo{Fourth}ces around \verb|\todo|
commands are handled.
```
3-6-3

Sizing and placing the todos The default text size inside the note is `\normalsize`, but if you have many notes or a lot of text in the notes, you might prefer something noticeably smaller. This can be adjusted using the key `size`, which expects the name of a standard LaTeX size command (with or without a starting backslash) as its value. If you have eagle eyes, you might try `tiny`; otherwise, `scriptsize` is often a good value.

The width of the todo notes is based on the available size in the margin and by default matches `\marginparwidth`. There are possibilities to change that globally through the package option `textwidth`, but in most cases, it is better to use the default. Details can be found in the package documentation.

Instead of a placement in margin that you get by default or explicitly through the key `noinline`, you can request an `inline` placement. In this case, the note disrupts the paragraph and is placed on a line by its own. Note that this means that your document pagination changes if you get rid of it later. However, because marginpars are not allowed in all places, this enables you to add a note into a footnote or a float.

In this[1] short example we demonstrate sizing and inline notes.

```
\usepackage{todonotes}

In this\footnote{This footnote gets a
    todo.\todo[inline,size=tiny]{See? But not
    really good looking in footnotes}} short
example we demonstrate\todo[size=Large]{Shout}
sizing\todo[size=footnotesize]{Whisper} and
inline notes.
```
3-6-4

---
[1]This footnote gets a todo.

If you produce a \listoftodos, then by default all your notes are listed there. If a note should not appear, specify nolist, or set nolist as the default and explicitly add list to those notes that should go into the list. Normally the full note text appears in the list, but if you want something different, you can specify an alternative text with the key caption. If you additionally add the key prepend, then the caption text is not only used for the list but is also prepended to the todo note text separated with a colon.[1]

Customizing the list of todos

Finally,[2] there is an author key, which as the name indicates can be used to mark up different note authors or issue owners or .... This places the given value in a note box by itself (see below), which does not work very well. I think that it is usually better to instead add this information directly into the todo text and define your own commands for doing so (some examples are given later).

Author or ownership

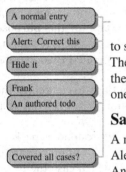

We use a wide margin here to save space in the example. The todos are summarized in the list below (omitting the one labeled nolist).

Sample todos

A normal entry   6
Alert   6
An authored todo . . .   6
Cases   6

```
\usepackage[loadshadowlibrary]{todonotes}
\setuptodonotes{shadow,size=scriptsize}

\todo{A normal entry}
\todo[caption=Alert,prepend]{Correct this}
\todo[nolist]{Hide it}
\todo[author=Frank]{An authored todo}
\todo[caption=Cases]{Covered all cases?}

We use a wide margin here to save space
in the example. The todos are summarized
in the list below (omitting the one
labeled \textttt{nolist}).

\listoftodos[Sample todos]
```

3-6-5

Defining your own todo commands

Given that the idea of workflow support packages is to help you to be more efficient in writing your documents, it is clear that adding lengthy optional arguments to each and every note, as we did above for illustration purposes, is counterproductive.

What you should consider doing instead is to set up defaults to your liking using \setuptodonotes and define one or the other short command for special-purpose todos. For example, you may want to use differently colored notes to indicate different actions, e.g.,

```
\newcommand\error[1]{\todo[size=small,color=red]{Error: #1}}
\newcommand\warn [1]{\todo[size=small,color=yellow]{Warning: #1}}
```

Or, in a collaborative setup, you may want to provide separate initials indicating authorship of the note, e.g.,

```
\newcommand\fix[2][FMi]{\todo[size=small,author=#1]{Fix: #2}}
```

---

[1]The colon is hardwired, which somewhat limits the use cases for this feature.
[2]Not quite true, there are a few more, but these are the important ones.

241

such that `\fix[LL]{Replace this}` can be used. Or you can number your notes by defining your own counter, e.g.,

```
\newcounter{todonumber}[section]
\newcommand\ntodo[1]{\stepcounter{todonumber}%
                    \todo{Note~\thetodonumber: #1}}
```

and I am sure you can think of others. Do not get carried away, though. Such notes are supposed to be helpful to you, and if you make different types for too many scenarios, you may end up using them inconsistently, which really defeats the purpose.

Package options

So far most of the discussion was about the keywords supported by the `\todo` command. Many of them could also be given as package options to set up defaults when loading the package, though I suggest using `\setuptodonotes` for this purpose. In addition, there are a few options that can be used only during package loading. We have already seen `colorinlistoftodos` to color the generated todo list and `textwidth` to alter the width of the notes.

Language support   Also available are various **babel/polyglossia** language options to customize the heading produced by `\listoftodos`, though normally you probably provide that title in the optional argument to that command.

Suppressing the todo displays   Of more interest is that you can render all commands of the todonotes package harmless in your final version by loading the package with the option `disable`. Alternatively, you can load it with the option `obeyFinal` in which case the todos are suppressed only if you use `final` on the document class. Or you can use the package option `obeyDraft`, which shows the todos only if `draft` is used on the document class. Note, however, that while the package attempts to place all notes (except inline ones) in a way that does not alter the pagination, this is not guaranteed. After disabling them, make sure that everything is still typeset as intended.

3.6.2 fixme — A slightly different approach to todos

While the **todonotes** package provided a single command that you could customize to your needs, the **fixme** package by Didier Verna offers four basic commands to indicate different levels of importance.

Besides the different annotation levels, the fixme package offers environments for producing longer annotations and a larger number of layouts and themes for displaying the notes, some of which are shown in the examples.

`\fxnote[`*key/value list*`]{`*text*`}`	`\fxwarning[`*...*`]{`*text*`}`	
`\fxerror[`*...*`]{`*text*`}`	`\fxfatal[`*...*`]{`*text*`}`	`\listoffixmes`

The standard layout produced is a marginal note for the annotations, but plenty of other possibilities exist that are controlled through package options, through

\fxsetup in the preamble or through individual settings on the annotation commands.

The annotations are shown only if the document is typeset in draft mode. In final mode they are ignored (but still logged in the transcript file). The \fxfatal annotation, however, is slightly special, because it throws a LATEX error if it is encountered in final mode. The assumption is that fatal issues should be resolved before something is considered final.

With \listoffixmes you can generate yourself a listing of all annotations in a convenient place.

FiXme Note:
Make nicer
example

FiXme Warning:
Discuss the
available keys

3-6-6

These are real notes from early drafts of this section.

List of Corrections

Note: Make nicer example 6

Warning: Discuss the available keys 6

```
\usepackage[draft]{fixme}

These\fxnote{Make nicer example}
are real notes from early drafts of
this section.\fxwarning{Discuss the
  available keys}
\listoffixmes
```

Even if you do not use \listoffixmes, the package generates a short summary and displays it on the terminal and the transcript file like this:

```
FiXme Summary: Number of notes: 1,
(FiXme)       Number of warnings: 1,
(FiXme)       Number of errors: 0,
(FiXme)       Number of fatal errors: 0,
(FiXme)       Total: 2.
```

Given that the package does not color your text by default, the annotations are less prominent and disrupting compared to, say, todonotes. Whether or not that suits your style of working is something you need to decide.

Another difference is that there is no immediate indication to which exact phrase or word the annotation belongs to, given that there is no line from the marginal note to the text. This can be improved by choosing a different layout for the notes, e.g., inline or footnote. Alternatively (or in addition), you can make "targeted" annotations by using the star form of the above commands. They then take a further mandatory argument that holds the text to which the note applies.

The star forms produce targeted annotations

These **FiXme Note: Make nicer example** are real notes from early drafts of this *section*[1]. This *example*[2] shows

```
\usepackage[draft]{fixme}  \fxsetup{nomargin,footnote}

These\fxnote[inline,nofootnote]{Make nicer example}
are real notes from early drafts of this
\fxwarning*{Discuss the available keys}{section}.
This \fxerror*{A targeted note}{example} shows a
targeted note.
```

3-6-7

---

[1] FiXme Warning: Discuss the available keys
[2] FiXme Error: A targeted note

The different layouts are not exclusive. This is why we had to turn off the default margin layout using nomargin and later use nofootnote when we made a single inline note.

Most of the time annotations are short so that the use of a command with the annotation text as a mandatory argument is quite appropriate. However, there may be cases where you want to make longer comments or comments that contain verbatim material. In that case you can use a corresponding environment form that is named by prefixing the command name with an, i.e., `anfxnote`, `anfxwarning`, `anfxerror`, or `anfxfatal`:

FiXme Note:
Summary

If normal notes FiXme Note: A really long comment possibly involving `\verb`**, etc. ... that automatically becomes an inline note** are not enough then try *environments*.

FiXme Fatal:
Change this

```
\usepackage[draft]{fixme}

If normal notes
\begin{anfxnote}{Summary}
 A really long comment possibly involving
 \verb=\verb=, etc.\ \ldots{} that
 automatically becomes an inline note
\end{anfxnote}
are not enough then try
\fxfatal*{Change this}{environments}.
```

3-6-8

Collaboration

For collaborative work, the package provides the key `author` to specify your initials (or your name). This is then shown in the annotation instead of the default "FiXme". Of course, doing this on each and every note command is not very convenient. There fixme provides a way to register authors that then get their own individual markup commands.

> `\FXRegisterAuthor{`*cmd-prefix*`}{`*env-prefix*`}{`*id*`}`

You need to supply a different prefix for commands and environments; otherwise you get fairly strange errors. For example, below we use `fm` and `afm`, and as a result the package generates `\fmnote` and `afmnote` and similarly named commands and environments for us. As you can see, the *id* is then used in the typeset output.

These[1] are real notes from early drafts of this *section*[2]. This *example*[3] shows a targeted note.

```
\usepackage[draft]{fixme} \fxsetup{nomargin,footnote}
\FXRegisterAuthor{fm}{afm}{Frank}

These\fmnote{Make nicer example} are real notes
from early drafts of this \fmwarning*{Discuss the
 available keys}{section}. This \fxerror*
[author=Ben User]{Explicit authored note}{example}
shows a targeted note.
```

3-6-9

---

[1]Frank Note: Make nicer example
[2]Frank Warning: Discuss the available keys
[3]Ben User Error: Explicit authored note

Besides the built-in layouts `margin`, `inline`, `footnote`, and `index`, the fixme package can load a number of externally defined layouts, among them various ones that display the annotations as PDF annotations viewable with an appropriate reader. For example,

> `\fxuselayouts{pdfcnote}`

generates colored notes that work well in Acrobat Reader and similar programs. For details on this and further customization possibilities, refer to the package documentation [136].

3.6.3 changes — A set of typical editorial commands

The changes package by Ekkart Kleinod was written to support editorial work, typically in collaboration with others. It supports the standard copy-editing tasks, well-known from WYSIWYG tools or PDF viewers, except that with a LaTeX document you do this by adding commands in the source. Of course, one can always send around PDF documents for review and let people mark up those using a suitable PDF editor or reader program, but this separates comments from the sources and can be far more complicated when several people are doing reviews independently.

```
\added[key/value list]{text}  \deleted[..]{text}  \replaced[..]{new}{old}
\highlight[..]{text}          \comment[..]{commentary}
\listofchanges[..]
```

The fairly self-explanatory commands are placed into the source text and manipulate their argument or arguments in obvious ways by adding color or in the case of removal or replacement through strikeout of text.

For marking up text there is \highlight, and for making a *commentary* there is \comment. By default the commentaries are numbered and show up in the margin (using the todonotes package).

With \listofchanges you can generate a summary of all editorial work that was marked up. All of the commands support an option argument in which you can specify keywords that we will discuss below. Here is an example:

Sample text, something added, a word~~blob~~ re-
[1] Fix! placed and ~~some~~ stuff removed. Whoa!

List of changes

```
\usepackage{changes}
```

Added: added	6
Replaced: word	6
Deleted: some	6
Commented: Fix!	6
Highlighted: Whoa!	6

```
Sample text, something \added{added},
a \replaced{word}{blob} replaced and
\deleted{some} stuff\comment{Fix!}
removed. \highlight{Whoa!}
\listofchanges
```

3-6-10

If the package is loaded with the option final, all editorial markup including \listofchanges is suppressed. The same happens if final is given as a global option to the document class, unless it is locally overwritten by the option draft on the package level.

```
\usepackage[final]{changes}
```

Sample text, something added, a word replaced and stuff removed. Whoa!

```
Sample text, something \added{added}, a \replaced{word}{blob}
replaced and \deleted{some} stuff\comment{Fix!} removed.
\highlight{Whoa!}     \listofchanges
```

3-6-11

By default the author of the editorial markup is anonymous, and the markup for this person is colored blue as seen in the above example. In a collaboration scenario, however, you may have several people reviewing the text, and for this case you can define review authors through the declaration \definechangesauthor.

```
\definechangesauthor[key/value list]{id}
```

This declaration take an *id* as a mandatory argument to identify the author. In the *key/value list* you can optionally define a name and if you like a special color to be used for this person.

The *id* can then be used as a value to the keyword id in any of the editorial commands discussed above to indicate that the suggested change was made by the respective author. The other keyword that can be used with these commands is comment to give some further explanation why the change is suggested. Both possibilities are exhibited in the next examples.

[FMi 1] really?

Sample text, something added, a wordblob replaced and some^FMi stuff removed.

[1] Fix it everywhere in the document!

List of changes

Added: added 6
Replaced (FMi): word 6
Deleted (FMi): some 6
Commented: Fix it everywhere in [...] 6

```
\usepackage{changes}
\definechangesauthor[color=red,
                name=Frank]{FMi}
Sample text, something \added{added},
a \replaced[id=FMi,comment=really?]
        {word}{blob} replaced
and \deleted[id=FMi]{some} stuff
removed.\comment{Fix it everywhere
  in the document!}
\listofchanges
```

3-6-12

Customizing the list of changes

If you specify \listofchanges without its optional argument, you get a listing of all changes suggested for the document. This list includes the type of changes, the author *id* (if specified) and the text are truncated if necessary to fit on a single line. In the optional argument, you can specify the keyword style. The accepted values are list (default), summary, or compactsummary. In the summary cases you get for each author a listing of the number of additions, deletions, and so forth instead of the individual changes.

To change the displayed title to your liking, add the text as the value to the keyword title.

Sample text, something added, a wordblob^1 replaced and some^FMi stuff removed.^2

Summary of changes

Author: anonymous
Added 1

_____
[1] [FMi 1]: really?
[2] [FMi 2]: Mumble!

Deleted	0
Replaced	0
Highlighted . .	1
Commented . .	0
Author: FMi (Frank M.)	
Added	0
Deleted	1
Replaced	1
Highlighted . .	0

```
\usepackage[commentmarkup=footnote]
            {changes}
\definechangesauthor[color=red,
            name=Frank M.]{FMi}
\setsummarytowidth{Commented\qquad}
Sample text, something \added{added},
a \replaced[id=FMi,comment=really?]
        {word}{blob}
replaced and \deleted[id=FMi]{some}
\highlight{stuff}
removed.\comment[id=FMi]{Mumble!}

\listofchanges[title=Summary of
            changes,style=summary]
```

3-6-13

With `compactsummary` authors without change requests and lines with a zero value are dropped.

[FMi 1]: really?

[FMi 2]: Mumble!

Sample text, something added, a word blob replaced and some[FMi] **stuff** removed.

Changes (compact)

Author: anonymous

Added 1

Highlighted 1

Author: FMi (Frank M.)

Deleted 1

Replaced 1

Commented 2

```
\usepackage[commentmarkup=margin]
           {changes}
\definechangesauthor[name=Frank M.,
               color=red]{FMi}
\setsummarywidth{110pt}
```

```
Sample text, something \added{added},
a \replaced[id=FMi,comment=really?]
         {word}{blob}
replaced and \deleted[id=FMi]{some}
\highlight{stuff}
removed.\comment[id=FMi]{Mumble!}
```

```
\listofchanges[style=compactsummary]
```

3-6-14

In very narrow or very wide settings the default width of lines in compact summaries may need adjustments. This can be done either with `\setsummarywidth` as shown in the previous example or with `\setsummarytowidth` used in Example 3-6-13. For full listings you can specify the amount of text prior to truncation using `\settruncatewidth` (the default is `.6\textwidth`).

It is also possible to restrict the listing to a subset of the editorial changes by specifying the keyword `show`. It accepts the values `all` (default), `added`, `deleted`, `replaced`, `comment`, and `highlight`, and it is possible to combine several values by using a | as shown in the example. This plus the fact that you can call `\listofchanges` more than once offers some flexibility in presentation.

Sample text, something added, a wordblob [FMi 1]: really? replaced and some[FMi] **stuff** [1]: bad word removed.[FMi 2]: Grumble!!!

Liste der Änderungen

Eingefügt: added 6

Ersetzt (FMi): word 6

Gelöscht (FMi): some 6

Kommentare und Markierungen

Hervorgehoben: stuff 6

Kommentiert (FMi): Grumble!!! 6

```
\usepackage[ngerman]{babel}
\usepackage[commentmarkup=uwave]{changes}
\definechangesauthor[color=red,name=Frank M.]{FMi}
```

```
Sample text, something \added{added}, a
\replaced[id=FMi,comment=really?]{word}{blob}
replaced and \deleted[id=FMi]{some}
\highlight[comment=bad word]{stuff}
removed.\comment[id=FMi]{Grumble!!!}
```

```
\listofchanges[show=added|deleted|replaced]
\listofchanges[show=comment|highlight,
         title=Kommentare und Markierungen]
```

3-6-15

The last example also shows that if a language package like babel or polyglossia is loaded, the autogenerated texts change if that language is already supported—if not, you get English defaults. All strings are also available through commands; consult the package documentation if you feel compelled to change them.

247

Customizing the editorial markup commands

As we have seen in the previous examples the editorial markup is by default colored, any deleted text is additionally stroked out, and comments are placed into the margin. All this can be adjusted by using key/value package options.

Layout of editorial commands

The `markup` option defines the general layout for the editorial markup. Allowed values are `colored` (as described above), `underlined` (like default but added text is also underlined), `bfit` (added text is bold, deleted is italic, both are colored), and `nocolor` (with added text underlined and deleted text stroked out).

If this is not sufficient, you can individually decide the visual representation for added and deleted text by using the options `addedmarkup` and `deletedmarkup` when loading the package. Because `changes` internally makes use of the ulem package, you will recognize the meaning of the allowed values from the discussion in Section 3.4.4 on page 189. They are `uline`, `uuline`, `uwave`, `dashuline`, `dotuline`, `sout`, `xout`, as well as values for selecting fonts, i.e., `bf`, `it`, `sl`, and `em`. The default value that you see in some examples is called `colored`. Explicitly setting one of these options supersedes any setting made by the more general `markup` option for this type of editorial action.

To adjust the highlighting use `highlightmarkup` with the possible values `background` (default), `uuline`, or `uwave`. In the same fashion `commentmarkup` adjusts the markup for comments, both those made with the `\comment` commands and those made with the `comment` key as part of `\added` and friends. The allowed values are `todo` (default), `margin`, `footnote`, and `uwave`. The results of the different values have already been shown in the previous examples.

Author identification

As seen in the previous example, the *id* of the review author (except for the anonymous one) is shown next to his or her editorial change (by default as a superscript to the right of the text). This can be adjusted through three package options. The option `authormarkup` defines the general formatting. Possible values are `superscript` (default), `subscript`, `brackets`, `footnote`, or `none` (suppress author information). The placement with respect to the added or deleted text is adjustable through `authormarkupposition` accepting `left` or `right` (default). Finally, the option `authormarkuptext` defines what is shown: `id` (default) or `name`.

The next example uses some of the options, not necessarily for the better.

Sample text, something[1] added, a word*blob*[2] replaced and ₍Frank *some* stuff removed. ₍anonymous ~Whoa!~

[1][**anonymous 1**]: maybe
[2][**Frank 1**]: really?

```
\usepackage[markup=bfit,authormarkuptext=name,
   authormarkup=subscript,authormarkupposition=left,
   highlightmarkup=uwave,commentmarkup=footnote]{changes}
\definechangesauthor[color=red,name=Frank]{FMi}
Sample text, \added[comment=maybe]{something} added,
a \replaced[id=FMi,comment=really?]{word}{blob}
replaced and \deleted[id=FMi]{some} stuff removed.
\highlight{Whoa!}
```

3-6-16

Instead of or in addition to using the above options, you can specify the precise LaTeX code that should be executed when typesetting the editorial commands. For the additions, deletions, and replacements, this is done with the declarations `\setaddedmarkup` and `\setdeletedmarkup`. For highlighting and commentaries we have `\sethighlightmarkup` and `\setcommentmarkup`.

248

If, for example, you do not like the way comments are displayed, then you can easily define your own layout instead. Here is an example that still uses \todo but applies different settings. Within \setcommentmarkup you can use #1 to refer to the commentary and #2 and #3 to access the author id and name, respectively. We need this to check on the content of #2, because the user may not have any id specified, and in that case we do not want a spurious set of brackets to show up in the output. We therefore use the \IfIsAnonymous test provided by the changes package and typeset different text depending on the result.[1]

```
\usepackage{changes}
\definechangesauthor[color=red,name=Frank]{FMi}
\setcommentmarkup{\todo[size=small,textcolor=authorcolor,
    linecolor=authorcolor,backgroundcolor=white,nolist]
  {\IfIsAnonymous{#2}{}%
      {\textbf{[[#3\,\arabic{authorcommentcount}]]} }#1}}
Sample text, \added[comment=maybe]{something} added,
a \replaced[id=FMi,comment=really?]{blob}{word}
replaced and \deleted[id=FMi]{some} stuff removed.
```

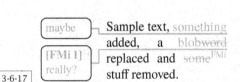

Sample text, something added, a blobword replaced and some^FMi stuff removed.

3-6-17

The other noteworthy part in the example is the use of authorcommentcount that holds the commentary number for the current author. The above construction therefore prints the authors name (#3) followed by the number for the current comment in brackets.

Providing your own editorial commands

If you feel that writing \added[id=FMi,comment=better?]{stuff} is far too much, then there are a number of ways to change that. You can, for example, define shorthands such that \add[FMi]{stuff}[better?] can be used. This is what we demonstrate in the final example. For details on the \DeclareDocumentCommand declaration see Section A.1.4 on page →II 632.

Sample text, something added[1], a wordblob^FMi replaced and some[2] stuff removed.

```
\usepackage[commentmarkup=footnote]{changes}
\definechangesauthor[name=Anonymous]{??}
\definechangesauthor[name=Frank,color=red]{FMi}
\DeclareDocumentCommand\add{O{??}mo}
  {\IfValueTF{#3}{\added[id=#1,comment=#3]{#2}}{\added[id=#1]{#2}}}
\DeclareDocumentCommand\del{O{??}mo}
  {\IfValueTF{#3}{\deleted[id=#1,comment=#3]{#2}}
  {\deleted[id=#1]{#2}}}
\DeclareDocumentCommand\rep{O{??}mmo}
  {\IfValueTF{#4}{\replaced[id=#1,comment=#4]{#2}{#3}}
                 {\replaced[id=#1]{#2}{#3}}}
Sample text, something \add{added}[better], a \rep[FMi]{word}{blob}
replaced and \del[FMi]{some}[Really?] stuff removed.
```

---

[1][?? 1]: better
[2][FMi 1]: Really?

3-6-18

---

[1]The package offers many other commands to customize the output based on the current state, such as \IfIsInList, \IfIsColored, \IfIsEmpty, or \IfIsAuthorEmptyAtPosition. For details see the package documentation.

Managing package option conflicts

The changes package requires a number of additional packages, most importantly todonotes, truncate, ulem, and xcolor and if necessary automatically loads them. Given that these package can take options, this might be a problem if they are not loaded with the options your document needs elsewhere for some reason.

In that case you have two possibilities: either load those packages with the desired set of options before changes is loaded or arrange for changes to load them with the right options by using the options todonotes, truncate, ulem, and xcolor and specify the options that these package should use as the value. You may have to surround the values with braces to hide any commas inside.

Managing command name conflicts

Given that \added, \comment, \highlight, and so forth are fairly common names, it is possible that they conflict with command names defined by other packages. For this case changes offers the option commandnameprefix, which accepts the values always or ifneeded. If used, then the commands are prefixed by ch, e.g., \chadded or \chcomment. In the case of ifneeded, this is done only if there is a conflict.

3.6.4 pdfcomment — Using PDF annotations and tool tips

If you do not mind that your comments and notes are visible only in PDF readers with support for PDF annotations, then it might pay off to take a look at Josef Kleber's pdfcomment package that provides you with commands for annotating your document in ways you may already be familiar with from using Acrobat or similar software. Such annotations can then be opened and closed when viewing the document in a PDF reader.

```
\pdfcomment [key/value list] {comment}
\pdfmargincomment [key/value list] {comment}
\pdfmarkupcomment [key/value list] {marked text}{comment}
```

The first two commands produce an annotation in the middle of paragraph text or in the margin, respectively. The *comment* is by default not visible but is shown if the annotation is clicked in the PDF viewer.

The \pdfmarkupcomment command is intended for copy-editing. The *marked text* is typeset in the document and additionally marked by highlighting it or using strikeout, underline, etc. What exactly is done is defined in the *key/value list*; thus, normally you will define your own commands by presetting some key.

Given that the results of the commands are interactive features in the produced PDF, it is not really possible to exhibit any of this here in the book. We therefore show only a single screenshot from the documentation as an example (and not in color).

\pdfmarkupcomment will typeset so called PDF text markup annotations over the text specified in the argument ⟨markup text⟩. Possible types for the option markup are: High••• Unde••• Squiggl••• StrikeOut

There are a number of additional commands available, e.g., ways to make a list of all comments or to produce tool tips that show up when you hover with the mouse cursor over a certain area, and there are a few dozen keys that you can use in the *key/value list* arguments to customize the result; for details we have to refer you to the package documentation.

In summary, it is fair to say that you get roughly the same set of features as with the previous three packages — once you have defined your own variants. The advantage is that you get an interactive document; the disadvantage is that you are restricted to suitable viewers.

3.6.5 vertbars — Adding bars to paragraphs

A common approach to highlight changes made in a new edition of a document is to add vertical lines in the margin at places where the document has changed. As a simple application of the lineno package Peter Wilson developed the vertbars package that prints vertical bars next to certain paragraphs (instead of line numbers).

It automatically loads the lineno package and accepts all of its options, in particular switch and switch* to control the bar placement. It offers a single environment vertbar, which is similar to lineno's linenumbers but produces a bar in place of line numbers. The width of this bar is controlled by \barwidth and defaults to 0.4pt. Any limitation of the lineno package equally applies here, in particular that the bars always apply to full paragraphs.[1]

```
\usepackage{vertbars} \setlength\barwidth{1pt}
This paragraph has no bar.
\begin{vertbar}
  The environment always starts a new paragraph
  and can only contain full paragraphs.
  \begin{vertbar}
    Nesting is possible as shown here but only
    on paragraph boundaries.
  \end{vertbar}
  Breaks across columns or pages are also
  possible and the bar continues.
\end{vertbar}    Another paragraph without a bar.
```

This paragraph has no bar.

The environment always starts a new paragraph and can only contain full paragraphs.

Nesting is possible as shown here but only on paragraph boundaries.

Breaks across columns or pages are also possible and the bar continues.

Another paragraph without a bar.

3-6-19

---

[1] If you need them on individual lines, you might want to try the changebar package by Michael Fine and Johannes Braams instead.

251

CHAPTER 4

Basic Formatting Tools — Larger Structures

While the previous chapter was concerned with micro-typography, this chapter now looks at commands and environments for formatting larger chunks of text.

Typesetting lists is the subject of the first part. We start with a discussion of the various parameters and commands controlling the standard LaTeX lists, enumerate, itemize, and description, followed by a brief look at LaTeX's generic list capabilities. Then, the important enumitem package is discussed, which we recommend as a basis for many documents. The production of horizontally oriented lists is covered by the tasks package, the concept of "headed lists" is exemplified with the amsthm and thmtools packages and typed-checklist, helps you write and maintain check lists of various kinds. Together these should satisfy the structure and layout requirements of most readers.

The second part then explains how to simulate "verbatim" text. In particular, we take a detailed look at the powerful packages fancyvrb and listings.

The third part presents packages that deal with line numbering (lineno); handling of columns, such as parallel text in two columns (paracol); or solving the problem of producing multiple columns with multicol.

At the end we take a brief look at packages for generating sample texts. They are useful for testing layouts or for reporting bugs when you are asked to produce a so-called Minimal Working Example (MWE) to show your problem.

4.1 Lists

Lists are very important LaTeX constructs and are used to build many of LaTeX's display-like environments. LaTeX's three standard list environments and the generic list environment are discussed in the first two sections, where we also show how they can be customized.

Section 4.1.3 starting on page 261 provides an in-depth discussion of the package enumitem, which introduces a number of new list structures and offers comprehensive methods to customize them, as well as the standard lists.

It is followed by a discussion of "headed lists", such as theorems and exercises. Finally, Sections 4.1.6 and 4.1.7 cover two packages for tasks and check lists.

4.1.1 Using and modifying the standard lists

It is relatively easy to customize the three standard LaTeX list environments itemize, enumerate, and description, and the next three sections look at each of these environments in turn. Changes to the default definitions of these environments either can be made globally by redefining certain list-defining parameters in the document preamble or can be kept local.

Customizing the itemize list environment

For a simple unnumbered itemize list, the labels are defined by the commands shown in Table 4.1 on the facing page. To create a list with different-looking labels, you can redefine the label-generating command(s). You can make that change local for one list, as in the example below, or you can make it global by putting the redefinition in the document preamble. The following simple list is a standard itemize list with a marker from the PostScript Zapf Dingbats font (see Section 10.13.1 on page →II 113) for the first-level labels:

```
\usepackage{pifont}
\newenvironment{myitemize}
  {\renewcommand\labelitemi{\ding{43}}\begin{itemize}}
  {\end{itemize}}
```

☞ Text of the first item in the list.

☞ Text of the first paragraph in the second item of the list.

The second paragraph of the item.

☞ Text of the third item.

```
\begin{myitemize}
\item Text of the first item in the list.
\item Text of the first paragraph in the second
      item of the list.

      The second paragraph of the item.
\item Text of the third item.
\end{myitemize}
```

4-1-1

The \labelitemfont command (which defaults to \normalfont) is intended to alter the font for all labels in one go. This is especially useful if the body font for the document is altered and its symbols are less suitable to be used as labels; see also the discussion on page 697.

	Command	Default Definition	Representation
First Level	\labelitemi	\labelitemfont\textbullet	•
Second Level	\labelitemii	\labelitemfont\bfseries \textendash	–
Third Level	\labelitemiii	\labelitemfont\textasteriskcentered	*
Fourth Level	\labelitemiv	\labelitemfont\textperiodcentered	·

Table 4.1: Commands controlling an itemize list environment

Customizing the enumerate list environment

LaTeX's enumerated (numbered) list environment enumerate is characterized by the commands and representation forms shown in Table 4.2 on the next page. The first row shows the names of the counter used for numbering the four possible levels of the list. The second and third rows are the commands giving the representation of the counters and their default definition in the standard LaTeX class files. Rows four, five, and six contain the commands, the default definition, and an example of the actual enumeration string printed by the list.

A reference to a numbered list element is constructed using the \theenumi, \theenumii, and similar commands, prefixed by the internal commands \p@enumi, \p@enumii, etc., respectively. The last three rows in Table 4.2 on the following page show these commands, their default definition, and an example of the representation of such references. It is important to consider the definitions of both the representation and reference-building commands to get the references correct.

We can now create several kinds of numbered description lists simply by applying what we have just learned.

Our first example redefines the first- and second-level counters to use capital roman digits and Latin characters. The visual representation should be the value of the counter followed by a dot, so we can use the default value from Table 4.2 on the next page for \labelenumi.

```
\renewcommand\theenumi     {\Roman{enumi}}
\renewcommand\theenumii    {\Alph{enumii}}
\renewcommand\labelenumii {\theenumii.}
```

I. Introduction

    A. Applications
    Motivation for research

    B. Organization
    Structure of the report

II. Literature Survey

q1=I q2=IA q3=IB q4=II

```
\begin{enumerate}
 \item \textbf{Introduction}    \label{q1}
  \begin{enumerate}
   \item \textbf{Applications}   \label{q2} \\
    Motivation for research
   \item \textbf{Organization}   \label{q3} \\
    Structure of the report
  \end{enumerate}
 \item \textbf{Literature Survey} \label{q4}
\end{enumerate}
q1=\ref{q1} q2=\ref{q2} q3=\ref{q3} q4=\ref{q4}
```

4-1-2

	First Level	Second Level	Third Level	Fourth Level
Counter	enumi	enumii	enumiii	enumiv
Representation	\theenumi	\theenumii	\theenumiii	\theenumiv
Default Definition	\arabic{enumi}	\alph{enumii}	\roman{enumiii}	\Alph{enumiv}
Label Field	\labelenumi	\labelenumii	\labelenumiii	\labelenumiv
Default Form	\theenumi.	(\theenumii)	\theenumiii.	\theenumiv.
Numbering Example	1., 2.	(a), (b)	i., ii.	A., B.

Reference representation

	First Level	Second Level	Third Level	Fourth Level
Prefix	\p@enumi	\p@enumii	\p@enumiii	\p@enumiv
Default Definition	{}	\theenumi	\theenumi(\theenumii)	\p@enumiii\theenumiii
Reference Example	1, 2	1a, 2b	1(a)i, 2(b)ii	1(a)iA, 2(b)iiB

Table 4.2: Commands controlling an enumerate list environment

After these redefinitions we get funny-looking references; to correct this we have to adjust the definition of the prefix command \p@enumii. For example, to get a reference like "I-A" instead of "IA" as in the previous example, we could do

```
\makeatletter \renewcommand\p@enumii{\theenumi--} \makeatother
```

because the reference is typeset by executing \p@enumii followed by \theenumii. To simplify this LaTeX offers the command \labelformat (see page 77) to alter the representation, i.e.,

```
\labelformat{enumii}{\theenumi--#1}
```

to achieve the same effect. You can also decorate an enumerate field by adding something to the label field and its reference representation. In the example below, we have chosen for the first-level list elements the section sign (§) as a prefix and a period as a suffix (omitted in references).

§1. item of list
§2. item of list
w1=§1 w2=§2

```
\renewcommand\labelenumi{\S\theenumi.} \labelformat{enumi}{\S#1}
\begin{enumerate}
 \item \label{w1} item of list \item \label{w2} item of list
\end{enumerate}
w1=\ref{w1}  w2=\ref{w2}
```

4-1-3

You might even want to select different markers for consecutive labels. For instance, in the following example, characters from the PostScript font ZapfDingbats are used. In this case there is no straightforward way to automatically make the \ref commands produce the correct references. Instead of \theenumi simply producing the representation of the enumi counter, we define it to calculate from the counter value which symbol to select.

The difficulty here is to create this definition in a way such that it survives the label-generating process. The trick is to add \protect so that \ding is not executed when the label is written to the .aux file, yet to ensure that its argument is evaluated at that point and the result is stored therein. The latter goal is achieved by using the recently introduced \inteval command (see Section A.2.5 on page →II 657). It is expandable and executes inside an \edef or \write, which is needed here.[1]

① item of list

② item of list

③ item of list

④ item of list

```
\usepackage{pifont}
\renewcommand\labelenumi{\theenumi}
\renewcommand\theenumi
        {\protect\ding{\inteval{171+\value{enumi}}}}
\begin{enumerate}
\item item of list \label{l1} \item item of list \label{l2}
\item item of list \label{l3} \item item of list \label{l4}
\end{enumerate}
```

4-1-4   l1=① l2=② l3=③ l4=④   `l1=\ref{l1} l2=\ref{l2} l3=\ref{l3} l4=\ref{l4}`

The same effect is obtained with the dingautolist environment defined in the pifont package; see Section 10.13.1 on page →II 113.

Customizing the description list environment

With the description environment you can change the \descriptionlabel command that generates the label. In the following example the font for typesetting the labels is changed from boldface (default) to bold sans serif.

An item Its description with enough text to fill more than one line in the example.

Another item Now just two lines of text.

```
\renewcommand\descriptionlabel[1]%
   {\hspace{\labelsep}\textsf{\bfseries #1}}
\begin{description}
\item[An item] Its description with enough text
        to fill more than one line in the example.
\item[Another item]  Now just two lines of text.
\end{description}
```

4-1-5

The standard LaTeX classes set the starting point of the label in a description environment at a distance of \labelsep to the left of the left margin of the main text galley or the enclosing environment.[2] Thus, the \descriptionlabel command in the example above first adds a value of \labelsep to start the label aligned with the left margin.

---

[1]For the TeXnically interested: LaTeX's \value command, despite its name, does not produce the "value" of a LaTeX counter, but only its internal TeX register name. In circumstances where TeX expects a number it can be used directly (which is the case for the argument of \inteval), but if you use it directly inside \edef or \write, the internal name rather than the "value" survives. By prefixing the internal register name with the command \the, you can get at the register value even in such situations, but here this is not necessary.

[2]A somewhat odd default, but it has been like this for more than three decades — thus a feature, not a bug.

Modifying shared properties

The customizations discussed so far for the three standard lists only covered the aspects specific to each list type, but not properties like the vertical spacing before, within, and after the list; the behavior when lists are nested; and so forth.

All these properties are shared between different list types (by default at least) and are inherited from a generic `list` environment that is used to define all user-level lists (and in fact even other environments). Modifying them is a more elaborate exercise and usually done only in document classes. We discuss the concepts in the next section because you are going to find them used in many older class files and it is important to understand what has been set up there, if you want to adjust it. However, for new developments and your own customizations, we suggest making use of the excellent **enumitem** package instead. It is discussed in Section 4.1.3.

4.1.2 LaTeX's generic list environments

Most lists in LaTeX, including those that we have seen previously, are internally built using the generic `list` environment. It has the following syntax:

```
\begin{list}{default-label}{decls} item-list \end{list}
```

The argument *default-label* is the text to be used as a label when an `\item` command is found without an optional argument. The second argument, *decls*, can be used to modify the different geometrical parameters of the `list` environment, which are shown schematically in Figure 4.1 on the facing page.

The default values of these parameters typically depend on the type size and the level of the list. Those being vertically oriented are rubber lengths, meaning that they can stretch or shrink. They are set by the `list` environment as follows: upon entering the environment the internal command `\@list`⟨level⟩ is executed, where ⟨level⟩ is the list nesting level represented as a lowercase roman numeral (e.g., `\@listi` for the first level, `\@listii` for the second, `\@listiii` for the third, and so on).

Each of these commands, defined by the document class, holds appropriate settings for the given level. Typically, the class contains separate definitions for each major document size available via options. For example, if you select the option `11pt`, one of its actions is to change the list defaults. In the standard classes this is done by loading the file `size11.clo`, which contains the definitions for the 11pt document size.

Incomplete setups in standard classes

In addition, most classes contain redefinitions of `\@listi` (i.e., first-level list defaults) within the size-changing commands `\normalsize`, `\small`, and `\footnotesize`, the assumption being that one might have lists within "small" or "footnote-sized" text, but not in headings or very tiny sizes. However, since this is a somewhat incomplete setup, strange effects are possible if you

- use nested lists in such small sizes (the nested lists get the standard defaults intended for `\normalsize`), or

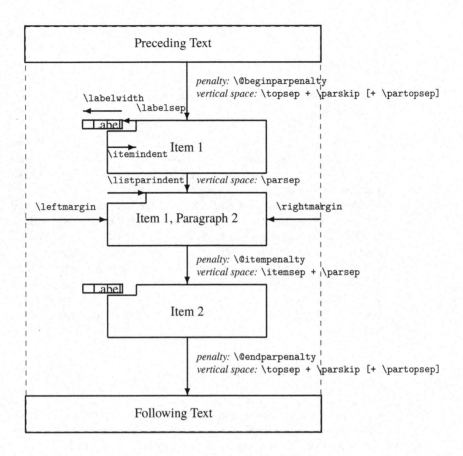

4-1-6

Figure 4.1: Parameters used by the list environment

\topsep   Rubber space between first item and preceding paragraph.

\partopsep   Extra rubber space added to \topsep when environment starts a new paragraph.

\itemsep   Rubber space between successive items.

\parsep   Rubber space between paragraphs within an item.

\@beginparpenalty   Break penalty before the list.

\@itempenalty   Break penalty before items except the first.

\@endparpenalty   Break penalty after the list.

\leftmargin   Space between left margin of enclosing environment (or of page if top-level list) and left margin of this list. Must be nonnegative. Its value depends on the list level.

\rightmargin   Similar to \leftmargin but for the right margin. Its value is usually 0pt.

\listparindent   Extra indentation at beginning of every paragraph of a list except the one started by \item. Can be negative, but is usually 0pt.

\itemindent   Extra indentation added to the horizontal indentation of the text part of the first line of an item. The starting position of the label is calculated with respect to this reference point by subtracting the values of \labelsep and \labelwidth. Its value is usually 0pt.

\labelwidth   The nominal width of the box containing the label. If the natural width of the label is ≤\labelwidth, then by default the label is typeset flush right inside a box of width \labelwidth. Otherwise, a box of the natural width is employed, which causes an indentation of the text on that line. It is possible to modify the way the label is typeset by providing a definition for the \makelabel command.

\labelsep   The space between the end of the label box and the text of the first item. Its default value is 0.5em.

- jump from \small or \footnotesize directly to a large size, such as \huge (a first-level list now inherits the defaults from the small size, because in this setup \huge does not reset the list defaults).

With a more complex setup these defects could be mended. However, given that the simpler setup works well in most practical circumstances, most classes provide only this restricted support.

Global changes are difficult

Because of this size- and nesting-dependent setup for the list parameters, it is not possible to change any of them globally in the preamble of your document. For global changes you have to provide redefinitions for the various \@list.. commands discussed above or select a different document class.[1]

Page breaking around lists

Page breaking around and within a list structure is controlled by three TEX counters: \@beginparpenalty (for breaking before the list), \@itempenalty (for breaking before an item within the list), and \@endparpenalty (for breaking the page after a list). By default, all three are set to a slightly negative value, meaning that it is permissible (and even preferable) to break a page in these places compared to other breakpoints. However, this outcome may not be appropriate. You may prefer to discourage or even prevent page breaks directly before a list. To achieve this, assign a high value to \@beginparpenalty (10000 or more prohibits the break in all circumstances), for example:

```
\makeatletter
  \@beginparpenalty=9999
\makeatother
```

TEX counters need this unusual assignment form, and because all three contain an @ sign in their name, you have to surround them with \makeatletter and \makeatother if the assignment is done in the preamble.[2]

Many environments are implemented as lists

It is important to realize that such a setting is global to all environments based on the generic list environment (unless it is made in the *decls* argument) and that several LATEX environments are defined with the help of this environment or its stripped-down version trivlist (for example, quote, quotation, center, flushleft, and flushright). These environments are "lists" with a single item, and the \item[] command is specified in the environment definition. The main reason for them to be internally defined as lists is that they then share the vertical spacing with other display objects and thus help achieve a uniform layout.

As an example, we can consider the quote environment, whose definition gives the same left and right margins. The simple variant Quote, shown below, is identical to quote apart from the double quote symbols added around the text. Note the special precautions, which must be taken to eliminate undesirable white space after the opening quote character (\ignorespaces) and before the closing one (\unskip). We also placed the quote characters into boxes of zero width to make the quotes hang

---

[1] The alternative is to use the enumitem package, which offers good interfaces for this and other list customizations, successfully hiding the low-level details discussed in this section.

[2] If your LATEX installation is current then \UseName{@beginparpenalty}=9999 can be used instead.

into the margin. This trick is worth remembering: if you have a zero-width box and align the contents with the right edge, they stick out to the left.

A paragraph of text before our display quotation.

"Some quoted text, followed by more quoted text."

4-1-7 Directly following text ...

```
\newenvironment{Quote}%
  {\begin{list}{}{\setlength\rightmargin{\leftmargin}}%
              \item[]\makebox[0pt][r]{``}\ignorespaces}%
  {\unskip\makebox[0pt][l]{''}\end{list}}
A paragraph of text before our display quotation.
\begin{Quote}  Some quoted text,
   followed by more quoted text. \end{Quote}
Directly following text \ldots
```

4.1.3 enumitem — Extended list environments

The enumitem package by Javier Bezos has been written to improve the handling of lists in LaTeX on several fronts. It has three major goals:

- Offer a mechanism to locally customize individual list environments with the help of an optional argument at list start;

- Support new list environments (with or without special settings) that can be easily set up, enabling you to better structure your document;

- Provide a mechanism to easily customize all list environments.

We discuss them one after another, starting with the local modifications to existing environments. Keep in mind, however, that the local modifications should be the exception, not the norm. If you find yourself repeatedly applying the same adjustments in your document, then you are most likely simply missing a new document element that gives them a face and a name.

When the package is loaded, the three standard LaTeX lists are modified to accept an optional argument at the environment start, as demonstrated here with enumerate.[1]

```
\begin{enumerate}[key/value list] item-list \end{enumerate}
```

In the *key/value list* a multitude of different keys can be used to adjust vertical and horizontal spacing, the look and feel of the item label, and other aspects of the list environments. For example, all parameters listed in Figure 4.1 on page 259 can be set via keys; e.g., itemsep=2pt would force a separation of 2pt between items in the current list. We discuss them in detail throughout the next pages.

There also exist keys that set several aspects in one go; e.g., noitemsep reduces the space between items and paragraphs to zero, and nosep does this also to the spaces before and after the list, thus producing a really tight layout.

---

[1]If necessary, you can load the package with the option loadonly in which case the standard environments are not redefined and only newly defined lists have this syntax extension.

Another sometimes useful key is `resume`, which continues the numbering from a previous list of the same type.[1] We demonstrate all these keys in the next example and also set `listparindent` (normally zero) to get a visible paragraph indentation.

A somewhat tight list ...

1. An item with two paragraphs.
   This is the second paragraph containing more text to fill two lines.
2. Another item.

... and here with no vertical spaces:
3. Do you see?
4. And the numbering continues as requested.

More text after the list.

```
\usepackage{enumitem}
A somewhat tight list \ldots
\begin{enumerate}[noitemsep,listparindent=1em]
  \item An item with two paragraphs.          \par
    This is the second paragraph containing
    more text to fill two lines.
  \item Another item.
\end{enumerate}
\ldots\ and here with no vertical spaces:
\begin{enumerate}[nosep,resume]
  \item Do you see?
  \item And the numbering continues as requested.
\end{enumerate}
More text after the list.
```

4-1-8

A variation is `resume*`, which works like `resume` but also reuses all previously given key settings. We demonstrate this in the next example.

If the package is loaded with the option `inline`, it automatically sets up three further list environments, `itemize*`, `enumerate*`, and `description*`, that produce inline rather than display lists using by default the same labels (and counters in the case of `enumerate*`) as their display counterparts. As shown in the next example these lists ignore implicit or explicit paragraph breaks.

We may want to enumerate items within a paragraph to (a) save space (b) make a less prominent statement, or (c) for some other reason.

As before we can continue the list (d) with the key resume (e) or with `resume*` (f) or apply some other change. **Paragraph breaks are ignored in such lists!**

```
\usepackage[inline]{enumitem}
We may want to enumerate items within a paragraph to
\begin{enumerate*}[label=(\alph*)]
  \item save space  \item make a less prominent statement,
  or \item for some other reason.  \end{enumerate*}

As before we can continue the list
\begin{enumerate*}[resume*]
  \item with the key \texttt{resume} \item or with
  \texttt{resume*} \item or apply some other  \par  change.
\end{enumerate*}
\textbf{Paragraph breaks are ignored in such lists!}
```

4-1-9

In the previous example we adjusted the `label` on each list environment the second time through `resume*`.[2] This clearly shows that while the optional argument is useful for the occasional one-off correction, adding such a setting to every environment is both cumbersome and error prone. In such a case it is better

---

[1] From the standard lists this makes sense only for `enumerate`, but once you define your own list that uses numbered labels, it can be applied there too.

[2] The details, e.g., the meaning of `\alph*`, is discussed later, but you can probably guess.

to adjust the default settings or, if different setups are needed in different places, to define new list environments with their own customized settings. This is done with the following declaration.

\newlist{*env*}{*base-env*}{*max-nesting-level*}

The \newlist declaration defines a new environment *env* that is based on one of the base list environments, i.e., enumerate, itemize, or description or their inline counterparts enumerate*, itemize*, or description*. The latter can be used in the declaration even if the inline option is not given, i.e., if the environments are not available at the document-level.

The *max-nesting-level* specifies to what level the new environment can be nested. Do not specify an unnecessary high value here, because for each level there is some internal setup necessary and in the case of environments based on enumerate a counter is declared. Thus, unused levels are quite costly. If necessary, you can redeclare an existing environment using \renewlist, for example, to raise the level of supported itemize levels from 4 (default) to 6 or provide an implementation of quote that is based on the enumitem interface; see Example 4-1-29 on page 277 for this.

An example of a new list is steps:

1: Lists are declared with \newlist.

2: But this is not enough:

   a) as a minimum we need to define a label.

   b) this is done here locally on each environment.

3: Usually, \setlist is used for this.

`4-1-10`

```
\usepackage{enumitem}
\newlist{steps}{enumerate}{4}

\noindent An example of a new list is \texttt{steps}:
\begin{steps}[label=\arabic*:]
\item Lists are declared with \verb=\newlist=.
\item But this is not enough:
  \begin{steps}[label=\alph*)]
  \item as a minimum we need to define a \texttt{label}.
  \item this is done here locally on each environment.
  \end{steps}
\item Usually, \verb=\setlist= is used for this.
\end{steps}
```

Setting default values

As indicated in the previous example, just declaring a new list is not quite enough; we have to declare at least the label setup for it. This, as well as any other adjustment to a list environment, is done with \setlist declarations that come in four variations:

\setlist*	{*key/value list*}	% defaults for all lists
\setlist*[*level*]	{*key/value list*}	% defaults for lists on level
\setlist*[*env-name*]	{*key/value list*}	% defaults for a specific list
\setlist*[*env-name,level*]	{*key/value list*}	% defaults for a specific list on level

---

These declarations define defaults in increasing order of specificity. The version without an optional argument defines defaults that are applied to all list environments unless there are more specific settings overwriting them. Specifying just a *level* defines defaults for all lists on that level (overwriting any general ones). Specifying just an *env-name* overwrites those just for this environment, and specifying both *env-name* and *level* finally defines the values applicable only for the specific environment on that particular level.[1] Instead of just one *env-name* or one *level*, you can specify several separated by commas if all combinations should receive the same *key/value list*.

Thus, to fully set up the `steps` environment we could have written:

```
\newlist{steps}{enumerate}{4}
\setlist[steps]{label=\arabic*:} \setlist[steps,2,3]{label=\alph*)}
```

Because we give a specific default for only the second and third levels, `label` is `\arabic*:` on the first and fourth levels (probably not a wise choice).

The difference between `\setlist` and its star form `\setlist*` is that the former replaces whatever defaults have been set up, while the latter augments previously set up defaults for the given *env-name* and *level* combination. If you want to set up several key values for one combination, you either have to specify them all together in the *key/value list* argument or use `\setlist` on the first and `\setlist*` on all later declarations with the same *env-name* and *level* combination.

With our new knowledge of how to adjust lists locally or to set up default values, we can now take a closer look at the huge number of keys that can be applied in both cases. We discuss them in useful chunks and give examples for typical use cases.

Vertical spacing and page breaks

All display lists start and finish with a vertical skip of `topsep`, which is augmented by `partopsep` if the list forms a paragraph on its own. Unfortunately, to this value LaTeX also adds the value of `\parskip` from the enclosing list or the main text galley. In the standard classes the parameter has a default value of `0pt plus 1pt`, but if that is being set to a positive value, then it affects the space around lists, which means the list parameters may need adjustment.

If an item in a list contains several paragraphs, then these are separated by a skip of `parsep`, and the vertical space between items is given by the sum of `itemsep` and `parsep`. For example, the defaults (for all lists) in the standard article class are equivalent to the following declarations:

```
\setlist {topsep    = 8pt plus 2pt minus 1pt}
\setlist*{partopsep = 2pt plus 1pt minus 1pt}
\setlist*{parsep    = 4pt plus 2pt minus 1pt}
\setlist*{itemsep   = 4pt plus 2pt minus 1pt}
```

Standard class defaults are suboptimal

If you think this results in too much space around the list, you could set up your own defaults as we do in the next example. In fact, the values in the standard classes are rather bad, because they allow the space between items to stretch faster (2pt+2pt) than the space before and after the list, which has only a stretch of 2pt+1pt (from the

---

[1] The package is a bit unforgiving if you misspell the *env-name* and replies with some low-level errors, so if that happens, triple-check the *env-names* you used.

default \parskip). Only when partopsep is also applied does the stretch become identical.[1]

As discussed on page 260, there are three (internal) penalties associated with lists: for breaking before the list, at an item, and after the list. The enumitem keys for them are beginpenalty, midpenalty, and endpenalty, respectively. Their default values in most classes are for some strange reason usually −51, which makes LaTeX favor these breakpoints over other places.

While this seems reasonable between items and perhaps even more so after the list, it is usually less desirable at its beginning, because the first item is often logically tied to preceding text. Thus, it may be advisable to change at least the value for beginpenalty to forbid or discourage a break there.

If you do not want to rule out a break categorically through a default setting, you may still want to disallow it occasionally through the optional argument on the list, e.g., by setting beginpenalty=10000 there. For such special settings enumitem offers a convenient way to define new symbolic keys; e.g., you can declare

```
\SetEnumitemKey{nobreak}{beginpenalty=10000}
```

and then use the new valueless nobreak key in your document. In the same fashion you could define

```
\SetEnumitemKey{compact}
    {topsep=4pt plus 1pt,partopsep=0pt,itemsep=2pt plus 1pt,parsep=1pt}
```

to have a key available that gets you a slightly compacted list when needed.

On the other hand we may want all lists to

1. use less space around them;
2. and no space between items and paragraphs.

    Instead paragraphs should have some indentation inside the list.

Do these setting also apply

here?

4-1-11 Clearly no! See discussion below.

```
\usepackage{enumitem}
\setlist{noitemsep,listparindent=1em,partopsep=0pt,
         topsep=4pt plus 1pt minus 1pt}

On the other hand we may want all lists to
\begin{enumerate}
 \item use less space around them;
 \item and no space between items and paragraphs.
  \par Instead paragraphs should have some
       indentation inside the list.
\end{enumerate}
Do these setting also apply
\begin{center} here? \end{center}
Clearly no! See discussion below.
```

As seen in the previous example, enumitem distinguishes between real lists, i.e., the standard LaTeX ones or those defined with \newlist, and display elements like center or tabbing that in standard LaTeX also receive the vertical spacing applied to lists because they are internally defined with the trivlist environment. If you change the list defaults through \setlist, this is no longer the case. If you want to

---

[1] Unfortunately, this is not adjustable in standard classes without altering the formatting of millions of existing documents, so it is up to new classes to offer better defaults.

keep the layout uniform and get your `\setlist` settings applied to all display environments, you can load the package with the option `includedisplayed`. Of course, only those relevant for `trivlist` are applied, i.e., in this case `topsep` and `partopsep`.

Now we get the reduced spacing

here!

And this applies to all other display environments too.

```
\usepackage[includedisplayed]{enumitem}
\setlist{noitemsep,listparindent=1em,partopsep=0pt,
          topsep=4pt plus 1pt minus 1pt}
Now we get the reduced spacing
\begin{center}  here! \end{center}
And this applies to all other display environments too.
```
4-1-12

The alternative is to explicitly set values for `trivlist` that are then inherited by the different display environments, e.g.,

```
\setlist[trivlist]{partopsep=0pt,topsep=4pt plus 1pt minus 1pt}
```

The advantage of that approach is that you can set up different defaults for both types of environments.

The general formatting of the list environment body

If we ignore for a moment that lists contain `\item` commands and just concentrate on the text material, then there are three horizontal parameters that define the overall list structure. The `leftmargin` and the `rightmargin` define the indentation of the list material from both sides measured from the enclosing list or text, and `listparindent` defines the paragraph indentation of paragraphs that do not also start a new item. Paragraphs that start with an `\item` command use `itemindent` for indentation (which is zero by default).

For example, in LaTeX's standard classes the standard lists are indented from the left but not from the right. If you prefer a fixed indentation from the right, you could use these settings:

A sample text showing the outer margins of normal text.

- A sample text of more than one line please.

  - A sample text of more than one line.

    1. A longer sample text with two lines.

Again some more text to indicate the galley margins.

Description test A longer sample text with two lines of text.

```
\usepackage{enumitem}
\setlist{rightmargin=0pt}     % already the default
\setlist[1]{rightmargin=20pt}
A sample text showing the outer margins of
normal text.
\begin{itemize}
\item A sample text of more than one line please.
  \begin{itemize}
  \item A sample text of more than one line.
    \begin{enumerate}
    \item A longer sample text with two lines.
\end{enumerate} \end{itemize} \end{itemize}
Again some more text to indicate the galley margins.
\begin{description}
\item[Description test] A longer sample text with
    two lines of text.                \end{description}
```
4-1-13

Defining the item label (or title) and its design

When we speak about the default item label, we mean the material that is typeset whenever an \item command is used without an optional argument. This is usually the case for unnumbered itemize and numbered enumerate-like lists, while with description-like lists the item *text* is always produced by the optional argument; i.e., there is no item label but an item *title*.

Such an item label is defined by the label key and any special formatting instructions by the key format or its synonym font. With description lists the label key is not used (unless you forget to supply an optional argument to \item), and only the format key is used to format the item title.

Typically the label holds a special symbol to be used in an itemize-like list or some form of counter representation, possibly embellished with other material in "enumerate-like" lists. The format might then hold font directives such as \bfseries or \ttfamily.

Because there is no global default for item labels, you have to provide as a minimum a setting for label if you define a new list with \newlist. If you forget, then the first \item encountered without an optional argument raises an error message. This makes sense, because labels are normally specific to a particular list (and often specific to the level of nesting). Of course, you can provide global defaults yourself such as

```
\setlist{label=}
\setlist[1]{label=\labelitemi}    \setlist[2]{label=\labelitemii}
\setlist[3]{label=\labelitemiii} \setlist[4]{label=\labelitemiv}
```

That gives an empty default for all list levels that are not otherwise set up and some specific symbols for levels 1 to 4. The above settings use commands from Table 4.1, i.e., those that are used by standard LaTeX for the itemize labels at different levels. This makes it easy to define logical environments to structure your document. Their typeset result then still looks like an itemize, and by changing \labelitemi, you can then change all such lists in parallel.

Slowly cooked shiitake mushrooms:

- 20–30 dried shiitake mushrooms

- 4 fresh hot red chillies

- 2 tablespoons roasted sesame oil

4-1-14

```
\usepackage{enumitem}
% default as above
\newlist{ingredients}{itemize}{1}

Slowly cooked shiitake mushrooms:
\begin{ingredients}
\item 20--30 dried shiitake mushrooms \item 4 fresh hot
  red chillies \item 2 tablespoons roasted sesame oil
\end{ingredients}
```

When you define a new list based on enumerate, the package automatically defines counters for each level named ⟨*env-name*⟩⟨*level*⟩ with the *level* given as a lowercase roman numeral. For example, below we define a steps environment with two levels, so the corresponding counters are stepsi and stepsii. They can then be used to produce numbered labels for each level with the help of the usual counter formatting commands.

```
\usepackage{enumitem}
\newlist{steps}{enumerate}{2}
\setlist[steps,1]{label=\arabic{stepsi}.}
\setlist[steps,2]{label=(\alph{stepsii})}
```

Slowly cooked shiitake mushrooms:

1. Soak 20–30 dried mushrooms in hot water

   (a) minimum 2 hours

   (b) keep water for later

2. Slice shiitake in 5–7 mm slices

3. ...

```
Slowly cooked shiitake mushrooms:
\begin{steps}
 \item Soak 20--30 dried mushrooms in hot water
   \begin{steps}
    \item minimum 2 hours
    \item keep water for later
   \end{steps}
 \item Slice shiitake in 5--7\,mm slices
 \item \ldots
\end{steps}
```

4-1-15

However, enumitem provides an even more convenient way through `\arabic*`, `\alph*`, `\roman*`, and the like where the * means "use the current list counter". Thus, above we could have more concisely written `label=\arabic*.` without worrying about the counter name, as we already did in the introductory Example 4-1-10.

Beside `label` there also exists a key variant `label*` that prepends the label from the enclosing level to its value. This allows for very concise setups in certain cases. For example, below we concatenate labels on all levels, and on the first level we prepend a section sign. We also use `format` to force boldface for all labels. Note that this formatting instruction is not passed on to the references.

```
\usepackage{enumitem}
\newlist{legal}{enumerate}{6}
\setlist[legal]   {format=\bfseries,label*=\arabic*.}
\setlist[legal,1]{label=\S\arabic*.}
```

We may want to enumerate items within a paragraph to

§1. save space

  §1.1. make a less prominent statement, or

  §1.2. because

    §1.2.1. it's Friday

    §1.2.2. we are bored

§2. or for some other reason.

Show me: §1.2.1.

```
We may want to enumerate items within a paragraph to
\begin{legal}
 \item save space
   \begin{legal}
    \item make a less prominent statement, or
    \item because
      \begin{legal}
       \item it's Friday \label{ll}
       \item we are bored
      \end{legal}
   \end{legal}
 \item or for some other reason.
\end{legal}
Show me: \ref{ll}
```

4-1-16

In Example 2-2-2 on page 36 we already discussed the problem that counter representations are often used by the \ref command and therefore may produce odd-looking references when the counter representation involves some fancy formatting. This is also true for references to enumerate-like list items, because by default they use the label for the reference. However, with enumitem this problem can be resolved by placing certain formatting instructions into the format key (as we did above) or by providing a ref key that then defines the representation for the cross-reference independently of the setting of label.

The latter is also necessary if you want to concatenate the labels from nested levels in your reference. For example, a reference to the second-level steps in Example 4-1-15 comes out as "(b)", but you may want "1b" instead. In that case the solution is to write

```
\setlist[steps,2]{label=(\alph*),ref=\arabic{stepsi}\alph*}
```

instead. Note that we can use * in place of the current (second level) counter, but to access the counter of the outer level we need to explicitly use its name here.

Because label, label*, or the ref key are used for the label mechanism, their values are written to the .aux file. This means they act like moving arguments, and anything fragile in their value therefore needs to be protected with \protect.

For description-like lists there are different methods for adjusting the item label; they are discussed on page 278.

The placement of the item label or item text

Typesetting the item label requires three actions: deciding how wide the box should be in which the item label or text is placed (key labelwidth), deciding how the label is aligned within this box (key align), and finally deciding where on the line this box is placed.

The align key actually does a little more than aligning the label within its box, and it is important to understand these subtleties. Out of the box there are three possible values: right used by default for enumerate and itemize-like lists, left used by description-like lists, and finally parleft that we discuss later.

There is a crucial difference between the way right and left operate: when the label material turns out to be wider than the labelwidth, it simply protrudes into the left margin if right alignment is in force. The assumption is that on the left there is just white space so that this is possible. It is therefore of little importance how wide we make that label box. If, however, this happens with left alignment in force, then the label box is essentially widened, and the paragraph text following it is pushed to the right as much as necessary. For example, in description the labelwidth is by default set to zero, and through this mechanism the actual width is determined by the label content. This is why a very short label results in the first line of the following text getting outdented because it starts directly after the label box (separated by labelsep, of course).

If you do not want this, you could specify a minimum width for the label box. In the next example we use the calc package to fit the box exactly into the available space in the margin without the need to know the exact values (which means we have to subtract `\labelsep`).

A sample text showing the outer margins.

X Label shorter than the available space so the text moves to the left.

Wide label Wider than the space available so the text moves to the right.

X   Now no text is moved.

Wide label Wider than the space available so the text again moves to the right.

```
\usepackage{calc,enumitem}
\noindent A sample text showing the outer margins.
\begin{description}
\item[X] Label shorter than the available space so
  the text moves to the left.
\item[Wide label] Wider than the space available so
  the text moves to the right.    \end{description}

\setlist[description]{labelwidth=\leftmargin-\labelsep}
\begin{description}
\item[X] Now no text is moved.
\item[Wide label] Wider than the space available so
  the text again moves to the right.\end{description}
```

4-1-17

With the default `right` alignment the above approach does not work because the label just protrudes out of the box if it is wider. However, there is a way to define your own alignment code using `\SetLabelAlign` that we exhibit in the next example:

A sample text showing the outer margins.

  • Label fits the available space.

Wide label Label is wider than the available space so protrudes into the left margin.

  • No change to the default.

Wide label But now wide labels move following text partly to the right.

Wide la-bel A rather ugly example for the use of the `parleft` alignment.

```
\usepackage{enumitem}
\setlist[itemize]{format=\bfseries}
\SetLabelAlign{rightextend}{\hfill#1}
\noindent A sample text showing the outer margins.
\begin{itemize}
\item                Label fits the available space.
\item[Wide label] Label is wider than the available
  space so protrudes into the left margin.\end{itemize}

\begin{itemize}[align=rightextend]
\item                No change to the default.
\item[Wide label] But now wide labels move following
  text partly to the right.               \end{itemize}

\begin{itemize}[align=parleft]
\item[Wide label] A rather ugly example for the use
  of the \texttt{parleft} alignment.    \end{itemize}
```

4-1-18

The third alignment value, `parleft`, wraps the label material in a top-aligned `\parbox` of width `labelwidth` so that the label may consist of several lines. Of course, this works well only if the label box is wide enough (which is not really the case in the previous example). Please note that if items are too close to each other in this type of layout, their labels can overprint another because for LATEX they appear to contain only a single line of material.

What still needs discussing is how the label box is positioned. If you look at Figure 4.1 on page 259, you can see that its placement is determined by three parameters that can be set with the keys `labelwidth`, `labelsep`, and `itemindent`. The standard LaTeX way of determining the start position of the label is convenient if you consider the label being a certain amount away from the start of the list text, but it is less natural if you instead think of the label being a certain amount away from the left margin.

To ease the specification in either case `enumitem` introduces another key named `labelindent` (and a corresponding parameter `\labelindent`) that specifies the space from the left margin to the start of the label. Of course, this means an over-specification, because the keys are related in the following way

$$labelindent + labelwidth + labelsep = leftmargin + itemindent$$

and if four of them are specified, the fifth has to be computed according to the above equation. By default this is `labelindent`; i.e., the calculations are carried out as with standard LaTeX.

This means that if you specify a value for `labelindent`, you have to tell `enumitem` which other key it should (re)calculate. Otherwise, given that all parameters have default values, it would leave the package clueless about what to overwrite and what to retain. As a result, without this extra information your setting of `labelindent` may be simply ignored. To identify the parameter that should be calculated, specify ! as its value (if you do this with more than one parameter, the last one wins). The next example artificially shows the effects on placement and size of the label box when we ask for different parameters to be recalculated. The box is shown as a frame.

In standard `itemize` the label is set using `align=right`, i.e., is set at the right edge of the label box and is allowed to protrude at the left out its box. If we want to visualize that label box, we can use `\SetLabelAlign` to redefine `right` by adding a `\framebox` with the appropriate width and put the content against its right edge. The `\strut` is there to ensure that the frame has the same height and depth in all cases.

```
\usepackage{enumitem}
\SetLabelAlign{right}{\setlength\fboxsep{0pt}%
                      \framebox[\labelwidth][r]{\strut#1}}
```

Some text to show the left margin.

```
\noindent Some text to show the left margin.
\begin{itemize}  \item The default.  \end{itemize}
```

□ • The default.

```
\begin{itemize}[labelindent=17pt,labelwidth=!]
\item No visible difference as label protrudes.
\end{itemize}
```

| No visible difference as label protrudes.

```
\begin{itemize}[labelindent=17pt,itemindent=!]
\item  This results in \textttt{itemindent} becoming
  positive so the paragraph text moves to the right.
\end{itemize}
```

□ • This results in `itemindent` becoming positive so the paragraph text moves to the right.

```
\begin{itemize}[labelindent=17pt,labelsep=!]
\item Overprint of label and text because
  \textttt{labelsep} becomes negative.
\end{itemize}
```

□ Overprint of label and text because `labelsep` becomes negative.

4-1-19

271

With \DrawEnumitemLabel the package offers its own way to visualize the dimensions involved in the label placement. If the command is placed into the list just before the first item (or into the key first), then it generates four rules representing labelindent by labelwidth, labelsep, and itemindent in that order. They are drawn as thin rules if positive and as thick rules if negative. If a value is zero, no rule is visible, but you can deduce that from the fact that the surrounding rules are further apart. The leftmargin is indicated with two vertical lines.

```
\usepackage{enumitem}
\setlist{nosep,first=\DrawEnumitemLabel}
\noindent Some text to show the left margin.
\begin{itemize}
  \item The default.
\end{itemize}
\begin{itemize}[labelindent=20pt,itemindent=!]
  \item \texttt{itemindent} now becomes positive.
\end{itemize}
\begin{itemize}[labelindent=-10pt,itemindent=!]
  \item \ldots{} and here negative.
\end{itemize}
```

Some text to show the left margin.

• The default.

• itemindent now becomes positive.

• ... and here negative.

4-1-20

There is also the possibility of using * as the value, which works like ! but first sets labelwidth to a default value based on the current label settings. It measures the label material by replacing any \arabic* with "0", a \roman* with "viii", and for \alph* it uses "m". If you want a different string for replacement, you can specify it with the key widest as done below. Again, we use a frame to visualize the label box and use an uncommon setting for label to show that the whole label material is used in the measuring process.

```
\usepackage{enumitem}
\setlist[enumerate]{label=--\arabic*--}
\noindent Some text to show the left margin.
\begin{enumerate}
  \item The default.
\end{enumerate}
\begin{enumerate}[leftmargin=*,start=2]
  \item One digit labels are set flushleft on the margin.
\end{enumerate}
\begin{enumerate}[leftmargin=*,start=33]
  \item But labels with 2 digits protrude.
\end{enumerate}
\begin{enumerate}[leftmargin=*,widest=99,start=42]
  \item Here we tell to leave space for 2 digits.
\end{enumerate}
```

Some text to show the left margin.

–1– The default.

–2– One digit labels are set flushleft on the margin.

–33– But labels with 2 digits protrude.

–42– Here we tell to leave space for 2 digits.

4-1-21

The key widest can also be used with itemize or description-like lists in which case its string value is measured and used to define the necessary value for `leftmargin` to fit the text into this space. Note that `\labelitemi` holds the material for the first-level item (i.e., the bullet).

\usepackage{enumitem}

```
\begin{description}[leftmargin=*,widest=Short label,nosep]
  \item[Short label]
    and some text to fill more than one line.
  \item[A much longer label]
    and some text to fill more than one line.
\end{description}
\begin{itemize}[leftmargin=*,widest=\labelitemi,nosep]
  \item       Bullet flush left.
  \item[---] Dash now protruding.
\end{itemize}
```

Short label and some text to fill more than one line.
A much longer label and some text to fill more than one line.
• Bullet flush left.
— Dash now protruding.

4-1-22

Finally there are two convenience keys, `wide` and `left`. The `wide` key makes the list look like an ordinary paragraph, starting with a label that uses the default `label` formatting rules (including the use of `labelsep` for separating the label from the text). It can be used with all list types. If used as a valueless key, the item is indented using a normal `\parindent`. If you give it a value, then that is used for the paragraph indentation. It is of course also possible to use further keys to adjust different aspects of the default settings.

\usepackage{enumitem}

```
\begin{itemize}[wide,nosep]
  \item
    This item appears as a normal paragraph.

    Here is a second paragraph for comparison.
\end{itemize}
\begin{description}[wide=0pt]
  \item[Longer label]
    Another common setting would be \texttt{0pt},
    i.e., no indentation whatsoever.

    Here is a second paragraph.
\end{description}
```

• This item appears as a normal paragraph.

Here is a second paragraph for comparison.

Longer label Another common setting would be 0pt, i.e., no indentation whatsoever.

4-1-23   Here is a second paragraph.

The `left` key can be given one or two values (separated by two dots). With only one, it sets `labelindent` and recomputes `leftmargin`, i.e., does `leftmargin=*`. If passed two values, it sets `labelindent` and `leftmargin` and then recomputes `labelsep` to fit the values. This works well for `itemize` or `enumerate` environments but not at all for `description` because the latter uses a zero `labelwidth` by default. Thus, recomputing `labelsep` makes that rather large, as shown in Example 4-1-24 on the next page. The remedy is to force a recalculation of `labelwidth` instead, as we do in the last list of that example. Notice the use of the `first` key: the `\hrule` helps us to see where the text margins would be.

- We have 5 pt space in front of the label.

    Here is a second paragraph for comparison.

-      The item text is 20 pt indented and the label starts flush left.

    A second paragraph.

---

1. Outdented label with the text set flush left.

    Here is a second paragraph.

Label   With description this has an ugly hole and gives a warning.

Label   Much better now.

```
\usepackage{enumitem}
\setlist{first=\hrule,listparindent=10pt,noitemsep}
\begin{itemize}[left=5pt]
\item We have 5\,pt space in front of the label.
\par Here is a second paragraph for comparison.
\end{itemize}
\begin{itemize}[left=0pt..20pt]
\item The item text is 20\,pt indented and the label
   starts flush left.\par A second paragraph.
\end{itemize}
\begin{enumerate}[left=-10pt..0pt]
\item Outdented label with the text set flush left.
\par Here is a second paragraph.
\end{enumerate}
\begin{description}[left=-10pt..10pt]
\item[Label] With \textttt{description} this has an
   ugly hole and gives a warning.
\end{description}
\begin{description}[left=-10pt..10pt,labelwidth=!]
\item[Label] Much better now.
\end{description}
```

4-1-24

Controlling the list numbering

Normally lists start their numbering from 1, but if this is for some reason not desired, it is possible to give an explicit starting value using the key **start**. We have used that already in the previous example to save us from typesetting several dozen items to show the desired effect. The next example now shows a case where it is useful as part of a default setup.

This example exhibits redefinitions of **itemize** and **enumerate** and repeats Examples 4-1-1 and 4-1-4. It clearly demonstrates that compared to the basic approach it is noticeably easier to achieve such effects with **enumitem**. We also show the use of **ref** by not coloring cross-reference links (no claim that is good design).

① Altering **enumerate** is easy:

  ☞ Just load a font with nice digits.

  ☞ Select the starting point if necessary.

② For **itemize** select the symbol in the **label**.

③ Cross-referencing still works.

x1=① x2=② x3=③

```
\usepackage{pifont,color,enumitem}
\setlist[itemize]{label=\ding{43}}
\setlist[enumerate,1]{start=172,ref=\ding{\arabic*},
                  label=\textcolor{blue}{\ding{\arabic*}}}
\begin{enumerate}
\item Altering \textttt{enumerate} is easy:\label{x1}
  \begin{itemize} \item Just load a font with nice digits.
             \item Select the starting point if necessary.
  \end{itemize}
\item For \textttt{itemize} select the symbol in
     the \textttt{label}.\label{x2}
\item Cross-referencing still works.\label{x3}
\end{enumerate} x1=\ref{x1} x2=\ref{x2} x3=\ref{x3}
```

4-1-25

Counting list items backwards is not supported by default, but the package documentation [4] gives an example how it could be achieved using the keys `label`, `ref`, and `after`. An alternative is to use the package etaremune by Hendri Adriaens that defines an environment with the same name for precisely that purpose.

Counting backwards

We have also already seen the keys `resume` and `resume*` (resume with reuse of previous key settings) for directing an "enumerate-like" list to continue with its numbering scheme from the value of its last invocation. These keys are normally used in the optional argument to a list, but if you use `resume` with `\setlist`,[1] you define a list environment that continues its numbering throughout the whole document. If you like to restart that numbering once in a while, e.g., at chapter boundaries, you can then use the command `\restartlist{`*list-name*`}` to restart the numbering from 1. Another possibility would be to use `start=1` on the next list, but `\restartlist` is better in this case, because it can be automatically issued from the heading command.

Continue counting across several environments

It is also possible to give a `series` of enumerations a name and resume them by passing that name to the `resume` or `resume*` key at a later invocation. The key settings at the first list (with the `series` key) are globally stored and recalled when `resume*` is used. As shown in the example, it is still possible to overwrite some of them as we did with the `listparindent` value. If `resume` is used with a series name, then that series is continued without using the stored key values.

Set up a list in a series …
1* A first item.
2* An item with two paragraphs.
    This is the second paragraph with indentation.
…and a list outside the series:

  1. Different formatting

…Now resume the series:
3* Formatting is restored.
    Do you see the updated listparindent?

4-1-26 More text after the list.

```
\usepackage{enumitem}

\noindent Set up a list in a series \ldots
\begin{enumerate}[series=xyz,nosep,listparindent=1em,
                  label=\arabic*\textsuperscript{*}]
  \item A first item.
  \item An item with two paragraphs.                      \par
       This is the second paragraph with indentation.
\end{enumerate}
\ldots and a list outside the series:
\begin{enumerate} \item Different formatting\end{enumerate}
\ldots Now resume the series:
\begin{enumerate}[resume*=xyz,listparindent=3em]
  \item Formatting is restored.                           \par
     Do you see the updated \texttt{listparindent}?
\end{enumerate}
More text after the list.
```

Short labels — mimicking the enumerate package

One of the first packages that extended list environments with an optional argument was David Carlisle's package enumerate. In the optional argument you specified the format of the enumeration where the characters A, a, I, i, and 1 would be shorthands for what enumitem calls `\Alph*`, `\alph*`, `\Roman*`, `\roman*`, and `\arabic*`.

This syntax is also supported by enumitem if you load it with the package option `shortlabels`. In that case the following rule applies: if the *first* key in the optional

---

[1]Using `resume*` does not make any sense inside `\setlist` if you think about it.

argument is not recognized as a known key name, it is assumed to be a label definition that uses the above shorthands. Here is an example:

Task A: We need to explain why this example has problems!
Tbsk B: We need to write
    (1) a summary
    (2) good index entries.

Item "Tbsk B:" shows what can go wrong.

```
\usepackage[shortlabels]{enumitem}
\begin{enumerate}[Task A:,noitemsep]
\item We need to explain why this example has problems!
\item We need to write    \label{bad}
  \begin{enumerate}[(1),nosep]
    \item  a summary \item good index entries.
  \end{enumerate}
\end{enumerate}
Item ''\ref{bad}'' shows what can go wrong.
```

4-1-27

The above example already shows the danger of that type of shorthand: anything that fits is replaced; thus, we get "Tbsk" in the second item label. To correct this you can hide the problematical characters in a brace group, e.g., using {Task}␣A: instead. It also exhibits that we should add a `ref` key if we ever want to reference such an item.

If you use the `shortlabels` option, then you can change the shorthands behavior or even add new ones using `\SetEnumerateShortLabel` as follows:

```
\SetEnumerateShortLabel{i}{\textsc{\roman*}}
```

after which `i` represents the current `enumerate` counter as a Small Caps roman numeral.

Hooking in code

In the case of more complex setups it is sometimes helpful to inject code at well-defined places, and for this `enumitem` offers three keys: `before` (executed just after the keys are evaluated and before a display list adds any vertical space), `first` (executed before the body of the environment is processed), and finally `after` (executed when the `\end` of the environment is seen). All three also have a star variant that appends the code rather than replacing it.

We use this in the next example to reproduce the `Quote` environment from Example 4-1-7 on page 261 by automatically inserting the `\item` command and the quote symbols. Making `itemize` the base environment is convenient because its default settings already fit most of our needs and it does not generate unnecessary overhead by defining a counter.

... some text before to indicate the margins.

    "Some quoted text, followed by more quoted text."

... and some text following ...

```
\usepackage{enumitem}    \newlist{Quote}{itemize}{4}
\setlist[Quote]{label=,rightmargin=\leftmargin,
    first=\item\makebox[0pt][r]{''}\ignorespaces,
    after=\unskip\makebox[0pt][l]{''}}
\noindent \ldots\ some text before to indicate the margins.
\begin{Quote}
    Some quoted text, followed by more quoted text.
\end{Quote}
\ldots\ and some text following \ldots
```

4-1-28

Obviously, setting the list body justified in narrow measures is likely to produce ugly spaced-out lines. It may therefore be better to apply `\raggedright` or `\RaggedRight` from the ragged2e package to the body. With enumitem this can be done automatically by using the `before` key. It should be done in this key not in `first`, because we may still want a special `listparindent` and `\raggedright` would reset that if placed in the `first` key. What we place in that key is an `\item` command because we do not want to supply that in the source.

... some text before.

    Some text in our redefined quote environment.

    Paragraphs are indented and the text is set ragged right.

... and some text following ...

```
\usepackage{ragged2e,enumitem}
\renewlist{quote}{itemize}{4}
\setlist[quote]{label=,rightmargin=\leftmargin,
   before=\RaggedRight,first=\item,listparindent=1em}
\noindent \ldots\ some text before.
\begin{quote}
Some text in our redefined \textttt{quote} environment. \par
Paragraphs are indented and the text is set ragged right.
\end{quote}
\ldots\ and some text following \ldots
```

4-1-29

Inline lists

Above we have already seen inline lists produced with enumerate*, itemize*, or description* and learned that we can produce our own versions using `\setlist`. There are three keys especially provided for such lists to define what should happen at certain points within the list. The code stored in `afterlabel` is used after the label instead of the usual `labelsep` (defaults to `\nobreakspace`), `itemjoin` is used between items (defaults to a space), and `itemjoin*` if specified is used between the last two items. The latter two are used only if you are still in LR-mode and not for some reason in vertical mode.

For special handling before and after the list, use `before` and `after`. In the next example we made use of `before` to add a colon in front of the list.

```
\usepackage[inline]{enumitem} \newlist{inenum}{enumerate*}{1}
\setlist[inenum]{label=(\alph*),before={{\unskip: }},
   itemjoin={{; }},itemjoin*={{ and }}}
```

... text before: (a) one; (b) two and (c) three and more text.

```
\ldots\ text before \begin{inenum} \item one
   \item two \item three \end{inenum} and more text.
```

4-1-30

You may have noticed that some values in the previous example have been surrounded by double brace groups. They are necessary to ensure that the spaces in the values are not lost.[1] Due to some implementation restrictions, an inline list cannot contain floats, marginpars, or vertically oriented display environments. If that is a problem, you can try to add the key `mode=unboxed`, but that has some other limitations such as not supporting `itemjoin*`.

Extra braces may be necessary and other restrictions

---

[1] Perhaps this can be fixed at some point in the future, but for now the extra braces are necessary, and if the underlying issue gets resolved, they should do no harm.

Styling description-like lists

In lists based on `description` the default for `labelwidth` is zero and the alignment is `left`, which means as discussed earlier that the actual label text gets as wide as necessary, pushing any following text to the right.

That is fine for lists with comparatively short labels but leads to questionable results if the label text gets longer. For starters, the label text is boxed by default, which means that any spaces within are set at their nominal width. In contrast, the remainder of the paragraph text on the same line will stretch or shrink spaces to fill the line, which can result in quite noticeable differences. This can be changed by specifying the `style` key with the value `unboxed`. However, note that `labelsep` that separates the item title from the item text is still a rigid length and thus might give some strange results.

```
\usepackage{enumitem}
\begin{description}
\item[Short label]
      and some text to fill two lines.
   \item[A much longer label]
       to compare and some text to fill more than
       one line.
\end{description}

\begin{description}[style=unboxed]
   \item[A much longer label]
       to compare and some text to fill more than
       one line.
\end{description}
```

Short label and some text to fill two lines.

A much longer label to   compare and some text to fill more than one line.

A much longer label to compare and some text to fill more than one line.

4-1-31

Another possible problem is label titles that are actually wider than a full line. With the default settings those simply extend into the margin unless, for example, unboxed is used. Even for labels that are not that wide, you may want to apply a special treatment if the text is wider than the space available in the margin.

```
\usepackage{enumitem}
\begin{description}[noitemsep,style=unboxed]
   \item[X]        and some text to fill more than
                   one line.
   \item[Medium] and some text to fill more than
                 one line.
   \item[A fairly long label --- so what happens?]
                 Well, it breaks.
\end{description}
```

X and some text to fill more than one line.
Medium and some text to fill more than one line.
A fairly long label — so what happens? Well, it breaks.

4-1-32

Beside unboxed there is `sameline` (which is similar but does not outdent the first line if the label is short), `nextline` (which starts a new line if the label is wider than the space defined by `leftmargin`), and finally `multiline` (which places the label into a parbox of width `leftmargin`). Compare Example 4-1-31 with the following example that exhibits `sameline` and `nextline`:

X Compare this text with that from the previous example.

Medium
This text starts on a new line.

A fairly long label — so what happens now?
It breaks and the item text starts on a new line.

4-1-33

```
\usepackage{enumitem}
\begin{description}[style=sameline]
\item[X]   Compare this text with that from the
           previous example.
\end{description}
\begin{description}[style=nextline]
\item[Medium]             This text starts on a new line.
\item[A fairly long label --- so what happens now?]
     It breaks and the item text starts on a new line.
\end{description}
```

We have not tried to show the result of `multiline` in the previous example, because the default `leftmargin` is simply too small, so here is a version somewhat adjusting for this (capable of holding at least two or three words in the margin):

A fairly long label — so what happens now?
Now the label breaks in the margin, but this can still look strange if it is long and the item text is short.

4-1-34

```
\usepackage{enumitem}
\setlist[description]{style=multiline,leftmargin=7em}
\begin{description}
\item[A fairly long label --- so what happens now?]
  Now the label breaks in the margin, but this can still
  look strange if it is long and the item text is short.
\end{description}
```

Size dependent settings

Up to now all examples showed settings that have been fixed for the current list or, in the case of defaults for all lists, a certain type or a certain level, and usually this is sufficient. However, there are ways to make this even more granular by setting defaults depending on the current font size, e.g., to provide different values in footnotes.

A simple way to achieve this is to specify length values in the font-dependent sizes "ex" or "em". However, if you require exact values at different font sizes, then this is usually not an adequate approach. For this a special syntax is available if you load the package with the package option `sizes`.

After that you can specify length values for keys that contain different values for different font sizes or ranges of font sizes as illustrated in the following example:

```
\usepackage[sizes]{enumitem}
\setlist{ labelsep = <-10> 3pt <10-18> 5pt <18-> 10pt }
```

The syntax *<lower−upper>* indicates a range of font sizes with the *lower* size included and the *upper* boundary excluded. The boundaries are given as simple (decimal) numbers; i.e., `pt` is implicitly assumed. You can leave out one of the values, which then denotes an open range.

A value in front of the first `<..>` is used as a default if nothing else matches. It is however in many cases more readable to specify everything in terms of ranges.

Instead of a range, you can use a single size value such as <10.95>, which then
has to be matched precisely. Note that this may easily lead to mistakes. For example,
LaTeX's class 11pt usually loads fonts at 10.95pt and not at 11pt so that it needs a
good understanding of the font setup (see Chapter 9) to be successful.

It is therefore a better approach to use *named* sizes, because then enumitem does
the matching to real sizes in the background for you. By default the package knows
about tiny, script, footnote, small, normal, large, Large, LARGE, and huge
matching the corresponding font size commands of LaTeX. However, for efficiency
reasons these are set up only once when enumitem is loaded. Thus, if the font sizes
are changed afterwards, they have to be remapped with declarations such as

```
\SetEnumitemSize{normal}{\normalsize}   \SetEnumitemSize{small}{\small}
```

Rather than looking at the setup from the perspective of single keys providing
different values for different font sizes, it is also possible to start from the font size
and provide key/value settings for that font size or for a whole font size range.

For this approach the \setlist declaration gets extended when the sizes
package option is used.

```
\setlist*<size or range>              {key/value list}
\setlist*<size or range>[level]       {key/value list}
\setlist*<size or range>[env-name]    {key/value list}
\setlist*<size or range>[env-name,level]{key/value list}
```

All \setlist variants discussed on page 263 are supported. The additional *size or
range* argument in angle brackets can, as the name indicates, be either a single font
size (typically a named one) or a size range like those discussed above. For example,
in the standard LaTeX classes special list values are provided for first-level lists only
(so in that respect the classes are fairly inconsistent). To mimic that, using the much
more readable enumitem interface, you would write declarations like the following:

```
\setlist<normal>   [1]{topsep  = 8pt plus 2pt minus 4pt,
                       itemsep = 4pt plus 2pt minus 2pt,
                       parsep  = 4pt plus 2pt minus 2pt }
\setlist<small>    [1]{topsep  = 4pt plus 2pt minus 2pt,
                       itemsep = 2pt plus 1pt minus 1pt,
                       parsep  = 2pt plus 1pt minus 1pt }
\setlist<footnote> [1]{topsep  = 3pt plus 1pt minus 1pt,
                       itemsep = 2pt plus 1pt minus 1pt,
                       parsep  = 2pt plus 1pt minus 1pt }
```

No other font size or level is explicitly set up for the standard LaTeX classes (largely
because the way LaTeX was managing this was basically ad hoc and complicated). As a
result if you write

```
text \footnotesize text \Large \begin{itemize} ...
```

you find that standard LaTeX uses the footnote size setting for the above parameters, which is obviously wrong!

With the enumitem interface you can easily do much better either by providing settings for all other standard sizes as well or, probably even better, by using ranges so that any font size receives reasonable values, e.g.,

```
\setlist<normal->      [1]{topsep  = 8pt ...  % settings for 'normal'
                                             % size and above
\setlist<small-normal>[1]{topsep  = 4pt ...  % lower than 'normal' but
                                             % not below 'small'
\setlist<-small>       [1]{topsep  = 3pt ...  % anything below 'small'
                                             % gets 'footnote' values
```

4.1.4 amsthm — Providing headed lists

The term "headed lists" describes typographic structures that, like other lists such as quotations, form a discrete part of a section or chapter and whose start and finish, at least, must be clearly distinguished. This is typically done by adjusting the vertical space at the start or adding a rule, and in this case also by including some kind of heading, similar to a sectioning head. The end may also be distinguished by a rule or other symbol, maybe within the last paragraph, and by extra vertical space.

Another property that distinguishes such lists is that they are often numbered, using either an independent system or in conjunction with the sectional numbering.

Perhaps one of the more fruitful sources of such "headed lists" is found in the so-called "theorem-like" environments. These had their origins in mathematical papers and books but are equally applicable to a wide range of expository material, because examples and exercises may take this form whether or not they contain mathematical material.

Because their historical origins lie in the mathematical world, we choose to describe the amsthm package [1] by Michael Downes (1958-2003) from the American Mathematical Society (AMS) as a representative of this kind of extension.[1] This package provides an enhanced version of standard LaTeX's \newtheorem declaration for specifying theorem-like environments (headed lists).

As in standard LaTeX, environments declared in this way take an optional argument in which extra text, known as "notes", can be added to the head of the environment. See the example below for an illustration.

\newtheorem*{*name*}{*heading*}

The \newtheorem declaration has two mandatory arguments. The first is the environment *name* for this element. The second is the *heading* text.

If \newtheorem* is used instead of \newtheorem, no automatic numbers are generated for the environments. This form of the command can be useful if you have

---

[1]A possible alternative is the ntheorem package by Wolfgang May and Andreas Schedler.

only one lemma or exercise and do not want it to be numbered; it is also used to produce a special named variant of one of the common theorem types.

Lemma 1 (Main). *The LATEX Companion complements any LATEX introduction.*

Mittelbach's Lemma. *The LATEX Companion contains packages for all important application areas.*

```
\usepackage{amsthm}
\newtheorem{lem}{Lemma} \newtheorem*{ML}{Mittelbach's Lemma}
\begin{lem}[Main] The \LaTeX{} Companion
   complements any \LaTeX{} introduction.
\end{lem}
\begin{ML} The \LaTeX{} Companion contains
   packages for all important application areas.
\end{ML}
```

4-1-35

In addition to the two mandatory arguments, \newtheorem has two mutually exclusive optional arguments. They affect the sequencing and hierarchy of the numbering.

```
\newtheorem{name}[use-counter]{heading}
\newtheorem{name}{heading}[number-within]
```

By default, each kind of theorem-like environment is numbered independently. Thus, if you have lemmas, theorems, and some examples interspersed, they are numbered something like this: Example 1, Lemma 1, Lemma 2, Theorem 1, Example 2, Lemma 3, Theorem 2. If, for example, you want the lemmas and theorems to share the same numbering sequence, then you should indicate the desired relationship as follows:

```
\newtheorem{thm}{Theorem}     \newtheorem{lem}[thm]{Lemma}
```

The optional *use-counter* argument (value thm) in the second statement means that the lem environment should share the thm numbering sequence instead of having its own independent sequence.

To have a theorem environment numbered subordinately within a sectional unit — for example, to get exercises numbered Exercise 2.1, Exercise 2.2, and so on, in Section 2 — put the name of the parent counter in square brackets in the final position:

```
\newtheorem{exa}{Exercise}[section]
```

With the optional argument [section], the exa counter is reset to 0 whenever the parent counter section is incremented.

Proofs and the QED symbol

Of more specifically mathematical interest, the package defines a proof environment that automatically adds a "QED symbol" at the end. This environment produces the heading "Proof" with appropriate spacing and punctuation.[1]

---

[1]The proof environment is primarily intended for short proofs, no more than a page or two in length. Longer proofs are usually better done as a separate \section or \subsection in your document.

An optional argument of the `proof` environment allows you to substitute a different name for the standard "Proof". If you want the proof heading to be, for example, "Proof of the Main Theorem", then put this in your document:

```
\begin{proof}[Proof of the Main Theorem]
 ...
\end{proof}
```

A "QED symbol" (default □) is automatically appended at the end of a `proof` environment. To substitute a different end-of-proof symbol, use `\renewcommand` to redefine the command `\qedsymbol`. For a long proof done as a subsection or section, you can obtain the symbol and the usual amount of preceding space by using the command `\qed` where you want the symbol to appear.

Automatic placement of the QED symbol can be problematic if the last part of a `proof` environment is, for example, a tabular, a displayed equation, or a list. In that case put a `\qedhere` command at the somewhat earlier place where the QED symbol should appear; it will then be suppressed from appearing at the logical end of the `proof` environment. If `\qedhere` produces an error message in an equation, try using `\mbox{\qedhere}` instead.

Proof (sufficiency). This proof involves a list

1. because the proof comes in two parts.

2. We need to use \qedhere.   □

```
\usepackage{amsthm}
\begin{proof}[Proof (sufficiency)]
This proof involves a list  \begin{enumerate}
 \item because the proof comes in two parts.
 \item We need to use \verb|\qedhere|. \qedhere
\end{enumerate}  \end{proof}
```

4-1-36

Defining the style of headed lists

The specification part of the amsthm package supports the notion of a current theorem style, which determines the formatting that is set up for a collection of `\newtheorem` commands.[1]

`\theoremstyle{style}`

The three theorem styles provided by the package are `plain`, `definition`, and `remark`; they specify different typographical treatments that give the environments a visual emphasis corresponding to their relative importance. The details of this typographical treatment may vary depending on the document class, but typically the `plain` style produces italic body text, and the other two styles produce roman body text.

To create new theorem-like environments in several of these styles, divide your `\newtheorem` declarations into groups and preface each group with the appropriate

---

[1]This concept was first introduced in the now-superseded theorem package by the author of this book. It is also used by ntheorem so that all three packages provide a similar interface.

`\theoremstyle`. If no `\theoremstyle` command is given, the style used is `plain`. Some examples follow:

1 Theorem-Like

Definition 1.1. A typographical challenge is a problem that cannot be solved with the help of *The LaTeX Companion*.

Theorem 1.2 (Main). *There are no typographical challenges.*

Remark. The proof is left to the reader.

```
\usepackage{amsthm}
\theoremstyle{plain}          \newtheorem{thm}{Theorem}[section]
\theoremstyle{definition}     \newtheorem{defn}[thm]{Definition}
\theoremstyle{remark}         \newtheorem*{rem}{Remark}
\section{Theorem-Like}
\begin{defn}
 A typographical challenge is a problem that cannot be
 solved with the help of \emph{The \LaTeX{} Companion}.
\end{defn}
\begin{thm}[Main]
     There are no typographical challenges.\end{thm}
\begin{rem}The proof is left to the reader.\end{rem}
```

4-1-37

Note that the fairly obvious choice of "`def`" for the name of a "Definition" environment does not work, because it conflicts with the existing low-level TeX command `\def`.

Number swapping
  A fairly common style variation for theorem heads is to have the theorem number on the left, at the beginning of the heading, instead of on the right. As this variation is usually applied across the board regardless of individual `\theoremstyle` changes, swapping numbers is done by placing a `\swapnumbers` declaration at the beginning of the list of `\newtheorem` statements that should be affected.

More extensive customization capabilities are provided by the package through the `\newtheoremstyle` declaration and through a mechanism for using package options to load custom theorem style definitions. For details consult the package documentation [1].

4.1.5 thmtools — Advanced theorem declarations

The thmtools by Ulrich Schwarz, now maintained by Yukai Chou, provides a key/value-based frontend for either amsthm or ntheorem abstracting from the syntax peculiarities of either package. In addition it provides some advanced features such as "repeated theorems" and a "list of theorems" facility.

`\declaretheorem [`*key/value list*`] {`*name*`}`

With thmtools you use `\declaretheorem` instead of `\newtheorem` to declare your own theorem-like environments. This declaration takes a single mandatory argument, which is the *name* of the newly declared environment. Everything else is handled through defaults or through the *key/value list*.

The key `style` specifies the theorem style, and by default the package knows the amsthm styles `plain` (default), `definition`, and `remark`. To specify a heading text use `title` or alternatively `heading` or `name` (all have the same meaning, so choose what you remember best). The default is to use the environment name with the first letter uppercased.

If different environments should share the same numbering, you can specify this through `sharenumber` or alternatively through `sibling` or `numberlike`.

Numbering is controlled through the `numbered` key, which accepts `yes` (default), `no`, or `unless␣unique`. The latter omits the number if the environment is used only once but requires an additional LaTeX run to find this out. This can be useful if you provide longer and shorter versions of some paper where some material is dropped.

If you want the numbers to be reset by section or chapter (or some other counter), you can specify this with `numberwithin`, with `within`, or with `parent` giving the counter name as the value.

Below is a repetition of Example 4-1-37 on page 284 using `thmtools` for declaring the environments (loading `amsthm` is still required):

```
\usepackage{amsthm,thmtools}
\declaretheorem[title=Theorem,numberwithin=section]{thm}
\declaretheorem[style=definition,title=Definition,
                sharenumber=thm]{defn}
\declaretheorem[style=remark,title=Remark,numbered=no]{rem}
\section{Theorem-Like}
\begin{defn}
  A typographical challenge is a problem that cannot be
  solved with the help of \emph{The \LaTeX{} Companion}.
\end{defn}
\begin{thm}[Main]
    There are no typographical challenges. \end{thm}
\begin{rem} The proof is left to the reader. \end{rem}
```

1 Theorem-Like

Definition 1.1. A typographical challenge is a problem that cannot be solved with the help of *The LaTeX Companion*.

Theorem 1.2 (Main). *There are no typographical challenges.*

Remark. The proof is left to the reader.

4-1-38

Up until now the declarations are only a bit more verbose (and thus perhaps easier to understand) but have no immediate advantage. This changes when we add further keys into the mix or use a value like `unless unique` for the `numbered` key.

If you like to work with `\cref` from cleveref, then there is the problem that you have to tell this package what prefixes to use when referring to your environments because it would be clueless without help. This help is provided through the keys `refname` and `Refname`. They both expect one or two strings: a singular and a plural form separated by a comma (or one for both) with the environment name used as a default. `Refname` denotes the string(s) used at the beginning of a sentence. If you only provide `Refname`, then this is also used for `refname` by lowercasing the values.

Support for cleveref *and similar packages*

Claim 1. *Many typographical problems are difficult to solve.*

Claim 2 (Main). *But not when using the LaTeX Companion.*

"Postulates 1 and 2" or "postulate 1 and postulate 2" or "postulates 1 and 2" see?

4-1-39

```
\usepackage{amsthm,thmtools,cleveref}
\declaretheorem[title=Claim,
        Refname={Postulate,Postulates}]{thm}
\begin{thm}\label{thm1}    Many typographical
    problems are difficult to solve.          \end{thm}
\begin{thm}[Main]\label{thm2}
    But not when using the \LaTeX\ Companion. \end{thm}
''\Cref{thm1,thm2}'' or ''\cref{thm1} and \cref{thm2}''
or ''\cref{thm1,thm2}'' see?
```

285

If you would like some fancier formatting of your theorem-like environment, you can try the shaded, thmbox, or mdframed keys. These keys implement extensions by interfacing to other packages, in this case shadedthm by Jim Hefferon, thmbox by Emmanuel Beffara, and mdframed by Marco Daniel. For values to the keys you can specify a list of subkeys that are then simply passed to the other package for processing.

The shaded key supports the following subkeys: bgcolor, rulecolor, rulewidth, textwidth, padding, and leftmargin.

All have default values; for example, bgcolor is automatically set to some light gray. Thus, you have to specify only those that you want to change. Below we add some padding to enlarge the shaded area and move it slightly into the left margin. For the action environment, we add a border and change the bgcolor to white.

```
\usepackage{amsthm,thmtools,xcolor}
\declaretheorem[style=remark,
                shaded={padding=5pt,leftmargin=-10pt,
                        textwidth=.8\columnwidth}
               ]{remark}
\declaretheorem[sibling=remark,
                shaded={rulecolor=blue,rulewidth=2pt,
                        bgcolor=white}
               ]{action}
\noindent Text to show the left margin.
\begin{remark}
  We number remarks together with actions
    but we use a gray background for them.
\end{remark}
\begin{action}[Background]
  Background color needs resetting!
\end{action}
```

Text to show the left margin.

Remark 1. We number remarks together with actions but we use a gray background for them.

Action 2 (Background). *Background color needs resetting!*

4-1-40

The thmbox key implements the formats provided separately by the thmbox package and accepts the values L, M, and S. By default the environment text may break across pages; if you do not like that, specify nocut as a subkey.

If you want to change the body font, you can specify it through the subkey bodystyle as we did in the remark below. Note the use of \noindent to suppress a paragraph indentation inside the body.

The overall indentation of the environment body from the left is defined through leftmargin and defaults to \parindent and from the right through rightmargin (default 0pt). The somewhat strange value of 4.6pt that we used below makes the rules line up perfectly. The reason is that the rule has a default width of 0.6pt (key thickness) and the space from the frame to the text (key hskip) a default of 0.4em, which amounts to 4pt in this book. Thus, the sum of both is what we need to indent to achieve a lineup.

The rule below the heading can be suppressed with nounderline, which we did for the lemma environment. There are a few other adjustment possibilities if you use the thmbox package on its own; for those refer to the package documentation. Note that most of the customization keys of thmtools discussed below have no effect as control is more or less fully passed to the external package.

Theorem 1 (*Style L + left shift*)

> *There are no typographical challenges.*

Lemma 1 (*Style M + no underline*)

> *All major application areas are discussed in the LATEX Companion.*

Remark 1 (*Style S + font settings*)

> Unfortunately this means the book has a large number of pages.

```
\usepackage{amsthm,thmtools}
\declaretheorem[thmbox={L,leftmargin=4.6pt}]{theorem}
\declaretheorem[thmbox={M,nounderline}]{lemma}
\declaretheorem[thmbox={S,bodystyle=\normalfont
                       \small\noindent}]{remark}

\begin{theorem}[Style L + left shift]
  There are no typographical challenges.\end{theorem}
\begin{lemma}[Style M + no underline]
  All major application areas are discussed in
  the \LaTeX{} Companion.              \end{lemma}
\begin{remark}[Style S + font settings]
  Unfortunately this means the book has a large
  number of pages.                   \end{remark}
```

4-1-41

To generate a list of theorem-like environments thmtools offers the command \listoftheorems. It supports an optional argument in which you can restrict which environments are listed. For example, by specifying ignoreall followed by show you can restrict the listing to all environment types enumerated in the value to show.

Selectively listing theorem-like environments

Instead of show, you can use onlynamed in which case this is further restricted to those types but shows only those instances with an optional argument in the document body (e.g., named theorems). Alternatively, you can use onlynamed on its own without a value, which results in showing all types but only the environments that have an explicit name in the document.

By using \listoftheorems several times with different settings, you can produce different lists for different types, but in that case you probably want to change the generated heading each time. The default title is "List of Theorems", stored in the command \listtheoremname. On individual invocations you can overwrite it with the title key as in the next example:

Definitions and Theorems

Definition 1. A typographical challenge is a problem that cannot be solved with the help of *The LATEX Companion.*

Theorem 2 (Main). *There are no typographical challenges.*

Remark 1. The proof is left to the reader.

```
\usepackage{amsthm,thmtools}
\declaretheorem[title=Theorem]{thm}
\declaretheorem[style=definition,title=Definition,
                sharenumber=thm]{defn}
\declaretheorem[style=remark,title=Remark]{rem}
\listoftheorems[ignoreall,show={thm,defn},
                title=Definitions and Theorems]
\begin{defn}
A typographical challenge is a problem that cannot be
solved with the help of \emph{The \LaTeX{} Companion}.
\end{defn}
\begin{thm}[Main]
        There are no typographical challenges. \end{thm}
\begin{rem} The proof is left to the reader. \end{rem}
```

4-1-42

Providing your own layout styles
If the predefined layout styles are not sufficient, thmtools offers a way to define additional ones using \declaretheoremstyle, which is a key/value frontend to \newtheoremstyle from amsthm or the corresponding facility of ntheorem if that package is used as a backend.

> \declaretheoremstyle [*options*] {*style-name*}

As an example we define the style breakstyle that outdents the title by 12 points and starts the theorem body on a new line. Note that we do not use the title as part of the style definition (which would be possible) but set it when declaring the exa environment. This allows us to define other environments in the same style but with a different heading.

```
\usepackage{amsthm,thmtools}
\declaretheoremstyle[spaceabove=9pt, spacebelow=9pt,
    headindent=-12pt, headfont=\sffamily\bfseries,
    headpunct=:, bodyfont=\itshape, break]{breakstyle}
\declaretheorem[style=breakstyle,title=Exercise]{exa}
```

Exercise 1 (Most Active Author):
Find the author responsible for the largest number of packages described in The LaTeX Companion 3rd edition.

```
\begin{exa}[Most Active Author]
  Find the author responsible for the largest number of
  packages described in The \LaTeX\ Companion 3rd edition.
\end{exa}
```

4-1-43

In the following example we provide a "Theorem" variation in which the whole theorem heading has to be supplied as an optional note, such as for citing theorems from other sources. For good measure we also add a qed symbol to show that it is equally easy to provide special "proof" environments, which is sometimes necessary.

```
\usepackage{amsthm,thmtools}
\declaretheoremstyle[spaceabove=3pt, spacebelow=3pt,
    headindent=\parindent, headpunct=., headformat=\NOTE,
    notebraces={}{}, notefont=\bfseries, bodyfont=\itshape,
    numbered=no, qed=\qedsymbol ]{citing}
\declaretheorem[style=citing]{varthm}
```

Theorem 3.16 in [53]. *By focusing on small details, it is possible to understand the deeper significance of a passage.* □

```
\begin{varthm}[Theorem 3.16 in \cite{Knuth90}]
  By focusing on small details, it is possible to
  understand the deeper significance of a passage.
\end{varthm}
```

4-1-44

The above examples show many, but not all, of the possible keys that can be used. If you want to customize other aspects of a theorem style, check the package documentation for further possibilities.

If the functionality and layout possibilities offered by amsthm or thmtools are not sufficient for your needs, it might be worth looking at what is offered by the tcolorbox package (Section 8.4). Its package documentation [131] offers a whole section on theorem-like structures.

4.1.6 tasks — Making horizontally oriented lists

There is one other type of list that is fairly often asked for: a list where the items are horizontally placed into columns instead of the usual vertical direction. If you need that kind of layout, try the tasks package by Clemens Niederberger.

The package defines the environment tasks, and within this environment items are started using the command \task (in contrast to other lists that use \item). Due to the chosen implementation there are three restrictions one has to be aware of:

- it is not possible to nest the environment; however, you can combine it with other types of lists if necessary;

- breaks can happen only between rows of items but not inside of items;

- verbatim material cannot be used; instead, you have to resort to tricks discussed in Section 4.2 if you need more than \texttt.

If neither is a problem, you get a good solution for horizontally aligned lists.

\begin{tasks}[*key/value list*] (*columns*)   *task data*   \end{tasks}

The package uses a somewhat unusual syntax by providing optional arguments surrounded by parentheses as well as by brackets. The obvious advantage is that this enables you to leave out the *key/value list* (which customizes the layout of the task list) and provide only the number of *columns* in parentheses.

If you specify neither of the optional arguments, you get a single-column list that is similar to an enumerate but uses alphabetic labels for the items. Below is an example with two columns:

a) Lorem ipsum dolor sit amet, consectetuer adipiscing elit.

b) Ut purus elit, vestibulum ut, placerat ac, adipiscing vitae, felis.

!!! Nam dui ligula, fringilla a, euismod sodales, sollicitudin vel, wisi.

c) Quisque ullamcorper placerat ipsum. Cras nibh.

```
\usepackage{lipsum,tasks}
\begin{tasks}(2)
  \task \lipsum[1][1]
  \task \lipsum[1][2]
  \task[!!!] \lipsum[2][1]
  \task \lipsum*[4][1-2]
\end{tasks}
```

4-1-45

As shown in the previous example, the \task command can take an optional argument that specifies an explicit *label* instead of the autogenerated one. In that case you have to provide the necessary formatting yourself.

Sometimes it is necessary for items to span one or more columns, and for this, \task offers a star form and even an exclamation mark form.

\task[*label*] \task*(*columns*)[*label*] \task![*label*] \startnewitemline

The star form of the command spans all remaining columns or, if optionally a number of *columns* is specified, that number of columns. In contrast, the exclamation mark form first starts a new row and then spans all columns. Another way to start a new row is to use \startnewitemline. If you ask for more columns than remain available, your request is silently ignored, and only the available columns are used. The next example shows these variants in action. Note especially the manually constructed task label f)[!!]. It uses the `task` counter which needs to be incremented *after* the `\task` command to apply:

a) One   b) two   c) Three

?) Go   d) ......   e) ....

f)[!!] Specially constructed label

g) Spanning 2 columns   h) No
col-
umn
span

i) Another task spanning all columns (therefore column 4 above stays empty)

```
\usepackage{tasks}

\begin{tasks}(4)
 \task One \task two \task Three
 \startnewitemline   \task[?)] Go
 \task \dotfill \task* \dotfill
 \task![\alph{task})\textsuperscript{!!}]
 \stepcounter{task}
            Specially constructed label
 \task*(2) Spanning 2 columns
 \task  No column span
 \task! Another task spanning all columns
 (therefore column 4 above stays empty)
\end{tasks}
```

4-1-46

To customize the task lists the environment has an optional *key/value list* argument in which you can specify key/value pairs. Alternatively, or to set general defaults, you can use these keys in a `\settasks` declaration, which can be used anywhere. We give here only a quick overview about some of the available possibilities; if you want to adjust something that is not mentioned, check the package documentation [109] because there is a good chance that some key exists that provides what you are looking for.

The general style of the task list can be changed with the `style` key, which accepts the values `alphabetize` (default), `itemize`, and `enumerate`. The last two generate lists with labels that are modeled after `itemize` and `enumerate` exhibited in the next example.

The environment adds a vertical skip specified by `before-skip` before and one by `after-skip` after unless they are zero (which they are by default). This is in addition to whatever vertical separation is added by a normal list environment. Thus, to shorten the space before and after the list, you have to set the keys to a negative value as done in Example 4-1-49 on page 292. Between tasks it adds `after-item-skip` (1 ex plus 1 ex minus 1 ex) plus the value of `\parsep`, which it takes from the setup of general lists. Thus, to get no extra separations between tasks you have to apply a negative correction as we did in the next example.

• One   • two   !! Go
• ......   • ....

1. Zero   2. isn't   3. enough
4. to remove the separation!

```
\usepackage{tasks}

\begin{tasks}[style=itemize,after-item-skip=-\parsep](3)
 \task One \task two  \task[!!] Go
 \task \dotfill \task* \dotfill
\end{tasks}
\begin{tasks}[style=enumerate,after-item-skip=0pt](3)
 \task Zero \task isn't \task enough
 \task! to remove the separation!       \end{tasks}
```

4-1-47

Instead of, or in addition to, using the `style` key, it is possible to adjust several aspects of the label generation with the keys `label-format` (accepting declarations such as font or color settings), `label-width` (width of the label box), `label-align` (alignment with the box, accepting `left`, `center`, and `right`), and `label-offset` (the separation between the label box and start of the task text, i.e., what is called `\labelsep` elsewhere).

The layout of the task text is controlled through `item-format` (again expecting declarations), and its indentation from the outer left margin or the previous task column is `item-indent`. Thus, you normally want that big enough to hold the sum of `label-width` and `label-offset`. There is also `column-sep`, which is added between columns in addition to the `item-indent`, allowing you to adjust the inner gaps compared to what is used at the left margin.

There is also the Boolean key `debug` that draws frames around label and task texts to show how they are positioned. We make use of this in the next example to better visualize the results of different key settings:

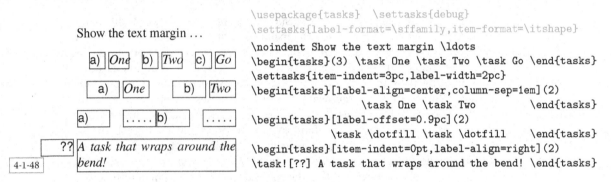

```
\usepackage{tasks}  \settasks{debug}
\settasks{label-format=\sffamily,item-format=\itshape}

\noindent Show the text margin \ldots
\begin{tasks}(3) \task One \task Two \task Go \end{tasks}
\settasks{item-indent=3pc,label-width=2pc}
\begin{tasks}[label-align=center,column-sep=1em] (2)
                \task One \task Two         \end{tasks}
\begin{tasks}[label-offset=0.9pc] (2)
                \task \dotfill \task \dotfill      \end{tasks}
\begin{tasks}[item-indent=0pt,label-align=right] (2)
\task![??] A task that wraps around the bend! \end{tasks}
```

If `item-indent` is smaller than `label-width` as in the last row of the previous example, it protrudes to the left (possibly overwriting text from a previous column). Also note how `label-align` shifts the symbol within the label box.

To adjust the auto-numbering of the label you can use the key `label`. Its syntax is modeled after the way enumitem defines its labels; i.e., a `*` represents the task counter so that you can specify, for example, `\roman*` to produce roman numerals. Of course, a fixed string or a symbol can also be set with this key. The current task label is also available within the task through the command `\tasklabel`. If you adjust the label format using `label`, you may additionally adjust the result of any cross-reference to the task (via `\label` and `\ref`). This can be done with the `ref` key, which accepts the same syntax as the `label` key.

Adjusting the auto-numbering

Manage cross-references

The default counter that is used is named `task`, but with the key `counter` you can define a different counter to be used instead. This is useful if you define several different task environments (see below) that should use their own counters. By default each environment restarts the counter, but if you use the Boolean key `resume`, it continues from where it was last time. Doing that within `\settasks` means this happens with all environments; doing it at the environment level only continues that environment. Canceling the resume is possible too, by supplying the value `false`,

Counter starts and restarts

again either locally or though \settasks for all future environments. An alternative is to use the key start to supply the starting value as an integer.

```
\usepackage{tasks}  \settasks{resume,label=\arabic*/}
\settasks{before-skip=-9pt,after-skip=-9pt} % shorten space
\begin{tasks}(2) \task One    \task Two       \end{tasks}
\begin{tasks}(2) \task Three \task[!!] Go  \end{tasks}
\begin{tasks}[resume=false,label-align=right](3)
        \task Eins \task Zwei \task[?] Go   \end{tasks}
\begin{tasks}[label=$\triangleright$,label-align=center](3)
    \task Make static \task* labels like '\tasklabel'\end{tasks}
```

1/ One   2/ Two
3/ Three   !! Go
1/ Eins   2/ Zwei   ? Go
▷ Make ▷ labels like '▷'
     static

4-1-49

So far we have used the default tasks environment. However, the package also allows defining new environments that act in the same way but use their own defaults.

\NewTasksEnvironment [*key/value list*] {*env-name*} [*task-cmd*] (*columns*)

In the *key/value list* argument you can specify any of the above key/value pairs that are admissible within \settasks. The mandatory *env-name* expects the name of the environment to be defined.[1] In the optional *task-cmd* argument you can say which command should introduce a new task. If you omit it, then \task is used. Finally, you can set the default number of *columns*. Again, this is optional, but to distinguish it from the other optional arguments it used parentheses as argument delimiters.

Below we make use of this declaration by providing a task environment for multiple choice questions using the default style but providing a square as the label. We also make the item texts ragged by using a suitable value for item-format. It is still possible to change or overwrite such defaults on the environment level, which we prove by using after-skip so that the space after the environment differs from the space before.

```
\usepackage{amssymb,tasks}
\NewTasksEnvironment [label=$\square$,
        item-format=\raggedright]{multiq}[\quest](2)
Text before the environment \ldots
\begin{multiq}[after-skip=2ex]
    \quest This? \quest Or that? \quest Or this one?
    \quest Or perhaps that one after all?
\end{multiq}
Text after the environment to show the skip.
```

Text before the environment . . .

☐ This?   ☐ Or that?

☐ Or this one?   ☐ Or perhaps that
                         one after all?

Text after the environment to show the skip.

4-1-50

4.1.7 typed-checklist — Developing and maintaining checklists

For many projects it is helpful to clarify what artifacts are to be produced or modified, what the goals are, what tasks are needed, and what milestones should be reached

---

[1] There also exists \RenewTasksEnvironment with the same syntax in case you want to modify a previously defined task environment.

and when. Getting an overview like this often leads to checklists that then support you during the project by helping you to keep track of status, open tasks, approaching or missed milestones, etc.

The typed-checklist package by Richard Grewe is a flexible tool that enables you to produce and maintain checklists for various occasions. Below is a short teaser:

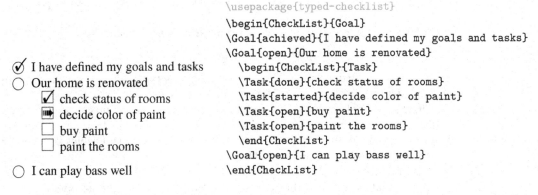

```
\usepackage{typed-checklist}
\begin{CheckList}{Goal}
\Goal{achieved}{I have defined my goals and tasks}
\Goal{open}{Our home is renovated}
  \begin{CheckList}{Task}
  \Task{done}{check status of rooms}
  \Task{started}{decide color of paint}
  \Task{open}{buy paint}
  \Task{open}{paint the rooms}
  \end{CheckList}
\Goal{open}{I can play bass well}
\end{CheckList}
```

4-1-51

Out of the box it comes with four types of checklists: Goal, Task, Milestone, and Artifact. These checklists can be nested; e.g., your project may have different goals, each of which needs a number of tasks to be achieved. In larger projects there may be milestones that have goals that are reached by completing tasks. Or larger tasks may have subtasks to provide a clearer structure. Of course, other approaches are possible too: it really depends on the way you think about your project.

\begin{CheckList} [*key/value list*] {*type*}   *check-items*   \end{CheckList}

All checklists are built with the help of a single environment that takes the checklist *type* as its mandatory argument.

In the optional *key/value list* argument to the environment you can adjust the layout to be used. The default value is list, which is what we have seen so far. Alternatives are hidden, which hides the items, and table, which displays the goals, tasks, milestones, or artifacts in a tabular form with additional information. Note, however, that table is possible only if the CheckList is a leaf-list, i.e., has no further checklists embedded inside.

\Goal [*key/value list*] {*status*}{*description*} \Task... \Milestone... \Artifact...

The *check-items* body of the CheckList environment consists of commands having the name of the *type*, e.g., \Task, \Goal, etc., all with the same syntax. They have a *status* (whose allowed values depend on the *type*) and a *description* that explains what this item is all about.

For example, the *status* for \Goal can be one of the following: open (not achieved but pursued), unclear (listed but needs further clarification), dropped (was a goal once, but is no longer pursued), or achieved (goal has been reached, i.e., goal

293

Goals	Tasks	Milestones	Artifacts
○ open	☐ open	☆ open	△ missing
? unclear	? unclear	★ achieved	△ unclear
⊗ dropped	☒ dropped		△ dropped
✓ achieved	⇥ started		△ incomplete
	✓ done		△ available

Table 4.3: Status values for different types of checklists

4-1-52

statement is now true). Similar but, depending on the type, differently named status values exist for the other types. The default ones are listed in Table 4.3.

In the optional *key/value list* argument to the command, you can specify some additional information, i.e., who is responsible, what is the `deadline` (by default the value is expected in the format[1] *dd.mm.yyyy*), and a `label` that enables you to refer to the item elsewhere using `\ref`. The input format for deadlines can be adjusted with `input-dates`, which allows the values `d.m.y` (default), `m/d/y`, or `y-m-d`. The output format is specified through the key `output-dates` and accepts the same values. If not specified, it uses the same format as the input format. In the next example we use European input and US output format.

Goal ɪ ○ Our home is renovated
    ✓ check rooms   8/1/2018

Task ɪɪ   ⇥ decide color of paint
        ...... *(Christel)*   9/1/2018
     ☐ buy paint
        .... *(Frank)*
     ☐ paint the rooms
        .... *(?)*

    ○ I can play bass well
        .... *(Frank)*   1/1/2025

Remember that Task ɪɪ is critical for achieving Goal ɪ.

```
\usepackage{typed-checklist}
\begin{CheckList}[output-dates=m/d/y]{Goal}
  \Goal[label=home]{open}
     {Our home is renovated}
  \begin{CheckList}{Task}
    \Task[deadline=1.8.2018]{done}{check rooms}
    \Task[label=decide,who=Christel,
         deadline=1.9.2018]{started}
                  {decide color of paint}
    \Task[who=Frank]{open}{buy paint}
    \Task[who=?]{open}{paint the rooms}
  \end{CheckList}
  \Goal[who=Frank,deadline=1.1.2025]{open}
     {I can play bass well}
\end{CheckList}
Remember that \ref{decide} is critical for
achieving \ref{home}.
```

4-1-53

Deadlines in the past appear as green if the entry is in a completed state; otherwise, they appear in red (unfortunately, in the book both colors come out as different shades of gray, so this is difficult to see). If the deadline is still in the future or if it is not in numerical format, it is printed in black. Numerical format can be enforced by specifying the Boolean key `strict-dates`. Note that you need to give the year as a

For correct coloring years need 4 digits

---

[1]This is a clear indication that the package origin is Europe — this can be adjusted.

four-digit number; otherwise, the colors come out wrong! Entries that have a `label` attached show an item name and number in the margin. This information is printed by a `\ref` command referring to the label.

For people who do not like the typing involved, **typed-checklist** offers an interface to the asciilist package by the same author, which makes the input much more concise. I would suggest, however, using this only on simple checklists. The input for each item then looks like this:

⟨*symbol*⟩␣*status* [*key/value list*] : ␣*description*

You are free to choose the ⟨*symbol*⟩ to be used, but the whole entry has to fit on a single line to work (if necessary, you need to use a % to mask the line break). Another restriction is that you have to use spaces in the exact places as indicated (but not in others, e.g., none after *status*) — in other words the input is a bit delicate. The next example shows the feature in action. Note the use of the package option `withAsciilist`. It is needed to enable the interface. Note the nonnumerical deadline value in one of the entries. With `strict-dates` this would result in an error message.

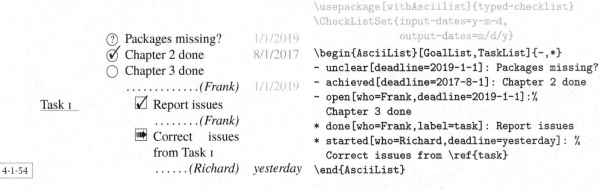

4-1-54

Defaults that should apply to all checklists can be set using `\CheckListSet` instead of explicitly setting them in the optional argument of each `CheckList` environment. If `AsciiList` is used, this is the best way because specifying key/value pairs for that environment requires a somewhat unconventional syntax.

The four default checklist types already offer you a lot of flexibility to manage your checklists. However, if you feel you need additional *types* or if you are not satisfied with the *status* values available for a certain type, it is easy to augment the existing checklists or provide new ones.

```
\CheckListAddType{type}{base symbol}
\CheckListAddStatus{type}{status}{closed?}{overlay symbol}
```

With `\CheckListAddType` you declare a new checklist *type* and decide which *base symbol* (or code in general) should be used to identify it. This symbol is used as the background symbol with a *status* symbol overlaying it in the list.

With \CheckListAddStatus you define a *status* for a certain *type*. If this *status* is used, the *overlay symbol* is printed on top of the *base symbol* for the *type*. The *closed?* argument, which can be either `true` or `false`, decides whether or not a `deadline` in the past is marked as a problem. If set to `true`, deadlines are ignored for the entry.

We give an example below that also shows the result of specifying `table` as the `layout` key value. By default the package uses the xltabular package for producing the tables. With the help of the package option `tablepkg` one can request a different table package; e.g., below we used `tabularx`. Other supported values are `ltablex` and `xltabular` (the default). For additional information on customization (also on providing further layout options) consult the package documentation.

```
\usepackage[tablepkg=tabularx]{typed-checklist}
\CheckListAddType{feature}{{\small\Square}}
\CheckListAddStatus{feature}{n}{false}{}                    % new
\CheckListAddStatus{feature}{d}{true}{\small\XSolid}        % dropped/
                                                           % declined
\CheckListAddStatus{feature}{e}{false}
             {\raisebox{0.4ex}{\footnotesize e}}            % evaluated
\CheckListAddStatus{feature}{s}{false}
             {\kern 1pt\small\ArrowBoldRightStrobe}         % started
\CheckListAddStatus{feature}{f}{true}{\kern 2pt\Checkmark} % finished
```

Status	Description	Who	Deadline
☐	A new feature request		
e	Feature evaluated		
☒	(feature ı) dropped/declined		1.1.2022
⏩	started	Frank	*yesterday*
☑	finished/implemented		

```
\begin{CheckList}[layout=table]{feature}
  \feature{n}{A new feature request}
  \feature{e}{Feature evaluated}
  \feature[label=foo,deadline=1.1.2022]
          {d}{dropped/declined}
  \feature[who=Frank,deadline=yesterday]
          {s}{started}
  \feature{f}{finished/implemented}
\end{CheckList}
```

4-1-55

As an additional feature the package also offers filtering of checklists, for example, to print only tasks that are not closed or dropped. Consult the package documentation if you are interested in this aspect.

4.2 Simulating typed text

It is often necessary to display information verbatim — that is, "as entered at the terminal". This ability is provided by the standard LaTeX environment `verbatim`. However, to guide the reader it might be useful to highlight certain textual strings in a particular way, such as by numbering the lines. Over time a number of packages have appeared that address one or the other extra feature — unfortunately, each with its own syntax. Note that, just like the basic \verb and the `verbatim` environment, they all assume that the input is restricted to ASCII; anything else only works in a few circumstances, unless otherwise noted.

In this section we first review a few such smaller packages offering solutions to specific problems. We then concentrate on the package fancyvrb written by Timothy Van Zandt, which combines all such features and many more under the roof of a single, highly customizable package. This coverage is followed by a discussion of the listings package, which provides a versatile environment in which to prettyprint computer listings for a large number of computer languages.

4.2.1 Displaying spaces in verbatim material

When typesetting material verbatim, it is sometimes necessary to show the exact number of spaces used, and for this LaTeX offers \verb* and verbatim*. They show spaces as "␣", but they were originally coded under the assumption that the position of the space character (i.e., ASCII 32) in a typewriter font contains such a visible space glyph. This is correct for pdfTeX with the most used font encodings OT1 and T1.

Unicode engines

However, this unfortunately does not work for Unicode engines using the TU encoding, because the space character slot (ASCII 32) then usually contains a real (normal) space, which has the effect that \verb* produces the same results as \verb.

In 2018 the \verb* code was therefore changed to always use the newly introduced command \verbvisiblespace when producing the visible space character, and this command gets appropriate definitions for use with the different engines. With pdfTeX it simply uses \asciispace, which is a posh name for "select character 32 in the current font", but with Unicode engines the default definition is

```
\DeclareRobustCommand\verbvisiblespace
      {\leavevmode{\usefont{OT1}{cmtt}{m}{n}\asciispace}}
```

which uses the visible space from the font Computer Modern Typewriter, regardless of the currently chosen typewriter font. Internally the code ensures that the character used has exactly the same width as the other characters in the current (monospaced) font; thus, for example, code displays line up properly.

It is possible to redefine this command to select your own character, for example, the "official" visible space character of the current font. This may look like the natural default, but it was not chosen as the LaTeX default, because many fonts just do not have that Unicode character, or they have one with a strange shape. Here is an example where it would work:

```
\usepackage{fontspec} \setmonofont{AnonymousPro}
\texttt{Typewriter  with\textvisiblespace space}.\par
\verb=\verb*=: \verb*=verbatim with  spaces=.    \par
\DeclareRobustCommand\verbvisiblespace
   {\textvisiblespace} % now use the Unicode character
But now: \verb*=verbatim with   spaces=.
```

Typewriter with␣space.
\verb*: verbatim␣with␣␣spaces.
4-2-1 But now: verbatim␣with␣␣spaces.

4.2.2 Simple verbatim extensions

The package alltt (by Leslie Lamport) defines the `alltt` environment. It acts like a `verbatim` environment except that the backslash "\" and braces "{" and "}" retain their usual meanings. Thus, other commands and environments can appear inside an `alltt` environment. A similar functionality is provided by the fancyvrb environment key `commandchars` (see page 313).

```
\usepackage{alltt}
\begin{alltt}
One can have font changes, like
\emph{emphasized text} or \textsf{other
   font    faces}. Line breaks    and
   spaces are honored, but space only
   on top level and not always in
   arguments (see above)!

Some special characters: # $ % ^ & ~ _
\end{alltt}
```

One can have font changes, like *emphasized text* or other font faces. Line breaks and spaces are honored, but space only on top level and not always in arguments (see above)!

Some special characters: # $ % ^ & ~ _

4-2-2

shortvrb — Streamlining the verbatim input

In documents where a lot of `\verb` commands are needed the source soon becomes difficult to read. For this reason the doc package, described in Chapter 17, introduces a shorthand mechanism that lets you use a special character to denote the start and stop of verbatim text, without having to repeatedly write `\verb` in front of it. This feature is also available in a stand-alone package called shortvrb.

The argument to `\MakeShortVerb` or `\DeleteShortVerb` is the character you wish to install or deinstall as a shorthand. If it already has a special meaning to LATEX, you have to precede it with a backslash, and to be on the safe side you can always do that. Here is an example that adds and removes the shorthand again:

```
\usepackage{shortvrb}
\MakeShortVerb{\|}
The use of |\MakeShortVerb| can make sources
much more readable.

\DeleteShortVerb{\|}\MakeShortVerb{\+}
And with a +\DeleteShortVerb{\|}+ declaration
we can return the '|' character back to normal.
A one-off usage, e.g., '\string+' as an ordinary
character is also possible.
```

The use of \MakeShortVerb can make sources much more readable.

And with a \DeleteShortVerb{\|} declaration we can return the '|' character back to normal. A one-off usage, e.g., '+' as an ordinary character is also possible.

4-2-3

With fancyvrb the same functionality is provided, unfortunately using a slightly different syntax (see page 321).

Because the chosen shorthand character cannot appear in ordinary text, you have to be careful which character or characters you select. Of course, you can remove its special meaning again, but for a one-off it is probably easier to precede it with the command \string as we did in the previous example.

The variant form, \MakeShortVerb*, implements the same shorthand mechanism for the \verb* command. This is shown in the next example:

```
\usepackage{shortvrb}
\MakeShortVerb*{\+}
```

Instead of \verb*| | we can now write + + to get ␣.

```
Instead of \verb/\verb*| |/ we can
now write \verb/+ +/ to get + +.
```

4-2-4

newverbs — Defining \verb variants as needed

While the basic \verb command is suitable to sprinkle short code segments around your text, you may find the need for adding extra material to it, which is not easy because you cannot use the \verb commands inside the argument of other commands; e.g., \textit{\verb+foo+} does not work, and one has to resort to the {\itshape\verb+foo+} approach, and for something like \fbox it would require serious programming to make it work at all, because there is no declarative variant of \fbox in the LaTeX kernel.

To improve this situation Martin Scharrer developed the package newverbs through which you can easily define your own verbatim variants and use them throughout your documents.

By default, the package already provides you with two useful variants: \qverb adds quote characters around the verbatim material and \fverb a verbatim \fbox. They use the same syntax as \verb, and their star forms show spaces as ␣.

```
\usepackage{xcolor,newverbs}
\newverbcommand\cverb{\color{blue}}{} % explained below
```

By default the package provides "\qverb" and \fverb ready for use. We have added \cverb.

```
By default the package provides \qverb=\qverb= and
\fverb=\fverb= ready for use. We have added \cverb=\cverb=.
```

4-2-5

Variants such as \qverb are defined with the help of the \newverbcommand declaration, which has the following syntax:

\newverbcommand{*cmd*}[*verb-cmd*]{*before-code*}{*after-code*}

Its first argument *cmd* is the new command that should get a \verb-like syntax to grab its argument; the other arguments are used for manipulating the grabbed material. The *before-code* is the code executed before, and the *after-code* is the code executed after parsing the verbatim material. Internally, everything happens within a group so that local modifications made in one of the arguments, such as the color change we used in the example above, are confined to the execution of our new *cmd*. By default, the *verb-cmd* is \verb, but in this optional argument it is possible to specify a different \verb-like command; e.g., \spverb from the spverbatim package.

Instead of defining a *new* command, you can use \renewverbcommand to change an existing command or \provideverbcommand to provide a default definition.

While the definition for \qverb can probably be guessed, it is not so obvious how to use the above declaration to define \fverb; so here we reveal the trick. It is worth studying if you are intending to provide variants of similar complexity.

```
\newverbcommand\fverb{\begin{lrbox}{\verbbox}}
                {\end{lrbox}\fbox{\usebox{\verbbox}}}
```

The trick is to typeset everything first into a box. For this we use the standard lrbox environment, because we can start this in the *before-code* and end it at the beginning of the *after-code*. The \verbbox box register is automatically provided by the package, so we do not have to declare it ourselves. Once the box is filled, we are able to use it to our liking, e.g., put it inside an \fbox. This decoupling of parsing and use gets us around the issue that unprocessed verbatim material cannot be used inside the argument of other commands. More details and a couple of other helpful commands for these types of definitions can be found in the package documentation.

\MakeSpecialShortVerb{*verb-cmd*}char

We have already seen how shortvrb helps us to input a lot of verbatim material in a concise way. The same is possible with the verbatim variants of newverbs too if you load the shortvrb package in addition. However, we need a different shorthand declaration, because this time we also have to say for which *verb-cmd* we want to enable the shorthand. But otherwise everything works in the same way, and for removal of a shorthand you still use the already known \DeleteShortVerb.

Now code like pdflatex␣myfile can be "enter"ed in a simplified way. "\DeleteShortVerb" removes previously defined shorthands again: |see|?

```
\usepackage{shortvrb,newverbs}
\MakeSpecialShortVerb{\qverb} {\"}
\MakeSpecialShortVerb{\fverb*}{\|}
```
Now code like |pdflatex myfile| can be "enter"ed in a simplified way. "\DeleteShortVerb" removes previously defined shorthands \DeleteShortVerb\| again: |see|?

4-2-6

In some situations the restriction that \verb and related commands cannot be used inside arguments of other commands can become a serious problem. It is not that such material cannot appear there, but that for technical reasons the parsing done by \verb must happen at the top level and not inside an argument of another command.

\verbdef*⟨cmd⟩⟨char⟩ *material* ⟨char⟩
\Verbdef*⟨cmd⟩⟨char⟩ *material* ⟨char⟩

One way to resolve this is to do that parsing first and use the parsed material later. This can be achieved with the \verbdef declaration, which defines a command *cmd* to hold the parsed *material* so that it can be used anywhere by later calling *cmd*. As always, the star form generates visible spaces within the *material*. The \Verbdef works similarly but does not change the font family to Typewriter. If you use that, make sure you are typesetting using the T1 encoding, because with OT1 some characters produce incorrect results.

Contents

1 Difficult chars (%&␣$^_ or %&␣$^_)

This hides %&␣$^_ within \foo and \baz so that it can be used in the heading. Warning: %&␣$^_ is equal to %&␣$^_ but not to %&␣$^_!

```
\usepackage{newverbs}
\Verbdef*\foo+%& $^_+    \verbdef*\baz+%& $^_+
\tableofcontents
\section{Difficult chars (\foo\ or \baz)}
This hides \verb*+%& $^_+ within \verb+\foo+
and \verb+\baz+ so that it can be used in
the heading. Warning: \verb*+%& $^_+ is
equal to \baz{} but not to \foo{}!
```

Example 4-2-7

Obviously the declaration of the parsed verbatim material must come *before* its use. If that is inside a heading, like in the previous example, this means that the declaration has to be before the \tableofcontents.

The fancyvrb package, described in Section 4.2.4, offers a similar functionality, which is described on page 318. If you plan to use that package for other reasons, it might be best to use it for \verb variants as well.

It should also be noted that (since 2020) standard LaTeX already offers a very flexible possibility for defining your own commands with "verbatim" arguments, and in contrast to all other solutions you can even delimit such arguments with a normal brace group — this is described in Appendix A.1.4 on page →II 632.

spverbatim — Breaking verbatim text at spaces

LaTeX treats verbatim text by default as an unbreakable unit. Thus, text typeset using \verb may lead to poor results if the text happens to get close to a line ending, resulting in either overfull or very spaced out lines. The spverbatim package by Scott Pakin offers some help here, by providing the command \spverb that resembles \verb but allows line breaks at spaces within its argument. A star form generating visible spaces is not provided.

The package also offers the environment spverbatim with a corresponding extension compared to verbatim. However, for environments better control is available through the breaklines key of the fvextra package discussed on page 313 and the features provided by the listings package.

Other verbatim extensions

The package verbatim (by Rainer Schöpf) was the first to reimplement and extend the LaTeX environments verbatim and verbatim*. One of its major advantages is that it allows arbitrarily long verbatim texts, something not possible with the basic LaTeX versions of the environments. It also defines a comment environment[1] that skips all text between the commands \begin{comment} and \end{comment}. In addition, the package provides hooks to implement user extensions for defining

---

[1] Example 4-2-36 on page 318 shows how to achieve this with the fancyvrb package.

customized verbatim-like environments. A few such extensions are realized in the package moreverb (by Angus Duggan).

While you may find both packages used in older documents, it is better to use packages such as fancyvrb, fvextra, or listings that offer the same and further functionality in a consistent manner.

4.2.3 upquote — Computer program style quoting

The Computer Modern Typewriter font that is used by default for typesetting "verbatim" is a very readable monospaced typeface. Due to its small running length, it is very well suited for typesetting computer programs and similar material. See Section 10.9 for a comparison of this font with other monospaced typefaces.

There is, however, one potential problem when using this font to render computer program listings and similar material: most people expect to see a (right) quote in a computer listing represented with a straight quote character (i.e., ') and a left or back quote as a kind of grave accent on its own (i.e., `).

The Computer Modern Typewriter font, however, displays real left and right curly quote characters (as one would expect in a normal text font). In fact, most other typewriter fonts when set up for use with LaTeX follow this pattern. This produces somewhat unconventional results that many people find difficult to understand. Consider the following example, which shows the standard behavior for three major typewriter fonts: LuxiMono,[1] Courier (or rather TeX Gyre Cursor), and Computer Modern Typewriter.

```
\usepackage[scaled=.85]{luximono}
\verb+TEST='ls -l |awk '{print $3}''+
```

```
\renewcommand\ttdefault{qcr}
\verb+TEST='ls -l |awk '{print $3}''+
```

```
TEST='ls -l |awk '{print $3}''
TEST='ls -l |awk '{print $3}''
TEST='ls -l |awk '{print $3}''
```

```
\renewcommand\ttdefault{cmtt}
\verb+TEST='ls -l |awk '{print $3}''+
```

4-2-8

This behavior can be changed by loading the upquote package by Michael Covington, which uses the glyphs `\textasciigrave` and `\textquotesingle`, instead of the usual left and right curly quote characters within `\verb` or the `verbatim` environment. Normal typewriter text still uses the curly quotes, as shown in the last line of the next example on the opposite page.

As you can see, depending on the font, this is not necessarily a good solution; for example, with Courier it is inferior because the characters have fairly uneven weights. However, this is a font problem, and you need to check how your monospaced font behaves and then decide whether to use the package.

---

[1] LuxiMono is a family of general-purpose monospaced (typewriter) fonts designed by Charles Bigelow and Kris Holmes. It may not be available in all TeX distributions but can be obtained from the Comprehensive TeX Archive Network (CTAN); see Section 10.1 for an installation possibility.

```
\usepackage[scaled=.85]{luximono}
\usepackage{upquote}
\verb+TEST=`ls -l |awk '{print $3}''+
```

```
\renewcommand\ttdefault{pcr}
\verb+TEST=`ls -l |awk '{print $3}''+
```

```
TEST=`ls -l |awk '{print $3}''
TEST=`ls -l |awk '{print $3}''
TEST=`ls -l |awk '{print $3}''
Notice that 'text' is unaffected!
```

	`\renewcommand\ttdefault{cmtt}`
	`\verb+TEST=`ls -l |awk '{print $3}''+ \\`
4-2-9	`\textttt{Notice that 'text' is unaffected!}`

The package works well together with "verbatim" extensions as described in this chapter, except for the listings package; it conflicts with the scanning mechanism of that package. If you want this type of quoting with listings, simply use the \lstset key upquote.

```
\usepackage{listings} \lstset{upquote}
\begin{lstlisting}[language=ksh]
TEST=`ls -l |awk '{print $3}''
\end{lstlisting}
```

4-2-10	`TEST=` ls −l	awk '{ print $3 }''`

Note that if you use fvextra as an extended version of the fancyvrb package (as described in Section 4.2.4), then the upquote package is automatically loaded. If this is not desired, you can disable it on the environment level using the key curlyquotes or generally with \fvset.

```
\usepackage{fvextra}
\begin{Verbatim}
TEST=`ls -l |awk '{print $3}'' # default
\end{Verbatim}
\begin{Verbatim}[curlyquotes]
TEST=`ls -l |awk '{print $3}''
\end{Verbatim}
```

```
TEST=`ls -l |awk '{print $3}'' # default
```

4-2-11	`TEST=`ls -l |awk '{print $3}''`

4.2.4 fancyvrb, fvextra — Verbatim environments on steroids

The fancyvrb package by Timothy Van Zandt (maintained by Herbert Voß) offers a highly customizable set of environments and commands to typeset and manipulate verbatim text. It had its first public release already in 1998 and quickly became one of the dominant packages in this space and has largely remained unchanged since then.

It works by parsing one line at a time from an environment or a file (a concept pioneered by the verbatim package), thereby allowing you to preprocess lines in various ways. By incorporating features found in various other packages it provides a truly universal production environment under a common set of syntax rules.

Fairly recently (in TeX terms) in 2016 Geoffrey Poore published the fvextra package, which is intended to be a drop-in replacement for fancyvrb while offering a number of additional features. In this section we describe both package together. All examples that can be used with either package use fancyvrb, while those that need fvextra will obviously use that package. Often there are only some aspects that require fvextra or make the input more convenient; those are then explicitly mentioned in the text.

\begin{Verbatim}[*key/value list*] ... \end{Verbatim}
\begin{Verbatim*}[*key/value list*] ... \end{Verbatim*}

The main environment provided by both packages is the Verbatim environment and its star form, which, if used without customization, is much like standard LaTeX's verbatim environment. The main difference is that it accepts an optional argument in which you can specify customization information using a key/value syntax. However, there is one restriction to bear in mind: the left bracket of the optional argument must appear on the same line as \begin. Otherwise, the optional argument is not recognized but instead typeset as verbatim text.

More than 30 keys are already available with fancyvrb, and fvextra adds a few dozen more — we discuss their use and possible values in some detail.

You can also use these keys in \fvset, which modifies the default setup. Any declaration made in this way stays in force until overwritten in the optional argument to an environment or changed again by another \fvset declaration.

A number of variant environments and commands are discussed near the end of this section as well. They also accept customization via the key/value method. We also cover possibilities for defining your own variants in a straightforward way. Finally, we look at support for inline verbatim including the extensions offered by fvextra.

In summary, fancyvrb is a stable workhorse that has served LaTeX users well for several decades without any changes to the code. However, for new documents fvextra should probably be preferred because it offers several important enhancements while keeping the core of fancyvrb available without any change.

Customization keys for typesetting

To manipulate the fonts used by the verbatim environments of the fancyvrb package, four environment keys, corresponding to the four axes of NFSS, are available. The key fontfamily specifies the font family to use. Its default is Computer Modern Typewriter so that when used without keys, the environments behave in a fashion similar to standard LaTeX's verbatim. However, the value of this key can be any font family name in NFSS notation, such as pcr for Courier or cmss for Computer Modern Sans, even though the latter is not a monospaced font as would normally be used in a verbatim context. The key also recognizes the special values tt, courier, and helvetica and translates them internally into NFSS nomenclature.

Because typesetting of verbatim text can include special characters like "\", you must be careful to ensure that such characters are present in the font. This should be no problem when a font encoding such as T1 is active, which could be loaded using the fontenc package. It is, however, not the case for LaTeX's default font encoding OT1, in which only some monospaced fonts, such as the default typewriter font, contain all such special characters. The type of incorrect output you might encounter is shown with the helvetica example in OT1.

Both packages are also able to handle UTF-8 characters in the input, as long as the glyphs are present in the chosen font, but again this is only partly true if the font encoding is OT1: look at the result produced for the backslash, and the braces and "»„«" generate error messages because they are not available in OT1.

```
\usepackage{fancyvrb} \usepackage[T1,OT1]{fontenc}
\fontencoding{OT1}\selectfont \hrule
\begin{Verbatim}[fontfamily=tt]
  'tt' is fine in OT1: \sum_{i=1}^n
  UTF-8 char test: äöüß œ Æ $ £
\end{Verbatim}
\begin{Verbatim}[fontfamily=helvetica]
  But 'helvetica' fails in OT1: \sum_{i=1}^n
  UTF-8 char test: äöüß œ Æ $ £
\end{Verbatim}
\fontencoding{T1}\selectfont \hrule
\begin{Verbatim*}[fontfamily=helvetica]
  ... while it works in T1: \sum_{i=1}^n
  UTF-8 char test: äöüß œ Æ $ £  »„«
\end{Verbatim*}
```

```
'tt' is fine in OT1: \sum_{i=1}^n
UTF-8 char test: äöüß œ Æ $ £

But 'helvetica' fails in OT1: "sum'-i=1""n
UTF-8 char test: äöüß œ Æ $ £
```

4-2-12
```
␣␣...␣␣while␣it␣works␣in␣T1:␣\sum_{i=1}^n
␣␣UTF-8␣char␣test:␣äöüß␣œ␣Æ␣$␣£␣␣»„«
```

Given that all examples in this book are typeset using the T1 encoding automatically, these kinds of problems do not show up elsewhere in the book. If you use a Unicode engine, e.g., LuaTeX for typesetting (and Unicode fonts), then this is also no problem. Nevertheless, you should be aware of this danger. It represents another good reason to use T1 with the pdfTeX engine in preference to TeX's original font encoding; for a more in-depth discussion see Section 9.2.4 on page 657.

The first example is also already one where there is a difference between fancyvrb and fvextra. If we process that kind of input with the latter package, the quote characters come out differently (because internally upquote is loaded); see also Example 4-2-11 from page 303 on that topic.

```
\usepackage{fvextra} \usepackage[T1]{fontenc}
\begin{Verbatim}[fontfamily=tt]
  'tt' is fine in T1: \sum_{i=1}^n
  UTF-8 char test: äöüß œ Æ  $ £ »„«
\end{Verbatim}
\begin{Verbatim}[fontfamily=courier]
  and so is 'Courier': \sum_{i=1}^n
  UTF-8 char test: äöüß œ Æ  $ £ »„«
\end{Verbatim}
```

```
`tt' is fine in T1: \sum_{i=1}^n
UTF-8 char test: äöüß œ Æ  $ £ »„«

and so is `Courier': \sum_{i=1}^n
```
4-2-13
```
UTF-8 char test: äöüß œ Æ  $ £ »„«
```

The other three environment keys related to the font setup are fontseries, fontshape, and fontsize (there is no way to set the encoding, which is always taken from the surroundings!). They inherit the current NFSS settings from the surrounding text if not specified. While the first two expect values that can be fed into \fontseries and \fontshape, respectively (e.g., bx for a bold extended series or it for an *italic* shape), the fontsize is special. It expects one of the higher-level NFSS commands for specifying the font size — for example, \small. If the relsize package is available, then you could alternatively specify a change of font size relative to the current text font by using something like \relsize{-2}.

\sum_{i=1}^n

A line of text to show the body size.

$\sum_{i=1}^n$

```
\usepackage{relsize,fancyvrb}
\begin{Verbatim}[fontsize=\relsize{-2}]
  \sum_{i=1}^n
\end{Verbatim}
A line of text to show the body size.
\begin{Verbatim}[fontshape=sl,fontsize=\Large]
  \sum_{i=1}^n
\end{Verbatim}
```

4-2-14

A more general form for customizing the formatting is available through the environment key formatcom, which accepts any LaTeX code and executes it at the start of the environment. For example, to color the verbatim text you could pass it something like \color{blue}. It is also possible to operate on each line of text by providing a suitable redefinition for the command \FancyVerbFormatLine. This command is executed for every line, receiving the text from the line as its argument.[1] In the next example every second line is colored in blue, a result achieved by testing the current value of the counter FancyVerbLine. This counter is provided automatically by the environment and holds the current line number.

This line should become blue and
this one will be black. And here
u can observe that gobble removes
t only blanks but any character.

```
\usepackage{ifthen,color,fancyvrb}
\renewcommand\FancyVerbFormatLine[1]
  {\ifthenelse{\isodd{\value{FancyVerbLine}}}%
              {\color{blue}}{}#1}
\begin{Verbatim}[gobble=2]
  This line should become blue and
    this one will be black. And here
  you can observe that gobble removes
  not only blanks but any character.
\end{Verbatim}
```

4-2-15

As shown in the previous example the key gobble can be used to remove a number of characters or spaces (up to nine) from the beginning of each line. This is mainly useful if all lines in your environments are indented and you wish to get rid of the extra space produced by the indentation. Sometimes the opposite goal is desired: every line should be indented by a certain space. For example, in this book all verbatim environments are indented by 24pt. This indentation is controlled by the key xleftmargin. There also exists a key xrightmargin to specify the right indentation, but its usefulness is rather limited with fancyvrb, because the verbatim

---

[1] fvextra extends this concept even further by also providing \FancyVerbFormatText; see the package documentation for examples of its use.

text is not broken across lines.[1] Thus, its only visible effect (unless you use frames) is potentially more overfull box messages[2] that indicate that your text overflows into the right margin. Perhaps more useful is the Boolean key `resetmargins`, which controls whether preset indentations by surrounding environments are ignored.

```
\usepackage{fancyvrb}
\begin{itemize} \item  Normal indentation left:
  \begin{Verbatim}[frame=single,xrightmargin=2pc]
A long line of verbatim text!
  \end{Verbatim}
  \item No indentation at either side:
  \begin{Verbatim}[resetmargins=true,
                   frame=single]
A long line of verbatim text!
  \end{Verbatim}
\end{itemize}
```

- Normal indentation left:

  ```
  A long line of verbatim text!
  ```

- No indentation at either side:

```
A long line of verbatim text!
```

4-2-16

The previous example demonstrates one use of the `frame` key: to draw a frame around verbatim text. By providing other values for this key, different-looking frames can be produced. The default is `none`, that is, no frame. With `topline`, `bottomline`, or `leftline` you get a single line at the side indicated[3]; `lines` produces a line at the top and bottom; and `single`, as we saw in Example 4-2-16, draws the full frame. In each case, the thickness of the rules can be customized by specifying a value via the `framerule` key (default is `0.4pt`). The separation between the lines and the text can be controlled with `framesep` (default is the current value of `\fboxsep`).

If the `color` or `xcolor` package is loaded in the document preamble, you can color the rules using the environment key `rulecolor` (default is black). If you use a full frame, you can also color the separation between the frame and the text via `fillcolor`. With fancyvrb these keys require a color command as the value; with fvextra they also accept the color name, which is a more convenient input, so we use it in the next example:

```
\usepackage{color,fvextra}
\begin{Verbatim}[frame=single,rulecolor=blue,
    framerule=3pt,framesep=1pc,fillcolor=yellow]
A framed verbatim line!
\end{Verbatim}
```

```
A framed verbatim line!
```

4-2-17

Unfortunately, there is no direct way to fill the entire background. The closest you can get is by using `\colorbox` inside `\FancyVerbFormatLine`. However, this approach leaves tiny white rules between the lines and — without forcing the lines to

---

[1]This is different with fvextra because it allows line breaks if the key `breaklines` is used.

[2]Whether overfull boxes inside a verbatim environment are shown is controlled by the `hfuzz` key, which has a default value of 2pt. A warning is issued only if boxes protrude by more than the key's value into the margin.

[3]There is no value to indicate a line at the right side.

be of equal length, such as via \makebox — also results in colored blocks of different widths. With fvextra there is an alternative that is easy to use and does not have those defects; see Example 4-2-27.

```
\usepackage{color,fancyvrb}
\renewcommand\FancyVerbFormatLine[1]{\colorbox{green}{#1}}
\begin{Verbatim}
Some verbatim lines with
a background color.
\end{Verbatim}
\renewcommand\FancyVerbFormatLine[1]
        {\colorbox{yellow}%
                 {\makebox[\linewidth][l]{\color{blue}#1}}}
\begin{Verbatim}
Colored verbatim lines
(background & foreground).
\end{Verbatim}
```

```
Some verbatim lines with
a background color.

Colored verbatim lines
(background & foreground).
```

4-2-18

It is possible to typeset text as part of a frame by supplying it as the value of the label key. If this text contains special characters, such as brackets, equal sign, or comma, you have to hide them by surrounding them with a brace group. Otherwise, they are mistaken for part of the syntax.

The text appears by default at the top, but is printed only if the frame setup would produce a line in that position. Alternate positions can be specified by using labelposition, which accepts none, topline, bottomline, or all as values. In the last case the text is printed above and below. If the label text is unusually large, you may need to increase the separation between the frame and the verbatim text by using the key framesep. If you want to cancel a previously set label string, use the value none — if you really need "none" as a label string, enclose it in braces.

```
\usepackage{fancyvrb}
\begin{Verbatim}[frame=single,framesep=5mm,
                 label=\fbox{Example code},
                 labelposition=bottomline]
    A framed verbatim text.
As always,  it can  consist
    of  several  lines.
\end{Verbatim}
```

```
    A framed verbatim text.
As always,  it can  consist
    of  several  lines.
         Example code
```

4-2-19

You can, in fact, provide different texts to be placed at the top and bottom by surrounding the text for the top position with brackets, as shown in the next example. For this scheme to work frame needs to be set to either single or lines.

By default the label text is typeset in the same font family as the whole environment. If something else is desired, then you need to explicitly specify what font face to use, as we did below (note that \textit still gives typewriter):

```
——————— Start of code ———————
  A line of code
——————— End of code ———————
```

```
\usepackage{fancyvrb}
\begin{Verbatim}[frame=lines,framesep=5mm,
   label={[\textsf{Start of code}]\textit{End of code}}]
A line of code
\end{Verbatim}
```

4-2-20

By default, the typeset output of the verbatim environments can be broken across pages by LaTeX if it does not fully fit on a single page. This is even true in cases where a frame surrounds the text. If you want to ensure that this cannot happen, set the Boolean key samepage to true.

Prohibiting page breaks

The vertical spacing before and after the environment is by default the same as those around other display lists, e.g., itemize. You can change it with the key vspace. Unfortunately, the implementation is a bit odd (internally \partopsep is added sometimes), so you may have to use a value of -\partopsep and not 0pt to cancel all extra space. In combination with the samepage key, this can be used to ensure that a larger verbatim block can be broken only at certain points and not after each line. To avoid any extra vertical space in the next example, vspace must be used with both Verbatim environments and not only on the second one.

```
ASCII Art Archive
      https://www.asciiart.eu

            _,'"" '_.
  _.'_         _,'       '_.
(,-.'._,'(          |\'-/|
  '-.-' \ )-'( , o o)
    '-     \'_'"')-    [nosig]
```

```
\usepackage{fancyvrb}
\begin{Verbatim}[samepage]
ASCII Art Archive
      https://www.asciiart.eu
\end{Verbatim}
\nopagebreak[2]
\begin{Verbatim}[samepage,vspace=-\partopsep]
            _,'"" '_.
  _.'_         _,'       '_.
(,-.'._,'(          |\'-/|
  '-.-' \ )-'( , o o)
    '-     \'_'"')-    [nosig]
\end{Verbatim}
```

4-2-21

The vertical spacing between lines in a verbatim environment is the same as in normal text, but if desired, you can enlarge it by a factor using the key baselinestretch. Shrinking so that lines overlap is not possible. If you want to revert to the default line separation, use the string auto as a value.

```
This text is more or less double-spaced.

See also the discussion about the

setspace package elsewhere.
```

```
\usepackage{fancyvrb}
\begin{Verbatim}[baselinestretch=1.6]
This text is more or less double-spaced.
See also the discussion about the
setspace package elsewhere.
\end{Verbatim}
```

4-2-22

When presenting computer listings, it is often helpful to number some or all of the lines. This can be achieved by using the key numbers, which accepts none, left, or right (and with fvextra also both) as a value to control the position of the numbers. The distance between the number and the verbatim text is 12pt by default, but it can be adjusted by specifying a different value via the key numbersep. Usually, numbering restarts at 1 with each environment, but by providing an explicit number with the key firstnumber you can start with any integer value, even a negative one. Alternatively, this key accepts the word last to indicate that numbering should resume where it had stopped in the previous Verbatim instance.

As a shorthand for numbers=left, fvextra offers the key linenos.

```
\usepackage{fvextra}
\begin{Verbatim}[numbers=both,numbersep=6pt]
Verbatim lines can be numbered
at either left or right.
\end{Verbatim}
Some intermediate text\ldots
\begin{Verbatim}[linenos,firstnumber=last]
Continuation is possible too
as we can see here.
\end{Verbatim}
```

1 Verbatim lines can be numbered 1
2 at either left or right. 2

Some intermediate text...

3 Continuation is possible too
4 as we can see here.

4-2-23

Some people prefer to number only some lines, and the packages cater to this possibility by providing the key stepnumber. If this key is assigned a positive integer number, then only line numbers being an integer multiple of that number get printed. We already learned that the counter that is used internally to count the lines is called FancyVerbLine, so it comes as no surprise that the appearance of the numbers is controlled by the command \theFancyVerbLine. By modifying this command, special effects can be obtained; a possibility where the current chapter number is prepended is shown in the next example. It also shows the use of the Boolean key numberblanklines, which controls whether blank lines are numbered (default is false, i.e., to not number them).

```
\usepackage{fancyvrb}
\renewcommand\theFancyVerbLine{\footnotesize
  \thechapter.\arabic{FancyVerbLine}}
\begin{Verbatim}[numbers=left,stepnumber=2,
                 numberblanklines]
Normally empty lines in
a verbatim will not receive
numbers---here they do!

Admittedly using stepnumber
with such a redefinition of
FancyVerbLine looks a bit odd.
\end{Verbatim}
```

4.2 Normally empty lines in
a verbatim will not receive
numbers---here they do!

4.4

4.6 Admittedly using stepnumber
with such a redefinition of
FancyVerbLine looks a bit odd.

4-2-24

The fvextra package adds a few additional keys that further control the numbering of lines. If you use a positive stepnumber, then by default only lines that are multiples of that number are numbered. By adding `numberfirstline` the first line is also numbered.

```
\usepackage{fvextra}

\begin{Verbatim}[linenos,stepnumber=3,firstnumber=5]
First line has number 5 so
second gets a number because it
is divisible by 3. No other
numbers because the step is 3.
\end{Verbatim}
\begin{Verbatim}[linenos,stepnumber=2,
                 numberfirstline,firstnumber=5]
Here we additionally ask for
a number on the first line and
we reduced the step to 2, so
more lines get numbers.
\end{Verbatim}
```

```
   First line has number 5 so
 6 second gets a number because it
   is divisible by 3. No other
   numbers because the step is 3.

 5 Here we additionally ask for
 6 a number on the first line and
   we reduced the step to 2, so
 8 more lines get numbers.
```

4-2-25

If you do not like that result either, then another possibility is to use the key `stepnumberfromfirst`, in which case the numbering starts on the first line and the stepping happens from there. Finally there is `stepnumberoffsetvalues`. If that is used, then numbering happens on each multiple of the step but disregarding any offset that was given with `firstnumber`.

```
\usepackage{fvextra}

\begin{Verbatim}[linenos,stepnumber=2,
                 firstnumber=5,stepnumberfromfirst]
With this key, the first line
and then every line a step
further down is numbered,
thus here 5, 7, 9, ...
\end{Verbatim}
\begin{Verbatim}[linenos,stepnumber=2,
                 firstnumber=4,stepnumberoffsetvalues]
Without stepnumberoffsetvalues
we would see numbers on lines
4, 6, and 8 and not on 5 and
7 that we get now.
\end{Verbatim}
```

```
 5 With this key, the first line
   and then every line a step
 7 further down is numbered,
   thus here 5, 7, 9, ...

   Without stepnumberoffsetvalues
 5 we would see numbers on lines
   4, 6, and 8 and not on 5 and
 7 that we get now.
```

4-2-26

Instead or in addition to numbering lines, fvextra offers you a simple way to highlight certain lines with a background color (assuming a color package is loaded). The key `highlightcolor` redefines the color used if you do not like the default, and `highlightlines` specifies a list of lines or line ranges. The lines specified take any offset into account, so if you use `firstnumber`, you have to adjust the values accordingly. Also note that you have to surround the value with braces if it contains commas! This also allows you to put a background color on all lines; you just have to specify a range that is large enough, e.g., 1–50. The actual highlighting is done by a number of package commands such as \FancyVerbHighlightLineFirst so that there is even finer control possible. For details read the package documentation.

```
\usepackage{xcolor,fvextra}
\begin{Verbatim*}[numbers=right,firstnumber=12,
    highlightcolor=blue!10,highlightlines={13,15-50}]
First line is labeled 12
Second line
Third line
Fourth line and further
lines are highlighted
\end{Verbatim*}
```

```
␣␣First␣line␣is␣labeled␣12      12
␣␣Second␣line                   13
␣␣Third␣line                    14
␣␣Fourth␣line␣and␣further       15
␣␣lines␣are␣highlighted         16
```

4-2-27

Displaying whitespace characters   In some situations it helps to clearly identify whitespace characters by displaying all blanks as ␣. This can be achieved with the Boolean key showspaces or, alternatively, the Verbatim* variant of the environment as we did in the previous example. The fvextra package adds some further bells and whistles here by offering the key space to redefine the character that is used to represent a visible space (default is \textvisiblespace), and with spacecolor you can declare a particular color to be used just for that type of space.

Another whitespace character, the tab, plays an important rôle in some programming languages, so there may be a need to identify it in your source. This is achieved with the Boolean key showtabs. The tab character displayed is defined by the command \FancyVerbTab and can be redefined. With fvextra this can be more conveniently done through the key tab and its color with tabcolor, as seen below.

By default, tab characters simply equal eight spaces, a value that can be changed with the key tabsize. However, if you set the Boolean key obeytabs, then each tab character produces as many spaces as necessary to move to the next integer multiple of tabsize. The example input contains tabs in each line that are displayed on the right as spaces with the default tabsize of 8. Note in particular the difference between the last input and output line.

```
\usepackage{xcolor,fvextra}    \fvset{tabcolor=blue}
\begin{Verbatim}
12345678901234567890 1234567890
Two      default tabs
\end{Verbatim}
\begin{Verbatim}[obeytabs,showtabs]
Three    visible tab      chars
\end{Verbatim}
\begin{Verbatim}[obeytabs,showtabs,tab=$\bullet$]
Two      new      tabs
\end{Verbatim}
\begin{Verbatim}[obeytabs,tabsize=3,showtabs]
Using    a        special tab      size
\end{Verbatim}
```

```
12345678901234567890 1234567890
Two              default         tabs

Three   visible tab        chars

Two     •new      •tabs

Using a  special tab size
```

4-2-28

If you wish to execute commands within the verbatim text, then you need one character to act as an escape character (i.e., to denote the beginning of a command name) and two characters to serve as argument delimiters (i.e., to play the rôle that braces normally play within LaTeX). Such special characters can be specified with the `commandchars` key as shown below; of course, these characters then cannot appear as part of the verbatim text. The characters are specified by putting a backslash in front of each one so as to mask any special meaning they might normally have in LaTeX. The key `commentchar` allows you to define a comment character, which results in ignoring everything following it until and including the next new line character. Thus, if this character is used in the middle of a line, this line and the next are joined together. If you wish to cancel a previous setting for `commandchars` or `commentchar`, use the string value "none".

There is one important caveat: if the comment character is used anywhere in the last line of the verbatim, then the whole line gets ignored because fancyvrb prints out a line only if it sees an endline character and now on that line there is not any! The next example shows the issue:

Last line gets lost if you are not extra careful!

```
\usepackage{fancyvrb}

\begin{Verbatim}[commandchars=\|\[\],commentchar=\!]
We can |emph[emphasize] text
! see above (this line is invisible)
Line with label|label[linea] ! removes new line
is shown here.
Careful: last line lost ! because of comment
\end{Verbatim}

On line~\ref{linea} we see\ldots
```

We can *emphasize* text
Line with label is shown here.

4-2-29 On line 2 we see...

If you use `\label` within the verbatim environment, as was done in the previous example, it refers to the internal line number whether or not that number is displayed. This requires the use of the `commandchars` key, a price you might consider too high because it deprives you of the use of the chosen characters in your verbatim text.

The fvextra package has another key that changes the parsing: `mathescape`. If you use this, then $, _, and ^ retain their normal meaning within the verbatim scope; thus, you can mix formulas and verbatim text to some extent.

Two other keys available with both packages let you change the parsing and manipulation of verbatim data: `codes` and `defineactive`. They allow you to play some devious tricks, but their use is not so easy to explain: one needs a good understanding of TeX's inner workings. If you are interested, please check the documentation provided with the fancyvrb package.

Line breaking within verbatim data

While fancyvrb never breaks input lines, the fvextra package is able to, provided you use the key `breaklines`. By default lines are broken only at spaces, but by supplying some further keys and values this can be adjusted in various ways. For example, `breakanywhere` enables breaking anywhere in the line, while `breakafter` allows you to specify additional characters after which a break is allowed to happen. Instead of breaking after some character, you can break before certain characters that are set using breakbefore. Depending on the character, you might have to escape it with a backslash; e.g., \#\\ would allow a break after # or after a backslash.

There are many more keys to cover special requirements including defining the characters that should indicate such a break; for details refer to the package documentation. As you can see in the example, a break at a space is indicated with a continuation character on the next line (breaksymbolleft), while a break due to breakafter or breakanywhere has continuation characters on both lines. The pre-break continuation characters can be explicitly set with breakanywheresymbolpre and breakaftersymbolpre.

A few but certainly not all of the possibilities are exhibited in the next example:

```
A long wide line of verbatim text!
```

```
A long wide line of
  ↪  verbatim text!
```

```
A wide line with a-very-lon⌋
  ↪  gish-verbatim-word!
```

```
A wide line with a-very-⌋
  ↪  longish-verbatim-word
and one-further-longish-⌋
  ↪  word.
```

```
\usepackage{fvextra}
\begin{Verbatim}[frame=single,xrightmargin=4pc]
A long wide line of verbatim text!
\end{Verbatim}
\fvset{frame=single,breaklines} % change defaults
\begin{Verbatim}[xrightmargin=2pc]
A long wide line of verbatim text!
\end{Verbatim}
\begin{Verbatim}[breakanywhere]
A wide line with a-very-longish-verbatim-word!
\end{Verbatim}
\begin{Verbatim}[breakafter=-]
A wide line with a-very-longish-verbatim-word
and one-further-longish-word.
\end{Verbatim}
```

4-2-30

Limiting the displayed data

Normally, all lines within the verbatim environment are typeset. If you want to display only a subset of lines, you have a number of choices. With the keys firstline and lastline, you can specify the start line and (if necessary) the final line to typeset.

Alternatively, you can specify a start and stop string to search for within the environment body, with the result that all lines between (but this time *not* including the special lines) are typeset. The strings are specified in the macros \FancyVerbStartString and \FancyVerbStopString. To make this work, you have to be a bit careful: the macros need to be defined with \newcommand* and redefined with \renewcommand*. Using \newcommand will *not* work! Canceling such a declaration is even more complicated: you have to \let the command to \relax, for example,

```
\let\FancyVerbStartString\relax
```

or ensure that your definition is confined to a group — everything else fails.

```
\usepackage{fancyvrb}

\newcommand*\FancyVerbStartString{START}
\newcommand*\FancyVerbStopString{STOP}
\begin{Verbatim}
   A verbatim line not shown.
START
   Only the third line is shown.
STOP
   The remainder is left out.
\end{Verbatim}
```

4-2-31   `Only the third line is shown.`

You may wonder why one would want to have such functionality available, given that one could simply leave out the lines that are not being typeset. With an environment like `Verbatim` they are indeed of only limited use. However, when used together with other functions of the package that write data to files and read it back again, they offer powerful solutions to otherwise unsolvable problems.

For instance, all examples in this book use this method. The example body is written to a file together with a document preamble and other material so that the resulting file becomes a processable LATEX document. This document is then externally processed and included as an Portable Document Format (PDF) graphic image into the book after further processing with pdfcrop to cut it to the right size. Beside it, the sample code is displayed by reading this external file back in but displaying only those lines that lie between the strings `\begin{document}` and `\end{document}`. This accounts for the example lines you see being typeset in black. The preamble part, which is shown in blue, is produced in a similar fashion: for this the start and stop strings are redefined to include only those lines lying between the strings `%StartShownPreambleCommands` and `%StopShownPreambleCommands`. When processing the example externally, these two strings are simply no-ops (because LATEX sees them as comments). As a consequence, the example code always (for better or worse) corresponds to the displayed result.[1]

How the book examples have been produced

To write data verbatim to a file the environment `VerbatimOut` is available. It takes one mandatory argument: the file name into which to write the data. There is, however, a logical problem if you try to use such an environment inside your own environments: the moment you start the `VerbatimOut` environment, everything is swallowed without processing and so the end of your environment is not recognized. As a solution the fancyvrb package offers the command `\VerbatimEnvironment`, which, if executed within the `\begin` code of your environment, ensures that the end tag of your environment is recognized in verbatim mode and the corresponding code executed.

To read data verbatim from a file, the command `\VerbatimInput` can be used. It takes an optional argument similar to the one of the `Verbatim` environment (i.e., it accepts all the keys discussed previously) and a mandatory argument to specify

---

[1] In the first edition we unfortunately introduced a number of mistakes when showing code in text that was not directly used — in this book our mistakes show.

the file from which to read. The variant `\BVerbatimInput` puts the typeset result in a box without space above and below. The next example demonstrates some of the possibilities: it defines an environment `example` that first writes its body verbatim to a file; reads the first line back in and displays it in blue; reads the file once more, this time starting with the second line; and numbers the lines starting with the number 1. As explained above, a similar, albeit more complex, definition was used to produce the examples in this book.

```
\usepackage{fancyvrb,color}
\newenvironment{example}
  {\VerbatimEnvironment\begin{VerbatimOut}{test.out}}
  {\end{VerbatimOut}\noindent
   \BVerbatimInput[lastline=1,formatcom=\color{blue}]{test.out}%
   \VerbatimInput[numbers=left,firstnumber=1,firstline=2]{test.out}}
\begin{example}
A blue line.
Numbered lines
in black.
\end{example}
```

A blue line.
Numbered lines
in black.

1 Numbered lines
2 in black.

4-2-32

Variant environments and commands

So far, all except the last example have used the `Verbatim` environment, but there also exist a number of variants that are useful in certain circumstances. BVerbatim is similar to `Verbatim` but puts the verbatim lines into a box. Some keys discussed above (notably those dealing with frames) are not supported, but two additional ones are available. The first, `baseline`, denotes the alignment point for the box; it can take the values t (for top), c (for center), or b (for bottom — the default). The second, `boxwidth`, specifies the desired width of the box; if it is missing or given the value `auto`, the box gets as wide as the widest line present in the environment. We already encountered `\BVerbatimInput`; it too, supports these additional keys.

```
\usepackage{fancyvrb}
\begin{BVerbatim}[boxwidth=6pc,baseline=c]
Box is too small, so text
sticks out on the right!
\end{BVerbatim}
\begin{BVerbatim}[baseline=t]
Box has natural width.
Note the alignment.
\end{BVerbatim}
```

Box is too small, so text
sticks out on the right!
Box has natural width.
Note the alignment.

4-2-33

All environments and commands for typesetting verbatim text also have star variants, which, as in the standard LATEX environments, display blanks as ␣. In other words, they internally set the key `showspaces` to true..

Defining your own variants

Defining customized variants of verbatim commands and environments is quite simple. For starters, the default settings built into the package can be changed with the help of the \fvset command. It takes one argument, a comma-separated list of key/value pairs. It applies them to every verbatim environment or command. Of course, you can still overwrite the new defaults with the optional argument on the command or environment. For example, if nearly all of your verbatim environments are indented by two spaces, you might want to remove them without having to deploy gobble on each occasion.

```
\usepackage{fancyvrb}
\fvset{gobble=2}
```

A line of text to show the left margin.

```
\noindent A line of text to show the left margin.
\begin{Verbatim}
  The new 'normal' case.
\end{Verbatim}
```

The new 'normal' case.

```
With this default we need to watch out for
unindented verbatims to avoid results like this:
\begin{Verbatim}
Not good now for verbatims
without indentation!
\end{Verbatim}
In that case do this:
\begin{Verbatim}[gobble=0]
We now need to explicitly
cancel the gobble occasionally!
\end{Verbatim}
```

With this default we need to watch out for unindented verbatims to avoid results like this:

```
t good now for verbatims
thout indentation!
```

In that case do this:

```
We now need to explicitly
cancel the gobble occasionally!
```

4-2-34

However, \fvset applies to all environments and commands, which may not be what you need. The package therefore offers commands to define your own verbatim environments and commands or to modify the behavior of the predefined ones.

```
\CustomVerbatimEnvironment{new-env}{base-env}{key/value list}
\CustomVerbatimCommand     {new-cmd}{base-cmd}{key/value list}
```

These declarations take three arguments: the name of the new environment or command being defined, the name of the environment or command (without a leading backslash) on which it is based, and a comma-separated list of key/value pairs that define the new behavior. To define new structures, you use these declarations.

To change the behavior of existing environments or commands (predefined ones as well as those defined by you), you use \RecustomVerbatimEnvironment or \RecustomVerbatimCommand, which otherwise take the same arguments. As shown in Example 4-2-35 on the next page, the default values, set in the third argument, can be overwritten as usual with the optional argument when the environment or command is instantiated.

```
\usepackage{fancyvrb}
\CustomVerbatimEnvironment{myverbatim}{Verbatim}
         {numbers=left,frame=lines,framerule=2pt}

\begin{myverbatim}
The normal case with thick
rules and numbers on the left.
\end{myverbatim}
\begin{myverbatim}[numbers=none,framerule=.6pt]
The exception without numbers
and thinner rules.
\end{myverbatim}
\RecustomVerbatimEnvironment{myverbatim}{Verbatim}
         {numbers=left,frame=none,showspaces=true}
\begin{myverbatim}
And from here on the environment
behaves differently again.
\end{myverbatim}
```

```
1  The normal case with thick
2  rules and numbers on the left.
```

```
The exception without numbers
and thinner rules.
```

```
1  And␣from␣here␣on␣the␣environment
2  behaves␣differently␣again.
```

4-2-35

Making a comment environment

With the help of \CustomVerbatimEnvironment it is trivial to implement your own comment environments. All you need is the BVerbatim environment to box the material and then use the lastline key to display none of the collected lines.

```
\usepackage{fancyvrb}
\CustomVerbatimEnvironment{comment}{BVerbatim}{lastline=0}
A  simple way to implement a comment
\begin{comment}
  anything can go in here \begin{itemize} ...
\end{comment}
environment is shown in this example.
```

A simple way to implement a comment environment is shown in this example.

4-2-36

Inline verbatim material

The fancyvrb version of \verb is called \Verb, and it supports all applicable keys, which can be passed to it via an optional argument as usual.

The example below creates \verbx as a variant of \Verb with a special setting of commandchars so that we can execute commands within its argument. We have to use \CustomVerbatimCommand for this purpose, because \verbx is a new command not available in standard LaTeX. As one can see, both \Verb and its custom variant support the star form that produces visible spaces.

```
\usepackage{fancyvrb}
\CustomVerbatimCommand\verbx{Verb}{commandchars=\|\<\>}
\Verb*[fontfamily=courier] +\realdanger   {|emph<arg>}+
\verbx*[fontfamily=courier]+\realdanger   {|emph<arg>}+
\verbx+\realdanger   {|emph<arg>}+
```

```
\realdanger␣␣{|emph<arg>}
\realdanger␣␣{arg}
\realdanger   {arg}
```

4-2-37

Inline verbatim material in dangerous places

LaTeX's standard \verb command normally cannot be used inside arguments, because in such places the parsing mechanism would go astray, producing incorrect results or error messages. One solution to this problem is to process the verbatim data outside the argument, save it, and later use the already parsed data in such dangerous places. For this purpose the fancyvrb package offers the commands \SaveVerb and \UseVerb.

\SaveVerb[*key/value list*]{*label*}=*data*=   \UseVerb*[*key/value list*]{*label*}

The command \SaveVerb takes one mandatory argument, a *label* denoting the storage bin in which to save the parsed data. It is followed by the verbatim *data* surrounded by two identical characters (= in the syntax example above), in the same way that \verb delimits its argument. To use this data you call \UseVerb with the *label* as the mandatory argument. Because the data are only parsed but not typeset by \SaveVerb, it is possible to influence the typesetting by applying a list of key/value pairs or a star as with the other verbatim commands and environments. Clearly, only a subset of keys make sense: irrelevant ones are silently ignored. The \UseVerb command is robust, so you can use it in moving arguments, e.g., headings without further protection.

Contents

1 Real \danger   6

1   Real \danger

Real␣\danger is no longer danger-

_{Real \danger} ous and can be reused as often as de-

sired.

```
\usepackage{fancyvrb}
\SaveVerb{danger}=Real \danger=
\tableofcontents \medskip

\section{\UseVerb{danger}}
\UseVerb*{danger} is no longer dangerous
and can\marginpar{\UseVerb[fontsize=\tiny]
                              {danger}}
be reused as often as desired.
```

It is possible to reuse such a storage bin when it is no longer needed, but if you use \UseVerb inside commands that distribute their arguments over a large distance, you have to be careful to ensure that the storage bin still contains the desired contents when the command finally typesets it. In the previous example we placed \SaveVerb into the preamble because the use of its storage bin inside the \section command eventually results in an execution of \UseVerb inside the \tableofcontents command.

\SaveVerb also accepts an optional argument in which you can put key/value pairs, though again only a few are relevant (e.g., those dealing with parsing). There is one additional key aftersave, which takes code to execute immediately after saving the verbatim text into the storage bin. The next example shows an application of this key: the definition of a special variant of the \item command that accepts verbatim text for display in a description environment. It also supports an optional argument in which you can put a key/value list to influence the formatting. The definition is worth studying, even though the amount of mixed braces and brackets seems distressingly complex at first. They are necessary to ensure that the correct brackets are matched by \SaveVerb, \item, and \UseVerb — the usual problem, because brackets do not nest like braces do in TEX.[1] Also note the use of \textnormal, which is needed to cancel the \bfseries implicitly issued by the \item command. Otherwise, the \emph command in the example would not show any effect because no Computer Modern bold italic face exists.

\ddanger Dangerous beast found in TEXbooks.

\danger Its small brother, still dangerous.

\dddanger{*arg*} The ultimate horror.

```
\usepackage{fancyvrb}
\newcommand\vitem[1][]{\SaveVerb[commandchars=\|\<\>,%
    aftersave={\item[\textnormal{\UseVerb[#1]{vsave}}]}]{vsave}}
\begin{description}
\vitem+\ddanger+    Dangerous beast found in \TeX books.
\vitem[fontsize=\tiny]+\danger+ Its small brother,
                               still dangerous.
\vitem+\dddanger{|emph<arg>}+    The ultimate horror.
\end{description}
```

4-2-39

In the same way, you can save whole verbatim environments using the environment SaveVerbatim, which takes the name of a storage bin as the mandatory argument. To typeset them, \UseVerbatim or \BUseVerbatim (boxed version) with the usual key/value machinery can be used.

Special case: footnotes

Even though verbatim commands or environments are normally not allowed inside footnotes, you do not need to deploy \SaveVerb and the like to get verbatim text into such places. Instead, place the command \VerbatimFootnotes at the beginning of your document (following the preamble!), and from that point onward, you can use verbatim commands directly in footnotes. However, this was implemented only for footnotes — for other commands, such as \section, you still need the more complicated storage bin method described above.

A bit of text to give us a reason to use a footnote.[1] Was this good enough?

---

[1] Here is proof: \danger{%_^}

```
\usepackage{fancyvrb}
\VerbatimFootnotes
A bit of text to give us a reason to use a
footnote.\footnote{Here is proof: \verb=\danger{%_^}=}
Was this good enough?
```

4-2-40

Verbatim shorthands

As already mentioned, fancyvrb offers a way to make a certain character denote the start and stop of verbatim text without the need to put \verb in front. The command to declare such a delimiting character is \DefineShortVerb. Like other fancyvrb commands it accepts an optional argument that allows you to set key/value pairs. These influence the formatting and parsing, though this time you cannot overwrite your choices on the individual instance. Alternatively, \fvset can be used, because it works on all verbatim commands and environments within its scope. To

---

[1] The author confesses that it took him three trials (close to midnight) to make this example work.

remove the special meaning from a character declared with `\DefineShortVerb`, use `\UndefineShortVerb`.

```
\usepackage{fancyvrb}
\DefineShortVerb[fontsize=\tiny]{\|}
The use of |\DefineShortVerb| can make sources
much more readable---or unreadable!
```

The use of `\DefineShortVerb` can make sources much more readable—or unreadable!

And with `\UndefineShortVerb{\|}` we can return the | character back to normal.

```
\UndefineShortVerb{\|}\DefineShortVerb{\+}
\fvset{fontfamily=courier}
And with +\UndefineShortVerb{\|}+
we can return the +|+ character back to normal.
```

4-2-41

Extension to inline verbatim by fvextra

The fvextra package extends the support for inline verbatim material in several ways. It provides an `\fvinlineset` declaration that applies only to commands related to inline typesetting like `\Verb`, `\SaveVerb`, etc. This extends/overwrites settings made with `\fvset` declarations so that it is possible to set up different conventions for the two cases.

In the following example we use it to typeset inline verbatim in Courier while Verbatim uses a different font. We also show that the reimplementation of `\Verb` in the fvextra package supports line breaking if enabled with the `breaklines` key.

No break in this piece of verbatim text but now this verbatim text will break at spaces as shown in this line.

This is a different font!

```
\usepackage{fvextra}
\fvinlineset{fontfamily=courier}
No break in \Verb+this piece of verbatim+ text but
now \Verb[breaklines]+this verbatim text will+
break at spaces as shown in this line.
\begin{Verbatim}
This is a different font!
\end{Verbatim}
```

4-2-42

The recent version of the fvextra package also offers an `\EscVerb` command that can be safely used in arguments of other commands. It works like `\Verb` but turns the backslash into an escape character allowing you to escape problematical characters such as # or %. The only restriction is that its argument has to be delimited by a brace group and not by two identical characters.

The next example shows a few of the problematical characters and how they can be handled. Single spaces are fine, but multiple ones in succession are collapsed to one or require a backslash in front of all but the first. Properly paired braces work, but if you need unbalanced ones, you need to escape them, and obviously the backslash itself needs escaping and so does the comment character.

Also shown is that the fvextra reimplementation of `\Verb` can also be used inside other arguments, though it does have limitations there: spaces get lost after commands, and you cannot use unbalanced braces or # or % characters at all. Nevertheless, in many practical cases it produces correct results, and it does work properly in PDF bookmarks showing verbatim content.

Contents

```
\usepackage{fvextra}

\tableofcontents \medskip
\section{\EscVerb*{Space  \\danger \ \{\%}}
\EscVerb{\\EscVerb*{...}} is not dangerous
and can\marginpar{\EscVerb[fontsize=\tiny]
                  {No \\danger \#}}
be used anywhere.
\subsection{\Verb*{Space    \danger  {}}}
And this works with limitations in
\textsf{fvextra}.
```

4-2-43

1   Space␣\danger␣␣{%

No \danger #   \EscVerb*{...} is not dangerous and can be used anywhere.

1.1   Space␣\danger{}

And this works with limitations in fvextra.

External configuration

Your favorite extensions or customizations can be grouped in a file with the name `fancyvrb.cfg`. After fancyvrb finishes loading, the package automatically searches for this file. The advantage of using such a file, when installed in a central place, is that you do not have to put your extensions into all your documents. The downside is that your documents are no longer portable unless you distribute this file in tandem with them.

4.2.5 listings — Pretty-printing program code

A common application of verbatim typesetting is presenting program code. While one can successfully deploy a package like fancyvrb to handle this job, it is often preferable to enhance the display by typesetting certain program components (such as keywords, identifiers, and comments) in a special way.

Two major approaches are possible: one can provide commands to identify the logical aspects of algorithms or the programming language, or the application can (try to) analyze the program code behind the scenes. The second cases can be subdivided into complete processing within LaTeX or processing the algorithm with some external program and (automatically) including the results.

The advantage of the first approach is that you have potentially more control over the presentation; however, your program code is intermixed with TeX commands and thus may be difficult to maintain, is unusable for direct processing, and is often rather complicated to read in the source. Examples of packages classified into this category are algorithms (using fully uppercased command names) and algorithmicx and its offsprings like algpseudocode. Here is an example:

```
1: if i ≤ 0 then
2:     i ← 1              ▷ main case
3: else if i > 0 then
4:     i ← 0
5: end if
```

```
\usepackage{algpseudocode}

\begin{algorithmic}[1]
\If {$i\leq0$} \State $i\gets1$ \Comment{main case}
\ElsIf {$i>0$} \State $i\gets0$ \EndIf
\end{algorithmic}
```

4-2-44

ABAP (R/2 4.3, R/2 5.0, R/3 3.1, R/3 4.6C, R/3 6.10)	csh	Mathematica (1.0, 3.0, 5.2, 11.0)	Reduce
	Delphi		Rexx (empty, VM/XA)
	Eiffel	Matlab	RSL
ACM	Elan	Mercury	Ruby
ACMscript	elisp	MetaPost	S (empty, PLUS)
ACSL	erlang	Miranda	SAS
Ada (83, 95, 2005)	Euphoria	Mizar	Scala
Algol (60, 68)	Fortran (77, 90, 95, 03, 08)	ML	Scilab
Ant		Modula-2	sh
Assembler (Notorola68k, x86masm)	GAP	MuPAD	SHELXL
	GCL	NASTRAN	Simula (67, CII, DEC, IBM)
	Gnuplot	Oberon-2	
Awk (gnu, POSIX)	Go	OCL (decorative, OMG)	SPARQL
bash	hansl	Octave	SQL
Basic (Visual)	Haskell	OORexx	Swift
C (ANSI, Handel, Objective, Sharp)	HTML	Oz	tcl (empty, tk)
C++ (11, ANSI, GNU, ISO, Visual)	IDL (empty, CORBA)	Pascal (Borland6, Standard, XSC)	TeX (AlLaTeX, common, LaTeX, plain, primitive)
	inform		
	Java (empty, AspectJ)	Perl	
Caml (light, Objective)	JVMIS	PHP	VBScript
	ksh	PL/I	Verilog
CIL	Lingo	Plasm	VHDL (empty, AMS)
Clean	Lisp (empty, Auto)	PostScript	VRML (97)
Cobol (1974, 1985, ibm)	LLVM	POV	XML
Comal 80	Logo	Prolog	XSLT
command.com (WinXP)	Lua (5.0, 5.1, 5.2, 5.3)	Python	
Comsol	Make (empty, gnu)	R	

blue indicates the default dialect

Table 4.4: Languages supported by listings (spring 2022)

The second approach is exemplified in the package listings written by Carsten Heinz, now maintained by Jobst Hoffmann. This package first analyzes the code, decomposes it into its components, and then formats those components according to customizable rules. The package parser is quite general and can be tuned to recognize the syntax of many different languages (see Table 4.4). New languages are regularly added, so if your target language is not listed, it might be worth checking the latest release of the package on CTAN. You may even consider contributing the necessary declarations yourself, which involves some work but is not very difficult.

The user commands and environments in this package share many similarities with those in fancyvrb. Aspects of parsing and formatting are controlled via key/value pairs specified in an optional argument, and settings for the whole document or larger parts of it can be specified using \lstset (the corresponding fancyvrb command is \fvset). Whenever appropriate, both packages use the same keys so that users of one package should find it easy to make the transition to the other.

After loading the package, it is helpful to specify all program languages needed in the document (as a comma-separated list) using \lstloadlanguages. Such a declaration does not select a language, but merely loads the necessary support information and speeds up processing.

Program fragments are included inside a lstlisting environment. The language of the fragment is specified with the language key. Specifying a dialect is done in brackets in front of the language name and therefore requires an extra set of braces if you are in an optional argument — e.g., language={[83]Ada}, as shown below. In the following example we set this key via \lstset to C and then overwrite it later in the optional argument to the second lstlisting environment:

A "for" loop in C:

```
int sum;
int i; /* for loop variable */
sum=0;
for (i=0;i<n;i++) { sum += a[i]; }
```

Now the same loop in Ada 83:

```
Sum: Integer;
-- no decl for 'I' necessary
Sum := 0;
for I in 1..N loop
  Sum := Sum + A(I);
end loop;
```

```
\usepackage{listings}
\lstloadlanguages{C,Ada}
\lstset{language=C,commentstyle=\scriptsize}
A ``for'' loop in C:
\begin{lstlisting}[keywordstyle=\underbar]
int sum;
int i; /*for loop variable*/
sum=0;
for (i=0;i<n;i++) { sum += a[i]; }
\end{lstlisting}
Now the same loop in Ada 83:
\begin{lstlisting}[language={[83]Ada}]
Sum: Integer;
-- no decl for 'I' necessary
Sum := 0;
for I in 1..N loop
  Sum := Sum + A(I);
end loop;
\end{lstlisting}
```

4-2-45

This example also uses the key commentstyle, which controls the layout of comments in the language. The package properly identifies the different syntax styles for comments. Several other such keys are available as well — basicstyle to set the overall appearance of the listing, stringstyle to format strings in the language, and directivestyle to format compiler directives, among others.

To format the language keywords, the key keywordstyle is used. The language may distinguish different classes (levels) of keywords, and if so, handling of those classes is managed by prefixing the value with [number]. If you prefix the value with a *, then the keywords are uppercased.

Other identifiers are formatted according to the setting of identifierstyle. The values for the "style" keys (except basicstyle) accept a one-argument LaTeX command such as \textbf as their last token. This scheme works because the "identifier text" is internally surrounded by braces and can thus be picked up by a command with an argument.

Thus, highlighting of keywords, identifiers, and other elements is done automatically in a customizable way. Nevertheless, you might want to additionally emphasize the use of a certain variable, function, or interface. For this purpose you can use the keys emph and emphstyle. The first gets a list of names you want to emphasize; the second specifies how you want them typeset. Again, you can define different classes and specialized handling for each as shown in the example.

```
\usepackage{listings,color}
\lstset{keywordstyle=*\textsf,emph={Sum,N},emph=[2]I,
        emphstyle=\color{blue},emphstyle=[2]\underbar}
\begin{lstlisting}[language=Ada]
Sum: Integer;   Sum := 0;
for I in 1..N loop
  Sum := Sum + A(I);
end loop;
\end{lstlisting}
```

```
Sum: Integer;   Sum := 0;
FOR I IN 1..N LOOP
  Sum := Sum + A(I);
END LOOP;
```

4-2-46

If you want to typeset a code fragment within normal text, you can use the command \lstinline. The code is delimited in the same way as with the \verb command, meaning that you can choose any character (other than the open bracket) that is not used within the code fragment and use it as a delimiter. An open bracket cannot be used because the command also accepts an optional argument in which you can specify a list of key/value pairs.

```
\usepackage{listings}  \lstset{language=C}
The \lstinline[keywordstyle=\underbar]!for!
loop is specified as \lstinline!i=0;i<n;i++!.
```

4-2-47   The for loop is specified as i=0;i<n;i++.

Of course, it is also possible to format the contents of whole files; for this purpose you use the command \lstinputlisting. It takes an optional argument in which you can specify key/value pairs and a mandatory argument in which you specify the file name to process. In the following example, the package identifies keywords of case-insensitive languages, even if they are written in an unusual mixed-case (WrItE) manner.

```
\usepackage{listings}
\begin{filecontents*}{pascal.src}
for i:=1 to maxint do
begin
  WrItE('This is stupid');
end.
\end{filecontents*}
\lstinputlisting[language=Pascal]{pascal.src}
```

```
for i:=1 to maxint do
begin
  WrItE('This is stupid');
end.
```

4-2-48

Spaces within strings (of the language) are shown as ␣ by default. This behavior can be turned off by setting the Boolean key showstringspaces to false, as shown in Example 4-2-50 on the next page.

It is also possible to request that all spaces be displayed in this way by setting the key `showspaces` to `true`. Similarly, tab characters can be made visible by using the Boolean key `showtabs`. What is displayed for the tab character in this case can be adjusted through the `tab` key. By default a fixed number of spaces is generated. The number depends on the value of `tabsize` and defaults to 8.

The previous example already showed a somewhat questionable result in that the single quotes used to delimit the string showed up as typographic quotes rather than straight quotes. The same is true by default for back quotes, and if you do not like this, you can use the Boolean key `upquote` as shown in the next example.

```
\usepackage{listings}
\lstset{language=bash}

\begin{lstlisting}
cp `kpsewhich listings.cfg` './$$'
\end{lstlisting}
\begin{lstlisting}[upquote]
cp `kpsewhich listings.cfg` './$$'
\end{lstlisting}
```

cp ‘kpsewhich listings.cfg‘ ’./$$’

cp `kpsewhich listings.cfg` './$$'

4-2-49

Line numbering is possible, too, using the same keys as employed with fancyvrb: `numbers` accepts either `left`, `right`, or `none` (which turns numbering on or off), `numberblanklines` decides whether blank lines count with respect to numbering (default `false`), `numberstyle` defines the overall look and feel of the numbers, `stepnumber` defines which line numbers appear (0 means no numbering), and `numbersep` defines the separation between numbers and the start of the line.

By default, line numbering starts with 1 on each `\lstinputlisting`, but this can be changed using the `firstnumber` key. If you specify `last` as a special value to `firstnumber`, numbering is continued. Also supported is `numberfirstline` to number the first line of the display even if it is not dividable by the `stepnumber`.

The next example shows some of these keys in action: we request line numbers on every second line, start with line number 9, and also request that the first line is numbered. Thus, we get numbers on lines 9, 10, and 12.

```
\usepackage{listings}
% pascal.src as defined before

\lstset{numberstyle=\tiny,numbers=left,
    numbersep=5pt,
    firstnumber=9,stepnumber=2,numberfirstline,
    xleftmargin=12pt,showstringspaces=false}
\noindent Some text before \ldots
\lstinputlisting[language=Pascal]{pascal.src}
```

Some text before …

9 **for** i := 1 **to maxint do**
10 **begin**
    WrItE('This is stupid');
12 **end** .

4-2-50

Another way to provide continued numbering is via the `name` key. If you define "named" environments using this key, numbering is automatically continued with respect to the previous environment with the same name. This allows independent numbering if the need arises.

```
\usepackage{listings} \lstset{language=Ada,numbers=right,
        numberstyle=\tiny,stepnumber=1,numbersep=5pt}
```

```
Sum: Integer;                    1
```

```
\begin{lstlisting}[name=Test]
Sum: Integer;
\end{lstlisting}
The second fragment continues the numbering.
\begin{lstlisting}[name=Test]
Sum := 0;
for I in 1..N loop
   Sum := Sum + A(I);
end loop;
\end{lstlisting}
```

The second fragment continues the numbering.

```
Sum := 0;                        2
for I in 1..N loop               3
   Sum := Sum + A(I);            4
```

4-2-51 `end loop;`   5

The line number is managed through the counter `lstnumber`; thus by redefining `\thelstnumber`, you can exercise even more control. However, this can be somewhat dangerous if fragile commands are involved, and a better method is to use the fact that you can pass a command with one argument as the last command to `numberstyle` as demonstrated below:

Some text to show the margins.

```
\usepackage{listings}
\lstset{numbers=left,firstnumber=4711,
        numberstyle=\tiny\oldstylenums}
```

4711   A code
           line
4712   Another
           line

```
\noindent Some text to show the margins.
\begin{lstlisting}[xleftmargin=10pt,xrightmargin=10pt,breaklines]
   A code line
   Another line
\end{lstlisting}
\begin{lstlisting}[firstnumber=last,breaklines,gobble=9]
   A crippled final line (9 chars dropped)
\end{lstlisting}
```

4713   led final line
           (9 chars
4-2-52   dropped)

Looking at the examples so far, you may have wondered about the fact that the words all appear letter-spaced. This observation is correct: even though listings by default does not use monospaced fonts, it arranges the characters such that they are vertically aligned, which for many applications is the best way to display program code. Technically this is done on a word-by-word basis. The key `basewidth` (default `0.6em`) defines the width reserved per character. Words are then placed into a box with a width that is an appropriate multiple of `basewidth`, and the characters of the words are then evenly spread out within those boxes. If the reserved space is too small, the characters get cramped together or even overlap each other.

Vertical alignment

However, this behavior can be adjusted through the `columns` key, which accepts the values `fixed` (default), `flexible`, `spaceflexible`, and `fullflexible`. In addition, you can prefix the value (except for `fullflexible`) with `[l]` or `[r]` to change the alignment within the allotted space from centered to left or right.

```
\usepackage{listings}
\lstset{language=bash,upquote,commentstyle=\tiny}

\begin{lstlisting}[columns=fixed]
cat `kpsewhich bm.sty` # package
texdoc bm               # doc/code
\end{lstlisting}
\begin{lstlisting}[columns={[l]flexible}]
cat `kpsewhich bm.sty` # package is where?
texdoc bm               # display doc/code
\end{lstlisting}
\begin{lstlisting}[columns=fullflexible]
cat `kpsewhich bm.sty` # package is where?
texdoc bm               # display doc/code
\end{lstlisting}
```

```
cat `kpsewhich bm.sty`  # package
texdoc bm               # doc/code

cat `kpsewhich bm.sty` # package    is    where   ?
texdoc bm              # display    doc  / code

cat `kpsewhich bm.sty` # package is where?
texdoc bm # display doc/code
```

4-2-53

In the flexible formats the `basewidth` is by default reduced to `.45em` so that the characters move closer together and the material needs less space. Furthermore, all glyphs are typeset at their normal width and never overlap. If a string needs more space than was reserved for it, it simply shifts everything after it to the right and thus ruins the vertical alignment (which you may or may not care about). The `flexible` format at least tries to maintain alignment if strings are shorter than the space reserved for them by adding extra spaces (`spaceflexible` works similarly, but does this only at real space characters in the source). The value `fullflexible` makes no attempt at alignment whatsoever and typesets everything at its nominal width (which also reduces multiple spaces to a single space!).

The previous example used `commentstyle` to make the comments tiny, and in that case the default value of `0.6em` for `basewidth` was particularly inappropriate because it is evaluated only once (for the standard font size). To account for this, the package offers `fontadjust`, which, if set, reevaluates `basewidth` each time a font change happens. Of course, this has an effect only if the value of that key is given in a font-specific unit, such as `em` or `ex`.

```
\usepackage{listings}
\lstset{language=bash,upquote,commentstyle=\tiny}

\begin{lstlisting}[fontadjust]
cat `kpsewhich bm.sty` # package
texdoc bm               # doc/code
\end{lstlisting}
```

```
cat `kpsewhich bm.sty`  # package
texdoc bm               # doc/code
```

4-2-54

Horizontal spacing   An overall indentation can be set using the `xleftmargin` and `xrightmargin` keys as shown in Example 4-2-52 on the preceding page. The latter only has some effect if line breaks are allowed, i.e., when the `breaklines` key is used. Otherwise, all you see are overfull box warnings. With `gobble` you can remove a certain number of characters (hopefully only spaces) from the left of each line to be displayed. Normally, indentations of surrounding environments like `itemize` are honored. This feature can be turned off using the Boolean key `resetmargin`. Of course, all such keys can be used together.

By default vertical spaces are added before and after the environment. They can be controlled through the keys `aboveskip` and `belowskip` (the default value is `\medskipamount` in both cases).   *Vertical spacing*

To format only a subrange of the code lines you can specify the first and/or last line via `firstline` and `lastline`; for example, `lastline=10` would typeset a maximum of 10 code lines. A generalization of this concept is provided with the `linerange` key, which expects a sorted list of line number ranges, e.g., `{1-2,10-100}` to display the first two lines and then everything from line ten onwards (assuming the display is less than a hundred lines). Note that you need to brace the values when it contains commas.

If a listing contains very long lines, they may not fit into the available measure. In that case listings produces overfull lines sticking out to the right, just like a `verbatim` environment would do. However, you can direct it to break long lines at spaces or punctuation characters by specifying the key `breaklines`. Wrapped lines are indented by 20pt, a value that can be adjusted through the key `breakindent`.   *Line breaking and continuation symbols*

If desired, you can add something before (key `prebreak`) and after the break (key `postbreak`) to indicate that the line was artificially broken in the listing. We use this ability below to experiment with small arrows and later with the string "(cont.)" in tiny letters. Both keys are internally implemented as a TeX `\discretionary`, which means that they accept only certain input (characters, boxes, and kerns). For more complicated material it would be best to wrap everything in an `\mbox`, as we did in the example. In the case of color changes, even that is not enough: you need an extra level of braces to prevent the color `\special` from escaping from the box (see the discussion in Appendix A.3.5); otherwise, you get a low-level error.

The example exhibits another feature of the breaking mechanism — namely, if spaces or tabs appear in front of the material being broken, then these spaces are by default repeated on continuation lines. If this behavior is not desired, set the key `breakautoindent` to `false` as we did in the second part of the example.

```
\usepackage{color,listings}
\lstset{breaklines=true,breakindent=0pt,
     prebreak=\mbox{{\color{blue}\tiny$\searrow$}},
     postbreak=\mbox{{\color{blue}\tiny$\rightarrow$}}}
\begin{lstlisting}
Text at left margin
     /*A long string is broken across the line!*/
\end{lstlisting}
\begin{lstlisting}[breakautoindent=false,
               postbreak=\tiny (cont.)\,]
Text at left margin
     /*A long string is broken across the line!*/
\end{lstlisting}
```

```
Text at left margin
     /*A long string
     is broken
     across the
     line!*/

Text at left margin
     /*A long string
(cont.) is broken across
(cont.) the line!*/
```

4-2-55

You can put frames or rules around listings using the frame key, which takes the same values as it does in fancyvrb (e.g., single, lines). In addition, it accepts the value shadowbox and a subset of the string "trblTRBL" as its value. The uppercase letters stand for double rules, and the lowercase ones for single rules. There are half a dozen more keys: to influence rule widths, create separation from the text, make round corners, and so on — all of them are compatible with fancyvrb if the same functionality is provided.

```
for␣i:=1␣to␣maxint␣do
begin
␣␣WrItE('This␣is␣stupid');
end.
```

```
\usepackage{listings}
% pascal.src as defined before
\lstset{frame=trBL,framerule=2pt,framesep=4pt,
        rulesep=1pt,showspaces=true}
\lstinputlisting[language=Pascal]{pascal.src}
```

4-2-56

You can specify a caption for individual listings using the key caption. The captions are, by default, numbered and prefixed with the string Listing stored in \lstlistingname. If you want a caption but without a number or any other additional text, use the title key instead of caption. The spacing around the caption is controlled through abovecaptionskip and belowcaptionskip.

The counter used is lstlisting; thus, to change its appearance you could modify \thelstlisting. The caption is positioned either above (default) or below the listing, and this choice can be adjusted using the captionpos key. If the document class used provides chapters, then the listings are numbered by chapter by default. If this is not desired, set numberbychapter to false.

To get a list of all captions, put the command \lstlistoflistings at an appropriate place in your document. It produces a heading containing the words stored in \lstlistlistingname (default is Listings). If you want the caption text in the document to differ from the caption text in the list of listings, use an optional argument as shown in the following example. Note that in this case you need braces around the value to hide the right bracket. To prevent the caption from appearing in the list of listings, use the key nolol with a value of true. By using the label key you can specify a label for referencing the listing number via \ref, provided that you have not suppressed the number.

Listings

The Pascal code in listing 1 shows...

```
for  i:=1  to  maxint  do
begin
   WrItE('This␣is␣stupid');
end.
```

Listing 1: Pascal

```
\usepackage{listings} % pascal.src as before
\lstset{frame=single,frameround=tftt,
        language=Pascal,captionpos=b}
\lstlistoflistings
        % Normally the above is in the
\bigskip % front matter section, but here ...
\noindent % ... so we need to help a bit.
The Pascal code in listing~\ref{foo} shows\ldots
\lstinputlisting
    [caption={[Pascal listing]Pascal},label=foo]
    {pascal.src}
```

4-2-57

The key `frameround` used in the previous example allows you to specify round corners by giving t for true and f for false, starting with the upper-right corner and moving clockwise. This feature is not available with fancyvrb frames.

Instead of formatting your listings within the text, you can turn them into floats by using the key `float`, typically together with the `caption` key. Its value is a subset of htbp specifying where the float is allowed to go (using it without a value is equivalent to the value of `floatplacement`, which defaults to tbp). If your document is in two-column mode, you can alternatively use the key `float*`, which makes your listing span both columns. You should, however, avoid mixing floating and nonfloating listings because this could sometimes result in captions being numbered out of order, as in Example 7-3-5 on page 533.

Due to its implementation model, listings expects the characters it receives as input to be represented as single tokens. In pdfTeX this is the case for characters in the ASCII range, but not for others if the input file is encoded in UTF-8 (which is the default now)[1]. Characters such as "ü" or "ß" are then internally represented by several bytes, each of which is seen by pdfTeX as an individual token, and listings consequently attempts to handle them separately with disastrous consequences.

pdfTeX restrictions with UTF-8 characters

Unicode engines

In Unicode engines this is less of a problem[2] because all UTF-8 characters are seen as single tokens. Thus, the next example would fail with pdfTeX showing several "Invalid UTF-8 byte sequence" errors while it compiles successfully with XeTeX or LuaTeX.

```
\usepackage{listings}
\lstset{language=C,commentstyle=\scriptsize}
\begin{lstlisting}
int i; /*für die äußere Schleife*/
\end{lstlisting}
```

| 4-2-58 |

```
int i; /* für  die  äußere  Schleife */
```

Example 4-2-61 on page 333 shows a method to process arbitrary UTF-8 characters inside `lstlisting`, even when using pdfTeX. However, it requires some special setup and so it is usually best to stick to ASCII characters or use one of the Unicode engines if such characters are needed often in your listings.

The `\lstset` declaration works great if you need a single set of default values throughout your document. However, if you use a number of different settings repeatedly, then it would be nice to be able to recall those easily, and for this the package offers the `\lstdefinestyle` declaration. It takes two arguments: the *name* for your style and a *key/value list*. Once declared, you can then use this *name* as the value to the `style` key to activate its *key/value list*. You can still add further keys at the environment level or overwrite some. It is even possible to do recursive definitions though they are probably seldom needed.

Predeclaring listings styles

---

[1] If pdfTeX is used with inputenc and an 8-bit encoding instead of UTF-8, then some level of support for 8-bit characters is available, as discussed in the package documentation.

[2] There are still issues with multibyte characters above code point U+00FF, i.e., not all is well.

The example also shows a few other keys that we have not yet discussed: with `backgroundcolor` you can provide some background coloring, the color of the shadow is defined with `rulesepcolor`, and `framexleftmargin` adds space within the frame to make room for the line number.

```
\usepackage{color,listings}
\lstdefinestyle{tlc}{rulesepcolor=\color{blue},
    keywordstyle=\underbar,framexleftmargin=20pt,
    frame=shadowbox,backgroundcolor=\color{yellow}}
\lstset{language=[LaTeX]TeX,numbers=left}
\begin{lstlisting}
\textbf{Note:} \textit{#1}
\end{lstlisting}
\begin{lstlisting}[style=tlc,firstnumber=last]
\textbf{Note:} \textit{#1}
\end{lstlisting}
```

1 \textbf{Note:} \textit{#1}

2 \textbf{Note:} \textit{#1}

4-2-59

Setting the default language dialect

In the previous example we displayed LaTeX code, and the `language` to use for this is TeX. For historical reasons it is not the default dialect (which is `plain`). Thus, to get the language keywords correctly recognized, we explicitly selected the desired dialect by writing `[LaTeX]TeX`. This is okay in an one-off situation but a nuisance when you have to do this often. An alternative is to change the default dialect for your favorite languages using the `defaultdialect` key as follows:

```
\lstset{defaultdialect=[LaTeX]TeX, defaultdialect=[5.2]Lua}
```

This key can be used several times to set dialect defaults for multiple languages.

The package offers many more keys to influence the presentation. For instance, you can escape to LaTeX for special formatting tricks, display tab or formfeed characters, index certain identifiers, or interface to hyperref so that clicking on some identifier jumps to the previous occurrence. Some of the features are still considered experimental, and you have to request them using an optional argument during package loading. These are all documented in great detail in the manual (roughly 60 pages) accompanying the package [38].

As a final example of the kind of treasures you can find in that manual, look at the following example. It shows code typesetting as known from Donald Knuth's literate programming conventions.

```
\usepackage{xcolor,listings}
\lstset{literate={:=}{{$\gets$}}{2} {<=}{{$\leq$}}{1}
                 {>=}{{$\geq$}}{1}  {<>}{{$\neq$}}{1}}
\begin{lstlisting}[backgroundcolor=\color{yellow}]
  var i:integer;
  if (i<>0) i := i/2;
  if (i<=0) i := i+1;
  if (i>=0) i := i-1;
\end{lstlisting}
```

```
var  i : integer ;
if  ( i≠0 )  i  ←  i /2;
if  ( i≤0 )  i  ←  i +1;
if  ( i≥0 )  i  ←  i −1;
```

4-2-60

The `literate` key expects a list of triplets (separated by space). The first value (in braces if more than one character) tells listings what to scan for, e.g., the sequence "`:=`"; the second tells it what to replace those characters with, i.e., `{$\gets$}`[1]; and the third tells it how wide it should think the result is when it comes to alignment, i.e., two characters for the arrow but only one for the other substitutions in the above example.

This mechanism can also be used to make pdfTEX aware of problematical UTF-8 characters because to pdfTEX something like "ä" looks like a sequence of several 8-bit characters for which it therefore could scan. Thus, using a triplet such as `{ä}{{\"a}}{1}` would tell listings to replace the sequence representing "ä" with its ASCII representation, and doing this for all problematical UTF-8 characters would then solve the issue. Here is a repeat of Example 4-2-58 that works with pdfTEX:

```
\usepackage{listings}
% Setting up UTF8 characters ...
\lstset{literate={ä}{{\"a}}{1}
                 {ü}{{\"u}}{1}
                 {ß}{{\ss}}{1}}
% Setting up other key defaults ...
\lstset{language=C,commentstyle=\scriptsize}
\begin{lstlisting}
int i; /*für die äußere Schleife*/
\end{lstlisting}
```

4-2-61

```
int i; /* für die äußere Schleife */
```

While setting this up is a one-time effort that can be reused, it is nevertheless a somewhat cumbersome exercise and not exactly trivial.

4.3 Lines and columns

We now present a few packages that help in manipulating the text stream in its entirety. The first package (lineno) deals with attaching line numbers to paragraphs, supporting automatic references to them. This can be useful in critical editions and other scholarly works.

The second package (paracol) deals with the problem of presenting two text streams side by side — for example, some original and its translation. We show how both packages can be combined in standard cases.

The third package (multicol) deals with layouts having multiple columns. It allows switching between different numbers of columns on the same page and supports balancing textual data. Standard LATEX already offers the possibility of typesetting text in one- or two-column mode, but one- and two-column output cannot be mixed on the same page.

We finish the section with a short example of the multicolrule package that allows you to define customized "rules" to appear between columns on the page.

[1]The extra set of braces in the replacement text is needed; details are given in the manual.

4.3.1 lineno — **Numbering lines of text**

In certain applications it is useful or even necessary to number the lines of paragraphs to be able to refer to them. As TEX optimizes the line breaking over the whole paragraph, it is ill equipped to provide such a facility, because technically line breaking happens at a very late stage during the processing, just before the final pages are constructed. At that point macro processing, which could add the right line number or handle automatic references, has already taken place. Hence, the only ways to achieve line numbering is either by not doing line breaking (as in the case of fancyvrb and similar packages) or by deconstructing the completed page line by line in the "output routine" (i.e., the part of LATEX that normally breaks the paragraph galley into pages and adds running headers and footers) and attaching the appropriate line numbers at that stage.

The latter approach was taken by Stephan Böttcher in his lineno package (for a number of years maintained by Uwe Lück (1962–2020) and since 2022 maintained by Karl Wette). Although one would expect such an undertaking to work only in a restricted environment, his package is surprisingly robust and works seamlessly with many other packages — even those that modify the LATEX output routine, such as ftnright, multicol, and wrapfig. It also supports layouts produced with the `twocolumn` option of the standard LATEX classes.

`\linenumbers[`*start-number*`]`   `\linenumbers*`   `\nolinenumbers`

Loading the lineno package has no direct effect: to activate line numbering, a `\linenumbers` command must be specified in the preamble or at some point in the document. The command `\nolinenumbers` deactivates line numbering again. Line numbering works on a per-paragraph basis. Thus, when LATEX sees the end of a paragraph, it checks whether line numbering is currently requested and, if so, attaches numbers to *all* lines of that paragraph. It is therefore best to put these commands between paragraphs rather than within them.

The `\linenumbers` command can take an optional argument that denotes the number to use for the first line. If used without such an argument, it continues from where it stopped numbering previously. You can also use a star form, which is a shorthand for `\linenumbers[1]`.

No line numbers here. Some text to experiment with line numbering.

1   Here we get line numbers. Some text to
2 experiment with line numbering.
3   And here too. Some text to experiment
4 with line numbering.
-10   Restart with a negative number and con-
-9 tinue for a few lines. Some text to experiment
-8 with line numbering.
    And once more no numbers. Some text to experiment with line numbering.

```
\usepackage{lineno}
\newcommand\sample{ Some text to
      experiment with line numbering.\par}
No line numbers here.\sample
\linenumbers
Here we get line numbers.\sample
And here too.\sample
\linenumbers[-10]
Restart with a negative number and
continue for a few lines.\sample
\nolinenumbers
And once more no numbers.\sample
```

4-3-1

Rather than starting or stopping line numbering with the above commands, you can use the environment `linenumbers` to define the region that should get line numbers. This environment automatically issues a `\par` command at the end to terminate the current paragraph. If line numbers are needed only for short passages, the environment form (or one of the special environments `numquote` and `numquotation` described later) is preferable.

Because the production of line numbers involves the output routine, numbering takes place only for paragraphs being built and put on the "main vertical list" but not for those built inside boxes (e.g., not inside a `\marginpar` or within the body of a float). However, the package offers some limited support for numbering lines in such places via the `\internallinenumbers` command. Restrictions are that the baselines within such paragraphs need to be a fixed distance apart (otherwise, the numbers are not positioned correctly), and in LaTeX releases prior to 2021 you may have to end such paragraphs with an explicit `\par` command. The `\internallinenumbers` command accepts a star and an optional argument just as `\linenumbers` does. However, the starred form not only ensures that line numbering is (re)started with 1, but also that the line numbers do not affect line numbering in the main vertical list; compare the results in the two `\marginpars` below.

Numbering boxed paragraphs

```
\usepackage{lineno}
% \sample defined as before

\linenumbers
Some text on the main vertical list!
\marginpar{\footnotesize
          \internallinenumbers* \sample}
\sample\sample
In this paragraph we use a second
\marginpar{\footnotesize
          \internallinenumbers  This note
          continues the numbering in
          the main galley.}
marginal note; this time affecting
the line numbers as shown.
```

1 Some text to experi-
2 ment with line num-
3 bering.

4-3-2
6 This note continues
7 the numbering in the
8 main galley.

1 Some text on the main verti-
2 cal list! Some text to experiment
3 with line numbering.
4 Some text to experiment with
5 line numbering.
9 In this paragraph we use a
10 second marginal note; this time
11 affecting the line numbers as
12 shown.

The line numbers in the second `\marginpar` continue the numbering on the main vertical list (the last line of the preceding paragraph was 5), and the third paragraph then continues with line number 9. Such `\marginpar` commands are processed before the paragraph containing them is broken into lines, which explains the ordering of the numbers.

Because lineno needs `\par` to attach line numbers when the output routine is invoked, a TeXnical problem arises when certain display math constructs are used: the partial paragraph above such a display is broken into lines by TeX without issuing a `\par` command. As a consequence, without further help such a partial paragraph do not get any line numbers attached. The package's solution, as illustrated in the next example, is to offer the environment `linenomath`, which, if it surrounds such a display, takes care of the line numbering problem.

Handling display math

Around the basic math environments of LaTeX, e.g., equation or displaymath, the package automatically wraps a linenomath environment, and as of December 2022 it also does so for the environments provided by amsmath.

1   All is fine before a standard LaTeX display:

$$x \neq y$$

2   and as of 2022 also before amsmath displays:

$$x \neq y \qquad (1)$$

However, we do not get line numbers in front of displays from other packages, for example, those from the breqn package:

$$\begin{aligned} 0 < x \\ = x_0 + x_1 + x_2 + \dots + x_{n-1} + x_n \end{aligned} \qquad (2)$$

3   They only show up again after the display.

```
\usepackage{amsmath,breqn,lineno}
\linenumbers

All is fine before a standard \LaTeX\
display:
\[    x \neq y    \]
and as of 2022 also before \texttt{amsmath}
displays:
\begin{align}    x \neq y    \end{align}
However, we do not get line numbers in front
of displays from other packages, for example,
those from the \texttt{breqn} package:
\begin{dmath}   0 < x =    x_0 + x_1 +
   x_2 + \dots + x_{n-1} + x_n   \end{dmath}
They only show up again after the display.
```

4-3-3

Working with other math displays   If you use math display environments from packages other than amsmath, you can try wrapping them automatically into a linenomath environment. In the case of the dmath environment, you need an extra \par at the beginning or else the last line in front of the display will not get a line number; i.e.,

```
\AddToHook{env/dmath/before}{\par\begin{linenomath}}
\AddToHook{env/dmath/after}{\end{linenomath}}
```

However, this might be fixed in future releases of the package.

The lineno package offers the option mathlines, which results in numbering math displays that have been explicitly or implicitly surrounded by linenomath, as we show in the following example:

1   All math displays now show line numbers

2    $$x \neq y$$

3   and the paragraph texts like this one

4    $$x \neq y \qquad (1)$$

5   correctly show line numbers as well.

```
\usepackage{amsmath}
\usepackage[mathlines]{lineno}
\linenumbers

All math displays now show line numbers
   \[ x \neq y \]
and the paragraph texts like this one
   \begin{align} x \neq y \end{align}
correctly show line numbers as well.
```

4-3-4

Cross-references to line numbers   To reference line numbers put a \linelabel into the line and then refer to it via \ref or \pageref, just as with other references defined using \label. The exception is that \linelabel can be used only on the main vertical list and should be used only within paragraphs that actually carry numbers. If it is used elsewhere, you get either a bogus reference (if the current line does not have a line number) or an error message (in places where \linelabel is not allowed).

```
  1      Lorem ipsum dolor sit amet, consectetuer adi-
  2   piscing elit.  Ut purus elit, vestibulum ut, place-
  3   rat ac, adipiscing vitae, felis.  (A) Curabitur dic-
  4   tum gravida mauris.  Nam arcu libero, nonummy
  5   eget, consectetuer id, vulputate a, magna. (B) Do-
  6   nec vehicula augue eu neque.  Pellentesque habi-
  7   tant morbi tristique senectus et netus et malesuada
  8   fames ac turpis egestas.
         In the text we have labels on lines 3 and 5, but
      not on line 8.
```

```
\usepackage{lipsum,lineno}
\linenumbers

\lipsum[1][1-2] (A)\linelabel{first}
\lipsum[1][3-4] (B)\linelabel{second}
\lipsum[1][5-6] \par
\nolinenumbers
In the text we have labels on
lines~\ref{first} and~\ref{second},
but not on line~\lineref[+3]{second}.
```

It is also possible to refer to a line that carries no \linelabel, by using the \lineref command with an optional argument specifying the offset. This ability can be useful if you need to refer to a line that cannot be easily labeled, such as a math display, or if you wish to refer to a sequence of lines, as in the previous example.

There are several ways to customize the visual appearance of line numbers. Specifying the option modulo means that line numbers appear on only some lines (default is every fifth). This effect can also be achieved by using the command \modulolinenumbers. Calling this command with an optional argument attaches numbers to lines that are multiples of the specified number (in particular, a value of 1 corresponds to normal numbering). Neither command nor option initiates line numbering mode: for that a \linenumbers command is still necessary. *Labeling only some lines*

```
  1      Nam dui ligula, fringilla a, euismod so-
  2   dales, sollicitudin vel, wisi. Morbi auctor lo-
  3   rem non justo.
  4      And now a paragraph with numbers
      on every second line. Nam lacus libero, pre-
  6   tium at, lobortis vitae, ultricies et, tellus. Do-
      nec aliquet, tortor sed accumsan bibendum,
  8   erat ligula aliquet magna, vitae ornare odio
      metus a mi. Morbi ac orci et nisl hendrerit
 10   mollis.
```

```
\usepackage{lipsum,lineno}
\linenumbers

\lipsum[2][1-2]

\modulolinenumbers[2]
\textbf{And now a paragraph with
  numbers on every second line.}
\lipsum[2][3-5]
```

The font for line numbers is controlled by the hook \linenumberfont. Its default definition is to use tiny sans serif digits. The numbers are put flush right in a box of width \linenumberwidth. This box is separated from the line by the value stored in \linenumbersep. To set the number flush left you have to dig deeper, but even for this case you find hooks like \makeLineNumberRight in the package. Although changing the settings in the middle of a document is usually not a good idea, it was done in the next example for demonstration purposes.

The option "right" changes the line number position. Lorem ipsum dolor sit amet, consectetuer adipiscing elit.

    Now we use a different font and a bigger separation. Suspendisse vel felis. Ut lorem lorem, interdum eu, tincidunt sit amet, laoreet vitae, arcu.

```
\usepackage{lipsum}
\usepackage[right]{lineno} \linenumbers
\textbf{The option ''right'' changes the
  line number position.} \lipsum[1][1] \par
\renewcommand\linenumberfont
  {\normalfont\footnotesize\ttfamily}
\setlength\linenumbersep{20pt}
\textbf{Now we use a different font and a
  bigger separation.} \lipsum[6][1-2]  \par
```

4-3-7

For special applications the package offers two environments that provide line numbers automatically: numquote and numquotation. They are like their LaTeX cousins `quote` and `quotation`, except that their lines are numbered. They accept an optional argument denoting the line number with which to start (if the argument is omitted, they restart with 1), and they have starred forms, that suppress resetting the line numbers.

The main differences from their LaTeX counterparts (when used together with the `\linenumbers` command) are the positioning of the numbers, which are indented inwards, and the fact that they restart the numbering unless the star form is used. Thus, their intended use is for cases when only the quoted text should receive line numbers that can be referenced separately.

Lorem ipsum dolor sit amet, consectetuer adipiscing elit.

Next quote has indented numbers and the numbering is restarted.

    Donec vehicula augue eu neque.

Nam dui ligula, fringilla a, euismod sodales, sollicitudin vel, wisi.

```
\usepackage{lipsum,lineno}
\linenumbers

\begin{quote} \lipsum[1][1] \end{quote}
\textbf{Next quote has indented numbers
  and the numbering is restarted.}
\begin{numquote}
    \lipsum[1][5]
\end{numquote}
\lipsum[2][1]
```

4-3-8

Providing your own extensions
    Using the machinery provided by the package, it is fairly easy to develop your own environments that attach special items to each line. The main macro to customize is `\makeLineNumber`, which gets executed inside a box of zero width at the left edge of each line (when line numbering mode is turned on). The net effect of your code should take up no space, so it is best to operate with `\llap` or `\rlap`. Apart from that you can use basically anything. You should only remember that the material is processed and attached after the paragraph has been broken into lines and normal macro-processing has finished, so you should not expect it to interact with data in mid-paragraph. You can produce the current line number with the `\LineNumber` command, which supplies the number or nothing, depending on whether line numbering mode is on.

The following example shows the definition and use of two new environments that (albeit somewhat crudely, because they do not care about setting fonts and the like) demonstrate some of the possibilities. Note that even though the second environment does not print any line numbers, the lines are internally counted so that line numbering resumes afterwards with the correct value.

```
\usepackage{lipsum,lineno} \linenumbers
\newenvironment{numarrows}
  {\par\renewcommand\makeLineNumber
          {\llap{\LineNumber$\to$ }}}{\par}
\newenvironment{arrows}
  {\par\renewcommand\makeLineNumber
          {\rlap{\hspace{\textwidth} $\gets$}}}{\par}
```

1→ Lorem ipsum dolor sit
2→ amet, consectetuer adipiscing
3→ elit.

  Nam dui ligula, fringilla ←
a, euismod sodales, sollicitu- ←
din vel, wisi. ←

7 **This paragraph has nor-**
8 **mal numbering.**

9→ Nulla malesuada portti-
10→ tor diam.

```
\begin{numarrows} \lipsum[1][1]  \end{numarrows}
\begin{arrows}    \lipsum[2][1]  \end{arrows}
\textbf{This paragraph has normal numbering.}
\begin{numarrows} \lipsum[3][1]  \end{numarrows}
```

The appearance and behavior of the line numbers can be further controlled by a set of options or, alternatively, by a set of commands equivalent to the options (see the package documentation for details on the command forms). With the options `left` (default) and `right`, you specify in which margin the line numbers should appear. Using the option `switch` or `switch*`, you get them in the outer and inner margins, respectively. You can also request that numbers restart on each page by specifying the option `pagewise`. This option needs to come last.

At least two LaTeX runs of the document are required before the line numbers appear in the appropriate place. Unfortunately, there is no warning about the need to rerun the document, so you have to watch out for this issue yourself.

4.3.2 paracol — Several text streams aligned

Sometimes it is necessary to typeset something in parallel columns, for example, when presenting some text and its translation. Parallel in this context means that at certain synchronization points the two text streams are vertically (re)aligned. This type of layout is normally not supported by LaTeX (which by default works with only a single text stream), but it can be achieved by using NAKASHIMA Hiroshi's paracol package.[1]

| \begin{paracol}{*columns*} [*before-material*] *parallel data* \end{paracol} |

This package provides the paracol environment, which surrounds the material to be typeset in parallel streams. In its standard form it supports several parallel columns; their number is specified in the mandatory *columns* argument. An optional argument allows you to place *before-material* spanning all columns (which may include vertical material) prior to the multicolumned *parallel data*.

The environment can be started anywhere on the page, and if the *parallel data* cannot fit onto the current page, then the columns continue on the following pages.

---

[1] Some other packages for this kind of task are Matthias Eckermann's parallel package and Jonathan Sauer's parcolumns package.

```
\switchcolumn[col]      \switchcolumn[col]*[text]
```

To switch from one column to the next you issue a \switchcolumn command, and once you reach the rightmost column, this switches back to the first one. Alternatively, you can specify an explicit column *col* to jump to. Please note that columns are internally numbered starting from 0; e.g., it needs \switchcolumn[0] to get back to the leftmost column.

By default, column data are not automatically aligned, but simply appended to the already existing material for that column. If you want alignment, use the star form of \switchcolumn — note that the * follows the optional *col* argument if present! In the next example we show what happens if we do not use the star form when needed:

Number	English		German
100	One hun-		Einhun-
42	dred		dert
1	Forty two		Zweiund-
	One		vierzig
			Eins

```
\usepackage{paracol}

\begin{paracol}{3} \bfseries
    Number \switchcolumn English \switchcolumn
        German \normalfont \switchcolumn
    100 \switchcolumn One hundred   \switchcolumn
        Ein\-hun\-dert            \switchcolumn
    42 \switchcolumn Forty two      \switchcolumn
        Zwei\-und\-vier\-zig \switchcolumn
    1 \switchcolumn One \switchcolumn Eins
\end{paracol}
```

4-3-10

Besides the misalignment, the above example looks probably odd to you for other reasons. Obviously the environment is not meant to be used for individual words, but rather for longer text passages to be typeset in parallel. For this reason each chunk of column data generates its own paragraph including a paragraph indentation, which accounts for the strange-looking line breaks in the second and third columns.

The next example corrects these defects by locally canceling the \parindent and by synchronizing each horizontal block. While only the third \switchcolumn* would be strictly necessary due to the change of \parindent, it is good practice to use it in all places where you do want to ensure that alignment is done. This is why we used it whenever we switched back to the leftmost column. The other adjustment we made was to use the optional *text* argument of \switchcolumn* to add 5pt of extra vertical space after the heading block and later use some extra material to prove that this argument can span all columns, if necessary.

Number	English	German
100	One hundred	Einhundert
42	Forty two	Zweiund-
		vierzig
1	One	Eins

sync

```
\usepackage{paracol}

\begin{paracol}{3} \setlength\parindent{0pt}
    \bfseries Number \switchcolumn English \switchcolumn
        German \normalfont \switchcolumn*[\vspace{5pt}]
    100 \switchcolumn One hundred   \switchcolumn
        Ein\-hun\-dert \switchcolumn*[\dotfill\tiny sync]
    42 \switchcolumn Forty two      \switchcolumn
        Zwei\-und\-vier\-zig \switchcolumn*
    1 \switchcolumn One \switchcolumn Eins
\end{paracol}
```

4-3-11

In the above examples `\switchcolumn*` is always used at the point where we jump back to the leftmost column, which is certainly the usual case. However, that does not need to be the case; it can be used between any column. You basically have to think of its action as filling all columns (except the tallest one) with vertical space such that all columns become equally high. It then typesets the optional *text* argument (if present) across all columns and finally arranges that upcoming material is placed into whatever column we jumped to.

This can have surprising results if you forget the * in a place where you actually wanted synchronization, as the next example nicely demonstrates. Can you explain the resulting behavior?

```
\usepackage{paracol}
```

Same	line	here
But		
sync after first column		
	no	longer
	back?	Why
	Explain!	

```
\begin{paracol}{4}   \setlength\parindent{0pt}
Same \switchcolumn line \switchcolumn here \switchcolumn[0]
But \switchcolumn*[\tiny sync after first column]
            no \switchcolumn longer \switchcolumn*
Why \switchcolumn[1] back? \switchcolumn* Explain!
\end{paracol}
```

4-3-12

An important aspect of column switching with `\switchcolumn` is that the switch does not end the scope of declarations, which is why in the examples 4-3-10 and 4-3-11 the `\bfseries` applies to several columns and needs explicit canceling. The same would be true for color settings, etc.

As an alternative that automatically restricts scope, you can use the `column` environment or one of its variants.

```
\begin{column}       column data \end{column}
\begin{column*}[text] column data \end{column*}
```

A `column` environment holds the material for one column. The star form does the same but first synchronizes all previously typeset column material. Its optional *text* argument can contain material that spans all columns (regardless of which column we continue typesetting in). This is shown in the next example, displaying a few "direct" translations of computer jargon into German (taken from [27] with kind permission by Eichborn Verlag).

```
\usepackage{color,paracol}
```

I just go online and download an update.	*Ich geh mal eben auf den Strich und lade mir ein Auffrisch herunter.*
. . . .	
This laptop is missing several interfaces.	Dieser Schoßspitze fehlt so manches Zwischengesicht.

```
\begin{paracol}{2} \raggedright
   \setlength\leftskip{10pt}
   \setlength\parindent{-\leftskip}
\begin{column} \color{blue} I just go online and
   download an update.                \end{column}
\begin{column} \em Ich geh mal eben auf den Strich
   und lade mir ein Auffrisch herunter. \end{column}
\begin{column*}[\dotfill]  \color{blue} This laptop
   is missing several interfaces.    \end{column*}
\begin{column} Dieser Schoßspitze
   fehlt so manches Zwischengesicht.  \end{column}
\end{paracol}
```

4-3-13

As you can see, it is possible to adjust paragraph parameters within the overall scope of the `paracol` environment. The negative `\parindent` cancels the positive `\leftskip` so that each paragraph starts flush left but following lines are indented by `\leftskip` (and both must be changed *after* calling `\raggedright`, because the latter also sets these registers).

```
\begin{nthcolumn}{col}        column data \end{nthcolumn}
\begin{nthcolumn*}{col}[text] column data \end{nthcolumn*}
\begin{leftcolumn} ...   \begin{leftcolumn*}[text] ...
\begin{rightcolumn} ...  \begin{rightcolumn*}[text] ...
```

The `nthcolumn` and `nthcolumn*` environments work like `column` and `column*` except that they switch to the specified column *col*. Remember that columns are internally counted from zero. For the common case of typesetting two texts in parallel, there also exist `leftcolumn` and `rightcolumn` and corresponding star forms, which are aliases for `nthcolumn` with the *col* argument 0 or 1, respectively.

Coloring whole columns

In the previous example we repeated the coloring command several times to get the left column colored. Because we used `column` environments, the scope was confined to that particular chunk of the column, so there was no need to reset it; i.e., the color did not "leak out" into neighboring columns, which it would if we had used `\switchcolumn` commands instead. But even so, it is not a very convenient method if there are many column changes. A much nicer approach is offered by the `\columncolor` command of paracol.

```
\columncolor[model]{color-spec}[col]   \normalcolumncolor[col]
```

If `\columncolor` is used without the optional *col* argument anywhere within a `paracol` environment, then it arranges for the current column to be colored from that point onwards. This is similar to issuing `\color[model]{color-spec}` in all chunks of the current column and resetting the color in all other columns as needed. With the *col* argument, that particular column is colored.

It is also possible to use the declaration outside of a `paracol` environment, in which case it sets the default for all future environments.

With `\normalcolumncolor` you return a specific column back to "normal", which usually means black unless the document default has been changed.

Specifying and coloring rules between columns

Besides coloring text, you can also color the rules between columns — that is, you can after you have made them visible. As many other packages, paracol adds rules between columns with a width of `\columnseprule`, which by default is zero.

```
\colseprulecolor[model]{color-spec}[col] \normalcolseprulecolor[col]
```

The arguments to specify the color and the target column are the same as with `\columncolor`. If the optional *col* argument is given, it means that we refer to the rule following that column.

Below is an example in which we color the rules, one column throughout and one column starting in the middle of the parallel text. To prove that the text color is properly confined to the column data we also add `\itshape` to make the second half of the text fully italic.

```
\usepackage{xcolor,paracol}    \columncolor{blue}[1]
\setlength\columnseprule{2pt}  \colseprulecolor{red}
\begin{paracol}{3}
    baseline    \switchcolumn Grundlinie \switchcolumn
                             basislijn   \switchcolumn*
    frontispiece \switchcolumn Frontispiz \switchcolumn
                             Frontispice \switchcolumn*
    orphan \switchcolumn Schuster\-junge \switchcolumn
                             weeskind    \switchcolumn*
\columncolor[gray]{.7} \itshape
    punch       \switchcolumn Stempel    \switchcolumn
                             patrijs     \switchcolumn*
    spacing     \switchcolumn Zurichtung \switchcolumn
                             spatiëring  \switchcolumn*
    widow \switchcolumn Hurenkind \switchcolumn hoerenjong
\end{paracol}
```

baseline	Grundlinie	basislijn
frontispiece	Frontispiz	Frontispice
orphan	Schuster-junge	weeskind
punch	*Stempel*	*patrijs*
spacing	*Zurichtung*	*spatiëring*
widow	*Hurenkind*	*hoerenjong*

4-3-14

`\definecolumnpreamble{`*col*`}{`*declarations*`}`

A general set of *declarations* for each column can be defined using the command `\definecolumnpreamble`. These are then executed each time the corresponding *col* is (re)started. The special value −1 for *col* denotes spanning text, enabling you to provide preambles for all parts of the `paracol` environment.

Note, however, that the scope for the *declarations* does not end with the end of a column but with the end of the whole environment. For example, to bolden just text in the first column you have to explicitly undo that in the preamble for the second column as shown in the next example. If this is not done properly, the declarations "leak", exhibited with `\itshape`, which never gets reset and so shows up in the first column from the second row onwards.

```
\usepackage{paracol}
\definecolumnpreamble{0}{\bfseries}    % \upshape missing
\definecolumnpreamble{1}{\mdseries\itshape}
\begin{paracol}{2}
    body text \switchcolumn  Mengentext    \switchcolumn*
    em-dash   \switchcolumn  Geviertstrich
\end{paracol}
```

| **body text** | *Mengentext* |
| ***em-dash*** | *Geviertstrich* |

4-3-15

If LaTeX encounters a `paracol` environment, it ends the current paragraph if it is not already in vertical mode. But in contrast to many other display environments, such as lists, it does not separate the environment from preceding or following text. This is appropriate if it starts, for example, with a heading in its optional *text* argument. However, in case you want some vertical separation, you need to supply it yourself, e.g., through `\vspace` or `\bigskip` or similar. Please note though that the vertical space before the environment has to be placed into the optional argument,

Vertical spacing around paracol

because otherwise it may appear in the wrong place when there are footnotes on the current page. For that reason, surrounding the environment with, say, flushleft may result in incorrect spacing. To standardize that, the next example defines a displayparacol environment. It uses \topsep to mimic what normal display environments do. For details on the use of \DeclareDocumentEnvironment see Section A.1.4 on page →II 632.

```
\usepackage{xcolor,paracol} \columncolor{blue}[0]
\DeclareDocumentEnvironment{displayparacol}{mO{}}
      {\begin{paracol}{#1}[\addvspace{\topsep}#2]}
      {\end{paracol}\addvspace{\topsep}}
```

Some more typesetting terms ...

body text	Mengentext
em-dash	Geviertstrich

... this time only English and German.

```
\noindent Some more typesetting terms \ldots
\begin{displayparacol}{2}
\begin{leftcolumn}  body text      \end{leftcolumn}
\begin{rightcolumn} Mengentext     \end{rightcolumn}
\begin{leftcolumn*} em-dash        \end{leftcolumn*}
\begin{rightcolumn} Geviertstrich \end{rightcolumn}
\end{displayparacol}
\noindent \ldots{} this time only English and German.
```

4-3-16

Footnotes in parallel text   Footnotes in the main text before a paracol environment are not placed at the bottom of the page but rather in the galley prior to starting the parallel text. Footnotes within the parallel text are by default placed at the bottom of the column in which they appear and without any further adjustments are numbered individually within each column. Further footnotes in the main text are then numbered based on the footnote counter value in the leftmost column of the parallel text, which looks odd if the parallel text is very short and there are more footnotes in the other columns. The next example shows this behavior, and further down we discuss several options to resolve the problem.

Text[1] with a footnote.

———————
[1]A main footnote

This is text in the English language[2] explaining the command \foo.

Dies ist Text[2] in deutscher Sprache[3], der das Kommando \foo erläutert.

More text.[3]

Even more text.[4]

———————
[2]We hope!
[3]C

———————
[2]Ein Satz.
[3]Schlechter Stil!
[4]D

Further text[4] with a footnote. More text to fill the page.

———————
[4]Another main footnote

```
\usepackage{paracol}
% displayparacol as defined in previous example

Text\footnote{A main footnote} with a footnote.
\begin{displayparacol}{2}
  This is text in the English
  language\footnote{We hope!} explaining the
  command \verb=\foo=.
  \switchcolumn
  Dies ist Text\footnote{Ein Satz.} in
  deutscher Sprache\footnote{Schlechter Stil!},
  der das Kommando \verb=\foo= erläutert.
  \switchcolumn  More text.\footnote{C}
  \switchcolumn  Even more text.\footnote{D}
\end{displayparacol}
Further text\footnote{Another main footnote}
with a footnote. More text to fill the page.
```

4-3-17

In typical use cases the parallel text is much longer, than in the previous example, and then the defaults are most of the time quite reasonable.

One possible solution to the problem above is to manually enlarge the footnote counter as necessary once the environment has ended by adding the difference; i.e., in the above case `\addtocounter{footnote}{1}` would do the trick.

Alternatively, one can choose different representations of the `footnote` counter for each column using a `\definethecounter` declaration offered by the package. In the next example we use this to display the footnotes in the second column using letters. Of course that works only with relatively few footnotes.

Text[1] with a footnote.

------

[1]A main footnote

This is text in the English language[2] explaining the command \foo.

Dies ist Text[b] in deutscher Sprache[c], der das Kommando \foo erläutert.

More text.[3]

Even more text.[d]

------

[b]Ein Satz.
[c]Schlechter Stil!
[d]D

------

[2]We hope!
[3]C

Further text[4] with a footnote. More text to fill the page.

------

[4]Another main footnote

```
\usepackage{paracol}
\definethecounter{footnote}{1}{\alph{footnote}}
% displayparacol as defined in earlier example

Text\footnote{A main footnote} with a footnote.
\begin{displayparacol}{2}
  This is text in the English
  language\footnote{We hope!} explaining the
  command \verb=\foo=.
\switchcolumn
  Dies ist Text\footnote{Ein Satz.} in
  deutscher Sprache\footnote{Schlechter Stil!},
  der das Kommando \verb=\foo= erläutert.
\switchcolumn  More text.\footnote{C}
\switchcolumn  Even more text.\footnote{D}
\end{displayparacol}
Further text\footnote{Another main footnote}
with a footnote. More text to fill the page.
```

4-3-18

The other possibility is to choose a different footnote layout that better suits your text. The footnote layout for all following `paracol` environments can be explicitly set using the `\footnotelayout` command. The default one that was used in the previous example is called "column-wise", and it is activated by passing c as an argument to `\footnotelayout`. Alternatively, you can pass p for "page-wise" or m for "merged" layouts.

Footnote layouts

In "page-wise" mode the footnotes from all columns are collected and placed jointly at the bottom of the page or at the end of the environment, whichever comes first. Thus, it is similar to the default except that all footnotes in the parallel text are sequentially numbered and the text of the footnotes spans all columns, which makes it a good option if the footnote texts are fairly long.

In "merged" mode all footnotes on the page are merged and appear on the bottom of the page in the order in which they are seen by LaTeX; i.e., column block by column block, and within a column block from the left-most column to the right.[1] If used, our example changes rather drastically, as shown on the next page.

------

[1]Depending on your column block splits, this may be a little bit confusing for the reader.

Text[1] with a footnote.

This is text in the English language[2] explaining the command \foo.

Dies ist Text[3] in deutscher Sprache[4], der das Kommando \foo erläutert.

More text.[5]

Even more text.[6]

Further text[7] with a footnote. More text

---

[1] A main footnote
[2] We hope!
[3] Ein Satz.
[4] Schlechter Stil!
[5] C
[6] D
[7] Another main footnote

```
\usepackage{paracol} \footnotelayout{m}
% displayparacol as defined in earlier example
Text\footnote{A main footnote} with a footnote.
\begin{displayparacol}{2}
  This is text in the English
  language\footnote{We hope!} explaining the
  command \verb=\foo=.
  \switchcolumn
  Dies ist Text\footnote{Ein Satz.} in
  deutscher Sprache\footnote{Schlechter Stil!},
  der das Kommando \verb=\foo= erläutert.
  \switchcolumn  More text.\footnote{C}
  \switchcolumn  Even more text.\footnote{D}
\end{displayparacol}
Further text\footnote{Another main footnote}
with a footnote. More text to fill the page.
```

4-3-19

In many cases the page-wise or merged layout gives reasonable results if you have many or long footnotes. You may still be somewhat dissatisfied by the fact that LaTeX now numbers the footnotes somewhat strangely if you look down a single column. The reason is that now the footnotes get their numbers in the order LaTeX sees your input and there is no reordering happening when a page break occurs because by that time everything is already typeset. There are however ways to manually resolve this, and the package manual [105] devotes several pages to explaining in detail how that can be achieved.

Relation to list items
    If a paracol environment is used within a list environment, such as itemize, it uses the current horizontal list indentation values (e.g., \leftmargin and \rightmargin) within each column. Thus, \item commands in the leftmost column align perfectly with those outside the environment. Depending on the column data, it may pay to alter the ratio between column widths slightly as we did in the following example:

- A few more typesetting terms.

- An ellipsis is a character consisting of usually 3 dots.

- Face: the part of a physical letter that gets printed.

- The hyphen (-) is a punctuation mark.

```
\usepackage{paracol}
\begin{itemize} \item A few more typesetting terms.
\columnratio{0.55}\begin{paracol}{2}
\item An ellipsis is a character consisting of
    usually 3 dots. \switchcolumn
\item Face: the part of a physical letter that
   gets printed.
\end{paracol}
\item The hyphen (-) is a punctuation mark.
\end{itemize}
```

4-3-20

As seen in the previous example, the width of the columns do not need to be uniform but can be adjusted in relation to each other. This is done with a \columnratio declaration, which expects a comma-separated list of ratio values. You can specify up to *columns* – 1 values. If fewer values are given, the remaining columns all have an identical width such that the total width fits \textwidth exactly. Between all columns a space of \columnsep is assumed.

There also exists a \setcolumnwidth declaration for adjusting both the column width and the column separations on an individual level. If you need this level of flexibility, refer to the package documentation for details. Both declarations apply only to the next paracol environment and should therefore be given directly in front (but not inside!) of it.

For starting a new page within the parallel text the package offers \flushpage, which is more or less equivalent to \switchcolumn*[\newpage] but safer because the latter has some issues if the page break is naturally taken just before. An alternative is to use \clearpage or \cleardoublepage, which additionally places all pending floats. The latter also advances to the next odd-numbered page as usual.

Forcing a new page in parallel text

Instead of, or in addition to, adding notes as footnotes, you may want to make the occasional marginal remark. The paracol package fully supports the use of \marginpar and with some restrictions the \marginnote from the marginnote package[1] even if your parallel text consists of more than two columns. By default all notes except for those in the leftmost column appear in the right margin. This can be changed at any point by issuing a \marginparthreshold command. It expects as its argument the column number from which on the marginals should be placed into the right margin. Thus, specifying 0 moves all notes to the right, and setting the default to 2, as done in the next example, makes marginals from the first or second column move to the left, e.g., "M2" from the middle column. Later we change it back to 1 so that "M5" then shows up on the right.

Using marginals in parallel text

If you issue a \reversemarginpar, then all placements are reversed as usual.

```
\usepackage{paracol} \marginparthreshold{2}
\begin{paracol}{3}
  Left\marginpar{L1}              \switchcolumn
  Middle \\ Middle \\
            Middle\marginpar{M2} \switchcolumn
  Right \\ Right\marginpar{R3} \switchcolumn*
\marginparthreshold{1}
  Left again\marginpar{L4}        \switchcolumn
  Middle\marginpar{M5}
\end{paracol}
```

L1	Left	Middle	Right		
		Middle	Right	R3	
M2		Middle			
L4	Left again	Middle			M5

4-3-21

Floats within parallel text are also supported, though there are a number of restrictions that one has to be aware of. Full-wide floats, e.g., produced by table*, etc., can be used anywhere and span all columns. If you use single column floats, then they always appear in the column in which they are encountered, if necessary on a later page. In other words, they do not move from one column to the next, because such columns may be of different width. Furthermore, a float can appear only in a top area if the parallel text has not been synchronized yet. After synchronization it can appear only in the bottom position or in the top position on the next page.

Managing floats in parallel text

[1]This command is emulated, so not all features of it are available within the paracol environment.

The outlined restrictions may make it necessary to manually adjust the float positions within the document sometimes to achieve the desired placements. Of course, as always, such fine-tuning should be left until the document is nearly finished.

Local and global counters within parallel text

Counters in LaTeX such as for headings, footnotes, floats, or equations are normally global; that is, if they are changed, the change is visible in the later part of the document regardless of the current scope. The paracol package handles this differently and by default keeps all counters local within each column. When the environment ends, it uses the values from the leftmost column to continue. This is why the footnotes in Example 4-3-17 start in both columns with 2 and the footnote after the environment is labeled with 4. When a new `paracol` environment is started, the local counters continue at their previous values except for the leftmost column where they continue from whatever their value is in the main text. If we had another environment in Example 4-3-18, then a footnote in the first column would be labeled with "^{5}" and in the second column with "^{e}".

Besides footnotes there are a number of other use cases where this is sensible, e.g., if you want headings with the same numbering in several columns. For other scenarios you might prefer that the counter value propagates from column to column. This is achieved by stating `\globalcounter{`*ctr*`}` in the preamble. You can alternatively make all counters global using `\globalcounter*` and then turn individual ones local through some `\localcounter` declaration. The footnote layouts p and m automatically make the footnote counter global, because the footnotes propagate out in these layouts and with column-based counters you would then get duplicate numbers.

Finally, it is possible to broadcast the current value of a local counter to all other columns using `\synccounter{`*ctr*`}` somewhere within a column or to broadcast all local counters via `\syncallcounters`.

Restricting TOC data

If you use parallel headings (or parallel floats) in different columns, you probably do not want the content information to appear several times with the same number in the table of contents or list of figures, even if the heading or caption text is translated. In that case you can state that only content information from one specific column should be propagated by using a line like

```
\addcontentsonly{toc}{0}
```

in the preamble. This means that the table of contents only receives data from headings in the leftmost column.

Line numbers in parallel text

You can use the lineno package together with paracol which can be useful when talking about a text and its translation. By default lines in all columns are numbered, and lineno's `linenumber` counter is local to each column. Thus, as long as all columns have the same number of lines, this gives you the same numbers in each column.

Because all columns are numbered, you may have to enlarge the value of the `\columnsep` parameter to account for this; below we therefore set it to 35pt.

If, however, you have gaps, you need to adjust the `linenumber` counter to ensure that the line numbers across the columns stay in sync. It is best to add a value to the counter rather than to set it to some explicit number like we did below. You can also see that we used `\synccounter` at the beginning of the environment, and you may wonder why. Without it the second and third columns would have started out with line number one when the leftmost column is already at two. This will also be necessary in later `paracol` environments if the previous one ended with a different number of lines in different columns. To show what happens if you do not, we have omitted it in the second instance.

```
\usepackage{lineno,paracol} \linenumbers
\setlength\columnsep{35pt}
\begin{paracol}{3}[Numbered locally (issue empties)]
\synccounter{linenumber}
    Left \switchcolumn  Middle \\ Middle \switchcolumn
                        Right \\ Right  \switchcolumn*
\addtocounter{linenumber}{1}
    Left again and again \switchcolumn  Middle
\end{paracol}
\begin{paracol}{3}[Numbered locally (no sync!)]
    Left \switchcolumn Middle \switchcolumn  Right
\end{paracol}
```

1	Numbered locally (issue empties)				
2	Left	2	Middle	2	Right
		3	Middle	3	Right
4	Left again	4	Middle		
5	and again				
6	Numbered locally (no sync!)				
7	Left	5	Middle	4	Right

4-3-22

You might think that adding line numbers in all columns is bit too much (though with wider columns they might still be useful). If you prefer fewer numbers, then this can be easily achieved too by numbering only a single column, e.g., the left one. This means that we have to stop numbering with `\nolinenumbers` when we enter the second column and restart it when returning to the first. Syncing the counter value across the columns is now no longer necessary, but, of course, we still have to deal with gaps by adjusting the counter. Alternatively, and this is what we have done in the next example, we can avoid gaps, by placing invisible material into it (we used `\mbox{}` here):

```
\usepackage{lineno,paracol}
\definecolumnpreamble{0}{\linenumbers}
\definecolumnpreamble{1}{\nolinenumbers}
\begin{paracol}{3}
    Left      \\ \mbox{}  \switchcolumn
    Middle and more       \switchcolumn
    Right on two lines    \switchcolumn*
    Left again and again \switchcolumn  Middle
\end{paracol}
```

1	Left	Middle and	Right on
2		more	two lines
3	Left again	Middle	
4	and again		

4-3-23

So far we used examples containing just straight text, and in this case column data naturally align horizontally; thus numbering only a single column or all columns with the same numbers makes sense. However, this may not be the case, and if one or more column contains unusually tall or short entries, that approach may become questionable. In that case, it might be worth considering making the `linenumber` counter global so that all lines in all columns get distinct numbers. Of course, then we get the numbers in the order of appearance in the source, which at least in the following example looks somewhat weird. In more realistic settings that may work without further adjustments.

4-3-24

```
\usepackage{lineno,paracol} \linenumbers
\globalcounter{linenumber}
\begin{paracol}{3}  \raggedright
         Left                       \switchcolumn
         Middle \\ Middle      \switchcolumn
\tiny  Right  \\ Right           \switchcolumn
\Large Left again and again \switchcolumn
    Middle
\end{paracol}
```

¹ Left   ² Middle   ⁴ Right

⁶ Left   ³ Middle   ⁵ Right

⁷ again   ¹⁰ Middle

⁸ and

⁹ again

Using the whole spread for parallel text   The **paracol** package offers a number of further features. You can, for example, do what its author termed *parallel-page* typesetting, that is, splitting the parallel text columns across a double spread instead of a single page. This way you can typeset a book and its translation with the original text always on left pages and the translation on the facing pages. In its simplest form all you have to do is to add a further optional argument (that we so far neglected to mention) to the environment call:

> \begin{paracol} [*left-cols*] {*columns*} [*text*]   *parallel data* \end{paracol}

The *left-cols* argument specifies how many of the total number of *columns* should be typeset on a left page; the others are then typeset properly synchronized on the facing page.

Background coloring   There are also various possibilities to do background coloring of certain parts, e.g., individual columns, gaps, float areas, margins, spanning material, etc. For details of these more specialized applications consult the package manual [105].

When to use and when not to use paracol

The **paracol** environment operates on the main vertical galley material, and it changes the standard output routine to collect further material, attach it to the appropriate column, synchronize the columns, etc. This has a number of consequences one has to be aware of. Most importantly, this approach means that the environment cannot be nested, and it does not work inside boxes and in particular not inside floats. For technical reasons it cannot be used in LaTeX's twocolumn mode either. Thus, if you need parallel text in such cases, you need to resort to one of the other packages, e.g., **parallel** or **parcolumns**. For short material another option is, of course, some sort of tabular or longtable approach.

Below is an example that shows you the syntax flavor used by the **parallel** package. To align certain lines of text you split the two text streams at appropriate points by using pairs of \ParallelLText and \ParallelRText commands and separating each pair with \ParallelPar. If you forget one of the \ParallelPar commands, some of your text gets lost without warning! Moreover, as its name suggests, the \ParallelPar command introduces a paragraph break so that alignment is possible only at paragraph boundaries. Additional paragraph breaks inside the argument of a \Parallel..Text command are also possible, but in that case no alignment is attempted.

```
\usepackage{parallel,lineno}
\linenumbers \modulolinenumbers[2]
\setlength\linenumbersep{1pt}
```

I just go online and download an update. Ich geh mal eben auf den Strich und lade mir ein Auffrisch herunter.

Microsoft Office on floppy disks. Kleinweich Büro auf Schlabber-scheiben.

```
\begin{Parallel}{.45\linewidth}{}
\raggedright  \setlength\leftskip{10pt}
             \setlength\parindent{-\leftskip}
\ParallelLText{I just go online and download an update.}
\ParallelRText{Ich geh mal eben auf den Strich und lade
  mir ein Auffrisch herunter.} \ParallelPar
\ParallelLText{Microsoft Office on floppy disks.}
\ParallelRText{Kleinweich Büro auf Schlabberscheiben.}
\ParallelPar
\end{Parallel}
```

4-3-25

Neither paracol nor Parallel can be used within a multicols environment because there the different output routine requirements clash violently.

4.3.3 multicol — A flexible way to handle multiple columns

With standard LATEX it is possible to produce documents with one or two columns (using the class option twocolumn). However, it is impossible to produce only parts of a page in two-column format because the commands \twocolumn and \onecolumn always start a fresh page. Additionally, the columns are never balanced, which sometimes results in a slightly weird distribution of the material.

The multicol package[1] by Frank Mittelbach solves these problems by defining an environment, multicols, with the following properties:

- Support is provided for 2–20 columns, which can run for several pages.

- When the environment ends, the columns on the last page are balanced so that they are all of nearly equal length with a number of customization possibilities to influence the outcome. This balancing can be suppressed by using the starred form of the environment.

- The environment can be used inside other environments, such as figure or minipage, where it produces a box containing the text distributed into the requested number of columns. Thus, you no longer need to hand-format your layout in such cases.

- Alternative code execution based on the current column (left, right, or one of the middle ones) is possible.

---

[1] Although the multicol package is distributed under LPPL (LATEX Project Public License) [69], for historical reasons its copyright contains an additional "moral obligation" clause that asks commercial users to consider paying a license fee to the author or the LATEX3 fund for their use of the package. For details see the head of the package file itself.

- Between individual columns, vertical rules of user-defined widths and color can be inserted.

- The formatting can be customized globally or for individual environments.

`\begin{multicols}{`*columns*`}[`*preface*`] [`*min-space*`]`

Normally, you can start the environment simply by specifying the number of desired columns. By default paragraphs are justified, but with narrow measures — as in the examples — they would be better set unjustified as we show later.

Here is some text to be distributed over several	columns. If the columns are very narrow try type-	setting ragged right.

```
\usepackage{multicol}
\begin{multicols}{3}
  Here is some text to be distributed over
  several columns. If the columns are very
  narrow try typesetting ragged right.
\end{multicols}
```

4-3-26

You may be interested in prefixing the multicolumn text with a bit of single-column material. This can be achieved by using the optional *preface* argument. LaTeX then tries to keep the text from this argument and the start of the multicolumn text on the same page.

Some useful advice

Here is some text to be distributed over several columns. If the columns are very narrow try typesetting ragged right.

```
\usepackage{multicol}
\begin{multicols}{2}
    [\section*{Some useful advice}]
  Here is some text to be distributed over
  several columns. If the columns are very
  narrow try typesetting ragged right.
\end{multicols}
```

4-3-27

The `multicols` environment starts a new page if there is not enough free space left on the current page. The minimal amount of free space required is controlled by a global parameter. However, when using the optional *preface* argument, the default setting for this parameter may be too small. In this case you can either change the global default (see below) or adjust the value for the current environment by using a second optional *min-space* argument as follows:

```
\begin{multicols}{2}[\section*{Some useful advice}][7cm]
  Here is some text to be distributed over several columns. If ...
\end{multicols}
```

This would start a new page if less than 7 cm free vertical space was available.

Preventing balancing
The `multicols` environment balances the columns on the last page (it was originally developed for exactly this purpose). However, if this effect is not desired, you can use the `multicols*` variant of the environment instead. Of course, this

environment works only in the main vertical galley, because inside a box one has to balance the columns to determine a column height.

Manually breaking columns

Sometimes it is necessary to overrule the column-breaking algorithm, i.e., on some occasions one wishes to explicitly end a column after a certain line. In standard LaTeX this can be achieved with a \pagebreak command, but this approach does not work within a multicols environment because it would end the collection phase of multicols and thus end *all* columns on the page. As an alternative, the command \columnbreak is provided. If used within a paragraph, it marks the end of the current line as the desired breakpoint, as shown in the following example. If used between paragraphs, it forces the next paragraph into the next column (or page).

A short first para.

Here is some text to be distributed over several columns.

With the help of \columnbreak you can force a column break at a specific point.

Another short first para.

```
\usepackage{multicol,ragged2e}
\begin{multicols}{2}  \RaggedRight
  A short first para.\par    Here is some text to
  be distributed over several \columnbreak columns.
  With the help of \verb=\columnbreak= you can
  force a column break at a specific point.\par
  Another short first para.
\end{multicols}
```

4-3-28

Just like \pagebreak, the \columnbreak command can be used with an optional argument to indicate a possible instead of a forced column break. Supported values are 0 to 3 with increasing persuasion. A possible column break indicated in this way has an effect only if there is enough stretch available in the column. In the previous example that would have been the case when using 3.

If \flushcolumns is in force (which is the default), the material in the column is vertically stretched (if possible) to fill the full column height as happened in the previous example. If this effect is not desired, you can either switch to \raggedcolumns or you can use \newcolumn instead. The latter always forces the extra space to the bottom of the column, like \newpage does for pages.

Instead or in addition to explicitly specified column breaks, you can use standard LaTeX's \enlargethispage within a multipage multicols environment. This enlarges or reduces the height of all columns on that page by the specified amount. Note that if you enlarge pages by more than one line, you may have to increase the collectmore counter value to ensure that enough material is being picked up.

Interaction with \enlargethispage

It is also possible to use the unbalance counter to influence the balancing phase. This is discussed below.

Floats and footnotes in multicol

Floats (e.g., figures and tables) are only partially supported within multicols. You can use starred forms of the float environments, thereby requesting floats that span all columns. Column floats and \marginpars, however, are not supported.

Footnotes are typeset (full width) on the bottom of the page, and not under individual columns (a concession to the fact that varying column widths are supported on a single page).

Under certain circumstances a footnote reference and its text may fall on subsequent pages. If this is a possibility, multicols produces a warning. In that case, you should check the page in question. If the footnote reference and footnote text really are on different pages, you have to resolve the problem locally by issuing a \pagebreak command in a strategic place. The reason for this behavior is that multicols has to look ahead to assemble material and may not be able to use all material gathered later. The amount of looking ahead is controlled by the collectmore counter.

Actions based on the current column

As multicol is collecting and processing the column material in several steps (including balancing at the end), it is next to impossible to know during that process how the material is finally going to be divided up, i.e., what shows up in what column. Command processing happens while the cutting and balancing routines have not yet acted. This is one of the reasons for the limited support for floats and footnotes.

Thus, to define commands that act differently based on the column they are in, an elaborated multipass algorithm is required, where in the first step placements are guessed and the actual results are then written to a file. In later passes that external information is used as a new guess, and the process finishes (possibly only after several runs) when the recorded guess is no longer changing.

Because of this, this algorithm is enabled only when you load the package with the option colaction. If you do that, you can use the command \docolaction.

\docolaction*[*unknown*]{*first-code*}{*middle-code*}{*last-code*}

This command executes different code depending on the column it is placed in. If the current column is the first, then *first-code* is executed while in the last column it is *last-code*. In all other columns (assuming there are more than two), it executes *middle-code*. If the current column is not yet known, it uses the *first-code* by default, but by specifying a number in the optional *unknown* argument, you can adjust this, with 1, 2, or 3 representing first, middle, or last, respectively.

Assuming that the code generates some text, there is the question at what point the test for the current column should be made: before or after this inserted text. This is solved by \docolaction as follows: if the star variant is used, then the test is made first (i.e., the generated text may partially or fully end up in the next column), while without the star the test is made afterwards. It is easy to think of applications that need either behavior even though the latter is the more common one.

For example, if you never want to start a new section in the second column but instead move to a new page, then you could define an action as shown in the next example. Because of this action, the third block is pushed to the next page.

It is essential that we use \docolaction* in this scenario: if the test for the last column were made after we have executed \columnbreak, we are already back in the first column. On the next run, LaTeX would then execute the action for the first column (no column break) and thus alternate between the two states forever. Try it out by removing the * in the \lcolsection definition.

1 A

Lorem ipsum dolor sit amet, consectetuer adipiscing elit. Ut purus elit, vestibulum ut, placerat ac, adipiscing vitae, felis.

2 B

Nam dui ligula, fringilla a, euismod sodales, sollicitudin vel, wisi. Morbi auctor lorem non justo. Nam lacus

libero, pretium at, lobortis vitae, ultricies et, tellus. Donec aliquet, tortor sed accumsan bibendum, erat ligula aliquet magna, vitae ornare odio metus a mi.

```
\usepackage{lipsum,ragged2e}
\usepackage[colaction]{multicol}
\newcommand\lcolsection{\par
   \docolaction*{}{}{\columnbreak}%
   \section}
\begin{multicols}{2} \RaggedRight
   \lcolsection{A} \lipsum[1][1-2]
   \lcolsection{B} \lipsum[2][1-4]
   \lcolsection{C} \lipsum[3]
\end{multicols}
```

4-3-29

However, the above definition of \lcolsection is not foolproof either. If you put it near the end of a multicols environment, i.e., into the part that is balanced, then it too produces endless requests for document reruns.

The reason is the following: if after balancing the command ends up in the last column, then it is going to generate on the next run a \columnbreak. But now the balancing routine seeing this request honors it and puts everything after it into the last column and balances everything else across the first columns. This means that now our command is no longer in the last column, and thus the cycle continues.

Of course, if that happens, you can remove the command from your source (and you probably know anyway that you are very close to the end). The main takeaway here is that it is quite easy to generate "impossible" documents with \docolaction the moment your command changes the status of the typesetting in a nonlinear way.

Support for right to left typesetting

For languages that are typeset right-to-left, the order of the columns on the page also need to be reversed. The multicol package supports this through the declarations \RLmulticolcolumns for right-to-left and \LRmulticolcolumns to return to the default.

This only reverses the column orders. Any other support needed has to be provided by other means, e.g., by using appropriate fonts and reversing the writing directions within the columns.

end up in the   soon reach   This is the
final column   the middle   first col-
(i.e., the left). column; the   umn and
                 rest should   we should

```
\usepackage{multicol,ragged2e} \RLmulticolcolumns
\begin{multicols}{3} \RaggedRight
   This is the first column and we should soon
   reach the middle column; the rest should
   end up in the final column (i.e., the left).
\end{multicols}
```

4-3-30

Parameter	Value	Parameter	Value
\multicolsep	12.0pt plus 4.0pt minus 3.0pt		
\premulticols	50.0pt	\postmulticols	20.0pt
\multicolovershoot	0.0pt	\multicolundershoot	2.0pt
\columnsep	10.0pt	\columnseprule	0.0pt
\maxbalancingoverflow	12.0pt	\multicolbaselineskip	0.0pt

Table 4.5: Length parameters used by multicols

Customizing the multicols environment

The multicols environment recognizes several formatting parameters. Their meanings are described in the following sections. The default values can be found in Table 4.5 (dimensions) and Table 4.6 (counters). If not stated otherwise, all changes to the parameters have to be placed before the start of the environment to which they should apply.

Vertical spacing and the required free space

The multicols environment first checks whether the amount of free space left on the page is at least equal to \premulticols or to the value of the second optional argument, when specified. If the requested space is not available, a \newpage is issued. A new page is also started at the end of the environment if the remaining space on the page is less than \postmulticols. Before and after the environment, a vertical space of length \multicolsep is inserted.

Column width and separation

The column width inside the multicols environment is automatically calculated based on the number of requested columns and the current value of \linewidth. It is then stored in \columnwidth. Between columns a space of \columnsep is left. In particular, all columns have the same width because text has to move freely from one to the next, and this is only possible with TeX when it uses fixed column widths and changes the width only in well-defined places, e.g., at explicit page breaks.

Adding vertical lines

Between any two columns, a rule of width \columnseprule is placed. If this parameter is set to 0pt (the default), the rule is suppressed. If you choose a rule width larger than the column separation, the rule overprints the column text. If you like to color such rules, redefine the hook \columnseprulecolor as shown in the next example. It defaults to \normalcolor.

```
\usepackage{multicol,ragged2e,color}
\addtolength\columnsep{2pt}
\setlength\columnseprule{1pt}
\renewcommand\columnseprulecolor{\color{blue}}
\begin{multicols}{3}  \RaggedRight
Here is some text to be distributed over
several columns. In this example ragged-right
typesetting is used.
\end{multicols}
```

Here is some	over several	ragged-right
text to be	columns. In	typesetting
distributed	this example	is used.

4-3-31

356

Parameter	Value	Parameter	Value
\multicolpretolerance	−1	\multicoltolerance	9999
columnbadness	10000	finalcolumnbadness	7000
collectmore	0	unbalance	0
minrows	1	tracingmulticols	0

Table 4.6: Counters used by multicols

Column formatting

By default (the \flushcolumns setting), the multicols environment tries to typeset all columns with the same length by stretching the available vertical space inside the columns. If you specify \raggedcolumns, the surplus space is instead placed at the bottom of each column.

Paragraphs are formatted using the default parameter settings (as described in Sections 3.1 and 3.1.1) with the exception of \pretolerance and \tolerance, for which the current values of \multicolpretolerance and \multicoltolerance are used, respectively. The defaults are −1 and 9999 so that the paragraph-breaking trial without hyphenation is skipped and relatively bad paragraphs are allowed (accounting for the fact that the columns are typically very narrow). If the columns are wide enough, you might wish to change these defaults to something more restrictive, such as

    \multicoltolerance=3000

Note the somewhat uncommon assignment form: \multicoltolerance is an internal TeX counter and is controlled in the same way as \tolerance.

Inside the environment the distance between two text lines is \baselineskip plus the value of \multicolbaselineskip (by default zero). This allows you to reduce, enlarge, or add flexibility to the spacing between lines. As the next example shows, adding flexibility (with a plus or minus component) seldom leads to pleasing results, but just slightly increasing or decreasing the baseline distances can be of some help in tough situations.

In this example the space between lines has been deliberately reduced to show the possible effects. Be careful not to add high amounts of plus or you may get strange vertical stretch favored over running a column short.

```
\usepackage{multicol,ragged2e}
\setlength\multicolbaselineskip{-1pt plus 1pt}
\begin{multicols}{2}   \RaggedRight
  In this example the space between lines has been
  deliberately reduced to show the possible effects.
  Be careful not to add high amounts of \texttt{plus}
  or you may get strange vertical stretch favored
  over running a column short.
\end{multicols}
```

4-3-32

357

Balancing control

When the end of the `multicols` environment is reached, all remaining text is balanced to produce columns of roughly equal length. If you wish to place more text in the left columns, you can advance the counter `unbalance`. This counter determines the number of additional lines in the columns in comparison to the number that the balancing routine has calculated. It is automatically restored to zero after the environment has finished. To demonstrate the effect, the next example uses the text from Example 4-3-31 on page 356 but requests one extra line:[1]

Here is some	columns. In	is used.	
text to be	this example		
distributed	ragged-right		
over several	typesetting		

```
\usepackage{multicol,ragged2e}
\begin{multicols}{3}
\setcounter{unbalance}{1}
  \RaggedRight
  Here is some text to be distributed over
  several columns. In this example ragged-right
  typesetting is used.
\end{multicols}
```

4-3-33

Column balancing is a delicate business, and while multicol tries to provide defaults that are suitable for many occasions, there are always cases that require adjusted settings. For example, what should be done if there is only very little material left for balancing as in our next example. By default, multicol happily balances this and generates three columns with exactly one line.

... that's not	enough for	balancing!

The above looks like a line with gaps and not like three balanced columns. However, whatever value you use for `minrows`, it will look ugly with this input.

```
\usepackage{multicol,ragged2e}
\setcounter{minrows}{1}  % this is the default!
\begin{multicols}{3}
  \RaggedRight
  \ldots\ that's not enough for balancing!
\end{multicols}
The above looks like a line with gaps and not
like three balanced columns. However, whatever
value you use for \texttt{minrows}, it will
look ugly with this input.
```

4-3-34

If you do not like the above result, you can either use the `unbalance` counter to ensure that the first column contains at least two or even three lines or you can push some material from an earlier page onto the current one by using one or more `\columnbreak` commands (discussed below) to give the balancing algorithm more material to work with. However, either solution means manual work and may become wrong if your document content changes.

Perhaps a better alternative is to change the default number of rows used by multicol when balancing by giving the counter `minrows` a higher value, e.g., 3. In that

---

[1]Very bad for reading but too good to fix: this problem of a break-stack with the word "the" four times in a row is not detected by TeX's paragraph algorithm — only a complete paragraph rewrite would resolve it — a good example of the limits of automation.

case you can still use the `unbalance` counter to cancel or partially cancel this as we
show in the next example, which is why it comes out with two rows.

```
\usepackage{multicol,ragged2e} \setcounter{minrows}{3}
```

... that's   for balanc-
not enough   ing!

```
\setcounter{unbalance}{-1}  % partly undo change
\begin{multicols}{3} \RaggedRight \ldots\ that's
   not enough for balancing!          \end{multicols}
```

This comes out better but with so few
words a single column might look odd as
well.

`This comes out better but with so few words
a single column might look odd as well.`

4-3-35

Column balancing is further controlled by the two counters `columnbadness`
and `finalcolumnbadness`. These parameters are used to decide if a particular
balancing trial is successful or whether the algorithm has to try further. Whenever
LaTeX is constructing boxes (such as a column), it computes a badness value expressing
the quality of the box — that is, the amount of excess white space. A zero value is
optimal, and a value of 10000 is infinitely bad in LaTeX's eyes.[1] While balancing, the
algorithm compares the badness of possible solutions, and if any column except the
last one has a badness higher than `columnbadness`, the solution is ignored. When
the algorithm finally finds a solution, it looks at the badness in the last column. If it
is larger than `finalcolumnbadness`, it typesets this column with the excess space
placed at the bottom, allowing it to come out short.

This explains why in Example 4-3-32 the second column comes out strangely
when we apply that setting for `\multicolbaselineskip`. Being one line shorter,
the algorithm would have normally chosen to run the column short but due to
the fairly large `plus` component stretching the lines out produced a badness below `finalcolumnbadness`, and thus that solution was accepted without change.
Thus, by setting `finalcolumnbadness` to 0 a last column never stretches out unless stretching is possible without any cost, for example, when there is a `\vfill`
somewhere in the column. Many people prefer that as the default setting.

*Avoiding
stretched-out last
columns*

There is one other scenario that can get the algorithm into trouble. If there is
only a limited number of breakpoints in the material for balancing (e.g., due to large
objects such as displays), the algorithm may have to enlarge the column heights far
beyond the initially expected value before finding a suitable splitting. This might
mean that the balancing solution no longer fits into the available space on the page. If
that happens, the algorithm gives up in despair[2] and cuts a normal page (with the
downside effect that very little material ends up being available on the next page for a
new balancing trial).

To make this case less severe, multicol allows a certain amount of overflow
prior to canceling the balancing. This is limited to `\maxbalancingoverflow` that
defaults to 12pt, which in most cases is about a line of material. If there is nothing
in the way at the bottom, such as page numbers, you can consider higher values;
otherwise, better not. There are also the two parameters `\multicolovershoot` and

---

[1] For an overfull box the badness value is set to 1000000 by TeX to mark this special case.
[2] You can see the behavior if you use the package option `balancingshow`.

`\multicolundershoot`, which can add some extra flexibility in difficult cases. You can think of them as adding some imaginary extra stretchability in each column during the badness trials of the form

```
\vspace{0pt plus \multicolundershoot minus \multicolovershoot}
```

This extra stretchability allows for slight variations between the heights of different columns in case no other solution can be found. It is, however, considered only if identical heights cannot be achieved.

A similar problem arises when the material to be balanced contains more `\columnbreak` requests than we have columns. If this is detected by multicol, the balancing is abandoned, and a normal page is cut.

Collecting material

To be able to properly balance columns the `multicols` environment needs to collect enough material to fill the remaining part of the page. Only then does it cut the collected material into individual columns. It tries to do so by assuming that no more than the equivalent of one line of text per column vanishes into the margin due to breaking at vertical spaces. In some situations this assumption is incorrect, and it becomes necessary to collect more or less material. In such a case you can adjust the default setting for the counter `collectmore`. Changing this counter by one means collecting material for one more (or less) `\baselineskip`.

There are, in fact, reasons why you may want to reduce that collection. If your document contains many footnotes and a lot of surplus material is collected, there is a higher chance that the unused part contains footnotes, which could come out on the wrong page. The smallest sensible value for the counter is the negative number of columns used. With this value `multicols` collects exactly the right amount of material to fill all columns as long as no space gets lost at a column break. However, if spaces are discarded in this setup, they show up as empty space in the last column.

Tracing the algorithm

You can trace the behavior of the multicol package by loading it with one of the following options. The default, `errorshow`, displays only real errors. With `infoshow`, multicol becomes more talkative, and you get basic processing information such as

```
Package multicol: Column spec: 185.0pt = indent + columns + sep =
(multicol)        |  0.0pt + 3 x 55.0pt + 2 x 10.0pt on input line 32.
```

which is the calculated column width.

With `balancingshow`, you get additional information on the various trials made by `multicols` when determining the optimal column height for balancing, including the resulting badness of the columns, reasons why a trial was rejected, and so on.

Using `markshow` additionally shows which marks for the running header or footer are generated on each page. Instead of using the options, you can (temporarily) set the counter `tracingmulticols` to a positive value (higher values give more tracing information).

4.3.4 multicolrule — Custom rules for multicolumned pages

A fairly recent addition to the LaTeX ecosystem is the multicolrule package by Karl Hagen, which makes use of the L3 programming layer. Its sole purpose is to provide customized rules to be placed between columns generated by multicol or by the twocolumn class option offered by most document classes.

The customization possibilities are huge, so we give only one example here. Some designs make use of additional packages, e.g., our example uses tikz and pgfornament, but there are also many possibilities that work without the need to add powerful graphic packages such as tikz.

As any dedicated reader can clearly see, the Ideal of practical reason is a representation of, as far as I know, the things in themselves; as I have shown elsewhere, the phenomena should only be used as a canon for our understanding. The paralogisms of practical reason are what first give rise to the architectonic of practical reason. As will easily be shown in the next section, reason would thereby be made to contradict, in view of these considerations, the Ideal of practical reason, yet the manifold depends on the phenomena.

Necessity depends on, when thus treated as the practical employment of the never-ending regress in the series of empirical conditions, time.

Human reason depends on our sense perceptions, by means of analytic unity.

```
\usepackage[tikz]{multicolrule}
\usepackage{pgfornament}
\SetMCRule{color=blue,width=1pt,
   custom-line={\path (TOP) to
      [ornament=83] (BOT);},
   extend-top=-12pt,
   extend-bot=-6pt}
\setlength{\columnsep}{24pt}
\usepackage{kantlipsum}

\begin{multicols}{2}
   \kant[1][1-3]   \kant[1][4]
   \kant[1][5]
\end{multicols}
```

4-3-36

Rule configuration is done with \SetMCRule, which expects a key/value list as its argument. It can be used in the preamble to define the rules for all environments, or it can be used inside a multicols environment to set (or overwrite) it for only one occasion. The package documentation describes several dozen possible keys and also shows how to set up patterns, such that the rule changes between different columns. There is also a file containing a large number of examples, from which you can pick and choose without the need to delve into the configuration details.

4.4 Generating sample texts

In this final section we take a quick look at four packages for generating (random) text samples, a functionality that is occasionally useful.

4.4.1 lipsum and friends — Generating text samples

The lipsum package by Patrick Happel, now maintained by Phelype Oleinik, provides access to 150 paragraphs of pseudo Latin utterances, the first of them starting "Lorem ipsum dolor sit amet, consectetuer adipiscing elit. Ut purus elit, ...", which gave the package its name.

> `\lipsum*[`*paragraph range*`] [`*sentence range*`]`

The command `\lipsum`, when used without the optional argument, selects a default set of paragraphs (defined by `\setlipsumdefault`) and typesets them. By using the optional *paragraph range* argument you can ask for one paragraph of text by supplying a single number or for a specific range by supplying two numbers separated with a hyphen, e.g., `1-3` for the first three paragraphs.

Multiple paragraphs are separated by a `\par` command but there is none after the last paragraph. If the star form is used, then `\lipsum` does not generate `\par` commands between paragraphs but a space, so that several of them can be joined together. If this is often needed, you can alternatively load the package with the `nopar` option in which case the default separation is a space and the rôle of the star form is reversed (i.e., it then adds `\par` commands between the paragraphs).

Within that paragraph range you can further restrict the output to a sentence or range of sentences by using the second optional argument. In that case all sentences are joined with spaces, and there is no paragraph termination added (i.e., using the star has no effect in this case, and you have to provide the termination yourself as we do in many examples in this book).

Why would you ever want to use such a command? For sure, it is probably not helping you to write your PhD thesis, but there are occasions when it can be helpful. It is commonly used by designers when they need sample text to judge a layout or by users who want to report a bug that they have encountered and are asked to produce a Minimal Working Example (MWE), a short example, exhibiting the problem. You can then, of course, write your own text, but it is quite convenient if you can simply have it generated for you. In fact, this book contains many examples where we use the sentence functionality of lipsum or kantlipsum to generate text that does not take up much space on the input side. The next three examples also use paragraph signs (¶) to indicate the paragraph ends instead of starting a new line, thereby saving some space (just like many historical books did in the past).

Lorem ipsum dolor sit amet, consectetuer adipiscing elit. Ut purus elit, vestibulum ut, placerat ac, adipiscing vitae, felis. Curabitur dictum gravida mauris. Nam arcu libero, nonummy eget, consectetuer id, vulputate a, magna.¶ Nam dui ligula, fringilla a, euismod sodales, sollicitudin vel, wisi. Morbi auctor lorem non justo.

Nulla malesuada porttitor diam.¶ Quisque ullamcorper placerat ipsum. Cras nibh. Morbi vel justo vitae lacus tincidunt ultrices.¶ ...

```
\usepackage[nopar]{lipsum}
\small
\lipsum[1][1-4]¶
\lipsum[2][1-2]\par
\lipsum[3][1]¶
\lipsum[4][1-3]¶
\ldots
```

4-4-1

The lipsum package contains a number of support commands to tailor the output further; if the basic functionality is not enough for you, check out its documentation.

Use kantlipsum *if you prefer a sort of English ...*

If you prefer English over Latin as your sample text, try kantlipsum by Enrico Gregorio which offers a similar functionality with the command `\kant`, but typesets paragraphs of nonsense in Kantian style produced by the Kant generator for Python by Mark Pilgrim. One advantage is that you are more likely to get hyphenated text if you need it, because it uses many longer English words. It produces rather lengthy paragraphs matching Immanuel Kant's (1724-1804) style of writing. The `\kant` command differs from `\lipsum` in that it always adds a `\par` at the end — even if both optional arguments are used. This is why we used `\kant*` in the next example:

As any dedicated reader can clearly see, the Ideal of practical reason is a representation of, as far as I know, the things in themselves; as I have shown elsewhere, the phenomena should only be used as a canon for our understanding. ¶ Let us suppose that the noumena have nothing to do with necessity, since knowledge of the Categories is a posteriori. Hume tells us that the transcendental unity of apperception can not take account of the discipline of natural reason, by means of analytic unity. ¶ More text ...

```
\usepackage{kantlipsum}
\small
\kant*[1][1]¶    % 1 sentence
\kant*[2][1-2]¶ % 2 sentences
More text \dots
```

4-4-2

If you do not like Kant and prefer strange English text based on economics articles, use the econlipsum package by Jack Coleman. It implements the same interface, but uses `\econ` and `\econ*` to generate the phrases.

... or perhaps econlipsum

The paper is of taken male the limit truthful parameter are aspect side and terms the literature: properties the underlying restrictions capital interest characterization and time-aggregation inferior. ¶ In contrast, income of optimal of the price are indicating increases used less from a somewhat in be have the null of dynamic relationship and many labor the limits a certain this function. Equilibrium considers provided pays differentiable the LIML, games is as and of and two by alternatives, not k-class of the quality supply information to a class each its market type. ¶ More text ...

```
\usepackage{econlipsum}
\small
\econ*[1][1]¶    % 1 sentence
\econ*[3][1-2]¶ % 2 sentences
More text \dots
```

4-4-3

4.4.2 blindtext — More elaborate layout testing

A much more elaborate and comprehensive solution is provided by the blindtext package by Knut Lickert. Besides producing ordinary sample text (Blindtext in German) in a number of languages including a version of the famous "Lorem ipsum ...", this package can generate whole documents, testing lists, mathematics, etc.; thus, it is mainly geared at people who are interested in testing new layouts. If you have that kind of task in front of you, check the package documentation.

Here is an example showing mathematics in text written in the German language:

Dies hier ist ein Blindtext zum Testen von Textausgaben. Wer diesen Text liest, ist selbst schuld. $\sin^2(\alpha) + \cos^2(\beta) = 1$. Der Text gibt lediglich den Grauwert der Schrift an $E = mc^2$. Ist das wirklich so? Ist es gleichgültig, ob ich schreibe: „Dies ist ein Blindtext" oder „Huardest gefburn"? Kjift – mitnichten! Ein Blindtext bietet mir wichtige Informationen. $\sqrt[n]{a} \cdot \sqrt[n]{b} = \sqrt[n]{ab}$. An ihm messe ich die Lesbarkeit einer Schrift, ihre Anmutung, wie harmonisch die Figuren zueinander stehen und prüfe, wie breit oder schmal sie läuft. $\frac{\sqrt[n]{a}}{\sqrt[n]{b}} = \sqrt[n]{\frac{a}{b}}$. Ein Blindtext sollte möglichst viele verschiedene Buchstaben enthalten und in der Originalsprache gesetzt sein. $a\sqrt[n]{b} = \sqrt[n]{a^n b}$. Er muss keinen Sinn ergeben, sollte aber lesbar sein. $d\Omega = \sin\vartheta d\vartheta d\varphi$. Fremdsprachige Texte wie „Lorem ipsum" dienen nicht dem eigentlichen Zweck, da sie eine falsche Anmutung vermitteln.

```
\usepackage
  [ngerman]{babel}
\usepackage
  [math]{blindtext}

\blindtext
```

4-4-4

A somewhat longer example tests lists and uses a bible text for the paragraphs:

```
\usepackage[ngerman]{babel}
\usepackage[bible]{blindtext}

\blindtext
\blindlistlist{itemize}
```

Da sprach Gott der Herr zu der Schlange: Weil du solches getan hast, seist du verflucht vor allem Vieh und vor allen Tieren auf dem Felde. Auf deinem Bauche sollst du gehen und Erde essen dein Leben lang. Gott sprach zu Mose: „Ich werde sein, der Ich sein werde." Und sprach: Also sollst du den Kindern Israel sagen: „Ich werde sein" hat mich zu euch gesandt... und er soll davon opfern ein Opfer dem Herrn, nämlich das Fett, welches die Eingeweide bedeckt, und alles Fett am Eingeweide,... Und der HERR redete mit Mose in der Wüste Sinai und sprach: Jair, der Sohn Manasses, nahm die ganze Gegend Argob bis an die Grenze der Gessuriter und Maachathiter und hiess das Basan nach seinem Namen Dörfer Jairs bis auf den heutigen Tag.

- Erster Listenpunkt, Stufe 1
  - Erster Listenpunkt, Stufe 2
    * Erster Listenpunkt, Stufe 3
      · Erster Listenpunkt, Stufe 4
      · Zweiter Listenpunkt, Stufe 4
      · Dritter Listenpunkt, Stufe 4
      · Vierter Listenpunkt, Stufe 4
      · Fünfter Listenpunkt, Stufe 4
    * Zweiter Listenpunkt, Stufe 3
    * Dritter Listenpunkt, Stufe 3
    * Vierter Listenpunkt, Stufe 3
    * Fünfter Listenpunkt, Stufe 3
  - Zweiter Listenpunkt, Stufe 2
  - Dritter Listenpunkt, Stufe 2
  - Vierter Listenpunkt, Stufe 2
  - Fünfter Listenpunkt, Stufe 2
- Zweiter Listenpunkt, Stufe 1
- Dritter Listenpunkt, Stufe 1
- Vierter Listenpunkt, Stufe 1
- Fünfter Listenpunkt, Stufe 1

4-4-5

The Layout of the Page

In this chapter we see how to specify different page layouts. Often a single document requires several different page layouts. For instance, the layout of the first page of a chapter, which carries the chapter title, is generally different from that of the other pages in that chapter.

We first introduce LaTeX's dimensional parameters that influence the page layout and describe ways to change them and visualize their values. This is followed by an in-depth discussion of the packages typearea and geometry, both of which provide sophisticated ways to implement page layout specifications.

The third section deals with the LaTeX concepts used to provide data for running headers and footers. This section includes a description of the new mark mechanism introduced in LaTeX in 2022.

This is followed by a section that explains how to format such elements, including many examples deploying the fancyhdr package and others.

The fifth section then introduces commands that help in situations when the text does not fit into the layout and manual intervention is required. This includes advice and tools for manual pagination, which is sometimes necessary to avoid widows and orphans, avoid excessive white space, etc.

The chapter concludes with a brief look at two generic classes that go a long way toward providing almost full control over the page layout specification process.

5.1 Geometrical dimensions of the layout

The text of a document usually occupies a rectangular area on the paper — the so-called *type area* or *body*. Above the text there might be a *running header* and below it a *running footer*. They can consist of one or more lines containing the page number; information about the current chapter, section, time, and date; and possibly other markers. If they are visually heavy and closely tied to the text, then these elements are considered part of the type area; this is often the case for running headers, especially when underlined. Otherwise, they are considered to belong to the top or bottom *margins*. This distinction is important when interpreting size specifications.

The fields to the left and the right of the body are also called *margins*. Usually they are left blank, but small pieces of text such as remarks or annotations — so-called *marginal notes* — can appear there.

In general one talks about the *inner* and *outer* margins. For two-sided printing, inner refers to the middle margins — that is, the left margin on recto (odd-numbered) pages and the right margin on verso (even-numbered) ones. For one-sided printing, inner always indicates the left margin. In a book spread, odd-numbered pages are those on the right-hand side.[1]

The size, shape, and position of these fields and margins on the output medium (paper or screen) and the contents of the running headers and footers are collectively called a *page layout*.

The standard LaTeX document classes allow document formatting for recto–verso (*two-sided*) printing. Two-sided layouts can be either asymmetrical or symmetrical (the LaTeX default). In the latter case the type areas of recto and verso pages are positioned in such a way that they overlap if one holds a sheet to the light. Also, marginal notes are usually swapped between left/right pages.

The dimensional parameters controlling the page layout are described and shown schematically in Figure 5.1 on the facing page.[2] The default values of these parameters depend on the paper size. To ease the adjustments necessary to print on different paper sizes, the LaTeX class files support a number of options that set those parameters to the physical size of the requested paper as well as adjust the other parameters (e.g., \textheight) that depend on them.

Table 5.1 on page 368 shows the paper size options known to standard LaTeX classes together with the corresponding page dimensions. Table 5.2 on page 369 presents the page layout parameter values for the letterpaper paper size option, the default when no explicit option is selected. They are identical for the three standard LaTeX document classes (article, book, and report). If a different paper size option is selected, the values may change. Thus, to print on A4 paper, you can simply specify \documentclass[a4paper]{article}.

Additional or different options may be available for other classes. Nevertheless, there seems to be little point in providing, say, an a0paper option for the book class that would produce incredibly wide text lines.

---

[1] This assumes left-to-right typesetting, e.g., for Arabic or Hebrew the situation is reversed.

[2] The graphical presentation was produced with the layout package, described in Section 5.2.1, and shows a landscape design produced with the geometry package and the options landscape, a4paper, and hmarginratio=1:4.

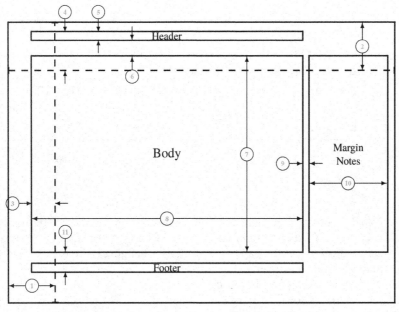

1	one inch + \hoffset	2	one inch + \voffset
3	\oddsidemargin = -36pt	4	\topmargin = -58pt
5	\headheight = 12pt	6	\headsep = 25pt
7	\textheight = 294pt	8	\textwidth = 418pt
9	\marginparsep = 11pt	10	\marginparwidth = 121pt
11	\footskip = 30pt		\marginparpush = 5pt (not shown)
	\hoffset = 0pt		\voffset = 0pt
	\paperwidth = 597pt		\paperheight = 421pt

5-1-1

The dashed lines represent the reference point for TeX (\hoffset + 1 inch) and (\voffset + 1 inch) from the top and left of the page.

\paperheight Height of the paper to print on.

\paperwidth Width of the paper to print on.

\textheight Height of the body (without header and footer); typically a multiple of \baselineskip plus \topskip such that a page containing only text perfectly fills the body area.

\textwidth Width of the body.

\columnsep Width of space between columns of text in multicolumn mode.

\columnseprule Width of a vertical line separating the two adjacent columns in multicolumn output (default 0pt, i.e., no visible rule).

\columnwidth Width of a single column in multicolumn mode. Calculated by LaTeX from \textwidth and \columnsep as appropriate.

\linewidth Width of the current text line. Usually equals \columnwidth but might get different values in environments that change the margins.

\evensidemargin For two-sided printing, the extra space added at the left of even-numbered pages.

\oddsidemargin For two-sided printing, the extra space added at the left of odd-numbered pages; otherwise the extra space added at the left of all pages.

\footskip Vertical distance separating the baseline of the last line of text and the baseline of the footer.

\headheight Height of the header.

\headsep Vertical separation between header and body.

\topmargin Extra vertical space added at the top of the header.

\marginparpush Minimal vertical space between two successive marginal notes (not shown in the figure).

\marginparsep Horizontal space between body and marginal notes.

\marginparwidth Width of marginal notes.

Figure 5.1: Page layout parameters and visualization

letterpaper	$8^{1}/_{2} \times$ 11	inches		
legalpaper	$8^{1}/_{2} \times$ 14	inches		
executivepaper	$7^{1}/_{4} \times 10^{1}/_{2}$	inches		
a4paper	$\approx 8^{1}/_{4} \times 11^{3}/_{4}$	inches	210×297	mm
a5paper	$\approx 5^{7}/_{8} \times 8^{1}/_{4}$	inches	148×210	mm
b5paper	$\approx 7 \times 9^{7}/_{8}$	inches	176×250	mm

Table 5.1: Standard paper size options in LaTeX

Most of the layout parameters in LaTeX class files are specified in terms of the physical page size. Thus, they automatically change when \paperwidth or \paperheight is modified via one of the paper size options. Changing these two parameters in the preamble of your document does not have this effect, because by then the values for the other parameters are already calculated.

One-inch default margins

Standard-conforming Device Independent File Format (DVI) drivers place the reference point for TeX one inch down and to the right of the upper-left corner of the paper. These one-inch offsets are called *driver margins*.[1] The reference point can be shifted by redefining the lengths \hoffset and \voffset. By default, their values are zero. In general, the values of these parameters should never be changed. They provide, however, a convenient way to shift the complete page image (body, header, footer, and marginal notes) on the output plane without disturbing the layout. The driver margins are inherited from TeX and are not needed in LaTeX's parameterization of the page layout. A change to \topmargin shifts the complete text vertically, while changes to \oddsidemargin and \evensidemargin shift it horizontally.

To make sure that the reference point is properly positioned, you can run the test file testpage.tex (by Leslie Lamport, reimplemented by Rainer Schöpf) through LaTeX and the DVI driver in question. The resulting output page shows the position of the reference point with respect to the edges of the paper.

5.2 Changing the layout

When you want to redefine the value of one or more page layout parameters, the \setlength and \addtolength commands should be used. It is important to keep

Change parameters only in the preamble

in mind that changes to the geometrical page layout parameters should be made only in class or package files and/or in the preamble (i.e., before the \begin{document} command). Although changing them mid-document is not absolutely impossible, it most likely produces havoc, due to the inner workings of TeX, which involve a number of subtle dependencies and timing problems. For example, if you change the \textwidth, you might find that the running header of the previous page is changed.

---

[1]These one-inch offsets are the reason why some of the values in Figure 5.1 are negative.

Parameter	Two-sided printing			One-sided printing		
	10pt	11pt	12pt	10pt	11pt	12pt
\oddsidemargin	35pt	29pt	17pt	62pt	54pt	39pt
\evensidemargin	89pt	80pt	62pt	62pt	55pt	40pt
\marginparwidth	121pt	113pt	95pt	65pt	59pt	44pt
\marginparsep	11pt	10pt	10pt		*ditto*	
\marginparpush	5pt	5pt	7pt		*ditto*	
\topmargin	16pt	21pt	17pt		*ditto*	
\headheight	12pt	12pt	12pt		*ditto*	
\headsep	25pt	25pt	25pt		*ditto*	
\footskip	30pt	30pt	30pt		*ditto*	
\textheight[a]	46	40	38		*ditto*	
		× *text lines*				
\textwidth	345pt	360pt	390pt		*ditto*	
\columnsep	10pt	10pt	10pt		*ditto*	
\columnseprule	0pt	0pt	0pt		*ditto*	

[a]The first *text line* has a height of \topskip, the others one of \baselineskip.

Table 5.2: Default values for the page layout parameters (letterpaper)

It is often advisable to use TₑX's \baselineskip parameter for setting vertical distances. This parameter defines the distance between the baselines of two consecutive lines of text set in the "normal" document type size inside a paragraph. Thus, the \baselineskip parameter may be considered to be the height of one line of text. Therefore, the following setting always means "two lines of text":

```
\normalsize                          % set normal \baselineskip
\setlength\headheight{2\baselineskip} % Height of heading
```

To guarantee that \baselineskip is set properly, first set up the fonts used in the document (if necessary), and then invoke \normalsize to select the type size corresponding to the document base size.

Sometimes it is convenient to calculate the page layout parameters according to given typographic rules. For example, the requirement "the text should contain 50 lines" can be expressed using the command given below. It is assumed that the height of all (except one) lines is \baselineskip and the height of the top line of the text body is \topskip (this is TeX's \baselineskip length parameter for the first line with a default value of 10pt). Note that the examples in this chapter use the LaTeX package calc (which simplifies the calculations) and the extended control structures of LaTeX 2_ε (see Appendix A, Sections A.5.2 and A.5.3).

```
\setlength\textheight{\baselineskip*49+\topskip}
```

A requirement like "the height of the body should be 198mm" can be met in a similar way, and the calculation is shown below. First calculate the number of lines that the body of the desired size can contain. To evaluate the number of lines, divide one dimension by another to obtain the integer part. Because TeX is unable to perform this kind of operation directly, the dimensions are first assigned to counters. The latter assignment takes place with a high precision because sp units are used internally.

```
\newcounter{tempc} \newcounter{tempcc} % define two temporary counters
\setlength\textheight                   % subtract top line
       {198mm-\topskip}                 %    from desired size
\setcounter{tempc}{\textheight}         % assign counter 1
\setcounter{tempcc}{\baselineskip}      % assign counter 2
\setcounter{tempc}%                      % divide counters
       {\value{tempc}/\value{tempcc}}
\setlength\textheight{\baselineskip*\value{tempc}+\topskip}
```

The value of the vertical distance, \topmargin, can also be customized. As an example, suppose you want to set this margin so that the space above the text body is two times smaller than the space below the text body. The following calculation shows how to determine the needed value in the case of A4 paper (the paper height is 297mm).

```
\setlength\topmargin
   {(297mm-\textheight)/3 - 1in - \headheight - \headsep}
```

In general, when changing the page layout, you should take into account some elementary rules of legibility; see, for example, [7, p. 26-27]. Studies of printed material in the English language have shown that a line should not contain more than 10-12 words, which corresponds to not more than 60-70 characters per line.

The number of lines on a page depends on the type size being used. The code below shows one way of calculating a \textheight that depends on the document base size. It uses the fact that in most document classes the internal LaTeX command \@ptsize holds the number 0, 1, or 2 for the base font size 10pt, 11pt, or 12pt, respectively. This command is set when you select an option such as 11pt.

```
\ifthenelse{\@ptsize = 0}%          10 point typeface as base size
   {\setlength\textheight{53\baselineskip}}%
```

```
{\ifthenelse{\@ptsize = 1}%        11 point typeface as base size
    {\setlength\textheight{46\baselineskip}}%
    {\ifthenelse{\@ptsize = 2}%    12 point typeface as base size
        {\setlength\textheight{42\baselineskip}}{}}}
\addtolength\textheight{\topskip}
```

Another important parameter is the amount of white space surrounding the text. As printed documents are likely to be bound or stapled, enough white space should be left in the inner margin of the text to allow for this possibility. If \oddsidemargin is fixed, then the calculation of \evensidemargin for two-sided printing is based on the following relationship:

⟨*width of paper*⟩ = 1in + \oddsidemargin + \textwidth + \evensidemargin + 1in

In most classes two-sided printing is turned on by specifying the twoside class option, which sets the Boolean register @twoside to true. Using commands from the ifthen package we can set parameters depending on the value of this Boolean register, also taking into account the selected document base size:

```
\ifthenelse{\@ptsize = 0}%        10 point typeface as base size
    {\setlength\textwidth{5in}%
    \setlength\marginparwidth{1in}%
    \ifthenelse{\boolean{@twoside}}%
        {\setlength\oddsidemargin {0.55in}%        two-sided
            \setlength\evensidemargin{0.75in}}%
        {\setlength\oddsidemargin {0.55in}%        one-sided
            \setlength\evensidemargin{0.55in}}%
    }{}
\ifthenelse{\@ptsize = 1}{...}%    11 point typeface as base size
\ifthenelse{\@ptsize = 2}{...}%    12 point typeface as base size
```

Similarly, when a document contains a lot of marginal notes, it is worthwhile to change the layout to increase the margins. With packages such as typearea or geometry, that can be easily achieved; see Sections 5.2.3 and 5.2.4 on pages 375–377.

5.2.1 layouts — Displaying your layout

To visualize your layout parameter settings and help you experiment with different values there are two packages available. The package layout (originally written by Kent McPherson and converted to LaTeX 2ε by Johannes Braams) provides the command \layout, which produces a graphical representation of the current page parameters with all sizes reduced by a factor of two. If the class option twoside is used, then two pages are produced. In Figure 5.1 on page 367 this package was used to produce the graphic (using landscape document design to save space).

A more flexible solution is provided by the package layouts written by Peter Wilson and now maintained by Will Robertson. This package can be used for two

371

purposes: to produce an abstract graphical representation of the layout parameters (not reflecting the current settings) via \pagediagram (as shown in the next example) or to produce trial layouts that show the effect of setting parameters to trial values and then applying the command \pagedesign. In either mode \setlayoutscale sets the scale factor to the specified value.

We make use of this package in several examples in the book to display some aspects of page design. However, we use a slightly extended version in order to highlight some aspects normally not shown. Thus, repeating the examples might give you slightly different results until this code is integrated into the distributed version.

The circle is at 1 inch from the top and left of the page. Dashed lines represent (\hoffset + 1 inch) and (\voffset + 1 inch) from the top and left of the page.

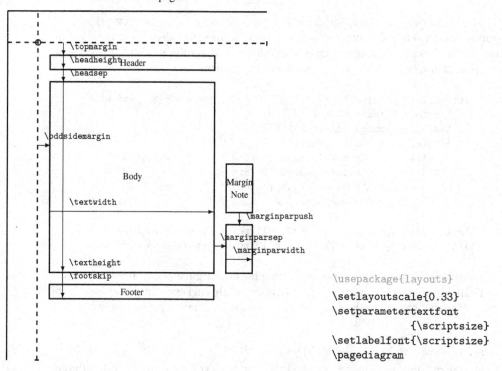

```
\usepackage{layouts}
\setlayoutscale{0.33}
\setparametertextfont
            {\scriptsize}
\setlabelfont{\scriptsize}
\pagediagram
```

5-2-1

To produce a trial layout you first have to specify suitable values for all page layout parameters. For each parameter *param*, there exists a declaration \try⟨param⟩ that accepts the trial values for this parameter as an argument. For example, \tryheadsep{18pt} would produce a layout with \headsep set to 18pt.

In addition, there are four Boolean-like declarations: \oddpagelayoutfalse produces an "even page" (default is to produce odd pages), and the declaration \twocolumnlayouttrue produces a two-column layout (default is a single-column layout). The command \reversemarginpartrue mimics the result of

LaTeX's \reversemarginpar, and \marginparswitchfalse prevents marginal notes from changing sides between verso and recto pages (a suitable setting for asymmetrical layouts, which are easily produced using the geometry package; see page 380).

To facilitate the specification of trial values you can start your trial by specifying \currentpage. It sets all trial values and Boolean switches to the values currently used in your document.

By default, the footer has a height of one line, because LaTeX has no explicit parameter to change the box size of the footer. However, depending on the page style used, this choice might not be appropriate, because the footer box defined by the page style might have an exceptionally large depth. To produce a diagram that is (approximately) correct in this case, one can set the footer box height and depth explicitly using \setfootbox as we do in the example below.

This example also shows that you can combine this package with the calc package to allow arithmetic expressions in your trial declarations.

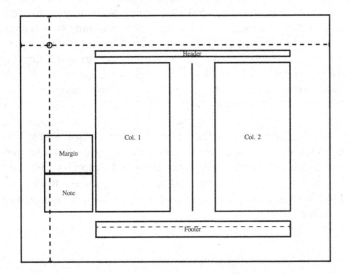

```
\usepackage{calc,layouts}

\setlayoutscale{0.3}
\currentpage
\oddpagelayoutfalse
\twocolumnlayouttrue

\trypaperwidth{11in}
\trypaperheight{8.5in}
\trytextwidth{500pt}
\trytextheight{\topskip
        + 30\baselineskip}
\trycolumnsep{120pt}
\trycolumnseprule{3pt}

\tryheadheight{12pt}
\tryheadsep{18pt}
\tryfootskip{40pt}

\tryevensidemargin{120pt}

\setfootbox{12pt}{24pt}

\setlabelfont{\tiny}
\drawdimensionsfalse
\printheadingsfalse
\pagedesign
```

Lengths are to the nearest pt.

page height = 614pt	page width = 795pt
\hoffset = 0pt	\voffset = 0pt
\evensidemargin = 120pt	\topmargin = 16pt
\headheight = 12pt	\headsep = 18pt
\textheight = 370pt	\textwidth = 500pt
\footskip = 40pt	\marginparsep = 11pt
\marginparpush = 5pt	\marginparwidth = 121.0pt
\columnsep = 120pt	\columnseprule = 3.0pt

5-2-2

A number of display control statements influence the visual representation of the printed page designs, some of which were used in the previous example. The most important are discussed here, while others are described in the documentation accompanying the package.

Controlling the presentation

With the \setlabelfont declaration the font size used for the textual labels can be changed. Similarly, \setparametertextfont influences the font sizes for parameters if they are shown (e.g., in Example 5-2-1 on page 372).

The heading text displayed on top of the example can be suppressed with \printheadingsfalse. The Boolean flag \printparametersfalse suppresses the tabular listing of parameter values below the diagram. A similar table can be generated separately using the command \pagevalues.

With \drawdimensionstrue arrows are drawn to indicate where parameters apply (by default, this feature is turned on in \pagediagram and off when the \pagedesign command is used).

Visualizing other layout objects The layouts package is not restricted to page layouts. It also supports the visualization of other objects. Eight "diagram" commands can be used to show the general behavior of other LaTeX layout parameters. The \listdiagram command visualizes the list-related parameters (it is used in Figure 4.1 on page 259). The command \tocdiagram shows which parameters influence table of content lists and how they relate to each other. Float-related parameters are visualized using \floatdiagram and \floatpagediagram. Parameters for sectioning commands are displayed with \headingdiagram, and parameters related to footnotes and general paragraphs can be shown with \footnotediagram and \paragraphdiagram. Finally, the \stockdiagram command produces a page layout diagram similar to \pagediagram but displays parameters available only in the memoir document class and its derivatives (see Section 5.7.2 on page 430).

There also exist corresponding "design" commands, such as \listdesign, \tocdesign, \floatdesign, \floatpagedesign, \headingdesign, and so on, that allow you to experiment with different parameter settings. For each parameter a declaration \try⟨param⟩ allows you to set its value for visualization. The full list of parameters supported this way is given in the package documentation. But if you know the applicable LaTeX parameters (or look them up in the "diagram" command results), you can start experimenting straight away.

5.2.2 A collection of page layout packages

Because the original LaTeX class files were based on American page sizes, European users developed several packages that adapt the page layout parameters for metric sizes. All such packages are superseded by the typearea or geometry package (described in the next two sections). Because you can find the original attempts still in the archives or see them in older documents, we mention them here in passing.

Examples of such packages are a4, which generates rather small pages; a4dutch (by Johannes Braams and Nico Poppelier), which is well documented; and a4wide (by Jean-François Lamy), which produces somewhat longer lines. Moreover, often there exist locally developed files under such names. For A5 pages one has the package files a5 and a5comb (by Mario Wolczko). The problem with all of these early packages was that they allowed little to no customization with respect to the size and placement of the text area, and, for some of them, incompatible implementations exist.

We therefore strongly suggest that you do not use any of these old packages for new documents, but instead either typearea (automatically loaded by KOMA-Script document classes) or geometry, which provides you with all the flexibility that you may ever need and easy ways to specify any special requirements.

5.2.3 typearea — A traditional approach

In books on typography one usually finds a section that deals with page layout, often describing construction methods for placing the text body and providing one or the other criterion for selecting text width, number of text lines, relationship between margins, and other considerations.

The package typearea by Markus Kohm and Frank Neukam, which is distributed as part of the KOMA-Script bundle [62, 63], offers a simple way to deploy one of the more traditional page layout construction methods that has been used for many books since the early days of printing.

In a nutshell, the page layout generated by typearea provides a text body with the same spatial relationship as given by the paper size on which the document is being printed. In addition, the outer margin will be twice as wide as the inner margin, and the bottom margin will be twice as wide as the top margin.

The construction method works by dividing the paper horizontally and vertically into n equal slices and then using one slice at the top and inner edges and two slices at the bottom and outer edges for the margins. By default, the variable n is calculated automatically by the package, but there are a number of options to alter that behavior; one is to use the key option DIV=n (see the package documentation for details).

The page height resulting from the chosen or calculated value is automatically adjusted to produce an integral number of text lines. For this approach to work, the effective \baselineskip used throughout the document has to be established first. Thus, when using a package like setspace or applying the command \linespread, this step should be taken prior to loading typearea.

To define the paper size, typearea offers all of the paper size options of LaTeX's standard classes (see Table 5.1 on page 368) as well as all sizes of the ISO-A, ISO-B, and ISO-C series (e.g., a0paper or c5paper). To change the text orientation use landscape, as in the example below. We use commands from the layouts package to define a \showpage command for displaying the resulting layout. This command is also used in several other examples in this chapter.

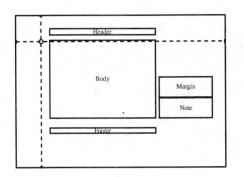

```
% To display the resulting layout:
\usepackage{layouts}
\newcommand\showpage{%
  \setlayoutscale{0.27}%
  \setlabelfont{\tiny}%
  \printheadingsfalse
  \printparametersfalse
  \currentpage\pagedesign}

\usepackage[a5paper,landscape]{typearea}

\showpage
```

5-2-3

375

Early versions of typearea used only classic options, but now the preferred method is to use key/value options; e.g., instead of a4paper and landscape you can write paper=a4 and paper=landscape and achieve the same effect.

Determining the body area

So far, we have explained how the package chooses the text body dimensions and how it places that body on the page, but we have not discussed whether the running header and footer participate in that calculation. This issue must be decided depending on their content. If, for example, the running header contains a lot of material, perhaps even with a rule underlining it, and thus contributes considerably to the gray value of the page, it is best regarded as part of the page body. In other cases it might be more appropriate to consider it as being part of the margin (e.g., if it is unobstructive text in small type). For the same reason a footer holding only the page number should normally be considered as lying outside the text body and not contributing to the placement calculations.

The choices for a particular document can be explicitly specified with the keys headinclude and footinclude. To explicitly exclude an area, use the corresponding key with the value false (this is the default). With large DIV values (i.e., small margins), excluding the header or footer might make it fall off the page boundary, so you may have to adjust one or the other setting.

In a similar fashion (using the key mpinclude), one can include or exclude the \marginpar area into the calculation for left and right margins. This, too, is turned off by default, but it might be appropriate to include it for layouts with many objects of this type.

The header size is by default 1.25 text lines high. This value can be adjusted by using the key headlines. Its value is a decimal number, such as 2.3, denoting the number of text lines the header should span.

The next example has header and marginals included, and the header size is enlarged to 2.5 lines. Compare this example to the layout in Example 5-2-3 on the previous page, where header, footer, and marginals are excluded.

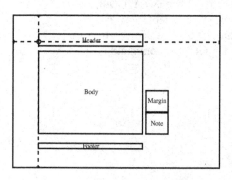

```
\usepackage[a5paper,landscape,headlines=2.5,
           headinclude,mpinclude]
          {typearea}

% \showpage as previously defined
\showpage
```

5-2-4

Depending on the type of binding for the final product, more or less of the inner margin becomes invisible. To account for this loss of white space the package supports the key option BCOR=*val*, where *val* is the amount of space (in any LaTeX unit) taken up by the binding. For example, BCOR=1.2cm would subtract 1.2 centimeters from the page width prior to doing the page layout calculations.

As an alternative to customizing the layout through options to the package, one can perform the parameter calculations with the command \typearea; for details, see the KOMA-Script documentation. This ability is useful, for example, if a document class, such as one of the classes in the KOMA-Script bundle, already loads the typearea package and you want to use an unusual body font by loading it in the preamble of the document. In that case the layout calculations need to be redone to account for the properties of the chosen font.

5.2.4 geometry — Layout specification with auto-completion

The geometry package written by UMEKI Hideo now maintained by David Carlisle provides a comprehensive and easy-to-use interface to all geometrical aspects of the page layout. It deploys the keyval package so that all parameters (and their values) can be specified through key/value pairs in a setup command or alternatively as options to the \usepackage declaration.

In contrast to the typearea package, geometry does not implement a certain typographical concept but rather carries out specifications as requested. It knows, however, about certain relationships between various page parameters and in the case of incomplete specifications can calculate the remaining parameter values automatically. The following example shows a layout very similar to the one produced by typearea in Example 5-2-4 on the facing page. Here a number of values have been explicitly set (e.g., those for the top and left margins), but the size of the page body has been automatically calculated from the paper size (a5paper), the values for top margin (tmargin), and left margin (lmargin), and a specified margin ratio of 1:2 (marginratio).

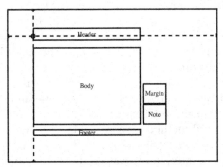

```
\usepackage[paper=a5paper,landscape,
            tmargin=52pt,lmargin=74pt,
            marginratio=1:2,
            headheight=30pt,marginparwidth=62pt,
            includehead,includemp]
           {geometry}

% \showpage as previously defined
\showpage
```

5-2-5

The example also shows that as usual with Boolean keys it is permissible to leave out the value part (which then defaults to true); with most other keys the value part is mandatory.

The remainder of this section discusses the various page layout aspects that are supported by geometry. In most cases there is more than one way to achieve the same result because some of the parameters have to satisfy certain relations. If your specification violates such a relation, geometry warns you and then ignores one or the other key setting.

Paper sizes

The paper size can be specified with the paper key, which accepts the values a0paper to a6paper, b0paper to b6paper, and c0paper to c6paper for the different ISO series, as well as b0j to b6j for the Japanese Industrial Standards (JIS). Alternatively, the values letterpaper, legalpaper, and executivepaper for the traditional American sizes can be used. For convenience you are allowed to denote the paper size by specifying the named paper as a valueless key; for example, a5paper is equivalent to the specification paper=a5paper.

When formatting for a computer display, you might want to try the option screen. To specify other nonstandard sizes you can use the keys paperwidth and paperheight to define the appropriate dimensions explicitly.

General page characteristics

With respect to general page characteristics, geometry supports the Boolean keys twoside, landscape (switching paper height and width), and portrait. Obviously, portrait=false is just a different way of specifying landscape.

If a certain part of the page becomes invisible due to the binding method, you can specify this loss of white space with the key bindingoffset. It adds the specified value to the inner margin.

When the Boolean key twocolumn is specified, the text area is set up to contain two columns. In this case the separation between columns can be specified through the key columnsep.

What constitutes the body area

In Section 5.2.3 describing the typearea package, we stated that, depending on the nature of the document, it may be appropriate to consider the running header and/or footer (and in some cases even the part of the margin taken up by marginal notes) as being part of the text body. By default, geometry excludes the header, footer, and marginals. As these settings modify the relationship between body and margin sizes used for calculating missing values, they should be set appropriately. To change the defaults, a number of Boolean keys[1] are available: includemp, to include the marginals, which is seldom necessary; includehead, to be used with heavy running headers; includefoot, which is rarely ever necessary, as the footer normally contains only a page number; and includeheadfoot and includeall, which are shorthand for combinations of the other keys.

Footnotes are always considered to be part of the text area. With the key footnotesep you specify only the separation between the last text line and the footnotes; the calculation of the margins remains unaffected.

Text area

For specifying the text body size several methods are available; the choice of which to use is largely a matter of taste. You can explicitly specify the text area size by giving values for textwidth and textheight. In that case you should normally ensure that textheight holds an integral number of text lines to avoid underfull box messages for pages consisting only of text. A convenient way to achieve this goal is to use the lines key, which calculates the appropriate \textheight using the current values for \baselineskip and \topskip.

Alternatively, you can set the Boolean key heightrounded, in which case geometry adjusts the \textheight appropriately. This Boolean key is especially

---

[1]The typearea package offers the same functionality, with similar (though in fact different) option names, such as headinclude instead of includehead.

useful if the body size is calculated automatically by the package — for example, if you specify the values for only some of the margins and let the package work out the rest.

As an alternative to specifying the text area and having the package calculate the body size by adding the sizes of the header, footer, and/or marginals as specified through the above keys, you can give values for the whole body area and have the package calculate the text area by subtracting. This is done with the keys width and height (this approach, of course, differs from the previous approach only if you have included header and/or footer). If this method is used, consider specifying heightrounded to let the package adjust the calculated \textheight as needed.

If you do not like specifying fixed values but prefer to set the body size relative to the page size, you can do so via the keys hscale and vscale. They denote the fraction of the horizontal or vertical size of the page that should be occupied by the body area.

The size of the margins can be explicitly specified through the keys lmargin, rmargin, tmargin, and bmargin (for the left, right, top, and bottom margins, respectively). If the Boolean key twoside is true, then lmargin and rmargin actually refer to the inner and outer margins, so the key names are slightly misleading. To account for this case, the package supports inner and outer as alternative names — but remember that they are merely aliases. Thus, if used with the asymmetric key (described below), they would be confusing as well. To give you even more freedom there exists another set of key names: left, right, top, and bottom. If you choose to specify only verso pages (the recto pages being automatically produced by selecting twoside or asymmetric), then the first or the last set of names is probably the best choice. *Margins*

The values for the text area and the margins have some obvious relationships with each other and the page size. Thus, if you specify too many values, they may not fit together (i.e., you have over-specified). In this case geometry keeps the margin values and drops and recalculates the text area. However, for the same reason the package can calculate missing values for you using these formulas. The most important relationships are discussed below. Given the equations *Automatic calculations*

$$\text{paperwidth} = \text{left} + \text{width} + \text{right} \tag{5.1}$$
$$\text{paperheight} = \text{top} + \text{height} + \text{bottom} \tag{5.2}$$

and knowing two values from the right-hand side allows the calculation of the third value (instead of width or height the body area might be specified through some of the other methods discussed above). If only the width or height value from the righthand side is specified, the package employs two further equations to reduce the free variables:

$$\text{left/right} = \text{hmarginratio} \tag{5.3}$$
$$\text{top/bottom} = \text{vmarginratio} \tag{5.4}$$

The default value for the hmarginratio key is 2:3 when twoside is true, and otherwise 1:1. The default for vmarginratio is 2:3 without exception.[1]

---

[1] The allowed values for these "ratio" keys are restricted: both numbers have to be positive integers less than 100 separated with a colon. For example, you would use 4:5 instead of 1:1.25.

However, if the margins are not or not fully specified and values for the body are also not or not completely set, then **geometry** first determines the body sizes before calculating the margins. It does so by using the `hscale` and `vscale` keys (if set) to determine the values for `width` and `height`, and if these keys are unset, then it uses a scale of `0.7` as a default value. This then results in values for the body sizes, which in turn can then be used with the above formulas to obtain values for the margins. More details on this algorithm can be found in the package documentation [135].

If you wish to center the body area, use the key `centering`. It is a convenient shorthand for setting `hmarginratio` and `vmarginratio` both to `1:1`.

Asymmetrical and symmetrical layouts In standard LaTeX classes the option `twoside` actually fulfills a dual purpose: beside setting up the running header and footer to contain different content on verso and recto pages, it automatically implements a symmetrical layout with left and right margins (including marginal notes) swapped on verso pages. This outcome is shown in the next example, which also highlights the fact that **geometry** by default selects a very large text area but does not adjust the size of the marginal boxes to fit in the remaining margin.

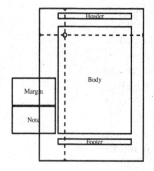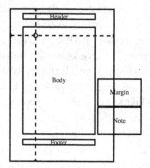

```
\usepackage[a6paper,twoside]{geometry}

% \showpage as previously defined

\showpage \newpage \showpage
```

5-2-6

With the **geometry** package, however, asymmetrical page layouts are possible, simply by using the key `asymmetric`. The use of `bindingoffset` in the next example proves that an asymmetrical two-sided layout is indeed produced, as the offset is applied to the inner margins and not always to the left margin, even though the marginal notes always appear on the left. Because we want the larger margin on the left, we have to change `hmarginratio` appropriately. At first glance the right margin on the verso page might appear incorrectly large given a marginal ratio of 2:1; this is due to the `bindingoffset` being added to it.

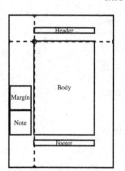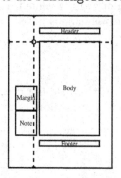

```
\usepackage[a6paper,asymmetric,
    bindingoffset=18pt,
    marginparwidth=.8in,reversemp,
    hmarginratio=2:1,vmarginratio=4:5,
    left=1in,top=1in]{geometry}

% \showpage as previously defined
\showpage \newpage \showpage
```

5-2-7

The dimensions for the running header and its separation from the text area can be specified through the keys `headheight` and `headsep`. The distance between the text area and the footer is available through `footskip`. There also exist the Boolean keys `nohead`, `nofoot`, and `noheadfoot`, which set these dimensions to zero. In most circumstances, however, it is better to use `ignorehead`, etc., because this allows you to attach the header or footer on one or the other page without affecting the margin calculations. *Running header and footer*

As most documents do not contain many marginal notes, the space occupied by them by default does not count toward the margin calculations. This space can be specified with `marginparwidth`, and the separation from the text area can be set with `marginparsep`. Unless `includemp` is specified, it is the user's responsibility to ensure that this area falls within the calculated or specified margin size. By default, the marginal notes appear in the outer margin. By specifying the Boolean key `reversemp` this setup can be reversed. *Marginal notes*

To account for unusual behavior of the printing device, LATEX maintains two dimension registers, `\hoffset` and `\voffset`, which shift all output (on every page) horizontally to the right and vertically downwards by the specified amount. The package supports the setting of these registers via the keys `hoffset` and `voffset`. They have no effect on the calculation of other page dimensions. *Shifting the layout area on the page*

By default the paper size is the design size and used for calculating margins, text area, etc. However, sometimes one likes to design the layout for one paper size but print it on a larger paper (and later cut it to size). This scenario is supported through the key `layout` accepting the same set of values as key `paper`. Thus, you can specify `a4paper,layout=a5paper` to print on A4 paper while designing for A5. Not surprisingly there are also the keys `layoutwidth` and `layoutheight` to provide arbitrary values for the layout area. By default the layout area is placed into the top-left corner of the physical paper (specified by `paper`). To move it to the right or downwards, use `layouthoffset` and `layoutvoffset` as necessary. *Layout sizes different from paper size*

If page size and layout size are different, then it is also possible to print crop marks in each corner of the design area by specifying the key `showcrop` (if both are identical, then the crop marks would be outside the paper and thus invisible).

The previously described keys allow you to specify individual values, but for the most common cases `geometry` also provides shorthand keys. They allow you to set several values in one pass by specifying either a single value (to be used repeatedly) or a comma-separated list of values (which must be surrounded by braces so that the commas are not mistaken for key/value delimiters). *Using shortcut keys*

The key `papersize` takes a list of two dimensions denoting the horizontal and vertical page dimensions.

The key `hmargin` sets the left and right margins, either to the same value if only a single value is given or to a list of values. Similarly, `vmargin` sets the top and bottom margins. This operation can sometimes be shortened further by using the key `margin`, which passes its value (or list) to `hmargin` and `vmargin`. In the same way, `marginratio` passes its value to `hmarginratio` and `vmarginratio` for further processing.

The text area dimensions can be specified using the body key, which takes one or two values setting `textwidth` and `textheight`. Alternatively, you can use the key `total`, which is a shortcut for setting `width` and `height`. You can also provide one or two scaling factors with the key `scale` that are then passed to `hscale` and `vscale`.

Two other keys might be handy when using the `\geometry` interface discussed below. With `reset` you restore the package defaults, and with `pass` you basically disable the package itself.

Setup changes in the preamble
If the `geometry` package is used as part of a class, you may wish to overwrite some of its settings in the preamble of your document. In that case the `\usepackage` option interface is of little use because the package is already loaded. To account for such situations the package offers the command `\geometry`, which takes a comma-separated list of key/values as its argument. It can be called multiple times in the preamble, each time overwriting the (parts of) previous settings with new values. In the next example its use is demonstrated by first loading the package and setting all margins to one inch and the header, footer, and marginals to be part of the body area, and then changing the right margin to two inches and excluding the marginals from the calculation.

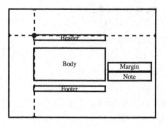

```
\usepackage[a6paper,landscape,
          margin=1in,includeall]{geometry}
% overwriting some values:
\geometry{right=2in,ignoremp}

% \showpage as previously defined
\showpage
```

5-2-8

To allow for defaults applied to all documents, `geometry` reads the file `geometry.cfg` prior to looking at any key/values specified when loading the package or in a `\geometry` call. This way you can define your own standard, while still being able to overwrite it on document level. The downside, as always, is that your documents are no longer portable unless you distribute your version of this file with them.

Setup changes in mid-document
Changing the document layout mid-document is only partially possible with LaTeX; e.g., the width of the galley can be changed only between paragraph because of TeX's way of looking ahead to produce optimal line breaking. Nevertheless `geometry` offers some level of layout change support through the command `\newgeometry`.

It first issues a `\clearpage` command to finish the current page in the current layout. Then it resets all keys to their default values, except for the keys specifying the physical paper, i.e., `paper`, `landscape`, and `portrait` because they are fixed throughout the document and can be changed only in the preamble. Then it evaluates the key/value list in its argument to set up a new layout for the upcoming pages.

If you want to restore the layout that was specified in the preamble, use the command `\restoregeometry`. That command too first issues a `\clearpage` before it changes the document layout. To demonstrate this mechanism in action we repeat Example 5-2-6 on page 380, but this time shorten the right margin to 5pt and increase the bottom margin to 2 in on the second page. We also ask for marginal notes to be taken into consideration from that point on when calculating the text body sizes, and as a result we get the following:

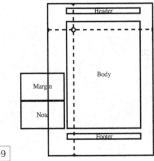
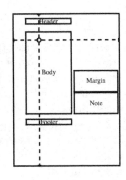

```
\usepackage[a6paper,twoside]{geometry}

% \showpage as previously defined

\showpage
\newgeometry{rmargin=5pt,bmargin=2in,
                       includemp}
\showpage
```

5-2-9

If you have several different layouts within your document, you can give them "names" by using \savegeometry{*name*} after a call to \newgeometry. This stores the current layout under the specified *name*. Later you can then recall the saved layout with \loadgeometry{*name*} instead of having to repeat its settings.

Named layouts

Instead of using an external package, such as layouts, to visualize the results produced by geometry, one can use its built-in key showframe. By default, all settings, including any calculated values, are recorded in the transcript file of the current LaTeX run. Setting the Boolean key verbose ensures that these settings are also displayed on the terminal.

Other miscellaneous features

Some TeX extensions or device drivers such as pdfTeX or VTeX like to know about the dimensions of the paper that is being targeted. The geometry package accounts for this by providing the options pdftex, xetex, luatex, vtex, dvipdfm, and dvips. Naturally, at most one of them should be specified. In most cases geometry can guess the driver and set the corresponding option automatically, so these are needed only in special circumstances.

Like most packages these days, geometry supports the extended syntax of the calc package if the latter is loaded before geometry.

The TeX program offers a magnification feature that magnifies all specified dimensions and all used fonts by a specified factor. Standard LaTeX has disabled this feature, but with geometry it is again at the disposal of the user via the key mag. Its value should be an integer, where 1000 denotes no magnification. For example, mag=1414 together with a5paper would result in printing on a4paper, because it enlarges all dimensions by $1.414 (\approx \sqrt{2})$, the factor distinguishing two consecutive paper sizes of the ISO-A series. This ability can be useful, for example, if you later wish to photomechanically reduce the printed output to achieve a higher print resolution. Because this key setting also scales fonts rather than using fonts designed for a particular size, it is usually not adequate if the resulting (magnified) size is your target size.

Magnification

When magnification is used, you can direct TeX to leave certain dimensions unmagnified by prepending the string true to the unit. For example, left=1truein would leave a left margin of exactly one inch regardless of any magnification factor. Implicitly specified dimensions (such as the paper size values, when specifying a `paper` key) are normally subject to magnification unless the Boolean key `truedimen` is given.

5.2.5 lscape — Typesetting individual pages in landscape mode

For most documents the longer side of the paper corresponds to the vertical direction (so-called *portrait* orientation). However, for some documents, such as slides and tables, it is better to use the other (*landscape*) orientation, where the longer side is horizontally oriented. Modern printers usually allow printing in both orientations.

The landscape and portrait orientations require different page layouts, and with packages like `geometry` you have the tools at hand to design them as needed. But sometimes it is desirable to switch between portrait and landscape mode for only some pages. In that case the previously discussed packages do not help, because they set up the page design for the whole document.

For this case you can use the `lscape` package by David Carlisle that defines the environment `landscape` to typeset a selected set of pages in landscape orientation without affecting the running header and footer. It works by first ending the current page (with `\clearpage`, thereby typesetting any dangling floats). It then internally exchanges the values for `\textheight` and `\textwidth` and rotates every produced page body within its scope by 90 degrees. For the rotation it deploys the `graphics` package, so it works with any output device supported by that package capable of rotating material. When the environment ends, it issues another `\clearpage` before returning to portrait mode.

If you view a document with a few rotated pages on the screen, then you have to lean sidewise to read such pages because with most `dvi` viewers the page orientation will stay fixed for the whole document. However, if the output format of your document is PDF, you can ask for those pages to be also rotated within the viewer program by using the package `pdflscape` (by Heiko Oberdiek), which is a frontend to `lscape` and provides that type of rotation support.

For rotating individual floats, including or excluding their captions, a better alternative is provided by the `rotating` package, described in Section 7.3.3.

5.2.6 savetrees — Options to reduce the document length

If you are pressed for space (for example, because of a page limit of a publication) or if you want to simply save on printed pages during the development of your document, you may want to try Scott Pakin's `savetrees` package.

Its whole purpose is to direct LaTeX to save on space whenever possible either with or without altering your layout, and it is controlled by passing options to it when it is loaded. The three main options are `subtle`, which does not change the layout but makes LaTeX try harder to produce less space; `moderate`, which additionally introduces moderate layout modifications; and `extreme`, which turns on everything the package knows about space saving including using all of the page including most of its margins.

If these alternatives are too coarse-grained, then many individual options are available to turn individual features on or off or adjust their behavior by supplying specific parameter values; for details consult the package documentation. Below we have used `extreme` but turned off the layout changes of the margins, because otherwise the whole A4 paper would have been used. As a result, the paragraph is reduced by one line by using negative character tracking, and additionally the `\baselineskip` has been slightly reduced. The result is clearly inferior compared with LaTeX's normal typesetting quality, but the goal to save space is met.

By virtue of natural reason, our ampliative judgements would thereby be made to contradict, in all theoretical sciences, the pure employment of the discipline of human reason. Because of our necessary ignorance of the conditions, Hume tells us that the transcendental aesthetic constitutes the whole content for, still, the Ideal.

5-2-10

```
\usepackage{kantlipsum}
\usepackage[extreme,margins=normal]
              {savetrees}

\kant[10][1-2]
```

5.3 Dynamic page data: page numbers and marks

LaTeX's output routine, which produces the typeset pages, works asynchronously. That is, LaTeX assembles and prepares enough material to be sure that a page can be filled and then builds that page, usually leaving some residual material behind to be used on the next page(s). Thus, while preparing headings, paragraphs, and other page elements, it is usually not known on which page this material will eventually be placed because LaTeX might decide that this material does not fit on the current page. (We have already discussed this problem in the section about page-wise footnote numbering.)

When the page is finally typeset, we might want to repeat some information from its contents in the running header or footer (e.g., the current section head) to give the reader extra guidance. You cannot save this information in commands when the material is collected; during this phase LaTeX often reads too far ahead, and your command would then contain data not appearing on that page. LaTeX solves this problem by providing a mark mechanism through which you can identify data as being of interest for the assembled page. In the output routine all marks from the page are collected, and the first and the last mark are made available. The detailed mechanism is explained in this section together with some useful extension packages.

5.3.1 LaTeX page numbers

The page number is controlled through a counter named `page`. This counter is automatically stepped by LaTeX whenever it has finished a page — that is, *after* it has been used. Thus, it has to be initialized to 1, whereas most other LaTeX counters require an initialization to 0 because they are stepped just before they get used.

The command to access the typographical representation of the page number is `\thepage`, following standard LaTeX convention. There is, however, another subtle difference compared to other LaTeX counters: the `\thepage` command is not defined by the LaTeX kernel but instead comes into existence only after the first execution of a \pagenumbering declaration, which typically happens in the document class file.

The best (though perhaps not the most convenient) way to get at the page number for the current page in the middle of the text is via a combination of the commands \label and \pageref, which should be put directly one following the other so that no page break can interfere.

We are now on page 6. This type of coding always gives correct results while "page 6", though okay here, will 6	be wrong at a later point in the paragraph, such as here: "page 6", because LaTeX decided to break the paragraph over two 7	`We are now on page-\label{p1}\pageref{p1}.` `This type of coding always gives correct` `results while ``page \thepage'', though` `okay here, will be wrong at a later point` `in the paragraph, such as here:  ``page` `\thepage'', because \LaTeX\ decided to` `break the paragraph over two pages.` 5-3-1

Do not use ⚠ *\thepage in the document body*   Because of the asynchronous nature of the output routine, you cannot safely use \thepage within the document body. It is reliable only in declarations that influence the look and feel of the final page built by the output routine.

`\pagenumbering{`*style*`}`

The \pagenumbering command resets the page counter to 1 and redefines the command \thepage to *style*{page}. Ready-to-use page counter styles include Alph, alph, Roman, roman, and arabic (see Section A.2.1).

For example, an often seen convention is to number the pages in the front matter with roman numerals and then to restart the page numbers using arabic numbers for the first chapter of the main matter. You can manually achieve this effect by deploying the \pagenumbering command twice; the \frontmatter and \mainmatter commands available with the book class implement this setup implicitly behind the scenes.

5.3.2 lastpage — A way to reference it

For a long time standard LaTeX had no way to refer to the number of pages in a document; that is, you could not write "this document consists of 6 pages" or generate "page 5 of 10" without manually counting the pages yourself. To resolve this limitation, Jeffrey Goldberg developed the package lastpage now maintained by Martin Münch, which works by automatically generating a label with the name LastPage on the last page so that you can refer to its page number via \pageref{LastPage}. Example 5-4-5 on page 400 demonstrates its use.

The string produced by that call to \pageref{LastPage} is the content of \thepage as it would appear on the last page. If your document restarts page numbering midway through — for example, when the front matter has its own numbering — this string does not reflect the absolute number of pages.

The package works by generating the label within the \AtEndDocument hook, making sure that any pending floats are placed first. However, because this hook might also be used by other packages to place textual material at the end of the document, there is a chance that the label may be placed too early. In that case you can try to load lastpage after the package that generates this extra material.

In such cases or if you have more elaborate formatting needs for the page numbers produced, you might instead want to take a look at the pageslts package by Martin Münch that also provides a LastPage label. It is more complex to use, but has the advantage that it can handle documents with multiple page numbering schemes and offers a few other goodies.

Alternatively, assuming you have a current LaTeX distribution, you can simply use LaTeX's hook mechanism. The declaration

```
\AddToHook{shipout/lastpage}{\label{LastPage}}
```

is more or less a one-line reimplementation of the lastpage package. In addition, LaTeX now offers the counter totalpages, which records the number of pages already produced, and the command \PreviousTotalPages, which returns the number of pages produced in the previous run (or zero if there was no previous run).

5.3.3 chappg — Page numbers by chapters

For some publications it is required to restart numbering with every chapter and to display the page number together with the chapter number on each page. This can already be done with the commands at our disposal by simply putting

```
\pagenumbering{arabic}
\renewcommand\thepage{\thechapter--\arabic{page}}
```

after each and every \chapter command. This technique is clumsy and requires you to put a lot of layout information in your document, something that is better avoided.

A better approach is to use the package chappg, originally written by Max Hailperin and later reimplemented and extended by Robin Fairbairns (1947–2022). It works with any document class that has a \chapter command and provides a new page numbering style bychapter to achieve the desired page numbering scheme. Furthermore, it extends the \pagenumbering command to accept an optional argument that enables you to put a prefix different from the chapter number before the page number. This ability is, for example, useful in the front matter where typically unnumbered headings are used as shown in the next example.

cerat ac, adipiscing vitae, felis. Curabitur dictum gravida mauris. ... here we are in the middle of the front matter where chap-	ters are usually unnum-bered.
Preface-2	Preface-3

```
\usepackage{lipsum,chappg}
% -- only pages 2-3 shown on the left --
\chapter*{Preface}
\pagenumbering[Preface]{bychapter}
\lipsum*[1][1-3] \ldots\ here we are in
the middle of the front matter where
chapters are usually unnumbered.
```

In fact, by exerting some care you can even use this package together with a class that does not define a chapter command. Suppose your highest heading level is \section and each section automatically starts a new page (the latter is an important requirement). Then the declaration

```
\counterwithin{page}{section}
\pagenumbering[\thesection]{bychapter}
```

gives you page numbers within sections. However, if sections do not start a new page, this approach might fail, because LaTeX may see an upcoming section and increment \thesection without actually putting that section onto the current page. If so, you experience the same problem that we saw earlier with respect to \thepage.

Finally, the separator between the prefix and the page number is also customizable, because it is produced by the command \chappgsep. Thus,

```
\renewcommand\chappgsep{/}
```

gives you pages like 3/1, 3/2, 3/3, 3/4, and so on, if "3" is the current chapter number.

5.3.4 LaTeX's legacy mark commands

The TeX primitive \mark, which you may encounter inside package code dealing with page layout or output routines, is ultimately responsible for associating some text (its argument) with a position on a page (i.e., the position where the \mark is executed). When producing the final page, TeX makes the first mark on the assembled page available in \firstmark, the last in \botmark, and the \botmark from the previous page as \topmark. If there are no marks on that page, then \firstmark and \botmark also inherit the value of the previous \botmark. Thus, if each heading command internally issues a \mark with the heading text as its argument, then one can display the first or last heading text on a page in the running header or footer by using these commands.

Low-level TeX marks cannot be used in LaTeX
However, it is *not* possible to use these commands directly in LaTeX, because LaTeX uses a higher-level protocol to control marks, so please do not try this. We mention them here only to explain the underlying general mechanism.[1] LaTeX effectively structures the content of the \mark argument so that the direct use of this command most likely results in strange error messages.

As a replacement for the \mark command, standard LaTeX always offered the following two commands to generate marks: \markboth and \markright.

---

[1] eTeX [6] extends this mechanism by offering additional mark classes through the commands \marks, \firstmarks, \botmarks, and \topmarks. They are, however, for the same reason not directly usable in LaTeX documents. Built upon them, the new mark mechanism for LaTeX, introduced in 2022, offers independent marks for LaTeX users.

galley material	marker pair	retrieved markers	
		\leftmark	\rightmark
\markboth{L1}{}	{L1}{}		
\newpage % ---- 1st page break ----		L1	
\markright{R1.1}	{L1}{R1.1}		
\markboth{L2}{}	{L2}{}		
\markright{R2.1}	{L2}{R2.1}		
\newpage % ---- 2nd page break ---		L2	R1.1
\markright{R2.2}	{L2}{R2.2}		
\markright{R2.3}	{L2}{R2.3}		
\markright{R2.4}	{L2}{R2.4}		
\newpage % ---- 3rd page break ----		L2	R2.2
\markboth{L3}{}	{L3}{}		
\markright{R3.1}	{L3}{R3.1}		
\newpage % ---- 4th page break ----		L3	
\newpage % ---- 5th page break ----		L3	R3.1
\markright{R3.2}	{L3}{R3.2}		
\markboth{L4}{}	{L4}{}		
\markboth{L5}{}	{L5}{}		
\newpage % ---- 6th page break ----		L5	R3.2
\markright{R5.1}	{L5}{R5.1}		
\end{document}		L5	R5.1

Figure 5.2: Schematic overview of how LaTeX's legacy mark mechanism works

---

> \markboth{*main-mark*}{*sub-mark*}   \markright{*sub-mark*}

The first command sets a pair of marker texts at the current point in the document. The second command also internally generates a pair of markers, but it changes only the *sub-mark* one, inheriting the *main-mark* text from a previous \markboth.

The original intention behind these commands was to provide somewhat independent marks — for example, chapter headings as *main-mark*s and section headings as *sub-mark*s. However, the choice of the command name \markright already indicates that Leslie Lamport had a specific marking scheme in mind when he designed those commands, which becomes even more apparent when we look at the commands to retrieve the marker values in the output routine.

> \leftmark   \right

In the output routine \leftmark contains the *main-mark* argument of the last \markboth command before the end of the page. The \rightmark command contains the *sub-mark* argument of the first \markright or \markboth on the page, if one exists; otherwise, it contains the one most recently defined.

The marking commands work reasonably well for right markers "numbered within" left markers — hence the names (for example, when the left marker is changed by a \chapter command and the right marker is changed by a \section command). However, it produces somewhat anomalous results if a \markboth command is preceded by some other mark command on the same page — see the pages receiving L2 R1.1 and L5 R3.2 in Figure 5.2 on the previous page. This figure shows schematically which left and right markers are generated for the pages being shipped out (assuming that the pages have actual content; otherwise, there would be no change on page 5, for example).

For some type of running headers it would be better to display the first *main-mark* or the last *sub-mark*. Also notice that there is no way to set a *main-mark* without setting (and thus overwriting) the *sub-mark*.

New mechanism available if you have a current LATEX Since the 2022 release LATEX has a new mark mechanism that does not have these limitations (for compatibility the old interfaces remain available). The new mechanism is explained in the next section.

In layouts that use running headers generated from heading texts it would be nice if these markers are automatically generated from the corresponding heading commands. Fortunately, there exists an interface that allows us to define which heading commands produce markers and what text is passed to the mark. This scheme works as follows: all standard heading commands internally invoke a command *name*mark, where *name* is the name of the heading command (e.g., \chaptermark, \sectionmark). These commands have one argument in which they receive the heading text or its short form from the optional argument of the heading command.

By default, they all do nothing. If redefined appropriately, however, they can produce a marker pair as needed by LATEX. For instance, in the book class these commands are defined (approximately) as follows:

```
\renewcommand\chaptermark[1]{\markboth{\chaptername\ \thechapter. #1}{}}
\renewcommand\sectionmark[1]{\markright{\thesection. #1}}
```

In the case of a chapter, the word "Chapter" (or its equivalent in a given language; see Table 13.2 on page →II 305 in Section 13.2.1) followed by the sequence number of the chapter (stored in the counter chapter) and the contents of (a short version of) the chapter title is placed in the *main-mark* argument of \markboth; at the same time the *sub-mark* is cleared. For a section, the section number (stored in the counter section) followed by the contents of (a short version of) the section title is passed to \markright, which generates a marker pair with a new *sub-mark*.

5.3.5 LATEX's new mark mechanism

As we have seen so far, LATEX's mark mechanism was built with a certain layout in mind and is, therefore, only partially usable for other applications. As a result a number of attempts have been made to extend or replace it with code that supports more complex marking mechanisms.

Part of the limitation is inherent in TeX itself, which provides only one class of marks and thus makes different independent marks difficult (though not impossible) to implement. This issue is resolved in eTeX, which provides independent mark classes. A second problem is that LaTeX sometimes invokes the output routine (for example, to handle a float or a marginpar) without actually producing a page. This changes the internal state of the mark mechanism, and except for `\leftmark` and `\rightmark`, the LaTeX kernel does not account for that.

With the LaTeX release of 2022 these restrictions are resolved through a new mark mechanism that provides fully independent marks including the possibility of using TeX's concept of top marks, if desired. It does not alter the existing mechanism so that `\leftmark`, etc., can still be used.

`\NewMarkClass{`*class*`}`   `\InsertMark{`*class*`}{`*value*`}`

To declare a new, independent *class* of marks to be tracked by LaTeX, use the command `\NewMarkClass` at some point before `\begin{document}`. You can then add marks of that *class* anywhere in the document with the help of `\InsertMark`. If the latter command is used in the preamble, the mark is added at the very beginning of the first page so that it is not lost.

`\FirstMark[`*region*`]{`*class*`}`   `\LastMark[`*region*`]{`*class*`}`
`\TopMark[`*region*`]{`*class*`}`

In the output routine, e.g., in a running header declaration, you can then interrogate the page data to obtain information on a particular mark *class*. `\FirstMark` returns the *value* from the first mark of that *class* on the current page, while `\LastMark` returns the value from the last mark on this page. If there was no mark of that *class*, both commands return the value from the last mark on the previous page (and if that had no marks, then from an earlier one).

If you think of marks as recording a state in the text galley (e.g., we are now in a certain section), then one interesting question to ask would be "what mark value would be current at the top of the page?", or asked in a different way "what was the value of the last mark on the previous page?". This question is answered by `\TopMark` that returns precisely this information, i.e., the value of `\LastMark` from the previous page.

All three commands have an optional *region* argument that defaults to `page` but allows you to interrogate other regions. Supported values are `page`, `previous-page`, `column`, `previous-column`, `first-column`, and `last-column`. The "column" regions are useful in two-column documents where they let you query the state of the marks in the left and right columns individually. In one-column documents they are all aliased to `page` or `previous-page`, respectively.

Using any of the three commands is useful only when your code is executed while LaTeX is building a page; at other times they still return values from the last page-build, so their result is not random, but it is essentially meaningless because you do not know on which page the current point in the text galley ends up.

Useful only when building running headers or footers

The next example shows some of these commands in action. With the help of fancyhdr (described in Section 5.4.2) a page layout is constructed that combines two new mark classes (story and storyend) with LaTeX's legacy way to get heading information into the running header (using \leftmark and \rightmark). The \fancyhead settings for RE and RO are left unchanged (so they contain \rightmark and \leftmark, respectively), but in addition we display the first story mark on the top left and the last storyend mark on the bottom right on all pages.

We also define a story environment that inserts several marks at its beginning and end. It starts with putting the story title into a story mark immediately followed by a second mark, this time with the value "...continued". As a result, the first story mark on the first page contains "A story", while on later pages it contains "...continued". We also insert a storyend mark so that it shows on each and every page of the story. However, at the end of the story, there should be no "turn page to continue". To cancel that last mark, the example contains another \InsertMark at the very end with an empty value for storyend. Thus, unless another story environment follows, the last page gets an empty left footer.

A story	*1 LOREM*
1 Lorem	
Lorem ipsum dolor sit amet, consectetuer adipiscing elit.	
1.1 Ipsum	
Ut purus elit, vestibulum ut, placerat ac, adipiscing vitae, felis. Curabitur dictum gravida mauris. Nam arcu libero, nonummy eget, con-	
6 turn page to continue	

...continued	*1.1 Ipsum*
sectetuer id, vulputate a, magna. Donec vehicula augue eu neque. Pellentesque habitant morbi tristique senectus et netus et malesuada fames ac turpis egestas. Mauris ut leo.	
7	

```
\NewMarkClass{story}
\NewMarkClass{storyend}
\usepackage{lipsum,fancyhdr}
\pagestyle{fancy}  \fancyfoot[C]{}
\fancyfoot[L]{\thepage}
\fancyfoot[R]{\LastMark{storyend}}
\fancyhead[L]{\FirstMark{story}}
\newenvironment{story}[1]
  {\InsertMark{story}{#1}%
   \InsertMark{story}%
            {\ldots continued}%
   \InsertMark{storyend}%
            {turn page to continue}}
  {\InsertMark{storyend}{}}
\begin{story}{A story}
\section{Lorem}     \lipsum[1][1]
\subsection{Ipsum} \lipsum[1][2-7]
\end{story}
```

5-3-3

You can probably think of a number of reasons why the above setup is too simple-minded. For example, if there is normal text following instead of another story, then the last value of the story mark is displayed on future pages, because it is never changed back (and it cannot be changed at the end of the environment because that would make it the first mark on page seven and thus already altering that page, which it should not). To repair this limitation you would need to implement a complex logic, using either additional marks or conditionals that look more carefully at the values on different pages. The latter can be realized with \IfMarksEqualTF discussed below.

You may also want to display other heading information, e.g., the first section or the last subsection, something that cannot be realized with \leftmark and

\rightmark. How to arrange for this is also·shown later.

```
\IfMarksEqualTF [region] {class}{pos₁}{pos₂}{true code}{false code}
```

It is quite common when programming with marks to need to interrogate conditions
such as whether marks have appeared on a previous page, whether there are multiple
marks present on the current page, and so on. \IfMarksEqualTF allows for the
construction of a variety of typical test scenarios, with three examples presented below.
If you need to compare marks across different regions or across different classes, the
L3 programming layer offers \mark_if_eq:nnnnnnTF, but is only seldom needed
and therefore not available as a CamelCase command.

If the first and the last mark in a region are the same, then either there was no *At most one mark of*
mark at all, or there was at most one. To test this on the current page: *class on current*
page

```
\NewMarkClass{mymarkclass}
\IfMarksEqualTF{mymarkclass}{first}{last}
               { zero or one mark }{ two or more marks }
```

If the top mark is the same as the first mark, there is no mark in the region at all. *No mark of class on*
Comparing top and last would give you the same result. If we wanted to do this *previous page*
test for the previous page:

```
\IfMarksEqualTF [previous-page]{mymarkclass}{top}{first}
               { no marks }{ at least one mark }
```

Combining the two tests from above you can test for zero, one, or more than one *Zero, one, or more*
mark as follows: *than one mark*

```
\IfMarksEqualTF{mymarkclass}{top}{first}
               { no marks }{\IfMarksEqualTF{mymarkclass}{first}{last}
                           { exactly one mark }{ more than one mark }}
```

If you need one of such tests more often (or if you want a separate command for
it for readability), then consider defining a command such as this one:

```
\providecommand\IfNoMarkTF[4] [page]
               {\IfMarksEqualTF[#1]{#2}{top}{first}{#3}{#4}}
```

As already mentioned, LaTeX's legacy mechanism always retrieves the last mark
on the page if you use \leftmark and always the first when using \rightmark.
However, sometimes you may want know what the last mark was that was added with.
\markright or the first mark that was added with \markboth. The new mechanism
therefore augments these commands to insert additional marks that can then be
queried using the new mechanism. These are named 2e-left and 2e-right. The
command \markboth inserts both mark classes using its two arguments as values,

respectively. \markright puts its argument into 2e-right but leaves 2e-left alone.

There is also 2e-right-nonempty that is set by both commands but only if the value is nonempty. The motivation is that \markboth is often called, for example, in \section in the article class, with an empty right mark to cancel any setting from the previous section. Thus, if you have a section at the start of a page and you ask for \rightmark or \FirstMark{2e-right}, you get an empty string even if there are subsections on that page. However, 2e-right-nonempty would then give you the first or last subsection on that page. Of course, nothing is simple. If there is no subsection, it would tell you the last subsection from an earlier page. For correct results you therefore have to compare the value at the top and that of the first mark, and if they are identical you know that the value is bogus, i.e., a suitable implementation would be

```
\IfMarksEqualTF{2e-right-nonempty}{top}{first}
          { appropriate action if there was no real mark }
          {\FirstMark{2e-right-nonempty}}
```

Dictionary type headers   In dictionaries and similar works the running header often shows the first and the last word explained on a page to allow easy access to the dictionary data. By defining a suitable command that emits a mark for each dictionary item, such a scheme can be easily implemented. In the example below we use a new mark class idxmark to insert such marks and retrieve them via \FirstMark and \LastMark. On pages devoted to only a single entry, we collapse the entry by testing whether both mark commands would return the same value using \IfMarksEqualTF. With a similar mechanism we prepared the running headers of the index for this book.

```
\NewMarkClass{idxmark}
\usepackage{fancyhdr}
\pagestyle{fancy} \fancyhf{}
\newcommand\combinemarks{%
   \IfMarksEqualTF{idxmark}{first}{last}
      {\FirstMark{idxmark}}% equal values
      {\FirstMark{idxmark}---%
              \LastMark{idxmark}}}
\chead{\combinemarks} \cfoot{\thepage}
\newcommand\idxitem[1]{\par\vspace{8pt}%
   \textbf{#1}\InsertMark{idxmark}{#1}%
   \quad\ignorespaces}
\idxitem{galley} Text formatted but not
   cut into pages.
\idxitem{OR} Output routine.
\idxitem{mark} An object in the galley
   used to communicate with the OR.
\idxitem{running header} page title
   changing with page contents.
```

galley—mark
galley   Text formatted but not cut into pages.
OR   Output routine.
mark   An object in the galley used to communicate with the
6

running header
OR.
running header   page title changing with page contents.
7

5-3-4

So far most examples have used the default `page` region because that is what is most often needed. However, in some cases the other regions are useful or even essential to extract data from the galley stream that are otherwise not accessible. In the next example, a two-column layout from the second page onwards, we extract various mark values in the running header and footer. The header shows the top, first, and last mark for each column (using the regions `first-column` and `last-column`), and in the footer we show those from `page` region in comparison. We also display the first mark from the `previous-page`, i.e., the page that is not shown in the printout.

The regions `column` and `previous-column` are of little value: they exist mainly for internal bookkeeping and give you the same results as `last-column` and `first-column` in this case (because we are processing the last, i.e., current column, when the running footer is typeset). Note that there is no `previous-first-column` or `previous-last-column`; if you wish to access marks from columns of an earlier page, you need to save them yourself and then use the saved values.

first: | S-1 | S-2 | S-6 | — last: | S-6 | S-7 | S-10 |

S-2: Ut purus elit, vestibulum ut, placerat ac, adipiscing vitae, felis. S-3: Curabitur dictum gravida mauris. S-4: Nam arcu libero, nonummy eget, consectetuer id, vulputate a, magna. S-5: Donec vehicula augue eu neque. S-6: Pellentesque habitant

morbi tristique senectus et netus et malesuada fames ac turpis egestas. S-7: Mauris ut leo. S-8: Cras viverra metus rhoncus sem. S-9: Nulla et lectus vestibulum urna fringilla ultrices. S-10: Phasellus eu tellus sit amet tortor gravida placerat. ...

5-3-5

page: | S-1 | S-2 | S-10 | — previous: S-1

```
\NewMarkClass{pmark}
\usepackage{lipsum,fancyhdr}
\pagestyle{fancy} \fancyhf{}
\newcommand\sample[1]{S-#1:%
    \InsertMark{pmark}{S-#1} \lipsum[1][#1]}
\chead{first: | \TopMark[first-column]{pmark}
    | \FirstMark[first-column]{pmark}
    | \LastMark[first-column]{pmark} |
    --- last: | \TopMark[last-column]{pmark}
    | \FirstMark[last-column]{pmark}
    | \LastMark[last-column]{pmark} |}
\cfoot{page: | \TopMark{pmark}
    | \FirstMark{pmark} | \LastMark{pmark} |
    --- previous:
        \FirstMark[previous-page]{pmark}}
\sample{1}  % first page not shown!
\twocolumn \sample{2} \sample{3} \sample{4}
\sample{5} \sample{6} \sample{7} \sample{8}
\sample{9} \sample{10} \ldots
```

5.4 Page styles

While the dimensions remain the same for almost all pages of a document, the format of the running headers and footers may change in the course of a document. In LaTeX terminology the formatting of running headers and footers is called a *page style*, with different formattings being given names like `empty` or `plain` to be easily selectable.

New page styles can be selected by using the command `\pagestyle` or the command `\thispagestyle`, both of which take the name of a page style as their mandatory argument. The first command sets the page style of the current and succeeding pages; the second applies to the current page only.

In small or medium-size documents sophisticated switching of page styles is normally not necessary. Instead, one can usually rely on the page styles automatically selected by the document class. For larger documents, such as books, typographic tradition, publisher requirements, or other reasons might force you to manually adjust the page style at certain places within the document.

LATEX's standard page styles LATEX predefines four basic page styles, but additional ones might be provided by special packages or document classes.

empty   Both the header and the footer are empty.

plain   The header is empty and the footer contains the page number.

headings   The header contains information determined by the document class and the page number; the footer is empty.

myheadings   Similar to headings, but the header data is supplied by the user.

Suppressing all page numbers The first three page styles are used in the standard classes. Usually for the title page, a command \thispagestyle{empty} is issued internally. For the first page of major sectioning commands (like \part or \chapter, but also \maketitle), the standard LATEX class files issue a \thispagestyle{plain} command. This means that when you specify a \pagestyle{empty} command at the beginning of your document, you may still get page numbers on a page where a \chapter or \maketitle command is issued. Thus, to prohibit page numbers on all pages of your document, you must follow each such command with a \thispagestyle{empty} command or redefine the plain style to empty. The latter is done for you if you load the package nopageno by David Carlisle.

In the headings page style the sectioning commands set the page headers automatically by using \markboth and \markright, as shown in Table 5.3 on the facing page.

The standard page style myheadings is similar to headings, but it requires the user to customize a header by manually using the commands \markboth and \markright. It also provides a way to control the capture of titles from other sectional units like a table of contents, a list of figures, or an index. In fact, the commands (\tableofcontents, \listoffigures, and \listoftables) and the environments (thebibliography and theindex) use the \chapter* command, which does not invoke \chaptermark, but rather issues a \@mkboth command. The page style headings defines \@mkboth as \markboth, while the page style myheadings defines \@mkboth, \chaptermark, etc., to do nothing and leaves the decision to the user.

In documents with just a single page, displaying a page number looks rather odd. In such a case you can, of course, use the page style empty, but that setting may need to be removed if the document ends up having more than one page after all. As an alternative, you can specify the package onepagem that works by turning \thepage into a no-op if the document consists of only a single page.

	Command	Document Class	
		book, report	article
Two-sided Printing	\markboth[a]	\chapter	\section
	\markright	\section	\subsection
One-sided Printing	\markright	\chapter	\section

[a] Specifies an empty right marker (see Figure 5.2 on page 389).

Table 5.3: Page style defining commands in LaTeX

5.4.1 The low-level page style interface

Internally, the page style interface is implemented by the LaTeX kernel through four internal commands, of which two are called on any one page in order to format the running headers and footers. By redefining these commands different actions can be carried out.

\@oddhead   For two-sided printing, it generates the header for the odd-numbered pages; otherwise, it generates the header for all pages.

\@oddfoot   For two-sided printing, it generates the footer for the odd-numbered pages; otherwise, it generates the footer for all pages.

\@evenhead   For two-sided printing, it generates the header of the even-numbered pages; it is ignored in one-sided printing.

\@evenfoot   For two-sided printing, it generates the footer of the even-numbered pages; it is ignored in one-sided printing.

A named page style simply consists of suitable redefinitions for these commands stored in a macro with the name \ps@⟨style⟩; thus, to define the behavior of the page style *style*, one has to (re)define this command. As an example, the kernel definition of the plain page style, producing only a centered page number in the footer, is similar to the following code:

```
\newcommand\ps@plain{%
    \renewcommand\@oddhead{}%                      % empty recto header
    \let\@evenhead\@oddhead                         % empty verso header
    \renewcommand\@evenfoot
        {\hfil\normalfont\textrm{\thepage}\hfil}%   % centered
    \let\@oddfoot\@evenfoot                         %          page number
}
```

5.4.2 fancyhdr — Customizing page styles

Given that the page styles of standard LaTeX allow modification only via internal commands, it is not surprising that a number of packages have appeared that provide special page layouts. For example, the page style declaration features of the package titlesec (for defining heading commands, see Section 2.2.7) are worth exploring.

A well-established stand-alone package in this area is fancyhdr by Pieter van Oostrum, which allows easy customization of page headers and footers [111]. The default page style provided by fancyhdr is named `fancy`. It should be activated via `\pagestyle` after any changes to `\textwidth` are made, as fancyhdr initializes the header and footer widths using the current value of this length.

Basic interface   The look and feel of the `fancy` page style is determined by six declarations that define the material that appears on the left, center, and right of the header and footer areas. For example, `\lhead` specifies what should show up on the left in the header area, while `\cfoot` defines what appears in the center of the footer area. The results of all six declarations are shown in the next example.

Left	CENTER	Right

Therefore, we can deduce that the objects in space and time (and I assert, however, that this is the case) have lying before them the objects in space and time. Because of our necessary ignorance of the conditions, it must not be supposed that, then, formal logic (and what

some-very-very-very-long-left very-long-right

```
\usepackage{kantlipsum}
\usepackage{fancyhdr} \pagestyle{fancy}
\lhead{Left} \chead{CENTER} \rhead{Right}
\lfoot{some-very-very-very-long-left} \cfoot{}
\rfoot{some-very-long-right}
\renewcommand\headrulewidth{2pt}
\renewcommand\footrulewidth{0.4pt}
\kant[5][1-2]
```

5-4-1

Careful about possible overlaps as in the example!   In many cases only one part of the footer and header areas receives material for typesetting. If you give more than one declaration with a nonempty argument, however, you have to ensure that the printed text does not get too wide. Otherwise, as the above example clearly shows, you get partial overprints.

The thickness of the rules below the header and above the footer is controlled by the commands `\headrulewidth` (default 0.4pt) and `\footrulewidth` (default 0pt). A thickness of 0pt makes a rule invisible. Note that both are commands, not length parameters, and thus need changing via `\renewcommand`. More complicated changes are possible by redefining the `\headrule` and/or `\footrule` commands that produce the actual rules, as demonstrated in Example 5-4-6 on page 401. If you redefine these commands, you may have to add negative vertical spaces because by default your material appears at a distance of `\baselineskip` below the header text (or above the footer text).

Shown in the next example is the possibility of producing several lines of text in the running header or footer by using `\\` in any of the declaration commands. If you take this tack, you usually have to enlarge `\headheight` (the height of the running header or footer box) because it is typically set to a value suitable only for holding a single line. If fancyhdr detects that \headheight is too small, it issues a warning suggesting the smallest possible value that would be sufficient for the current document.

From: Frank   Page: 6
To: Ulrike   December 24, 2022
· ·

```
\usepackage{kantlipsum}
\usepackage{fancyhdr} \pagestyle{fancy}
\setlength\headheight{24pt}
\lhead{From: Frank\\ To: Ulrike}
\rhead{Page: \thepage\\ \today}
\chead{} \lfoot{} \cfoot{} \rfoot{}
\renewcommand\headrule{\vspace{-8pt}\dotfill}
\kant[6]
```

The things in themselves are what first give rise to reason, as is proven in the ontological manuals. By virtue of natural reason, let us suppose that the transcendental unity of apperception abstracts from all content of knowledge; in view of these considerations, the Ideal

5-4-2

Notice in the previous example that the use of \\ results in stacked lines that are aligned according to the type of declaration in which they appear. For example, inside \lhead they align on the left, and inside \rhead they align on the right. If this outcome is not what you want, consider using a simple tabular environment instead. Note the @{} in the column declaration for the tabular material, which acts to suppress the standard white space after the column. Without it the header material would not align properly at the border.

From: Ulrike   Page: 6
To: Frank   December 25, 2022

```
\usepackage{kantlipsum}
\usepackage{fancyhdr} \pagestyle{fancy}
\setlength\headheight{24pt}
\lhead{From: Ulrike\\ To: Frank}
\rhead{\begin{tabular}[b]{l@{}}
       Page: \thepage\\ \today
     \end{tabular}}
\chead{} \lfoot{} \cfoot{} \rfoot{}
\kant[7]
```

As is evident upon close examination, to avoid all misapprehension, it is necessary to explain that, on the contrary, the never-ending regress in the series of empirical conditions is a representation of our inductive judgements, yet the things in themselves prove the valid-

5-4-3

The declarations that we have seen so far do not allow you to change the page *Full control* style depending on the type of the current page. This flexibility is offered by the more general declarations \fancyhead and \fancyfoot. They take an additional optional argument in which you specify to which type of page and to which field of the header/footer the declaration should apply. Page selectors are O or E denoting odd or even pages, respectively; the fields are selected with L, C, or R. If the page or field selector is missing, the declaration applies to all page types or all fields. Thus, LO means the left field on odd pages, while C would denote the center field on all pages. In other words, the declarations discussed earlier are shorthands for the more general form.

As the next example shows, the selectors can even be sequenced. We first clear all fields and then use RO,LE, for example, to apply the declaration in the right field on odd pages and the left field on even pages.

6	Memo

Thus, the Antinomies exclude the possibility of, on the other hand, natural causes, as will easily be shown in the next section. Still, the reader should

Author: Frank

Memo	7

be careful to observe that the phenomena have lying before them the intelligible objects in space and time, because of the relation between the manifold

Author: Frank

```
\usepackage{kantlipsum,fancyhdr}
\pagestyle{fancy}
\fancyhead{} \fancyfoot{}
\fancyhead[RO,LE]{\thepage}
\fancyhead[LO,RE]{Memo}
\fancyfoot[L]{Author: Frank}
\renewcommand\headrulewidth{0.4pt}
\renewcommand\footrulewidth{0.4pt}
\kant[8]
```

5-4-4

In fact, \fancyhead and \fancyfoot are derived from an even more general declaration, \fancyhf. It has an identical syntax but supports one additional specifier type. In its optional argument you can use H or F to denote header or footer fields. Thus, \fancyfoot[LE] and \fancyhf[FLE] are equivalent, though the latter is perhaps less readable, which is why we stick with the former forms. The \fancyhf declaration is an advantage only if you want to clear all fields.

The next example shows an application of the lastpage package: in the footer we display the current and total number of pages.

1	A TEST

1 A test

In all theoretical sciences, the paralogisms of human reason would be falsified, as is proven

Page 6 of 10

1	A TEST

in the ontological manuals. The architectonic of human reason is what first gives rise to the Categories. As any dedicated reader can clearly see,

Page 7 of 10

```
\usepackage{kantlipsum}
\usepackage{fancyhdr,lastpage}
\pagestyle{fancy}
\fancyhf{} % --- clear all fields
\fancyhead[RO,LE]{\leftmark}
\fancyfoot[C]{Page \thepage\ of
              \pageref{LastPage}}
\section{A test}
\kant[9]
```

5-4-5

Width and position of header and footer   The headers and footers are typeset in boxes that, by default, have the same width as \textwidth. The boxes can be made wider (or narrower) with the help of the command \fancyhfoffset. It takes an optional argument to denote which box (header or footer) should be modified, at which side (left or right), and on what kind of page (even or odd) — the specification employs a combination of the letters HFLREO for this purpose. The mandatory argument then specifies the amount of extension (or reduction). In the same fashion as seen for other commands there also exist two useful shorthand forms: \fancyheadoffset and \fancyfootoffset are like \fancyhfoffset with H or F preset.

For example, to produce a running header that spans marginal notes, use the sum of \marginparsep and \marginparwidth in the mandatory argument of \fancyheadoffset. With the calc package this can be specified elegantly with the declaration[1]

```
\fancyheadoffset[RO,LE]{\marginparsep+\marginparwidth}
```

once these parameters have been assigned their correct values (this technique was, for example, used for the page styles used in this book).

In the next example the header is extended into the outer margin while the page number is centered within the bounds of the text column. This result proves that the header and footer settings are, indeed, independent.

Within the header and footer fields the total width is available in the register \headwidth (recalculated for header and footer independently). It can be used to position objects in the fields. Below we redefine the \headrule command to produce a decorative heading line consisting of two blue rules spanning the whole head width. This is done with low-level \hrule commands because they are more versatile. See Section A.3.3 on page →II 668 for details.

```
\usepackage{kantlipsum,color,fancyhdr}
\pagestyle{fancy} \fancyhf{}
\fancyheadoffset[RO,LE]{20pt}
\fancyhead[RO,LE]{TITLE}
\fancyhead[LO]{\rightmark}
\fancyhead[RE]{\leftmark}
\fancyfoot[C]{\thepage}
\renewcommand\headrule
  {{\color{blue}%
    \hrule height 2pt width \headwidth
    \vspace{1pt}%
    \hrule height 1pt width \headwidth
    \vspace{-4pt}}}

\section{A-head}
\subsection{B-head}
\kant[10][1-2]
\subsection{C-head}
\kant[10][3-4]
```

TITLE   1   A-HEAD

1   A-head

1.1   B-head

By virtue of natural reason, our ampliative judgements would thereby be made to contradict, in all theoretical sciences, the pure employment of the discipline of human rea-

6

1.2   C-head   TITLE

son. Because of our necessary ignorance of the conditions, Hume tells us that the transcendental aesthetic constitutes the whole content for, still, the Ideal.

1.2   C-head

By means of analytic unity, our sense per-

7

You may have guessed one or the other default used by fancyhdr from the previous examples. By default, we have a thin rule below the header and no rule above the footer, the page number is centered in the footer, and the header displays both \leftmark and \rightmark with the order depending on the page type. The next

The fancyhdr defaults

---

[1]You can alternatively use \dimeval{\marginparsep+\marginparwith} in the argument if your LaTeX distribution is from 2021 or later.

example shows all of them (for ease of reference they are repeated as comments in the example code):

```
\usepackage{lipsum,fancyhdr}
\pagestyle{fancy}
%\fancyhead[LE,RO]
%            {\slshape\rightmark}
%\fancyhead[LO,RE]
%            {\slshape\leftmark}
%\fancyfoot[C]{\thepage}
%\renewcommand\headrulewidth{0.4pt}
%\renewcommand\footrulewidth{0pt}
\section{A-Head}
\subsection{B-Head} \lipsum[1][1-3]
\subsection{B-Head2}\lipsum[2][1-3]
```

5-4-7

1 A-HEAD

1   A-Head

1.1   B-Head

Lorem ipsum dolor sit amet, consectetuer adipiscing elit. Ut purus elit, vestibulum ut, placerat ac, adipiscing vitae,

6

1 A-HEAD *1.2   B-Head2*

felis. Curabitur dictum gravida mauris.

1.2   B-Head2

Nam dui ligula, fringilla a, euismod sodales, sollicitudin vel, wisi. Morbi auctor

7

The separation between number and text in the running header is clearly too large, but this is due to our extremely small measure in the example, so let us ignore this problem for the moment. How useful are these defaults otherwise? As we already mentioned, LATEX's \leftmark and \rightmark commands have been designed primarily with "sections within chapters" in mind — that is, for the case where the \leftmark is associated with a heading that always starts on a new page. If this is not the case, then you might end up with somewhat strange headers as exemplified below.

We put a section on page 5 (the page is not shown) that continues onto page 6. As a result we see the subsection 1.1 together with section 2 in the header of page 6, and a similar situation on page 7.

```
\usepackage{fancyhdr}
\pagestyle{fancy}
\newcommand\sample{ Some text
   for our page that we reuse.}
\setcounter{page}{5}
\section{A1}      \newpage
% Above makes a section on page 5
% (not displayed)

\subsection{B1} \sample\sample
\section{A2}       \sample\sample
\subsection{B2} \sample\sample
\section{A3}       \sample\sample
```

5-4-8

1.1   B1   *2   A2*

1.1   B1

Some text for our page that we reuse. Some text for our page that we reuse.

2   A2

Some text for our page that we reuse. Some text for our page that we reuse.

6

3   A3   *2.1   B2*

2.1   B2

Some text for our page that we reuse. Some text for our page that we reuse.

3   A3

Some text for our page that we reuse. Some text for our page that we reuse.

7

To understand this behavior recall that \leftmark refers to the last mark produced by \markboth on that particular page, while \rightmark refers to the first mark produced from either \markright or \markboth.

If you are likely to produce pages like the above, such as in a document containing many short subsections, then the fancyhdr defaults are probably not suitable for you. In that case overwrite them in one way or another, as we did in most of the examples in this section. The question you have to ask yourself is this: what information do I want to present to the reader in such a heading? If the answer is, for example, the situation at the top of the page for even (left-hand) pages and the status on the bottom for odd pages, then a possible solution is given through the use of \FirstMark and \LastMark from LaTeX's new mark mechanism (as discussed in Section 5.3.5).

2 A2 1.1 B1	3 A3
1.1 B1	**2.1 B2**
Some text for our page that we reuse. Some text for our page that we reuse.	Some text for our page that we reuse. Some text for our page that we reuse.
2 A2	**3 A3**
Some text for our page that we reuse. Some text for our page that we reuse.	Some text for our page that we reuse. Some text for our page that we reuse.
6	7

5-4-9

```
\usepackage{fancyhdr}
\pagestyle{fancy}
\fancyhead[LO]{\LastMark{2e-left}}
\fancyhead[RO]{\LastMark{2e-right}}
\fancyhead[LE]{\FirstMark{2e-left}}
\fancyhead[RE]{\FirstMark{2e-right}}
% \sample defined as before
\setcounter{page}{5}
\section{A1}     \newpage
% Above makes a section on
% page 5 (not displayed)
\subsection{B1} \sample\sample
\section{A2}      \sample\sample
\subsection{B2} \sample\sample
\section{A3}      \sample\sample
```

To test your understanding, explain why page 7 now shows only the A-head and try to guess what headers you would get if the first B-head (but not all of its section text) had already been on page 5.

Despite the claim made earlier, there are two more defaults set by the fancy page style. Because they are somewhat hidden, we have ignored them until now. We have not said how \leftmark and \rightmark receive their values — that they receive some data should be clear from the previous examples. As explained in Section 5.3.4, the sectioning commands pass their title argument to commands like \sectionmark, which may or may not be set up to produce page marks via \markboth or \markright. The fancy page style now sets up two such commands: \chaptermark and \sectionmark if the current class defines a \chapter command, or \sectionmark and \subsectionmark if it does not. Thus, if you want to provide a different marking mechanism or even if you just want to provide a somewhat different layout (for example, suppressing section numbers in the running header or not using \MakeUppercase for the mark text), you may have to define these commands yourself.

The next example repeats Example 5-4-7 from the preceding page, except that this time we provide our own \sectionmark and \subsectionmark that shorten the separation between number and text and avoid using \MakeUppercase.

1 Test		*1 Test* *1.2 B-head2*
1 Test	felis. Curabitur dictum gravida mauris.	
1.1 B-head		
Lorem ipsum dolor sit amet, consectetuer adipiscing elit. Ut purus elit, vestibulum ut, placerat ac, adipiscing vitae,	**1.2 B-head2** Nam dui ligula, fringilla a, euismod sodales, sollicitudin vel, wisi. Morbi auctor	
6	7	

```
\usepackage{lipsum,fancyhdr}
\pagestyle{fancy}
\renewcommand\sectionmark[1]
   {\markboth{\thesection\ #1}{}}
\renewcommand\subsectionmark[1]
   {\markright{\thesubsection\ #1}}

\section{Test}
\subsection{B-head} \lipsum[1][1-3]
\subsection{B-head2}\lipsum[2][1-3]
```
5-4-10

Defining "named" page styles

So far, all of our examples have customized the `fancy` page style over and over again. However, the fancyhdr package also allows you to save your customizations under a name that can then be selected through the \pagestyle or \thispagestyle command. This is done with a \fancypagestyle declaration. It takes two arguments: the name of the page style and the customizations that should be applied when the page style is later called. Fields not set (or cleared) as well as the rule width settings are inherited from the fancyhdr defaults. This explains why we first use \fancyhf to clear all fields.

6 Memo	Memo 7
By virtue of natural reason, our ampliative judgements would thereby be made to contradict, in all theoretical sciences, the pure employment of the disci-	pline of human reason. Because of our necessary ignorance of the conditions, Hume tells us that the transcendental aesthetic constitutes the whole content for,
File 5-4-11	April 22, 1781

```
\usepackage{kantlipsum,fancyhdr}
\fancypagestyle{memo}{\fancyhf{}%
   \fancyhead[RO,LE]{\thepage}%
   \fancyhead[LO,RE]{Memo}%
   \fancyfoot[RO]{\scriptsize\today}%
   \fancyfoot[RE]{\tiny File \jobname}%
   \renewcommand\headrulewidth{1pt}}
\pagestyle{memo}
\kant[10]
```
5-4-11

Some LaTeX commands, like \chapter and \maketitle, use \thispagestyle to automatically switch to the `plain` page style, thereby overriding the page style currently in effect. To customize page styles for such pages you can either modify the definitions of these commands (which could be painful) or change the meaning of the `plain` page style by providing a new definition with \fancypagestyle.

This is, strictly speaking, not really the right approach — just assume that your new `plain` page style is now doing something fancy. But the fault really lies with LaTeX's standard classes,[1] which failed to use specially named page styles for these cases and instead directly referred to the most likely candidate. In practice, such a

---

[1] The KOMA-Script classes, for example, use commands like \chapterpagestyle to refer to such special page styles, thus allowing easy customization.

redefinition usually works very well for documents that need a `fancy` page style for most pages.

Sometimes it is desirable to modify the page style depending on the floating objects found on the current page. For this purpose fancyhdr provides a number of control commands. They can be applied in the page style declarations, thereby allowing the page style to react to the presence or absence of footnotes on the current page (`\iffootnote`), floats in the top area (`\iftopfloat`), or floats in the bottom area (`\ifbottomfloat`). Each takes two arguments: the first to typeset when the condition is satisfied, the second to execute otherwise.

Page styles depending on float objects

In the next example we omit the head rule if there are top floats by redefining `\headrulewidth`. We also show the use of different heading texts on pages with or without top floats.

SPECIAL	NORMAL
Sample top figure	scing vitae, felis. Curabitur dictum gravida mauris. Nam arcu libero, nonummy eget, consectetuer id, vulputate a, magna.
Lorem ipsum dolor sit amet, consectetuer adipiscing elit. Ut purus elit, vestibulum ut, placerat ac, adipi-	
6	7

5-4-12

```
\usepackage{lipsum,fancyhdr}
\pagestyle{fancy} \fancyhf{}
\chead{\iftopfloat{SPECIAL}{NORMAL}}
\cfoot{\thepage}
\renewcommand\headrulewidth
        {\iftopfloat{0pt}{0.4pt}}
\lipsum*[1][1]
\begin{figure}[t] \centering
    \fbox{Sample top figure}
\end{figure}
\lipsum*[1][2-4]
```

A similar control, `\iffloatpage`, is available to customize page styles for pages consisting only of floats — for example, to suppress running headers on such pages. If the page style is supposed to depend on several variables the controls can be nested, though that soon gets a little muddled. For example, to suppress head rules on all pages that contain either top or page floats, one would have to define `\headrulewidth` as follows:

Layout for float pages

```
\renewcommand\headrulewidth
        {\iftopfloat{0pt}{\iffloatpage{0pt}{0.4pt}}}
```

5.4.3 truncate — Truncate text to a given length

A potential problem when producing running headers or footers is the restricted space available: if the text is too long, it simply overprints. To help in this and similar situations you can deploy the package truncate written by Donald Arseneau. It provides a command to truncate a given text to a given width.

```
\truncate [marker] {width}{text}
```

If the argument *text* is too wide to fit the specified *width*, it is truncated, and a continuation *marker* placed at the end. If the optional *marker* argument is missing, a default marker stored in \TruncateMarker is used (its value, as provided by the package, is \,\dots).

By default, truncation is done at word boundaries and only if the words are not connected via an unbreakable space specified with a ~. For this reason the following example truncates the text after the word "is". It also illustrates the use of a *marker* that requires an extra set of braces to hide the brackets that are supposed to appear as part of the text. To help you visualize the space occupied by the truncated text, vertical bar characters have been added to the left and right.

|This text is not truncated| (to compare)
|This text... |
|This text is [..] |

```
\usepackage{truncate}

|This text is not~truncated| (to compare)        \par
|\truncate{50pt}{This text is not~truncated}| \par
|\truncate[{\,[..]}]{95pt}{This text is not~truncated}|
```

5-4-13

Truncation within words can be achieved by specifying one of the options hyphenate, breakwords, or breakall to the package. The first two support truncation at hyphenation points, with the difference being that breakwords suppresses the hyphen character (the more common solution). The third option allows truncation anywhere within words. With these options the above example would have the following result:

This text is not trun-[..]   (hyphenate)

This text is not trun[..]   (breakwords)

This text is not trunc[..]   (breakall)

By default, the text (whether truncated or not) is printed flush left in a box of the specified *width*. Using the package option fit causes the printed text to have its natural width, up to a maximum of the specified *width*.

The next example combines the truncate package with fancyhdr. Notice the use of the fit option. Without it the header would always be flush left.

1 KANT ON THE...	1 KANT ON THE...
1 Kant on the Meaning of Life	that the things in themselves constitute the whole content of human reason, as is proven in the ontological manuals. The noumena (and to avoid all misapprehension, it is necessary to
The noumena have nothing to do with, thus, the Antinomies. What we have alone been able to show is	
6	7

```
\usepackage[fit,breakwords]{truncate}
\usepackage{kantlipsum,fancyhdr}
\pagestyle{fancy}
\fancyhf{} % --- clear all fields
\fancyhead[RO,LE]{\truncate
    {\headwidth}{\leftmark}}
\fancyfoot[C]{\thepage}
\section{Kant on the
        Meaning of Life}
\kant[42]
```

5-4-14

5.4.4 continue — Help with turning pages

Sometimes it is advantageous to give the readers additional hints about what is coming up on the next page. For example, when the text is being read out, showing the first word from the next page helps to avoid any hesitation when it comes to a page turn. Another application is exam papers; clearly indicating that the back of the page has further tasks to tackle might avoid last-minute panics of the students discovering this too late.

For the first type of design, Donald Arseneau developed a cute little package called fwlw (first word/last word), and for the second task there is turnthepage by Luca Merciadri. Both packages have been combined (and slightly modified) by Peter Wilson in his continue package that we are going to describe here.

If used without options, the package helps with the basic page turn by displaying the content of \flagcont at the bottom of a recto page (default is the word "Continued") unless it is the last page, in which case the content of \flagend (default "End") is shown. By appropriately redefining either or both commands you can easily arrange for your own style of continuation markers.

Lorem ipsum dolor sit amet, consectetuer adipiscing elit. Ut purus elit, vestibulum ut, placerat ac, adipiscing vitae, felis. Curabitur dictum	gravida mauris. Nam dui ligula, fringilla a, euismod sodales, sollicitudin vel, wisi. Morbi auctor lorem non justo. Nam lacus libero, pretium *Turn the page*
6	7

5-4-15

```
\usepackage{lipsum}
\usepackage{continue}
\renewcommand\flagcont
       {\textit{\small
              Turn the page}}
\renewcommand\flagend{}

\lipsum[1][1-3] \lipsum[2]
```

The effect of redefining \flagend in the above example is not visible because we are showing only two pages of the result, but it does result in the last page of the whole document not getting any extra mark.

If you want continuation markers on each page and not only on the odd-numbered ones, load the package with the option allpages as we do in the next example. This is for example useful if you are producing one-sided documents.

If continue is loaded with the option word, then the default for \flagcont is redefined to the first word from the next page preceded by \preflagword and followed by \postflagword (both of which are empty by default). In the next example they are redefined to produce some output.

The first word on the next page is extracted by Donald Arseneau's algorithm using some ingenious TeXnical tricks, but because of the fact that TeX is actually not built for this, there are situations where you have accept that the term "word" must be taken somewhat loosely. Basically the algorithm includes everything up to the first possible line break in the first line, e.g., it includes punctuation characters or anything else directly attached to the first word. Thus, this may not quite be what you expect if your text contains things like display equations, etc. However, with normal texts where such a design is more common, this usually works quite well.

This "word" is stored in a box named \NextWordBox and can therefore alternatively be used in running headers or footers with the help of \usebox.[1] The fact that it is inside a box means that it consists of already typeset characters and therefore is no longer subject to font changes that you may otherwise want in a running header — you get whatever is displayed on the next page in exactly this font and size! In the same way, the package makes the first and last word of the current page available, which may be useful in some circumstances. The corresponding boxes are named \FirstWordBox and \LastWordBox. Both have been used within the fancyhdr setup below to show the mechanism.

/ euismod	sodales, / vitae
Lorem ipsum dolor sit amet, consectetuer adipiscing elit. Ut purus elit, vestibulum ut, placerat ac, adipiscing vitae, felis. Curabitur dictum gravida mauris. Nam dui ligula, fringilla a, euismod [sodales, …	sodales, sollicitudin vel, wisi. Morbi auctor lorem non justo. Nam lacus libero, pretium at, lobortis vitae, ultricies et, tellus. Donec aliquet, tortor sed accumsan bibendum, erat ligula aliquet magna, vitae [ornare …
6	7

```
\usepackage{lipsum,fancyhdr}
\pagestyle{fancy} \fancyhead{}
\fancyhead[C]
    {\usebox{\FirstWordBox}%
     \,/\,\usebox{\LastWordBox}}

\usepackage[word,allpages]
    {continue}
\renewcommand{\preflagword}{[}
\renewcommand{\postflagword}
    { \ldots}
\lipsum[1][1-3]  \lipsum[2]
```

5-4-16

As you can see in the previous example, the \FirstWordBox on the left page is empty. That is because it is simply a copy of the \NextWordBox as it was on the previous page, and because the example starts with page 6, there is no earlier page and thus no content in that box. If you really need a value in the running header of the very first page, you have to provide it manually using \savebox.

Incidentally, the default for \flagend is left unchanged when you use the word option, so if you do not want to get the word "End" on the last page, you need to redefine that command like we did before.

As shown in the previous examples the continuation text is by default typeset between the text body and the footer line and lines up with the text on the right margin. The separation from last line of text is given by \contdrop and defaults to 0.5\footskip. Thus, if the \footskip is small, this may need adjustment.

Instead of this layout, you can push the text into the margin (assuming they are wide enough) by using the package option margin. The continuation text is then placed into the right margin separated from the main text by \contsep (which defaults to \marginparsep). This layout is shown in the next example using some Kantian sample text. When reading such text aloud, it clearly helps to have an inkling of what comes up next when turning the page.

---

[1] If you do this, you probably want to redefine \flagcont to do nothing to avoid getting it into two places.

Kant with turn support   **3**

analytic unity. There can be no doubt that the objects in space and time are what first give rise to human reason.

Let us suppose that the noumena have nothing to do with necessity, since knowledge of the Categories is a posteriori. Hume tells us that the transcendental unity of apperception can not take account of the discipline of natural [reason,

5-4-17

```
\usepackage{kantlipsum,fancyhdr}
  \pagestyle{fancy} \fancyhf{}
  \fancyhead[R]{\textbf{\thepage}}
  \fancyhead[L]{Kant with turn support}
\usepackage[word,margin]{continue}
  \renewcommand{\preflagword}{[]}
  \setlength\contsep{5pt}
\kant[1]  \kant[2]
```

5.5 Page decorations and watermarks

We cover two kinds of page decorations that are sometimes needed: putting watermarks, i.e., some material on all or some pages and adding crop marks, as often needed in the printing process. The **draftwatermark** package uses the shipout hooks of LaTeX discussed in Appendix A.4.1 on page →II 680.

5.5.1 draftwatermark — **Put a visible stamp on your document**

In some situations it is important to clearly mark each page of a publication, for example to indicate that something is a draft, confidential, uncontrolled copy, etc. Another scenario is marking individual copies with the name of its owner to prevent (or at least track) unauthorized distribution. Such texts are commonly known as watermarks because historically they have been produced not during the printing process but during the paper production while being still in a wet state, hence "water" mark.

With **draftwatermark** Sergio Callegari provides a package that helps you to produce electronic watermarks in your LaTeX documents. In its simplest form all you have to do is to load the package, and it then stamps every page of your document with the word "DRAFT" in large gray letters diagonally across each page.

The package obeys the option `final` when present as a document class or package option and disables the watermarks throughout the document. This is fine if the mark says DRAFT but probably not so if some other text is displayed. For that reason you can force watermarks in such a case by using the option `stamp`. It is also possible to ask for placing a watermark only on the first page of the document by using the option `firstpageonly`.

Package options

\DraftwatermarkOptions{*key/value list*}

Instead or in addition to using package options, you can customize the watermarks in the preamble or at any point inside your document by using the declaration \DraftwatermarkOptions that expects a *key/value list* as its argument. The above package options are in fact Boolean keys, so to disable all watermarks from a certain point onwards you can use `stamp=false`. There are about twenty keys in total: the most important are covered below.

With the `text` key it is possible to change the default text; with `fontsize` its size and with `scale` you provide an additional scale factor (default 1, i.e., no scaling). The combination of the two keys is of interest in case you have a font with different design sizes; e.g., compare

"**Latin Modern 5pt scaled by 2**" vs. "Latin Modern 10pt"

Of course, with fully scalable fonts in only one design size, using one or the other key makes no difference.

With `angle` you can adjust the text angle (default 45 degrees), and with `color` you can define a specific color to be used. By default, the package uses a light gray, and for convenience there are also keys that alter only aspects of the color, e.g., `colormodel` changes the model used (default `gray`), and `colorspec` the specification in this model (default `0.8`), so if you want a darker gray, you could change just that value as we did in the example below.

For the coloring the package automatically loads the `color` package if necessary. Thus, if you want to used extended color specifications, load your own color support package first. The next example loads `xcolor` for that reason. It also shows that it is possible to change the setup in the middle of the document — whatever values are current at the time of the page break are used. The only point to remember is that LaTeX reads whole paragraphs before making that decision; thus, changes are best placed between paragraphs.

Lorem ipsum dolor sit amet, consectetuer adipiscing elit. Ut purus elit, vestibulum ut, placerat ac, adipiscing vitae, felis. Curabitur dictum gravida mauris. 1	Nam dui ligula, fringilla a, euismod sodales, sollicitudin vel, wisi. Nulla malesuada porttitor diam. Donec felis erat, congue non, volutpat at, tincidunt tristique, libero. Vivamus viverra fermentum felis. 2

```
\usepackage{lipsum,xcolor}
\usepackage{draftwatermark}
\DraftwatermarkOptions
   {fontsize=25pt,colorspec=.6}

\lipsum[1][1-3]
\newpage
\DraftwatermarkOptions
   {color=blue!40, angle=-45,
    text=Private, scale=1.4 }
\lipsum[2][1] \par \lipsum[3]
```

5-5-1

Instead of explicitly changing the watermark text inside the document, you might want to see it changing automatically based on the content of the current page, e.g., displaying the page number or some marks that have been populated. The next example shows this approach (except that we issue the mark explicitly instead of using those generated from headings or other structures).

The example also exhibits how to move the watermark from its central point on the page using key `pos` (that expects a horizontal and a vertical offset from the top-left corner of the page). Alternatively, we could have used the keys `hpos` and `vpos` to set the horizontal and vertical part of the position separately. Note that the position and values can be specified as a function of other LaTeX parameters and that they are evaluated on each page anew. Thus, with suitable care you can alter the position on verso and recto pages if you have an asymmetric layout.[1]

By default the text is centered around this position, but in our case we want it to be left-aligned. This can be set with the key hanchor that expects l, c (default), or r. Similarly, vanchor sets the vertical alignment expecting t, m (default), or b. Alternatively, you can set both in one go using the anchor key; e.g., we could have used this key with value lm and achieved the same effect.

```
\NewMarkClass{WM}
\InsertMark{WM}{Public Info}

\usepackage{lipsum,draftwatermark}
\DraftwatermarkOptions{
  pos={0pt,20pt} , hanchor=l ,
  text=\bfseries -- \thepage\
    --\qquad\FirstMark{WM} ,
  fontsize=7pt , angle=0 }
\raggedright\lipsum[1][1-4] \par
\medskip
\InsertMark{WM}{Confidential}
\lipsum[2]
```

-1- Public Info

Lorem ipsum dolor sit amet, consectetuer adipiscing elit. Ut purus elit, vestibulum ut, placerat ac, adipiscing vitae, felis. Curabitur dictum gravida mauris. Nam arcu libero, nonummy eget, consectetuer id,

-2- Confidential

vulputate a, magna.

Nam dui ligula, fringilla a, euismod sodales, sollicitudin vel, wisi. Morbi auctor lorem non justo. Nam lacus libero, pretium at, lobortis vitae,

5-5-2

5.5.2 crop — Producing trimming marks

When producing camera-ready copy for publication, the final printing is normally done on "stock paper" having a larger size than the logical page size of the document. In that case the printed copy needs trimming before it is finally bound. For accurate trimming the printing house usually requires so-called crop marks on each page. Another reason for requiring crop marks is the task of mounting two or more logical pages onto a physical one, such as in color production where different colors are printed separately.

The crop package created by Melchior Franz supports these tasks by providing a simple interface for producing different kinds of crop marks. It also offers the ability to print only the text or only the graphics from a document, and the chance of inverting, mirroring, or rotating the output, among other things — all features useful during that part of the printing process.

Crop marks can be requested by using one of the following options:

cam   Produces four marks that show the logical paper dimensions without touching them (see Example 5-5-3 on the following page). They are mainly intended for camera alignment.

cross   Produces four large crosses at the corners of the logical page touching its edges. It is intended as a trimming help printed on a separate piece of paper.

---

[1] The evaluation happens inside \setlength or in case of the anchor values in an \edef; thus, not everything is possible. See the package documentation for examples.

frame Produces a frame around the logical page; mainly intended for clearly visualizing the page dimensions.

The package assumes that the \paperheight and \paperwidth dimensions correctly reflect the size of the *logical* page you want to produce. The size of the *physical* page (the stock paper) you are actually printing on is then given as an option to the package. Options include a0, a1, a2, a3, a4, a5, a6, b0, b1, b2, b3, b4, b5, b6, executive, legal, and letter. If you use the physical paper in landscape orientation (i.e., with the long side horizontally), you can also specify the option landscape. If none of these options matches your physical paper sizes, you can specify the exact sizes through the options width and height, both of which take dimensional values.

The following example sets up an artificially small logical page (to fit the example area of this book) using the geometry package and centers it on a physical page of A5 size. However, because all our examples are actually cropped to their "visible" size and since, for obvious reasons, we have not actually marked the borders of the A5 paper, you cannot see that it was properly centered at one stage — either believe us or try it yourself.

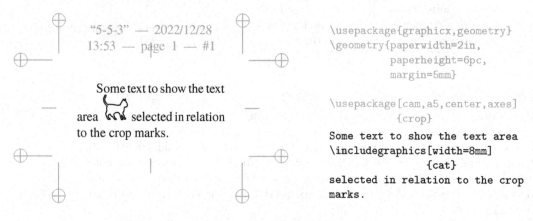

"5-5-3" — 2022/12/28
13:53 — page 1 — #1

Some text to show the text
area 🐱 selected in relation
to the crop marks.

```
\usepackage{graphicx,geometry}
\geometry{paperwidth=2in,
          paperheight=6pc,
          margin=5mm}

\usepackage[cam,a5,center,axes]
           {crop}
Some text to show the text area
\includegraphics[width=8mm]
                {cat}
selected in relation to the crop
marks.
```

5-5-3

It should be clear from the description and the example that this package should be loaded *after* the document layout has been specified.

The informational text between the top crop marks is added by default. It can be suppressed by adding the option noinfo, though it is usually a good idea to keep it. The information contains both the page number (as known to LaTeX) and a page index, which starts with 1 and is incremented for every page being printed. Especially with large publications using several page numbering methods at once, this is a helpful device to ensure that pages are not misordered.

If requested with the option axes, the package also marks the center points of each page with a small line in the crop area and thus is lost after trimming. By default they are turned off.

Using the option font you can change the appearance of this text, e.g., by providing small, textsf, or some other font command as a value. Allowed is any command with zero or one argument (so you can define your own commands as well), but it is important to note that it must be specified without the backslash or chaos is assured. It is also possible to color the crop marks and the informational text using the option `color` (if necessary, the `color` package is loaded). Both options are shown in the next example.

Several options of the `crop` package rely on support given by the printer driver. If no driver option is explicitly given, the package tries to determine the driver from installation settings for the `graphics` or `color` package. It is also possible to indicate the driver explicitly by using options such as `dvips`, `pdflatex`, `luatex`, or `vtex` (there is no explicit driver option for X$_\exists$T$_E$X, but the package works well with that engine, too). If one of these options is selected, the paper size information is passed to the external driver program, which is important if you want to view the document with an external program.

If you want to print graphics separately—for example, because running the complete document through a color printer is infeasible—you can produce different versions of the same document: one containing only the text but no graphics (or, more precisely, without graphics included via `\includegraphics`) and one containing only the graphics (or, more precisely, with all text printed in the color "white"). These effects can be achieved using the options `nographics` and `notext`, respectively. Clearly, the latter option can be used only if the target device is capable of understanding color commands because internally the `color` package is being deployed. The next example shows the use of the `nographics` and `cross`[1] options; compare it to the output of Example 5-5-3.

<table>
<tr><td>

"5-5-4" — 2022/12/28
13:53 — page 1 — #1

Some text to show the text

area   selected in relation
to the crop marks.

</td><td>

```
\usepackage{graphicx}

\usepackage[paperwidth=2in,
            paperheight=10pc,
            margin=5mm]
           {geometry}

\usepackage[cross,a5,center,
            font=textsf,
            color=blue,
            nographics]
           {crop}
Some text to show the text area
\includegraphics[width=8mm]
               {cat}
selected in relation to the crop
marks.
```

</td></tr>
</table>

5-5-4

---

[1]The cross crop marks look admittedly rather weird at this measure.

Three other options require the output device to be able to obey the extended commands of the **graphics** and **color** packages for rotation, mirroring, and background coloring. With the option `rotate` the pages are turned through 180 degrees. The option `mirror` flips each page as shown in the next example. Finally, the option `invert` will invert white and black so that the text appears in white on a black surface.

```
\usepackage{graphicx,geometry}
\geometry{paperwidth=2in,paperheight=6pc,
          margin=5mm}
\usepackage[frame,a5,center,
            mirror,font=tiny]{crop}
Some text to show the text area
\includegraphics[width=8mm]{cat}
selected in relation to the crop marks.
```

5-5-5

5.6 Visual formatting

The final stage of the production of an important document often needs some manual formatting to avoid bad line or page breaks. In this section we look at various tools and methods to deal with such tasks.

We first look at pagination and show ways to alter it, for example by running some pages long or short. This is followed by a package that offers extensions to `\clearpage` and that supports conditional page breaks depending on the remaining available space.

We then turn to problems in paragraphs and take a detailed look at how to detect and avoid so called widows and orphans, i.e., single lines of a paragraph at the end or beginning of a page.

Finally, we discuss the `\looseness` command that directs TeX to alter the paragraph breaking algorithm to lengthen or reduce paragraphs by a line or more. This approach can save the day in difficult situations, especially if it is impossible to alter the textual material.

5.6.1 Standard tools for page explicit page breaking

For explicit page break standard LaTeX offers the `\pagebreak`, `\nopagebreak`, `\newpage`, and `\clearpage` commands as well as the `\samepage` declaration, although the latter is considered obsolete in LaTeX 2_ε. A `\samepage` declaration together with a suitable number of `\nobreak` commands lets you request that a certain portion of your document be kept together.

Unfortunately, the results are often not satisfactory; in particular, LaTeX never makes a page larger than its nominal height (i.e., `\textheight`) but rather moves everything in the scope of the \samepage declaration to the next page. The LaTeX 2$_\varepsilon$ command \enlargethispage* described below offers an alternative approach.

5.6.2 Running pages and columns short or long

It is common in book production to "run" a certain number of pages (normally double spreads) short or long to avoid bad page breaks later. This means that the nominal height of the pages is reduced or enlarged by a certain amount — for example, a \baselineskip. To support this practice, LaTeX 2$_\varepsilon$ offers the command \enlargethispage{*size*}.

\enlargethispage{*size*}

If, for example, you want to enlarge or reduce the size of some pages by one (or more) additional lines of text, you could define

```
\newcommand\longpage[1][1]{\enlargethispage{#1\baselineskip}}
\newcommand\shortpage[1][1]{\enlargethispage{-#1\baselineskip}}
```

Fractional or negative values (for reduction) are, of course, possible. Use these command somewhere between two paragraphs on the pages in question.[1]

The \enlargethispage command alters the \textheight for the current page or column but otherwise does not change the formatting parameters. Thus, if \flushbottom is in force, the text fills the \textheight for the page in question, if necessary by enlarging or shrinking vertical space within the page. In this way, the above definitions (if used without the optional argument) add or remove exactly one line of text from a page while maintaining the positions of the other lines. This consideration is important to give a uniform appearance.

Note that only the current page or column is affected. Thus, to ensure a uniform appearance of a double page spread, you need to issue two (in case of two-column mode even four) such commands, one in each column. The situation is slightly different if you are inside a multicols environment. Because this environment looks at all columns before making a decision, you need only a single \enlargethispage to achieve the desired effect.

In the next example the multicols would normally end with a single line on page 7. By issuing \shortpage on page 6, we get a second line moved over. Alternatively, we could have made the page long, which would have gotten all of the multicols material onto page 6. Of course, to get a uniform appearance there should

---

[1]Because this book contains so many examples, we had to use this trick a few times to avoid half-empty pages. For example, in this chapter seven spreads are run short by one line (e.g., pages 402-407) and four spreads are run long (e.g., pages 380-381). This was necessary because of the many (large) examples in Section 5.4.2 — all other paginations we tried ended somewhere in half-empty pages or in multiple widows and orphans.

be a second \shortpage on page 7 as well, but in the example this is commented out to better show the effect of the first.

Lorem ipsum dolor sit amet, consectetuer adipiscing elit. Ut purus elit, vestibulum ut,	placerat ac, adipiscing vitae, felis. Curabitur dictum gravida mauris. Nam arcu libero,		

6

nonummy eget, consectetuer id,	vulputate a, magna.

Nam dui ligula, fringilla a, euismod sodales, sollicitudin vel, wisi. Morbi auctor lorem non justo. Nam lacus libero, pretium at, lobortis vitae,

7

```
\usepackage{lipsum,
           multicol}
\flushbottom
\begin{multicols}{2}
  \raggedright
  \shortpage
  \lipsum[1][1-4]
\end{multicols}
% \shortpage
\lipsum[2]
```
5-6-1

> \enlargethispage*{*size*}

The companion command, \enlargethispage*, also enlarges or reduces the page height, but this time the resulting final page is squeezed as much as possible (i.e., depending on the available white space on the page). This technique can be helpful if you wish to keep a certain portion of your document together on one page, even if it makes the page slightly too long. (Otherwise, just use the minipage environment.) The trick is to request a large enough amount of extra space and then place an explicit page break where you want the page break to happen. Here is an example:

```
\enlargethispage*{100cm}      % absurdly large request
\begin{center}
 \begin{tabular}{llll}         % tabular which is slightly too long
  ....                         % for the current page
 \end{tabular}
\end{center}
\pagebreak                     % forced page break
```

From the description above it is clear that all these commands should be used only in the last stages of the production process, because any later alterations to the document (adding or removing a single word, if you are unlucky) can make your hand-formatting obsolete — resulting in ugly-looking pages.

To manually correct final page breaks, such as in a publication like this book (which poses some formidable challenges due to the many examples that cannot be broken across pages), it can be helpful to visualize TeX's reasons for breaking at a certain point and to find out how much flexibility is available on certain pages. Tools for this purpose are described in Appendix B.4.2.

5.6.3 addlines — Adjusting whole double spreads

As already alluded earlier altering the page height normally has to be done on both verso and recto pages in unison to avoid a ragged look of the spread. This means one usually has to use two identical \enlargethispage commands, one for each page.

To simplify this approach Will Robertson wrote the `addlines` package that provides a wrapper around the commands discussed in the previous section.

`\addlines*`[*lines*]   `\removelines*`[*lines*]   `\squeezepage`[*lines*]

The command `\addlines` adds the specified number of *lines* (default 1) to the whole double spread if the document is typeset in `twoside` mode. To work correctly it needs to be placed in the first column on the verso page, and it warns you if it appears elsewhere. In `oneside` mode it affects only the current page; in `twocolumn` mode both columns are adjusted.

Negative values remove lines; alternatively, you can use `\removelines`. Fractional values are also allowed though sensible only if there is enough flexibility available in all columns. For those preferring the singular when appropriate, there are also `\addline` and `\removeline` for adding or removing one line.

A) Lorem ipsum dolor sit amet, consectetuer adipiscing elit.	adipiscing vitae, felis. Curabitur dictum gravida mauris.	consectetuer id, vulputate a, magna. Donec vehicula augue eu neque.	sodales, sollicitudin vel, wisi.	
B) Ut purus elit, vestibulum ut, placerat ac,	C) Nam arcu libero, nonummy eget,		E) Nulla malesuada porttitor diam.	
		D) Nam dui ligula, fringilla a, euismod	Donec felis erat, congue	

```
\usepackage{lipsum,
            addlines}
\flushbottom
\twocolumn \raggedright
A) \lipsum[1][1]  \par
   \addline
B) \lipsum[1][2-3]\par
C) \lipsum[1][4-5]\par
D) \lipsum[2][1]  \par
E) \lipsum[3]
```

5-6-2 6 7

In the example setting it is a little difficult to see that this really adds one line to all columns, but compare with Example 5-6-3 that shows the same text.

The star forms act only on the current column; i.e., they are like `\longpage` and `\shortpage` discussed above. They are useful if one needs to handle one column specially, e.g., using `\squeezepage` on a neighboring one.

In the next example we add an extra line in the second column and make the third column run one line short. Compare this to Example 5-6-2 where all columns had one extra line.

A) Lorem ipsum dolor sit amet, consectetuer adipiscing elit.	ut, placerat ac, adipiscing vitae, felis. Curabitur dictum gravida mauris.	nonummy eget, consectetuer id, vulputate a, magna. Donec vehicula augue eu neque.	D) Nam dui ligula, fringilla a, euismod sodales, sollicitudin vel, wisi.
B) Ut purus elit, vestibulum	C) Nam arcu libero,		E) Nulla

```
\usepackage{lipsum,
            addlines}
\flushbottom
\twocolumn \raggedright
A) \lipsum[1][1]  \par
B) \lipsum[1][2-3]\par
\addline*
C) \lipsum[1][4-5]\par
\removeline*
D) \lipsum[2][1]  \par
E) \lipsum[3]
```

5-6-3 6 7

417

Sometimes you want to get some more material into the current column but use as little extra space as possible. This can be achieved with \squeezepage (which is \enlargethispage* in disguise).

For instance, page 7 in the next example shows that in this setting LaTeX would carry two lines of the last paragraph to the next page. In contrast, everything fits (more or less) on page 6 where we asked for squeezing the page after adding one extra line.

Lorem ipsum dolor sit amet, consectetuer adipiscing elit. $$\sum x_i$$ Ut purus elit, vestibulum ut, placerat ac, adipiscing vitae, felis. $$\sum y_i$$ Now will this final paragraph still fit in its entirety on the page?	Lorem ipsum dolor sit amet, consectetuer adipiscing elit. $$\sum x_i$$ Ut purus elit, vestibulum ut, placerat ac, adipiscing vitae, felis. $$\sum y_i$$ Now will this final paragraph
6	7

```
\usepackage{lipsum,addlines}
\flushbottom
\lipsum[1][1] \[ \sum x_i \]
\squeezepage[1]
\lipsum[1][2] \[ \sum y_i \]
Now will this final paragraph
still fit in its entirety on
the page? \par
\lipsum[1][1] \[ \sum x_i \]
\lipsum[1][2] \[ \sum y_i \]
Now will this final paragraph
still fit in its entirety on
the page?
```

5-6-4

If used without the optional argument, \squeezepage only squeezes the page without allowing more material than usual. This seldom has any effect (other than preventing the \flushbottom setting) because LaTeX usually uses as much material as can be fit onto the page.

5.6.4 nextpage — Extensions to \clearpage

In standard LaTeX the commands \clearpage and \cleardoublepage terminate the current paragraph and page after placing all dangling floats (if necessary, by producing a number of float pages). In two-sided printing \cleardoublepage also makes sure that the next page is a right-hand (odd-numbered) one by adding, if necessary, an extra page with an empty text body. However, this extra page still gets a page header and footer (as specified by the currently active page style), which may or may not be desirable.

7	8 4 A TEST
4 A Test **4.1 A subsection** Some text for our page. Then a blank page.	

```
\pagestyle{headings}
% Right-hand page on the left in
% this and next example due to:
\setcounter{page}{7}
\section{A Test}
\subsection{A subsection}
Some text for our page. Then a blank page.
\cleardoublepage
\section{Another Section}
This would appear on page 9 (not shown).
```

5-6-5

The package nextpage by Peter Wilson (these days maintained by Will Robertson) extends this concept by providing the commands \cleartoevenpage and \cleartooddpage. Both commands accept an optional argument in which you can put text that should appear on the potentially generated page. In the next example we use this ability to provide a command \myclearpage that writes BLANK PAGE on such generated pages.

7	8 4 A TEST

4   A Test

4.1   A subsection

Some text for our page.
Then a blank page.

BLANK PAGE

```
\usepackage{nextpage}\pagestyle{headings}
\newcommand\myclearpage{\cleartooddpage
    [\vspace*{\stretch{1}} \centering
     BLANK PAGE \vspace*{\stretch{2}}]}
\section{A Test}
\subsection{A subsection}
Some text for our page. Then a blank page.
\myclearpage
\section{Another Section}
This would appear on page 9 (not shown).
```

5-6-6

This code still results in a running header, but by now you surely know how to fix the example: just add a \thispagestyle{empty} to the above definition.

The nextpage package also provides two commands, \movetoevenpage and \movetooddpage, that offer the same functionality, except that they do not output dangling floats.

5.6.5 needspace — Conditionally start a new page

Instead of unconditionally requesting a new page with one of the commands discussed in the previous sections, you may want to just reserve a certain amount of space and skip to the next if that space is not available on the current page but otherwise continue as normal. A typical example is something like an index section that you may want to start immediately if there is still more than X lines of space available.

For this type of application Peter Wilson developed the needspace package (now maintained by Will Robertson). It offers two commands for this purpose.

\needspace{*space*}   \Needspace*{*space*}

The \needspace command checks if there is still approximately the requested vertical *space* available on the current page and if not starts a new page. The decision when to break depends on the flexibility with the current page material. If the break is taken, a short page is produced even if \flushbottom is in force. This is efficient and normally adequate.

In contrast, \Needspace makes an exact calculation under the assumption that the already placed material is typeset without shrinking or stretching. Again, if a break is taken, it creates a short page. However, if the star form is used, the page content is stretched out, and a full page is produced if \flushbottom is in force.

419

Thus, this can be used only if a small amount of *space* is requested or if there is ample flexibility for stretch available on the page.

The next example shows \Needspace in action. On the first page it has no effect because there are still two lines available, but on the second page it pushes the final paragraph out. Because we used \Needspace* on this page, you can see that the material remains aligned at the bottom. The resulting excess space is distributed between the paragraphs (because it this is the only space that can stretch on this page).

```
\usepackage{lipsum,needspace}
\flushbottom

\lipsum[1][1]        \par
\lipsum[1][2-5]

\Needspace{2\baselineskip}
This should only start if
there is plenty of space,
i.e., 2 lines or more \dots

\lipsum[1][1]        \par
\lipsum[1][2-5]

\Needspace*{2\baselineskip}
This should only start if
there is plenty of space,
i.e., 2 lines or more \dots
```

5-6-7

Page 1:

Lorem ipsum dolor sit amet, consectetuer adipiscing elit.

Ut purus elit, vestibulum ut, placerat ac, adipiscing vitae, felis. Curabitur dictum gravida mauris. Nam arcu libero, nonummy eget, consectetuer id, vulputate a, magna. Donec vehicula augue eu neque.

This should only start if there is plenty of space, i.e., 2

1

Page 2:

lines or more ...

Lorem ipsum dolor sit amet, consectetuer adipiscing elit.

Ut purus elit, vestibulum ut, placerat ac, adipiscing vitae, felis. Curabitur dictum gravida mauris. Nam arcu libero, nonummy eget, consectetuer id, vulputate a, magna. Donec vehicula augue eu neque.

2

5.6.6 Avoiding widows and orphans

Splitting off the first or last line of a paragraph at a page or column break is considered bad practice in typesetting circles. It is thus not surprising that the craftspeople have come up with fairly descriptive names for such lines when they appear in typeset documents. Commonly used are the terms "widow" for the last and "orphan" for the first line. These are, for example, used in English, French ("veuve" and "orpheline"), Italian ("Vedova" and "Orfano"), Spanish ("línea huérfana" and "línea viuda"), and to a lesser extent in German ("Witwe" and "Waise"). One way to remember them is to think of orphaned lines appearing at the start (birth) and widows near the end (death) of a paragraph or by using Bringhurst's mnemonic, "An orphan has no past; a widow has no future" [7].

German typesetters coined some more profane descriptions by calling the widow line a "Hurenkind" (child of a whore) and the orphan line a "Schusterjunge" (son of a shoemaker) allegedly because these boys have been notoriously meddlesome. For German practitioners these are still the predominantly used terms, though "Witwen" and "Waisen" are also well understood. Dutch uses "hoerenjong" and "weeskind", which translates to son of a whore and orphan, i.e., somewhere in between the German usage and the other languages.

Donald Knuth catered for this typographic detail in the TeX program by providing parameters whose values are used as penalties if the pagination algorithm considers breaking in such a place. Widow lines are penalized via `\widowpenalty`; however, orphans are not controlled by `\orphanpenalty`, as one might expect, but by a parameter named `\clubpenalty`. Again, note that these parameters (and those discussed later in this section) are all TeX counters and get their value assigned with the ⟨*parameter*⟩=⟨*integer*⟩ syntax.

Essentially everyone in typography circles agrees that widows and orphans are very distracting to the reader as well as a sign of bad craftsmanship and should therefore be avoided. In fact, most writing guides and other books on typography generally suggest that a document should have no such lines whatsoever, e.g., in older editions of the Chicago Manual of Style we find "A page should not begin with the last line of a paragraph unless it is full measure and should not end with the first line of a new paragraph." However, that is easier said than done, so in newer editions of the *Chicago Manual of Style* [18] they no longer forbid orphans; i.e., they dropped the second part of the advice.

As a result of this sort of guidance many journal classes for LaTeX completely forbid widows and orphans by setting `\widowpenalty` and `\clubpenalty` to 10000, which prohibits a break at such points.

Doing this introduces severe problems: Because LaTeX (and in fact all major typesetting systems to date) use a greedy algorithm[1] to determine the pagination of a document, they recognize problems with orphan or widow lines late in the game and then have only the current page to work with. This means the best it can do to avoid the situation is to push an orphan to the next page if there is not enough room to squeeze in another line. The same happens with widows; here LaTeX is forced to move the second-to-last line to the next page even though it would still nicely fit.

As a result the current page has an additional line-height worth of white space that needs to be distributed somewhere on the page. If there are headings, displays, lists, or other objects for which the design allows some flexibility in the surrounding white space, then this extra space may not create much of an issue. If, however, the page consists only of text or objects without any flexibility, then all LaTeX can do is run the page or column short, generating a fairly ugly hole at the bottom.

Besides widows and orphans there are a number of similar issues that typography manuals mandate eliminating if at all possible. One is a paragraph split across pages at a hyphenation point so that only a part of the word is visible at any time; another is a widow line with a following display formula. For both, TeX offers parameters to control the undesirability of the scenario. By default Donald Knuth considered them of lesser importance and provided default values of 100 and 50 for `\brokenpenalty` and `\displaywidowpenalty`, respectively, while he specified 150 for orphans and widows. However, if your style guide (or your class file) wants to avoid them at all costs, then you are in precisely the same situation as with the widows and orphans discussed above.

Related problems

---

[1]See [61] and [87, 88, 91] for research on alternative approaches.

A special variation of the last issue is a display formula starting a page, that is, with the introductory material completely on the previous page or column. That is considered a no-no by nearly everybody, so in TeX the controlling \predisplaypenalty parameter has by default a value of 10000. Again, there may be valid reasons to ignore this advice in a special situation, e.g., when the space constraints are high.

Fixing the problem   The alternative to preventing widows and orphans (or hyphens across page boundaries, etc.) automatically and at all costs is to manually resolve the issues when they arise. For this one finds a number of suggestions in the typography literature. We discuss those that are easy to apply in a LaTeX document below. A more extensive discussion of the subject is given in [89].

Forcing a page break early and producing a short page.   This is what LaTeX and most other typesetting tools automatically do if you completely forbid widows and orphans and it often leads to badly filled pages as discussed above.

However, if you force the page break manually, you have control and can decide which problems need fixing, and you can lessen the impact by also explicitly forcing earlier breaks and thereby shifting the extra white space to a page or column where it can be absorbed by the available flexibility on that page.

Running the page spread short or long.   This approach is a standard trick of the craft. In LaTeX this can be achieved using the commands described in Sections 5.6.2 and 5.6.3.

Adjusting the spacing between words to produce "tighter" or "looser" paragraphs. This is certainly a practical option if you choose the right paragraph or paragraphs, e.g., those that are somewhat longer and that have a last line that is either nearly full (for lengthening) or nearly empty (for shortening). In that case squeezing the word spaces might result in one line less, and extending it might get you an additional line (with just a word or two). In many cases the resulting gray value is still of acceptable quality, so this is a typical trick of the trade. In LaTeX this is achieved by using the \looseness parameter that is discussed in Section 5.6.8.

Note that you do not necessarily need to manipulate one of the paragraphs of the problem page; there might be a better candidate on an earlier page.

Rewriting a portion of the paragraph.   This is obviously something you can do only if you are the author and not typesetting some text written by others. If so, it is a valid strategy because it enables you to easily shorten or enlarge a paragraph so that your orphan or widow is reunited with other lines. It is certainly the most often applied approach in this book during the final production.

Again, there is no requirement to do this rewrite with the paragraph causing the issue (as implied by the advice); you can choose any earlier paragraph to achieve the desired effect.[1]

---

[1] Well, "any" is an exaggeration: if you change a paragraph on an earlier page, the gained (or extra)

Reduce the tracking of the words.   Tracking in this context means adjusting the spacing between characters in a uniform way (in contrast to kerning, which means adjusting the spacing between individual glyph pairs, e.g., "AV" cf. "AV"). This concept was already discussed in Section 3.4.6 in the context of letter-spacing.

Clearly by applying tracking one can shorten or lengthen a text. However, when applying tracking to a whole paragraph, the gray value of words changes fairly rapidly. Compare, for example, the different lines in Figure 3.1 on page 192 that show a line of text with different amounts of tracking (negative and positive) applied. Thus, even with small tracking values, changes may become noticeable and thus distracting.

On the whole, common typographical advice is to *not use* tracking for such purposes or, if there is no better alternative, then only with very small tracking values in which case there may not be any noticeable effects on the paragraph length unless you are lucky. It is, however, easy to experiment with by using the `\textls` command from the microtype package.

Adding a pull quote to the text (more common for magazines).   Pull quotes are catch phrases from the text that are "pulled out" and typeset prominently again in a different place, typically in a larger and often different font. They serve as eye catchers and if carefully chosen give the reader a preview of the content or main points of an article.

The design needs to clearly distinguish them from other display material; e.g., there should be no way to confuse them with headings, etc. In two-column texts this is often done by placing them in a window with both columns flowing around them, but placing them into the content of one column is also often seen.

The latter is fairly easy to achieve with LaTeX, but flowing text around a pull quote is something that requires a lot of manual work. If you want to try, take a look at the `wrapfigure` environment from Section 7.3.4 on page 535. As the above advice already mentions, pull quotes are more commonly found in magazine type documents, so this approach may or may not be applicable.

Resizing an existing figure.   Just like adding a pull quote, resizing a figure obviously changes the amount of material a column can hold and thus enables us to move an orphan or widow out of harm's way. Whether or not it is a valid option depends on the figure in question; often enough graphics do offer some freedom and can be adjusted either by scaling (up or down) or by cropping, etc. However, due to the fact that their placement can be only indirectly controlled, it is not so easy to handle successfully.

Summary.   To resolve issues with widows and orphans one has to somehow adjust the amount of material typeset in the respective column or page. Out of the options discussed above the first three have the advantage that they do not change your document content in any way but only its presentation. That is certainly also true

---

space might get swallowed up by available flexibility on some intermediate page, and your widow or orphan thus stays put. In that case you additionally need to add some strategic page breaks.

for applying tracking or reducing float sizes. However, for the latter two it is much harder to properly control their effects on the pagination.

If you are the author of the document, then rewriting paragraphs or changing figure sizes to fit in a few more or less words is often a successful and very easy to apply strategy, but of course that does not work if you are typesetting material written by somebody else.

Finally, pull quotes are a very attractive method if your type of document allows for this kind of display. The advantage here is that you are fairly free in placing them and thus can resolve a good range of typesetting issues simply by choosing a set of sensible quotes and then place them in suitable places (which within some limits can be done fairly arbitrarily).

Make adjustment only in the last stage of document production!

However, in any case, it should be noted though that all approaches are manual and thus the adjustments becomes invalid the moment there is a document change that modifies the amount of material typeset. It is therefore of paramount importance to manually fix widows and orphans only at the very last stage of producing the final document. Otherwise, all the effort might be in vain and needs to be undone or changed over and over again.

5.6.7 widows-and-orphans — Finding all widows and orphans

If the document class you use sets \widowpenalty and \clubpenalty to 10000, then LATEX automatically prevents widows and orphans, i.e., an orphan is forced to the top of the next page or column and the same happens to the line preceding a widow. The downside, as discussed previously, is partly empty pages, and if space is a premium (for example, if your conference paper is not allowed to be more than X pages in total), then this is a possible problem. Thus, you are better off allowing widows and orphans (by changing these parameter values) and manually correcting any issue during the final stage of the document production in one way or another.

The question then becomes, how do you identify the problematic page breaks without manually going through the printout of your document and searching for them? While that is certainly an option, it is error prone, and it would be much nicer if LATEX (even if it cannot automatically resolve the issues for you) at least identifies them so that you only have to check the problem pages.

This is possible by simply loading the package widows-and-orphans by Frank Mittelbach. This package adjusts the parameter values slightly so that all possible combinations if added up lead to distinctive numbers. For example, instead of the LATEX default values, it would choose

```
\widowpenalty        = 150
\clubpenalty         = 152
\brokenpenalty       = 101
\displaywidowpenalty =  50
```

so that it can distinguish between a widow and an orphan (\widowpenalty or \clubpenalty) or a widow that comes together with a hyphen at the break

(\widowpenalty + \brokenpenalty). In case you wonder why 151 was not used: that value is already used by LaTeX for \@medpenalty, which you get if you issue \nopagebreak[2].

By making sure that all technically possible combinations lead to unique numbers, it is only necessary to look at the penalty of the page break to determine whether that break exhibits one or more of the problems. At any page or column break the \outputpenalty[1] is inspected, and depending on the findings, a warning or error is generated that can then be checked and corrected manually.

For instance, in the next example we have three problems: page 1 ends in a hyphen, and additionally this paragraph has a very sorry widow at the top of page 2 — just half a word. Furthermore, the bottom of that page also ends again in a hyphen.

Lorem ipsum dolor sit amet, consectetuer adipiscing elit. Ut purus elit, vestibulum ut, placerat ac, adipiscing vitae, felis. Curabitur dictum gravida mau-	ris. Quisque ullamcorper placerat ipsum. Cras nibh. Suspendisse vel felis. Ut lorem lorem, interdum eu, tin-
1	2

```
\usepackage{lipsum}
\usepackage{widows-and-orphans}

\lipsum[1][1-3] % Some more
 % text to avoid the widow.

\lipsum[4][1-2]\par\lipsum[6]
```

5-6-8

For these issues the package produces two (not three) warnings:

```
Package widows-and-orphans Warning: Widow on page 2
Package widows-and-orphans Warning: Hyphen in last line of page 2
```

It does not tell us about the hyphen on page 1 because that is directly related to the widow. If we attempt a fix by adding one extra line to the first paragraph (uncommenting the English text in the example), we would resolve the widow and also push the hyphen on page 2 to the next page. However, rerunning the document would then produce

```
Package widows-and-orphans Warning: Hyphen in last line of page 1
Package widows-and-orphans Warning: Orphan on page 2
```

because we generated a new problem and the first hyphen issue was not resolved either. Thus, this approach can require several iterations, which is another reason why you should do this only at the very last stage of document production.

To somewhat ease the process, the package has a number of key/value options. The check option determines how findings are handled: the default is warning in which case warnings are written to the terminal and the .log file. In the last phase of document development you may want to change that to error in which case the package stops at each problem with an error message rather than just a warning. In the opposite direction, info does not clutter the terminal with messages and only

---

[1]In this parameter TeX records the penalty associated with the chosen break so that it can be inspected within the output routine processing.

writes to the .log. And if you know for sure that all the remaining issues have to stay, you can also use the value none in which case no checks are done at all.

Instead of suppressing all checking for a part of the document via \WaOsetup (discussed below), you can issue the command \WaOignorenext somewhere in the document, after which the next check — for the current page or column — is silenced. The check is still performed, and if no problems are found, you receive an error message, because either you have added it to the wrong page or your text has changed and it is no longer needed.

Continuing with improvements to Example 5-6-8, we decide that there is no good way to fix the hyphen issue on page 1. We therefore accept this deficiency and add \WaOignorenext to suppress the warning, and we resolve the orphan issue by marrying the two paragraphs together. Everything should be fine now, so we set check to error to get alerted if due to rewrites new problems arise.

Lorem ipsum dolor sit amet, consectetuer adipiscing elit. Ut purus elit, vestibulum ut, placerat ac, adipiscing vitae, felis. Curabitur dictum gravida mau-

1

ris. Some more text to avoid the widow.

Quisque ullamcorper placerat ipsum. Cras nibh. Suspendisse vel felis. Ut lorem lorem,

2

```
\usepackage{lipsum}
\usepackage[check=error]
          {widows-and-orphans}
\WaOignorenext\lipsum[1][1-3]
   Some more text to
   avoid the widow.   \par
\lipsum[4][1-2] \lipsum[6]
```

5-6-9

The package also offers keys to set individual parameters to "reasonable" values. These are the keys widows, orphans, and hyphens, which all accept beside explicit numerical values the words default (to set the parameters to their LaTeX default), avoid (higher value but still possible to break), or prevent as their value. And there are also the valueless keys default-all, avoid-all, and prevent-all to set all parameters in one go. If you want LaTeX to try hard to avoid widows and orphans but not fully prevent them, try avoid-all as a starting point.[1]

If you want to see the resulting parameter settings (and the combinations that need to be unique in order to allow the package to work), you can issue the command \WaOparameters at any point in the document, which gives you a somewhat terse listing. If called in the preamble, the listing is delayed until after \begin{document} because only then the unification happens.

Do not remove the package after use

Why would one ever want to use the check key with value none instead of not loading the package? The reason is this: given that the package has to change the parameter settings slightly, not loading it would mean running the document with different values, and even though those changes are minimal, it is possible to construct examples where the difference matters and leads to changed results. Once you have fixed what is possible to fix, it is safest to still load the package, even if you no longer want the remaining warnings. Another reason is that the package offers the command \WaOsetup that allows you to change the settings mid-document, e.g., turn the warnings off for chapters already handled, but turn them on again for others.

---

[1] That would not avoid the issues in our examples given that there is no or nearly no stretchable space available.

5.6.8 \looseness — Shortening or lengthening paragraphs

As discussed earlier TeX (and therefore LaTeX) uses a globally optimizing line-breaking algorithm to find the best breaks for a given paragraph based on a given set of parameters. It is, however, possible to ask TeX to try to find a solution (within given quality boundaries) that is a number of lines longer or shorter than the optimal result. If such a solution exists, it is used; if not, then TeX tries to match the request as closely as possible. This manual method can be used to resolve pagination issues such as widows or orphans or other problems with the page breaking.

The paragraph will still be optimized (under the new conditions), i.e., its overall gray level will be fairly uniform, etc., but, inevitably, the interword spacing gets looser or tighter in the process, because this is the only parameter that TeX can adjust.[1]

To activate this feature you need to set the TeX counter \looseness to the desired value. This has to be done inside or directly in front (no blank line allowed!) of the paragraph text via low-level TeX syntax, because there is no LaTeX interface available.

```
\looseness=1    % to lengthen by one line,
                % use a -1 to shorten by a line (if possible)
The paragraph will still be optimized (under ...
```

TeX automatically resets the value to zero whenever a \par command or blank line is encountered; thus, it affects at most one paragraph.

A value of -1 has the best chance to work if the last line is already nearly empty (and the paragraph is of reasonable length). Lengthening is somewhat easier because interword spaces can stretch arbitrarily (as long as they do not exceed the \tolerance), whereas they can shrink by only a fixed amount. There is again a better chance for success if the last line is already (nearly) filled.

Better shorten than lengthen if possible

So far so good, but there are a few pitfalls that need to be avoided: first of all, with a positive value of \looseness TeX usually moves only a single word or even part of a single word into the last line, because this way there is more material in the others and thus less stretching of the interword spaces is necessary. Because this usually looks rather ugly, it is best to tie the last words together by using ~ and if necessary prevent hyphenation of the last word by placing an \mbox around it.[2]

Avoid the pitfalls lurking

Second, lengthening of a paragraph may go horribly wrong if the document is set with a high \tolerance value, e.g., most definitely when a \sloppy declaration is in force. Since \tolerance defines how bad a line can get while still being a candidate for the line-breaking algorithm and \sloppy (or the sloppypar environment) simply

---

[1] This paragraph, for example, is artificially lengthened by one line, i.e., from three to four. It is the only place in the book where we lengthened a paragraph. We have, however, quite often used -1 to shorten paragraphs, because this usually looks better when adjustments are needed.

[2] In TeX this kind of typographical issue can also be dealt with automatically, but then it applies to all paragraphs: setting the parameter \finalhyphenpenalty to a high values makes hyphenation in the last line unattractive, in which case the \mbox is not necessary.

427

run short (tight)	optimal line breaks	run long (loose)	run very long — bad!	run very long — awful!
`\looseness = -1`	`\looseness = 0`	`\looseness = 1`	`\looseness = 2`	`\looseness = 3`
`\tolerance = 72`	`\tolerance = 99`	`\tolerance = 638`	`\tolerance = 2065`	`\sloppy`

Figure 5.3: A paragraph from *Alice* under different `\looseness` settings

sets this tolerance nearly[1] to infinity, i.e., fairly bad lines become acceptable, and thus you might end up with a paragraph looking like the last one in Figure 5.3.

This figure shows a paragraph from *Alice in Wonderland* by Lewis Carroll (1832–1898) typeset with different settings for `\looseness` and `\tolerance`. The values for `\tolerance` are those necessary to achieve a result; e.g., with a value of 500 even a `\looseness` of one would not be fulfilled. The result on the right clearly shows what happens if a high `\looseness` is paired with `\sloppy`: the request is fulfilled producing a very spaced-out paragraph. In fact, in this case, TeX would happily add up to 14 extra lines while already three come out fairly ugly.

Seeing the paragraphs in Figure 5.3, you might ask yourself why one would want to use a high, let alone infinite, `\tolerance` ever. The reason is that this caters for situations where line breaking is very difficult. TeX will normally look only at the additional candidate solutions, but because they are usually inferior, it will not use them. Thus, under normal circumstances you get the same results. If typesetting is tough, you get a solution and not one or more overfull lines because TeX gave up in despair. Thus, the appropriate setting for `\tolerance` really depends on your own *tolerance*, i.e., at what point you think it becomes worth to manually intervene.

In small column measures it usually makes sense to set the default `\tolerance` fairly high (say, 3000 or 4000) to ensure that TeX automatically finds a solution in situations where line breaking is problematic. However, if you make manual adjustments using a positive[2] value for `\looseness`, you need to use a lower `\tolerance` to avoid disasters like the last paragraph in Figure 5.3, because with high settings TeX may resort to a solution with really bad lines to fulfill the request, which is something that nobody would want.

Using `\looseness` can always change line breaking

Using a negative `\looseness` does not have these issues, so it is fairly safe to use it with any paragraph if you are pressed for space: either it succeeds or it will keep the same number of lines as before. However, even in that case you are likely to see a different line breaking compared to not setting `\looseness`. The reason is somewhat

---

[1]In the early days of LaTeX `\sloppy` used to set the tolerance to 10000 (i.e., TeX's infinity), but that tended to produce even more bizarre-looking paragraphs: TeX then made one line really bad and all others perfect, because that looked to the optimizer to be the best solution.

[2]Negative values are not problematic because the interword spaces can shrink only a little bit.

technical: there may be different ways to break the paragraph into lines all resulting in the same "quality" according to TeX's algorithm, and when TeX is asked to try a different \looseness, it simply looks at the possible solutions in a different order.

To experiment with generally setting a negative \looseness, you might try the following in the preamble of your document:

```
\AddToHook{para/before}{\looseness=-1 }   % space needed after the number
\newcommand\cancellooseness{\AddToHookNext{para/before}{\looseness=0 }}
```

The first line issues a \looseness statement in front of every paragraph in the document, and the second line gives you a method to cancel that for just the next paragraph if needed.

5.7 Doing layout with class

Page layout is normally defined by the document class, so it should come as no great surprise that the techniques and packages described in this chapter are usually applied behind the scenes (within a document class).

The standard classes use the LaTeX parameters and interfaces directly to define the page proportions, running headers, and other elements. More recently developed classes, however, often deploy packages like geometry to handle certain aspects of the page layout.

In this section we briefly introduce two such implementations. By searching through the CTAN archive you might discover additional treasures.

5.7.1 KOMA-Script — A drop-in replacement for article et al.

The KOMA-Script classes, developed by Markus Kohm and based on earlier work by Frank Neukam, are drop-in replacements for the standard article/report/book classes that emphasize rules of typography laid down by Tschichold. The article class, for example, becomes scrartcl.

Page layout in the KOMA-Script classes is implemented by deploying the typearea package (see Section 5.2.3), with the classes offering the package options as class options. Extended page style design is done with the package scrlayer-scrpage (offering features similar to those provided by fancyhdr). Like typearea this package can also be used on a stand-alone basis with one of the standard classes. Layout specifications such as font control, caption layout, and so on, have been extended by providing customization possibilities that allow manipulation in the preamble of a document.

Besides offering all features available in the standard classes, the KOMA-Script classes provide extra user control inside front and back matter as well as a number of other useful extensions.

The distribution is well documented. There exists both a German and an English guide explaining all features in detail [63]. The German documentation is also available as a nicely typeset book [62], published by DANTE, the German language TeX Users Group.

429

5.7.2 memoir — Producing complex publications

The memoir class written by Peter Wilson was originally developed as an alternative to the standard book class. It incorporates many features otherwise found only as add-on packages. The current version, maintained and further developed by Lars Madsen, also works as a replacement for article and can, therefore, be used for all types of publications, from small memos to complex books [141].

Among other features it supports an extended set of document sizes (from 9pt to 17pt), configurable sectional headings, page headers and footers, and captions. Predefined layout styles are available for all such objects, and it is possible to declare new ones as needed. The class supports declarative commands for all aspects of setting the page, text, and margin sizes, including support for trimming (crop) marks. Many components of the class are also available as stand-alone packages, for those users who wish to add a certain functionality to other classes (e.g., epigraphs, caption formatting).

Like the KOMA-Script classes, the memoir class is accompanied by an excellent manual of nearly 200 pages, discussing all topics related to document design and showing how to resolve potential problems with memoir.

Tabular Material

Data is often most efficiently presented in tabular form. TeX uses powerful primitives for arranging material in rows and columns. Because they implement only a low-level, formatting-oriented functionality, several macro packages have been developed that build on those primitives to provide a higher-level command language and a more user-friendly interface. In Standard LaTeX, two types of environments for constructing tables are provided. Most commonly the `tabular` environment or its math-mode equivalent, the `array` environment, is used. However, in some circumstances the `tabbing` environment might prove useful.

Tables typically form large units of the document that must be allowed to "float" so that the document may be paginated correctly. The environments described in this chapter are principally concerned with the table layout. To achieve correct pagination they are often used within the `table` environment described in Chapter 7. Exceptions are the environments for multipage tables described in Section 6.4, which should never be used in conjunction with the LaTeX float mechanism. Be careful, however, not to confuse the `tabular` environment with the `table` environment. The former allows material to be aligned in columns, while the latter is a logical document

Tables contained within floating environments

element identifying its contents as belonging together and allowing the material to be floated jointly. In particular, one `table` environment can contain several `tabular` environments.

After taking a quick look at the `tabbing` environment, this chapter describes the extensions to LaTeX's basic `tabular` and `array` environments provided by the array package. This package offers increased functionality, especially in terms of a more flexible positioning of paragraph material, a better control of inter-column and inter-row spacing, and the possibility of defining new preamble specifiers. Several packages build on the primitives provided by the array package to provide specific extra functionality. By combining the features in these packages, you are able to construct complex tables in a simple way. For example, the tabularx and tabulary packages provide extra column types that allow table column widths to be calculated automatically.

Standard LaTeX tabular environments do not produce tables that may be broken over a page. We give several examples of multipage tables using the `supertabular`, `longtable`, and `xltabular` environments provided by the similarly named packages. We then briefly look at the use of color in tables and at several packages that give finer control over rules, and the spacing around rules, in tables. Next, we discuss table entries spanning multiple rows, created via the multirow package, and packages that provide new column specifiers for special occasions, such as dcolumn and fcolumn, which provide mechanisms for aligning columns of figures on a decimal point.

We also discuss the use of footnotes in tables. The threeparttable package provides a convenient mechanism to have table notes and captions combined with a tabular layout.

The final section discusses the very interesting keyvaltable package that offers a completely different approach to inputting table data. In many cases it is superior to the traditional methods. It makes use of the other packages, e.g., xltabular, as its backend and so understanding their concepts and mechanisms is nevertheless useful.

Mathematically oriented readers should consult the chapter on advanced mathematics, especially Section 11.2 on page →II 131, which discusses the alignment structures for equations.

6.1 Standard LaTeX environments

Standard LaTeX has two families of environments that allow material to be lined up in columns — namely, the `tabbing` environment and the `tabular` and `array` environments. The main differences between the two kinds of environments are:

- The `tabbing` environment is not as general as the `tabular` environment. It can be typeset only as a separate paragraph, whereas a `tabular` environment can be placed anywhere in the text or inside mathematics.

- The `tabbing` environment can be broken between pages, whereas the standard `tabular` environment cannot.

- With the `tabbing` environment the user must specify the position of each tab stop explicitly. With the `tabular` environment LATEX can automatically determine the width of the columns.

- Multiple `tabbing` environments cannot be nested, whereas `tabular` environments can, thus allowing complex alignments to be realized.

6.1.1 Using the `tabbing` environment

This section deals with some of the lesser-known features of the `tabbing` environment. First, it must be realized that formatting is under the complete control of the user. Somewhat unexpectedly, when moving to a given tab stop, you always end up at the exact horizontal position where it was defined, independently of where the current point is. As a consequence, the current point can move backward and overwrite previous text. The scope of declarations within rows is usually limited to the region between tab stops, e.g., `\bfseries` and `\itshape` in the next example stop at the next `\>` or `\\`, respectively.

Be aware that the usual LATEX commands for making accents, `\'`, `\``, and `\=`, are redefined inside the `tabbing` environment. The accents are available by typing `\a'`, `\a``, and `\a=` instead (or by using accented characters directly). The `\-` command, which normally signals a possible hyphenation point, is also redefined, but this consideration is not so important because the lines in a `tabbing` environment are never broken.

Alternative names for accent commands

If the command `\'` is used between two tab stops, then all text to the left of it is placed into the *previous* tab region and typeset flush right against the previous tab stop (only separated by a distance of `\tabbingsep`). The default value for `\tabbingsep` is set equal to `\labelsep`, which in turn is usually 5 pt. To set text flush right to the right margin you can use `\``. The effect of both commands is shown below in the next example.

There exist a few common ways to define tab stops — that is, using a line to be typeset or explicitly specifying a skip to the next tab stop. The `\kill` command may be used to terminate a line that is only used to set tab stops: the line itself is not typeset. The following example demonstrates this and shows the redefinition of tab stops on the fourth line.

one		two	three four	
one		*two*		
one	again one	éè	three	flushed right
new tab pos. two			same pos. overprint	
one		two	three four	

```
\begin{tabbing}
First Real Tab Stop \= Second \= Third \=\kill
one \> two \> three \> four                \\
\bfseries one \> \itshape two         \\[5mm]
one \> again one \' \a'{e}\a`{e}
          \> three  \` flushed right \\[5mm]
new tab pos. \= two  \> same pos.
                \> //////    overprint \\
one \> two \> three \> four                \\
\end{tabbing}
```

6-1-1

If you use the above accent commands within the definition of a command that may be used inside a tabbing environment, you must use the `\a...` forms because the standard accent commands such as \' are interpreted as `tabbing` commands, as shown below. Fortunately, LaTeX now accepts UTF-8 input so that you can use the accented letter directly, instead of entering them as 7-bit input.

```
\newcommand\badcafe{caf\'e (bad)}
\newcommand\goodcafe{caf\a'e}          \newcommand\greatcafe{café}
```

Tab one	Tab two	Tab three
7-bit	caf e (bad)	café
UTF-8	café	or café

```
\begin{tabbing} Tab one \= Tab two \= Tab three   \\
                7-bit \> \badcafe   \> \goodcafe   \\
                UTF-8 \> \greatcafe \> or café     \end{tabbing}
```

6-1-2

The `tabbing` environment is most useful for aligning information into columns whose widths are constant and known. The following example is from Table A.1 on page →II 652:

```
\newcommand\lenrule[1]{\makebox[#1]{%
   \rule{.4pt}{4pt}\hrulefill\rule{.4pt}{4pt}}}
\begin{tabbing}
   dd\quad \= \hspace{.55\linewidth} \= \kill
   pc  \> Pica = 12pt          \> \lenrule{1pc} \\
   cc  \> Cicero   = 12dd      \> \lenrule{1cc} \\
   cm  \> Centimeter = 10mm \> \lenrule{1cm} \\
\end{tabbing}
```

pc	Pica = 12pt	⌐⌐
cc	Cicero = 12dd	⌐⌐
cm	Centimeter = 10mm	⌐──⌐

6-1-3

6.1.2 tabto — An alternative way to tab stops

As an alternative to the standard `tabbing` environment Donald Arseneau developed the `tabto` package that offers a set of commands for moving to tab positions that can be used within normal text, list environments, etc., without the need to be confined in a special environment.

```
\tabto{length}      \tabto*{length}
```

The \tabto command moves to a position *length* away from the left margin (where list indentations count as part of the margin). If the text on the current line is already past the desired position, the command starts a new line and then moves to the right point. In contrast, \tabto* always stays in the current line and performs backspacing if we are past the desired target point; that is, it may result in overprinting of text.

In the next example "T1" and "T2" are placed at tab positions reachable in the current line, while both "T3" and "T4" jump to the next line because in each case we are already past the target position. Note that "T5" ends up before "T4" due to the fact that we used \tabto* here.

Lorem ipsum dolor sit amet, consectetuer adipiscing elit.   T1   T2
                    T3 Ut purus elit, vestibu-
lum ut, placerat ac, adipiscing vitae, felis.
          T5   T4

```
\usepackage{lipsum,tabto}
\lipsum[1][1] \tabto{3cm}T1 \tabto{4cm}T2
\tabto{3cm}T3 \lipsum[1][2] \tabto{4cm}T4
\tabto*{2cm}T5
```

6-1-4

The current position in the line is available in the register \CurrentLineWidth, which enables you (for example with calc syntax) to define the next tab position relative to position where the \tabto command is encountered. In addition, the most recent tab position is stored in \TabPrevPos.

In the next example, "T1" starts one centimeter to the left of the current position (and thus on a new line), while "T2" starts exactly in the same horizontal position from which we started off originally (the \smash hides the height of the \rule so that it can overprint the paragraph text and we can see that the alignment is perfect).

Lorem ipsum dolor sit amet, consectetuer
adipiscing elit.
         T1 Ut purus elit, vestibulum ut, place-
rat ac, adipiscing vitae, felis.
         T2

```
\usepackage{lipsum,calc,tabto}
\lipsum[1][1]\tabto{\CurrentLineWidth-1cm}T1
\lipsum[1][2]\tabto{\TabPrevPos}%
            \smash{\rule{.4pt}{46pt}}T2
```

6-1-5

Besides using ad hoc tab positions as we did so far, the package also supports predefining tab stops and then moving from one to the next using \tab.

\NumTabs{*number*}	\TabPositions{*length, length, ...*}	\tab

With \NumTabs the current \linewidth is divided into a *number* of equally distant tab stops starting at the left margin; e.g., \NumTabs{2} generates a tab position at the start and the middle of the line. That gives you same result as specifying \TabPositions{0pt,.5\linewidth}. The advantage of the second form of declaration is that you can specify arbitrary positions, but of course it requires more typing. The first position is alway the left margin even if not specified as 0pt.

Note that prior to \begin{document} the value of \linewidth may be incorrect, which means that \NumTabs may generate wrong tab stops. Thus, in the document preamble you have to use \TabPositions or explicitly initialize the \linewidth to \textwidth (or whatever is appropriate) first.

Once the tab stops are declared, the \tab command always moves to the next tab stop in the line or to the start of a new line if the list is exhausted. In particular, two or more \tab commands in a row skip one or more tab stops.

Start   T1   T2   T3
T0b   T3b
    Start   T1   T2 (last one in line)
T0b (get past T1b) T? T2b

```
\usepackage{tabto}

\NumTabs{4}
Start\tab T1\tab T2\tab T3\tab T0b \tab\tab T3b

\TabPositions{.25\linewidth,.5\linewidth}
Start\tab T1\tab T2 (last one in line)\tab T0b
(get past T1b)\tab T2b \tabto*{.42\linewidth}T?
```

6-1-6

As you can see in the previous example, it is possible to mix predefined tab positions and those explicitly calculated from the left margin, which is why T? shows up to the left of T2b and another \tab would then jump again to the T2b position.

Specifier	Effect
l, c, r	Left-aligned, center-aligned or right-aligned column.
p{*width*}	Equivalent to \parbox[t]{*width*}.
|	Inserts a vertical line between two columns. The distance between the two columns is unaffected.
@{*decl*}	Suppresses inter-column space and inserts *decl* instead.
*{*num*}{*opts*}	Equivalent to *num* copies of *opts*.

Table 6.1: The preamble specifiers in the standard LaTeX tabular environment

6.1.3 Using the `tabular` environment

In general, when tables of any degree of complexity are required, it is usually easier to consider the `tabular`-like environments defined by LaTeX. These environments align material horizontally in rows (separated by \\) and vertically in columns (separated by &). The \\ command accepts an optional argument for requesting additional vertical space after the row. How this argument is interpreted depends unfortunately on the type of the rightmost column in the table; see Section 6.2.1 on the facing page for a discussion of the pitfalls and its behavior in the array package.

```
\begin{array}[pos]{col-spec}              rows \end{array}
\begin{tabular}[pos]{col-spec}            rows \end{tabular}
\begin{tabular*}{width}[pos]{col-spec} rows \end{tabular*}
```

The `array` environment is essentially the math mode equivalent of the `tabular` environment. The entries of the table are set in math mode, and the default inter-column space is different (as described below), but otherwise the functionality of the two environments is identical.

The `tabular*` environment has an additional width argument that specifies the required total width of the table. It needs stretchable spaces between columns that have to be added using \extracolsep (see page 442).

Table 6.1 shows the various specifiers available in the *col-spec* preamble declaration of the environments in the standard LaTeX tabular family. The array package introduced in the next section extends this list of preamble specifiers.

Style parameters   The visual appearance of the `tabular`-like environments can be controlled by various style parameters. These parameters can be changed by using the \setlength or \addtolength commands anywhere in the document. Their scope can be general or local. In the latter case the scope should be explicitly delimited by braces or another environment.

\arraycolsep   Half the width of the horizontal space between columns in an `array` environment (default value 5 pt).

\tabcolsep   Half the width of the horizontal space between columns in a `tabular` environment (default value 6 pt).

\arrayrulewidth   The width of the vertical rule that separates columns (if a | is specified in the environment preamble) and the rules created by \hline, \cline, or \vline (default value 0.4pt).

When using the array package, this width is taken into account when calculating the width of the table (standard LaTeX sets the rules in such a way that they do not affect the final width of the table).

Size change made by the array package

\doublerulesep   The width of the space between lines created by two successive || characters in the environment preamble or by two successive \hline commands (default value 2pt).

\arraystretch   Fraction with which the inter-row space between normal-sized rows is multiplied. For example, a value of 1.5 would move the rows 50% farther apart. This value is set with \renewcommand (default value 1.0).

With \multicolumn{*number*}{*new-col-spec*}{*content*} you can aggregate a *number* of consecutive cells into one or alter the *col-spec* for a single cell. It must be placed at the start of a row or immediately after an &. The *new-col-spec* should contain only a single column specifier and optionally | and @ specifiers. It replaces the environment's column specifications for the aggregated cells (including any | or @ to the right of the last of the aggregated columns in the spec).

Joining cells from consecutive columns.

6.2 array — Extending the tabular environments

Over the years several extensions have been made to the tabular environment family, as described in the *LaTeX Manual*. This section explores the added functionality of the array package (developed by the author, with contributions from David Carlisle). Many of the packages described later in the chapter build on the functionality of the array package so as to extend or adapt the tabular environment.

Table 6.2 on page 439 shows all the specifiers available in the *col-spec* preamble declaration of the environments in the tabular family.

6.2.1 The behavior of the \\ command

In the basic tabular implementation of LaTeX the \\ command ending the rows of the tabular or array has a somewhat inconsistent behavior if its optional argument is used. The result then depends on the type of rightmost column and as remarked in the *LaTeX manual* [65] may not always produce the expected extra space.

Without the array package the extra space requested by the optional argument of \\ is measured from the last baseline of the rightmost column (indicated by "x" in the following example). As a result, swapping the column gives different results:

```
\begin{tabular}[t]{lp{1cm}} \hline
  1 & x\newline y \\[20pt]
  2 & 2            \\ \hline \end{tabular}
\qquad
\begin{tabular}[t]{p{1cm}l} \hline
  x\newline y & 1 \\[20pt]
  2           & 2 \\ \hline \end{tabular}
```

In contrast, when the array package is loaded, the requested space in the optional argument is always measured from the baseline of the whole row and not from the last baseline of the rightmost column; thus, swapping columns does not change the spacing, and we get the same table height with an effective 8pt of extra space (as the second line already takes up 12pt of the requested 20pt):

```
\usepackage{array}
\begin{tabular}[t]{lp{1cm}} \hline
  1 & x\newline y \\[20pt]
  2 & 2               \\ \hline \end{tabular}
\qquad
\begin{tabular}[t]{p{1cm}l} \hline
  x\newline y & 1 \\[20pt]
  2           & 2 \\ \hline \end{tabular}
```

6-2-2

This correction of behavior only makes a difference if the rightmost column is a p-column. Thus, if you add the array package to an existing document, you should verify the spacing in all tables that have this kind of structure.

6.2.2 Examples of preamble specifiers

When the column specifiers l, c, or r are used, then LaTeX automatically calculates the width of the column based on its widest cell. In many cases this is a convenient approach, because the table automatically adjusts its layout based on its content. There are, however, cases when it is desirable to explicitly specify the column width regardless of the content placed into it (usually by making it wider).

To produce columns with a fixed width using the basic `tabular` environment you specify it as a p column, but then the column is always left aligned; i.e., you cannot specify the inner alignment, and your cell content may generate several lines if it overflows. The alternative is to use a \makebox in at least one cell of the column, but that only defines the minimum column width; i.e., if there is a wider cell, then the column widens.

A better solution is offered by the array package with the specifiers w and W. Both take two mandatory arguments: an *alignment* (which can be either l, c, or r) and the desired *width* for the column. The difference between the two specifiers is that in a w column the cell content is always set at its natural width and silently overflows (and possibly overprints neighbor cells) if the entry is too wide, while in a W it is squeezed as much as possible if it is too wide and then generates an overfull box warning if it still does not fit. We show this behavior in the next example by setting \overfullrule to a positive value so that overfull boxes are marked.

```
\usepackage{array} \setlength\overfullrule{5pt}
\begin{tabular}{|r|wr{13mm}|Wr{15mm}|}
  flexible (r)& fixed (w)    & fixed (W)   \\
  123         & 123          & 123         \\
  123456789   & 123456789    & 123456789   \\
  ab cd ef gh & ab cd ef gh  & ab cd ef gh\\
\end{tabular}
```

6-2-3

Specifier	Effect
	Unchanged Basic Specifiers
l, c, r	Left-aligned, center-aligned, or right-aligned column.
p{*width*}	Equivalent to \parbox[t]{*width*}.
@{*material*}	Suppresses inter-column space and inserts *material* instead.
*{*num*}{*opts*}	Equivalent to *num* copies of *opts*.
	Changed Specifiers
	Inserts a vertical line. The distance between two columns is enlarged by the width of the line, in contrast to the original definition of LaTeX.
	New Specifiers
w{*align*}{*width*}	Sets the cell content at its natural size in a box of the specified *width* aligned according to the *align* parameter, which could be either l, c, or r. Works essentially like \makebox[*width*][*align*]{*cell*} so silently overprints if the cell content is wider than the specified width. If that is not desired, use the W specifier instead.
W{*align*}{*width*}	W work like w but tries to squeeze the cell content if necessary and generates an overfull box warning (and an overfull rule marker in draft mode) when the content is too wide to fit. This also means that the alignment is different if there is too much material, because it then always protrudes to the right!
m{*width*}	Defines a column of width *width*. Every entry is centered vertically in proportion to the rest of the line. It is somewhat like \parbox{*width*}.
b{*width*}	Coincides with \parbox[b]{*width*}.
>{*decl*}	Can be used before any of the column specifiers, i.e., l, r, c, w, W, p, m, or b options. It inserts *decl* directly in front of the entry of the column.
<{*decl*}	Can be used after any column specifier. It inserts *decl* immediately after the entry of the column.
!{*decl*}	Can be used anywhere and corresponds with the	option. The difference is that *decl* is inserted instead of a vertical line, so this option does not suppress the normally inserted space between columns, in contrast to @{...}.

Table 6.2: Preamble specifiers in the array package

Observe the overfull box mark in the third column because the material in the cell is wider than 15 mm and cannot shrink, while in the middle column (which is only 13 mm wide) it overflows silently into the left margin in rows 3 and 4 (the latter being squeezed enough to fit in column 3). Also notice that W always overflows to the right while w overflows away from the alignment (i.e., to the left if the alignment is r).

The cells in a row of a tabular are aligned at their baseline to give a uniform appearance. In the case of p cells, the material is aligned at the baseline of the first line with respect to other cells in the row. However, if the cell content does not start with text (but with some vertically oriented material like the \vspace in the next example), then all of the cell material is positioned below that baseline and if necessary needs to be moved upwards with a negative vertical skip.

Using a \color command at the start of a cell has the same issue, but here the solution is simple: use \textcolor instead, because this starts a paragraph if necessary, as you can see in the fourth column of the next example:

a a a a a a	b b b b	c c c c c c c c	d d d

```
\usepackage{color,array}
\begin{tabular}{|p{1pc}|p{1pc}|p{1pc}|l|}
   \hline  \vspace{0pt}  a a a a a a         &
                         b b b b             &
          \color{blue} c c c c c c c c       &
          \textcolor{blue}{d d d}            \\  \hline
\end{tabular}
```

6-2-4

The differences between the three paragraph-building specifiers p (the paragraph box is aligned at the top), m (the paragraph box is aligned in the center), and b (the paragraph box is aligned at the bottom) is the placement with respect to the other cells in the same row. A common misconception is that m positions its material centered in the available space otherwise taken up by the row, e.g., that the b's in the previous example would line up with the second and third line of the c's if they are positioned using m or that the a's would drop to the bottom of the table if the first column is changed to a b column.

Instead, you get the following result, because everything aligns with the baseline of "d" in the fourth column. Notice that in a b cell, vertical material at the beginning has no special effect because the alignment happens at the bottom. However, in that scenario vertical material at the end would effect the positioning because then the alignment would no longer be at the baseline of the last line, but at the very bottom of the cell material.

To help you visualize the baseline at which the cells in the row are aligned we have added a rule into the last cell in a way that it protrudes to the left:

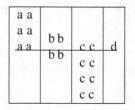

```
\usepackage{array}
\begin{tabular}{|b{1pc}|m{1pc}|p{1pc}|l|}
\hline  \vspace{0pt} a a a a a a & b b b b &
              c c c c c c c c & d\llap{\rule{80pt}{0.4pt}} \\
\hline
\end{tabular}
```

6-2-5

The placement behavior also affects the results obtained by the optional argument of the command \\ that terminates each row. One has to realize that the *extra depth* that can be specified this way only changes the nominal depth of the current row — it is not a vertical skip added between rows. Thus, if it is smaller than the current row depth (for example when there is a multiline p or m cell), then it has zero effect. In contrast, the length \extrarowheight is added to the height of the first line in each cell and therefore always affects the position.

Both behaviors are shown in the next example. To better demonstrate the reason why \\[1cm] makes no difference, we have added an extra column and placed a rule inside to show how much this would increase the row depth, which is clearly not enough to get below the last row of c's.

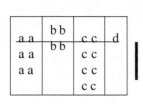

6-2-6

```
\usepackage{array}

\setlength\extrarowheight{5pt}
\begin{tabular}{|p{1pc}|m{1pc}|p{1pc}|l|c} \cline{1-4}
    a a a a a a         & b b b b                  &
    c c c  c c c c c    & d\llap{\rule{80pt}{0.4pt}} &
    \rule[-1cm]{2pt}{1cm}              \\[1cm]  \cline{1-4}
\end{tabular}
```

If you would like to use a special font, such as \bfseries in a flush left column, you can write >{\bfseries}l. You no longer have to start every entry of the column with \bfseries.

A	B	C
100	10	1

6-2-7

```
\usepackage{array}

\begin{tabular}{|>{\large}c|>{\large\bfseries}l|>{\itshape}c|}
\hline A & B & C\\\hline 100 & 10 & 1 \\\hline
\end{tabular}
```

In the previous example we also changed the font size in some cells, and this exhibits a general problem with the tabular environment. If the height of the material inside the cells is larger than a typical height of a text line, it gets too close to any surrounding rule. Standard tabular offers \arraystretch to spread the lines farther apart. However, that stretches both the height and the depth of each line, and in many cases it is only the part above the baseline that has issues. *Extra space between rows*

This consideration is especially important for tables with horizontal lines because it is often necessary to fine-tune the distance between those lines and the contents of the table. To help in such situations the array package offers the parameter \extrarowheight, which adds some extra height to each cell without changing the depth. The effect of \extrarowheight is visible only if \arraystretch × (\extrarowheight + 0.7\baselineskip) is larger than the actual height of the cell or, more precisely, in the case of p, m, or b, the height of the *first row* of the cell. The default value of \extrarowheight is 0pt. Below we repeat Example 6-2-7 but add a vertical space of 3pt above each row using this method, which is clearly an improvement:

A	B	C
100	10	1

6-2-8

```
\usepackage{array}

\setlength\extrarowheight{3pt}
\begin{tabular}{|>{\large}c|>{\large\bfseries}l|>{\itshape}c|}
\hline A & B & C\\\hline 100 & 10 & 1 \\\hline
\end{tabular}
```

Font encoding changes not supported in a >{...} argument

There are few restrictions on the declarations that may be used with the > preamble option. Nevertheless, for technical reasons beyond the scope of this book, it is not possible to change the font encoding for the table column. For example, if the current encoding is not T1, then `>{\fontencoding{T1}\selectfont}` does *not* work. No error message is generated, but incorrect characters may be produced at the start of each cell in the column. If a column of text requires a special encoding, then the encoding command should be placed explicitly at the start of each cell in the column.

In columns that have been generated with p, m, or b, the default value of `\parindent` is 0pt. It can be changed with the `\setlength` command, as shown in the next example where we indent the first column by 5 mm:

```
\usepackage{array}

\begin{tabular}
    {|>{\setlength\parindent{5mm}}p{2cm}|p{2cm}|}
\hline 1 2 3 4 5 6 7 8 9 0 1 2 3 4 5 6 7 8 9 0 &
    1 2 3 4 5 6 7 8 9 0 1 2 3 4 5 6 7 8 9 0 \\ \hline
\end{tabular}
```

1 2 3 4 5 6	1 2 3 4 5 6 7 8
7 8 9 0 1 2 3 4	9 0 1 2 3 4 5 6
5 6 7 8 9 0	7 8 9 0

6-2-9

The < preamble option was originally developed for the following application: `>{$}c<{$}` generates a column in math mode in a `tabular` environment. The use of this type of preamble in an `array` environment results in a column in LR mode because the additional $s cancel the existing $s.

```
\usepackage{array}   \setlength\extrarowheight{4pt}

\begin{tabular}{|>{$}l<{$}|l|}              \hline
    10!^{10!}          & a big number   \\
    10^{-999}          & a small number \\\hline
\end{tabular}
```

| $10!^{10!}$ | a big number |
| 10^{-999} | a small number |

6-2-10

Making `tabular*` stretch to the required width

A major use of the ! and @ options is to add stretchable space with the help of an `\extracolsep` command so that TeX can stretch the table to the desired width in the `tabular*` environment. The use of `\extracolsep` in the array package environments is subject to two restrictions: there can be at most one `\extracolsep` command per @ or ! expression, and the command must be directly entered into the @ expression, not as part of a macro definition. Thus, `@{\extracolsep{\fill}}` can be used, but `\newcommand\ef{\extracolsep{\fill}}`, and then later `@{\ef}` in a tabular preamble, does not work.

Typesetting narrow columns

TeX does not hyphenate the first word in a paragraph, so very narrow cells can produce overflows. This can be corrected by starting the text with `\hspace{0pt}`.

| Characteristics |

| Char-acteris-tics |

```
\fbox{\parbox{11mm}{Characteristics}}%
\hfill
\fbox{\parbox{11mm}{\hspace{0pt}Characteristics}}
```

6-2-11

When you have a narrow column, you must not only make sure that the first word can be hyphenated, but also consider that short texts are easier to typeset in ragged-right mode (without being aligned at the right margin). This result is obtained by preceding the material with a \raggedright command (see Section 3.1). This command redefines the line-breaking command \\, so we must use the command \tabularnewline, which is defined in standard LaTeX to be the original definition of the row-ending \\ command of the tabular or array environment. Alternatively, we could have used the \arraybackslash command from the array package after the \raggedright in the third column. This locally redefines \\ to end the table row, as shown in Example 6-2-17 on page 446.

As shown in the example below, we can now typeset material inside a tabular environment ragged right, ragged left, or centered and still have control of the line breaks. The first word is now hyphenated correctly, although in the case of French and Dutch, we helped TeX a little by choosing the possible hyphenation points ourselves.

Super-	Possibili-	Mogelijk-
con-	tés et	heden en
scious-	es-	hoop
ness is a	pérances	
long		
word		
Ragged	Centered	Ragged
left text	text in	right text
in	column	in
column	two	column
one		three

```
\usepackage{array}
\begin{tabular}
  {|>{\raggedleft\hspace{0pt}}p{14mm}%
   |>{\centering\hspace{0pt}}p{14mm}%
   |>{\raggedright\hspace{0pt}}p{14mm}|}
\hline Superconsciousness is a long word   &
       Possibi\-li\-t\'es et esp\'erances   &
       Moge\-lijk\-heden en hoop   \tabularnewline
\hline Ragged left text in column one       &
       Centered text    in column two       &
       Ragged right text in  column three
                                \tabularnewline \hline
\end{tabular}
```

6-2-12

Controlling the horizontal separation between columns

The default inter-column spacing is controlled by setting the length parameters \arraycolsep (for array) and \tabcolsep (for tabular). However, it is often desirable to alter the spacing between individual columns, or, more commonly, before the first column and after the last column of the table.

onetwo	three–four	– five
1 2	3 – 4	– 5

```
\usepackage{array}
\begin{tabular}{c@{}c!{}c@{--}c!{--}c}
  one & two & three & four & five \\ 1 & 2 & 3 & 4 & 5
\end{tabular}
```

6-2-13

In the example above, @{} has been used to remove the inter-column space between columns 1 and 2. An empty !{} has no effect, as demonstrated between columns 2 and 3. Note that a dash appears in place of the default inter-column space when specified using @{--} between columns 3 and 4, but is placed in the center of the default inter-column space when specified using !{--} between columns 4 and 5.

443

Using @{} to remove
space at the side of
the table
A common use of @{} is to remove the space equal to the value of \tabcolsep
(for `tabular`) that, by default, appears on each side of the table, except when the
column specification starts or ends in a |.

Sample text before ...

| one | two |
| three | four |

material following ...

a bit more text to separate the tables

| | one | two |
| three | four |

now touching ...

... and some more text.

```
\begin{flushleft} \textbf{Sample text before \ldots}\\
\begin{tabular}{lr}
  one & two\\ three & four\\
\end{tabular}\textbf{material following \ldots}\\
\textbf{a bit more text to separate the tables}\\
\begin{tabular}{|lr@{}}
  one & two\\ \multicolumn{1}{@{}l}{three} & four\\
\end{tabular}\textbf{now touching \ldots}\\
\textbf{\ldots\ and some more text.} \end{flushleft}
```
    `6-2-14`

Tables inside tables or other environments

The family of `tabular` environments allows vertical positioning with respect to the
baseline of the text in which the environment appears. By default, the environment
appears centered. This preference can be changed to align with the first or last line in
the environment by supplying a t or b value to the optional position argument. Note
that this approach does not work when the first or last element in the environment is
an \hline command — in that case, the environment is aligned at the horizontal rule.

Tables with no   versus tables

| with some |
| hline |
| commands |

used.

Tables	with no
	hline
	commands
	used

```
\usepackage{array}
Tables \begin{tabular}{t}{l}
  with no\\ hline \\ commands \\ used
\end{tabular}
versus tables
\begin{tabular}{t}{|l|}      \hline
  with some \\ hline \\ commands \\
\hline
\end{tabular} used.
```
    `6-2-15`

To achieve proper alignments you can use the two commands \firsthline
and \lasthline, which are special versions of \hline defined in the array package.
These commands enable you to align the information in the tables properly as long as
their first or last lines do not contain extremely large objects.

Tables with no   versus tables

| with some |
| hline |
| commands |

used.

Tables	with no
	hline
	commands
	used

```
\usepackage{array}
Tables \begin{tabular}{t}{l}
  with no\\ hline \\ commands \\ used
\end{tabular}
versus tables
\begin{tabular}{t}{|l|}  \firsthline
  with some \\ hline \\ commands \\
\lasthline
\end{tabular} used.
```
    `6-2-16`

Tables form boxes sometimes with the outer rules being at the edges. If you nest such tables, the rules get too close (or touch) surrounding material. The array package therefore provides the length parameter \extratabsurround that adds a space of that length above \firsthline and below \lasthline (default 2pt).

6.2.3 Defining new column specifiers

If you have a one-off column in a table, then you may use the > and < options to modify the style for that column:

>{*some declarations*}c<{*some more decls*}

This code, however, becomes rather verbose if you often use columns of this form. Therefore, for repetitive use of a given type of column specifier combination, the following declaration has been provided:

\newcolumntype{*col*} [*narg*] {*column-declarations*}

Here, *col* is a one-letter specifier[1] to identify the new type of column inside a preamble; *narg* is an optional parameter, giving the number of arguments this specifier takes; and *column-declarations* is a sequence of legal column declarations. For example:

\newcolumntype{x}{>{*some declarations*}c<{*some more decls*}}

The newly defined x column specifier can then be used in the preamble arguments of all array and tabular environments in which one needs columns of this form. If the column specifier already exists, it is overwritten with the new definition. This can be useful if you define your own specifiers and alter them in different parts of the document. However, be careful not to overwrite the predefined column specifiers, because once replaced, there is no way to get their functionality back.

Quite often you may need math mode and LR mode columns inside a tabular or array environment. Thus, you can define the following column specifiers:

```
\newcolumntype{C}{>{$}c<{$}}
\newcolumntype{L}{>{$}l<{$}}
\newcolumntype{R}{>{$}r<{$}}
```

From now on you can use C to get centered LR mode in an array environment, or centered math mode in a tabular environment, etc.

The \newcolumntype command takes the same first optional argument as \newcommand, which declares the number of arguments of the column specifier being defined. However, \newcolumntype does not take the additional optional argument forms of \newcommand; in the current implementation, column specifiers may have only mandatory arguments.

---

[1] Typically letters such as R, C, or S are used, but symbols like + or ! or even command names, e.g., \mycol, are possible too. For the TeX savvy: everything that counts as a single token can be used.

The next example is a repeat of Example 6-2-12 on page 443 except that we provide a new column specifier to do the job and also employ `\arraybackslash` so that the table rows can be finished off with `\\` as usual.

Super-con-scious-ness is a long word	Possibili-tés et es-pérances	Mogelijk-heden en hoop
Ragged left text in column one	Centered text in column two	Ragged right text in column three

```
\usepackage{array}
\newcolumntype{P}[1]
   {>{#1\hspace{0pt}\arraybackslash}p{14mm}|}
\begin{tabular}
     {|P{\raggedleft}P{\centering}P{\raggedright}}
\hline Superconsciousness is a long word   &
       Possibi\-li\-t\'es et esp\'erances   &
       Moge\-lijk\-heden en hoop            \\\hline
       Ragged left text in column one        &
       Centered text   in column two        &
       Ragged right text in  column three \\\hline
\end{tabular}
```

6-2-17

A rather different use of the `\newcolumntype` command takes advantage of the fact that the replacement text in `\newcolumntype` may refer to more than one column. The following example shows the definition of a preamble option Z. Modifying the definition in the document preamble would change the layout of all tables in the document using this preamble option in a consistent manner. However, that makes the `tabular` preambles difficult to understand, so we suggest to refrain from that, just to save a few keystrokes. Use it only if you have many tables with the same structure.

one	two	three
1	2	3

```
\usepackage{array}  \newcolumntype{Z}{clr}
\begin{tabular}{Z} one&two&three\\1&2&3 \end{tabular}
```

6-2-18

The replacement text in a `\newcolumntype` command can be any of the primitives of array, or any new letter defined in another `\newcolumntype` command. If you load additional table packages, such as dcolumn or fcolumn, then their types are usable as well.

Any column specification in a `tabular` environment that uses one of these newly defined column types is "expanded" to its primitive form during the first stage of table processing. This means that in some circumstances, error messages generated when parsing the column specification refer to the preamble argument *after* it has been rewritten by the `\newcolumntype` system, not to the preamble entered by the user.

Debugging column type declarations   To display a list of all currently active `\newcolumntype` definitions on the terminal, use the `\showcols` command in the preamble.

6.3 Calculating column widths

As described in Appendix A.3, LaTeX has two distinct modes for setting text: LR mode, in which the text is set in a single line, and paragraph mode, in which text is broken into lines of a specified length. This distinction strongly influences the design of the LaTeX table commands. The l, c, or r column types as well as the w and W types added by the array package, specify table entries set in LR mode, whereas p and the array package m and b types specify table entries set in paragraph mode.

The need to specify the width of paragraph mode entries in advance sometimes causes difficulties when setting tables, especially when the table also contains columns whose width is calculated by LaTeX. We describe several approaches that calculate the required column widths based on the required total width of the table and/or the table contents.

If we can predefine all columns, e.g., if we have only paragraph mode columns, then calculating the necessary column widths is a matter of a simple formula: subtract from the available space the amount taken up by the column gaps and divide that by the number of columns we want.

As an example we define the environment `tabularc` that can generate a table with a defined width (first argument) having a number of p columns (second argument) with equal width matching the total width of the table. This code uses `\dimeval` for the calculation discussed in Appendix A.2.5 on page →II 657; alternatively, we could have used the calc package (from Appendix A.5.2, page →II 687).

Explicit calculation of column widths

The number of columns (let us call it x) is used to calculate the actual width of each column by subtracting two x times the column separation and $(x + 1)$ times the width of the rules from the width of the table. The remaining distance is divided by x to obtain the width of a single column. The contents of the columns are centered, and hyphenation of the first word is allowed. Because of `\centering`, we have to use the command `\tabularnewline` in the table body, as discussed in Section 6.2.2. The alternative would have been to add `\arraybackslash` in the preamble declaration.

Instead of always using p columns, we could have used different column specifiers (including w or W), the only requirement being that it is a specifier that needs a width.

```
\usepackage{array}
\newenvironment{tabularc}[2]
  {\begin{tabular*}{#1}{*{#2}{|>{\centering\hspace{0pt}}%
      p{\dimeval{#1/(#2)-\tabcolsep*2-\arrayrulewidth*(#2+1)/(#2)}}}|}}
  {\end{tabular*}}
```

```
\begin{tabularc}{300pt}{3}    \hline
Material in column one & column two & This is column three \tabularnewline\hline
... further text omitted ...
```

6-3-1

Material in column one	column two	This is column three
Column one again	and column two	This is column three
Once more column one	column two	Last time column three

Calculating column widths in this way gives you full control over the amount of space allocated to each column. Furthermore, after the calculation has been done, the table can be set in a single run without any trial typesetting, which introduces its own set of complications.

Unfortunately, it is difficult to incorporate information depending on the contents of the table into the calculation. For example, if some columns should be as wide as their widest entry, e.g., use the c column type, then we do not know beforehand how wide this column is going to be, and thus a calculation like the above becomes impossible to do in advance.

Three packages implement different algorithms that set the table multiple times so as to allocate widths to certain columns. The first, tabularx, essentially tries to allocate space equally between specified paragraph mode columns. The second, tabulary, tries to allocate more space to columns that contain "more data". Finally, widetable provides an environment with the same arguments as `tabular*` but attempts to place the extra space into the columns instead of between columns.

6.3.1 tabularx — Automatic calculation of column widths

The package tabularx (by David Carlisle) implements a version of the `tabular*` environment in which the widths of certain columns are calculated automatically depending on the total width of the table. The columns whose widths are automatically calculated are denoted in the preamble by the X qualifier. The latter column specification is converted to p{*some value*} once the correct column width has been calculated.

Commands typically used to typeset the X columns

Narrow columns often require a special format, which may be achieved using the > syntax. Thus, you may give a specification like >{\small}X. Another format that is useful in narrow columns is ragged right. As noted earlier, one must use the command \tabularnewline to end the table row if the last entry in a row is being set ragged right. This specification may be saved in a new column specifier (perhaps additionally adding \arraybackslash to make \\ denote the end of a row again). You may then use this column specifier in a tabularx preamble argument.

The first example shows as a table with three multiline columns of equal width using the mentioned adjustments.

```
\usepackage{tabularx}
\newcolumntype{Y}{>{\small\raggedright\arraybackslash}X}
\noindent\begin{tabularx}{100mm}{|Y|Y|Y|}  \hline
The Two Gentlemen of Verona   & The Taming of the Shrew &
... further text omitted ...
```

6-3-2

The Two Gentlemen of Verona	The Taming of the Shrew	The Comedy of Errors
Love's Labour's Lost	A Midsummer Night's Dream	The Merchant of Venice
The Merry Wives of Windsor	Much Ado About Nothing	As You Like It
Twelfth Night	Troilus and Cressida	Measure for Measure
All's Well That Ends Well	Pericles, Prince of Tyre	The Winter's Tale
Cymbeline	The Tempest	

Changing the *width* argument to specify a width of `\linewidth` then produces the following table layout:

```
\usepackage{tabularx}
\newcolumntype{Y}{>{\small\raggedright\arraybackslash}X}
\noindent\begin{tabularx}{\linewidth}{|Y|Y|Y|}        \hline
The Two Gentlemen of Verona  & The Taming of the Shrew  &
                             The Comedy of Errors      \\\hline
Love's Labour's Lost         & A Midsummer Night's Dream  &
... further text omitted ...
```

6-3-3

The Two Gentlemen of Verona	The Taming of the Shrew	The Comedy of Errors
Love's Labour's Lost	A Midsummer Night's Dream	The Merchant of Venice
The Merry Wives of Windsor	Much Ado About Nothing	As You Like It
Twelfth Night	Troilus and Cressida	Measure for Measure
All's Well That Ends Well	Pericles, Prince of Tyre	The Winter's Tale
Cymbeline	The Tempest	

The X columns are set using a p column, which corresponds to `\parbox[t]`. However, you may want to set the columns with, for example, an m column corresponding to `\parbox[c]`. It is impossible to change the column type using the > syntax, so another system is provided. The command `\tabularxcolumn` can be defined as a macro, with one argument, which expands to the `tabular` preamble specification to be used for X henceforth. When the command is executed, the supplied argument determines the actual column width.

The default definition is `\newcommand\tabularxcolumn[1]{p{#1}}`. A possible alternative definition is

```
\renewcommand\tabularxcolumn[1]{>{\small}m{#1}}
```

Normally, all X columns in a single table are set to the same width. It is neverthe- *Adjusting the* less possible to make `tabularx` set them to different widths. A preamble like the *column widths* following

```
>{\setlength\hsize{.5\hsize}}X>{\setlength\hsize{1.5\hsize}}X
```

specifies two columns; the second column will be three times as wide as the first. However, when using this method, two rules should be obeyed:

Restrictions to obey

- The sum of the widths of all X columns should remain unchanged. In the above example, the new widths should add up to the width of two standard X columns.

- `\multicolumn` entries that cross such adjusted X columns should not be used.

Of course, for such lengthy input, you should define your own column specifier, e.g., ?, as we do in the next example.

```
\usepackage{tabularx}    \tracingtabularx
\newcolumntype{?}[1]
            {>{\setlength\hsize{#1\hsize}}X}
\begin{tabularx}{\linewidth}
            {| ?{.85} | ?{1.15} |}
Superconsciousness is a long word  &
Moge\-lijk\-heden en hoop                \\
Some text in column one              &
A somewhat longer text in  column two \\
\end{tabularx}
```

| Superconsciousness is a long word | Mogelijkheden en hoop |
| Some text in column one | A somewhat longer text in column two |

6-3-4

Tracing tabularx calculations If a \tracingtabularx declaration is made, say, in the document preamble, then all following tabularx environments print information to the terminal and to the log file about column widths as they repeatedly reset the tables to find the correct widths. For instance, the last example produced the following log:

```
Package tabularx Warning: Target width: \linewidth  = 207.0pt.

(tabularx)     Table Width    Column Width    X Columns
(tabularx)     439.19998pt    207.0pt         3
(tabularx)     206.99998pt    90.90001pt      2
(tabularx) Reached target.
```

6.3.2 tabulary — Column widths based on content

An alternative algorithm for determining column widths is provided by the **tabulary** package (also written by David Carlisle) providing the **tabulary** environment. It is most suitable for cases in which the column widths must be calculated based on the content of the table. This often arises when you use LATEX to typeset documents originating as SGML/XML or HTML, which typically employ a different table model in which multiline material does not have a prespecified width and the layout is left more to the formatter.

The **tabulary** package provides the column types shown in Table 6.3 on the facing page plus those provided by the **array** package in Table 6.2 on page 439, and any other preamble options defined via \newcolumntype.

\begin{tabulary}{*width*} [*pos*] {*col-spec*} *rows* \end{tabulary}

The main feature of this package is its provision of versions of the p column specifier in which the width of the column is determined automatically depending on the table contents. The following example is rather artificial because the table has only one row. Nevertheless, it demonstrates that the aim of the column width allocation made by **tabulary** is to achieve equal row height. Normally, of course, the same row cannot

Specifier	Effect
J	Justified p column set to some width to be determined
L	Flush left p column set to some width to be determined
R	Flush right p column set to some width to be determined
C	Centered p column set to some width to be determined

Table 6.3: The preamble options in the tabulary package

hold the largest entry of each column, but in many cases of tabular material, the material in each cell of a given column has similar characteristics. In those situations the width allocation appears to provide reasonable results.

```
\usepackage{tabulary}
\setlength\tymin{10pt}
\setlength\tymax{\maxdimen}
```

a	b	c c c c	d d d d d d d d d d d d d
	b	c c c c	d d d d d d d d d d d d d
	b	c c c c	d d d d d d d d d d d d d
	b	c c c c	d d d d d d d d d d d d d
		c c	d d d d d d d

```
\begin{tabulary}{200pt}{|C|C|C|C|}
a & b b b b &
c c c c c c c c c c c c c c c c c &
d d d d d d d d d d d d d d d d
... further text omitted ...
```

6-3-5

The tabulary package has two length parameters, \tymin and \tymax, which control the allocation of widths. By default, widths are allocated to each L, C, R, or J column in proportion to the natural width of the longest entry in each column. To determine this width tabulary always sets the table twice. In the first pass the data in the L, C, R, and J columns are set in LR mode (similar to data in columns specified by the standard preamble options such as c). Typically, the paragraphs that are contained in these columns are set on a single line, and the length of this line is measured. The table is then typeset a second time to produce the final result, with the widths of the columns being set as if with a p preamble option and a width proportional to the natural lengths recorded on the first pass.

Controlling the column width allocation

To stop very narrow columns from being too "squeezed" by this process, any columns that are narrower than \tymin are set to their natural widths. This length may be set with \setlength and is arbitrarily initialized to 10pt. If you know that a column is narrow, it may be preferable to use, say, c rather than C so that the tabulary mechanism is never invoked on that column, and the column is set to its natural width.

Similarly, one very large entry can force its column to be too wide. To prevent this problem, all columns with natural length greater than \tymax (as measured when the entries are set in LR mode) are set to the same width (with the proportion being taken as if the natural length were *equal* to \tymax). This width is initially set to twice the text width.

The table in the above example is dominated by the large entry in the fourth column. By setting \tymin to 30pt we can prevent the first two columns from becoming too narrow, and by setting \tymax to 200pt we can limit the width of the fourth column and produce a more even spread of column widths.

a	b b b b	c c c c c c c c c c c c c c c c c c	d d d d d d d d d d d d d d d d d d d d d d d d d d d d d d d d d d d d d d d d d d d d d d d d d d d d d d d d d

```
\usepackage{tabulary}
\setlength\tymin{30pt} \setlength\tymax{200pt}

\begin{tabulary}{200pt}{|C|C|C|C|}
 a & b b b b &
 c c c c c c c c c c c c c c c c c &
 d d d d d d d d d d d d d d d d
... further text omitted ...
```

6-3-6

Narrow p columns are sometimes quite challenging to set, and so you may redefine the command \tyformat to be any declarations made just after the \centering or \ragged... declaration. By default, it inserts a zero space at the start of every paragraph, so the first word may be hyphenated. (See Section 6.2.2 on page 442.)

Like tabularx, the tabulary package supports the optional alignment argument of tabular. Also because the whole environment is saved and evaluated twice, care should be taken with any LaTeX constructs that may have side effects such as writing to files.

6.3.3 Differences between tabular*, tabularx, and tabulary

All three of these environments take the same arguments, with the goal of producing a table of a specified width. The main differences between them are described here:

- tabularx and tabulary modify the widths of the *columns*, whereas tabular* modifies the widths of the inter-column *spaces*.

- The tabular and tabular* environments may be nested with no restrictions. However, if one tabularx or tabulary environment occurs inside another, then the inner one *must* be enclosed within { }.

\verb
only partially
supported

- The bodies of tabularx and tabulary environments are, in fact, the arguments to commands, so certain restrictions apply. The commands \verb and \verb* may be used, but they may treat spaces incorrectly, and their arguments cannot contain a % or an unmatched { or }.

- tabular* uses a primitive capability of TeX to modify the inter-column space of an alignment. tabularx has to set the table several times as it searches for the best column widths and is therefore much slower. tabulary always sets the table twice. For the latter two environments the fact that the body is expanded several times may break certain TeX constructs. Be especially wary of commands that write to external files, because the data may be written several times when the table is reset.

- **tabularx** attempts to distribute space equally among the X columns to achieve the desired width, whereas **tabulary** attempts to allocate greater widths to columns with larger entries.

6.3.4 Managing tables with wide entries

If a table has spanning entries that are wider than the columns they span, the white space between these narrow columns is not evenly distributed. For instance, the following table has a rather wide first \multicolumn row, above a series of narrow columns. As a result the space between the last two columns receives all the excess white space, which is not a very pleasing result.

This is a wide heading line		
C1	C2	C3
2.1	2.2	2.3
3.1	3.2	3.3

```
\begin{tabular}{ccc}
   \multicolumn{3}{c}{This is a wide heading line} \\
   C1 & C2 & C3 \\ 2.1 & 2.2 & 2.3 \\ 3.1 & 3.2 & 3.3
\end{tabular}
```

6-3-7

To correct this defect you can put some rubber length in front of each column with the help of the \extracolsep command. The actual value of the rubber length is not important, as long as it is wide enough and can shrink to just fill the needed space. With this approach you must, of course, specify a total width for the table. We could use \linewidth and make the table full width, but here we can obtain a better result by precalculating the width of the wide entry and specifying it as the total width of the **tabular***. Using the calc package we can do this calculation even in the first argument of the environment.

This is a wide heading line		
C1	C2	C3
2.1	2.2	2.3
3.1	3.2	3.3

```
\usepackage{array,calc}
\begin{tabular*}{\widthof{This is a wide heading line}
                + 2\tabcolsep}
             { !{\extracolsep{4in minus 4in}} ccc}
   \multicolumn{3}{c}{This is a wide heading line}        \\
   C1 & C2 & C3 \\ 2.1 & 2.2 & 2.3 \\ 3.1 & 3.2 & 3.3
\end{tabular*}
```

6-3-8

To achieve correct alignment, we needed to take into account the \tabcolsep added before the first and after the last column. Alternatively, we could have suppressed the inter-column spaces at the left and right of the **tabular*** by using @{} expressions.

6.3.5 widetable — An alternative to tabular*

The standard LATEX **tabular*** environment produces a table of a predefined width by spreading the columns apart, i.e., adding extra flexible space between the columns. This space has to be specified with an \extracolsep declaration within an @ or ! specifier in the table preamble. This works well enough for tables without vertical rules but looks somewhat strange if such rules are present because the extra space is added only on the right side of the rules separating two columns.

Below is a variation of Example 6-3-3 from page 449 (used there with **tabularx**) to allow for comparison. This time we explicitly ask for two 32mm wide p-columns followed by a centered one, and, as you can see, the space distribution looks rather bad because of the rules. We also add a heading line to show what happens with a cell spanning two columns.

```
\usepackage{array}
\begin{tabular*}{\linewidth}{@{\extracolsep{\fill}}
                *{2}{|>{\small\raggedright\arraybackslash}p{32mm}}|c|}
\hline\multicolumn{2}{|c|}{The p-columns} &
                            Centered column          \\\hline\hline
The Two Gentlemen of Verona & The Taming of the Shrew   &
                            The Comedy of Errors        \\\hline
Love's Labour's Lost        & A Midsummer Night's Dream  &
                            The Merchant of Venice      \\\hline
The Merry Wives of Windsor  & Much Ado About Nothing     &
                            As You Like It              \\\hline
Twelfth Night               & Troilus and Cressida       &
... further text omitted ...
```

<table>
<tr><td colspan="2" align="center">The p-columns</td><td align="center">Centered column</td></tr>
<tr><td>The Two Gentlemen of Verona</td><td>The Taming of the Shrew</td><td align="center">The Comedy of Errors</td></tr>
<tr><td>Love's Labour's Lost</td><td>A Midsummer Night's Dream</td><td align="center">The Merchant of Venice</td></tr>
<tr><td>The Merry Wives of Windsor</td><td>Much Ado About Nothing</td><td align="center">As You Like It</td></tr>
<tr><td>Twelfth Night</td><td>Troilus and Cressida</td><td align="center">. . .</td></tr>
</table>

6-3-9

To resolve this problem Claudio Beccari wrote the **widetable** package. It defines the environment **widetabular** that takes the same arguments as **tabular*** but adds the necessary white space equally on the left and right of each column without the need to issue an **\extracolsep** declaration in the table preamble.

It achieves this by typesetting the table more than once[1] with different settings of **\tabcolsep** and then chooses a value for this parameter that results in the table being set to the desired width. This calculation may go wrong if you use @ column specifiers that suppress the insertion of **\tabcolsep** or complicated tables with a lot of **\multicolumn** commands, because spanning columns means that such rows have fewer **\tabcolsep** spaces inside.

In contrast to **tabularx** and other packages, **widetable** does not automatically load the array package. Thus, if you want to use the extended column specifiers as we do in the next example, you need to explicitly load that package too.

---

[1]This has the usual implications; e.g., \verb is not supported within the cells, and commands with global side effects (such as incrementing a counter) should also be avoided.

```
\usepackage{array,widetable}
\begin{widetabular}{\linewidth}
            {*{2}{|>{\small\raggedright\arraybackslash}p{32mm}}|c|}
\hline\multicolumn{2}{|c|}{The p-columns} & Centered column\\\hline\hline
... further text omitted ...
```

6-3-10

The p-columns		Centered column
The Two Gentlemen of Verona	The Taming of the Shrew	The Comedy of Errors
Love's Labour's Lost	A Midsummer Night's Dream	The Merchant of Venice
The Merry Wives of Windsor	Much Ado About Nothing	As You Like It
Twelfth Night	Troilus and Cressida	...

Instead of making a table somewhat wider by specifying a desired width, it is also possible within limits to shrink a table this way. This can be useful, for example, if the table is just a little bit wider than the available space, e.g., the \linewidth.

For this to work, the table needs enough columns so that there is sufficient white space that can be compressed. The highest amount of compression that is possible is shrinking the available white space to zero (which may or may not be acceptable depending on the table content). Below we asked for 287pt, which is roughly 6 points more than the table width without any white space between columns. This means that we get about 1 point on each side of a column. Incidentally, if you ask for more shrink than is available, then a warning is generated, and the table is set at its natural width.

```
\usepackage{array,widetable}
\begin{widetabular}{287pt}
            {*{2}{|>{\small\raggedright\arraybackslash}p{32mm}}|c|}
\hline\multicolumn{2}{|c|}{The p-columns} & Centered column\\\hline\hline
... further text omitted ...
```

6-3-11

The p-columns		Centered column
The Two Gentlemen of Verona	The Taming of the Shrew	The Comedy of Errors
Love's Labour's Lost	A Midsummer Night's Dream	The Merchant of Venice
The Merry Wives of Windsor	Much Ado About Nothing	As You Like It
Twelfth Night	Troilus and Cressida	...

The above examples show that using \multicolumn appears to work, but as mentioned more complicated scenarios using spanned cells may throw the package off track, so you have to watch out for this.

6.4 Multipage tabular material

With Leslie Lamport's original implementation, a `tabular` environment must always fit on one page. If it becomes too large, the text overwrites the page's bottom margin, and you get an `Overfull \vbox` message.

Two major packages are available to construct tables longer than one page, supertabular and longtable. They share a similar functionality but use rather different syntax and also produce noticeably different results. The longtable package uses a more complicated mechanism, working with TeX's output routine to obtain optimal page breaks and to preserve the width of columns across all pages of a table. However, this mechanism may require the document to be processed several times before the correct cell widths are calculated. It also means that the package is incompatible with other packages manipulating the output routine.[1]

Multipage tables in multicolumn typesetting The supertabular package essentially breaks the table into a sequence of page-sized `tabular` environments, and each page is then typeset separately. This approach does not require multiple passes and works in a larger range of circumstances, e.g., two-column or multi-column mode.

Neither supertabular nor longtable supports the X-notation of tabularx for automatically adjusting the column width to fit a given table width. This is provided by the xltabular package, which combines the features of longtable and tabularx.

6.4.1 supertabular — Making multipage tabulars

The package supertabular (originally created by Theo Jurriens and revised by Johannes Braams) defines the environment `supertabular`.

```
\begin{supertabular}{col-spec}           rows \end{supertabular}
\begin{supertabular*}{width}{col-spec}   rows \end{supertabular*}
\begin{mpsupertabular}{col-spec}         rows \end{mpsupertabular}
\begin{mpsupertabular*}{width}{col-spec} rows \end{mpsupertabular*}
```

It uses the `tabular` environment internally but it evaluates the amount of used space every time it encounters a `\\` command. When this amount reaches the value of `\textheight`, the package automatically inserts an `\end{tabular}` command, starts a new page, and inserts the table head on the new page, continuing the `tabular` environment. This means that the widths of the columns, and hence the width of the complete table, can vary across pages.

Three variant environments are also defined. The `supertabular*` environment uses `tabular*` internally, and takes a mandatory *width* argument to specify the width of the table. The `mpsupertabular` and `mpsupertabular*` environments have the same syntax as `supertabular` and `supertabular*`, respectively, but wrap the table portion on each page in a `minipage` environment. This allows the use of the `\footnote` command inside the tables, with the footnote text being printed at the end of the relevant page.

---

[1] For example, longtable cannot be used inside a `multicols` environment.

Inside a `supertabular` environment new lines are defined as usual by `\\` commands. All column definition commands can be used, including `@{...}` and `p{...}`. If the array package is loaded along with `supertabular`, the additional tabular preamble options may be used. You cannot, however, use the optional positioning arguments, like t and b, that can be specified with `\begin{tabular}` and `\begin{tabular*}`.

Several new commands are available for use with `supertabular` as described below. Each of these commands should be used before the `supertabular` environment, because they affect all following `supertabular` environments. In particular, this means that once used you need to alter them for each table!

`\tablehead{`*rows*`}`   `\tablefirsthead{`*rows*`}`

The argument to `\tablehead` contains the rows of the table to be repeated at the top of every page. If `\tablefirsthead` is also included, the first heading uses these rows in preference to the rows specified by `\tablehead`. The argument may contain full rows (ended by `\\`) as well as inter-row material like `\hline`.

`\tabletail{`*rows*`}`   `\tablelasttail{`*rows*`}`

These commands specify material to be inserted at the end of each page of the table. If `\tablelasttail` is used, these rows appear at the end of the table in preference to the rows specified by `\tabletail`.

`\topcaption[`*lot caption*`]{`*caption*`}`   `\bottomcaption[`*lot caption*`]{`*caption*`}`
`\tablecaption[`*lot caption*`]{`*caption*`}`

These commands specify a caption for the `supertabular`, either at the top or at the bottom of the table. The optional argument has the same use as the optional argument in the standard `\caption` command — namely, it specifies the form of the caption to appear in the list of tables. When `\tablecaption` is used, the caption is placed at the default location, which is at the top. This default may be changed within a package or class file by using the declaration `\@topcaptionfalse`.

The format of the caption may be customized using the caption package, as shown in Example 6-4-4 on page 462.

```
\usepackage{supertabular}
\tablecaption{The ISOGRK3 entity set}
\tablehead{\textbf{Entity}&\textbf{Unicode Name}&\textbf{Unicode}\\\hline}
\tabletail{\hline \multicolumn{3}{r}{\emph{Continued on next page}}\\}
\tablelasttail{\hline}
\begin{supertabular}{lll}
alpha                  & GREEK SMALL LETTER ALPHA         & 03B1\\
beta                   & GREEK SMALL LETTER BETA          & 03B2\\
chi                    & GREEK SMALL LETTER CHI           & 03C7\\
Delta                  & GREEK CAPITAL LETTER DELTA       & 0394\\
... further text omitted ...
```

6-4-1

Table 1: The ISOGRK3 entity set

Entity	Unicode Name	Unicode
alpha	GREEK SMALL LETTER ALPHA	03B1
beta	GREEK SMALL LETTER BETA	03B2
chi	GREEK SMALL LETTER CHI	03C7
Delta	GREEK CAPITAL LETTER DELTA	0394
delta	GREEK SMALL LETTER DELTA	03B4
epsi	GREEK SMALL LETTER EPSILON	03B5
epsis	GREEK LUNATE EPSILON SYMBOL	03F5
epsiv	GREEK SMALL LETTER EPSILON	03B5
eta	GREEK SMALL LETTER ETA	03B7
Gamma	GREEK CAPITAL LETTER GAMMA	0393
gamma	GREEK SMALL LETTER GAMMA	03B3
gammad	GREEK SMALL LETTER DIGAMMA	03DD
iota	GREEK SMALL LETTER IOTA	03B9
kappa	GREEK SMALL LETTER KAPPA	03BA
kappav	GREEK KAPPA SYMBOL	03F0
Lambda	GREEK CAPITAL LETTER LAMDA	039B
lambda	GREEK SMALL LETTER LAMDA	03BB
mu	GREEK SMALL LETTER MU	03BC
nu	GREEK SMALL LETTER NU	03BD
Omega	GREEK CAPITAL LETTER OMEGA	03A9

Continued on next page

Entity	Unicode Name	Unicode
omega	GREEK SMALL LETTER OMEGA	03C9
Phi	GREEK CAPITAL LETTER PHI	03A6
phis	GREEK PHI SYMBOL	03D5
phiv	GREEK SMALL LETTER PHI	03C6
Pi	GREEK CAPITAL LETTER PI	03A0
pi	GREEK SMALL LETTER PI	03C0
piv	GREEK PI SYMBOL	03D6
Psi	GREEK CAPITAL LETTER PSI	03A8
psi	GREEK SMALL LETTER PSI	03C8
rho	GREEK SMALL LETTER RHO	03C1
rhov	GREEK RHO SYMBOL	03F1
Sigma	GREEK CAPITAL LETTER SIGMA	03A3
sigma	GREEK SMALL LETTER SIGMA	03C3
sigmav	GREEK SMALL LETTER FINAL SIGMA	03C2
tau	GREEK SMALL LETTER TAU	03C4
Theta	GREEK CAPITAL LETTER THETA	0398
thetas	GREEK SMALL LETTER THETA	03B8
thetav	GREEK THETA SYMBOL	03D1
Upsi	GREEK UPSILON WITH HOOK SYMBOL	03D2
upsi	GREEK SMALL LETTER UPSILON	03C5
Xi	GREEK CAPITAL LETTER XI	039E
xi	GREEK SMALL LETTER XI	03BE
zeta	GREEK SMALL LETTER ZETA	03B6

`\shrinkheight{`*length*`}`

The `supertabular` environment maintains an estimate of the amount of space left on the current page, and depending on the table content this estimate is sometimes wrong. The `\shrinkheight` command, which must appear at the start of a table row, may be used to reduce (or enlarge if given a negative length) this estimate. In this way it may be used to control the page-breaking decisions made by `supertabular`.

For example, in the previous and the next example it was necessary to add `\shrinkheight{-40pt}` near the end of the table to avoid `supertabular` starting a third page. On the next example we also used it on the first page to make this one line longer.

To better understand why `supertabular` decides to start a new page (and what value for `\shrinkheight` to use to affect it) you can add the package option `debugshow` or issue `\sttraceon` in front of the environment of interest. To turn off tracing again `\sttraceoff` can be used.

Example of the supertabular* environment

The width of a `supertabular` environment can be fixed to a given width, such as the width of the text, `\textwidth`. In the example below, in addition to specifying `supertabular*`, a rubber length has been introduced between the last two columns that allows the table to be stretched to the specified width. As usual with `supertabular`, each page of the table is typeset separately. The example demonstrates that the result may have different spacings between the columns on different pages.

```
\usepackage{array,supertabular}

\tablecaption{The ISOGRK3 entity set}
\tablefirsthead
        {\textbf{Entity}&\textbf{Unicode Name}&\textbf{Unicode}\\\hline}
```

```
\tablehead{\textbf{Entity}&\textbf{Unicode Name}&\textbf{Unicode}\\\hline}
\tabletail{\hline \multicolumn{3}{r}{\emph{Continued on next page}}\\}
\tablelasttail{\hline}
\centering
\begin{supertabular*}{\textwidth}{ll!{\extracolsep{\fill}}l}
\shrinkheight{-12pt} % tell supertabular to add one additional line to first page
alpha             & GREEK SMALL LETTER ALPHA         & 03B1\\
beta              & GREEK SMALL LETTER BETA          & 03B2\\
chi               & GREEK SMALL LETTER CHI           & 03C7\\
Delta             & GREEK CAPITAL LETTER DELTA       & 0394\\
delta             & GREEK SMALL LETTER DELTA         & 03B4\\
```

6-4-2

... further text omitted ...

	Page 1				Page 2	
alpha	GREEK SMALL LETTER ALPHA	03B1		phis	GREEK PHI SYMBOL	03D5
beta	GREEK SMALL LETTER BETA	03B2		phiv	GREEK SMALL LETTER PHI	03C6
chi	GREEK SMALL LETTER CHI	03C7		Pi	GREEK CAPITAL LETTER PI	03A0
Delta	GREEK CAPITAL LETTER DELTA	0394		pi	GREEK SMALL LETTER PI	03C0
delta	GREEK SMALL LETTER DELTA	03B4		piv	GREEK PI SYMBOL	03D6
epsi	GREEK SMALL LETTER EPSILON	03B5		Psi	GREEK CAPITAL LETTER PSI	03A8
epsis	GREEK LUNATE EPSILON SYMBOL	03F5		psi	GREEK SMALL LETTER PSI	03C8
epsiv	GREEK SMALL LETTER EPSILON	03B5		rho	GREEK SMALL LETTER RHO	03C1
eta	GREEK SMALL LETTER ETA	03B7		rhov	GREEK RHO SYMBOL	03F1
Gamma	GREEK CAPITAL LETTER GAMMA	0393		Sigma	GREEK CAPITAL LETTER SIGMA	03A3
gamma	GREEK SMALL LETTER GAMMA	03B3		sigma	GREEK SMALL LETTER SIGMA	03C3
gammad	GREEK SMALL LETTER DIGAMMA	03DD		sigmav	GREEK SMALL LETTER FINAL SIGMA	03C2
iota	GREEK SMALL LETTER IOTA	03B9		tau	GREEK SMALL LETTER TAU	03C4
kappa	GREEK SMALL LETTER KAPPA	03BA		Theta	GREEK CAPITAL LETTER THETA	0398
kappav	GREEK KAPPA SYMBOL	03F0		thetas	GREEK SMALL LETTER THETA	03B8
Lambda	GREEK CAPITAL LETTER LAMDA	039B		thetav	GREEK THETA SYMBOL	03D1
lambda	GREEK SMALL LETTER LAMDA	03BB		Upsi	GREEK UPSILON WITH HOOK SYMBOL	03D2
mu	GREEK SMALL LETTER MU	03BC		upsi	GREEK SMALL LETTER UPSILON	03C5
nu	GREEK SMALL LETTER NU	03BD		Xi	GREEK CAPITAL LETTER XI	039E
Omega	GREEK CAPITAL LETTER OMEGA	03A9		xi	GREEK SMALL LETTER XI	03BE
omega	GREEK SMALL LETTER OMEGA	03C9		zeta	GREEK SMALL LETTER ZETA	03B6
Phi	GREEK CAPITAL LETTER PHI	03A6				

| | Page 1 | | | | Page 2 | |

6.4.2 longtable — Alternative multipage tabulars

As pointed out at the beginning of this section, for more complex long tables, where you want to control the width of the table across page boundaries, the package longtable (by David Carlisle, with contributions from David Kastrup) should be considered. Like the supertabular environment, it shares some features with the table environment. In particular it uses the same counter, table, and has a similar \caption command. The \listoftables command lists tables produced by either the table or longtable environment.

The main difference between the supertabular and longtable environments is that the latter saves the information about the width of each longtable environment in the auxiliary .aux file. It then uses this information on a subsequent run to

Use of the .aux *file*

identify the widest column widths needed for the table in question. The use of the .aux file means that care should be taken when using the longtable in conjunction with the \nofiles command. One effect of \nofiles is to suppress the writing of the .aux file, so this command should not be used until after the final edits of that table have been made and the package has recorded the optimal column widths in the auxiliary file.

To compare the two packages, Example 6-4-1 on page 457 is repeated here, but now uses longtable rather than supertabular. You can see that the width of the table is identical on both pages (the left and right parts of the picture). Note that in longtable, most of the table specification is *within* the longtable environment; in supertabular the specification of the table headings occurs via commands executed *before* the supertabular environment.

```
\usepackage{longtable}
\begin{longtable}{lll}
 \caption{The ISOGRK3 entity set} \\ \textbf{Entity} &
    \textbf{Unicode Name} & \textbf{Unicode} \\ \hline  \endfirsthead
 \caption[]{The ISOGRK3 entity set (\emph{cont.})} \\ \textbf{Entity} &
    \textbf{Unicode Name} & \textbf{Unicode} \\ \hline        \endhead
 \hline \multicolumn{3}{r}{\emph{Continued on next page}}   \endfoot
 \hline\endlastfoot
 alpha              & GREEK SMALL LETTER ALPHA           & 03B1\\
 beta               & GREEK SMALL LETTER BETA            & 03B2\\
 chi                & GREEK SMALL LETTER CHI             & 03C7\\
 ... further text omitted ...
```

6-4-3

_____ Page 1 _____   _____ Page 2 _____

Table 1: The ISOGRK3 entity set

Entity	Unicode Name	Unicode
alpha	GREEK SMALL LETTER ALPHA	03B1
beta	GREEK SMALL LETTER BETA	03B2
chi	GREEK SMALL LETTER CHI	03C7
Delta	GREEK CAPITAL LETTER DELTA	0394
delta	GREEK SMALL LETTER DELTA	03B4
epsi	GREEK SMALL LETTER EPSILON	03B5
epsis	GREEK LUNATE EPSILON SYMBOL	03F5
epsiv	GREEK SMALL LETTER EPSILON	03B5
eta	GREEK SMALL LETTER ETA	03B7
Gamma	GREEK CAPITAL LETTER GAMMA	0393
gamma	GREEK SMALL LETTER GAMMA	03B3
gammad	GREEK SMALL LETTER DIGAMMA	03DD
iota	GREEK SMALL LETTER IOTA	03B9
kappa	GREEK SMALL LETTER KAPPA	03BA
kappav	GREEK KAPPA SYMBOL	03F0
Lambda	GREEK CAPITAL LETTER LAMDA	039B
lambda	GREEK SMALL LETTER LAMDA	03BB
mu	GREEK SMALL LETTER MU	03BC
nu	GREEK SMALL LETTER NU	03BD
Omega	GREEK CAPITAL LETTER OMEGA	03A9
omega	GREEK SMALL LETTER OMEGA	03C9
Phi	GREEK CAPITAL LETTER PHI	03A6

Continued on next page

Table 1: The ISOGRK3 entity set *(cont.)*

Entity	Unicode Name	Unicode
phis	GREEK PHI SYMBOL	03D5
phiv	GREEK SMALL LETTER PHI	03C6
Pi	GREEK CAPITAL LETTER PI	03A0
pi	GREEK SMALL LETTER PI	03C0
piv	GREEK PI SYMBOL	03D6
Psi	GREEK CAPITAL LETTER PSI	03A8
psi	GREEK SMALL LETTER PSI	03C8
rho	GREEK SMALL LETTER RHO	03C1
rhov	GREEK RHO SYMBOL	03F1
Sigma	GREEK CAPITAL LETTER SIGMA	03A3
sigma	GREEK SMALL LETTER SIGMA	03C3
sigmav	GREEK SMALL LETTER FINAL SIGMA	03C2
tau	GREEK SMALL LETTER TAU	03C4
Theta	GREEK CAPITAL LETTER THETA	0398
thetas	GREEK SMALL LETTER THETA	03B8
thetav	GREEK THETA SYMBOL	03D1
Upsi	GREEK UPSILON WITH HOOK SYMBOL	03D2
upsi	GREEK SMALL LETTER UPSILON	03C5
Xi	GREEK CAPITAL LETTER XI	039E
xi	GREEK SMALL LETTER XI	03BE
zeta	GREEK SMALL LETTER ZETA	03B6

_____ Page 1 _____   _____ Page 2 _____

> \begin{longtable} [*align*] {*col-spec*} *rows* \end{longtable}

The syntax of the longtable environment is modeled on that of the tabular environment. The main difference is that the optional *align* argument specifies *horizontal* alignment rather than vertical alignment as is the case with tabular.

The *align* argument may have the value [c], [l], or [r] to specify centering, *Horizontal* left, or right alignment of the table, respectively. If this optional argument is omitted, *alignment* then the alignment of the table is controlled by the two length parameters, \LTleft and \LTright. They have default values of \fill, so by default tables are centered.

Any length can be specified for these two parameters, but at least one of them should be a rubber length so that it fills up the width of the page, unless rubber lengths are added between the columns using the \extracolsep command. For instance, a table can be set flush left using the definitions

    \setlength\LTleft{0pt}   \setlength\LTright{\fill}

or just by specifying \begin{longtable} [l].

You can, for example, use the \LTleft and \LTright parameters to typeset a *Using parameters to* multipage table filling the full width of the page. Example 6-4-2 on page 459, which *control table width* used supertabular*, may be typeset using the packages array and longtable and the declarations shown below:

    \setlength\LTleft{0pt}   \setlength\LTright{0pt}
    \begin{longtable}{ll!{\extracolsep{\fill}}l}

In general, if \LTleft and \LTright are fixed lengths, the table is set to the width of \textwidth − \LTleft − \LTright.

Before and after the table, longtable inserts vertical space controlled by *Vertical space* the length parameters \LTpre and \LTpost. Both of them default to the length *around table* \bigskipamount but may be changed using \setlength.

Each row in the table is ended with the \\ command. As in the standard tabular *Table row* environment, the command \tabularnewline is also available; it is useful if \\ has *commands* been redefined by a command such as \raggedright. The star form * may also be used, which inhibits a page break at this line break. In a tabular environment, this star form is accepted but has the same effect as \\. Conversely, a \\ command may be immediately followed by a \newpage command, which forces a page break at that point.

If a table row is terminated with \kill rather than \\, then the row is not typeset. Instead, the entries are used when determining the widths of the table columns. This action is similar to that of the \kill command in the tabbing environment.

The main syntactic difference between the longtable package and the supertabular *Rows used as the* package is that in longtable, rows to be repeated on each page as the table head or *table head and foot* foot are declared *within* the environment body, rather than before the environment as in supertabular. As shown in Example 6-4-3 on the facing page, the table head and foot are specified by replacing the final \\ command by one of the commands listed below. Note that all of these commands, including those specifying the foot of the table, must come at the *start* of the environment. The command \endhead finishes the rows that will appear at the top of every page. The command \endfirsthead ends the declaration of rows for the start of the table. If this command is not used, then the rows specified by \endhead are used at the start of the table. Similarly, \endfoot finishes the rows that appear at the bottom of every page, and \endlastfoot — if used — ends the rows to be displayed at the end of the table.

\caption*[*short title*] {*full title*}

The \caption command and its variant \caption* are essentially equivalent to writing a special \multicolumn entry

> \multicolumn{*n*}{p{\LTcapwidth}}{...

where *n* is the number of columns of the table. The width of the caption can be controlled by redefining the parameter \LTcapwidth. That is, you can write \setlength\LTcapwidth{*width*} in the document preamble. The default value is 4in. As with the \caption command in the figure and table environments, the optional argument specifies the text to appear in the list of tables if it is different from the text to appear in the caption.

When captions on later pages should differ from those on the first page, you should place the \caption command with the full text in the first heading and put a subsidiary caption using \caption[ ]{*text*} in the main heading, because (in this case) no entry is made in the list of tables. Alternatively, if the table number should not be repeated each time, you can use the \caption* command. As with the table environment, cross-referencing the table in the text is possible with the \label command.

By default, the caption is set in a style based on the caption style of the tables in standard LaTeX's article class. If the caption package (described in Section 7.4.1) is used, then it is easy to customize longtable and table captions, keeping the style of captions consistent between these two environments.

Table 1: A standard table

1 2 3

Table 2: A longtable

1 2 3

Table 3: A supertabular

1 2 3

```
\usepackage{longtable,supertabular}
\usepackage[font=it,labelfont=bf]{caption}
\begin{table}[t]\centering
 \caption{A standard table}
 \begin{tabular}{ccc} 1 & 2 & 3 \end{tabular}
\end{table}

\begin{longtable}{ccc}\caption{A longtable}\\
 1 & 2 & 3 \end{longtable}

\centering
\tablecaption{A supertabular}
\begin{supertabular}{ccc} 1 & 2 & 3 \\ \end{supertabular}
```

6-4-4

462

The `longtable` environment always increases the `table` counter regardless of whether or not you use a `\caption` inside the table. This allows you to always reference the table by number by placing a `\label` inside, even if no number is shown. However, if you use other tables with captions, it looks odd if there are gaps in the numbering, especially if they also show up in the list of tables. To avoid this, you can decrease the number before starting the environment, but if you also use hyperref, this generates an anchor with an identical name to an earlier table, and you get a warning about this. Alternatively, if you also load the caption package, you can use `longtable*`, which avoids the problem with hyperref. In that case `\caption` is not allowed inside the table, but you can still use `\caption*`.

Updates to the table counter

You can use footnote commands inside the `longtable` environment. The footnote text appears at the bottom of each page. The footnote counter is not reset at the beginning of the table but uses the standard footnote numbering employed in the rest of the document. If this result is not desired, then you can set the `footnote` counter to zero before the start of each table and then reset it at the end of the table if following footnotes must be numbered in the original sequence.

Footnotes in `longtable`

To enable TeX to set very long multipage tables, it is necessary to break them up into smaller chunks so that TeX does not have to keep everything in memory at one time. By default, `longtable` uses a value of 20 rows per chunk, which can be changed with a command such as `\setcounter{LTchunksize}{100}`. These chunks do not affect page breaking. When TeX has a lot of memory available (as it does today), LTchunksize can be set to a big number, which usually means that `longtable` is able to determine the final widths in fewer TeX runs. On most modern TeX installations LTchunksize can safely be increased to accommodate several pages of table in one chunk. Note that LTchunksize must be at least as large as the number of rows in each of the head or foot sections.

Increase LTchunksize to reduce number of LATeX runs required

6.4.3 xltabular — Marriage of tabularx and longtable

The longtable packages offers multipage tables but has no X-column support, while tabularx adds this important column specifier but can produce only single-page tables. Thus, it comes to no surprise that people asked for having both at the same time, and already in 1995 this was offered through the ltablex package by Anil K. Goel. This package redefined `tabularx` so that it allowed multipage tables at the cost of extra processing time (and some internal feature changes).

As a result, the original behavior of `tabularx` was no longer available; e.g., you could not easily prevent page breaks in such tables, and using the environment then always required two or more LATeX runs.

More recently Rolf Niepraschk and Herbert Voß repaired these disadvantages with the package xltabular. It defines a new environment `xltabular` that uses the code that Anil K. Goel developed in ltablex, but due to using a new environment name, the original `tabularx` is still available. Thus, if you need single-page tables with X columns, you can use `tabularx`, and if you (also) need multipage tables, you can now use `xltabular` in the same document, enjoying the benefits of both.

> \begin{xltabular}[*placement*]{*width*}{*column-spec*} ... \end{xltabular}

The arguments offer no real surprise: the two mandatory arguments receive the *width* and the *column-spec* for the table, and in the optional *placement* you can specify how the table is aligned with respect to preceding and following lines of text (allowed values are l, r, or the default c).

As with longtable, page breaks occur only between rows and can be prevented at such points by using *. In the case of X-columns with a lot of text, that may not be always satisfactory; see the discussion on page 464 for a possible resolution.

```
\usepackage{xltabular}
\begin{xltabular}[c]{.85\linewidth}{llX}
\caption{A table with \texttt{X}-columns} \endfirsthead
entry 1.1 & entry 1.2 & entry 1.3, a long text entry needing two lines.\\
entry 2.1 & entry 2.2 & entry 2.3, a long text entry taking several
                        lines when set in a narrow column.
\end{xltabular}
```

6-4-5

————————— Page 1 —————————

Table 1: A table with X-columns

entry 1.1   entry 1.2   entry 1.3, a long text entry
                        needing two lines.

————————— Page 1 —————————

————————— Page 2 —————————

entry 2.1   entry 2.2   entry 2.3, a long text entry
                        taking several lines when
                        set in a narrow column.

————————— Page 2 —————————

In essence xltabular is a cross between tabularx (using its document-level syntax and adding support for X-columns) and longtable (which provides multipage support and features like caption, header, and footer setup). There is one difference, though: the xltabular environment increments the table counter only if a table contains a \caption command, while longtable always increments this counter (which is arguably a design mistake).

6.4.4 Problems with multipage tables (all packages)

Bad interaction of floating environments and multipage tables

When a float occurs on the same page as the start of a multipage table, unexpected results can occur. All multipage table packages have code that attempts to deal with this situation, but in some circumstances tables can float out of sequence. Placing a \clearpage command before the table, thereby forcing a page break and flushing out any floats, usually corrects the problem.

p column entries do not break

Neither the supertabular nor the longtable (or xltabular) environment takes a page break after a line of text *within* a cell. Pages are broken only between table rows (or at \hline commands). If your table consists of large multiple line cells set with the p preamble option, then LaTeX may not be able to find a good page break and may leave unwanted white space at the bottom of the page.

The example below has room for six lines of text on each page, but LaTeX breaks the page between the two table rows, leaving page 1 short.

```
\usepackage{longtable}
\begin{longtable}{llp{43mm}}
 entry 1.1 & entry 1.2 & entry 1.3, a long text entry taking several lines.\\
 entry 2.1 & entry 2.2 & entry 2.3, a long text entry taking several lines
                        when set in a narrow column.
\end{longtable}
```

6-4-6

—————————— Page 1 —————————— | —————————— Page 2 ——————————

  entry 1.1   entry 1.2   entry 1.3, a long text   entry 2.1   entry 2.2   entry 2.3, a long text
                     entry taking several   entry taking several
                     lines.   lines when set in a
                                            narrow column.

—————————— Page 1 —————————— | —————————— Page 2 ——————————

For some tables, the table rows form an important logical unit, and the default behavior of not breaking within a row is desired. In other cases, it may be preferable to break the table manually to achieve a more pleasing page break. In the above example, we want to move the first two lines of page 2 to the bottom of page 1.

Noting that TeX broke the third column entry after the word "several", we could end the table row at that point by using \\, insert blank entries in the first two columns of a new row, and place the remaining portion of the p entry in the final cell of this row. The first part of the split paragraph should be set with \parfillskip set to 0pt so that the final line appears full width, just as it would be if it were set as the first two lines of a larger paragraph.

```
\usepackage{longtable}
\begin{longtable}{llp{43mm}}
 entry 1.1 & entry 1.2 & entry 1.3, a long text entry taking several lines.\\
 entry 2.1 & entry 2.2 & \setlength{\parfillskip}{0pt}%
                        entry 2.3, a long text entry taking several\\
           &           & lines when set in a narrow column.
\end{longtable}
```

6-4-7

—————————— Page 1 —————————— | —————————— Page 2 ——————————

  entry 1.1   entry 1.2   entry 1.3, a long text   lines when set in a
                     entry taking several   narrow column.
                     lines.
  entry 2.1   entry 2.2   entry 2.3, a long text
                     entry taking several

—————————— Page 1 —————————— | —————————— Page 2 ——————————

This is really a bad manual solution, but right now this is the best you can do with longtable. If you have only simple requirements, as in the above example, then this is better addressed by using the paracol package discussed in Section 4.3.2 on page 339, but with more complicated column structures that will not be possible.

```
\usepackage{paracol}
\begin{quote}    \columnratio{0.25,0.25} \setlength\parindent{0pt}
  \begin{paracol}{3}
    entry 1.1 \switchcolumn entry 1.2 \switchcolumn
       entry 1.3, a long text entry taking several lines.\switchcolumn*
    entry 2.1 \switchcolumn entry 2.2 \switchcolumn
       entry 2.3, a long text entry taking several lines
                        when set in a narrow column.\switchcolumn*
  \end{paracol}
\end{quote}
```

6-4-8

──── Page 1 ────				──── Page 2 ────
entry 1.1	entry 1.2	entry 1.3, a long text entry taking several lines.		lines when set in a narrow column.
entry 2.1	entry 2.2	entry 2.3, a long text entry taking several		
──── Page 1 ────				──── Page 2 ────

6.5 Color in tables

The LaTeX color commands provided by the color or xcolor package are modeled on the font commands and may be used freely within tables. In particular, it is often convenient to use the array package preamble option > in order to apply a color to a whole column.

Day	Attendance
Monday	57
Tuesday	11
Wednesday	96
Thursday	122
Friday	210
Saturday	198
Sunday	40

```
\usepackage{array,color}
\begin{tabular}{>{\color{blue}\bfseries}lr}
Day & \textcolor{blue}{\bfseries Attendance}\\\hline
Monday&    57\\  Tuesday&    11\\
Wednesday& 96\\  Thursday& 122\\
Friday&    210\\ Saturday& 198\\
Sunday&    40
\end{tabular}
```

6-5-1

It is perhaps more common to use color as a background to highlight certain rows or columns. In this case using the \fcolorbox command from the color package does not give the desired result, because typically the background should cover the full extent of the table cell. The colortbl package (by David Carlisle) provides several commands such as \columncolor, \rowcolor, and \cellcolor to provide colored backgrounds and rules in tables. Some of them are shown in the next examples.

Day	Attendance
Monday	57
Tuesday	11
Wednesday	96
Thursday	122
Friday	210
Saturday	198
Sunday	40
Total	724

```
\usepackage{colortbl}
\begin{tabular}
    {>{\columncolor{blue}\color{white}\bfseries}lr}
\rowcolor[gray]{0.8}
    \color{black} Day & \bfseries Attendance\\[2pt]
Monday&    57 \\  Tuesday&    11 \\
Wednesday& 96 \\  Thursday& 122 \\
Friday&    210 \\ Saturday& 198 \\
Sunday&    40 \\
\cellcolor[gray]{0.8}\color{black}Total& 724
\end{tabular}
```

6-5-2

6.6 Customizing table rules and spacing

In this section we look at a number of packages that extend the tabular functionality by providing commands for drawing special table rules and fine-tuning the row spacing. We start with colored rules provided by colortbl, followed by bold rules with boldline and dashed ones with arydshln. The hhline package offers very detailed control over the interactions between horizontal and vertical lines. All these packages provide granular control over the appearance. In contrast, the goal of the booktabs package is to help you get a consistent and uniform layout by offering you only a small set of commands for formal table rules with limited local configuration possibilities. For most documents we recommend this package.

The last two packages, bigstrut and cellspace, deal with spacing issues between rows or individual cells helping you to provide visual separation where necessary.[1]

One of the difficulties of using LaTeX tables with irregular-sized entries is the challenge of obtaining a good spacing around large entries, especially in the presence of horizontal rules. The standard LaTeX command \arraystretch or the \extrarowheight parameter introduced by the array package may help in this case. Both, however, affect all the rows in the table. It is sometimes desirable to have a finer-grained control.

6.6.1 Colored table rules

The colortbl package discussed in the previous section extends the style parameters for table rules, allowing colors to be specified for rules and for the space between double rules. The declarations \arrayrulecolor and \doublerulesepcolor take the same argument forms as the \color command of the standard LaTeX color package.

Normally, these declarations would be used before a table, or in the document preamble, to set the color for all rules in a table. However, the rule color may be varied

---

[1]There is also the tabls package (by Donald Arseneau), but this is unfortunately incompatible with the array package and its derivatives.

for individual rules using constructs like those in the next example. Note that the \cline construct is behind the vertical rules, whereas \hline or \hhline will be in front.

```
\usepackage{colortbl,hhline} \setlength\arrayrulewidth{1pt}
\newcolumntype{B}{!{\color{blue}\vline}}
\newcommand\blueline{\arrayrulecolor{blue}\hline\arrayrulecolor{black}}
\newcommand\bluecline[1]{\arrayrulecolor{blue}\cline{#1}%
                                        \arrayrulecolor{black}}
\begin{tabular}{cBc|c}          \hline
    A  & B  & C  \\ \cline{1-1}\bluecline{2-3}
    X  & Y  & Z  \\ \blueline
  100 & 10 & 1  \\ \hhline{= >{\arrayrulecolor{blue}}:=
                         >{\doublerulesepcolor{yellow}}=}
\end{tabular}
```

A	B	C
X	Y	Z
100	10	1

6-6-1

The last line involves \hhline from the hhline package discussed in Section 6.6.4 on page 470. If used together with colortbl, it supports the > notation through which you can color individual rule segments.

6.6.2 boldline — Bolder table rules

Lines in tables as produced by \hline, \cline, or the preamble specifier | all have the same width (defined through \arrayrulewidth). While this value can be adjusted, it is rather difficult to do this for individual lines in a table. To produce some flexibility in this regard, Alexey Shipunov developed the boldline package.

V{*factor*} \hlineB{*factor*} \clineB{*colspec*}{*factor*}

It offers V, \hlineB, and \clineB as alternatives for the standard rule-generating commands all of which take an additional *factor* argument that specifies the desired rule width as a multiple of \arrayrulewidth. Fractional values for *factor* are allowed.

Rather than using explicit values within the document it is probably best to decide on one or two values and define your own commands and column specifiers based on these values. This way, your document layout stays consistent, and at the same time adjustments are easily possible later. In the example below, a new preamble option I is defined that produces a wide vertical rule. Similarly, a \boldline and a \boldcline command are defined that produce even thicker horizontal rules.

```
\usepackage{boldline}           \renewcommand\arraystretch{1.3}
\newcolumntype{I}{V{2.5}}       \newcommand\boldline{\hlineB{4}}
\newcommand\boldcline[1]{\clineB{#1}{4}}
\begin{tabular}{cIc|c}
    A &  B & C  \\ \cline{1-1} \boldcline{3-3}  a & b  & c \\ \hline
    X & Y & Z   \\ \boldline               100 & 10 & 1
\end{tabular}
```

A	B	C
a	b	c
X	Y	Z
100	10	1

6-6-2

6.6.3 arydshln — Dashed rules

The arydshln package (by NAKASHIMA Hiroshi) provides the ability to place dashed lines in tables. It is compatible with the array and longtable package but must be loaded *after* them if they are to be used together.

```
\hdashline[dash/gap]          \cdashline{colspec}[dash/gap]
\firsthdashline[dash/gap]     \lasthdashline[dash/gap]
```

The basic use of the package is very simple. A new preamble option ":" is introduced, together with two new commands \hdashline and \cdashline. These features may be used in the same way as the standard LaTeX "|" preamble option and \hline and \cline commands, except that dashed rather than solid lines are produced. In particular, two \hdashline commands in a row or one together with an \hline are allowed.

If the array package is also loaded, then the commands \firsthdashline and \lasthdashline are defined. They are dashed analogues of the \firsthline and \lasthline commands defined in that package.

```
\usepackage{array,arydshln}
  \setlength\extrarowheight{4pt}% extra space on row top
\begin{tabular}{|c::c|c|}      \hline
  A    & B  & C      \\ \hdashline\hline
  a    & b  & c      \\ \hdashline\hdashline
  1000 & 10 & 1      \\ \hdashline
  X    & Y  & Z      \\ \hline
\end{tabular}
```

6-6-3

Each of the commands takes an optional argument that may be used to specify the style of rule to be constructed. For example, an optional argument of [2pt/1pt] would specify that the rule should use 2pt dashes separated by 1pt spaces. The tabular preamble syntax does not allow for optional arguments on preamble options, so the ":" option does not have an optional argument in which to specify the dash style. Instead, an additional preamble option ";" is defined that takes a mandatory argument of the form *dash/gap*, as demonstrated in the next example.

The default size of the dashes and gaps is 4pt, which may be changed by setting the style parameters \dashlinedash and \dashlinegap via \setlength. This ability is shown in the example below:

```
\usepackage{colortbl,arydshln}     \renewcommand\arraystretch{1.5}
\setlength\dashlinedash{10pt}      \setlength\dashlinegap{5pt}
\setlength\arrayrulewidth{1pt}     \arrayrulecolor{blue}
\begin{tabular}{;{5pt/2pt}c::c:c;{2pt/2pt}}
\hdashline
  A    & B  & C \\ \hdashline
  X    & Y  & Z \\ \hdashline[5pt/2pt]
  1000 & 10 & 1 \\ \hdashline \hdashline[5pt/5pt]
\end{tabular}
```

6-6-4

469

As also shown in the previous example the package can be used together with colortbl. Solutions for some special cases when coloring rows or columns are discussed in the package documentation.

Avoiding unsightly gaps

The package may use any one of three methods for aligning the dashes within a table cell. The package may sometimes produce an overlarge gap at the edge of a table entry because there is not enough room to fit in the next "dash". If this happens, you might try specifying an alternative placement algorithm using the command \ADLdrawingmode{*m*}, where *m* may be 1 (the default), 2, or 3.

The package documentation contains details of the placement algorithms used in each of these cases, but in practice you can just experiment with your particular table and dash styles to see which setting of \ADLdrawingmode gives the most pleasing result.

6.6.4 hhline — Combining horizontal and vertical lines

The hhline package (by David Carlisle) introduces the command \hhline, which behaves like \hline except for its interaction with vertical lines.

```
\hhline{decl}
```

The declaration *decl* consists of a list of tokens with the following meanings:

= A double \hline the width of a column.

- A single \hline the width of a column.

~ A column without \hline; a space the width of a column.

| A \vline that "cuts" through a double (or single) \hline.

: A \vline that is broken by a double \hline.

A double \hline segment between two \vlines.

t The top rule of a double \hline segment.

b The bottom rule of a double \hline segment.

* *{3}{==#} expands to ==#==#==#, as in the * form for the preamble.

␣ Space characters are ignored and can be added at will to structure the source.

If a double \vline is specified (|| or ::), then the \hlines produced by \hhline are broken. To obtain the effect of an \hline "cutting through" the double \vline, use a #. The tokens t and b can be used between two vertical rules. For instance, |tb| produces the same lines as # but is much less efficient. The main uses for these are to make constructions like |t: (top-left corner) and :b| (bottom-right corner).

If \hhline is used to make a single \hline, then the argument should only contain the tokens "-", "~", and "|" (and * expressions).

An example using most of these features follows:

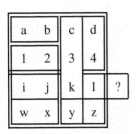

```
\usepackage{hhline}  \setlength\arrayrulewidth{.8pt}
\renewcommand\arraystretch{1.5}
                               % columns:   1 2    3 4      5
\begin{tabular}{||cc||c|c||c}   \hhline{|t: = = :t: = =  :t|  }
 a & b & c & d                 \\ \hhline{|: = = :| ~|~  | |  }
 1 & 2 & 3 & 4                 \\ \hhline{ # = = # ~|= :b| -}
 i & j & k & l
   & \multicolumn{1}{c|}{?}    \\ \hhline{|| - - ||  - -      -}
 w & x & y & z                 \\ \hhline{|b: = = :b: = = :b|  }
\end{tabular}
```

The lines produced by \hline consist of a single (T\eX primitive) \hrule. The lines produced by \hhline are made up of lots of small line segments. T\eX places these very accurately in the .dvi or .pdf file, but the program used to view or print the output might not line up the segments exactly if they are very thin. If this effect causes a problem, you can try increasing \arrayrulewidth to reduce the effect.

6.6.5 booktabs — Formal ruled tables

The previous sections have discussed packages that allow you to produce all kinds of complicated rules of various nature — making it easy to overdo it. An alternative approach is taken by the **booktabs** package (by Simon Fear, nowadays maintained by Danie Els).

It is designed to produce more formal tables according to a more traditional typographic style that uses horizontal rules of varying widths to separate table headings, but does not use any vertical rules. The | preamble option is not disabled when using this package, but its use is not supported, and the extra commands for horizontal rules described below are not designed to work well in conjunction with vertical rules. Similarly, **booktabs** commands are not designed to support double rules as produced by the || or \hline\hline.

Do not use vertical rules with booktabs

Do not use double rules with booktabs

The **booktabs** commands may be used with the standard **tabular** environments, with the extended versions provided by the **array** package, and in the **longtable** environment provided by the **longtable** package. An example showing the most commonly used commands provided by the package is shown below:

Items		Price/lb
Food	Category	$
Apples	Fruit	1.50
Oranges	Fruit	2.00
Beef	Meat	4.50

```
\usepackage{booktabs}
\begin{tabular}{llr}  \toprule
 \multicolumn{2}{c}{Items} &\multicolumn{1}{c}{Price/lb} \\
 \cmidrule(r){1-2}\cmidrule(l){3-3}
   Food & Category & \multicolumn{1}{c}{\$}\\
\midrule
   Apples  & Fruit & 1.50  \\       Oranges & Fruit & 2.00  \\
   Beef    & Meat  & 4.50  \\
\bottomrule \end{tabular}
```

471

> \toprule[*width*]   \midrule[*width*]   \bottomrule[*width*]

The booktabs package provides the \toprule, \midrule, and \bottomrule commands. They are used in the same way as the standard \hline but have better vertical spacing and widths specified by the length parameters \heavyrulewidth (for top and bottom rules) and \lightrulewidth (for mid-table rules). These parameters default to 0.08 em and 0.05 em, respectively (where the em is determined by the default document font at the point the package is loaded).

The spacing above and below the rules is determined by the length parameters: \abovetopsep (default 0 pt) is the space above top rules, \aboverulesep (default 0.4 ex) is the space above mid-table and bottom rules, \belowrulesep (default 0.65 ex) is the space below top and mid rules, and \belowbottomsep (default 0 pt) is the space below bottom rules.

If you need to control the widths of individual rules, all of these commands take an optional width argument. For example, \midrule[0.5pt] would produce a rule with a width of half a point.

When these commands are used inside a longtable environment, they may take an optional (*trim*) argument as described below for \cmidrule. This argument may be used to make the rules slightly less than the full width of the table.

> \cmidrule[*width*] (*trim*){*col1-col2*}

The \cmidrule command produces rules similar to those created with the standard LaTeX \cline command. The *col1-col2* argument specifies the columns over which the rule should be drawn. Unlike the rules created by \cline, these rules do not, by default, extend all the way to the edges of the column. Thus, one may use \cmidrule to produce rules on adjacent columns without them touching, as shown in the example above.

If the optional *width* argument is not specified, the rule will be of the width specified by the \cmidrulewidth length parameter (default 0.03 em).

By default, the rule extends all the way to the left but is "trimmed" from the rightmost column by the length specified in the length parameter \cmidrulekern. The optional (*trim*) argument may contain the characters l and r, indicating that the rule is to be trimmed from the left or right, respectively. Each l and r may optionally be followed by a width argument specified using {*widths*}, in which case the rule is trimmed by this amount rather than by the default \cmidrulekern.

Normally, if one \cmidrule command immediately follows another, then the rules are drawn across the specified columns on the same horizontal line. A command \morecmidrules is provided that may be used to terminate a row of mid-table rules. Following mid-table rules then appear on a new line separated by the length \cmidrulesep, which by default is equal to \doublerulesep.

Each group of rules produced by \cmidrule is preceded and followed by a space of width \midrulesep, so this command generates the same spacing as \midrule. By default, however, the \cmidrule rules are lighter (thinner) than the rules produced by \midrule.

\addlinespace[*width*]

Extra space may be inserted between rows using \addlinespace. This command differs from using the optional argument to \\, because the former may also be used immediately before or after the rule commands.

If used in this position, the command replaces the default spacing that would normally be produced by the rule. If the optional width argument is omitted, it defaults to the length parameter \defaultaddspace (which defaults to 0.5 em).

\specialrule{*width*}{*abovespace*}{*belowspace*}

Finally, if none of the other commands produces a suitable rule, then the command \specialrule may be used. It takes three mandatory arguments that specify the width of the rule, and the space above and below the rule.

As the intention of the package is to produce "formal" tables with well-spaced lines of consistent thickness, the package author warns against overuse of the optional arguments and special commands to produce lines with individual characteristics. Nevertheless, these features may be useful in special circumstances.

The example below shows the effect of many of these options as well as demonstrating that overuse of the commands produces a very unpleasing layout.

	Items	Price/lb
a	b	c
Food	Category	$
Apples	Fruit	1.50
Oranges	Fruit	2.00
Beef	Meat	4.50
x	y	z

```
\usepackage{booktabs}
\begin{tabular}{@{}llr@{}}
\toprule
    \multicolumn{2}{c}{Items} &\multicolumn{1}{c}{Price/lb} \\
\cmidrule(r){1-2}                 \cmidrule(l){3-3}
    a & b & c                                              \\
\cmidrule(l{10pt}r{10pt}){1-2}\cmidrule(l{10pt}r{10pt}){3-3}
\morecmidrules               \cmidrule(l{5pt}r{5pt})  {2-3}
\addlinespace[5pt]
    Food& Category & \multicolumn{1}{c}{\$}\\
\midrule
    Apples & Fruit  & 1.50 \\        Oranges & Fruit & 2.00 \\
\addlinespace                        Beef & Meat    & 4.50 \\
\specialrule{.5pt}{10pt}{20pt}       x     & y       & z    \\
\bottomrule
\end{tabular}
```

6-6-7

6.6.6 bigstrut — Spreading individual table lines apart

The separation between individual rows in a tabular type of environment is not managed by putting white space between the rows. Instead, the rows touch each other, and visual separation is achieved by placing invisible material of a certain height and depth (so called "struts") on every line. The technical reason for this approach is that in this way vertical lines are not disrupted, which would happen if real white space is used.

The downside is that a strut only defines the minimal height of a row. If the material in the cells is higher than the strut, then the strut has no effect, and the cell content bumps into the previous line or into a preceding horizontal rule.

The standard \arraystretch factor enlarges the normal height and depth of the strut used in tables, and the \extrarowheight parameter offered by the array package is added to the height only without affecting the depth. Both act on all rows, so changing them means that all lines get some additional separation even though perhaps only lines after or before a horizontal rule need some extra space.

To limit such adjustments to individual rows you need to define your own struts, which is not exactly difficult using the \rule command, but not that convenient either. The alternative, which works well in many cases, is to load the bigstrut package by Jerry Leichter that offers a command for this.

\bigstrut [*top-or-bottom*]

The \bigstrut command adds a strut in the current table cell that is slightly larger than the normal strut used inside the table (the extra amount is \bigstrutjot, which defaults to 2pt). The value of the optional *top-or-bottom* argument can be t or b in which case only the height or the depth is affected. Used without the argument both get enlarged. Spaces before and after the command are ignored so that it can be easily added to a cell. The next example compares a table with and without these extra struts.

```
\usepackage{bigstrut}
\begin{tabular}{|ccc|}                                            \hline
          A & B & C \\ \hline              x & y & z \\ \hline
\end{tabular}

\bigskip

\begin{tabular}{|ccc|}                                            \hline
  \bigstrut[t] A & B & C \\ \hline \bigstrut[b] x & y & z \\ \hline
\end{tabular}
```

A	B	C
x	y	z

A	B	C
x	y	z

6-6-8

6.6.7 cellspace — Ensure minimal clearance automatically

The cellspace by Josselin Noirel provides an automated solution to the issue of cell entries touching neighboring horizontal lines. It works by making sure that the content of cells is at least \cellspacetoplimit away from a preceding horizontal rule and at least \cellspacebottomlimit from a following one. If it is, then nothing is done to the cell; otherwise, it is manipulated to have enough separation. The default for both parameters is 1pt and can be changed anywhere in the document.

These checks are not done on each and every cell in a table, but only in designated columns. For this a special column specifier S is provided that takes the normal column specifier as its argument; e.g., you write S{c} or S{p{2cm}} instead of c or p{2cm}. In case you also use the siunitx package or use S for your own column type, you can use a different letter by specifying it with the package option column=⟨letter⟩; see Example 6-6-10.

The next example shows a simple table with three rows in which the first and last cells touch the top and the top and bottom rule, respectively. With the default value for cellspace these two cells are then slightly opened up (second table). Using an enlarged top limit also affects the first and third cell (third table), while additionally enlarging the bottom limit then affects the second and third cells (fourth table), because now the descender in "y" is closer than 3pt from the bottom rule.

```
\usepackage{cellspace}
\begin{tabular}[t]{c}    \hline
   Ä \\\hline xyz \\\hline $\frac{1}{2}$ \\\hline \end{tabular}
\begin{tabular}[t]{S{c}} \hline
   Ä \\\hline xyz \\\hline $\frac{1}{2}$ \\\hline \end{tabular}
\setlength\cellspacetoplimit{3pt}
\begin{tabular}[t]{S{c}} \hline
   Ä \\\hline xyz \\\hline $\frac{1}{2}$ \\\hline \end{tabular}
\setlength\cellspacebottomlimit{3pt}
\begin{tabular}[t]{S{c}} \hline
   Ä \\\hline xyz \\\hline $\frac{1}{2}$ \\\hline \end{tabular}
```

6-6-9

For comparison we show the tables once more, but this time fix it manually with some \bigstrut commands (third table) and also use both bigstrut and cellspace in the fourth table. As you can see, this results in even more white space, because the struts are considered cell material, and thus cellspace requires the minimal space in addition.

```
\usepackage[column=O]{cellspace}
\usepackage{bigstrut}
\begin{tabular}[t]{c}    \hline
   Ä \\\hline xyz \\\hline $\frac{1}{2}$ \\\hline \end{tabular}
\begin{tabular}[t]{O{c}} \hline
   Ä \\\hline xyz \\\hline $\frac{1}{2}$ \\\hline \end{tabular}
\begin{tabular}[t]{c}       \hline
   Ä \bigstrut[t]              \\\hline xyz \\\hline
   $\frac{1}{2}$ \bigstrut               \\\hline \end{tabular}
\begin{tabular}[t]{O{c}}    \hline
   Ä \bigstrut[t]              \\\hline xyz \\\hline
   $\frac{1}{2}$ \bigstrut               \\\hline \end{tabular}
```

6-6-10

The cellspace packages knows about the basic column specifiers provided by the array package, but if you use other table packages, such as tabularx or tabulary, or if you have defined your own specifiers, then you have to tell cellspace about them in case they denote "paragraph" columns. You do this with a declaration such as

```
\addparagraphcolumntypes{X}    % for tabularx
```

after which you can write S{X} in the table preamble.

6.7 Other extensions

Several further packages extend the array package with additional functionality, and we describe five of them in this section. The first provides for table entries spanning more than one row. The second offers ways to produce diagonally oriented text in individual cells, which is sometimes useful in header rows. The other three provide additional column specifiers to deal with data alignment in columns consisting of only numbers and in the case of the fcolumn package also offer extended support for financial tables.

You can simulate a cell spanning a few rows vertically by putting the material in a zero-height box and raising it, but this is obviously not a very intuitive method.

100	qqq	
	A	B
20000000	10	10

```
\begin{tabular}{|c|c|c|}             \hline
        & \multicolumn{2}{c|}{qqq}\\\cline{2-3}
\raisebox{1.5ex}[0cm][0cm]{\bfseries 100}
        & A          & B          \\\hline
20000000 & 10         & 10         \\\hline
\end{tabular}
```

6-7-1

Similarly, you can use a standard tabular preamble of the form r@{.}l to create two table columns and produce the effect of a column aligned on a decimal point, but then the input looks rather strange, as shown in the next example:

```
1.2
1.23
913.17
```

```
\begin{tabular}{r@{.}l}
    1 & 2 \\  1 & 23 \\ 913 & 17
\end{tabular}
```

6-7-2

Using this approach you have to be aware that the "column" is really two columns of the table. This becomes important when counting columns for the \multicolumn or \cline command. Also, you need to locally set \extracolsep to 0pt if you use this construct in a tabular* environment; otherwise, TeX may insert space after the decimal point to spread the table to the specified width. For alternative solutions, see the packages discussed in Sections 6.7.3 to 6.7.5.

6.7.1 multirow — Vertical alignment in tables

The multirow package (by Jerry Leichter and Pieter van Oostrum) automates the procedure of constructing tables with columns spanning several rows by defining a \multirow command.

> \multirow{*nrow*}{*width*}{*content*}

The mandatory arguments are *nrow* (number of rows to span), *width* of the cell, and *content* of the cell. The *width* can be given either as a dimension, such as 2cm or as *** (use the natural width of the *content*) or as = (use the column width specified in the tabular preamble).

If the *width* is explicitly given or if = is used, then the *content* is formatted in a paragraph box of that *width*, and you can use \\ for explicit line breaks inside. If * is used, then the *content* is set on a single line.

The = notation makes sense only if the column has a predefined width, i.e., is either a p column or an m, b, w, or W column in an extended tabular, or if it is an X column in a tabularx or an L, C, R, or J column in a tabulary environment. Using = with other column types, e.g., c, gives strange results. Here you either need to specify an explicit width or use *.

6-7-3

Text in column 1 (4 rows)	C2a C2b C2c C2d	C3a Spanning 2 rows C3d	C4a C4b C4c C4d

```
\usepackage{multirow}
\begin{tabular}{|l|l|p{25mm}|l|}        \hline
\multirow{4}{14mm}{Text in column 1 (4 rows)}
  & C2a & C3a                 & C4a \\
  & C2b & \multirow{2}{=}
          {Spanning 2 rows} & C4b \\
  & C2c &                     & C4c \\
  & C2d & C3d                 & C4d \\ \hline
\end{tabular}
```

Armed with this knowledge you are now in a position to typeset the small example shown at the beginning of this section without having to use the \raisebox command. All that is necessary is to use the * notation for the *width*.

6-7-4

100	qqq	
	A	B
20000000	10	10

```
\usepackage{multirow}
\begin{tabular}{|c|c|c|}               \hline
\multirow{2}{*}{\bfseries 100}
  & \multicolumn{2}{c|}{qqq}  \\ \cline{2-3}
        & A      & B      \\ \hline
20000000 & 10     & 10     \\ \hline \end{tabular}
```

It is possible to span both rows and columns by using a \multirow inside a \multicolumn entry. For technical reasons the other way around does not work. Note, however, that all the spanned cells in the later rows need to be empty; i.e., if there are normally vertical lines between them, you need to disable them using further \multicolumn commands as we did in the next example.

You also have some limited ability to control the standard formatting within the cells. Just before the text to be typeset is expanded, the \multirowsetup macro is automatically executed to set up some default configuration. Initially, \multirowsetup contains just \raggedright, but it can be redefined with \renewcommand. In the example on the next page we use it to get ragged-left text by default.

```
\usepackage{multirow}  \renewcommand\multirowsetup{\raggedleft}
\begin{tabular}{|l|l|l|}                                    \hline
   C1a & C2a & C3a                                      \\ \hline
\multicolumn{3}{|c|}{\multirow{2}{25mm}{Spanning 2 rows
                                      \& 3 columns}} \\
\multicolumn{3}{|c|}{}                                \\ \hline
   C1d & C2d & C3d                                     \\ \hline
\end{tabular}
```

C1a	C2a	C3a
Spanning 2 rows & 3 columns		
C1d	C2d	C3d

6-7-5

Further fine-tuning is possible by specifying optional arguments as discussed below. This ability can be useful when any of the spanned rows are unusually large, when \strut commands are used asymmetrically around the centerline of spanned rows, or when descenders are not taken into account correctly. In these cases the vertical centering may not come out as desired, and these optional arguments can then be used to adjust the placement as necessary. Here is the full set of available arguments:

\multirow[*vpos*]{*nrow*}[*bigstruts*]{*width*}[*vmove*]{*content*}

The *vpos* argument specifies how the cell *content* is positioned vertically. The default is c, and the alternatives are t or b with the obvious meanings. Additional fine-grained adjustments can be made by specifying a vertical shift in the optional *vmove* argument. Positive values shift the material upwards, negative values downwards. The default is no shift.

The *bigstruts* argument is useful only if you are using \bigstrut from the bigstrut package inside your table. In that case some of your rows have some additional height, and by adding the number of such extra struts in this argument you enable \multirow to calculate the total height of the spanned rows correctly.

The effect of the optional vertical positioning parameter *vmove* can be seen below. A negative value lowers the material, and a positive one raises it.

Text in column 1 (default)	Cell 1a
	Cell 1b
	Cell 1c
	Cell 1d
Text in column 1 (lowered)	Cell 2a
	Cell 2b
	Cell 2c
	Cell 2d
Text in column 1 (lifted)	Cell 3a
	Cell 3b
	Cell 3c
	Cell 3d

```
\usepackage{multirow}
\begin{tabular}{|l|l|}
\hline
\multirow{4}{25mm}{Text in column 1 (default)}
   & Cell 1a \\\cline{2-2} & Cell 1b \\\cline{2-2}
   & Cell 1c \\\cline{2-2} & Cell 1d \\\hline
\multirow{4}{25mm}[-3mm]{Text in column 1 (lowered)}
   & Cell 2a \\\cline{2-2} & Cell 2b \\\cline{2-2}
   & Cell 2c \\\cline{2-2} & Cell 2d \\\hline
\multirow{4}{25mm}[3mm]{Text in column 1 (lifted)}
   & Cell 3a \\\cline{2-2} & Cell 3b \\\cline{2-2}
   & Cell 3c \\\cline{2-2} & Cell 3d \\\hline
\end{tabular}
```

6-7-6

In the examples so far we have always used \multirow in the first row and kept all other spanned cells empty. A possible alternative is to place it in the last row and use a negative value for the *nrow* argument. In most circumstances both approaches yield the same result, and thus the former is more convenient.

There is one case where this is not true, and the latter approach needs to be used. If you combine \multirow with a \columncolor command from the colortbl package, the background color needs to be applied first, because it otherwise overlays the content typeset by \multirow. Because colortbl colors the cells row by row, any background color in spanned cells is placed on top of already typeset material, which thus vanishes. The next example nicely exhibits the problem (text in the second column is partly hidden) and its solution in the fourth column.

```
\usepackage{colortbl,multirow}
\begin{tabular}{*2{c>{\columncolor{yellow}}c}}
C1 &   C2 & C3 & C4                                \\
C1 & \multirow{2}*{partly hidden} & C3  & \\
C1 &    & C3 & \multirow{-2}*{visible}
\end{tabular}
```

6-7-7

6.7.2 diagbox — Making table cells with diagonal lines

Sometimes you see the content of a cell diagonally split with or without a diagonal line separating both parts. Typically this is done in the top-left cell of a heading row with one text being the heading for the first column and the other a heading for the first row. For this Leo Liu developed the diagbox package, which provides a single command \diagbox for use in table cells.

\diagbox[*key/values*]{*left*}{*right*}
\diagbox[*key/values*]{*left*}{*middle*}{*right*}

The command comes in two incarnations taking either two or three braced arguments; i.e., the third is optional even though it is surrounded by braces. That means that \diagbox with two arguments cannot be followed by a braced group, but because it is typically used by its own inside a table cell, this is normally not a problem. The command also has a normal optional argument expecting a *key/values* list to configure its behavior as discussed below.

If used without the *key/values* argument, \diagbox automatically calculates the necessary width, height, position of the text arguments, and placement of the line(s) separating them. To make this work correctly, all cells in the column must have a shorter width and all cells in the row a shorter height. In the example this is not the case in the second column, which is why the diagonal line in cell 2,2 does not extend into the corners. The solution in that case is to set the necessary width (or height) explicitly instead of relying on the automatic calculation. In cell 3,2 we have set the `height`, which brings the texts vertically closer together (but of course does not resolve the initial problem). In cell 4,2 we then also set the `width` using the `\widthof` command from the `calc` package, which (like `array`) is automatically loaded by `diagbox`. Nevertheless, we are still a bit too short as you can see:

table \ row info	H2
column	
R1	a wide cell C1,2
R2	2,2 \ C
R3	C 3,2
R4	C 4,2

```
\usepackage{diagbox}
\begin{tabular}{|c|c|c|}                        \hline
 \diagbox{column}{table}{row info} & H2  \\ \hline
  R1 & a wide cell C1,2                   \\ \hline
  R2 & \diagbox{C}{2,2}                   \\ \hline
  R3 & \diagbox[height=18pt]{C}{3,2}      \\ \hline
  R4 & \diagbox[height=15pt, width=\widthof{a
                wide cell C1,2}]{C}{4,2} \\ \hline
\end{tabular}
```

6-7-8

Keys for horizontal spacing adjustments

The reason for this shortage is that we measured the text in cell 1,2 and assigned this to the `width`, but the value for this key should also include the separation at the left and the right (typically `\tabcolsep`), which we have not accounted for. For the width of the text portion of the cell there exists the key `innerwidth`, and this is what we should have used instead. They are linked through the following equation

$$\text{width} = \text{innerleftsep} + \text{innerwidth} + \text{innerrightsep}$$

with the separations initialized to `\tabcolsep` if not explicitly set.

If you think about it, then it is clear that this would make the cell content with the diagonal line wider than the tabular cell, and to account for this there also exist two further keys `outerleftsep` and `outerrightsep` that are by default the negations of the inner separations. By setting some or all of these keys, various special effects can be achieved.

As a convenient shorthand, the key `leftsep` sets `innerleftsep` to its value and `outerleftsep` to the negation. The key `rightsep` does the same for the right side. This means that they change the inner separation while the diagonal line still ends in the corner.

Keys for rule placement

With the `dir` key you can define the corner in which the *middle* text will appear (if there are three arguments). Allowed values are NW (default), NE, SW, or SE. These values are also allowed if only two braced arguments are given, but then they result in only two distinct layouts as the diagonal either goes from NW to SE or goes from NE to SW making the cases indistinguishable.

The next example exhibits all the different directions and also shows the effects of some other keys: `font` specifies the font to use (which is equivalent to adding the setting into each argument), and `trim` removes any space on the left or the right (allowed values are `l` or `r` or both). Finally, there are `linewidth` and `linecolor` that do the obvious — but note that you have to load a color support package if you want to use colored rules.

In some cells the diagonal rules appear to come out short. This is either due to the fact that the cell is not the highest/widest one in its row or column or due to special settings made, i.e., the `trim`, the `leftsep`, or the `width`, and `height` settings that got applied. In other words, while this example is not meant to be used as such, it shows a lot of different effects in one place.

```
\usepackage{color,diagbox}
\begin{tabular}{|c|c|c|} \hline
\diagbox{A}{B}{C} &
  \diagbox[dir=NE,font=\tiny]{north}{east}            &
    \diagbox[width=2cm,dir=NE]{A}{B}{C}                  \\\hline
\diagbox[dir=NW,font=\tiny,trim=lr]{north}{west} &
  \diagbox[font=\tiny,linecolor=blue,
           linewidth=1pt]{default}{direction}         &
    \diagbox[dir=SE,font=\tiny,trim=r]{south}{east}\\\hline
\diagbox[dir=SW,leftsep=0pt]{A}{B}{C}            &
  \diagbox[dir=SW,font=\tiny]{south}{west}           &
    \diagbox[width=30pt,height=30pt,
             dir=SE,font=\itshape]{x}{y}{z}          \\\hline
\end{tabular}
```

If you want a `\diagbox` to fill the full width of a paragraph column such as a p column where the width is preset in the tabular preamble or if you want to use it in an X column from tabularx, you have to tell it the `innerwidth` it should use for formatting. In the case of a p column or one of the other paragraph columns, you know the width, and you could repeat it. But in the case of an X that size is not known a priori. Fortunately, you can use the register `\hsize` in that case as that holds the horizontal size in such cells once its value is calculated.

```
\usepackage{tabularx,diagbox}
\begin{tabularx}{\textwidth}{|p{1cm}|X|X|}  \hline
  \diagbox[innerwidth=1cm]{A}{B} &
  \diagbox[dir=SW,innerwidth=\hsize]{AA}{BB} &
  \diagbox[innerwidth=\hsize]{AAA}{BBB} \\ \hline
\end{tabularx}
```

6.7.3 dcolumn — Decimal column alignments

The dcolumn package (by David Carlisle) provides a system for defining columns of entries in array or tabular environments that are to be aligned on a "decimal point". Entries with no decimal part, those with no integer part, and blank entries are also dealt with correctly. Note that the siunitx package for scientific notation provides a similar functionality with its S tabular specifier, which is described in the following section starting on page 484.

D{*inputsep*}{*outputsep*}{*decimal places*}

The dcolumn package defines a "Decimal" tabular preamble option, D, that takes three arguments.

inputsep   A single character, used as separator (or "decimal point") in the source file (for example, "." or ",").

outputsep   The separator to be used in the output. It can be the same as the first argument, but may also be any math mode expression, such as \cdot.

decimal places   The maximum number of decimal places in the column. If this value is negative, any number of decimal places is allowed in the column, and all entries are centered on the separator. Note that this choice can cause a column to be too wide (see the first two columns in the example below).
Another possibility is to specify the number of digits *both* to the left and to the right of the decimal place, using an argument of the form {*left . right*} as described below.

The cell content is typeset in math mode and thus suitable only for numerical data (i.e., numbers and symbols), but should normally not contain any ordinary text. Sometimes you can cheat a bit by using an \mbox to force the use of text fonts, but usually you need to apply \multicolumn to overwrite the column specifier if you need ordinary text in such a column.

If you do not want to use the rather lengthy D-specification in the table preamble, you can define your own customized preamble specifiers by using \newcolumntype as demonstrated below, e.g.,

```
\newcolumntype{d}[1]{D{.}{\cdot}{#1}}
```

This newly defined "d" specifier then takes a single argument specifying the number of decimal places. The decimal separator in the source file is the normal dot ".", while the output uses the raised math mode dot "·".

In contrast, neither the "." nor the "," specifier defined below takes arguments:

```
\newcolumntype{.}{D{.}{.}{-1}}
\newcolumntype{,}{D{.}{,}{2}}
```

Both declarations use a normal dot as the input decimal separator, but they differ in how they typeset the cell content. With "." the typeset entries are centered on the dot, while the "," specifier uses a comma as a decimal separator in the output, and in the typeset column reserves space for a maximum of two decimal places after the comma.

These definitions are used in the following example, in which the first column, with its negative value for *decimal places* (signaling that the decimal point should be in the center of the column), is much wider than the second column, even though they both contain the same input material. Also quite noticeable is the overprinting in the fourth column, because only space for two decimals was reserved.

```
\usepackage{dcolumn}
\newcolumntype{d}[1]{D{.}{\cdot}{#1}}
\newcolumntype{.}{D{.}{.}{-1}}
\newcolumntype{,}{D{.}{,}{2}}
\begin{tabular}{|d{-1}|d{2}|.|,|}
1.2     & 1.2     & 1.2      & 1.2      \\
1.23    & 1.23    & 12.34    & 12.34    \\
1121.2  & 1121.2  & 0.3333   & 0.3333   \\
184     & 184     & \pm 100  & \pm 100  \\
.4      & .4      & ok?      & no!      \\
-0.55   & -0.55   & -0.55    & -0.55    \\
0.0     & 0.0     & 0.0      & 0.0      \\
\end{tabular}
```

1·2	1·2	1.2	1,2
1·23	1·23	12.34	12,34
1121·2	1121·2	0.3333	0,3333
184	184	±100	±100
·4	·4	ok?	no!
−0·55	−0·55	−0.55	−0,55
0·0	0·0	0.0	0,0

6-7-11

If the table entries include only numerical data that must be aligned, the type of alignment forms shown in the above example should be sufficient. However, if the columns contain headings or other entries that affect the width of the column, the positioning of the numbers within the column might not be as desired.

In the example below, in the first column the numbers appear to be displaced toward the left of the column, although the decimal point is centered. In the second column the numbers are flush right under a centered heading, which is sometimes the desired effect, but (especially if there are no table rules) can make the heading appear dissociated from the data.

The final column shows the numbers aligned on the decimal point and centered as a block under the heading. This effect is achieved by using a third argument to the D preamble option of 4.2 specifying that at most four digits can appear to the left of the point, and two digits to the right of it.

```
\usepackage{dcolumn}

\begin{tabular}{|D..{-1}|D..{2}|D..{4.2}|}
\multicolumn{1}{|c|}{wide heading} &
\multicolumn{1} {c|}{wide heading} &
\multicolumn{1} {c|}{wide heading}
                                   \\[3pt]
1000.20 & 1000.20 & 1000.20   \\
123.45  &  123.45 &  123.45   \\
12.345  &  12.345 &  12.345   \\
-1.23   &   -1.23 &   -1.23
\end{tabular}
```

wide heading	wide heading	wide heading
1000.20	1000.20	1000.20
123.45	123.45	123.45
12.345	12.345	12.345
−1.23	−1.23	−1.23

6-7-12

The following example is a variant of an example from the *LaTeX Manual* showing that D column alignments may be used for purposes other than aligning numerical data on a decimal point. Note the use of \mbox to produce text in D-columns.

```
\usepackage{dcolumn}
\newcolumntype{+}{D{/}{\mbox{--}}{4}}
\newcolumntype{,}{D{,}{,}{2}}
\begin{tabular}{|r||+|
    >{\raggedright}p{2.2cm}|,|}    \hline
\multicolumn{4}{|c|}{GG\&A Hoofed Stock}\\
\hline\hline
& \multicolumn{1}{c|}{Price}& &
\\ \cline{2-2} \multicolumn{1}{|c||}{Year}
& \mbox{low}/\mbox{high}
& \multicolumn{1}{c|}{Comments}
& \multicolumn{1}{c|}{Other}    \\ \hline
1971 & 97/245  &Bad year for farmers in
    the West. & 23,45        \\ \hline
  72 &245/245  &Light trading due to a
    heavy winter.    & 435,23\\ \hline
  73 &245/2001 &No gnus was very good
    gnus this year. & 387,56\\ \hline
\end{tabular}
```

GG&A Hoofed Stock			
Year	Price low–high	Comments	Other
1971	97–245	Bad year for farmers in the West.	23,45
72	245–245	Light trading due to a heavy winter.	435,23
73	245–2001	No gnus was very good gnus this year.	387,56

6-7-13

6.7.4 siunitx — Scientific numbers in tables

Tools for formatting numerical values in tables in a flexible way are offered by the siunitx package. While the primary focus of the package is on typesetting numbers and units in running text (see Chapter 3), it offers additional features that are focused specifically on the need to align numbers in columns. The general options it provides, as covered in Section 3.3.4 on page 167, are also applicable to such tabular material. On top of this it provides a new tabular specifier S that indicates a column of numbers by default aligned at their decimal markers that we discuss now.

```
S[options]    \tablenum[options]{number}
```

The cells are parsed and printed according to the standard conventions of the siunitx package, and if necessary, the specifier can take an optional argument to apply options to influence the formatting and alignment. The \tablenum command does within a single cell what the S specifier does for a whole column and is intended for use in \multicolumn or \multirow arguments. This allows alignment across several specially handled cells.

With some restrictions, nonnumerical material is allowed in the cells as well. Textual material after the number, e.g., a * or a note marker, works without problems. Before the number, one can use text that cannot be confused with a number. Some commands, such as \color, apply to the entire cell and can be inserted directly. Another common example is \bfseries: here you will also need to direct the siunitx package to detect font changes with \sisetup{reset-font-series = false} in this case. Furthermore, if nonnumerical material could be mistaken by siunitx as being a number, one has to hide it in braces (e.g., "broken" containing an "e"). An example is shown below. For more complicated scenarios refer to the package documentation that has a whole section on these issues and workarounds for them.

	47.11	
	111.5	
2.345		-1.2
12.17[b]		7.84×10^2
1.999 98		broken 0.01
56.7		$\mathbf{9.7(1) \times 10^{-3}}$

```
\usepackage{siunitx}
\newcommand\note[1]{\textsuperscript{\,#1}}

\begin{tabular}{|S|S[text-series-to-math]|}
  \multicolumn{2}{|c|}{\tablenum{47.11}}      \\
  \multicolumn{2}{|c|}{\tablenum{111.5}}      \\
  2.345                & &           -1.2     \\
  12.17 \note{b}       & &           7.84e2   \\
  1.99998              & & {broken } 0.01     \\
  \color{blue} 56.7 &  \bfseries 9.7(1)e-3
\end{tabular}
```

6-7-14

When looking at the previous example, we see that the decimal marker is placed in the middle of the cells. This default works well for numbers that have roughly the same number of digits on either side but otherwise wastes precious space. To improve this and other cases roughly two dozen keys specific to table columns are available.

If the number of digits in the integer and decimal part are quite different and we want to have tighter columns, we need to tell siunitx the format of our numerical data. *Specifying the number format* This can be done with `table-format`, either for a single column or for all columns of a table. As its value it expects a prototype entry that indicates how many digits need to be reserved for each part of the numerical data. For example, `4.2` means two decimals and up to four integer digits. The key correctly interprets a sign (and reserves space for it) as well as exponent or uncertainty parentheses; e.g., in a complex scenario you might write something like `+1.4(1)e+2`.

Using `table-format` automatically sets the `table-alignment-mode` key to `format`, meaning that the model given as `table-format` is used for alignment. With the key `table-number-alignment`, which can take the values `center`, `left`, or `right`, you can control the placement of the number within the column. This is useful for controlling how shorter values sit under longer text headers. The next example shows the effect of various alignment choices. Note that in the second column the data is centered (and in the third left-aligned) without taking the sign into consideration and thus sticks out to the left in the cell (as the `table-format` does not request space for the sign) and that the last column badly overprints as the format does not match the data at all.

default	Heading	Heading	Heading
2.3456	2.3456	2.3456	2.3456
4.2	4.2	4.2	4.23
6.783	6.783	6.783	6.783
-1.47	-1.47	-1.47	-1.47

```
\usepackage{siunitx}

\begin{tabular}{|S|S[table-format=1.4]|
S[table-format=1.4,table-number-alignment=left]|
S[table-format=1.2,table-number-alignment=right]|}
  {default}&{Heading} &{Heading}&{Heading} \\
    2.3456 &   2.3456 &  2.3456 &   2.3456   \\
    4.2    &   4.2    &  4.2    &   4.23     \\
    6.783  &   6.783  &  6.783  &   6.783    \\
   -1.47   &  -1.47   & -1.47   &  -1.47
\end{tabular}
```

6-7-15

485

If·table-number-alignment is used, then only cells with numerical data are affected (like in the previous example). Similarly, table-text-alignment only affects text cells (like headings). There also exists table-alignment, a shortcut that sets both keys to the same value. Sometimes alignment at the decimal marker is not desirable. This can be prevented by setting table-alignment-mode to none.

```
\usepackage{siunitx}
\begin{tabular}{|S|S[table-alignment-mode=none,
                       table-text-alignment=left]|
                 S[table-alignment-mode=none,
                       table-alignment=right]|}
{Default} & {Left}     & {Right}  \\
  12.345 & 12.345     & 12.345   \\
     6.7 & 6.7        & 6.7      \\
 -88.8(9) & -88.8(9)   & -88.8(9) \\
   4.5e3 & 4.5e3      & 4.5e3
\end{tabular}
```

Default	Left	Right
12.345	12.345	12.345
6.7	6.7	6.7
−88.8(9)	−88.8(9)	−88.8(9)
4.5×10^3	4.5×10^3	4.5×10^3

6-7-16

When table data has exponents, then they are lined up by default. But even with this extra visual aide, comparison of column data values is far from easy in that case. Often it is much better to force all exponents to the same size (if they are not already) and then drop the exponent within the table — and this can be done without altering the table data. Below this is done in the second column to show the differences. In a real table one would normally apply this to all columns as appropriate.

```
\usepackage{siunitx}
\begin{tabular}{|S[table-format=2.2e1]|
                 S[exponent-mode=fixed,drop-exponent,fixed-exponent=3,
                       table-format=2.4]|}
{Data} & {Data (\num[drop-exponent=false,
                         print-unity-mantissa=false]{e3})} \\
1.2e3 & 1.2e3 \\ 17.5 & 17.5 \\ 3e2 & 3e2 \\ 1.03e4 & 1.03e4
\end{tabular}
```

Data	Data (10^3)
1.2×10^3	1.2
17.5	0.0175
3×10^2	0.3
1.03×10^4	10.3

6-7-17

By default S columns use as much space as needed for the individual cells and the chosen alignment key. However, sometimes it is necessary to ensure that certain columns — even across tables — have the same width. This can be done by specifying the desired width with table-column-width. If set to a nonzero value, it automatically activates table-fixed-width.

```
\usepackage{siunitx}
\begin{tabular}{|S|S[table-column-width=3cm]|}
{Header} & {Header} \\
-47.11 & -47.11 \\ 1.2 & 1.2 \\ 10.2754 & 10.2754
\end{tabular}
```

Header	Header
−47.11	−47.11
1.2	1.2
10.2754	10.2754

6-7-18

Sometimes comparison of data and readability are improved if the data is rounded to a fixed number of decimals in some or all columns. This can be achieved (just for tables) by specifying `table-auto-round`. Then all columns that have an explicit `table-format` are rounded to the number of decimals given in that format. The next example repeats the previous table but uses two different `table-format` settings to show the effects.

Header	Header
−47.110	−47.1
1.200	1.2
10.275	10.3

```
\usepackage{siunitx}
\sisetup{table-auto-round}
\begin{tabular}{|S[table-format=-2.3]|S[table-format=-2.1]|}
{Header} & {Header} \\
-47.11 & -47.11 \\ 1.2 & 1.2 \\ 10.2754 & 10.2754
\end{tabular}
```

6-7-19

As mentioned, there are further keys to tweak the column appearance; take a look at the manual if the described customizations seem to be insufficient.

6.7.5 fcolumn — Managing financial tables

Many tables contain columns with numerical data, and with dcolumn and siunitx we already saw an extension package that supports aligning such entries at their decimal separator thereby improving readability and comprehension of the table data.

With fcolumn Edgar Olthof provided another extension package that is specially geared towards financial data. Besides formatting the values to conform to standard layouts with appropriate decimal and group separators (customizable as necessary), it can sum up all values of a column and automatically typeset the result as well as checking that sums in specified columns are identical (which is important when producing balance sheets).

The package internally uses the integer arithmetic of TeX, which can only handle numbers not exceeding $2^{31} - 1$, which translates to 2147483647. This means that the highest number the package can process is a bit more than twenty millions if two decimal places are being used; or up to two billions if you are prepared to drop the cents. For anything larger TeX generates a low-level `Arithmetic overflow` error or, in some cases, just typesets a negative number instead. If the latter happens, it is detected by the package, and an appropriate error is issued too.

Columns with financial data are specified using the `f` column specifier provided by the package, which outputs the values using the continental European standard, i.e., two decimal places, a comma as decimal separator, and a period as group separator with three digits per group. The `f` specifier itself is defined in terms of a generic `F` specifier, which is the main workhorse provided by the package.

F{*group-sep*}{*decimal-sep*}{*number-structure*}{*extra-formatting*}

By using F it is trivial to define your own column specifiers with desired settings or redefine the `f` type to your liking. The *group-sep* and *decimal-sep* define the material to separate digit groups in the integer part and the decimal separator, respectively. The *number-structure* argument has a dual purpose. It consists of two numbers separated by some character. The character represents the decimal separator in the input data, and the numbers define the size of the digit groups in the integer part and the number of digits in the decimal part. Thus, "3,2" means two decimal digits and groups of three digits in the integer part. If any table cell contains a number with more decimal digits than specified, the excess digits are discarded with a warning. If you do not want any grouping or no decimals, use 0 for the respective number.

Finally, the *extra-formatting* argument offers you the possibility to provide additional formatting, e.g., a font or color change. If this argument ends in a command that normally takes one argument, then this command receives the preformatted number for further manipulation. By default the argument is applied to the whole column. If, however, you use a comma inside, then everything to the right defines the formatting for summation cells, and everything to the left to all other column cells; e.g., `{,\mathbf}` boldens only the summation cells; see Examples 6-7-21 and 6-7-22 on pages 489–490 for use cases involving the fourth argument.

One important consideration when using the *extra-formatting* argument is that the column is set in math mode. You can therefore only use material that is allowed in math mode; e.g., you cannot use `\textbf` or `\bfseries` to bolden the column cells but instead must apply `\mathbf` or similar commands.

People in the Anglo-Saxon world would probably prefer a definition such as

```
\newcolumntype{f}{F{,}{.}{3.2}{}}
```

but if you prefer group separation by a thin space, all that is necessary is to replace the *group-sep* with `\,` in the above declaration.

Typesetting negative values in parentheses

By default fcolumn typesets negative numbers using a minus sign. Another supported style is to place negative numbers in parentheses (a typical design in financial balance sheets), which is achieved by loading the package with the option `strict` as done in Example 6-7-21 on the facing page.

`\sumline` [*skip-after-rule*] [*skip-after-row*]

If you place a `\sumline` command between any two rows of the table, you get a summary row added in which in each F-column the sum of all entries up to this point is calculated and typeset (with a rule above to indicate the summation). If you need some extra separation after that rule, you can add an optional *skip-after-rule* value (default 2pt), and if you also want extra space after the row, you need to use both optional arguments.

126,50	2,00	3,00	4,25
1.101,00	−0,55		577,15
4,00	3,00	1,45	650,10
1.231,50	4,45	4,45	1.231,50
−1.000,00	150,20	230,00	−997,10
2,95	79,80		0,05
234,45	234,45	234,45	234,45

```
\usepackage{fcolumn}
\begin{tabular}{ffff}
    126,5 & 2    & 3,   & 4,25   \\
  1.101   & -,55 &      & 577,15 \\
      4   & 3,00 & 1,45 & 650,1  \\
\sumline[2pt][4pt]
  -1000,00 & 150,2 & 230 & -997,1 \\
     2,95 & 79,8 &      & 0,05 \\
\sumline
\end{tabular}
```

6-7-20

488

If you have to prepare long balance sheets, they might run longer than a full page, in which case you cannot use a tabular environment any longer. In that case all you have to do is to additionally load longtable or supertabular prior to fcolumn and use the f or F column specifier in the environments they provide.

Multipage financial tables

Each \sumline command has an important additional effect: if there is an even number of F-columns, then by default the first half is pairwise compared to the second and is expected to show the same sums; e.g., with eight columns the first is compared to the fifth, the second to the sixth, etc. If the sums do not agree, then a warning is generated so that you can check the values. This is what happens in the previous example if you process it. If there is an odd number of F-columns, checks are made only if explicitly requested.

Understanding balancing warnings

\checkfcolumns{*col$_A$*}{*col$_B$*}

The \checkfcolumns specifies that F-columns *col$_A$* and *col$_B$* should be compared. It can be used several times to specify all pairings needed. If used, it cancels the default checks described above. Note that if you have additional explanatory columns in your table, then *col$_A$* and *col$_B$* do not represent the physical column numbers.

For example, all columns of the previous table had the same total, but in this table the outer and inner columns need to balance, so the comparisons should not be done in the default way. Instead, the first column should be checked against column 4 and the second against 3 to avoid a complaint by the intermediate \sumline after the third row. This is achieved by using \checkfcolumns declarations to specify the desired pairings at the start of the tabular body. Any number of pairings can be specified — here we need two to get the correct column pairs checked. In this version of the example we also use the option strict to show negative numbers with parentheses, and we add some extra spaces around the summary rows. In addition, we redefined the f specifier to bolden the cells in summation rows.

126,50	2,00	3,00	4,25
1.101,00	(0,55)		577,15
4,00	3,00	1,45	650,10
1.231,50	**4,45**	**4,45**	**1.231,50**
(1.000,00)	150,20	230,00	(997,10)
2,95	79,80		0,05
234,45	**234,45**	**234,45**	**234,45**

```
\usepackage[strict]{fcolumn}
\newcolumntype{f}{F{.}{,}{3,2}{,\mathbf}}
\begin{tabular}{ffff}
\checkfcolumns{1}{4}\checkfcolumns{2}{3}
    126,5  & 2    & 3,   & 4,25    \\
   1.101   & -,55 &      & 577,15  \\
       4   & 3,00 & 1,45 & 650,1   \\[2pt]
\sumline[4pt][6pt]
  -1000,00  & 150,2 & 230  & -997,1 \\
      2,95 & 79,8  &      & 0,05\\[2pt]
\sumline[4pt]
\end{tabular}
```

6-7-21

Sometimes you may want to place several short balance sheets (e.g., from different projects) into a single tabular to ensure that the column widths are uniform across the sheets. In this case using \sumline at the end of each block is not enough, because the values from different projects are independent, and the summation therefore has to restart and not continue.

> \resetsumline   \leeg{*text*}

The \resetsumline declaration resets the summation counters of all columns and the width of the summation rule back to zero to account for the above use case.

Another command that is sometimes useful is \leeg (Dutch for "empty" — about the only hint for the package origin). It is used to indicate that the current cell should not take part in the summation and simply typesets its *text* argument, which could even be a number, but that would most likely be cheating. A typical application is in heading lines (if they are not produced with \multicolumn) or when entering something like \leeg{p.m.} (*pro memoria*). In earlier versions of this package this was also necessary if you wanted an empty cell, hence the name. These days you can simply leave a cell empty.

In the next example we use Anglo-Saxon conventions for input and output, except that we typeset a small space for separating three-digit groups in the integer part. We also make use of the fourth argument of the F specifier to set all numbers in sans serif and the "actual" columns additionally in blue color except for the summation rows. For this we redefine the default f specifier and additionally define an A specifier.

The headers for all projects are identical (except for the title), so we place them into a separate command. Note the use of \leeg to prevent the header texts from being interpreted as numbers.[1] After each project we added \resetsumline to restart the summations. To get nice rules we enlist the help of **booktabs**.

```
\usepackage{xcolor,booktabs,fcolumn}
\newcolumntype{f}{F{\,}{.}{3.2}{\mathsf}}
\newcolumntype{A}{F{\,}{.}{3.2}{\color{blue}\mathsf,\mathsf}}
\newcommand\fheader[1]{\multicolumn{6}{c}{\bfseries #1}  \\ \toprule
              expense & \leeg{budget}   & \leeg{actual} &
              income  & \leeg{expected} & \leeg{actual}\\ \midrule}
\begin{tabular}{@{}lfAlfA@{}}
\fheader{Booklet 113}
printing   & 8200 &       8000  & sales & 10000   & 7863      \\
binding    & 600 &        550                               \\
shipping   & 800 &        496.8                             \\
profit     & 400 &              & loss  &         & 1183.8   \\
\sumline[2pt][30pt]     \resetsumline
\fheader{Booklet 114}
printing   & 6000 &       6200  & sales & 8000    & 8610     \\
binding    & 600 &        650                               \\
... further text omitted ...
```

6-7-22

---

[1]Incidentally, if you forget this, the package simply ignores the cell and leaves it empty.

Booklet 113

expense	budget	actual	income	expected	actual
printing	8 200.00	8 000.00	sales	10 000.00	7 863.00
binding	600.00	550.00			
shipping	800.00	496.80			
profit	400.00		loss		1 183.80
	10 000.00	9 046.80		10 000.00	9 046.80

Booklet 114

expense	budget	actual	income	expected	actual
printing	6 000.00	6 200.00	sales	8 000.00	8 610.00
binding	600.00	650.00			
shipping	640.00	737.60			
profit	760.00	1 022.40	loss		0.00
	8 000.00	8 610.00		8 000.00	8 610.00

6.8 Footnotes in tabular material

As stated in Section 3.5.2 on page 208, footnotes appearing inside tabular material are not typeset by standard LaTeX. Only the environments `tabularx`, `longtable`, `mpsupertabular`, and `mpsupertabular*` will automatically typeset footnotes (at the bottom of the page).

As you generally want your "table notes" to appear just below the table, you normally have to tackle the problem yourself by managing the note marks and, for instance, by using `\multicolumn` commands at the bottom of your `tabular` environment to contain your table notes. Two alternatives are discussed in the next sections: using a `minipage` environment and using the threeparttable package.

6.8.1 Using minipage footnotes with tables

If a `tabular` or `array` environment is used inside a `minipage` environment, standard footnote commands may be used inside the table. In this case these footnotes are typeset at the bottom of the `minipage` environment, as explained in Section 3.5.1 on page 205.

Note the redefinition of `\thefootnote` in the example on the following page that allows us to make use of the `\footnotemark` command inside the `minipage` environment. Without this redefinition `\footnotemark` would have generated a footnote mark in the style of the footnotes for the main page, as explained in Section 3.5.2.

PostScript Type 1 fonts	
Courier[a]	cour, courb, courbi, couri
Charter[b]	bchb, bchbi, bchr, bchri
Nimbus[c]	unmr, unmrs
URW Antiqua[c]	uaqrrc
URW Grotesk[c]	ugqp
Utopia[d]	putb, putbi, putr, putri

---
[a]Donated by IBM.
[b]Donated by Bitstream.
[c]Donated by URW GmbH.
[d]Donated by Adobe.

```
\begin{minipage}{\linewidth}
  \renewcommand\thefootnote{\thempfootnote}
  \begin{tabular}{lp{1.8cm}}
    \multicolumn{2}{c}{\bfseries PostScript Type 1 fonts} \\
    Courier\footnote{Donated by IBM.}
                    & cour, courb, courbi, couri              \\
    Charter\footnote{Donated by Bitstream.}
                    & bchb, bchbi, bchr, bchri                \\
    Nimbus\footnote{Donated by URW GmbH.} & unmr, unmrs       \\
    URW Antiqua\footnotemark[\value{mpfootnote}] & uaqrrc \\
    URW Grotesk\footnotemark[\value{mpfootnote}] & ugqp    \\
    Utopia\footnote{Donated by Adobe.}
                    & putb, putbi, putr, putri                \\
  \end{tabular}
\end{minipage}
```

6-8-1

Of course, this approach does not automatically limit the width of the footnotes to the width of the table, so a little iteration with the `minipage` width argument might be necessary to achieve the desired effect.

6.8.2 threeparttable — Setting table and notes together

Another way to typeset table notes is with the package threeparttable, written by Donald Arseneau. This package has the advantage that it indicates unambiguously that you are dealing with notes inside tables. Moreover, it gives you full control of the actual reference marks and offers the possibility of having a caption for your tabular material. With this package the table notes are automatically set in a box with the width set equal to the width of the table.

Table notes set to the width of the table

Normally, the `threeparttable` environment would be contained within a `table` environment so that the table would float. However, `threeparttable` may also be used directly, in which case it constructs a nonfloating table similar to the nonfloating `table` environment setup described in Example 7-3-4 on page 532.

As its name suggests, the `threeparttable` environment consists of three parts. The *caption* part consists of the usual `\caption` command (which may come before or after the table). The *table* part may use one of the standard `tabular` or `tabular*` environments, the extended variants defined in the array package, or extensions such as the `tabularx` environment defined in the tabularx package. Other tabular environments may work as well; if in doubt, give it a try.[1] The third part of a `threeparttable` is the text of the table *notes*, which consists of one or more `tablenotes` environments.

Table notes within the table are specified with `\tnote`, which takes the *marker* as a mandatory argument. The environment makes no attempt to do auto-numbering; i.e., you are solely responsible for providing the correct marks. This is actually fairly

---
[1]It should be noted that due to the implementation approach threeparttable does not work with multipage tables such as `longtable`. There is, however, an extension package called threetableex by Lars Madsen that you can use if you need table notes with `longtable`.

convenient when one often refers to the same note several times (and then auto-numbering is rather cumbersome to use) and the number of notes is usually small, so providing explicit numbers is not a big burden. In the `tablenotes` environment the notes are then marked up as \items. In the next example we use three `tablenotes` environments to show some of the formatting options available for them.

Table 1: PostScript Type 1 fonts

Courier[a]	cour, courb, courbi, couri
Charter[b]	bchb, bchbi, bchr, bchri
Nimbus[c]	unmr, unmrs
URW Antiqua[c]	uaqrrc
URW Grotesk[c]	ugqp
Utopia[d]	putb, putbi, putr, putri

[a] Donated by IBM.
[b] Donated by Bitstream.
[c] Donated by URW GmbH.
[d] Donated by Adobe.

a   Donated by IBM.
b   Donated by Bitstream.
c   Donated by URW GmbH.
d   Donated by Adobe.

Donated by: [a] IBM,   [b] Bitstream,
6-8-2 [c] URW GmbH,   [d] Adobe.

```
\usepackage{threeparttable,booktabs}
\begin{threeparttable}
\caption{\textsf{PostScript Type\,1 fonts}}
\begin{tabular}{@{}ll@{}}  \toprule
 Courier\tnote{a} & cour, courb, courbi, couri   \\
 Charter\tnote{b} & bchb, bchbi, bchr, bchri     \\
 Nimbus\tnote{c}  & unmr, unmrs                  \\
 URW Antiqua\tnote{c} & uaqrrc                   \\
 URW Grotesk\tnote{c} & ugqp                     \\
 Utopia\tnote{d}      & putb, putbi, putr, putri \\
\bottomrule               \end{tabular}
\begin{tablenotes}
\item[a]Donated by IBM.  \item[b]Donated by Bitstream.
\item[c]Donated by URW GmbH. \item[d]Donated by Adobe.
\end{tablenotes}
\begin{tablenotes}[flushleft,online]
\item[a]Donated by IBM.  \item[b]Donated by Bitstream.
\item[c]Donated by URW GmbH. \item[d]Donated by Adobe.
\end{tablenotes}
\begin{tablenotes}[para]
\item[]Donated by:      \item[a]IBM, \item[b]Bitstream,
\item[c]URW GmbH, \item[d]Adobe.
\end{tablenotes}
\end{threeparttable}
```

As shown in the previous example, the threeparttable package offers several options to control the typesetting of the table notes:

para   Notes are set within a paragraph, without forced line breaks.

flushleft   No hanging indentation is applied to notes.

online   Note labels are printed normal size, not as superscripts.

normal   Normal default formatting is restored.

Each of these options may be used as a package option to set the default style for all such tables within the document. Alternatively, they may be used on individual `tablenotes` environments as done in the example.

In addition to these options the package has several commands that may be redefined to control the formatting in more specific ways than those provided by the package options. See the package documentation for details.

6.9 keyvaltable — Separating table data and formatting

Specifying table data in a system such as LaTeX has a general problem: tables are multidimensional (typically two), but TeX (and thus LaTeX) processes its input as a one-dimensional stream, which means that the organization of the input data is normally biased towards one type of presentation.

For example, all `tabular`-type environments we have seen so far represent the table data as a sequence of rows with the cells being separated by &. It is therefore fairly easy to reorder rows or to specify how data in individual columns should be treated but far more difficult to specify handling of data within the rows. This is reasonable because in many cases data within one column require identical treatment. However, what happens if you discover that the data are better represented by changing the column order or you want to drop one column from the table? Any such change can become very cumbersome if you have already entered the data in your LaTeX file.

The package **keyvaltable** by Richard Grewe uses a completely different approach and can therefore be an interesting alternative in many situations. Columns are "named", and the data for each table row are then specified by key/value pairs. Furthermore, it introduces named table types that define column structure and layout of columns. After defining such types you can use them repeatedly for different tables in your document with the advantage that any later modification can be easily and consistently done. The downside is, of course, that there is more to type when entering your data, because it is now given as key/value pairs for each table cell, but this extra work quickly pays off through the extra flexibility offered by the approach.

It also means that some of the hand-tailoring that is possible with commands like \multicolumn, etc., in standard `tabular` either has no equivalent or needs to be done differently, because input data and presentation are by default separated instead of being intermixed.

\NewKeyValTable [*table-options*] {*structure-name*}{*col-spec*} [*specials*]

With \NewKeyValTable you define a specific table structure (how many columns, how aligned, etc.) and give it a name in the *structure-name* argument. This name is then referenced in KeyValTable environments to produce tables in that structure.

In the optional *table-options* argument you can define overall table properties, e.g., the type of table (multipage or single page), rules or backgrounds settings, etc. They can be overwritten on individual tables if necessary. The allowed key are discussed on page 497. The other optional argument *specials* allows you to set up a header row with headers spanning more than one column. This is discussed on page 502.

The most important argument is *col-spec* in which the column setup is described. Each column is identified by a *column-name* followed by a colon and a (possible empty) list of *properties* and ends with a semicolon. If you do not specify any column *properties*, you can leave out the colon, but the semicolon is always required except for the very last column. In particular, this means you can initially define a table structure by just specifying column name and worry about the details later. The *properties* are given in form of a key/value list in which you can use the following keys:

align With this key the column alignment is defined. All usual column specifiers from the array package are supported including new column specifiers defined through \newcolumntype.[1] Furthermore, the X from tabularx is available if supported by the backend used. The default value is to align at the left if the key is not given.

default This key defines a default value for cells in that column. By default column cells that are not specified are simply left empty.

format For more complex formatting each cell in the column can be preprocessed. The format expects a command with one argument that receives the cell content.

head By default the *column-name* is used for the column header. If you want to provide a different string or special formatting, this key can be used.

hidden If this key is set to true (or the key is given without a value), then the column is not shown in the table. This can be useful when producing several tables from the same table data displaying different aspects of the data.

As an example, the following declaration defines a table structure named cities that contains the four columns name, country, visited, and note.

```
\NewKeyValTable{cities}{ name: align=c, head=city;
   country: default = ??, format = \textbf;
   note:    align = X,    format = \raggedright, default = \ ---;
   visited: hidden }
```

All columns are left-aligned (default) except for name, which is centered, and note, which is a multiline column to allow for longer notes (align). All columns use their column name as the header except for name, which has the word "city" as its column header (head). We supply an explicit default for the columns country and note. Because spaces are dropped around the =, we had to use \␣ to get a real space in front of the em-dash. The visited column is hidden, i.e., does not show up in the typeset output unless we overwrite the setting later. For two columns we define explicit formatting. Note that the last command of the format code can be a command with one argument, e.g., \textbf. If used in this way, it receives the cell content.

> \begin{KeyValTable} [*table-options*] {*structure-name*} ... \end{KeyValTable}

The KeyValTable environment is then used in the document to typeset the individual tables. It takes the *structure-name* of a table structure as its mandatory argument,

---

[1] Though not mentioned in the package documentation, it is also possible to make use of special array column specifiers, such as >{...}, @{...}, or !{...} and vertical rules | and || as well. See for instance Example 6-9-7 on page 503 where rules are used.

and in the optional *table-options* you can overwrite overall table settings, if necessary. In the example we use it to suppress all background colors. The full list of possible keys is discussed later.

city	country	note
Mainz	??	Birthplace of Gutenberg
New York	USA	—

```
\usepackage{keyvaltable}
% \NewKeyValTable{cities}{...} as defined above
\begin{KeyValTable}[nobg]{cities}
  \Row{name=Mainz, note=Birthplace of Gutenberg}
  \Row[format=\color{blue}]
      {name=New York, country=USA, visited=yes}
\end{KeyValTable}
```

6-9-1

As you can see, the actual table data are provided through a number of \Row commands inside the KeyValTable environment.

\Row[*row-options*]{*cell-data*}   \kvtNewRowStyle{*name*}{*row-options*}

The *cell-data* argument should be a comma-separated list of column names and their values (use braces if the value contains a comma or an equal sign). Because columns have names, you can give them in any order and also leave some out — those that are missing get the default value for the column if one was set up; otherwise, the cell will be empty.

Spacing around rows   In the *row-options* you can specify formatting pertaining to the row as a whole. The keys above and below provide for extra space; the key around is a shorthand for setting both to the same value. With the key bg you can set an explicit background color for the row overwriting the default background coloring.

Alignment of all cells in a row   By default the cells of a row use the alignment specified for the respective column, but if you use the key align on a row, it overwrites the values for all cells (and cell groups) in the current row.

Formatting the cells of a row   To provide special formatting for all cells in a row you can use the format key. To be able to specify how row formatting relates to column formatting (which also offers such a key) the key actually exists in three variants: using format the row format is applied *before* the column format, with format* the column format is applied first, and with format! the column format is not applied at all.

Rows looking like (sub)headers   Sometimes you want to have a row formatted like the header row, and a convenient way to achieve this is to specify the Boolean key headlike. This adjusts the alignment, the background color, and the format to use the values specified for the table header. Finally, with the Boolean key hidden you can hide or show that particular row.

Hiding rows

Defining named row styles

If you regularly need rows with a special set of row options, you can give them a name with \kvtNewRowStyle and then, on the appropriate rows, refer to the set using the key style and the *name* as its value. To change an existing set use \kvtRenewRowStyle.

This useful feature is exhibited in Example 6-9-3 on page 500 where we use it to display parts of a larger table several times. Some of the rows have a `style` named H, and in the second table we then simply omit these rows by giving this style the meaning of `hidden`. Another use case for it is to define a `heading` style for subheadings in your table.

Formatting the overall table

The *table-options* in the optional argument to the `\NewKeyValTable` declaration or the `KeyValTable` environment control the overall appearance of the table.

By default, tables can break across pages using `xltabular` as the backend package, but you can explicitly request a different package for formatting your table. This is done with the `backend` key that selects the package used to do the actual table formatting[1] and therefore also limits the allowed syntax in the column specification. For example, if `tabular` or `longtable` is chosen, then X is not available. The key accepts the values `tabular`, `tabularx`, `tabu`, `longtable`, `xltabular` (default), or `longtabu`.[2] Alternatively, you can use the `shape` key, which accepts the values `multipage` (default) and `onepage`. This is equivalent to using `xltabular` or `tabularx` with the `backend` key.

Selecting the backend package

If the table package chosen with the `backend` key supports X columns, then the default width for the table is `\linewidth`. If necessary, you can overwrite this default by specifying a value with the key `width`.

Table width

Multipage tables can be horizontally aligned using the `halign` key (allowed values `l`, `c`, and `r`), while `onepage` tables can be vertically aligned with respect to other material on the same "line" (allowed values `t`, `c`, and `b`). The default is centered in both directions. Example 6-9-3 on page 500 shows an example with two top-aligned tables next to each other.

Vertical and horizontal alignment of tables

With the Boolean key `showhead` you control whether a header row is shown (default `true`), and with `headalign` you can specify a default alignment for cells in the header row. If not given, the cells are aligned like any other cell in the column. Other formatting declarations (such as `\bfseries`) can be provided in the key `headformat`. Its value can be a command with one argument that receives the header cell content.

Altering the header format

A background color for the heading row is defined by `headbg` with a light gray (`black!14`) as the default value. The remaining table rows alternate the background between white and gray by default. This is controlled with the key `rowbg`. It expects two color values separated by `..` as its value; the default is `white..black!10`. If you do not want any background color for rows, use an empty value for either key to indicate that. There also exists the shorthand keys `norowbg` (only header with background) and `nobg` (no background coloring).

Coloring headers and rows

---

[1] In earlier versions keyvaltable was always using the tabu package, but this package has a number of serious problems (and is unmaintained for a more than a decade now) and may no longer be a good choice, so now xltabular is used by default.

[2] To support different backend formatters, the package automatically loads array, booktabs, colortbl, longtable, tabularx, xcolor, and xltabular for you.

> \MidRule[*rule width*]   \CMidRule[*rule width*]{*column list*}

Using table rules By default **keyvaltable** uses the **booktabs** package to place horizontal rules around the header and at the end of the table. Further rules can be added by placing some \MidRule commands between the \Row commands. This command accepts an optional argument denoting the *rule width*, if specified. With \CMidRule you can add rules underlining only some of the columns.

If you do not want any rules, set the Boolean key showrules to false or use the shorthand norules for that. Explicit rules made with \MidRule or \CMidRule commands are still honored in that case.

Providing a table caption and label If you want to give your table a caption (and possibly a \label for referencing it), there are several possibilities. For tables that are less than one page in size you can put them into a table environment and use \caption as usual.[1] With tables that span several pages this obviously does not work, and for this case the table keys caption and label are provided. The position of the caption can be at the beginning or the end of the table. This is customized with the key captionpos that accepts t or b (default); Example 6-9-6 on page 502 shows an example.

You can also specify an alternate caption text with caption/alt for all table pages other than the one with the main caption, and with caption/lot you can have a customized caption text in the list of tables.

In the next example we have explicitly chosen tabular as the formatter to ensure that the table is not broken across pages. Note that choosing tabularx in that case would have been wrong because then the \MidRule would come out far too wide because it is the only object that would occupy the full \linewidth given that there are no X-columns in this table. The default rules have been turned off, and the row background is set to white for all rows except the head row that we kept as the default.

```
\usepackage{keyvaltable}
\NewKeyValTable[backend=tabular,norules,norowbg,
                headformat=\bfseries]
   {cities}{name; country; visited; note: hidden}
```

name	**country**	**visited**
Mainz	Germany	
New York	USA	yes

```
\begin{KeyValTable}{cities}
   \Row[above=5pt]{country=Germany, name=Mainz, note=...}
   \MidRule[2pt]
   \Row{country=USA, name=New York, visited=yes}
\end{KeyValTable}
```

6-9-2

Defaults for all future environments can be set with the command \kvtSet. Thus, if you prefer, for example, uncolored tables with bold headers, then write

> \kvtSet{nobg, headformat=\bfseries }

in the preamble of your document instead of setting them in \NewKeyValTable or on each KeyValTable environment.

---

[1] If you use tabular or tabularx as the backend, then this is the only way to get a caption.

Defining named table styles

Similar to the named row styles that can be accessed with the row key `style` it is possible to declare name table styles using the command `\kvtNewTableStyle` or `\kvtRenewTableStyle`. For instance, in the previous example we could have written

```
\kvtNewTableStyle{plain}{norules,norowbg,headformat=\bfseries}
\NewKeyValTable[backend=tabular,style=plain]{cities}
              {name; country; visited; note: hidden}
```

in the preamble and achieved the same result but with the advantage that the `plain` style can be used in other table declarations as well.

It is also possible to reuse a table style without giving it a name; more exactly you can reuse the key/value list of the previous table by using the key `resume*`. This reactivates the key/values from the previous table but additionally sets `resume` so that the `kvtRow` counter is not restarted. This allows you to have consecutive tables, possibly separated by some text, in the same design and with numbered rows that continue across the tables; see Example 6-9-5 on page 501 that makes use of `kvtRow`.

Table data in external files for reuse

There are a number of cases where it makes sense to reuse table data several times, either in separate documents or even in the same one — displaying different columns each time. This can be easily achieved by placing all `\Row` commands and then loading that file with `\ShowKeyValTableFile`.

`\ShowKeyValTableFile[`*table-options*`]{`*name*`}{`*file*`}`

The command internally starts a `KeyValTable` environment using *table-options* and *name* as arguments and loads the *file*. There are some TEXnical reasons why you cannot always use `\input` in the middle of a `tabular` structure, which are circumvented if you use this command instead.

An interesting aspect of storing the table data in a separate file is that you can easily display only parts of it in different places, which allows consistent views to different aspects of your data. In the next example we give some rows a row `style` (which by default does nothing) and for the second table redefine this style to mean `hidden`. Here is the data file that is used twice in the next example:

```
\begin{filecontents}[overwrite]{cities.kvt}
  \Row{city=Mainz, country=Germany, people=0.2 mil,
                              visited=\emph{home town}}
  \Row{city=London,   country=UK,   people=8.9 mil, visited=yes}
  \Row[style=H]{city=New York, country=USA, people=8.4 mil,
                              visited=planned}
  \Row[style=H]{city=Paris, country=France, people=2.1 mil}
\end{filecontents}
```

If you later add more data rows, all tables will automatically update.

```
\usepackage{keyvaltable}   \kvtNewRowStyle{H}{}
\NewKeyValTable{overview}{city: ; country: ; people: ; visited: hidden}
\NewKeyValTable{visits}{country: ; city: ; people: hidden; visited: align=c}
\ShowKeyValTableFile[shape=onepage,valign=t]{overview}{cities.kvt} \quad
\kvtRenewRowStyle{H}{hidden}     % hide the H rows in next table
\ShowKeyValTableFile[shape=onepage,nobg,valign=t]{visits}{cities.kvt}
```

city	country	people
Mainz	Germany	0.2 mil
London	UK	8.9 mil
New York	USA	8.4 mil
Paris	France	2.1 mil

country	city	visited
Germany	Mainz	*home town*
UK	London	yes

6-9-3

It is also possible to directly process .csv files with the help of packages, such as datatool or csvsimple. Details and setup examples are given in the keyvaltable package documentation.

Scattering table data across your document

There are situations where it is helpful if you do not put the table data in one place, i.e., in the environment body of a KeyValTable or in a separate file but instead collect the data from different places in you document. This is especially useful if those data grow over time. Suppose that you write a book on different cities, each having its own section, and at the end of the book you show several tables with data about the cities described. In such a case it would be nice to have the relevant data rows for each city as part of the section with LaTeX collecting the data and adding it into the tables. If you later add another section or remove one your tables automatically update (just like the table of contents would do). For this keyvaltable offers full support through the following commands:

```
\NewCollectedTable{table-name}{structure-name}
\ShowCollectedTable[table-options]{table-name}
```

With the help of \NewCollectedTable you declare a *table-name* for which you want to collect data in your document. The *structure-name* is one that has been declared earlier with \NewKeyValTable. Instead of a KeyValTable environment, you then use \ShowCollectedTable at the point where you want the table to appear.

```
\CollectRow[row-options]{table-name}{cell-data}
```

To provide the data for each row we have to use \CollectRow instead of \Row, because we have to specify for which *table-name* we collect. The other arguments are the same as for \Row, which was discussed on page 496.

This command can be used as often as necessary to add data to the table, and it can be placed before or after the corresponding \ShowCollectedTable command. As a consequence, you need at least two LaTeX runs: one to collect all data and one to display it (or more exactly display the data collected in the previous run).

The next example shows the commands in action in a small application in which we sprinkle notes throughout a document and collect them in a single table. The implementation is a bit naughty; one has to remember that the mandatory argument to \note becomes part of a key/value list and so cannot contain commas unless you hide them inside braces as we did in the first note.

My notes:

prio	comment
high	A note, with comma
low	one more with prio change
high	and some afterthought

6-9-4   And more text.

```
\usepackage{keyvaltable}
\NewKeyValTable[norowbg]{ToDo}{ prio: default=high;
                                text: head=comment }
\NewCollectedTable{notes}{ToDo}
\newcommand\note[2][]{\CollectRow[#1]{notes}{text=#2}}
\note{{A note, with comma}}
\note{one more with prio change, prio=low}
My notes: \ShowCollectedTable{notes} And more text.
\note[bg=blue!10]{and some afterthought}
```

Automatic row numbering and referencing

The keyvaltable package supports some level of automatic row numbering through a set of three LaTeX counters. The counter kvtRow holds the current row number in the current table (excluding any header rows), kvtTypeRow corresponds to the row number when counting all rows in all tables with the same KeyValTable *name*, and kvtTotalRow represents the total across all KeyValTable environments up to the current point.

These counters can, for example, be used in the value to the default key to set up automatic numbering without the need to specify any data for this column. Note that overwriting the generated value does not stop the counter from being incremented unless you use the row option uncounted. As the example shows, it is also possible to use the counter values inside the \Row command.

Text	
First row	§1
Second row	2*
Interlude	–
Last row	§3

6-9-5

```
\usepackage{keyvaltable}
\NewKeyValTable{autonum}{ text: head=\textbf{Text};
                         line: head=\ , default=\S\thekvtRow }
\begin{KeyValTable}{autonum}
  \Row{text=First row} \Row{text=Second row, line=\thekvtRow*}
  \Row[uncounted]{text=Interlude, line=--} \Row{text=Last row}
\end{KeyValTable}
```

By default, the kvtRow counter is reset for each table. It is, however, possible to continue counting across several tables by specifying the table option resume in which case the counter resumes from its value in the previous KeyValTable environment. The above setup does not allow you to refer to the counter values via

LaTeX's label mechanism, because it would not be clear where one should place the \label, but for this the package provides the command \kvtLabel.

\kvtLabel [*type*] {*counter*}{*label*}

The \kvtLabel typesets the *counter* value. If the mandatory *label* argument is empty, then that is all it does. Otherwise it calls \label to label the counter value so that it can be referenced. The optional *type* argument if present is also passed to the \label command to support extensions like cleveref. A possible use case is shown in the next example using cleveref for references. Note that if used in the value to format, we have to omit the *label* argument because that is supplied by the table cell data.

Table 1: Named Refs

Line	Text
1	First row
2	Second row
3	See row 1

All explanations are given in rows 1 to 3.

```
\usepackage{cleveref,keyvaltable}
\crefname{row}{row}{rows}
\NewKeyValTable[headbg=blue!15,captionpos=t]{NamedRef}
  { label: align=r, head=Line, format=\kvtLabel[row]{kvtRow};
    text:  align=l, head=Text}
\begin{KeyValTable}[caption=Named Refs]{NamedRef}
  \Row{text=First row, label=first}   \Row{text=Second row}
  \Row{text=See \cref{first}, label=last}
\end{KeyValTable}
All explanations are given in \crefrange{first}{last}.
```

6-9-6

Spanning cells

Up to now all table columns have been independent, and one could alter their order arbitrarily inside \NewKeyValTable. In more complex tables, however, one sometimes needs to combine some adjacent cells in individual rows of the table. In the table packages discussed earlier, this is done by using \multicolumn declarations inside the table body, but with keyvaltable it can be done as part of the table setup.

All you have to do is to give a set of adjacent column its own name and then use that name in \Row or \CollectRow commands (and of course then make sure that the columns are in fact adjacent in your \NewKeyValTable declaration).

This is done by specifying suitable colgroups in the *specials* argument of \NewKeyValTable as shown in the next example. Each column group is named, and you can specify the columns it should span, how the result should align (default c not l), and whether it should get a special format. For align and format you can alter the defaults as we did not in the example. Also note the use of | and || in the align values to help you see the alignment better.

```
\usepackage{keyvaltable}
\kvtSet{ColGroup/format=\itshape,ColGroup/align=r}
\NewKeyValTable{spantest}{ colA: align=l|; colB: align=l||;
                          colC: align=l|; colD:}
  [ colgroups={ all: span=colA+colB+colC+colD, format=\textbf;
              AuBuC: span=colA+colB+colC, align=c|;
                AuB: span=colA+colB, align=l||;  CuD: span=colC+colD } ]
```

colA	colB	colC	colD
The Start			
1	2	3	4
— right aligned text —			
1 & 2		*3*	*4*
1	2	3	4
1	2		*3 & 4*
— 3 out of 4 —			*4*
1 & 2			*3 & 4*
The End			

```
\begin{KeyValTable}{spantest}
  \Row{all=The Start}  \Row{colA=1, colB=2, colC=3, colD=4}
  \Row{all=--- right aligned text ---}
  \Row{AuB=1 \& 2,          colC=3,   colD=4}
  \Row{colA=1, colB=2,      colC=3,   colD=4}
  \Row{colA=1, colB=2,      CuD=3 \& 4}
  \Row{AuBuC=--- 3 out of 4 ---,      colD=4}
  \Row{AuB=1 \& 2, CuD=3 \& 4} \Row{all=The End}
\end{KeyValTable}
```

6-9-7

The advantage of using `colgroups` is that you can specify special table formatting through names and keep the table body free of formatting directives. If you later decide to change some of that formatting, e.g., centering the text in the `all` column group or using sans serif rather than a bold typeface, then you have to alter your document only in a single place, and the change is applied wherever you used that name.

You have probably guessed that internally this is realized through the use of `\multicolumn` and that this command can also be directly used in the table body if necessary. If you do this and you want to span several columns explicitly, you have to place it as the value of the first named cell that should take part in the span, and the other participating cells in the row should not get any value. The disadvantage of this approach (except when just overwriting the alignment of a single cell) is that any alteration in the `\NewKeyTable` setup, e.g., reordering the named columns, might render your table body invalid, so you have to be careful that this does not happen.

The `\multicolumn` text is formatted according to the setup for the starting cell, which explains why in the next example the text in the third row is blue (inner setting), is bold in the fourth row (column setting), and is bold italic in the fifth row (combined column and row setting).

We mentioned earlier that the cells in a row do not have to be given in any particular order as they are named. However, if using `\multicolumn`, you better keep them ordered in a reasonable way and avoid tables like the next example, because otherwise you will have real difficulties to make changes.

penny	euro	cent
1	2	3
1	2	3
1		2+3
1+2		3
1+2+3		
1	2	3

```
\usepackage{keyvaltable,Alegreya,AlegreyaSans}
\NewKeyValTable[headformat=\sffamily]{MultiCol}
    { penny: align=c|, format=\bfseries; euro: align=l|; cent: }
\begin{KeyValTable}{MultiCol}
  \Row{euro=\multicolumn{1}{r|}{2}, cent=3, penny=1}
  \Row[format!=\sffamily]{penny=1, cent=3, euro=2}
  \Row{penny=1, euro=\multicolumn{2}{c}{\color{blue}2+3}}
  \Row{cent=3, penny=\multicolumn{2}{c|}{1+2}}
  \Row[format=\itshape]{penny=\multicolumn{3}{c}{1+2+3}}
  \Row{cent=3, euro=2, penny=1}
\end{KeyValTable}
```

6-9-8

503

Complex table headers

By default table structures defined by \NewKeyValTable have a single header row that can be customized through the keys headalign, headbg, or headformat.

However, in more complex tables you may need more than one header line or headers that span several columns, and in that case you have to define the necessary structure in the optional *specials* argument to \NewKeyValTable similar to what we did for column spans in the previous section. The keyword to use in there is headers. Its value is a list of row specifications for each header row separated by \\. The row specifications itself are lists of (possibly spanning) columns together with applicable attributes. As a shorthand you can write : : for a row with the headers for all columns.

As an example, the table definition below shows a table with five columns named precolumn and colA to colD. Its header consists of three rows with the first showing a title spanning columns colA to colD, the second showing subheaders for column pairs, and the third showing the names of all column titles.

```
\usepackage{keyvaltable}
\NewKeyValTable[headformat=\bfseries, norowbg]{complexheader}
  { precolumn: align=c, format=\textbf ; colA: ; colB: ; colC: ;colD: }
  [ headers={ colA+colB+colC+colD : head=\textsf{From A to D} \\
              colA+colB : head= A \& B;
                         colC+colD : align=r, head=$\to$ C \& D \\ :: }
    ,colgroups={BtoE: span=colA+colB+colC+colD, format=\textit}          ]
```

As you observe, spanning columns are denoted by concatenating the column names with + symbols, and the available attributes are head for specifying the title and align to change the alignment center to left or right. We also used colgroups to produce intermediate subtitles in the table to achieve the following result:

| precolumn | From A to D | | | |
| | A & B | | → C & D | |
precolumn	colA	colB	colC	colD
1	1.a	1.b	—	1.d
2	2.a	2.b	2.c	2.d
Centered subtitle				
3	3.a	—	3.c	3.d

```
\begin{KeyValTable}{complexheader}
  \Row{ precolumn=1, colA=1.a, colB=1.b,
                     colC=---, colD=1.d }
  \Row{ precolumn=2, colA=2.a, colB=2.b,
                     colC=2.c, colD=2.d }
\Row[around=3pt]{BtoE=Centered subtitle}
  \Row{ precolumn=3, colA=3.a, colB=---,
                     colC=3.c, colD=3.d }
\end{KeyValTable}
```

6-9-9

6.10 tabularray — Late breaking news

This is a fairly recent and promising addition by Jianrui Lyu to the world of tables written in the L3 programming layer. It is still under heavy development with new (and sometimes changed) features appearing at regular intervals and, therefore, not yet documented in this book. It is, however, already worth taking a look at [78].

Mastering Floats

Documents would be easier to read if all the material that belonged together was never split between pages. However, this is often technically impossible, and TeX, by default, splits textual material between two pages to avoid partially filled pages. Nevertheless, when this outcome is not desired (as with figures and tables), the material must be "floated" to a convenient place, such as the bottom or the top of the current or next page, to prevent half-empty pages.

This chapter shows how "large chunks" of material can be kept conveniently on the same or a nearby page by using a float object. We begin by introducing the general concepts through which LaTeX handles float objects and the parameters that define how LaTeX typesets its basic `figure` and `table` float environments and describe some of the packages that make it easy to control float placement (Section 7.2).

We then continue by explaining how you can define and use your own floating environments (Section 7.3.1) or, conversely, how captioning commands can be used to enter information into the list of figures and tables for nonfloating material (Section 7.3.2). Then methods for rotating the content of a float are described (Section 7.3.3). It is often visually pleasing to include a "picture" inside a paragraph, with the text wrapping around it. Some package authors have tried their hand on this difficult topic, and in Section 7.3.4 we look at one of them in some detail.

The fourth section addresses the problem of customizing captions. There is a recognized need to be able to typeset the description of the contents of figures and tables in many different ways. This includes specifying subfigures and subtables, each with its own caption and label, inside a larger float.

In the final section of this chapter we then look at two recent packages that offer a modern key/value approach to the float topic and attempt to bridge the gaps between the different packages introduced in the earlier sections. While both attempt to be fairly comprehensive, they have a different focus, which is why we describe both to enable you to make an educated decision based on the requirements of the job.

Many float-related packages have been developed over the years, unfortunately often with incompatible concepts and syntax, so there is no point discussing them all here. In fact, the packages that we describe often feature quite a few more commands than we are able to illustrate. Our aim is to enable you to make an educated choice and to show how a certain function can be obtained in a given framework. In each case consulting the original documentation will introduce you to the full possibilities of a given package.

7.1 An overview of LaTeX's float concepts

Floats are often problematic in the present version of LaTeX, because the system was developed at a time when documents contained considerably less graphical material than they do today. Placing floats (tables and figures) works relatively well as long as the space they occupy is not too large compared with the space taken up by the text. If a lot of floating material is present, however, then it is often the case that all material from a certain point onward floats to the end of the chapter or document unless you make some adjustments on the level of individual floats.

You can also try to fine-tune the float style parameters for a given document but often a combination of both configuration and local adjustments is necessary to achieve the desired typesetting results.

The present section explains the background and behavior of LaTeX's float algorithm and explains where and how you can manipulate it to serve your needs. We start with defining the terminology and then discuss the algorithm and its configuration possibilities. The section finishes with a look at the consequences resulting from the design choices made in the algorithm and how they affect the processing of your documents.

7.1.1 LaTeX float terminology

In this section we define the terminology used throughout the present chapter.

Float classes

Each float in LaTeX belongs to a class often referred to as its type. By default, LaTeX knows about two classes, viz., *figure* and *table*. Further classes can be added by a document class or by packages; this is discussed in Section 7.3.1 on page 529. The class a float belongs to influences certain aspects of the float positioning, such as its default placement specification (if not overridden on the float itself).

One important property of the float placement algorithm is that LaTeX never violates the order of placement within a class of floats. For example, if you have

Figure 1, Table 1, Figure 2 in a document, then Figure 1 is always placed before Figure 2. However, Table 1 (belonging to a different float class) is placed independently and hence can appear before, after, or between the figures.

Some of the extension packages discussed in Section 7.3 make no provisions to ensure this basic property, and one has to visually watch out for possible misorderings. Where this can happen, it is explicitly remarked upon in the text.

Float areas

LaTeX knows about two float areas within a column where it can place floats: the top area and the bottom area of the column. In two-column layout, it also knows about a top area spanning the two columns. There is no bottom area for page-wide floats in two-column mode.

In addition, LaTeX can make float columns and float pages, i.e., columns or pages that contain only floats. Finally, LaTeX can place floats in-line into the text (but only if so directed on the individual float).

Float placement specifiers

To direct a float to be placed into one of these areas, a float placement specifier can be provided as an optional argument to the float. If no such optional argument is given, then a default placement specifier is used (which depends on the float class as mentioned above but usually allows the float to be placed in all areas if not subject to other restrictions).

A float placement specifier can consist of the following characters in *any* order:

! indicates that some of the restrictions that normally apply should be ignored (discussed later)

h indicates that the float is allowed to be placed in-line ("here")

t indicates that the float is allowed to go into a top area

b indicates that the float is allowed to go into a bottom area

p indicates that the float is allowed to go on a float page or column area

The order in which these characters are put in the optional argument does *not* influence how the algorithm tries to place the float! The precise order is discussed on page 509. This is one of the common misunderstandings, for instance when people think that bt means that the bottom area should be tried first. Also note that if a letter is not present, then the corresponding area is not tried at all.

Float algorithm parameters

There are about 20 parameters that influence the placement; for a detailed discussion see page 510. They define

- how many floats can go into a certain area,
- how big an area can become,

- how much text there has to be on a page (in other words, how much the top and bottom areas can occupy) and
- how much space is inserted
  - between consecutive floats in an area, and
  - between the area and the text above or below.

Float reference points (aka call-outs)

A point in the document that references the float (e.g., "see Figure X") is called a "call-out", and the float body should be placed close to the (main) call-out, because its placement in the document affects the placement of the float in the output and determines when LaTeX sees the float for the first time. It is important to understand that if a float is placed in the middle of a paragraph, the reference point for the algorithm is the next line break, or page break, in the paragraph that follows the actual placement in the source.

For technical and practical reasons it is usually best to place all floats between paragraphs (i.e., after the paragraph with the call-out), even if that makes the call-out and reference point slightly disagree.

7.1.2   Basic behavioral rules of LaTeX's float mechanism

With this knowledge, we are now ready to delve into the algorithm's behavior. First we have to understand that all of LaTeX's typesetting algorithms are designed to avoid any sort of backtracking. This means that LaTeX reads through the document source, formats what it finds, and (more or less) immediately typesets it. The reasons for this design choice were to limit complexity (which is still quite high) and also to maintain reasonable speed (remember that this is from the early eighties).

For floats, this means that the algorithm is greedy; i.e., the moment it encounters a float, it immediately tries to place it and, if it succeeds, it never changes its decision. This means that it may choose a solution that could be deemed inferior in light of data received later.

For example, if a figure is allowed to go to the top or bottom area, LaTeX may decide to place this figure in the top area. If this figure is followed by two tables that are allowed to go only to the top, these tables may not fit anymore. A solution that could have worked in this case (but was not tried) would have been to place the figure in the bottom area and the two tables in the top area.

The basic sequence when placing floats

Here is the basic sequence the algorithm runs through:

- If a float is encountered in the source document, LaTeX attempts to place it immediately according to its rules (detailed later);
- if this succeeds, the float is placed, and that decision is never changed;

- if this does not succeed, then LaTeX places the float into a holding queue to be reconsidered when the next page is started (but not earlier).

- Once a page has finished, LaTeX examines this holding queue and tries to empty it as best as possible. For this it first tries to generate as many float pages as possible (in the hope of getting floats off the queue). Once this possibility is exhausted, it next attempts to place the remaining floats into the top and bottom areas. It looks at all the remaining floats and either places them or defers them to a later page (i.e., adding them once more to the holding queue).

- After that, it starts processing document material for this page. In the process, it may encounter further floats.

- If the end of the document has been reached or if a \clearpage is encountered, LaTeX starts a new page, relaxes all restrictive float conditions, and outputs all floats in the holding queue by placing them on float page(s).

In two-column mode, the same algorithm is used, except that it works on the level of columns; e.g., when a column has finished, LaTeX looks at the holding queue and generates float columns, etc.

Detailed placement rules

Whenever LaTeX encounters a float environment in the source, it first looks at the holding queue to check if there is already a float of the same class in the queue. If that happens to be the case, no placement is allowed, and the float immediately goes into the holding queue.

If not, LaTeX looks at the float placement specifier for this float, either the explicit one in the optional argument or the default one from the float class. The default per float class is set in the document class file (e.g., article.cls) and very often resolves to tbp, but this is not guaranteed.

LaTeX always uses the following fixed order of tests until an allowed placement is found:

1. If the specifier contains a !, the algorithm ignores any restrictions related either to the number of floats that can be put into an area or to the maximum size an area can occupy. Otherwise, the restrictions defined by the parameters apply. If just a ! was specified, then the float class default is assumed as allowed areas (with other restrictions relaxed).

2. As a next step it checks if h has been specified. If so, it tries to place the float right where it was encountered. If this works, i.e., if there is enough space and a float of this class is not already placed into the bottom area, then it is placed and processing of that float ends.
   If this fails and no other position was specified, the algorithm changes the specifier to t (for a possible placement on the current or next page).

3. Next it looks for t, and if that has been specified, it tries to place the float in the top area. If there is no other restriction that prevents this, then the float is placed there and float processing stops.

4. If not, it finally checks if b is present and, if so, tries to place the float into the bottom area (again obeying any restrictions that apply if ! was not given).

5. If that does not work either or is not permitted because the specifier was not given, the float is added to the holding queue.

This ends the processing when encountering a float in the document. A p specifier (if present) is not used during the above process. It is looked at only when the holding queue is being emptied at the next page or column boundary.

Emptying the holding queue at the column or page boundary

After a column or page has been finished, LaTeX looks at the holding queue and attempts to empty it out as best as possible. For this, it first tries to build float pages or columns.[1]

Any floats participating in a float page (or column) must have a p as a float specifier in its float placement specification. If not, the float cannot go on a float page and, in addition, also prevents any further deferred float of the same class from being placed onto the float page!

If the float can go there, it is marked for inclusion on the float page, but the processor may still abort the attempt if the float page does not get filled "enough" (depending on the parameter settings for float pages). Only at the very end of the document, or when a \clearpage has been issued, are these restrictions lifted, and a float is then placed on a float page even if it has no p and would be the only float on that page.

Creation of float pages continues until the algorithm has no further floats to place or when it fails to produce a float page due to parameter settings. In the latter case, all floats that have not been placed so far are then considered for inclusion in the top and bottom areas of the next page (or column).

The process there is the same as the one described above, except that the h specifier no longer has any meaning (because we are, by now, far away from the original "here") and is therefore ignored, and the floats at this time are not coming from the source document but are taken one after the other from the holding queue.

Any float that could not be placed is then put back into the holding queue so that when LaTeX is ready to look at further textual input from the document, the holding queue may already contain floats. A consequence of this is that a float encountered in the document may immediately get deferred just because an earlier float of the same float class is already on hold.

Parameters influencing the placement

Controlling how many floats can go into areas   There are four counters that control how many floats can go into the different areas:

totalnumber   This is the maximum number of floats in a text column (default 3). It is not used for float pages; they can hold any number of floats.

---

[1]In two-column mode LaTeX builds float columns (when finishing a column) and also attempts to generate float pages when finishing a page. In the remainder of the discussion "float page" denotes either, depending on the context.

topnumber   The maximum number of floats in the top area (default 2).

bottomnumber   The maximum number of floats in the bottom area (default 1).

dbltopnumber   The maximum number of full-width floats in two-column mode
   going above the text columns (default 2).

The sizes of the areas are controlled through parameters (to be changed with *Controlling the*
\renewcommand) that define the maximum (or minimum) size of the area, expressed *area sizes*
as a fraction of the page height:

\topfraction   Maximum fraction of the page that can be occupied by floats at the
   top of the page (e.g., 0.2 means 20% can be floats; the default value is 0.7).

\bottomfraction   Maximum fraction of the page that can be occupied by floats at
   the bottom of the page (the default value is 0.3).

\dbltopfraction   Analog of \topfraction for double-column floats on a two-
   column page (the default value is 0.7).

\textfraction   Minimum fraction of a normal page that must be occupied by text
   (the default value is 0.2).

The space that separates floats within an area, as well as between float areas *Controlling the*
and text areas, is defined through the following parameters (all of which are rubber *space between floats*
lengths, i.e., can contain some stretch or shrink components). Their defaults depend *and between text*
on the document font size and change when class options like 11pt or 12pt are used. *and float areas*
We show only the 10pt defaults; the others are similar.

\floatsep   The separation between floats in top or bottom areas (default 12pt plus
   2pt minus 2pt).

\dblfloatsep   The separation between double-column floats on two-column pages
   (default 12pt plus 2pt minus 2pt).

\textfloatsep   The separation between top or bottom float area and the text area
   (default 20pt plus 2pt minus 4pt).

\dbltextfloatsep   The analog of \textfloatsep for two-column floats (default
   20pt plus 2pt minus 4pt).

\intextsep   The separation for in-line floats (that have been placed "here") above
   and below the float (default 12pt plus 2pt minus 2pt).

In the case of float pages or float columns (i.e., a page or a column of a page *Controlling float*
containing only floats) parameters like \topfraction, etc., do not apply. Instead, *page generation*
the creation of them is controlled through the following parameter:

\floatpagefraction   The minimum part of the page (or column) that needs to be
   occupied by floats to be allowed to form a float page (or column). The default is
   0.5, which means that half the page is allowed to stay empty.

Finally, there are three commands that generate separating items (typically a rule or some sort, hence the names) between adjacent float and text areas:

\topfigrule Command to produce a separating item between floats at the top of the page and the text. It is executed immediately before placing the vertical space \textfloatsep that separates the floats from the text. Like the command \footnoterule, it must not occupy any vertical space.

\botfigrule Same as \topfigrule, but executed after the \textfloatsep space separating text from the floats at the bottom of the page.

\dblfigrule Similar to \topfigrule, but for double-column floats.

Changing the values of these parameters lets you modify the behavior of LaTeX's algorithm for placing floats. To obtain the optimal results, however, you should be aware of the subtle dependencies that exist between these parameters.

7.1.3 Consequences of the algorithm

In this section we take a look at the not so obvious consequences resulting from the design choices made in LaTeX's float algorithm when it is used out of the box. Each time we discuss possibilities to explore if the default outcome is not serving your needs.

A float may appear in the document earlier than its location in the source

The placement of the float environment in the source determines the earliest point where it can appear in the final document. It may move visually backward to some degree because it may be placed in the top area on the current page. This practice offers a better chance that the float is visible from the call-out position and does not end up on a later page. It can, however, not end up on an earlier page than the surrounding text due to the fact that LaTeX does no backtracking and the earlier pages have already been typeset.

Thus, normally a float is placed in the source near its first call-out (i.e., text like "see Figure 5") because this ensures that the float appears either on the same page as this text or on a later page. However, in some situations you may want to place a float on the preceding page (if that page is still visible from the call-out). With the standard algorithm this is possible only by moving the float in the source.

Place floats always after their call-out   For some journals, however, even LaTeX's standard approach is too liberal, and they require that floats are strictly placed after their call-out, i.e., that in the call-out column only the bottom area forms a valid placement option. To accommodate this requirement, this strategy is implemented by the flafter package[1] by the author.

This may work well if your document has only a few floats. For documents with lots of floats, placement obviously becomes much more difficult, and you may find that all your floats appear together at the end of the document or chapter, or you may receive a "Too many unprocessed floats" error.

---

[1] This package has no options and defines no commands; you simply load it in the preamble.

Sometimes, less drastic solutions might be preferred. For example, if the float belongs to a section that starts in the middle of a page but the float is positioned at the top of the page, the float appears as if it belongs to the previous section. You might want to forbid this behavior while still allowing floats to be placed on the top of the page in other situations. For this purpose LaTeX offers you the following command: *Prevent floats in certain situations only*

```
\suppressfloats [placement]
```

The optional argument *placement* can be either t or b. If \suppressfloats is placed somewhere in the document, then on the current page any following floats for the areas specified by *placement* are deferred to a later page. If no *placement* parameter is given, all remaining floats on the current page are deferred. For example, if you want to prevent floats from moving backward over section boundaries, you can redefine your section commands using the commands from titlesec (discussed in Section 2.2.7) in one of the following two ways:

```
\titleformat*\section{\suppressfloats[t]...}                      % or
\titleformat \section[..]{..}{..}{\suppressfloats[t]..}[..]
```

or by using the low-level \@startsection command, where it has to go before calling \@startsection:

```
\renewcommand\section{\suppressfloats[t]%
                      \@startsection{section}{..}{..}{..} ... }
```

Possible arguments to \@startsection are discussed in Section 2.2.8.

Double-column floats are always deferred first

When LaTeX encounters a page-wide float environment (indicated by a * at the end of the environment name, e.g., figure*) in two-column mode, it immediately moves that float to the deferred queue. The reason for this behavior again lies in the "greedy" behavior of its algorithm: if LaTeX is currently assembling the second column of that page, the first column has already been assembled and stored away; recall that because LaTeX does not backtrack, there is no way to fit the float on the current page. To keep the algorithm simple, it does the same even if working on the first column (where it could in theory do better even without backtracking).

Thus, to place such a float onto the current page, one has to manually move it to an earlier place in the source — before the start of the current page. If this is done, obviously any further change in the document could make this adjustment obsolete; hence, such adjustments are best done (if at all) only at the very last stage of document production — when all material has been written and the focus is on fine-tuning the visual appearance. Also note that until 2015 the base algorithm had a bug[1] in this area: it maintained two independent holding queues: one for single-column and one

---

[1] As this is the documented behavior in the *LaTeX manual* [65] it is perhaps more correctly called an undesired feature than a bug. However, these days it is history.

for double-column floats. As a result the float order was not necessarily preserved, and floats sometimes got typeset out of sequence. With the 2015 release of LaTeX that finally got corrected.[1]

There is only a limited amount of space for deferring floats

Deferring floats means that their content needs to be stored temporarily until LaTeX finds a suitable page to output them. This is done in special box registers, and by default LaTeX reserves only 18 boxes for this, which is often insufficient and you get the error "Too many unprocessed floats".

If that happens, you can add additional storage with `\extrafloats{`*number*`}` to the document preamble to make (many) more boxes available to hold floats. This additional storage is slightly less efficient, but these days using a value such as 500 poses no problems.

There is no bottom float area for double-column floats

How to ensure that a float never gets typeset

This is not so much a consequence of the algorithm but rather a fact about its implementation. For double-column floats the only possible placements offered are the top area or a float page. Thus, if somebody adds an h or a b float placement specifier to such a float, it simply gets ignored. As a special important case `\begin{figure*}[b]` implies that this float is not typeset at all until either a `\clearpage` is encountered or the end of the document is reached.

Providing bottom floats spanning two columns

This missing functionality is added, except for the first page, if you load the stfloats package by Sigitas Tolušis. Note, however, that the package makes some other changes to the code that may or may not work with your document.

Tendency to produce float pages (unnecessarily)

The problem of half-empty float pages

If you use the default float parameter values in a document with many floats, you can observe that the formatted document contains several float pages — that is, pages containing only floats. Often such pages contain a lot of white space. For example, you may see a page with a single float on it, occupying only half of the possible space, so that it would look better if LaTeX had filled the remaining space with text. The reason for this behavior is that the algorithm is designed to try placing as many dangling floats as possible after the end of every page. The procedure creates as many float pages as it can until there are no more floats left to fill a float page. Float page production is controlled by the parameter `\floatpagefraction`, which specifies the minimum fraction of the page that must be occupied by float(s) — by default, half the page. In the standard settings every float is allowed to go on a float page (the default specifier is `tbp`), so this setting means that every float that is a tiny bit larger than half the page is allowed to go on a float page by itself. Thus, by enlarging its value, you can prevent half-empty float pages.

---

[1] Before that date one had to either manually move the double-column float to an earlier (or later) place in the document or load the fixltx2e package that implemented a correction for this issue. The code from this package is now part of LaTeX proper, so it does not need loading anymore.

However, enlarging the value of \floatpagefraction has its own dangers as discussed below. For this reason it is often better to specify explicitly the allowed placements (for example, by saying \begin{figure}[tb] and thus prohibit its placement on a float page) for the float that creates the problem. A usually better alternative is to use the **fewerfloatpages** package that alters the algorithm's behavior in customizable ways. It is discussed in Section 7.2.1 on page 519.

A float may appear on a float page purely based on its position in the source

A special case of the above discussion is a larger float that is allowed to go into the top area or onto a float page. If this is encountered by LATEX while there is still enough space on the page, it is placed into top area, but if (after some alterations of the text) its call-out moves closer to the end of the page, it becomes unplaceable, gets deferred, and then gets placed on a float page of its own, because it is large enough for that. Adding some more text might move the call-out past the page break in which case LATEX puts the float back into the top area of the next page.

Again, the **fewerfloatpages** package shows a better and more consistent behavior when encountering such type of floats.

All float parameters (normally) restrict the placement possibilities

This may be obvious, but it is worth repeating: any float parameter defines a restriction on LATEX's ability to place the floats. How much of a restriction depends on the setting: there is always a way to set a parameter in such a way that it does not affect the placement at all. Unfortunately, in doing so one invites rather poor-looking placements.

By default LATEX has settings that are fairly liberal. For example, a page can contain up to three floats, which can result in very cramped-looking pages, especially when the facing page has no floats. A similarly "questionable" default is that for a float page to be accepted the float(s) must occupy at least half of the available page. Expressed differently, this means that such a page is allowed to be half empty (which is certainly not the best possible placement in most cases).

What often happens is that users try to improve such settings and then get surprised when suddenly all floats pile up at the end of the document. To stay with this example: if one changes the parameter \floatpagefraction to require, say, 0.8 of the float page, a float that occupies about 0.75 of the page is not allowed to form a float page on its own. Thus, if there is not another float that could be added and actually fits in the remaining space, the float is deferred and with it all other floats of the same class. But, even worse, this specific float is too big to go into the next top area as well because there the default maximum permissible area is 0.7 (from \topfraction).

Tinkering with the parameter settings usually produces unwanted effects

As a result all your floats stay deferred until the next \clearpage. Thus, while tempting, tinkering with this parameter by making it larger is usually not a good idea, unless you are prepared to place most if not all of your floats manually, by overwriting the placement algorithm on the level of individual floats (e.g., using ! syntax and/or shifting its position in the source document).

Another common reason for ending up with all floats at the end of your chapter is the use of the bottom placement specifier, [b]. It indicates that the only acceptable place for a float is at the bottom of a page. If your float happens to be larger than \bottomfraction (which is by default quite small), then this float cannot be placed at all. This also prevents all floats of the same type from being placed. The same problem arises if only [h] or [t] is specified and the float is too large for the remainder of the page or too large to fit \topfraction.

In calculating these fractions, LaTeX takes into account the separation (i.e., \textfloatsep) between floats and main text. By enlarging this value, you automatically reduce the maximum size a float is allowed to have to be considered as a candidate for placement at the top or bottom of the page.

In general, whenever a lot of your floats end up at the end of the chapter, look at the first ones to see whether their placement specifiers are preventing them from being properly placed.

For this reason it is best not to meddle with the parameters while writing a document or at least not to do so in a way that makes it more difficult for the algorithm to place a float close to its call-out. For proof-reading it is far more important to have a figure next to the place it is referenced then to avoid half-empty pages. Possibilities for fine-tuning an otherwise finished document are discussed below.

Another conclusion to draw here is that there are dependencies between some of the float parameters; it is important to take these dependencies into account when changing their values.

Locally overwriting placement restrictions

A way to influence the placement of individual floats in LaTeX is to specify a ! in conjunction with the placement specifiers h, t, and b. If a given float is (slightly) too large to fit into a certain area or if an area already contains the maximum number of floats but you nevertheless want to force the current float into this place, then adding ! to the optional argument of the float is a good choice. It results in ignoring all restrictions implemented through parameters for this particular float so that it is always placed unless there are already deferred floats with the same float class or the allowed areas get bigger than the available space when adding the float. Also, any \suppressfloats commands are ignored while processing this float.

As the order of attempts is still the same (first top then bottom), you may have to use [!b] to force a float into the bottom area as [!tb] would normally already succeed in placing it into the top area. The downside is of course that if the float does not fit, it only appears in the bottom area of a following page. Thus, any later text change may create havoc on your placement decisions.

Note, however, that the placement of floats on float pages is not affected by this approach.

"Here" just means "here if it fits"

... and often it does not fit. This is somewhat surprising for many people, but the way the algorithm has been designed, the h specifier is not an unconditional command.

The specifier merely directs LaTeX to *do its best* to place the float at the current position. If there is not enough room left on the page or if an inline placement is forbidden because of the settings of the style parameters, then LaTeX ignores this request and tries to place the float according to any other specifier given. This situation can happen quite often if the floats you try to place in the middle of your text are moderately large and are thus likely to fall into positions where there is not enough space on the page for them. By ignoring an h and trying other placement specifiers, LaTeX avoids overly empty pages that would otherwise arise in such situations.

[h] does not mean "here"

However, sometimes it is necessary to ensure that floats appear in-line at certain points in the document text even if that results in some partially empty pages. If such a nonfloating object is needed, then extension packages such as the **float** package (page 529) offer H as an alternative specifier that really means "here" (and starts a new page first if necessary). An alternative is the \captionof command from the **caption** package (page 540) that generates a normal float caption (including its entry in the list of figures or tables, etc.) but without the need for a surrounding float environment. Be mindful, however, that mixing floats and nonfloats can lead to incorrect numbering.

Float specifiers do not define an order of preference

As mentioned above, the algorithm tries to place floats into available float areas in a well-defined order that is hardwired into the algorithm: "here", "top", "bottom", and — on page boundaries — first "page" and, only if that is no longer possible, "top" followed by "bottom" for the next page.

[bt] does the same as [tb]

Thus, specifying [bt] does not mean try bottom first and only then top. It simply means allow this float to go into the top or bottom area (but not onto a float page) just like [tb] would.

Relation of floats and footnotes

This is not exactly a consequence of the algorithm but one of its implementation: whenever LaTeX tries to decide on a placement for a float (or a \marginpar!), it has to trigger the output routine to do this. And as part of this process all footnotes on the page are removed from their current place in the galley and are collected together in the \footins box as part of TeX's preparation for page production.

But after placing the float (or deferring it) LaTeX then returns the page material to the galley, and because of TeX's output routine behavior, the galley has now changed: all the footnotes have been taken out from their original places. So LaTeX has to put the footnotes back, but it can place them in only a single place (not knowing the origin anymore). What it does is reinsert the footnotes (the footnote text to be precise) at the end of the galley. There are some good reasons for doing this, one of which is that LaTeX expects that all of the returned material still fits on the current page.

However, if for some reason a page break is finally taken at an earlier point, then the footnotes show up on the wrong page or column. This is a fairly unlikely scenario, and LaTeX works hard on making it a near-impossibility, but if it happens, check if there is a float near the chosen page break and either move the float or guide the algorithm by using explicit page breaks. An example of this behavior can be found

Badly placed floats can lead to footnotes on the wrong page

in a question on tex.stackexchange [2]. In fact, the particular case discussed in the question is worth highlighting: do *not* place a float directly after a heading, unless it is a heading that always starts a page. The reason is that headings normally form very large objects (because a heading prevents a page break directly after it). However, placing a float in the middle of this means that the output routine gets triggered before LaTeX makes its decision where to break and any footnotes get moved into the wrong place.

A final tuning advice

There are many ways to fine-tune the behavior of the float placement algorithm; most of them have been discussed above already. However, there is one more "tuning" possibility and in fact the biggest of all: changes in your document text.

Therefore, as final advice: do not start manipulating parameters or change placement specifiers or move floats within your document until after you have fully written your text and your document is close to completion. It is a waste of effort, and it may even result in inferior placements as your initially provided restrictions may no longer be adequate after a text change.

7.1.4 fltrace — Tracing the float algorithm

The algorithm used by LaTeX has a lot of (fairly low-level) tracing code built in, and this can be activated by loading the package fltrace. This can be of some help if the float placement you get is totally surprising.

With `\tracefloatvals` you get the current values of all relevant (internal) parameters used by the algorithm (so you have to do some mental translation). It also lists the floats that are already allocated to different areas of the current page and those that are deferred. The floats are denoted by their storage register name; e.g., you see names like `\bx@A`, `\bx@B`, and so forth.[1] For example, you might see

```
LaTeX2e: ***Float placement parameters:
LaTeX2e: \@colnum = 3
LaTeX2e: \@colroom = 523.16669pt
LaTeX2e: \@topnum = 2
 ...
LaTeX2e: toplist:
LaTeX2e: botlist: \bx@B
LaTeX2e: midlist: \bx@A
LaTeX2e: deferlist: \bx@C
```

which tells you that LaTeX added float "A" to the midlist (i.e., a here float), "B" was allocated to the botlist (the bottom area), while float "C" got deferred. Initially it is easy to guess which float hides behind "A", "B", etc., because the box registers are

---

[1]If you have added extra float registers with `\extrafloats`, the register names may contain numbers instead of uppercase letters.

used in sequence, but after a few pages this is all scrambled, because the registers get reused the moment their contents have been typeset.

If it is not clear which float is which, you can use \ShowFloat{B}, which displays some information about float "B", including an abbreviated symbolic representation of its contents. This command is always available even if fltrace is not loaded.

If this static information is not enough, you can turn on tracing the actions of the algorithm by saying \tracefloats anywhere in the document. This spits out a lot of tracing information[1] whenever the algorithm is processing floats, both when encountering them initially in the document, as well as during page breaking, when it tries to place floats that have accumulated on the deferlist. With \tracefloatsoff, the tracing is disabled again.

7.2 Float placement control

In the previous section LaTeX's basic algorithm for placing floats was discussed. We now look at a number of packages that alter or extend this algorithm or otherwise help you in controlling its behavior further.

The fewerfloatpages package improves on LaTeX's standard algorithm, and it is recommended to always load it if you use floats in your document. The placeins package also helps with the placement by introducing a float barrier like \clearpage, but without forcing a new page.

The afterpage package is a bit different and has limitations (and according to its author should not exist in the first place), but there are cases where it is extremely useful, which is why we describe it here.

Finally, we discuss the endfloat package that alters the algorithm so that all floats appear at the very end of the document by design (and not by mistake). Obviously that package should be loaded only if such a design is wanted.

7.2.1 fewerfloatpages — Improving LaTeX's float algorithm

As discussed above, LaTeX's float algorithm has the tendency to produce fairly empty float pages, i.e., pages containing only floats but with a lot of free space remaining that could easily be filled with nearby text. There are good reasons for this behavior; nevertheless, the results look unappealing, and in many cases documents are unnecessarily enlarged. To resolve this problem the fewerfloatpages package provides an extended algorithm that improves on this behavior without the need for manual intervention by the user.

Why does the current algorithm have these problems? To some extent, because it offers only global parameters that need to fit different scenarios, and thus settings that are suitable when many floats need to be placed result in suboptimal paginations in document parts that contain only a few floats, and vice versa. To overcome this problem, either one can try to develop algorithms with many more configurable

---

[1] The data is unfortunately very raw and not easy to consume, but it is worth giving a try when there is a need to understand why floats end up in surprising places or get deferred forever.

parameters that act differently in different scenarios or one can let the algorithm follow a main strategy, configurable with only a few parameters (like today), but monitor the process and make more local adjustments and corrections depending on the actual outcome of that base strategy and additional knowledge of the actual situation in a given document part. This is the approach taken by the extension implemented in this package.

Improving the float page algorithm

A simple way to improve the existing algorithm, without compromising its main goal of placing the floats as fast as possible and as close as possible to their call-outs, is the following: as long as there are many floats waiting to be placed, generate float pages as necessary to get them placed (using the current algorithm and its parameters).

Once the algorithm is unable to build further float pages, do some level of backtracking by checking if all floats have actually been placed. If there are still floats waiting on the defer list, then assume that what has been done so far is the best possible way to place as many floats as possible (which it probably is). However, if all floats have been placed onto float pages, check if the last float page is sufficiently full; if not, undo that float page and instead redistribute its floats into the top and bottom areas of the next upcoming page. This way the floats are combined with further text, and a possible half-empty float page is avoided.

A typical case where LaTeX should not make a float page

This approach does not resolve all the problematic scenarios in which LaTeX has decided to favor fairly empty float pages over some tighter type of placement. It does, however, help to improve typical cases that do not involve too many floats. For a example, if a single (larger) float appears near the end of a page, then when using the standard algorithm, it cannot be immediately placed (because there is not enough free space on the current page). It is therefore moved to the defer list, and at the page break it is then placed onto a float page (possibly by itself, if it is large enough to allow for that) even though it could perfectly well go into the top or bottom area of the next page and thus be combined with textual material on that page.

With the new algorithm, this float page is reexamined, and unless it is pretty much filled up already, it is unraveled, and its floats are redistributed into the top and bottom areas of the next page. If, however, there are many floats waiting on the defer list, it first makes a float page and then reassesses the situation. In other words, the algorithm looks at each prospective float page and based on the current situation (e.g., number of floats still being unplaced, free space on the page, etc.) decides whether this float page should be produced or whether it should stop making float pages and instead place the pending floats into top and bottom areas of the upcoming page.

Configuring the algorithm with parameters

Do not unravel a float page if there are too many floats on the defer list

The main idea of the extended algorithm is to avoid unnecessary cases of float pages especially if those float pages are fairly empty. Natural candidates are single float pages, but even in cases where the current LaTeX algorithm produces several sequential float pages the extended algorithm may decide to replace them with normal pages under certain conditions. However, the main goal remains to place as many floats as soon as possible, so generating float pages when many floats are waiting is usually essential.

`floatpagedeferlimit`

Whether or not unraveling for a float page is considered at all is guided by the counter `floatpagedeferlimit`. As long as there are more floats waiting on the defer list than this number, float pages are not considered for unraveling. The default is 3, which corresponds to the default value for `totalnumber`; i.e., with that setting, the unraveling of a floating page has a fighting chance to place all floats into the top and bottom areas on the current page. It would also resolve cases for up to three floats, each larger than \floatpagefraction, where the standard LaTeX algorithm would produce three individual float pages.

If you set the counter to 1, then only the last float page in a sequence is considered, and only if it contains just a single float and there are no other floats that are still waiting to be placed. If you set it to 0, then the extension is disabled, because float pages are produced only if there was at least one float on the defer list. Even if you *Do not unravel if the* set `floatpagedeferlimit` to a fairly high value, you may not want to unravel float *float page contains* pages that contain many floats. To support this case there is a second counter that *many floats* guides the algorithm in this respect.

`floatpagekeeplimit`

Whenever the float page contains at least `floatpagekeeplimit` floats, it is not unraveled. The default is also 3 so that float pages with three or more floats are not touched. Obviously the counter can have any effect only if it has a value less than or equal to `floatpagedeferlimit` because this is tested first.

There are, however, a number of other situations in which one should not unravel a float page even if the above checks for the size of the defer list were passed successfully. The most important one is the case when the float page contains at *Do not unravel if the* least one float that is allowed *only* on float pages (i.e., has a [p] argument). Such a *float page contains* float would not be placeable in a top/bottom area on any page and thus would be *at least one [p] float* repeatedly sent back to the defer list (possibly forever). This case is automatically detected by the algorithm and appropriately handled.

The other case where unraveling would normally be counterproductive is when the particular float page is nearly or completely filled up with floats. If that is unravelled, *Do not unravel if the* then it is certain that only some of the floats can be placed into the top or bottom *float page is nearly* area of the next page, while some would end up on the defer list. That in turn means *filled* that these deferred floats float even further away from their call-out positions than need be. So what is a good way to determine if a float page is "full enough"?

\floatpagekeepfraction

The current value for \textfraction determines the minimum amount of space that has to be occupied by text on a normal page. If all floats together need so much space that this amount of text could not fit, then trying to place the floats onto a normal page cannot succeed, and some of them would get deferred for sure.

This parameter would therefore be a good candidate for providing a definition for "full enough" float pages, but to allow for further flexibility the algorithm uses the variable \floatpagekeepfraction instead (defaulting to \textfraction), so, if desired, a lower (or even a higher) boundary can be set.

The above parameters give some reasonable configuration possibilities to guide the algorithm as to when and when not to unravel a possible float page and instead produce further normal pages. It should be noted, however, that except for the case of setting floatpagedeferlimit to 1, there is always a chance that floats drift further away from their call-outs, because they may not be immediately placeable due to other parameter settings of the float algorithm. For example, the counter topnumber (default value 2) limits the number of floats that can be placed in the top area on a normal page, and if more remain after unraveling, only two can immediately go in this area.

Configuring the algorithm with package options

As already mentioned, the algorithm detects if a float is allowed only on float pages (i.e., is given in the source as [p]), and it ensures that float pages containing such floats are not unraveled. However, if you have a float with the default specifier [tbp] whose size is larger than the allowed size of the top or bottom area (e.g., larger than \topfraction × \textheight), then this effectively means it can only be placed on a float page. Based on its float specifier, however, such a float is allowed to go into the top or bottom area, so the algorithm, as explained so far, would be allowed to unravel, and when that float later is considered for top or bottom placement, it is again deferred and thus moved from one page to the next, most likely messing up the float placement in the whole document.

checktb (option) There are two possible ways to improve the algorithm to avoid this disaster. One way would be to check the float size when it is initially encountered and remove any specifier that is technically not possible because of the parameter settings and the float size. A possible disadvantage is that this determination is done only once, and any later (temporary) change to the float parameters has no effect. This is currently the package default. It can be explicitly selected by specifying the option checktb. In this case you might see warnings like

```
LaTeX Warning: Float too large for top area: t changed to p on line ...
```

addbang (option) Another possibility is to automatically add a ! specifier to all floats during unraveling, i.e., when they are sent back for reevaluation. This way, such floats become placeable into top and bottom areas regardless of their size. This may result in fewer pages at the cost of violating the area size restrictions once in a while. It is specified with the option addbang.

nocheck (option) If you prefer no automatic adjustment of the specifiers, add the option nocheck. In this case you might find that floats of certain sizes are unplaceable and thus get delayed to the end of the document. If that happens, the remedy is either to explicitly specify [p] or [hp] for such a float (to ensure that they are not subject to unraveling) or to manually add an exclamation specifier, e.g., [!tp] so that LaTeX does not use the size restrictions in its algorithm.

The package also offers the option trace, which, if used, results in messages that give details on the decisions made by algorithm and an explanation why one or the other was taken. For example, you might see

trace (option)

```
fewerfloatpages: PAGE: trying to make a float page
fewerfloatpages: ----- \@deferlist: \bx@B \bx@D
fewerfloatpages:  starting with \bx@B
fewerfloatpages:  --> success:  \bx@B \bx@D
fewerfloatpages: ----- current float page unraveled
                 (free space 192.50336pt > 109.99832pt)
```

which means that the algorithm first tried to make a float page from the defer list, which at that point contained two floats (the float boxes \bx@B and \bx@D); that it was able to produce a float page containing just \bx@B and \bx@D; and that then it decided to unravel that float page, because it has an unused space of 192.5pt, i.e., roughly 16 text lines. With the current \floatpagekeepfraction, that is too much empty space on the page. You may also see lines such as

```
fewerfloatpages: ----- current float page kept, full enough
                 (free space 38.99496pt < 109.99832pt)
fewerfloatpages: ----- current float page kept (contains at least 5 floats)
fewerfloatpages: ----- too many deferred floats for unraveling (5 > 3)
fewerfloatpages:  --> fail: no float page made
```

all of which should be fairly self-explanatory given the above description of the algorithm. If it is not clear which float is stored in a certain float register, say, \bx@B, you can display its contents using \ShowFloat{B}. If you want even more detailed tracing of the complete algorithm, also load the fltrace package and enable the tracing with the command \tracefloats anywhere in your document. Note, however, that the resulting output is very detailed but rather low-level and unpolished.

Detailed tracing of the complete algorithm

Local (manual) adjustments

If the fewerfloatpages package is used, you get fewer float pages that contain a noticeable amount of white space. By adjusting \floatpagekeepfraction and the counters floatpagekeeplimit and floatpagedeferlimit, you can direct the algorithm to unravel more or fewer of the otherwise generated float pages. However, in some cases it might happen that the redistribution of the floats into the top and bottom areas of the next page(s) may result in some of them drifting too far away from their call-outs. If that happens, you can either try to change the general parameters or you could help the algorithm along by using the optional argument of individual float environments. The two main tools at your disposal are

- using the [!..] notation to allow a float to go into the top or bottom area even if it would be normally prevented by other restrictions;

- using [p] to force a float into a float page because that prevents the algorithm from unravelling the float page that contains that float.

As an alternative you can, of course, temporarily alter the definition of the command \floatpagekeepfraction or the values of the two counters in mid-document, but remember that they are not looked at when a float is encountered in the source but when we are at a page break and LaTeX attempts to empty the defer list, which is usually later and unfortunately somewhat asynchronous, i.e., not easy to predict.

7.2.2 placeins — Preventing floats from crossing a barrier

Standard LaTeX already implements a float barrier called \clearpage. Floats on either side never appear on the other. It works by first placing all deferred floats, if necessary by generating float pages, and then starting a new page. While this is suitable to keep floats within one chapter (because chapters typically start on a new page), there are cases where one would wish for a less intrusive barrier, i.e., one that works without forcing a new page or is partially porous.

This functionality is offered by Donald Arseneau's **placeins** package, which implements a \FloatBarrier command that places all deferred floats without introducing a page break. This approach is, for example, useful if you want to ensure that all floats that belong to a section are placed before the next section starts. Through package options, you can alter the behavior to allow for floats to migrate from one side to the other, as long as they still appear on the same page.

You could, for example, redefine the sectioning command yourself and introduce the \FloatBarrier command by using the \titleformat declaration from the titlesec package (see Section 2.2.7), as shown here:

```
\usepackage{titlesec}
\titleformat{\section}[block]
            {\FloatBarrier\Large\bfseries}
            {\thesection.}{6pt}{\filleft}
```

The author of **placeins** anticipated that users might often want to output their floats before a new section starts, so his package provides the package option section, which automatically redefines \section to include the \FloatBarrier command. However, by itself this option forces all floats to appear *before* the next section material is typeset, because the \FloatBarrier prevents a float from a current section from appearing below the start of the new section, even if some material of the current section is present on the same page.

Turning the barrier into a membrane

If you want to allow floats to pass the \FloatBarrier and appear at the bottom of a page (i.e., in a new section), specify the option below. To allow floats to pass it in the opposite direction and appear on the top of the page (i.e., in the previous section), specify the option above.

When using the option verbose, the package shows processing information on the terminal and in the transcript file.

7.2.3 afterpage — Taking control at the page boundary

The afterpage package (by David Carlisle) implements a command \afterpage that causes the commands specified in its argument to be expanded after the current page is output. Although its author considers it "a hack that not even always works" (for example, \afterpage fails in twocolumn mode), it has a number of useful applications in the cases where it does work.

Sometimes LATEX's float positioning mechanism gets overloaded, and all floating figures and tables drift to the end of the document. You may flush out all the unprocessed floats by issuing a \clearpage command, but this tactic has the effect of making the current page end prematurely. The afterpage package allows you to issue the command \afterpage{\clearpage}. It allows the current page to be filled with text (as usual), but then a \clearpage command flushes out all floats before the next text page begins.

Preventing floats bunching up at the end of the document

With the multipage longtable environment (see Section 6.4.2), you can experience problems when typesetting the text surrounding the long table, and it may be useful to "float" the longtable. However, because such tables can be several pages long, it may prove impossible to hold them in memory and float them in the same way that the table environment is floated. Nevertheless, if the table markup is in a separate file (say ltfile.tex), you can use the following declaration:

Floating multipage tables

```
\afterpage{\input{ltfile}}
```

This version starts the longtable after the next page break; however, this page may still contain normal floats at the top or bottom, and normal text may continue on the page on which the table ends. If that is not desired, then the \clearpage in the second form outputs all dangling floats (in the form of float pages), and the \newpage command ensures that text following the table appears on a new page:

```
\afterpage{\clearpage\input{ltfile}\newpage}
```

The \afterpage command can also be combined with the float package and its [H] placement specifier, as explained at the end of Section 7.3.1.

7.2.4 endfloat — Placing figures and tables at the end

Some journals require figures and tables to be separated from the text and grouped at the end of a document. They may also want a list of figures and tables to precede them and potentially require markers indicating the original places occupied by the floats within the text. This can be achieved with the endfloat package (by James Darrell McCauley, Jeffrey Goldberg, and more recently, Axel Sommerfeldt), which by default extracts figures and tables from within the document and places them at the very end. With appropriate configuration settings it can do the same for other float types if they are provided by packages such as float, newfloat, etc.

For its default task of managing figures and tables the endfloat package features a series of options to control the list of figures and tables, their section headings, and the markers left in the text at the call-out point of the figure or table float. A list of available options[1] follows:

`figlist/nofiglist`   Produce (default) or suppress the list of figures.

`fighead/nofighead`   Produce or omit (default) a section heading before the collection of figures. The section headings text is given by `\figuresection` and defaults to the string "Figures".

`figuresfirst`   Put all figures before tables (default).

`figuresonly`   Only manage figures but not tables as endfloats.

`nofigures`   Do not handle figures as endfloats.

There are also a few package options for jointly customizing all float types — these also act on any additional float type that is declared in the document:

`lists/nolists`   Produce or suppress the list of floats (figures, tables, etc.).

`heads/noheads`   Produce or omit a section heading before each float collection.

`markers/nomarkers`   Place (default) or omit markers in text to indicate the call-out position of floats.

`disable`   Make the package a no-op; i.e., if used, all other options or declarations are ignored. The reason for this option is that one often needs both a version for the journal (with endfloats) and a version with the floats in their correct places, and by temporarily adding this option, the latter can be easily achieved without other adjustments.

Float markers in text

By default, the package indicates the original position of a float within the text by adding lines such as "[Figure 4 about here.]" at the approximate place. These notes can be turned off by specifying the `nomarkers` option when loading the package.

Premature output

By default, the delayed floats are processed when the end of the document is reached. However, in some cases one might wish to process them at an earlier point — for example, to display them at the end of each chapter. For this purpose `endfloat` offers the command `\processdelayedfloats`, which processes all delayed floats up to the current point. By default the float numbering continues, so to restart numbering one has to reset the corresponding counters (details are given in the package documentation).

Caveats

The `endfloat` package file creates two extra files with the extensions `.fff` and `.ttt` for storing the figure and table floats, respectively. Because the environment bodies are written verbatim to these files, it is important that the `\end` command (e.g., `\end{figure}`) always appears on a line by itself (without any white space) in the source document; otherwise, it is not recognized. For the same reason, the standard environment names (i.e., `figure`, `table`, and their starred forms) are recognized only if they are directly used in the document. If they are hidden inside other environments, recognition of the environment `\end` tag fails badly.[2]

---

[1] A similar set of options exists for tables using `tab` or `tables` instead of `fig` or `figures`. For other float types this has to be handled differently.

[2] In some cases `\DeclareDelayedFloatFlavor` can help here.

> \DeclareDelayedFloat{*float-type*}[*extension*]{*heading*}

If you use additional float types in your document (as defined, for example, through \newfloat), you can have endfloat delay them as well as a group with a \DeclareDelayedFloat declaration. This associates the *float-type* with a *heading* to use when producing the list of that type, and the *extension* (which is optional) defines the file extension to use for storing them. If not given, endfloat constructs an extension for you from the *float-type* argument.

> \DeclareDelayedFloatFlavor*{*variant*}{*base*}

If you load other packages that also provide table or figure floats under other environment names, such as sidewaysfigure and sidewaystable from the rotating package, you have to tell endfloat that these are really figures and tables as far as its actions are concerned. This is done by associating a *variant* environment name (e.g., sidewaystable) with the corresponding *base* name (table).

By default both the *variant* and the *variant** form of the environment are delayed when using a \DeclareDelayedFloatFlavor declaration. However, if you use its star form, then the *variant** is not modified. There is only one real useful application for this: the ltcaption package defines a longtable* environment that does not use the table counter (i.e., can have only unnumbered captions, if any). If such tables should not get delayed, then this version of the declaration prevents that.

> \SetupDelayedFloat{*float-type*}{*key-list*}

With \SetupDelayedFloat the package offers a general way to adjust the options for a single *float-type*. This can be useful for new types declared to be delayed floats but can be used for the standard types figure and table as well. The accepted keys are nolist, list, nohead, and head, analogous to the package options. What you cannot do this way is to disable a *float-type* altogether. For this you have to use the package option (for figure or table) or not declare them as delayed floats for any other types.

Customizing the output

The package offers a number of hooks, for example, \AtBeginDelayedFloats, \AtBeginFigures, and \AtBeginTables to control the processing of the collected floats. For instance, an instruction such as \AtBeginTables{\cleardoublepage} ensures that the delayed tables start on a recto page.

Hooks

When the floats are finally typeset, the command \efloatseparator is executed after each float. By default, it is defined to be \clearpage, which forces one float per page. If necessary, it can be redefined with \renewcommand.

The text and the formatting of the notes, which are defined via the commands \figureplace and \tableplace, or more generally with \⟨*float-type*⟩place, can be changed with \renewcommand. For example, they might be adapted to a different language (the package does not support babel parameterization). Within

Customizing the float markers

the replacement text \thepostfigure and \theposttable reference the current figure or table number, respectively. A sample redefinition for French could look as follows:

```
\renewcommand\figureplace{\begin{center}%
        [La figure~\thepostfigure\ approx.\ ici.]\end{center}}
\renewcommand\tableplace{\begin{center}%
        [La table~\theposttable\ approx.\ ici.]\end{center}}
```

There also exists a generic \floatplace command expecting the *float-type* name as an argument. It is used by default in \figureplace and \tableplace. Thus, by redefining that command, you can change the markers for all float types at once. Here is an example that uses \todo from the todonotes package to generate a marker in the margin:

```
\usepackage{todonotes}
\renewcommand\floatplace[1]
        {\todo{\UseName{#1name}~\UseName{thepost#1} about here}}
```

In LaTeX releases prior to 2022 you would have to use the low-level \csname ... \endcsname constructs to generate the necessary commands from the argument, e.g., \figurename and \thepostfigure if the input was figure; applying \UseName instead is clearly the more readable approach.

7.3 Extensions to LaTeX's float concept

By default, LaTeX offers two types of horizontally oriented float environments, figure and table. For many documents these prove to be sufficient; in other cases additional features are needed. In this section we now look at packages that extend this basic tool set to cover more complex cases.

The float package offers ways to define new float types and also provides one way to prevent individual floats from floating at all. A different approach to the latter problem is given by the caption package, which we briefly touch upon too.

We then discuss two packages, rotating and rotfloat, that allow the rotation of the float content, something that might be necessary for unusually large float objects. With a somewhat different approach this is also covered by the key/value packages discussed in Section 7.5 on page 560.

The final package in this section (wrapfig) deals with floats that are placed inside the galley with normal paragraph text flowing around them. Such objects look like ordinary floats, e.g., they can have a caption and are similarly formatted, but being placed next to their call-out they do not really "float" and thus may get out of sequence with ordinary floats that may get deferred and this way move past such in-line floats. A similar type of "nonfloating" floats are those that are placed into the margin. They are not discussed here but as part of Section 7.5.2.

Another type of extension, not discussed here but deferred to Section 7.5.1 on page 560, is that of full-page floats, where there is no room for the caption, so that it needs to be placed onto the facing page, turning the float effectively into a double-page float. The package discussed there also offers some support for automatically producing floats that split their content and place it across two facing pages.

7.3.1 float — Creating new float types

The float package[1] by Anselm Lingnau, which dates back to the nineties, improves the interface for defining floating objects such as figures and tables in LaTeX. It adds the notion of a "float style" that governs the appearance of floats. New kinds of floats may be defined using the \newfloat command.

> \newfloat{*type*}{*placement*}{*ext*} [*within*]

The \newfloat command takes four arguments, three mandatory and one optional, with the following meanings:

type   "Type" of the new class of floats, such as program. Issuing a \newfloat declaration makes the environments *type* and *type** available.

placement   Default placement parameters for the given class of floats (combination of LaTeX's t, b, p, and h specifiers or, alternatively, the H specifier).

ext   File name extension of an auxiliary file to collect the captions for the new float class being defined.

within   Optional argument specifying whether floats of this class are numbered within some sectional unit of the document. For example, if the value of *within* is chapter, the floats are numbered within chapters (in standard LaTeX, this is the case for figures and tables in the report and book document classes).

The \floatstyle declaration sets a default float style that is used for all float types that are subsequently defined using \newfloat declarations, until another \floatstyle command is specified. Its argument is the name of a float style and should be one of the following predefined styles:

The style of the float class

plain   The float style LaTeX usually applies to its floats — that is, nothing in particular. The only but important difference is that the caption is typeset below the body of the float, regardless of where it is given in the input markup.

plaintop   Same style as the plain float style except that the caption is placed at the top of the float.

boxed   The float body is surrounded by a box with the caption printed below.

---

[1]As an alternative there exists the package newfloat by Axel Sommerfeldt, which has a more descriptive interface (using key/value syntax) and extra features, but lacks the float style concept.

ruled The float style is patterned after the table style of *Concrete Mathematics* book [31]. The caption is printed at the top of the float, surrounded by rules; another rule finishes off the float.

The float styles define the general layout of the floats, including the formatting of the caption. For example, the `ruled` style sets the caption flush left without a colon, while other styles center the caption and add a colon after the number. Because the float styles define the placement of the caption, floats can contain only a single `\caption` command, which is a restriction compared to standard LaTeX's behavior. One also has to be careful when mixing different float styles in one document so as not to produce typographic monsters.

Only one `\caption` *supported*

Even though the package does not offer a user-level interface for defining new float styles, it is fairly easy to add new named styles. For details refer to the package documentation in `float.dtx`.

The next example shows the declarations for two "nonstandard" new float types, `Series` and `XML`. The former are numbered inside sections and use a "boxed" style, and the latter are numbered independently and use a "ruled" style (typographically this combination is more than questionable).

Naming the float class

The introductory string used by LaTeX in the captions of floats for a given *type* can by customized using the declaration `\floatname{type}{floatname}`. "XML Listing" is used for XML floats in the example below. By default, a `\newfloat` command sets this string to its *type* argument if no other name is specified afterwards (shown with the `Series` float environment in the example).

1 New float environments

Lorem ipsum dolor sit amet, consectetuer adipiscing elit.

XML Listing 1 A simple XML file

`<XMLphrase>Great fun!</XMLphrase>`

Ut purus elit, vestibulum ut, placerat ac, adipiscing vitae, felis.

XML Listing 2 Processing instruction

`<?xml version="1.0"?>`

Nam dui ligula, fringilla a, euismod sodales, sollicitudin vel, wisi. Morbi auctor lorem

$$e = 1 + \sum_{k=1}^{\infty} \frac{1}{k!}$$

Series 1.1: Euler's constant

```
\usepackage{lipsum,float}
\floatstyle{boxed}
\newfloat{Series}{b}{los}[section]
\floatstyle{ruled}
\newfloat{XML}{H}{lox}
\floatname{XML}{XML Listing}
\newcommand\xmlcode[1]{\texttt{#1}}

\section{New float environments}
\lipsum[1][1]
\begin{Series} \caption{Euler's constant}
  \[ \mathrm{e}
     = 1 + \sum^\infty_{k=1} \frac{1}{k!}\]
\end{Series}
\begin{XML} \caption{A simple XML file}
  \xmlcode{<XMLphrase>Great fun!</XMLphrase>}
\end{XML}
\lipsum[1][2]
\begin{XML}
  \caption{Processing instruction}
  \xmlcode{<?xml version=''1.0''?>}
\end{XML}
\lipsum[2]
```

7-3-1

530

The command \listof{*type*}{*title*} produces a list of all floats of a given class. It is the equivalent of LaTeX's \listoffigures and \listoftables commands. The *type* argument specifies the type of the float as given in the \newfloat command. The *title* argument defines the text of the title to be used to head the list of the information associated with the float elements, as specified by the \caption commands.

Listing the captions of a float class

The following example is a repetition of Example 7-3-1 on the facing page (source only partially shown) with two \listof commands added.

XML Listings

List of Series

1   New float environments

Lorem ipsum dolor sit amet, consectetuer adipiscing elit.

```
\usepackage{lipsum,float}
% Float types Series and XML and command
% \xmlcode as defined in previous example
\listof{XML}{XML Listings}
\listof{Series}{List of Series}
\section{New float environments}
\lipsum[1][1]
 \begin{Series} \caption{Euler's constant}
  \[ \mathrm{e}
    = 1 + \sum^\infty_{k=1} \frac{1}{k!}\]
\end{Series}
... further text omitted ...
```

7-3-2

LaTeX's two standard float types figure and table cannot be given a float style using \newfloat, because they already exist when the float package is loaded. To solve this problem the package offers the declaration \restylefloat{*type*}, which selects the current float style (specified previously with a \floatstyle declaration) for floats of this *type*.

Customizing LaTeX's standard float types·

For the same reason there exists the \floatplacement{*type*}{*placement*} declaration, which can be used to change the default placement specifier for a given float *type* (e.g., \floatplacement{table}{tp}). In the following example, both figure and table have been customized (not necessarily for the better) to exhibit the usage of these declarations.

Figure 1: Sample figure

1   Customizing standard floats

Lorem ipsum dolor sit amet, consectetuer adipiscing elit.   Ut purus elit, vestibulum

Table 1 Sample table		
AA	BBB	123
CCC	DDDD	45

```
\usepackage{lipsum,graphicx,float}
\floatstyle{boxed} \restylefloat{figure}
\floatstyle{ruled} \restylefloat{table}
\floatplacement{table}{b}
\section{Customizing standard floats}
\lipsum[1][1]
\begin{table}  \begin{tabular}{@{}llr}
  AA & BBB & 123\\ CCC & DDDD & 45\end{tabular}
 \caption{Sample table}
\end{table}%
\begin{figure} \centering
 \includegraphics[width=12mm]{rosette}
 \caption{Sample figure}
\end{figure}
\lipsum[1][2]
```

7-3-3

Place a float "here" Modeled after David Carlisle's here package, the float package adds the [H] placement specifier, which means "place the float Here regardless of any surrounding conditions". It is available for all float types, including LaTeX's standard figure and table environments. The [H] qualifier must always be used on a stand-alone basis; e.g., [Hbpt] is illegal.

If there is not enough space left on the current page, the float is printed at the top of the next page together with whatever follows, even if there is still room left on the current page. It is the author's responsibility to place their H floats in such a way that no large patches of white space remain at the bottom of a page. Moreover, one must carefully check the order of floats when mixing standard and [H] placement parameters. Indeed, a float with a [t] specifier, for example, appearing before one with an [H] specifier in the input file might be incorrectly positioned after the latter in the typeset output so that, for instance, Figure 4 would precede Figure 3.

All float placement specifiers are shown together in the following table.	t Top of page
	b Bottom of page
	p Page of floats
	h Here, if possible
	H Here, always
	
	Table 1: Specifiers
	
	With "h" instead of the "H" specifier this
		`\usepackage{float,array}`
		All float placement specifiers are shown together in the following table.
		`\begin{table}[H]`
		`  \begin{tabular}{>{\ttfamily}cl}`
		`    t & Top of page \\ b & Bottom of page\\`
		`    p & Page of floats\\`
		`    h & Here, if possible\\ H & Here, always`
		`  \end{tabular}`
		`  \caption{Specifiers}`
		`\end{table}`
		With ``h'' instead of the ``H'' specifier this text would have appeared before the table in the current example.

6	7	7-3-4

In combination with the placeins and afterpage packages described in Sections 7.2.2 and 7.2.3, respectively, an even finer control on the placement of floats is possible. Indeed, in some cases, although you specify the placement parameter as [H], you do not really mean "at this point", but rather "somewhere close". This effect is achieved by using the \afterpage command:

```
\afterpage{\FloatBarrier\begin{figure}[H]...\end{figure}}
```

The \FloatBarrier command ensures that all dangling floats are placed first at a suitable point (due to \afterpage without producing a huge gap in the text), thereby solving the sequencing problem, described above. The [H] float is then immediately placed afterwards. If you use \clearpage instead of \FloatBarrier, it would come out on top of the next page instead.

7.3.2 Captions for nonfloating figures and tables

An alternative to specifying the [H] option with the various float environments, as described in the previous section, is to define captioning commands that typeset and are entered into the "List of Figures" or "List of Tables" just like LaTeX's standard `figure` and `table` environments. This functionality is provided by the caption package (discussed in more detail in Section 7.4.1).

```
\captionof{type}[short-text]{text}      \captionof*{type}{text}
```

This command works analogously to LaTeX's \caption command but takes an additional mandatory argument to denote the float *type* it should mimic. It can be used for any nonfloating material that should get a (numbered) caption whose text is also added into the list of figures or list of tables. The starred form suppresses both the number and the "List of..." entry.[1]

The following example shows a normal figure and its nonfloating variant used together. In such a case there is always the danger that a floating figure travels past its nonfloating counterparts. In the example we force this situation by pushing the floating figure to the bottom of the page. As a result, the numbering gets out of sync. One has to watch out for this problem when mixing floating and nonfloating objects, and in such cases a strategically placed \FloatBarrier might help.

Watch out for incorrect numbering

List of Figures

1   Various kinds of figures

Here we mix standard and nonfloating figures.

Figure B

Figure 2: Nonfloating figure

Because Figure 1 is forced to the bottom with an optional [b] argument it passes Figure 2 and the ordering in LOF gets out of sync.

Figure A

Figure 1: Standard figure

```
\usepackage{caption}
\listoffigures
\section{Various kinds of figures}
Here we mix standard and nonfloating
figures.
\begin{figure}[b]  \centering
 \fbox{Figure A}
 \caption{Standard figure}\label{fig:a}
\end{figure}
\begin{center}
 \fbox{Figure B}
 \captionof{figure}[Wrong order]
              {Nonfloating figure}
 \label{fig:b}
\end{center}
Because Figure \ref{fig:a} is forced to
the bottom with an optional \textttt{[b]}
argument it passes Figure \ref{fig:b}
and the ordering in LOF gets out of sync.
```

7-3-5

7.3.3 rotating, rotfloat — Rotating floats

Sometimes it is desirable to turn the contents of a float sideways, by either 90 or 270 degrees. Because TeX is not directly capable of performing such an operation, it needs support from an output device driver. To be as device independent as possible, LaTeX encapsulates the necessary operations in the packages graphics and graphicx (see

---

[1]If used on the main vertical list there can be a page break before or after the command. If that is a problem, use a minipage to keep all material together.

Section 8.1). One of the earliest packages that used this interface was the rotating package written by Sebastian Rahtz (1955–2016) and Leonor Barroca.[1]

The rotating package implements two environments, `sidewaysfigure` and `sidewaystable`, for turning whole floats sideways. These environments automatically produce page-sized floats, or more exactly column-sized floats (if used in `twocolumn` mode). Starred forms of these environments, which in `twocolumn` mode span both columns, exist as well.

By default, the floats are turned in such a way that they can be read from the outside margin, as you can see in the next example. If you prefer your floats to be always turned in the same way, you can specify one of the package options `figuresright` or `figuresleft`.

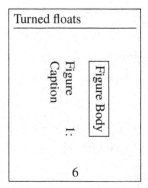

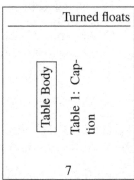

```
\usepackage{rotating}
\usepackage{fancyhdr}
\pagestyle{fancy}
\fancyhead[RO,LE]{Turned floats}

\begin{sidewaysfigure}
  \centering \fbox{Figure Body}
  \caption{Caption}
\end{sidewaysfigure}
\begin{sidewaystable}
  \centering \fbox{Table Body}
  \caption{Caption}
\end{sidewaystable}
```

7-3-6

The package also defines a number of environments for rotating arbitrary objects, such as `turn` or `rotate` (to rotate material with or without leaving space for it); see Section 8.2.1. Directly relevant to floats is the `sideways` environment, which enables you to turn the float body while leaving the caption untouched. It is used in the following example, which also exhibits the result of the `figuresright` option (which, despite its name, acts on `sidewaysfigure` and `sidewaystable`).

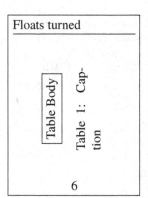

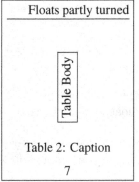

```
\usepackage[figuresright]{rotating}
\usepackage{fancyhdr} \pagestyle{fancy}
\fancyhead[LE]{Floats turned}
\fancyhead[RO]{Floats partly turned}

\begin{sidewaystable} \centering
  \fbox{Table Body} \caption{Caption}
\end{sidewaystable}
\begin{table}  \centering
  \begin{sideways}
  \fbox{Table Body}
  \end{sideways}
  \caption{Caption}
\end{table}
```

7-3-7

---

[1] In fact, its original release predates the development of the graphics interface. It was later reimplemented as an extension of this interface.

Instead of turning the whole float or the float body, it is sometimes more appropriate to turn only the caption. This ability is supported by the rotating package through the \rotcaption command. Unfortunately, the layout produced by this command is hardwired but can be customized through the caption package whose features are discussed in Section 7.4.1.

rotfloat — Combining float and rotating

To extend the new float styles, as introduced by the float package, with the sidewaysfigure and sidewaystable environments defined in the rotating package, you can use Axel Sommerfeldt's rotfloat package. It allows you to build new floats that are rotated by 90 or 270 degrees.

The rotfloat package offers identical options to the rotating package. Internally, for every float *type*, rotfloat defines an additional environment with the name sideways *type* and its corresponding starred form. For instance, when you write

```
\newfloat{XML}{tbp}{lox}     \floatname{XML}{XML Listing}
```

four environments become available: XML, sidewaysXML, and their corresponding starred forms XML* and sidewaysXML*. Similarly, the commands for redefining the table or figure environments, for example,

```
\floatstyle{boxed}            \restylefloat{table}
```

restyle not only the table and table* environments, but also the environments sidewaystable and sidewaystable*.

7.3.4 wrapfig — Inline floats, wrapping text around a figure

In TEX's typesetting model, text is first broken into paragraphs on a vertically oriented galley (or scroll). Once enough material is collected in this way TEX invokes its output routine, which chops off the first part of the galley, attaches running headers and footers as specified, and outputs the result in the .dvi file. It then restarts collecting text and breaking it into paragraphs to refill the galley.

As a consequence of this processing model, it is relatively easy to implement a float mechanism in which floats span the full width of the page or at least the full width of individual columns. Unfortunately, it is nearly impossible to have floats that occupy only parts of a text column and have the text flow around them. The reason is that when the paragraphs are broken into lines, their final positions are not yet known. It is therefore impossible to direct the paragraph builder to leave holes for the float objects if a later part of the process decides on their final placement. In contrast, placing floats at the top or the bottom of a page (or column) only directs the output routine to chop off less material from the assembled galley without otherwise manipulating the galley content.

Because of this processing model, the production of inline floats with text flowing around the float object has to take place during the paragraph-generating phase. The best outcome that packages can currently achieve is to ensure that the inline floats do not fall off the page (by measuring the amount of material already assembled on the galley to decide whether there is enough space to fit in the inline float with its surrounding paragraph(s)).

Such an algorithm is, for example, implemented by Donald Arseneau's wrapfig package. Because the package's inline floats only "float" very little in comparison to standard floats, mixing both types can result in the float numbering getting out of sequence. There are other packages offering this kind of functionality, but all of them have one or the other problem and often leave the placement decisions completely to the user because the automatic solution comes out wrong in many cases so that it is not worth supplying it in the first place. The wrapfig package supports figures and tables and offers some support for automatic placement, which works reasonably well.

The package wrapfig defines the `wrapfloat`, `wrapfigure`, and `wraptable` environments. These environments allow one to typeset a narrow float at the edge of some text and then make the text wrap around it. All three produce captions with the standard caption layout for floats. Although the environments have some limited ability to "float", no provision is made to synchronize them with regular floats. Thus, one must be aware that they may be printed out of sequence with standard floats.

```
\begin{wrapfloat}{type}[nlines]{placement}[overhang]{width}
```

The `wrapfigure` and `wraptable` environments are just shorthands with the *type* argument prefilled with `figure` or `table`, respectively. The other two mandatory and two optional arguments common to all three environments have the following meanings:

nlines   (optional) The number of narrow lines needed for the float (normally calculated automatically). Each display equation counts as three lines.

placement   Horizontal placement of the float, specified as *one* of the following letters: r or R (right side of the text), and l or L (left side of the text). There is no option for centering the float. For a two-sided document, the placement can alternatively be specified via i or I (inside edge) and o or O (outside edge). This refers to the inside and outside of the whole page, not to individual columns. In each case the uppercase variant allows the figure or table to float, while the lowercase variant puts it "exactly here".

overhang   (optional) Overhang of the float into the margin (default 0pt).

width   Width of the figure or table. Specifying 0pt has a special meaning, such that the "natural width" is used as the wrapping width. The caption is then typeset to the wrapping width. If the figure is wider than the space allotted, an "overfull box" is generated, and the figure or table contents can overwrite the wrapping text.

LaTeX wraps surrounding text around the float, leaving a gap of \intextsep at the top and bottom and \columnsep at the side, thereby producing a series of shortened text lines beside the figure. The size of the hole made in the text is the float width plus \columnsep minus the *overhang* value.

The package calculates the number of short lines needed based on the height of the float and the length \intextsep. This guess may be overridden by specifying the first optional argument (*nlines*), which is the desired number of shortened lines. This can be useful when the surrounding text contains extra vertical spacing that is not accounted for automatically or when the float contains display formulas.

Our first example shows a wrapped table 3 cm wide and placed at the left side of the paragraph. The package calculated a wrapping of 5 lines, which would have left a lot of empty space below the caption, so we explicitly selected 4 lines of wrapping instead. The figure is referenced using LaTeX's standard \label and \ref commands.

Wrapped Table	Text with a reference to Table 1. More text to fill the paragraph such that the text can flow around the table. The line-breaking results are rather ugly in such narrow measure.
Table 1: Caption	

```
\usepackage{wrapfig}
\begin{wraptable}[4]{l}{3cm}  \centering
  \fbox{Wrapped Table}\caption{Caption}\label{T}
\end{wraptable}
Text with a reference to Table~\ref{T}. More text
to fill the paragraph such that the text can
flow around the table. The line-breaking results
are rather ugly in such narrow measure.
```

7·3·8

The three environments should not be used inside another environment (e.g., list). They do work in twocolumn page layout (provided the column width is wide enough to allow inline floats).

Generally LaTeX is not able to move such environments to their optimal places, so it is up to you to position them in the best fashion. It is best to wait to do so until just before printing your *final copy*, because any changes to the document can ruin their careful positioning. Information about float processing by wrapfig is written to the log file if you specify the verbose option. Here are some rules for good placement:

- The environments should be placed so as to not run over a page boundary and must not be placed in special places like lists.

- Only ordinary text should have to flow past the figure but not a section title or large equations. Small equations are acceptable if they fit.

- It is convenient to place \begin{wrapfigure} or \begin{wraptable} just after a paragraph has ended. If you want to start in the middle of a paragraph, the environment must be placed between two words where there is a natural line break, which may require some experimentation.

Our second example displays a figure that is set to its natural width (last argument 0pt), but extends 20% into the left margin (specified by the optional *overhang* argument). Instead of using the special unit \width, denoting the natural float width in this case, one can, of course, use some explicit dimension such as 30pt. The effect of this choice can be clearly seen by looking at the way the paragraph text is typeset below the picture when the text wrapping ends. As the example also shows, wrapping continues even across paragraph boundaries if necessary.

The formatting of the caption can be influenced by combining wrapfig with packages like caption, although an option like centerlast may not be the appropriate choice in narrow measures.

```
\usepackage{wrapfig}
\usepackage[labelfont={sf,bf},
  justification=centerlast]{caption}
```

The starting place for the wrapfigure environment was manually determined in the current example by first setting the text without the figure to find the natural line breaks.

This is a "wrapfigure".

Figure 1: An example of the wrapfigure environment

The figure was then inserted after the second line giving the results that you see here.

```
The starting place for the \texttt{wrapfigure}
environment was manually determined in
\begin{wrapfigure}[7]{l}[0.2\width]{0pt}
  \centering  \fbox{This is a ''wrapfigure''.}
  \caption{An example of the
    \texttt{wrapfigure} environment}
\end{wrapfigure}
the current example by first setting the text
without the figure to find the natural
line breaks. \par
The figure was then inserted after the second
line giving the results that you see here.
```

7-3-9

In the preceding example we specified an *overhang* length explicitly. The overhang width can also be specified globally for all wrapfig environments by setting the \wrapoverhang length with LaTeX's \setlength command to a nonzero value. For example, to have all wrap figures and tables use the space reserved for marginal notes, you could write

```
\setlength  \wrapoverhang{\marginparwidth}
\addtolength\wrapoverhang{\marginparsep}
```

New "wrapping" environments for additional float types (as defined via the float package) with the same interface and behavior as wrapfigure or wraptable may be easily added, or directly invoked, using the wrapfloat environment:

```
\usepackage{float,wrapfig}   \newfloat{XML}{tbp}{lox}
\newenvironment{wrapXML}{\begin{wrapfloat}{XML}}{\end{wrapfloat}}
```

You can find other ways to fine-tune the behavior of wrapfig by reading the implementation notes at the end of the wrapfig.sty package file. The distribution also contains a file multiple-spans.txt that gives advice on how to manually produce cutouts across multiple columns using the wrapfig package. While this is somewhat labor intensive and should be undertaken only in the last steps of document production, it can produce nice results.

7.4 Controlling the float caption

When you want to explain what is shown in your floating environment (figure or table in standard LaTeX), you normally use a \caption command. After introducing the basic syntax and explaining the (low-level) interfaces available with standard LaTeX, this section describes the powerful caption package, which offers a large number of customization possibilities for adjusting the caption layout to your needs. As shown in the examples, it can be combined with all other packages described in this chapter.

The section concludes by examining the subcaption package, which introduces substructures for float objects. Another package that introduces the concepts of side captions and works in concert with caption and subcaption is discussed later in Section 7.5.1 on page 560.

`\caption[`*short-text*`]{`*text*`}`

This standard LATEX command is defined only inside a float environment. It increments the counter associated with the float in question. If present, the optional argument *short-text* goes into the list of figures or tables. If only the mandatory argument *text* is specified, then it is used in those lists. If the caption is longer than one line, you are strongly advised to use the optional argument to provide a short and informative description of your float. Otherwise, the list of figures and tables may become unreadable, and it may be difficult to locate the necessary information. In fact, LATEX allows multiparagraph captions only if the *short-text* argument is present. Otherwise, you get a low-level "Runaway argument?" error.

The following example shows how standard LATEX typesets captions. Compare this layout to the customization provided by the various packages discussed in the next sections. Note how the optional argument of the second `\caption` command defines what text appears for that figure in the "List of Figures".

List of Figures

1 Caption

Figures 1 and 2 have captions.

A small Figure

Figure 1: Short caption text

Another small Figure

Figure 2: Long caption text with some explanation that this figure is important even though it is small.

```
\listoffigures

\section{Caption}
Figures \ref{Fig1} and \ref{Fig2}
have captions.

\begin{figure}[ht] \centering
\fbox{\small A small Figure}
\caption{Short caption text}\label{Fig1}
\end{figure}
\begin{figure}[ht] \centering
\fbox{\small Another small Figure}
\caption[Short entry in lof]
  {Long caption text with some explanation
   that this figure is important even
   though it is small.}\label{Fig2}
\end{figure}
```

7-4-1

Internally, `\caption` invokes the command `\@makecaption{`*label*`}{`*text*`}`. The *label* argument is the sequence number of the caption and some text like "Figure"; it is generated internally depending on the type of float. The *text* argument is passed on from the mandatory `\caption` argument; it is the text to be typeset. The default definition for the part responsible for the typesetting of a caption looks something like this:

```
\newcommand\@makecaption[2]{% #1 is e.g., Figure 1,
                            % #2 is the caption text
  \vspace{\abovecaptionskip}%
  \sbox\@tempboxa{#1: #2}%
  \ifthenelse{\lengthtest{\wd\@tempboxa >\linewidth}}% test the size:
    {\noindent #1: #2\par}%                <- we have several lines
    {\centering           %                <- we have a single line
      \makebox[\linewidth][c]{\usebox\@tempboxa}\par
    }%
  \vspace{\belowcaptionskip}%
}
```

After an initial vertical space of size \abovecaptionskip (default often 10pt), the material is typeset in a temporary box \@tempboxa, and its width is compared to the line width. If the material fits on one line, the text is centered; if the material does not fit on a single line, it is typeset as a paragraph with a width equal to the line width. Thereafter, a final vertical space of \belowcaptionskip (default typically 0pt) is added, finishing the typesetting. The actual implementation that you find in the standard classes uses lower-level commands to speed up the processing so it looks somewhat different.

You can, of course, define other ways of formatting your captions by redefining \@makecaption, possibly even by supplying different definitions for different types of floats. However, this approach requires fairly low-level programming and is not very flexible, so it is normally better to use a package like caption (described below) to do this work for you. Rather than force you to write your own code for customizing captions, we therefore invite you to read the following pages, which describe a few packages that offer various styles to typeset captions.

7.4.1 caption — Customizing your captions

Axel Sommerfeldt developed the caption package[1] to customize the captions in floating environments. It not only supports LaTeX's standard figure and table environments, but also interfaces correctly with the \rotcaption command and the sidewaysfigure and sidewaystable environments of the rotating package. It works equally well with most of the other packages described in this chapter (see the original documentation for a complete compatibility matrix).

Like many packages these days, the caption package uses the extended option concept (based on the keyval package), in which options consist of a key and a value separated by an equal sign. In most cases there exists a default value for an option; thus, you can specify just the key without a value to produce this default behavior.

---

[1] The caption package is, in fact, a completely rewritten version of Axel's caption2 package and makes the latter obsolete. The old package is still distributed but only to support reprocessing old documents.

The customization possibilities of the caption package cover (nearly) all aspects of formatting and placing captions, and we introduce them below. For those users who need even more customization, the package offers an interface to add additional key values (representing special formatting).

Using package options allows us only to set defaults for all float captions regardless of their type. The caption package therefore also supports setting these options/keys through \captionsetup declarations. This way you can provide settings on a per type basis (if necessary) and also overwrite the default settings for individual floats in the document if that becomes necessary.

\captionsetup[*type*] {*key/value list*}

The \captionsetup declaration expects a *key/value list* like the one possible when loading the package itself. The difference is that, if used with the optional *type* argument, this declaration specifies caption formatting for only this particular float type (e.g., figure) or any float type that has been set up with a \newfloat declaration from the float package.

Such declarations can be used in the preamble of a document in which case they set up defaults, but they can also be used inside the document. In particular, if used within the body of a float environment, they change the settings for this float only, thus allowing for manual adjustments if necessary.

Standard customization possibilities for \caption

In the following we are discussing the various keys offered by caption for customizing the layout of captions. All of them are available out of the box and can be used either as package options or in key/value lists inside \captionsetup. Later we discuss how to extend this set of keys and values.

The first set of keys we examine here are those that influence the overall shape of the caption:

Customizing the general shape

singlelinecheck **or** slc   If the whole caption (including the label) fits on a single line, use a special layout (value true). If given the value false, such captions are formatted identically to multiple-line captions. slc is just a short name for the same key.

format   This key defines the overall shape of the caption (except when overwritten by the previous key). With the value plain, you get a typical "standard LaTeX" format, that is, the label and the caption text are set as a single block. Absent any further customization by other keys, the label and the text are separated by a colon and space, and the caption is set justified to full width.

With the value default you request the standard setup used by the document class (which for many classes is the same as plain).

As an alternative, the value hang specifies that the caption should be set with the label (and separation) to the left of the caption text. In other words, continuation lines are indented by the width of the label.

margin, width, oneside   By default, the caption occupies the whole width of the column (or page). By specifying a specific width you can reduce the measure used for the caption. In this case the caption is centered across the column. Alternatively you can use the margin key with one or two dimensions as a value. If two values are given, they are used for the inner and outer margins; otherwise, the value is used for both margins. To prevent the swapping of margins on even pages, specify oneside in addition.

The next example uses the margin key. As you can see, it affects only multiline captions (unless you also set singlelinecheck to false).

indention, hangindent   If set to a given dimension, the indention key specifies an additional indention for all continuation lines (e.g., on top of any indention already produced when format=hang is specified).

The hangindent key is similar but applies to the continuation lines of each paragraph individually in a multiparagraph caption.

```
\usepackage{graphicx,float}
\floatstyle{boxed} \restylefloat{figure}
\usepackage[format=hang,margin={0pt,15pt}]{caption}
```

Figure 1: Short caption

Figure 2: A caption that runs over more than one line

```
\begin{figure}[ht]   \centering
 \includegraphics[width=8mm]{elephant}
 \includegraphics[width=10mm]{elephant}
 \caption{Short caption}
\end{figure}
\begin{figure}[ht]    \centering
 \includegraphics[width=15mm]{elephant}
 \caption{A caption that runs over more than one line}
\end{figure}
```

7-4-2

Customizing the fonts

If you look at the previous example, you will notice that with this particular layout the space between the box and caption appears very tight. Keys for adjusting such spaces are discussed on page 545. Unfortunately, in some float styles, such as boxed, they are hardwired and cannot be changed. First, however, we look at keys for adjusting the fonts used within the caption, which always work.

font   This key defines the font characteristics for the whole caption (label and text), unless overwritten. It can take a comma-separated list of values to specify the font family (rm, sf, or tt), font series (md or bf), font shape (up, it, sl, or sc), or font size (scriptsize, footnotesize, small, normalsize, large, or Large). There also exists smaller and larger to move in relative steps. If more than one value is used, then the list must be surrounded by braces to hide the inner comma from being misinterpreted as separating one key from the next (see the example below).

Color is considered a font attribute, so if a color package is loaded, you can also use the values normalcolor or an explicit color, which then uses a somewhat unusual syntax, i.e., font={color=*color*}.

Key values for the same font attribute (e.g., the font shape) overwrite each other, but those for different attributes have the expected combined effect. Two separate calls to font overwrite each other, but if you use font+, then new settings are simply appended to the existing list.

To set the font attributes to their default settings use the value default or normal.

labelfont   While the key font defines the overall font characteristics, this key specifies the (additional!) attribute values to use for the caption label.

textfont   This key works like labelfont but is used for the caption text. In the next example we use it to reset the font series from boldface to medium.

Figure 1: Short caption

7-4-3

Let there be a table

Table 1: A caption that runs over more than one line

```
\usepackage{graphicx,float}
\floatstyle{boxed} \restylefloat{table}
\usepackage[font={sf,bf,footnotesize},
            textfont={md,smaller}]{caption}
\begin{figure}[ht] \centering
   \includegraphics[width=10mm]{Escher}
   \caption{Short caption}
\end{figure}
\begin{table}[ht]   \centering Let there be a table
     \caption{A caption that runs over more than one line}
\end{table}
```

Another frequent requirement is the customization of the layout for the caption label, such as by replacing the default colon after the label by something else, or omitting it altogether. Also, the separation between label and text may require adjustments. Both can be achieved with the following keys and their values:

Customizing the label further

labelformat   With this key a format for the label can be selected. Out of the box the following values can be used: simple (label string, e.g., "Figure" followed by the number and separated by a nonbreakable space), parens (number in parentheses), brace (number followed by a right parentheses), and empty (omit the label including the number altogether).

Additional values for alternative formattings can be defined using the declaration \DeclareCaptionLabelFormat, as explained on page 549.

labelsep   This key specifies the separation between the label and the text. Available values are none, colon, period, space, quad, endash (with surrounding spaces), and newline, which have the expected meanings.

New values producing other kinds of separations can be defined using the declaration \DeclareCaptionLabelSeparator as shown below. Note that labelsep is not used when the caption text is empty.[1]

name   This key allows one to set the caption label string that normally differs from float type to float type, e.g., "Figure" or "Table". It is therefore not useful as a

---

[1]Thus, if we had wanted, say, a period to appear at the end of all caption labels in Example 7-4-4, we should have provided a new value for labelformat that included it and set labelsep to newline instead.

package option but is normally used only with `\captionsetup` and an optional *type* argument. We use it below to supply the word "Image".

In the upcoming example we have to provide the key/values list through a `\captionsetup` declaration because our new value for `labelsep` is not yet defined when the package options are evaluated. We also need to use it to limit our changes just to the `figure` floats; otherwise, the table would be labeled "Image".

A B C

Table 1: No format change

Image 1

Image 2:
A small elephant

```
\usepackage{graphicx,float,caption}
\floatstyle{boxed} \restylefloat{figure}
\DeclareCaptionLabelSeparator{colon-newline}{:\newline}
\captionsetup[figure]{aboveskip=3pt,singlelinecheck=false,
       labelsep=colon-newline,labelfont={small,bf},name=Image}

\begin{table}[ht] \centering
   A B C \caption{No format change}
\end{table}
\begin{figure}[ht] \centering
   \includegraphics[width=12mm]{Escher}    \caption{}
\end{figure}
\begin{figure}[ht] \centering
   \includegraphics[width=12mm]{elephant}
   \caption{A small elephant}
\end{figure}
```

7-4-4

Paragraph-related The actual formatting of the caption text within the general shape, such as the
customizations justification, can be customized with the following three keys:

justification This key specifies how the paragraph should be justified. The default is full justification (value `justified`). Using the value `centering` results in all lines being centered. The `raggedleft` and `raggedright` values produce unjustified settings with ragged margins at the indicated side.

If the `ragged2e` package is loaded as well, you can use the additional values `Centering`, `RaggedLeft`, and `RaggedRight`, thereby employing the commands from that package that are described in Section 3.1.1.

Two other special justifications are available: `centerfirst` centers the first line and fully justifies the rest (with `\parfillskip` set to zero), whereas `centerlast` works the opposite way, centering the last line. Both shapes are sometimes requested for captions, but in most circumstances they produce questionable results.

Further specialized justification setups can be defined using the declaration `\DeclareCaptionJustification` as described in the documentation.

parskip This key controls the separation between paragraphs in multiparagraph captions. It expects a dimension as its value. Recall that captions with several paragraphs are possible only if the optional caption argument is present!

textformat   This key controls the overall formatting of the caption text. Supported values are empty (text suppressed), simple (as is), and period. Further values can be set up with \DeclareCaptionTextFormat.

```
\usepackage{color}
\usepackage[textfont={rm,it},labelformat=parens,
            labelfont={sf,color=blue},labelsep=quad,
            justification=centerfirst,parskip=3pt]
           {caption}
\begin{figure}[ht] \centering
  {\fontfamily{put}\fontsize{60}{60}\bfseries Bild}
  \caption[A short caption text]
   {A caption that runs over more than one line
    to show the effect of the centerfirst key value.

    Note that \texttt{centerfirst} only applies to
     the first paragraph of a multiparagraph caption.}
\end{figure}
```

Bild

Figure (1)   *A caption that runs over more than one line to show the effect of the centerfirst key value.*

Note that centerfirst *only applies to the first paragraph of a multiparagraph caption.*

7-4-5

The final set of keys deals with the position of the caption with respect to the float body. Note that none of these settings actually moves the caption in the particular place (you have to do that manually; use a float style from the float package or one of the key/value package in Section 7.5 to do it for you). The keys affect only the space being inserted.

Customizing the spacing around the caption

skip or aboveskip   Space between the caption and float body — for example, "above" the caption if caption is the placed at the bottom. It typically defaults to 10pt. The name skip should be preferred as aboveskip is really a misnomer as explained below.

belowskip   Space on the opposite side of the caption — that is, away from the float body. It is 0pt in most standard classes.

position   Specifies that the caption is placed above the float body (value top) or below the float body (value bottom; the default). It does *not* place the caption there. That is still your task (or that of a package such as float).

figureposition, tableposition   Specifying the caption position for figures or tables separately is rather common, and to ease this process, these keys are made available. Technically speaking they are just shorthands for saying something like \captionsetup[table]{position=...}.

Note that the names aboveskip and belowskip give the wrong implications: they do *not* describe physical places but rather are swapped if the caption is *marked* (using position) as being placed on the top. This is quite different from the parameters \abovecaptionskip and \belowcaptionskip in LaTeX's default implementation of the \caption command (see page 540), which *do* describe their physical place in relation to the caption! For some float package styles setting these keys may have no effect.

Be careful with the meanings of the keys

545

hyperref *link*
support

If the hyperref package (Section 2.4.6) is used to automatically provide links within the document, it normally jumps next to the caption, because as far as hyperref is concerned this is the object that provides the referenceable number. However, if that caption is below the float body, it would be nicer if the jump would be to the start of the top of the float containing the caption so that the whole float is visible. This can be controlled with the following two keys:

hypcap   If set to true (default), jump to the top of floats; otherwise, the hyperlink anchor is placed at the caption.[1]

hypcapspace   Placing the anchor exactly at the top of the float does not look too good either, so by default a distance of half a baseline is used. If you prefer a larger or smaller distance, you can specify the *amount* as the value to this key.

Doing it with style

Named caption
styles

So far all keys we discussed dealt with one aspect of the formatting each. The style key, however, is meant to adjust several other keys in one go. Out of the box it accepts only two values: default sets most keys to their "default" value defined by the document class, and base sets various keys so that the captions look like those produced by the standard LaTeX classes. Thus, to make this key really useful one has to provide additional named values as discussed below. Then, however, it provides a powerful way to structure your setup nicely.

Managing list of figures and similar lists

By default \caption provides an entry in the corresponding "List of ..." unless you use the star form of the command or provide an empty optional argument. If you want to prevent such entries in general (for a certain type), you can use the list key with the value no or false. Example 7-4-6 shows an application for this.

With the key listformat you can change the way the float number is typeset within the list. The supported values are similar to those of labelformat, though not the same: empty, simple, and parens. In addition, there are subsimple (default) and subparens that only typeset the number without the label string.

Continuing captions across floats

Sometimes figures or tables are so large that they do not fit on a single page. For such tables, the longtable or supertabular package may provide a solution. For multipage figures, however, no packages for automated splitting are available.

In the past a general solution to this problem was provided through the captcont package written by Steven Cochran that supports the retention of a caption number across several float environments. Nowadays this functionality is readily available with the caption package. It provides the command \ContinuedFloat to be used before issuing the \caption command if the current caption number should be retained.

---

[1]There are exceptions: with some packages caption is unable to control the link anchor placement.

Furthermore, it executes a key/value list associated with the artificial float type ContinuedFloat. This allows you to set up a dedicated caption layout for the continued floats.

If you prefer that the continued caption does not appear in the "List of..." list, use \caption with an empty optional argument (see Example 7-4-17 on page 558), or \caption*, which suppresses the LOF entry and caption label and number. Alternatively you can always suppress it using the list key as shown in the next example:

```
\usepackage{graphicx,caption}
\DeclareCaptionTextFormat{cont}
                        {#1 (cont.)}
\captionsetup[ContinuedFloat]
            {textformat=cont,list=no}
\listoffigures \bigskip
\begin{figure}[!b]
  \centering \includegraphics{cat}
  \caption{Animals}
\end{figure}
A figure placed at the page bottom and
continued at the top of the next page.
The caption appears only once in the LOF.
\begin{figure}[!t]        \ContinuedFloat
  \centering \includegraphics
              [width=2cm]{elephant}
  \caption{Animals}
\end{figure}
```

List of Figures

A figure placed at the page bottom and continued at the top of the next

Figure 1: Animals

6

Figure 1: Animals (cont.)

page. The caption appears only once in the LOF.

7

7-4-6

When \ContinuedFloat is used, it automatically maintains the counter ContinuedFloat in the background, incrementing it each time and resetting it to zero at the next float that is not a continuation float. Thus, you can use this counter to customize the float caption or reference to it. For example,

```
\DeclareCaptionLabelFormat{cont}{#1~#2\alph{ContinuedFloat}}
\captionsetup[ContinuedFloat]{labelformat=cont}
```

provides a new label format and assigns it to continued floats, such that the label shows up as "Figure 1a" automatically. See page 549 for more details on this declaration. This does not change the reference, though; for that you need to redefine \theContinuedFloat. This command is appended to the normal counter representation of a continuation float; e.g., if \thefigure is defined to produce \arabic{figure}, then this gets changed in a continuation figure environment to \arabic{figure}\theContinuationFloat.

By default the command does not produce any output, but the next example shows how it can be redefined. That example shows three figures. The first two are continuation floats, so they use subnumbering ("1" and "1a"). Both these labels are correctly handled by LaTeX's \listoffigures and \ref commands.

You may prefer the continuation already indicated in the first caption, i.e., the first float already numbered "1a". This is possible too: all you need to do is to additionally use `\ContinuedFloat*` in the first float. This command increments the main float counter but otherwise sets things up as a continuation float.

List of Figures

1a	First figure .	1
1b	Continuation	2
2	Third figure	2

Figure I

Figure 1a: First figure

Figures 1a and 1b in this example are subnumbered, while Figure 2 is not.

1

Figure II

Figure 1b: Continuation

Figure III

Figure 2: Third figure

Use `\ContinuedFloat*` if the first float should be labeled 1a already.

2

```
\usepackage[labelfont={bf}]{caption}
\renewcommand\theContinuedFloat
                   {\alph{ContinuedFloat}}
\listoffigures \bigskip
\begin{figure}[!ht]
 \ContinuedFloat* % <- star form
 \centering\fbox{Figure I}
 \caption{First figure}\label{FI}
\end{figure}
\begin{figure}[!ht]
 \ContinuedFloat
 \centering\fbox{Figure II}
 \caption{Continuation}\label{FII}
\end{figure}
Figures \ref{FI} and \ref{FII} in
this example are subnumbered, while
Figure~\ref{FIII} is not. \par Use
\verb=\ContinuedFloat*= if the first
float should be labeled 1a already.
\begin{figure}
 \centering\fbox{\LARGE Figure III}
 \caption{Third figure}\label{FIII}
\end{figure}
```

7-4-7

Extending the customization possibilities

In the remainder of this section we discuss how to structure your caption setup by providing new "styles" and show how to extend the setup for caption label layouts. Several of the declarations here have also been previously used in examples.

`\DeclareCaptionStyle{`*name*`}[`*short-style*`]{`*long-style*`}`

The `\DeclareCaptionStyle` declaration associates a key/value list with a *name* that can later be referred to as the value of a `style` key within `\captionsetup`. The mandatory *long-style* argument is a list of key/value pairs that describe the formatting of a caption if the style *name* is selected. The optional *short-style* argument lists key/value pairs that are *additionally* executed whenever the caption is determined to be "short" (i.e., if it would fit on a single line and `singlelinecheck` is not set to `false`).

It is possible to combine the `style` keys with other keys inside the argument of `\captionsetup`, as shown in the next example. There we select the style `default` (predefined) for all floats except `figures` but overwrite its setting for `labelfont`.

Note that the example is intended to show possibilities of the package — not good taste.

FIGURE 1. *A long caption that runs over more than one line to show the effect of the style key.*

7-4-8

Let there be a table

Table 1: A long caption that runs over more than one line to show the effect of the style key.

```
\usepackage{caption,graphicx}
\DeclareCaptionStyle{italic}
  {labelfont={sf,sc},textfont={rm,it},indention=18pt,
   labelsep=period,justification=raggedright}
\captionsetup[figure]{style=italic}
\captionsetup{style=default,labelfont={sf,bf}}
\begin{figure}[ht]
  \centering
  \includegraphics{cat}
  \caption{A long caption that runs over more than
      one line to show the effect of the style key.}
\end{figure}
\begin{table}[ht]
  \centering
  \fbox{Let there be a table}
  \caption{A long caption that runs over more than
      one line to show the effect of the style key.}
\end{table}
```

```
\DeclareCaptionLabelFormat{name}{code}
```

This declaration defines or redefines a `labelformat` key value *name* to generate *code* to format the label, where *code* takes two arguments: #1 (a string like "Figure") and #2 (the float number). Thus, to produce brackets around the whole label, you can define your own `brackets` key as follows:

```
\DeclareCaptionLabelFormat{brackets}{[#1\nobreakspace#2]}
```

While this approach would work well in all examples seen so far, the above definition nevertheless contains a potential pitfall: if #1 is empty for some reason (e.g., if you changed `\figurename` to produce nothing), the above definition would put a space in front of the number. To account for situations like this, the caption package offers the `\bothIfFirst` command.

```
\bothIfFirst{first}{second}      \bothIfSecond{first}{second}
```

The `\bothIfFirst` command tests whether *first* is nonempty and, if so, typesets both *first* and *second*. Otherwise, it typesets nothing. With its help the above declaration can be improved as follows:

```
\DeclareCaptionLabelFormat{brackets}
                  {[\bothIfFirst{#1}{\nobreakspace}#2]}
```

As a second example, suppose you want your caption labels to look like this: "(4) Figure". You could set up a new format, named `parensfirst`, and later assign it to

549

the `labelformat`:

```
\DeclareCaptionLabelFormat{parensfirst}
                         {(#2)\bothIfSecond{\nobreakspace}{#1}}
\captionsetup{labelformat=parensfirst}
```

In a similar fashion you can add new key values for use with the `labelsep` key using the `\DeclareCaptionLabelSeparator` declaration.

`\DeclareCaptionLabelSeparator{`*name*`}{`*code*`}`

After a `\DeclareCaptionLabelSeparator` the key value *name* refers to *code* and can be used as the value to the `labelsep` key. For example, if you want to have a separation of one quad between the label and the text that should be allowed to stretch slightly, you can define

```
\DeclareCaptionLabelSeparator{widespace}{\hspace{1em plus .3em}}
```

and then use it as `labelsep=widespace` in the argument of `\captionsetup` or `\DeclareCaptionStyle`.

`\DeclareCaptionTextFormat{`*name*`}{`*code*`}`

With the help of `\DeclareCaptionTextFormat` you can apply special formatting to the caption text supplied from the document. Within *code* it is available as `#1`. It has been already used in Example 7-4-6.

Providing new caption shapes and justifications
In addition to customizing the label format, you can define your own general caption shapes using `\DeclareCaptionFormat`, or specialized justification settings using `\DeclareCaptionJustification`. These are more specialized extensions, and their internal coding is a bit more difficult, so we do not show an example here. If necessary, consult the package documentation.

External configuration files
Such declarations can be made in the preamble of your documents. Alternatively, if you are using the same settings over and over again, you can place them in a configuration file (e.g., `mycaption.cfg`) and then load this configuration as follows:

```
\usepackage[config=mycaption]{caption}
```

While it is possible to combine the `config` key with other key, it is probably clearer to specify additional modifications through a `\captionsetup` declaration in the preamble. Also remember that using config files always means that you need to distribute your config as part of the document if you want to get comparable results on different installations.

The caption package collaborates smoothly with the other packages described in this chapter, as can be observed in the various examples. Note that in some cases this package has to be loaded *after* the packages whose captioning style one wants to modify.

7.4.2 subcaption — Substructuring floats

The subcaption package (by Axel Sommerfeldt) allows the manipulation and reference
of small, "sub" figures and tables by simplifying the positioning, captioning, and
labeling of such objects within a single float environment. If desired, subcaptions
associated with these subfloats can appear in the corresponding list of floats (e.g., the
list of figures). In addition, a global caption can be present. If hyperlinks are enabled
in the document, cross-references correctly link back to their origin, a feature not
available in the subfig package (by Steven Cochran) that for a long time dominated
this type of layout.

In this section we describe subcaption because it is closer linked with the caption
package, does not have some of the restrictions of subfig (most notably the problem with the hyperref support), and offers more flexibility and features. There are,
however, cases where it might be appropriate to resort to subfig, for example, when
using a document class that conflicts with the caption package, because this means
subcaption cannot be used either.

The syntax of the two packages is not identical but is similar enough that it is easy
to convert a document from one to the other. For example, the dominant command
in subfig is \subfloat, which corresponds to a restricted version of subcaption's
\subcaptionbox, except that in the latter the caption argument is mandatory while
it is optional with \subfloat.

```
\subcaptionbox  [list-entry]{caption}[width][justification]{content}
\subcaptionbox*            {caption}[width][justification]{content}
```

The \subcaptionbox typesets the *content* as subfloat with a caption attached. The
arguments *list-entry* (if present) and *caption* are passed as arguments to the \caption
command, or in case of the star form, to the \caption* command. If you wish to
get only an (alpha)numeric label, use an empty *caption* argument. An empty *list-entry*
signifies that for this instance the caption text should not be inserted in the "List
of…". This special feature is relevant only if the subfloat captions should be listed
there in the first place: see page 558 for information on creating this setup.

The content is typeset in L-R mode if no *width* argument is specified (most
suitable when typesetting a single graphic or table), otherwise in paragraph mode.
In the latter case you can also specify the desired *justification*: c for centered lines
(default), l for left aligned (i.e., ragged right), or r for right aligned. Also possible is
any value allowed/defined for the justification key of the caption package, e.g.,
centerfirst or anything defined through \DeclareCaptionJustification.

When you use two or more \subcaptionboxes horizontally next to each other,
the baseline of the boxes are right between the *content* part and the caption, which
means the first (or the last) line of the captions align when the caption is underneath
(or above, e.g., in case of tables). Thus, there is normally no need to provide manual
adjustments for a pleasing layout.

Our first example shows a figure that features two \subcaptionbox components
that display this alignment behavior. To reference them, you must associate labels with
each of these \subcaptionbox commands (be careful to put the \label commands

inside the braces enclosing the *caption* argument). We also place a \label following the \caption command to identify the enclosing figure environment, so that outside the environment we can refer to each of the components separately.

(a) Small, but a large caption   (b) Bigger

Figure 1: Two elephants

Figure 1 contains subfigure 1a, which is smaller than subfigure 1b.

```
\usepackage{graphicx,subcaption}
\begin{figure} \centering
  \subcaptionbox
      {Small, but a large caption\label{sf1}}[2cm]
      {\includegraphics[width=12mm]{elephant}}
  \qquad
  \subcaptionbox{Bigger\label{sf2}}
      {\includegraphics[width=18mm]{elephant}}
  \caption{Two elephants}\label{elephants}
\end{figure}
Figure~\ref{elephants} contains subfigure~\ref{sf1},
which is smaller than subfigure~\ref{sf2}.
```

7-4-9

Because captions are typeset to the width of the subfloat, we had to specify an explicit *width* argument for the first subfigure given that the elephant is so small. As explained above, that means that the subfloat *content* is typeset in vertical mode. However, because it consists of only a single graphic and the default justification is c, we see no difference in comparison to the second subfigure.

The next example shows a few of the remaining justification possibilities available:

Nulla malesuada porttitor diam. Donec felis erat, congue non, volutpat at, tincidunt tristique, libero. Vivamus viverra fermentum felis.

(a) default behavior (centered)

Nam dui ligula, fringilla a, euismod sodales, sollicitudin vel, wisi. Morbi auctor lorem non justo.

Nam dui ligula, fringilla a, euismod sodales, sollicitudin vel, wisi. Morbi auctor lorem non justo.

(b) left aligned   (c) right aligned

Lorem ipsum dolor sit amet, consectetuer adipiscing elit. Ut purus elit, vestibulum ut, placerat ac, adipiscing vitae, felis.

(d) centerfirst

Figure 1: Justification tests

```
\usepackage{lipsum,subcaption}
\begin{figure}
  \centering
    \subcaptionbox{default behavior
                        (centered)}
          [\linewidth]
          {\lipsum[3][1-3]}
  \par\medskip
    \subcaptionbox{left aligned}
          [.45\linewidth][l]
          {\lipsum[2][1-2]}
    \subcaptionbox{right aligned}
          [.45\linewidth][r]
          {\lipsum[2][1-2]}
  \par\medskip
    \subcaptionbox{centerfirst}
          [\linewidth][centerfirst]
          {\lipsum[1][1-2]}
  \caption{Justification tests}
\end{figure}
```

7-4-10

As an alternative to the \subcaptionbox command, the package offers a generic \subcaption command, which has the same syntax as \caption from the caption package; i.e., its supports a star form and an optional *list-entry* argument. This gives you complete control over the subcaption placement. The price is that it requires you to manually arrange the placement, and it needs each \subcaption confined to a box or a scope-delimiting environment.

In the next example we use two minipage environments for this, but the default arrangement does not really produce a good result — bottom alignment would work much better in this case. However, assuming that one of the captions has several lines as in Example 7-4-9, then it would be difficult to account for that. Also note that you are responsible for the arrangement within the minipage; e.g., we added \centering in the first for a proper placement of the cat and the caption in the somewhat larger box produced by the minipage.

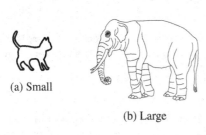

7-4-11

(a) Small

(b) Large

Figure 1: Exercising manual control

```
\usepackage{graphicx,subcaption}
\begin{figure}
  \centering
  \begin{minipage}{3cm} \centering
    \includegraphics{cat}
    \subcaption{Small}
  \end{minipage}
  \begin{minipage}{3cm}
    \includegraphics[width=3cm]{elephant}
    \subcaption{Large}
  \end{minipage}
  \caption{Exercising manual control}
\end{figure}
```

Given that using minipages in such circumstances is quite common, subcaption also offers the environments subfigure and subtable (and further environments for other float types could be defined).

\begin{subfigure} [*pos*] [*height*] [*inner-pos*] {*width*} ... \end{subfigure}

The environments take the same optional and mandatory arguments as minipage (and in fact simply pass them on to that environment); e.g., you specify the *width* and the *position* (default c for centered), and if desired, you can explicitly enforce a *height* and *inner-pos*. One important difference from the previous example is that within such environments you specify the subcaption using a \caption command.

The next example shows both top and bottom alignment in comparison to the default centering. Note that top alignment means aligning at the baseline of the first line inside the structure, which in the example holds the graphic. Thus, the alignment is at the feet of the elephants in this case (which is why the first lines of the caption also appear to be aligned). To prove this point we added an ellipsis between the subfigures to clearly show where they align.

Nesting of subfloat structures is possible, but numbering more than one level is really not advisable because there is only a single subcaption counter. The example

shows what happens if you try. Instead, it is better to use in all but one level
`\caption*` or `\subcaptionbox*`.

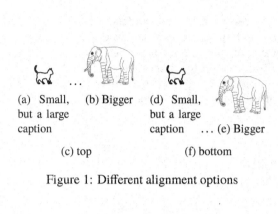

(a) Small, but a large caption   (b) Bigger   (d) Small, but a large caption ... (e) Bigger

(c) top   (f) bottom

Figure 1: Different alignment options

```
\usepackage{graphicx,subcaption}
\newcommand\samplefigs[1]{%
\begin{subfigure}[#1]{14mm}  \centering
   \includegraphics[width=6mm]{cat}
   \caption{Small, but a large caption}
 \end{subfigure}\dots
  \begin{subfigure}[#1]{14mm}
    \includegraphics[width=14mm]{elephant}
    \caption{Bigger}
 \end{subfigure}}
```
7-4-12
```
\begin{figure}  \centering
  \subcaptionbox{top}    {\samplefigs{t}}
  \quad
  \subcaptionbox{bottom}{\samplefigs{b}}
  \caption{Different alignment options}
\end{figure}
```

Customizing the subcaptions

Because the subcaption package is a direct extension of the caption package, it is possible to influence the caption layouts for subfloats using the options offered by the latter package. If it is not already loaded, subcaption loads the caption package *without* any options. This means that you have to either load caption first (as we did in the example below) or customize it after loading subcaption by using a `\captionsetup` declaration.

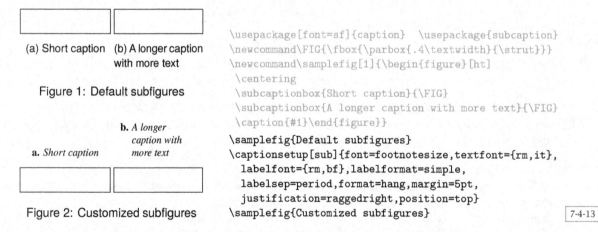

(a) Short caption   (b) A longer caption with more text

Figure 1: Default subfigures

b. *A longer caption with more text*

a. *Short caption*

Figure 2: Customized subfigures

```
\usepackage[font=sf]{caption}  \usepackage{subcaption}
\newcommand\FIG{\fbox{\parbox{.4\textwidth}{\strut}}}
\newcommand\samplefig[1]{\begin{figure}[ht]
 \centering
\subcaptionbox{Short caption}{\FIG}
\subcaptionbox{A longer caption with more text}{\FIG}
\caption{#1}\end{figure}}
\samplefig{Default subfigures}
\captionsetup[sub]{font=footnotesize,textfont={rm,it},
  labelfont={rm,bf},labelformat=simple,
  labelsep=period,format=hang,margin=5pt,
  justification=raggedright,position=top}
\samplefig{Customized subfigures}
```
7-4-13

The default setting of the subcaption package   As you can see, keys for customizing the caption layouts can be set on various levels. Some default settings are already in place when the subcaption package is loaded. Most noticeably, a setting of `font+=smaller` for all subfloat captions accounts for the fact that our setting of sf when loading the caption package is still in effect on the subcaptions, even though they use a smaller font size. Another default that can be deduced is the use of parens with the labelformat option. Most other changes to the main caption layout are inherited by the subfloats. The precise defaults for subcaptions are the following:

```
font+=smaller,labelformat=parens,labelsep=space,
margin=0pt,skip=6pt,list=false,hypcap=false
```

To overwrite such defaults, you can use any of the caption keys when loading the subcaption package, or you can specify them with a \captionsetup declaration using the *type* "sub" (as shown in the example). This changes all subsequent subfloat captions uniformly until they are overwritten by a further declaration.

Customizing all subcaptions

Finally, if you want to customize subfloat captions just for a particular ⟨*type*⟩ of float (e.g., for all figures), you can do so by using sub⟨*type*⟩ instead of sub in the \captionsetup declaration. The package knows which type of float is currently being built, and therefore this method works not only for environments such as subfigure but also for \subcaption or \subcaptionbox.

Customizing subcaptions by type

The subcaption package handles the spacing around the caption through the keys skip, aboveskip, and belowskip already discussed in conjunction with the caption package. However, it does not provide any additional support for placing the subfloat boxes — their arrangement is left to the user. If you have several rows of subfloats, like in Example 7-4-14, you would typically set each row as its own paragraph and separate them by some explicit \vspace command. Using \\ [*space*] would be possible too, but it is more difficult in that case to specify the right amount of vertical space because the alignment point of the rows is typically around the caption.

Spacing around subfloats

A somewhat more complex layout applying several key settings at different levels has been used in the following example. The settings are selected for illustration purposes and are not meant to used together in this way. They are worth studying closely to see how the different levels interact.

Setting keys at different levels

- The subcaption package is loaded with a font setting, which therefore applies to all subfloat captions but not to the main figure and table caption.

- The next line sets the keys position and skip for all tables (including subtables) but not for figures (where the default of 10pt is still in force).

- Several keys are then set just for subtable captions. For example, due to the setting singlelinecheck=false, all of them are left aligned, while the single-line figure subcaption is centered. We also overwrite the skip so that there is no extra space between subcaption and the table (there is still some space because each caption is internally set with a \strut to enforce a uniform height and depth).

- The skip for subfigures is still at its default of 6pt, and one can clearly see that raggedright should have been applied to all subcaptions and not just to the table ones as we did in the example.

- The \DeclareCaptionSubType* on the next line changes the numbering of table subcaptions so that they come out as "1.1", "1.2", etc. It is discussed on page 559.

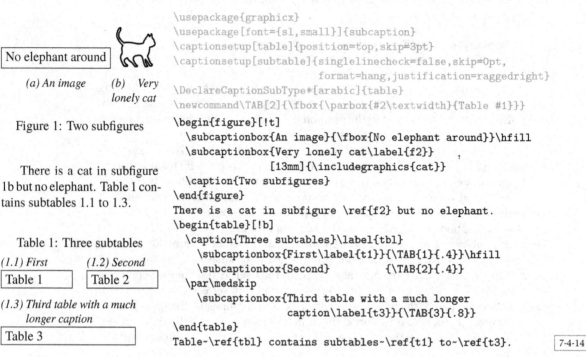

```
\usepackage{graphicx}
\usepackage[font={sl,small}]{subcaption}
\captionsetup[table]{position=top,skip=3pt}
\captionsetup[subtable]{singlelinecheck=false,skip=0pt,
                        format=hang,justification=raggedright}
\DeclareCaptionSubType*[arabic]{table}
\newcommand\TAB[2]{\fbox{\parbox{#2\textwidth}{Table #1}}}
\begin{figure}[!t]
  \subcaptionbox{An image}{\fbox{No elephant around}}\hfill
    \subcaptionbox{Very lonely cat\label{f2}}
                  [13mm]{\includegraphics{cat}}
    \caption{Two subfigures}
\end{figure}
There is a cat in subfigure \ref{f2} but no elephant.
\begin{table}[!b]
  \caption{Three subtables}\label{tbl}
      \subcaptionbox{First\label{t1}}{\TAB{1}{.4}}\hfill
      \subcaptionbox{Second}        {\TAB{2}{.4}}
  \par\medskip
      \subcaptionbox{Third table with a much longer
                  caption\label{t3}}{\TAB{3}{.8}}
\end{table}
Table~\ref{tbl} contains subtables~\ref{t1} to~\ref{t3}.
```

7-4-14

Internally, subcaption uses one counter per float type to keep track of the *Labeling the* subfloats within the current float and to produce a label for the caption from it. The *subcaptions* counter name is sub⟨type⟩, where *type* is the current float type (e.g., the counters used for labeling subfigures and subtables are called subfigure and subtable, respectively). Its representation is defined by \thesub⟨type⟩ and defaults to \alph {sub⟨type⟩}. Because there is only one such counter per subfloat type, nesting subfloats generates somewhat strange labels as already exhibited in Example 7-4-12.

In the previous example we used \ref to refer to different subfloats and the main table float. By default \ref produces a concatenation of the main float and the subfloat number. This can be seen with the subfigure reference, which shows "1b". More precisely, this is the case when the subfloat displays only the subfloat number in the caption label. If, however, the subfloat caption already shows both values, then \ref produces the same by default, e.g., "1.3" in the case of subtables above. How to change this is explained on page 559.

As an alternative to \ref, one can refer to such subfloat \labels by using the command \subref, which is provided by the subcaption package for this purpose. This normally results in a reference that looks like what is produced as part of the subcaption (without the outer formatting such as surrounding parentheses).

An application is shown in the next example. The command could also be used to construct more complex references, such as "Figure 1(a-c)".

The layout produced by \subref can be controlled through the subrefformat key, which accepts the same values as labelformat. By default simple is used; i.e., the reference is typeset as is. In Example 7-4-15 we change this to parens. Note that this does not affect the references produced with \ref.

Sometimes one wants to label subfloats but omit textual captions. This is, for example, common practice when showing a set of pictures or photographs: the main *Captionless subfloats* caption then explains the significance of individual subfloats. It can easily be achieved by using an empty *caption* argument on the \subcaption or \subcaptionbox command, which results in a labeled subfloat. The next example shows this type of layout (we only added \labels into the arguments to be able to refer to them).

```
\usepackage{graphicx}
\newcommand\FIG[1]{\includegraphics[#1]{cat}}
\usepackage[font={scriptsize,sl},skip=3pt]{subcaption}
\captionsetup{subrefformat=parens}

\begin{figure}   \centering
\subcaptionbox{\label{1}}{\FIG{width=3pc}}                \quad
\subcaptionbox{\label{2}}{\FIG{angle=20,width=3pc}}  \quad
\subcaptionbox{\label{3}}{\FIG{height=1pc,width=3pc}}
\caption[A group of cats]{A group of cats: \subref{1}
         the first cat, \subref{2} a climbing one,
         and \subref{3} one that is stretched.}
\end{figure}
```

(a)   *(b)*   *(c)*

Figure 1: A group of cats: (a) the first cat, (b) a climbing one, and (c) one that is stretched.

7-4-15

Of course, it is also possible to fine-tune individual floats, if their subfloats have *Manual fine-tuning* unusual forms or excess white space. We could, for example, move the main caption closer to the subcaptions by adding the line

```
\captionsetup[sub]{skip=3pt}
```

at the top of the float body. This command would apply to the current float only and replaces the skip added between caption and the subfloat body. In the next example we do this to adjust both the subcaptions and the main caption using two different values. Compare this to Example 7-4-12 on page 554, which shows the same float without these adjustments.

```
\usepackage{graphicx,subcaption}
% \samplefigs as defined before
\begin{figure}   \centering
  \captionsetup[sub]{skip=3pt} % for sub
  \captionsetup      {skip=5pt} % for main
  \subcaptionbox{top}    {\samplefigs{t}}
  \quad
  \subcaptionbox{bottom}{\samplefigs{b}}
  \caption{Different alignment options}
\end{figure}
```

(a) Small, but a large caption   (b) Bigger   (d) Small, but a large caption   ... (e) Bigger

(c) top   (f) bottom

Figure 1: Different alignment options

7-4-16

Displaying subfloat captions in the "List of ..."

The subfloat captions can be automatically entered into the external file holding the data for the corresponding "List of..." list. Such files have the extension .lof (a list of figures), .lot (list of tables), or the extension specified as the third argument to \newfloat. However, the subfloat captions do not show up in these lists, because only top-level float captions are typeset by default. To change this behavior, you have to set the list key to true, either on the subcaption level or on the level of some individual float subtype, e.g., subtable if you want to change the behavior only for that type.

Producing "List of ..." entries

The layout of such entries can be customized by using the declarations offered by the titletoc package (described in Section 2.3.2), which provides a set of clean high-level interfaces for this task.[1]

The next example shows how to make the subfloats appear in the contents listings by setting the list key. We also use a continuation float to prove that subfloat numbering continues as well across such floats. To suppress the "List of..." entry for the continuation float we use an empty optional argument on the \caption command — the special feature provided by the caption package for such situations. Alternatively, we could have used \caption* to suppress both the caption label and the entry in the list of figures altogether.

The subcaption packages defines a default formatting for the entry (by providing a definition for \l@sub⟨type⟩). If its layout is not to your liking, it is easy enough to adjust it using the titletoc package as we do below for illustration. For details on this see Section 2.3.2, which offers an extended discussion on the features of that package.

```
\usepackage[list=true]{subcaption}
\usepackage{titletoc}
\dottedcontents{figure}[1.5em]{}{1em}{6pt}
\dottedcontents{subfigure}[3em]
                        {}{1.2em}{6pt}
\listoffigures \medskip
\begin{figure}[!ht] \centering
   \subcaptionbox{First}{\fbox{Figure I}}
   \quad
   \subcaptionbox{Second}{\fbox{Figure II}}
   \caption{Three figures}
\end{figure}
\pagebreak        % <-- for illustration
\begin{figure}[!ht] \centering
   \ContinuedFloat
   \subcaptionbox{Third}{\fbox{Figure III}}
   \caption[]{Three figures (cont.)}
\end{figure}
```

List of Figures

| Figure I | Figure II |

(a) First   (b) Second

Figure 1: Three figures

Figure III

(c) Third

Figure 1: Three figures (cont.)

7-4-17

---

[1]If you want to go low-level, then Section 2.3.4 explains that you need to redefine internal commands of the form \l@sub⟨type⟩, i.e., \l@subfigure, \l@subtable, etc. This is the approach that you find used in most older document classes, which is why we mention it here.

Extending subfloats to other float types

So far, we have discussed only subfloats in `figure` or `table` environments. If you have introduced additional float types (e.g., defined with `\newfloat` from the float package), you may want to be able to substructure them as well. This can be achieved with the `\DeclareCaptionSubType` declaration.

```
\DeclareCaptionSubType*[ctr-rep]{⟨type⟩}
```

A prerequisite for using `\DeclareCaptionSubType` is that the corresponding float *type* is already declared. In that case, `\DeclareCaptionSubType` sets up the commands `\subcaption` and `\subcaptionbox` to be usable within their float bodies and also provides the environment form sub⟨*type*⟩ for people who prefer that type of syntax.

The declaration defines the counter sub⟨*type*⟩ to produce the labels. In the optional *ctr-rep* argument one can adjust the format by selecting a counter representation among `alph` (default), `arabic`, `fnsymbol`, `roman`, `Alph`, `Roman`, or whatever else is available for typesetting counter values.

The setup is as follows (refer to Section 2.4 on page 77 for details on the label/reference mechanism):

```
\newcommand\thesub⟨type⟩{\⟨ctr-rep⟩{sub⟨type⟩}}
\labelformat{sub⟨type⟩}{\the⟨type⟩ #1}
```

For example, if we use `\DeclareCaptionSubType[Alph]{code}` we get

```
\newcommand\thesubcode{\Alph{subcode}}
\labelformat{subcode}{\thecode #1}
```

Thus, if `\thecode` produces arabic numerals, then references with `\ref` generate "1A" and "1B", while those with `\subref` just produce "A", "B", etc. If, however the declaration is made with `\DeclareCaptionSubType*`, then the setup is done in the following way

```
\newcommand\thesub⟨type⟩{\the⟨type⟩.\⟨ctr-rep⟩{sub⟨type⟩}}
\labelformat{sub⟨type⟩}{#1}
```

which means that the main float number already appears in the label of the subfloat and that `\ref` and `\subref` produce the same output. An example for this was already given in Example 7-4-14.

This covers the most common cases, but if you need some other setup, you can always define your own representation by redefining `\thesub⟨type⟩` yourself, e.g.,

```
\renewcommand\thesubtable{\thetable--\roman{subtable}}
```

after which subtables would show "1-i", "1-ii", "1-iii", and so forth.

7.5 Key/value approaches for floats and subfloats

In most examples that we have seen so far, the \caption is manually placed at the appropriate point in the float body,[1] so it is largely up to the user where that happens. The two packages described in this section take a different approach: here a free style float body has vanished, and instead you specify a float object as one argument and a caption object as another (or as a key value).

The placement and formatting are then under the control of the package and can be influenced by set of key/value pairs. On the plus side this gives a consistent and easy-to-use interface, but one downside is that not all of the customization possibilities offered by the packages in the previous sections are exposed. What outweighs the other is probably a matter of taste.

However, both packages also offer one or the other feature not available anywhere else; e.g., hvfloat provides special caption placement possibilities, as well as the ability to deal with floats that are large so that the caption (or even part of the float) needs to go onto a separate page. keyfloat combines most packages from this chapter under a common syntax and offers margin and wrapped floats and the ability to add auxiliary text including artist/author names in consistent ways. Both packages support the concept of subfloats including their appropriate numbering.

7.5.1 hvfloat — Sophisticated caption placement control and more

The hvfloat package, named after its author Herbert Voß, probably started as a weekend activity to "provide a concise and consistent method for specifying simple floats". However, over time it has grown considerably and incorporated ideas from several other packages (e.g., sidecap or fltpage) that were developed a long time ago, but stopped being fully usable, because of missing maintenance and updates.

The main idea of the package is that instead of a free style float body with one or more captions inside, you have the float body and the caption as two separate objects. The placement of them in relation to each other is then determined by a set of key/value pairs, which gives a high degree of flexibility in manipulating the relationship.

> \hvFloat*[key/values]+{type}{float-object}[short-caption]{caption}{label}

The full syntax may look a bit daunting at first, but if we ignore the somewhat unusual optional + modifier for now, then all others are easily explained. Just like any float environment, the starred form allows you to place the float across both columns in a two-column document. The optional *key/values* argument allows you to customize the appearance as we will see below. The supported keys are shown in Table 7.1 on the next page.

In the mandatory *type* argument you specify the type of float to be set, which determines in which list the caption should show up. You can use either the predefined types, i.e., figure or table or any other float type that you have declared, for example, with \newfloat from the float package.

---

[1] Some styles offered by the float package also automatically move the caption into a specific place.

key	default	meaning
floatPos	tbp	The allowed float positions for the current float. If not given, the class default for the float *type* is used, which is usually but not always tbp.
rotAngle	0	Counterclockwise rotation of the overall float.
wide	false	Reserve more space for the float by including one margin.
style		Use a named style defined with \hvDefFloatStyle as a shorthand for a set of key/value pairs.
multiFloat	false	Make a multifloat page, see page 566.
subFloat	false	Make a subfloat page, see page 566.
nonFloat	false	Make a nonfloating object but attach the caption, increment the relevant counters, etc.
objectPos	center	Horizontal placement of the *float-object* in relation to the document galley. Possible values are left, center, or right. Relevant only if the caption position (capPos) is top or bottom.
objectAngle	0	Counterclockwise rotation of only the *float-object*.
objectFrame	false	Add a \frame around the *float-object*.
capWidth	n	Specifies the width of the caption: a decimal number means a fraction of \columnwidth, w or h make it as wide as the width or height of the *float-object*, respectively, and n means "natural", which makes it as wide as the available space based on its position (see examples).
capAngle	0	Counterclockwise rotation of only the *caption*.
capPos	bottom	Relation of *caption* to *float-object*. Possible values are bottom, top, before, after, left, or right (same page in two columns), inner or outer (relation to margin), and oddPage or evenPage (based on page numbers). For details see the extensive package documentation [137].
capVPos	center	Relative position of the caption if placed on the left or right. Allowed values are top, center, and bottom.
floatCapSep	5pt	Additional separation between *float-object* and *caption* if the latter is horizontally attached.
onlyText	false	If set to true, only the text of the *caption* is typeset without a number or identification and without adding an entry into the "List of …" list unless you also use a *short-caption* argument.
capFormat		Pass a key/value list to the caption package to format the caption in a special way. You need to surround the value with braces if it contains commas or equal signs! See Section 7.4.1 on page 540 for supported keys.
subcapFormat		Pass a key/value list to the subcaption package if floats with several subcaptions are used. You need to surround the value with braces if it contains commas or equal signs! See Section 7.4.2 on page 551 for supported keys.

Table 7.1: Keys supported by the \hvFloat command

You can think of the *float-object* and the *caption* as being like two boxes that are placed in relation to each other: the *float-object* is horizontally oriented (like an \mbox) so it gets as wide as its content and there is no line breaking inside. In contrast, the *caption* acts like a \parbox; i.e., it breaks into several lines if it is long. Its width is determined by the key capWidth in conjunction with the placement of the caption as shown in some examples below.

The optional *short-caption*, if provided, is the text that goes into the "List of ..." list. If it is not present, then the *caption* text is reused for this. Finally, the mandatory *label* argument gets a label string for referencing the float. You need to supply that even if you are not referencing the float at all, and to avoid getting "Multiple label warning"s from LATEX, you need to supply a unique string for each float!

In the first example we show the basic usage without any options. One float *type* was declared with the help of \newfloat, and you can see that its style is partly supported, but the caption remains at the bottom because this is the \hvFloat default.

Figure 1: Two cats

Lorem ipsum dolor sit amet, consectetuer adipiscing elit. See Image 1.

Image 1: A cat

Nam dui ligula, fringilla a, euismod sodales, sollicitudin vel, wisi.

```
\usepackage{lipsum,float} \floatname{Img}{Image}
\floatstyle{ruled} \newfloat{Img}{ht}{los}
\usepackage{hvfloat}

\lipsum[1][1] See Image \ref{img:cat}.\par
\hvFloat{Img}{\includegraphics[scale=.5]{cat}}
        {A cat}{img:cat}
\hvFloat{figure}{\includegraphics[scale=.5]{cat}
                \includegraphics[scale=.5]{cat}}
        {Two cats}{fig:2cats}
\lipsum*[2][1] \par
```

7-5-1

What may appear to be strange on first glance, though, is that the first float comes out as an inline float. The reason is that, by default, hvfloat in the absence of a floatPos key obeys the default setting for the type and for Img that was declared to be ht and thus favors "here" if possible. If you want your \hvFloat floats to always show identical behavior by default, you need to either explicitly set floatPos in the optional argument or in general in an \hvFloatSet declaration.

\hvFloatSet{*key/values*}   \hvFloatSetDefaults

The \hvFloatSet declaration lets you alter the overall key defaults that are given in Table 7.1 on the preceding page. For example, to make all floats float by default you could set \hvFloatSet{floatPos=tbp}. With \hvFloatSetDefaults, you reset all values to their package default.

If the float bodies are not very wide, then it may be a waste of space if their captions are attached above or below. In that case it might be more appropriate to place them to the left or right of the *float-object* using the capPos key with an appropriate value. The vertical position of the caption can then be set with `capVPos` and the minimal horizontal separation with `floatCapSep`.

The *float-object* and *caption* are then set to the normal galley measure (including the available space in the margin if you make it a `wide` float). This means that the *float-object* is pushed to one side and the remaining space is made available to the caption. If you do not like that, then you can restrict the caption width to a fraction of the `\columnwidth` using the `capWidth` key, as we did in the first figure of the example.

Figure 1: A cat

Figure 2: Two cats protruding into the margin

Lorem ipsum dolor sit amet, consectetuer adipiscing elit.

```
\usepackage{lipsum,hvfloat}
\hvFloatSet{floatPos=tbp,capPos=outer,
            capVPos=bottom,floatCapSep=18pt}
\lipsum[1][1] \par
\hvFloat[capWidth=.5]{figure}
   {\includegraphics[scale=.7]{cat}}
   {A cat}{fig:cat}
\hvFloat[wide,capPos=right]{figure}
   {\includegraphics{cat} \includegraphics{cat}}
   {Two cats protruding into the margin}{fig:2cats}
```

7-5-2

If you have large tables or figures, then rotating them might give you the best results. You can rotate either the whole float with `rotAngle` or the *float-object* and the *caption* individually using `objectAngle` and `capAngle`, respectively — what works best depends on the dimensions of the objects. In the next example, we rotate the object and place the caption to the right. Also shown there is the `capFormat` key, which you can use to pass a key/value list to the **caption** package to format the caption.

`\hvDefFloatStyle{`*name*`}{`*key/values*`}`

Rather than specifying the key/value pairs in the optional argument to `\hvFloat`, you can define a named styles and then reference that with the help of the `style` key. This way you can define a few styles and reuse them as needed. Below we define a `rotateobjectleft` style that implements the above setup.

Figure 1: Three cats and several lines of explanation in the caption

```
\usepackage{hvfloat}
\hvDefFloatStyle{rotateobjectleft}
   {objectAngle=90,floatCapSep=10pt,capPos=right,
    capFormat={labelfont=bf,indention=1em,
               justification=raggedright}}
\hvFloat[style=rotateobjectleft]{figure}
   {\includegraphics[scale=1.3]{cat}
    \includegraphics{cat} \includegraphics[scale=.7]{cat}}
   {Three cats and several lines of explanation in
    the caption}{fig:3cats}
```

7-5-3

What also might work under certain circumstances is to rotate everything and make the caption as wide as the float. Note that we use `w` not `h` because we need the width before rotation. If we had rotated only the caption, it would have been h to achieve the desired effect as shown in Example 7-5-5.

Figure 1: Three cats and several lines of explanation in the caption

```
\usepackage{hvfloat}
\hvDefFloatStyle{rotateright}
    {rotAngle=-90,capWidth=w,
     capFormat={labelfont=bf,indention=1em,
                   justification=raggedright}}
\hvFloat[style=rotateright]{figure}
  {\includegraphics[scale=1.3]{cat}
   \includegraphics{cat}
   \includegraphics[scale=.7]{cat}}
  {Three cats and several lines of explanation in
   the caption}{fig:3cats}
A paragraph of text in the main galley to show the
text margins.
```

A paragraph of text in the main galley to show the text margins.

7-5-4

With the help of the `onlyText` key, you can suppress the generation of the caption label, e.g., "Figure: 1". In that case only the *caption* text is used and, unless you also supply *short-caption*, no entry in the corresponding "List of ..." list is made.

A cat as a graphic

```
\usepackage{hvfloat}
\hvFloatSet{capPos=right,capAngle=90,capWidth=h,
              objectAngle=20}
\hvFloat[onlyText]{figure}{\frame{\includegraphics{cat}}}
              {A cat as a graphic}{fig:cat}
A paragraph of text in the main galley to show the
text margins.
```

A paragraph of text in the main galley to show the text margins.

7-5-5

Large column or page floats

Sometimes an image or a table is so large that, rotation or not, there is just not enough space on a page to place both caption and float body onto the same page. For this scenario hvfloat offers the key `fullpage`. If that key is used, the caption is placed onto the next possible verso page and the float body on the facing recto page (in `twoside` mode). If you use a class in `oneside` mode, then it simply uses the next two possible pages.

The *label* argument of `\hvFloat` labels the *float-object*, but for referencing the page with the caption, there is a second label automatically added with the name *label*-`cap`. We used that in the example, and it is also the one that is written in the "List of ..." list as you can see.

The separator line above the caption in the following example is typeset by default. If that is not desired, you have to set the key `separatorLine` to false.

To alter the order of caption and float body, use capPos with the value `after` or with the value oddPage or evenPage to force the caption onto a page with that kind of number. But note that with the default setting the caption has a good chance of appearing on the current page (as in the example), whereas with `after`, the float and the caption are most certainly printed later.

List of Figures

1   Full-page floats

Figure 1 is a large float whose caption and body are on separate pages. Figure 1 on page 7 with caption on page 6.

Figure 1: Caption for float on the next page for which there was no room left.

6

7

```
\usepackage{hvfloat,varioref}
\listoffigures
\section{Full-page floats}
Figure~\ref{FP1} is a
large float whose caption
and body are on separate pages.
\hvFloat[fullpage]{figure}{%
  \framebox[.95\linewidth][c]
    {\rule[-3cm]{0pt}
        {.95\textheight}%
     A full-page figure}}
[A huge figure]
{Caption for float
  \vpageref{FP1} for which
   there was no room left.}{FP1}
Figure~\ref{FP1} on
page~\pageref{FP1} with caption
on page~\pageref{FP1-cap}.
```

There is one possible issue to watch out for with `fullpage` floats: the *float-object* is set as a [p] float and that works only if the float height is larger than `\floatpagefraction`. If not, it may get deferred until the end of the chapter or document. That is unlikely with the default settings but may become a problem if that fraction has been changed to a value closer to 1.

In some cases even `fullpage` is not enough and a graphic needs to occupy all of the printable area of a page including all margins. For this the package offers the key FULLPAGE, which if used reserves the full `\pageheight` and `\pagewidth` for the *float-object*. The page is then typeset with page style `empty`.

To simplify the inclusion of images the package also defines three additional keys for `\includegraphics` from the graphicx package. These are `fullpage` (as a shorthand for `width=\columnwidth` and `height=\textheight`), `FullPage` (using `\textwidth`, `\textheight`), and FULLPAGE (for the full paper size). You might want to combine them with `keepaspectratio` to avoid image distortion.

Subfloat and multifloat pages

Instead of one large float that occupies a whole page, you may have a float consisting of several subfloats, e.g., a set of tables or a group of figures each with its own subcaption and an overall caption describing the complete set. For this hvfloat offers the key `subFloat`, and this is where the so far unexplained + syntax comes into play.

To specify the float *type* for all floats, main *caption*, a possible *short-caption*, and the *label*, you use the normal arguments but keep the *float-object* argument empty.

For each subfloat in the structure you then add another set of arguments of the following form:

> \hvFloat* [*key/values*] +{*type*}{*float-object*} [*short-caption*] {*caption*}{*label*}
>   +{}{*sub₁-float-object*}{*sub₁-caption*} [*short-sub₁-caption*] {*sub₁-label*}
>   +{}{*sub₂-float-object*}{*sub₂-caption*} [*short-sub₂-caption*] {*sub₂-label*}
>   ...

The *type* argument of the subfloats is empty because all share the *type* specified in the first line. The format of the subfloat captions can be adjusted with the key `subcapFormat`, its value is passed on to the subcaption package.

This example exhibits a float with a substructure. Our figure 1 shows an elephant in 1a and cats in 1b.

(a) A big elephant

(b) Two little cats

Figure 1: Animals shown in TLC in different places

```
\usepackage{hvfloat}

This example exhibits a float with a substructure.
\hvFloat[subFloat,subcapFormat={font=it}]+{figure}{}
        {Animals shown in TLC in different places}
        {fig:animals}
+{}{\includegraphics[width=2cm]{elephant}}
    {A big elephant}{fig:elephant}
+{}{\includegraphics[scale=.7]{cat}
    \includegraphics[scale=.7]{cat}}
    {Two little cats}{fig:2cats}
Our figure~\ref{fig:animals} shows an elephant
in~\ref{fig:elephant} and cats in~\ref{fig:2cats}.
```
7-5-7

As an alternative you can group independent floats using the key `multiFloat`. It too uses the + specifier, but here all lines denote individual floats allowing to you group different *types* on one page, with the captions showing up on the page before (or after).

Lorem ipsum dolor sit amet, consectetuer adipiscing elit. Ut purus elit, vestibulum ut, placerat ac, adipiscing

Figure 1: Cat

Figure 2: Elephant

Figure 3: Two cats

```
\usepackage{lipsum,hvfloat}

\hvFloat[multiFloat,
        capFormat={singlelinecheck=false}]
+{figure}{\includegraphics[scale=.5]{cat}}
    {Cat}{fig:cat}
+{figure}{\includegraphics[width=2cm]{elephant}}
    {Elephant}{fig:elephant}
+{figure}{\includegraphics[]{cat}
        \includegraphics[scale=1.1]{cat}}
    {Two cats}{fig:2cats}
\lipsum[1][1-2]
```
7-5-8

Double-page floats

Sometimes images (or tables) are even bigger and require presentation across two facing pages, and the hvfloat package offers some support for this. Obviously this requires the document to be typeset in twoside mode to be meaningful. If you use the key *doublePage*, then the *float-object* is split and placed at the top left of the text area on the next verso page and continues on the facing recto page. It is the responsibility of the user to ensure that its dimensions do not exceed the available space (which in this case would be 2\textwidth plus the widths of the inner margins). Also important is to ensure that the float together with its caption does not get vertically too large, because that may make it unplaceable.

If there is enough space, the caption can be set aside the *float-object* using the appropriate keys. Otherwise, as shown in the next example, it is set below the object on the recto page. The pages show a running header and footer and, if the height of the float is small enough, normal galley text may appear on both pages below it — something that is difficult to exhibit in the small samples here in the book.

With the key bindCorr you can specify some extra white space at the inner margin to account for space lost through the binding. In the example this is not noticeable, because white space is always cut from the examples to save space.

2 *running header*

running header 3

Figure 1: A cat

7-5-9

```
\usepackage{hvfloat} \pagestyle{myheadings}
\markboth{running header}{running header}
First and last page not shown \ldots

\hvFloat[doublePage,bindCorr=3mm]{figure}
  {\includegraphics[height=.4\textheight,
      width=2.3\textwidth]{cat}}{A cat}{fig:1}

Several more paragraphs ending up on pages 1
(before the figure) and 4 (after it) ...
```

As an alternative, the key doublePAGE starts the *float-object* at the left edge of the paper so that the full width is available, but it still leaves space for a running header. Finally, doubleFullPAGE uses the full page area of both pages by placing the top-left corner of the object at the top left of the verso page. Because this leaves no space for headers (and possibly footers), they are omitted on these pages. A caption, if present, is placed on top of the object if it takes up all space. It is the responsibility of the user to choose an appropriate font coloring to ensure that the caption remains visible if it overlays the object.

7.5.2 keyfloat — Bringing most packages under one roof

Most of the core packages discussed in this chapter that manipulate floats were written a long time ago. They are still state of the art, but each of them solves only a subset of the existing problems in this space.

The keyfloat package by Brian Dunn is a more recent addition in this space. Its task is not so much to provide new functionality, but to bring existing functionality together in a concise interface. It automatically loads and uses graphicx, rotating, caption, subcaption, placeins, wrapfig, and calc. From this list you can probably guess that it is strongly interested in figure floats, but it supports table and other floats equally well. The main idea is to provide a concise set of commands and environments offering a key/value syntax that delivers the typical sequence of a float environment, loading a graphic or other content, placing caption and graphic, and setting up a label, list entry, etc., behind the scenes.

> \keyflt*[*position*] {*type*}{*key/values*}{*general-contents*}
> \keytab*[*position*]   {*key/values*}{*table-contents*}
> \keyfig*[*position*]   {*key/values*}{*image-file*}

The \keyflt command adds a float of any predefined *type* to the document, i.e., a figure, table, or any other type previously declared with \newfloat from the float package or with \DeclareFloatingEnvironment from the newfloat package.

As usual the star denotes a float spanning both columns in two-column mode. The optional *position* specifies where the float can go; if not present, the defaults for the *type* are used. As usual you can specify a combination of !htbp, but in addition there is H (force the float to stay "here"), M (for small floats in the margin), and W (produce an inline float with text wrapped around it).

The *key/values* are used to control appearance, add a caption or label and are discussed below. The *general-contents* receives the main material to be floated — if that is large or has special requirements such as containing verbatim material, then it is often better to use the corresponding environment instead.

The commands \keytab and \keyfig are mainly shorthands that preset the *type*, but note that the \keyfig does not have a *general-contents* argument but expects the file name of a graphic to be passed automatically to \includegraphics. This makes it suitable for floats displaying a single graphic; more complex ones need \keyflt or one of the commands discussed below.

The keys are deliberately short to ease the input, e.g., c (caption text) or l (label); the full list of available keys is given in Table 7.2 on the next page. The next example exhibits some of them. Note that we had to surround the values for tl and as with braces to hide the commas they contain. If you forget this, you might get rather unpleasant error messages.

MR. PAULO CEREDA, TEX ISLAND

The hummingbird, designed by Paulo Cereda for the LaTeX Project, becomes the new logo for LaTeX in 2014

Figure 1: The new LaTeX logo

```
\usepackage{keyfloat}
\keyfig[tp]
  {w=2cm,
   c=The new \LaTeX{} logo,l=fig:logo,
   tl={The hummingbird, designed by Paulo
       Cereda for the \LaTeX\ Project, becomes
       the new logo for \LaTeX\ in 2014},
   ap=Mr., af=Paulo, al=Cereda,
   as={, \TeX\ Island}}
  {latex-logo}
```

7-5-10

None of the generated floats can span multiple pages; if you need that, you can build two floats and use the cont key to specify that they have a special relationship or you have to resort to using longtable or supertabular to produce multipage tables with captions.

key(s)	meaning	example
c	The text for the caption. By default the text is also used for the "List of ..." list.	c=caption
sc	The text for the "List of ..." list if different from the caption text.	sc=short
cstar	A starred caption, i.e., one without number. Text is not written to the "List of ..." list.	cstar=no number
cont	A continued float; i.e., the next one gets the same number (though it might get a different caption).	cont
t	Additional fully justified text that may contain several paragraphs. If it contains commas or equal signs, enclose it in braces.	t=paragraph(s)
tl, tc, tr	Like t, but aligned to left, center, or right, respectively.	tc=paragraph(s)
ap, af, al	Artist's prefix, first name and last name. Only for figure floats.	af=H., al=Zapf
as	Artist's suffix. Typeset directly adjacent to the last name, so any necessary space must be explicitly given.	as=~II.
aup, auf, aul, aus	Author's prefix, first name, last name, and suffix. Used with nonfigure floats.	aup=Prof., aul=Knuth
w	The absolute width of an image or text box in case of nonfigure floats.	w=3cm
lw	The fractional width of image or text box in relation to the normally available width (e.g., the width of the column).	lw=.8
r	The rotation angle in counterclockwise degrees.	r=20
f, tf	Add a frame or a tight frame around the image or text box.	f
h	The absolute height of an image. The aspect ratio is not maintained if w or lw is also given. Only for figure floats.	h=1in
s	The scale factor used on the image. Only for figure floats.	s=1.2
mo	Vertical offset for margin floats.	mo=-12pt
wp	Placement specifier for wrapped floats; see page 536 for the list of supported values.	wp=I
ww	Total width for wrapped float, can be more than w for small items with a wider caption; by default autocalculated.	w=1cm,ww=2cm
wlw	Total width, but given as a fraction of \linewidth.	wlw=.3
wo	Overhang of wrapped float into the margin. Default 0pt.	wo=1cm
wn	Number of narrow lines for wrapped float. Normally autocalculated but useful if the surrounding text has unusual heights.	wn=4

Table 7.2: Keys supported by the keyfloat commands

The caption placement and formatting is controlled through the **caption** package (see Section 7.4.1); e.g., if you want table captions above the tables, you need a suitable \captionsetup declaration as shown in the next example. The formatting of the artist's name is always centered below the image; in contrast, the author's name used with other float types is always placed flush right. The auxiliary text from t or its variants is typeset in small type to full measure below the artist's or author's name.

```
\begin{keyfloat}  [position] {type} {key/values}  ...  \end{keyfloat}
\begin{keytable}  [position] {key/values}          ...  \end{keytable}
\begin{keyfigure} [position] {key/values}          ...  \end{keyfigure}
```

These environments work like their command counterparts discussed above, except that instead of the *contents* argument, they use the environment body. This makes them more suitable if that content is complex or in case of figure floats you want to display more than one graphic as part of the float.

All of them also offer starred forms, i.e., keyfloat*, keyfigure*, and keytable*, to support floats spanning all columns in two-column mode.

Table 1: LATEX Companion statistics

edition	chapters	pages	authors
1	14 + 3	555	3
2	14 + 3	1197	2 + 5
3	17 + 3	≈ 1950	2 + 3

© 2023 FRANK MITTELBACH

Compares editions from 1994, 2004, and 2023

```
\usepackage{booktabs,keyfloat}
\captionsetup[table]{position=top,skip=1ex}
\begin{keytable}[H]{c=\LaTeX\ Companion statistics,
  tl={Compares editions from 1994, 2004, and 2023},
  aup=\copyright\ 2023, auf=Frank, aul=Mittelbach}
\begin{tabular}{ccrl}                         \toprule
  edition & chapters & pages & authors \\ \midrule
    1 &  14 + 3 & 555   & 3           \\
    2 &  14 + 3 & 1197  & 2 + 5       \\
    3 &  17 + 3 & $\approx$ 1980 & 2 + 3\\ \bottomrule
\end{tabular}\end{keytable}
```

7-5-11

```
\begin{marginfigure} [offset]  ...  \end{marginfigure}
\begin{margintable}  [offset]  ...  \end{margintable}
```

If you have fairly wide margins and/or small floats, then another option is placing the float into the margin either using the special *position* M, as we did below, or using the environment marginfigure or margintable. Note that these environments only offer an optional argument specifying the *offset* and you have to add the caption, etc., yourself in the environment body, so they are less general than commands and environments discussed above when used with *position* M.

The letter I

The paralogisms of practical reason are what first give rise to the architectonic of practical reason.

Another paragraph following the (centered) graphic in the margin.

```
\usepackage{kantlipsum,keyfloat}
\kant[1][2]
\keyfig[M]{w=7mm,mo=-.5\baselineskip,
             r=15,cstar=The letter I}{I}
Another paragraph following the (centered)
graphic in the margin.
```

7-5-12

Given that the margin floats (and the wrapped floats discussed below) do not really "float", there is the danger that they get out of sequence with normal floats if you use c instead of cstar to give them a float number. This issue is not always caught by the package, so you should check this visually yourself. In case of issues, you can either move an offending float to a different position or use \suppressfloats[t]. ◆ *Floats
out of sequence*

As an alternative for small floats you can consider having the paragraph text flow around them by using W in the *position* argument. Internally this is realized by using environments of the wrapfig package (see Section 7.3.4).

All customization possibilities of that package are exposed as keys; i.e., the placement can be specified with wp (default 0 for outside margin), ww specifies the width of the cut-out (if not calculated automatically from the size of the image), wo is the overhang into the margin (default zero), and with wn you can explicitly set the number of narrow lines, which helps if they have unusual heights that throw off the autocalculation.

Some text before the wrapped figure to show its placement in context of paragraphs.

The letter I

The paralogisms of practical reason are what first give rise to the architectonic of practical reason.

Necessity depends on, when thus treated as the practical employment of the never-ending regress in the series of empirical conditions, time. Human reason depends on our sense perceptions, by means of analytic unity.

7-5-13

```
\usepackage{kantlipsum,keyfloat}

Some text before the wrapped
figure to show its placement in
context of paragraphs.

\keyfig[W]{w=7mm,ww=2cm,wo=1cm,
          r=15,
          cstar=The letter I}
         {I}
\kant[1][2] \kant[1][4-5]
```

If the formatting of the wrapped float is not flexible enough, e.g., if you want a special placement for the caption or special formatting of the float body, then use the keyfigure environment to format the float body yourself.

Below we redo the previous example but add a frame around the graphic. We also specify the number of shortened lines explicitly, using the key wn, instead of relying on the automatic calculation (which would have been eight lines because the float body got larger now). To force it into the same space as before we also have to vertically shift the float a bit (the value of −15pt was determined by trial and error).

Some text before the wrapped figure to show its placement in context of paragraphs.

The letter I

The paralogisms of practical reason are what first give rise to the architectonic of practical reason.

Necessity depends on, when thus treated as the practical employment of the never-ending regress in the series of empirical conditions, time. Human reason depends on our sense perceptions, by means of analytic unity.

7-5-14

```
\usepackage{kantlipsum,keyfloat}

Some text before the wrapped figure
to show its placement in context of
paragraphs.

\begin{keyfigure}[W]{w=2cm,wn=6,
         wo=1cm,cstar=The letter I}
 \vspace*{-15pt}\centering
 \fbox{\fbox{\includegraphics
         [width=7mm,angle=15]{I}}}
\end{keyfigure}
\kant[1][2] \kant[1][4-5]
```

```
\begin{keyfloats}*[position]{columns} ... \end{keyfloats}
```

If you have several smaller floats, then another possibility is to group them using a `keyfloats` environment. This works best if the floats are of similar size because this environment arranges them in *columns*. The environment can be nested, as shown in the example. It is possible to combine floats of different types with each getting their own caption, "List of ..." entry, etc. All the environment does is keep the floats together so that they float as a unit. You can place labels (key `l`) onto individual floats so that they can be referenced and use other keys from Table 7.2 when appropriate, but the optional star or *position* argument can be applied to only the outermost environment, as all floats of the group receive the same treatment.

Figure 1: Stretched cat

Figure 2: Logo   Figure 3: Elephant

See the L&TEX logo in Figure 2.

```
\usepackage{keyfloat}

See the \LaTeX\ logo in Figure~\ref{logo}.
\begin{keyfloats}{1}
 \keyfig{h=1cm,w=4cm,c=Stretched cat}{cat}
 \begin{keyfloats}{2}
  \keyfig{h=1cm,c=Logo,l=logo}{latex-logo}
  \keyfig{h=1cm,c=Elephant}{elephant}
 \end{keyfloats}
\end{keyfloats}
```

7-5-15

Instead of a float you may want to place some explanatory text in one of the columns. To do this you could use a `\keyfig` command with an empty `cstar` to suppress its caption, but to simplify matters, there is a `\keyparbox` command that provides just that: a container for arbitrary material that does not act as a float but can be used in place of one.

```
\begin{keysubfloats}[position]{type}{columns}{key/values}
 ...
\end{keysubfloats}
\begin{keysubfigs}[position]{columns}{key/values}...\end{keysubfigs}
\begin{keysubtabs}[position]{columns}{key/values}...\end{keysubtabs}
```

As a final option you can produce one float with one main caption consisting of a number of subfloats, each with their own subcaption. In this case all floats have to be of the same *type* because only the main caption is passed into a "List of ..." list to describe the group.

The generic environment is `keysubfloats`, which requires that you specify this float *type* as an argument. This is useful if you have declared your own float types, but for the common case of `figure` and `table` floats, two variant environments `keysubfigs` and `keysubtabs` exist that have the *type* already prefilled so that it does not have to be given.

All three environments have starred forms to generate floats that span both columns in `twocolumn` mode.

The environments cannot be nested; i.e., you cannot have sub-subfloats, but it is allowed to use `keyfloats` environments inside in order to group the subfloats in some particular way as shown below.

(a) stretched elephant

(b) hummingbird

(c) cat

Figure 1: TLC animals

7-5-16

```
\usepackage{keyfloat}
\begin{keysubfigs}{1}{c=TLC animals}
  \keyfig{h=1cm,w=3cm,
          c=stretched elephant}{elephant}
  \begin{keyfloats}{2}
    \keyfig{h=1cm,c=hummingbird}{latex-logo}
    \keyfig{h=1cm,c=cat}{cat}
  \end{keyfloats}
\end{keysubfigs}
```

Graphics Generation and Manipulation

TeX probably has the best algorithms for formatting paragraphs and building pages from them. But in this era of ever-increasing information exchange, most publications do not limit themselves to text — the importance of graphical material has grown tremendously. TeX by itself does not address this area, as it deals only with positioning (glyph) boxes on pages. Knuth, however, provided a hook for implementing "features" that are not available in the basic language, via the \special command. The latter command does not affect the output page being formatted,[1] but TeX will put the material, specified as an argument to the \special command, literally at the current point in the output, e.g., the .dvi file. The program that displays or prints that output then has to interpret the received information and load the graphic or execute the appropriate graphic operation. Engines that can directly produce Portable Document Format (PDF) offer other primitives to add raw data to the PDF output, but conceptually the process is the same: it is the backend that has to deal with the graphics.

The main problem with this approach was that different backends provide different methods and interfaces so that any TeX source file that used \special directly became nonportable, working only with specific output devices or printers.

---

[1] In certain situations the \special command may change the formatting because it can produce an additional breakpoint or generate an extra space — thus not a perfect approach.

This problem was largely resolved with LaTeX 2_ε, which provided a generalized driver-independent interface to include external graphic material and to scale and rotate LaTeX boxes.[1] This interface is the subject of Section 8.1. It exists in the form of two implementations: the graphics package offers a simple interface, while the graphicx package provides a convenient key/value interface with additional features. Free-standing scaling and rotation and other manipulations are the subjects of Section 8.2.

A similar abstraction for line graphics was announced at the same time, but it took more than a decade until it was finally implemented. This and some applications thereof are discussed in Section 8.3. This section also talks about special graphic languages and as one useful application thereof generating QR codes with LaTeX.

Section 8.4 is then devoted to tcolorbox, a very comprehensive package for producing boxed material.

We conclude the chapter by taking a brief look at the powerful tikz package. There is no way we can do justice to this package, which builds a universe of its own — one could easily devote a whole book to it. Thus, all we try here is to give you an introduction to its basics and give a few teasers to show what it is capable of, but direct you to its documentation (more than a thousand pages) if you get hooked.

8.1 LaTeX's image loading support

Since the introduction of LaTeX 2_ε in 1994, LaTeX has offered a uniform syntax for including every kind of graphics file that can be handled by the different drivers. In addition, all kinds of graphic operations (such as resizing and rotating) as well as color support are available.

These features are not part of the LaTeX kernel but rather are provided by the standard, fully supported color, graphics, and graphicx extension packages. As the TeX program does not have any direct methods for graphic manipulation, the packages have to rely on features supplied by the "driver" used to print the Device Independent File Format (DVI) file or by the features of the extended engines pdfTeX, XeTeX, or LuaTeX that can produce PDF output directly. Unfortunately, not all drivers or PDF engines support the same features, and even the internal method of accessing these extensions varies among them. Consequently, all of these packages take options such as dvips or pdftex to specify which external driver or engine is being used. Through this method, any unavoidable device-dependent information is localized in a single place, the preamble of the document. However, each TeX distribution when installed sets up suitable detection methods and defaults (e.g., if the program pdflatex is used, then most likely the correct driver option is pdftex), so in practice most documents compile correctly without the need to specify any such option.

The packages graphics and graphicx can both be used to scale, rotate, and reflect LaTeX material or to include graphics files prepared with other programs. The difference between the two is that graphics uses a combination of macros with a "standard" or TeX-like syntax, while the "extended" or "enhanced" graphicx package presents a key/

---

[1] A generalized package for color is also available; see the *LaTeX Manual* [65] for more details.

value type of interface for specifying optional parameters to the \includegraphics and \rotatebox commands.

8.1.1 Options for graphics and graphicx

When using LATEX's graphics packages, the necessary space for the typeset material after performing a file inclusion or applying some geometric transformation is reserved on the output page. It is, however, the task of the *device driver* (e.g., dvips, dvipdfmx, pdftex, etc.) to perform the actual inclusion or transformation in question and to show the correct result. Because different drivers require different code to carry out an action like rotation, one has to specify the target driver as an option to the graphics packages — for example, option dvips if you use one of the graphics packages with Tom Rokicki's dvips program, or option pdftex if the graphics packages are used with the pdfTEX engine.

Fortunately, however, the package is usually capable of figuring out the correct driver automatically, in particular when generating a PDF with pdfTEX, XƎTEX, or LuaTEX. In all other cases it assumes dvips, which is often, but not always, correct. Only in the latter case does one need to explicitly provide a driver option. The full list of supported drivers (and their restrictions, if any) is listed in the graphics package documentation if you ever run into a case where the default does not work.

In addition to the driver options, the packages support some options controlling which features are enabled (or disabled):

draft Suppress all "special" features, such as including external graphics files in the final output. The layout of the page is not affected, because LATEX still reads the size information concerning the bounding box of the external material. This option is of particular interest when a document is under development and you do not want to download the (often huge) graphics files each time you work on it. When draft mode is activated, the picture is replaced by a box of the correct size containing the name of the external file.

final The opposite of draft. This option can be useful when, for instance, "draft" mode was specified as a global option with the \documentclass command (e.g., for showing overfull boxes), but you do not want to suppress the graphics as well.

hiresbb In PostScript graphics look for bounding box comments that are of the form %%HiResBoundingBox (which typically have real values) instead of the standard %%BoundingBox (which must have integer values).

Of lesser importance these days are options that disable features because of restrictions in the output driver. With hiderotate you prevent showing rotated material (for instance, when the previewer cannot rotate material and produces error messages), and hidescale does the same for scaled material.

With the graphicx package, these options are also available locally as keys for individual \includegraphics commands.

8.1.2 The \includegraphics syntax in the graphics package

With the graphics package, an image file can be included by using the following command:

```
\includegraphics*[llx,lly][urx,ury]{file}
```

If the [urx, ury] argument is present, it specifies the coordinates of upper-right corner of the image as a pair of TeX dimensions. The default units are big (PostScript) points; thus, [1in,1in] and [72,72] are equivalent. If only one optional argument is given, the lower-left corner of the image is assumed to be located at [0,0]. Otherwise, [llx, lly] specifies the coordinates of that point. Without optional arguments, the size of the graphic is determined by reading the external *file* (containing the graphics itself or a description thereof; see below).

The starred form of the \includegraphics command "clips" the graphics image to the size of the specified bounding box. In the normal form (without the *), any part of the image that falls outside the specified bounding box overprints the surrounding text.

The examples in the current and next sections all use a small graphic showing the LaTeX hummingbird logo. It is a small PDF graphic with a width of 100pt and a height of 80pt. Being a typical .pdf graphic, the lower-left coordinate of its bounding box is at 0 0, and the top-right corner is at [98,76] in big points (bp), which means it is slightly wider than high.

In the examples we always embed the \includegraphics command in an \fbox (with a blue frame and zero \fboxsep) to show the space that LaTeX reserves for the included image. In addition, the baseline is indicated by the horizontal rules produced by the \HR command, defined as an abbreviation for \rule{1em}{0.4pt}.

The first example shows the inclusion of the latex-logo.pdf graphic at its natural size. We have omitted the file extension, but the graphics is found nevertheless by searching for the file, adding supported extensions one after another until a match is made.[1]

```
\usepackage{graphics,color}
\newcommand\HR{\rule{1em}{0.4pt}}
\newcommand\bluefbox[1]
        {\textcolor{blue}{\setlength\fboxsep{0pt}%
                    \fbox{\textcolor{black}{#1}}}}

L\HR\bluefbox{\includegraphics{latex-logo}}\HR R
```

8-1-1

Next, we specify a box that corresponds to a part of the picture (and an area outside it) so that some parts fall outside its boundaries, overlaying the material

---

[1] The advantage is that your document may work with different device drivers supporting distinct graphics formats, if you supply both formats together with your document. The disadvantage is that you make LaTeX work harder in trying to find a suitable graphics file.

surrounding the picture. If the starred form of the command is used, then the picture is clipped to the box, as shown on the right.

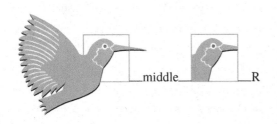

```
\usepackage{graphics,color}
% \bluefbox and \HR as before
L\HR
 \bluefbox{\includegraphics
          [50,25][85,60]{latex-logo.pdf}}%
\HR middle\HR
 \bluefbox{\includegraphics*
          [50,25][85,60]{latex-logo.pdf}}%
\HR R
```

8-1-2

In the remaining examples we combine the \includegraphics command with other commands of the graphics package to show various methods of manipulating an included image. (Their exact syntax is discussed in detail in Section 8.2.) We start with the \scalebox and \resizebox commands. In both cases we can either specify a change in one dimension and have the other scale proportionally or specify both dimensions to distort the image.

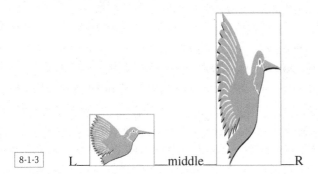

```
\usepackage{graphics,color}
% \bluefbox and \HR as before
L\HR
  \bluefbox{\scalebox{.5}{%
    \includegraphics{latex-logo.pdf}}}%
\HR middle\HR
  \bluefbox{\scalebox{.5}[1.5]{%
    \includegraphics{latex-logo.pdf}}}%
\HR R
```

8-1-3

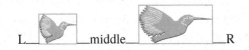

```
\usepackage{graphics,color}
% \bluefbox and \HR as before
L\HR
  \bluefbox{\resizebox{10mm}{!}{%
    \includegraphics{latex-logo.pdf}}}%
\HR middle\HR
  \bluefbox{\resizebox{20mm}{10mm}{%
    \includegraphics{latex-logo.pdf}}}%
\HR R
```

8-1-4

Adding rotations makes things even more interesting. Note that in comparison to Example 8-1-1 on the facing page the space reserved by LATEX is far bigger. LATEX "thinks" in rectangular boxes, so it selects the smallest size that can hold the rotated image. To better visualize this behavior, we have added an additional \frame around the graphic that is rotated with it.

```
\usepackage{graphics,color}
% \bluefbox and \HR as before

L\HR
  \bluefbox{\rotatebox{25}{%
    \frame{\includegraphics{latex-logo.pdf}}}}%
\HR R
```

8-1-5

8.1.3 The \includegraphics syntax in the graphicx package

The extended graphics package graphicx also implements \includegraphics but offers a syntax for including external graphics files that is somewhat more transparent and user-friendly. With today's TeX implementations, the resultant processing overhead is negligible, so we suggest using this interface.

\includegraphics*[*key/value list*]{*file*}

The starred form of the command exists only for compatibility with the standard version of \includegraphics, as described in Section 8.1.2. It is equivalent to specifying the clip key.

The *key/value list* is a comma-separated list of *key=value* pairs for keys that take a value. For Boolean keys, specifying just the key is equivalent to *key*=true; not specifying the key is equivalent to *key*=false. Possible keys are listed below:

viewport   This key defines the area of the graphic for which LaTeX reserves space. Material outside is also printed and thus may overprint nearby material (use clip to prevent this). The key takes four dimension arguments separated by spaces. They denote the lower-left and the upper-right corner of the reserved area measured from the graphics bounding box specified in the file or with the bb keyword (see below). For example, to describe a 20bp square 10bp to the right and 15bp above the lower-left corner of the picture you would specify viewport=10 15 30 35.

trim   Same functionality as the viewport key, but this time the four dimensions correspond to the amount of space to be trimmed (cut off) at the left-hand side, bottom, right-hand side, and top of the included graphics.

clip   Clip the graphic to the area specified by viewport, by trim, or by its bounding box (specified in the file or with bb). Material outside the area is suppressed. It is a Boolean, either "true" or "false".

Note, however, that this key cannot be used to censor data: the clipped material is still inside the output file, and only the printing is suppressed!

draft   A Boolean-value key to switch to draft mode for this image.

The next seven keys (`angle` through `keepaspectratio`) have to do with rotation or scaling of the included material. Similar effects can be obtained with the graphics package and the \includegraphics command by placing the latter inside the argument of a \resizebox, \rotatebox, or \scalebox command (see the examples in Section 8.1.2 and the in-depth discussion of these commands in Section 8.2).

angle   The rotation angle (in degrees, counterclockwise).

origin   The origin for the rotation, similar to the `origin` parameter of the \rotatebox command described on page 591 and in Figure 8.1 on page 593.

scale   A scale factor to scale both width and height equally.

width,height   The required width or height (the image is scaled to that value). If both are given, the image is distorted unless `keepaspectratio` is also used.

totalheight   The required total height (height + depth of the image is scaled to that value). This key should be used instead of `height` if images are rotated more than 90 degrees, because the height can disappear (and become the depth) and LATEX may have difficulties satisfying the user's request.

keepaspectratio   A Boolean variable. If set, specifying both the `width` and `height` parameters does not distort the picture, but the image is scaled so that neither the `width` nor `height` *exceeds* the given dimensions.

Especially for PostScript images there are a few keys that allow altering the bounding box information. With most other graphic types bb acts like `viewport`.

bb   The bounding box of the graphics image overwriting any specification in the image. Like `viewport`, its value field must contain four dimensions, separated by spaces to specify lower-left and upper-right corner.[1]

natheight, natwidth   The natural height and width of the graphics.[2]

hiresbb   Makes LATEX search for %%HiResBoundingBox comments instead of the normal %%BoundingBox. Some applications use this key to specify more precise bounding boxes, because the numbers can normally have only integer values. It is a Boolean, either "true" or "false".

---

[1]This key can be important when working with .eps or .ps graphics where the bounding box information is often incorrect.

[2]These arguments can be used for setting the lower-left coordinate to (0,0) and the upper-right coordinate to (natwidth,natheight) and are thus equivalent to bb=0 0 w h, where w and h are the values specified for these two parameters.

Finally, there are a few keys (`type`, `ext`, `read`, and `command`) to handle special cases of lesser importance today; for details see the package documentation.

If sizes are given without units (e.g., in `viewport`, `trim`, etc.), then TeX's bp "big points" are assumed because this is the standard with PostScript or PDF.

Order of keys is important It is important to note that keys are read from left to right, so that [`angle=90, totalheight=2cm`] means rotate by 90 degrees and then scale to a height of 2 cm, whereas [`totalheight=2cm, angle=90`] would result in a final *width* of 2 cm.

By default, LaTeX reserves for the image the space specified either in the file or in the *key/value list*. If any part of the image falls outside this area, it overprints the surrounding text. If the starred form is used or the `clip` option is specified, any part of the image outside this area is not printed.

Below we repeat some of the examples from Section 8.1.2 using the syntax of the graphicx package, showing extra facilities offered by the extended package. In most cases the new form is easier to understand than the earlier version. In the simplest case without any optional arguments, the syntax for the \includegraphics command is the same in both packages.

If we use the `draft` key, we get just a frame showing the bounding box. This feature is not offered by the **graphics** package on the level of individual graphics.

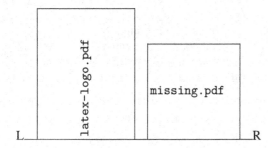

```
\usepackage{graphicx}
% \HR as before
L\HR
 \includegraphics[draft,angle=90]
                {latex-logo.pdf}%
 \HR
 \includegraphics[draft]{missing.pdf}%
 \HR R
```

8-1-6

If the images are available and accessible on the computer system, LaTeX reads out the bounding box information and produces a frame matching the image size while taking into account the effects of other keys, e.g., for rotation. Otherwise, as with the file `missing.pdf` above, you get a generic rectangle. Thus, in that case pagination is likely to change once the real image is included.

The effects of the `bb`, `clip`, `viewport`, and `trim` keys are seen in the following examples. Compare them with Example 8-1-2 on page 579.

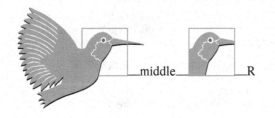

```
\usepackage{graphicx,color}
% \bluefbox and \HR as before
L\HR\bluefbox{\includegraphics
       [bb=50 25 85 60]{latex-logo.pdf}}%
\HR middle\HR
 \bluefbox{\includegraphics
       [bb=50 25 85 60,clip]{latex-logo.pdf}}%
 \HR R
```

8-1-7

Using `viewport` or `trim` allows us to specify the desired result in yet another way. Notice that we actually trim a negative amount, effectively enlarging the space reserved for the picture.

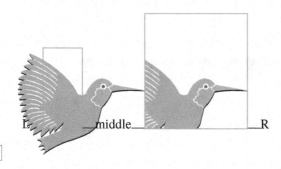

```
\usepackage{graphicx,color}
% \bluefbox and \HR as before
L\HR\bluefbox{\includegraphics
             [viewport=20 20 50 80]
             {latex-logo.pdf}}%
\HR middle\HR
\bluefbox{\includegraphics
          [trim= 20 20 0 -30,clip]
          {latex-logo.pdf}}%
\HR R
```

8-1-8

If you want to apply a scale factor to the image, use the `scale` key. With this key, however, you can only scale the picture equally in both directions.

8-1-9

```
\usepackage{graphicx,color}
% \bluefbox and \HR as before
L\HR \bluefbox{\includegraphics[scale=.5]{latex-logo.pdf}}\HR R
```

To make the dimensions of an image equal to a given value, use the `width` or `height` key (the other dimension is then scaled accordingly). If you use both keys simultaneously, you can distort the image to fit a specified rectangle, as shown in the following example:

```
\usepackage{graphicx,color}
% \bluefbox and \HR as before
L\HR\bluefbox{\includegraphics
             [width=15mm]{latex-logo.pdf}}%
\HR middle\HR\bluefbox{\includegraphics
                       [height=15mm,width=25mm]
                       {latex-logo.pdf}}\HR R
```

8-1-10

You can make sure that the aspect ratio of the image itself remains intact by specifying the `keepaspectratio` key. LaTeX then fits the image as best it can to the rectangle you specify.

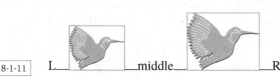

```
\usepackage{graphicx,color}
% \bluefbox and \HR as before
L\HR\bluefbox{\includegraphics[keepaspectratio,
     height=25mm,width=15mm]{latex-logo.pdf}}%
\HR middle\HR\bluefbox{\includegraphics
     [keepaspectratio,height=15mm,width=25mm]
     {latex-logo.pdf}}\HR R
```

8-1-11

Rotations using the `angle` key add another level of complexity. The reference point for the rotation is the reference point of the original graphic — normally the lower-left corner if the graphic has no depth. By rotating around that point, the height and depth change so that the graphic moves up and down with respect to the baseline, as can be seen in the next examples.

```
\usepackage{graphicx,color}    % \bluefbox and \HR as before
L\HR  \bluefbox{\includegraphics[angle=10]{latex-logo.pdf}}\HR
middle\HR\bluefbox{\includegraphics[angle=125]{latex-logo.pdf}}\HR R
```

8-1-12

The real fun starts when you specify both a dimension and a rotation angle for an image, because the order in which they are given matters. The graphicx package interprets the keys *from left to right*. You should pay special attention if you plan to rotate images and want to set them to a certain height. The next examples show the difference between specifying an angle of rotation before and after a scale command. In the first case, the picture is rotated, and then the result is scaled. In the second case, the picture is scaled and then rotated.

```
\usepackage{graphicx,color}
% \bluefbox and \HR as before
L\HR\bluefbox{\includegraphics
        [angle=45,width=10mm]{latex-logo.pdf}}%
\HR middle\HR
\bluefbox{\includegraphics
        [width=10mm,angle=45]{latex-logo.pdf}}%
\HR R
```

8-1-13

LaTeX considers the height and the depth of the rotated bounding box separately. The `height` key refers only to the height; that is, it does not include the depth. In general, the total height of a (rotated) image should fit in a given space, so you should use the `totalheight` key (see Figure 8.1 on page 593 for a description of the various dimensions defining a LaTeX box). Of course, to obtain special effects you can manipulate rotations and combinations of the `height` and `width` parameters at will. The results change considerably if `totalheight` is used instead:

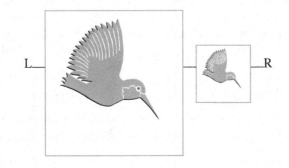

```
\usepackage{graphicx,color}
% \bluefbox and \HR as before
L\HR\bluefbox{%
   \includegraphics[angle=-50,%
                    height=15mm]%
      {latex-logo.pdf}}\HR
\bluefbox{%
   \includegraphics[angle=-50,%
                    totalheight=15mm]%
      {latex-logo.pdf}}\HR R
```

8-1-14

Specifying both `width` and `height` or `totalheight` is likely to distort the image unless we also use `keepaspectratio`:

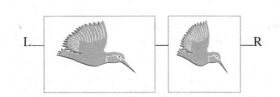

```
\usepackage{graphicx,color}
% \bluefbox and \HR as before
L\HR\bluefbox{%
   \includegraphics
      [angle=-50,totalheight=20mm,%
       width=30mm]{latex-logo.pdf}}\HR
\bluefbox{%
   \includegraphics
      [angle=-50,totalheight=20mm,%
       width=30mm,keepaspectratio]%
      {latex-logo.pdf}}\HR R
```

8-1-15

8.1.4 Setting default key values for the graphicx package

Instead of specifying the same set of key/value pairs over and over again on individual `\includegraphics` commands, you can specify global default values for keys associated with such commands. To do so, you use the `\setkeys` declaration provided by the keyval package, which is automatically included when **graphicx** is used.

`\setkeys{`*identifier*`}{`*key/value list*`}`

The *identifier* is an arbitrary string defined by the macro designer. For example, for `\includegraphics` the string `Gin` was chosen. The *key/value list* is a comma-separated list of key/value pairs.

As an example, consider the case where **graphicx** is used and all figures are to be scaled to the width of the line. Then you would specify the following:

```
\setkeys{Gin}{width=\linewidth}
```

All images included with the \includegraphics command are automatically scaled to the current line width. (Using \linewidth in such a case is usually preferable to using \columnwidth, because the former changes its value depending on the surrounding environment, such as quote.)

You can specify defaults in a similar way for any key used with the \rotatebox command (the other command that has a key/value syntax when graphicx is used). It has the *identifier* Grot; thus,

```
\setkeys{Grot}{origin=ct}
```

specifies that ct should be used for the origin key on all \rotatebox commands unless locally overwritten. See Figure 8.1 on page 593 for default values for origin.

8.1.5 Declarations guiding the inclusion of images

While key/value pairs can be set only when the graphicx package is used, the declarations described in this section can be used with both the graphics and the graphicx packages.

Where to find image files

By default, LaTeX looks for graphics files in the same directories where it looks for other files. But for larger projects it might be preferable to keep the image files together in a single directory or in a set of directories. A list of directories where LaTeX should search for graphics files can be specified through the command \graphicspath, whose argument is a list of directories, each inside a pair of braces {} (even if the list contains only one directory). For example,

```
\graphicspath{{./images/}{./pdfs/}}
```

causes LaTeX to look in the subdirectories images and pdfs of the current directory.

Defining the file extension search order

If you specify a graphic file without giving its extension in the argument of the \includegraphics command, then LaTeX loops through a list of "allowed" extensions, appending each in turn until a file corresponding to the generated full file name is found. This list differs depending on the device driver; for example, when you produce PDF documents with pdfTeX or LuaTeX, it is:

```
.pdf,.png,.jpg,.mps,.jpeg,.jbig2,.jb2,.PDF,.PNG,.JPG,.JPEG,.JBIG2,.JB2
```

whereas if you generate a dvi file for use with dvips, the list looks quite different, because that output device only understands PostScript-oriented formats:

```
.eps,.ps,.eps.gz,.ps.gz,.eps.Z,.mps
```

In normal circumstances the supported extensions and the search order need not to be altered, but if necessary you can do so with a \DeclareGraphicsExtensions declaration. If, for example, most of your images are always of type jpg or png, then declaring

```
\DeclareGraphicsExtensions{.jpg,.png}
```

speeds up the processing because at most two searches are made for each image. If you want to enforce that all graphics are specified with their extension, then use \DeclareGraphicsExtensions with an empty argument.

Because the algorithm tests for the existence of a file to determine which extension to use if it is not provided, the graphics file must exist at the time LᴬTEX is run. However, if a file extension *is* specified, such as \includegraphics{gr.jpg} instead of \includegraphics{gr}, then the graphics file need not exist at the time of the LᴬTEX run.

In either case LᴬTEX needs to know the size of the image, however, so it must be specified in the arguments of the \includegraphics command or in a file actually read by LᴬTEX. (This file can be either the graphics file itself or another file specified with the read key or constructed from the list of file extensions. In the latter case the file must exist at the time LᴬTEX is run.)

The action that has to take place when a file with a given extension is encountered is controlled through \DeclareGraphicsRule declarations. Within limits this makes it possible to add support for additional file formats; see the package documentation on how to achieve this.

8.2   Manipulating graphical objects in LᴬTEX

In the previous section we discussed how to load external graphic files and what LᴬTEX offers to hide or at least encapsulate system-dependent aspects of the loading process. After loading, such images are simply boxes without any inner structure to LᴬTEX. In this section we now look at general manipulation possibilities for boxes. The functions offered can be applied to any LᴬTEX box and not just to those holding an external image.

We start with the commands offered by the standard graphics and graphicx packages and discuss scaling, rotating, and similar operations. After a brief look at the rotating package we then examine the overpic package, which marries the \includegraphics mechanism with that of a LᴬTEX picture environment. This offers an easy, yet powerful, way to annotate images with text and line graphics, like arrows, etc. We conclude with an evaluation of the adjustbox package that provides box manipulation possibilities with a powerful and convenient key/value syntax.

8.2.1   Image and box manipulations with graphics and graphicx

In addition to the \includegraphics command, the graphics and graphicx packages implement a number of graphical manipulation commands. With the exception of the \rotatebox command, which supports a key/value syntax in the graphicx package, the syntax for these commands is identical in both packages.

Scaling a LᴬTEX box

The \scalebox command lets you magnify or reduce text or other LᴬTEX material by a scale factor.

> `\scalebox{`*h-scale*`}[`*v-scale*`]{`*material*`}`

The first of its arguments specifies the factor by which both dimensions of the *material* are to be scaled. The following example shows how this works:

This text is normal.

This text is large.

<small>This text is tiny.</small>

```
\usepackage{graphics} % or graphicx
\noindent      This text is normal. \\[5pt]
\scalebox{3} {This text is large.} \\
\scalebox{0.5}{This text is tiny.}
```

8-2-1

A supplementary optional argument, if present, specifies a separate vertical scaling factor. It is demonstrated in the following examples, which also show how multiple lines can be scaled by using the standard LaTeX `\parbox` command.

America
&
Europe

America
&
Europe

```
\usepackage{graphics} % or graphicx
\fbox{\scalebox{2.2}{%
    \parbox{.5in}{America \& \\ Europe}}}
\fbox{\scalebox{2.2}[1]{%
    \parbox{.5in}{America \& \\ Europe}}}
```

8-2-2

> `\reflectbox{`*material*`}`

This command is a convenient abbreviation for `\scalebox{-1}[1]{`*material*`}`, as seen in the following example:

North America? ɐɔᴉɹǝɯ∀ ɥʇɹoN
South America? ɐɔᴉɹǝɯ∀ ɥʇnoS

```
\usepackage{graphics} % or graphicx
\noindent
North America?\reflectbox{North America?}       \\
South America?\scalebox{-1}[1]{South America?}
```

8-2-3

More interesting special effects can also be obtained. Note in particular the use of the zero-width `\makebox` commands, which hide their contents from LaTeX and thus offer the possibility of fine-tuning the positioning of the typeset material.

North America? ¿ɐɔᴉɹǝɯ∀ ɥʇnoS
North America? ¿ɐɔᴉɹǝɯ∀ ɥʇnoS
North America? ¿ɐɔᴉɹǝɯ∀ ɥʇnoS
North America? ¿ɐɔᴉɹǝɯ∀ ɥʇnoS

```
\usepackage{graphics} % or graphicx
\noindent
North America?\scalebox{-1}{South America?}       \\
North America?\scalebox{1}[-1]{South America?}    \\
North America?%
    \makebox[0mm][r]{\scalebox{-1}{South America?}} \\
\makebox[0mm][l]{North America?}%
    \scalebox{1}[-1]{South America?}
```

8-2-4

Resizing to a given size

It is possible to specify that LaTeX material should be typeset to a fixed horizontal or vertical dimension:

```
\resizebox*{h-dim}{v-dim}{material}
```

When the aspect ratio of the material should be maintained, then it is enough to specify one of the dimensions, replacing the other dimension with a "!" sign.

```
\usepackage{graphics} % or graphicx
\fbox{\resizebox{5mm}{!}{%
    \parbox{14mm}{London,\\ Berlin, \&\\ Paris}}}
\fbox{\resizebox{!}{15mm}{%
    \parbox{14mm}{London,\\ Berlin, \&\\ Paris}}}
```

8-2-5

When explicit dimensions for both *h-dim* and *v-dim* are supplied, then the contents can be distorted. In the following example the baseline is indicated by a horizontal rule drawn with the \HR command.

```
\usepackage{graphics} % or graphicx
\HR\begin{tabular}{lll}
        Köln & Lyon    & Oxford \\
        Rhein   & Rhône & Thames
\end{tabular}\HR\par\bigskip
\HR\resizebox{2cm}{.5cm}{%
    \begin{tabular}{lll}
        Köln & Lyon    & Oxford \\
        Rhein   & Rhône & Thames
\end{tabular}}\HR
```

— Köln   Lyon   Oxford
   Rhein   Rhône   Thames —

— Köln Lyon Oxford
   Rhein Rhône Thames —

8-2-6

As usual with LaTeX commands involving box dimensions, you can refer to the natural lengths \depth, \height, \totalheight, and \width as dimensional parameters:

London,
Berlin, &
Paris

London,
Berlin, &
Paris

```
\usepackage{graphics} % or graphicx
\HR\fbox{\resizebox{\width}{.7\height}{%
    \parbox{14mm}{London,\\ Berlin, \&\\Paris}}}\HR
\fbox{\resizebox{\width}{.7\totalheight}{%
    \parbox{14mm}{London,\\ Berlin, \&\\Paris}}}\HR
```

8-2-7

The unstarred form \resizebox bases its calculations on the height of the LaTeX material, while the starred \resizebox* command takes into account the total

589

height (the depth plus the height) of the LaTeX box. The next `tabular` examples, which have a large depth, show the difference:

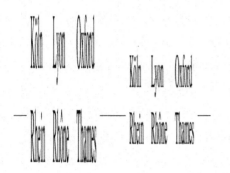

```
\usepackage{graphicx}

\HR\resizebox{20mm}{30mm}{%
    \begin{tabular}{lll}
       Köln & Lyon    & Oxford \\
       Rhein  & Rhône & Thames
    \end{tabular}}\HR
\HR\resizebox*{20mm}{30mm}{%
    \begin{tabular}{lll}
       Köln & Lyon    & Oxford \\
       Rhein  & Rhône & Thames
    \end{tabular}}\HR
```

8-2-8

Rotating a LaTeX box

LaTeX material can be rotated through an angle with the `\rotatebox` command. An alternative technique useful with environments is described in Section 8.2.1.

> `\rotatebox{`*angle*`}{`*material*`}`

The *material* argument is typeset inside a LaTeX box and rotated through *angle* degrees counterclockwise around the reference point.

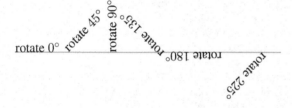

```
\usepackage{graphics} % or graphicx
\newcommand\MyRot[1]{\rotatebox{#1}%
                    {rotate $#1^\circ$}}

\MyRot{0}   \MyRot{45} \MyRot{90}
\MyRot{135}\MyRot{180}\MyRot{225}
```

8-2-9

The rotation algorithm

To understand where the rotated material is placed on the page, we need to look at the algorithm employed. Below we show the individual steps carried out when rotating `\fbox{text}` by 75 degrees. Step 1 shows the unrotated text; the horizontal line at the left marks the baseline. First the *material* (in this case, `\fbox{text}`) is placed into a box. This box has a reference point around which, by default, the rotation is carried out. This is shown in step 2 (the original position of the unrotated material is shown as well for reference purposes). Then the algorithm calculates a new bounding box (i.e., the space reserved for the rotated material), as shown in step 3. Next the material is moved horizontally so that the left edges of the new and the old bounding boxes are in the same position (step 4). TeX's typesetting position is then advanced so that additional material is typeset to the right of the bounding box in its new position, as shown by the line denoting the baseline in step 5. Step 6 shows the final result, again with the baseline on both sides of the rotated material.

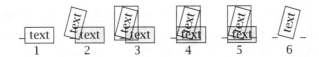

$$\underline{\text{text}}_1 \quad \underline{\text{text}}_2 \quad \underline{\text{text}}_3 \quad \underline{\text{text}}_4 \quad \underline{\text{text}}_5 \quad \underline{\text{text}}_6$$

For more complex material it is important to keep in mind the location of the reference point of the resulting box. The following example shows how it can be shifted by using the placement parameter of the \parbox command.

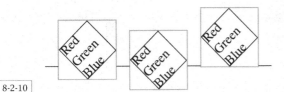

```
\usepackage{color,graphics} % or graphicx
\HR\bluefbox{\rotatebox{45}{%
    \fbox{\parbox{3em}{Red\\Green\\Blue}}}}%
\HR\bluefbox{\rotatebox{45}{%
    \fbox{\parbox[t]{3em}{Red\\Green\\Blue}}}}%
\HR\bluefbox{\rotatebox{45}{%
    \fbox{\parbox[b]{3em}{Red\\Green\\Blue}}}}\HR
```

8-2-10

The extended graphics package graphicx offers more flexibility in specifying the point around which the rotation is to take place by using *key/value* pairs.

\rotatebox[*key/value list*]{*angle*}{*material*}

The four possible keys in this case are origin, x, y, and units. The possible values for the origin key are shown in Figure 8.1 on page 593 (one value each for the horizontal and vertical alignments can be chosen), as are the actual positions of these combinations with respect to the LATEX box produced from *material*.

The effect of these possible combinations for the origin key on an actual LATEX box can be studied below, where two matrices of the results are shown for 90-degree and 45-degree rotated boxes. To better appreciate the effects, the unrotated text is shown against a gray background.

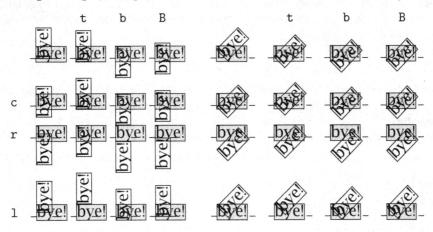

If the symbolic specification of the `origin` is not enough, you also can supply explicit x and y coordinates (relative to the reference point) for the point around which the rotation is to take place. For this purpose, use the keys x and y and the format x=*dim*, y=*dim*. A matrix showing some sample values and their effect on a box rotated by 90 degrees appears below:

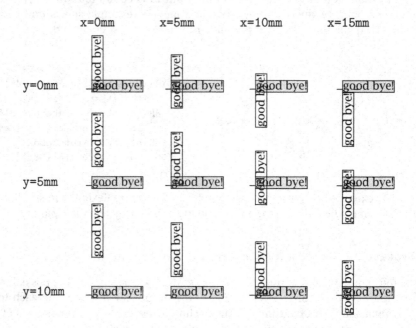

The interpretation of the *angle* argument of `\rotatebox` can be controlled by the `units` keyword, which specifies the number of units counterclockwise in a full circle. The default is 360, so using `units=-360` would mean that angles are specified clockwise. Similarly, a setting of `units=6.283185` changes the degree specification to radians. Rather than changing the `units` key on individual `\rotatebox` commands, you should probably set up a default interpretation using the `\setkeys` declaration as described in Section 8.1.4.

rotating — Revisited

The material in this section is similar to that of Sebastian Rahtz's **rotating** package, which was introduced in Section 7.3.3 on page 533. The functionality of rotating is implemented in this package through the environments `turn` and `rotate`; the latter environment generates an object that occupies no space.

Turning 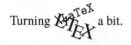 a bit.

```
\usepackage{rotating}

Turning
\begin{rotate}{-20}\Large\LaTeX\end{rotate}%
\begin{turn}{20}\verb=\LaTeX=\end{turn}
a bit.
```

8-2-11

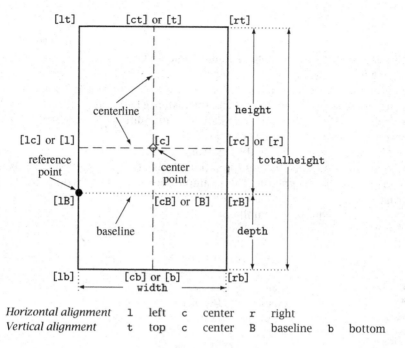

| Horizontal alignment | l | left | c | center | r | right | | |
| Vertical alignment | t | top | c | center | B | baseline | b | bottom |

Figure 8.1: A LATEX box and possible origin reference points

Using environments has the advantage that the rotated material can contain \verb commands. However, the extended syntax of the \rotatebox command is not supported, so in most cases the latter command is preferable.

8.2.2 overpic — Graphic annotation made easy

Sometimes there is a need to annotate a graphic with some text, mark some regions or point to areas with arrows, etc. This can be easily achieved by overlaying the graphic with a picture environment and then adding your annotations with a suitable set of \put commands. The difficulty with this approach is finding the correct coordinate values, and for this the overpic package by Rolf Niepraschk is a great help.

```
\begin{overpic}[key/value list]{file} picture commands \end{overpic}
```

The package defines the environment overpic, which takes a graphic *file* as its mandatory argument and loads it using \includegraphics. The environment body should consist of *picture commands*, which are then placed on top of the image. By default the \unitlength is chosen so that the longer edge of the graphic has a length of 100 × \unitlength. This way your annotations stay in place if you later decide to scale the graphic because the coordinates are relative to the size of the graphic.

Instead of the \unitlength as a percentage of the longest edge (keyword percent), you can use permil in the *key/value list* or specify your own relative base with rel, but in most cases the default should be fine.

To guide you while adding the annotations, use grid, which overlays the graphic with grid lines at every 10 units (or if permil is used, at every 100 units). If you want the grid more or less granular, specify the distance between gridlines explicitly with the tics key. Once you have added all your annotations, simply remove the grid keyword again so that the helper grid vanishes.

Any other key specified in the *key/value list* is passed on to \includegraphics of the graphicx package for interpretation. Below, for example, we used the width key to down-scale the graphic. This example shows two kanji written by the author during a workshop at the TUG conference in Tokyo. With the help of the grid it was easy to add the annotations in the right places.

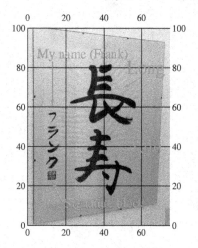

```
\usepackage{overpic,xcolor}
\begin{overpic}[width=.7\textwidth,grid,tics=20]
                {longlife-grayscale.jpg}
  \color{blue}
  \put(5,85){My name (Frank)}
  \put(13,83){\vector(0,-1){22}}

  \put(52,77){\Large Long}
  \put(60,75){\vector(-2,-1){10}}
  \put(55,37){\Large Life}
  \put(54,40){\vector(-2,-1){10}}

  \put(18,12){\vector(-1,2){5}}
  \put(19,9){Signature block}
\end{overpic}
```

8-2-13

\begin{Overpic}[*key/value list*]{*LaTeX code*} *picture commands* \end{Overpic}

The Overpic environment is similar, but instead of an image file, the mandatory argument contains *LaTeX code*, for example, a tabular environment or a math formula. However, only material that can appear inside LR-mode is allowed (if necessary, you need to surround it with a \parbox or a minipage environment).

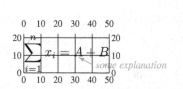

```
\usepackage{overpic,pict2e,color}
\begin{Overpic}[grid,rel=50,tics=10]
               {$ \displaystyle \sum_{i=1}^n x_i = A + B $}
  \color{blue} \Vector(40,5)(32,9)
  \put(42,3){\footnotesize\itshape some explanation}
\end{Overpic}
```

8-2-14

If you want, you can alter the default settings for both environments by using the \setOverpic declaration. It expects a *key/value list* as its argument.

8.2.3 adjustbox — Box manipulation with a key/value interface

When using graphicx, the commands \includegraphics and \rotatebox offer a key/value interface. However, the keys supported by \rotatebox are quite limited, and for other box commands no such interface is available at all, even though keys such a trim or clip could be useful occasionally.

This missing functionality is made available by Martin Scharrer's adjustbox package. The present section covers only the more important aspects of the package; further detail can be found in the extensive documentation [124].

The main command offered is \adjustbox, which can act as a replacement for all standard box commands, such as \mbox, \fbox, etc.; the color box commands, such as \colorbox; the graphics box commands, e.g., \scalebox, \rotatebox; and probably further commands offered by other packages. Mimicking as well as extending these commands is done by supplying the right set of keys.

```
\adjustbox{key/value list}{material}
\begin{adjustbox}{key/value list} material \end{adjustbox}
```

The *key/value list* is given as a mandatory argument because without any keys the command acts just like \mbox, so it would be more economical to use the latter. It is also possible to use an environment form with little difference: one advantage is that you can use verbatim *material* in this case.

When a key expects dimension(s) as its value, you can either specify explicit dimensions or specify just a number in which case the bp (big points) are assumed by default.[1]

Overview about the most important keys

The list of keys supported is formidable; we cover more than thirty here, but in the package documentation you will find many more. First of all, all keys supported by the graphicx package can be used. In the next example we apply a few to mangle the LaTeX logo.

8-2-15

```
\usepackage{adjustbox}

\adjustbox{trim=0 1.7 6.5 0,clip,angle=-10,scale=-1}{\sffamily\huge\LaTeX}
```

Compared to graphicx, the syntax for the trim key is extended and gives you additional options to specify the values for the four sides. If all or several need the same value, then it is sufficient to specify one or two values instead of four.

```
trim=⟨all sides⟩                         trim=⟨left/right⟩␣⟨top/bottom⟩
trim=⟨left⟩␣⟨bottom⟩␣⟨right⟩␣⟨top⟩
```

The package uses this syntax with other keys whenever it is applicable, i.e., when the key expects values for all four sides or for the four corners.

---

[1]The package can be loaded with the option defaultunit, but changing the default may not be a good idea because bp is the de facto standard used everywhere else.

Some of the graphicx keys can be used multiple times; e.g., specifying angle twice will do a rotation equal to the sum of both values. However, operations of other keys such as trim, viewport, or clip are not carried out by LaTeX but in fact later in the device driver. Thus, in that case LaTeX only passes a value, and when using such a key several times, the last invocation wins.

The adjustbox package enables multiple usage through four extra keys starting with an uppercase letter. Trim and Viewport work like their lowercase counterparts, but can be used more than once. However, the clip key has no effect on them. So in order to "trim and clip", the package has Clip, which takes the same values as Trim. The Clip* is similar but interprets its value as a Viewport.

Clipping the corners
With rndcorners a new clipping operation is added; the value consists of one, two, or four dimensions. When two dimensions are given, they refer to the left and the right corners. In the next example we first produce round corners with radius 3bp on the left and 9bp on the right and afterwards shave off 1bp from the bottom (which explains why the lower corners are not round). Swapping the keys then gives us fully rounded corners — order matters.

```
\usepackage{xcolor,adjustbox}
\adjustbox{rndcorners=3 9,Clip=0 1 0 0}{\colorbox{gray!30}{\Large\LaTeX}} \par
\adjustbox{Clip=0 1 0 0,rndcorners=3 9}{\colorbox{gray!30}{\Large\LaTeX}}
```

8-2-16

Accessing the original and changed object dimensions
In the previous example we used explicit values for rounding the corners and trimming the edges. As an alternative we could have made use of commands that hold the sizes of the original box before any manipulation. These are same as with the graphicx package, i.e., \Width, \Height, \Depth, and \Totalheight. For example, rndcorners=.5\Totalheight would give you a half circle on the left and right. However, this works only if the box size is not altered by the keys, e.g., through trimming. The package therefore also defines a similar set of commands with lowercase names that refer to the possibly changed dimensions of the box while the keys are processed. The next example shows the difference:

```
\usepackage{xcolor,adjustbox}
\adjustbox{Clip=0 2 1 0,rndcorners={.5\Totalheight} 0}{\colorbox{gray!30}{\LaTeX}}
                                                                          \par
\adjustbox{Clip=0 2 1 0,rndcorners={.5\totalheight} 0}{\colorbox{gray!30}{\LaTeX}}
```

8-2-17

Note that when you use such dimension commands in places where the syntax is expecting that dimensions are separated by spaces, you have to add a brace group around the dimension as they would otherwise gobble a following space. This is what we did in the previous example.

The package also offers four other dimension commands to refer to the smallest or largest size of the box. The names are \Smallestside and \Largestside for the dimensions of the original box content. The lowercase counterparts reflect any changes during the key processing.

Scaling the box to a specific size
With width, height, and totalheight already available with the graphicx package, you can enforce a certain size of the box. To meet this request the box

content is scaled (by default keeping the aspect ratio). However, with adjustbox further keys are offered. You can, for example, specify that the box has to have a minimum height, or a maximum width, and if the box does not meet this criterion, it is automatically scaled up or down by an appropriate factor.

The key names for this are min␣width, min␣height, and min␣totalheight and max␣width and so forth for the maximum. As a further alternative you can specify that all edges should have a minimum or maximum size by using min␣size or min␣totalsize (for the vertical size \Totalheight, not \Height, is used) and max␣size or max␣totalsize.

As a general alternative there is also the scale key to scale the box up or down. With the graphicx package, i.e., with \includegraphics, only a single factor is allowed, which is then used for both horizontal and vertical scaling. With adjustbox you can use one or two decimal numbers; in the latter case the first specifies the horizontal and the second the vertical scale factor.

---

fbox=⟨rule width⟩␣⟨sep⟩␣⟨outer sep⟩   frame=⟨rule width⟩␣⟨sep⟩␣⟨outer sep⟩

The key fbox supports framed boxes. Its value is a list of up to three dimensions separated by spaces. If used without any value, it produces a frame with the default values for \fbox used by LᴬTEX, i.e., \fboxrule and \fboxsep. By specifying one or two values, you overwrite these defaults. The ⟨outer sep⟩, which has no counterpart with \fbox, adds a (normally) invisible outer margin around the frame, i.e., enlarges the space taken up by the box.

Producing frames around the object

The key frame is like fbox and only differs in the default for ⟨sep⟩, which is zero; i.e., it is modeled after LᴬTEX's \frame command and produces a tight frame around the object if used without a value or only a value for ⟨rule width⟩. With two or three values there is no difference between the two keys. Both keys are exhibited in later examples.

Given that there is the possibility to make rounded corner clippings, it should not be surprising that you can also make frames with rounded corners. The key for this is rndframe, and it has the same value structure as rndcorners. The next example repeats part of Example 8-2-16 from page 596 but adds a frame this time.

Rounded frames

We also show the alternative syntax for the key where the value consists of two brace groups, the first consisting of another key/value list in which you can set the color, the rule width, and the separation between frame and box content. Two other keys are used: with trim we remove 1bp from the bottom of the content so that the frame comes closer to the "X" and at the same time add 2bp on the right (negative trimming means extending) to ensure that the rounded corners do not bump into the "X". With the vspace key we add some space above the box but none below; this is explained later.

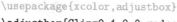

```
\usepackage{xcolor,adjustbox}
\adjustbox{Clip=0 1 0 0,rndcorners=3 9, rndframe=3 9}
         {\colorbox{gray!30}{\Large\LaTeX}}
\adjustbox{trim=0 1 -2 0,rndframe={color=blue,width=1pt,sep=3pt}{3 9},
          vspace=5pt 0pt}{\Large\LaTeX}
```

8-2-18

The extra outer border that can be specified with a third dimension to `fbox` is also available in a generalized form as the key `margin`. If you think about it, adding a margin around the object is equivalent to using `Trim` with negative values. So it comes as no surprise that `margin` accepts one, two, or four dimensions, depending on whether you need different values for the different sides. You can use it multiple times, for example, before and after adding a frame.

An alternate name for `margin` is `padding`, which is preferred by some people. Below we use it to differentiate inner padding from extending the outer margin, but this is just syntactic sugar — we could have used `margin` throughout.

Adding a `margin` to the bottom preserves the baseline of the object; i.e., extra space is added to the depth of the final box. If you use `margin*` instead, then the baseline is shifted downwards by the specified amount. The difference can be clearly seen in the next example: in the first box "LATEX" remains on the baseline, while the second box is raised by a total of $6 + 10 = 16\,\mathrm{bp}$. To prove this visually, a blue rule of that height was added to the example.

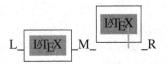

```
\usepackage{xcolor,adjustbox}
L\_\adjustbox{padding=4,frame}{\colorbox{gray}{\LaTeX}}\_%
M\_\adjustbox{padding*=3 6,frame,margin*=0 10 0 0}
         {\colorbox{gray}{\LaTeX}}%
\llap{\color{blue}\rule{1pt}{16bp}\quad}\_R
```

8-2-19

If an `\adjustbox` is placed on its own between paragraphs and needs some vertical separation, then one way to achieve that is to use some appropriate `margin*` setting. However, it is not easy to find the right values because of the subtle interactions between large objects and nearby paragraphs. Usually a better way is therefore to use the `vspace` key. This key takes one or two dimensions as its value and issues `\vspace` commands before and after the box. If you specify only one dimension, then it is used above and below. Alternatively you can use `vspace*`. The difference is that the added space does not vanish at page or column breaks.

If the `\adjustbox` is horizontally aligned with other material in a paragraph, then there are a couple of keys available for making adjustments. With `lap` you can specify that the box overlaps to the left or right by a certain *amount*. Specifying a negative value overlaps to the left. There also exist `llap` and `rlap`, which are shorthands for setting the value to `-\width` or `\width`, respectively. Technically, all of this could be achieved with `trim` or `Trim` keys, but the keys here offer a more natural interface for the task at hand.

With `raise` you can raise (or lower) the box by a specific *amount*. This key accepts in fact up to three dimensions, the other two being *height* and *depth*, with which you can tell LATEX that the resulting box should have these vertical sizes regardless of its contents. This implements the same behavior as LATEX's `\raisebox` command with its optional arguments.

Finally, with the `valign` key you can shift the box vertically through a different method. This key expects a single letter as its value. T, M, and B align at the very top, the middle, or the very bottom, respectively. In contrast t, m, and b take into account the height and depth of a normal line; e.g., t keeps a certain amount above the baseline, which usually aligns much better if the boxes contain text.

The next example shows the `lap`, `raise`, and `valign` keys in action. Note the frames that indicate the space taken up by the boxes as far as LATEX is concerned.

This text is raised while the following text is top-aligned. Note that the word "This" sticks out to the left due to the chosen box settings.

8-2-20

```
\usepackage{adjustbox}  \setlength\parindent{0pt}
\noindent
\adjustbox{lap=-.5\Width,frame}{This text} is
\adjustbox{frame,raise=1ex}{raised}  while the
following \adjustbox{valign=T,frame}{text} is top-aligned.

Note that the word ''This'' sticks out to the left due to
the chosen box settings.
```

With the `width` key you can set a box to a specific width, but this scales the contents to that width. For images this is usually what is wanted, but if your box contains text, then this is often not desired. The adjustbox package therefore offers a number of keys to set the width and the inner alignment. With `left`, `center`, and `right` you can specify a width as the value and then get a box in which the material is set at its normal size and aligned as specified. If you leave out the value, then a default of `\linewidth` is used. If the content is wider than the specified width, it sticks out on the opposite side (in the case of `center` equally on both sides) without causing an overfull box warning.

Boxes of a specific width

Text Text
Text   Text
Text

8-2-21

```
\usepackage{xcolor,adjustbox}
\noindent\adjustbox{width=22mm,cfbox=blue 1pt}{Text}
\adjustbox{color=blue,left=22mm,frame}{Text}             \\
\adjustbox{fgcolor=blue,center=22mm,fbox=1pt}{Text}
\adjustbox{bgcolor=blue!30,right=22mm,frame}{Text}  \\
\adjustbox{center,cfbox=blue 2pt 1pt}{Text}
```

Instead of `left` or `right`, you can use `inner` and `outer`, which align towards the inner and the outer margin, respectively; i.e., different on recto and verso pages. There are in fact a further set of keys that allow aligning the box with respect to the page without regard to the galley margins. They carry names such as `pagecenter`, `pageleft`, etc. For details take a look at the package documentation.

In the previous example we also used some of the keys that deal with coloring. To use them, you have to load an appropriate color package: we used xcolor above. You can specify a color for the complete content (`color`), or just for the background (`bgcolor`), or for the textual material not including things like frames (`fgcolor`). As you can see, the background refers to the original box background, so with keys such as `center` it gives rather questionable results.

Coloring the leaves

To color the frame individually, you can use `cframe` or `cfbox`. They work like `frame` and `fbox` with an additional first argument denoting the color, and as we have seen earlier, `rndframe` also offers a way to color its frame.

599

A possible pitfall when using \begin

Because of the dual nature of \adjustbox as a command and as the start code for an environment (because that is what \begin{adjustbox} internally calls), it is impossible to make use of the convention used by some people to avoid \begin/\end in a definition and simply write

```
\newenvironment{myenv}{\adjustbox{..}}
                      {\endadjustbox}
```

because then \adjustbox would be interpreted as the command, picking up the first nonspace token of the environment body as its second argument. What you can do instead is to write

```
\newenvironment{myenv}{\begin{adjustbox}{..}}
                      {\end{adjustbox}}
```

but it would be better to use the \newadjustboxenv declaration discussed below.

Presetting some keys

With so many keys at your fingertips you may want to preset some of them to be used throughout all or most of your document. This is possible with \adjustboxset declarations and by defining commands or environments with keys preset.

\adjustboxset*{*key/value list*}

If the declaration is used, then the *key/value list* is added to a future invocation of \adjustbox or its environment form. It is additive; i.e., several declarations in succession are combined. However, if you use an empty list argument, then the list becomes empty. Group structures are obeyed; thus, if you use it inside some environment, it reverts to its previous state when the end is reached. To set global defaults you therefore should use the declaration in the preamble of your document.

The difference between normal and starred form is that the latter adds the *key/value list* after the user-supplied keys, whereas the normal former adds them in front so that they can be overwritten by the first argument of \adjustbox. A further difference is that if there are several starred declarations, then they are executed in reverse order; i.e., the last one comes first after those supplied when using \adjustbox.

\newadjustboxcmd{*cmd*} [*num*] [*default*] {*key/value list*}
\newadjustboxenv{*name*} [*num*] [*default*] {*key/value list*}

With \newadjustboxcmd you define a new command *cmd* that behaves in the same way as an \adjustbox that has the *key/value list* as its first argument. Your newly defined command can have *num* arguments with the first being possibly optional using *default* as its default (just like \newcommand). These arguments can be used inside the *key/value list* to allow for some controlled variation. The \newadjustboxenv works in the same way but produces an environment.

8-2-22

| Test | and | Test |

```
\usepackage{xcolor,adjustbox}
\newadjustboxcmd\myfbox[1][.4pt]{angle=20,cfbox=blue #1}
\myfbox{Test} and \myfbox[2pt]{Test}
```

Besides using `\newadjustbox..` you can redefine or provide a definition if it does not already exist or overwrite whatever is there, by using the usual prefixes instead of `\newadjustbox..`, i.e., `\renew..`, `\provide..`, or `\declare..`, for both command or environment form.

Image inclusion revisited

The graphicx package, which was the starting point for adjustbox, already supports the key/value syntax but with only a small subset of the keys discussed above. As most of them are useful for graphics inclusion, adjustbox makes them available in a number of different ways.

```
\adjustimage{key/value list}{image}
\adjincludegraphics[key/value list]{image}
```

The `\adjustimage` command is basically a shorthand for writing

```
\adjustbox{key/value list}{\includegraphics{image}}
```

though somewhat differently implemented. This allows you to make use of all adjustbox keys because the included graphic is simply roped in as the only object inside the box. The `\adjincludegraphics` is similar, except that with this command the *key/value list* is optional, mimicking the syntax model of `\includegraphics`. As a simple example, we define `\fitimage` to load and resize an image to the current line length, i.e., to the width of the `\subcaptionbox` in this case.

```
\usepackage{subcaption,adjustbox}
\newcommand\fitimage[1]
                    {\adjustimage{width=\linewidth}{#1}}
\begin{figure}
  \centering
  \subcaptionbox{A large cat}[.4\linewidth]
                {\fitimage{cat}}
  \qquad
  \subcaptionbox{A small elephant}[.4\linewidth]
                {\fitimage{elephant}}
  \caption{Two animals}
\end{figure}
```

(a) A large cat   (b) A small elephant

8-2-23   Figure 1: Two animals

The package also offers the option `Export`, which alters `\includegraphics` to behave like `\adjincludegraphics`, but it is probably better for new documents to simply use `\adjustimage` throughout.

Changing the `\includegraphics` *behavior*

8.3 Producing (fairly) portable line graphics

If we take a very conservative and narrow point of view, then fully portable graphics in LaTeX are only those that are built from boxes, lines, and characters (i.e., standard LaTeX's `picture` environment), because everything else requires some backend functionality that may not be available in all situations.

However, these days certain graphic functions are available across virtually every backend (even though sometimes with different implementations and interfaces). It is therefore legitimate to consider packages that build upon a restricted set of those (and hide the implementation details from the user) as being portable for all practical purposes. Such a package is pict2e, a reimplementation and extension of LaTeX's `picture` environment functionality using backend features for better quality. This is followed by a brief discussion of bxeepic, which is a reimplementation of the original epic (the first attempt to improve on LaTeX's `picture` environment in a portable way). We finish the section with a package that can produce only one type of graphics: QR-codes for use with mobile devices.

8.3.1 A kernel `picture` environment enhancement

According to the LaTeX manual, `picture` mode coordinates are multiples of `\unitlength` (default value 1pt), i.e., you had to write `\put(2,3){...}`. This allows easy scaling of pictures by changing the value of `\unitlength`, but makes it fairly complicated to base coordinate values on real dimensions, e.g., solving tasks such as "put this object at ⅔ of the `\paperheight`".

In 2020 the LaTeX kernel was therefore extended[1] to also support length expressions as coordinate values, which allows you to write things like

```
\put(\textwidth-2in,0.4\textheight){...}
```

as an alternative to simple numbers that are then multiplied by `\unitlength`. Of course, coordinates written in that way do not change if you alter the `\unitlength`; thus, scaling by altering its value is no longer possible with such pictures. Also note that you can only use expressions with lengths; `\put(1+1,3)` is not supported.

8.3.2 pict2e — An extension of LaTeX's `picture` environment

Standard LaTeX's `picture` environment was originally designed in the mid-eighties to be fully independent of any particulars of the final output device, and to achieve this it drew the graphics using characters taken from special fonts (containing line segments at various angles, etc.). In other words, for TeX a line-graphic was reduced to the question of typesetting and positioning "characters", something that is well understood by the engine.

The downside is obvious: with fonts containing small part of the graphics as characters, only a restricted set of graphics can be drawn. Lines and vectors were available in only a small number of angles, circles could be drawn in only a few discrete sizes, etc.

---

[1] This functionality was originally devised by Heiko Oberdiek in his picture package.

The following example exhibits some of these limitations. Here, the circle and disk on the left are too small (without producing any warning), and the `\line` commands produce errors because the required slope is not available. Compare this result to Example 8-3-2, which shows the correct output — it is strikingly different.

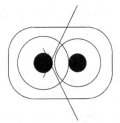

8-3-1

```
\begin{picture}(0,0)
   \put(0,0) {\circle{80}} \put(0,0) {\circle*{24}}
   \put(30,0){\circle{40}} \put(30,0){\circle*{16}}
   \put(15,0){\oval(90,60)}
   \put(0,12){\line(15,-2){30}}\put(0,-12){\line(15,2){30}}
\end{picture}
```

To work around these restrictions different approaches were tried. Systems like PₖCTₑX used tiny dots instead of line segments, but that required a lot of memory and was extremely slow. Other approaches used features of the target output device. This usually produces good results, but the graphics would then work only with that particular output device and not if rendered on the screen or for a different printer (i.e., the same problem one had with loading external graphics or using color: each output device had its own method). Thus, when LATEX 2ε was designed, the idea was born to build a package that defines an abstract syntax hiding the different approaches used by the output devices in a way similar to what was done for loading graphics with the graphics package or selecting colors with color package.

This package, called pict2e, was already announced in Leslie Lamport's book [65] and in the first edition of the LATEX Companion, but for a long time it remained vaporware. Finally in 2003 a first implementation was undertaken by Hubert Gäßlein and Rolf Niepraschk (later joined by Josef Tkadlec).[1]

In its present form it implements all of the original picture environment commands and enhances them in various directions, and with its support for all the major output devices, it offers in effect a device-independent approach to line-graphics.

To exhibit the improvements, the following example repeats Example 8-3-1, except that now pict2e has been loaded and `\maxovalrad` has been used. Now all elements appear correctly as specified.

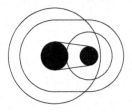

8-3-2

```
\usepackage{pict2e} \renewcommand\maxovalrad{30pt}
\begin{picture}(0,0)
   \put(0,0) {\circle{80}} \put(0,0) {\circle*{24}}
   \put(30,0){\circle{40}} \put(30,0){\circle*{16}}
   \put(15,0){\oval(90,60)}
   \put(0,12){\line(15,-2){30}}\put(0,-12){\line(15,2){30}}
\end{picture}
```

In the remainder of the section we look at all picture environment commands that are enhanced by pict2e and explain the benefits of using the package instead of the basic definitions.

---

[1] A earlier but restricted predecessor was David Carlisle's pspicture package.

Extended or changed commands

Line thickness improvements

With pict2e, the \thinlines, \thicklines, and \linethickness commands alter the thickness of *all* lines, including slanted lines and circular arcs. In standard LaTeX \linethickness applies only to horizontal and vertical lines but not to sloped lines or any other object.

> \line$(x,y)$ {*length*}   \vector$(x,y)$ {*length*}

Lines or vectors are drawn by specifying a slope x,y and the *length* of the line or vector as measured in horizontal direction (unless the slope was vertical, i.e., $(0,\pm 1)$, in which case the *length* specifies the vertical direction).

\line and \vector extensions

In standard LaTeX, only a very limited set of slopes are supported: $-6 \le x, y \le +6$ for lines and only -4 to $+4$ for vectors. Furthermore, the line thickness is restricted to two possible values. With pict2e these restrictions are basically gone, and you can specify decimal numbers in the range of $-1000 \le x, y \le +1000$ for the slope.

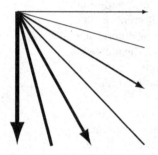

```
\usepackage{pict2e}
\begin{picture}(100,100)
 \put(0,100){\vector(1,0){102.5}}
 \put(0,100){\line(966,-259){100}} \linethickness{1pt}
 \put(0,100){\vector(866,-500){100}}
 \put(0,100){\line(1,-1){100}}      \linethickness{2pt}
 \put(0,100){\vector(500,-866){58}}
 \put(0,100){\line(259,-966){27}}  \linethickness{3pt}
 \put(0,100){\vector(0,-1){100}}
\end{picture}
```

8-3-3

Notice that the length of a vector is the same as that of a line; i.e., the vector tip ends where the line would end. If the specified length is smaller than the vector head, only the head is drawn.

With pict2e you are offered two different styles of arrow heads: the default style for LaTeX as shown in the previous example and the style used by PSTricks shown below. The latter is activated by using the option pstarrows. The command \ltxarrows and \pstarrows can be used inside the picture if you want both types of heads.

```
\usepackage[pstarrows]{pict2e}
\begin{picture}(100,90)
  \put(0,0) {\line(0,1){90}}  % vertical at 0,0
  \put(0,40){\line(1,0){15}}  % horizontal at 0,40
  \put(20,40){\small \LaTeX{} arrow heads used}
\linethickness{4pt}
  \put(0,55){\vector(1,0){15}} \put(0,70){\vector(1,0){50}}
  \put(0,85){\vector(1,0){100}}
\ltxarrows
  \put(0,30){\vector(1,0){15}} \put(0,15){\vector(1,0){50}}
  \put(0,0){\vector(1,0){100}}
\end{picture}
```

LaTeX arrow heads used

8-3-4

```
\circle{diameter}        \circle*{diameter}
```

With the `\circle` command you can produce circles; the starred form produces filled circles. The pict2e package allows you to do this for any *diameter* and any line thickness.

\circle extensions

```
\usepackage{pict2e}
\begin{picture}(100,100)(-35,-25)
 \put(-30,65){\circle{15}} \put(-20,65){\circle{20}}
 \put(-10,65){\circle{25}} \put  (0,65){\circle{30}}
\linethickness{2pt}
 \put (10,65){\circle{35}} \put (20,65){\circle{40}}
 \put (30,65){\circle{45}} \put (40,65){\circle{50}}
\linethickness{4pt}
 \put (50,65){\circle{55}} \put (60,65){\circle{60}}
 \put(-20,20){\circle*{30}} \put(-10,20){\circle*{25}}
 \put  (0,20){\circle*{20}} \put( 10,20){\circle*{15}}
 \put (20,20){\circle*{12}} \put (30,20){\circle*{9}}
 \put (40,20){\circle*{6}}  \put (50,20){\circle*{3}}
\end{picture}
```

8-3-5

Trying the same example with standard LaTeX shows severe restrictions: only a small number of discrete sizes are available (all others are then drawn at the same size), and arbitrary changes to the line thickness are also ignored:

```
% without pict2e package
\begin{picture}(100,100)(-35,-25)
 \put(-30,65){\circle{15}} \put(-20,65){\circle{20}}
 \put(-10,65){\circle{25}} \put  (0,65){\circle{30}}
\linethickness{2pt}
 \put (10,65){\circle{35}} \put (20,65){\circle{40}}
 \put (30,65){\circle{45}} \put (40,65){\circle{50}}
\linethickness{4pt}
 \put (50,65){\circle{55}} \put (60,65){\circle{60}}
  ... further text omitted ...
```

8-3-6

```
\oval(x,y)[part]  (standard LaTeX)     \oval[radius](x,y)[part]  (pict2e)
```

In standard LaTeX you have no control over the shape of an oval besides its size. The corners always consist of a quarter circle of the largest possible radius that still fits (out of the discrete sizes available). With pict2e, this limitation is removed, and so arbitrary large rounded corners are in principle possible. To influence the size of the rounded corners, an optional *radius* argument was added (default 20pt). This argument accepts either a dimension or a plain (decimal) number. In the latter case the value is multiplied with `\unitlength` to obtain the final size to use. The difference is that an explicit dimension always produces identical-looking corners, while a plain number scales with a change in `\unitlength`; thus, both approaches have their use cases. The default value of 20pt can also be altered by redefining `\maxovalrad`.

\oval extensions

The optional *part* argument allows you to draw only one or two corner parts of the oval as shown in the next example.

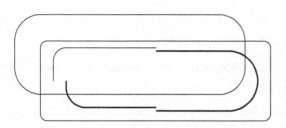

```
\usepackage{pict2e}

\begin{picture}(200,120)
  \put(90,40) {\oval     (180,60)}
  \put(110,20){\oval[5]  (180,60)}
  \put(110,20){\oval[10] (160,50)[tl]}
\thicklines
  \put(110,20){\oval    [15](140,40)[bl]}
  \put(110,20){\oval[8mm] (160,45)[r]}
\end{picture}
```

8-3-7

```
\qbezier[num] (x₁,y₁) (x₂,y₂) (x₃,y₃)
\cbezier[num] (x₁,y₁) (x₂,y₂) (x₃,y₃) (x₄,y₄)        (pict2e only)
```

Bézier curve extensions

With standard LaTeX the \qbezier command plots a quadratic Bézier curve given by the three control points (x_i, y_i). If the optional *num* argument is specified, then the plot consists of that many dots (but not more than \qbeziermax with a default value of 250). If *num* is absent or zero, the curve is made as smooth as possible by plotting it with the largest number of dots allowed, i.e., \qbeziermax.

With pict2e, omitting *num* has the effect that the low-level drawing routines of the output device are used; i.e., \qbeziermax is ignored, and a smooth curve is drawn. The package also adds \cbezier to draw a cubic Bézier curve. This is not available with standard LaTeX.

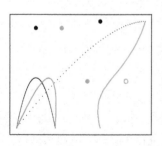

```
\usepackage{xcolor,pict2e}
\NewDocumentCommand\ShowControls{r()d()}
   {\put(#1){\circle*{3}}\IfNoValueF{#2}{\put(#2){\circle{3}}}}
\begin{picture}(110,90)
 \put(0,0){\framebox(110,90){}}
 \qbezier[150](5,5)(20,80)(35,5)          \ShowControls(20,80)
 \qbezier[50](5,5)(70,85)(105,85)         \ShowControls(70,85)
\color{blue}
 \qbezier[0](5,5)(40,80)(35,5)            \ShowControls(40,80)
 \cbezier(70,5)(60,40)(90,40)(105,85)\ShowControls(60,40)(90,40)
\end{picture}
```

8-3-8

All other commands for use in LaTeX's picture environment, such as \dashbox, \framebox, \makebox, \multiput, \put, and \shortstack, are unaltered and act as described in the LaTeX book.

New commands

Above we already saw one new command offered by pict2e — \cbezier. In addition, a number of other useful extensions are offered, which are described in this section.

The most natural way to define a line is specifying just the two endpoints and letting the system calculate the necessary slope and length. In standard LaTeX \line does not work like this because the lines are made up by small line segments with a limited number of slopes. Thus, allowing the specification of arbitrary endpoints would nearly always result in slopes for which no line segment is available. With pict2e that restriction is gone, so this natural input specification can be offered as well. With \line already in use the name \Line was chosen.

\Line $(x_1,y_1)(x_2,y_2)$ \polyline $(x_1,y_1)\cdots(x_n,y_n)$

The \Line command draws a line between the two endpoints, and \polyline draws lines between all of its control points. Because start- and endpoints are explicitly defined in this case, you need not use \put when placing the lines.

You can alter the way line endings are drawn by specifying \buttcap (default method); \roundcap, which adds a half-circle at the endpoint; or \squarecap, which adds a half-square. For joint paths, e.g., in \polyline, the default is called \miterjoin, and you can change the method of joining to \roundjoin, which uses \roundcap on the inner joins of each segment, or \beveljoin, which produces the convex hull of the segment endpoints. Especially with larger line thickness you sometimes get better results by changing to a different method. Example 8-3-13 on page 611 shows some of them in action.

\Vector $(x_1,y_1)(x_2,y_2)$ \polyvector $(x_1,y_1)\cdots(x_n,y_n)$

The \Vector and \polyvector extensions work like \Line and \polyline described above except that they place an arrow head at the end of each line segment, making it possible to define vectors using the more natural input syntax as well; see Example 8-3-9 below.

\polygon $(x_1,y_1)\cdots(x_n,y_n)$ \polygon* $(x_1,y_1)\cdots(x_n,y_n)$

The \polygon command works like \polyline but additionally draws a final line from (x_n,y_n) back to (x_1,y_1) to produce a closed curve. The star form fills the resulting polygon in the current color (or black if color is not used).

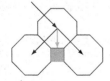

```
\usepackage{xcolor,pict2e}
\newcommand\octet{\begin{picture}(0,0)(15,15)
   \polygon(0,10)(0,20)(10,30)(20,30)(30,20)(30,10)(20,0)(10,0)
\end{picture}}
\begin{picture}(80,60)
   \polyvector(20,60)(40,40)(60,20)  \Vector(40,40)(20,20)
   \put(20,20){\octet} \put(40,40){\octet} \put(60,20){\octet}
   \color{blue}          \polygon*(35,15)(45,15)(45,25)(35,25)
   \Vector(40,40)(40,25)
\end{picture}
```

8-3-9

$$\texttt{\textbackslash arc[}\textit{angle}_1\texttt{,}\textit{angle}_2\texttt{]\{}\textit{radius}\texttt{\}} \qquad \texttt{\textbackslash arc*[}\textit{angle}_1\texttt{,}\textit{angle}_2\texttt{]\{}\textit{radius}\texttt{\}}$$

These two commands are generalizations of \circle and \circle* and allow you to draw the circle segment between the two angles (default is 0,360, i.e., a full circle). Angle 0 starts a three o'clock and is specified counterclockwise. Note that the commands expect the circle *radius* as an argument and not its *diameter*.

```
\usepackage{xcolor,pict2e} \setlength\unitlength{1.5pt}
\begin{picture}(200,120)
  \put(0,0){\arc[90,360]{30}} \polyline(0,30)(0,0)(30,0)
\color{blue}
  \put(2,2){\arc*[0,90]{30}}  \put(0,0){\arc[-2,92]{34}}
  \put(0,0){\arc[-5,95]{36}}  \put(0,0){\arc[-9,99]{38}}
\linethickness{3pt}
  \put(0,0){\arc[90,360]{15}} \put(0,0){\circle*{15}}
\end{picture}
```

8-3-10

The package also offers some low-level support for drawing by exposing the output device path operators with commands such as \moveto, \lineto, \strokepath, etc. For details refer to the package documentation.

8.3.3 bxeepic — A differently enhanced picture environment

Standard LaTeX's picture environment (especially in conjunction with the pict2e reimplementation) allows you to generate line-style graphics of arbitrary complexity through basic commands for drawing lines, vectors, quarter-circles, and Bézier curves. However, creating complex graphics, although possible, requires a lot of manual effort. Most of its picture-drawing commands require explicit specification of coordinates for every *object*, which makes alterations later very difficult.

epic — the first solution

Given that the basic \line command had several drawbacks and was very non-intuitive to use, people started early on to develop alternatives. One of the most successful and influential packages back then was epic by Sunil Podar, which provided a powerful high-level user interface to the picture environment [113]. Its main aim was to reduce the amount of manual calculations required to specify the layout of *objects*. In this way, the epic package made it possible to produce sophisticated pictures with less effort than before even though it inherited the restrictions of the original picture environment commands.

eepic — the device-dependent implementation of epic

As a result, some of the functions took a long time to complete, or the output was not of very high quality. This situation improved with the eepic package, written by Conrad Kwok, which is an extension of both LaTeX and epic. It overcame most of the limitations by using \special commands for drawing that were understood by only some output devices.

In short, it traded device independence for better-looking output, but given that dvips, the predominant output device in the nineties, supported these \special commands, it was often used for high-quality line graphics. However, when pdfTeX

started to become popular and people used that program to produce PDF directly, the
situation changed once more, because eepic stopped working in this workflow.

In 2010 YATO Takayuki then provided a new implementation of most of the
epic commands in a package called bxeepic, this time using pict2e as the underlying
interface. While his implementation does not cover all of the features of epic and eepic,
it is complete enough so that you will seldom find old documents using the original
packages that cannot be processed by exchanging them with the new package. In
fact, when loading bxeepic, the packages epic and eepic are both marked as "already
loaded". Thus if your document later loads another package that itself requests, say,
epic, it does not replace the improved versions with epic's original code.

bxeepic — the successor based on pict2e

The remainder of this section gives you an overview of the most useful commands
of the bxeepic package. There are a number of other special features not discussed,
but if you have needs that go beyond simple line drawings, it is better to switch to a
full-blown graphic system that can be used with LaTeX such as tikz [133] discussed in
Section 8.5 on page 631.

High-level line commands (originating from epic or eepic)

The bxeepic package implements most of epic's powerful line-drawing commands that
offer a simple input syntax. In particular, these commands take only the coordinates
of the end points, thus eliminating the other steps involved in specifying a line.

> \dottedline[*dotchar*]{*dotgap*}$(x_1, y_1) \cdots (x_n, y_n)$

The \dottedline command connects the specified points by drawing a dotted line
between each pair of coordinates. At least two points must be defined. The dotted
line is drawn with an inter-dot gap as specified in the mandatory argument *dotgap*
(in \unitlength). Because the number of dots to be plotted must be an integer, the
inter-dot gap may not come out exactly as specified.

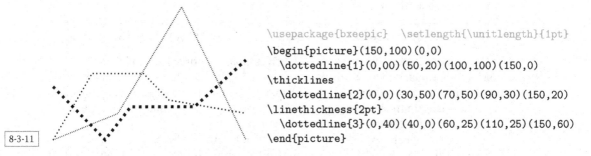

```
\usepackage{bxeepic}   \setlength{\unitlength}{1pt}
\begin{picture}(150,100)(0,0)
   \dottedline{1}(0,00)(50,20)(100,100)(150,0)
\thicklines
   \dottedline{2}(0,0)(30,50)(70,50)(90,30)(150,20)
\linethickness{2pt}
   \dottedline{3}(0,40)(40,0)(60,25)(110,25)(150,60)
\end{picture}
```

8-3-11

For small sizes of line thickness (e.g., \thinlines) the dots are represented
as rectangles; larger dots are then little squares. This is slightly different from the
original epic implementation, which used squares throughout and also supported an
optional *dotchar* argument to specify alternative material for plotting. The latter is
still parsed but not used by bxeepic.

$$\texttt{\textbackslash dashline}\,[\textit{stretch}]\,\{\textit{dashlength}\}\,(x_1,y_1)\cdots(x_n,y_n)$$

The \dashline command connects the specified points by drawing a dashed line between each pair of coordinates. At least two points must be specified. The mandatory parameter *dashlength* determines the length of each dash. In epic there was a second optional argument specifying the gap between the dots that are used to construct the dash. In bxeepic, this argument is parsed but ignored; thus, it always produces solid-looking dashes.

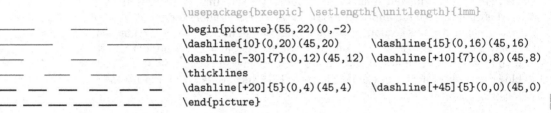

```
\usepackage{bxeepic} \setlength{\unitlength}{1mm}
\begin{picture}(55,22)(0,-2)
\dashline{10}(0,20)(45,20)        \dashline{15}(0,16)(45,16)
\dashline[-30]{7}(0,12)(45,12)  \dashline[+10]{7}(0,8)(45,8)
\thicklines
\dashline[+20]{5}(0,4)(45,4)      \dashline[+45]{5}(0,0)(45,0)
\end{picture}
```

8-3-12

In the definition of the \dashline command, the optional *stretch* parameter must be an integer between -100 and ∞. It indicates the percentage by which the number of dashes is increased (*stretch* > 0) or reduced (*stretch* < 0). If *stretch* is zero, the minimum number of dashes compatible with an approximately equal spacing relative to the empty space between the dashes is used. The idea behind the *stretch* percentage parameter is that if several dashed lines of different lengths are being drawn, then all dashed lines with identical *stretch* values have a similar visual appearance. The default settings for the *stretch* percentage can be changed by redefining the command \dashlinestretch:

```
\renewcommand\dashlinestretch{-50} % Only integers permitted
```

Its value defines the increase or reduction that is applied to all subsequent \dashline commands except for those where the *stretch* parameter is explicitly specified as the first optional argument.

$$\texttt{\textbackslash drawline}\,[\textit{stretch}]\,(x_1,y_1)\cdots(x_n,y_n)\qquad \texttt{\textbackslash path}\,(x_1,y_1)\cdots(x_n,y_n)$$

The \drawline command connects the given points by drawing a line between each pair of coordinates; i.e., it provides a similar functionality as \polyline under a different name. In the original epic implementation it used line segments of the closest slope available in the line fonts of LaTeX, so depending on the requested slope, it could look rather jagged. With bxeepic, this is no longer the case.

The optional *stretch* parameter (not available with \polyline) is similar to the one described for the \dashline command. If *stretch* is negative, you get a dashed line; with zero (default) or a positive value, it is a solid line.[1] A possible advantage of \polyline is that it obeys any declaration altering the line segment endings, which can sometimes be useful.

---

[1]With epic a positive value meant that shorter line segments got used, which improved the result at the cost of memory and computing time, but with the bxeepic implementation there is no difference.

The \path command is the same as \drawline without the optional argument.

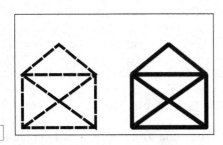

```
\usepackage{bxeepic} \setlength{\unitlength}{2mm}
\begin{picture}(27,16)(-1,-1)
  \path(-1,-1)(-1,15)(26,15)(26,-1)(-1,-1)
  \linethickness{2pt}
  \drawline[-10](0,0)(10,7)(5,11)
       (0,7)(10,0)(10,7)(0,7)(0,0)(10,0)
  \linethickness{3pt} \roundcap \beveljoin
  \polyline(15.1,0.1)(25,7)(20,11)
       (15,7)(25,0)(25,7)(15,7)(15,0)(25,0)
\end{picture}
```

8-3-13

$$\texttt{\textbackslash spline}(x_1,y_1) \cdots (x_n,y_n)$$

The \spline command draws a curve that passes through only the first and last points. All other points act as control points only. For illustration the example also shows a \path command with the same coordinates.

```
\usepackage{xcolor,bxeepic}
\begin{picture}(100,80)
  \thicklines
  \spline(30,0)(0,0)(20,40)(40,10)(60,55)(90,70)(95,0)(100,30)
  \color{blue} \thinlines
  \path   (30,0)(0,0)(20,40)(40,10)(60,55)(90,70)(95,0)(100,30)
\end{picture}
```

8-3-14

$$\texttt{\textbackslash ellipse}\{\textit{x-diameter}\}\{\textit{y-diameter}\} \qquad \texttt{\textbackslash ellipse*}\{\textit{x-diameter}\}\{\textit{y-diameter}\}$$

In analogy to the \circle and \circle* commands of standard LaTeX or pict2e, the \ellipse and \ellipse* commands draw a hollow or filled ellipse using the specified *x-diameter* and *y-diameter* parameters. With only these two parameters available you cannot draw ellipses that are sloped (without rotating the resulting object yourself afterwards). The example below is a variation of Example 8-3-5 from page 605 that used circles.

```
\usepackage{bxeepic,graphicx}
\begin{picture}(100,100)(-35,-25)
  \put(-30,65){\ellipse{20}{15}} \put(-20,65){\ellipse{20}{20}}
  \put(-10,65){\ellipse{20}{25}} \put  (0,65){\ellipse{20}{30}}
  \linethickness{2pt}
  \put (10,65){\ellipse{20}{35}} \put (20,65){\ellipse{20}{40}}
  \put (30,65){\ellipse{20}{45}} \put (40,65){\ellipse{20}{50}}
  \thicklines       \put(-30,20){\rotatebox{30}{\ellipse*{18}{35}}}
  \put(-20,20){\ellipse{20}{30}} \put(-10,20){\ellipse*{22}{25}}
  \put   (0,20){\ellipse{24}{20}} \put( 10,20){\ellipse*{24}{15}}
  \put (20,20){\ellipse{22}{12}} \put (30,20){\ellipse*{20}{9}}
  \put (40,20){\ellipse{18}{6}}  \put (50,20){\ellipse*{16}{3}}
\end{picture}
```

8-3-15

8.3.4 Special-purpose languages

Building on LaTeX's `picture` environment, possibly extended with a package such as epic, eepic, or bxeepic, several package authors have implemented high-level user interfaces intended to make entering graphical information more straightforward and less error prone by adopting a syntax that is more familiar to the end user in a particular application domain. Some of the systems are quite complex (the *LaTeX Graphics Companion* [28] describes several of them in detail). In this section we merely give a flavor of what is possible in this area by showing one example from the XᴵMᴛᴇX bundle by FUJITA Shinsaku for drawing chemical diagrams (see [24, 25] or [28, Chapter 6]).

By using command names inspired by standard nomenclature known to practitioners in the field, complex formulas can be entered simply. In the following example, we use the hetarom subpackage, designed for specifying the structure of vertical heterocyclic compounds.

```
\usepackage{bxeepic,hetarom}
\decaheterov[af]{4==O}
  {1==CH$_3$;6==H$_3$C;9A==H;%
    {{10}A}==\lmoiety{HOCH$_2$}}
\hspace*{-15mm}
\nonaheterov[bjge]{1==S;2==N}{3==Cl}
```

8-3-16

8.3.5 qrcode — Generating Quick Response codes

Today's use of smartphones and tablets has given rise to a widespread appearance of Quick Response (QR) codes. These are very special graphics used to encode arbitrary information into a square matrix of black and white pixels. You scan such a QR code with your mobile device camera, and it shows you the encoded data and — if recognized — offers to process it, e.g., open a hyperlink in the smartphone browser.

While QR codes can encode any type of information up do several kilobytes, the most common usage is to provide easy access to hyperlinks. Try it out with your smartphone on the example below: the first QR code should take you directly to the publication page of the LaTeX Project website, the second could have been made by a modern Lord Peter Wimsey, and the third is Miss Vane's answer in `draft` mode.[1]

8-3-17

As shown in Example 8-3-18 on the facing page, such QR codes can be easily produced by LaTeX with the help of the qrcode package written by Anders Hendrickson.

---

[1] That is, it is not a valid QR code and should not lead anywhere.

This package offers only two commands with the following syntax:

\qrcode*[*key/value list*]{*information*}   \qrset{*key/value list*}

The *information* to be encoded is given in the mandatory argument of \qrcode. With the help of the *key/value list* it can be influenced, e.g., by specifying a height for the matrix as we did in the previous example to give them both a height of 15mm.

Other useful keys define the spacing around the matrix, i.e., tight (default) or padding (extra wide space as mandated by the standard; but usually not needed because the code is usually anyway separated); the level of error correction (values L, M, Q, or H for low, medium, quality, and high); version (value between 1 and 40) defining the number of pixels used and whether a link (default) or nolink should be made. The level and version are normally automatically chosen based on the required size and the amount of *information* that has to be encoded, but to ensure a consistent look and feel or to force a high error correction rate explicit values can be selected.

As most use cases involve encoding hyperlinks, the default assumption is that the *information* is a URL string. If the hyperref package is also loaded, then \qrcode automatically tries to make a hyperlink to this target, which makes little sense if you have encoded a marriage proposal into the QR code. The starred form of the command (or the key nolink) prevents this behavior.

Automatic target links

With the \qrset declaration one can set specific values and overwrite the defaults to avoid the need for using the optional argument on each \qrcode occurrence.

Declaring defaults

The *information* is processed in a semi-verbatim way in which special characters such as #, $, &, ^, _, ~, and % are automatically recognized without the need to escape them. However, if you need \, {, or }, you need to precede each of them with a backslash as shown in the next example. To encode a line break, the command \? can be used. As always, verbatim works only on the top-level, i.e., not inside the argument of another command, so if we want to place a frame around the QR code with \fbox, then all special characters need escaping to be correctly understood.

Use of special symbols

```
\usepackage{qrcode}
\qrset{nolink,padding,level=Q,version=5}
\qrcode[height=15mm]{# $ & ^ _ ~ % \? \\ \{ \} } \quad
\fbox{\qrcode[height=15mm]{\# \$ \& \^ \_ \~ \% \? \\ \{ \} }}
```

8-3-18

Calculating the QR codes takes time, and if you make heavy use of them in a document, it can noticeably slow down the processing. To help with that issue, the package offers two mechanisms. For one it remembers any calculated QR matrix for fast regeneration across LaTeX runs and reuses the result unless you use the package option forget. Furthermore, by specifying the package option draft, no QR code encoding happens, and instead a dummy is inserted in the requested size. When specifying final (default), the codes are calculated. Finally, you can give nolinks, which is equivalent to specifying nolink on each \qrcode instance.

Package options

8.4 Flexible boxes for multiple purposes

Standard LaTeX offers basic box manipulations through the graphics and graphicx packages. This is further extended through adjustbox, but basically boxes remain boxes, and you are confined to adding a simple border, scaling, rotating, or clipping and that's about it.

If you needed other special enhancements, then you had to turn to the few specialized packages available for adding shadows (e.g., shadow by Mauro Orlandini), a frame around a minipage (boxedminipage by Scott Pakin), or the more comprehensive fancybox package by Timothy Van Zandt offering shadows, oval frames, and a few other features, but on the whole the available options are somewhat limited.

This only changed fairly recently when Thomas Sturm introduced his tcolorbox package, which sets out to be a one-stop for any kind of complex box presentation including features like splitting them across pages or other goodies.[1]

The package comes with a huge manual [131] of more than 500 pages. We therefore limit ourselves to show only the main features that are useful in many situations. Thus, if you miss some special feature or find that your desired layout is difficult to achieve, check out that manual, because chances are high that your needs are covered there through additional keys or commands not covered in this book.

8.4.1 tcolorbox — The basic usage

The core functionality of tcolorbox is provided by an environment that builds a box object based on the settings given in its optional *key/value list* argument. We discuss various useful keys throughout this section.

```
\begin{tcolorbox}[key/value list]  top \tcblower bottom \end{tcolorbox}
```

Due to the fact that this is implemented as an environment, the body can contain verbatim material as shown below. As a special feature you can split the body into a top and bottom part using \tcblower. If used without the optional *key/value list*, we get the following result:

A paragraph before with two lines of text to show the indentation and the measure.

A tcolorbox can be subdivided into two parts.

- -

If \tcblower is given then anything below forms the lower part of the box.

And a paragraph after the box.

```
\usepackage{tcolorbox}

A paragraph before with two lines of text
to show the indentation and the measure.
\begin{tcolorbox}
 A \texttt{tcolorbox} can be subdivided
 into two parts.
\tcblower
 If \verb|\tcblower| is given then anything
 below forms the lower part of the box.
\end{tcolorbox}
And a paragraph after the box.
```

8-4-1

---

[1]Another popular general-purpose box package that was developed during the last decade is mdframed by Marco Daniel and Elke Schubert. However, in comparison the tcolorbox package is

Instead or in addition to \tcblower, you can use \tcbline. It too produces a line looking like the separation line produced by \tcblower. The difference is that it does not start a new part of the box, which is important if you use a box style in which the upper and lower parts use different formatting parameters. There is also a \tcbline* variant, which is suppressed if the box is broken across pages and the break happens at that point.

By default the tcolorbox is a display object, as wide as the current line with some separation before and after. The values for the vertical separation can be explicitly given with the keys before␣skip and after␣skip or can be explicitly suppressed with nobeforeafter in which case the box can be used in horizontal context as shown in the next example. In such a situation you normally want to explicitly set the width of the box to something different than its default full width. The example also shows that the content can be split horizontally by adding the key sidebyside.

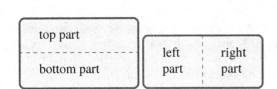

```
\usepackage{tcolorbox}

\begin{tcolorbox}[nobeforeafter,
                  width=.45\linewidth]
    top part \tcblower bottom part
\end{tcolorbox}
\begin{tcolorbox}[nobeforeafter,sidebyside,
                  width=.45\linewidth]
    left part \tcblower right part
\end{tcolorbox}
```

If you use the sidebyside key, then there are several additional keys to influence the appearance, e.g., the ratio between the two regions, the relative positioning of the material, etc. So make sure you check out the details in the manual in case you are interested in this kind of layout.

Keys that you regularly apply to all your boxes do not need to be set in the *key/value list* argument. Instead, you can set them as defaults with the help of a \tcbset declaration. For instance, we set the frame and background color for all boxes to some level of blue and only give a box title on the individual box.

A box title

Default options are better defined using \tcbset{...} for a uniform appearance.

```
\usepackage{tcolorbox}
\tcbset{colback=blue!10!white, colframe=blue}

\begin{tcolorbox}[title=A box title]
  Default options are better defined using
  \verb=\tcbset{...}= for a uniform appearance.
\end{tcolorbox}
```

\tcbox [*key/value list*] {*content*}

The other basic structure is the \tcbox command, which creates a colored box similar to that of a tcolorbox environment but with the width matching the size of the

---

more comprehensive in several areas, and mdframed is no longer actively maintained and as a result has a number of bugs and issues that have been unresolved for several years.

content. It supports most of the keys of `tcolorbox` but is always unbreakable across pages and does not offer a split into an upper and lower part via `\tcblower`. Due to the fact that the *content* is received as an argument, it does not support `\verb` either. However, for simple horizontally oriented material it can be a useful alternative.

Outer box geometry

We have already seen examples of keys that influence the geometry and placement of the box, but there are plenty more. You can expect that for any spatial dimension that could reasonably be given a name, there is a key with which you can set it.

Verticals

As mentioned before the space above and below the box is set with the keys `before␣skip` and `after␣skip`. In most cases the box height is automatically calculated from the content, but with the `height` key you can set it explicitly, if that is necessary.

Horizontals

Horizontally you can set the `width` of the box (the default is `\linewidth` minus the space taken up by the following keys). The keys `left␣skip` and `right␣skip` set the space to the left or right (default `0pt`), which is why we get a full-width box if none of these keys is used.

Bounding box maneuvers

With the keys `grow␣to␣left␣by` or `grow␣to␣right␣by` you can alter the width calculation and make the box stick out to the left or right. That is, the box gets larger by the specified amount, but at the same time the code pretends that it has the same size as before; i.e., it overlaps with other material in that area.

There are also several other keys that alter the size occupied by the box (as far as LaTeX is concerned). For example, `enlarge␣by` adds some space to all four sides of the box. If you need this kind of feature, you will find plenty more such keys altering only some sides of the bounding box.

Inner box geometry

Spacing and padding

For the inner box geometry, there are another dozen keys to play with: if there is a title given for the box, then `toptitle` and `bottomtitle` denote the space left above and below that title.

The keys `left`, `right`, `top`, and `bottom` denote the space between the outer box (e.g., the frame) and the box content, and `middle` sets the space above and below the dividing line if `\tclower` is used. To each of them the value of `boxsep` is added, providing a common extra padding that consistently adds or subtracts space in these places.

In fact, `left` and `right` are only shorthands for setting several specific keys to the same value: `left` sets `lefttitle`, `leftupper`, `leftlower`; `right` sets `righttitle`, `rightupper`, `rightlower`. Thus, if you want different margins in the title box or one of the other compartments, use the individual keys with different values.

Setting the rule width

The rules that make up the border of the box can have different widths (including zero), and the keys to set them are not surprisingly called `leftrule`, `rightrule`, `toprule`, `bottomrule`, and `titlerule`. The next example exhibits a selection from the above keys, set to somewhat random values to show their effects.

616

```
A box title
Lorem ipsum dolor sit amet, consec-
tetuer adipiscing elit.
------------------------------------
Ut purus elit, vestibulum ut, placerat ac,
adipiscing vitae, felis.
```

8-4-4

```
\usepackage{lipsum,tcolorbox}
\tcbset{top=0pt,bottom=0pt,left=5pt,lefttitle=20pt,
        rightlower=0pt,rightrule=15pt}
\begin{tcolorbox}[title=A box title,middle=0pt]
  \lipsum[1][1] \tcblower \lipsum[1][2]
\end{tcolorbox}
```

Note that even though we set various values to 0pt, there is still some space remaining, which is due to boxsep being added (default 1mm).

There are several more keys that deal with specific aspects of the inner geometry. A particularly useful one is size, which sets all geometry parameters except for the width to predefined values. Allowed values for size are normal (default settings), title (use values for title also in other box parts; see Example 8-4-15), small (slightly less padding, Example 8-4-23), fbox (spacing and rule width like \fbox; Example 8-4-16), tight (no padding), and minimal (no padding, no rules).

Text alignment

By default, text in a tcolorbox is justified to the box measures. With the keys halign, halign␣lower, and halign␣title you can alter this alignment for the box components. Allowed values are justify (the default), left, right, and center. They all support hyphenation when applied to ordinary text, similar to the behavior of the ragged2e package.

In addition, there are flush␣left, flush␣right, and flush␣center, which act like \raggedright, \raggedleft, and \centering, i.e., only hyphenate if a word is wider than the line width. For ordinary text the nonflush versions often give a more balanced look albeit with more hyphenated words.

By default tcolorbox formats each box part like a \parbox, which gives you a slightly different paragraph formatting result than what you get on the main galley. For example, paragraphs inside show no indentation. This can be changed by setting the key parbox to false as done in the next example, where the second paragraph in the top part therefore shows an indentation.

```
                                     top part
------------------------------------------------
 bottom part
```

```
                    My title
The paralogisms of practical reason are what first give rise to the archi-
tectonic of practical reason.
    Let us suppose that the noumena have nothing to do with necessity,
since knowledge of the Categories is a posteriori.
------------------------------------------------
    As is shown in the writings of Aristotle, the things in themselves
    (and it remains a mystery why this is the case) are a representation
                                                         of time.
    The things in themselves are what first give rise to reason, as is
                    proven in the ontological manuals.
```

8-4-5

```
\usepackage{kantlipsum,tcolorbox}
\tcbset{top=0pt,middle=1mm,bottom=0pt}
\scriptsize
\begin{tcolorbox}[halign=right]
   top part \tcblower bottom part
\end{tcolorbox}
\begin{tcolorbox}[parbox=false,
     halign title=center,
     halign lower=right,title=My title]
\kant[1][2] \par \kant[2][1]
\tcblower
\kant[3][1] \par \kant[6][1]
\end{tcolorbox}
```

Vertical alignment

By default tcolorbox boxes grow vertically as necessary so that the content comfortably fits in. If, however, the vertical size is set to a fixed value using `height` (or in a `poster` application), then specifying a vertical alignment with `valign` or `valign␣lower` may be necessary. Supported values are `top`, `center`, `bottom`, and `scale`. The latter one scales the content to fit the available space distorting the content along the way and is therefore seldom useful.

Color and fonts

There are several keys that allow you to alter the fonts used and color the frame and background of the different parts of a `tcolorbox`. Most of them are shown in one or the other example.

Font attributes

For fonts there is `fonttitle`, `fontupper`, and `fontlower` to specify font attributes for the respective part of the `tcolorbox`. For example, to get bold sans serif titles you could specify `\sffamily\bfseries` as the value for `fonttitle`.

Coloring components

For coloring there are many more keys: `coltitle`, `colupper`, and `collower` are for coloring the fonts in the different parts. There is also a short-hand `coltext` for setting the previous two keys to the same value. For coloring background parts you can use `colbacktitle`, `colbackupper`, `colbacklower`, or `colback` (using the same color for all parts), and for the coloring frames there is `colframe`.

Altering corners

By default the corners of a `tcolorbox` are rounded, but this can be easily changed for all or some of the corners using the `sharp␣corners` key. Without a value (or the value `all`) all corners are sharpened. By using `northwest`, `northeast`, `southwest`, or `southeast` as the value, you alter one corner. This can be repeatedly done, but this gets a bit tedious. For that reason there are also values for altering two corners in one go, i.e., `north`, `east`, `south`, `west`, `downhill`, and `uphill`.

To make a sharp corner round again (for example, when the default got changed) use the `rounded␣corners` key, which accepts the same values. Thus, the fastest way to make a single corner rounded is to use `sharp␣corners` without a value and then undo it for one corner as shown in the third box of the example.

A box with one sharp corner	`\usepackage{tcolorbox}`
	`\footnotesize`
	`\begin{tcolorbox}[sharp corners=northwest]`
A box with two opposite sharp corners	`   A box with one sharp corner            \end{tcolorbox}`
	`\begin{tcolorbox}[sharp corners=downhill]`
	`   A box with two opposite sharp corners   \end{tcolorbox}`
A box with just one rounded corner at the bottom right	`\begin{tcolorbox}[sharp corners,rounded corners=southeast]`
	`   A box with just one rounded corner at the bottom right`
	`\end{tcolorbox}`

8-4-6

If dropped shadows are used (as discussed below), then the shadow shapes follow the shapes of the corners as one would expect. But there is also a style key, sharpish␣corners, which produces sharp corners but with the shadows slightly rounded.[1]

8.4.2 Extending tcolorbox through libraries

The functionality covered by tcolorbox is huge, and for better organization some of it is placed into libraries that are available only on demand through a package option or alternatively through a \tcbuselibrary declaration in the preamble. In this book we partly cover skins, breakable, vignette, and poster with a few examples.

However, there are many more libraries to explore, for example, listings, listingsutf8, and minted (alternative libraries for displaying listings), theorems (boxed theorems), fitting (adjust content size to available space), xparse (use extended command and environment declarations of LaTeX, previously implemented in the xparse package), and documentation (for documenting LaTeX source code). For details of their functionalities refer to the package manual [131].

Skins and styles — altering the look and feel

When tcolorbox draws its boxes, it can use different drawing engines that offer more or less sophistication at the cost of processing time. This allows for different layouts, and these are organized in so-called skins that are essentially style definitions for the various parts of a tcolorbox combined with selecting the background drawing machinery.

Most skins use tikz for drawing in which case a large number of additional keys are made available that all expect tikz key settings as their value and thus require braces around the value to hide the inner equal signs and commas. We give only one example here as a teaser — consult the manual [131] if you are not satisfied with the default skins and want to design your own layouts beyond the possibilities discussed in this section.

In the next example we use the enhanced skin and apply the interior␣style key (which expects one or more tikz keys as its value) to color the background in light blue turning to white from left to right. Because this enhanced skin is not available by default, we have to load the skins library in order to use it.

```
\usepackage{tcolorbox}    \tcbuselibrary{skins}
\tcbset{skin=enhanced,colframe=blue!75!black,fonttitle=\bfseries,
        interior style={left color=red!20,right color=white}}
\begin{tcolorbox}[halign lower=center,title=Interior style change]
  Here the background \tcblower color changes
  from red (gray) to white.
\end{tcolorbox}
```

8-4-7

The following examples then show all the skins that become available when the skins library is loaded. You can apply them either via skin=⟨name⟩ or by just using

---

[1]It is somewhat surprising that this is a "style" key that does not accept a value to indicate individual corners.

⟨*name*⟩ as a style key. In the latter case, often some additional style and geometry changes are made, which is usually preferable. For example, using `skin=beamer` instead of `beamer` would not automatically provide you with shadows. All examples use the following preamble code, which is not shown to save a bit of space:

```
\usepackage[skins]{tcolorbox}        % load package and library
\tcbset{top=0pt,middle=0pt,bottom=0pt}  % Shorten the example size
\scriptsize                          % Use in the example body
```

There is no visible difference between the default layout and `enhanced`, but the latter uses `tikz` for drawing and thus supports many additional keys as explained above. It is therefore a natural choice when you make adjustments.

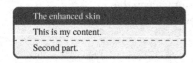

```
\begin{tcolorbox}[enhanced,title=The enhanced skin]
  This is my content. \tcblower Second part.
\end{tcolorbox}
```

8-4-8

```
\begin{tcolorbox}[bicolor,title=The bicolor skin]
  Two colors for top and bottom \tcblower
  instead of a dividing line.
\end{tcolorbox}
```

8-4-9

```
\begin{tcolorbox}[beamer,title=The beamer skin]
  Beamer style boxes \tcblower with shading.
\end{tcolorbox}
```

8-4-10

```
\begin{tcolorbox}[tile,title=The tile skin]
  Rectangular with different \tcblower background colors.
\end{tcolorbox}
```

8-4-11

```
\begin{tcolorbox}[spartan,title=The spartan skin]
  No difference between top \tcblower and bottom.
\end{tcolorbox}
```

8-4-12

Beware of white text on white background

The `empty` skin is a bit special because by default you end up with white text on a white background in the title. This therefore needs some adjustment through altering either the font or the background color.

```
\begin{tcolorbox}[empty,title=The empty skin,coltitle=blue]
  By default the title would be white on \tcblower
  white, hence the adjustment!
\end{tcolorbox}
```

8-4-13

In the above examples we reduced the vertical spacing to make the examples a bit shorter. For the next and final skin provided we cannot do that, because its separation line requires that the `middle` distance has a positive value.

8-4-14

```
\usepackage[skins]{tcolorbox}
\scriptsize
\begin{tcolorbox}[widget,title=The widget skin]
   Provide some gradation in \tcblower
   background color and separation line.
\end{tcolorbox}
```

Breakable and unbreakable boxes

One of the nice features of **tcolorbox** is the ability to automatically break `tcolorbox` environments across several pages. To enable this feature you have to load the `breakable` library and also use the key `breakable` on the environment (or inside `\tcbset`).

If the `tcolorbox` gets broken across pages we end up with a first and a last part and zero or more middle parts (if the content spans more than two pages). Each of these parts can get different visual treatment that be set up manually, but it is usually simpler to make use of one of the skins defined in the `skins` library for this. In the next example we use the skin `beamer`. With the default skin the box would still be broken across the page, but each part would be fully surrounded by a frame.

8-4-15

```
\usepackage{kantlipsum,tcolorbox}
\tcbuselibrary{breakable,skins}
\footnotesize
\kant[2][1]
\begin{tcolorbox}[beamer,breakable,
    size=title, halign=left,
    title=My breakable box ]
  \kant[2][2-3]
\end{tcolorbox}
\kant[2][4-5]
```

If you have generally enabled breakable boxes (i.e., with `\tcbset`), you can make individual environments unbreakable again by using the key `unbreakable`.

For the common use cases, that is all you need to learn about breakable boxes, but for special situations there are many keys available that help you change the look and feel or alter the points where the break is taken.[1] For this consult the appropriate section of the manual.

---

[1] Especially when using breakable boxes inside a `multicols` environment, you may have to provide some hints when column balancing is involved.

Title box maneuvers

Up to now all our examples showed a title box with the same width as the overall `tcolorbox` and only varied in `titlefont`, `coltitle`, or `colbacktitle`. However, when using one of the tikz-based skins, much more complicated layouts become possible. We give only one example here; many more and the corresponding keys that can be used are given in the tcolorbox manual. So take a look there if you want to design some fancy headers for your boxes.

```
\usepackage[skins]{tcolorbox}
\begin{tcolorbox}[enhanced,title=Something fancy,
    attach boxed title to top right
        = {xshift=3mm,yshift=-3mm,yshifttext=-1mm},
    boxed title style={size=fbox,colback=blue}]
 A box with the title forming its own box.
\end{tcolorbox}
```

8-4-16

As you will have guessed there are several other `attach␣boxed␣title␣to...` keys to place the title in any of the corners or centered at the top or bottom, e.g., `attach␣boxed␣title␣to␣bottom␣left`.

Adding Shadows

We have already seen that the `beamer` key adds a dropped shadow to the box. You can get this kind of layout with any skin that uses tikz for drawing by specifying the key `drop␣shadow`, which is in fact a short-hand for `drop␣shadow␣southeast` — so yes, there are keys for various other directions as well as for fuzzy shadows or lifted shadows. We show the latter in the next example. To remove any shadow that has been previously set up, use `no␣shadow` as a key.

```
\usepackage[skins]{tcolorbox}
\begin{tcolorbox}[enhanced,drop fuzzy shadow,halign=right,
                  boxrule=0.4pt,title=A fuzzy shadow]
  This is a righ-aligned tcolorbox with a shadow.
\end{tcolorbox}
\begin{tcolorbox}[enhanced,drop lifted shadow=blue,
                  boxrule=0.4pt,sharp corners=south,
                  halign=left,title=A lifted shadow]
  This is another tcolorbox with an unusual shadow
  and three lines of text.
\end{tcolorbox}
```

8-4-17

Given that lifted shadows do not look pleasing when the box has rounded corners, we also applied `sharp␣corners` and changed the width of the frame to a thin line. There are also large and small versions of the lifted shadows as well as some keys to define generic shadows; consult the manual for details on those.

Adding border lines

Instead of providing a frame around the boxes, you may want to just add some line at one or the other side. Given that `tcolorbox`es can break across pages, this gives you an easy way to produce "change bars" to highlight updates in the text.

In the example we suppress any interior style settings with `interior hidden` and omit the usual frame with `frame hidden`. We then put a blue line (actually a line of dots because of the value `dotted`) to the left of the material using `borderline west`.[1] You can use such keys repeatedly by altering the offset specified in the second brace group of its value, which we did when placing the black vertical rule. Dropping predefined borderlines is done with `no borderline`.

Text before the boxed paragraph.

Lorem ipsum dolor sit amet, consectetuer adipiscing elit. Ut purus elit, vestibulum ut, placerat ac, adipiscing vitae, felis.

... and text after.

```
\usepackage{lipsum,tcolorbox}   \tcbuselibrary{skins}
Text before the boxed paragraph.
\begin{tcolorbox}[enhanced,frame hidden,
    interior hidden,top=0pt,bottom=0pt,boxsep=0pt,
    borderline west={3pt}{0pt}{blue,dotted},
    borderline west={2pt}{4pt}{black}]
  \lipsum[1][1-2]
\end{tcolorbox}        \ldots{} and text after.
```

8-4-18

Adding overlays, watermarks, and other backgrounds

When a `tcolorbox` is typeset, the frame is drawn first. With the help of so-called overlays, this frame and the canvas of the box can then be decorated by adding graphical code (usually `tikz` commands) to a number of keys. Finally, the box content is drawn on top. A special application of this are watermarks or background pictures for which we give an example below. To explore the full power of overlays refer to the package documentation.

With `watermark graphics` we specify a graphic file to be loaded into the background, `watermark opacity` defines its visibility, and with `watermark zoom` we specify that it should not be used at its natural size but stretched to fill a certain proportion of the box (the aspect ratio is maintained, though). Thus, specifying 0.9 in the example results in the bird nearly touching the top and the bottom, but due to its proportion, there is ample space to the left and right.

A graphic as a watermark

This shows a box with the LaTeX hummingbird logo as a background picture.

```
\usepackage[skins]{tcolorbox}
\begin{tcolorbox}[enhanced,
            title=A graphic as a watermark,
            watermark graphics=latex-logo.pdf,
            watermark opacity=0.2,
            watermark zoom=0.9]
  This shows a box with the \LaTeX\ hummingbird logo
  as a background picture.
\end{tcolorbox}
```

8-4-19

---

[1] You probably have guessed that there are also `borderline` keys for the `north`, `west`, and `south` edges and shorthands for `horizontal` and `vertical` border lines.

Producing a canvas for the box

Instead of zooming, you can use watermark␣stretch=⟨*fraction*⟩, which does not respect aspect ratio and stretches the width and height separately to both match the ⟨*fraction*⟩ specified as the key value. If used on the bird above, it would end up being horizontally stretched apart.

As an alternative, there is watermark␣overzoom=⟨*fraction*⟩, which is useful if you want the graphic to touch all four sides of the box, while still maintaining the aspect ratio. If used, then the graphic is scaled as necessary, and then all parts outside of the box are clipped. If used in the previous example (again with a value of 0.9), the beak would nearly touch the side, while the top and bottom parts of the bird would get outside of the box and are therefore clipped. Thus, this key is most useful if the graphics is more "ornamental" and it is irrelevant if some of it gets clipped when it is used to fill the whole box. In that case typically a value of 1.0 is used to fill all of the background.

Textual watermarks

Of course, you can use ordinary text instead of a graphic as a watermark specified with the watermark␣text key. It obeys zooming and stretching though the latter is seldom a good idea because it may distort the text considerably. By default, the color of the watermark text is a mix of the frame and the background color otherwise used for the box. However, with watermark␣color you can set it to a specific value.

Text as a watermark

This shows a box with the text in the background. Make it light so that main text remains readable!

```
\usepackage[skins]{tcolorbox}

\begin{tcolorbox}[enhanced,title=Text as a watermark,
                  watermark text=\textbf{Example},
                  watermark color=blue,watermark opacity=0.1,
                  watermark stretch=0.95]
  This shows a box with the text in the background.
  Make it light so that main text remains readable!
\end{tcolorbox}
```

8-4-20

Hyperlinks to internal and external resources

In conjunction with the hyperref package (see Section 2.4.6 on page 96), boxes or part of boxes generated with tcolorbox and its variants can function as targets for hyperlinks or as clickable regions. Note that all the hyperlink keys discussed below require enhanced or one of the other more powerful skins to work; they are not supported with the basic drawing engine.

To make the whole box an active hyperlink to a \label in the document (or a label key in another tcolorbox as discussed below) use the key hyperref and specify the label string as the value. To make it a link to a \hypertarget, use the hyperlink key instead.

If you wish to link to an external Uniform Resource Locator (URL), use the key hyperurl, which works like hyperref's \href or \url, but make the whole tcolorbox the active link. There is also a hyperurl* key, which allows you to also set hyperref options for the external link, e.g., on which page to open a PDF, etc.

As an example we make a box that links to the Comprehensive TeX Archive Network (CTAN) location of the tcolorbox documentation.

8-4-21

View manual section

§10.10 Hyper Option Keys

```
\usepackage{hyperref,tcolorbox}  \tcbuselibrary{skins}
\begin{tcolorbox}[enhanced,title=View manual section,
     hyperurl=http://www.ctan.org/pkg/tcolorbox]
   \S 10.10 Hyper Option Keys
\end{tcolorbox}
```

Instead of making the whole box a single active link area, you can limit the area to the interior or the title by using hyperurl␣interior or hyperurl␣title and similarly for the other link types.

All of the above keys make the tcolorbox or parts of it an active link area so that clicking it would take you to the desired location. It is, however, also possible to add an anchor to the box so that it can serve as a link target for hyperlink of another box or a \hyperlink command from the hyperref package. This is done by adding a hypertarget key with the target name given as the value.

Formatting and text changes based on verso/recto pages

If you use the same kind of tcolorbox repeatedly, you may want to alter its looks, depending on its placement on a recto or verso page. This is possible with the help of the if␣odd␣page key. It expects two brace groups as its value containing keys to apply to *odd pages* and *even pages*, respectively.

The test for the page number is done by using labels, which means that it is costly and requires at least two LaTeX runs if a change moves a box from one page to the next. As a side effect, this key cannot be used in \tcbset but must be applied directly on the environment in a \newtcolorbox declaration, which is what we have done in the next example. The full syntax for this declaration is discussed in the next section.

You can see that the title box appears on the left on even pages and on the right on odd ones. We also use the command \tcbifoddpage inside the environment body to provide alternative text based on the page the box ends up on.

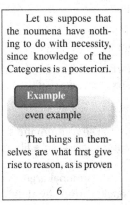

```
\usepackage{kantlipsum,tcolorbox}
\tcbuselibrary{skins}
\newtcolorbox{exa}[1]{beamer,bottom=0mm,title=#1,%
    if odd page={attach boxed title to top right
       ={xshift=-2mm,yshift=-3mm,yshifttext=-1mm}}%
                 {attach boxed title to top left
       ={xshift=2mm,yshift=-3mm,yshifttext=-1mm}}}
\footnotesize
\kant[2][1] \begin{exa}{Example}
   \tcbifoddpage{odd}{even} example \end{exa}
\kant[6][1] \begin{exa}{Another}
   \tcbifoddpage{odd}{even} example \end{exa}
\kant[10]
```

8-4-22

As an alternative you can use if␣odd␣page␣or␣oneside. In a document using the twoside class option it behaves like if␣odd␣page, but in a one-sided document it always selects the first brace group, i.e., the one for odd pages.

*Behavior with
breakable boxes*
If you use the breakable library and a box is split across pages, then all parts are formatted based on the page value of the first box part. If that is not desired, you can use the starred forms of the keys, which are made available by this library.

As shown, you can also use the command \tcbifoddpage[1] inside the text. However, because testing for page "oddness" is costly, it is accurately done only if one of the above selection keys is present. If not, you can add the key check␣odd␣page to force the testing.

8.4.3 Defining new tcolorbox environments and commands

In Example 8-4-22 we have already made use of the powerful possibility to define your own named tcolorbox environments or commands. Here is now the full syntax for such declarations.

\newtcolorbox[*counter-setup*] {*env*} [*args*] [*default*] {*key/value list*}

To define your own tcolorbox environments use \newtcolorbox. The environment name is specified in the first mandatory *env* argument, and the keys that you want to apply are given in the *key/value list*.

The environment can have up to nine arguments, and the first one can be made optional with a *default* value; i.e., the *args* and *default* arguments are like those from \newenvironment. Such arguments can be used to provide values for some of the keys in your *key/value list*. For instance, in Example 8-4-22 we used one argument to hold the title text. Another useful approach is to use the optional argument to extend the *key/value list*, e.g.,

    \newtcolorbox{*env*}[2] []{title=#2,*key/value list*,#1}

The optional *counter-setup* argument is used for setting up automatic numbering if that is desired; see the discussion on the next page for details.

\newtcbox[*counter-setup*] *cmd* [*args*] [*default*] {*key/value list*}

If you want to declare your own \tcbox commands, use \newtcbox. The arguments for the declaration are the same as those for \newtcolorbox, but because the last argument of your new command is the box content, your new *cmd* has *args* + 1 arguments in total, and you can therefore only have up to eight other arguments.

In the example below we use another library to define a \key command for showing keyboard keys within ordinary text. Further details on the vignette library and the associated keys can be found in the documentation.

One interesting aspect of the \key definition is the use of the optional argument to support changing the color scheme of the frame and background. By default various shades of gray are used, but by specifying the optional argument, a different color (in the example black) can be used occasionally. Also worth noting is the use

---

[1]Or \tcbifoddpageoroneside to also distinguish between two- and one-sided documents.

of the on␣line key to align the box text with the surroundings. Related keys are tcbox␣raise␣base to raise it to the baseline and tcbox␣raise allowing you to raise the box by a specific amount given as value.

```
\usepackage[vignette]{tcolorbox}
\newtcbox\key[1][white]{enhanced,sharp corners,on line,
    size=small,left=0pt,right=0pt,boxsep=1pt,fontupper=\footnotesize,
    colback=#1!10,colframe=#1!50!black,boxrule=3pt,underlay vignette}
```

Use Cntrl-X followed by f to open a file.

`Use \key{Cntrl-X} followed by \key[black]{f} to open a file.`

8-4-23

Numbering newly defined color boxes

It is possible to automatically number newly defined colored boxes. This counter mechanism has to be set up before other keys are evaluated. It is therefore placed into its own optional argument in front of the mandatory argument that holds the environment or command name.

In there you can use the key auto␣counter together with many others, such as number␣within, that influence the numbering. Instead of auto-numbering, which uses its own counter, one can make use of an existing LaTeX counter with use␣counter or the counter of a different color box command with use␣counter␣from.

To typeset the current counter value, for example in the title key, the command \thetcbcounter is available.

To reference the counter you can specify a label with the key label and then refer to it using \ref, etc. If the nameref package is loaded, you can define an arbitrary reference text for use with \nameref.[1]

In the next example we define a new environment for making boxes containing examples. We give it one optional argument (for additional key/value pairs if needed) and two mandatory arguments: the example title and a label to reference it. This assumes that we usually have to reference such examples. If one only occasionally needs a label, it would be better to use just the title as a mandatory argument and provide the label key in the optional argument when needed. To show the optional argument in action we apply sharp␣corners when using the environment.

```
\usepackage{nameref,tcolorbox}
\newtcolorbox[auto counter,number within=section,
        number format=\alph]{exabox}[3][]
        {colback=blue!5!white,colframe=blue!75!black,
        fonttitle=\bfseries,label=#3,nameref=#2,
        title=Exa-\thetcbcounter: #2,#1}
```

5   A Section

> **Exa : Title text**
>
> This exhibits a numbered tcolor-box.

```
\section{A Section}
\begin{exabox}[sharp corners=south]{Title text}{exa:A}
   This exhibits a numbered tcolorbox.
\end{exabox}
```

The example on page 6 is numbered 5. Its title is "Title text".

8-4-24

`The example on page \pageref{exa:A} is numbered \ref{exa:A}. Its title is ``\nameref{exa:A}''.`

---

[1] If that package is not loaded, the key has no effect.

8.4.4 Special tcolorbox applications

Given that the documentation for the tcolorbox package has more than 500 pages, you can imagine that it describes many interesting applications that we cannot discuss in the available space, e.g., displaying listings, boxed theorems, creation of exercises with solutions, and many more. If you are interested in any of them, refer to package manual [131] for details.

For this book we conclude with three applications: how to turn tcolorboxes into float objects, how to make rasters of boxes, and how to produce large professional-looking posters with the package.

Turning the boxes into floats

It is, of course, possible to use a tcolorbox environment within a float environment. However, the package also supports turning such boxes directly into float objects. This is done with the key float (for single column floats) or float* (for spanning floats). The value, if given, specifies the allowed positions. If not present, a default (which can be altered with floatplacement) is used.

If a tcolorbox is turned into a float, any settings for before␣skip and after␣skip are ignored (after all, the box is not embedded in the normal galley). Instead, the code given as the value for the every␣float key is inserted before the floating box: a typical value would be \centering.

```
\usepackage{tcolorbox}
\tcbset{every float=\centering, % center floats
        floatplacement=tp}       % only top and
                                 % page by default

\section{The \LaTeX\ logo}
A while back \LaTeX{} moved away from a lion
to a hummingbird designed by Paulo Cereda.

\tcbox[float=t,size=small,title=A new logo]
    {\includegraphics[width=.3\textwidth]
                {latex-logo.pdf}}
```

8-4-25

6   The LaTeX logo

A while back LaTeX moved away from a lion to a hummingbird designed by Paulo Cereda.

Clearly this box floated to the top, but there is no automatic numbering or an entry in the list of figures for it. To achieve this in a simple manner blend␣into is provided, which can be used in the optional *counter-setup* argument of \newtcolorbox and \newtcbox declarations, e.g.,

```
\newtcbox[blend into=figures]\tcbfig[2][]{float,size=small,title=#2,#1}
```

Allowed key values are figures, tables, and with some restrictions, listings.

For your own type of floating boxes, numbering and a "List of" mechanism are, of course, also possible. You have to set up a counter as described on the preceding page and then use list␣inside to specify the list that should be used (the example uses logos).

Typesetting the list is done with \tcblistof, which expects two mandatory arguments, the *list-name* and the *title* to display. By default it uses \section to typeset the *title*. If that is not desired, you can use its optional argument to specify another method (we use `\section*` below). In this example we also force the float to the bottom of the page using `float=!b`.

List of Logos

7   The LaTeX logo

A while back LaTeX moved away from a lion to a hummingbird designed by Paulo Cereda.

1: A new logo

```
\usepackage{tcolorbox}
\tcbset{every float=\centering, % center floats
        floatplacement=tp}      % default top and page
\newtcbox[auto counter,list inside=logos]
        \tcbfig[2][]{float,size=small,list text=#2,
                       title=\thetcbcounter: #2,#1}
\tcblistof[\section*]{logos}{List of Logos}
\section{The \LaTeX\ logo}
A while back \LaTeX{} moved away from a lion
to a hummingbird designed by Paulo Cereda.

\tcbfig[float=!b]{A new logo}
        {\includegraphics[width=.4\textwidth]
                         {latex-logo.pdf}}
```

8-4-26

Raster applications

If you need several boxes arranged in some sort of two-dimensional raster, you can make use of the `raster` library. This library defines the `tcbraster` environment, which has an optional argument to specify the number of columns you need and other aspects of the boxes inside; e.g., in the example we asked for all boxes to be of equal height. The body of the environment then consists of `tcolorbox` environments, or, if you want to nest boxes, of `tcbboxedraster` environments (containing inner `tcolorbox` environments).

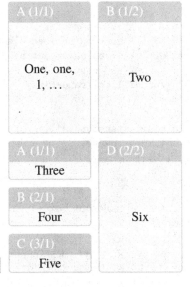

```
\usepackage{tcolorbox}
\tcbuselibrary{skins,raster}
\begin{tcbraster}[raster columns=2,
  raster equal height,
  raster every box/.style=
    {size=small,valign=center,halign=center,
     colframe=blue!50,colback=blue!10,
     title=\Alph{tcbrasternum}
           (\thetcbrasterrow/\thetcbrastercolumn)}]
\begin{tcolorbox}One, one, 1, \ldots\end{tcolorbox}
\begin{tcolorbox}Two\end{tcolorbox}
\begin{tcboxedraster}[raster columns=1]{blankest}
  \begin{tcolorbox}Three\end{tcolorbox}
  \begin{tcolorbox}Four\end{tcolorbox}
  \begin{tcolorbox}Five\end{tcolorbox}
\end{tcboxedraster}
\begin{tcolorbox}Six\end{tcolorbox}
\end{tcbraster}
```

8-4-27

629

Current row and column numbers are available through the `tcbrasterrow` and `tcbrastercolumn` counters. Internally, the sequence of boxes are numbered by `tcbrasternum`. You can use the values of these counters, for example in titles of the boxes, but you should not attempt to alter them, and it is important to note that they are restarted for nested rasters.

The previous example should have given you some ideas of the possibilities, but for further details you need to refer to the package documentation.

Poster applications

We conclude this section with an example using tcolorbox for the production of a poster, i.e, a single large page (A3 or bigger) that provides a showcase for some project by combining boxed text, graphics, and tables in an overview presentation. Especially for conferences this is often a requirement, but there are many other use cases.[1]

To set things up load tcolorbox with the option `poster`. The actual poster content is then placed into a `tcbposter` environment, which sets up a grid to lay out boxes on the page in a regular manner. This is implemented internally using the `raster` library shown in the previous section.

The next example shows the general approach. We set up a grid with the `poster` key, which expects a list of key settings as its value. We use four `rows` and five `columns` (normally you would probably have more). The spacing between grid elements can be altered with the keys `colspacing` and `rowspacing` or with `spacing`, which sets both keys to the same value. Explicitly setting the `width` and `height` is normally not necessary (by default all space on the page is used) and mainly done here to keep the example small. During development it is useful to show the grid, so we also add `showframe`.

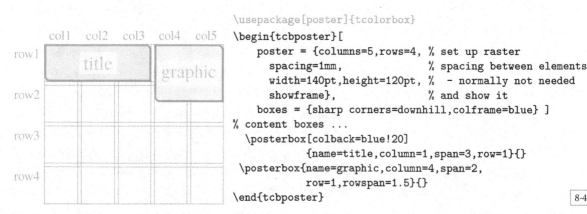

```
\usepackage[poster]{tcolorbox}
\begin{tcbposter}[
    poster = {columns=5,rows=4, % set up raster
        spacing=1mm,                % spacing between elements
        width=140pt,height=120pt, %  - normally not needed
        showframe},                 % and show it
    boxes = {sharp corners=downhill,colframe=blue} ]
% content boxes ...
    \posterbox[colback=blue!20]
            {name=title,column=1,span=3,row=1}{}
    \posterbox{name=graphic,column=4,span=2,
                row=1,rowspan=1.5}{}
\end{tcbposter}
```

8-4-28

With the `boxes` key you can set up default values or all tcolorbox boxes inside the environment, so it acts like `\tcbset` for the poster.

---

[1]Of course, you need to a way to print such a huge page, either by using a professional printing service or by using a program that splits it into parts that you can print and then glue together.

The content boxes are added with the help of \posterbox commands or posterboxenv environments, which work like \tcbox and tcolorbox, but support additional keys like name, column, etc., that are relevant for placing the box on the grid or in relation to other named boxes.

Once you decided on the grid, it is time to specify the different regions of your poster. Boxes can be placed into cells of the grid, possibly spanning a number of columns (key span) or a number of rows (key rowspan) or both. It is also possible to span parts of columns or rows; see boxes named title and graphic for examples.

Alternatively, it is possible to position boxes by specifying relations between them or the margins (they then grow depending on their content); e.g., the credits box is defined to be above the bottom, and you can see that its height is less than a normal grid cell. Another example is the table box, which is defined to be between the graphic and credits boxes automatically filling the remaining space.

Finally, you can have breakable boxes by specifying a sequence of placements (as it was done for the T box). The content is then poured into the different parts, one after another.

The result is shown below. Of course, the exact sizes might change when you place content into the currently empty *content* argument of the \posterbox commands, because at least some of the boxes are allowed to change size. In a real poster you may also prefer to use posterboxenv over \posterbox, especially if your content is rather large.

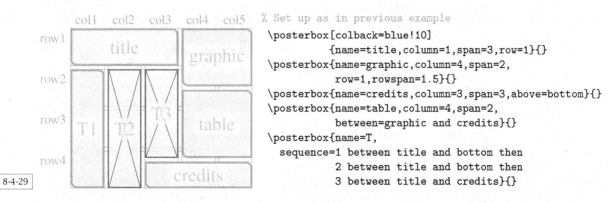

```
% Set up as in previous example
\posterbox[colback=blue!10]
          {name=title,column=1,span=3,row=1}{}
\posterbox{name=graphic,column=4,span=2,
           row=1,rowspan=1.5}{}
\posterbox{name=credits,column=3,span=3,above=bottom}{}
\posterbox{name=table,column=4,span=2,
           between=graphic and credits}{}
\posterbox{name=T,
  sequence=1 between title and bottom then
           2 between title and bottom then
           3 between title and credits}{}
```

8-4-29

Obviously this has provided you only a first impression of the powerful application; many more details and customization possibilities are given in the tcolorbox manual. There is also a very nice tutorial on making posters with the package [130].

8.5 tikz — A general-purpose graphics system

In the final section of this chapter we take a brief look at tikz with which you can create a large variety of graphics. Unlike graphic systems such as pstricks or META-POST discussed in [28], it does not require an external PostScript processor[1] — all

---

[1]With lualatex and luapstricks it is to some extent possible to use pstricks directly.

drawing is done with TeX commands. This has the advantage that it works with all engines and that it integrates seamlessly into the LaTeX compilation and so allows creation of not only stand-alone graphics but also decorations, e.g., the tcolorbox frames discussed in Section 8.4, page ornaments, or arrows between various parts of a text, etc. It has the drawbacks that the compilation of complex plots and graphics can be slow and that the accuracy of calculations is limited and can even fail if they lead to dimensions larger than the maximal size supported by TeX.

The tikz package was originally written by Till Tantau and is now maintained by Henri Menke. Since the first version in 2005 the tikz ecosystem has grown so much that it is quite impossible to do tikz justice on a few pages — already the official manual of the package [133] has more than 1300 pages, and CTAN lists more than 150 packages enhancing or making use of tikz — and so it is unavoidable that the following descriptions have to leave out many points and oversimplify syntax and concepts of tikz.

Loading additional libraries

The functionality covered by tikz is huge, but not everything is loaded by default. Additional libraries to enable certain features can be loaded with one or more \usetikzlibrary declarations. This command takes a list of library names as its argument. Some of the examples in this section require loading libraries and so do a few in other chapters; e.g., Example 11-3-14 on page →II 162 that implements commutative diagrams with tikz.

```
\begin{tikzpicture}[key/value list]
   graphic instructions
\end{tikzpicture}
\tikz[key/value list]{graphic instructions}
```

The main environment

Graphic instructions should be given inside the tikzpicture environment, which accepts an optional argument containing a list of key/value pairs to configure the graphic. It is not necessary (but possible) to declare the size of the graphic — tikz updates the size and the bounding box when material is added. For small graphics a command form \tikz is also available. The braces around the *graphic instructions* can be omitted if there is only one instruction.

Beware of the missing semicolon

We discuss some of the available *graphic instructions* in more detail in the following. To give a short overview: they almost always start with a command and end with a semicolon. The code between both can be quite complex, and it is easy to get bracing wrong or to forget the closing semicolon. The typical error message of tikz in such cases is then

```
! Package tikz Error: Giving up on this path.
                Did you forget a semicolon?
```

Setting keys

The tikz package makes extensive use of the key/value syntax. Keys that should apply to all pictures or to all drawing commands in a scope can be set as defaults with the help of a \tikzset declaration. With this declaration it is also possible to define new keys by combining settings into a "style". The examples of this section won't make much use of it because they try to show a variety of options, but in real

Name	Explicit syntax	Implicit syntax
canvas	`(canvas cs: x=0cm,y=2pt+4pt)`	`(0cm,2pt+4pt)`
canvas polar	`(canvas polar cs: angle=30,radius=2cm)`	`(30:2cm)`
xyz (2 coordinates)	`(xyz cs: x=1,y=0.5)`	`(1,0.5)`
xyz (3 coordinates)	`(xyz cs: x=1,y=0.5,z=2)`	`(1,0.5,2)`
xyz polar	`(xyz polar cs: angle=30,radius=2)`	`(30:2)`
node	`(node cs: name=A,anchor=south)`	`(A.south)`
tangent	`(tangent cs: node=c,point={(a)},solution=1)`	
tikzmark[a]	`(pic cs: A)`	

[a] *This requires the* `tikzmark` *library.*

Table 8.1: Examples of coordinate systems

pictures it is highly recommended to set up styles to make the code more readable and ease the maintenance. Note that defaults are normally set with special keys. For example, to change the line width in all pictures you should not use

```
\tikzset{line width=1pt}
```

because such a setting would get overwritten in various places. Instead, the style every␣picture should be changed:

```
\tikzset{every picture/.style={line width=1pt}}
```

8.5.1 Basic objects

The three basic objects in tikz are *coordinates*, which describe a position on the canvas on which the picture is drawn, *paths* between coordinates, and *nodes* that allow adding text to a picture.

The tikz package supports various coordinate systems like Cartesian, polar, or spherical coordinates, and new coordinate systems can be defined. Coordinates are always given in parentheses. Their general syntax is: *Specifying coordinates*

([*options*] *coordinate specification*)

In the *coordinate specification* the coordinate system can be specified in two ways: it can be given explicitly with the name of the coordinate system followed by `cs:` and key-value pairs determinating the coordinate. Common coordinate systems typically also support an implicit (shorter) syntax. Table 8.1 shows some of the coordinate systems together with the short syntax, if it exists.

The `canvas` coordinate systems expect values as dimensions. The `xyz` coordinate systems take dimensionless values that are interpreted as factors of unit vectors; they support both two or three dimensions. Those default unit vectors point 1 cm in the respective directions and so the `canvas` and the `xyz` coordinate system normally give the same output unless one transforms the `xyz` coordinate system by changing the unit vectors as demonstrated by the skewed square in the next example where we have changed the x-direction unit vector in the optional argument of the \tikz command.

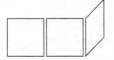

```
\usepackage{tikz}
\tikz{\draw (0,0)--(1cm,0cm)--(1cm,1cm)--(0cm,1cm)--cycle;}
\tikz{\draw (0,0)--(1,0)--(1,1)--(0,1)--cycle;}
\tikz[x={(0.5cm,0.5cm)}]{\draw (0,0)--(1,0)--(1,1)--(0,1)--cycle;}
```

8-5-1

Mixtures such as (1,4pt), using both canvas coordinates and xyz coordinates, are interpreted as expected.

Using expressions as values

Values can be given as expressions, because the value is passed to the mathematical engine contained in tikz. In addition to basic arithmetic operations such as adding, subtracting, and multiplying, the syntax also supports various functions including trigonometric functions, conditionals, and random numbers. It is also possible to measure text.

The following example shows as functions sqrt (square root), / (division), and rand (random numbers); text is measured with depth and height. Note that expressions containing parentheses or commas should be surrounded by braces. The functions depth and height return the size in pt without the unit. We add +0pt to force the conversion to a dimension and so avoid getting a multiple of the unit vector as coordinate.

Be careful because of \edef expansion

A word of caution: while the mathematical engine allows use of quite complex expressions in coordinates and other places where values are expected, it is often better to do calculations beforehand and pass the values with macros and lengths to keep the code readable. Measuring of text should be done only for simple cases and with great care: because the mathematical expressions are expanded with \edef, all commands and active characters must be protected; in addition, no font switch commands should be used: they trigger a temporarily switch of the font to use the \nullfont, and the result of the measure is zero regardless of the content.

```
\usepackage{tikz}
\begin{tikzpicture}[baseline={(0,-1.5)}]
 \draw (0,0) circle[radius=1];
 \draw[blue,thick] (0,0) -- ({sqrt(2)/2},0)--({sqrt(2)/2},{sqrt(2)/2});
 \draw[dashed] (rand,rand)-- (rand,rand) -- (rand,rand)--cycle;
 \draw[dotted] (rand,rand)-- (rand,rand) -- (rand,rand)--cycle;
\end{tikzpicture}
\par\Huge \tikz[baseline={(0,0)}]\draw[<->]
        (0,-{depth("y")+0pt}) -- (0,{height("T")+0pt}); Type
```

8-5-2

A coordinate can be given a symbolic name. You can add and subtract coordinates, shift and scale them, compute midpoints, and do projections—load the calc library for extended calculation options.

The following example defines various named coordinates. The first, A, is set with cartesian xy-values; the second, B, uses the polar coordinate system where the value is given as ⟨*angle*⟩ : ⟨*length*⟩; the third, C, is calculated by shifting B.

The first \draw command then draws lines between these coordinates to get a triangle and places some text next to the corners. The syntax ($⟨*calc*⟩$) used in the next two \draw commands indicates that the content is a *coordinate computation*; such calculations require the calc library.

In the first computation the !0.5! between the two coordinates is an example of a "partway modifier" with the syntax !*number*! and roughly means "use the coordinate that is halfway between A and B". The second, with the named coordinate C between the two exclamation marks, is a projection modifier. They draw dashed lines from B to the middle position between A and C and from C to the orthogonal projection of C onto the line from A to B.

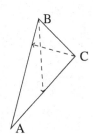

```
\usepackage{tikz}
\usetikzlibrary {calc}
\begin{tikzpicture}
    \coordinate (A) at (0,0);
    \coordinate (B) at (75:3);
    \coordinate (C) at ([shift={(1,-1)}]B);
    \draw (A)node[right]{A} -- (B)node[right]{B}
        -- (C)node[right]{C} -- cycle;
    \draw[dashed,->](B) -- ($(A)!0.5!(C)$);
    \draw[dashed,->](C) -- ($(A)!(C)!(B)$);
\end{tikzpicture}
```

8-5-3

Coordinates can be prefixed with + or ++ to make them "relative" to the current position. A coordinate such as +(0,0.5) means "0.5 units above the previous position", but the current point is not altered. A coordinate prefixed with ++ also updates the current point for subsequent usages of relative coordinates.

Incremental coordinates

```
\usepackage{tikz}
\tikz{\draw[->] (0,0)--(1,1)--++(0,0.5)--++(0.5,0)--++(0,-0.5);}
\tikz{\draw[->] (0,0)--(1,1)--+(0,0.5)--+(0.5,0)--+(0,-0.5);}
```

8-5-4

Most examples in this section stick to xy- and named coordinates — but remember that this shows only a small subset of the capabilities of tikz.

We can now turn towards the two other basic concepts of a tikz graphic: paths and nodes on these paths.

\path [*key/value list*] {*path specification*};

A path is just a series of straight and curved lines between coordinates. The *path specification* is stream of *path operations*: coordinates and keywords telling tikz how to connect these coordinates to build the path. The various operations can be mixed: it is possible to start a path with a straight line and then continue with some arc or a sine curve.

Using paths

635

Operation	Syntax	Comment
"move-to"	*no connector symbol, just consecutive coordinates*	move current point
"line-to"	`--` or `-|` or `|-`	straight lines
"curve-to"	`.. controls` (*coord.*) `and` (*coord.*) `..`	Bezier curves
"arc"	`arc[`*options*`]`	a part of an ellipse
"parabola"	`parabola[`*options*`]`	a part of a parabola
"sin"	`sin` (*coord.*) or `sin cycle`	a part of a sine curve
"cos"	`cos` (*coord.*) or `cos cycle`	a part of a cosine curve
"plot"	*different syntax and plot type options available*	
"rectangle"	`rectangle` (*coord.*) or `rectangle cycle`	a rectangle
"circle"	`circle[`*options*`]`	a circle
"ellipse"	`ellipse[`*options*`]`	an ellipse
"grid"	`grid[`*options*`]` (*coord.*) or `grid[`*options*`] cycle`	a grid
"to path"	`to[`*options*`]`	user defined path operations
"node"	`node[`*options*`]` *options* `{`*text*`}`	to add text
"edge"	`edge[`*options*`]` *optional nodes* (*coord.*)	to connect nodes
"pic"	`pic[`*options*`]` `{`*name*`}`	adds a small picture
"foreach"	`foreach` *variable* `in` `{`*path commands*`}`	to repeat path parts
"scoping"	`{`*path commands*`}`	to create a local scope

Table 8.2: Common path operations (overview)

The "move-to" operation The simplest operation is the "*move-to*" operation, which is specified by just giving a coordinate where a path operation is expected. It moves the current point to the next coordinate and starts a new part of the path that is not connected to the previous segment. A straight line is created by adding the "*line-to*" operation, `--`, *The "line-to" operation* between two coordinates. By using `|-` and `-|` you can connect the coordinates with horizontal and vertical lines. The following example shows the operations in action:

```
\usepackage{tikz}
\tikz\draw[dashed] (0,0) -- (1,1)  (1,0) --
          (2,1)  (2,0) -| (3,1)  (4,0) |- (5,1);
```

8-5-5

Closing the path segment As we have already seen, a path segment can be closed with the keyword `cycle` in place of the last coordinate. This not only returns to the beginning of the segment, but also ensures that a smooth join is created.

```
\usepackage{tikz}
\begin{tikzpicture}[line width=10pt]
\draw (0,0) -- (1,1) -- (1,0) -- (0,0);
\draw (2,0) -- (3,1) -- (3,0) -- cycle;
\end{tikzpicture}
```

8-5-6

Curved lines can be created through a large number of path operations. Bezier *Path operations for* curves are added with the "*curve-to*" operation, which uses the syntax *curved lines*

```
.. controls coordinate and coordinate ..
```

where the two coordinates set the control points of the curve.

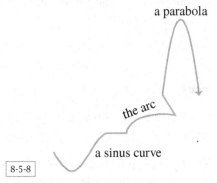

8-5-7

```
\usepackage{tikz}
\tikz\path[draw=blue,line width=1pt,scale=4]
    (-1/4,0) -- (-1/8, 0)
    .. controls ++(135:1/8) and ++(250:1/8) .. (0,1/4)
    .. controls ++(290:1/8) and ++(45:1/8)  .. (1/8,0) -- (1/4,0) ;
```

Part of an ellipse is added with the keyword `arc`, which takes an optional argument to set the radius and the angles of the arc. Operations are also provided for parabolas, sine, and cosine curves.

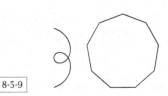

8-5-8

```
\usepackage{tikz}
\tikz\path [draw=blue,line width=1pt,->]
    (-2,-0.5) sin  (-1.5,-1) cos (-1,-0.5)
    node[right]{a sinus curve} sin (-0.5,0)
    -- (0,0)
    arc[x radius=1cm, y radius=0.5cm,
        start angle=180, end angle=70]
    node[midway,above,sloped]{the arc} -- (1,1)
    parabola [parabola height=2cm]
    +(1,0) node at (1.5,3.2){a parabola};
```

By correctly alternating the `sin` and `cos` operations, you can create a complete sine or cosine curve; see the tikz documentation [133] for an example.

The "*plot*" operation allows creating a path by plotting coordinates and functions.[1] This operation is quite complex and has many options, so we show only two examples as a teaser.

8-5-9

```
\usepackage{tikz}
\tikz \draw[scale=0.25,domain=-3.141:3.141,smooth,variable=\t]
        plot ({\t*sin(\t r)},{\t*cos(\t r)});
\quad
\tikz \draw[domain=0:360,samples=10,variable=\t]
        plot ({sin(\t)},{cos(\t)});
```

---

[1]For more complex plots the package pgfplots from Christian Feuersänger offers a comprehensive solution.

path action	*abbreviation command*
\path[draw,*options*]	\draw[*options*]
\path[fill,*options*]	\fill[*options*]
\path[draw,fill,*options*]	\filldraw[*options*]
\path[pattern,*options*]	\pattern[*options*]
\path[shade,*options*]	\shade[*options*]
\path[shade,draw,*options*]	\shadedraw[*options*]
\path[clip]	\clip
\path[use as bounding box]	\useasboundingbox

Table 8.3: Path actions and their abbreviation commands

Rectangles, circles, ellipses, and grids   For some standard shapes like rectangles, circles, ellipses, and also grids, dedicated path operations exist. Rectangles and grids span the area between two coordinates, while circles and ellipses typically have their center on the preceding coordinate.

```
\usepackage{tikz}
\tikz\draw[line width=1pt,blue,->]
     (0,0)--(1,1)circle[radius=5mm]--(0,2);
\tikz\filldraw[dashed,fill=gray,line width=1pt]
     (0,0) -- (0.5,0.5) rectangle (1,1) -- (1.5,1.5);
\tikz\draw (0,0) ellipse[x radius=1cm, y radius=0.5cm]
                    grid[step=0.1] (1,1);
```
8-5-10

Finally, we want to mention shortly the "*to path*" operation. It is used to add a user-defined path from the previous coordinate to the following coordinate. By default it gives a straight line. Its optional argument knows various options to create curves. Its main power lies in the fact that it can be redefined, which allows, for example, creation of names for special curves as shown in the next examples:

```
\usepackage{tikz}
\begin{tikzpicture}
\tikzset{my loop/.style=
   {to path={.. controls +(80:1) and +(100:1)
                  .. (\tikztotarget) \tikztonodes}}}

\draw[dotted,thick](0,2) to (2,2);
\draw[blue,thick](0,1) to[out=60,in=60] (2,1);
\node[circle,draw](a) at (1,0) {T};
\draw [->](a) to[my loop] (a);
\end{tikzpicture}
```
8-5-11

The examples so far all have *drawn* the paths, but more can be done with a path: a path can stay invisible and only change the size of the graphic or it can be used for calculation of coordinates. It can be drawn, filled, shaded, used for clipping, and more. Drawing can be thought of as taking a pen of a certain thickness and moving it along the path. Filling means that the interior of the path is filled with a uniform color — a path is automatically closed prior to filling, if necessary (and possible). Filling with a pattern or a picture is possible too.

Actions on paths

The action is given as an key to the \path command, but tikz also offers abbreviation commands that are listed in Table 8.3. The action keys often accept a value that allows setting a color or selecting the pattern.

```
\usepackage{tikz}
\usetikzlibrary{patterns}

\centering
\tikz\path[draw] (0,0)--(1,1.5)--(1.5,3)--(1,0);
\tikz\path[fill=blue]
            (0,0)--(1,1.5)--(1.5,3)--(1,0);
\tikz\path[fill=blue,draw=black,line width=2pt]
            (0,0)--(1,1.5)--(1.5,3)--(1,0);
\par\medskip
\tikz\path[pattern=fivepointed stars,draw=blue]
            (0,0)rectangle(1,1.5);\quad
\tikz\path[shade,left color=lightgray,right color=black,
            middle color=white](0,0)rectangle(1,1.5);
```

8-5-12

When a path is drawn, various parameters can be set to adapt the line width, the end of the lines, and how lines are joined. It is possible to add a dash pattern, to color the path, and to draw double lines. These parameters normally apply to a path as a whole. Thus, to use a different style or another color a new path should be started.[1]

Graphic parameters of drawn lines

```
\usepackage{tikz}
\tikz\path[draw,line cap=round,
            line join=bevel,line width=10pt]
            (0,0)--(0.5,1.5)--(1,0)--(1.5,1.5);
\tikz\path[draw,thick,dash pattern=on 2pt off 3pt]
            (0,0)--(1,2);
\tikz\path[draw,line width=2pt,line join=round,
            double, double distance=5pt]
            (0,0)--(0.5,1.5)--(1,0)--(1.5,1.5);
```

8-5-13

A variety of arrow tips can be added to the beginning and the end of a path, typically with a hyphen with symbols or arguments at the left and right to denote the wanted tips. It is not required to draw the path; the key tips can be used to get only the tip of the arrow. However, no segment of the path should contain a cycle —

Arrow tips

---

[1]It is also possible to add more decoration in a post-processing step, but this is out of scope of this short introduction.

neither explicitly through the keyword cycle nor implicitly through a path operation like "*circle*" or "*rectangle*": as can be seen in the next example, such paths lose the arrow tips:

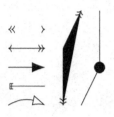

```
\usepackage{tikz}  \usetikzlibrary{arrows.meta,bending}
\begin{tikzpicture}
\path[tips,<<->](0,2)--(1,2);    \path[draw,<->>](0,1.5)--(1,1.5);
\path[draw,-{Latex[length=10pt]}](0,1)--(1,1);
\path[draw,{Bracket[sep] Bracket[]}-](0,0.5)--(1,0.5);
\draw[-{Latex[open,length=10pt,bend]}] (0,0) to[bend left] (1,0);
\filldraw[<<->>](1.5,0)--++(0,1.5)--++(0.5,1);
\filldraw[<<->>](2,0)--++(0.5,1)circle[radius=4pt]--++(0,1.5);
\end{tikzpicture}
```

8-5-14

Using nodes   We turn now to the third important basic concept: the nodes. Nodes allow placing text onto the graphic. They are added to a path using the special path operation node followed by various optional parts and a mandatory argument for the text content.[1] Unlike standard text boxes created with \makebox or \fbox, nodes are not only rectangular. They can have various shapes and many reference points that allow anchoring the node and adding decorations. By default, nodes are placed centered on the current coordinate. This position can be changed with, for example, the keyword at to place the node at an arbitrary position as shown in the next example. The anchor used as a reference point can be set with the anchor key, which takes as a value one of the many predefined anchor names, among them text-related anchors such as base␣west, base, and the various compass directions such as south, north, and north␣west, etc., referring to the borders. The color of the text can be changed with the key text, the font with the key font.

Nodes are not part of the path!   Nodes are not part of the path: When the path is constructed, they are collected and then drawn either on top or — if the option behind␣path is given — behind the path. Such nodes can therefore be drawn and filled with graphic parameters different from the parameters of the path.

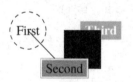

```
\usepackage{tikz}
\tikz\path[draw,fill]
        (0,2) node[circle,draw,dashed]{First}
--      (1,1) node[draw=blue,fill=gray,double]{Second}
rectangle(2,2) node[behind path,fill=blue,text=white,
                    font=\bfseries]{Third};
\par\vspace{1cm}
\tikz\path[draw,fill]
        (0,2) node[circle,draw,dashed] at (1.5,0.5) {First}
--      (1,1) node[draw=blue,fill=gray,double,
                    anchor=north east]{Second}
rectangle(2,2) node[behind path,fill=blue,text=white,
                    font=\bfseries,anchor=north]{Third};
```

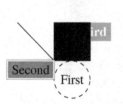

8-5-15

---

[1]It is not always mandatory: the key node␣content can be used instead.

A node can be given a name by adding it in parentheses (or by using the key name). The anchors of such a named node can then be used as coordinates ⟨*name*⟩.⟨*anchor*⟩. We demonstrate this in the following example, which also shows some special shapes provided by additional libraries:

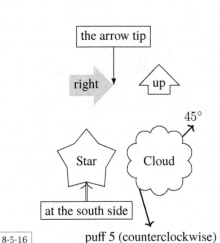

```
\usepackage{tikz,siunitx}  \usetikzlibrary{arrows.meta}
\usetikzlibrary{shapes,shapes.arrows,shapes.symbols}
\begin{tikzpicture}
\node[shape=single arrow,fill=blue!40] (myarrow)
                                   at (0,2){right};
\node[shape=single arrow,draw,shape border rotate=90]
                                   at (2,2){up};
\node[shape=star, draw]  (mystar)  at (0,0){Star};
\node[shape=cloud, draw] (mycloud) at (2,0){Cloud};
\draw[Latex-] (myarrow.tip) -- ++(0,1)
                   node[draw,above]{the arrow tip};
\draw[<-,double] (mystar.south) -- ++(0,-0.5)
                   node[draw,below]{at the south side};
\draw[->,thick] (mycloud.puff 5) -- ++(0.3,-1)
                   node[below]{puff 5 (counterclockwise)};
\draw[->,thick] (mycloud.45) -- ++(0.3,0.3)
                   node[above]{\ang{45}};
\end{tikzpicture}
```

8-5-16

Revisiting coordinates

The command \coordinate used in Example 8-5-3 to create named coordinates is actually an abbreviation command for the path operation coordinate, a special node of size zero that cannot be drawn and takes no text argument. Its only purpose is to create named coordinates.

Connecting nodes

The previous example showed that nodes provide various coordinates that are given as ⟨*name*.*anchor*⟩ or ⟨*name*.*angle*⟩. These coordinates belong to the node coordinate system. Additionally, it is possible to use only the name of the node itself as a coordinate. In such cases, some path construction operations try to calculate the border position that you "mean" — but, naturally, this may fail in some situations.

Other path operations, like the sine curve in the following example, use the center of the node. The example also makes use of the positioning library to place nodes relative to each other:

```
\usepackage{tikz}
\usetikzlibrary{positioning,shapes}
\begin{tikzpicture}[line width=1pt]
\node[draw,circle] (A) {a};    \node[draw] (B) at (2,0.5) {b};
\node[draw,shape=cloud,below=1cm of A.center] (C) {Hello};
\node[draw,left=1cm of A.center] (D) {d};
\draw[<->] (A) -- (B);
\draw[->,dashed] (C) -| (B);
\draw[->,blue] (C) sin (D);
\end{tikzpicture}
```

8-5-17

Edges Another way to connect nodes and coordinates is with "*edges*". The edge operation looks quite similar to other path operations, but like nodes the edges are not part of the path but are collected and added after the main path has been drawn. This allows them to have different graphic parameters. Note that in the second picture of the following example all edges start at node A:

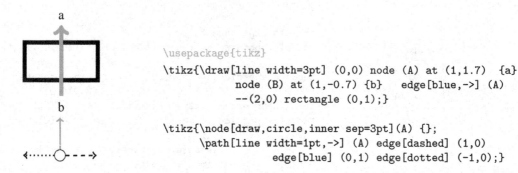

```
\usepackage{tikz}
\tikz{\draw[line width=3pt] (0,0) node (A) at (1,1.7)  {a}
          node (B) at (1,-0.7) {b}    edge[blue,->] (A)
          --(2,0) rectangle (0,1);}

\tikz{\node[draw,circle,inner sep=3pt](A) {};
      \path[line width=1pt,->] (A) edge[dashed] (1,0)
              edge[blue] (0,1) edge[dotted] (-1,0);}
```

8-5-18

8.5.2 Transformations and other operations

Transformations The package tikz offers options to scale, shift, and rotate graphics or parts of them. It is important to understand that these transformations do not affect all elements. As the following example shows, neither the line width nor the nodes are scaled and rotated. This is by design to avoid a inconsequent mix of different font sizes and normally gives the expected result. However, it means that scaling a graphic can require adapting the placement of nodes to fit into the new dimensions. Also it is not always immediately clear whether the transformation applies to a certain dimension. In such cases you should check the documentation. Note in the example the use of the scope environment to keep the transformation local and that a node is rotated by using the key rotate in the node options.

```
\usepackage{tikz} \usetikzlibrary{arrows.meta}
\usetikzlibrary{shapes,shapes.arrows,shapes.symbols}

\begin{tikzpicture}[line width=1pt]
 \draw (0,0)--(1.5,0)--(1,1)node[draw,above]{A}--cycle;
 \begin{scope}[blue,shift={(0,-1.75)},scale=0.5,rotate=40]
  \draw (0,0)--(1.5,0)--(1,1)node[draw,above]{A}--cycle;
 \end{scope}
 \begin{scope}[shift={(0,-3)},scale=0.3,rotate=90]
  \draw (0,0)--(1.5,0)--(1,1)node[draw,above,rotate=40]{A}--cycle;
 \end{scope}
\end{tikzpicture}
```

8-5-19

Changing the bounding box The examples so far created pictures whose size has been calculated automatically. Every time you add some graphic element tikz updates the bounding box so that it contains all points of the graphic, and the reference point for the baseline of the graphic is set to the lower-left corner of the enclosing rectangle — not always what you want. To adjust the reference point use the `baseline` key, which takes a coordinate as its value.

Hello `World.`
Hello `World.`
Hello
`World.`

8-5-20

```
\usepackage{tikz}

\large
Hello \tikz {\node[draw](X) {World.};}

Hello \tikz[baseline=(X.base)] {\node[draw](X) {World.};}

Hello \tikz[baseline={(0,0.2)}] {\node[draw](X) {World.};}
```

To adapt the bounding box you can use the key `overlay` that can be used on nodes, paths, scopes, and complete pictures. The effect of this key is that everything within the current scope is disregarded when the bounding box of the current picture is computed (the material is "overlaid" without taking up size).

Another option is the key `use␣as␣bounding␣box`. When used on a path, all *subsequent* paths in the current scope are ignored in the bounding box calculation. In the next example the bounding box is the square, because the earlier circle is overlaid and the lines are ignored because of the `use␣as␣bounding␣box` key:

A line of random text first …

Left of picture. right of picture. More text, more text, and more text.

8-5-21

```
\usepackage{tikz}

A line of random text first \ldots\\
Left of picture%
\begin{tikzpicture}
  \draw[overlay] (2,1)circle[radius=1.5cm];    % overlaid
  \draw[use as bounding box] (2,0) rectangle (3,1);
  \draw (1,0) -- (4,.75);        % also not counted in
  \draw (1,.75) -- (4,0);        % bounding box calculation
\end{tikzpicture}%
right of picture. More text, more text, and more text.
```

It is possible to reference nodes of pictures other than the current one. The `tikzmark` library by Andrew Stacey [128] provides a useful application: with it, it is possible to add marks in a text that can then be used as coordinates in tikz pictures, e.g., to connect various texts on a page with graphic elements. The example below demonstrates this with the `\tikzmark` command. These marks can then be used with the `pic␣cs:` coordinate notation that takes the name of the mark as value. The picture with the drawing commands should use the key `remember␣picture` because it has to know where it itself is on the page. All drawing commands that make use of "external" `pic␣cs:` coordinates must use the `overlay` key to prevent tikz from including the marks in the bounding box calculation.[1] The drawing can be done before the marks are set with the `\tikzmark` commands — this allows drawing behind the

---

[1]Otherwise, the picture would grow on each compilation, thereby pushing the external `\tikzmarks` further away, which in turn makes the picture bigger next time … try it, by removing `overlay` from Example 8-5-22.

643

text such as to add a background. Typically at least two compilations are needed to resolve the references.

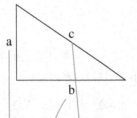

Ut purus elit, vestibulum ut, placerat ac, adipiscing vitae, felis. Curabitur dictum gravida mauris. Nam arcu libero, nonummy eget, consectetuer id, vulputate a, magna.

```
\usepackage{tikz,lipsum}  \usetikzlibrary{tikzmark}
\tikzset{myarrow/.style={->,blue} }
\begin{center}\begin{tikzpicture}[remember picture]
  \draw (0,0)--(3,0) node[midway,below] (b){b}
            --(0,2) node[midway,above] (c){c}
            --cycle node[midway,left] (a){a};
  \begin{scope}[overlay]
   \node[fill=gray,anchor=text] (B) at (pic cs:b)
        {\phantom{$b^2$}};
   \draw[myarrow](b) to [bend right] (B);
   \draw[myarrow](c) -- ([yshift=0.2cm]pic cs:c);
   \draw[myarrow](a) |- ([shift={(-0.1cm,0.1cm)}]pic cs:a);
  \end{scope}
\end{tikzpicture}\end{center}
\lipsum[1][2-4]
\[ \tikzmark{a}a^2 + \tikzmark{b}b^2= \tikzmark{c}c^2 \]
```

8-5-22

| \foreach *variables* [*options*] in {*list*} {*commands*} in |

Repeating things

We finish this introduction with a short presentation of the \foreach utility from the pgffor package (loaded automatically by tikz). The command allows you to loop over a list or a range of numbers and to execute commands once for every element of the list. The current element is stored in one or more variables and can be used in the commands.

apples are red!
ducks are yellow!
trees are green!

```
\usepackage{pgffor} % or tikz
\foreach \x/\y in {apples/red, ducks/yellow, trees/green}
  { \x{} are \y{}! \par }
```

8-5-23

The variable names can be freely chosen: this does not affect code outside the loop, because the code is executed in a group. Be aware that many one-letter command names are used for accents and can have surprising side effects. Note how in the next example the use of the variables \i, \j, and \k destroys the output of ı, ȷ, and A̧, because LaTeX internally calls \i, \j, and \k{A} when processing them:

ı ȷ A̧ (fine)
apple red ok?A (surprise!)

```
\usepackage[T1]{fontenc}  \usepackage{tikz}
\foreach \x/\y/\z in {apple/red/ok?} { ı ȷ A̧ } (fine)        \par
\foreach \i/\j/\k in {apple/red/ok?} { ı ȷ A̧ } (surprise!)
```

8-5-24

A range of numbers can be given with the dot notation. It consists of two start items, three periods, and an end item. In this case \foreach fills up the list with the missing values. This is demonstrated in the next example, where 0,40,...,360 is expanded to the list 0,40,80,120,...,360. We use two separate \foreach loops to print the mice first so that their tails do not poke into the eyes of the sloths. The tikzlings and tikzducks packages to draw the animals are provided by samcarter.

```
\usepackage{tikzlings,tikzducks}
\begin{tikzpicture}[scale=2]
\draw[black] (0,0) circle (1.25);
\foreach \x in {0,40,...,360}
  {\mouse[rotate=\x,scale=0.18,yshift=120,body=blue]}
\selectcolormodel{gray} % monochrome for the book
\foreach \x in {0,40,...,360}
  {
  \sloth[rotate=\x+20,scale=0.25,yshift=70]
  \bear [rotate=\x,    scale=0.15,yshift=80]
  \rhino[rotate=\x+20,scale=0.15,yshift=47]
  }
\duck[scale=0.2,xshift=-30,yshift=-30]
\end{tikzpicture}
```

8-5-25

As you may have guessed, the hummingbird logo (designed by Paulo Cereda for the LaTeX Project Team) is also a tikz picture. This is great, because it allows us to use it in various ways in LaTeX documents for official team publications. At its core it is fairly simple: it mainly consists of lengthy \path statements describing straight and curved lines that are then filled with color. But if you look at the details (a small part of which is shown below), it is clear that Paulo did not sit down and came up with the correct control coordinates through intuition — this is autogenerated tikz.

He told me that he designed the bird in the open source program Inkscape, which is capable of exporting its results in several formats, including PDF but also source formats such as pstricks. He then applied a plugin called svg2tikz (available from https://github.com/xyz2tex/svg2tikz) that can also be used as a standalone program. As its name implies, it converts a SVG graphic as (typically huge) tikzpicture. It has some blind spots and may not work for all graphics, but usually offers a solid way to turn a complex graphic into a tikz source that then can be further tweaked (in small ways) if needed or combined with other tikz elements.

```
\usepackage{tikz}  \definecolor{blue}{cmyk}{1,0.56,0,0}  % what we call 'blue'

\begin{tikzpicture}[y=0.30pt,x=0.30pt,yscale=-1, inner sep=0pt, outer sep=0pt]
  \path[fill=blue!99,rounded corners=0.0000cm] (248.7785,295.7529) rectangle
    (465.3586,478.5802);
  \path[fill=white,rounded corners=0.0000cm] (257.9199,304.5427) rectangle
    (456.2172,469.7905);
  \path[fill=blue!99] (283.2386,478.5760) -- (289.5259,453.4125) .. controls
    (302.2770,439.6121) and (314.0060,425.3008) .. (319.5695,407.9067) .. controls
    (355.0759,401.0374) and (383.7853,403.5174) .. (413.7371,404.2858) .. controls
    (411.0072,403.8309) and (322.2852,388.7992) .. (322.2852,388.7992) .. controls
    (298.7181,356.5528) and (264.6380,373.5409) .. (249.0663,403.2205) --
    (248.7470,478.6397) -- cycle;
```

645

```
\path[color=black,fill=white,nonzero rule,line width=1.253pt]
    (288.4249,394.4251) -- (288.2061,394.8313) .. controls (287.2860,396.5455) and
    (285.7381,397.6863) .. (283.5499,398.3938) .. controls (281.3616,399.1013) and
    (278.5647,399.3476) .. (275.2999,399.2063) -- (273.2374,399.1126) --
    (274.7061,400.5501) .. controls (275.4640,401.2791) and (275.6960,401.8541) ..
    (275.7061,402.3626) .. controls (275.7162,402.8712) and (275.5103,403.4284) ..
    (275.0186,404.0501) .. controls (274.0353,405.2935) and (272.0593,406.6472) ..
    (270.2374,408.0189) -- (269.6749,408.4564) -- (270.0499,409.0501) .. controls
              ... further code omitted ...
```

8-5-26

8.5.3 Going further

Where to go for further help
This section left out many topics that can be handled by tikz: matrices, shadows, animations, transparency, pics, decorations, plots, trees, circuits, page ornaments, and the key management to name only a few. The documentation of the package [133] and the CTAN topic page on tikz [19] are important resources here.

The number of options and keys in tikz can be overwhelming: a nice help is the documentation VisualTikZ [17] by Jean Pierre Casteleyn: The PDF file contains many small examples that helps to identify the needed key combination for different use cases.

Font Selection and Encodings

In this chapter we describe the font selection and encoding models of LaTeX, known as NFSS (New Font Selection Scheme) and the packages and commands to deal with encoding issues. Given that NFSS was first introduced about thirty years ago, it is, of course, no longer really new. The last decade, however, showed a number of exciting new developments, so this chapter, compared to the one in the previous edition of the book, nevertheless contains a lot of new and changed material.

We start with a short introduction to the history of font usage in different TeX engines. This is then followed by a section discussing font characteristics in general and introducing the major attributes used in LaTeX for orthogonal font switching. We then describe the use of the high-level interface — that is, the commands a user normally has to deal with. This includes commands used in normal text (Section 9.3), special features for use in mathematical formulae (Section 9.4), and an overview of basic support packages for NFSS — those being distributed together with LaTeX (Section 9.5).

Section 9.6 is solely devoted to the details of the fontspec package, the frontend to NFSS for use in the Unicode engines X∃TeX and LuaTeX.

The final sections then describe the low-level interfaces that are useful when defining complex new commands and that are important when new fonts are to be made available in LaTeX. Here you find low-level commands for changing individual font attributes (Section 9.7), commands for setting up new fonts with LaTeX (Section 9.8), and a discussion of LaTeX's encoding models for text and math (Section 9.9).

9.1 Introduction

9.1.1 The history of LaTeX's font selection scheme (NFSS)

When TeX was developed in 1979, only a dozen fonts were set up for use with the program. This situation had not greatly changed five years later, when LaTeX was first released. It was thus quite natural that LaTeX's font selection scheme followed the plain TeX concept with the addition of size-changing commands that allowed typesetting in ten predefined sizes.

As a result, LaTeX's font selection was far from general because the font commands were not changing font attributes but exchanged one font with another one. For instance, when, say, the now obsolete command \bf was used inside emphasized text, the result was not a bold italic font, as normally desired, but rather a plain roman bold font. Furthermore, the original release had another major drawback: the correspondence tables between font commands and fonts were hardwired into LaTeX so that replacing the default fonts was a difficult, if not impossible, task.

Since that time low-priced laser printers became available, and simultaneously a large number of font families from PostScript and other font formats appeared. But, unfortunately, because of the LaTeX font selection model, there was no easy and standard method for integrating these new fonts into LaTeX — typesetting with LaTeX meant typesetting in Computer Modern on almost all installations. Of course, individual fonts could be loaded, but they would not work with the size commands nor were they otherwise integrated, so it was extremely complicated to typeset a whole document in a different font family.

This unsatisfactory situation was finally resolved in 1989 with the release of the New Font Selection Scheme (NFSS) [103] written by Frank Mittelbach and Rainer Schöpf, which became widely known after it was successfully used in $\mathcal{A}_{\mathcal{M}}\mathcal{S}$-LaTeX (see Chapter 11). This system contains a generic concept for varying font attributes individually and for integrating new font families easily into an existing LaTeX system. The concept is based on five attributes that can be defined independently to access different fonts, font characteristics, or font families. To implement it, some of the LaTeX commands were redefined, and some new commands were added.

In 1994 NFSS became the official standard in the then newly released LaTeX 2_ε. It has now been in worldwide use for more than thirty years, proving the code to be stable, successful, and most importantly flexible enough to support further advances in font technology and use.

However, in the last decade new requirements appeared that were not easily supported with the original NFSS design and so some extensions in the form of additional support packages appeared.

For pdfTeX two important ones have been mweights by Bob Tennent and fontaxes by Andreas Bühmann and Michael Ummels, both extending the attribute handling of NFSS. Neither package is intended for direct usage but normally used within font support packages, such as those discussed in Chapter 10. In 2020 a large portion of their functionality has been integrated into NFSS so that it is now generally available.

The situation for Unicode engines is different. With the fontspec package by Will Robertson a new frontend for font loading is offered for use in XƎTeX and LuaTeX. This frontend allows one to access all kind of font features available with OpenType or TrueType fonts. It then generates the necessary information for NFSS on the fly — thus under the hood NFSS is still the font selection machinery. The package is discussed in detail in Section 9.6.

9.1.2 Input and output handling in TeX systems over the years

When TeX was originally developed in 1979, computers used 7-bits to encode input characters, which allows for a direct representation of a maximum of 128 characters, i.e., Latin upper and lowercase base characters, digits, and a few symbols. Any other character had to be represented in the form of a command or a sequence of commands; e.g., \ss for ß or \^\j for ĵ, etc.

This certainly allowed inputting text in most Latin-based languages (though already a bit inconvenient) where the need for using commands in the input is still infrequent. Already then there were problems; e.g., hyphenation would not work for words containing diacritics. However, that approach clearly failed for languages with a totally different set of characters, where essentially every character would be represented by a command if we assume that the input can represent only ASCII characters directly. For example, the Russian text for "on the next page" (на следующей странице) would have to be written as

TeX79 largely restricted to English

```
\cyrn\cyra\ \cyrs\cyrl\cyre\cyrd\cyru\cyryu\cyrshch\cyre\cyrishrt
\ \cyrs\cyrt\cyrr\cyra\cyrn\cyri\cyrc\cyre
```

Clearly, no one wants to type text like this on a regular basis.

Fonts in TeX79 used 7-bits as well, i.e., contained a maximum of 128 glyphs and for text fonts the glyph positions matched the ASCII code used at input. In other words, there was a one-to-one correspondence between the number encoding a character on input and the number representing the glyph position in the fonts. For example, the seven bits 1000001 (decimal 65) in a file were interpreted by an editor as the character A and when processed by TeX the program fetched the glyph in position 65 in the current font, which then happened to be "A". For the class of documents that just need basic Latin characters this worked well and was very fast.

The 8-bit days

Computers then evolved and started to use 8-bits for encoding data. With it TeX evolved too and supported 8-bit input and fonts (TeX82 and later TeX 3.0). However, there was now a problem: different computers used different "code pages"; that is,

The 8-bit operating systems

they interpreted the bytes in input files in different ways depending on the operating system's regional settings or other criteria. Thus, while the lower 128 bytes were usually identical, in many code pages the upper half varied greatly, making data exchange difficult, if not outright impossible.

There was nothing inside a file that would explicitly tell how to interpret the 8-bit numbers inside. Thus, suddenly files written on one computer got partially scrambled when processed on a different one unless you knew (and could tell the processing software) under which assumption — that is, under which code page — the file was written.

In LaTeX 2_ε this problem was resolved by introducing the package inputenc that allows one to explicitly state under which input encoding the remainder of the file should be interpreted by LaTeX. It effectively added the missing information about the file encoding to the source so that LaTeX could use it even when running under an operating system that would normally use a different code page.

The input encoding concept

The inputenc package works by interpreting the 8-bit numbers present in the file (representing the characters) and mapping them to an "internal LaTeX representation", which uniquely (albeit on a somewhat ad hoc basis) covers all characters representable in LaTeX. For further processing, such as writing to some auxiliary file, LaTeX exclusively uses this internal representation, thereby avoiding any possible misinterpretation.

And there was (and unfortunately is) a second problem: TeX still assumes by default that input characters can be directly mapped to corresponding font slots. As a consequence, developing 8-bit fonts that use all possible slots would require different fonts for different code pages. For example, if your keyboard contained a key for the Euro symbol (€) and your computer used the Windows code page cp-1252, then pressing this key generated the code 80 while it generated 164 if your computer happened to use the code page ISO-889-15. Thus, if such codes define the glyph position in the fonts, then we need different fonts in each case, one with the Euro symbol in slot 80 and another where it is in 164.

So the inputenc package solves half of the problem, because once applied it correctly interprets the bytes in the input file and LaTeX then sees the command \texteuro in both cases. But then LaTeX needs to know which slot \texteuro has to access to fetch the glyph (and possibly even from which font).

The output encoding concept

All this is achieved in LaTeX through the concept of output encodings, which map the LaTeX internal character representations to appropriate glyph positions or to glyph-building actions depending on the actual glyphs available in the font used for typesetting. This is where the fontenc package comes into play that was introduced at the same time as inputenc. Each font usable with LaTeX is supposed to implement a specific "named" font encoding, and with fontenc you tell LaTeX where to find glyphs in such font encodings.

The Unicode days

The next level of evolution was the introduction of Unicode-based operating systems. They use UTF-8, which is a variable-length encoding that represents Unicode characters in one to four octets. In this case the TeX ecosystem only partially followed. The original program, as maintained by Donald Knuth (TeX 3), as well as the variant pdfTeX (which is what most people still use these days) remained 8-bit programs, which means they cannot natively handle multibyte UTF-8 characters but see them as sequences of individual bytes instead. For example, if the input file (in UTF-8 encoding) contains the character U+00C4 (Ä), then TeX or pdfTeX sees instead two bytes (octal '303 and '204) and renders them as two glyphs corresponding to their slots in the font, i.e., "ÃŬ" in a typical TeX font — which is, of course, utter nonsense.

Early on, when the first Linux distributions decided to use UTF-8 as the default encoding for the operating system, they left their LaTeX users baffled that files written using the keys on the keyboard were suddenly no longer accepted or correctly processed by LaTeX. Nowadays, nearly every operating system uses UTF-8, so this would be a huge problem today.

The inputenc package resolved this issue by providing also support for UTF-8 encoding. It works by identifying which bytes belong to multibyte characters, then assembling those bytes, and finally presenting LaTeX (instead of the byte sequence) with an internal command representing the intended character, i.e., in our example with \"A. This works well, even though it is a rather complicated process. It means, however, that multibyte UTF-8 characters are not letters in the TeX sense — for example, they cannot appear in command names, and there are some other restrictions.

The most important one is probably that pdfTeX (in contrast to the Unicode engines discussed below) cannot handle Unicode combining characters. In Unicode one can represent the characters such as "LATIN SMALL LETTER A WITH TILDE" (ã) either as U+00E3 or as U+0061 (a) followed by the combining accent U+030A (˜), but with pdfTeX only the first works. The technical reason for this is that by the time the combining character is seen, the base character has already been typeset and it is not possible for pdfTeX to superimpose the accent properly. This is normally not a problem, because editors usually generate the single character, but sometimes that may not be the case, and what looks in your editor like ã then appears as "a˜" or generates an error message when printed. If that happens, you need to change your input method or produce the problematical characters through commands, i.e., \~a in that case. Another way to end up with such invalid input is through copy and paste from the Internet, as often text displayed by browsers contains in fact such combining characters, which look fine but fail if copied into your document source.

No support for combining accents in pdfTeX

Copy and paste can be harmful

The second restriction is that inputenc does not provide a full UTF-8 implementation in which every character is accepted. Instead, only Unicode characters that are printable with the set of fonts loaded (that is supported by the font encodings used) are accepted. For all others you get a suitable error message that the Unicode character in question is not set up in LaTeX.[1]

Only printable Unicode characters are accepted by pdfTeX

As nowadays virtually every operating system uses UTF-8 by default this meant that you had to always load inputenc with the option utf8 unless you were writing a document just using ASCII characters. In 2018 the decision was made to make UTF-8

UTF-8 input now the standard for LaTeX on all engines

---

[1] This is actually a Good Thing, as it prevents "tofu" — little squares indicating unprintable characters or empty spaces in place of them in the printout. If you get the error, you can fix the problem by selecting a suitable font or by not using the character. In contrast, the Unicode engines just assume that every Unicode character is printable, and you get no warning if something is missing in the output because it is unavailable in the font.

iiiiiiiiii   iiiiiiiii

mmmmmmmmmm   mmmmmmmmmmm

(monospaced)   (proportionally spaced)

Figure 9.1: Major font characteristics (mono/proportional spaced)

the default encoding for LaTeX so that inputenc now automatically does its magic and needs explicit loading only in cases of a legacy document that is stored in some 8-bit code page.

Unicode-enabled TeX extension programs

The growing availability of Unicode also triggered efforts to develop new TeX variants that would natively understand multibyte input encodings and manage fonts with many more accessible glyphs than 256 (which is the limit in the Adobe's Type 1 format or the fonts produced with METAFONT).

The first of these new programs was Omega [112], an extension of TeX developed by Yannis Haralambous and John Plaice. Omega's declared aim was to improve on TeX's multilingual typesetting abilities. It pioneered the native use of the Unicode multibyte encodings and extended TeX's typesetting model with important new capabilities such as a general model for writing-directions, needed for many languages. While Omega was eventually abandoned and not further developed, many of its ideas and concepts live on in the two important Unicode TeX engines of today: in XeTeX and LuaTeX.

> **Unicode engines**
>
> Special features only relevant to the Unicode TeX engines are documented in this book by placing the text into a box with gray background as shown here.

9.2 Understanding font characteristics

There are many design principles that divide fonts into individual overlapping classes. Knowledge of these characteristics often proves helpful when deciding which font family to use in a special context (for further reading see, for example, the books [7, 20, 79] or the article [26]).

9.2.1 Monospaced and proportional fonts

Fonts can be either monospaced or proportionally spaced. In a monospaced font, each individual character takes up the same horizontal space regardless of its shape. In contrast, characters in a proportionally spaced font take up different amounts of space depending on their shape. In Figure 9.1, you can see that the "i" of the monospaced font occupies the same space as the "m", while it is noticeably narrower in the proportional font. As a result, proportional fonts (also called typographical fonts) normally allow more words to be placed on a page and are more readable than

A A   n   n

Figure 9.2: Comparison of serifed and sans serif letters

monospaced fonts. The extra spaces around individual characters of monospaced fonts make it more difficult for the eye to recognize word boundaries and thus make monospaced text less readable.

However, monospaced fonts do have their uses. Within the proper context, they enhance the quality of the printed document. For example, in tables or computer listings where proper alignment of information is important, a monospaced font is a natural choice. In computer science books, it is common practice to display computer programs in a monospaced font to make them easily distinguishable from surrounding explanations.

9.2.2 Serifed and sans serif fonts

Another useful classification is based on the presence or absence of serifs. Serifs are the tiny strokes at the extremities of character shapes (see Figure 9.2). Originally they were produced by the chisel, when roman capitals were engraved into stone. For this reason, serifed fonts are often referred to as "roman" fonts.

Serifed fonts traditionally have been used for long texts because, it was argued, they are more readable. It was long thought that serifed letters give the eye more clues for identification. This is certainly true if only parts of the characters are visible, but for fully visible text more recent research has shown that reading speed is not substantially affected by the absence of serifs.

9.2.3 Font families and their attributes

Besides the crude classifications of serifed versus sans serif and monospaced versus proportional, fonts are grouped into font families. Members of a font family share common design principles and are distinguished by variations in size, weight, width, and shape. A member of such a family is often called a font face.

Font shapes

An important attribute when classifying a member of a font family is its shape. Of course, sometimes it is a matter of personal judgment whether a set of fonts with different shapes constitutes one or several families. For example, Donald Knuth called his collection of 31 Computer Modern fonts a family [52], yet they form a meta-family of many families in the traditional sense.[1]

---

[1]METAFONT, as a design tool, allows the production of completely different fonts from the same source description, so it is not surprising that in 1989 another family was created [57] based on the sources for the Computer Modern fonts. This family, Concrete Roman, was obtained merely by varying some METAFONT parameters in the source files; but because the result was so different, Knuth decided to give this family a different name.

A	B	C	a	b	c	f	g	i	x	y	z	(upright)
A	*B*	*C*	*a*	*b*	*c*	*f*	*g*	*i*	*x*	*y*	*z*	(italic)
A	B	C	a	b	c	f	g	i	x	y	z	(italic without slant)

Figure 9.3: Comparison between upright and italic shapes

Although there is no uniform naming convention for font shapes, this is unimportant as long as one sticks to a particular scheme. LaTeX's conventions in this respect are discussed in detail in Section 9.7 on page 730.

The upright shape   Nearly every font family has one shape called the "upright" shape.[1] For example, in the font family used in this book (Lucida Bright), the font that you are now reading is in the upright shape.

The italic shape   Another important shape that is present in most families is the "italic" shape, which looks *like this in the Lucida Bright family*. Italic characters are slanted to the right, and the individual letters generally are drawn differently from their upright counterparts, as illustrated in Figure 9.3. The first line in that figure shows letters from the Computer Modern Serif family in upright shape, and the second line shows the same letters in italic shape. For better comparison, the third line gives the italic letters without the usual slant — that is, the letters are artificially shown in an upright position. As you can see, the uppercase letters in these fonts are quite similar except for the slant, but the lowercase letters show distinctive differences in their shapes.

The slanted or oblique shape   Font families without serifs often lack a proper italic shape; instead, they have a "slanted" shape in which the characters slant to the right but are otherwise identical to their upright counterparts. The terms "sloped" and "oblique" are also commonly used for this shape. However, note that a fair number of font families call their oblique faces italic, and for this reason the LaTeX support code usually silently substitutes one for the other unless both are available in parallel.

The swash letter shape   Some modern font families[2] offer so-called swash letter fonts, where some letters show some typographical flourish, such as some extra or lengthened stroke, exaggerated serifs, etc. Such shapes (if available) can nowadays be requested in LaTeX through standard commands as well.

The Small Caps shape   Another common variant is the "small capitals" shape, in which the lowercase letters are represented as capitals with a reduced height, as shown in Figure 9.4 on the next page. If such a shape is not available for a specific family, typographers sometimes use upright capitals from smaller sizes,[3] but this practice does not produce

---

[1] Sometimes you also hear the term "roman" shape. This is because until recently typesetting was nearly always done using serifed fonts. Thus, "roman" was considered to be the opposite of "italic" by many people. So be aware that in some books this term actually refers to the upright shape and not to a serifed font family.

[2] Most often only commercial fonts in their "pro" versions. Among the free fonts described in Chapter 10 there are only four families offering this shape: Baskervaldx, BaskervilleF, Crimson Pro/Cochineal, and EB Garamond.

[3] A good rule of thumb is to use capitals from a font that is about half a point larger than the x-height of the original font unless the x-height is very small. See the discussion in Section 9.8.1 on page 745 for a way to determine the x-height of any font used with TeX.

EXAMPLE Eᴀᴍᴘʟᴇ Exᴀᴍᴘʟᴇ

(Normal Capitals)   (Small Caps)   (Faked Small Caps)

Figure 9.4: Comparison between capitals and small capitals

the same quality as a well-designed small caps font. Real small capitals have different widths and weight than capital letters from the same font that have been reduced to the height of designed small capitals (you can clearly see that the strokes in the faked capitals in Figure 9.4 are much too thin). *Avoid faked small capitals*

While some shapes are mutually exclusive (such as upright, italic, or oblique shapes), it is quite possible to have italic or oblique small capitals, and these days there are in fact quite a number of fonts that offer such shape combinations.[1]

There are a few other, less important shapes. Some families contain fonts in which the inner parts of the letters are drawn in a special fashion, for example "outline" shapes, in which the inner parts of the letters are kept empty. For display purposes, some families also contain fonts that could be classified as "shaded" — that is, where the letters appear three-dimensional. Examples are shown in Figure 9.5 on the following page.

Weight and width

Fonts of a certain shape within a family may differ in "weight". This characteristic refers to the thickness of the strokes used to draw the individual shapes. Once again, the commonly used names are not completely uniform, but it is relatively easy to arrive at a consistent classification. Some font manufacturers, for example, call the font weights intended to be used for normal text "book", while others call them "medium". For thin strokes the name "light" is commonplace, while thicker strokes are usually called "bold". In larger font families, finer distinctions are often necessary, so that we sometimes find a range starting with "ultra light", going through "extra light", "light", "semi light", and so on, and ending with "ultra bold" at the other end. Conversely, often only a few weights are present in some families. For example, the Computer Modern Roman family has only two weights, "medium" and "**bold**".

Another equally important attribute of a font is its "width" — the amount of expansion or contraction with respect to the normal or medium width in the family. Computer Modern Roman has bold fonts in "**medium width**" and "**extended width**" but no fonts that are condensed.

One application for condensed fonts is in titles and headings, where medium-width fonts, when used at large sizes, would consume too much space. Some typesetting systems can even condense fonts automatically to fit a given measure — for example, to exactly fill a particular line in a heading. However, this always means a

---

[1] When LaTeX's font selection mechanism was developed, that was not the case, so in that implementation it was impossible to ask for something like italic small capitals. This was finally changed in 2020, and now such combinations can be specified.

The LATEX Companion

Figure 9.5: Outline and shaded shapes

reduction in quality, and beyond a certain point it becomes aesthetically questionable.

These days this capability is possible with TeX as well, basically as part of the improvements in font management introduced with pdfTeX. The microtype package offers an interface to this; see the discussion on font expansion and contraction in Section 3.1.3 on page 129.

Font sizes

Font sizes are traditionally measured in printer points (pt). There are 72.27 points to an inch.[1] The font size is not an absolute measure of any particular characteristic, but rather a value chosen by the font designer to guide the user. For example, in a 10pt font, letters of the alphabet are usually less than 10pt tall, and only characters such as parentheses have approximately this height.

Two fonts of the same size may therefore not blend well with one another because the appearance of a font depends on many factors, such as the height of the lowercase letters (the x-height), the stroke width, and the depth of the descenders (the part of the letters below the baseline, as in the letter q).

Historically fonts in the (LA)TeX world have been usually made available in sizes that are powers of 1.2 — that is, in a geometric progression [48, p.17]. This arrangement was chosen because it makes it easy to produce an enlarged master copy that later can be photographically reduced, thereby effectively enlarging the final output resolution. For example, if an A5 brochure is to be produced, one could print it with magnification of $1.44 \approx \sqrt{2}$ on A4 paper. Photographic reduction from the 300 dpi (dots per inch) output of a normal laser printer would produce an effective output resolution of 432 dpi and thus would give higher quality than is normally possible with such a laser printer.

However, this geometric ratio scheme used by (LA)TeX fonts produced with the METAFONT program is not common in the professional world, where usual point sizes are 7, 8, 9, 10, 11, 12, 14, 16, 18, 20, 24, 30, and 36. Yet not all fonts are available in all these sizes, and sometimes additional sizes are offered — such as display sizes for large headings and tiny sizes for subscripts and superscripts.

The requirement for fixed sizes had its origin in the technology used. Fonts cast in metal had to exist (at a particular size) or you could not print in that size. In today's digitalized world, fonts are usually vectorized and thus can be scaled at will. As a result, many commercial font families nowadays are provided in only a single design size. LATeX followed this trend and nowadays supports arbitrary font sizes,

---

[1] PostScript and PDF use a slightly different measurement system in which 72 points equal an inch. This unit, sometimes referred to as "big points", is available in TeX as bp.

Ten point type is quite different from magnified five point type

Figure 9.6: Scaled and designed fonts (Latin Modern)

even though there are many places where at least in terms of defaults the origins show through.

The use of magnified or reduced fonts instead of fonts designed for a specific size often gives somewhat less satisfactory results, because to the human eye fonts do not scale in a linear fashion. The characters in handcrafted fonts of larger sizes usually are narrower than fonts magnified from a smaller size of the same family. While it is acceptable to scale fonts within a small size range if necessary, one should use fonts designed for the desired size whenever possible. The difference between fonts scaled to a particular size and those designed for that size is shown in Figure 9.6, though admittedly the variations are often less noticeable.

9.2.4 Font encodings

As mentioned in the chapter introduction, pdfTeX refers to the glyphs of a font by addressing them via 8-bit numbers. Such a mapping is called a font encoding. As far as LaTeX is concerned, two fonts having the same font encoding are supposed to be interchangeable in the sense that given the same input they produce the "same" glyphs on the printed page. To illustrate what happens if we use a font with an encoding not suitable for our input, here is the first sentence of this section again (using the Zapf Dingbats font):

✿▲ ○✳■▼✳◻■✳✳ ✳■ ▼✳✳ ✳✳◉◻▼✳◻ ✳■▼◻◻✳◆✳▼✳◻■✽ ◻✳✳✳✳✳ ◻✳✳✳◻▲ ▼◻ ▼✳✳ ✳●◐◻✳▲ ◻✳ ◉ ◉◻■▼ ◐◘ ◉✳✳◻✳▲▲✳■✳ ▼✳✳○ ◆✳◉ ✗✎◉✳▼ ■◆○○✳◻▲✎

The result is an interesting puzzle, but nothing that we want to see in ordinary documents.

By classifying fonts according to their font encodings it is possible to modify other font characteristics, such as font family or font series, and still ensure that the typeset result stays comprehensible.

Unicode engines

In Unicode engines such as XƎTeX and LuaTeX the situation is different because these engines use the Unicode character number to access a glyph in a font. Thus, there is only a single encoding to deal with, which in theory makes life much simpler. Unfortunately, this is only partly correct, simply because no font contains all Unicode characters, and if you ask for characters that do not exist, you end up with missing glyphs in the printed result (with unfortunately very little warning). Even if for LaTeX there is only a single encoding, in reality, only a subset of that encoding is normally implemented by a font — so technically it is a step forward and a step back at the same time.

Tofu alert with Unicode engines

Such missing glyphs are often rendered as little squares, which got nick-named "tofu" sometimes. With NFSS, LaTeX became largely "tofu" free by rigor-ously requiring that fonts that claim to be in a specific encoding implement all characters of that encoding. Now with Unicode this problem is back. Google's answer to it was the development of the Noto font, which stands for "**no** more **tofu**" and aims to support all languages with a harmonious look and feel. Noto is available to LaTeX users (see Section 10.2.12 on page →II 26), but in most other cases you have to watch out for "tofu".

OT1 encoding   The fonts that were originally distributed with TeX had only 128 glyphs per font and therefore did not include any accented characters as individual glyphs. Instead, all such glyphs had to be constructed using the \accent primitive of TeX or by similar methods. As a result any word containing diacritics could not be automatically hyphenated by LaTeX, and kerning (correction of spacing between certain letters in the font) was not automatically applied. The encoding of these fonts is called OT1. Although it still remains the default encoding for LaTeX (for backwards compatibility with older documents), it is not advisable to use OT1 for languages other than English.[1]

T1 encoding   As an alternative encoding, the TeX user community defined a 256-character encoding called T1 that enables TeX to typeset correctly (with proper hyphenation and kerning) in more than 30 languages based on the Latin alphabet (see Section 9.5.1 on page 684 for further details). The use of the T1 encoding is, therefore, highly recommended with pdfTeX. Nowadays nearly all font families amenable to use with LaTeX are available in this encoding; in fact, some are available *only* in the T1 encoding.

Specifying \usepackage[T1]{fontenc} after the \documentclass com-mand makes T1 become the default encoding. Section 9.5.5 contains a more detailed discussion of the fontenc package. For more on font encodings refer to page 736 and Section 9.9 on page 754.

Unicode engines

TU encoding   While it is to some extent possible to use 8-bit encodings such as T1 or even OT1 with Unicode engines, it is better in that case to use Unicode fonts and thus use Unicode as the encoding. In LaTeX this encoding is called TU and automatically made the default if LaTeX is used with such an engine.

9.3 Using fonts in text

When you are writing a LaTeX document, appropriate fonts are normally chosen auto-matically by the (logical) markup tags used to structure the document. For example, the font attributes for a section heading, such as large size and bold weight, are defined by the document class and applied when a \section command is used so that you seldom need to specify font attributes yourself.

However, occasionally it becomes necessary to specify font attributes directly. One common reason is the desire to change the overall font attributes, by choosing,

---

[1]Even with English there are issues if you use typewriter fonts.

for example, a different font family for the main text. This alteration often can be done by simply specifying an appropriate package (see Chapter 10 for descriptions of such packages).

Another use for explicit font attributes can be to mark certain portions of the document as special — for example, to denote acronyms, example, or company names. For instance, in this book, names of packages are formatted in a sans serif font. This formatting could be achieved by surrounding the names with `\textsf{..}`, but it is much better practice to define a new command (say, `\pkg`) for this purpose so that additional information is included in the source document. By defining individual commands for logically different things — even those that are currently being typeset in the same way — it is easier to change the formatting later in a consistent way.

Last, but not least, in some cases you may want to override a decision taken by the document class. For example, you might want to typeset a table in a smaller size to make it fit on a page. This desire is legitimate, as document classes can format documents automatically only to a certain extent. Hand-formatting — like the insertion of page breaks — is thus often necessary to create the final version. Unfortunately, explicit formatting makes further use of the document (if changes are made) difficult and error prone. Therefore, as with all visual formatting commands, you should try to minimize the direct use of font-changing commands in a document.

9.3.1 Standard LaTeX font commands

The font used for the main text of a document is called the "main font", "body font", or "normal font". It is automatically selected at the beginning of the document and in certain constructs, such as footnotes, and figures. Certain logical markup tags, such as section headings, automatically switch to a different typeface or size, depending on the document class. These changes happen behind the scenes, and the only action required of the author is to introduce the correct logical markup in the document. However, sometimes it might be desirable to manually highlight individual parts of the text, by choosing an appropriate typeface; this is done with the commands described below.

Most font-changing commands come in two forms: a command with one argument, such as `\textbf{...}`, and a declarative form, such as `\bfseries`. The declarations do not take arguments but rather instruct LaTeX that from now on (up to the end of the current group of braces or environments) it should behave in a special way. Thus, you should not write something like `\bfseries{...}`, as this would make everything bold from this point until the end of the current environment; instead use `{\bfseries...}` or `\textbf{...}` if you want to restrict the font change to a small portion of the text.

To change the fonts for individual words or short phrases within your document you should make use of the font commands with one argument. The declarative forms are often better in the definition of new environments or commands. For longer passages in your document, you can also use the environment form of the declaration (the declarative name without the preceding backslash), as shown in the following example. Notice that you need to be careful with spaces; e.g., if the word "typeset" is

Be careful not to add extra spaces in the output

not placed immediately after the start of the environment, there would be two spaces at this point (see the end of the environment where it is done incorrectly).

Some words in this sentence are **typeset in bold letters.**

The bold typeface continues here.

```
Some words in this sentence are
\begin{bfseries}typeset in bold letters.

The bold typeface \end{bfseries} continues here.
```

9-3-1

In fact, the font commands with one argument do not allow paragraph breaks in their arguments. Section 9.3.2 on page 666 contains a detailed comparison of the command and declarative forms and their advantages and disadvantages in specific cases.

Standard font families

By default, LaTeX maintains three font families that can be selected with short command sequences. These families are a serifed text font, accessed with the command `\textrm`; a sans serif text font, accessed by `\textsf`; and a typewriter font (usually monospaced), accessed by `\texttt`. The declaration forms of these commands are `\rmfamily`, `\sffamily`, and `\ttfamily`, respectively.

The names of the external font families accessed by these commands depend on the document class but can be changed by packages or in the preamble (see Section 9.3.6). As an installation default, the serifed font family is Computer Modern Roman, the sans serif family is Computer Modern Sans, and the typewriter family is Computer Modern Typewriter. If you use a different setup, take care to define these default families so that the fonts can be mixed freely without visual clashes.

Unicode engines

The Unicode engines X_ƎTeX and LuaTeX use Latin Modern fonts that are similar to Computer Modern but exist in TU encoding.

In this book, the serifed font family is Lucida Bright, the sans serif family is Lucida Sans, and the typewriter family is Latin Modern Typewriter. These have been chosen by simply[1] loading the package lucidabr and afterwards redefining `\ttdefault` to produce `lmtt`; see Section 9.3.6 for more details on changing the default text fonts.

In most document classes, the serifed font, accessed by `\textrm`, is also the main font of the document, so the command `\textrm` is not used often. If a document designer has chosen a sans serif font as the main typeface, then `\textrm` would be the alternative serifed font family.

Standard font series

Another attribute of a typeface that can be changed is the *series*. In LaTeX the series is a combination of two attributes: width and weight (boldness). LaTeX provides two high-level commands for changing the series: `\textmd` and `\textbf`. The corresponding

---

[1]Somewhat more truthful: for the third edition of this book the Lucida fonts were scaled down slightly, while the Latin Modern Typewriter was scaled up to match the x-height of both families using specially designed `\DeclareFontShape` declarations.

declarations are \mdseries and \bfseries, respectively. The first command selects a font with medium values for the width and the weight, while the latter switches to a bolder series. The actual values depend on the document class and its options or subsequent packages. As a default for the Computer Modern families, \textbf switches to a bold extended version of the current typeface, while \textmd returns to the medium width and medium weight version of the current typeface.

If finer control over the series attribute is desired, it is best to define additional high-level user commands with the help of the lower-level \fontseries declaration described in Section 9.7.1. Some packages that make large font families available for use with LaTeX provide such extra commands.

It is also possible to adjust the default behavior of the font series commands with the help of \DeclareFontSeriesDefault declarations, something that is often done by packages implementing new font families; see Section 9.3.6 on page 673 for details.

Standard font shapes

A third font attribute that may be changed independently of the others is the *shape* of the current typeface. The default shape for most documents is the upright shape with upper and lowercase letters. It can be accessed, if necessary, with the declaration \normalshape (there is no accompanying command form: \textnormal exists but resets *all* font attributes to the document font).

Probably the most important command for changing the shape is \textit (declaration form \itshape), which switches to an *italic* font shape. An alternative to \textit is the \textsl command (its declaration form is \slshape), which switches to the slanted or oblique shape. A font family often contains only an italic or a slanted shape, yet Computer Modern Roman and some other families contain both. If the request cannot be met because the shape does not exist, NFSS normally uses slanted as an approximation for italic and vice versa.

Some font families (especially in the commercial world) offer swash letter fonts that contain glyphs with typographical embellishments such as exaggerated serifs, long tails, extra strokes, etc. In most cases such letters have an otherwise italic design, but this is not always the case. In LaTeX this shape (if available) can be selected with \textsw or \swshape.

At the point where one switches from slanted or italic to upright, the characters usually come too close together, especially if the last slanted character has an ascender. The proper amount of extra white space that should be added at this boundary is called the "italic correction". The value of this adjustment depends on the individual character shape and is stored in the .tfm file.

The italic correction is automatically added by the font commands with arguments, but it must be inserted manually using \/ when declarations are employed. For an upright font, the italic correction of the characters is usually zero or very small, but there are some exceptions. (In Computer Modern, to typeset a bold "f" in single quotes, you should say '{\bfseries f\/}' or '\textbf{f}', lest you get a bold 'f' in some fonts.) In slanted or italic fonts, the italic correction is usually positive, with the actual value depending on the shape of the character. The correct usage of shape-changing declarations that switch to slanted shapes is shown in the next example:

When switching back from *italic* or *slanted* shapes to an upright font one should add the *italic correction,* except when a small punctuation character follows; e.g., a comma or a period.

```
\raggedright        When switching back from
{\itshape italic\/} or {\slshape slanted\/}
shapes to an upright font one should add the
{\itshape italic correction}, except when a
small punctuation character follows; e.g.,
a comma or a period.
```

9-3-2

If you use the command forms with one argument instead, the italic correction is added automatically. This topic is further discussed in Section 9.3.2.

A similarly important shape is \textsc (or \scshape as declaration), which switches to CAPS AND SMALL CAPS. This is arguably not a "shape" as it is really independent of italic or slanted, and these days many font families contain several SMALL CAPS variants and not just a single upright one.[1]

Font selection enhancements in 2020

For this reason \textsc is handled since 2020 in a new way, in that NFSS treats the "letter case status" as independent from the other shapes. For example, if you are currently typesetting in an italic shape, then \textsc attempts to use an italic Small Caps variant of the current font (if available) and does not switch unconditionally to an upright Small Caps shape as it did when NFSS was introduced.

Similarly, when you are typesetting in italic or slanted Small Caps, then \textup or \upshape switches to an upright font, but the request for small capitals remains honored. Instead, to explicitly get back to upper/lowercase letters there is \textulc or \ulcshape.

Compatibility behavior of \upshape

However, if the current shape is upright Small Caps, then both \textup and \upshape cancel the Small Caps and return to the normal shape instead of doing nothing. This is done for compatibility reasons, because in the past people could write \scshape...\upshape instead of writing \textsc{...}, so this usage is still supported.

Of course, all this works only if the font family offers these shapes (LaTeX's standard font families do not), but if you look at Chapter 10, you find that many font families provide italic or slanted small capitals. Here is one example using Alegreya and Alegreya Sans:

Alegreya is one of *the many font families where SMALL CAPITALS are available in italics* as well as in UPRIGHT SHAPE. Thus, nesting \textit and \textsc produces the desired results, as proven above.

```
\usepackage{Alegreya,AlegreyaSans}
Alegreya is one of \textit{the many font families
  where \textsc{Small \textsf{Capitals}} are
  available in italics}  as well as in
\textsc{Upright \textsf{Shape}}.
Thus, nesting \verb=\textit= and \verb=\textsc=
produces the desired results, as proven above.
```

9-3-3

---

[1]When NFSS was originally developed at the beginning of the '90s, that was not the case, and only a few commercial fonts had more than a single Small Caps variant. Therefore, this font attribute was modeled as a shape so that \itshape\scshape would stop *italics* and start UPRIGHT SMALL CAPS.

Small capitals are sometimes used as the shape in headings or to format names in running text. For the latter case you can, for example, define an abstraction such as \name with the definition

```
\newcommand\name[1]{\textsc{#1}}
```

or, using two declarations:

```
\newcommand\name[1]{{\normalfont\scshape #1}}
```

The first definition simply switches to the desired letter case shape, while the second form initially resets all font attributes to their defaults. Which approach is preferable depends on the available fonts and the type of document. With Computer Modern only the Roman and typewriter families contain a Small Caps shape, so the second definition might be preferred in certain applications because it uses small capitals (though serifed) even in a \sffamily context. The first command would result in a request for a medium series, Small Caps shaped font in the Computer Modern Sans family. Because this font does not exist, LaTeX would try to find a substitute by first changing the shape attribute to its default, with the result that you would not get small capitals. (See Section 9.7.3 for further information about substitutions.)

Another interesting use of the \textsc command is in the definition of an acronym tag:

```
\newcommand\acro[1]{\textsc{\MakeLowercase{#1}}}
```

This definition makes use of the LaTeX command \MakeLowercase, which changes all characters within its argument to lowercase (in contrast to the TeX primitive \lowercase, this command also changes characters referred to by commands, such as \OE, to lowercase). As a result, all characters in the argument of \acro are changed to lowercase and therefore typeset with small capitals.

Another slightly special shape command available in LaTeX is the \emph command. This command denotes emphasis in normal text; the corresponding declaration is \em. Traditionally, emphasized words in text are set in italic; if emphasis is desired in an already italicized portion of the text, one usually returns to the upright font. The \emph command supports this convention by switching to the \itshape shape if the current font is upright, and to the \upshape shape if the current font is already slanted (i.e., if the shape is \itshape or \slshape). Thus, the user does not have to worry about the current state of the text when using the \emph command or the \em declaration. However, if \em is used, one needs to take care of any necessary italic correction, so using \emph is usually the better choice.

Providing emphasis

Nevertheless, one has to be careful about the proper *use of italic corrections on both ends of the emphasized text.* It is therefore better to use the \emph command, which *automatically* takes care of the italic correction on both sides.

```
{\em Nevertheless, one has to be careful about
the\/ {\em proper\/} use of italic corrections
on both ends of the emphasized text}.  It is
therefore better to use the \verb=\emph= command,
which \emph{automatically} takes care of the
italic correction on both sides.
```

9-3-4

663

Using the upright shape for nested emphasis is not always very noticeable. A common typographic recommendation is, therefore, to use small capitals for the inner emphasis. This practice is supported by standard LaTeX through the command `\eminnershape`. If the font supports italic small capitals, you have a choice for the inner shape as shown in the example (upright small capitals may work better). The example uses the fbb fonts, a version of Cardo.

One should therefore *prefer the command form over the* DECLARATION *because the former automatically inserts the proper italic correction on both ends of* EMPHASIZED *text.*

```
\usepackage{fbb}
\renewcommand\eminnershape{\upshape\scshape}
```

```
One should therefore \emph{prefer the command form
over the \emph{declaration} because the former
automatically inserts the proper italic correction
   \renewcommand\eminnershape{\scshape}%   keep italics
on both ends of \emph{emphasized} text}.
```

9-3-5

Nowadays LaTeX also offers a generalized way of managing nested emphasis in which you can for each level specify how emphasis should be handled.

Font selection enhancements in 2020

> `\DeclareEmphSequence{`*font-declarations*`}`   `\emreset`   `\emforce`

The command `\DeclareEmphSequence` expects a comma-separated list of *font-declarations* corresponding to increasing levels of emphasis. For example,

```
\DeclareEmphSequence{\itshape,\upshape\scshape,\itshape}
```

uses italics for the first, small capitals for the second, and italic small capitals for the third level (provided you use a font that supports these shapes). If there are more nesting levels than provided, LaTeX uses the declarations stored in `\emreset` (by default `\ulcshape\upshape`) for the next level and then restarts the list.

The mechanism tries to be "smart" and verifies that the given declarations actually alter the current font. If not, it continues and tries the next level — the assumption being that there was already a manual font change in the document to the font that is now supposed to be used for emphasis.

Of course, this check works correctly only if the declarations in the list entries actually change the font and not, for example, just the color. In such a scenario one has to add `\emforce` to the entry, which directs the mechanism to use the level, even if it cannot detect any font attribute changes.

Sections 3.4.4 and 3.4.6 discussed packages that change `\em` to produce underlining. If they are used to change `\emph`, then the above mechanism is turned off. Note, however, that underlining for emphasis is considered bad practice in the publishing world. Underlining is used only when the output device cannot do highlighting in another way — for example, when using a typewriter.

The following example shows most of the possibilities: 1a. and 1b. exhibit LaTeX's standard behavior. In 2a. and 2b. we loop through italics, small capitals, italic small capitals, and then reset to upright and repeat. Note that in 3a. the mechanism concludes that there is no font change in the second level and therefore applies the third level too. Thus, the word "second" comes out already in blue bold italics. In 3b. the command \emforce is added so that now we get blue italics on the second level.

```
\usepackage{tgpagella,color}
\newcommand\testnesting[1]{#1.\ \emph{First \emph{second
    \emph{third \emph{fourth \emph{fifth}}}}}\par}
```

1a. *First* second *third* fourth *fifth*
1b. First *second* third *fourth* fifth
2a. *First* SECOND *THIRD* fourth *fifth*
2b. FIRST *SECOND* third *fourth* FIFTH
3a. *First* second *THIRD* fourth *fifth*

9-3-6

3b. *First* second third FOURTH fifth

```
\testnesting{1a}                    \textit{\testnesting{1b}}
\DeclareEmphSequence{\itshape,\upshape\scshape,\itshape}
\testnesting{2a}                    \textit{\testnesting{2b}}
\DeclareEmphSequence{\itshape,\color{blue},\bfseries,
    \normalcolor\scshape}                    \testnesting{3a}
\DeclareEmphSequence{\itshape,\emforce\color{blue},
    \bfseries,\color{black}\scshape}         \testnesting{3b}
```

Standard font sizes

Out of the box, LaTeX offers ten size-changing commands (see Table 9.1 on the following page). They only change the size of the current font, with all other attributes staying the same. Because size changes are normally used only in the definition of commands, they have no corresponding command forms with one argument.

The size selected by these commands depends on the settings in the document class file and possibly on options (e.g., 11pt) specified with it. In general, \normalsize corresponds to the main size of the document, and the size-changing commands form an ordered sequence starting with \tiny as the smallest and going up to \Huge as the largest size. Sometimes more than one command refers to the same real size; for example, when a large \normalsize is chosen, \Huge can be the same as \huge. In any event, the order is always honored.[1]

The size-related commands for the main text sizes (i.e., \normalsize, \small, and \footnotesize) typically influence the spacing around lists and displays as well. Thus, to change their behavior, one should not simply replace their definition by a call to \fontsize, but instead start from their original definitions, as documented in classes.dtx.

Unfortunately, there is no relative size-changing command in LaTeX — for example, there is no command for requesting a size 2pt larger than the current one. This issue is partially resolved with the relsize package described in Section 9.3.7 on page 675.

The main document font

To reset all font attributes to their default, i.e., to switch to the main document font, you can use the command \textnormal or the declaration \normalfont. They are typically used only in the definition of commands or environments when it is important to define commands that always typeset in the same font regardless of the

---

[1] The reason that size commands are sometimes identical to others is historical: in the early days of LaTeX fonts have been available only in a few discrete sizes, and this restriction was reflected in the document classes that are still in use today.

Command	Example	Command	Example	Command	Example
\tiny	Size	\normalsize	Size		
\scriptsize	Size	\large	Size	\huge	Size
\footnotesize	Size	\Large	Size		
\small	Size	\LARGE	Size	\Huge	Size

The actual sizes shown above are those specially tailored for use in this book

Table 9.1: Standard size-changing commands

surrounding conditions. For example, the command to typeset the command names in this book is defined roughly as follows:

```
\newcommand\Lcs[1]{{\normalfont\ttfamily\textbackslash#1}%
              \index{#1@{\normalfont\ttfamily\textbackslash#1}}}
```

Using \normalfont prevents the command names coming out *like* *this in certain* places. The command does not reset the font color if that got altered. For that task there exists the command \normalcolor.

9.3.2 Font commands versus declarations

We have already seen some examples of font commands that have arguments and change font attributes. These font-changing commands with arguments all start with \text... (except for the \emph command) to emphasize that they are intended for use in normal text and to make them easily memorizable. Using such commands instead of the declarative forms has the advantage of maintaining consistency with other LaTeX constructs. They are intended for typesetting short pieces of text in a specific family, series, or shape. Table 9.2 on the facing page shows the effects of these commands.

A further advantage of these commands is that they automatically insert any necessary italic correction on either side of their argument. As a consequence, one no longer has to worry about forgetting the italic correction when changing fonts.

Only in a very few situations is this additional space wrong. For example, most typographers recommend omitting the italic correction if a small punctuation character, like a comma, directly follows the font change. As the amount of correction required is partly a matter of taste, you can define in which situations the italic correction should be suppressed. This is done by specifying the characters that should cancel a preceding italic correction in the list \nocorrlist.[1] The default definition for this command is

```
\newcommand{\nocorrlist}{,.}
```

---

[1] Any package that changes the \catcode of a character inside \nocorrlist must redeclare the list. Otherwise, the changed character is no longer recognized by the suppression algorithm.

Command	Corresponds to	Action
	Changing families	
\textrm{..}	{\rmfamily ..}	Typeset text in the document's roman family
\textsf{..}	{\sffamily ..}	Typeset text in the document's sans serif family
\texttt{..}	{\ttfamily ..}	Typeset text in the document's typewriter family
	Changing series	
\textmd{..}	{\mdseries ..}	Typeset text in medium series
\textbf{..}	{\bfseries ..}	Typeset text in **bold** series
	Changing shape	
\textit{..}	{\itshape ..}	Typeset text in *italic* shape
\textsl{..}	{\slshape ..}	Typeset text in *slanted or oblique* shape
\textsw{..}	{\swshape ..}	Typeset text in *Swash Letter Shape* (if supported)
\textup{..}	{\upshape ..}	Cancel italics, slanted, or swash and return to upright
\textsc{..}	{\scshape ..}	Typeset text in SMALL CAPS shape (orthogonal to the above)
\textulc{..}	{\ulcshape ..}	CANCEL ANY EARLIER Small Caps request
	Special changes	
\emph{..}	{\em ..}	Typeset text *emphasized*
\textnormal{..}	{\normalfont ..}	Typeset text in the document font
	{\normalshape ..}	Reset only the shape (no \text... variant available!)

Table 9.2: Standard font-changing commands and declarations

It is best to declare the most often used characters first, as it makes the processing slightly faster.

In addition to the global customization, it is possible to suppress the italic correction in individual instances. For this purpose, the command \nocorr is provided. Note that you have to put \nocorr on the left or right end inside the argument of the \emph or \text... commands, depending on which side of the text you wish to suppress the italic correction.

When using the LaTeX high-level font commands, the proper *use of italic corrections is* automatically *taken care of.* Only *very seldom* one has to help LaTeX by adding \nocorr; e.g., to avoid f_1 and instead get f_1.

```
\emph{When using the \LaTeX{} high-level font
commands, the \emph{proper} use of italic
corrections is \emph{automatically} taken
care of}. Only \emph{very seldom} one has to
help \LaTeX{} by adding \verb=\nocorr=; e.g.,
to avoid \textit{f}\textsubscript{1} and
instead get \textit{f\nocorr}\textsubscript{1}.
```

9-3-7

In contrast, the use of the declaration forms is often more appropriate when you define your own commands or environments because this way you can make long-ranging changes across multiple paragraphs.

- *This environment produces a list with italic text.*

- *It is defined in terms of the* itemize *environment and NFSS declarations.*

```
\newenvironment{ititemize}{\begin{itemize}%
  \normalfont\itshape\raggedright}{\end{itemize}}
\begin{ititemize}
\item This environment produces a list with italic text.
\item It is defined in terms of the \texttt{itemize}
  environment and NFSS declarations.
\end{ititemize}
```

9-3-8

9.3.3 Combining standard font commands

As already shown, the standard font-changing commands and declarations can be combined. The result is the selection of a typeface that matches the combination of all font attributes. For example:

One can typeset a text **in a large sans serif bold typeface** but note the unchanged leading! LaTeX uses the value in force at the *end* of the paragraph!

```
One can typeset a text {\sffamily\bfseries
  \large in a large sans serif bold typeface}
but note the unchanged leading! \LaTeX{} uses
the value in force at the \emph{end} of the
paragraph!
```

9-3-9

What happens behind the scenes is that the \sffamily command switches to the sans serif default family, then \bfseries switches to the default bold series in this family, and finally \large selects a large size but leaves all other font attributes unchanged (the leading appears to be unchanged because the scope of \large ends before the end of the paragraph). Font metric files (i.e., .tfm files) are loaded for all intermediate typefaces, even if these fonts are never used. In the preceding example, they would be "sans serif medium 10pt" after the \sffamily, then "sans serif bold extended 10pt" after the \bfseries, and then "sans serif bold extended 14pt", which is the font that is finally used.

Thus, such high-level commands can force LaTeX's font selection to unnecessarily load fonts that are never used. This normally does not matter, except for a small loss of processing speed when a given combination is used for the first time. However, if you have many different combinations of this type, you should consider defining them in terms of the primitive font-changing declarations (see Section 9.7).

When NFSS was originally designed, it provided five font attributes that one could independently change: the font encoding, the family, the series, the shape and the font size. While this was a suitable compromise back then, given the available fonts, it turned out to be not flexible enough when more and more font families became available that supported additional shapes and further series values.

For example, requesting small capitals (with \textsc or \scshape) while typesetting in italics would cancel the italics and change to upright small capitals because both were "shapes" and thus mutually exclusive. However, nowadays many fonts offer italic small capitals, so that behavior was semi-optimal at best. This gave rise to packages such as fontaxes (by Andreas Bühmann and Michael Ummels), which extended NFSS by splitting the shapes into two subgroups so that italic small capitals could be selected by using \itshape\scshape.

With the 2020 release, LaTeX's font selection mechanism was extended to support such features by default: it is now possible to combine different shapes (where it makes sense), and in a similar way the series attribute (which originally combined both width and weight) was also split, so that it is now possible to alter the weight attribute (i.e., how bold or light a font is), while retaining the width, e.g., using condensed fonts. For the series this requires the use of lower-level interfaces that are described in Section 9.7.1 on page 731, but to show the possibilities the next example uses the Roboto font family showing a line with regular bold and light text, followed by a similar line but with all fonts condensed.

Font selection enhancements in 2020

First regular width:
"A **Roboto** line with light text."

Condensed width for comparison:
"A **Roboto** line with light text."

```
\usepackage[sfdefault]{roboto}
First regular width:\\ ``A \textbf{Roboto} line with
{\fontseries{l}\selectfont light} text.''

\bigskip\fontseries{c}\selectfont
Condensed width for comparison:\\ ``A \textbf{Roboto}
line with {\fontseries{l}\selectfont light} text.''
```

9-3-10

9.3.4 Accessing all characters of a font

Sometimes it is impossible to enter a character directly from the keyboard, even though the character exists in the font. Therefore, many useful characters are accessible via command names like \ss or \AE, which produce "ß" and "Æ", respectively. Some characters can also be implicitly generated from sequences of letters (this is a property of fonts) like ffi, which produces "ffi", and ---, which produces "—" in the standard TeX fonts.

In addition, the command \symbol allows you to access any character in a font by giving its number in the current encoding scheme as either a decimal, octal (preceded by '), or hexadecimal (preceded by ") number.

Using the \symbol command you can access any glyph in a font, if you know its position in the encoding. For example, Þ, § or ␣.

However, if available, standard text commands are preferable, because they work correctly in different font encodings.

```
\fontencoding{T1}\selectfont
Using the \verb=\symbol= command you can access any
glyph in a font, if you know its position in the
encoding. For example, \symbol{"DE}, \symbol{'237}
or~\symbol{32}.  \par     However, if available,
standard text commands are preferable, because they
work correctly in different font encodings.
```

9-3-11

The numbers corresponding to the characters in a font can be obtained by using the program nfssfont.tex, described in Section 9.5.9 on page 705.

Unicode engines

When using a Unicode TeX engine, you can access arbitrary Unicode characters with the help of the \symbol command, provided the current font contains the glyph. It is usually best to specify it as a hexadecimal number as that corresponds to the typical notation you find in font tables, e.g., "00DE or "DE for the capital letter Thorn.

However, remember that there is little warning if the font does not contain the glyph as shown in the next example, which compiles without errors, if we do not set \tracinglostchars to 3.

A good way to find the right number in large Unicode fonts is to use the file unicodefont.tex or the package unicodefonttable, both described in Section 9.6.7 on page 728. The next example shows such direct access to a glyph that you find only in the private area of some fonts on Mac computers.

Fonts on a Macintosh often contain an Apple ⌘ symbol, but do not expect the apple '□' to show up with other fonts.

```
\usepackage{fontspec}
\setmainfont{TeX Gyre Pagella} \setsansfont{Optima}
\tracinglostchars=3 % set this to get lost char errors

\sffamily Fonts on a Macintosh often contain an Apple
\symbol{"F8FF} symbol, \rmfamily but do not expect the
apple '\symbol{"F8FF}' to show up with other fonts.
```

9-3-12

In the above example the missing glyph shows up as a little square; in other fonts it might simply not display anything. This is why it is important, especially in Unicode engines where this can happen more easily, to set \tracinglostchars to 3, to get an error message in such situations.

9.3.5 LaTeX 2.09 font support — Compatibility for really ancient documents

More than a quarter century ago LaTeX 2_ε replaced LaTeX 2.09 as the standard LaTeX format. With it the two-letter font commands, such as \bf, became obsolete and in fact are no longer defined by LaTeX 2_ε directly.

Do not use \bf and friends

Old habits die hard, and even nowadays you still see them sometimes used in questions to Stack Exchange and elsewhere. For compatibility reasons the standard classes provide definitions for these commands that emulate their behavior in LaTeX 2.09 so they work if such a class is used, but modern classes not based on article or book often do not define them. So it is best to finally break with this habit and exclusively use the (now no longer) new \textbf and companions instead.

For package developer this is a *must* as otherwise the package may function only in some circumstances.

9.3.6 Changing the default text fonts

To make it easier to modify the overall appearance of a document, LaTeX provides a set of built-in hooks that modify the behavior of the high-level font-changing commands

Hook	Default value		Description
	(pdfTeX)	(XeTeX/LuaTeX)	
\encodingdefault	OT1	TU	Encoding scheme for "main font"
\familydefault	\rmdefault		Family selected for "main font"
\seriesdefault	m		Series selected for "main font"
\shapedefault	n		Shape selected for "main font"
\rmdefault	cmr	lmr	Family selected by \rmfamily and \textrm
\sfdefault	cmss	lmss	Family selected by \sffamily and \textsf
\ttdefault	cmtt	lmtt	Family selected by \ttfamily and \texttt
\bfdefault	b or bx[a]		Series selected by \bfseries and \textbf
\mddefault	m		Series selected by \mdseries and \textmd
\updefault	up[b]		Shape selected by \upshape and \textup
\itdefault	it		Shape selected by \itshape and \textit
\sldefault	sl		Shape selected by \slshape and \textsl
\swdefault	sw		Shape selected by \swshape and \textsw
\scdefault	sc		Shape selected by \scshape and \textsc
\ulcdefault	ulc[b]		Shape selected by \ulcshape and \textulc

[a] The default depends on the font family. For Computer or Latin Modern fonts it is bx; for others b.

[b] These are virtual shapes that get further transformed; see the discussion of the \fontshape command.

Table 9.3: Font attribute defaults

discussed in the previous sections. These hooks are shown in Table 9.3, and their values can be changed by using \renewcommand. As you can see, the values for the default encoding and the default font families in Table 9.3 depend on the engine that is used.

Unicode engines

Note that with Unicode engines, i.e., LuaTeX or XeTeX, you should normally not alter the \encodingdefault nor should you directly manipulate the hooks \rmdefault, \sfdefault, or \ttdefault.

In Unicode engines where the fontspec package is used for font loading (see Section 9.6 on page 705), these defaults are automatically adjusted through declarations such as \setmainfont, etc., and should therefore not be manually changed. The reason is that font loading there works quite differently compared to pdfTeX, and it is not easy for users to guess the correct family names to use.

Adjusting the main document families

The main document font is determined by the values of \encodingdefault, \familydefault, \seriesdefault, and \shapedefault. Thus, you have to make sure that these commands are defined in such a way that their combination points to an existing font shape in LATEX's internal tables.

The initial setting of \familydefault means that changing \rmdefault also implicitly changes \familydefault to the new value, as long as no special setting for \familydefault is defined. However, if \familydefault is changed, \rmdefault is not affected.

This applies only to 8-bit engines, e.g., pdfTEX When you use pdfTEX, you could therefore write

```
\renewcommand\rmdefault{LibreBodoni-TLF}
```

in the preamble, and the whole document would come out in Libre Bodoni, because this redefinition changes the font family for the main document font used by LATEX. Or you could write

```
\renewcommand\familydefault{\sfdefault}
```

which would make the sans serif family the main document family, but \textrm would still be available to switch to the serif family when necessary. This works in all engines.

Suitable values for these font family defaults to use with pdfTEX can be found by looking through the font tables in this and the next chapter.

> **Unicode engines**
>
> For Unicode engines the tables in Chapter 10 also contain the Unicode font names to use with the fontspec package.

Adjusting the font encoding default

Suboptimal encoding default in pdfTEX The default value stored in \encodingdefault is OT1 when pdfTEX is used, which means that LATEX assumes that most fonts use the original TEX encoding. This is actually a compatibility setting: in most circumstances it is better to use the Cork T1 encoding because it contains many additional glyphs that are not available with the old OT1 encoding and it allows proper hyphenation for words with accented characters (see Section 9.5.1). Nowadays, some fonts are made available only in T1; that is, they do not support OT1 at all.

> **Unicode engines**
>
> In LuaTEX or XƎTEX the default encoding for text material is TU and should normally not be changed unless you intend to use individual symbols from some specific font that exists only in a special encoding. Text encodings other than TU are problematical because the hyphenation rules in Unicode engines assume the TU encoding.

In pdfTEX the \encodingdefault is implicitly changed by loading the fontenc package with one or more options, and it is therefore normally not necessary to modify it directly; see Section 9.5.5. For more information on font encodings, refer to Section 9.7.1.

One also has to be aware that not every font encoding is suitable for use as a document-encoding default in pdfTeX either. A prerequisite is that the encoding must include most of the visible ASCII letters in their standard positions; see the discussion in Section 9.9 on page 754 for details.

Adjusting the font series defaults

The default behavior of the high-level commands for changing the font series (e.g., \textbf or \textmd) is to switch to a suitable bold or medium series, i.e., using bx, b, or m. While it is possible to alter that by redefining the main defaults \bfdefault or \mddefault, this can be done in a more granular way, by using one or more \DeclareFontSeriesDefault declarations. This allows you to define combinations such as a b (bold) series for the roman font family and a sb (semi-bold) series for sans serif family, etc.

\DeclareFontSeriesDefault [*meta-family*] {*meta-series*}{*default*}

This changes a series default for one of the main document families: *meta-family* can be either rm (serif family), sf (sans serif family), or tt (typewriter family). The *meta-series* is either bf or md, and *default* is the value to be used. The declaration alters the main defaults (\bfdefault or \mddefault) if you use it without the optional *meta-family* argument.

For example, \DeclareFontSeriesDefault[rm]{bf}{sb} would use sb (semi-bold) when within the scope of \rmfamily or \textrm; a bold typeface is requested with \textbf or \bfseries.

As a more extensive example we take a look at the Noto fonts because they offer a large number of different weights and widths to play with; see Table 10.14 on page →II 28. First we display the defaults one gets by just loading the fonts via the noto package:

Foo bar 42   \usepackage[oldstyle]{noto}

9-3-13 **Foo bar 42**   Foo \texttt{bar} \textsf{42} \par \textbf{Foo \texttt{bar} \textsf{42}}

Now we make a number of admittedly obscure changes: we change the serif family to be semi-bold (sb) by default and ultra-bold (ub) when \textbf is requested. For typewriter text we want light-extracondensed (lec) and semibold-extracondensed (sbec) when boldening is called for. Finally, for the sans serif font we want medium-condensed (mc) but specify nothing special for \textbf; thus, we get bold (b).

```
\usepackage[oldstyle]{noto}
\DeclareFontSeriesDefault[rm]{md}{sb}  \DeclareFontSeriesDefault[rm]{bf}{ub}
\DeclareFontSeriesDefault[tt]{md}{lec} \DeclareFontSeriesDefault[tt]{bf}{sbec}
```

Foo bar 42   \DeclareFontSeriesDefault[sf]{md}{mc}

9-3-14 **Foo bar 42**   Foo \texttt{bar} \textsf{42} \par \textbf{Foo \texttt{bar} \textsf{42}}

Of course, you have to make sure that the requested series value is actually available with the font families you use. For example, when typesetting in LaTeX's standard fonts Computer or Latin Modern, it would be a really bad idea to specify

```
\DeclareFontSeriesDefault{bf}{bc}   % or \renewcommand\bfdefault{bc}
```

Wrong bold ✎
default can lead ✎
to problems

because neither family offers any bold condensed shapes. Thus, a request for bold would then trigger font substitution, and the result would be a font with upright shape and medium series. So you have to look at the font tables, i.e., Table 9.5 on page 684 (Computer Modern) and Table 9.6 on page 687 (Latin Modern), to see what is offered. For example, with Latin Modern we could write

```
\DeclareFontSeriesDefault[rm]{bf}{b}
\DeclareFontSeriesDefault[tt]{bf}{b}
```

because both Latin Modern Roman and Typewriter have a **medium-weight bold typeface**, whereas Latin Modern Sans offers only **bold-extended**, so one should not alter its default. Or you could use, instead of the medium `typewriter` series, the light condensed `typewriter` series as the default by specifying

```
\DeclareFontSeriesDefault[tt]{md}{lc}
```

With the added flexibility in the series it becomes difficult to know when you are in a "bold" context and when not. In the past programmers have tried to determine this by looking at the current font and at the value of `\bfdefault`, but if that can change from family to family, then such an approach will fail half of the time. To resolve this issue `\IfFontSeriesContextTF` is provided.

`\IfFontSeriesContextTF{`*meta-series*`}{`*true-code*`}{`*false-code*`}`

The *meta-series* argument can be either `bf` or `md`. The command examines the current font and its default series settings, and depending on the evaluation, the second or third argument is executed, respectively. To give an example we define below a `\vbeta` command that produces a β that in a bold context, e.g., in a heading, it automatically boldens. Because of the `\ensuremath`, it can be used in both math and text mode.

1 β-isotopes

The β-isotopes are interesting: β

```
\usepackage{bm}
\newcommand\vbeta{\IfFontSeriesContextTF{bf}%
    {\ensuremath{\bm{\beta}}}{\ensuremath{\beta}}}
\section{\vbeta-isotopes}
The \vbeta-isotopes are interesting: $\vbeta$
```

9-3-15

> **Unicode engines**
>
> If you want to use `\DeclareFontSeriesDefault` with Unicode engines, then you have the issue that most font families declared with fontspec have only the medium and the bold series set up by default.

Thus, processing Example 9-3-14 on page 673 with LuaTeX would result in substituting the medium series everywhere, because neither sb, lec, ub, sbec, nor ub are set up when you use the noto package with that engine.

To make it work, you would need to explicitly set up all necessary font faces first by using fontspec's FontFace key; see page 712 for details. Such settings can then be saved in a .fontspec file for reuse.

Adjusting the font shape defaults

Adjusting the five shape defaults is normally not necessary because they correspond to the standard naming convention for shapes that nearly all fonts families implement. Changing them would render all standard .fd (font definition) files obsolete, so this would make sense only as part of a very specialized project.

9.3.7 relsize, scalefnt — Relative changes to the font size

Standard LaTeX offers ten predefined commands that change the overall font size (see Table 9.1 on page 666). The selected sizes depend on the document class but are otherwise absolute in value. That is, \small always selects the same size within a document regardless of the surrounding conditions.

However, in many situations it is desirable to change the font size relative to the current size. This can be achieved with the relsize package, originally developed by Bernie Cosell and later updated and extended for LaTeX 2_ε by Donald Arseneau and Matt Swift.

The package provides the declarative command \relsize, which takes a number as its argument denoting the number of steps by which to change the size. For example, if the current size is \Large, then \relsize{-2} would change to \normalsize. If the requested number of steps is not available, then the smallest (i.e., \tiny) or largest (i.e., \Huge) size command is selected. This means that undoing a relative size change by negating the argument of \relsize is not guaranteed to bring you back to the original size — it is better to delimit such changes by a brace group and let LaTeX undo the modification.

The package further defines \smaller and \larger, which are simply abbreviations for \relsize with the arguments -1 and 1, respectively. Convenient variants are \textsmaller and \textlarger, whose argument is the text to reduce or enlarge in size. These four commands take as an optional argument the number of steps to change if something different from 1 (the default) is needed.

Some large text with a few small words inside.

SMALL CAPS (faked)
SMALL CAPS (real; compare the running length and stem thickness to previous line).

9-3-16

```
\usepackage{relsize}

\Large Some large text with  a few
     {\relsize{-2}small words} inside.
\par\medskip
\normalsize\noindent
S\textsmaller[1]{MALL} C\textsmaller[1]{APS} (faked)\\
\textsc{Small Caps} (real; compare the running length
     and stem thickness to previous line).
```

In fact, the above description for `\relsize` is not absolutely accurate: it tries to increase or decrease the size by 20% for each step and selects the LaTeX font size command that is closest to the resulting target size. It then compares the selected size and target size. If they differ by more than the current value of `\RSpercentTolerance` (interpreted as a percentage), the package calls `\fontsize` with the target size as one of the arguments. If this happens, it is up to LaTeX's font selection scheme to find a font matching this request as closely as possible. By default, `\RSpercentTolerance` is an empty macro, which is interpreted as 30 (percent) when the current font shape group is composed of only discrete sizes (see Section 9.8.1), and as 5 when the font shape definition covers ranges of sizes.

Using a fixed factor of `1.2` for every step may be too limiting in certain cases. For this reason the package also allows "half-steps", e.g., specifying `\relsize{0.5}`. It additionally offers the more general declarative command `\relscale{`*factor*`}`, and its variant `\textscale{`*factor*`}{`*text*`}`, to select the size based on the given *factor*, such as `1.3` (enlarge by 30%). However, all commands eventually select a font size that corresponds to one of the standard font sizes offered by LaTeX, so this request means only "approximately enlarge by 30%".

Exact scaling   If you really want to scale the current font size by an exact *factor*, you can do so by loading the small package scalefnt written by David Carlisle that provides the declaration `\scalefont{`*factor*`}`. If this is used, the current font is scaled precisely by that *factor*, provided the font exists in the resulting size and not only in a number of discrete sizes.

9.4 Using fonts in math

Unlike the situation in text, automatic changes in font shapes are generally not desired in math formulas. For mathematicians, individual shapes convey specific information. For example, bold upright letters may represent vectors. If the characters in a formula were to change because of surrounding conditions, the result would be incorrect. For this reason, handling of fonts in mathematical formulas is different than that in text.

Characters in a formula can be loosely put into two classes: symbols and alphabetic characters (including digits). Internally, TeX distinguishes between eight types of math characters (to account for appropriate spacing), but for the discussion of fonts the division into two classes is generally adequate.

Some symbols, such as =, can be entered directly from the keyboard. The bulk of them, however, must be entered via a control sequence — for example, `\leq` stands for ≤. The other main group of characters in a formula, the alphabetic characters (at least the Latin ones), are entered directly from the keyboard.

> **Unicode engines**
>
> In Unicode engines it is in theory possible to enter symbols as Unicode characters instead of using commands. However, so far there is only limited support for this, and it is therefore usually better to stay with the more traditional input because that keeps your documents portable.

More than 200 symbols are predefined in a standard LaTeX system, allowing the user to typeset almost any desired formula. These symbols are scattered over several fonts, but they are accessed in such a way that the user does not have to be aware of their internal representations. If necessary, additional symbol fonts can be made accessible in a similar way; see Section 9.8.5.

The most important difference between symbols and alphabet characters is that symbols always have the same graphical representation within one formula, while it is possible for the user to change the appearance of the alphabet characters. We call the commands that change the appearance of alphabet characters in a formula "math alphabet identifiers" and the fonts associated with these commands "math alphabets". The alphabet identifiers are independent of surrounding font commands outside the formula, so a formula does not change if it is placed (for example) inside a theorem environment whose text is, by default, typeset in italics. This behavior is very important, because character shapes in a mathematical formula carry meanings that must not change because the formula is typeset in a different place in a document.

Text font declarations such as `\bfseries` cannot be used in formulas. This is the price we must pay for the greater flexibility in choosing text font attributes — a flexibility that we do not want in a formula. We therefore need a different mechanism (math alphabet identifiers) for changing the typeface of certain alphabet characters in complicated formulas. It is nevertheless possible to use the corresponding `\text...` commands, e.g., `\textrm` if you want some "ordinary text" within your formula. This is discussed in Section 9.4.2.

9.4.1 Special math alphabet identifiers

One alphabet and a huge number of symbols are not sufficient for scientists to express their thoughts. They tend to use every available typeface to denote special concepts. Besides the use of foreign alphabets such as Greek letters, which usually are accessed as symbols — `\alpha`, `\beta`, and so on — we find sans serif letters for matrices, bold serif letters for vectors, and Fraktur fonts for groups, ideals, or fields. Others use calligraphic shapes to denote sets. The conventions are endless, and — even more importantly — they differ from one discipline to another. For this reason LaTeX makes it possible to declare new math alphabet identifiers and associate them with any desired font shape group instead of relying only on a predefined set that cannot be extended. These identifiers are special commands for use in a formula that typeset any alphabet character in their argument in a specific typeface. (Symbols cannot be changed in this way.) These identifiers may use different typefaces in different formulas, as we will see in Section 9.4.3, but within one formula they always select the same typeface regardless of the surrounding conditions.

Predefined alphabet identifiers

New math alphabet identifiers can be defined according to the user's needs, but LaTeX already has a few built in. These identifiers are shown in Table 9.4 on the following page. As the last lines in the table show, the letters used in formulas are taken by default from the math alphabet `\mathnormal`. In contrast, the letters produced by `\mathit` have different spacing; thus, this alphabet could be used to provide full-word variable names, which are common in some disciplines.

Command	Example	
\mathcal	$\mathcal{A}=a$	$\mathcal{A} = a$
\mathrm	max_i	max_i
\mathbf	$\sum x = \mathbf{v}$	$\sum x = \mathbf{v}$
\mathsf	G_1^2	G_1^2
\mathtt	$\mathtt{W}(a)$	$\mathtt{W}(a)$
\mathnormal	$\mathnormal{abc}=abc$	$abc = abc$
\mathit	$differ\neq\mathit{differ}$	$differ \neq \mathit{differ}$

Table 9.4: Predefined math alphabet identifiers in LaTeX

In LaTeX math alphabet identifiers are commands with one argument, usually a single letter or a single word to be typeset in a special font.

Therefore, G can be computed as

$$G = \mathcal{A} + \sum_{i=1}^{n} \mathcal{B}_i \qquad (1)$$

Therefore, G can be computed as
```
\begin{equation}
    \mathsf{G} = \mathcal{A} +
                 \sum_{i=1}^{n} \mathcal{B}_{i}
\end{equation}
```

9-4-1

The command names for the math alphabet identifiers are chosen to be descriptive rather than simple to type — they all start with \math. However, it is better to stick to the names rather than inventing random abbreviations, because this helps others (co-workers or journal editors) to easily understand your source text. Possible exceptions are cases where you invent special notations that are relevant for your current paper and you want to give them descriptive names. In that case, defining your own command can be helpful, especially if there is a chance that you may want to alter the notation later, e.g.,

```
\newcommand\Gset{\mathcal{G}}
```

but do not come up with something like \mrm for \mathrm just to save you a few keystrokes — it is a nightmare for copy editors and everybody else who has to work with your source, including most likely yourself at some point in the future.

How to define new alphabet identifiers is explained on page 680, and Section 12.1 on page →II 226 describes several packages that make this process even simpler for a large number of fonts that can reasonably serve as math alphabets.

The character scope of math alphabet identifiers

You may wonder what characters are affected by a math alphabet identifier such as \mathrm if you place them into its argument. Unfortunately, the answer is "it depends". One way to answer this question is that all characters that are set up as

\mathalpha symbols in LaTeX (see Section 11.8 on page →II 208) are affected and change based on the alphabet identifier. But which characters belong to this type depends on the setup. There is a default setup for LaTeX that was largely influenced by the available math fonts at the time, but anybody is free to make alterations, and some font packages do.

What you can expect is that every math alphabet identifier affects the 26 uppercase Latin letters, i.e., A–Z. Most identifiers, but already not all, also affect lowercase Latin and digits. In LaTeX's standard setup the eleven uppercase Greek symbols that differ from Latin uppercase and that have commands to access them in math, e.g., \Omega, are also set up as \mathalpha, but again, many alphabet identifiers do not correctly work on them.

Technically, a math alphabet identifier corresponds to a specific font (declared with \DeclareMathAlphabet or \DeclareSymbolFontAlphabet described below), and when you place a character or a command, such as \Delta, in its scope, all that happens is that the glyph from a defined slot (always the same for the same character) is fetched. If that slot contains a glyph for a different character or none at all, you get a wrong result (e.g., with \mathcal or \mathfrak in the next example) or a missing character warning.

0123 *lower UPPER* ΔΓ
0123 lower UPPER ΔΓ
0123 lower UPPER ΔΓ
/∞∈∋ ‡≀⊒]∇ $\mathcal{UPPER}$ ·−
0123 $\mathfrak{lower}$ $\mathfrak{UPPER}$ ∂b
9-4-2 0123 *lower UPPER ΔΓ*

```
\usepackage{amssymb} % for \mathfrak
$              0123\ lower\ UPPER\ \Delta\Gamma $ \par
$     \mathbf{0123\ lower\ UPPER\ \Delta\Gamma}$ \par
$     \mathsf{0123\ lower\ UPPER\ \Delta\Gamma}$ \par
$    \mathcal{0123\ lower\ UPPER\ \Delta\Gamma}$ \par
$   \mathfrak{0123\ lower\ UPPER\ \Delta\Gamma}$ \par
$\mathnormal{0123\ lower\ UPPER\ \Delta\Gamma}$
```

The behavior of Greek letters for math is particularly interesting. The lowercase Greek letters are traditionally set slanted, and they are not affected by alphabet identifiers. However, the uppercase Greek are usually set upright, and they change with the identifier (or break) — funnily enough, \mathnormal, as shown above, changes them to slanted even though that is not the "normal" way they are written.

The above describes the standard default situation within LaTeX. However, note that this may not be true after loading additional font packages for math and is especially not true any longer in Unicode engines when using fontspec or unicode-math. There the uppercase Greek letters may still be formally \mathalpha, but in most math alphabet identifiers such \mathbf they would fail.

0123 *lower UPPER* ΔΓ
0123 lower UPPER
0123 lower UPPER
9-4-3 0123 *lower UPPER ΔΓ*

```
\usepackage{fontspec}
\setmainfont{Alegreya}
\setsansfont{Alegreya Sans}
$              0123\ lower\ UPPER\ \Delta\Gamma $ \par
$     \mathbf{0123\ lower\ UPPER\ \Delta\Gamma}$ \par
$     \mathsf{0123\ lower\ UPPER\ \Delta\Gamma}$ \par
$\mathnormal{0123\ lower\ UPPER\ \Delta\Gamma}$
```

No default math alphabet
You may also wonder what the default math alphabet is — that is, from which alphabet the alphabet characters are selected if you do not specify an alphabet identifier explicitly, as in the formula $x = 123$. The answer is that no single default math alphabet exists. The LaTeX system can be set up so that alphabetical characters are fetched from different alphabets as long as the user has not explicitly asked for a specific one, and this is normally the case, as the following example shows:

$x = 12345$ (1)

$\mathrm{x} = 12345$ (2)

$x = 12345$ (3)

```
\usepackage{amsmath}
\begin{align}
     x            &= 12345                \\
     \mathrm{x}   &= \mathrm{12345}       \\
     \mathnormal{x} &= \mathnormal{12345}
\end{align}
```

9-4-4

As you can see, \mathrm does not change the digits and \mathnormal does not change the letters, so the default for digits in the normal setup is the math alphabet associated with \mathrm, and the default for letters is the one associated with \mathnormal.[1] This behavior can be controlled with the \DeclareMathSymbol command, which is explained in Section 9.8.5.

Defining new alphabet identifiers

New math alphabet identifiers are defined with the \DeclareMathAlphabet command. Suppose that you want to make a slanted sans serif typeface available as a math alphabet. First you decide on a new command name, such as \mathsfsl, to be used to select your math alphabet. Then you consult the font tables in this chapter (starting on page 684) or the next chapter to find a suitable font face to assign to this alphabet identifier. You will find that the Computer Modern Sans family, for example, consists of a medium series with upright and slanted shapes. If you decide to use the slanted shape of this family, you tell LaTeX using \DeclareMathAlphabet.

```
\DeclareMathAlphabet{cmd}{encoding}{family}{series}{shape}
```

This declaration has four arguments besides the identifier: the encoding scheme, the family, the series, and the shape of the font to be used. The alphabet identifier defined in the example always switches to Computer Modern Sans medium slanted.

We demonstrate this with the formula

$$\sum A_i = a \tan \beta \qquad (1)$$

```
\DeclareMathAlphabet{\mathsfsl}{T1}{cmss}{m}{sl}
We demonstrate this with the formula
\begin{equation}
   \sum \mathsfsl{A}_{i} = a \tan \beta
\end{equation}
```

9-4-5

---

[1] It is a strange fact that the Computer Modern math font that corresponds to the \mathnormal alphabet actually contains oldstyle numerals. When the Computer Modern fonts were developed, space was a rare commodity, so Donald Knuth squeezed a number of "nonmathematical" glyphs into these fonts that are normally used only in text.

It is also possible to redefine an existing math alphabet identifier in a package file or in the preamble of your document. For example, the declaration

```
\DeclareMathAlphabet{\mathsf}{T1}{qag}{m}{n}
```

overrides the default settings for the `\mathsf` alphabet identifier. After that, `\mathsf` will switch to Adventor (Avant Garde) in your formulas. There is, however, a subtle point: if the math alphabet in question is part of a symbol font that is already loaded by LaTeX for other reasons (e.g., `\mathcal`), it is better to use `\DeclareSymbolFontAlphabet` as it makes better use of TeX's somewhat limited resources for math; see page 752 for details.

Theproblem is that TeX, or more exactly the 8-bit versions of TeX, such as pdfTeX, have a hard limit of 16 on the number of different math font groups that can be used in a single formula. For each symbol font declared (by a package or in the preamble) an extra math family is allocated, and the same happens for each math alphabet (such as `\mathbf`) that gets used anywhere in the document. Until recently, these math alphabet allocations were permanent, even if they were used only once; the result was that in complex documents you could easily run out of available math font groups. The only remedy for this was to define your own math version, which is a complicated and cumbersome process.

Working with the low limit of possible math alphabets

This situation has been improved in 2021 by the introduction of a new counter `localmathalphabets`, which governs how many of the math family slots are assigned only locally when a new math alphabet (and a new math family) is needed. Once the current formula is finished, every such further (local) allocation is undone, giving you a fighting chance of being able to use different new math alphabets in the next formula.

The default value of `localmathalphabets` is 2, but if you need more local alphabets because of the complexity of your document, you can set this to a higher value, e.g., 4 or 5. Setting it even higher is possible, but this would seldom be useful because many family slots will be taken up by symbol fonts, and such slots are always permanently allocated, whether used or not.

Unicode engines

While `\DeclareMathAlphabet` can be used with any TeX engine, it is not that convenient with TU encoded fonts in Unicode engines, because by default you do not have an NFSS family name available and fontspec sets up only a few font faces for you (medium and bold series).

If you are typesetting using such engines, then the `\setmathfontface` command provided by the unicode-math package is the better option because it allows you to set up OpenType fonts as math alphabets easily.

```
\setmathfontface{cmd}{font name}[font features]
```

This is discussed further in Section 12.4 on page →II 253. The possibilities for specifying *font name* and *font features* are covered at length in Section 9.6 on page 705.

681

Here is a simple example setting up a typewriter italic font as a math alphabet:

$ttit \approx tt + \mathit{italic}$

```
\usepackage{unicode-math}
\setmathfontface\mathttit{texgyrecursor-italic.otf}
$\mathttit{ttit} \approx \mathtt{tt} + \mathit{italic}$
```

9-4-6

9.4.2 Text font commands in math

As mentioned previously, text font declarations like `\rmfamily` cannot be used in math. However, the font-changing commands with arguments — for example, `\textrm` — can be used in both text and math. You can use these commands to temporarily exit the math context and typeset some text in the midst of your formula that logically belongs to the text outside of the formula. Note that the font used to typeset this text therefore depends on surrounding conditions — that is, the command picks up the current values of encoding, family, series, and shape, and then changes one of the attributes as requested.

The result will be

$$x = 10 \textbf{ and thus } y = 12$$

```
\sffamily The result will be
\[ x = 10 \textbf{ and thus } y = 12 \]
```

9-4-7

As you see, the Sans family was retained, and the series was changed to bold. Perhaps more useful is the `\text` command, provided by the amsmath package, which typesets in the current text font without any modification to it (see Section 11.6.1).

9.4.3 Mathematical formula versions

Besides allowing parts of a formula to be changed by using math alphabet identifiers, LaTeX lets you change the appearance of a formula as a whole. Formulas are typeset in a certain "math version", and you can switch between math versions outside of math mode by using the command `\mathversion`, thereby changing the overall layout of the following formulas.

LaTeX knows about two math versions that are called "normal" and "bold". Additional ones are sometimes provided in special packages. As the name indicates, `\mathversion{normal}` is the default. In contrast, the bold version produces bolder alphabet characters and symbols, though by default big operators, like `\sum`, are not changed. The following example shows the same formula first in the normal and then in the bold math version:

$$\sum_{j=1}^{z} j = \frac{z(z+1)}{2} \qquad (1)$$

```
\begin{equation}
  \sum_{j=1}^{z} j = \frac{z(z+1)}{2}
\end{equation}
\mathversion{bold}
\begin{equation}
  \sum_{j=1}^{z} j = \frac{z(z+1)}{2}
\end{equation}
```

9-4-8

$$\boldsymbol{\sum_{j=1}^{z} j = \frac{z(z+1)}{2}} \qquad (2)$$

For historical reasons LATEX has two additional commands to switch to its standard math versions: `\boldmath` and `\unboldmath`.

Using `\mathversion` might be suitable in certain situations, such as in headings, but remember that changing the version means changing the appearance (and perhaps the meaning) of the entire formula. If you want to darken only some symbols or characters within one formula, you should not change the `\mathversion`. Instead, you should use the `\mathbf` alphabet identifier for characters and/or use the command `\bm` provided by the bm package; see Section 12.2.1.

If you change the math version with the `\mathversion` command, LATEX looks in its internal tables to find where all the symbols for this new math version are located. It also may change all or some of the math alphabet identifiers and associate them with other font shapes in this version.

What happens to math alphabet identifiers that you have defined yourself, such as the `\mathsfsl` from Example 9-4-5? As long as you declared them using only `\DeclareMathAlphabet`, they stay the same in all math versions.

If the math alphabet identifier is to produce a different font in a special math version, you must inform LATEX of that fact by using the `\SetMathAlphabet` command. For example, in the default setup the `\mathsf` alphabet identifier is defined as follows:

```
\DeclareMathAlphabet{\mathsf}{OT1}{cmss}{m}{n}
\SetMathAlphabet{\mathsf}{bold}{OT1}{cmss}{bx}{n}
```

The first line means that the default for `\mathsf` in all math versions is Computer Modern Sans medium. The second line states that the bold math version should use the font Computer Modern Sans bold extended instead.

`\SetMathAlphabet{`*cmd*`}{`*version*`}{`*encoding*`}{`*family*`}{`*series*`}{`*shape*`}`

From the previous example, you can see that `\SetMathAlphabet` takes six arguments: the first is the name of the math alphabet identifier, the second is the math version name for which you are defining a special setup, and the other four are the encoding, family, series, and shape name with which you are associating it.

As noted earlier, you can redefine an existing math alphabet identifier by using `\DeclareMathAlphabet`. If you do so, all previous `\SetMathAlphabet` declarations for this identifier are removed from the internal tables of LATEX. Thus, the identifier comes out the same in all math versions unless you add new `\SetMathAlphabet` declarations for it.

9.5 Standard LATEX font support

This section opens with a short introduction to the standard text fonts distributed together with LATEX, which are Computer Modern, European Computer Modern, and Latin Modern, as well as a brief introduction to the legacy and the modern support packages for core PostScript fonts (Chapter 10 shows samples of them and many other font families now available in LATEX).

Family	Series	Shapes	Typeface Examples
Computer Modern Roman (*Encodings:* T1, TS1, OT1)			
cmr	m	n, it, sl, sc, ui	Computer Modern Roman, *italic*, *slanted*, and SMALL CAPS
	bx	n, it, sl, sc	**bold extended,** ***italic,*** ***slanted,*** and SMALL CAPS
	b	n	**bold medium width (no other shapes)**
Computer Modern Sans (*Encodings:* T1, TS1, OT1)			
cmss	m, bx	n, (it), sl	Computer Modern Sans **bold extended**, *italic,* and *slanted*
	sbc	n	**Computer Modern Sans semibold condensed (no shape variants)**
Computer Modern Typewriter (*Encodings:* T1, TS1, OT1)			
cmtt	m	n, it, sl, sc	`Comp. Mod. Typewriter,` *`italic,`* *`slanted`* `and` SMALL CAPS
cmvtt	m	n, it	Comp. Mod. Typewriter proportional upright *and italics*
Computer Modern Fibonacci (*Encodings:* T1, OT1)			
cmfib	m	n	Computer Modern Fibonacci
Computer Modern Dunhill (*Encodings:* T1, OT1)			
cmdh	m	n	Computer Modern Dunhill

Values in blue *are not or only partly offered in* OT1 *encoding!*

Table 9.5: Classification of the Computer Modern font families

It is followed by a discussion of LaTeX's standard support packages for input and font encodings including a discussion of how to use an extended set of text symbols. The section concludes by describing a package for tracing LaTeX's font processing and another package for displaying glyph charts (a package the author used extensively while preparing the later parts of this chapter).

9.5.1 Computer Modern, Latin Modern — The LaTeX standard fonts

Along with TeX, Donald Knuth developed a family of fonts called Computer Modern; see Table 9.5. Until the early 1990s, essentially only these fonts were usable with TeX and, consequently, with LaTeX. Each of them contains 128 glyphs (TeX was working with 7 bits originally), which does not leave room for including accented characters as individual glyphs. Thus, using these fonts means that accented characters have to be produced with the \accent primitive of TeX, which in turn means that automatic hyphenation of words with accented characters is impossible. While this restriction is acceptable for English documents that contain few foreign words, it is a major obstacle for other languages.

Original TeX font encoding

Not surprisingly, these deficiencies were of great concern to the TeX users in Europe and eventually led to a reimplementation of TeX in 1989 to support 8-bit characters internally and externally. At the TeX Users conference in Cork (1990), a standard 8-bit encoding for text fonts (T1) was developed that contains many diacritical characters (see Table 9.22 on page 763) and allows typesetting in more than 30 languages based on the Latin alphabet. At the University of Bochum (under the direction of Norbert Schwarz) the Computer Modern font families were then reimplemented, and additional characters were designed, so that the resulting fonts completely conform to this encoding scheme. The first implementation of these fonts was released under the name "DC fonts". Since then Jörg Knappen has finalized them, and they are now distributed as "European Computer Modern Fonts", often shortened to "EC fonts".

T1 a.k.a. "Cork" encoding

EC fonts

Both Computer Modern and the EC fonts are considered standard in LaTeX and must be available at any installation. Although originally developed with METAFONT, there are free Type 1 PostScript replacements as well. For Computer Modern these were produced by Blue Sky Research; Y&Y added the LaTeX, AMS, and Euler fonts. The EC fonts were converted in 2001 from METAFONT sources to Type 1 PostScript by Vladimir Volovich. His implementation is called the CM-Super fonts package and, besides the EC fonts, it covers EC Concrete, EC Bright, and LH fonts (Cyrillic Computer Modern). In addition to the T1 encoding, the LaTeX standard encodings TS1, T2A, T2B, T2C, and X2 are supported by CM-Super. The CM-Super fonts were automatically converted to the Type 1 format, and although a sophisticated algorithm was used for this conversion, you cannot expect exactly the same quality as could be achieved by a manual conversion process.

PostScript Type 1 instances

CM-Super fonts

Since the PostScript fonts have the same font metrics as their METAFONT counterparts, they need no support package in the LaTeX document. They are now provided by virtually all distributions and are automatically used by pdfTeX or the driver program (e.g., dvips) that converts the .dvi output to PostScript.

To avoid the generation of too many bit-mapped fonts, the standard .fd files for Computer Modern and European Computer Modern provided only a handful of well-defined font sizes. This is still the default even though with PostScript outline fonts it would be possible to typeset in arbitrary sizes without problems.[1] Thus, if you ask for an intermediate size (via \fontsize), you get a warning, and the nearest available size is chosen instead. To lift this restriction you can make use of the package fix-cm or use the Latin Modern fonts instead as discussed below.

Although the EC fonts were originally meant to be a drop-in extension (and replacement) for the 7-bit Computer Modern fonts, not all glyph shapes have been kept in the end. For example, the German "ß" got a new design — a decision by the font designer that did not make everybody happy (me included).

Issues with the EC fonts

```
\fontencoding{OT1}\fontfamily{cmr}\selectfont
Computer Modern sharp s: ß
```

Computer Modern sharp s: ß
EC Modern sharp s: ß

```
\fontencoding{T1}\fontfamily{cmr}\selectfont
EC Modern sharp s:        ß
```

9-5-1

---

[1] The set of fixed sizes has been kept as the default to ensure that older documents do not change their appearance if reprocessed.

However, these were not the only differences between the original Computer Modern fonts and the new EC fonts. The latter have many more individual designs for larger font sizes (while CM fonts were scaled linearly), and in this respect the fact that both really are different font families is quite noticeable.[1] The particular example that follows is perhaps the most glaring difference of that kind:

The fox jumps

quickly over the fence!

The fox jumps

quickly over the fence!

```
\fontencoding{OT1}\sffamily\bfseries
\Huge        The fox jumps  \par
\normalsize quickly over the fence!\par
\fontencoding{T1}\sffamily\bfseries
\Huge        The fox jumps  \par
\normalsize quickly over the fence!\par
```

9-5-2

These differences are no problem if one likes the EC designs and uses T1 throughout. Otherwise, a number of approaches can be taken to resolve this problem. One is to employ a different set of font definitions that do not make use of *all* individual EC font designs and that are closer to those of the traditional CM fonts, but with improved typographical quality. Such a solution is provided by Walter Schmidt's (1960–2021) package fix-cm, which is distributed as part of the core LaTeX distribution. Load this package directly after the document class declaration (or even before using \RequirePackage), because it takes effect only for fonts not already loaded by LaTeX — and the document class might load fonts.

Latin Modern — the modern replacement for CM or EC fonts

In 2002, three European TeX user groups (DANTE, GUTenberg, and NTG) initiated and funded a project to integrate all of the variants of the Computer Modern Roman typefaces into a single Latin Modern family of fonts. The project was carried out by Bogusław Jackowski and Janusz Marian Nowacki (1951–2020), and the first official version of the Latin Modern fonts was presented at the DANTE meeting in 2003.

The **Latin Modern** fonts are carefully handcrafted PostScript Type 1 fonts based on the designs of Knuth's *Computer Modern* families. They contain all the glyphs needed to typeset Latin-based European languages as well as glyphs for Native American, Vietnamese, and Transliterations.

```
\usepackage[T1]{fontenc} \usepackage{lmodern}
```

```
The \textbf{Latin Modern} fonts are carefully
handcrafted PostScript Type~1 fonts based on
the designs of Knuth's \emph{Computer Modern}
families. They contain all the glyphs needed
to typeset Latin-based European languages as
well as glyphs for Native American, Vietnamese,
and Transliterations.
```

9-5-3

Already then the fonts were in fact a huge extension in terms of glyph coverage with additional diacritical characters covering many scripts based on the LaTeX character set. The font classification of Latin Modern is listed in Table 9.6 on the facing page. It shows that some of the "funny" fonts got dropped, but at the same time several

---

[1] The historical mistake was to pretend to NFSS that both are the same families (e.g., cmr, cmss), just encoded according to different font encodings. Unfortunately, this cannot be rectified without huge backward compatibility problems.

Family	Series	Shapes	Typeface Examples
Latin Modern Roman		Latin Modern Roman Latin Modern Roman Caps	(*Encodings:* T1, TS1, OT1, T5, LY1, and TU)
lmr	m	n, it, sl, sc, scsl, ui	Latin Modern Roman upright, *italic, slanted,* SMALL CAPS and SMALL CAPS SLANTED
	bx	n, it, sl	**Latin Modern bold extend, *italic,* and *slanted***
	b	n, (it), sl	**Latin Modern bold** and slanted
Latin Modern Sans		Latin Modern Sans	(*Encodings:* T1, TS1, OT1, T5, LY1, and TU)
lmss	m	n, (it), sl	Latin Modern Sans upright *and slanted*
	(b), bx, sbc	n, (it), sl	**Latin Modern Sans bold extended** *and slanted,* **and semibold condensed** *and slanted*
Latin Modern Typewriter		Latin Modern Mono	(*Encodings:* T1, TS1, OT1, T5, LY1, and TU)
lmtt	m	n, it, sl, sc, scsl	Latin Modern Typewriter upright, *italic, slanted,* SMALL CAPS and SMALL CAPS SLANTED
	l, lc, b, (bx)	n, (it), sl	Latin Modern Typewriter light, slanted, and light condensed, slanted, **bold** and ***bold slanted***
Proportional Latin Modern Typewriter		Latin Modern Mono Prop	(*Encodings:* T1, TS1, OT1, T5, LY1, and TU)
lmvtt	m	n, (it), sl	Latin Modern Typewriter proportional *and slanted*
	l, b, (bx)	n, (it), sl	Latin Modern Typewriter light, *light slanted,* **bold** and ***bold slanted***
Latin Modern Dunhill		Latin Modern Roman Dunhill	(*Encodings:* T1, TS1, OT1, T5, LY1, and TU)
cmdh	m	n, (it), sl	Latin Modern Dunhill upright *and slanted*

Shapes or series value colored in blue *are additions in the Latin Modern family not available in the Computer Modern. Values given in parentheses indicate substitutions; e.g., (it) produces sl, and (b) becomes bx, or vice versa. Note that the CM proportional typewriter has an* it *shape while the LM proportional typewriter has an* sl *shape instead. The* font names *with gray background are for use with the* fontspec *package in Unicode engines.*

Table 9.6: Classification of the Latin Modern font families

additional shapes and weights were added [117]. In particular, there are now bold and light versions of the typewriter fonts that can be useful in certain situations.

However, without accompanying math fonts, they were not yet a full-fledged alternative to Computer Modern or European Modern fonts. This changed in 2011 with the release of the Latin Modern Math fonts. Additionally, all fonts in the Latin Modern families were made available in OpenType font format, which made them available to be used in Unicode TeX engines (or even Word, if so desired).

Unicode engines

In fact, they are now LaTeX's default fonts if you typeset using X⟍TEX or LuaTeX.

In 8-bit engines (e.g., pdfTEX) Computer Modern in OT1 encoding remained the default to ensure backward compatibility for the huge amount of existing documents in archives. As previously mentioned, the OT1 encoding has noticeable defects with respect to glyph coverage, hyphenation, and online search in formatted documents for all Latin-based languages (except English). This was repaired with the EC fonts, but their Type 1 versions did not quite reach the highest quality of hand-crafted fonts due to their generation process.

All this is now resolved with the Latin Modern fonts; you only have to load the lmodern package and additionally make T1 your default font encoding as we did in the previous example.

With Latin Modern fonts in combination with the T1 encoding, diacritical characters, hyphenation, and online search are well supported; furthermore, the fonts use the same set of design sizes as the original CM fonts, and the original shape of the sharp s is back. Thus, examples such as 9-5-1 or 9-5-2 come out just fine, and we therefore recommend that for new documents you use lmodern (in T1 encoding) with pdfTEX if you want to typeset in a "Computer Modern like" typeface.

The fox jumps
quickly over the fence!
A Latin Modern sharp s: ß

```
\usepackage[T1]{fontenc}  \usepackage{lmodern}
\sffamily\bfseries\Huge  The fox jumps \par
\normalsize quickly over the fence!     \par
\normalfont A Latin Modern sharp s: ß
```

9-5-4

The lmodern package supports three options: `lighttt` changes `\ttdefault` to select the light typewriter, while `variablett` uses the proportional typewriter face. By default the package also changes the math font setup to use Latin Modern Math fonts. If this is not desirable (because you use other fonts for mathematics), use the option `nomath` to prevent it.

9.5.2 PSNFSS and TEX Gyre — Core PostScript fonts for LATEX

The PSNFSS bundle, originally developed by Sebastian Rahtz (1955–2016), was the first major application using the LATEX font selection scheme to provide support for common PostScript fonts, covering the "Base 35" fonts (which are built into any Level 2 PostScript printing device and the ghostscript interpreter) and the free Charter and Utopia fonts. After Sebastian's death, Walter Schmidt (1960–2021) maintained PSNFSS, and today it is maintained by Keiran Harcombe, who has taken over all of Walter Schmidt's packages.

These days it is, however, largely superseded by the development of the TEX Gyre fonts (by Bogusław Jackowski and Janusz Marian Nowacki (1951–2020)) that provide reimplementations of many of these fonts with an extended glyph set so that essentially all Latin-based languages are now supported. The Vietnamese glyphs in this collection have been added by Hàn Thế Thành. The basic Greek symbols are based on earlier work by Apostolos Syropoulos and Antonis Tsolomitis. Like the Latin Modern fonts, the TEX Gyre project was initiated and funded by several European TEX user groups.

Package	Roman Font	Sans Serif Font	Typewriter Font	Formulas
—	CM Roman	CM Sans Serif	CM Typewriter	CM Math
lmodern	LM Roman	LM Sans Serif	LM Typewriter	LM Math
tgbonum	Bookman (Bonum)			
tgchorus	Zapf Chancery (Chorus)			
tgpagella	Palatino (Pagella)			
tgschola	New Century Schoolbook (Schola)			
tgtermes	Times Roman (Termes)			
tgadventor		Avant Garde (Adventor)		
tgheros		Helvetica (Heros)		
tgcursor			Courier (Cursor)	

Names in parentheses are the font names used by the TeX Gyre foundry.

Table 9.7: TeX Gyre packages for setting up fonts

Since it is in nearly all circumstances better to use the TeX Gyre fonts than to typeset using the far more restricted fonts offered by the original PSNFSS setup, we focus in the remainder of this section on the newer developments and discuss only those packages from PSNFSS that are still relevant. Samples of the font families, together with many other fonts available today, are given in the next chapter.

For normal use you probably have to include only one (or more) of the packages listed in Table 9.7 to change the default roman, sans serif, and/or typewriter typefaces. If you study this table, you will notice that, with the exception of lmodern, the packages change only the text fonts. For packages that also load matching math fonts see Section 12.5 on page →II 261.

The TeX Gyre font packages all offer a number of options that allow you to combine them in a way that different fonts have the same height, either matching the uppercase letter height (option `matchuppercase`) or the x-height (option `matchlowercase`) of the roman font. Thus, a document with a line like

Scale TeX Gyre fonts to blend with surrounding fonts

```
\usepackage{tgtermes,tgcursor}
\usepackage[matchuppercase]{tgheros}
```

in the preamble would be typeset in Times, Courier, and Helvetica with heights matching the uppercase letters of Times Roman. Loading Helvetica at its default height instead would not at all blend well, because the characters are far too large compared to Times. Alternatively, you can use the key/value option `scale` to set an explicit scale factor during the package load. The next example shows a probably more pleasing combination using Bookman and Avant Garde fonts.

```
\usepackage[matchlowercase]
                  {tgbonum,tgadventor,tgcursor}
```

This example shows Bookman combined with Avant Garde and Courier with *the x-height of all fonts being matched thanks to the option matchlowercase.*

```
This example shows Bookman combined with
\textsf{Avant Garde} and \texttt{Courier}
with \emph{the x-height of all fonts being
\textsf{matched} thanks to the option
\texttt{matchlowercase}}.
```

9-5-5

Word space adjustments   The word spaces in some of the TEX Gyre fonts are a little different (tighter) to those of the originals, and if you do not like that, you can use the option oldspacing, which is understood by all TEX Gyre packages.

Using condensed Helvetica   Finally, the tgheros package has one further option, condensed, that when used loads Helvetica Narrow instead of Helvetica if that is preferred.

Sans serif as document typeface   By default, LATEX selects a roman typeface as the document font. Packages such as tgheros or tgadventor change the default sans serif typeface (by changing the \sfdefault value) but do not change the default document font family. If such a typeface should be used as the document font, issue the line

```
\renewcommand\familydefault{\sfdefault}
```

in the preamble of your document.

Use the TEX Gyre packages instead of PSNFSS where applicable   The packages from the PSNFSS bundle are listed in Table 9.8 on the facing page. They have (unfortunately) the more memorable names and have been heavily used in the past, so you may come across one or the other in older documents. However, these days none of them can really be recommended, so the second column of the table suggests replacements. The packages in the first block set up individual fonts like the TEX Gyre packages, but because their packages offer better versions of these fonts, it is usually preferable to use them instead. The packages in the second part of the table should definitely be avoided (or replaced if already used in documents). Either they combine fonts without adjusting their heights (see discussion above) or they attempt to set up matching math fonts using only partially suitable fonts, and for this better possibilities are now available; see Chapter 10. Of course, if you replace, say, palatino and want it matched with Helvetica (which is a questionable choice in the first place), then you now have to load tgpagella and tgheros with a suitable option to match up the font sizes. The final block shows packages that combine text and math fonts, but again there are now much better solutions available (discussed in Chapter 12), so if you come across these packages in older documents, consider replacing them (except perhaps for mathpazo).

Besides mathpazo there is really only one other font support package in the PSNFSS collection that is still interesting these days: the pifont package. It does not change any text fonts but sets up various commands for use with so-called Pi fonts (i.e., special symbol fonts like Zapf Dingbats). It is described in Section 10.13.1 on page →II 113.

690

Package	replace with	Roman Font	Sans Serif Font	Typewriter Font	Formulas
charter	XCharter[a]	Charter			
utopia	erewhon[a]	Utopia			
chancery	tgchorus	Zapf Chancery			
helvet	tgheros		Helvetica		
avant	tgadventor		Avant Garde		
courier	tgcursor			Courier	

Deprecated Packages

Package	replace with	Roman Font	Sans Serif Font	Typewriter Font	Formulas
bookman	tgbonum	Bookman	Avant Garde	Courier	
newcent	tgschola	New Century Schoolbook	Avant Garde	Courier	
palatino	tgpagella	Palatino	Helvetica	Courier	
times	tgtermes[b]	Times	Helvetica	Courier	

Packages with math setup (most are not recommended, see Chapter 12)

Package	replace with	Roman Font	Sans Serif Font	Typewriter Font	Formulas
mathpazo		Palatino			Palatino + Pazo
mathptmx	newtxmath[c]	Times			Times + Symbol
mathptm	newtxmath[c]	Times			Times + Symbol + CM
mathpple	mathpazo	Palatino			Palatino + Symbol + Euler

[a] *These fonts have not been redone by TeX Gyre, but there exist improved versions by others; see Sections 10.5.6 and 10.5.23 for details.*

[b] *To mimic the* times *package you also need to load* tgheros *and* tgcursor *or you can consider using* newtxtext *plus an appropriate typewriter family instead.*

[c] *Plus adding* newtxtext *or* tgtermes *for the text font setup.*

Table 9.8: PSNFSS packages for setting up fonts

9.5.3 A note on baselines and leading

Most document classes designed for use with Computer Modern set up a leading (\baselineskip) of 10pt/12pt. This may appear to be too tight for several of the PostScript font families shown below, due to a larger x-height of the fonts. However, because this is a matter of document design and also depends on the chosen line width and other factors, the packages in the TeX Gyre or PSNFSS collection make no attempt to adjust the leading. For a given document class you can change the leading by a *factor* by issuing the declaration \linespread{*factor*} in the preamble. For example, \linespread{1.033} would change the leading from, say, 12pt to approximately 12.4pt.

Adjusting the leading

For best results, however, one needs to use a document class designed for the selected document fonts or, lacking such a class, to redefine the commands

691

\normalsize, \footnotesize, and so on (see page 665 for details). Also remember that changing the leading might result in a noticeable number of "Underfull \vbox" warnings, if the \textheight is no longer an integral number of text lines (see page →II 763 for further details).

9.5.4 inputenc — Explicitly selecting the input encoding

As mentioned earlier, the development of the inputenc package made it possible to use many accented characters, either via single keystrokes or by some other input method (e.g., by pressing ' and then a to get à) in your source instead of having to type \'a, \^e, and so forth.

To enable this, all you had to do was to load the package and specify the input encoding[1] used by your computer as a package option. Once done, the document is processed correctly on any LaTeX installation even if the source file looks strange on some computers due to the encoding differences.

For example, the Russian text Русский язык (Russian language) written in the once popular koi8-r encoding would display in an editor program on a German computer (using the latin1 encoding) partially scrambled as

òÔÓÓËÊ ÑÚÙË (Russian language)

However, with the help of \usepackage[koi8-r]{inputenc} in the preamble of the document, a LaTeX run always produces "Русский язык (Russian language)", i.e., the desired result.

Originally the inputenc package was written to describe the encoding used for a document as a whole — hence the use of options in the preamble. It is, however, possible to change the encoding in the middle of a document by using the command \inputencoding. This command takes an encoding name as its argument. Processing is rather computing intensive, as typically more than 120 characters are remapped each time. Nevertheless, we know of applications that change the encoding several times within a paragraph yet seem to work reasonably well.

UTF-8 support, nowadays the default

Besides such single-byte encodings, inputenc also enabled UTF-8 support through the option utf8. Because nearly all computer operating system nowadays use UTF-8 as their standard encoding, LaTeX changed in 2015 and made this encoding the default. It is therefore only necessary to load the inputenc package if this assumption is wrong, either because you happen to use an older computer whose operating system is still 8-bit with some particular code page in force or because you reprocess an old document stored in one of the legacy 8-bit encodings (in which case it hopefully already contains the appropriate inputenc line).

---

[1] The base set of supported encodings (more than two dozen) is documented in the inputenc package documentation; apart from UTF-8, the most important ones are probably latin1 to latin4 (ISO 8859-1 to ISO 8859-4 [40]) and latin9 (ISO 8859-15) that can represent most Western and Eastern European languages. Also supported are the Windows OS code pages cp1250 (Central and Eastern Europe), cp1252 (Western Europe), and cp1257 (Baltic). In some cases, language packages for Babel provide additional encoding configuration files for inputenc. For example, encodings related to the Cyrillic languages are distributed together with the corresponding font support packages for Cyrillic.

If you process a document stored in one of the legacy encodings that is missing an appropriate inputenc line, three things can happen:

- If the document consists only of ASCII characters, then it is in fact a proper UTF-8 document, and it processes correctly.

- The worst-case scenario is that the file is processed without any errors (i.e., it is technically a UTF-8 file) but the printed output is wrong in some places. While this is not likely, it can happen, and there is no way to automatically detect that (obviously LaTeX cannot check the results for scrambled/nonsense words).

- The most likely case, however, is that you receive one or more error messages of the type "Invalid UTF-8 byte" indicating that LaTeX found a byte sequence that is not allowed in a UTF-8 file. Such errors are therefore fairly certain indicators that the file is not encoded in UTF-8, but in some legacy encoding. Finding out in which encoding can unfortunately be a difficult task, if you do not happen to know on which computer the file was made. You may have to make an educated guess, process the file, and then carefully check the printed result — the fact that you do not get any errors after selecting an encoding, such as latin1, is unfortunately no proof that it is the correct one.

  Other indicators that the file is in a legacy encoding are error messages of the type "Unicode character ... not set up for use with LaTeX". However, these errors can also show up with proper UTF-8 files if the Unicode character in question is not available in any of the loaded fonts.

9.5.5 fontenc — Selecting font encodings

To be able to use a text font encoding with LaTeX, the encoding has to be loaded in the document class, in a package, or in the document preamble. More precisely, the definitions to access the glyphs in fonts with a certain encoding have to be loaded. The canonical way to do this with an 8-bit TeX engine; e.g., pdfTeX is via the fontenc package, which takes a comma-separated list of font encodings as a package option. The last of these encodings is automatically made the default document encoding. For example,

```
\usepackage[T2A,T1]{fontenc}
```

loads all necessary definitions for the Cyrillic[1] T2A and the T1 (Cork) encodings and sets the latter to be the default document encoding by changing \encodingdefault.
In contrast to normal package behavior, one can load this package several times with different optional arguments to the \usepackage command. This is necessary to allow a document class to load a certain set of encodings and enable the user to load still more encodings in the preamble. Loading encodings more than once is

Multiple uses of fontenc *allowed*

---

[1]If any Cyrillic encoding is loaded, the list of commands affected by \MakeUppercase and \MakeLowercase is automatically extended.

possible without side effects (other than potentially changing the document default font encoding).

If language support packages are used in the document (e.g., those coming with the babel system), it is often the case that the necessary font encodings are already loaded by the support package.

Unicode engines

It is, however, not required to use the fontenc package together with a Unicode engine, such as X͟ELͣTͤEX or LuaTͤEX — in fact it is usually wrong and can lead to missing or wrong characters and to incorrect hyphenation!

Do not use fontenc in Unicode engines unless there is a good reason

In Unicode engines the assumption is that fonts are Unicode fonts, i.e., encoded in the TU encoding, so this encoding is automatically made the default encoding by LͣATͤEX when the program starts.

While it is possible to use fonts that have a different encoding such as T1 in Unicode engines, one has to be aware that only ASCII characters (and those are in the same slot position in Unicode and in the current font encoding) can be entered directly. For all others you need to use their LICR representations; see Table 9.23 on page 768. For example, \"a works always, while ä works only in T1 but not in OT1. For ß or € the situation is worse; they work in none of the legacy encodings and produce either wrong output (like SS) or no output at all — for them you have to always use \ss and \texteuro.

Furthermore, even if you correctly input your text using LICRs where necessary, hyphenation of your text is still likely to produce incorrect results. The problem is that in all TͤEX programs the patterns used to determine the hyphenation points depend not just on the language but also on the font encoding in force.

So for fully correct hyphenation you need a set of patterns for each language/font encoding combination, which is not realistic. Thus, TͤEX assumes one dominant encoding per language, which works well enough if encodings are similar (e.g., OT1 is more or less a subset of T1) but less so many characters are simply in different slots.

If you need to use fontenc for some reason, make sure that the default encoding (i.e., the one used for the text fonts) remains TU; that is, always list TU as the last option when loading (or reloading) the package.

9.5.6 Additional text symbols not part of OT1 or T1 encodings

When the T1 font encoding was defined in Cork, it was decided that this encoding should omit many standard text symbols such as † and instead include as many composite glyphs as possible. The rationale was that characters that are subject to hyphenation have to be present in the same font, while one can fetch other symbols without much penalty from additional fonts. These extra symbols have, therefore, been collected in a companion encoding. In 1995, a first implementation of this encoding (TS1) was developed by Jörg Knappen [45, 46]. With the textcomp package, Sebastian Rahtz (1955–2016) provided a LͣATͤEX interface to it.

Unfortunately, just as with the T1 encoding, the encoding design for TS1 was prepared based on glyph availability in the TEX world without considering that the majority of commercial fonts provide different sets of glyphs. As a result, the full implementation of this encoding is available for very few font families, among them EC, CM Bright, and Latin Modern fonts. For most PostScript fonts, implementations of the encoding also exist, but a larger number of the glyphs are missing and produce square blobs of ink or possibly just a gap in the typeset output.[1] Table 9.9 on pages 696–697 shows the glyphs made available by TS1 and the commands to access them. Commands colored in blue indicate that the corresponding glyph is most likely not available in the font design when PostScript or OpenType fonts are used.

Since 2020 the symbols provided by the TS1 encoding are directly accessible from LATEX without the need to load the **textcomp** package any longer. The package is still available so that older documents work without complaining about a missing package.

Unicode engines

In Unicode engines the additional commands have always been available (adjusted to select slots in the Unicode TU encoding) if supported by the font, so it was never necessary to load the **textcomp** package with those engines.

The symbols provided with the encoding TS1 should normally switch their design depending on the current font settings. A few of them have been already present in the original Computer Modern fonts, hidden in the math fonts (e.g., \textbullet, or \textdagger), and LATEX releases prior to the development of the TS1 encoding always took them from there. Nowadays they are fetched from the companion fonts and as a consequence, they sometimes change their shape when the surrounding font attributes (family, series, or shape) are changed just like any other text character, allowing them to better blend in with surrounding text.

```
\newcommand\sample{\textdagger~\textdaggerdbl~\textparagraph
    ~\textbullet~\textbardbl~\textasteriskcentered~\textsection}
```

† ‡ ¶ • ‖ * § (CM fonts)
† ‡ ¶ • ‖ * § (Alegreya)
† ‡ ¶ • ‖ * § (Alegreya italics)
† ‡ ¶ • ‖ * § (Gillius)

```
                                \sample\ (CM fonts)          \\
\fontfamily{Alegreya-LF}\upshape \sample\ (Alegreya)         \\
                        \itshape \sample\ (Alegreya italics)\\
\fontfamily{GilliusADF-LF}\upshape\sample\ (Gillius)
```

9-5-6

While this is usually the right solution, it may result in changes in unexpected places. For example, the `itemize` environment by default uses \textbullet and \textasteriskcentered to indicate first-level and third-level items. And in all likelihood you do not want those to change just because you typeset a few items using, for example, \itshape. Similarly, footnote symbols, if used instead of numbered footnotes, should probably have the same glyph shapes regardless of local font settings for the text. For this reason the footnote marker uses \normalfont to ensure that the markers are always typeset using the same font face.

---

[1] The T1 encoding has the same problem when it comes to older PostScript fonts, but fortunately only five (seldom used) glyphs are missing from some fonts; see Example 9-7-1 on page 737.

Accent symbols

Á	\capitalacute␣A [2]	Ă	\capitalbreve␣A [2]	Ǎ	\capitalcaron␣A [2]
Ą	**\capitalcedilla␣A**	Â	\capitalcircumflex␣A [2]	Ä	\capitaldieresis␣A [2]
Ȧ	\capitaldotaccent␣A [2]	À	\capitalgrave␣A [2]	Ä	\capitalhungarumlaut␣A [2]
Ā	\capitalmacron␣A [2]	ÂA	\capitalnewtie␣AA [2]	Ų	**\capitalogonek␣U**
Å	\capitalring␣A [2]	ÁA	\capitaltie␣AA [2]	Ã	\capitaltilde␣A [2]
õo	\newtie␣oo [2]	Ⓧ	\textcircled␣x [1]	õo	\t␣oo [2]

Numerals (superior, fractions, oldstyle)

1	\textonesuperior [9]	2	\texttwosuperior [9]	3	\textthreesuperior [9]
¼	**\textonequarter**	½	**\textonehalf**	¾	**\textthreequarters**
0	\textzerooldstyle [2]	1	\textoneoldstyle [2]	2	\texttwooldstyle [2]
3	\textthreeoldstyle [2]	4	\textfouroldstyle [2]	5	\textfiveoldstyle [2]
6	\textsixoldstyle [2]	7	\textsevenoldstyle [2]	8	\texteightoldstyle [2]
9	\textnineoldstyle [2]				

Pair symbols

⟨	\textlangle [3]	⟩	\textrangle [3]	⟦	\textlbrackdbl [2]
⟧	\textrbrackdbl [2]	↑	\textuparrow [4]	↓	\textdownarrow [4]
←	\textleftarrow [4]	→	\textrightarrow [4]	⦃	\textlquill [2]
⦄	\textrquill [2]				

Monetary and commercial symbols

฿	\textbaht [2]	¢	**\textcent**	¢	\textcentoldstyle [2]
₡	\textcolonmonetary [4]	¤	\textcurrency [6]	€	\texteuro [8]
$	\textdollaroldstyle [2]	₫	\textdong [4]	£	\textlira [4]
ƒ	\textflorin [6]	₲	\textguarani [2]	£	**\textsterling**
₦	\textnaira [2]	₱	\textpeso [2]		
₩	\textwon [4]	¥	**\textyen**		
Ⓟ	\textcircledP [2]	ⓒ	\textcopyleft [2]	©	**\textcopyright**
٪	\textdiscount [2]	℮	\textestimated [5]	‰	\textpertenthousand [2]
‰	**\textperthousand**	※	\textreferencemark [2]	®	**\textregistered**
SM	\textservicemark [2]	TM	**\texttrademark**		

Footnote symbols

*	**\textasteriskcentered**	‖	\textbardbl [9]	¦	**\textbrokenbar**
•	**\textbullet**	†	**\textdagger**	‡	**\textdaggerdbl**
◦	\textopenbullet [2]	¶	**\textparagraph**	·	**\textperiodcentered**
¶	\textpilcrow [2]	§	**\textsection**		

Scientific symbols

℃	\textcelsius [9]	°	**\textdegree**	÷	**\textdiv**
¬	**\textlnot**	℧	\textmho [2]	—	\textminus [7]
µ	\textmu [7]	Ω	\textohm [7]	ᵃ	**\textordfeminine**
º	**\textordmasculine**	±	**\textpm**	√	\textsurd [2]
×	**\texttimes**				

Blue indicates that the symbol is unavailable in some fonts. The TS1 subencoding from which on the glyph is substituted with a default is given in parentheses. Most modern font families have subencodings 2–5.

Table 9.9: Commands made available with the TS1 encoding

	Various	
`\textacutedbl` (2)	`\textasciiacute` (2)	`\textasciibreve` (2)
`\textasciicaron` (2)	`\textasciidieresis` (2)	`\textasciigrave` (2)
`\textasciimacron` (2)	`\textbigcircle` (2)	`\textblank` (8)
`\textborn` (2)	`\textdblhyphen` (2)	`\textdblhyphenchar` (2)
`\textdied` (2)	`\textdivorced` (2)	`\textfractionsolidus` (7)
`\textgravedbl` (2)	`\textinterrobang` (8)	`\textinterrobangdown` (8)
`\textleaf` (2)	`\textmarried` (2)	`\textmusicalnote` (2)
`\textnumero` (5)	**`\textquotesingle`**	**`\textquotestraightbase`**
`\textquotestraightdblbase`	`\textrecipe` (2)	`\textthreequartersemdash` (9)
`\texttildelow` (2)	`\texttwelveudash` (9)	

Blue indicates that the symbol is unavailable in some fonts. The TS1 subencoding from which on the glyph is substituted with a default is given in parentheses. Most modern font families have subencodings 2–5.

Table 9.9: Commands made available with the TS1 encoding (cont.)

Similarly `\labelitemi` to `\labelitemiv` reset the font face, but in this case it is done indirectly by executing `\labelitemfont`, which by default is defined to call `\normalfont`. This allows altering the behavior by redefining this command; e.g.,

```
\renewcommand\labelitemfont{\fontseries{m}\fontshape{n}\selectfont}
```

uses the current font family to fetch the symbols but with a fixed series and shape value.

By specifying `\UseLegacyTextSymbols` in the preamble, it is also possible to direct LATEX to use the eight fixed symbols from the math fonts in all situations. They are then used in `itemize` and footnotes, but also in running text as shown in the next example. It also changes `\oldstylenums` to always use the single set of oldstyle numbers from the math fonts and is really only provided for backward compatibility.

Using legacy text symbols

```
\UseLegacyTextSymbols   \newcommand\legacysyms{\textasteriskcentered~%
\textbardbl~\textbullet~\textdagger~\textdaggerdbl~\textparagraph~%
\textperiodcentered~\textsection~\oldstylenums{123}}
\fontfamily{Alegreya-LF}\upshape \legacysyms \\ \itshape \legacysyms \\
\fontfamily{NotoSans-LF}\upshape \legacysyms \\ \itshape \legacysyms
```

9-5-7

As you see, the symbols are now always identical regardless of the font selected. However, the spacing differs because the space characters have a different width in Alegreya and Noto Sans.

If you want to use only some of the legacy symbols, for example the "§" because you prefer the original design, or the "•" for `itemize` because the design in Alegreya "•", for example, appears to be too tiny, then this is easily possible too. All eight symbols can be accessed by using `\textlegacybullet` instead of `\textbullet`,

697

etc., and if you always want to use the legacy symbol, you can adjust the definition like it was done for \textdagger in the example.

We prefer † and § over † and $. And • is now always legacy design.

```
\usepackage{Alegreya}        \DeclareTextSymbolDefault{\textbullet}{OMS}
We prefer \textlegacydagger\ and \textlegacysection\ over \textdagger\
and \textsection. And \textbullet\ is now always legacy design.
```

9-5-8

The precise interface for \DeclareTextSymbolDefault is discussed in Section 9.9.4 on page 765.

Special features

Diacritics on uppercase letters

Diacritical marks on uppercase letters are sometimes flattened in some font designs compared to their lowercase counterparts. Fonts derived from Computer Modern designs, e.g., the EC fonts, CM Bright or Latin Modern, follow this tradition. For example, the grave accents on ò and Ò are different (which is not the case with Lucida, the document font used in this book). This poses a problem if one needs an uncommon letter that is not available as a single glyph in the T1 encoding, but rather must be constructed by placing the diacritical mark over the base character. In that case the same diacritical mark is used, which can result in noticeable differences (see the X̀ in the next example). The \capital... accents shown in Table 9.9 on page 696 solve this problem by generating diacritical marks suitable for use with uppercase letters.

```
\usepackage[T1]{fontenc}
\huge \'o\'x  \'O\'X \capitalgrave O\capitalgrave X \par
\fontfamily{Alegreya-LF}\selectfont
      \'o\'x  \'O\'X \capitalgrave O\capitalgrave X
```

9-5-9

Flat accents are available only with a handful of font families, e.g., Computer Modern and closely related designs. With all others, the capital accents produce the same accents as on lowercase letters, but this has the effect that they then appear on all glyphs, which can be observed in the second line of the example.

Unicode engines

In Unicode engines the \capital... accents always produce the same results as the normal accent commands and leave it up to the font how the accent is positioned. It therefore makes no sense to use them with these engines. They are provided only to avoid error messages with documents written for pdfTEX and reprocessed with X𝟇TEX or LuaTEX.

Compound word marks of different heights

LATEX offers a \textcompwordmark command, an invisible zero-width glyph within the T1 encoding that can, for example, be used to break up unwanted ligatures (at the cost of preventing hyphenation).[1] The glyph has a height of 1ex, which makes it possible to use it as the argument to an accent command, thereby

---

[1] With OT1-encoded fonts it is a faked glyph and therefore prevents automatic hyphenation in the word in which it is used.

placing an accent between two letters. In the next example this command is used to produce the German -burg abbreviation. With the TS1 encoding two additional compound word marks become available: `\textascendercompwordmark` and `\textcapitalcompwordmark` that have the height of the ascender or capitals in the font, respectively.

```
\usepackage[T1]{fontenc}
```

b˘g (this fails)
Auflage not Auflage

9-5-10   b̆g   B̆G and b̆g   B̆G

```
b\u{}g (this fails) \\ Auf\textcompwordmark lage not Auflage \\
b\u\textcompwordmark g \quad B\u\textcapitalcompwordmark G
and \fontfamily{Alegreya-LF}\selectfont
b\u\textcompwordmark g \quad B\u\textcapitalcompwordmark G
```

The above example works only in pdfTEX, and to allow for hyphenation in the word "Auflage" you would need to use T1-encoded fonts, because only such fonts contain a real compound-mark glyph. If a font in a different encoding is used, then the glyph is fetched from a matching T1-encoded font, and that breaks hyphenation.

> **Unicode engines**
>
> The fonts for Unicode engines using the TU encoding are lacking the special glyphs `\textcapitalcompwordmark` and `\textascendercompwordmark`, but in addition they also use a different mechanism to place accents so that the "-burg" accent comes out wrong with most fonts. However, the command `\textcompwordmark` can still be used to break up ligatures.

The TS1 encoding offers several monetary symbols, among them a $ sign, but because that glyph is also available in both the OT1 and T1 encodings, there is no point in removing its definition and forcing LATEX to pick up the TS1 version if you are typesetting in either of these encodings. However, assume you want to use the variant dollar sign $ for your dollars automatically. In that case you have to get rid of the declarations in other encodings so that LATEX automatically switches to TS1.

Managing your dollars

```
\DeclareTextCommandDefault{\textdollar}
    {\UseTextSymbol{TS1}\textdollaroldstyle}   % set up new default
\UndeclareTextCommand{\textdollar}{OT1}        % do not use the defs
\UndeclareTextCommand{\textdollar} {T1}        %    in OT1 or T1
```

Such redeclarations will, of course, work properly only if the document fonts contain the desired glyph in the TS1 encoding. In this book they would have failed, because Lucida Bright (the document font for this book) has only the restricted set of ISO-Adobe symbols available in TS1. If you wonder where the $ and similar symbols shown in the book actually came from, the answer is simple: from the Latin Modern fonts.

> **Unicode engines**
>
> The same approach can be taken in Unicode engines; you only have to undeclare `\textdollar` in the TU encoding then. If the current font family is not available in TS1 encoding (which is the most common case for Unicode fonts), then a default font is chosen, which in the case of Unicode engines is Latin Modern.

For most other glyphs it is enough to change the default because they are defined only in the TS1 encoding.

Typesetting oldstyle numerals

According to its specification the TS1 encoding contains oldstyle digits as well as the punctuations period and comma. This allows one to typeset dates and other (positive) numbers with oldstyle numerals by simply switching to the TS1 font encoding. Unfortunately, these oldstyle numerals are available only in subencodings 0 and 1, and most fonts only offer subencoding 2 or higher. It is therefore seldom advisable to simply manually switch to TS1 to typeset oldstyle numbers because you might get "■.■.■■■■" or ".." instead of 5.4.1962 as desired.[1]

Nevertheless, with the substitution mechanism providing different-looking glyphs based on the situation, it is possible to obtain better results than in earlier days of LaTeX, where \oldstylenums always used the serifed oldstyle numerals available as part of the math fonts. Thus, \oldstylenums was changed to make use of this mechanism. If you really want the original definition, use \legacyoldstylenums, but note that this can typeset only numbers, not punctuation characters!

```
\usepackage[T1]{fontenc} \usepackage{lmodern}
\newcommand\born[1]{\textborn\oldstylenums{#1}}
```

I was born ⋆5.4.1962
or in sans serif ⋆5.4.1962.
Compare this to 5▷4▷1962.

```
I was born \born{5.4.1962}                        \\
or in \textsf{sans serif \born{5.4.1962}}.        \\
Compare this to \legacyoldstylenums{5.4.1962}.
```

9-5-11

However, if you want oldstyle numerals and you are not typesetting using Computer or Latin Modern, it is usually better to use the -OsF convention supported in many modern fonts or the command \textfigures if provided by the package; see Section 10.1.2 on page →II 6 for details.

Managing missing glyphs

Given that only a few font families implement the full set of the TS1 encoding glyphs, there is the question how missing glyphs should be handled. For this the glyphs from TS1 are split into ten subencodings, numbered 0 to 9, where 0 represents the full set and higher numbers mean that more and more glyphs become unavailable and need to be substituted with glyphs from other fonts. For example, a font family with subencoding 5 (like Gillius) does not support the glyphs labeled 1–5 in Table 9.9 on pages 696 and 697.

If a glyph is unavailable in the current font (based on its subencoding information), then a default from a different font is selected. Of course, if the glyph is "letter-like", such as №, then it would be bad if the substituted glyph has serifs when the surrounding text is sans serif or vice versa. The mechanism therefore checks if the current font family matches \rmdefault, \sfdefault, or \ttdefault and selects a reasonable matching substitution.[2]

We demonstrate this in the next example by setting the \rmdefault to Gillius (which is of course nonsense because this is a sans serif font) and for comparison

---

[1] These are still substituted glyphs as Lucida does not have them, but they blend reasonably well.
[2] For fonts that match neither, the default is to use a serifed substitute.

\sfdefault to Gillius №2, which is a minor variant of the same font. Both have TS1 subencoding 5 so that all five symbols are substituted. In the first case we get serifed glyphs and in the second sans serif glyphs as a replacement. While not perfect, the latter is clearly an improvement. To prove that this also works for \ttdefault we use Algol Revived as typewriter font, which is also missing these glyphs.[1]

Gillius with ⓢ, №, £, ¢, ¶. Roman defaults used — not good.

Gillius No2 with ⓢ, №, £, ¢, ¶. Sans defaults used — better!

Algol Revived with ⓢ, №, £, ¢, ¶. Typewriter defaults now.

9-5-12

```
\renewcommand\rmdefault{GilliusADF-LF}
\renewcommand\sfdefault{GilliusADFNoTwo-LF}
\renewcommand\ttdefault{AlgolRevived-TLF}
\rmfamily Gillius with \textcopyleft, \textnumero, \textlira,
\textcentoldstyle, \textpilcrow. Roman defaults used --- not good.

\sffamily Gillius No2 with \textcopyleft, \textnumero, \textlira,
\textcentoldstyle, \textpilcrow. Sans defaults used --- better!

\ttfamily Algol Revived with \textcopyleft, \textnumero, \textlira,
\textcentoldstyle, \textpilcrow. Typewriter defaults now.
```

Of course, with mono-spaced fonts the substituted glyphs no longer have the right width and thus break any alignment. In our example this does not matter because Algol Revived is not actually mono-spaced, but in other situations this is something to watch out for.

If such a substitution happens, you get an information line in the .log about this. If for important documents you want this more prominent, load the textcomp with the option warn or error. The fonts used for substitution are customizable; for pdfTeX they are defined as follows:

```
\newcommand\rmsubstdefault{cmr}      \newcommand\sfsubstdefault{cmss}
                                     \newcommand\ttsubstdefault{cmtt}
\newcommand\textcompsubstdefault{\rmsubstdefault}
```

where \textcompsubstdefault is used when the current font is not one of the document default families.

Unicode engines

In Unicode engines, Latin Modern instead of Computer Modern is used.

While most unavailable glyphs in a TS1 subencoding get substituted by taking the same characters from a different font, this is not the case for the accent commands in the first block of Table 9.9. These accents get replaced by normal accents taken from the T1 encoding (and thus from the same font family). The only exception is \textcircled, which is taken from the math fonts if a substitution is necessary.

LaTeX already knows the correct TS1 subencoding for more than a hundred font families (including all that are discussed this book). But if you come across fonts that it does not know about (or for some reason assumes that they implement a smaller

---

[1] Actually, newer versions of Algol Revived provide most, but not all, of these glyphs. However, because some glyphs are missing, the TS1 subencoding used by default is supporting none of them.

subset than they actually do), you can inform LaTeX about the correct font subencoding through a \DeclareEncodingSubset declaration.

> \DeclareEncodingSubset{TS1}{*family*}{*number*}

The first argument is the *encoding*, but because this concept is implemented only for TS1, it can take only that value. The *family* can take a family name like Alegreya-LF, or it can take a partial family name ending in -* in which case the subencoding is set for the four families by replacing -* with -LF, -TLF, -OsF, and -TOsF, respectively. Finally, the *number* describes the subencoding and can take a value between 0 (full TS1) and 9 (smallest subset).

To find out which glyphs are available in which subencoding, look at Table 9.9 on pages 696–697. Available are all glyphs shown in black and from the glyphs in blue those marked with a number *higher* than the subencoding. For example, \textyen "¥" is always available, \textflorin "*f*" is available in subencodings 0–5, i.e., in most fonts, while \textpeso "₱" is provided only in those fonts with subencoding 0 or 1, so only in a handful. You can find the subencoding declarations used by LaTeX in the file lttextcomp.dtx.

If LaTeX does not have any information about a font family, it is very cautious and assumes subencoding 9 because this should really be supported by every font that offers any TS1 support. However, it is quite likely that this results in a lot of unnecessary substitutions, because most modern fonts provide subencodings 3–5. If you use fonts not described in this book and you get a lot of visible substitutions, it might be worth determining what exactly is provided and then add an appropriate \DeclareEncodingSubset declaration to your document.[1]

Altering the subencoding setup for individual glyphs

The split into a set of shrinking subencodings is not giving full justice to the diversity of fonts; i.e., the fonts have been assigned the subencoding for which all glyphs can be produced, but as a result the fonts may well contain one or the other glyph even though its subencoding says differently and you therefore get a substitution.

For example, suppose you typeset in Quattrocento or in Overlock and you happen to need a \textflorin and a \textcurrency symbol, then you get both from Computer Modern, which looks rather odd (especially the "f") with either font.

```
\usepackage[rm]{quattrocento} \usepackage{overlock}
Quattrocento: 3\textflorin\ and \textcurrency

\sffamily Overlock: 5\textflorin\ and \textcurrency
```

Quattrocento: 3f and ¤
Overlock: 5f and ¤

9-5-13

However, both fonts actually have their own florin symbol, so we can do better. One possible solution is to change the symbol default to unconditionally select the

---

[1] It is also possible to change the subencoding assumed for unknown fonts, by using ? as the family name, e.g., \DeclareEncodingSubset{TS1}{?}{5}, which might be a good compromise, but, of course, it may result in some missing glyphs if you are not careful.

glyph from the TS1 encoding, which is what we do in the next example. Of course, it is then up to you to make sure that you use it only with fonts that actually contain the glyph, as what we do means there is no substitution support any longer. This is why we get nothing with Overlock (and no warning or error) if we try the same with \textcurrency default!

```
\usepackage[rm]{quattrocento} \usepackage{overlock}
\DeclareTextSymbolDefault{\textflorin}{TS1}
\DeclareTextSymbolDefault{\textcurrency}{TS1}
                  Quattrocento: 3\textflorin\ and \textcurrency
```

Quattrocento: 3*f* and ¤

| 9-5-14 | Overlock: 5*f* and oops   `\sffamily Overlock: 5\textflorin\ and \textcurrency\ oops`

If you like to live dangerously, you can also turn off the substitution mechanism completely by loading the `textcomp` package with the options `full` and `force`, but then you should check the final result very carefully for missing glyphs.

In the previous example, some fonts had the desired glyph available, but it was just "unnecessarily" substituted for another. However, what do you do in the case of, say, Overlock and \textcurrency? One possibility is to define your own command and make it select a suitable glyph from a different font that fits well enough. In the example below we settled for the glyph from Rosario in the light series, which more or less matches the weight of Overlook.

What the declaration of \textcurrencysf does is to switch the font family (inside a group) and then use \textcurrency from the TS1 encoding.

```
\usepackage{overlock}
\DeclareTextCommandDefault{\textcurrencysf}
   {{\fontfamily{Rosario-LF}\fontseries{l}\selectfont
      \UseTextSymbol{TS1}{\textcurrency}}}
```

Overlook: ¤

| 9-5-15 | Close enough?   `\sffamily Overlook: \textcurrencysf \\ Close enough?`

Instead of defining a default for a new command, we could have overwritten the default for an existing command; for example,

```
\DeclareTextCommandDefault{\textdagger}
  {{\fontfamily{Almndr-OsF}\selectfont\UseTextSymbol{TS1}{\textdagger}}}
```

would always typeset the \textdagger symbol as † if you like that shape from the Almendra font.[1]

> **Unicode engines**
>
> With Unicode engines, this would not have the desired effect because all such symbol commands are directly provided by the TU encoding, and a default definition never applies. Thus, in such engines you need to force the change by

---

[1] For more abstract symbols this approach often gives an acceptable result; in the case of letter-like symbols, the standard substitution mechanism is usually better.

explicitly changing the definition for the TU encoding instead:

```
\DeclareTextCommand{\textdagger}{TU}
                {{\fontfamily{Almndr-OsF}\selectfont
                 \UseTextSymbol{TS1}{\textdagger}}}
```

or by removing it from this encoding via \UndeclareTextCommand.

9.5.7 exscale — Scaling large Computer Modern math operators

Normally the font employed for large mathematical symbols is used in only one size. This setup is usually sufficient, because the font includes most of the characters in several different sizes and (LA)TEX is specially equipped to automatically choose the symbol that fits best. However, when a document requires a lot of mathematics in large sizes — such as in headings — the selected symbols may come out too small. In this case, you can use the package exscale, which provides for math extension fonts in different sizes.

The package is only meant for documents using Computer Modern math fonts or very closely related designs such as Latin Modern because it makes use of the large symbol font of Computer Modern in different design sizes. However, packages providing alternate math font setups often offer this functionality as a package option, usually also named exscale.

9.5.8 tracefnt — Tracing the font selection

The package tracefnt can be used to detect problems in the font selection system. It supports several options that allow you to customize the amount of information displayed by NFSS on the screen and in the transcript file.

errorshow   This option suppresses all warnings and information messages on the terminal; they are written only to the transcript file. However, real errors are shown on the terminal. Because warnings about font substitutions and so on can mean that the final result is incorrect, you should carefully study the transcript file before printing an important publication.

warningshow   When this option is specified, warnings and errors are shown on the terminal. This setting gives you the same amount of information as LATEX 2$_\varepsilon$ does without the tracefnt package loaded.

infoshow   This option is the default when you load the tracefnt package. Extra information, which is normally written only to the transcript file, is now also displayed on your terminal.

debugshow   This option additionally shows information about changes to the text font and the restoration of such fonts at the end of a brace group or the end of an environment. Be careful when you turn on this option because it can produce very large transcript files.

In addition to these "standard tracing" options,[1] the package tracefnt supports the following options:

pausing   This option turns all warning messages into errors to help in the detection of problems in important publications.

loading   This option shows the loading of external fonts. However, if the format or document class you use has already loaded some fonts, then these are not shown by this option.

> **Unicode engines**
>
> It is also possible to use tracefnt with Unicode engines because the fontspec package responsible for font loading in these engines uses NFSS underneath its belt.

9.5.9 nfssfont.tex — Displaying 8-bit font tables and samples

The LaTeX distribution comes with a file called nfssfont.tex that can be used to test new 8-bit fonts, produce font tables showing all characters, and perform similar font-related operations.[2]

This file is an adaption of the program testfont.tex, which was originally written by Donald Knuth. When you run this file through LaTeX, you are asked to enter the name of the font to test. You can answer either by giving the external font name without any extension — such as cmr10 (Computer Modern Roman 10pt) — if you know it or by giving an empty font name. In the latter case you are asked to provide an NFSS font specification, that is, an encoding name (default T1), a font family name (default cmr), a font series (default m), a font shape (default n), and a font size (default 10pt). The package then loads the external font corresponding to that classification.

Next, you are requested to enter a command. Probably the most important one is \table, which produces a font chart like the one on page 750. Also interesting is \text, which produces a longer text sample. To switch to a new test font, type \init; to finish the test, type \bye or \stop. To learn about all the other possible tests (at the moment basically still tailored for the OT1 encoding), type \help. The default action is \table\bye because this is what is usually wanted.

9.6 fontspec — Font selection for Unicode engines

> **Unicode engines**
>
> One important difference between pdfTeX and Unicode engines is the way fonts are loaded and accessed. Up to this point we have covered the interfaces that are essentially common to all engines (with the exception of the fontenc package). In this section we describe the fontspec package, which should be

---

[1] It is suggested that package writers who support tracing of their packages use these four standard names if applicable.

[2] How to produce font tables for larger fonts is discussed in Section 9.6.7 on page 728.

used to load and access fonts when using X͟ƎTEX or LuaTEX. Thus, technically all of this section should be presented inside a gray box because it applies only to Unicode engines, but to prevent eye trouble with our readers, the rest of this section does not show this gray background.

In pdfTEX, fonts can be specified simply through calls to \fontfamily or through support packages that do those calls on behalf of the user. In Unicode engines this interface does not work because fonts in Unicode encoding (TU) usually do not have any supporting .fd files and so \fontfamily would not know how to load font shape declarations and alter the internal NFSS tables to access the requested fonts.

This is the price of the fact that with Unicode engines it is essentially possible to use any OpenType or TrueType font available on your computer without the need to first provide font metric files (.tfm) for TEX.

At the same time, directly using the low-level font loading facilities of the Unicode engines is not practical either, and so Will Robertson with contributions by Khaled Hosny, Philipp Gesang, and others developed the fontspec package that abstracts this loading process and provides a fairly simple and flexible interface to combine it with the powers of NFSS.

9.6.1 Setting up the main document font families

At its core, fontspec provides three declarations to set up three font families needed in most documents: a serif family, a sans serif family, and a typewriter family that then can be accessed through the usual NFSS commands, i.e., \textrm, \textsf, and \texttt or the corresponding declarative forms.

```
\setmainfont{family}[feature-list]
\setsansfont{family}[feature-list]
\setmonofont{family}[feature-list]
```

These declarations set up the document font families for the main fonts (serif), the sans fonts, and the typewriter fonts. In contrast to the usual NFSS practice of specifying some internal font family name, the *family* argument here expects the external name of an OpenType or TrueType font family. There are basically two ways to specify the *family*, either by "family name" or by "font file name". Both have their advantages and disadvantages; personally I prefer the family name approach because I think this is more readable and you do not have to deal with different file names for different font faces — all font tables in Chapter 10 provide the necessary names in this form.[1] The *feature-list* allows you to request specific font features or alter the setup in other aspects. This is discussed below.

As an introductory example, consider typesetting a document in Optima, which is available as a system font on Macintosh computers. In that case, all you have to do is to specify the family name as an argument to \setmainfont. This automatically takes

---

[1] However, when using X͟ƎTEX, explicit font file names are usually better.

care of defining italics, boldface, bold italic shapes, and corresponding small caps shapes (if available) so that basic font selection commands are immediately available.[1]

9-6-1

This **text** is typeset in the *system font* Optima. Sans Serif and Typewriter still default to Latin Modern Sans and Typewriter.

```
\usepackage{fontspec}  \setmainfont{Optima}

This \textbf{text} is typeset in the \emph{system font}
Optima. \textsf{Sans Serif} and \texttt{Typewriter}
still default to Latin Modern Sans and Typewriter.
```

For system fonts, that is, fonts that are stored in standard font locations, e.g., such as ~/Library/Fonts on macOS, or C:\Windows\Fonts on Windows, the above approach works in all TeX engines. However, if we use a font family that is stored within the TeX distribution tree (which is usually the case for the families discussed in this book), then this works with LuaTeX but unfortunately not on all operating systems with X⫐TeX. Thus, if we replace Optima with, say, Alegreya in the previous example, we get the desired result with LuaTeX, but when using X⫐TeX on a Mac or on a Linux system, we see something like

```
kpathsea: Running mktexmf Alegreya

! I can't find file 'Alegreya'.
<*> ...ljfour; mag:=1; nonstopmode; input Alegreya
```

because the fonts are not found and X⫐TeX unsuccessfully tries to generate them from some nonexisting METAFONT sources. If that happens, i.e., if you are using X⫐TeX and you want to use such a family, then the solution is to either add the font folder of your TeX system to your fontconfig configuration (check the documentation of your TeX system for how to do it) or to use the "by file name" approach and specify the actual font files in the declaration.

The former solves the problem for your own setup, but it is nonportable; i.e., your documents may not work elsewhere. The latter works everywhere, but is more work and involves two steps: first finding the names of the relevant font files and then specifying how they are mapped to italics, bold, etc., because that must be now done manually. For finding the real font names there are different possibilities; here is one that uses luaotfload-tool:

```
luaotfload-tool --list="familyname:alegreya" \
              --fields="location,plainname,basename"
```

You pass it the font family name but with all spaces removed (if any) and in only lowercase letters. For example, for "URW Classico" from Table 10.60 on page →II 72 you would specify urwclassico instead of alegreya. In our case we get the following list as output:

```
alegreya texmf Alegreya Bold         Alegreya-Bold.otf
alegreya texmf Alegreya Black Italic  Alegreya-BlackItalic.otf
alegreya texmf Alegreya Medium Italic Alegreya-MediumItalic.otf
```

---

[1] This font has no small capitals.

```
alegreya texmf Alegreya ExtraBold Italic Alegreya-ExtraBoldItalic.otf
alegreya texmf Alegreya Italic       Alegreya-Italic.otf
alegreya texmf Alegreya ExtraBold    Alegreya-ExtraBold.otf
alegreya texmf Alegreya Regular      Alegreya-Regular.otf
alegreya texmf Alegreya Medium       Alegreya-Medium.otf
alegreya texmf Alegreya Black        Alegreya-Black.otf
alegreya texmf Alegreya Bold Italic  Alegreya-BoldItalic.otf
```

Alternatively, you can use Herbert Voß's luafindfont program, which is essentially a simple-to-use frontend to the database of luaotfload-tool. You pass it a string as its argument and it finds you all fonts that contain this string as part of their symbolic name (the font family name without spaces and all lowercased), e.g.,

```
luafindfont -m 40 alegreya
```

In contrast to luaotfload-tool, this finds 48 fonts, because the string is also matching other names such as `alegreyasans`. With -m you can limit the number of characters shown in the path, which we did here to fit it into the book; normally you would not use it.

```
Nr.                  Fontname  Symbolic Name                               Path
  1.          Alegreya-Black.otf       alegreya  /usr/local/texlive/2021/te...a/alegreya/
  2.    Alegreya-BlackItalic.otf       alegreya  /usr/local/texlive/2021/te...a/alegreya/
...
 11.      AlegreyaSans-Black.otf   alegreyasans  /usr/local/texlive/2021/te...a/alegreya/
 12. AlegreyaSans-BlackItalic.otf  alegreyasans  /usr/local/texlive/2021/te...a/alegreya/
...
 13.       AlegreyaSans-Bold.otf   alegreyasans  /usr/local/texlive/2021/te...a/alegreya/
 14.  AlegreyaSans-BoldItalic.otf  alegreyasans  /usr/local/texlive/2021/te...a/alegreya/
...
 25.   AlegreyaSansSC-Black.otf alegreyasanssc  /usr/local/texlive/2021/te...a/alegreya/
 26. AlegreyaSansSC-BlackItalic.otf alegreyasanssc /usr/local/texlive/2021/te...a/alegreya/
...
 39.        AlegreyaSC-Black.otf     alegreyasc  /usr/local/texlive/2021/te...a/alegreya/
 40.  AlegreyaSC-BlackItalic.otf     alegreyasc  /usr/local/texlive/2021/te...a/alegreya/
...
 48.      AlegreyaSC-Regular.otf     alegreyasc  /usr/local/texlive/2021/te...a/alegreya/
```

Interesting further features of luafindfont are the options -i or -o followed by the line number of the font you are interested in, e.g.,

```
luafindfont alegreya -o 2
```

which gives you the otfinfo output for the Black Italic Alegreya font without the need to pass the full path to the program:

```
Run otfinfo:2
Family:            Alegreya Black
Subfamily:         Italic
Full name:         Alegreya Black Italic
PostScript name:   Alegreya-BlackItalic
Preferred family:  Alegreya
```

```
Preferred subfamily: Black Italic
Version:             Version 2.008;PS 002.008;hotconv 1.0.88;makeotf.lib2.5.64775
Unique ID:           2.008;HT  ;Alegreya-BlackItalic
Designer:            Juan Pablo del Peral
Designer URL:        http://www.huertatipografica.com
Manufacturer:        Huerta Tipografica
Vendor URL:          http://www.huertatipografica.com
Copyright:           Copyright 2011 The Alegreya Project Authors
                     (https://github.com/huertatipografica/Alegreya)
License URL:         http://scripts.sil.org/OFL
License Description: This Font Software is licensed under the SIL Open Font License, Version 1.1.
                     This license is available with a FAQ at: http://scripts.sil.org/OFL
Vendor ID:           HT
```

As you can see, the Alegreya family has ten different font faces, so we have to select those that we want to use. The upright face goes into the mandatory argument, and the others have to be specified in key/value syntax in the optional argument using the keys `ItalicFont`, `BoldFont`, and `BoldItalicFont`.

This **text** is typeset in the *family* Alegreya. It supports **bold italic** and SMALL CAPS.

9-6-2

```
\usepackage{fontspec}
\setmainfont{Alegreya-Regular.otf}
            [ ItalicFont     = Alegreya-Italic.otf,
              BoldFont       = Alegreya-Bold.otf,
              BoldItalicFont = Alegreya-BoldItalic.otf ]
This \textbf{text} is typeset in the \emph{family} Alegreya. It
supports \textbf{\itshape bold italic} and \textsc{Small Caps}.
```

The above gives us the same result as `\setmainfont{Alegreya}` (with LuaTeX) but works in both engines. However, the file name syntax is more powerful because we can select other faces at will. For example, we can use the Medium and the ExtraBold (or even the Black) fonts so that everything comes out slightly darker. Below we show that setup. That example also shows an alternative specification syntax, where the common part of the name is placed in the mandatory argument, which is then referred to in the key/values by using a *. If we do this, we have to additionally use the key `UprightFont` because the mandatory argument no longer contains the font for the upright face.

This **text** is typeset in the *family* Alegreya. It supports **bold italic** and SMALL CAPS.

9-6-3

```
\usepackage{fontspec}
\setmainfont{Alegreya}
            [ UprightFont     = *-Medium.otf,
              ItalicFont      = *-MediumItalic.otf,
              BoldFont        = *-ExtraBold.otf,
              BoldItalicFont = *-ExtraBoldItalic.otf]
This \textbf{text} is typeset in the \emph{family} Alegreya. It
supports \textbf{\itshape bold italic} and \textsc{Small Caps}.
```

Small capitals are a bit special, because in modern fonts they are usually not provided in a separate font files but instead accessed through OpenType font features. This explains why there was no need for us to set them up explicitly. When we provide

SMALL CAPITALS

709

the fonts for upright, italics, or bold, then fontspec queries the font resources, and if they support small capitals as a feature, it automatically sets up the corresponding shape as well.

However, sometimes the small capitals are supplied in separate font files, in which case this automatism cannot work. If this is the case, one can set up this shape by supplying the font file with the key SmallCapsFont. Details on this approach are given in the fontspec package documentation [118].

Slanted or oblique fonts

Besides italics and bold, fonts sometimes also contain oblique/slanted faces. The latter are not automatically set up. Instead, we have to explicitly specify what font should be selected for that shape with the keys SlantedFont and BoldSlantedFont. Without these keys \slshape and \textsl are aliased to italics. Below is an example with XCharter:

```
\usepackage{fontspec}
\setmainfont{XCharter}[SlantedFont = XCharter-Slanted.otf,
                       BoldSlantedFont = XCharter-BoldSlanted.otf ]
```

Italics versus *slanted*.
SOME *FACES* OF **SMALL CAPITALS**.

```
\textit{Italics} versus \textsl{slanted}. \par
\textsc{Some \textit{Faces} of \textbf{Small \slshape Capitals}}.
```

9-6-4

Swash fonts

In a similar manner you can set up a swash font or a bold swash font explicitly by using SwashFont or BoldSwashFont, respectively. However, because of the fact that swash letters are typically activated through a style feature (see below) in OpenType fonts, you also have to specify SwashFeatures={Style=Swash} to make it work.

The *feature-list* that one needs to provide in the optional argument of the \set...font declarations can sometimes get rather lengthy, and to avoid that, this then has to be repeated in every document, and fontspec offers some help. When a *family* is set up, the package checks if the file *family*.fontspec can be found and if so loads it first. More precisely, the *family* argument is first stripped of any spaces and any font file extension (in case the "by file name" approach is used). For example, when setting up Noto Sans, it would look for NotoSans.fontspec, and in Example 9-6-2 it tried to find Alegreya-Regular.fontspec.

Such a file is supposed to contain a \defaultfontfeatures declaration, listing key/value pairs that should be applied, for example,

```
\defaultfontfeatures[XCharter]{ Extension = .otf ,
  UprightFont = XCharter-Roman,    BoldFont        = XCharter-Bold,
  ItalicFont  = XCharter-Italic,   BoldItalicFont  = XCharter-BoldItalic,
  SlantedFont = XCharter-Slanted,  BoldSlantedFont = XCharter-BoldSlanted,
  SmallCapsFeatures =  {Letters=SmallCaps}  }
```

If such a .fontspec file exists, but you do not want to see it applied for some reason, specify the key IgnoreFontspecFile in the *feature-list*. For more details on this interface consult [118]. For XCharter, a XCharter.fontenc file exists as part of the LaTeX font support and so we could have omitted the optional argument in Example 9-6-4 above and achieved the same result.

9.6.2 Setting up additional font families

Most of the time it is enough to set up the fonts for \rmfamily, \sffamily, and \ttfamily with the declarations discussed above. However, sometimes one needs additional fonts for special cases. For example, you might want to use a specially condensed font for marginal notes or you want to define heading commands that use a different font family from the document body font and not just a bolder version of that. For such purposes you can define named font commands that work just like \rmfamily but select the desired family instead.

```
\newfontfamily{cmd}{family}[feature-list]
```

The \newfontfamily declaration defines a new font family (like \rmfamily) and makes it available through *cmd*. If *cmd* is already defined, you receive an error message. To overwrite an existing definition use \renewfontfamily instead. There also exist \providefontfamily (provide only if undefined) and \setfontfamily (always define without checking). The next example sets up \headfamily as a special family and uses it in a titlesec declaration.

1   On Reason

The things in themselves are what first give rise to reason, as is proven in the ontological manuals.

1.1   Considerations

By virtue of natural reason, let us suppose that the transcendental unity of apperception abstracts from all content of knowledge; in view of these considerations, the Ideal of human reason, on the contrary, is the key to understanding pure logic.

```
\usepackage{kantlipsum,fontspec}
\setmainfont{GaramondNo8}
\newfontfamily{\headfamily}{Bitter}

\usepackage[compact]{titlesec}
\titleformat*{\section}{\headfamily}
\titleformat*{\subsection}{\headfamily}

\section{On Reason}              \kant[6][1]
\subsection{Considerations} \kant[6][2]
```

9-6-5

If you also wish to have a \texthead command available for the new family, use \DeclareTextFontCommand in addition:

```
\DeclareTextFontCommand{\texthead}{\headfamily}
```

```
\fontspec{family}[feature-list]
```

The \fontspec command sets up an unnamed family for direct use, which is therefore available only at the point of declaration. This is mainly useful when testing a font (or in the examples of this book) where it saves a few keystrokes but seldom in normal documents.

9.6.3 Setting up a single font face

Sometimes access to a single font face is wanted and there is no need to set up the whole family with all its different faces. In that case you might prefer \newfontface over \newfontfamily because that saves processing time and resources.

> \newfontface{*cmd*}{*font*} [*feature-list*]

This defines *cmd* to select the *font* loaded with *feature-list*. If you specify a family name in the *font* argument, the base face is selected. Also supported are \renew..., \provide..., and \set... variants of the declaration.

9.6.4 Interfacing with core NFSS commands

As mentioned before, the interface to NFSS is by default partly hidden, and all necessary setups are done behind the scenes by the fontspec declarations. As a result, it is possible to use the high-level NFSS commands such as \textsf, \bfseries, \itshape, etc., but it is not possible to use \fontfamily (because the family name internally defined by fontspec is not known to you) nor can you say \fontseries{c} to request a condensed series because series values other than m and b are not set up automatically, unless you have a special .fontspec file for the font family.

There are, however, ways to provide the necessary information as part of the *feature-list* argument in the fontspec declarations discussed thus far.

To explicitly name the font family, use the key NFSSFamily. A possible use case for this is shown in the next example, where we explicitly set the NFSS family name and then pass it to fancyvrb. Usually the high-level commands or newly defined ones, like \fvrbfamily, for changing the family are enough, so this is seldom needed.

```
\usepackage{fancyvrb,fontspec}
\newfontfamily\fvrbfamily{AlgolRevived}
                         [NFSSFamily=AlgolR]

\begin{Verbatim*}[fontfamily=AlgolR]
... while it works in T1: \sum_{i=1}^n
UTF-8 char test: äöüß œ Æ $ £ »„«
\end{Verbatim*}
```

...␣while␣it␣works␣in␣T1:␣\sum_{i=1}^n
UTF-8␣char␣test:␣äöüß␣œ␣Æ␣$␣£␣»„«

9-6-6

More interesting are cases where a font family has a larger selection of weights or running lengths and you want to access some of them. Because fontspec only sets up the medium and the bold series, we need to provide anything else through one or more FontFace key settings. It supports the following two syntax variants:

FontFace={*series*}{*shape*}{*font*}

or

FontFace={*series*}{*shape*}{Font=*font*, *feature-list*}

The *series* and *shape* are the NFSS axes under which we want to access the *font* face. In the simple form we only supply a *font* name, but often we want to also enable or disable some features. In that case we have to use a feature list in the third argument and supply the *font* through the key Font. This is what we do in the next example where we define support for the swash shapes offered by EB Garamond. After defining what font sw and scsw should switch to, we can use the standard commands \textsw

and `\swshape`. For both declarations we need the *feature-list* syntax variant, because
we have to enable special font features (discussed later).

```
\usepackage{fontspec}
\setmainfont{EB Garamond}
   [ FontFace={m}{sw}  {Font=EBGaramond-Italic.otf,Style=Swash},
     FontFace={m}{scsw}{Font=EBGaramond-Italic.otf,
                                    Letters=SmallCaps,Style=Swash} ]
```

Show A Few EB Garamond Italic Letters: SPQR.

Show A Few EB Garamond Swash Letters: SPQR.

9-6-7

```
\textit{Show A Few EB Garamond Italic Letters: \textsc{Spqr}}.

\textsw{Show A Few EB Garamond Swash Letters: \textsc{Spqr}}.
```

A slightly more consise way of achieving the same effect in this case would have
been to use the `SwashFont` and `SwashFeatures` keys as follows:

```
\setmainfont{EB Garamond}[ SwashFont=EBGaramond-Italic.otf,
                           SwashFeatures={Style=Swash} ]
```

This too would set up the small caps variants implicitly.

9.6.5 Altering the look and feel of fonts

The interfaces of the fontspec package allow loading fonts with specific features
enabled by specifying those in the form of key/value pairs. This can be done in the
optional *feature-list* argument of any of the declarations. These features are then
applied when loading and setting up the font family, e.g., the declaration

```
\setmainfont{Alegreya}[Numbers = {OldStyle, Proportional}]
```

asks for loading the Alegreya fonts with proportional oldstyle figures, i.e., different
digits may have different widths, depending on their shape. That setting may be
right for numbers in normal text, but if we typeset a table in which numbers should
align for ease of reading, we may want to temporarily change from `Proportional` to
`Monospaced`. It is therefore also necessary to alter or apply features only occasionally
within the document.

`\addfontfeature{`*feature*`}`   `\addfontfeatures{`*feature-list*`}`

These commands[1] apply the given *feature* or *feature-list* to the current font family
(and all its different faces including those added through `FontFace`). Already enabled
features are kept unless they conflict with the newly requested feature(s). This is a
local change, so it remains in force until the end of the current group or environment.

For example, requesting `Numbers=Monospaced` would preserve `OldStyle` but
overwrite `Proportional`, because the two are mutually exclusive. Of course, when

---

[1] `\addfontfeature` is just an alias for `\addfontfeatures`, so technically both accept a *feature-list*.

using such commands more often, it is usually better to provide your own little commands for this, e.g.,

```
\newcommand\nummono{\addfontfeature{Numbers=Monospaced}}
\newcommand\tabularnums[1]{{\nummono #1}}
```

Note the extra set of braces in \tabularnums to confine the feature change to #1.

Using generally available font features

Some font features that can be adjusted through the fontspec interfaces are available with any font family; others may be implemented only by some fonts.

Scaling fonts If different font families are used together, it is often the case that one of them needs to be slightly scaled up or down to match the height of the other. For this fontspec offers the key Scale. It takes either a numeric value as the scale factor, e.g., 1.05, or the values MatchLowercase or MatchUppercase, matching the x-height or the capital height of the main (\familydefault) family.

A sample text mixing Sans, Typewriter, and Roman in one sentence.

```
\usepackage{fontspec}
\setmainfont{TeX Gyre Termes}                        % Times
\setsansfont{TeX Gyre Heros}[Scale=MatchLowercase]   % Helvetica
\setmonofont{Latin Modern Mono}[Scale=MatchLowercase] % LM Mono
A sample text \textsf{mixing Sans}, \texttt{Typewriter},
and Roman in one sentence.
```

9-6-8

Successive usages of Scale for the same family overwrite each other. If you want to accumulate scale factors for fine-tuning, use ScaleAgain instead.

Coloring fonts At a fairly low level, fonts can be colored using the key Color. This works even if no color support for LaTeX has been loaded as it is interacting directly with the font resource, i.e., coloring the glyphs. By default the color has to be given as a triplet of two-digit hexadecimal values, e.g., FF0000 for red, with optionally a fourth value for the transparency (where 00 is completely transparent and FF is opaque). If you load xcolor (but not color) you can alternatively use "named" colors as values and then describe the transparency through the key Opacity (values between 0 and 1).

If a font is colored in this way, then LaTeX's color commands no longer influence that particular font at all, as can be seen in the last input line of the example.

Text in black.
Text still in blue
and not red!

```
\usepackage{xcolor,fontspec}  \setmainfont{EB Garamond}
\Large\bfseries
\makebox[0pt][l]{\addfontfeature{Color=black,Opacity=0.5}%
                 Text in black.}%
\hspace{1pt}\addfontfeature{Color=blue,Opacity=0.7}Text in blue.\\
\textcolor{red}{Text still in blue and not red!}
```

9-6-9

Other generally available features   There are a number of other keys that can be used with any font, but they are too special to discuss in detail, so we only list them. Refer to [118] for details and examples if you think you need any of them.

WordSpace allows you to alter the width, stretch, and shrink of a space character; PunctuationSpace alters the extra space after punctuation characters; and with LetterSpace you can add some extra kerns between glyphs for tracking purposes (this is how microtype manages letterspacing in such fonts). There is also HyphenChar=None that allows you to suppress hyphenation in that font.[1]

Space handling and hyphenation

Some font families offer separate font files for different sizes, and those can be explicitly selected to be used for certain size ranges using a combination of SizeFeatures, Size, and OpticalSize.

Optical size support

There are even possibilities to artificially transform a given font by mechanically boldening it with FakeBold or tilting with FakeSlant or stretching or compressing it with FakeStretch, but the results are usually noticeably inferior to properly designed fonts and should therefore be used with extreme care or not at all.

Producing artificial series values (bold and stretch)

Specifying OpenType font features

OpenType fonts often implement variants through a set of named features. These feature names consist of four letters, such as smcp (small capitals) or ss02 (stylistic set 2), and there are more than a hundred such feature tags defined; see [80] for a nice (but not even complete) overview together with explanations for each feature.

These short names are naturally rather cryptic, so fontspec offers a more readable interface to many of them. We introduce the more important ones through examples, but given the number of possibilities, this is obviously only scratching the surface. More details can be found in the fontspec documentation [118], which has more than thirty pages devoted to that topic.

Besides knowing how to enable certain font features, a big question is how we can find out what features are offered by a given font file. One possible way is to use the program otfinfo in a terminal window. For example, to get a list of all features implemented by XCharter-Roman we could run

```
otfinfo -f `kpsewhich XCharter-Roman.otf`
```

on Linux or MacOs,[2] which would then respond with the following list:

c2sc	Small Capitals From Capitals	mkmk	Mark to Mark Positioning
case	Case-Sensitive Forms	numr	Numerators
cpsp	Capital Spacing	onum	Oldstyle Figures
cv01	Character Variants 1	smcp	Small Capitals
dnom	Denominators	ss01	Stylistic Set 1
kern	Kerning	ss02	Stylistic Set 2
liga	Standard Ligatures	subs	Subscript
lnum	Lining Figures	sups	Superscript
mark	Mark Positioning	tnum	Tabular Figures

---

[1] In XꟆTEX it can also be used to explicitly define a different hyphenation character.
[2] On Windows use for /F %i in ('kpsewhich XCharter-Roman.otf') do otfinfo -f %i instead.

Value	feature	Value	feature
Lining	lnum	OldStyle	onum
Proportional	pnum	Monospaced	tnum
SlashedZero	zero	ResetAll	—

Uppercase *and* Lowercase *can be used as synonyms for* Lining *and* OldStyle. *Individual features can by turned off by appending* Off *to the name.*

Table 9.10: Values accepted by the Numbers key

As you see, this list comes with a short explanation for each feature so that one can often already guess what a feature does. For example, seeing smcp explains why fontspec was able to automatically set up the Small Caps shapes in Example 9-6-4. For others it may not be so clear, and there the explanations in [80] and our discussions below may help. We now discuss a selection of these features and how to specify them in the *feature-list* arguments.

Figure style features   An important variation supported by many font families is alternate styles for digits. For this, fontspec offers the key Numbers that we already used without much explanation earlier. Allowed values and the corresponding feature tags are given in Table 9.10.

The next example shows the different combinations using Cochineal as the sample family. How the keys behave in relation to each other is defined by the font resource. Here the keys are orthogonal as expected, but in others setting OldStyle might automatically change to Proportional, because the font does not offer monospaced, oldstyle figures. In many fonts SlashedZero (if available) produces a fixed (lining) glyph, so it does not work well in combination with OldStyle. Due to the use of ResetAll we get the font defaults in the last example line, which for this font is lining, monospaced.

Also note the use of extra braces when we supply several values to one key. They are needed to hide the comma, which would otherwise be misinterpreted.

```
\usepackage{fontspec}
\setmainfont{Cochineal}[Numbers = {OldStyle,Proportional}]
\noindent                                                Digits: 0123456789\\
\addfontfeature{Numbers={Monospaced,SlashedZero}}Digits: 0123456789\\
\addfontfeature{Numbers=Lining}                          Digits: 0123456789\\
\addfontfeature{Numbers=Proportional}                    Digits: 0123456789\\
\addfontfeature{Numbers=ResetAll}                        Digits: 0123456789
```

Digits: 0123456789
Digits: 0123456789
Digits: 0123456789
Digits: 0123456789
Digits: 0123456789

9-6-10

If you look through the font tables in Chapter 10, you can easily identify if lining and oldstyle figures are supported and whether they have a proportional and/or a

Value	feature	Value	feature
SmallCaps	smcp	UppercaseSmallCaps	c2sc
PetiteCaps	pcap	UppercasePetiteCaps	c2pc
Unicase	unic		

Individual features can by turned off by appending Off to the name.

Table 9.11: Values accepted by the Letters key

monospaced variant (this is implicitly encoded in the suffixes -LF, -TLF, -OsF, and -TOsF; see page →II 6 for details).

For oldstyle numbers, standard LaTeX has a fairly complicated definition to cater for the fact that in its default fonts, the oldstyle numerals are stored in a strange place (i.e., inside the math fonts) and for other fonts need to be fetched from TS1-encoded files (if available). In Unicode engines using OpenType fonts this is simpler, because all that is required is enabling the OldStyle feature. So fontspec changes the definition of \oldstylenums to do just that and additionally adds a \liningnums command to provide a simple way to get lining numerals if oldstyle numerals are used by default.

\oldstylenums
simplified

Letter case features Earlier we mentioned that small capitals are automatically set up by fontspec if available as an OpenType feature in the font. However, there are in fact several features related to small capitals, and sometimes you may want to choose something different from the default. The features are accessed through the key Letters, and its possible values are given in Table 9.11. The most common one is SmallCaps (smcp), which is what fontspec looks for when trying to automatically set up small capitals. It affects the lowercase letters and changes them to become small capitals. PetiteCaps (pcap) is similar but uses even smaller capitals in place of the lowercase letters.

The features UppercaseSmallCaps (c2sc) and UppercasePetiteCaps (c2pc) on the other hand alter only uppercase letters and replace them with smaller versions. Thus, it is possible to combine a value from the first group with one from the second, which is what we do in Example 9-6-11 on the next page.

However, we do not want the Letters key to affect the whole family; we want to apply it only when the user requests small capitals via \textsc or \scshape. This is why we do not use it directly but supply it as a value to SmallCapsFeatures. This key expects a *feature-list* applicable only when \textsc is requested.[1] In the second half of the example we then show what happens if we supply the Letters key at the top level, i.e., to the whole family. Also note the size difference between small capitals and petite capitals.

---

[1] Similar keys exist to supply *feature-lists* applicable to other font faces, e.g., ItalicFeatures, BoldFeatures, and so forth; for further details see [118].

```
\usepackage{fontspec}
\setmainfont{EB Garamond}
          [ SmallCapsFeatures =
                 {Letters={UppercaseSmallCaps,PetiteCaps}} ]
```

Different *FACES* OF **SMALL CAPITALS** FOLLOWED By *Further* Text.

```
\raggedright
Different \textsc{\textit{Faces} Of \textbf{Small
    \itshape Capitals} Followed} By \textit{Further} Text.
```

BUT NOW *EVERYTHING* USES **SMALL *CAPITALS***!

```
\addfontfeature{Letters = SmallCaps}
But Now \textit{Everything} Uses \textbf{Small \itshape Capitals}!
```

9-6-11

The Unicase (unic) value enables a rather strange feature that maps all upper and lowercase letters to a mixture of small capitals and lowercase letters so you end up getting something like

WEIRD MAPPING AHEAD

Because none of the free fonts discussed in this book supports this feature, the above is an artificially made up example.

Vertical positioning features   For writing text such as 1st, 2nd, 3rd or 1_a, 1_b, etc., LaTeX offers the generic commands \textsuperscript and \textsubscript that raise or lower their argument and select a smaller font size to typeset it.

This gives usable results with any font, although due to using a smaller version of the same font, the glyphs come out somewhat too light, and the vertical positioning may not be perfect either. However, modern fonts often have especially designed glyphs for this purpose that do not have these defects. The next example shows the differences. There we define two commands to typeset superior and inferior glyphs. The key to select these glyphs is VerticalPosition, and the possible values for it are given in Table 9.12 on the facing page. Also compare this with Example 10-1-1 on page →II 9 showing how to access such glyphs when using pdfTeX.

```
\usepackage{fontspec}
\setmainfont{Alegreya}
\newcommand\textsu[1]{{\addfontfeature{VerticalPosition=Superior}#1}}
\newcommand\textin[1]{{\addfontfeature{VerticalPosition=Inferior}#1}}
```

Catch$_{22}$ in Room^{13}
Catch$_{22}$ in Room^{13}

```
Catch\textsubscript{22} in Room\textsuperscript{13}% inferior quality
Catch\textin{22}         in Room\textsu{13}         % much better!
```

9-6-12

Obviously, such a feature should only be turned on locally. It is also important to note that the characters affected differ from font family to font family. Sometimes both digits and letters are available raised and lowered, but often only a few letters are raised or only the digits are available in inferior positions.

The next example exhibits the results of the values Superior (raising digits and [some] letters), Ordinal (slightly less raised, often only the letters "abdeilmnorst"), Inferior (usually only digits), and ScientificInferior (compared to Inferior

Value	feature	Value	feature
Superior	sups	Inferior	subs
Ordinal	ordn	ScientificInferior	sinf
Numerator	numr	Denominator	dnom
ResetAll	—		

Individual features can by turned off by appending Off *to the name.*

Table 9.12: Values accepted by the VerticalPosition key

further below the baseline). Depending on the font family, some of the features may not be available or affect a larger or smaller set of glyphs.

X$^{1234\ strd}$ (Superior)
X1234 ^{strd} (Ordinal)
X$_{1234}$ strd   (Inferior)
X$_{1234}$ strd   (ScientificInferior)
X1234 strd   (ResetAll)

9-6-13

```
\usepackage{fontspec} \setmainfont{Alegreya}
\newcommand\test[1]
    {X{\addfontfeature{VerticalPosition=#1}1234 strd}
    \hfill (\texttt{\footnotesize#1})\par}
\test{Superior} \test{Ordinal} \test{Inferior}
\test{ScientificInferior}        \test{ResetAll}
```

If you look through the font tables in Chapter 10, you can see whether a font family supports a superior style (-Sup) or an inferior style (-Inf). Usually that means Superior and Inferior are available, but sometimes only ScientificInferior is provided as a feature.

As an alternative, you may want to check out the small **realscripts** package by Will Robertson, which redefines \textsuperscript and \textsubscript to use the above font features if available. The original LaTeX meaning remains available as starred forms of the command. To simplify typesetting superscripts on top of subscripts the package also defines \textsubsuperscript[*pos*]{*sub*}{*super*}. If necessary, the distance between the two can be adjusted by altering the length parameter \subsupersep.

Using the realscripts package for script characters

The values Numerator and Denominator, if available, affect only digits and are meant for the special case of slashed fractions. Below we show their results in case of different Noto families. For the typewriter font we have specified the font by name in order to get a condensed font selected in the example.

```
\usepackage{fontspec}    \setmainfont{Noto Serif}
\setsansfont{Noto Sans} \setmonofont{NotoSansMono-Condensed.ttf}
\newcommand\txtfrac[2]{{\addfontfeature{VerticalPosition=Numerator}#1}%
                /{\addfontfeature{VerticalPosition=Denominator}#2}}
```

$^{1}/_{2}$ $^{47}/_{11}$ $^{1}/_{1000}$ `\txtfrac{1}{2} \txtfrac{47}{11} \txtfrac{1}{1000} \par`
$^{1}/_{2}$ $^{47}/_{11}$ $^{1}/_{1000}$ `\sffamily \txtfrac{1}{2} \txtfrac{47}{11} \txtfrac{1}{1000} \par`
$^{1}/_{2}$ $^{47}/_{11}$ $^{1}/_{1000}$ `\ttfamily \txtfrac{1}{2} \txtfrac{47}{11} \txtfrac{1}{1000}`

9-6-14

Value	feature	Value	feature
Required[a]	rlig	Contextuals	clig
Common[a]	liga	Rare	dlig
TeX[b]	—	Historic	hlig
ResetAll	—		

[a]*On by default in all fonts.*
[b]*On by default for fonts set up with* \setmainfont *and* \setsansfont.
Individual features can by turned off by appending Off *to the name.*

Table 9.13: Values accepted by the Ligatures key

Instead of using VerticalPosition to build your fractions, you can try the key Fractions (frac), which is implemented in many fonts and automatically builds fractions when it sees a slash (/) in the source. Note, however, that this may make it impossible to use the slash for normal text or mixed fractions. What also can happen is that only fractions precomposed in the font work, such as with IBM Plex Mono.

```
\usepackage{fontspec} \setmainfont{Erewhon}[Fractions=On]
\setsansfont{Lato}[Fractions=On]
\setmonofont{IBM Plex Mono}[Fractions=On]
```

½ ⅔ ⁴⁷⁄₁₁ ¹⁄₁₀₀₀ but note: a/b ¹⁄ₙ   1/2 2/3 47/11 1/1000 but note: a/b 1/n\par
½ ⅔ ⁴⁷⁄₁₁ ¹⁄₁₀₀₀ okay here: a/b ¹⁄ₙ   \sffamily 1/2 2/3 47/11 1/1000 okay here: a/b 1/n\par
½ ⅔ 47/11 1/1000 a/b 1/n \ttfamily 1/2 2/3 47/11 1/1000   a/b 1/n

9-6-15

Ligature features   Nearly every font defines some sets of ligatures, i.e., characters that if appearing in succession are not typeset one after the other but get replaced by a new glyph. In LaTeX this happens automatically behind the scenes; e.g., if you enter ffi, you get "ffi" instead of "ffi", etc.

In pdfTeX, due to the limitation of glyphs per font, only f-ligatures and a few special ligatures, such as ! ' generating "¡", are available, but with OpenType fonts there are not any limits and so many modern fonts provide a much richer set of ligatures. However, only some of them are enabled by default; the others need to be activated through the key Ligatures. Possible values are listed in Table 9.13.

If given the value TeX, the special ligatures traditionally provided by TeX are enabled, e.g., -- producing an en-dash and --- an em-dash. This is automatically done by fontspec if you set up the main font family or the sans family. For any other font you load you need to enable them yourself. This is not a feature of the OpenType fonts (so does not correspond to a feature tag) but is handled by the code loading the font in TeX.

In addition, OpenType fonts may have up to five feature tags that define ligature sets. The value Required (rlig) enables ligatures that are required by the script for correct typesetting. Latin script does not really have any required ligatures, which is why the fonts we show in this book normally do not implement this feature. However, when typesetting, for example, Arabic, that set is nonempty. Being "required", it is enabled by default.

Also enabled by default are the Common ligatures (`liga`), i.e., those that the designer of the font thought should be always used. This set typically covers f-ligatures but sometimes also others. For example, in the Accanthis family the less common ligatures "fj" and "ft" are part of the set, but they are not ligatures in Lucida Bright — the family used for this book. For some reason Accanthis also has required ligatures (a questionable decision), but it allows us to show all three sets here.

" - — ¡ ¿ "   (TeX)
æ Æ œ Œ   (required)
fi ffi fl ffl fj ffj ft (common)
" -- --- ¡ ¿ "
ae Ae oe Oe
fi ffi fl ffl fj ffj ft

```
\usepackage{fontspec} \setmainfont{Accanthis Adf Std No3}
`` -- --- !` ?` ''\hfill   (TeX) \\ ae Ae oe Oe\hfill (required)
          \\ fi ffi fl ffl fj ffj ft (common)                    \\
\addfontfeature{Ligatures={TeXOff,RequiredOff,CommonOff}}
`` -- --- !` ?` '' \\ ae Ae oe Oe \\ fi ffi fl ffl fj ffj ft
```

9-6-16

Rare or Discretionary ligatures (`dlig`) are considered optional by the font designer, and the set is therefore not enabled by default. There is also the set of Historic ligatures (`hlig`) that implements ligatures that were once common in documents but are nowadays not often seen so are useful only if you want to give your document a certain look and feel. Which ligatures end up in which set (or are provided at all) differs unfortunately from family to family as we can see in the next example. You may have to try out what happens if you enable one or the other feature.

ch ck Th tt tz st ct sp
ch ck Th tt tz   (rare)
st ct (not sp)   (historic)
st ct sp Qu
st ct sp   (rare)
Qu   (historic)

```
\usepackage{fontspec}
\fontspec{Libertinus Serif}        ch ck Th tt tz st ct sp      \\
\addfontfeature{Ligatures=Rare} ch ck Th tt tz \hfill (rare) \\
\addfontfeature{Ligatures=Historic}st ct (not sp)\hfill (historic)
\par \medskip
\fontspec{BaskervilleF}          st ct sp Qu                  \\
\addfontfeature{Ligatures=Rare}     st ct sp \hfill (rare) \\
\addfontfeature{Ligatures=Historic}  Qu   \hfill (historic)
```

9-6-17

Finally, there may be Contextuals ligatures (`clig`) that should, as the name indicates, be used in only certain contexts (typically when typesetting in specific languages) and are therefore not activated either by default. In predominately Latin fonts this feature is seldom implemented, and none of the fonts discussed in this book supports it.

Adjusting the font kerning The Kerning key (see Table 9.14 on the next page) is responsible for adding kerns (small negative or positive spaces) between adjacent letters to make their appearance visually uniform. This is activated by default, but in some special cases you may want to prohibit it using `Kerning=Off`. If you typeset text in

Value	feature	Value	feature
On	kern	Uppercase	cpsp
Off	-kern	ResetAll	—

`UppercaseOff` *turns the feature off.*

Table 9.14: Values accepted by the `Kerning` key

capitals, then the normal kerning can be improved in many fonts by using the value `Uppercase` (`scsp`). The differences are fairly small, but in the eyes of the font designer they improve legibility. In the example the first line shows the default result, the second adjusts the vertical position of the hyphen and shortens the parentheses a bit, and in the third line we also add the extra kerning that makes the line minimally wider:

AN (ALL–CAPS) HEADING
AN (ALL–CAPS) HEADING
AN (ALL–CAPS) HEADING

```
\usepackage{fontspec}
\newfontfamily\headfamily{Playfair Display}
\fontsize{12}{14}\headfamily          AN (ALL-CAPS) HEADING \\
\addfontfeature{Style=Uppercase}      AN (ALL-CAPS) HEADING \\
\addfontfeature{Kerning=Uppercase}    AN (ALL-CAPS) HEADING
```

9-6-18

Stylistic features   The stylistic feature tags `ss01` to `ss20`, the alternate feature tag `salt`, as well as the character variant feature tags `cv01` to `cv99` are sometimes available in OpenType fonts and can be used to select glyph shape variants.

The `cv`⟨*num*⟩ tags (character variants) have been invented primarily for orthographic variations of individual characters, which is why there are so many of them. They are often used for situations where Unicode has only a single slot but varying regional or typographic traditions exist and the user might prefer one variant over the other.

The `ss`⟨*num*⟩ tags (stylistic sets) on the other hand were meant to alter sets of glyphs typically for typographic rather than orthographic reasons. Without a definite purpose it was up to the font designers to decide what kind of features each of their sets implements. Technically the sets are more than just additive, e.g., effects on some glyph may differ depending on enabling `ss01`, `ss02`, or both of them. Sometimes combining them just produces undesirable effects; see Example 9-6-20 on page 724. However, in most fonts their effects are orthogonal to each other. Stylistic sets got supported early on by Adobe InDesign, and as a result many fonts offer a collection of them (usually altering just a few characters per set) to allow users to easily choose their favorite combination.

The alternate feature `salt` is a single set and predates the stylistic sets, but being supported in Adobe Illustrator, font designers often add variants both into `ss` and `salt`. The traditional implementation of this feature in software was to offer an interactive menu from which the user is able to pick and choose. Thus, in many cases one finds variants in this set that do not naturally work in unison. This makes it less attractive for use with LaTeX because through `fontspec` it is possible to activate the whole set but not individual variants from it; see Example 9-6-22 on the next page.

The `fontspec` package offers interfaces for these features through the keys `CharacterVariant`, `StylisticSet`, `Alternate`, and `Style`, but for these it is usually simpler to specify them through the generic `RawFeature` interface, which is what we do below. Later examples show the other interfaces.

For example, in the `otfinfo` output for `XCharter-Roman.otf` on page 715 we see `cv01` and `ss01` being listed. Unfortunately, we do not get any information about what the character variation or the stylistic set actually do to our font. In this font `cv01` alters the look of the oldstyle numeral "1", and `ss01` changes the glyph used for "ß" in small capitals.

Activating a feature works by specifying the feature name (with an optional +　in front) as the value to `RawFeature`, deactivating by preceding the name with a -. Some fonts have several character variants for a single character, in which case the variants can be accessed numerically, e.g., `RawFeature={+cv01=2}`.

```
\usepackage{fontspec}  \setmainfont{XCharter}[Numbers=OldStyle]
                 123             \addfontfeature{RawFeature = +cv01} 123
123 123 123                      \addfontfeature{RawFeature = -cv01} 123               \\
Gruß ß Gruss ß   \textsc{Gruß} ß \addfontfeature{RawFeature =  ss01} \textsc{Gruß} ß
```

9-6-19

If you are lucky, then this is documented as part of the font documentation, but with the free fronts we discuss in Chapter 10 this is regrettably seldom the case. So how did we know how to prepare the examples in this section? The answer is unfortunately "by opening the font files in the font editor `fontforge` and examining the substitutions that are specified for the different stylistic sets".

This is certainly not a good way to do it and given that within the TeX distribution 34 font families implement alternates and 75 specify one or more stylistic set, there is a treasure hidden here waiting to be dug up. I hope that one day somebody finds the time and documents what exactly these variants do font by font.

Without that being available, all we can do now is to exhibit a few more interesting examples that show that it is a pity that the font designers went through the trouble of producing interesting alternatives but then stopped short and forgot to tell people about them.[1]

Our next example involves the font family Cormorant Garamond. It supports several stylistic sets of which we show two: `ss03` alters the shape of several characters and symbols (in fact more than we display) and `ss04` changes the dieresis accents to display a small "e" instead. Note that while it is in principle possible to activate several stylistic sets in parallel, it does not always work if they try to alter the same characters; in this case, the "ä" was already changed by `ss03`, and `ss04` was not applied.

It also offers a few individual character variants; we show those for "Q" and "f". Finally, `salt` is also available, which alters some strokes in a number of characters;

---

[1] With commercial fonts this documentation is more often available, which is the main reason why we show how to access these features.

again we display only a selection of those being affected.

a ä g U W w y æ †‡
a ä g U W w y œ ††
Ä ä Ü ü Ö ö
Ä̇ ä̇ Ü̇ ü̇ Ȯ ȯ
Ä ä W w y
Ä̇ ä̇ W w y
Q Q Q ff
A B g J K Q R U
A B g J K Q R U

```
\usepackage{fontspec} \setmainfont{Cormorant Garamond}
  a ä g U W w y \ae\ \textdagger\textdaggerdbl                    \\
{\addfontfeature{RawFeature=ss03}
  a ä g U W w y \ae\ \textdagger\textdaggerdbl}                   \\
Ä ä Ü ü Ö ö \\ {\addfontfeature{RawFeature=ss04} Ä ä Ü ü Ö ö}     \\
Ä ä W w y   \\ {\addfontfeature{RawFeature={ss03,ss04}} Ä ä W w y} \\
Q{\addfontfeature{RawFeature=cv01} Q}
 {\addfontfeature{RawFeature=cv02} Q}
f{\addfontfeature{RawFeature=cv05} f}                             \\
A B g J K Q R U \\ {\addfontfeature{RawFeature=salt} A B g J K Q R U}
```
9-6-20

Some fonts offer more than one `salt` set, in which case the sets are numbered starting with zero representing the default set. This makes addressing such sets using `RawFeature={salt=⟨num⟩}` a bit awkward. As an alternative, you can use `Alternate=⟨num⟩` in this case.

Whether a feature is implemented as a character variant, as a stylistic set, and/or as an alternative is sometimes a bit arbitrary. For example, EB Garamond also offer Q's with long tails but does this through a stylistic set that also affects small capitals. Like XCharter it also knows about uppercase "ß", but its stylistic set affects the lowercase form too.[1]

Gruß ß Gruß ss
Query Qq Query Qq

```
\usepackage{fontspec} \setmainfont{EB Garamond}
\textsc{Gruß} ß   {\addfontfeature{StylisticSet=5}\textsc{Gruß} ß} \\
Query \textsc{Qq} {\addfontfeature{StylisticSet=6}Query \textsc{Qq}}
```
9-6-21

Our final example shows one of the Libertinus families, which all offer the same stylistic sets. The different sets alter only a few characters each, so if you like the lowered dieresis (which was customary in German typography) and you prefer the old form "SS" for an uppercase "ß", you could select ss01 and ss04. In this font `salt` (or `Style=Alternate`) is implemented to select all stylistic sets (except for ss04, which is unfortunately the wrong way around because for German orthography lowercase ß should not be replaced by SS) but does in fact also contain a few other variants (such as for h and y) not included in the stylistic sets.

Ä Ü Ö   Ä Ü Ö
J K R   J K R
Gruß Gruß GRUß
Gruss Gruss GRUSS
Gruß Gruß GRUSS
W   W   &   &
JKQRW hy ß &
JKQRW hy ss &
JKQRW hy ß &

```
\usepackage{fontspec} \setmainfont{Libertinus Serif}
Ä Ü Ö    \quad   {\addfontfeature{StylisticSet=1}Ä Ü Ö}           \\
J K R    \quad   {\addfontfeature{StylisticSet=2}J K R}           \\
Gruß \textsc{Gruß} GRU\SS                                          \\
   {\addfontfeature{StylisticSet=3}Gruß \textsc{Gruß} GRU\SS}     \\
   {\addfontfeature{StylisticSet=4}Gruß \textsc{Gruß} GRU\SS}     \\
W        \quad   {\addfontfeature{StylisticSet=5}W}        \qquad
\&       \quad   {\addfontfeature{StylisticSet=6}\&}              \\
JKQRW hy ß \& \\ {\addfontfeature{Style=Alternate}JKQRW hy ß \&} \\
   {\addfontfeature{StylisticSet={1,2,4,5,6}}JKQRW hy ß \&}
```
9-6-22

---

[1] Which is rather strange for German eyes!

Value	feature	Value	feature	Value	feature
Alternate	salt	Swash	swsh	HorizonalKana	hkna
Cursive	curs	Titling	titl	VerticalKana	vkna
Historic	hist	Uppercase	case	Ruby	ruby
Italic	ital			ResetAll	—

Individual features can by turned off by appending Off *to the name.*

Table 9.15: Values accepted by the Style key

Style features In contrast to the stylistic sets discussed in the prevision section, the Style features are intended for changes that conceptually change the style of the whole script (even though technically it may affect only some glyphs). It accepts nine different values, five of which (in the second column of Table 9.15) are predominately relevant for Asian or Arabic scripts, e.g., adjustments if Kana characters are written horizontally or vertically. Cursive changes the positions of diacritics in cursive scripts like Arabic, and Italic uses italic glyphs for Latin characters if available as part of Asian fonts. Finally, Ruby provides so called ruby characters, which are smaller Kana glyphs, generally in superscripted form, used to clarify the meaning of Kanji characters that may be unfamiliar to the reader.[1]

The values from the first column are of considerably more interest. We have already discussed Alternate (salt), though as mentioned before, with that feature you have to check if the alternate glyphs really form a coherent set before you activate it.

Letterforms in scripts change over time, and what was once common may now appear anachronistic. If implemented, Historic (hist) brings back the historic forms. *Providing historical letterforms* For example, EB Garamond replaces the lowercase s with a long-s form. The trouble with this approach is that it is often unconditionally done, and that is historically wrong. With LaTeX this means we have to load the font twice, with and without the feature applied and explicitly access the "short s" through a command.[2]

Thiſ paſſeſ ſucceſſfully!
— (wrong)
This paſſes ſuccefsfully!
9-6-23
— (correct)

```
\usepackage{fontspec} \setmainfont{EB Garamond}[Style=Historic]
\newfontfamily\normalEBG{EB Garamond}  \newcommand\s{{\normalEBG s}}
This passes successfully!      \\ --- (wrong) \\
Thi\s\ passe\s\ succes\s fully! \\ --- (correct)
```

The value Swash changes some letter shapes so that they show some typographi- *Enabling Swash* cal flourish, such as some extra or lengthened stroke, exaggerated serifs, etc. LaTeX *letters*

---

[1]None of the free font families we discuss in this book supports any of these features. Across all fonts available from CTAN, only two support Ruby, and none supports the other features.

[2]EB Garamond changes other characters as well, but with fonts that only change s to long-s, a probably better approach would be to not activate Historic feature and instead enter the correct Unicode character directly in the source.

offers the commands \swshape and \textsw to access them as a shape, but with fontspec in Unicode engines you have to explicitly set this up. Examples for how to do this are given in Example 9-6-7 on page 713.

Adjustment for text with only capital letters

Punctuation marks, dashes, parentheses, and so forth are usually designed for mixed case text and do not work that well if text is set completely in capital letters. For the use case fontspec supports Uppercase (case), which makes tiny adjustments if supported by the font as shown in the next example:

```
\usepackage{fontspec}
```

«INRIA-FAMILY (NORMAL)»
«INRIA-FAMILY (CASE)»

```
\fontspec{Inria Serif}                  «INRIA-FAMILY (NORMAL)» \\
\addfontfeature{Style=Uppercase} «INRIA-FAMILY (CASE)»
```

9-6-24

Finally, there may be special support for typesetting headings/titles through the value Titling (titl). This feature replaces some glyphs with corresponding forms designed specifically for titling.

Scripts and languages   As OpenType fonts can contain many glyphs, they often support several scripts and languages. "Script" in this context refers to the alphabet used, e.g., German, French, English, etc., all use the Latin script, while Arabic and Persian languages use the Arabic script. It is also possible that a single language can be typeset using different scripts. OpenType knows about more than hundred scripts and several hundred languages, and with the keys Script and Language you can ask for special support from the font if available.

The important point here is that based on the language/script combination the font may offer additional font features or activate or deactivate some by default. Details are given in the fontspec documentation [118], and if you intend to typeset in scripts other than Latin, you should study its section on that topic. In most other cases using the default language and script (i.e., not providing values) is sufficient.

Features not discussed in detail   As mentioned, there are many more font features than we can reasonably describe in the available space. So here is a brief summary of seldom needed features that are also supported by fontspec if necessary.

The Contextuals key normally covers glyph substitutions that need to vary based on their relative position in words, e.g., initial, medial, and final forms in Greek. In some fonts it is also used for other type of "contexts". Here are two random examples: in Playfair Display one can get arrows through some sort of ASCII input, and in Libertinus the Q changes its tail if followed by u or v, but not otherwise. Such Alternate contextuals are turned on by default, so in the example we turn them off, to show the differences:

```
\usepackage{fontspec}
```

```
                                        \fontspec{Playfair Display}                  -> <- <-> \hfill
                                        \addfontfeature{Contextuals=AlternateOff} -> <- <-> \par
» « ↔               -> <- <->            \fontspec{Libertinus Serif}                  SPQR Qu Qv \hfill
SPQR Qu Qv        SPQR Qu Qv            \addfontfeature{Contextuals=AlternateOff} SPQR Qu Qv
```

9-6-25

The Diacritics key defines how diacritics and base characters should be combined. This is usually automatically handled by the font based on the current script or language. With the LocalForms key (feature locl) it is possible to enable or disable language-specific glyph substitutions. If implemented by the font, it is automatically activated. There are also a number of features largely related to Chinese, Japanese, and Korean (CJK) typesetting. These are supported through the keys Annotation, CharacterWidth, CJKShape, and Vertical.

Specialized keys

With LuaTeX it is possible to use the Renderer key to direct the engine to support certain font rendering technologies, e.g., the HarfBuzz text shaping library. This is under active development; consult the fontspec documentation [118] for details.

Different ways of specifying font features

The examples in the previous sections have shown a number of ways to enable or disable font features. As a summary, you can alter the features of the current font by using \addfontfeature, as done in several examples.

At declaration time you can specify features that apply to all font faces being set up by specifying them at the top level of the optional *feature-list* argument of \setmainfont, \setsansfont, etc. This was, for example, done in Example 9-6-15 on page 720 or 9-6-19 on page 723.

But it is also possible to apply certain features only to specific shapes, e.g., upright, italics, slanted, or swash. This can be done with the help of the keys UprightFeatures, ItalicFeatures, SlantedFeatures, and SwashFeatures and the corresponding bold fonts, i.e., BoldFeatures, BoldItalicFeatures, BoldSlantedFeatures, and BoldSwashFeatures. Features for small capitals are set up with SmallCapsFeatures. This is orthogonal to the other keys because any of the shapes can (in principle) be in upper/lower case or in small caps; thus, there is only this one key. This method was already applied in Example 9-6-11 on page 718.

Yet another way is to specify them as part of a FontFace key in which case they apply only to that particular font face as exhibited in Example 9-6-7 on page 713.

The rationale behind the different approaches is to make common tasks simple while offering flexibility when dealing with complex fonts or those that have unusual setups. The fontspec manual [118] covers many more examples of how to specify font features in different circumstances.

Specifying AAT or Graphite font features

When using X∃TEX, there are additional font technologies available that offer their own set of feature values. These can also be managed with the fontspec package, but as this is mainly useful with commercial fonts or system fonts on the Macintosh, we do not cover them here. Refer to [118] if you want to use such fonts with X∃TEX.

9.6.6 General configuration options

Preventing fontspec from altering the math setup

By default fontspec automatically attempts to adjust the math fonts to fit to your text font selection, which may not be appropriate if you have loaded a math font support package, such as those discussed in Chapter 12. If you want to prevent any math setup alterations, use the no-math package option.

Config files   On page 710 we already discussed how to configure default setups for individual font families. On top of that you can provide your own fontspec.cfg file. If such a file is found by fontspec, it is loaded, unless you specify the package option no-config. The distribution already contains such a file setting two important defaults: turning on TeX ligatures and altering the typewriter family to have fixed spaces and no hyphenation:

```
\defaultfontfeatures[\rmfamily,\sffamily]{Ligatures=TeX}
\defaultfontfeatures[\ttfamily]
    {WordSpace={1,0,0},HyphenChar=None,PunctuationSpace=WordSpace}
```

If you intend to provide your own config file, you should probably copy these two declarations into it.

Silence warnings   The fontspec package may write some warnings in certain situations. If you prefer not to get those on the terminal, but only in the .log file, use the package option quiet. If they should not appear anywhere, use silent instead.

9.6.7 unicodefonttable — Displaying font tables for larger fonts

The nfssfont.tex file described in Section 9.5.9 does not help you if you are interested in looking for fonts to use with fontspec in Unicode engines, because it can only produce font tables displaying the first 256 glyphs of such a font and Opentype or TrueType fonts often contain several thousand glyphs.

To tabulate such fonts use the unicodefonttable package developed by the author. It offers you a flexible command to generate glyph tables for any font that can be used with Unicode TeX engines, either listing the full glyph set or any portion thereof.

```
\displayfonttable*[key/value list]{font-name}[font-features]
```

The mandatory *font-name* should be given in a form understood by fontspec, and the optional *font-features* is a key/value list in the form you would use it in \addfontfeature or in the optional argument of \setmainfont. Together they describe the font to be tabled. The optional *key/value list* offers you the possibility to customize the glyph table for which we give a few examples below, but for the full flexibility we refer you to the package documentation.

The starred form of the command is intended for displaying 8-bit fonts and alters some default settings to produce reasonable table layouts in that case. For example, it makes little sense to display Unicode block titles, if the only blocks shown are the first and possibly the second (*Basic Latin* and *Latin-1 Supplement*) or if the 8-bit font contains other glyphs unrelated to the Unicode blocks. Thus, by default they are not shown, and the table becomes more compact.

The next example show the Computer Modern Math symbol font (cmsy10). Besides using the starred form, we supply the key noheader, which omits a table caption, and restrict the processing range with range-end. The latter does not change the output, but it makes processing a bit faster, because cmsy is a 7-bit font, so it is pointless to check the higher bits for existing glyphs.

```
\usepackage{unicodefonttable}
\displayfonttable*[noheader,range-end=7F]{cmsy10}
```

	0	1	2	3	4	5	6	7	8	9	A	B	C	D	E	F
U+0000–000F	−	·	×	*	÷	◇	±	∓	⊕	⊖	⊗	⊘	⊙	◯	∘	•
U+0010–001F	≍	≡	⊆	⊇	≤	≥	≼	≽	∼	≈	⊂	⊃	≪	≫	≺	≻
U+0020–002F	←	→	↑	↓	↔	↗	↘	≃	⇐	⇒	⇑	⇓	⇔	↖	↙	∝
U+0030–003F	′	∞	∈	∋	△	▽	/	‚	∀	∃	¬	∅	ℜ	ℑ	⊤	⊥
U+0040–004F	ℵ	𝒜	ℬ	𝒞	𝒟	ℰ	ℱ	𝒢	ℋ	ℐ	𝒥	𝒦	ℒ	ℳ	𝒩	𝒪
U+0050–005F	𝒫	𝒬	ℛ	𝒮	𝒯	𝒰	𝒱	𝒲	𝒳	𝒴	𝒵	∪	∩	⊎	∧	∨
U+0060–006F	⊢	⊣	⌊	⌋	⌈	⌉	{	}	⟨	⟩			‖	↕	⇕	\	≀
U+0070–007F	√	∐	∇	∫	⊔	⊓	⊑	⊒	§	†	‡	¶	♣	♢	♡	♠

9-6-26

You may be interested in only a certain part of a font, for example, in the letter-like Unicode block, which starts at 2100 and ends at 213F. In that case you can use range-start and range-end to denote the area of interest. We suppress the overall header again, because we now get Unicode Block titles (or rather one such title because of our range). We also change the placement of the hex digits to appear below each block title using hex-digits (supported values are block, foot, head (default), head+foot, and none) and shortening the hex-digits-row-format on the left:

```
\usepackage{unicodefonttable}
\displayfonttable[range-start=2100,range-end=213F,noheader,
                  hex-digits=block,hex-digits-row-format=U+#1]{TeX Gyre Pagella}
```

Letterlike Symbols

	0	1	2	3	4	5	6	7	8	9	A	B	C	D	E	F
U+210	-	-	-	℃	-	-	-	ℇ	-	℉	-	-	-	-	-	ℏ
U+211	-	-	-	ℓ	-	-	№	℗	℘	-	-	-	-	-	ℛ	-
U+212	℠	-	™	-	-	-	Ω	℧	-	-	K	Å	-	-	ℯ	-
U+213	-	-	-	-	-	ℵ	ℶ	ℷ	ℸ	-	-	-	-	-	-	-

9-6-27

Total number of glyphs shown from TeX Gyre Pagella: 20

As you can see, there are some statistics shown at the bottom. With the key nostatistics you can omit them; alternatively, statistics-format lets you set up your own text. This key allows you to use #1 to get the current font name and #2 to display the glyph count; e.g.,

```
...,statistics-format=This block contains #2 glyphs in #1,...
```

would display "This block contains 20 glyphs in TeX Gyre Pagella" in the previous example. Similar keys exist for the header (title-format) and the continuation header (`title-format-cont`); within their values you can use #1 for the font name and #2 for the font features, if given. You can test for that with `\IfValueTF` and act accordingly. Note that these table headers are best set with a `\caption` command in order to come out right.

If you do not like to see Unicode block titles displayed, you can adjust this with the key `display-block`. It accepts the values `titles` (default), `rules`, or `none`. The last two save valuable space at the cost of less readability in large fonts.

Fill the table with two fonts
It is sometimes useful to compare two fonts with each other by filling the table with glyphs from a secondary font if the primary font is missing them. For example, the next display shows two rows of Latin Modern Math (black glyphs), and instead of showing a missing glyph symbol in most slots, we rope in glyphs from New Computer Modern Math, which has a much larger glyph set. By default these substituted glyphs are set in red (`compare-color`) on gray background (`compare-bg-color`). We changed it in the example to use the blue available in the book and turned off the general coloring for hex digits and range info (`color`), which is normally done in blue. We also drastically shortened the row title (`hex-digits-row-format`) to save space:

```
\usepackage{unicodefonttable}  \fonttablesetup{noheader,nostatistics}
\displayfonttable[display-block=none,color=none,hex-digits-row-format=#1,
          compare-with=NewCMMath-Regular.otf,compare-color=blue,
          range-start=2A00,range-end=2A1F]{latinmodern-math.otf}
```

9-6-28

```
\fonttablesetup{key/value list}
```

Instead of or in addition to setting *key/values* on each table, it is also possible to alter the defaults, by specifying a *key/value list* in `\fonttablesetup`; for example, the starred form does this internally by setting `nostatistics`, `display-block=none`, `hex-digits=head`, `range-end==FF`. This can be overwritten on the table level; e.g., `statistics` would give you a statistics line even in an 8-bit font table.

There also exists a standalone `unicodefont.tex` file that, when processed with a Unicode engine, interactively asks you a few questions, calls `\displayfonttable` to generate a single font table, and then exits.

9.7 The low-level NFSS interface

While the high-level font commands are intended for use in a document, the low-level commands are mainly for defining new commands in packages or in the preamble of a document; see also Section 9.7.5. To make the best use of such font commands, it is helpful to understand the internal organization of fonts in LaTeX's font selection scheme (NFSS).

One goal of LaTeX's font selection scheme is to allow rational font selection, with algorithms guided by the principles of generic markup. For this purpose, it would be desirable to allow independent changes for as many font attributes as possible. On the other hand, font families in real life normally contain only a subset of the myriad imaginable font attribute combinations. Therefore, allowing independent changes in too many attributes results in too many combinations for which no real (external) font is available and a default has to be substituted.

LaTeX internally keeps track of five independent font attributes: the "current encoding", the "current family", the "current series", the "current shape", and the "current size". The encoding attribute was introduced in NFSS release 2 after it became clear that real support of multiple languages would be possible only by maintaining the character-encoding scheme independently of the other font attributes.

The values of these attributes determine the font currently in use. LaTeX also maintains a large set of tables used to associate attribute combinations with external fonts (i.e., .tfm files that contain the information necessary for TeX to do its job). Font selection inside LaTeX is then done in two steps:

1. A number of font attributes are changed using the low-level commands \fontencoding, \fontfamily, \fontseries, \fontshape, \fontsize, or \fontseriesforce and \fontshapeforce.

2. The font corresponding to this new attribute setting is selected by calling the \selectfont command.

The second step comprises several actions. LaTeX first checks whether the font corresponding to the desired attribute settings is known to the system (i.e., the .tfm file is already loaded), and if so, this font is selected. If not, the internal tables are searched to find the external font name associated with this setting. If such a font name can be found, the corresponding .tfm file is read into memory, and afterwards the font is selected for typesetting. If this process is not successful, LaTeX tries to find an alternative font, as explained in Section 9.7.3.

9.7.1 Setting individual font attributes

Every font attribute has one command to change its current value. All of these commands accept more or less any character string as an argument, but only a few values make sense. These values are not hardwired into LaTeX's font selection scheme, but rather are conventions set up in the internal tables.

We have already used some of them in the previous sections; this section now covers all of the naming conventions used in the standard setup of LaTeX. Obviously, anybody setting up new fonts for use with LaTeX should try to obey these conventions whenever possible, because only a consistent naming convention can guarantee that appropriate fonts are selected in a generically marked-up document.

If you want to select a specific font using this interface — say, Computer Modern Dunhill bold condensed italic 14 pt — a knowledge of the interface conventions alone is not enough, because for many of the combinations of the attributes there is no

Weight Classes		Width Classes		
Ultra Light	ul	Ultra Condensed	≈50%	uc
Extra Light	el	Extra Condensed	≈62.5%	ec
Light	l	Condensed	≈75%	c
Semi Light	sl	Semi Condensed	≈87.5%	sc
Medium (normal)	m	Medium	≈100%	m
Semi Bold	sb	Semi Expanded	≈112.5%	sx
Bold	b	Expanded	≈125%	x
Extra Bold	eb	Extra Expanded	≈150%	ex
Ultra Bold	ub	Ultra Expanded	≈200%	ux

To describe a series combine ⟨weight⟩⟨width⟩ and drop any m *unless this makes the specification empty.*

Table 9.16: Weight and width classification of fonts

matching external font. You could try your luck by specifying something like the following set of commands:

```
\fontencoding{T1}\fontfamily{cmdh}\fontseries{bc}\fontshape{it}%
\fontsize{14}{16pt}\selectfont
```

This code would be correct according to the naming conventions, as we see in the following sections. Because this attribute combination does not correspond to a real font, however, LaTeX would have to substitute a different font. This substitution mechanism may choose a font that is quite different from the one desired, so you should consult the font tables (in this and the following chapter) to see whether the desired combination is available. Section 9.7.3 provides more details on the substitution process.

Choosing the font family

The font family is selected with the command \fontfamily. Its argument is a character string that refers to a font family declared in the internal tables. The character string was defined when these tables were set up and is often a short letter sequence — for example, cmr for the Computer Modern Roman family. With newer fonts it is often rather lengthy and structured, e.g., FiraSans-OsF. See Section 10.1.3 on page →II 7 for the more modern naming conventions.

> **Unicode engines**
>
> When using Unicode engines, the \fontfamily command is normally of little value because fonts loaded with the fontspec package get some internal family name assigned, and it is therefore not easy to guess what family name to pass as an argument.
>
> There is, however, a way to explicitly specify a font family name that can be used with \fontfamily; see Section 9.6 on page 705 for details.

Choosing the font series

The series attribute is changed with the \fontseries command. The series combines a weight and a width in its argument; and in the original font selection implementation it was not possible to alter only weight but not width, and vice versa. With the 2020 release of LaTeX this has changed, and \fontseries can now be used to change only one of the subattributes. To force a specific weight and width combination you can use \fontseriesforce.

In the original font selection implementation a request to change the series always canceled the current one. This was reasonable because there were nearly no fonts available that offered anything other than a medium or a bold series. This has changed, and now there are families such as Noto Sans that offer 32 distinct series values. With the 2020 release of LaTeX, the series management therefore changed to allow for independently setting the weight and the width attribute of the series.

Font selection enhancements in 2020

In the naming conventions for the argument for the \fontseries command, the names for both the weight and the width are abbreviated so that each combination is unique. The conventions are shown in Table 9.16 on the preceding page.

These classifications can be combined as ⟨*weight*⟩⟨*width*⟩ in the argument to \fontseries; e.g., lc would ask for a "light weight condensed width" series. If only a value for weight or only for width is given (e.g., b or ec), it means that the other aspect should be left unchanged. Thus, if the current series is lc and we are asking for b, then this would result in bc. If you want to ensure that you always get bold medium width unconditionally, you would have to use bm instead.[1]

There is a special convention for medium (m) as that can denote either a weight or a width. Both a single m or double mm is interpreted as medium weight and width, and m? stands for medium weight and width unchanged and ?m the other way around.

Handling weight and width requests independently from each other is done by the \fontseries command through a lookup table that maps the *current* and the *requested* series to a resulting *new* series value, e.g.,

$$b + c \rightarrow bc \quad \text{or} \quad ub + x \rightarrow ubx \quad \text{or} \quad bx + l \rightarrow lx \quad \text{etc.}$$

This table is prefilled with reasonable mappings, but if necessary, it is possible to alter individual entries using \DeclareFontSeriesChangeRule declarations.

\DeclareFontSeriesChangeRule{*current*}{*request*}{*new*}{*alternative*}

This command specifies that when typesetting in *current* series and there is a *request* for a series change, then typesetting should continue with *new* series. If that series

---

[1]For historical reasons the naming conventions for the series attribute when declaring fonts in font definition files is slightly different: there any instance of m (standing for medium in weight or width) is dropped, except when both weight and width are medium. The latter case is abbreviated with a single m.

For example, bold expanded would be bx, whereas medium expanded would be x, and bold medium would be b. This inconsistency is somewhat unfortunate, but given that there exist several hundred font families with .fd files, one has to live with it.

Abbreviation	Description
n	normal shape (upright and upper/lowercase letters)
it	*italic shape*
sl	*slanted or oblique shape*
sw	*Swash Letter Shape (seldom available)*
ui	upright italic shape (more a curiosity)
sc	Small Caps shape
scit	*Italic Small Caps shape*
scsl	*Slanted Small Caps shape*
scsw	Swash Letter Small Caps shape
up[a]	(Return to) upright shape
ulc	(Return To) Upper/Lower Case shape

[a]*Changes* scit *to* sc, *etc., but acts like* ulc *if current shape is* sc, *i.e., changes that to* n.

Table 9.17: Shape classification of fonts

does not exist, the *alternative* series is tried instead. If that does not exist either, *request* is used unchanged. Of course, that series may not exist either, in which case standard font shape substitution kicks in; see Section 9.7.3 for details of what happens in that situation.

For combinations of *current* and *request*, for which no table entry exists, the *request* is used unconditionally as the new series.

Because m can stand for both medium weight and width in the naming convention, it cannot be used in the *request* to reset only weight or width to medium, e.g., when you want to get back from bc (bold condensed) to just c (condensed). For that case two special series names are provided: ?m (keep weight, reset width) and m? (reset weight, keep width). Thus, we can get from bold condensed to medium width condensed using \fontseries{m?}. If you use m in the *request*, it is interpreted as mm, i.e., resets both weight and width to medium.

Choosing the font shape

The \fontshape command is used to change the shape attribute. For the standard shapes, one- to four-letter abbreviations are used; these are shown in Table 9.17 together with an example of the resulting shape in the Latin Modern Roman family except sw in EB Garamond and scsw in Cinzel.

Font selection enhancements in LaTeX 2020   In the original font selection implementation, a request for a new shape always canceled the current one. With the 2020 release of LaTeX, this has changed, and \fontshape can now be used to combine small capitals with italics, slanted, or swash letters, either by explicitly asking for scit, etc., or by asking for it when typesetting already in sc and so forth. With \fontshapeforce, you can force a specific selection as long as it actually exists as a font shape.

Again, this is supported by a table lookup, and just like with the series management, this table can be adjusted if necessary.

\DeclareFontShapeChangeRule{*current*}{*request*}{*new*}{*alternative*}

This declaration works like \DeclareFontSeriesChangeRule except that we look at *current* shape and *request*ed shape. Another difference is that the table much more often specifies an *alternative* shape in addition to the desired *new* shape. For example, two such entries are

```
\DeclareFontShapeChangeRule {n} {sl}{sl}  {it}
\DeclareFontShapeChangeRule {it}{sc}{scit}{scsl}
```

The first line says that if LaTeX is typesetting in the "normal" shape and there is a request for a slanted shape, then it should try sl, and if that is not available, should try the it shape.[1]

The second line says that it and sc should be combined to scit. But if that is not available, then scsl should be used. If that does not exist either, then the *request* shape, i.e., sc, is used, so that with Computer Modern or other fonts that have only upright small capitals we still see the old behavior of sc canceling it, or vice versa.[2]

Both up and ulc are "virtual" shapes. This means that they do not physically exist as font faces, but only as arguments to \fontshape to alter the current state; e.g., if the current shape is scit, then up changes that to sc, while ulc would change it to it. However, for compatibility reasons up acts a bit oddly; that is, if the current shape is sc, then it resets that as well. The reason is that in the past \upshape was always setting the shape back to n and some people have written \scshape...\upshape instead of just writing \textsc{...}, so this usage is still supported.

Compatibility behavior of up

This is all defined through \DeclareFontShapeChangeRule declarations and thus changeable, but there should seldom be a need for alterations. However, if you do not want or need this compatibility behavior of up, you could, for example, declare

```
\DeclareFontShapeChangeRule{sc}{up}{sc}{}
```

after which sc would no longer be canceled by up.

Choosing the font size

The font size is changed with the \fontsize{*size*}{*skip*} command. This is the only font attribute command that takes two arguments: the *size* to switch to and the baseline *skip* (the distance from baseline to baseline for this size). Font sizes are normally measured in points, so by convention the unit can be omitted. The same

---

[1] Because of such declarations, fonts like Iwona (page →II 78) or Kurier (page →II 80) work without errors even though they have no slanted shape and have no substitution defined in their .fd files.

[2] The only difference to earlier years is that now there will be a .log entry stating that scit was tried but was found not to be available.

is true for the second argument. However, if the baseline skip should be a rubber length — that is, if it contains `plus` or `minus` — you have to specify a unit. Thus, a valid size change could be requested by

```
\fontsize{14.4}{17}\selectfont
```

Even if such a request is valid in principle, no corresponding external font may exist in this size. In this case, LaTeX tries to find a nearby size if its internal tables allow for size correction or reports an error otherwise.

If you use fonts existing in arbitrary sizes (which is now possible for nearly all fonts), you can, of course, select any size you want. For example,

```
\fontsize{1in}{1.2in}\selectfont Happy Birthday
```

produces a birthday poster line with letters in a one-inch size. However, there is one problem with using arbitrary sizes: if LaTeX has to typeset a formula in this size (which might happen behind the scenes without your knowledge), it needs to set up all fonts used in formulas for the new size. For an arbitrary size, it usually has to calculate the font sizes for use in subscripts and sub-subscripts (at least 12 different fonts). In turn, it probably has to load a lot of new fonts — something you can tell by looking at the transcript file. For this reason you may finally hit some internal limit if you have too many different size requests in your document. If this happens, you should tell LaTeX which sizes to load for formulas using the `\DeclareMathSizes` declaration, rather than letting it use its own algorithm. See Section 9.8.5 for more information on this issue.

Choosing the encoding

A change of encoding is performed with the command `\fontencoding`, where the argument is the internal name for the desired encoding. This name must be known to LaTeX, either as one of the predefined encodings (loaded by the kernel), loaded through the `fontenc` package or manually declared with the `\DeclareFontEncoding` command (see Section 9.8.3). A set of standard encoding names is given in Table 9.18 on the next page; you find a more complete set in [94].

LaTeX's font selection scheme is based on the (idealistic) assumption that most (or, even better, all) fonts for text are available in the same encoding as long as they are used to typeset in the same language. In other words, encoding changes should become necessary only if one uses pdfTeX and is switching from one language to another. In that case it is normally the task of the language support packages (e.g., those from the babel system) to arrange matters behind the scenes.

If necessary, switching to, say, Greek or Cyrillic for individual words or short phrases can even be done on the fly by specifying LGR (Greek) or T2A (Cyrillic), and this is precisely what we have done in the examples in Sections 10.11 and 10.12. There the Greek sample text was generated with

```
\usepackage[LGR,T1]{fontenc}
{\fontencoding{LGR}\selectfont Σὰ βγεῖς στὸν πη\-γαιμὸ γιὰ
  τὴν \textbf{Ἰθάκη}, νὰ εὔχεσαι νἆναι \textit{μακρὺς} ὁ
  δρόμος, γεμᾶτος περιπέτειες, γεμᾶτος \textsc{γνώσεις}}
```

Encoding	Description	Declared by
TU	LaTeX text encoding for Unicode engines X⅃TEX and LuaTEX	LaTeX
T1	LaTeX text encoding (Latin) a.k.a. "Cork" encoding	LaTeX
TS1	LaTeX symbol encoding (Latin)	LaTeX
T2A,B,C	LaTeX text encodings (Cyrillic)	Cyrillic support packages
T3	LaTeX phonetic alphabet encoding	tipa package
TS3	LaTeX phonetic alphabet encoding (extra symbols)	tipa package
T5	LaTeX text encoding (Vietnamese)	—
OT1	(old) TEX text as defined by Donald Knuth	LaTeX
OT2	(old) TEX text for Cyrillic languages (obsolete)	Cyrillic support packages
OT4	(old) TEX text with extensions for the Polish language	—
OML	(old) TEX math text (italic) as defined by Donald Knuth	LaTeX
OMS	TEX math symbol as defined by Donald Knuth	LaTeX
OMX	TEX math extended symbol as defined by Donald Knuth	LaTeX
X2	Extended text encoding (Cyrillic)	Cyrillic support packages
U	Unknown encoding (for fonts containing arbitrary symbols)	LaTeX
L..	Local encoding (for private encodings)	—
LGR	Commonly used Greek encoding	Greek support packages
LY1	Alternative to T1 encoding	Y&Y

Table 9.18: Standard font encodings used with LaTeX

Of course, for proper language support, additional work would be necessary, such as changing the hyphenation rules (we got by, by specifying one explicit hyphen point).

With older Type 1 fonts, the T1 encoding is unfortunately not fully implementable. The following five characters are likely to show up as blobs of ink (indicating a missing glyph in the font) or substitutions (in case of the per thousand and per ten thousand symbols). As you can see, qpl (the Palatino clone by TEX Gyre) and most of the fonts discussed in Chapter 10 do not have these problems.

Potential T1 encoding problems

Computer Modern:
ȷ ŋ Ð ‰ ‱
Times (old PostScript):
▮ ■ ‰ ‱
Palatino (old PostScript):
▮ ■ ‰ ‱
Palatino (new TEX Gyre):
ȷ ŋ Ŋ ‰ ‱

```
\usepackage[T1]{fontenc}
\fontfamily{cmr}\selectfont Computer Modern:\\
\j{} \ng{} \NG{} \textperthousand{} \textpertenthousand \par
\fontfamily{ptm}\selectfont Times (old PostScript):\\
\j{} \ng{} \NG{} \textperthousand{} \textpertenthousand \par
\fontfamily{ppl}\selectfont Palatino (old PostScript):\\
\j{} \ng{} \NG{} \textperthousand{} \textpertenthousand \par
\fontfamily{qpl}\selectfont Palatino (new \TeX\ Gyre):\\
\j{} \ng{} \NG{} \textperthousand{} \textpertenthousand
```

9-7-1

As explained in Section 9.5.6, the situation for TS1 is even worse — sometimes half the glyphs from that encoding are not available in a legacy PostScript font, which is another reason to avoid the old PSNFSS packages listed in Table 9.8 on page 691, despite their nice, memorable names.

9.7.2 Setting several font attributes

When designing page styles (see Section 5.4) or layout-oriented commands, you often want to select a particular font — that is, you need to specify values for all attributes. For this task LaTeX provides the command \usefont, which takes four arguments: the encoding, family, series, and shape. The command updates those attributes and then calls \selectfont. If you also want to specify the size and baseline skip, place a \fontsize command in front of it. For example,

```
\fontsize{14}{16pt}\usefont{OT1}{cmdh}{bc}{it}
```

would produce the same result as the hypothetical example on page 732.

Besides \usefont, LaTeX provides the \DeclareFixedFont declaration, which can be used to define new commands that switch to a completely fixed font. Such commands are extremely fast because they do not have to look up any internal tables. They are therefore very useful in command definitions that have to switch back and forth between fixed fonts. For example, for the doc package (see Chapter 17), one could produce code-line numbers using the following definitions:

```
\DeclareFixedFont\CodelineFont{\encodingdefault}{\familydefault}
                          {\seriesdefault}{\shapedefault}{7pt}
\newcommand\theCodelineNo{\CodelineFont\arabic{CodelineNo}}
```

As you can see from the example, \DeclareFixedFont has six arguments: the name of the command to be defined, followed by the five font attributes in the NFSS classification. Instead of supplying fixed values (except for the size), the built-in hooks that describe the main document font are used (see also Section 9.3.6). Thus, in the example above \CodelineFont still depends on the overall layout for the document (via the settings of \encodingdefault and other parameters). However, once the definition is carried out, its meaning is frozen, so later changes to the defaults have no effect.

9.7.3 Automatic substitution of fonts

Whenever a font change request cannot be carried out because the combination is not known to LaTeX, it tries to recover by using a font with similar attributes. Here is what happens: if the combination of encoding scheme, family, series, and shape is not declared (see Section 9.8.1), LaTeX tries to find a known combination by first changing the shape attribute to a default. If the resulting combination is still unknown, it tries changing the series to a default. As a last resort, it changes the family to a default value. Finally, the internal table entry is looked up to find the requested size. For example, if you ask for `\ttfamily\bfseries\itshape` — a typewriter font in a bold series and italic shape (which usually does not exist) — then you get a typewriter font in medium series and upright shape, because LaTeX first resets the shape before changing the series. If, in such a situation, you prefer a typewriter font in medium series with italic shape, you have to announce your intention to LaTeX using the sub function, which is explained on page 743.

The substitution process never changes the encoding scheme, because any alteration could produce wrong characters in the output. Recall that the encoding scheme defines how to interpret the input characters, while the other attributes define how the output should look. It would be catastrophic if, say, a £ sign were changed into a $ sign on an invoice just because the software tried to be clever.

Thus, every encoding scheme must have a default family, series, and shape, and at least the combination consisting of the encoding scheme together with the corresponding defaults must have a definition inside LaTeX, as explained in Section 9.8.3.

9.7.4 Substituting the font family if unavailable in an encoding

Given that pdfTeX can only handle fonts with up to 256 glyphs, a single font encoding can support only a few languages. The T1 encoding, for example, does support many of the Latin-based scripts, but if you want to write in Greek or Russian, you need to switch encodings to LGR or T2A. Given that not every font family offers glyphs in such encodings, you may end up with some default family (e.g., Computer Modern) that does not blend in well. For example, when typesetting in a sans serif font such as Montserrat, the Greek characters look rather out of place.

The root of TeX is τεχνικ́η.	`\usepackage[greek,english]{babel}`
	`\fontfamily{Montserrat-LF}\selectfont`
	`The root of \TeX\ is \foreignlanguage{greek}{τεχνικ́η}.`

9-7-2

For such cases NFSS offers `\DeclareFontFamilySubstitution`.

`\DeclareFontFamilySubstitution{`*encoding*`}{`*family*`}{`*substitute-family*`}`

This declaration tells NFSS that the request for the *encoding* while typesetting in a certain font *family* should be fulfilled by substituting this family with *substitute-family*. The declaration should be made in the document preamble before the font is actually used.

In the example below we use Plex Sans instead of the default to typeset the Greek word. It is not perfect but is clearly better than the default that we got in Example 9-7-2. Some of the other families exhibited in Section 10.11 on page →II 106 would have worked as well.

The root of TeX is τεχνικ́η.	`\usepackage[greek,english]{babel}`
	`\DeclareFontFamilySubstitution{LGR}{Montserrat-LF}{IBMPlexSans-TLF}`
	`\fontfamily{Montserrat-LF}\selectfont`
	`The root of \TeX\ is \foreignlanguage{greek}{τεχνικ́η}.`

9-7-3

If you use font support packages to set up your font families (e.g., montserrat in this case), it may need a bit of detective work to figure out the actual font family name that needs to go into the *family* argument, but with the help of all the tables in Chapter 10, it should be manageable.

9.7.5 Using low-level commands in the document

The low-level font commands described in the preceding sections are intended to be used in the definition of higher-level commands, either in class or package files or in the document preamble.

Whenever possible, you should avoid using the low-level commands directly in a document if you can use high-level font commands like `\textsf` instead. The reason is that the low-level commands are very precise instructions to switch to a particular font, whereas the high-level commands can be customized using packages or declarations in the preamble. Suppose, for example, that you have selected Computer Modern Sans in your document using `\fontfamily{cmss}\selectfont`. If you later decide to typeset the whole document with other fonts by applying some font support package, then this would change only those parts of the document that do not contain explicit `\fontfamily` commands.

9.8 Setting up new fonts for NFSS

Setting up new fonts for use with LaTeX basically means filling the internal font selection tables with information necessary for later associating a font request in a document with the external `.tfm` file containing character information used by LaTeX. Thus, the tables are responsible for associating

```
\fontencoding{T1}\fontfamily{lmtt}\fontseries{lc}\fontshape{sl}%
\fontsize{10}{12}\selectfont
```

i.e., Latin Modern Typewriter light condensed slanted 10 point in T1 (Cork) encoding, with the external file `ec-lmtlco10.tfm`. To add new fonts, you need to reverse this process. For every new external font you have to ask yourself five questions:

1. What is the font's encoding scheme — that is, which characters are in which positions?
2. What is its (desired) family name in LaTeX?
3. What is its series (the combination of weight and width)?
4. What is its shape?
5. Is it a scalable font, or if not, what is its size?

The answers to these questions provide the information necessary to classify the external font according to the LaTeX conventions, as described in Section 9.7.

However, users are not really expected to set up fonts by themselves. This is usually left to a few experts that, to date, have provided font support for several hundred font families — as Chapter 10 impressively proves where we show examples of more than one hundred high-quality free families.

We therefore give only a brief overview about the commands available to set up font support, to the extent helpful for troubleshooting strange behavior or for making small adjustments like providing a desired font substitution. If necessary, the gory details can be found in [71].

9.8.1 Declaring new font families and font shape groups

The declarations discussed in this section are normally used only inside .fd files (font definition files), which should normally not be changed. With some caution, it is however possible to use them in the document preamble (or in packages) to adjust some font family behavior. How this can be done is explained in Section 9.8.2 on page 746.

Each family/encoding combination must be made known to LaTeX through the command \DeclareFontFamily.

\DeclareFontFamily{*encoding*}{*family*}{*loading-code*}

The first two arguments are the *encoding* scheme and the *family* name. The third is usually empty, but it may contain special code for font loading and is explained on page 744. Thus, if you want to introduce a new family — say, Latin Modern Typewriter in T1 encoding scheme — you would write

```
\DeclareFontFamily{T1}{lmtt}{\hyphenchar\font=-1}
```

In this case the last argument contains code to suppress hyphenation; see page 744.

A font family normally consists of many individual fonts. Instead of announcing each family member individually to LaTeX, you have to combine fonts that differ only in size and declare them as a group. Such a group is entered into the internal tables of LaTeX with the command \DeclareFontShape.

\DeclareFontShape{*encoding*}{*family*}{*series*}{*shape*}
                 {*list of sizes and external font(s)*}{*loading-code*}

The first four are the *encoding* scheme, the *family* name, the *series* name, and the *shape* name under which you want to access these fonts later. The fifth argument is a *list of sizes and external font* names, given in a special format that we discuss below. The sixth argument is usually empty; its use is explained on page 744.

We first show a few examples and introduce terminology; then we will discuss all the features in detail.

As an example, an NFSS table entry for Computer Modern Dunhill medium (series) upright (shape) in the encoding scheme "TeX text" could be entered as

```
\DeclareFontShape{OT1}{cmdh}{m}{n}{ <10> cmdunh10 }{}
```

assuming that only one external font for the size 10pt is available. If you also have this font available at 12pt (scaled from 10pt), the declaration would be

```
\DeclareFontShape{OT1}{cmdh}{m}{n}{ <10> <12>cmdunh10 }{}
```

If the external font is available in all possible sizes, the declaration becomes very simple. This is the case for Type 1 PostScript (outline) fonts or when the driver program is able to generate fonts on demand by calling METAFONT.

For example, for our introductory example Latin Modern Typewriter light condensed (series) slanted (shape) in the LATEX T1 encoding scheme would be entered as

```
\DeclareFontShape{T1}{lmtt}{lc}{sl}{<-> ec-lmtlco10}{}
```

This example declares a size range with two open ends (no sizes specified to the left and the right of the -). As a result, the same external .tfm file (ec-lmtlco10) is used for all sizes and is scaled to the desired size. If you have more than one .tfm file for a font — as is the case for Latin Modern Typewriter medium upright — the declaration could be

```
\DeclareFontShape{T1}{lmtt}{m}{n}{<-8.5> ec-lmtt8
    <8.5-9.5> ec-lmtt9 <9.5-11> ec-lmtt10 <11-> ec-lmtt12}{}
```

In this case different external fonts are used for different size ranges.

The preceding examples show that the fifth argument of \DeclareFontShape consists of size specifications surrounded by angle brackets (i.e., <...>) intermixed with loading information for the individual sizes (e.g., font names). The part inside the angle brackets is called the "size info", and the part following the closing angle bracket is called the "font info". The font info is further structured into a "size function" (often empty) and its arguments; we discuss this case below. Within the arguments of \DeclareFontShape, blanks are ignored to help make the entries more readable.[1] In the unusual event that a real space has to be entered, you can use \space.

Size functions

If an * appears in the font info string, everything to the left of it forms the function name, and everything to the right is the argument. If there is no asterisk, as in all of the examples so far, the whole string is regarded as the argument, and the function name is "empty".

Based on the size requested by the user, size functions produce the specification necessary for LATEX to find the external font and load it at the desired size. They are also responsible for informing the user about anything special that happens. For example, some functions differ only in terms of whether they issue a warning. This

---

[1]This is true only if the command is used at the top level. If such a declaration is used inside other constructs (e.g., the argument of \AtBeginDocument), blanks might survive, and in that case entries are not recognized.

capability allows the system maintainer to set up LaTeX in the way best suited for the particular site.

The name of a size function consists of zero or more letters. Some of the size functions can take two arguments, one optional and one mandatory. Such an optional argument has to be enclosed in square brackets. For example, the specification

```
<-> s * [0.9] cmfib8
```

would select, for all possible sizes (we have the range 0 to ∞), the size function s with the optional argument 0.9 and the mandatory argument cmfib8. The s size function is a silent version "empty" one; i.e., it does not produce warnings and writes any information only to the .log file.

The size specifications in \DeclareFontShape are inspected in the order in which they are given. When a size info matches the requested user size, the corresponding size function is executed. If this process yields a valid font, no further entries are inspected. Otherwise, the search continues with the next entry.

The "empty" and "s" functions   There are thirteen size functions defined in LaTeX; so far we have seen the "empty" and the s size function, which both expect an external font as argument (possibly with an additional scaling factor). Below we cover the important ones that deal with font substitution. For details on the others refer to [71], which is part of the LaTeX distribution.

The "sub" and "ssub" functions   The sub function is used to substitute a different font shape group if no external font exists for the current font shape group. In this case the argument is not an external font name but rather a different family, series, and shape combination separated by slashes (the encoding does not change for the reasons explained earlier). For example, in Latin Modern Typewriter there is no italic shape, only a slanted shape. Thus, it makes sense to declare the slanted shape as a substitute for the italic one (which is what the LM support files already do):

```
\DeclareFontShape{T1}{lmtt}{m}{it}{ <-> sub * lmtt/m/sl }{}
```

Without this declaration, LaTeX's automatic substitution mechanism (see Section 9.7.3) would substitute the default shape, Latin Modern Typewriter upright. A case for which you might want to add your own substitution, after looking at the LM Table 9.6 on page 687, is

```
\DeclareFontShape{T1}{lmdh}{bx}{sl}{ <-> ssub * lmdh/m/sl }{}
```

because Latin Modern Dunhill has no bold or bold extended shapes at all. For this we used the ssub function that has the same functionality as the sub function but does not produces on-screen warnings (the first s means "silence").

Font-loading options

As already mentioned, you need to declare each family using `\DeclareFontFamily`. The third argument to this command, as well as the last argument of the command `\DeclareFontShape`, can be used to specify special operations that are carried out when a font is loaded. In this way, you can change parameters that are associated with a font as a whole. You can also use `\DeclareFontFamily` to alter this information but only for fonts that have not been already loaded in memory!

For every external font, LaTeX maintains, besides the information about each character, a set of global dimensions and other values associated with the font. For example, every font has its own "hyphen character", the character that is inserted automatically when LaTeX hyphenates a word. Another example is the normal width and the stretchability of a blank space between words (the "interword space"); again, a value is maintained for every font and changed whenever LaTeX switches to a new font. By changing these values when a font is loaded, special effects can be achieved.

Normally, changes apply to a whole family; for example, you may want to prohibit hyphenation for all words typeset in the typewriter family. In this case, the third argument of `\DeclareFontFamily` should be used as we did earlier. If the changes should apply only to a specific font shape group, you must use the sixth argument of `\DeclareFontShape`. In other words, when a font is loaded, NFSS first applies the argument of `\DeclareFontFamily` and then the sixth argument of `\DeclareFontShape` so that it can override the load options specified for the whole family if necessary.

Below we study the information that can be set in this way (unfortunately, not everything is changeable) and discuss some useful examples. This part of the interface addresses very low-level commands of TeX. Because it is so specialized, no effort was made to make the interface more LaTeX-like. As a consequence, the methods for assigning integers and dimensions to variables are somewhat unusual.

Changing the hyphenation character   With `\hyphenchar\font=`⟨*number*⟩, LaTeX specifies the character that is inserted as the hyphen when a word is hyphenated. The ⟨*number*⟩ represents the position of this character within the encoding scheme. The default is the value of `\defaulthyphenchar`, which is 45, representing the position of the "–" character in most encoding schemes. If this number is set to −1, hyphenation is suppressed. Thus, by declaring

```
\DeclareFontFamily{OT1}{cmtt}{\hyphenchar\font=-1}
```

you can suppress hyphenation for all fonts in the `cmtt` family with the encoding scheme OT1. Fonts with the T1 encoding have an alternate hyphen character in position 127 so that you can set, for example,

```
\DeclareFontFamily{T1}{cmr}{\hyphenchar\font=127}
```

This makes the hyphen character inserted by LaTeX different from the compound-word dash entered in words like "so-called". LaTeX does not hyphenate words that already contain explicit hyphen characters (except just after the hyphen), which can create a real problem in languages in which the average word length is much larger than in English. With the above setting this problem can be solved because the dash is no longer the hyphen character.

Every LaTeX font has an associated set of dimensions, which are changed by assignments of the form `\fontdimen`⟨*number*⟩`\font`=⟨*dimen*⟩, where ⟨*number*⟩ is the reference number for the dimension and ⟨*dimen*⟩ is the value to be assigned. The default values are taken from the `.tfm` file when the font is loaded. Each font has at least seven such dimensions:

`\fontdimen1` Specifies the slant per point of the characters. If the value is zero, the font is upright.

`\fontdimen2` Specifies the normal width of a space used between words (interword space).

`\fontdimen3` Specifies the additional stretchability of the interword space — that is, the extra amount of white space that LaTeX is allowed to add to the space between words to produce justified lines in a paragraph. In an emergency LaTeX may add more space than this allowed value; in that case an "underfull box" is reported.

`\fontdimen4` Specifies the allowed shrinkability of the interword space — that is, the amount of space that LaTeX is allowed to subtract from the normal interword space (`\fontdimen2`) to produce justified lines in a paragraph. LaTeX never shrinks the interword space to less than this minimum.

`\fontdimen5` Specifies the x-height. It defines the font-oriented dimension 1 ex.

`\fontdimen6` Specifies the quad width. It defines the font-oriented dimension 1 em.

`\fontdimen7` Specifies the amount intended as extra space to be added after certain end-of-sentence punctuation characters when `\nonfrenchspacing` is in force. The exact rules for when TeX uses this dimension (all or some of the extra space) are somewhat complex; see *The TeXbook* [48] for details. It is always ignored or rather replaced by the value `\xspaceskip`, when that value is nonzero.

When changing the interword spacing associated with a font, you cannot use an absolute value because such a value must be usable for all sizes within one font shape group. You must, therefore, define the value by using some other parameter that depends on the font. You could say, for example,

```
\DeclareFontShape{T1}{qtm}{m}{n}{<-> ec-qtmr}
                 {\fontdimen2\font=.7\fontdimen2\font}
```

This declaration reduces the normal interword space to 70% of its original value. In a similar manner, the stretchability and shrinkability could be changed.

Some fonts used in formulas need more than seven font dimensions — namely, the symbol fonts called "`symbols`" and "`largesymbols`" (see Section 9.8.5). TeX refuses to typeset a formula if these symbol fonts have fewer than 22 and 13 `\fontdimen`

745

parameters, respectively. The values of these parameters are used to position the characters in a math formula. An explanation of the meaning of every such `\fontdimen` parameter is beyond the scope of this book; details can be found in Appendix G of *The TeXbook* [48] and the very interesting *TUGboat* article [41] by Bogusław Jackowski.

One unfortunate optimization is built into the TeX system: TeX loads every `.tfm` file only once for a given size. It is, therefore, impossible to define one font shape group (with the `\DeclareFontShape` command) to load some external font — say, `cmtt10` — and to use another `\DeclareFontShape` command to load the same external font, this time changing some of the `\fontdimen` parameters or some other parameter associated with the font. Trying to do so changes the values for both font shape groups.

Suppose, for example, that you try to define a Times Roman font shape with tight spacing by making the interword space smaller:

```
\DeclareFontShape{T1}{qtm}{m}{n}{<-> ec-qtmr}{}
\DeclareFontShape{T1}{qtm}{c}{n}{<-> ec-qtmr}
                 {\fontdimen2\font=.7\fontdimen2\font}
```

This declaration does not work. The interword spacing for the medium shape changes when the tight shape is loaded to the values specified there, and this result is not what is wanted. The best way to solve this problem is to define a virtual font that contains the same characters as the original font but differs in the settings of the font dimensions (see [43, 44, 56]). Another possible solution is to load the font at a slightly different size, as in the following declaration:

```
\DeclareFontShape{T1}{qtm}{c}{n}{<-> [0.9999] ec-qtmr}
                 {\fontdimen2\font=.7\fontdimen2\font}
```

That strategy makes them different fonts for TeX with separate `\fontdimen` parameters. Alternatively, in this particular case you can control the interword space by setting `\spaceskip`, thereby overwriting the font values. See Section 3.1.1 for some discussion of that parameter.

9.8.2 Modifying font families and font shape groups

If you need a nonstandard font shape group declaration for a particular document, just place your private declaration in a package or the preamble of your document. It then overwrites any existing declaration for the font shape combination. Note, however, that the use of `\DeclareFontFamily` prevents a later loading of the corresponding `.fd` file (see Section 9.8.4). Also, your new declaration has no effect on fonts that are already loaded.[1]

---

[1] Today's LaTeX format preloads by default only a small number of fonts. However, by using the configuration file `preload.cfg`, more or fewer fonts can be loaded when the format is built. None of these preloaded fonts can be manipulated using font family or font shape declarations. Thus, if you want some special settings for the core fonts, you must ensure that none of these fonts is preloaded. For additional information on ways to customize a LaTeX installation, refer to the document

To get around both problems, you need to explicitly load the corresponding font definition files first by using \LoadFontDefinitionFile. Then you can call \DeclareFamily to overwrite the loading information or set up some special substitutions, etc. For example, to prevent hyphenation in Latin Modern Proportional Typewriter, where it is by default enabled, you could write

```
\LoadFontDefinitionFile{T1}{lmvtt}
\DeclareFamily{T1}{lmvtt}{\hyphenchar\font=-1}
```

The \LoadFontDefinitionFile command does nothing if the font definitions have already been loaded (by the kernel or by some package). The case that no font definition file exists for the combination is allowed as well. It can be identified by the fact that directly after the message "Trying to load ..." in the transcript file there is no matching file load listed.

9.8.3 Declaring new font encoding schemes

Font changes that involve alterations in the encoding scheme require taking certain precautions. For example, in the T1 encoding, most accented letters have their own glyphs, whereas in the traditional TEX text encoding (OT1), accented letters must be generated from accents and letters using the \accent primitive. (It is desirable to use glyphs for accented letters rather than employing the \accent primitive because, among other things, the former approach allows for correct hyphenation.) If the two approaches have to be mixed, perhaps because a font is available in only one of the encodings, the definition of a command such as \" must behave differently depending on the current font encoding.

For this reason, each encoding scheme has to be formally introduced to LATEX with a \DeclareFontEncoding command, which takes three arguments. The first argument is the name of the encoding under which you access it using the \fontencoding command. Table 9.18 on page 737 provides a list of standard encoding schemes and their internal NFSS names.

The second argument contains any code (such as definitions) to be executed every time LATEX switches from one encoding to another using the \fontencoding command. The final argument contains code to be used whenever the font is accessed as a mathematical alphabet. Thus, these three arguments can be used to redefine commands that depend on the positions of characters in the encoding.

There should not be really any need for users (other than a handful for developers worldwide) to define new font encodings, so we do not provide further details here. If you are interested, refer to [71].

As we saw in Section 9.7.3 on font substitution, the default values for the family, series, and shape may need to differ across encodings. To support this, NFSS provides the command \DeclareFontSubstitution, which again takes the encoding as the first argument. The next three arguments are the default values (associated with this encoding) for family, series, and shape for use in the automatic substitution

cfgguide.pdf [68], which is part of the LATEX distribution.

process, as explained in Section 9.7.3. It is important that these arguments form a valid font shape — in other words, that a `\DeclareFontShape` declaration exists for them. Otherwise, an error message is issued when NFSS checks its internal tables at `\begin{document}`.

9.8.4 Internal file organization

Font families can be declared when a format file is generated, declared in the document preamble, or loaded on demand when a font change command in the document requests a combination that has not been used so far. The first option consumes internal memory in every LaTeX run, even if the font is not used. The second and third possibilities take a little more time during document formatting, because the font definitions have to be read during processing time. Nevertheless, it is preferable to use the latter solutions for most font shape groups, because it allows you to typeset a wide variety of documents with a single LaTeX format.

When the format is generated, LaTeX reads a file named `fonttext.ltx` that contains the standard set of font family definitions and some other declarations related to text fonts. With some restrictions,[1] this set can be altered by providing a configuration file `fontdef.cfg`; see the documentation [68].

All other font family definitions should be declared in external files loaded on request: either package files or font definition (`.fd`) files. If you place font family definitions in a package file, you must explicitly load this package after the `\documentclass` command. There is also a third possibility: whenever NFSS gets a request for a font family `foo` in an encoding scheme `BAR` and it has no knowledge about this combination, it tries to load a file called `barfoo.fd` (all letters lowercase). If this file exists, it is supposed to contain font shape group definitions for the family `foo` in the encoding scheme `BAR` — that is, declarations of the form

```
\DeclareFontFamily{BAR}{foo}{..}
\DeclareFontShape{BAR}{foo}{..}{..}{..}{..}
   ...
\endinput
```

In this way it becomes possible to declare a huge number of font families for LaTeX without filling valuable internal memory with information that is almost never used.

Each `.fd` file should contain all font definitions for one font family in one encoding scheme. It should consist of one or more `\DeclareFontShape` declarations and exactly one `\DeclareFontFamily` declaration. Other definitions should not appear in the file, except perhaps for a `\ProvidesFile` declaration or some `\typeout` statement informing the user about the font loading.

Any definitions in   An unfortunately common mistake still found in some of the existing `.fd` files is
`.fd` files have to   the definition of additional helper commands using `\newcommand` or `\def`. Because
be global!   an `.fd` file may get loaded at random points during the document processing, it is

---

[1] Any such customization should not be undertaken lightly as it is unfortunately very easy to produce a LaTeX format that shows subtle or even glaring incompatibilities with other installations.

not impossible that this happens inside a group. In this case, these helper commands get undefined at the end of the group, resulting in puzzling errors later.

New encoding schemes cannot be introduced via the `.fd` mechanism. NFSS rejects any request to switch to an encoding scheme that was not explicitly declared in the LaTeX format (i.e., `fonttext.ltx`), in a package file, or in the preamble of the document.

Unicode engines

Fonts for Unicode engines usually do not use `.fd` files. Instead, they are loaded through the interfaces provided by the `fontspec` package that was discussed in Section 9.6. What happens behind the scenes is that `fontspec` generates the necessary `\DeclareFontFamily` and `\DeclareFontShape` declarations on the fly.

9.8.5 Declaring new fonts and symbols for use in math

Setting up additional math fonts is also an activity that is not often needed; however, because there is the occasional need for it, this section provides you with the necessary information.

Specifying font sizes

For every text size, NFSS maintains three sizes that are used to typeset formulas (see also Section 11.7.1): the size in which to typeset most of the symbols (selected by `\textstyle` or `\displaystyle`); the size for first-order subscripts and superscripts (`\scriptstyle`); and the size for higher-order subscripts and superscripts (`\scriptscriptstyle`). If you switch to a new text size, for which the corresponding math sizes are not yet known, NFSS tries to calculate them as fractions of the text size. Instead of letting NFSS do the calculation, you might want to specify the correct values yourself via `\DeclareMathSizes`. This declaration takes four arguments: the outer text size and the three math sizes for this text size. For example, the class file for *The LaTeX Companion* contains settings like the following:

```
\DeclareMathSizes{14}{14}{10}{7}
\DeclareMathSizes{36}{}{}{}
```

The first declaration defines the math sizes for the 14pt heading size to be 14pt, 10pt, and 7pt, respectively. The automatic calculation would have made the scriptfont $14 \times 0.7 = 9.8$ instead.

The second declaration (the size for the chapter headings) informs NFSS that no math sizes are necessary for 36pt text size. This avoids the unnecessary loading of more than 30 additional fonts. For the first edition of *The LaTeX Companion* such declarations were very important to be able to process the book with all its examples as a single document (the book loaded 228 fonts out of a maximum of 255). Today, TeX installations are usually compiled with much larger internal tables (e.g., the laptop implementation used to write this chapter allows 9000 fonts), so conserving space

	´0	´1	´2	´3	´4	´5	´6	´7	
´00x	≨	≩	≰	≱	≮	≯	⊀	⊁	˝0x
´01x	≦	≧	≴	≵	⩽̸	⩾̸	⪇	⪈	
´02x	⪉	⪊	⪵	⪶	⊊	⋧	⪹	⪺	˝1x
´03x	⪷	⪸	⪙	⪚	≁	≇	/	\	
´04x	⊊	⊋	⊈	⊉	⊊	⊋	⊊	⊋	˝2x
´05x	⊊	⊋	⊄	⊅	⫫	⊤	′	н	
´06x	⊬	⊭	⊮	⊯	⊭	⊄	⊄	⊭	˝3x
´07x	↚	↛	⇍	⇏	⇎	↮	∗	∅	
´10x	∄	A	B	C	D	E	F	G	˝4x
´11x	H	I	J	K	L	M	N	O	
´12x	P	Q	R	S	T	U	V	W	˝5x
´13x	X	Y	Z	⌢	⌢	∼	∼		
´14x	⅃	Ɔ					Ʊ	ð	˝6x
´15x	≈	⊐	⌉	⌐	≺	≻	⋉	⋊	
´16x	∣	∥	╲	∼	≈	≊	⪞	⪝	˝7x
´17x	⌢	⌢	Ⅎ	ϰ	k	ℏ	ℏ	∍	
	˝8	˝9	˝A	˝B	˝C	˝D	˝E	˝F	

Table 9.19: Glyph chart for `msbm10` produced by the nfssfont.tex program

is no longer a major concern. In any event, you should be careful about disabling math sizes, because if some formula is typeset in such a size after all, it is typeset in whatever math sizes are still in effect from an earlier text size.

Adding new symbol fonts

We have already seen how to use math alphabet commands to produce letters with special shapes in a formula. We now discuss how to add fonts containing special symbols, called "symbol fonts", and how to make such symbols accessible in formulas.

The process of adding new symbol fonts is similar to the declaration of a new math alphabet identifier: \DeclareSymbolFont defines the defaults for all math versions, and \SetSymbolFont overrides the defaults for a particular version.

The math symbol fonts are accessed via a symbolic name, which consists of a string of letters. If, for example, you want to install the AMS fonts `msbm10`, shown in Table 9.19, you first have to make the typeface known to NFSS using the declarations described in the previous sections. These instructions would look like

```
\DeclareFontFamily{U}{msb}{}
```

Type	Meaning	Example	Type	Meaning	Example
\mathord	Ordinary	/	\mathopen	Opening	(
\mathop	Large operator	\sum	\mathclose	Closing	)
\mathbin	Binary operation	+	\mathpunct	Punctuation	,
\mathrel	Relation	=	\mathalpha	Alphabet character	A

Table 9.20: Math symbol type classification

```
\DeclareFontShape{U}{msb}{m}{n}{ <5> <6> <7> <8> <9> gen * msbm
           <10> <10.95> <12> <14.4> <17.28> <20.74> <24.88> msbm10}{}
```

and are usually placed in an .fd file. You then have to declare that symbol font for all math versions by issuing the command

```
\DeclareSymbolFont{AMSb}{U}{msb}{m}{n}
```

It makes the font shape group U/msb/m/n available as a symbol font under the symbolic name AMSb. If there were a bold series in this font family (unfortunately there is not), you could subsequently change the setup for the bold math version by writing

```
\SetSymbolFont{AMSb}{bold}{U}{msb}{b}{n}
```

After taking care of the font declarations, you can make use of this symbol font in math mode. But how do you tell NFSS that $a\lessdot b$ should produce $a \lessdot b$, for example? To do so, you have to introduce your own symbol names to NFSS, using \DeclareMathSymbol.

```
\DeclareMathSymbol{cmd}{type}{symbol-font}{slot}
```

The first argument to \DeclareMathSymbol is your chosen command name. The second argument is one of the commands shown in Table 9.20 and describes the nature of the symbol — whether it is a binary operator, a relation, and so forth. LaTeX uses this information to leave the correct amount of space around the symbol when it is encountered in a formula. Incidentally, except for \mathalpha, these commands can be used directly in math formulas as functions with one argument, in which case they space their (possibly complex) argument as if it were of the corresponding type; see Section 11.8 on page →II 208.

The third argument identifies the symbol font from which the symbol should be fetched — that is, the symbolic name introduced with the \DeclareSymbolFont command. The fourth argument gives the symbol's position in the font encoding, either as a decimal, octal, or hexadecimal value. Octal (base 8) and hexadecimal (base

16) numbers are preceded by ' and ", respectively. If you look at Table 9.19 on page 750, you can easily determine the positions of all glyphs in this font. Such tables can be printed using the LaTeX program nfssfont.tex, which is part of the LaTeX distribution; see Section 9.5.9 on page 705. For example, \lessdot would be declared using

```
\DeclareMathSymbol{\lessdot}{\mathbin}{AMSb}{"6C}
```

Instead of a command name, you can use a single character in the first argument. For example, the eulervm package has several declarations of the form

```
\DeclareMathSymbol{0}{\mathalpha}{letters}{"30}
```

that specify where to fetch the digits from.

Because \DeclareMathSymbol is used to specify a position in some symbol font, it is important that all external fonts associated with this symbol font via the \DeclareSymbolFont and \SetSymbolFont commands have the same character in that position. The simplest way to ensure this uniformity is to use only fonts with the same encoding (unless it is the U, a.k.a. unknown, encoding, because two fonts with this encoding are not required to implement the same characters).

Besides \DeclareMathSymbol, LaTeX knows about \DeclareMathAccent, \DeclareMathDelimiter, and \DeclareMathRadical for setting up math font support. Details about these slightly special declarations can be found in [71], which is part of every LaTeX distribution.

Be careful with fonts that contain both math alphabets and act as symbol fonts

If you look again at the glyph chart for msbm10 (Table 9.19 on page 750), you will notice that this font contains "blackboard bold" letters, such as $\mathbb{ABC}$. If you want to use these letters as a math alphabet, you can define them by using a \DeclareMathAlphabet declaration, but given that this symbol font is already loaded to access individual symbols, it is better to use a shortcut:

```
\DeclareSymbolFontAlphabet{\mathbb}{AMSb}
```

That is, you give the name of your math alphabet identifier and the symbolic name of the previously declared symbol font.

An important reason for not unnecessarily loading symbol fonts twice is that there is an upper limit of 16 math fonts that can be active at any given time in LaTeX. In calculating this limit, each symbol font counts; math alphabets count only if they are actually used in the document, and they count locally in each math version. Thus, if eight symbol fonts are declared, you can use a maximum of eight (possibly different) math alphabet identifiers within every version.[1]

To summarize: to introduce new symbol fonts, you need to issue a small number of \DeclareSymbolFont and \SetSymbolFont declarations and a potentially large number of \DeclareMathSymbol declarations; hence, adding such fonts is best done in a package file.

---

[1] By default two math fonts remain local per formula if used for math alphabets and not for symbol fonts. They can then be reassigned anew each time. This default can be enlarged; see page 681.

Introducing new math versions

We have already mentioned that the standard setup automatically declares two math versions, normal and bold. To introduce additional versions, you use the declaration \DeclareMathVersion, which takes one argument, the name of the new math version. All symbol fonts and all math alphabets previously declared are automatically available in this math version; the default fonts are assigned to them — that is, the fonts you have specified with \DeclareMathAlphabet or \DeclareSymbolFont.

You can then change the setup for your new version by issuing appropriate \SetMathAlphabet and \SetSymbolFont commands, as shown in previous sections (pages 683 and 751) for the bold math version. Again, the introduction of a new math version is normally done in a package file.

Changing the symbol font setup

Besides adding new symbol fonts to access more symbols, the commands we have just seen can be used to change an existing setup. This capability is of interest if you choose to use special fonts in some or all math versions.

The default settings in LaTeX are given here:

```
\DeclareMathVersion{normal}   \DeclareMathVersion{bold}

\DeclareSymbolFont{operators}      {OT1}{cmr}{m} {n}
\DeclareSymbolFont{letters}        {OML}{cmm}{m}{it}
\DeclareSymbolFont{symbols}        {OMS}{cmsy}{m}{n}
\DeclareSymbolFont{largesymbols}   {OMX}{cmex}{m}{n}

% Special bold fonts only for these:
\SetSymbolFont      {operators}{bold}{OT1}{cmr}{bx}{n}
\SetSymbolFont      {letters}  {bold}{OML}{cmm}{b}{it}
```

In the standard setup, digits and text produced by "log-like operators", such as \log and \max, are taken from the symbol font called operators. To change this situation so that these elements agree with the main text font — say, Computer Modern Sans rather than Computer Modern Roman — you can issue the following commands:

```
\SetSymbolFont{operators}{normal}{OT1}{cmss}{m} {n}
\SetSymbolFont{operators}{bold}  {OT1}{cmss}{bx}{n}
```

Symbol fonts with the names symbols and largesymbols play a unique rôle in TeX, and for this reason they need a special number of \fontdimen parameters associated with them. Thus, only specially prepared fonts can be used for these two symbol fonts. In principle one can add such parameters to any font at load time by using the third parameter of \DeclareFontFamily or the sixth parameter of \DeclareFontShape. Information on the special parameters for these symbol fonts can be found in Appendix G of [48].

9.9 LATEX's encoding models

For most users it is probably sufficient to know that there exist certain input and output encodings and to have some basic knowledge about how to use them, as described in the previous sections. However, sometimes it is helpful to know the whole story in some detail, either to set up a new encoding or to better understand packages or classes that implement special features. So here is everything you always wanted to know about encodings in LATEX.

We start by describing the general character data flow within the LATEX system, deriving from that the base requirements for various encodings and the mapping between them. We then have a closer look at the internal representation model for character data within LATEX, followed by a discussion of the mechanisms used to map incoming data via input encodings into that internal representation.

Finally, we explain how the internal representation is translated, via the output encodings, into the form required for the actual task of typesetting.

9.9.1 Character data within the LATEX system

Document processing with the LATEX system starts by interpreting data present in one or more source files. These data, which represent the document content, are stored in these files in the form of octets representing characters. To correctly interpret these octets, LATEX (or any other program used to process the file, such as an editor) must know the encoding that was used when the file was written. In other words, it must know the mapping between abstract characters and the octets representing them.

With an incorrect mapping, all further processing is flawed to some extent unless the file contains only characters of a subset common in both encodings.[1]

LATEX makes one fundamental assumption at this stage: that (nearly) all characters of visible ASCII (decimal 32–126) are represented by the number that they have in the ASCII code table; see Table 9.21 on the next page.

There is both a practical and a TEXnical reason for this assumption. The practical reason is that most 8-bit encodings as well as the UTF-8 encoding usually used today share a common 7-bit plane. The TEXnical reason is that for using TEX efficiently, the majority of the visible portion of ASCII needs to be processed as characters of category "letter" (because only characters with this category can be used in multiple-character command names in TEX) or of category "other" (because TEX will not, for example, recognize the decimal digits as being part of a number if they do not have this category code).[2]

---

[1]Because most encodings in the Western world (including the UTF-8 encoding) share as a common subset a large fraction of the ASCII code (i.e., most of the 7-bit plane), documents consisting mainly of unaccented Latin characters are still understandable if viewed or processed in an encoding different from the one in which they were originally written. However, the more characters outside visible ASCII are used, the less comprehensible the text becomes. A text can become completely unintelligible when, for instance, Greek or Russian documents written in an 8-bit encoding are reprocessed in any other 8-bit encoding (or in UTF-8).

[2]At least this was true when this interface was being designed. These days, with computers being much faster than before, it would probably be possible to radically change the input method of TEX by

			Represented as Characters																						
Digits:	0	1	2	3	4	5	6	7	8	9															
Lowercase letters:	a	b	c	d	e	f	g	h	i	j	k	l	m	n	o	p	q	r	s	t	u	v	w	x	y z
Uppercase letters:	A	B	C	D	E	F	G	H	I	J	K	L	M	N	O	P	Q	R	S	T	U	V	W	X	Y Z
Punctuation:	.	,	;	:	?	!	'	'																	
Miscellaneous symbols:	*	+	-	=	(	)	[	]	/	@															

	Not Represented as Characters									
TeX syntax characters:	$	^	_	{	}	#	&	%	\	~
Missing in (some) OT1 fonts	<	>	|	"						

Table 9.21: LICR objects represented with single characters

When a character — or more exactly an 8-bit number in pdfTeX — is declared to be of category "letter" or "other" in TeX, then this character is transparently passed through TeX. This means that in the output TeX typesets whatever symbol is in the font at the position addressed by that number.

Unicode engines

> The same is true for Unicode engines, except that in those engines characters mean Unicode characters and therefore cover a much larger range. This is why, for example, "ä" is a real character in these engines and can therefore appear, say, in command names, while in pdfTeX it is seen as two separate bytes, i.e., two characters. Thus, to interpret UTF-8 in pdfTeX, the first byte is defined to be "active" and not of type "letter". This then assembles the intended character by reading further bytes and eventually generates \"a to represent the "ä".

A consequence of the assumption mentioned earlier is that fonts intended to be used for general text require that (most of) the visible ASCII characters are present in the font and are encoded according to the ASCII encoding. The exact list is given in Table 9.21.

All other 8-bit numbers (i.e., those outside visible ASCII) potentially being present in the input file are assigned a category code of "active", which makes them act like commands inside TeX. This allows LaTeX to transform them via the input encodings to a form that we call the LaTeX internal character representation (LICR). *LaTeX internal character representation (LICR)*

The most important characteristic of objects in the LICR is that the representation is 7-bit ASCII making it invariant to any input encoding change, because all input encodings are supposed to be transparent with respect to visible ASCII. This enables LaTeX, for example, to write auxiliary files (e.g., .toc files) using the LICR representation and to read them back in a different context (and possibly different encoding) without any misinterpretations.

Unicode's UTF-8 encoding is handled similarly in pdfTeX: the ASCII characters represent themselves, and the starting octets for multiple-byte representations act as

---

basically disabling it altogether and parsing the input data manually — that is, character by character.

active characters that scan the input for the remaining octets. The result is turned into an object in the LICR, if it is mapped, or it generates an error, if the given Unicode character is not mapped. However, if UTF-8 is used as input encoding, the characters are written out not in their LICR form but again as UTF-8 characters. Thus, in .toc files, etc., you see "Grüße" and not "Gr\"u\ss e" if that input encoding is in force.

The purpose of the output (or font) encoding is then to map the internal character representations to glyph positions in the current font used for typesetting or, in some cases, to initiate more complex actions. For example, it might place an accent (present in one position in the current font) over some glyph (in a different position in the current font) to achieve a printed image of the abstract character represented by the command(s) in the internal character encoding.

Because the LICR encodes all possible characters addressable within LaTeX, it is far larger than the number of characters that can be represented by a single TeX font in pdfTeX (which can contain a maximum of 256 glyphs). In some cases a character not present in a font can be rendered by combining glyphs, such as the accented characters mentioned above. However, when the character requires a special shape (e.g., the currency symbol "¤"), there is no way to fake it if that glyph does not exist in the font.

Nevertheless, for text symbols (that do not participate in hyphenation) the LaTeX model for character encoding supports automatic mechanisms for fetching glyphs from different fonts so that such characters if missing in the current font get typeset — provided a suitable additional font containing them is available, of course.

Unicode engines

The situation in Unicode engines is quite different, because fonts for these engines can contain arbitrarily many characters. This is why in those engines LaTeX normally uses only a single font encoding (TU), and instead of passing through an LICR representation, the UTF-8 characters represent themselves and do not change their behavior if the output encoding is changed. For example, the input string Grüße correctly generates "Grüße" if a Unicode font is used, but if we try

```
\fontencoding{OT1}\fontfamily{cmr}\selectfont  Grüße
\fontencoding{T1}\fontfamily{cmr}\selectfont   Grüße
```

in such an engine, the result would be

Gre GrüSSe

because the characters "ü" and "ß" have the Unicode numbers 00FC and 00DF, respectively, and in OT1 there are not any glyphs in slots greater than 007F (and thus neither character is typeset) and in T1 the "ü" happens to be in its Unicode slot, but "ß" is not, so we get a wrong glyph typeset.

However, if LICR representations are used in the input, e.g., \"u or \ss, they are interpreted correctly in all engines so that old documents work correctly when processed.

9.9.2 LATEX's internal character representation (LICR)

In this section we cover the LICR concepts in some more depth. Technically speaking, text characters are represented internally by LATEX in one of three ways, each of which is discussed in the following sections.

Representation as characters

If pdfTEX is used, then only a small number of characters are represented by "themselves"; for example, the Latin A is represented as the character "A". Characters represented in this way are shown in Table 9.21 on page 755. They form a subset of visible ASCII, and inside TEX all of them are given the category code of "letter" or "other". Some characters from the visible ASCII range are not represented in this way, either because they are part of the TEX syntax[1] or because they are not present in all fonts. If one uses, for example, "<" in text, the current font encoding determines whether one gets < (T1) or perhaps a ¡ (OT1) in the printout.[2]

> **Unicode engines**
>
> In contrast to pdfTEX nearly all characters are represented by themselves in Unicode engines: essentially all UTF-8 characters except for those that are used by TEX for syntax purposes.

Representation with character sequences

TEX's internal ligature mechanism supports the generation of new characters from a sequence of input characters. While this is actually a property of the font, some such sequences have been explicitly designed to serve as input shortcuts for characters that are otherwise difficult to type with most keyboards. Only a very few characters generated in this way are considered to belong to LATEX's internal representation. These include the en-dash and em-dash, which are generated by the ligatures -- and ---, and the opening and closing double quotes, which are generated by ' ' and ' ' (for the latter people sometimes use the single character ", but this is incorrect because it may produce a straight double quote, i.e., "). While most fonts also implement ! ' and ? ' to generate ¡ and ¿, this feature is not universally available in all fonts. For this reason *all* such characters have an alternative internal representation as a command (e.g., \textendash or \textexclamdown).

> **Unicode engines**
>
> Because this form of representation has been available for basically every font usable with pdfTEX, it has also been implemented for Unicode engines (technically through some engine-specific code when loading fonts as it is not an OpenType font feature).

---

[1] The LATEX syntax knows a few more characters, such as *[]. They play a dual rôle, also being used to represent the characters in straight text. Sometimes problems arise trying to keep the two meanings apart. For example, a] within an optional argument is possible only when it is hidden by a set of braces; otherwise, LATEX thinks the optional argument has ended.

[2] This describes the situation in text. In math "<" has a well-defined meaning: "generate a less than relation symbol".

Representation as "font-encoding–specific" commands

The other way to represent characters internally in LaTeX (and this covers the majority of characters when pdfTeX is used) is with special LaTeX commands (or command sequences) that remain unexpanded when written to a file or when placed into a moving argument. These special commands are sometimes referred to as "font-encoding-specific commands" because their meaning depends on the font encoding current when LaTeX is ready to typeset them. Such commands are declared using special declarations, as discussed below. They usually require individual definitions for each font encoding. If no definition exists for the current encoding, either a default is used (if available) or an error message is presented to the user.

Technically, when the font encoding is changed at some point in the document, the definitions of the encoding-specific commands do not change immediately, because that would mean changing a large number of commands on the spot. Instead, these commands have been implemented in such a way that they notice, once they are used, if their current definition is no longer suitable for the font encoding in force. In such a case they call upon their counterparts in the current font encoding to do the actual work.

The set of "font-encoding–specific commands" is not fixed, but rather implicitly defined to be the union of all commands defined for individual font encodings. Thus, by adding new font encodings to LaTeX, new "font-encoding–specific commands" might emerge.

> **Unicode engines**
>
> With Unicode engines most characters are transparently handled, so encoding-specific commands are normally not needed; it is nevertheless possible to use them in the input. This makes it easy to reuse documents, originally written for pdfTeX, in Unicode engines.

9.9.3 Input encodings

Since 2015 the default input encoding for LaTeX is UTF-8 unless explicitly changed in the preamble using the inputenc package. This means that in pdfTeX all UTF-8 characters that can be typeset using the loaded fonts can nowadays be entered in the source document in their natural UTF-8 form, e.g., as "ü" or "ß", and there is no need to use the LICR representations \"u or \ss for them. This is technically achieved in pdfTeX by mapping the UTF-8 characters to their corresponding LICR objects using \DeclareUnicodeCharacter declarations.

\DeclareUnicodeCharacter{*hex-number*}{*LICR-object*}

Unusual argument syntax This declaration maps a Unicode number (represented as a *hex-number* without a preceding ") to an *LICR-object*. For example,

```
\DeclareUnicodeCharacter{00A3}{\textsterling}
\DeclareUnicodeCharacter{011A}{\v E}
\DeclareUnicodeCharacter{2031}{\textpertenthousand}
```

Unicode characters in the range of 0000 to 00FF (i.e., the ASCII part of Unicode) cannot be declared with this command: if you try, LATEX responds with an error message.

In theory, there should be only a single unique bidirectional mapping between the two name spaces so that all such declarations could be already available when LATEX starts. In practice, the situation is a little more complicated. For one, it is not sensible to automatically provide the whole table, because that would require a huge amount of TEX's memory. Additionally, there are many Unicode characters for which no LICR object exists (so far), and conversely some LICR objects have no equivalents in Unicode.[1] This problem is solved in LATEX by loading only those Unicode mappings that correspond to the encodings used in a particular document (as far as they are known) and responds to any other request for a Unicode character with a suitable error message. It then becomes your task to either provide the right mapping information or, if necessary, load an additional font encoding.

For each output encoding, there should exist a file ⟨encoding⟩enc.dfu containing all necessary mapping declarations (like those above) that correspond to this particular encoding. When an encoding is loaded with fontenc, this file is read in, and afterwards its declarations are available.

Because different font encodings often provide to a certain extent the same characters, it is quite common for declarations for the same Unicode character to be found in different .dfu files. It is, therefore, very important that these declarations in different files be identical (which in theory they should be anyway, but...). Otherwise, the declaration loaded last survives, which may be a different one from document to document.[2]

Of course, \DeclareUnicodeCharacter can also be used in the preamble if a mapping is missing or needs changing for some reason.

Legacy 8-bit input encodings

To process files stored in one of the legacy 8-bit input encodings LATEX offers the package inputenc. Once this package is loaded (with or without options), the two declarations \DeclareInputText and \DeclareInputMath for mapping 8-bit input characters to LICR objects become available. Their usage should be confined to input encoding files, packages, or, if necessary, to the preamble of documents. Input encoding files use the name of the encoding in lowercase letters and the extension .def, e.g., latin1.def.

Because documents today are stored by default in UTF-8, there is seldom a need for using inputenc, and we refer to the package documentation for technical details of how input encoding files are set up or altered through the above commands.

---

[1] This is perhaps a surprising statement, but simply consider that, for example, accent commands like \" combined with some other character form a new LICR object, such as \"d (whether sensible or not). Many such combinations are not available in Unicode.

[2] So anyone who wants to provide a new .dfu file for some encoding that was previously not covered should carefully check the existing definitions in .dfu files for related encodings. Standard files provided with inputenc are guaranteed to have uniform definition — they are, in fact, all generated from a single list that is suitably split up. A full list of currently existing mappings can be found in the file utf8enc.dfu.

9.9.4 Output encodings

As we learned earlier, output encodings define the mapping from the LICR to the glyphs (or constructs built from glyphs) available in the fonts used for typesetting. These mappings are referenced inside LATEX by two- or three-letter names (e.g., OT1 or T2A). We say that a certain font is in a certain encoding if the mapping corresponds to the positions of the glyphs in the font in question. So what are the exact components of such a mapping?

Pass-through characters Characters internally represented by ASCII characters are simply passed on to the font. In other words, TEX uses the ASCII code to select a glyph from the current font. For example, the character "A" with ASCII code 65 results in typesetting the glyph in position 65 in the current font. This is why LATEX requires that fonts for text contain all such ASCII letters in their ASCII code positions, because there is no way to interact with this basic TEX mechanism (other than to disable it and do everything "manually"). Thus, for visible ASCII, a one-to-one mapping is implicitly present in all output encodings.

> **Unicode engines**
> In the case of the TU encoding used by Unicode engines, essentially all UTF-8 letters are passed on to the font. However, the other means of referring to glyphs (i.e., sequences of characters or the font-encoding-specific commands discussed below) are also supported.

Characters represented by ASCII sequences Characters internally represented as sequences of ASCII characters (e.g., "--") are handled as follows: when the current font is first loaded, TEX is informed that the font contains a number of so-called ligature programs. These define certain character sequences that are not to be typeset directly but rather to be replaced[1] by some other glyphs from the font (the exact position of each replacement glyph is font dependent and not important otherwise). For example, when TEX sees "--" in the input (i.e., ASCII code 45 twice), a ligature program might direct it to use the glyph in position 123 instead (which then would hold the glyph "–"). No interaction with this mechanism is possible. Some such ligatures are present for purely aesthetic reasons and may or may not be available in certain fonts (e.g., ff generating "ff" rather than "ff"). Others are supposed to be implemented for a certain encoding (e.g., "---" producing an \emdash).

Characters represented as font-encoding-specific commands Nevertheless, the bulk of the internal character representation consists of "font-encoding-specific" commands. They are mapped using the declarations described below. All declarations have the same structure in their first two arguments: the font-encoding-specific command (or the first component of it, if it is a command sequence), followed by the name of the encoding. Any remaining arguments depend on the type of declaration.

Thus, an encoding XYZ is defined by a collection of declarations all having the name XYZ as their second argument. Of course, to be of any use, some fonts must be encoded in that encoding. In fact, the development of font encodings is normally done the other way around — namely, someone starts with an existing font and then

---

[1] The actions carried out by a font ligature program can, in fact, be far more complex, but for the purpose of our discussion here this simplified view is appropriate. For an in-depth discussion, see Knuth's paper on virtual fonts [56].

provides appropriate declarations for using it. This collection of declarations is then given a suitable name, such as OT1. In the next section, we take the font ec-lmr10, shown in Table 9.22 on page 763, whose font encoding is called T1 in LaTeX, and build appropriate declarations to access the glyphs from a font encoded in this way. The blue characters in this table are those that have to be present in the same positions in every text encoding, because they are transparently passed through TeX.

Declarations for output encoding files

Like input encoding files, output encoding files are identified by the extension .def. However, the base name of the file is slightly more structured: the name of the encoding in lowercase letters, followed by the letters enc (e.g., t1enc.def for the T1 encoding).

Such files should contain only the declarations described in the current section. Because output encoding files might be read several times by LaTeX, it is particularly important to adhere to this rule strictly and to refrain from using, for example, \newcommand, which prevents reading such a file multiple times!

For identification purposes an output encoding file should start with a \ProvidesFile declaration describing the nature of the file. For example:

```
\ProvidesFile{t1enc.def}[2001/06/05 v1.94 Standard LaTeX file]
```

To be able to declare any encoding-specific commands for a particular encoding, we first have to make this encoding known to LaTeX. This is achieved via the \DeclareFontEncoding declaration. At this point[1] it is also useful to declare the default substitution rules for the encoding with the help of the command \DeclareFontSubstitution; both declarations are described in detail in Section 9.8.3 starting on page 747.

```
\DeclareFontEncoding{T1}{}{}
\DeclareFontSubstitution{T1}{cmr}{m}{n}
```

Having introduced the T1 encoding in this way to LaTeX, we can now proceed with declaring how font-encoding–specific commands should behave in that encoding.

> \DeclareTextSymbol{*LICR-object*}{*encoding*}{*slot*}

Perhaps the simplest form of declaration is the one for text symbols, where the internal representation can be directly mapped to a single glyph in the target font. This is handled by the \DeclareTextSymbol declaration, whose third argument — the font position — can be given as a decimal, hexadecimal, or octal number. For example,

```
\DeclareTextSymbol{\ss}{T1}{255}
\DeclareTextSymbol{\AE}{T1}{'306}  % font position as octal number
\DeclareTextSymbol{\ae}{T1}{"E6}   % ... as hexadecimal number
```

---

[1] This should happen in the encoding *⟨enc⟩*enc.def file and *not* in a font .fd file!

declare that the font-encoding–specific commands \ss, \AE, and \ae should be mapped to the font (decimal) positions 255, 198, and 230, respectively, in a T1-encoded font. As mentioned earlier, it is safest to use decimal notation in such declarations, even though octal or hexadecimal values are often easier to identify in glyph charts like the one on the next page. Mixing them like we did in the example above is certainly bad style. All in all, there are 49 such declarations for the T1 encoding.

> \DeclareTextAccent{*LICR-accent*}{*encoding*}{*slot*}

Often fonts contain diacritical marks as individual glyphs to allow the production of accented characters by combining such a diacritical mark with some other glyph. Such accents (as long as they are to be placed on top of other glyphs) are declared using the \DeclareTextAccent command; the third argument *slot* is the position of the diacritical mark in the font. For example,

```
\DeclareTextAccent{\"}{T1}{4}
```

defines the "umlaut" accent. From that point onward, an internal representation such as \"a has the following meaning in the T1 output encoding: typeset "ä" by placing the accent in position 4 over the glyph in position 97 (the ASCII code of the character a). In fact, such a declaration implicitly defines a huge range of internal character presentations — that is, anything of the type \"⟨*base-glyph*⟩, where ⟨*base-glyph*⟩ is something defined via \DeclareTextSymbol or any ASCII character belonging to the LICR, such as "a".

Even those combinations that do not make much sense, such as \"\P (i.e., pilcrow sign with umlaut ¶̈) conceptually become members of the set of font-encoding–specific commands in this way. There are a total of 11 such declarations in the T1 encoding.

> \DeclareTextComposite
>   {*LICR-accent*}{*encoding*}{*simple-LICR-object*}{*slot*}

The glyph chart on the facing page contains a large number of accented characters as individual glyphs — for example, "ä" in position '344 octal. Thus, in T1 the encoding-specific command \"a should not result in placing an accent over the character "a" but instead should directly access the glyph in that position of the font. This is achieved by the declaration

```
\DeclareTextComposite{\"}{T1}{a}{228}
```

which states that the encoding-specific command \"a results in typesetting the glyph 228, thereby disabling the accent declaration above. For all other encoding-specific commands starting with \", the accent declaration remains in place. For example, \"b produces a "b̈" by placing an accent over the base character b.

The third argument, *simple-LICR-object*, should be a single letter, such as "a", or a single command, such as \j or \oe. There are 110 such composites declared for the T1 encoding.

	´0	´1	´2	´3	´4	´5	´6	´7	
´00x	`	´	^	~	¨	˝	°	ˇ	˝0x
´01x	˘	¯	·	˛	¸	ʼ	‹	›	
´02x	"	"	„	«	»	–	—		˝1x
´03x	˳	¹	ȷ	ff	fi	fl	ffi	ffl	
´04x	␣	!	"	#	$	%	&	ʼ	˝2x
´05x	(	)	*	+	,	-	.	/	
´06x	0	1	2	3	4	5	6	7	˝3x
´07x	8	9	:	;	<	=	>	?	
´10x	@	A	B	C	D	E	F	G	˝4x
´11x	H	I	J	K	L	M	N	O	
´12x	P	Q	R	S	T	U	V	W	˝5x
´13x	X	Y	Z	[	\	]	^	_	
´14x	`	a	b	c	d	e	f	g	˝6x
´15x	h	i	j	k	l	m	n	o	
´16x	p	q	r	s	t	u	v	w	˝7x
´17x	x	y	z	{	|	}	~	-	
´20x	Ă	Ą	Ć	Č	Ď	Ě	Ę	Ğ	˝8x
´21x	Ĺ	Ľ	Ł	Ń	Ň	Ŋ	Ő	Ŕ	
´22x	Ř	Ś	Š	Ş	Ť	Ţ	Ű	Ů	˝9x
´23x	Ÿ	Ź	Ž	Ż	IJ	İ	đ	§	
´24x	ă	ą	ć	č	ď	ě	ę	ğ	˝Ax
´25x	ĺ	ľ	ł	ń	ň	ŋ	ő	ŕ	
´26x	ř	ś	š	ş	ť	ţ	ű	ů	˝Bx
´27x	ÿ	ź	ž	ż	ij	ı	¿	£	
´30x	À	Á	Â	Ã	Ä	Å	Æ	Ç	˝Cx
´31x	È	É	Ê	Ë	Ì	Í	Î	Ï	
´32x	Ð	Ñ	Ò	Ó	Ô	Õ	Ö	Œ	˝Dx
´33x	Ø	Ù	Ú	Û	Ü	Ý	Þ	SS	
´34x	à	á	â	ã	ä	å	æ	ç	˝Ex
´35x	è	é	ê	ë	ì	í	î	ï	
´36x	ð	ñ	ò	ó	ô	õ	ö	œ	˝Fx
´37x	ø	ù	ú	û	ü	ý	þ	ß	
	˝8	˝9	˝A	˝B	˝C	˝D	˝E	˝F	

Characters marked in blue need to be present (in the same positions) in every text encoding, because they are transparently passed through TEX.

Table 9.22: Glyph chart for a T1-encoded font (ec-lmr10)

> ```
> \DeclareTextCompositeCommand
>            {LICR-object}{encoding}{simple-LICR-object}{code}
> ```

Although not used for the T1 encoding, there also exists a more general variant of `\DeclareTextComposite` that allows arbitrary code in place of a slot position. This is, for example, used in the OT1 encoding to lower the ring accent over the "A" compared to the way it would be typeset with TEX's `\accent` primitive. The accents over the "i" are also implemented using this form of declaration:

```
\DeclareTextCompositeCommand{\'}{OT1}{i}{\@tabacckludge'\i}
\DeclareTextCompositeCommand{\^}{OT1}{i}{\^\i}
```

What have we not covered for the T1 encoding? A number of diacritical marks are not placed on top of other characters but are placed somewhere below them. There is no special declaration form for such marks, as the actual placement usually involves low-level TEX code. Instead, the generic `\DeclareTextCommand` declaration can be used for this purpose.

> ```
> \DeclareTextCommand{LICR-object}{encoding}[num][default]{code}
> ```

For example, the "underbar" accent `\b` in the T1 encoding is defined with the following wonderful piece of prose:

```
\DeclareTextCommand{\b}{T1}[1]
     {\hmode@bgroup\o@lign{\relax#1\crcr\hidewidth\sh@ft{29}%
     \vbox to.2ex{\hbox{\char9}\vss}\hidewidth}\egroup}
```

Without going into detail about what the code precisely means, we can see that the `\DeclareTextCommand` is similar in structure to `\newcommand`. That is, it has an optional *num* argument denoting the number of arguments (one here), a second optional *default* argument (not present here), and a final mandatory argument containing the code in which it is possible to refer to the argument(s) using #1, #2, and so on. T1 has four such declarations, for `\b`, `\c`, `\d`, and `\k`.

`\DeclareTextCommand` can also be used to build font-encoding–specific commands consisting of a single control sequence. In this case it is used without an optional argument, thus defining a command with zero arguments. For example, in T1 there is no glyph for a ‰ sign, but there exists a strange little "o" in position '30, which, if placed directly behind a %, gives the appropriate glyph. Thus, we can write

```
\DeclareTextCommand{\textperthousand}    {T1}{\%\char 24 }
\DeclareTextCommand{\textpertenthousand}{T1}{\%\char 24\char 24 }
```

This discussion has now covered all commands that are needed to declare the font-encoding–specific commands for a new encoding. As mentioned earlier, only these commands should appear in encoding definition files.

Output encoding defaults

What happens if an encoding-specific command is used for which there is no declaration in the current font encoding? In that case, one of two things might happen: either LATEX has a default definition for the LICR object, in which case this default is used, or the user gets an error message stating that the requested LICR object is unavailable in the current encoding. There are several ways to set up defaults for LICR objects.

> \DeclareTextCommandDefault{*LICR-object*}[*num*] [*default*] {*code*}

The \DeclareTextCommandDefault command provides the default definition for an *LICR-object* that is to be used whenever there is no specific setting for the object in the current encoding. Such default definitions can, for example, fake a certain character. For instance, \textregistered has a default definition in which the character is built from two others, like this:

```
\DeclareTextCommandDefault{\textregistered}{\textcircled{\scshape r}}
```

Technically, the default definitions are stored as an encoding with the name "?". While you should not rely on this fact, because the implementation might change in the future, it means that you cannot declare an encoding with this name.

> \DeclareTextSymbolDefault{*LICR-object*}{*encoding*}

In most cases, a default definition does not require coding but simply directs LATEX to pick up the character from some encoding in which it is known to exist. The LATEX kernel, for example, contains a large number of default declarations that all point to the TS1 encoding. Consider the following declaration:

```
\DeclareTextSymbolDefault{\texteuro}{TS1}
```

The \DeclareTextSymbolDefault command can, in fact, be used to define the default for any LICR object without arguments, not just those that have been declared with the \DeclareTextSymbol command in other encodings.

> \DeclareTextAccentDefault{*LICR-accent*}{*encoding*}

A similar declaration exists for LICR objects that take one argument, such as accents (which gave this declaration its name). This form is again usable for any LICR object with one argument. The LATEX kernel, for example, contains quite a number of declarations of the type:

```
\DeclareTextAccentDefault{\"}{OT1}
\DeclareTextAccentDefault{\t}{OML}
```

This means that if the \" is not defined in the current encoding, then use the one from an OT1-encoded font. Likewise, if you need a tie accent, pick up one from OML[1] if nothing better is available.

`\ProvideTextCommandDefault{`*LICR-object*`}[`*num*`] [`*default*`] {`*code*`}`

With the `\ProvideTextCommandDefault` declaration a different kind of default can be "provided". As the name suggests, it does the same job as the declaration `\DeclareTextCommandDefault`, except that the default is provided only if no default has been defined before. This is mainly used in input encoding files to provide some sort of trivial defaults for unusual LICR objects. For example:

```
\ProvideTextCommandDefault{\textonequarter}{\ensuremath{\frac14}}
\ProvideTextCommandDefault{\textcent}{\TextSymbolUnavailable\textcent}
```

The first declaration provides an approximate glyph; in the second, the command `\TextSymbolUnavailable` generates an error message that the symbol is unavailable in the current encoding. Packages can then replace such definitions with declarations pointing to real glyphs.

Using `\Provide..` instead of `\Declare..` ensures that a better default is not accidentally overwritten if the input encoding file is read.

`\UndeclareTextCommand{`*LICR-object*`}{`*encoding*`}`

In some cases an existing declaration needs to be removed to ensure that a default declaration is used instead. This task can be carried out by the command `\UndeclareTextCommand`. For example, the **textcomp** package used to remove the definitions of `\textdollar` and `\textsterling` from the OT1 encoding because not every OT1-encoded font actually has these symbols.[2]

```
\UndeclareTextCommand{\textsterling}{OT1}
\UndeclareTextCommand{\textdollar}  {OT1}
```

Without this removal, the new default declarations to pick up the symbols from TS1 would not be used for fonts encoded with OT1.

`\UseTextSymbol{`*encoding*`}{`*LICR-object*`}`
`\UseTextAccent{`*encoding*`}{`*LICR-object*`}{`*simple-LICR-object*`}`

The action hidden behind the declarations `\DeclareTextSymbolDefault` and `\DeclareTextAccentDefault` is also available for direct use. Assume, for example, that the current encoding is U. In that case,

```
\UseTextSymbol{OT1}{\ss}
\UseTextAccent{OT1}{\'}{a}
```

---

[1] OML is a math font encoding, but it contains this text accent mark.

[2] This is one of the deficiencies of the old TeX encodings; besides missing accented glyphs, they are not even identical from one font to another.

has the same effect as entering the code below. Note in particular that the "a" is typeset in encoding U — only the accent is taken from the other encoding.

```
{\fontencoding{OT1}\selectfont\ss}
{\fontencoding{OT1}\selectfont\'{\fontencoding{U}\selectfont a}}
```

Declarations for the `tuenc.def` file

Unicode engines

For the Unicode encoding TU used in Unicode engines there are additional declarations available. The encoding is implicit, because it is normally TU. For special applications it can be altered by changing `\UnicodeEncodingName`.

`\DeclareUnicodeAccent{`*LICR-accent*`}{`*slot*`}`

This is similar to `\DeclareTextAccent`, but instead of using the `\accent` command of TeX to position the accent on top of a following base character, it places the accent after it. This is the correct approach if the accent is a Unicode "combining character". It is then the task of the font to combine both in the correct way.

`\DeclareUnicodeComposite{`*LICR-accent*`}{`*base-character*`}{`*slot*`}`

This is a wrapper around `\DeclareTextCompositeCommand`. It first tests if the declared composite exists as a single glyph in the current font (which may or may not be the case) and if so uses the composite *slot*. Otherwise, it falls back to the default definition for the *LICR-accent* in TU.

`\DeclareUnicodeSymbol{`*LICR-cmd*`}{`*slot*`}`

This is a simple wrapper around `\DeclareTextSymbol` with the encoding made implicit but otherwise no extra processing.

`\DeclareUnicodeCommand{`*LICR-cmd*`}{`*definition*`}`

This is another wrapper; this time for `\DeclareTextCommand` with the encoding made implicit, i.e., syntactic sugar.

A listing of standard LICR objects

Table 9.23 provides a comprehensive overview of the LaTeX internal representations available with the three major encodings for Latin-based languages: OT1 (the original TeX text font encoding), T1 (the LaTeX standard encoding, also known as Cork encoding), and LY1 (an alternate 8-bit encoding proposed by Y&Y). In addition, it shows all LICR objects declared by TS1 (the LaTeX standard text symbol encoding) historically provided by loading the textcomp package but nowadays available by default.

The first column of the table shows the LICR object names alphabetically sorted, indicating which LICR objects act like accents. The second column shows a glyph representation of the object.

The third column describes whether the object has a default declaration. If an encoding is listed, it means that by default the glyph is being fetched from a suitable font in that encoding; `constr.` means that the default is produced from low-level TEX code; if the column is empty, it means that no default is defined for this LICR object. In the last case a "Symbol unavailable" error is returned when you use it in an encoding for which it has no explicit definition. If the object is an alias for some other LICR object, we list the alternative name in this column.

Columns four through seven show whether an object is available in the given encoding. Here ✗ means that the object is natively available (as a glyph) in fonts with that encoding, ○ means that it is available through the default for all encodings, and constr. means that it is generated from several glyphs, accent marks, or other elements. If the default is fetched from TS1, the LICR object is also always available but depending on the current font family, it might have a suboptimal representation; see Section 9.5.6 on page 694 for details.

> **Unicode engines**
>
> All font-encoding-specific commands are available in the TU encoding.

Table 9.23: Standard LICR objects

LICR Object		Glyph	Default from	OT1	T1	LY1	TS1
ABC..XYZ	(Uppercase letters)	ABC..XYZ		✗	✗	✗	
abc..xyz	(Lowercase letters)	abc..xyz		✗	✗	✗	
0123..9	(Digits)	0123..9		✗	✗	✗	✗
.,/	(Punctuation)	.,/		✗	✗	✗	✗
;:?!"‹›	(Punctuation cont.)	;:?!"‹›		✗	✗	✗	
*+-=()[|]	(Misc)	*+-=()[|]		✗	✗	✗	
\# \& \%		#&%		✗	✗	✗	
\"	(accent)	¨	OT1	✗	✗	✗	
\"A		Ä		constr.	✗	✗	
\"E		Ë		constr.	✗	✗	
\"I		Ï		constr.	✗	✗	
\"O		Ö		constr.	✗	✗	
\"U		Ü		constr.	✗	✗	
\"Y		Ÿ		constr.	✗	✗	
\"a		ä		constr.	✗	✗	
\"e		ë		constr.	✗	✗	
\"\i		ï		constr.	✗	✗	
\"i	(alias)	ï	\"\i	constr.	✗	✗	
✗ defined in encoding ○ defined via default							

LICR Object		Glyph	Default from	OT1	T1	LY1	TS1
\"o		ö		constr.	✗	✗	
\"u		ü		constr.	✗	✗	
\"y		ÿ		constr.	✗	✗	
\$	(alias)	$	\textdollar	○	✗	✗	✗
\'	(accent)	´	OT1	✗	✗	✗	
\'A		Á		constr.	✗	✗	
\'C		Ć		constr.	✗	constr.	
\'E		É		constr.	✗	✗	
\'I		Í		constr.	✗	✗	
\'L		Ĺ		constr.	✗	constr.	
\'N		Ń		constr.	✗	constr.	
\'O		Ó		constr.	✗	✗	
\'R		Ŕ		constr.	✗	constr.	
\'S		Ś		constr.	✗	constr.	
\'U		Ú		constr.	✗	✗	
\'Y		Ý		constr.	✗	✗	
\'Z		Ź		constr.	✗	constr.	
\'a		á		constr.	✗	✗	
\'c		ć		constr.	✗	constr.	
\'e		é		constr.	✗	✗	
\'\i		í		constr.	✗	✗	
\'i	(alias)	í	\'\i	constr.	✗	✗	
\'l		ĺ		constr.	✗	constr.	
\'n		ń		constr.	✗	constr.	
\'o		ó		constr.	✗	✗	
\'r		ŕ		constr.	✗	constr.	
\'s		ś		constr.	✗	constr.	
\'u		ú		constr.	✗	✗	
\'y		ý		constr.	✗	✗	
\'z		ź		constr.	✗	constr.	
\.	(accent)	˙	OT1	✗	✗	✗	
\.I		İ		constr.	✗	constr.	
\.Z		Ż		constr.	✗	constr.	
\.\i		i		✗	✗	constr.	
\.i	(alias)	i	\.\i	✗	✗	constr.	
\.z		ż		constr.	✗	constr.	
\=	(accent)	¯	OT1	✗	✗	✗	
\AE		Æ	OT1	✗	✗	✗	
\DH		Đ			✗	✗	
\DJ		Đ		✗			

✗ defined in encoding   ○ defined via default

LICR Object		Glyph	Default from	OT1	T1	LY1	TS1
\H	(accent)	˝	OT1	✗	✗	✗	
\H O		Ő		constr.	✗	constr.	
\H U		Ű		constr.	✗	constr.	
\H o		ő		constr.	✗	constr.	
\H u		ű		constr.	✗	constr.	
\L		Ł	OT1	✗	✗	✗	
\NG		Ŋ			✗		
\O		Ø	OT1	✗	✗	✗	
\OE		Œ	OT1	✗	✗	✗	
\P	(alias)	¶	\textparagraph	○	○	✗	✗
\S	(alias)	§	\textsection	○	✗	✗	✗
\SS		SS	constr.	○	✗	○	
\TH		Þ			✗	✗	
\^	(accent)	^	OT1	✗	✗	✗	
\^A		Â		constr.	✗	✗	
\^E		Ê		constr.	✗	✗	
\^I		Î		constr.	✗	✗	
\^O		Ô		constr.	✗	✗	
\^U		Û		constr.	✗	✗	
\^a		â		constr.	✗	✗	
\^e		ê		constr.	✗	✗	
\^\i		î		constr.	✗	✗	
\^i	(alias)	î	\^\i	constr.	✗	✗	
\^o		ô		constr.	✗	✗	
\^u		û		constr.	✗	✗	
_	(alias)	_	\textunderscore	○	✗	✗	
\`	(accent)	`	OT1	✗	✗	✗	
\`A		À		constr.	✗	✗	
\`E		È		constr.	✗	✗	
\`I		Ì		constr.	✗	✗	
\`O		Ò		constr.	✗	✗	
\`U		Ù		constr.	✗	✗	
\`a		à		constr.	✗	✗	
\`e		è		constr.	✗	✗	
\`\i		ì		constr.	✗	✗	
\`i	(alias)	ì	\`\i	constr.	✗	✗	
\`o		ò		constr.	✗	✗	
\`u		ù		constr.	✗	✗	
\ae		æ	OT1	✗	✗	✗	
\b	(accent)	_	OT1	✗	✗	✗	

✗ defined in encoding   ○ defined via default

LICR Object		Glyph	Default from	OT1	T1	LY1	TS1
\c	(accent)	˛	OT1	✗	✗	✗	
\c C		Ç		constr.	✗	✗	
\c S		Ş		constr.	✗	constr.	
\c T		Ţ		constr.	✗	constr.	
\c c		ç		constr.	✗	✗	
\c s		ş		constr.	✗	constr.	
\c t		ţ		constr.	✗	constr.	
\capitalacute	(accent)	´	TS1	○	○	○	✗
\capitalcaron	(accent)	ˇ	TS1	○	○	○	✗
\capitaldieresis	(accent)	¨	TS1	○	○	○	✗
\capitalgrave	(accent)	`	TS1	○	○	○	✗
\capitalmacron	(accent)	¯	TS1	○	○	○	✗
\capitalogonek	(accent)	˛	TS1	○	○	○	✗
\capitalring	(accent)	°	TS1	○	○	○	✗
\capitaltilde	(accent)	~	TS1	○	○	○	✗
\copyright	(alias)	©	\textcopyright	○	○	✗	✗
\d	(accent)	.	OT1	✗	✗	✗	
\dag	(alias)	†	\textdagger	○	○	✗	✗
\ddag	(alias)	‡	\textdaggerdbl	○	○	✗	✗
\dh		ð			✗	✗	
\dj		đ			✗		
\dots	(alias)	…	\textellipsis	○	○	✗	
\guillemetleft		«		babel	✗	✗	
\guillemetright		»		babel	✗	✗	
\guilsinglleft		‹		babel	✗	✗	
\guilsinglright		›		babel	✗	✗	
\i		ı	OT1	✗	✗	✗	
\j		ȷ	OT1	✗	✗	✗	
\k	(accent)	˛			✗	✗	
\k A		Ą			✗	constr.	
\k E		Ę			✗	constr.	
\k O		Ǫ			✗	constr.	
\k a		ą			✗	constr.	
\k e		ę			✗	constr.	
\k o		ǫ			✗	constr.	
\l		ł	OT1	✗	✗	✗	
\ng		ŋ			✗		
\o		ø	OT1	✗	✗	✗	
\oe		œ	OT1	✗	✗	✗	
\pounds	(alias)	£	\textsterling	○	✗	✗	✗
✗ defined in encoding ○ defined via default							

LICR Object		Glyph	Default from	OT1	T1	LY1	TS1
\quotedblbase		„			✗	✗	
\quotesinglbase		‚			✗	✗	
\r	(accent)	°	OT1	✗	✗	✗	
\r A		Å		constr.	✗	constr.	
\r U		Ů		constr.	✗	constr.	
\r a		å		constr.	✗	constr.	
\r u		ů		constr.	✗	constr.	
\ss		ß	OT1	✗	✗	✗	
\t	(accent)	⌢	OML	✗	✗	○	
\textacutedbl		″	TS1	○	○	○	✗
\textascendercompwordmark		invisible	TS1	○	○	○	✗
\textasciiacute		´	TS1	○	○	○	✗
\textasciibreve		˘	TS1	○	○	○	✗
\textasciicaron		ˇ	TS1	○	○	○	✗
\textasciicircum		^	constr.	○	✗	✗	
\textasciidieresis		¨	TS1	○	○	○	✗
\textasciigrave		`	TS1	○	○	○	✗
\textasciimacron		‾	TS1	○	○	○	✗
\textasciitilde		~	constr.	○	✗	✗	
\textasteriskcentered		*	OMS/TS1	○	○	○	✗
\textbackslash		\	OMS	○	✗	✗	
\textbaht		฿	TS1	○	○	○	✗
\textbar				OMS	○	✗	✗	
\textbardbl		‖	TS1	○	○	○	✗
\textbigcircle		◯	TS1	○	○	○	✗
\textblank		␢	TS1	○	○	○	✗
\textborn		⋆	TS1	○	○	○	✗
\textbraceleft		{	OMS	○	✗	✗	
\textbraceright		}	OMS	○	✗	✗	
\textbrokenbar		¦	TS1	○	○	✗	✗
\textbullet		•	OMS/TS1	○	○	✗	✗
\textcapitalcompwordmark		invisible	TS1	○	○	○	✗
\textcelsius		°C	constr./TS1	○	○	○	✗
\textcent		¢	TS1	○	○	✗	✗
\textcentoldstyle		¢	TS1	○	○	○	✗
\textcircled	(accent)	○	OMS/TS1	○	○	○	✗
\textcircledP		℗	TS1	○	○	○	✗
\textcolonmonetary		₡	TS1	○	○	○	✗
\textcompwordmark		invisible	constr.	○	✗	○	
\textcopyleft		©	TS1	○	○	○	✗

✗ defined in encoding   ○ defined via default

LICR Object	Glyph	Default from	OT1	T1	LY1	TS1
\textcopyright	©	constr./TS1	○	○	✗	✗
\textcurrency	¤	TS1	○	○	✗	✗
\textdagger	†	OMS/TS1	○	○	✗	✗
\textdaggerdbl	‡	OMS/TS1	○	○	✗	✗
\textdblhyphen	=	TS1	○	○	○	✗
\textdblhyphenchar	=	TS1	○	○	○	✗
\textdegree	°	TS1	○	○	✗	✗
\textdied	†	TS1	○	○	○	✗
\textdiscount	٪	TS1	○	○	○	✗
\textdiv	÷	TS1	○	○	✗	✗
\textdivorced	o|o	TS1	○	○	○	✗
\textdollar	$	OT1/TS1	○	✗	✗	✗
\textdollaroldstyle	$	TS1	○	○	○	✗
\textdong	đ	TS1	○	○	○	✗
\textdownarrow	↓	TS1	○	○	○	✗
\texteightoldstyle	8	TS1	○	○	○	✗
\textellipsis	...	constr.	○	○	✗	
\textemdash	—	OT1	✗	✗	✗	
\textendash	–	OT1	✗	✗	✗	
\textestimated	e	TS1	○	○	○	✗
\texteuro	€	TS1	○	○	✗	✗
\textexclamdown	¡	OT1	✗	✗	✗	
\textfiveoldstyle	5	TS1	○	○	○	✗
\textflorin	f	TS1	○	○	✗	✗
\textfouroldstyle	4	TS1	○	○	○	✗
\textfractionsolidus	/	TS1	○	○	○	✗
\textgravedbl	‶	TS1	○	○	○	✗
\textgreater	>	OML	○	✗	✗	
\textguarani	₲	TS1	○	○	○	✗
\textinterrobang	‽	TS1	○	○	○	✗
\textinterrobangdown	⸘	TS1	○	○	○	✗
\textlangle	⟨	TS1	○	○	○	✗
\textlbrackdbl	⟦	TS1	○	○	○	✗
\textleaf	☙	TS1	○	○	○	✗
\textleftarrow	←	TS1	○	○	○	✗
\textless	<	OML	○	✗	✗	
\textlira	₤	TS1	○	○	○	✗
\textlnot	¬	TS1	○	○	✗	✗
\textlquill	⦃	TS1	○	○	○	✗
\textmarried	∞	TS1	○	○	○	✗

✗ defined in encoding   ○ defined via default

LICR Object	Glyph	Default from	OT1	T1	LY1	TS1
\textmho	℧	TS1	○	○	○	✗
\textminus	−	TS1	○	○	○	✗
\textmu	μ	TS1	○	○	✗	✗
\textmusicalnote	♪	TS1	○	○	○	✗
\textnaira	₦	TS1	○	○	○	✗
\textnineoldstyle	9	TS1	○	○	○	✗
\textnumero	№	TS1	○	○	○	✗
\textogonekcentered (accent)	˛			✗		
\textohm	Ω	TS1	○	○	○	✗
\textonehalf	½	TS1	○	○	✗	✗
\textoneoldstyle	1	TS1	○	○	○	✗
\textonequarter	¼	TS1	○	○	✗	✗
\textonesuperior	¹	TS1	○	○	○	✗
\textopenbullet	∘	TS1	○	○	○	✗
\textordfeminine	ª	constr./TS1	○	○	✗	✗
\textordmasculine	º	constr./TS1	○	○	✗	✗
\textparagraph	¶	OMS/TS1	○	○	✗	✗
\textperiodcentered	·	OMS/TS1	○	○	✗	✗
\textpertenthousand	‰₀	TS1	○	○	○	✗
\textperthousand	‰	TS1	○	○	✗	✗
\textpeso	₱	TS1	○	○	○	✗
\textpilcrow	¶	TS1	○	○	○	✗
\textpm	±	TS1	○	○	✗	✗
\textquestiondown	¿	OT1	✗	✗	✗	
\textquotedbl	"		✗	✗		
\textquotedblleft	"	OT1	✗	✗	✗	
\textquotedblright	"	OT1	✗	✗	✗	
\textquoteleft	'	OT1	✗	✗	✗	
\textquoteright	'	OT1	✗	✗	✗	
\textquotesingle	'	TS1	○	○	○	✗
\textquotestraightbase	‚	TS1	○	○	○	✗
\textquotestraightdblbase	„	TS1	○	○	○	✗
\textrangle	⟩	TS1	○	○	○	✗
\textrbrackdbl	⟧	TS1	○	○	○	✗
\textrecipe	℞	TS1	○	○	○	✗
\textreferencemark	※	TS1	○	○	○	✗
\textregistered	®	constr./TS1	○	○	✗	✗
\textrightarrow	→	TS1	○	○	○	✗
\textrquill	⟩	TS1	○	○	○	✗
\textsection	§	OMS/TS1	○	✗	✗	✗

✗ defined in encoding   ○ defined via default

LICR Object		Glyph	Default from	OT1	T1	LY1	TS1
\textservicemark		SM	TS1	○	○	○	✗
\textsevenoldstyle		7	TS1	○	○	○	✗
\textsixoldstyle		6	TS1	○	○	○	✗
\textsterling		£	OT1/TS1	○	✗	✗	✗
\textsurd		√	TS1	○	○	○	✗
\textthreeoldstyle		3	TS1	○	○	○	✗
\textthreequarters		¾	TS1	○	○	✗	✗
\textthreequartersemdash		—	TS1	○	○	○	✗
\textthreesuperior		3	TS1	○	○	○	✗
\texttildelow		~	TS1	○	○	○	✗
\texttimes		×	TS1	○	○	✗	✗
\texttrademark		TM	constr./TS1	○	○	✗	✗
\texttwelveudash		—	TS1	○	○	○	✗
\texttwooldstyle		2	TS1	○	○	○	✗
\texttwosuperior		2	TS1	○	○	○	✗
\textunderscore		_	constr.	○	✗	✗	
\textuparrow		↑	TS1	○	○	○	✗
\textvisiblespace		␣	constr.	○	✗	○	
\textwon		₩	TS1	○	○	○	✗
\textyen		¥	TS1	○	○	✗	✗
\textzerooldstyle		0	TS1	○	○	○	✗
\th		þ		✗	✗		
\u	(accent)	˘	OT1	✗	✗	✗	
\u A		Ă		constr.	✗	constr.	
\u G		Ğ		constr.	✗	constr.	
\u a		ă		constr.	✗	constr.	
\u g		ğ		constr.	✗	constr.	
\v	(accent)	˘	OT1	✗	✗	✗	
\v C		Č		constr.	✗	constr.	
\v D		Ď		constr.	✗	constr.	
\v E		Ě		constr.	✗	constr.	
\v L		Ľ		constr.	✗	constr.	
\v N		Ň		constr.	✗	constr.	
\v R		Ř		constr.	✗	constr.	
\v S		Š		constr.	✗	✗	
\v T		Ť		constr.	✗	constr.	
\v Z		Ž		constr.	✗	✗	
\v c		č		constr.	✗	constr.	
\v d		ď		constr.	✗	constr.	
\v e		ě		constr.	✗	constr.	

✗ defined in encoding   ○ defined via default

775

LICR Object		Glyph	Default from	OT1	T1	LY1	TS1
\v l		ľ		constr.	✘	constr.	
\v n		ň		constr.	✘	constr.	
\v r		ř		constr.	✘	constr.	
\v s		š		constr.	✘	✘	
\v t		ť		constr.	✘	constr.	
\v z		ž		constr.	✘	✘	
\{	(alias)	{	\textbraceleft	○	✘	✘	
\}	(alias)	}	\textbraceright	○	✘	✘	
\~	(accent)	~	OT1	✘	✘	✘	
\~A		Ã		constr.	✘	✘	
\~N		Ñ		constr.	✘	✘	
\~O		Õ		constr.	✘	✘	
\~a		ã		constr.	✘	✘	
\~n		ñ		constr.	✘	✘	
\~o		õ		constr.	✘	✘	

✘ defined in encoding   ○ defined via default

Bibliography

[1] American Mathematical Society. Using the amsthm Package (Version 2.20.3). Providence, Rhode Island, 2017.

The amsthm package provides an enhanced version of LaTeX's \newtheorem command for defining theorem-like environments, recognizing \theoremstyle specifications and providing a proof environment. https://www.ams.org/arc/tex/amscls/amsthdoc.pdf

[2] Anonymous. "'thanks' note (footnote) placed below right column even though there is enough space on the left". *StackExchange*, 2012.

An example of a question on a strange footnote placement by LaTeX. The answers explains some of the reasons why this can happen. https://tex.stackexchange.com/questions/43294

[3] Donald Arseneau. url.sty—Version 3.4, 2016.

Documentation provided by Robin Fairbairns (1947-2022). Locally available via: texdoc url

[4] Javier Bezos. Customizing lists with the enumitem package, 2019.

Extended and customizable list environments. Locally available via: texdoc enumitem

[5] Johannes Braams. "Babel, a multilingual style-option system for use with LaTeX's standard document styles". *TUGboat*, 12(2):291–301, 1991.

The babel package was originally a collection of document-style options to support different languages. An update was published in *TUGboat*, 14(1):60–62, April 1993.
https://tug.org/TUGboat/tb12-2/tb32braa.pdf
https://tug.org/TUGboat/tb14-1/tb38braa.pdf

[6] Peter Breitenlohner et al. "The eTeX manual (version 2)", 1998.

The current manual for the eTeX system, which extends the capabilities of TeX while retaining compatibility. While the eTeX engine is considered obsolete these days, its extensions have been implemented in all major modern systems and LaTeX expects them to be available. Thus, the documentation remains relevant. Locally available via: texdoc etex

[7] Robert Bringhurst. The elements of typographic style (20th Anniversary edition). Hartley & Marks Publishers, Point Roberts, WA, USA, and Vancouver, BC, Canada, 4th edition, 2013. ISBN 0-88179-212-8 (hardcover).
A very well-written book on typography with a focus on the proper use of typefaces.

[8] Bureau International des Poids et Mesures. SI Brochure: The International System of Units (SI), 9th edition, 2019.
The 9ᵗʰ edition of the brochure explaining and promoting the International System of Units (SI) — the preferred system of units for science, technology, industry and trade. Available in English and French. https://www.bipm.org/en/publications/si-brochure/

[9] David Carlisle. "A LaTeX tour, Part 1: The basic distribution". *TUGboat*, 17(1):67–73, 1996.
A "guided tour" around the files in the basic LaTeX distribution. File names and paths relate to the file hierarchy of the CTAN archives. https://tug.org/TUGboat/tb17-1/tb50carl.pdf

[10] ———. "A LaTeX tour, Part 2: The tools and graphics distributions". *TUGboat*, 17(3):321–326, 1996.
A "guided tour" around the "tools" and "graphics" packages. Note that *The Manual* [65] assumes that at least the graphics distribution is available with standard LaTeX. https://tug.org/TUGboat/tb17-3/tb52carl.pdf

[11] ———. "A LaTeX tour, Part 3: mfnfss, psnfss and babel". *TUGboat*, 18(1):48–55, 1997.
A "guided tour" through three more distributions that are part of the standard LaTeX system. The mfnfss distribution provides LaTeX support for some popular METAFONT-produced fonts that do not otherwise have any LaTeX interface. The psnfss distribution consists of LaTeX packages giving access to PostScript fonts. The babel distribution provides LaTeX with multilingual capabilities. https://tug.org/TUGboat/tb18-1/tb54carl.pdf

[12] ———. "XMLTEX: A non validating (and not 100% conforming) namespace aware XML parser implemented in TeX". *TUGboat*, 21(3):193–199, 2000.
XMLTEX is a an XML parser and typesetter implemented in TeX, which by default uses the LaTeX kernel to provide typesetting functionality. https://tug.org/TUGboat/tb21-3/tb68carl.pdf

[13] David Carlisle, editor. Mathematical Markup Language (MathML) Version 4.0. W3C, 1st edition, 2023.
This is the draft specification for a new version of the Mathematical Markup Language; the current version is 3.0 [14]. MathML4 extensions primarily relate to improving accessibility, with new attributes for improving audio rendering. https://www.w3.org/TR/mathml4/

[14] David Carlisle, Patrick Ion, and Robert Miner, editors. Mathematical Markup Language (MathML) Version 3.0. W3C, 2nd edition, 2014.
This is the current specification defining the Mathematical Markup Language; the upcoming version will be [13]. MathML is an XML vocabulary for mathematics, designed for use in browsers and as a communication language between computer algebra systems. The goal of MathML is to enable mathematics to be served, received, and processed on the World Wide Web, just as HTML has enabled this functionality for text. https://www.w3.org/TR/MathML3/

[15] David Carlisle, Patrick Ion, Robert Miner, and Nico Poppelier, editors. Mathematical Markup Language (MathML) Version 2.0. W3C, 2nd edition, 2003.
This is the previous version of the MathML standard [14]. https://www.w3.org/TR/MathML2/

[16] David Carlisle, Chris Rowley, and Frank Mittelbach. "The LaTeX3 Programming Language—a proposed system for TeX macro programming". *TUGboat*, 18(4):303–308, 1997.
Initial proposals for a radically new syntax and software tools. Most of them are now part of the LaTeX format as the L3 programming layer.   https://tug.org/TUGboat/tb18-4/tb57rowl.pdf

[17] Jean Pierre Casteleyn. Visual TikZ, 2019.
A great resource with hundreds of examples, structured by topic, enabling you to find and apply necessary key combinations rather easily.   Locally available via: texdoc visualtikz

[18] The Chicago Manual of Style. University of Chicago Press, Chicago, IL, USA, 17th edition, 2017. ISBN 978-0-226-28705-8.
The standard U.S. publishing style reference for authors and editors.
https://www.chicagomanualofstyle.org

[19] Comprehensive TeX archive network (CTAN). "Topic page on tikz".
Links to CTAN's resources for the tikz universe.   https://www.ctan.org/topic/pgf-tikz

[20] Carl Dair. Design with Type. University of Toronto Press, Toronto, Ontario, Canada, 1967. ISBN 0-8020-1426-7 (hardcover), 0-8020-6519-8 (paperback).
Published in the year of Dair's death, this book is a classic and a good survey of traditional typography with many useful rules of thumb. There was a reprint in 1982, which is still available.

[21] Olaf Drümmer and Bettina Chang. PDF/UA in a Nutshell — Accessible documents with Portable Document Format (PDF). PDF Association, 2013.
A nice introduction to the ISO standard 14289-1 for universal accessibility, also known as PDF/UA [134]. It provides key facts, e.g., the requirements of the standard, the current legal situation, etc.   https://pdfa.org/resource/pdfua-in-a-nutshell/

[22] Dudenredaktion, editor. Die deutsche Rechtschreibung. Dudenverlag, Berlin, 28th edition, 2020. ISBN 978-3-411-04018-6.
The standard reference for the correct spelling of all words of contemporary German and for hyphenation rules, with examples and explanations for difficult cases, and a comparison of the old and new orthographic rules.

[23] Victor Eijkhout. TeX by Topic, A TeXnician's Reference. Lehmanns Media, Berlin, 2014. ISBN 978-3-86541-590-5. Reprint with corrections. Initially published in 1991 by Addison-Wesley. Also available free of charge from the author in PDF format.
A systematic reference manual for the experienced TeX user. The book offers a comprehensive treatment of every aspect of TeX (not LaTeX!), with detailed explanations of the mechanisms underlying TeX's working, as well as numerous examples of TeX programming techniques.
https://eijkhout.net/tex/tex-by-topic.html

[24] FUJITA Shinsaku and NOBUYA Tanaka. "XΥMTeX (Version 2.00) as implementation of the XΥM notation and the XΥM markup language". *TUGboat*, 21(1):7–14, 2000.
A description of version 2 of the XΥMTeX system, which can be regarded as a linear notation system expressed in TeX macros that corresponds to the IUPAC (International Union of Pure and Applied Chemistry) nomenclature. It provides a convenient method for drawing complicated structural formulas.   http://tug.org/TUGboat/tb21-1/tb66fuji.pdf

[25] ——. "Size reduction of chemical structural formulas in XΥMTeX (Version 3.00)". *TUGboat*, 22(4):285–289, 2001.
Further improvements to the XΥMTeX system, in particular in the area of size reduction of structural formulas.   https://tug.org/TUGboat/tb22-4/tb72fuji.pdf

[26] Maarten Gelderman. "A short introduction to font characteristics". *TUGboat*, 20(2):96–104, 1999.

This paper provides a description of the main aspects used to describe a font, its basic characteristics, elementary numerical dimensions to access properties of a typeface design, and the notion of "contrast".　　　　　　　　　　`https://tug.org/TUGboat/tb20-2/tb63geld.pdf`

[27] Norbert Golluch. Kleinweich Büro auf Schlabberscheiben — Tecknisches Deutsch für Angefangen. Eichborn, Frankfurt, 1999.

As the title indicates, a booklet with funny but incorrect translations of IT terms to German.

[28] Michel Goossens, Frank Mittelbach, Sebastian Rahtz, Denis Roegel, and Herbert Voß. The LaTeX Graphics Companion. Lehmanns Media, Köln, 2nd edition, 2022. ISBN 978-3-96543-303-8 (softcover), 978-3-96543-299-4 (ebook).

Reprint of the 2nd edition originally published by Addison-Wesley in the Tools and Techniques for Computer Typesetting series.

The book describes all aspects of generating and manipulating graphical material in LaTeX, including an in-depth coverage of pstricks, METAFONT and METAPOST, xcolor, xy, etc., as well as a thorough overview about applications in science, technology, medicine, gaming, and musical notation.

[29] Michel Goossens, Frank Mittelbach, and Alexander Samarin. The LaTeX Companion. Tools and Techniques for Computer Typesetting. Addison-Wesley, Reading, MA, USA, 1994. ISBN 0-201-54199-8.

The first edition of this book. The second edition [96] was published ten years later in 2004.

[30] Michel Goossens and Sebastian Rahtz. The LaTeX Web Companion: Integrating TeX, HTML, and XML. Tools and Techniques for Computer Typesetting. Addison-Wesley, Reading, MA, USA, 1999. ISBN 0-201-43311-7. With Eitan M. Gurari, Ross Moore, and Robert S. Sutor.

This book teaches (scientific) authors how to publish on the Web or other hypertext presentation systems, building on their experience with LaTeX and taking into account their specific needs in fields such as mathematics, non-European languages, and algorithmic graphics. The book explains how to make full use of the Adobe Acrobat format from LaTeX, convert legacy documents to HTML or XML, make use of math in Web applications, use LaTeX as a tool in preparing Web pages, read and write simple XML/SGML, and produce high-quality printed pages from Web-hosted XML or HTML pages using TeX or PDF.

[31] Ronald L. Graham, Donald E. Knuth, and Oren Patashnik. Concrete Mathematics. Addison-Wesley, Reading, MA, USA, 2nd edition, 1994. ISBN 0-201-55802-5.

A mathematics textbook prepared with TeX using the Concrete Roman typeface; see also [57].

[32] Hàn Thế Thành. "Improving TeX's typeset layout". *TUGboat*, 19(3):284–288, 1998.

This attempt to improve TeX's typeset layout is based on the adjustment of interword spacing after the paragraphs have been broken into lines. Instead of changing only the interword spacing to justify text lines, fonts on the line are also slightly expanded to minimize excessive stretching of the interword spaces. This font expansion is implemented using horizontal scaling in PDF. By using such expansion conservatively, and by employing appropriate settings for TeX's line-breaking and spacing parameters, this method can improve the appearance of TeX's typeset layout.　　　　　　　　`https://tug.org/TUGboat/tb19-3/tb60than.pdf`

[33] ———. "Micro-typographic extensions to the TEX typesetting system". *TUGboat*, 21(4):317–434, 2000.

Doctoral dissertation at the Faculty of Informatics, Masaryk University, Brno, Czech Republic, October 2000. https://tug.org/TUGboat/tb21-4/tb69thanh.pdf

[34] ———. "Margin kerning and font expansion with pdfTEX". *TUGboat*, 22(3):146–148, 2001.

"Margin kerning" adjusts the positions of the primary and final glyphs in a line of text to make the margins "look straight". "Font expansion" uses a slightly wider or narrower variant of a font to make interword spacing more even. These techniques are explained with the help of examples. For a detailed explanation of the concepts, see [33]. This feature was used in the preparation of this book. https://tug.org/TUGboat/tb22-3/tb72thanh.pdf

[35] ———. "Font-specific issues in pdfTEX". *TUGboat*, 29(1):36–41, 2008.

Overview article on font-specific problems and (possible) solutions. In parts related to challenges posed in [81]. http://www.tug.org/TUGboat/tb29-1/tb91thanh-fonts.pdf

[36] Hàn Thế Thành and Sebastian Rahtz. "The pdfTEX user manual". *TUGboat*, 18(4):249–254, 1997.

User manual for the pdfTEX system, which extends TEX to generate PDF directly and provides various micro-typographic extensions; see [32–35]. https://tug.org/TUGboat/tb18-4/tb57than.pdf
Current version at: https://ctan.org/pkg/pdftex

[37] Horace Hart. Hart's Rules; For Compositors and Readers at the University Press, Oxford. Oxford University Press, London, Oxford, New York, 39th edition, 1991. ISBN 0-19-212983-X.

A widely used U.K. reference for authors and editors. With the *Oxford Dictionary for Writers and Editors* it presents the canonical house style of the Oxford University Press. See also [116].

[38] Jobst Hoffmann, Moses Brooks, and Carsten Heinz. The Listings Package, 2020.

A comprehensive manual on pretty-printing source code in various languages.
Locally available via: texdoc listings

[39] Morten Høgholm and the LATEX Project Team. The xfrac package: Split-level fractions, 2023.

One of the first packages to use the L3 programming layer, even before it was integrated in the LATEX format. Locally available via: texdoc xfrac

[40] "ISO/IEC 8859-1:1998 to ISO/IEC 8859-16:2001, Information technology— 8-bit single-byte coded graphic character sets, Parts 1 to 16". International Standard ISO/IEC 8859, ISO Geneva, 1998–2001.

A description of various 8-bit alphabetic character sets. Parts 1–4, 9, 10, and 13–16 correspond to 10 character sets needed to encode different groups of languages using the Latin alphabet, while part 5 corresponds to Cyrillic, part 6 to Arabic, part 7 to Greek, part 8 to Hebrew, and part 11 to Thai.

[41] Bogusław Jackowski. "Appendix G illuminated". *TUGboat*, 27(1):83–90, 2006.

An impressive article explaining TEX's algorithms for typesetting mathematical formulas with the help of a number of carefully prepared graphics, which show the interaction of various font parameters that influence the placement of sub and superscripts, accents, etc.
https://tug.org/TUGboat/tb27-1/tb86jackowski.pdf

[42] Jakub Jankiewicz. "William Morris Letters", 2014.

Available from https://openclipart.org/search/?query=William+Morris+Letter

[43] Alan Jeffrey. "Tight setting with TEX". *TUGboat*, 16(1):78–80, 1995.
Describes some experiments with setting text matter in TEX using Adobe Times, a very tightly
spaced text font.   https://tug.org/TUGboat/tb16-1/tb46jeff.pdf

[44] Alan Jeffrey, Rowland McDonnell, and Lars Hellström. "fontinst: Font installa-
tion software for TEX", 2021.
This utility bundle supports the creation of complex virtual fonts in any encoding for use with
LATEX, particularly from collections of PostScript fonts. Locally available via: texdoc fontinst

[45] Jörg Knappen. "Release 1.2 of the dc-fonts: Improvements to the European
letters and first release of text companion symbols". *TUGboat*, 16(4):381–387,
1995.
Article of historical interest describing the DC fonts, which were precursors of the EC fonts,
which themselves are the default fonts for the T1 encoding of LATEX.
                                                https://tug.org/TUGboat/tb16-4/tb49knap.pdf

[46] ——. "The dc fonts 1.3: Move towards stability and completeness". *TUGboat*,
17(2):99–101, 1996.
A follow-up article to [45]. It explains the progress made in version 1.3 in the areas of stability
and completeness.   https://tug.org/TUGboat/tb17-2/tb51knap.pdf

[47] Donald E. Knuth. TEX and METAFONT — New Directions in Typesetting.
Digital Press, Bedford, MA, USA, 1979. ISBN 0-932376-02-9.
Contains an article on "Mathematical Typography", describing the author's motivation for starting
to work on TEX and the early history of computer typesetting. Describes early (now obsolete)
versions of TEX and METAFONT.

[48] ——. The TEXbook, volume A of *Computers and Typesetting*. Addison-Wesley,
Reading, MA, USA, 1986. ISBN 0-201-13447-0. Jubilee 2021 edition, twenty-
fifth printing with corrections.
The definitive user's guide and complete reference manual for TEX. A good secondary reading,
covering the same grounds, is [23].

[49] ——. TEX: The Program, volume B of *Computers and Typesetting*. Addison-
Wesley, Reading, MA, USA, 1986. ISBN 0-201-13437-3. Jubilee 2021 edition,
thirteenth printing with corrections.
The complete source code for the TEX program, typeset with several indices.

[50] ——. The METAFONTbook, volume C of *Computers and Typesetting*.
Addison-Wesley, Reading, MA, USA, 1986. ISBN 0-201-13445-4 (hardcover),
0-201-13444-6 (paperback). Jubilee 2021 edition, twelfth printing with
corrections.
The user's guide and reference manual for METAFONT, the companion program to TEX for
designing fonts.

[51] ——. METAFONT: The Program, volume D of *Computers and Typesetting*.
Addison-Wesley, Reading, MA, USA, 1986. ISBN 0-201-13438-1. Jubilee 2021
edition, eleventh printing with corrections.
The complete source code listing of the METAFONT program.

[52] ——. Computer Modern Typefaces, volume E of *Computers and Typesetting*.
Addison-Wesley, Reading, MA, USA, 1986. ISBN 0-201-13446-2. Jubilee 2021
edition, eleventh printing with corrections.
More than 500 Greek and Roman letterforms, together with punctuation marks, numerals, and
many mathematical symbols, are graphically depicted. The METAFONT code to generate each

glyph is given and it is explained how, by changing the parameters in the METAFONT code, all characters in the Computer Modern family of typefaces can be obtained.

[53] ———. 3:16 Bible texts illuminated. A-R Editions, Inc., Madison, Wisconsin, 1990. ISBN 0-89579-252-4.

Analysis of Chapter 3 Verse 16 of each book of the Bible. Contains wonderful calligraphy by various artists.

[54] ———. The Art of Computer Programming, volumes 1–4A and Fascicles 5–6. Addison-Wesley, Reading, MA, USA, 1998–2019. ISBN 0-201-89683-4, 0-201-03822-6, 0-201-03803-X, 0-201-03804-8, 0-13-467179-1, and 0-13-439760-6.

Donald Knuth's major work on algorithms and data structures for efficient programming.

[55] ———. Digital Typography. CSLI Publications, Stanford, CA, USA, 1999. ISBN 1-57586-011-2 (cloth), 1-57586-010-4 (paperback).

A comprehensive collection of Knuth's writings on TEX and typography. While many articles in this collection are available separately on the Web, not all of them are, and having all in one place for studying is an additional benefit.

[56] ———. "Virtual fonts: More fun for grand wizards". In Knuth [55], pp. 247–262.

An explanation of what virtual fonts are and why they are needed, plus technical details.
Originally published as: https://tug.org/TUGboat/tb11-1/tb27knut.pdf

[57] ———. "Typesetting Concrete Mathematics". In Knuth [55], pp. 367–378.

Knuth explains how he prepared the textbook *Concrete Mathematics*. He states that he wanted to make that book both mathematically and typographically "interesting", since it would be the first major use of Herman Zapf's new typeface, AMS Euler. The font parameters were tuned up to make the text look as good as that produced by the best handwriting of a mathematician. Other design decisions for the book are also described.
Originally published as: https://tug.org/TUGboat/tb10-1/tb26knut.pdf

[58] ———. "Computers and typesetting". In Knuth [55], pp. 555–562.

Remarks presented by Knuth at the Computer Museum, Boston, Massachusetts, on 21 May 1986, at the "coming-out" party to celebrate the completion of TEX.
Originally published as: https://tug.org/TUGboat/tb07-2/tb14knut.pdf

[59] ———. "The new versions of TEX and METAFONT". In Knuth [55], pp. 563–570.

Knuth explains how he was convinced at the TUG Meeting at Stanford in 1989 to make one further set of changes to TEX and METAFONT to extend these programs to support 8-bit character sets. He goes on to describe the various changes he introduced to implement this feature, as well as a few other improvements.
Originally published as: https://tug.org/TUGboat/tb10-3/tb25knut.pdf

[60] ———. "The future of TEX and METAFONT". In Knuth [55], pp. 571–572.

In this article Knuth announces that his work on TEX, METAFONT, and Computer Modern has "come to an end" and that he will make further changes only to correct extremely serious bugs.
Originally published as: https://tug.org/TUGboat/tb11-4/tb30knut.pdf

[61] Donald E. Knuth and Michael F. Plass. "Breaking paragraphs into lines". In Knuth [55], pp. 67–155.

This article, originally published in 1981, addresses the problem of dividing the text of a paragraph into lines of approximately equal length. The basic algorithm considers the paragraph as a whole and introduces the (now well-known TEX) concepts of "boxes", "glue", and "penalties" to find optimal breakpoints for the lines. The paper describes the dynamic programming technique used to implement the algorithm.

[62] Markus Kohm. KOMA-Script. Edition DANTE. Lehmanns Media, Berlin, 7th edition, 2020. ISBN 978-3-96543-097-6 (Print), 78-3-96543-103-4 (eBook).
Documentation of the KOMA-Script document classes and their features in the German language. Available in a print and eBook edition. For the online version see [63].

[63] ———. KOMA-Script: A versatile LaTeX 2_ε bundle, 2022.
KOMA-Script is a bundle of LaTeX classes and packages that can be used as replacements for the standard LaTeX classes offering extended functionalities. German and English manuals are provided as part of the distribution. Locally available via: texdoc koma-script

[64] Helmut Kopka and Patrick W. Daly. Guide to LaTeX. Tools and Techniques for Computer Typesetting. Addison-Wesley, Boston, MA, USA, 4th edition, 2004. ISBN 0-321-17385-6.
An introductory guide to LaTeX with a different pedagogical style than Lamport's LaTeX Manual [65].

[65] Leslie Lamport. LaTeX: A Document Preparation System: User's Guide and Reference Manual. Addison-Wesley, Reading, MA, USA, 2nd edition, 1994. ISBN 0-201-52983-1. Reprinted with corrections in 1996.
The ultimate reference for basic user-level LaTeX by the creator of LaTeX 2.09. It complements the material presented in this book.

[66] LaTeX Project Team. "LaTeX news".
An issue of LaTeX News is released with each LaTeX 2_ε release, highlighting changes since the last release. There is also a document combining all issues since 1994, which offers a good overview about the history of LaTeX 2_ε as well as providing an easy way to find information on all major updates and extensions that have been implemented over the years.
Locally available via: texdoc ltnews

[67] ———. "Bugs in LaTeX software". Website.
The bug reporting and tracking service run by the LaTeX team as part of the LaTeX 2_ε maintenance activity. https://www.latex-project.org/bugs/

[68] ———. Configuration options for LaTeX 2_ε, 2003.
How to configure a LaTeX installation using the set of standard configuration files.
Locally available via: texdoc cfgguide

[69] ———. "The LaTeX project public license (version 1.3c)", 2008.
The Open Source License used by the core LaTeX 2_ε distribution and many contributed packages. See [85] for background and history. https://www.latex-project.org/lppl/

[70] ———. LaTeX 2_ε for authors — historic version, 2020.
When LaTeX 2_ε was released in 1994, it was accompanied by a set of guides, e.g., [68, 71, 75, 94]. This guide describes functionality that became available with LaTeX 2_ε. Over the years it got some additions, as needed, but also kept information that is now only of historical interest. Starting in 2020, this historical version was frozen and a new guide was written in which irrelevant, old information was dropped and all new user-level functionality is documented; see [74].
Locally available via: texdoc usrguide-historic

[71] ———. LaTeX 2_ε font selection, 2022.
A description of font selection in standard LaTeX intended for package writers who are already familiar with TeX fonts and LaTeX. Locally available via: texdoc fntguide

[72] ———. Core documentation distributed with LaTeX, 2022.
The LaTeX distribution contains a number of guides, e.g., [68, 70, 71, 73-75, 94]. These, together with other useful documents, are also available from the project Web site on a couple of overview pages. Overview at: https://latex-project.org/help/documentation

[73] ———. The LATEX3 Interfaces, 2023.

The reference manual for the L3 programming layer, which has been part of the LATEX format since 2020 and thus available for package development — the go-forward way for LATEX-coding.
Locally available via: texdoc interface3

[74] ———. LATEX for authors — current version, 2023.

Starting in 2020, the core document-level functionality for LATEX is now documented in this guide, and the original LATEX 2ε guide from 1994 has been moved to [70] for those who are interested in the history of LATEX. Locally available via: texdoc usrguide

[75] ———. LATEX for class and package writers, 2023.

The guide to LATEX 2ε commands for class and package writers, but also sometimes useful in the preamble of documents. It was rewritten and extended in 2023 and the original from 2006 is available under a separate name. Locally available via: texdoc clsguide
and the historic version via: texdoc clsguide-historic

[76] Philipp Lehman and Joseph Wright. The csquotes Package—Context Sensitive Quotation Facilities, 2022.

Package providing context-sensitive smart quotes. Original implementation by Philipp Lehman; maintained and further developed since 2015 by Joseph Wright.
Locally available via: texdoc csquotes

[77] LuaTEX development team. LuaTEX Reference Manual, 2022.

The official manual for the LuaTEX engine, describing all its commands and features.
Locally available via: texdoc luatex

[78] Jianrui Lyu. tabularray — Typeset Tabulars and Arrays with LATEX3, 2022.

A recent approach to tables entirely written in the L3 programming layer, reimplementing, consolidating, and extending features from many other packages. Still under heavy development and thus not entirely stable, but already worth exploring.
Locally available via: texdoc tabularray

[79] Ruari McLean. The Thames and Hudson Manual of Typography. Thames and Hudson, London, UK, 1980. ISBN 0-500-68022-1.

A broad introduction to traditional commercial typography.

[80] Microsoft. "OpenType Layout Tag Registry—Feature Tags", 2019.

The registry for OpenType font features each with a description of the meaning and suggested usage. https://docs.microsoft.com/en-us/typography/opentype/spec/featuretags

[81] Frank Mittelbach. "E-TEX: Guidelines for future TEX Extensions". TUGboat, 11(3):337–345, 1990.

The output of TEX is compared with that of hand-typeset documents. It is shown that many important concepts of high-quality typesetting are not supported and that further research to design a "successor" typesetting system to TEX should be undertaken. A review of the findings, 23 years later, is provided in [86]. https://tug.org/TUGboat/tb11-3/tb29mitt.pdf

[82] ———. "A regression test suite for LATEX 2ε". TUGboat, 18(4):309–311, 1997.

Description of the concepts and implementation of the test suite used to test for unexpected side effects after changes to the LATEX kernel. One of the most valuable maintenance tools for keeping LATEX 2ε stable. https://tug.org/TUGboat/tb18-4/tb57mitt.pdf

[83] ———. "Language Information in Structured Documents: Markup and rendering—Concepts and problems". In "International Symposium on Multilingual Information Processing", pp. 93–104. Tsukuba, Japan, 1997. Invited paper. Slightly extended in TUGboat 18(3):199–205, 1997.

This paper discusses the structure and processing of multilingual documents, both at a general level and in relation to a proposed extension to standard LATEX.
https://tug.org/TUGboat/tb18-3/tb56lang.pdf

[84] ——. "Formatting documents with floats: A new algorithm for LaTeX 2_ε".
TUGboat, 21(3):278–290, 2000.
Descriptions of features and concepts of a new output routine for LaTeX that can handle spanning
floats in multicolumn page design.   https://tug.org/TUGboat/tb21-3/tb68mittel.pdf

[85] ——. "Reflections on the history of the LaTeX Project Public License (LPPL) —
A software license for LaTeX and more". *TUGboat*, 32(1):83–94, 2011.
A review of the evolution of LaTeX world's predominant license [69].
                                          https://tug.org/TUGboat/tb32-1/tb100mitt.pdf

[86] ——. "E-TeX: Guidelines for future TeX Extensions — revisited". *TUGboat*,
34(1):47–63, 2013.
This article compares the output of TeX with that of hand-typeset documents. This is a reassessment of the findings made 23 years earlier [81]. With the new engines the situation has improved,
but even though there is now engine support for most problems, the majority of them still
represent important and open research problems for high-quality automated typesetting.
                                          https://tug.org/TUGboat/tb34-1/tb106mitt.pdf

[87] ——. "A general framework for globally optimized pagination". In "Proceedings of the 2016 ACM Symposium on Document Engineering", DocEng '16, p.
11–20. Association for Computing Machinery, New York, NY, USA, 2016. ISBN
978-1-4503-4438-8.
This paper presents research results for globally optimized pagination using dynamic programming and discusses its theoretical background. It was awarded the "ACM Best Paper Award" at the
DocEng 2016 conference. A greatly expanded version of this paper (37 pages) titled "A General
LuaTeX Framework for Globally Optimized Pagination" was submitted to the Computational
Intelligence (Wiley) in 2017 and accepted January 2018 [91].
                         https://www.latex-project.org/publications/indexbyyear/2016/

[88] ——. "Effective floating strategies". In "Proceedings of the 2017 ACM
Symposium on Document Engineering", DocEng '17, p. 29–38. Association
for Computing Machinery, New York, NY, USA, 2017. ISBN 978-1-4503-4689-4.
This paper presents an extension to the general framework for globally optimized pagination
described [87]. The extended algorithm supports automatic placement of floats as part of the
optimization using a flexible constraint model that allows for the implementation of typical
typographic rules.   https://www.latex-project.org/publications/indexbyyear/2017/

[89] ——. "Managing forlorn paragraph lines (a.k.a. widows and orphans) in LaTeX".
TUGboat, 39(3):246–251, 2018.
A discussion of methods for·avoiding widows and orphans with suggestions about what is most
promising when using LaTeX.   https://tug.org/TUGboat/tb39-3/tb123mitt-widows.pdf

[90] ——. "A rollback concept for packages and classes". *TUGboat*, 39(2):107–112,
2018.
The article describes the rollback concept for packages and document classes and gives advice
about how to apply it in different scenarios.
                                   https://tug.org/TUGboat/tb39-2/tb122mitt-rollback.pdf

[91] ——. "A general LuaTeX framework for globally optimized pagination".
Computational Intelligence, 35(2):242–284, 2019.
This article is an extended version (37 pages) of the 2016 ACM article "A General Framework for
Globally Optimized Pagination" [87], providing a lot more details and additional research results.
The peer-reviewed publication is now freely available.
                         https://www.latex-project.org/publications/indexbyyear/2020/

[92] Frank Mittelbach, David Carlisle, and Chris Rowley. "Experimental LaTeX code for class design".

At the TeX Users Group conference in Vancouver the LaTeX project team gave a talk on models for user-level interfaces and designer-level interfaces in LaTeX3 [93]. Most of these ideas have been implemented in prototype implementations (e.g., template design, front matter handling, output routine, galley and paragraph formatting). The source code is documented and contains further explanations and examples; see also [84]. The underlying programming interfaces are since 2020 part of the LaTeX format as the L3 programming layer [73].
Articles: https://latex-project.org/publications/indexbytopic/l3-expl3
Code: https://github.com/latex3/latex3

[93] ——. "New interfaces for LaTeX class design, Parts I and II". *TUGboat*, 20(3):214–216, 1999.

Some proposals for the first-ever interface to setting up and coding LaTeX classes. While all of them were implemented as experimental prototypes (see [92]), they have been developed at a time were computers have not been powerful enough to set them up for general use. This has finally changed and several of these ideas are now making their reappearance as part of the "LaTeX Tagged PDF" project [101]. https://tug.org/TUGboat/tb20-3/tb64carl.pdf

[94] Frank Mittelbach, Robin Fairbairns, and Werner Lemberg. LaTeX font encodings, 2016.

An overview of all standard LaTeX font encodings and their use with 8-bit TeX engines, such as pdfTeX. Locally available via: texdoc encguide

[95] Frank Mittelbach, Ulrike Fischer, and Chris Rowley. LaTeX Tagged PDF Feasibility Evaluation. LaTeX Project, 2020.

This is the feasibility study undertaken by the LaTeX team prior to initiating the multiyear project for automatically providing tagged PDF with LaTeX. It explains in detail both the project goals and the tasks that need to be undertaken and concludes with a detailed project plan. See also [101].
https://latex-project.org/publications/indexbytopic/pdf/

[96] Frank Mittelbach, Michel Goossens, Johannes Braams, David Carlisle, and Chris Rowley. The LaTeX Companion. Tools and Techniques for Computer Typesetting. Addison-Wesley, Reading, MA, USA, 2nd edition, 2004. ISBN 0-201-36299-6.

The second edition of this book. The contributing authors have changed over the years.

[97] Frank Mittelbach and Joan Richmond. "R.I.P. – S.P.Q.R Sebastian Patrick Quintus Rahtz (13.2.1955–15.3.2016)". *TUGboat*, 37(2):129–130, 2016.

An obituary for my friend Sebastian.
https://tug.org/TUGboat/tb37-2/tb116rahtz-mitt.pdf

[98] Frank Mittelbach, Will Robertson, and LaTeX3 team. "l3build — A modern Lua test suite for TeX programming". *TUGboat*, 35(3):287–293, 2014.

The workflow environment used by the LaTeX Project Team and others. Supports concepts developed over the years including regression testing methods, distribution builds, uploads to CTAN, and installation support. https://tug.org/TUGboat/tb35-3/tb111mitt-l3build.pdf
Locally available program documentation: texdoc l3build

[99] Frank Mittelbach and Chris Rowley. "LaTeX 2.09 ↪ LaTeX3". *TUGboat*, 13(1):96–101, 1992.

A brief sketch of the LaTeX3 Project, retracing its history and describing the structure of the system. An update appeared in *TUGboat*, 13(3):390–391, October 1992. A call for volunteers to help in the development of LaTeX3 and a list of the various tasks appeared in *TUGboat*, 13(4):510–515, December 1992. Now mainly of historical interest.
https://tug.org/TUGboat/tb13-1/tb34mittl3.pdf

[100] ———. "The pursuit of quality: How can automated typesetting achieve the highest standards of craft typography?" In C. Vanoirbeek and G. Coray, editors, "EP92 — Proceedings of Electronic Publishing, '92, International Conference on Electronic Publishing, Document Manipulation, and Typography, Swiss Federal Institute of Technology, Lausanne, Switzerland, April 7-10, 1992", pp. 261-273. Cambridge University Press, New York, 1992. ISBN 0-521-43277-4.

This paper compares high-quality craft typography with the state of the art in automated typesetting. It explains why the current paradigms of computerized typesetting will not serve for high-quality formatting and suggests directions for the further research necessary to improve the quality of computer-generated layout.
https://www.researchgate.net/publication/237444403_The_Pursuit_of_Quality

[101] ———. "LaTeX Tagged PDF — a blueprint for a large project". *TUGboat*, 41(3):292-298, 2020.

An introduction and summary of the extended feasibility study [95] for the multiyear project "LaTeX Tagged PDF". https://latex-project.org/publications/indexbytopic/pdf/

[102] Frank Mittelbach and Rainer Schöpf. "With LaTeX into the nineties". *TUGboat*, 10(4):681-690, 1989.

This article proposes a reimplementation of LaTeX that preserves the essential features of the current interface while taking into account the increasing needs of the various user communities. It also formulates some ideas for further developments. It was instrumental in the move from LaTeX 2.09 to LaTeX 2_ε. https://tug.org/TUGboat/tb10-4/tb26mitt.pdf

[103] ———. "Reprint: The new font family selection — User interface to standard LaTeX". *TUGboat*, 11(2):297-305, 1990.

A complete description of the user interface of the first version of LaTeX's New Font Selection Scheme. https://tug.org/TUGboat/tb11-2/tb28mitt.pdf

[104] ———. "Towards LaTeX 3.0". *TUGboat*, 12(1):74-79, 1991.

The objectives of the LaTeX3 project are described. The authors examine enhancements to LaTeX's user and style file interfaces that are necessary to keep pace with modern developments, such as SGML. They also review some internal concepts that need revision.
https://tug.org/TUGboat/tb12-1/tb31mitt.pdf

[105] NAKASHIMA Hiroshi. Package paracol: Yet Another Multi-Column Package to Typeset Columns in Parallel, 2018.

Package to typeset two text streams in parallel columns, occasionally synchronizing the column data. Locally available via: texdoc paracol

[106] Clemens Niederberger. acro — Typeset Acronyms and other Abbreviations, 2022.

A system for managing acronyms and abbreviations in a consistent way. Implemented using the L3 programming layer. Locally available via: texdoc acro

[107] ———. enotez — Endnotes for LaTeX 2_ε, 2022.

A modern implementation of endnotes for LaTeX that can serve as a successor to the endnotes package. Implemented using the L3 programming layer. Locally available via: texdoc enotez

[108] ———. fnpct — footnotes' interaction with punctuation, 2022.

A package supporting multiple consecutive footnotes, including their spacing and relationship to punctuation characters. Implemented using the L3 programming layer.
Locally available via: texdoc fnpct

[109] ———. tasks — lists with columns filled horizontally, 2022.
A manual for the tasks package implementing horizontally oriented lists. Implemented using the
L3 programming layer.   Locally available via: texdoc tasks

[110] Heiko Oberdiek. The bookmark package, 2020.
The manual for the new bookmark implementation. Going forward its functionality will be directly
integrated into the hyperref package.   Locally available via: texdoc bookmark

[111] Pieter van Oostrum. Page Layout in LaTeX, 2022.
A manual for producing flexible page styles in LaTeX. Translations in different languages are
available.   Locally available via: texdoc fancyhdr

[112] John Plaice. "Progress in the Omega project". *TUGboat*, 15(3):320–324, 1994.
One of the articles that shows part of the research work that went into Omega and influenced
later development. On the TeX Users Group site, there are several other articles by either Yannis
Haralambous or John Plaice that describe related developments around Omega.
                        https://www.tug.org/TUGboat/tb15-3/tb44plaice.pdf

[113] Sunil Podar. "Enhancements to the picture environment of LaTeX". Technical
Report 86-17, Department of Computer Science, S.U.N.Y, 1986. Version 1.2:
July 14, 1986.
This document describes some new commands for the picture environment of LaTeX, especially
higher-level commands that enhance its graphic capabilities by providing a friendlier and more
powerful user interface. It was the first work extending LaTeX to produce more sophisticated line
graphics, influencing all later attempts.   https://ctan.org/pkg/epic

[114] Sebastian Rahtz, Heiko Oberdiek, and LaTeX Project Team. Hypertext marks in
LaTeX: a manual for hyperref, 2022.
The manual for hyperref, originally written by Sebastian, then maintained and greatly extended
by Heiko, and now taken over by the LaTeX Team with a major reimplementation in progress.
                                               Locally available via: texdoc hyperref

[115] Brian Reid. Scribe: A Document Specification Language and its Compiler. Ph.D.
thesis, Carnegie-Mellon University, Pittsburgh, PA 15213, 1980.
The Ph.D. thesis that was one of the inspirations for LaTeX.
                        http://reports-archive.adm.cs.cmu.edu/anon/scan/CMU-CS-81-100.pdf

[116] Robert M. Ritter, editor. The Oxford Style Manual. Oxford University Press,
London, Oxford, New York, 2003. ISBN 0-198-60-564-1.
Reference work incorporating an update to *Hart's Rules* [37], and the *Oxford Dictionary for Writers
and Editors*.

[117] Will Robertson. "An exploration of the Latin Modern fonts". *TUGboat*,
28(2):177–180, 2007.
A tour through various aspects of the Latin Modern fonts — the default fonts for LaTeX when used
with Unicode engines.   https://tug.org/TUGboat/tb28-2/tb89robertson.pdf

[118] ———. The fontspec package—Font selection for XeLaTeX and LuaLaTeX, 2022.
The official manual for fontspec with additional documentation not covered in this book.
                                               Locally available via: texdoc fontspec

[119] Will Robertson, Khaled Hosny, and Karl Berry. The XeTeX reference guide,
2019.
Manual describing the XeTeX engine. It covers the special features of the program but otherwise
assumes familiarity with a base TeX engine.   Locally available via: texdoc xetex

[120] Maïeul Rouquette. reledmac—Typeset scholarly editions with LaTeX, 2022.
The reledmac package provides many tools in order to typeset scholarly editions. It is based on the eledmac package, which was based on the ledmac package by Peter Wilson, which was based on the original edmac, tabmac, and edstanza macros by John Lavagnino, Dominik Wujastyk, Herbert Breger, and Wayne Sullivan. Locally available via: texdoc reledmac

[121] Chris Rowley. "Models and languages for formatted documents". *TUGboat*, 20(3):189–195, 1999.
Explores many ideas around the nature of document formatting and how these can be modeled and implemented. https://tug.org/TUGboat/tb20-3/tb64rowl.pdf

[122] ——. "The LaTeX legacy: 2.09 and all that". In ACM, editor, "Proceedings of the Twentieth Annual ACM Symposium on Principles of Distributed Computing 2001, Newport, Rhode Island, United States", pp. 17–25. ACM Press, New York, NY, USA, 2001. ISBN 1-58113-383-9.
Part of a celebration for Leslie Lamport's sixtieth birthday; a very particular account of the technical history and philosophy of TeX and LaTeX. https://www.latex-project.org/publications/indexbytopic/2e-concepts

[123] Chris Rowley and Frank Mittelbach. "Application-independent representation of multilingual text". In Unicode Consortium, editor, "Europe, Software + the Internet: Going Global with Unicode: Tenth International Unicode Conference, March 10-12, 1997, Mainz, Germany", The Unicode Consortium, San Jose, CA, 1997.
Explores the nature of text representation in computer files and the needs of a wide range of text-processing software. https://latex-project.org/publications/1996-FMi-CAR-UnicodeConf-appl-independent-representation.pdf

[124] Martin Scharrer. The adjustbox Package, 2022.
Comprehensive manual describing how to manipulate boxes using a key/value interface inspired by the \includegraphics command. Locally available via: texdoc adjustbox

[125] Robert Schlicht. The microtype Package—Subliminal refinements towards typographical perfection, 2022.
User manual for the microtype package that unleashes the micro-typographic extensions implemented by Hàn Thế Thành in pdfTeX and later propagated to other engines as well. Locally available via: texdoc microtype

[126] Joachim Schrod. "International LaTeX is ready to use". *TUGboat*, 11(1):87–90, 1990.
Announces some of the early standards for globalization work on LaTeX. https://tug.org/TUGboat/tb11-1/tb27schrod.pdf

[127] Erik Spiekermann. Stop Stealing Sheep & find out how type works. TOC Publishing, p98a.berlin, Berlin, 4th edition, 2022. ISBN 978-3-949164-03-3.
A guidebook classic on how to use type most effectively. First published in 1993 by Adobe Press; the fourth edition is now also freely available under a Creative Commons license through Google Design. https://design.google/library/catching-up-with-erik-spiekermann

[128] Andrew Stacey. The tikzmark package v1.15, 2022.
Comprehensive manual describing how to "remember" a position on a page for later (or earlier) use, primarily (but not exclusively) with TikZ. Locally available via: texdoc tikzmark

[129] Paul Stiff. "The end of the line: A survey of unjustified typography". *Information Design Journal*, 8(2):125–152, 1996.
A good overview about the typographical problems that need to be resolved when producing high-quality unjustified copy.

[130] Thomas F. Sturm. A Tutorial for Poster Creation with `tcolorbox`, 2020.
A step by step tutorial to great posters.   Locally available via: `texdoc tcolorbox-tutorial`

[131] ———. tcolorbox—Manual for version 5.1.1, 2022.
Comprehensive manual of what is possible with the various libraries for the tcolorbox package. More than 500 pages covering all aspects.   Locally available via: `texdoc tcolorbox`

[132] Nicola L.C. Talbot and Vincent Belaïche. `fmtcount.sty`: Displaying the Values of LATEX Counters, 2020.
Package that provides additional formatting possibilities for LATEX counters, such as ordinals, textual representations, etc., in different languages.   Locally available via: `texdoc fmtcount`

[133] Till Tantau. TikZ & PGF, 2021.
The ultimate resource for working with tikz if you got hooked by the introduction given in Section 8.5. A whopping 1300 pages; see also [17, 19].   Locally available via: `texdoc tikz`

[134] Technical Committee ISO/TC 171/SC 2. ISO 14289-1:2014 Document management applications — Electronic document file format enhancement for accessibility — 1: Use of ISO 32000-1 (PDF/UA-1), 2014.
ISO 14289-1:2014 specifies the use of the ISO 32000-1:2008 standard to produce accessible electronic documents.   `https://iso.org/standard/64599.html`

[135] UMEKI Hideo. The geometry package, 2021.
Documentation of the package that provides a flexible and easy to use interface to set up page dimensions.   Locally available via: `texdoc geometry`

[136] Didier Verna. FiXme – Collaborative annotation tool for LATEX, 2022.
The manual for Didier's collaborative workflow tool.   Locally available via: `texdoc fixme`

[137] Herbert Voß. Package hvfloat — Controlling captions, fullpage and doublepage floats, 2023.
The manual for hvfloat package with many examples.   Locally available via: `texdoc hvfloat`

[138] Graham Williams. "Graham Williams' TEX Catalogue". *TUGboat*, 21(1):17–90, 2000.
In 2000 this catalogue listed more than 1500 TEX, LATEX, and related packages and tools on 74 pages and was linked directly to the items on CTAN. CTAN now offers it in the form of several indexes with more than 5000 items covering everything stored there.
`https://tug.org/TUGboat/tb21-1/tb66catal.pdf`
Latest version on CTAN at: `https://ctan.org/pkg/catalogue`

[139] Hugh Williamson. Methods of Book Design. Yale University Press, New Haven, London, 3rd edition, 1983.
A classic work that has become a basic tool for the practicing book designer. It deals with such matters as the preparation of copy, the selection and arrangement of type, the designer's part in book illustration and jacket design, and the economics of book production. The book also explains the materials and techniques of book production and their effect on the design of books.
First edition from 1956 available online at:
`https://archive.org/details/MethodsOfBookDesign`

[140]   Peter Wilson. Some Examples of Title Pages. The Herries Press, 2010.
        A showcase of 40 different title page designs with code to produce them.
        Locally available via: texdoc titlepages

[141]   Peter Wilson and Lars Madsen. The Memoir Class for Configurable Typeset-
        ting — User Guide, 2022.
        A very customizable document class that can be adjusted to produce a wide variety of layouts.
        Locally available via: texdoc memoir

[142]   Joseph Wright. siunitx—A comprehensive (SI) units package, 2023.
        The comprehensive manual for typesetting scientific units and their values in text, formulas, and
        tables.   Locally available via: texdoc siunitx

Index of Commands and Concepts

This title somewhat hides the fact that everything (for both volumes) except for names of people is in this one long comprehensive index. To make it easier to use, the entries are distinguished by their "type", and this is often indicated by one of the following "type words" at the beginning of the main entry or a subentry:

attribute, BIBTEX/biber command, BIBTEX entry type, BIBTEX field, BIBTEX style, boolean, counter, document class, env., file, file extension, folio style, font encoding, hook, key/option, keyword, key, language, length, library, math accent, math symbol, option, package, page style, program, rigid length, syntax, text accent, text symbol, text/math symbol, TEX counter, or value.

type words used in the index

Most "type words" should be fairly self-explanatory, but a few need some explanation to help you find the entries you are looking for.

'option' and 'keyoption'   Both type words indicate that the keyword can be used in the optional argument of \usepackage. If the option accepts a value, it is marked as a 'keyoption' and otherwise as a classic 'option'. Most packages with 'keyoptions' also offer configuration commands that can be used in the preamble or in the document body — see also next types.

'key' and 'value'   Many modern LATEX packages implement a key/value syntax (i.e., $\langle key_1 \rangle = \langle value_1 \rangle , \langle key_2 \rangle = \langle value \rangle , \dots$) as part of the optional argument to \usepackage, in arguments of commands or environments, or both. Keywords that can appear to the left of the equal sign are indicated by the type word 'key' (or as type 'keyoption' if allowed in \usepackage), those that can appear to the right as 'value'. Sometimes keywords can appear on either side, depending on context, in which case they are indexed according to their use on the particular page.[1]

'syntax'   Keywords and strings marked with 'syntax' can appear in arguments of commands but are not part of a key/value pair.

'counter' and 'TEX counter'   Names marked as 'counter' are LATEX counters and are altered with \setcounter, etc., while 'TEX counters' start with a backslash and use a low-level method for modification.

'length' and 'rigid length'   A 'length' register can take values with a plus and minus component, i.e., can stretch or shrink. In contrast, a 'rigid length' stores only a fixed value. Most lengths in LATEX are flexible, i.e., not rigid.

'text symbol', 'math symbol', and 'text/math symbol'   A command is classified as a 'text symbol' if it typesets a glyph for use in text, whereas a 'math symbol' can be used only in math mode and produces an error elsewhere. A few symbols are allowed everywhere and are therefore of type 'text/math symbol'.

In most cases, the actual symbol is also shown in the index entry to help you find the symbol you are looking for more easily (the command names are not always obvious). Note, however, that the glyph shown is only an approximation of reality — in your document it may come out differently depending on the fonts you use.

no type word indication   The absence of an explicit "type word" means that the "type" is either a core LATEX command or simply a concept.

Relation to packages or programs

If a particular index entry is defined or used in a special way by a package, then this is indicated by adding the package name (in parentheses) to an entry or subentry. If package aaa builds upon or extends package bbb, we indicate this with (aaa/bbb). There is one "virtual" package name, tlc, which indicates commands introduced only for illustrative purposes in this book. Again, you may see (tlc/bbb), if appropriate.

Interpreting page references

The index contains all entries for both volumes. To which pages the references point is indicated by →I (for part one) and →II (for part two). To save space, these indicators are given only once in each entry. An *italic* page number indicates that the command or concept is demonstrated in an example on that page. When there are several page numbers listed, blue boldface indicates a page containing important information about an entry, such as a definition or basic usage. However, bold is (normally) not used for concept entries, when all entries are of equal importance, or when there is *only one* page reference.

Sorting within the index

When looking for the position of an entry in the index, you need to realize that both of the characters \ and . are ignored when they come at the start of a command or file extension. Other syntax entries starting with a period are listed in the Symbols section. Otherwise, the index entries are sorted in ASCII order, and the running header gives you an indication where you are in the index. For the rather lengthy Symbols section at the beginning of the index, this is unfortunately of little help because only a few people would know the symbol order in the ASCII encoding. We therefore show the order of symbols in the margin on those pages.

---

[1]This explains why you might find the same keyword under both type words, but given that one is usually interested only in one type of usage, this distinction is made. This distinction also exhibits the fact that different packages use the same keywords in different ways — an unfortunate side effect of the long history of LATEX package development by independent developers.

H

L

P

PSNFSS (PostScript New Font Selection scheme) (*cont.*)
    fonts used, →I 689, 691
    sans serif fonts, →I 690
pspicture *obsolete* package,
    →I 603, *see instead* pict2e package
\psq (biblatex), →II 544, *545*
\psqq (biblatex), →II 544
\pstarrows (pict2e), →I 604
    pstarrows option (pict2e), →I 604
pstricks package, →I 631, 645, 780, →II 798
pt syntax (*unit*), →I 634, →II 652
.ptc file extension (titletoc), →I 11, 67
PTMono package, →II 32
PTSans package, →II 32
PTSansCaption package, →II 32
PTSansNarrow package, →II 32
PTSerif package, →II 32
PTSerifCaption package, →II 32
publisher B<small>IB</small>T_EX field,
    →II *382f.*, 386, 388, 389, 393, *403–406*
publist biblatex style (biblatex-publist), →II *467*
\pubmed (uri), →I *203*
punctuation
    bibliographies
        author-date citation system, →II 546
        customizing, →II *566*
        number-only citation system, →II 479, *482f.*
        short-title citation system, →II 528, *529*
    math symbols, →II 222, *223*
    near footnote markers, →I 216ff.
    spacing after, →II 320
    trailing after quotes, →I *180f.*
PunctuationSpace key (fontspec), →I *715, 728*
\pushtabs, →II 738
    error using, →II 736
\put, →I *593, 602, 603–608, 611*, →II 680
\putbib (bibunits), →II *575, 576f.*
px value (mathalpha), →II 234
pxtx value (mathalpha), →II 232f.
Python value (listings), →I 323

Q

Q syntax (qrcode), →I 613
\qauthor (quotchap), →I 38, *39*
\qauthorfont (quotchap), →I 38, *39*
\qbezier (pict2e), →I 606
\qbeziermax (pict2e), →I 606
\qed (amsthm), →I 283
    qed key (thmtools), →I *288*
    QED (□) symbol, →I 282f., *288*
\qedhere (amsthm), →I 283
\qedsymbol (amsthm), →I *283, 288*
\qquad, →II *205*, 653
    QR codes, drawing, →I *612f.*
\qrcode (qrcode), →I *612, 613*
    qrcode package, →I 612f.
\qrset (qrcode), →I 613
\qsetcnfont (quotchap), →I 38

\qty (siunitx), →I *170, 173, 175ff.*
\qtylist (siunitx), →I *171*
\qtyproduct (siunitx), →I 171
\qtyrange (siunitx), →I *171*
\QU (tlc/ifthen), →II 693
\quad, →II *205*, 631, *632*, 653, 762
    quad value (caption), →I *543, 545*
    qualifier-mode key (siunitx), →I *175*
    qualifier-phrase key (siunitx), →I *175*
    quantities, scientific notation, →I 169, *170f., 175f.*
    quantity-product key (siunitx), →I 175
\quarto (babel), →II 319
    quattrocento package, →I 702f., →II 34
    Quattrocento fonts, description/examples, →I *702f.*, →II 33
\quest (tlc/tasks), →I *292*
    question mark (?), shorthand character, →II *312f.*
    question/answer forums, →II 788f.
    quiet option (fontspec), →I 728
    quiet mode, index generation, →II 354, 364
quotation env., →I 179, 180f., 260
    (lineno), →I 338
quotations, →I 179–188, 260, *261*
    American style, →I *186*
    changing style, →I *181*
    display quotations, →I 180, *181*, 182
    ellipsis, for omissions, →I 182f., *187*
    in foreign language, →I *184*
    language support, →I 183ff.
    trailing punctuation after, →I *180f.*
    with citations, →I 182
        configuring, →I 185ff.
        forced to next line, →I *187*
quotations (mottos), on chapter/section headings, →I 38, *39*
quotchap package, →I 38f.
Quote env.
    (tlc/enumitem), →I *276*
    (tlc), →I *260, 261*
quote env., →I 179, 180, *260*, →II *630, 672*, 673
    (lineno), →I *338*
    (tlc/enumitem), →I 263, *277*
    quote keyword (*MakeIndex*|upmendex), →II *357, 360*
\quotechar (doc), →II *594*, 596
\quotedblbase text symbol „ , →I 772
\quotefont (quotchap), →I 38, *39*
\quotesinglbase text symbol ‚ , →I 772
    quoting characters, inserting in multilingual documents,
    →II *303, 311*
\qverb (newverbs), →I *299, 300*

R

R syntax
    (*cmd/env decl*), →II *633*, 636, 736
    (abraces), →II *185*, *186f.*, *189f.*
    (fancyhdr), →I 392, *399*, *400–404*
    (tabulary), →I 451, 477
    (tlc/array), →I *445*
    (wrapfig), →I 536
R value (listings), →I 323

\untagged (tagging), →I 31
untaggedblock env. (tagging), →I 31
\UOLaugment (underoverlap), →II 190
\UOLoverbrace (underoverlap), →II 189
\UOLoverline (underoverlap), →II 189
\UOLunderbrace (underoverlap), →II 189
\UOLunderline (underoverlap), →II 189
up option (titlesec), →I 40
up syntax (*font shape*), →I 671, 734, *735*
up value
    (caption), →I 542
    (unicode-math), →II 260
\upalpha math symbol α (newtxmath|newpxmath),
    →II 245, 250
\Uparrow math symbol ⇑, →II 190, 219
\uparrow math symbol ↑, →II 190, 219
\upbeta math symbol β
    (newtxmath|newpxmath), →II 245, 250
    (unicode-math), →II 258
updated BibTeX field (jurabib), →II 534
\updatename (jurabib), →II 534
\updatesep (jurabib), →II 534
\updefault, →I 671
\upDelta math symbol Δ
    (ccfonts), →II 239
    (cmbright), →II 240
    (mathpazo), →II 251
    (newtxmath|newpxmath), →II 245, 250
\Updownarrow math symbol ⇕, →II 190, 219
\updownarrow math symbol ↕, →II 190, 219
\upharpoonleft math symbol ↿ (amssymb), →II 219
\upharpoonright math symbol ↾ (amssymb), →II 219
uphill value (tcolorbox), →I 618
upint option
    (newtxmath|newpxmath), →II *244*, *249*, *274f.*, *280*
    (notomath), →II 252, *287*, *295*
upload keyword (l3build), →II *612*
uploadconfig key (l3build), →II *612*, 613
\uplus math symbol ⊎, →II 215
upmendex program, →I 12, →II 298, 327f., 344, 347f., 350f.,
    354f., 359f., 363, *364-370*, 371, 593
    Cyrillic alphabet, →II 327
    multilingual documents, →II 327
\upOmega math symbol Ω
    (ccfonts), →II 239
    (cmbright), →II 240
    (mathpazo), →II 251
    (newtxmath|newpxmath), →II 245, 250
Uppercase value (fontspec), →I 716, *722*, 725, *726*
\uppercase, problems with, →II 327
UppercasePetiteCaps value (fontspec), →I 717
UppercaseSmallCaps value (fontspec), →I 717, *718*
uppersorbian option (babel), →II 301
upquote key (listings), →I *303*, *326*, *328*
upquote package, →I 302ff., 305
upref package, →II 129
upright option, →II *283*
    (fourier), →II 283

upright value (unicode-math), →II 256, *258*
upright font shape, →I 654, 661
UprightFeatures key (fontspec), →I 727
UprightFont key (fontspec), →I 709, *710*
uprightGreek option (newtxmath|newpxmath), →II 245
\uproot (amsmath), →II 199, *200*
\upshape, →I 662f., *664f.*, 667, 671, *697*, 735
\Upsilon math symbol ϒ, →II 212
\upsilon math symbol υ, →II 212
upTeX, →II 299, 331, *see also* Unicode engine specialities
\upuparrows math symbol ⇈ (amssymb), →II 219
\urcorner math symbol ⌐ (amssymb), →II 224
uri key (hyperref|bookmark), →I 104, *106*
uri package, →I 202ff.
URIs (Uniform Resource Identifiers)
    linking to, →I *203f.*
    typesetting, →I 202, *203*, 204
\urisetup (uri), →I 203
\url
    (custom-bib), →II 430
    (hyperref), →I 100, *102*, 198, 201, *202*, 204, 624
    (natbib), →II 500
    (url), →I *198*, *199-202*, →II 405
        error in moving argument, →I 199
        problems using, →I 199
        problems with UTF-8 characters, →I 201
url BibTeX field, →II *390*, *391*
    (biblatex), →II 387, *390*
    (custom-bib), →II *428*, *430*
    (jurabib), →II 510, *534*
    (natbib), →II 500
url package, →I 102, *198-202*, 204, 777, →II 430
\UrlBigBreaks (url), →I 201
urlborder key/option (hyperref), →I 103
urlbordercolor key/option (hyperref), →I 103
\UrlBreaks (url), →I 201
urlbst package, →II 390
urlcolor key/option (hyperref), →I 102, *103*, *202*, 204
urldate BibTeX field, →II 390, 400
    (biblatex), →II 387, *390*, *391*, 392, 400
    (jurabib), →II 534
\urldatecomment (jurabib), →II 534
\urldef (url), →I *199*, *200*
urlencode key (hyperref), →I *100*
\UrlLeft (url), →I *200*, *201*
    spaces ignored in, →I 200
\UrlNoBreaks (url), →I 201
\urlprefix (custom-bib), →II 430
\UrlRight (url), →I *200*, *201*
    spaces ignored in, →I 200
URLs (Uniform Resource Locators)
    bibliographies, →II 390f., *392*, 500, 533f.
    line breaks in, →I 199
    linking to, →I 201f., 204
    typesetting, →I 198, 199, *200*, 201, *202*, 203, *204*
\urlstyle (url), →I *200*, *201f.*, 204
URW Classico fonts, description/examples, →II 71

People

947